9/06

D0621257

ENCYCLOPEDIA OF THE ARCTIC

Volume 3
O–Z
Index

Mark Nuttall, Editor

ROUTLEDGE
NEW YORK AND LONDON

Published in 2005

Routledge
270 Madison Avenue
New York, NY 10016
www.routledge-ny.com

Published in Great Britain by
Routledge
2 Park Square
Milton Park, Abingdon,
Oxon OX14 4RN U.K.
www.routledge.co.uk

Copyright © 2005 by Routledge.
Routledge is an imprint of the Taylor & Francis Group.

Printed in the United States of America on acid-free paper

All rights reserved. No part of this book may be reprinted or reproduced or utilized in any form or by any electronic, mechanical, or other means, now known or hereafter invented, including photocopying and recording, or in any information storage or retrieval system, without permission in writing from the publishers.

10 9 8 7 6 5 4 3 2 1

Library of Congress Cataloging-in-Publication Data
Encyclopedia of the Arctic / Mark Nuttall, editor.
P. cm.
ISBN 1-57958-436-5 (set: alk. paper) -- ISBN 1-57958-437-3 (volume 1 : alk. paper) -- ISBN 1-57958-438-1 (volume 2 : alk. paper) -- ISBN 1-57958-439-X (volume 3 : alk. paper) 1. Arctic regions -- Encyclopedias. I. Title: Arctic. II. Nuttall, Mark.
G606. E49 2005
909'.0913'03--dc22
2004016694

Cover Photos
Volume 1: Inuit hunters in kayaks return to shore towing a narwhal they have harpooned, Qaanaaq, Northwest Greenland. Copyright *Bryan and Cherry Alexander* Photography

Volume 2: Polar bear mother and cubs on new sea ice, Cape Churchill, Manitoba, Canada. Copyright *Bryan and Cherry Alexander* Photography

Volume 3: Northern lights, aurora borealis, over a Nenets reindeer herders camp, Yamal Peninsula, Western Siberia, Russia. Copyright *Bryan and Cherry Alexander* Photography

REF
909.0913
ENC
2005
V.3

BOARD OF ADVISERS

Dr. David G. Anderson
Department of Anthropology
University of Aberdeen
Scotland

Lawson Brigham
Deputy Director, US Arctic Research Commission
Arlington, Virginia

Prof. Terry V. Callaghan
Director, Abisko Scientific station
Royal Swedish Academy of Sciences
Abisko, Sweden

Dr. Torben R. Christensen
Department of Plant Ecology
Lund University
Sweden

Dr. Liz Cruwys
Scott Polar Research Institute
University of Cambridge
England

Prof. Louis-Jacques Dorais
Department of Anthropology
Laval University
Quebec, Canada

Prof. Julian Dowdeswell
Director, Scott Polar Research Institute
University of Cambridge
England

Dr. Niels Einarsson
Director
Stefansson Arctic Institute
Akureyri, Iceland

Mads Fægteborg
Arctic Information
Copenhagen
Denmark

Prof. Peter Johnson
Department of Geography
University of Ottawa
Ontario, Canada

Dr. Igor Krupnik
Arctic Studies Center
National Museum of Natural History
Smithsonian Institution
Washington DC

Dr. Molly Lee
University of Alaska Museum
University of Alaska Fairbanks

Dr. Hanne Petersen
Director, Danish Polar Center
Copenhagen, Denmark

Dr. Beau Riffenburgh
Scott Polar Research Institute
University of Cambridge
England

Dr. David Scrivener
Department of International Relations
University of Keele
Keele, England

Dr. Frank Sejersen
Department of Eskimology
University of Copenhagen
Denmark

Prof. Sergei Sutyrin
Department of World Economy
St. Petersburg University
Russia

Prof. Peter Wadhams
Department of Applied Mathematics and
Theoretical Physics
University of Cambridge
England

Prof. Gunter Weller
Cooperative Institute for Arctic Research
University of Alaska Fairbanks

Karla Jessen Williamson
Executive Director
Arctic Institute of North America
University of Calgary
Alberta
Canada

Prof. Robert G. Williamson
Arctic Institute of North America
University of Calgary
Alberta
Canada

Contents

Entries A-Z

Arctic Fox
Arctic Ground Squirrel
Arctic Hare
Arctic Haze
Arctic Leaders' Summit
Arctic Mid-Ocean Ridge
Arctic Ocean
Arctic Ocean Hydrographical Expedition, 1909–1915
Arctic Peoples' Conference
Arctic Pilot Project
Arctic Research Consortium of the United States
    (ARCUS)
Arctic Research Policy Act
Arctic Slope Regional Corporation (ASRC)
Arctic Small Tool Tradition
Arctic Waters Pollution Prevention Act (1971)
Arctic Woodland Culture
Arkhangel'sk
Arkhangel'skaya Oblast'
Arms Control
Armstrong, Terence
Arnasson, Ingolfur
Aron from Kangeq
Art and Artists (Indigenous)
Arutyunov, Sergei
Association Inuksiutit Katimajiit
Association of Canadian Universities for Northern
    Studies (ACUNS)
Association of World Reindeer Herders
Atassut
Athapaskan
Atlantic Layer
Atlasov, Vladimir
Auk
Aurora
Axel Heiberg Island

B

Back River
Back, Sir George
Badigin, Konstantin Sergeyevich
Baer, Karl von
Baffin Bay
Baffin Island
Baffin, William
Bang, Jette
Banks Island
Barents Council
Barents Region
Barents Regional Council
Barents Sea
Barents, Willem
Barentsburg

Barnacle Goose
Barrow
Barrow, Sir John
Bartlett, Robert
Bathurst Island
Bathurst Mandate
Bear Ceremonialism
Bear Island
Bearded Seal
Bears
Beaufort Gyre
Beaufort Sea
Beechey, Frederick
Belcher, Sir Edward
Bel'kachi Culture
Bellot, Joseph-René
Beluga (White) Whale
Bennett, James Gordon Jr
Bering Sea
Bering Strait
Bering, Vitus
Beringia
Bernier, Joseph-Elzéar
Bilibino
Bilibino Nuclear Power Plant
Billings, Joseph
Bioconcentration
Biodiversity
Biodiversity: Research Programmes
Biogeochemistry
Birch Forests
Birket-Smith, Kaj
Birnirk Culture
Birthplace Criteria
Bladder Ceremony
Blue Whale
Boas, Franz
Bogoraz, Vladimir Germanovich
Boothia Peninsula
Boreal Forest Ecology
Bourque, James W.
Bowhead (Greenland Right) Whale
Brent Geese
British Arctic Expedition, 1875–1876
Brooks Range
Bruce, W.S.
Brun, Eske
Bunge, Alexander von
Buntings and Longspurs
Bureau of Indian Affairs
Bureau of Land Management
Buryat Republic (Buryatiya)
Button, Sir Thomas

Volume 3

O

P

ENTRIES A-Z

O

OB' RIVER

The Ob' River basin in West Siberia is the largest in Russia (2,990,000 km² in area), with 85% situated in the West Siberian lowland and the rest in the Altai mountains. The left bank of the basin dominates. The Ob' is formed by the merger of the Biya and the Katun' rivers, originating in the Altai mountains and draining into the Obskaya Inlet of the Kara Sea. The Ob' River measures 3676 km long, or 5570 km if counted from the head of the Irtysh (the largest tributary). The river depth is 2–6 m in the headwaters and 4–10 m in the lower reaches. The Ob' has a very low gradient of 4.4 cm km^{-1} and forms numerous branches, meanders, and oxbows. The valley reaches 80–120 km width in places and the river incision is minor. The floodplain ranges in width from 5–7 km in the headwaters to 25–35 km in the lower reaches. The Ob' is the only river on Earth having spring floods that persist for more than 100 days. The water of the Ob' is mostly provided by snowmelt. Among the tributaries the Irtysh, the Biya, the Katun', and the Tchulym have the highest runoff. The mean Ob' runoff is 394 km³, and the mean discharge in the Salekhard area is 14,000 m³ s^{-1}.

The Ob' crosses steppe, taiga, and tundra; however, most of the basin is covered by bogs and fens. The mean annual air temperature ranges from −10.5°C in the north to 1–2°C in the south. Permafrost is continuous in the tundra and permafrost islands spread down to the latitude of 64° N. Fifty-five fish species dwell in the Ob' and the Obskaya Inlet, 20 of which are of commercial value (sturgeon, sterlet, inconnu, whitefish, and so on).

Indigenous people are Nenets in the tundra and forest-tundra; Khanty, Mansi, and Sel'kup in the taiga; and Siberian Tatars and Altaitsy (both Turkic people) in the steppe. Russians, currently constituting 87% of the population (*Goskomstat Rossii*, 2000), started to settle in the late 16th century following the gradual inclusion of Siberia in the Russian Empire. The Ob' basin belongs to Altaisky Kray, the Altai Republic, and five Oblasts of the Russian Federation, including Khanty-Mansi and Yamal-Nenets Autonomous Areas. The population density is 0.7 persons per sq km in the Yamal-Nenets, and 15.6–33.3 persons per sq km in the industrial areas adjacent to railways. Many large towns, such as Novosibirsk, Omsk, Tyumen', Tomsk, Surgut, Salekhard, and Khanty-Mansiisk are located on the banks of the Ob' and its large tributaries.

The Ob' is navigable throughout its extent, and is an important transportation route to the Kara Sea. Its basin plays an important role in Russian economy due to rich raw materials, and land and water resources. The main industries are oil, coal, metallurgy, timber, chemical, and mechanical engineering. More than half of Russian oil and gas condensate production comes from the Ob' basin. There are three hydroelectric power stations in the upper stream of the Ob' and the Irtysh. The south is an important agricultural area. Industrial development has resulted in the pollution of water bodies, 40% loss of breeding areas, and damage to fish population.

ELENA LAPTEVA

Further Reading

Brusinina, Irina N. (editor), *Izuchenie reki Obi i ee pritokov v sviazi s hoziaistvennym osvoeniem Zapadnoi Sibiri* [Studies on the Ob' river and its tributaries in connection with the economic development of West Siberia], Leningrad: GosNIORH, 1989

Domohitzky, Anatoly P., Raisa G. Dubrovina & Anna I. Isaeva, *Reki i ozera* Sovetzkogo *Souza* [Rivers and lakes of the USSR], Leningrad: Gidrometeoizdat, 1971

Golovnev, Andrei V., "The Khanty living world." *Anthropology & Archeology of Eurasia*, 32(2) (1993): 74–92

———, *Govoriashchie cultury: traditzii samodiitzev i ugrov* [Talking cultures: samoyed and ugrian traditions], Ekaterinburg: UrO RAN, 1995

Mikhailov, Nikolai I., Anatoly G. Voronov & I.E. Timashev (editors), *Priroda Sredinnogo regiona SSSR* [Nature of the Middle Region of the USSR], Moscow: MGU, 1980

Vilchek, G.E. & O.Y. Bykova, "The origin of regional ecological problems within the Northern Tyimen Oblast, Russia." *Arctic and Alpine Research*, 24(2) (1992): 99–107

OCEAN DUMPING

Ocean dumping refers to the deliberate disposal of waste at sea. The waste can include—but is not limited to—garbage, municipal and industrial wastes, oil, and radioactive wastes. There is a history of ocean dumping in the Arctic. It was the obvious solution for communities situated along the coast of the sea, where the isolation and harsh conditions made domestic and industrial waste disposal difficult and costly. Permafrost also makes conventional land filling difficult, if not impossible. Waste was often deposited directly into Arctic waters or hauled out onto the ice to sink to the ocean floor with the summer thaw. After World War II, intensified military activity and exploitation of resources in the Arctic led to an increasing concentration of military installations, mining operations, and oil exploration camps along the edge of the sea. This growth brought a corresponding increase in ocean dumping and a change in the nature of the material being discarded.

Extent

In the Canadian Arctic and Alaska, during the operation of the Distant Early Warning (DEW) Line radar stations and other military sites from the 1950s to the 1980s, there was extensive ocean dumping. Word-of-mouth accounts of such activities were not verified until 1993. The effects of ocean disposal were investigated in the harbor of the largest coastal community and former DEW Line site, Cambridge Bay, and in more exposed seas off the east coast of Baffin Island, near areas with histories of military activity. Debris found on the bed of Cambridge Bay included airplanes, vehicles, fuel barrels, and electric equipment containing traces of polychlorinated biphenyls (PCBs). Very little underwater debris was found near Baffin Island. In both locations, however, there were local PCB hotspots in the seabed and PCB accumulations in sea urchins and fish from the immediate vicinity. The PCB contamination in all cases was clearly attributable to local sources on the shore and not to the dumped material. Some metal chemical contamination

was detectable nearby but was localized and minimal. These studies suggest that ocean dumping in the Canadian Arctic has not affected the surrounding marine environment, except within a few meters of metal-containing objects.

The Soviet Union, over roughly the same period, dumped large quantities of radioactive and chemical waste at numerous sites in the Barents and Kara seas. In 1993, a report commissioned by the Russian government disclosed the full extent of nuclear dumping by the former USSR. The comprehensive document, referred to as the Yablokov Report, included a description of the ocean dumping program and the locations and contents of the dumping sites. Investigations by Russian, Norwegian, British, and American groups have subsequently verified the existence of much of the dumped material. Low-level liquid waste from reactor cooling systems such as those on board submarines, and from cleaning and decontamination operations at shipyards, was dumped in the Barents Sea. The main dumping site for high-level nuclear waste was the shallow water off the coast of Novaya Zemlya, in the Kara Sea. The most serious threat comes from reactors that were dumped with their spent nuclear fuel, and from spent fuel dumped separately in containers. Although some leakage is occurring, the contamination is limited to the immediate area of the dumped objects. At present, radiation from the dumped waste is not detectable in the open Kara Sea, but increased leakage is expected over time, as the containment material corrodes. There is consensus that the past ocean dumping of radioactive material is not an immediate threat to humans or the Arctic ecosystem. The main risks are for the long term, and this may also apply at any undiscovered dump sites. If leakage occurs, the effects are not likely to affect the general Arctic because of the patterns of ocean currents. The future risk from contained spent fuel contributes to the more significant risk from the high concentration of potential radiation sources in the Arctic, which include fuel stored on land and operating nuclear reactors.

Also during this time, the United States, Russia, Canada, and Norway began offshore oil exploration and production in the Arctic, discarding drill waste directly into the ocean. Lead and zinc mines in Greenland and heavy industries in Iceland dumped tailings and organic waste into deep coastal fjords. Oceans were viewed as a vast resource and the possibility that they could be harmed by relatively small quantities of waste was slow to gain acceptance.

Regulatory Control

The Convention on the "Prevention of Marine Pollution by Dumping of Wastes and Other Matter," known as the London Convention of 1972, is the primary international agreement controlling ocean dumping. It prohibits the dumping of specified items in the ocean and has grown increasingly restrictive. In 1993, 72 countries of the London Convention agreed to ban the disposal of industrial and low-level radioactive wastes at sea. The so-called "reverse list," introduced in 1996, specifies materials that may be considered for disposal at sea, with all others being prohibited. Permitted material includes dredged material, sewage sludge, industrial fish-processing waste, offshore man-made structures at sea, organic material of natural origin, and bulky items made of iron, steel, or concrete. Sewage and industrial outfall effluent, accidental oil spills, and routine discharges from vessels are regulated separately. Most of the eight Arctic countries have passed legislation prohibiting the dumping of hazardous materials. Only Russia has reported the dumping of industrial or radioactive wastes since 1990, but this practice ceased in 1993.

Outlook

Even though current risks would not appear to be increased as a result of past ocean dumping, future release rates and pathways to people remain to be evaluated, particularly in the Russian Arctic.

ENVIRONMENTAL SCIENCES GROUP, ROYAL MILITARY
COLLEGE OF CANADA

See also **Bioconcentration; Contaminants; Environmental Problems; Hydrocarbon Contamination; Local and Transboundary Pollution; Persistent Organic Pollutants (POPs); Polychlorinated Biphenyls; Radioactivity; Waste Management**

Further Reading

Arctic Council, AMAP *Assessment Report: Arctic Pollution Issues. A State of the Arctic Environment Report*, Oslo, Norway: Arctic Monitoring and Assessment Programme, 1997

Environmental Sciences Group, *Historical Ocean Disposal in the Canadian Arctic*, Ottawa, Ontario: Director General Environment, Department of National Defence, 1994

Jensen, J., K. Adare, & R. Shearer (editors), *Canadian Arctic Contaminants Assessment Report*, Ottawa, Ontario: Indian Affairs and Northern Development Canada, 1997

Kirk, Elizabeth J. (editor), *Ocean Pollution in the Arctic North and the Russian Far East: Proceedings from the Ocean Pollution Session of the Conference "Bridges of Science Between North America & the Russian Far East,"* Vladivostok, Russia, September 1, 1994 (45th Arctic Science Conference, 1994)

Office of Technology Assessment, *Nuclear Wastes in the Arctic: An Analysis of Arctic and Other Regional Impacts from Soviet Nuclear Contamination*, OTA-ENV-623, Washington, Distrcit of Columbia: US Government Printing Office, September 1995

OSPAR Commission for the Protection of the Marine Environment of the North-East Atlantic, *Quality Status Report 2000, Region I—Arctic Waters*, London: OSPAR Commission, 2000

Reimer, K.J., D.A. Bright, W.T. Dushenko, S.L. Grundy & J.S. Poland, *The Environmental Impact of the DEW Line on the Canadian Arctic*, Ottawa: Director General Environment, Department of National Defence, 1993

Yablokov, A.V. (editor), *Russian Arctic: At the Door of Disaster*, Russia: Center for Ecological Policy of Russia, 1996

Yablokov, A.V. et al., *Facts and Problems Connected with the Disposal of Radioactive Waste in the Seas Adjacent to the Territory of the Russian Federation*, Moscow: Administration of the President of the Russian Federation, February 1993

Zimmerman, W., E. Nikitina & J. Clem, "The Soviet Union and the Russian Federation: A Natural Experiment in Environmental Compliance." In *Engaging Countries: Strengthening Compliance with International Environment-al Accords*, edited by E. Brown Weiss & H. K. Jacobson, Cambridge, Massachusetts: MIT Press, 1998

OCEAN FRONTS

Ocean fronts are narrow zones of strong horizontal gradients of seawater properties (temperature, salinity, or nutrients) that separate broader zones of different stratification (vertical structure). Fronts occur on a variety of scales, from 100 m to 10,000 km along-front; and from 10 m to 100 km across-front; and from 1 m to 1 km down-front; their lifetime varies from hours to millions of years. Fronts separate water masses that might change little over many hundreds of kilometers, and yet frontal gradients of temperature and salinity might be as sharp as 10°C and 1 ppt, respectively, over a distance of 100 m. Some fronts are short-lived, but most fronts are quasistationary and seasonally persistent: they form (and disappear) in the same locations during the same season, year after year. The most prominent fronts are present year-round. Fronts play a key role in various processes that occur in the ocean and its interfaces with the atmosphere, sea ice, and ocean bottom:

(1) Fronts are accompanied by along-front oceanic jets or currents that transport the bulk of water, heat, and salt.

(2) Eddy variability peaks at fronts.

(3) Frontal meanders can close to form eddies or rings that carry the bulk of cross-frontal transport.

(4) Fronts are major biogeographical boundaries with enhanced biological productivity, driving the Arctic marine food chain.

(5) Atmospheric boundary layer parameters change abruptly across major ocean fronts.

(6) High-latitude fronts are related to sea ice cover.

(7) Fronts profoundly influence acoustic environment.

(8) Ocean sedimentation is largely determined by frontal pattern.

(9) Pollutants concentrate thousands of times in surface frontal zones.

Fronts are formed by various processes; accordingly, there are several major frontal types. Only those fronts that exist in the Arctic/Subarctic are described below, starting from the inshore fronts and proceeding offshore.

Estuarine (riverine) fronts occur between plumes of riverine freshwater outflow and the surrounding sea water. These salinity fronts are sometimes accompanied by a temperature gradient, for example, when riverine water is warmer than sea water. Riverine sediments (silt) make most estuarine fronts clearly visible from space as turbidity fronts owing to the distinct color and or transparency gradients across these fronts. Examples include the Mackenzie River Plume fronts (Carmack et al., 1989) and also poorly studied fronts of the Kara and Laptev seas resulting from discharges of Siberian rivers (Ob', Yenisey, Lena, and Khatanga).

Shelf fronts form over mid-shelf areas, well inshore of the continental shelfbreak. Their origin is sometimes related to the opposing currents over the shelf or two water masses separated by the front. Bottom relief (e.g., submerged terraces or paleo-shorelines) could play a role. Examples include the Labrador Shelf and Bering Sea Alaskan Shelf (Coachman, 1986).

Tidal mixing fronts develop between the completely mixed water column over the shallow depths and the stratified water column over the deeper bottom. Naturally, these fronts are best defined where tidal energy dissipation is a maximum. In the Arctic/Subarctic region, tides are relatively weak, except for a few areas such as the Sea of Okhotsk, with a robust tidal front around Kashevarov Bank (Kowalik and Polyakov, 1999), and Bering Sea, with tidal fronts around Pribilof Islands (Schumacher et al., 1979).

Shelfbreak fronts are collocated with the shelfbreak and separate the shelf water from the slope water. These fronts are typically stable owing to the topography that steers them. There is always a well-defined, narrow, and swift current (sometimes called "jet") along the shelfbreak fronts. Examples include the Beaufort Shelfbreak Front, East/West Greenland Polar Front (Paquette et al., 1985) and Labrador Front.

Marginal ice zone fronts form along the edge of the seasonal ice cover. Sea ice formation results in salt release (brine rejection) that causes haline convection. When sea ice melts, the ensuing superficial freshening gives rise to a salinity front between the fresh meltwater and the ambient water. The meltwater layer is more stable and therefore absorbs solar radiation more efficiently than the ambient water. This differential heating results in a temperature gradient (thermal front) across the initial salinity front. The marginal ice zone fronts exist in all of the Arctic marginal seas and are better studied in the Barents, Bering, Labrador, and Greenland seas.

Water mass fronts occur at the interface between two different water masses. For example, the Bering Strait inflow brings Pacific waters to the Arctic Ocean, resulting in a front in the Chukchi Sea, while the Atlantic water inflow creates a front in the Barents Sea. The boundary between the Pacific and Atlantic waters in the Arctic Ocean is observed as a well-defined front (McLaughlin et al., 1996; Morison et al., 1998). This front is known to have been located over the Lomonosov Ridge. Recently, however, the front has shifted and currently extends over the Mendeleyev Ridge and Alpha Ridge. This relocation represents a major change in the long-term balance between the Atlantic and Pacific water inflows into the Arctic Basin. It is not clear whether a reversal, if any, would occur in the foreseeable future.

Fronts are important in many applications. Marine transportation companies can use seasonally adjusted frontal locations to optimize ship routing. Due to enhanced biological productivity at ocean fronts (phytoplankton and zooplankton at the surface of the subducting water mass being concentrated in a narrow band at the surface), the fishing industry can efficiently manage fishery grounds of the most important species such as sardine, cod, tuna, swordfish, and salmon that straddle major ocean fronts. Climate change monitoring and prediction benefits from incorporating fronts in global circulation models as well as regional models of atmosphere-sea ice-atmosphere interaction. Marine mining operators need to know current patterns associated with fronts in the vicinity of oil and gas platforms and submarine pipes. Last but not least, submarine navigation is crucially dependent on the exact knowledge of location and parameters of fronts.

IGOR BELKIN

See also **Oceanography**

Further Reading

Belkin, I.M. Fronts. In Encyclopedia of Marine Sciences, New York: Grolier, 2002

Carmack, E.C., R.W. Macdonald & J.E. Papadakis, "Water mass structure and boundaries in the Mackenzie Shelf estuary." *Journal of Geophysical Research*, 94(C12) (1989): 18043–18055

Coachman, L.K., "Circulation, water masses, and fluxes on the southeastern Bering Sea shelf." *Continental Shelf Research*, 5(1/2) (1986): 23–108

Kowalik, Z. & I. Polyakov, "Diurnal tides over Kashevarov Bank, Okhotsk Sea." *Journal of Geophysical Research*, 104(C3) (1999): 5361–5380

McLaughlin, F.A., E.C. Carmack, R.W. Macdonald & J.K.B. Bishop, "Physical and geochemical properties across the Atlantic/Pacific water mass front in the southern Canadian basin." *Journal of Geophysical Research*, 101(C1) (1996): 1183–1197

Morison, J., M. Steele & R. Andersen, "Hydrography of the upper Arctic Ocean measured from the nuclear submarine U.S.S. Pargo." *Deep-Sea Research I*, 45(1) (1998): 15–38

Paquette, R.G., Bourke, R.H., J.F. Newton & W.F. Perdue, "The East Greenland Polar Front in autumn." *Journal of Geophysical Research*, 90(C3) (1985): 4866–4882

Schumacher, J.D., T.H. Kinder, D.J. Pashinski & R.L. Charnell "A structural front over the continental shelf of the eastern Bering Sea." *Journal of Physical Oceanography*, 9(1) (1979): 79–87

OCEANOGRAPHY

Introduction

The atmosphere and the world's oceans are an intimately coupled system that together determines our weather and climate. While both the atmosphere and the oceans transport heat and water on global scales, the atmosphere through prevailing winds and the oceans through currents, the transit times are quite different. For the atmosphere, transit times range from days to weeks, whereas for the oceans the transit times range from months to millennia.

Ocean currents transport heat from warmer regions of the Earth to colder ones. The Gulf Stream and North Atlantic Drift, for example, carry heat from the tropical North Atlantic Ocean to Northern Europe, which results in a climate there that is much milder than the climate at the same latitudes elsewhere in North America and Asia. This is dubbed the "Global Conveyor Belt" (Broecker, 1995). Figure 1 shows a highly schematic depiction of how the global ocean operates. The actual global circulation, the global thermohaline circulation, is much more complex (*see* **Thermohaline Circulation**). Global thermohaline circulation depends on processes that make surface water dense enough to sink. In the Northern Hemisphere, this happens in winter in the Nordic seas (Norwegian, Greenland, and Iceland seas) and in the Labrador Sea. The newly formed dense water flows at depth toward tropical regions, where it upwells and becomes warm. An analogous process occurs in Antarctic regions. The surface waters must be sufficiently dense for this process to be successful. If the salinity of the surface waters is decreased by a few percent, then winter cooling will produce sea ice, as occurs in the central Arctic Ocean, rather than producing deep water.

As part of the Global Conveyor Belt, the Arctic Ocean helps shape global thermohaline circulation in two ways. It contributes deep water formed within the Arctic Ocean to the northern part of the Global Conveyor Belt, a contribution that presently amounts to about 30% of the deep water overflowing from the Nordic seas (Anderson et al., 1999). Moreover, it influences the density of the water close to the surface in the Nordic and Labrador seas through the export of fresh water to these regions. There are three components of this freshwater export to the North Atlantic Ocean: relatively fresh sea water of Pacific origin, rivers flowing into the Arctic Ocean, and sea ice (in solid form and as meltwater). The Pacific contribution results from there being more evaporation than precipitation over the Atlantic Ocean, with the excess evaporated water from the Atlantic Ocean being transported by the atmosphere to fall as precipitation into the Pacific Ocean as well as over regions that drain into the Arctic Ocean. The Arctic Ocean thus provides the pathway for the return of this fresh water to the North Atlantic Ocean from the Pacific Ocean (*see* maps in **Arctic Ocean**) and also from rivers entering the Arctic Ocean to balance the budget.

The Arctic Ocean and Modern Exploration

Whalers and explorers provided the first knowledge of Arctic regions. These efforts were largely confined to the marginal seas: in the Eastern Hemisphere, the Norwegian, Greenland, and Barents seas, and in the Western Hemisphere, Hudson and Baffin bays, the Canadian Arctic Archipelago, and the Bering Sea, including limited penetration into the Arctic Ocean along the North American coast. At the end of the 19th century, Fridtjof Nansen led the earliest scientifically inspired exploration of the Arctic Ocean. From 1893 to 1896, Nansen's ship, *Fram*, was frozen into pack ice north of Siberia and drifted across two of the major basins (Amundsen and Nansen) of the Arctic Ocean, reaching a latitude of 86° N, but failing to drift far enough north to claim the North Pole (Nansen, 1902). Nevertheless, this bold venture provided the first real insight into the nature of the Arctic Ocean, obtaining a vast amount of information on an ocean region where virtually none had existed before. Soundings made by this expedition produced a comprehensive bathymetric map and showed that the Arctic Ocean had depths exceeding 4 km and consisted of a single elliptical basin. Nansen also obtained evidence for the theory of an east-west current in the Arctic Ocean. During Roald Amundsen's *Maud* expedition from 1918 to 1925, Norwegian scientist Harald Ulrik Sverdrup conducted valuable research on tides, currents, physical properties of sea water, and sea ice, which contributed to the publication of *The Oceans: Their Physics, Chemistry and*

Figure 1: Global Conveyor Belt representing global thermohaline circulation emphasizing the Arctic and Atlantic Oceans (courtesy of Greg Holloway). Warm water flows to Polar Regions, transporting heat and eventually becoming cooled and made dense enough to sink to deep waters and flow south. Upwelling in equatorial regions closes the loop.

General Biology in 1942, the first modern textbook in oceanography. These early scientific expeditions were followed by the former Soviet Union embarking on several surveys starting from 1930 to 1985. These were conducted from drifting ice camps, aircraft, and icebreakers. Much of these data were unavailable to the rest of the world until summarized in atlas form (Gorshkov, 1983). Much of these data provide a basis for assessing changes in the Arctic Ocean that have been taking place since the early 20th century. More recent Arctic Ocean exploration by western nations was carried out with a series of ice camps from the 1960s through the 1980s (*see* **Drifting Stations**).

Not until 1987 did a surface research vessel, the German icebreaker *Polarstern*, exceed the farthest north point in the *Fram* drift path, and then by only a few miles. This was the first transect of an Arctic Ocean Basin by a ship using modern instruments and sampling techniques to carry out such a transect. The next such survey took place in 1991 on board the Swedish icebreaker *Oden*, which together with *Polarstern* conducted a similar survey in the central Arctic Ocean. On September 7, 1991, the *Oden* and *Polarstern* became the

first fully dedicated research vessels to reach the North Pole. The expedition proved the feasibility of carrying out modern oceanographic surveys throughout most of the Arctic Basin in spite of the difficulties presented by the perennial ice cover, and to obtain data in previously sparsely sampled regions of the Arctic Ocean. Since then, several icebreaker and submarine expeditions have traversed many of the key regions of the Arctic Ocean, carrying out sonar mapping, geophysical surveys (e.g., gravity, magnetic), temperature and salinity measurements, radionuclide and chemical tracer studies, and water sampling of biological constituents. Data on concentration and dispersal of nutrients, chlorophyll, dissolved oxygen, dissolved organic carbon, and on the movement of chemical tracers (pollutants or naturally occurring) help determine carbon budget, water circulation time scales, tracer transport processes, and current levels of persistent pollutants. Many of these expeditions have been carried out under the umbrella of international organizations like the World Meteorological Organization, the Arctic Ocean Sciences Board, and the International Arctic Polynya Program (IAPP). One project particularly relevant to the Arctic Ocean is the Arctic

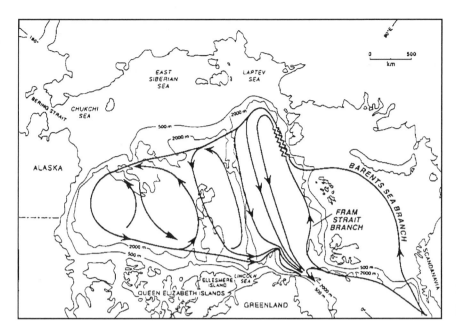

Figure 2: Mean circulation of the Atlantic Layer and Upper Polar Deep Water.

Climate System Study (ACSYS). In addition, there are many primarily national programs such as the Scientific Ice Expeditions (SCICEX), which explored the Arctic Ocean with US Navy submarines, Surface Heat Budget of the Arctic Ocean (SHEBA), Study of Environmental Arctic Change (SEARCH), Shelf Basin Interactions (SBI), and Joint Ocean Ice Studies (JOIS). All these have extensive websites that describe their work and results, and have links to many other relevant websites (*see* **Oceanography: Research Programs**).

Waters in the Arctic Ocean

The Arctic Ocean is not a homogeneous body of water. Ocean currents flow into the Arctic Ocean carrying water from the North Atlantic and Pacific oceans. Within the Arctic Ocean basins, currents carry, distribute, and mix waters from these and other sources, such as rivers and sea ice meltwater, with the result that water at different areas and different depths will have diverse properties. Throughout most of its volume, the

Arctic Ocean is stratified into somewhat arbitrarily defined layers that can be fairly well described by salinity and temperature (see Table 1). At the surface, there is a Polar Mixed Layer that contains water from both the Atlantic and Pacific oceans and from rivers. Beneath this layer are the halocline (water with a strong gradient in salinity and density) and the relatively warm Atlantic Layer. Intermediate-depth water, sometimes called Upper Polar Deep Water, is mostly of Atlantic origin coming from the Norwegian and Barents seas, as do the contributions to the deep and bottom water (*see* **Arctic Ocean; Cold Halocline; &Atlantic Layer**). In addition to salinity and temperature, there are several naturally occurring chemical constituents in unique combinations (e.g., nutrients, oxygen) that help to characterize or "fingerprint" specific water masses so that it then becomes possible to determine their sources and to trace their circulation. Anthropogenic (or man-made) materials (e.g., chlorofluorocarbons, radioactive tritium, and carbon-14 from bomb tests), which were introduced into the global

TABLE 1. Characteristics of Water in the Arctic Ocean

Water mass	Depth range (m)	Salinity*	Temperature	Residence time (years)
Polar Mixed Layer	0–50	30–33	Near −1.8°C	5–10
Halocline				
Upper Halocline	50–130	Near 33.1	Near −1.6°C	5–15
Lower Halocline	20–200	Near 34.2	Near −1.2°C	5–15
Atlantic Layer	200–600	34.8–34.95	0–3°C	Up to 25
Upper Polar Deep Water	600–1700	Near 34.9	0–0.5°C	20–40
Deep Water				
Eurasian Basin	1700–4400	34.92	−0.94°C	50–150
Canadian Basin	1700–4000	34.94	−0.5°C	Roughly 700

*Salinity is the ratio of the measured conductivity of sea water compared to a conductivity standard. The numerical values correspond closely to the salt content in parts per thousand.

environment including the ocean during the 20th century, provide information on how long it takes for water to move from one place to another or how long it takes for water in a deep basin to be renewed. Naturally produced radioactive carbon-14 helps to characterize older water. The times for water to traverse the upper half of the Arctic Ocean range from a few years up to a few decades. Deeper waters take from 100 to about 1000 years to be renewed.

About 75% of the water in the Arctic Ocean originates in the North Atlantic. Atlantic water enters through the Barents Sea (typically 200–300 m deep) and through Fram Strait (2500 m deep) between Greenland and Svalbard. This inflowing water provides a substantial portion of upper waters (Rudels et al., 1996) and almost all of the mid-depth (Rudels et al., 1994) and deep waters (Jones et al., 1995) (*see* **Arctic Ocean; Cold Halocline; Atlantic Layer**). Most of the rest of the water in the Arctic Ocean originating in the North Pacific enters through the narrow (80 km wide) and shallow (50 m deep) Bering Strait, and is largely confined to the upper layers in the Canadian Basin. While constituting a small fraction of all water entering the Arctic Ocean, large rivers, mostly from Siberia, introduce fresh water that strongly influences the properties of the near-surface waters and processes that occur within them. Water exits to the North Atlantic Ocean through Fram Strait and through the Canadian Arctic Archipelago and Baffin Bay. (Figure 7 of the Arctic Ocean entry shows these intermediate and deep circulations in map form, while Figure 2 of that entry shows freshwater fluxes into the Arctic Basin from major rivers.)

Ice formation in the Barents and Chukchi sea shelves is a major process in the formation and modification of the deeper waters of the Arctic Ocean. Brine excluded from ice as it forms produces dense water. This dense water flows along the bottom to the shelf edge, triggering shelf plumes, which then sink and entrain water as they flow off the continental shelf. These plumes carry some surface water and water from the warm Atlantic Layer into deeper regions of the Canadian Basin, making the deep water warmer and slightly fresher than it would otherwise be (Jones et al., 1995).

The Eurasian Basin Deep Water is slightly colder and fresher than the Canadian Basin Deep Water. These differences are small, but puzzling, because the major source of the Canadian Basin Water is presumed to be colder water from the Eurasian Basin overflowing the Lomonosov Ridge. An explanation again lies in the shelf plumes. In the Eurasian Basin, shelf plumes enter the Arctic Ocean via deep canyons, such as the St Anna Trough, at depths great enough to bypass the Atlantic Layer as they sink to depth. In contrast, the Canadian Basin continental shelves are generally shallower than those of the Eurasian Basin. Shelf plumes dense enough to reach deep waters in the Canadian Basin would have to pass through the warm Atlantic Layer, entraining warmer water and carrying heat to the deep water.

The Arctic Ocean and Global Climate

Until near the end of the last century, the Arctic Ocean was perceived as a quiet, steady-state ocean. Recently, a very different picture has emerged. The most dramatic of the observed changes has been the increased temperature of the Atlantic Layer (e.g., Quadfasel et al., 1991; Carmack et al., 1995; Morison et al., 1998). In 1990, Atlantic Layer temperatures in the Eurasian Basin were observed to be about 1°C warmer than those reported earlier. In 1993, warm Atlantic Layer water was observed in the Canadian Basin over the Mendeleyev Ridge, far removed from the earlier boundary between the warmer and colder parts of the Atlantic Layer. The warmer Atlantic Layer water, however, has not been observed in all parts of the Arctic Ocean near the Lomonosov Ridge. In the Canada Basin north of Alaska, the temperature, salinity, and density were almost identical in 1985 and 1997, and are consistent with the few earlier measurements in the region. It is expected that the warmer water in the Atlantic Layer will eventually make its way around the Arctic Ocean following the circulation pattern of Figure 2.

During this same period when warming of the Atlantic Layer was observed, there was also a redistribution of waters in the surface layer and halocline (McLaughlin et al., 1996; Newton and Sotirin, 1997; Smith et al., 1999) as well as changes in ice drift (Rigor et al., 2002). These changes correlate with changes in average wind fields (Swift et al., 1997), and models that calculate the effect of wind fields on ice drift seem to be consistent with these observations. Coincident with these changes in the water were significant changes in ice thickness observed at some locations (Rothrock et al., 1999). Some models suggest that changes in ice thickness may be mostly a result of changing wind fields rather than a loss of ice from increased melting.

In the context of global climate change associated with the increase of greenhouse gases (such as carbon dioxide) in the atmosphere, it is an open question whether the observed changes in the Arctic Ocean are part of a trend, perhaps associated with the predicted climate change. Generally, the circulation in the Arctic Ocean seems to be strongly influenced by basin structure, and this has not changed. Evidence from the extensive surveys carried out by the former Soviet Union indicates that similar changes have occurred in the past . There is an indication that ice drift may be returning to previous pathways (Rigor et al., 2002). Climate processes are driven in the first instance by heat and its transport throughout the globe. In a global perspective, the atmosphere and the ocean take up solar energy largely in the tropics, with lesser amounts being captured in temperate regions. By contrast, Arctic regions receive very little solar energy directly. Nevertheless, most climate change models predict larger temperature changes in Polar Regions than elsewhere. While fairly substantial changes have been observed in the Arctic Ocean, it is premature to conclude that these are the changes predicted by models.

A natural question is whether changes in the Arctic Ocean can have global change implications. Changes in the freshwater flow from the Arctic Ocean may have significant consequences for the climate and life on Earth. At the least, it could result in a cooling in northern regions if the thermohaline circulation in the North Atlantic Ocean is weakened (Aagaard and Carmack, 1989). More calamitous is the postulation that, in the past, changes in the thermohaline circulation, or a shutdown of the Global Conveyor Belt, may have been the cause of ice ages. We need to improve our ability to predict, with far greater certainty, the magnitude of such effects and the probability of their occurrence within a given time scale. Identifying where source waters come from and how they flow in Arctic regions is essential so that heat transport and freshwater budgets can be appropriately represented in models that describe global thermohaline circulation. Such models are vital to describing climate and predicting climate change.

E.P. JONES

See also **Arctic Ocean; Atlantic Layer; Climate: Research Programs; Cold Halocline; Marine Biology; North Atlantic Drift; Oceanography: Research Programs; Submarines in Arctic Exploration; Thermohaline Circulation**

Further Reading

Aagaard, K. & E.C. Carmack, "The role of sea ice and other freshwater in the Arctic circulation." *Journal of Geophysical Research,* 94 (1989): 14485–14498

Anderson, L.G., E.P. Jones & B. Rudels, "Ventilation of the Arctic Ocean estimated by a plume entrainment model constrained by CFCs." *Journal of Geophysical Research,* 104 (1999): 13423–13429

Broecker, W.S., "Chaotic climate." *Scientific American,* 273(5) (1995): 62–69

Carmack, E.C., R.W. Macdonald, R.G. Perkin, F.A. McLaughlin & R.J. Pearson, "Evidence for warming of Atlantic water in the southern Canadian Basin of the Arctic Ocean: results from the Larsen-93 expedition." *Geophysical Research Letters,* 22 (1995): 1061–1064

Gorshkov, S.G., *World Ocean Atlas,* Volume 3, Oxford: Pergamon Press, 1983

Jones, E.P., B. Rudels & L.G. Anderson, "Deep waters of the Arctic Ocean: origins and circulation." *Deep-Sea Research* 42 (1995): 737–760

McLaughlin, F., E.C. Carmack, R.W. Macdonald & J.K.B. Bishop, "Physical and geochemical properties across the Atlantic/Pacific water mass front in the southern Canadian Basin." *Journal of Geophysical Research,* 101 (1996): 1183–1197

Morison, J., M. Steele & R. Andersen, "Hydrography of the upper Arctic Ocean measured from the nuclear submarine U.S.S. *Pargo.*" *Deep-Sea Research,* 45 (1998): 15–38

Nansen, F., *Farthest North,* Volume 1 and 2, London: George Newnes, 1902

Newton, J.L. & B.J. Sotirin, "Boundary undercurrent and water mass changes in the Lincoln Sea." *Journal of Geophysical Research* 102 (1997): 3393–3403

Quadfasel, D., A. Sy, D. Wells & A. Tunik, "Warming in the Arctic." *Nature,* 350 (1991): 385

Rigor, I., J.M. Wallace & R. Colony, "Response of sea ice to the Arctic Oscillation." *Journal of Climate,* 15 (2002): 2648–2663

Rothrock, D.A., Y. Yu & G.A. Maykut, "Thinning of the Arctic sea-ice Cover." *Geophysical Research Letters,* 26 (1999): 3469–3472

Rudels, B., E.P. Jones, L.G. Anderson & G. Kattner, "On the intermediate Depth Waters of the Arctic Ocean." In *The Role of Polar Oceans in Shaping the Global Climate,* edited by O. M. Johannessen et al., Washington: American Geophysical Union, 1994, pp. 33–46

Rudels, B., L.G. Anderson & E.P. Jones, "Formation and evolution of the surface mixed layer and halocline of the Arctic Ocean." *Journal of Geophysical Research* 101 (1996): 8807–8821

Smith, J.N., K.M. Ellis & T. Boyd, "Circulation features in the central Arctic Ocean revealed by nuclear fuel reprocessing tracers from Scientific Ice Expeditions 1995 and 1996." *Journal of Geophysical Research* 104 (1999) 29663–29677

Swift, J.H., E.P. Jones, K. Aagaard, E.C. Carmack, M. Hingston, R.W. Macdonald, F.A. McLaughlin & R.G. Perkin "Waters of the Makarov and Canada basins." *Deep-Sea Research* 44 (1997): 1503–1529

OCEANOGRAPHY: RESEARCH PROGRAMS

The Arctic Ocean has been noted for its sensitive responses in relation to global climate change. There have been some critical environmental changes in recent decades in the Arctic Ocean such as significant reductions in sea ice extent (Parkinson et al., 1999) and a 43% reduction in average sea ice thickness (Rothrock et al., 1999). These substantial impacts on the Arctic Ocean environment may be the result of rapid change in the Arctic climate, possibly due to global warming. In order to understand the mechanisms controlling recent environmental changes in the Arctic Ocean and also the feedback effects within the Arctic Ocean ecosystem, a number of national and international research programs have been carried out based on field observations and simulation models. Major research programs relating to the Arctic Ocean environment, both previous and ongoing, are summarized below.

Arctic System Science Program (ARCSS) (http://www.nsf.gov/od/opp/arctic/system.htm)

ARCSS is a formal program in the Arctic Section of the National Science Foundation's (NSF) Office of Polar Program (OPP). Growing concern about the Arctic system's sensitivity to global change plus recognition of the Arctic as an agent of such change led to the creation of ARCSS in 1988. The ARCSS program is an interdisciplinary program, whose goal is (1) to understand the physical, geological, chemical, biological, and sociocultural processes of the Arctic system in the entire Earth system related to global change, and (2) to advance the scientific basis for predicting environmental change in a seasonal-to-centuries time scale, and for formulating policy options in response to the anticipated impacts of global change on humans and societal support systems.

Ocean-Atmosphere-Ice Interactions (OAII) (http://arcss-oaii.hpl.umces.edu/)

Ocean-Atmosphere-Ice Interactions (OAII) was established as a major ARCSS component in 1991 (Moritz et al., 1992). Near-term OAII activities will focus on the Surface Heat Budget of the Arctic Ocean (SHEBA), Shelf-Basin Interactions (SBI), and the Study of Environmental Arctic Change (SEARCH) projects, which grew into a multi-agency and international program. The following projects have been implemented under the ARCSS/OAII program.

Northeast Water Polynya Study (NEW), 1991–1995

The NEW experiment, part of the International Arctic Polynya Programme, examined a polynya located on the continental shelf off Northeast Greenland. This seasonally open water area is embedded in a high-latitude (~80° N) ice-covered unusually productive ecosystem, where opening of the ice pack by wind enhances phytoplankton productivity in spring. The focus of this project was improving predictions of how biological conditions and carbon cycling would change if warming increased the amount of open water at such high northern latitudes. In addition to the OAII, this project was supported by Canada, Germany, Denmark, and Greenland, and the research platforms included the US Coast Guard's icebreaker *Polar Sea* and Germany's *Polarstern* icebreaker research vessel. Data were successfully recovered from four moorings and provided the first suite of year-round oceanographic observations from the NEW polynya. The results suggested that high-latitude marine ecosystems are an efficient sink for atmospheric carbon dioxide (Yager et al., 1995), and that a low abundance of herbivorous zooplankton can be attributed to low advection of zooplankton onto the shelf in the polynya (e.g., Ashjian et al., 1997).

Investigations of the Western Arctic (IWA), 1992–1995

IWA was also known initially as the Western Arctic Moorings (WAM) experiment. As part of this project, an international effort to continue the monitoring of water transport through Bering Strait and Barrow Canyon regions was implemented. The results have helped to document the changes in the Bering Strait inflow to the Arctic Ocean, showing a remarkable freshening and warming of this inflow in recent years (Aagaard et al., 1999; Roach et al., 2000). For example, maximum salinities in the inflow have decreased by ~1.5‰. IWA also provided new information on the formation and transport of halocline waters formed in the Northeast Chukchi Sea (Weingartner et al., 1998) and on the flux and dispersal of fresh water carried onto this shelf in the Siberian Coastal Current (Weingartner et al., 1999). Several expeditions to the Bering/Chukchi/Beaufort region were also supported under the IWA program.

Arctic Ocean Section (AOS), 1994–1997

The AOS project was a bilateral US-Canadian effort that produced the first comprehensive treatment of the properties of the Canada Basin (including pollutants and the food chain). It also helped to document the major changes in the hydrography of the Arctic Ocean that have occurred in recent years. The AOS results suggested that many previous estimates of the biological productivity of the polar basin were too low, partly because of insufficient recognition of the role of ice algae (Gosselin et al., 1997). This project was comprehensive and included observations on geological structure, biogeochemical cycling, the Canada Basin sediments, tracer chemistry, biogeochemical cycling, and the microbial food chain. Many of the results are reviewed in a special issue of *Deep-Sea Research* (Wheeler, 1997).

Surface Heat Budget of the Arctic Ocean (SHEBA), 1995–2003 (http://sheba.apl.washington.edu)

SHEBA is a coordinated project to investigate the role of Arctic climate in global change. The primary goals of SHEBA are (1) to determine the ocean-ice-atmosphere processes that control the surface albedo and cloud-radiation feedback mechanisms over Arctic pack ice, and to use this information to demonstrably improve models of Arctic-ocean-atmosphere-ice interactive processes, and (2) to develop and implement models that improve the simulation of the present variability, utilizing coupled global climate models. The key processes include processes in the sea ice and upper ocean and Arctic cloud processes. The SHEBA fieldwork with a year-long observation from a frozen-in icebreaker as an operations base—the first such scientific frenzy-in for more than a century—helped to foster truly interdisciplinary activities. The thinning of the ice cover in the Arctic was reported during this experiment (e.g., Rothrock et al., 1999).

Western Arctic Shelf-Basin Interactions (SBI), 1999–2007 (http://utk-biogw.bio.utk.edu/SBI.nsf)

The fundamental goal of the SBI project is to understand the physical and biogeochemical link between the Arctic shelves, slope, and deep basins that could be influenced by global change. The initial focus of the SBI project is the western Arctic Ocean, particularly where the North Pacific waters are modified by shelf processes that exert significant influences on the biology and physics of the Arctic Ocean. Changes in either the balance of shelf processes that modify the Pacific waters, or in the slope processes that control exchange with the deep basin, will likely result in major alterations of the Arctic marine environment. The study area of the SBI project will be the outer shelf and continental slope area of the Chukchi/Beaufort seas. In addition to SBI mooring network, multidisciplinary survey and process studies are conducted across the shelf and slope regions during various fieldwork seasons (Phase I: 1998–2001; Phase II: 2002–2006).

Study of Environmental Arctic Change (SEARCH), 2000– (http://psc.apl.washington.edu/search/index.html and http://www.unaami.noaa.gov/)

SEARCH has been conceived as a broad, interdisciplinary, multiscale program with the core aim of understanding the complex of intertwined pan-Arctic changes occurring across terrestrial, oceanic, atmospheric, and human systems, the suite of recent and ongoing changes that is named *Unaami* (the Yup'ik word for "tomorrow"). Activities undertaken as part of SEARCH are guided by a series of hypotheses such as: (1) Unaami is related to or involves the Arctic Oscillation. (2) Unaami is a component of climate change. (3) Feedback among the ocean, the land, and the atmosphere are critical to Unaami. (4) The physical changes of Unaami have large impacts on the Arctic ecosystems and society. Various components of the SEARCH program are at different stages of readiness. Many of the long-term physical observations, for example, can be started immediately. Much of the application component has yet to be developed.

Arctic Climate System Study (ACSYS) (http://acsys.npolar.no/)

ACSYS was organized under the auspices of the World Climate Research Program (WCRP). The scientific goal of ACSYS is to investigate the role of the Arctic in global climate change by attempting to find answers to the following related questions: (1) What are the global consequences of natural or man-made change in the Arctic Climate system? (2) Is the Arctic climate system as sensitive to increased greenhouse gases as climate models suggest? ACSYS comprises the following six programs: (1) Arctic Ocean Circulation Program (including The Arctic Ocean Hydrographic Survey, The Arctic Ocean Shelf Studies, The Arctic Ocean Variability Project, The Historical Arctic Ocean Climate Database Project), (2) Arctic Sea Ice Program, (3) Arctic Atmosphere Program, (4) Hydrological Cycle in the Arctic Region, (5) ACSYS Modeling Program, and (6) Data Management and Information Panel (DMIP).

Arctic Environmental Observatory (AEO) (http://arctic.bio.utk.edu/AEO/index.html)

The aim of the project is to establish an onshore environmental observatory at Diomede Village, Alaska. The strategic location of this observatory on Little Diomede Island in the center of the Bering Strait will permit rapid, flexible collection of chemical, biological, and physical data on the transport of nutrient- and organic-rich waters of north Pacific origin into the Arctic Ocean through this narrow strait. The water sampling equipment was installed during the summer of 2000. Salinity, temperature, nitrate, nitrite, phosphate, and fluorometric proxies (chlorophyll *a*) of Bering Strait water will be measured continuously on a year-round basis.

Canadian Arctic Shelf Exchange Study (CASES) (http://www.cases.quebec-ocean.ulaval.ca/vessel.asp)

The main objective of CASES is to understand and model the response of biogeochemical and ecological cycles to atmospheric, oceanic, and continental forcing of sea-ice cover variability on the Mackenzie Shelf. The aim of the CASES field program is to study the fall and winter preconditioning of the Mackenzie Shelf/Amundsen Gulf ecosystem by the minimum fall and winter discharge of the Mackenzie River, and its spring and summer development in response to the intense freshet and the variable ice breakup. The field program (2002–2004) will provide a three-year interannual comparison of ecosystem maturation according to sea-ice cover variability and, for the first time ever, a year-round, highly integrated interdisciplinary research of an Arctic shelf ecosystem. The CASES network brings together investigators from 11 countries.

Climate of the Arctic: Modeling and Processes (CAMP)

CAMP has two main objectives, which are (1) to produce demonstrable improvements in simulations of Arctic climate by coupled models, and (2) to support the Arctic Climate Impact Assessment (ACIA) through state-of-the art scenario information on 21st-century Arctic climate. While CAMP involves global climate models in its activities, especially its support of ACIA, it also includes an Arctic Ocean Model Intercomparison Project (AOMIP) and an Arctic Regional Climate Model Intercomparison Project (ARCMIP). The CAMP modeling effort requires the best data input possible, based on both observations and data assembly. The lack of observational data places a major constraint on the ability to understand and model the processes involved. Thus, an observational project (Nansen and Amundsen Basins Observational System (NABOS)) has been undertaken as one of the CAMP-supporting projects based at the International Arctic Research Center (IARC), University of Alaska Fairbanks. The first few moorings were deployed in the Laptev Sea during 2002.

European Subpolar Ocean Programme (ESOP 2)

The goal of ESOP-2 (1996–1999) was to understand the thermohaline circulation in the Greenland Sea, its sensitivity, and impact on global ocean circulation, building on novel experimental techniques, modeling, and experience gained under ESOP-1 (1993–1996). Deepwater formation in the Nordic Seas drives the global "conveyorbelt," which is recognized to be relevant to climate and climate change. The program, a consortium of scientists from 21 laboratories in eight European countries, had the following specific objectives: (1) to understand the oceanic thermohaline circulation on meso and large scales and its dependence on surface fluxes of heat, fresh water, and momentum; (2) to follow the fate of newly formed waters as they flow into the Norwegian Sea, the Iceland Sea, and over the Denmark Strait, and their contribution to the global ocean circulation; (3) to study freshwater fluxes into and out of the central Greenland Sea region; (4) to evaluate the role of convection area in ocean-atmosphere gas exchange; and (5) to investigate the role of thermohaline circulation in Carbon dioxide transport.

Frontier (Observational) Research System for Global Change/International Arctic Research Center (http://www.frontier.iarc.uaf.edu/)

The Frontier (Observational) Research System for Global Change (FORSGC) located at the International Arctic Research Center at the University of Alaska, Fairbanks, was established in 1997 in order to elucidate the global-Arctic feedback mechanism and predict the impact of global climate change on the Arctic region. The research program is a collaboration with the Japan Marine Science and Technology Center (JAMSTEC). Frontier is comprised of two primary research groups: the Atmosphere-Ocean-Ice modeling group and the Multi-Disciplinary group (or observational biogeochemistry group). The goal of this program is to detect Arctic climate change and variability, understand basic mechanisms and feedbacks related to Arctic climate, investigate Arctic climate and regional climate models in the context of the global climate system, and understand basic biogeochemical processes that affect the Arctic.

International Arctic Buoy Program (IABP) (http://iabp.apl.Washington.edu/)

The objective of IABP is to establish and maintain a network of drifting buoys in the Arctic Ocean to provide meteorological and oceanographic data for real-time operational requirements and research purposes, including support to the World Climate Research Program (WCRP) and the World Weather Watch (WWW) Program. IABP maintains a network of automatic data buoys in the Arctic Basin, which monitor synoptic-scale fields of pressure, temperature, and ice motion. The operational area of the IABP includes the central Arctic Basin and its marginal seas, excluding the economic zone except where agreement of the coastal state has been obtained. A variety of maps and reports by season, and by year, are available from the IABP website. IABP buoy data are distributed in real time on Global Telecommunication System (GTS) circuits using the World Meteorological Organization (WMO) buoy format following the GTS headers.

International North Water Polynya Study (NOW) (http://www.fsg.ulaval.ca/giroq/now/)

Funded by the Natural Sciences and Engineering Research Council of Canada as part of the International Arctic Polynya Programme of the Arctic Ocean Science Board, the NOW programme selected the North Water polynya for fieldwork in 1997–1999. The North Water polynya, which forms each winter at the north end of Baffin Bay between Greenland and Ellesmere Island, is the largest Arctic polynya (about 150×80 km). The study aimed to address (1) the generation of the polynya, (2) the ecosystem of the polynya, and (3) the role of the polynya in the carbon dioxide flux.

Laptev Sea System 2000 (http://www.awipotsdam.de/www-pot/geo/laptev2000.html)

The Laptev Sea System (1994–1997) Russian-German project provided multidisciplinary synoptic studies of the entire Siberian Sea system. Detailed climatic reconstructions of the late Quaternary and important information concerning the complex modern system were obtained and form the basis for Arctic climate system models and the prediction of future climate changes. The Laptev Sea System 2000 project was supported by the Alfred Wegener Institute for Polar and Marine Research in Bremerhaven, Germany, the GEOMAR Research Center for the Marine Geosciences in Kiel, and the Arctic and Antarctic Research Institute in St Petersburg, Russia. Three terrestrial expeditions to the Lena Delta and the coastal region of the Laptev Sea were carried out from 1998 to 2000, to study seasonal changes in submarine permafrost, effects of environmental changes, terrestrial/marine interactions in coastal zones, and causes and impacts of climatic trends in the central Siberian Arctic.

North Pole Environmental Observatory (NPEO) (http://psc.apl.Washington.edu/northpole/index.html)

NPEO was established in 2000 to provide the types of long-term, multi-faceted research observations that are needed to understand how the Arctic is changing. More than a single installation, the NPEO includes a drifting observatory that is unmanned for most of the year, providing year-round automated data collection, a deep-sea instrument mooring that remains anchored to the seafloor near the North Pole at a depth of 4000 m and stretching to within 50 m of the surface, and yearly aerial surveys. Each spring, a group of buoys is deployed on drifting ice near the pole, and continuously records ocean, ice, and atmospheric variables such as water temperature and salinity, ice thickness, and solar radiation. Data are telemetered via satellite.

Russian American Initiative on Shelf-Land Environments in the Arctic (RAISE) (http://arctic.bio.utk.edu/RAISE/index.html)

RAISE is focused on the Russian Eurasian Arctic, where the world's largest continental shelves may play a key role in influencing the scope of global warming and other environmental changes on regional and global scales. The objective of this program, supported by the US National Science Foundation, Arctic System Science Program, and the Russian Foundation for Basic Research, is to facilitate collaborative research between Russian and American scientists in order to understand processes and events in terrestrial, shelf, and ocean environments in northern Eurasia in the context of a globally changing environment. RAISE participates in the international Arctic Science Committee's efforts to improve bilateral, international research in the Russian Arctic through its International Scientific Initiative in the Russian Arctic (ISIRA).

Science Ice Expeditions (SCICEX) http://www.ldeo.columbia.edu/SCICEX/

In 1993, scientists from several academic institutions were invited to participate in a US Navy submarine cruise under the Arctic sea-ice aboard the USS *Pargo* to explore using a submarine as a platform for scientific observations. This mission was so successful that it was expanded into a five-year program called SCICEX, or Science Ice Expeditions (1995–1999). The six SCICEX cruises across the Arctic Ocean have provided valuable insights into the circulation of the Arctic Basin, the recent state and dynamics of the sea ice cover, the carbon cycles within the Arctic Ocean system, and the structure and origin of the Arctic bathymetric features. A complete list of the SCICEX projects, project summaries, and the tracks of each submarine cruise can be found at the SCICEX home page.

KYUNG-HOON SHIN

See also **Climate: Research Programs; Oceanography**

Further Reading

Aagaard, K., D. Darby, K. Falkner, G. Flato, J. Grebmeier, C. Measures & J. Walsh, *Marine Science in the Arctic: A Strategy,* Fairbanks: Arctic Research Consortium of the USA (ARCUS), 1999; available at http://www.arcus.org/Marine_Science/

Ashjian, C., S. Smith, F. Bignami, T. Hopkins & P. Lane, "Distribution of zooplankton in the Northeast Water Polynya during summer 1992." *Journal of Marine Systems,* 10 (1997): 279–298

Gosselin, P.M., M. Levasseur, P.A. Wheeler, R. A. Horner & B. C. Booth, "New measurements of phytoplankton and ice algal production in the Arctic Ocean." *Deep Sea Research,* 44 (1997): 1623–1644

Morison, J.H. et al., "North Pole Environmental Observatory delivers early results." *EOS* 83(33) (2002): 360–361

Moritz, R.E., K. Aagaard, D.J. Baker, D. Clark, L.A. Codispoti, W. O. Smith, R. C. Tipper, J. R. Toggweiler & J. E. Walsh, Arctic System Science, Ocean-Atmosphere-Ice Interaction: Report of a Workshop held at the UCLA Lake Arrowhead Conference Center, March 12–16, 1990. Washington, District of Columbia: 1992, Joint Oceanographic Institutions

OAII Steering Committee, "Investigating the Arctic marine environment during a period of rapid change development, accomplishments and outlook for OAII." *Arctic Research of the United States,* Volume 11, 2003; available at http://www.nsf.gov/pubs/2003/nsf03048/nsf03048_2.pdf

Parkinson, C., D. J. Cavalieri, P. Gloersen, H.J. Zwally & J.C. Comiso, "Arctic sea ice extents, area, and trends, 1978–1996." *Journal of Geophysical Research*, 104 (1999): 20837–20856

Roach, A. T., K. Aagaard & T. Weingartner, "Recent changes in Bering Strait." *EOS*, 80 (2000)

Rothrock, D. A., Y. Yu & G. A. Maykut, "Thinning of the arctic sea-ice cover." *Geophysical Research Letters*, 26 (1999):1–5

Weingartner, T. J., D. J. Cavalieri, K. Aagaard & Y. Sasaki, "Circulation, dense water formation and outflow on the northeast Chukchi Sea Shelf." *Journal of Geophysical Research* 103 (1998): 7647–7662

Weingartner, T. J., S. Danielson, Y. Sasaki, V. Pavlov & M. Kulakov, "The Siberian Coastal Current: A wind and buoyancy-forced arctic coastal current." *Journal of Geophysical Research* 104 (1999): 29697–29713

Wheeler, P. A., "Preface: the 1994 Arctic Ocean section." *Deep Sea Research*, 44(8), (1997): 1483–1485 (volume 44(8) was a special issue on the Arctic Ocean edited by P.A. Wheeler)

Yager, P., D.W.R. Wallace, K.M. Johnson, W.O. Smith, P.J. Minnett & J.W. Deming, "The Northeast Water Polyna as an atmospheric CO_2 sink: a seasonal rectification hypothesis." *Journal of Geophysical Research*, 100 (1995): 4389–4398

ODDSSON, DAVID

David (Davíð) Oddsson has served as the mayor of Reykjavík, Iceland, the chairperson of the right-wing Independence party, and the longest-serving prime minister of Iceland (since 1991). Oddsson's record of holding high office exceeds that of any other politician in Iceland.

Oddsson studied law at Háskóli Íslands (the University of Iceland) in Reykjavík, and worked part-time for the Reykjavík theater company (Leikfélag Reykjavíkur, 1970–1972). He was also one of three writers and performers in a comic radio show, *Útvarp Matthildur*, which was broadcast on the country's only radio station. Active in the right-wing student union, Vaka, Oddsson also worked as a reporter for Reykjavík's largest newspaper, the conservative *Morgunblaðið*. In 1974, while still a student, Oddsson was elected to the city council of Reykjavík.

Although by the 1970s Oddsson had officially entered politics, he continued his literary career for some years, writing plays for the theater and television. Years later, as Iceland's prime minister, he wrote another teleplay and published a collection of novels, called *Nokkrir góðir dagar án Guðnýjar* (A few good days without Guðný, 1997).

Oddsson served on the Reykjavik City Council from 1974 to 1982. In 1980, he emerged as leader of the Independence party in Reykjavík and succeeded in recapturing a majority in the city council two years later. This was partly due to divisions within the left-wing coalition, but the forceful opposition of the new minority leader must have also played a role. Elected the city's mayor in 1982, Oddsoon served in that

capacity with a measure of both controversy and success. He was criticized for expensive building projects, such as the large city council house built in the heart of Reykjavík and a restaurant in Öskjuhlíð called the Pearl (today a Reykjavík landmark). However, Reykjavík enjoyed prosperity and growth, with an ever larger part of the Icelandic population moving to the capital and its environs. Under Oddsson's tenure, the Independence party maintained a strong majority in two successive elections (1986 and 1990). The result in 1990 was especially convincing, as the Independence party managed to gain 60% of the vote, and 10 out of 15 city council members.

In 1991, Oddsson was elected to the Icelandic parliament for the first time, whereby he was able to form a coalition government. As mayor, Oddsson had enjoyed the comfort of ruling through a strong single-party majority, but in the realm of national politics Oddsson was equally effective, especially in attracting coalition partners.

As prime minister since 1991, Oddsson has followed an economic policy that is consistently neoliberal, although hardly dogmatic. His first coalition government (with the Social Democratic Party, 1991–1995) oversaw structural reforms in economic management. Although Iceland joined the European Economic Area (EEA) in 1994, Oddsson has remained a staunch opponent of Iceland joining the European Union. His later coalition government (with the Progressive Party, from 1995 onwards) oversaw the privatization of state companies, most significantly the state banks and telecommunications. Under the auspices of Oddsson, the state took measures to facilitate the creation of a stock market. The position of Iceland's Central Bank was strengthened as it gained greater autonomy in setting interest rates.

After some initial resistance, Oddsson became a popular prime minister. His second term as a prime minister coincided with a stronger and more diversified economy.

Biography

David Oddsson was born in Reykjavík, Iceland, on January 17, 1948. His father, Oddur Ólafsson (1914–1977), was a doctor; his mother, Ingibjörg Kristín Lúðvíksdóttir (born 1922), was a secretary. They were never married. Oddsson did not come from a family with political connections. He spent his early years in the village of Selfoss, near his grandfather, but moved to Reykjavík with his single mother at the age of five. He married Ástríður Thorarensen , a nurse, in 1970. They had one son. He graduated from Reykjavik College in Iceland, 1970, and earned a law degree from the University of Iceland, 1976. Oddsson was a member of Reykjavik City Council from 1974 to 1982; a member of the Executive Committee of Reykjavik City Council from 1980 to 1991; and its chairperson from 1982 to 1991. He was assistant director and director of the Board of Health (Sjúkrasamlag) in Reykjavík 1976–1982, and became the city's mayor from 1982 to 1991. A member of Parliament from April 1991, he was elected prime minister of Iceland in 1991, a position he still holds.

SVERRIR JAKOBSSON

See also **Reykjavík**

Further Reading

"David Oddsson, Icelands Eurosceptic leader." *The Economist*, April 12, 2001

Eiríkur Jónsson, *Davíð. Líf og saga. Beysi kemur í bæinn*, *Reykjavík*, 1989

ODULOK, TEKKI

Tekki Odulok is the pen name of Nikolay Ivanovich Spiridonov, the first Yukagir writer and scientist from the indigenous peoples of the Russian Arctic. In 1921, he joined the Young Communist League in Srednekolymsk. He went to study in Yakutsk, but he was taken prisoner by Russian White Guards en route. After 11 months of capture, he arrived at Yakutsk in 1924, where he studied in the Soviet and Communist Party school.

In 1925, Odulok joined the Communist Party and was directed to study at Leningrad University. There he studied under Waldemar Bogoras (Vladimir Germanovich Bogoraz), a well-known ethnographer and specialist in Northern studies. He took an active part in the Committee for Assistance to the Indigenous Peoples of the North (Committee for the North) at the Presidium of the All-Union Central Executive Committee. Odulok went to Kolyma and Chukotka as a member of the expedition of the Far Eastern State Trade Organization as ordered by the Committee for Assistance to the Indigenous Peoples of the North. There he collected ethnographic materials for his future work.

In 1931, Odulok graduated from the Ethnographic Department of Leningrad University and, as advised by Bogoraz, entered the postgraduate course of the Leningrad Institute of the Indigenous Peoples of the North. Then he went to Chukotka as a member of the Organizing Committee of the Far Eastern Regional Executive Committee in order to establish the Chukotka national region. There he lived among the Chukchi, was in Anadyr, the Providenie, and St Laurent bays, and other nomadic camps for seven months. He worked under the Committee's orders, conducting cultural and educational activities among aboriginal people.

In May 1934, Odulok completed his postgraduate course and defended his dissertation with the theme "Forms of exploitation of Yukagir people from 18th century till the October revolution." Subsequently in 1934–1936, Odulok worked as head of the Ayano-Maysky Regional Party Committee. Then he was appointed as director of the national section of the Khabarovsk Department of the Writer's Union.

In 1936, he returned to Leningrad to defend his thesis for a doctoral degree. According to Odulok's wife, Olga Nikolaevna, he completed his defense but the confirming documents were lost. In June 1936, he worked in the Detgiz (Children Publishing House) at the Leningrad Department of the Writer's Union.

In 1937, Odulok and nine other well-known researchers of the Institute of the North were arrested on charges of espionage in favor of Japan. On March 17, 1938, Odulok and the other defendants were shot as punishment for their guilty sentence. As victims of Josef Stalin's totalitarian repression, the ten were buried at a memorial cemetery. Odulok's reputation was not reinstated in Russia until 1955.

In his lifetime, Odulok published many scientific and literary works such as *Na Kraynem Severe* (In the Far North), *Oduly (Yukagiry) Kolymskogo okruga* (Odul (Yukagir) of Kolyma District), *Yukagirs*, and other articles in the periodical press.

In *Na Kraynem Severe*, he described his impressions of Kamchatka, Chukotka, and the Kolyma River, and told of the history of these lands and these peoples. Odulok wrote his best-known work *Zhizn Imteurgina-starshego* (The life of elder Imteurgin) during his travel in Chukotka. In this work, he told about Chukchi life in czarist Russia. The work was awarded a special prize as one of the best children's books of that year. The book was republished three times during the lifetime of the writer, and was published in foreign countries. *Zhizn Imteurgina-starshego* was published in English in London by the title *The Snowmen*. It was reissued several times in Prague in the Czech language and was also published in France.

Odulok drew attention in his writing to his native people, who were on the verge of extinction and whose number was only several hundred individuals by the beginning of the 20th century. He described the tragic fate of the Yukagir people, writing about their poverty. Odulok suggested introducing the Yukagirs to a settled life. To accomplish this, he suggested organizing state-farms (*sovkhoz*), reindeer-breeding collective farms (*kolkhoz*), developing new branches of the economy, and establishing cultural and educational centers with schools, first-aid stations, libraries, and the like to help aboriginal people establish profitable branches of the economy.

Odulok further advocated establishing reservations for indigenous peoples so that these people could integrate into the new lifestyle. He called for the establishment of the Yukagir-Chuvan national region for his people, and claimed the position of plenipotentiary in this region for himself. But indigenous reservations were not established, because the authorities decisively denied this measure.

Two weeks before his arrest in a meeting of workers of the Detgiz (Children's Publishing House) — jointly with writers and artists of Moscow and Leningrad and with members of the Central Committee of Leninist Young Communist League of the Soviet Union—Odulok spoke of the problems of survival of the Yukagir people, the decrease of their numbers, and their extinction. After his death, the problems of the survival of the Yukagir peoples were largely forgotten until the late 1980s during Mikhail Gorbachev's perestroika (reformation) and democratization of the Soviet Union. In 1996, the first Yukagir national school in Russia in the village of Nelemnoe of the Upper Kolyma District, Republic of Sakha, was named after Tekki Odulok.

Biography

Tekki Odulok (née Nikolay Ivanovich Spiridonov) was born on May 22, 1906 in the Yukagir nomadic camp of Ottur-Kuel (in the Republic of Sakha (Yakutia). His father, Atylyakhan Ipolun, was a poor Odul hunter of the Cholghorodie tribe, which is translated as "hare's people." Yukagir people of the Upper Kolyma call themselves *Odul*, which translates as "strong" or "mighty." Parents had to make their children work for other people in order not to die of hunger. When Odulok (Spiridonov) was eight, his parents sent him to work for a rich herder from Nelemnoe, who later sold the boy to a Russian merchant from the town of Srednekolymsk. Having noticed the youth's talent, the owner sent him to study in a church school, where Odulok learned to read and write. Upon his death in 1937, Olga Nikolaevna Spiridonova, Odulok's wife, was exiled to Nolinsk, Kirovsky Oblast'.

ANDREY KAZAEV

See also **Bogoraz, Vladimir Germanovich; Literature, Russian**

Further Reading

Odulok, N. *Vnimanie yukhagiram* [Attention for Yukagir], Soviet Yakutia, 1930–1933 pp. S.111–118
Odulok, Tekki, *Na Kraynem Severe* [In the Far North], Moscow, 1933
———, *Zhizn Imteurgina starshego* [Life of elder Imteurgin], Leningrad, 1934 as Snow People, London: Methuen & Co., 1934

OFFICE OF POLAR PROGRAMS, NATIONAL SCIENCE FOUNDATION

The National Science Foundation (NSF) is the United States' national funding organization for research in the physical and social sciences. The Office of Polar Programs (OPP) supports a wide range of research in the Arctic and Antarctic, grounded in NSF's understanding of the polar regions as a "natural laboratory" (NSF, 2001). The OPP was reorganized in 1995 into three units: the Antarctic Sciences Section, the Arctic Sciences Section, and the Polar Research Support Section.

The office's current priorities reside in three broad research areas: the earth and its systems (climate, land, water, flora, and fauna); geography (multidisciplinary studies designed to advance science and education); and science enabled by the polar setting. The OPP supports individual and group projects in the United States and with teams of American and international scholars. The office publishes two journals: the *Antarctic Journal of the United States* and *Arctic Research of the United States*.

Although the overarching priorities of the NSF have historically been in the physical sciences, research in the social sciences has been gradually gaining ground, and increasingly includes ethical considerations. This is reflected in the OPP, which supports work in anthropology, archaeology, economics, geography, linguistics, political science, psychology, sociology, and other disciplines. The NSF, OPP, and the Social Sciences and Humanities Research Council of Canada (SSHRC) jointly review proposals for research.

One of the most important initiatives of the OPP was an inquiry into research ethics, which involved collaboration between NSF and the Arctic Research Consortium of the United States (ARCUS). Building on the 1989 document *Agenda for Action*, the participants drafted a document outlining priorities and methodologies for Arctic Social Science, and a set of "Principles for the Conduct of Research in the Arctic" (NSF Arctic Social Sciences Program, 1999). A fundamental principle is that of ethical responsibility "toward the people of the North, their cultures, and the environment." The focus on ethically responsible conduct reflects a national and international trend; moreover, in recent years, members of many disciplines have been developing codes of conduct and statements of principles for ethical, culturally sensitive research.

The current OPP programs grew out of the 1984 Arctic Research and Policy Act aimed at improving research on the Arctic. The Office established the US Arctic Research Commission and the Interagency Arctic Research Policy Committee to develop and implement policy. There has been a revolution in research methodology in the past two decades. In place of the old pattern in which researchers descended on Arctic communities and left with artifacts and information, today's physical and social scientific research is conducted in close collaboration with Arctic residents and sometimes has considerable impact on Arctic policy and community projects and programs.

VALERIE ALIA

See also **Arctic Research Consortium of the United States (ARCUS); Arctic Research and Policy Act**

Further Reading

National Science Foundation Arctic Social Sciences Program, *Arctic Social Sciences: Opportunities in Arctic Research*, Fairbanks, Alaska: Arctic Research Consortium of the United States (ARCUS), 1999

Office of Polar Programs website: http://www.nsf.gov/od/opp/start.htm

OIL EXPLORATION

Oil production is significant to the Arctic economy: oil revenues comprise about 80% of Alaska's state revenue, while in Siberia's largest oil reserves of the Yamal-Nenets Autonomous Okrug, over one-quarter of the working population are employed in the oil and gas extraction and transportation industry.

Most parts of the world display conditions for the successful formation of accessible oil and gas. The Arctic is no exception. Onshore, Alaska, the Mackenzie Delta, northern Russia, the Yamal Peninsula, Sakha Republic (Yakutia), and Sakhalin Island all include sedimentary basins known to contain recoverable oil and gas. Offshore, known fields exist under the Beaufort Sea, in the Canadian Arctic Archipelago, east of Labrador, west of Greenland, and under the Barents Sea west of Novaya Zemlya (Gudmestad et al., 1999). Not surprisingly, exploration focused first on areas where production could be economic if oil or gas were to be found, and the more difficult areas were left till later. Interesting but completely unexplored prospects remain east of Svalbard, north of Siberia, off West Greenland, and in the Canadian Arctic.

Many of the aforementioned fields have been known for a long time. Native Americans used the natural oil seeps near Cape Simpson on the Arctic coast of Alaska, and in the Alaska Peninsula in the south. A field at Katalla on the Gulf of Alaska coast was dis-covered in 1902 and produced oil for 30 years. The explorer Ernest Leffingwell observed seeps in the sea cliffs on the north coast of Alaska in 1905. A large area of northern Alaska was designated as Naval Petroleum Reserve 4 in 1923, and extensive exploration followed (Roderick, 1997). In the 1960s, significant oil development occurred on the Kenai Peninsula and in Cook Inlet, and then in 1968, what turned out to be one of the largest fields in North America was discovered around Prudhoe Bay on the Arctic coast. Oil production in Alaska's North Slope peaked in 1988—ten years after it was opened for production—and has since declined. Production from Alaska's North Slope comprised 970,000 barrels per day in 2001.

The Arctic's natural environment is vulnerable to damage and pollution. The environment's biological productivity is low; it is therefore slow to restore itself after interference. A single truck driven across the tundra damages the vegetation, interferes with the thermal regime in the active layer that thaws each summer, and can initiate long-lasting rutting and water pooling, which in turn can alter drainage patterns and initiate secondary erosion. In contrast, the same truck driven across a tropical grassland again induces immediate damage, but biological processes soon repair the damage. Researchers and environmentalists stress that any human activity must be planned and implemented with extraordinary sensitivity.

Concern for environmental damage has been a major factor in Arctic petroleum developments in Alaska and Arctic Canada, and will remain so (*see* **Hydrocarbon Contamination** for a discussion of pollution caused by oil in the Arctic). Under the reign of the Soviet Union, the government suppressed environmental protest, except in a few extreme instances; however, in post-Soviet Russia, a robust awareness of the issues (and of the damage that was done in the past) exists. Environmental controversy often becomes part of a much broader argument between those who value economic development and employment, and those who value wildlife and untouched wilderness. Arguments over caribou herds in the Arctic National Wildlife Refuge (ANWR) and near oil fields of Alaska's North Slope are tinged by historical guilt about the destruction of the buffalo 150 years earlier, and the cultural survival of the Gwich'in communities that depend on the Porcupine caribou herd. Each side has tended to oversimplify and characterize unfairly the stance of the other, resulting in negative terms such as "boosters" or "tree-huggers." As a result, constructive dialogue has suffered. A further factor is that sections of the environmental movement are viscerally opposed to any use of petroleum whatsoever, and oppose any development on principle, while others use environmental arguments as weapons in broader

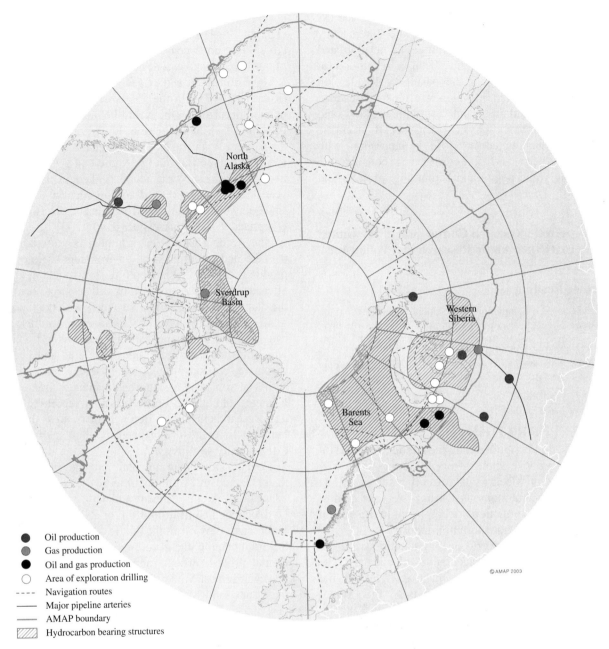

Oil production
Gas production
Oil and gas production
Area of exploration drilling
- - - - Navigation routes
——— Major pipeline arteries
——— AMAP boundary
Hydrocarbon bearing structures

Major areas of oil and gas development and potential development in the Arctic, and major shipping routes and possible new routes through Arctic waters. From *AMAP Assessment Report: Arctic Pollution Issues*, Arctic Monitoring and Assessment Programme, 1998. Reproduced with permission.

battles about capitalism and Native rights. Finally, the arguments are subject to shifts in fashion: environmentalists argued against the Rampart Dam on the ground that nuclear power was preferable, and against the Alaskan oil pipeline and for oil export by rail, on the ground that the pipeline would be temporary but a railroad would be permanent.

The discovery of the Prudhoe Bay fields in Alaska coincided with the growth of the power of the environmental movement, and many of the arguments crystallized around the export pipeline, and the possible alternatives of export by ship or by railroad.

Protest, litigation, and political argument seemed for a time likely to prevent the pipeline's construction altogether, but it finally won Congressional and State approval in the autumn of 1973. The political situation in the Middle East, the rising price of oil, and concern about the security of supply probably all contributed to the pipeline's passage. These types of arguments continue in the 21st century as regards oil exploration in the Arctic and elsewhere.

Construction of the pipeline from Prudhoe Bay to the port of Valdez went ahead, at a cost of eight billion dollars over a three-year period, and the line started

A pumping unit in the oil fields near Niznevartovsk, Khanty-Mansi Autonomous Okrug, Siberia.
Copyright Bryan and Cherry Alexander Photography

operation in June 1977 (Coates, 1991). Strict environmental and technical controls were imposed, and the industry came to concede that the line was better built than it would have been if the initial plan had been followed. On the other hand, the consensus opinions, fearing that the line would ruin Alaska, were very exaggerated, although a few remain irreconcilably opposed. From an early stage, some critics worried that marine transportation onward from Valdez might turn out to be the weak link, and their concerns were in part realized on March 24, 1989 when the tanker *Exxon Valdez* struck a reef in Prince William Sound and spilled 250,000 barrels, causing great damage to marine life.

Twenty-six trillion cubic feet (750 billion cubic meters) of gas remain locked in the Prudhoe Bay area, and recent rises in the gas price have prompted renewed discussion on how to export it. One option is a pipeline to a liquefied natural gas (LNG) plant south of the Bering Strait, from which the gas could be exported in LNG tankers such as those used elsewhere. One disadvantage of LNG, however, is that the processes of liquefaction and regasification consume nearly a third of the energy content. The leading gas pipeline schemes go south to the Fairbanks area, and thence along the Alaska Highway to Canada and the US, or alternatively offshore parallel to the coast as far as the Mackenzie Delta, and then up the Mackenzie Valley, tying in additional gas from the Delta and the Canadian Beaufort Sea, and perhaps also from the Canadian Arctic Islands, which has another 400 billion cubic meters. The choice of route remains extremely controversial.

Large petroleum-bearing sedimentary basins exist in northern Europe and Asia. The Russians have found large quantities of gas on the Yamal Peninsula in the Kara Sea and have built several large gas pipelines to bring the gas to Russian population centers and to export it into Europe. There is also gas offshore, notably the Shtockmannovskoye and Murmanskoye fields in the Barents Sea west of Novaya Zemlya (Gudmestad et al., 1999), oil onshore and offshore in several fields near the Pechora River (the Timan-Pechora province), oil further south in the Komi Republic and in Western Siberia in the Khanty-Mansi Autonomous Okrug, and huge but remote gas fields in the Sakha Republic.

Petroleum consists mostly of hydrocarbons, with small quantities of sulfur, oxygen, nitrogen, salt, and water that are removed during refining. Hydrocarbons range from light gases such as methane (the principal component of natural gas) to long-chain alkanes (such as paraffin) and ring molecules (such as benzene) that are liquids at ordinary temperatures. They are formed from marine organisms that were buried in sediments and subject to increasing heat and pressure as they became more deeply buried. Driven by density differences and by pressure, and over tens of millions of years, petroleum migrates from the source rock where it was formed through crevices and permeable rocks. Sometimes an overlying "cap" of impermeable rock prevents the petroleum from migrating further, and it remains in a reservoir that can be tapped by drilling. Gas rises to the top of the reservoir; below it lies the denser oil, and below that water. If no impermeable cap is present, the petroleum continues to rise up to the Earth's surface, where it creates a natural seep and is progressively lost to the atmosphere and to surface water.

The exploration, drilling, production, and transportation techniques applied onshore in the Arctic are essentially the same as those applied elsewhere, but there are some special problems. Permanently frozen soil (permafrost) extends downward, often for hundreds of meters, but an active layer at the surface thaws every summer. The frozen soil is hard, and can withstand almost any load, but the ground thaws if a surface structure alters the thermal regime, and the thawed soil is often weak and incapable of supporting loads. The first principle of construction on permafrost is to keep the ground frozen and this demands special measures such as insulated piles, open ventilated space under buildings, and active measures to suppress radiation and conduction from the base of buildings.

Permafrost influences drilling. Most petroleum reservoirs are several thousand meters below ground, below the base of the permafrost. Oil flowing up a well is hotter than the surrounding frozen soil, and heat conducted outward thaws a soil annulus around the well. The thawed soil is wet and mechanically weak, and tends to slump downward, dragging with it the steel casing that stabilizes the wellbore. In extreme cases, the casing buckles; insulated casing prevents this as does spacing the wells so that the thaw annuli around them cannot join up.

Offshore production in the Arctic must contend with sea ice. In the Canadian Arctic Archipelago, the continuous ice sheet is 2 m thick in late winter, and can include pressure ridges 30 m thick and drifting ice islands 50 m deep. These massive features exert huge forces on surface-piercing structures, and rule out the anchored floating production systems that applied with frequency in other areas.

Much research has been done to develop ice force models that can be applied confidently (see, e.g., Sanderson, 1988; Palmer and Sanderson, 1991; Dempsey et al., 2001), and to devise economic structures that can withstand the ice. The optimal solution in shallow water is an island built with gravel dredged from the seabed, and with its sides protected against wave and ice by riprap or concrete blocks. In deeper water, gravel islands are uneconomic because of the quantity of gravel required, and it is better to install a steel or concrete caisson platform, built in a protected dock, towed into position, and ballasted down onto a prepared gravel pad. In deeper water, the platform in turn becomes uneconomic. An alternative is to avoid the ice by building a self-contained and possibly robotic submerged system, founded on the seabed and not piercing the surface. These not-normally-manned seabed schemes pose formidable difficulties with supply, safety, reliability, maintenance, and transportation, and they will not be economically attractive until the price of petroleum rises far above its present level, in perhaps 50 years.

A second problem related to sea ice is that floating ice runs aground in shallow water, and drags along the bottom, driven by wind and current, cutting gouges that may be 5 m deep and 80 m wide (Woodworth-Lynas et al., 1996). The force that the ice applies to the bottom to create a gouge is immense; if instead it acted on a pipeline or a seabed wellhead, it would inflict severe damage. One solution is to trench and bury these systems in the seabed, to a depth well below the ice, although this is difficult and expensive over long distances. A further aspect is that the ice heavily deforms the seabed soil beneath it, so that a pipeline might be damaged even if it were set low enough for the ice to cross above it.

One new technology that will influence the shape of offshore oil and gas developments in the Arctic is extended-reach drilling, which makes it feasible to reach and produce from reservoirs at a substantial horizontal distance from the drilling site. The record horizontal distance is 10.7 km (nearly 7 miles), and there is no reason to suppose this as a physical limit. Extended-reach drilling makes it possible to access a large field from a single drilling site, sited at an optimal location to minimize environmental impact.

The petroleum resources of the Arctic exist if humankind wishes to exploit them. Many people believe that this can be done without unacceptable impact on the environment, and that when the resources are depleted the installations can be removed in a way that will leave no trace. Critics of oil exploration would not accept this view.

ANDREW PALMER

See also **Exxon Valdez; Gas Exploration; Hydrocarbon Contamination; Mackenzie Delta; North Slope; Pechora Basin; Prudhoe Bay; Trans-Alaska Pipeline; Yamal-Nenets Autonomous Okrug**

Further Reading

Coates, P.A., *The Trans-Alaska Pipeline Controversy,* Bethlehem, PA: Lehigh University Press, 1991

Dempsey, J.P., A.C. Palmer & D.S. Sodhi, "High pressure zone formation during compressive ice failure." *Engineering Fracture Mechanics*, 68 (2001): 1961–1974

Gudmestad, O.T., A.B. Zolotukhin, A.I. Ermakov, R.A. Jakobsen, I.T. Michtchenko, V.S. Vovk, S. Loeset & K.N. Shkhinek, *Basics of Offshore Petroleum Engineering and Development of Marine Facilities with Emphasis on the Arctic Offshore,* Moscow : Neft i gaz, 1999

Johnston, G.H., *Permafrost Engineering Design and Construction,* Toronto: John Wiley & Sons, 1981

Palmer, A.C. & T.J.O. Sanderson, "Fractal crushing of ice and brittle solids." *Proceedings of the Royal Society*, Series A, 433, (1991): 469–477

Roderick, J., *Crude Dreams,* Fairbanks, Alaska: Epicenter Press, 1997

Sanderson, T.J.O., *Ice Mechanics: Risks to Offshore Structures*, London: Graham, & Trotman, 1988

Tsytovich, N.A., *The Mechanics of Frozen Ground,* New York: McGraw-Hill, 1975

Woodworth-Lynas, C.M.L., J.D. Nixon, R. Phillips & A.C. Palmer, "Subgouge deformations and the security of Arctic marine pipelines." *Proceedings of the Twenty-Eighth Annual Offshore Technology Conference,* Volume 4, Houston, OTC8222 1996, pp. 657–664

OKALIK, PAUL

The first premier of the territory of Nunavut and one of only a few Inuit lawyers in Canada, Paul Okalik was chosen premier at the age of 34 in March 1999. In this position Okalik faced vast economic and social problems with a poise that surprised observers, considering his relative inexperience in politics.

Within Nunavut, alcoholism, drugs, lack of housing, domestic violence, and suicides rank above the national norm, while the employment rate is low and health facilities are in short supply compared to the rest of Canada. The territory depends upon the Canadian government for 90% of its revenues, and its social problems are among the most serious in Canada. Okalik has nonetheless managed to establish Nunavut as a unique jurisdiction in Canadian politics. He has enjoyed the support of his legislative colleagues in this endeavor, operating in a government-by-consensus manner that reflects Inuit culture, or *Inuit Qaujimajatuqangit* (traditional knowledge).

Eighty-five per cent of Nunavut's population of 26,000 are Inuit and this is reflected in the makeup of Okalik's cabinet, the majority of which is Inuit. Okalik has insisted upon decision-making that relies on true consensus among his colleagues. In selecting his cabinet, Okalik named Jack Anawak, his main competitor for the role of premier, to two of the most influential cabinet posts, Justice and Community Government, Housing and Transportation.

Despite the federal government's heavy financial influence upon Nunavut, Okalik lost little time after taking office in introducing measures that, although not usurping the powers of the senior level of government, did indicate the territory's desire to handle affairs in its own way. Among these measures was the signing of a cooperation agreement with the Home Rule government in Greenland in June 1999 and the establishment of a Law Reform Commission the same year. The agreement with Greenland calls for the two jurisdictions to work together on an ongoing basis on matters of mutual importance. The Law Reform Commission was enacted to ensure that Nunavut's laws reflect Inuit culture. In addition, Okalik made Inuktitut the working language of his cabinet.

In his first year as premier, Okalik and his cabinet drew up a 20-year plan for the territory, which they called the Bathurst Mandate. The plan was initiated at the cabinet's first retreat and was developed with input from organizations and individuals throughout the territory. The plan listed the government's immediate priorities, such as healthy communities, self-reliance, and improved education, and outlined a longer-term program calling for improved transportation and communication, affordable housing, a clean environment, and active participation in circumpolar affairs.

Another of Okalik's foremost priorities was the decentralization of government jobs out of the territorial capital, Iqaluit, and into ten other communities. However, the young Nunavut government has found this more difficult to implement than expected, mainly due to the difficulty of attracting qualified personnel to live in the smaller municipalities. Because of the lack of sufficient numbers of qualified, Inuit-born personnel, the new government has had to rely heavily on educated administrators from outside Nunavut, many of whom have been reluctant to work in the remote towns. The territorial government also faced competition for qualified personnel from both the federal government and Inuit organizations, many of which sprang up following the signing of the Nunavut Land Claims Agreement in 1993. This agreement led to Nunavut's independence as a territory separate from the Northwest Territories. Okalik's government also suffered an early setback over its unpopular decision to introduce one time zone for the far-flung territory to replace the three already in place. Residents in the western zone complained that the 2 h difference between their former time and the new one caused excessive disruption in their lives; therefore, after two years, Okalik ordered a reversion to the original three zones.

Nunavut possesses a host of mostly untapped natural resources, such as oil and gas and a broad range of minerals, and Okalik has shown an interest in their development. Along with his fellow northern premiers from the Northwest Territories and Yukon, he has attempted to convince the federal government to provide the territories with a larger share of the resource revenues. He has worked with the premiers of Canada's ten provinces, but his relations with the premiers of the other two territories have been closer than those with the provincial premiers due to the territories' subordinate status in the country's political hierarchy. To this end, the territorial premiers set up the northern leaders' forum to maintain good relations and increase their influence with the federal government.

Okalik and his government have also begun to exploit the possibilities for increased tourism in Nunavut. Currently curtailed by the high cost of transportation and services, the industry nevertheless is beginning to make its presence felt, and the premier has supported moves to see it flourish.

When federal Northern Affairs Minister Jane Stewart spoke at the inauguration of Nunavut in April 1999, she described Okalik as a man whose "strength of character, determination, personal skills and experience reflect the very nature and experience of the Inuit." One year later, John Amagoalik, one of the key proponents of the Nunavut Land Claims Agreement and a columnist for the Iqaluit-based weekly *Nunatsiaq News*, wrote: "The new government has been like a hunter on the floe edge, cautious of the ice he has been standing on" (Amagoalik, 2000: 11).

Biography

Paul Okalik was born on and raised in the Baffin Island hamlet of Pangnirtung on May 26, 1964. He began his education in Pangnirtung before moving to Iqaluit, now the capital of Nunavut, to attend high school. He briefly attended secondary school in Iqaluit, eventually obtaining a welder's certificate, and worked underground at the Nanisivik mine on Baffin Island for two years. He moved to Ottawa, the Canadian capital, in 1985 to join the Inuit Tapirisat of Canada as a researcher on the proposed Nunavut Land Claims Agreement. After returning to school in the 1990s, Okalik graduated from Carleton University, Ottawa, in 1993 with a bachelor of arts degree; four years later, he earned a law degree from the University of Ottawa. He was called to the bar in Iqaluit on February 12, 1999, and three days later he was elected to Nunavut's legislative assembly as a member for Iqaluit West. On March 5, 1999, he was chosen by his fellow legislators as Nunavut's first premier.

DAVE MULLINGTON

See also **Amagoalik, John; Nunavut**

Further Reading

Amagoalik, John, "My little corner of Canada." *Nunatsiaq News*, April 7, 2000, p. 10

Bourgeois, Annette, "Law grad Okalik never lost sight of dream." *Nunatsiaq News,* June 20, 1997

———, "Paul Okalik: first a lawyer, then an MLA." *Nunatsiaq News*, February 18, 1999

De Palma, Anthony, "In new land of Eskimos, a new chief offers hope.on." *The New York Times*, April 4, 1999

Duffy, Andrew, "Law school to give Inuit 'Tools to integrate change." *The Ottawa Citizen*, March 1, 2001

"First Canadians hold their ground." *The Economist*, London, July 24, 1999

McKibbon, Sean, "Okalik committed to decentralization, but not overnight." *Nunatsiaq News*, May 28, 1999

Okalik, Paul, "Premier Paul Okalik's sessional address: full text." *Nunatsiaq News*, May 21, 1999

Purvis, Andrew, "Nunavut gets ready." *Time Magazine*, March 29, 1999

Walker, Ruth, "A year later, 'our land' struggles." *Christian Science Monitor*, April 13, 2000

OKHOTSK, SEA OF

In 1639, Cossacks led by Ivan Moskvitin laid a course from Yakutsk across Siberia toward the east, "toward the Sun" to the mouth of the Okhota River. The sea into which the river fell was named "Okhotsky Sea," although to the Evenks, Even, and Yakuts it was known as *Lamu, Laamy, Namy,* or simply "the Sea."

This semienclosed marginal sea between the Russian coast, the Kamchatka Peninsula, Sakhalin Island, and the Kuril Islands opens to the Pacific Ocean. The Okhotsk Sea has a north-south length of 2445 km and an east-west length of 1407 km, an area of 1,583,000 km^2, an average depth of 777 m, and a maximum depth of 3846 m. Its large bays include Shelikhov Bay with Gizheinsky and Binzhinsky inlets, Tausky inlet on the northern coast at the northeast corner of the sea, Udsky inlet at the southwest corner of the sea, neighboring with the Tugursky, Ulbansky, Nikolayevsky gulfs, the Sakhalinsky Gulf and passing on to the Amursky estuary of Nevelsky (or Tartar) Strait, and at the southeastern corner of Sakhalin Island, the Aniva and Terpenia (Patience) gulfs. The Kuril Island arc on the southeast margin of the Sea of Okhotsk limits the exchange of matter and energy with the Pacific Ocean. From the northeast, the sea is isolated from the Pacific by the long Kamchatka Peninsula.

The coasts of the sea are mountainous in nearly all parts. There are numerous volcanoes, among them many active: 31 in the Kuril Islands and 19 in Kamchatka. The bottom relief of the Sea of Okhotsk is asymmetric. The northern part is mainly flat at about 200 m depth, sloping to the south. The southern part of the basin along a relatively narrow strip along the Kuril archipelago has deepwater areas reaching 3000 m. By the southwest shores, not far from the Shantarsky Islands and by northern and northeastern shores, the bottom relief is rather complicated.

The tectonic evolution of the basin and the Okhotsk Sea coast represents the transition zone of the Pacific Cenozoic geosyncline going through the primary phase of orogenesis, as evidenced by folded complexes (the Jugjuhr Ridge, Yudomsky, Kukhtuisky, and others). The eastern Sea of Okhotsk coast (the Kuril Islands and Kamchatka Peninsula) is intersected by the long Kurilo-Kamchatka subduction trench, and this part of the coast is mountainous and formed by the volcanic island arc complex. Relatively low-lying shores are characteristic of the western Kamchatka and Northern Sakhalin coasts, and of the river mouth areas.

The climate of the Sea of Okhotsk is influenced by the southeast Asia monsoon (warm and humid) in summer, and by the Subarctic (cold, dry, continental) climate of east and northeast Siberia. Subarctic features of the climate and ocean dominate. Winds from the cold continental interior blow nearly all year round, freezing the sea water. It is generally considered that the ice regime of the Sea of Okhotsk is more complex than that of the Bering Sea, with interannual and long-term variability. The sea is one of the coldest seas of Russia's Far East. Ice cover in the northeastern sea remains for about 280 days, and 120–130 days in the south. The inner waters of the Sea of Okhotsk—with depths of more than 100–150 m and the straits and shores of the Kuril Islands—remain free from permanent ice cover. The average air temperature in January in the northern and western parts of the sea reaches –20°C to 24°C, in the northeast of the sea –14°C to 20°C, and in the east and south –5°C to 7°C. The average temperatures in July, correspondingly, are 11–14°C, 10–12°C, and 11–18°C. Annual precipitation is significantly higher than that on the continent: 300–500 mm in the northern part of the sea, 600–800 mm in the western part, and more than 1000 mm in the southern and southeastern parts.

The most important impact on the water regime and water balance formation is from the exchange of water masses with the Pacific Ocean and the Japan Sea through the straits of the Kuril Islands and the La Perouse Strait. Precipitation, river flow, and evaporation are not significant in the water balance. Inflow of the waters of the Pacific from the south and southeast and from the rivers of the northeast, north, and west create slow cyclonic rotation of the sea waters with speeds of 2–10 cm s^{-1} in the open sea. Counterclockwise flows bring warm waters from the south in the eastern sector of the sea and cold waters from the western sector. Local rotations can also be observed by Shantarsky Islands, for instance. Pacific deepwater inflow with a temperature of 1.8–2.3°C and a salinity of 34.4–34.7 takes place all year round at depths below 1000–1300 m. The upper water layer temperature and salinity fluctuate, but is persistently cold (–1.8–2.0°C in winter and +1.5–15°C in summer; salinity 32.8–33.8%). It has a thickness from several tens of meters by the coast to 500 m in the open sea. An intervening layer of convection water wedges between the upper Sea of Okhotsk and the deep Pacific layers.

The Sea of Okhotsk is a highly productive ecosystem, a large marine ecosystem, and an important fisheries area. Species of commercial importance include walleye pollock, flounder, herring, Pacific salmon, halibut, crab, and shrimp, which are fished by Japan, Sakhalin Island, and Kamchatka. Overfishing may become a problem since the waters are unregulated. The rich fish population provides food for numerous birds (puffins, murres, Steller's sea eagle), and the sea is a significant stopover near Arctic breeding grounds for over a million migratory shorebirds. Marine mammals found in the area include minke whale, Steller's sea lion, northern fur seal, Dall's porpoise, and ribbon seals.

INNOKENTY ZHIRKOV

See also **Kamchatka Peninsula; North Pacific Ocean; Sakhalin Island**

Further Reading

Kuznetsov, V.V. et al., "Food Chains, Physical Dynamics, Perturbations, and Biomass Yields of the Sea of Okhotsk." In *Large Marine Ecosystems: Stress, Mitigation, and Sustainability*, edited by Kenneth Sherman et al., Washington,District of Columbia: American Association for the Advancement of Science, 1993, pp. 69–78

Nishimura, S., "Okhotsk Sea, Japan Sea, East China Sea." In *Ecosystems of the World, Estuaries and Closed Seas*, edited by B.H. Ketchum, Amsterdam and New York: Elsevier, 1983, pp. 375–402

Preller, R.H. & P.J. Hogan, "Oceanography of the Sea of Okhotsk and the Japan/East Sea." In *The Sea, Volume 11, The Global Coastal Ocean, Regional Studies & Syntheses*, edited by A.R. Robinson and K.H. Brink, New York: Wiley, 1998, pp. 429–482

OKLADNIKOV, ALEXEI

Alexei Okladnikov, a 20th-century Russian archaeologist and historian, specialized in Siberian prehistoric rock art. From 1928 to 1934, he worked as the head of the ethnographic department of Irkutsk Museum of Regional Studies. From 1929 to 1934, Okladnikov studied history at the Pedagogical Institute of Irkutsk. The future scholar's first forays into archaeology were guided under the mentorship of B.E. Petri, a forerunner of contemporary Siberian archaeology. He spent the next 25 years earning his doctoral degree from the Institute of History of the Material Culture in St Petersburg, working first as the director of the Leningrad branch of the Institute, and then as the head of the Institute's Paleolithic department.

The sphere of Okladnikov's scientific interests was inordinately wide. Archaeology, especially of the Stone Age, comprised the chief subject of his scholarship; however, all of his monographs regard archaeological materials within a historical perspective in connection with the ethnic history of the peoples and regions he studied. Other objects and fields of scientific study included medieval Siberian history and the historical discoveries of Siberia and the Arctic. Much of Okladnikov's research centered on the origin and development of art, especially ancient drawings, petroglyphs, and sculpture, to include the history of art from the Paleolithic to the Middle Ages. Some of his writings deal with the events of the discovery of Siberia by Russians, and the history of Siberia in the later period. One of his penultimate works was a biographical survey of Archbishop Innocent (Ivan Veniaminov).

Okladnikov was among the first researchers to conduct wide archaeological excavations in Siberia and the Russian Far East. In 1940, he began investigations in Yakutia; from 1947 to 1952, he conducted archaeological expeditions in Buryatia; and from 1951 to 1955, he investigated within the basin of the Angara River. Beginning in 1949, he took part in the work of Soviet archaeological expeditions in Mongolia. Okladnikov initiated some of the earliest archaeological excavations in the Far East, including the basin of Amur River, the coasts of the Okhotsk and Japanese seas, and in the Primorskiy Territory. He published the results of these researches in two texts dealing with the history of the Far East from the Stone Age to the Middle Ages.

In 1974, along with other Siberian archaeologists, Okladnikov participated in the archaeological expedition on the Aleutian Islands where American archaeologists were conducting researches.

Okladnikov's contribution to the archaeological and historical literature is immense. In the catalogue of Russian National Library, Okladnikov is mentioned as the author and editor of more than 120 books in addition to nearly 1000 articles, papers, notes, and newspaper articles. In addition to his scientific monographs, Okladnikov authored several popular books in archaeology and the history of Siberia. Okladnikov influenced the Siberian scientific school of archaeologists (followers of his theories and work) who continue investigations, excavations, and researches in Siberia and the Russian Far East. Representatives of this school today work in Blagoveshchensk, Vladivostok, Yuzhno-Sakhalinsk, Ulan-Ude, Yakutsk, and in other cities of Siberia.

Biography

Okladnikov was born on October 3, 1908, in the village Konstantinovshchina, Irkutsk Province (today Oblast') in Russia to a country teacher who had married a local peasant woman. He graduated from secondary school in the village of Anga, Irkutsk province, and in 1926–1934 attended the Irkutsk Pedagogical Institute. Okladnikov published his first scientific paper in 1926, when he was 18 years old. Having graduated from the Institute in 1934 in autumn of that same year, he arrived in Leningrad for postgraduate study at the State Academy of History of Material Culture. In 1938, he defended his thesis dealing with the Neolithic in the valley of Angara River. From 1938 to 1949, Okladnikov worked as senior research fellow in the Institute of History of the Material Culture; in 1949, he

became the director of the Leningrad branch of this Institute; and in 1951, he became the chief of the Paleolithic department. He defended his doctoral thesis "Essays on the History of Yakutia since the Paleolithic till the joining to the Russian State" in 1947. He later wrote the first volume of *The History of Yakutia* (1955) based on his doctoral work.

In 1961, Okladnikov arrived in Novosibirsk, where at that time the Academy of Sciences of the Soviet Union was in the midst of creating a new Siberian and other science departments. He assumed the post of chairperson of general history at Novosibirsk State University; in 1966, he became the director of the Institute of History under the auspices of the Siberian branch of the Academy of Sciences, where he worked until his death. In 1964, Okladnikov was elected as a member-correspondent of the Academy of Sciences of the Soviet Union, and in 1968 he received the title of academician.

Okladnikov's family played an important role in his research activity. His wife Vera Zaporozhskaya accompanied him on expeditions and assisted in the publication of his works; she is named as coauthor in some of his books on Siberian petroglyphs. Their only daughter, Yelena Okladnikova, born in 1951, took part in the expeditions with her parents. Today she works in the Museum of Anthropology and Ethnography of Russian Academy of Sciences (Kunstkamera). She also served as coauthor with her father on various texts dealing with the rock drawings of the ancient Altai. Okladnikov died on November 18, 1981 in Novosibirsk.

ALEXIS BURYKIN

See also **Archbishop Innocent (Ivan Veniaminov); Sakha Republic (Yakutia)**

Further Reading

"About Okladnikov [Obituary]," *Sovetskaya Arxeologiya*, 1982, No. 3, *Sovetskaya Etnografiya*, 1982, No. 2

Derevyanko, A.P., *V poiskax Olenya zolotyje roga* [In the Search of the Deer with Golden Antlers], Khabarovsk, 1978; 2nd edition, Moscow, 1980

Okladnikov, Aleksey Pavlovich, *Yakutiya do prisoyedineniya k Russkomu gosudarstvu* [Yakutia before joining to the Russian state], Moscow-Leningrad: Academy of Sciences Publishers, 1955

———, "The introduction of iron in the Arctic and in the Far East." *Folk*, 5(1963): 249–255

———, *Dalekoye proshloye Primorya*, Vladivostok, 1959; as *The Soviet Far East in Antiquity: An Archeological and Historical Study of the Maritime Region of the USSR*, Toronto: Toronto University Press, 1965

———, *Utro iskusstva* [The Dawn of Art], Leningrad: Iskusstvo, 1967

——— (editor), *Istoriya Sibiri* [The History of Siberia], Volumes.1–4, Leningrad: Nauka, 1968, Volime 5, Leningrad: Nauka, 1969

———, *Petroglify Nizhnego Amura* [The Petroglyphs of the Lower Amur], Leningrad: Nauka, 1971

———, *Petroglify Sredney Leny*. [The Petroglyphs of the Middle Lena], Leningrad: Nauka, 1972 (with V.D. Zaporozhskaya)

———, *Dalekoye proshloye Primorya i Priamurya* [The Far-Gone Past of Maritime Region and Amur Basin], Vladivostok: Primorskoye Knizhnoye Izdatel'stvo, 1973 (with A.P. Derevyanko)

———, *Petroglify Verxney Leny* [The Petroglyphs of the Upper Lena], Leningrad: Nauka, 1977 (with V.D. Zaporozhskaya)

———, *Drevniye risunki Kyzyi-Kyol'a* [The Ancient Drawings of Kyzyl-Kyol], Novosibirsk: Nauka, 1985 (with Ye.A. Oklandikova)

Vasilevskii, R.S., *Alexei Pavlovich Okladnikov*, Moscow: Nauka, 1981 (in Russian)

OLD BERING SEA CULTURE

Old Bering Sea is the term for an archaeological material culture found in the Bering Strait region, particularly on St Lawrence Island (190 km from the Alaska mainland) and the Siberian coast, around the beginning of the first millennium. In the 1920s, Diamond Jenness, best known for his expeditions of the Copper Inuit, named the Bering Sea culture, having recognized it as a distinctive phase of Arctic prehistory while excavating in the Diomede Islands. Henry B. Collins later thoroughly defined it in site reports and renamed it the "Old Bering Sea" (OBS) following his own excavations on St Lawrence Island. Okvik, which was once defined as a separate culture, is now commonly subsumed into OBS.

Important sites include Kukulik, Gambell, Miyowagh, and Hillside on St Lawrence Island, Okvik on Punuk Island, and Uelen and Ekven on the Siberian coast. No Old Bering Sea site has yet been found on the American mainland, despite a number of surveys over the years. Houses appear to have been small, square, semi-subterranean structures with stone floors. The walls consisted of horizontal logs, occasionally incorporating whale jaw bones, held in place by wooden or bone stakes supporting sod roofs. Inhabitants entered via a long passageway, sunk below the level of the house floor.

OBS was a highly specialized sea mammal hunting culture. Harpoon heads were often elaborately decorated and form the basis of a typology for northwest Alaska that remains in use today. Float equipment, such as float plugs and mouthpieces, which generally indicate sophisticated hunting techniques that allowed for open water hunting, and the taking of whales, has also been found. Atlatls (devices for throwing spears or darts) and models of kayaks and umiaks, as well as some individual parts, provide additional evidence. Archaeologists have excavated the remains of ringed seal, bearded seal, walrus, and whale from refuse areas. Birds and fish were also taken with multipronged spears. Arrowheads for hunting caribou and other large land animals derive from mainland Siberian sites. Plants and berries were probably consumed when available.

Artifact assemblages include both chipped stone but predominantly ground slate tools and weapons. Heavy and comparatively crude ceramics, sometimes decorated with a broad linear or check design, remain. A shift from fiber to gravel as temper occurred early in the period and remained characteristic of later Eskimo pottery. Apart from the harpoon heads, other diagnostic artifacts include the ulu knife, oil lamp, and snow goggles. Engraving tools with metal tips have been found, suggesting knowledge of and trade for iron. Inhabitants used small sleds and baleen toboggans for transportation across the ice, although there is no evidence that they harnessed dogs.

OBS culture is famed for its elaborate incised artwork and decoration, which often completely covers harpoon heads, socket pieces, and other tools and artifacts. OBS has been divided into three or four phases, originally thought to be sequential: Okvik, OBS I, OBS II, and OBS III are primarily based upon styles of decoration. Later excavations, analysis, and radiocarbon dates suggest that these three artistic "phases" were in fact largely contemporaneous. Common iconographic elements include circles, dots, and raised bosses. Although the general composition of such graphic motifs is similar—often following the shape of the artifact—OBS I is based upon a design of uninterrupted spurred lines. OBS II is based upon dotted lines, and OBS III is characterized by broken and unbroken parallel lines. Okvik, which is most closely linked with OBS I, is somewhat distinct in its use of simpler, more deeply cut geometric elements. Carvings of human figures, torsos without arms or legs, and heads are relatively common, and may be highly stylized or naturalistic, as might animal carvings. Winged objects, which were apparently used as darting harpoon counterweights, were elaborately embellished. As in the Ipiutak culture, decorative chains were carefully carved out of ivory, including "seams" that mimicked those on metal chains.

Archaeologists have identified OBS burials from the East Asian sites at Uelen and Ekven, which both include large cemeteries comparable to that at Ipiutak on the Alaskan mainland. The burial chambers incorporated wooden floors and roofs, stone walls, and whalebone supports. Although there is some variation, human skeletons were generally supine and extended, and were often accompanied by beautifully decorated grave goods. The culture conducted both single and multiple burials. Evidence suggests that some double burials were vertically arranged, the skeletons one above the other, sometimes separated by a wooden floor and/or ceiling.

The antecedents to OBS culture are not thoroughly understood. Once thought to be ancestral to all Eskimo people, archaeologists today cite the OBS as contemporaneous with the Norton and Ipiutak cultures, and believe that the three cultures share a number of similarities, particularly in artistic style and pottery. Scholars have proposed three "ancestral streams": from the Aleutians, from Asia, and from mainland Alaska, which coalesced to create the OBS culture as a unified entity. Whereas inland groups strongly influenced cultures on the mainland, OBS evolved a more purely maritime way of life. Many OBS sites are overlain with Punuk culture material, strongly suggesting that by around 1500 BP, OBS had evolved into the Punuk culture, which was later to become the Thule culture, and was thus ancestral to today's Inupiaq people.

JENNIFER I.M. NEWTON

See also **Collins, Henry B.; Ipiutak Culture; Jenness, Diamond; Norton Culture; Thule Culture**

Further Reading

Collins, Henry B., *Archaeology of St Lawrence Island*, Washington: Smithsonian Miscellaneous Collections, 1937

Dumond, Don E., *The Hillside Site, St Lawrence Island, Alaska: An Examination of Collections from the 1930s*, Eugene: University of Oregon Anthropological Papers 55, 1998

————, "The Legacy of Henry B. Collins." *Archaeology in the Bering Strait Region*, Eugene: University of Oregon Anthropological Papers 59, 2002

Leskov, A.M. & H. Müller-Beck, *Artische Waljäger vor 3000 Jarhren: Unbekannte sibirsche Kunst*, Mainz-München: v. Hase & Koehler Verlag, 1993

Rainey, Froelich, *Eskimo Prehistory: The Okvik Site on the Punuk Islands*. Anthropological Papers of the American Museum of Natural History 37(4), 1941

Wardwell, Allen, *Ancient Eskimo Ivories of the Bering Strait*, New York: Hudson Hills Press in association with the American Federation of Arts, 1986

OLD CROW FLATS

The Old Crow Flats is a vast flat wetland, over 4000 square kilometers in extent, forming the floor of a huge bowl-shaped structural depression in the northern Yukon. Known as the Old Crow Basin, this depression formed some 60 million years ago as a result of the final phase of mountain building in the area. The rim of the Basin is formed by the summits of the surrounding mountains; the floor of the Basin is the Old Crow Flats. Underlying the vegetation and the lakes and ponds of the Flats are many layers of sediments. The thin top layer is of relatively recent sediments: clay, silt, and sand. Under this layer are thick sequences of much older sedimentary rocks. Studies suggest that these older layers may be up to 4000 m thick. The layers of rock that form the mountains and basin originated as layers of sediments formed at the bottom of ancient seas some 600 million years ago.

The Old Crow Flats fall within the drainage basin of the Porcupine River which joins the Yukon River near Fort Yukon in Alaska, making it part of the vast trans-border Yukon River Basin. The Old Crow River meanders through the Flats collecting water from the creeks that drain the mountains and hills that form the sides of the Old Crow Basin, and then flows south to join the Porcupine River near the village of Old Crow. The Old Crow Flats, the Old Crow River, and the settlement of Old Crow were all named after a revered Gwich'in Chief, Te-Tshim-Gevtik or "Walking Crow," who died in the 1870s.

The Old Crow Flats contain hundreds of lakes. Many of the lakes are square or rectangular and are oriented in a northwest-southeast direction. Groups of small, irregular lakes are usually the remnants of earlier large, square lakes that have become infilled with organic deposits. Many of these lakes are perched up on a level above the Old Crow River. In contrast, there are also many lakes formed by river action. The slow-moving Old Crow River has cut down 30–50 m into the fine-grained sediments of the Old Crow Flats to form a valley that is up to 3 km wide in places. The spectacular meanders of the Old Crow River have formed numerous lakes as the river course changes, isolating a part of the river bed to form many series of oxbow lakes. The northern limit of trees runs east-west across the northern parts of the Flats.

As one of the few areas in Canada untouched by glaciation during the Pleistocene Ice Ages, the Old Crow Flats area was a refuge for many ice-age plants and animals. Hundreds of thousands of fossil remnants of ice-age plants and animals were preserved in the layers of silt and clay. The Old Crow River, in eroding down into the sediments, has exposed bluffs that hold long-buried fossils of animals such as horses, giant beaver, camels, and mammoths. Paleontologists have declared this area to be one of the most promising and productive areas in Canada for uncovering evidence of the prehistoric past. Artifacts found in the Flats and the nearby Bluefish Caves are important traces of some of the earliest people to make their way into North America, possibly as long ago as an estimated 35,000 years.

The Old Crow Flats wetlands are also of great local, national, and international importance because of the wildlife they support. The Old Crow Flats provide important wetland habitat for many truly aquatic species, and also for other life forms that depend on water for special habitats, especially waterfowl, moose, mink, and muskrat. One half million birds use this area for nesting or as a staging station before migrations along the major North American flyways. The waterfowl are more concentrated here than at other locations

the Chukotka Peninsula coast south of the Anadyr River estuary to the Kamchatka Peninsula, at the extreme northeast limit of the distribution of the Old Koryak culture (*see* **Old Koryak Culture**).

The investigation of different archaeological objects by Orekhov (1999) formed the basis for recognizing the Lakhtin culture, which is characterized by material complexes related to a specifically maritime economy. The cultural traditions of the stone and bone industry of the bearers of the Lakhtin culture, their mode of life, construction of their houses and altars, as well as their ceramics, are manifested in the ethnographic culture that leads up to the ancestors of the present-day Kerek people.

Orekhov divided the total Lakhtin-related sequence into separate parts. The Pre-Lakhtin period (second millennium BC) was characterized by remnants of blades using both prismatic and less formal cores, and lacked ceramics. There were a few tools fashioned by grinding. Chipped tools are also infrequent, and bone artifacts were few. The Early Lakhtin period (the first half of the first millennium BC) was defined by similar artifacts with the addition of ceramics and polish-ed slate and an increase in bone artifacts. The "Paleometal" Lakhtin period dates from possibly as early as 2300 BP. Semi-subterranean sod houses often had square fireplaces demarcated by upright stone slabs. Ceramics of spherical shape included some decorated with comb striations, linear stamping, or cord marking. Polished slate knifes were common. Axes or adzes had polished parts. Many bone tools were made from walrus tusks.

Orekhov considers that the Lakhtin people did not adopt the harpoon complex for marine mammal hunting, thought to be associated with the influence of Paleo-Eskimo culture. But recently, harpoon heads were found on the Gavriila Bay coast. This testifies to the need to investigate this culture more thoroughly.

The Neolithic complexes have been dated from the second millennium BC to the 5th or 3rd centuries BC. However, it would have been more correct to define the lower boundary of the date as the middle of the second millennium BC since the two earliest radiocarbon dates available belong to the second half of the second millennium BC.

To date, the earliest stage of the Old Kerek culture has been studied only superficially. The Beringian (or Lakhtina) sites have mixed material and were found to be very damaged. Materials of this site and others (Etchun II, Orianda I) are very poor.

Researchers have noted the archaic appearance of the stone implements in the early stage of the Old Kerek culture. The primitive technique of reworking stone tools attests to a degradation of the stone industry. Orekhov had noted this, although he was inclined to attribute this primitiveness to the fact that the Kerek culture goes back genetically to the earliest relict cultural stratum. Such degrading of the stone-working technique is observed in most cultures of the Pacific coast in the first millennium BC (end of the Neolithic to the Early Metal period), including apparently the northwestern Bering Sea.

In the variety of the tool configuration, as well as in multifunctional tools, Orekhov sees archaic features, which, in his opinion, reflects a low level of development of productive forces. It is difficult to agree with this, because functionalism, which is inherent in the aboriginal population of many cultures of the Stone Age and especially of the Remnant Neolithic of the northeast, apparently played a definite role in the existence of these tools.

With respect to the sources of the Old Kerek (Lakhtin) culture, the assumption is that it goes back to the Sumnagin and Maltan Mesolithic traditions. This conclusion is postulated without any supporting evidence. A huge chronological break between the earliest stage of the Old Kerek culture and the presently only superficially represented Mesolithic complexes in the basin of the Khatyrka River contradicts this assumption. Meanwhile on the Bering Sea, archaeological sites of the Early and Developed Neolithic are lacking, which makes identification of the genetic sources of the Old Kerek culture difficult.

It should be noted that the modern Kerek people are one of the isolated and original subdivisions of northeastern Paleo-Asiatic tribes, possibly related to the Koryak and greatly influenced by the Eskimos, Itel'men, and Chukchi.

A.I. LEBEDINTSIV

See also **Old Bering Sea Culture; Tokareva Culture**

Further Reading

Orekhov, A.A. "The development of maritime adaptation among the early populations of the northwest Bering Sea region." *Arctic Anthropology*, 35(1) (1998): 263–280
——, *An Early Culture of the Northwest Bering Sea*, Anchorage: National Park Service, 1999

OLD KORYAK CULTURE

The Old Koryak Culture existed on the northern coast of the Sea of Okhotsk in the first to mid-second millennium AD covering the area from Shelting Bay near Magadan to Kamchatka. Studies of the Old Koryak were pioneered by Vladimir Iokhel'son (Jochelson) in 1901; later on, in the early 1960s, it was significantly defined and researched by R. Vasilyevsky. Over 100 Old Koryak sites and settlements have been found.

The basis for the Old Koryak Culture was the Tokarev Culture of the second to first millenia BC.

The Tokarev tool assemblage contained a number of stone tools. Already in the first millenium BC, the people of the Okhotsk Coast specialized in marine mammal hunting and had a developed harpoon complex and boats. The share of bone tools (harpoons, leister—a forklike fishing harpoon) increased, with the appearance of metal artifacts.

The Old Koryak Culture lived through several stages: Zavialov Stage (5th–8th centuries AD), Boguchan Stage (9th–10th centuries AD), Atargan Stage (10th–13th centuries AD), Lengenval' Stage (13th–15th centuries AD), and the Old Koryak settlements of 16th–17th centuries AD. The stages were distinguished primarily by site stratigraphy and Old Koryak materials correlation with those from the neighboring cultures. So far, there are only a few radiocarbon dates on the Old Koryak Culture.

In the early Zavialov Stage, stone tool processing still bore many Neolithic features: small, carefully retouched subtriangular scrapers; leaf-shaped points; and large ground oval axes. From the Boguchan Stage onward, tools became rougher, with silicious shale mostly being used. Since the Atargan Stage, the number of lithic tools was significantly reduced as well as the retouch quality. Rough spear points and axes were still used, but smaller scrapers, arrow points, and perforators almost disappeared, being replaced with metal and bone tools. The production of the latter became easier with the introduction of metal. Only for skin scraping were massive, roughly retouched subtriangular scrapers produced. By the mid-15th century, only rough stemmed spear points, large harpoon endblades for whale hunting, and rough, unmodified oval scrapers on large pebble spolls for skin scraping were used; these were retained in the Old Koryak Culture up to the 19th century.

Bone tools played an important role in the Old Koryak Culture. From the Zavialov Stage, the share of bone tools increased: these included ice picks, mattock shovels for shell and seaweed picking, hooks, arrow points, harpoons, perforators, spoons, and knives. Compound harpoons were still used and developed; the most typical were toggling harpoons that appeared on the Okhotsk Coast in the second half of the first millennium BC. In the Boguchan Stage, the harpoon complex as well as whale hunting continued to develop. Whale bones were used for the construction of houses. In the Atargan Stage, the toggling harpoons with metal endblades appeared and remained until the Russians came to the Okhotsk Coast.

Metal, which began to be used on the Okhotsk Coast at the end of the first millennium BC, had originally been scarce; therefore, it was valued and used only for making endblades for toggling harpoons, perforators, blades for knives with bone handles, and burins. On the Atargan Site, some slags were found,

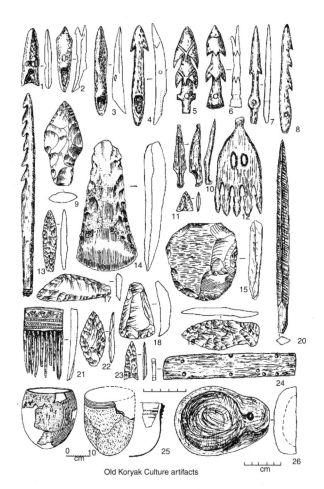

Old Koryak Culture artifacts

Old Koryak Culture artifacts: 1–4—toggling harpoon heads; 5–8, 16—barbed harpoon heads; 9, 11, 13, 20, 22, 23—points; 10—fishhook; 12—leister point; 14—adze; 15, 18—scrapers; 17, 19—knives; 21—comb; 24—armor plate; 25—pots; 26—oil lamp. 1–8, 10, 12, 16, 20, 21, 24—bone, 9, 11, 13–15, 17–19, 22, 23, 26—stone, 25—ceramic.

but there is no direct evidence of metal work at that time. By the end of the 15th century AD, the number of Old Koryak metal tools increased; they almost completely replaced stone and bone tools.

In the course of the Old Koryak Culture development, its pottery was changing as well. Old Koryak pots were originally round, with thin walls covered with a textile pattern. Later on, the even-walled vessels with plastic rolls appeared. In the Atargan Stage, pots became spherical, with a smooth surface. Along the rim, several rows of rolls with cross notches were placed. The size of pots increased to 30–35 cm in diameter. Already in the Lengenval' Stage, the use of ceramics significantly reduced, while wooden dishes and even baleen vessels were widely utilized. Metal pans might have appeared, but there is no evidence of this.

The main activity of the Old Koryaks was marine mammal, mostly seal, hunting. In the early stages, it was significantly complemented with hunting continental animals (reindeer, mountain ram) and fishing. However, from the Atargan Stage onward, marine mammal (mostly various seals) hunting dominated. Various hunting methods were used. In the spring and fall period, hunting was conducted both on the shore, at rookeries, or on the ice. In the summertime, they hunted with harpoons from boats in the sea. Net hunting in the coastal zone might have also existed, which has been testified by the findings of stone hammers to kill seals caught in the nets. According to ethnographic materials, the marine mammal nets were most probably made of mammalian leather bands. Whale hunting techniques developed during the Boguchan Stage peaked during the Lengenval' Stage: the remains of more than 200 whales found at the Sredny Settlement exclude gathering bodies on the coast. Evidence of fishing comes from leister points, various types of hooks, and fish bones and scales found at the sites. Stone and bone net sinkers indicate that nets (probably made of nettle fibers) were also used in fishing. Shell mounds show the importance of clam gathering. Besides, the findings of dog bones in dwellings and meat pits of the Atargan settlements testify to Old Koryak dog breeding. Dogs were supposedly used for sledding, because runners and other sled equipment were found.

Sea mammal hunting determined why Old Koryak people settled on the Okhotsk Coast. Iron provided its development: marine mammal hunting tools became more sophisticated and reliable. This increased the number of Old Koryak settlements and caused the changes in dwelling sizes. Originally, dwellings were semi-subterranean (25–50 cm deep) wooden structures faced with sod. They were round, 7–8 m in diameter, with side entrances and rectangular hearths, made of vertically laid stone plates, in the middle. Later, in the Atargan and Lengenval' stages, dwellings were bigger, either rounded quadrangular or octangular with side corridors. Whale bones were widely used in construction. Dwellings reached 20–30 m in diameter. The change in size must have also reflected certain social changes, exposed in the composition of findings from different dwellings, fortified settlements, bone armor plates, and compound long-range bows.

In the 16th–17th centuries, the number of settlements on the Okhotsk Coast reduced significantly, and they became smaller in size (to 3–4 dwellings), their territory limited within that of the Shelikhov Bay. Stone tools and ceramics almost completely disappeared, while the number of wooden artifacts increased. Bone tools became scarce, which was probably associated with the use of metal tools. The reduction of the Old Koryak Culture area is most probably connected with the spread of the Tungus tribes and reindeer herding on the Okhotstk Coast.

SERGEI SLOBODIN

See also **Iokhel'son, Vladimir Il'ich; Koryak; Tokarev Culture**

Further Reading

Johelson, Waldemar, *The Koryak*, The Jesup North Pacific Expedition, Volume VI, Leiden: Brill, and New York: Stechert, 1908
———, *Archaeological Investigations in Kamchatka*, Publication 388, Washington, District of Columbia: Carnegie Institution, 1928
Lebedintsev, Aleksandr, "Maritime cultures of the north coast of the Sea of Okhotsk," *Arctic Anthropology*, 35(1) (1998): 296–320
———, *Early Maritime Cultures of Northwestern Priokhot'e*, Anchorage: National Park Service, 2000
Vasil'evskii, Ruslan, "Ancient Koryak culture," *American Antiquity*, 30(1) (1964): 19–24
———, "A contribution to the history of the ancient culture of the Okhotsk coast," *Arctic Anthropology*, 6(1) (1969): 165–170
———, "The origin of the ancient Koryak culture on the northern Okhotsk coast." *Arctic Anthropology*, 6(1) (1969): 150–164
———, *Proiskhozhdeniye drevney kul'tury koryakov [The Origins and the Old Culture of the Koryak]*, Novosibirsk: Nauka, 1971

OLD SETTLERS—*See* RUSSIAN "OLD SETTLERS"

OLEARIUS, ADAM

Adam Olearius was a German 17th-century scholar and mathematician who traveled widely. He is known for his monumental descriptions of Persia and Russia, where some of the earliest reliable accounts of West Greenlandic Inuit culture and language were given.

Olearius, originally named after his father Adam Öhlschleger, began to use the Latin form of his name from his student days in Leipzig. In 1633, he left Leipzig to become secretary to an embassy sent by Friedrich III (1597–1659), the Duke of Schleswig-Holstein-Gottorp, to establish an overland trade route with Persia via Russia. The duke dispatched the first embassy to Moscow in 1633–1634 to secure the Russian Czar's permission. The second embassy arrived in Isfahan (present-day Esfahan, Iran) from Moscow in 1635–1639 to negotiate with the Shah of Persia. In total, Olearius spent six years traveling between Germany, Russia, and Persia. Even though the two missions failed commercially—neither the Czar nor the shah were convinced of the project—the voyages were a scientific success. Commissioned by Duke Friedrich III, Olearius had gathered an incredible amount of information about the geography and ethnography of the interior Russian and Persian empires, from which he compiled an exhaustive account in the coming years.

After returning to Schleswig-Holstein in 1639, Olearius continued in the duke's services at Gottorp Castle. Olearius had turned down the Russian Czar's appointment as royal astronomer in order to become the German duke's court mathematician. Consequently, in 1649 Friedrich III appointed Olearius as head librarian in charge of his *Kunstkammer* (museum of curiosities). Olearius expanded both the court library and the museum into leading collections in northern Europe. In 1650, Olearius acquired the Dutch collection of Bernhard Paludanus, a private museum located in Enkhuizen with notable Near Eastern objects from Paludanus's travels, for Friedrich III. The acquisitions substantially enriched the Gottorp collections, which later became part of the National Museum in Copenhagen. The same year, Olearius supervised the construction of the new church in Friedrichstadt, and in 1651 he began to plan one of his greatest achievements in astronomy: the design of the Gottorp Globe, an early form of the planetarium that measured about 4 m in diameter, weighed over 3 tons, and could seat several persons inside on a circular bench. In addition to his work in astronomy, Olearius built a telescope and a microscope, perfected the manufacture of lenses, wrote German and Latin poetry, made copper engravings, and translated Persian literature.

In 1647, Olearius published the first edition of his exhaustive travel account *Offt begehrte Beschreibung der newen orientalischen Reise* (translated in English as *The Travels of Olearius in Seventeenth-Century Russia in 1967)*. In 1656, the second and enlarged edition, *Vermehrte Moscowitische und Persianische Reysebeschreibung*, was published, reprinted in numerous editions from 1661 to 1971, and translated into many languages including Dutch, French, Italian, Russian, and English—indication of the book's international reputation. Among the many editions, not all contained the scope of Olearius's travel. The Italian translation, for example, contains only the Russian part and the English translations lack the chapter on the Greenlanders, which David Scheffel translated in 1987. In any event, Olearius's text provides the first detailed description of Persia since classical antiquity, and a portrayal of Russia that not only spans many generations but meticulously describes the Russian Empire.

In the Russian section of *Vermehrte Moscowitische und Persianische Reysebeschreibung,* Olearius devoted a brief chapter to the appearance of the northern peoples, including the Samoyeds, based in part on his own observations. Olearius used an accidental meeting with some Samoyeds in Moscow to interview them about their home country. Most noteworthy is the chapter "Von den Grünländern" (About the Greenlanders) that Olearius incorporated into the revised edition of 1656. After a general introduction to Greenland's history, Olearius describes the physical appearance, facial tattoos, language, clothing, dwellings, boats, fishing, hunting, whaling, food, beverages, eating and drinking habits, temperament, and religion of the Greenlanders whom he considered closely related to the Tartars and Samoyeds he had met in Russia. Olearius also lists 100 Greenlandic words, including some loan-words from Danish or Norwegian. In 1721, the Danish missionary Hans Egede relied on Olearius's list in his mission work in West Greenland.

Olearius's written observations were largely based on first-hand information he had gathered with the help of three captive West Greenlandic Inuit in Gottorp in 1654. From Olearius's account, scholars know that the group consisted of four Inuit, one man (Ihiob as described by Olearius) and three women (Kuneling, aged 45; Kabelau, aged 25; and the 13-year-old girl called Sigoko), who had been kidnapped by Captain David Urbanus Dannel in the Nuuk fjord in the summer of 1654. But Kabelau's father, Ihiob, had died on the way from Bergen in Norway to Copenhagen. An oil painting in the collection of the National Museum in Copenhagen and two illustrations from Olearius's travel account depict the entire group. The three women were presented to the Danish king, who during the plague of Copenhagen kept court in Flensburg, Germany, and thereafter to his cousin, the Duke of Gottorp. Olearius happily used the unexpected opportunity to more closely examine the Inuit in 1655. He met with them on several occasions, and incorporated their portraits in his description of the Gottorp *Kunstkammer.*

Although critics of Olearius's approach have claimed that he relied upon a few meetings with only four Inuit from which to extrapolate an entire chapter on the West Greenlanders, his work remains the earliest insightful description of the Inuit culture and language nearly a century before the ethnographic works of Hans Egede and David Crantz.

Biography

Adam Olearius was born on August 16, 1599 as the son of a tailor, Adam Oehlschlegel, in Aschersleben in the German state of Anhalt. From 1620 to 1627, Olearius studied theology at the University of Leipzig, where he received a master's degree in theology (1627) and in natural sciences (1629). In 1630, Olearius taught Latin grammar, poetry, mathematics, and German writing at the Nikolaischool in Leipzig. Thereafter, he taught as a member of the philosophy faculty at the University of Leipzig. After returning from his six-year voyage to Russia and Persia,

Olearius married Katharina Müller from Reval, Germany, with whom he had four children. He died in 1671 and was buried in the cathedral at Schleswig-Holstein, Germany.

VERENA TRAEGER

See also **Crantz, David; Egede, Hans; Greenland**

Further Reading

Holwein, Johan, *Gottorffische Kunst-Kammer*, Schleswig: Gottfriedt Schultzen, 1674

Lohmeier, Dieter, "Adam Olearius. Leben und Werke." *Vermehrte Newe Beschreibung Der Muscowitischen und Persischen Reyse*, reprinted, Tübingen: Niemeyer, 1971, pp. 3–42

Olearius, Adam, *Offt begehrte Beschreibung der newen orientalischen Reise* [first published in 1647 and translated as *The Travels of Olearius in Seventeenth-Century Russia*, edited by Samuel H. Bason, Stanford, California: Stanford University Press, 1647

———, *Vermehrte Moscowitische und Persianische Reysebeschreibung*, Schleswig, Germany: 1656 [translated into English by John Davies as *The Voyages and Travels of the Ambassadors sent by Frederick, Duke of Holstein, to the Great Duke of Muscovy and the King of Persia*, London: J. Starkey, and T. Basset, 1669]

Scheffel, David, "Adam Olearius 'About the Greenlanders'." *Polar Record*, 23(147) (1987): 701–711

OLENEK RIVER

The Olenek River is the longest river in the northwest of Yakutia (Sakha Republic), and drains into the Arctic Ocean west of the Lena River. Its annual discharge of about 35 km³ makes it one of the largest freshwater inputs to the Laptev Sea. The river has a length of 2292 km and a basin area of 220,000 km². The source is located in Krasnoyarsk Kray in the northern border of the Viluisky Plateau near the small mountain Yankan (Boukochan mountain ridge). On flowing into Olenek Bay of the Laptev Sea, the river forms a small delta with an area of 475 km², and two main channels: Ulakhan Yos (left) and Koubalaakh (right).

Along almost its entire length, the river flows in a steep-sided valley making abrupt sudden turns at rocky outcrops of the hard, crystalline Anabar shield and Olenek massif. After the Kystyk Plateau, the river valley broadens as the river flows through the North Siberian lowland, although on the east side the river bank encounters spurs of the Chekanovsky mountain ridge. The river has many tributaries draining large areas west from the lower Lena to the basin of the Anabar River. The left tributaries are (from the upper reaches to the estuary) Argaa Salaa, Senku, Oukoukit, Birekte, Nekekit, Kuoyka, Beenchime, Buur, and Buolkalaakh; the right tributaries are Verkhnyaya (Upper) Tomba, Nizhnyaya (Lower) Tomba, Alakit, Siligir, Merchimden, Kuytingde, and Khorbousuonka.

Annual precipitation is about 340 mm. The river is fed mainly by snowmelt and has a maximum spring flood discharge of 20,400 m³ s⁻¹. Summer flood discharge caused by rain is 8470 m³ s⁻¹, and minimum winter discharge is less than 0.09 m³ s⁻¹.

In the upper reaches, the river freezes over for on average eight months in winter. During unfavorable years, the river also freezes over in the lower reaches for a short period of time (one month). Ice breakup in the upper reaches in spring may be accompanied by ice jams lasting up to four days and flooding, due to blockages in the lower reaches along the meandering riverbed.

The maximum water level during ice blockage at the estuary of the Buur River was 20.43 m, and 21.82 m near the village Tymyaty. The water level rise during ice jams can be catastrophic: 8.5 m in 24 h (at the estuary of the Buur River). The level can also be normalized very quickly if the blockage is destroyed. At the estuary, the tidal range usually reaches 0.6 m.

The Olenek River is navigable for 970 km from the estuary up to the village of Soukhana. It is rich in commercially valuable species of fish, particularly in the lower reaches (white salmon, sturgeon).

INNOKENTY ZHIRKOV

See also **Laptev Sea**

Further Reading

Chistyakov, G.E., *Vodnye resoursy rek Yakutii* [Water resources of the rivers of Yakutia], Moscow: Nauka, 1964

Resoursy poverkhnostnykh vod SSSR, tom 17, Leno-indigirsky rayon [Resources of surface water of the USSR, Volume 17, Leno-Indigirsky region], Leningrad: Gydrometeoizdat, 1972

OLSEN, JØRGEN

Jørgen Clemens Valdemar Frederik Olsen was an influential Greenlandic politician of the post-World War II era. For almost four decades, Olsen was active as a politician in Greenland. From 1942 he was a member of the local council of Sisimiut, and from 1955 a member of the Provincial Council, a position he left in 1978 on account of poor health. Olsen, an outspoken and sometimes blunt leader, promoted Greenlandic independence and self-government. His efforts to this end earned him the nickname "Greenland's Lumumba" after the first prime minister of the independent Republic of Congo. Like Patrice Lumumba, nine years his junior, Olsen devoted his work to the greater world, educating himself in other cultures, their practices, and beliefs. He also admired Western politicians and scientists such as Abraham Lincoln and Albert Einstein. Fundamentally, Olsen believed in education and enlightenment as the means to progress and national Greenlandic independence.

Olsen often severely criticized the moral character of his fellow Greenlanders in general, and cited excessive drinking, laziness, and indulgence as some of the worst enemies of Greenlandic self-government. While he did not acquit the Greenlanders of their responsibility, he attributed these weaknesses to the impact of Danish colonialism and paternalism. However, according to Olsen, the Greenlanders must first liberate themselves from the colonial mentality to become free. Far from complying with the usual stereotype of the shy and soft-spoken Greenlander prevalent in the 1950s and 1960s, Olsen presented himself and was perceived as being a severe and unrestrained critic of the authorities and, not least, of his fellow Greenlanders. In this capacity, Olsen often made enemies, as when, in 1959 in an interview with the Danish paper *Information*, quoted in the Danish and Greenlandic radio news on August 4, he suggested that Greenland should have the same status as the Faroe Islands, that is, Home Rule. In the same interview, he called his predecessors in the provincial council "weak puppets" of the council chairperson, the Danish governor, and products of colonial times (Fleischer, 2000).

Olsen further directed criticism toward the Danish government's administration and development policy. He was one of the strongest opponents of the provision that allowed local native Greenlandic state officials, such as telegraph operators, clergymen, and teachers, to be paid 25% less than their Danish (nonnative) counterparts in Greenland according to the so-called rule of birthplace criterion. Although a member of the so-called G-60 commission, a program that outlined the development policy for Greenland in 1964, he reluctantly accepted the policy. As a member of the Regional Council, he continued to counter what he perceived as economic discrimination of the Greenlanders.

One of the policies of the 1960s that Olsen advocated was the so-called "concentration policy," which would later become a detested symbol of Danish colonialism. In brief, the policy meant concentrating the strongest human and economic resources in the larger towns of central West Greenland where sea ice did not prevent fishing on a year-round basis: Sisimiut, Maniitsoq, Nuuk, and Paamiut. Although born and raised in a village, Olsen was convinced that investments and the population ought to be allocated in a relatively modest number of places. Having experienced firsthand the severe hardships and poverty of the old Greenland, material development, such as better housing and health and education facilities, remained a high priority for Olsen. As he stated in the Provincial Council at a meeting on October 3, 1967, the state exchequer was not inexhaustible and the money must be spent where the prospects of profitability were best, and that

such population concentration policies occurred throughout the world. Olsen was far from being the only person supporting the concentration policy. Most of the members of the Provincial Council as well as many ordinary citizens until the early 1970s supported the policy until it became a symbol of Danish oppression.

Olsen was the first member of the Greenlandic Provincial Council to suggest that its chairperson be elected from and by its own members. When he made the suggestion in 1958, it seemed premature, and his fellow members rejected his suggestion. However, the development was in favor of enhanced Greenlandic participation and influence, and the council adopted the suggestion eight years later, in 1966. At the assembly in the spring of 1967—chaired for the first time by a Greenlander, Erling Høegh—Olsen gave the opening speech in his capacity as senior member and thus acting chairperson.

A Greenlandic nationalist and an experienced, outspoken politician, Olsen served as a mentor for the young, nationalist politicians of the new Greenlandic left wing in the 1970s, including the founders of the Siumut (Forward) Party (who included Olsen's nephew, Moses Olsen), the first prime minister of Greenland's Home Rule government, Jonathan Motzfeldt, and Motzfeldt's successor and rival, Lars Emil Johansen. Jørgen Olsen had not shied away from stating his opinion even when ill-perceived or going against the current political trends such as his 1958 call for a Home Rule arrangement like the one in the Faroe Islands. Although he was doubtlessly one of the key inspirations of Greenlandic Home Rule, Olsen did not run for the Greenlandic Home Rule parliament, the Landsting, in 1979. This was probably because the political scene had changed radically: Greenland now maintained three political parties and a host of energetic young politicians, many of whom propagated the same policy as Olsen himself. Olsen explained his withdrawal from politics as due to poor health. Like many other Greenlanders growing up in small crowded houses, he had suffered severely from tuberculosis in his youth, and was hospitalized for a year in Denmark, where he also underwent an operation that nearly cost him his life. It may be true that Olsen's health had become too weak to allow him to continue the difficult life of a Greenlandic politician, almost constantly on the move by boat, helicopter, and plane in Greenland and back and forth across the North Atlantic between Denmark and Greenland.

Biography

Jørgen Clemens Valdemar Frederik Olsen was born in 1916 in the small and impoverished village of Qerrortusoq in central West Greenland near the town of Sisimiut. He was the son of an uneducated cate-chist; his mother died when he was four. Olsen was raised by his grandmother in poverty. A bright pupil, he was singled out for further education and sent to Sisimiut, where he became a telegraph operator at the age of 16. In 1942, he was elected to the local council of Sisimiut and the same year he became its chairper-son. In 1944, Olsen married Andrea Poulsen from the village of Atammik, and they adopted a number of children. From 1944 to 1950, with the help of his wife, he wrote, duplicated, and distributed the local periodi-cal, *Piniartoq* (The Hunter), which published political critique. Olsen died in December 1985 in Sisimiut, the town he had represented for so many years in the Provincial Council. He was honored with a statue put up by his fellow-townspeople in Sisimiut in 1991.

SØREN FORCHHAMMER

See also **Birthplace Criteria; Høegh, Erling; G-60; Greenland Home Rule Act; Johansen, Lars Emil; Motzfeldt, Jonathan; Olsen, Moses**

Further Reading

Fleischer, Jørgen, *Grønlands Lumumba*, Nuuk: Forlaget Atuagkat, 2000
Lidegaard, Mads, "Olsen, Jørgen Clemens Valdemar Frederik." In *Dansk Biografisk Leksikon*, Copenhagen: Gyldendal, 1984

OLSEN, MOSES

Simon Johansínguaq Moses Valdemar Olsen stands among the generation of politicians who paved the road for Greenland's Home Rule government in the 1970s and 1980s.

As a student in Copenhagen in the 1960s, Olsen became a leading member of two associations of Greenlanders in Copenhagen—vice chairperson of *Peqatigît Kalâtdlit* (1960–1963) and cofounder and chairperson of *Kalâdtlit Inûsugtut Peqatigît* (1965–1968). In the 1960s and 1970s, the associations were vital fora for young Greenlanders receiving their further training in Denmark, among them many who were to constitute the political elite in Greenland in the 1970s and 1980s, and here basic principles of a new socialist and nationalist policy were shaped.

Like many of his contemporaries of the late 1960s and the 1970s, Olsen opposed the Danish and Greenlandic authorities and politicians as well as the policies they had developed and implemented in Greenland in the 1950s and 1960s. In particular, Olsen critically focused on the educational system that was implemented in Greenland in the 1960s. In the 1950s and 1960s, Danish as well as Greenlandic politicians and authorities wanted to intensify education in the Danish language and otherwise prepare Greenlandic

youth for secondary education in Denmark. To accom-plish this goal, many young children were sent to schools in Denmark, where they lived with Danish fam-ilies. According to Greenlandic and Danish authorities of the time, these policies were designed to improve conditions in Greenland, educate the Greenlandic pop-ulation, and enable the Greenlanders to take care of their own affairs. In Olsen's view, the new Greenlandic school system was detrimental to Greenlanders because it signified a loss of "Greenlandic" identity and an acceptance of one's "complete alienation" from his or her cultural background, as he described it in an article in the Danish newspaper *Politiken* (August 24, 1969). The school system implied that "Greenlandic youth must have a Danish education" and thus forced them to "become Danish." Olsen's political project from the late 1960s onward was to make the Greenlanders turn away from the "Danification" policy as he called it (ibid.). Instead, Greenlanders should recognize the intrinsic cultural values, the essential "Greenlandicness" of the Greenlander.

In an interview with the Danish newspaper *Information* (October 23, 1972), Olsen argued that any policy in Greenland must devolve from the "specific Greenlandic conditions." To Olsen, Greenlandic con-ditions were inherent in nature, but they were forgot-ten or repressed by the bilingual Greenlanders who, like Olsen himself, had received a formal education in the Danish-shaped school system. In Olsen's opinion, such Greenlanders were often even more Danish than many Danes. To retrace the specific Greenlandic con-ditions, one had to look to the monolingual Greenlanders who had not received much formal train-ing, preferably those living in villages and remote dis-tricts where Danish influence had been minimal, those who had been marginalized.

Olsen also argued that the Greenlandic language, whereby he meant West Greenlandic, comprised a crit-ical part of Greenlandic identity. In other words, to be an indigenous Greenlander one must speak Greenlandic as your first language. In contrast to this polarization of Danish and Greenlandic speakers, in later years Olsen amended his polemic, advocating the view that both Greenlandic-and Danish-speaking Greenlanders enjoy similar rights and privileges.

In 1971, in what was then called a political "new wave" and Greenlandic youth revolt, two of Olsen's political peers with whom he would later found and lead the Siumut (Forward) party, Jonathan Motzfeldt and Lars Emil Johansen, entered the Provincial Council. Olsen himself entered the Danish parliament as a dark horse the same year. Inspired by the ideas of the European and American youth revolt, and by anti-colonialist and anti-imperialist ideals and rhetoric, Olsen adopted a political strategy far more aggressive and provocative to the politicians and authorities of Denmark, as well as to the general public, than his predecessors. In 1972, when a new government was to be formed, the two sides of parliament were equal in number; Olsen found himself in a situation where he had the power to decide which parties could form the government when his vote was included. When he benefited from the situation and demanded concessions in favor of Greenland, it prompted a wave of hostility against him in Denmark. Legal experts and prominent Danish politicians even suggested limiting the Greenlanders' right to elect members to the Danish parliament.

After leaving the Danish Parliament in 1973, Olsen returned to Greenland. In close collaboration with his peers, he prepared ground for a new Home Rule government through his work with the nascent left-wing and nationalist political movement that led to the formation of the Siumut Party in 1977. Olsen became known as the main ideologist of the movement and party in the 1970s.

During the 1970s and the early years of Home Rule, Olsen argued for cooperatives to play an important role in Greenland's economy based on his skepticism that the free sway of market forces would lead to societal equality and unity for all Greenlanders. However, in the mid-1980s, when he was Home Rule Minister of Commerce, he abandoned that policy in favor of one that centralized economic power in the hands of the Home Rule government. The Danish state had relinquished the fish production division of the Royal Greenland Trade Company (KGH) to the Greenlandic Home Rule authorities. With its fleet of large, modern fishing vessels and its vast number of big land-based fish production facilities, the Trade Company was an economic giant in Greenland. This action led to the Home Rule government's eventual takeover of the cooperative fish-processing plants that were now competitors.

Biography

Moses Olsen was born in Sisimiut, Greenland, on June 6, 1938, a nephew of the legendary Greenlandic politician Jørgen Olsen. He finished primary school at the public boarding school in Nuuk in 1959 and graduated from high school in Copenhagen in 1962. He studied Icelandic language, literature, and history at the University of Iceland from 1963 to 1964. In 1968, he graduated as a translator in Copenhagen and from that year worked as a translator in the Ministry for Greenland. In 1964 and 1965, Olsen briefly returned to Sisimiut, and from 1970 to 1972 taught at the folk high school in Sisimiut. He became the head of the secretariat of the Fishers and Hunters Organization from 1972, and town clerk in Sisimiut in 1978. He also engaged himself in social work and was a cofounder of Pooq, the consultancy for Greenlanders in Copenhagen, in 1967. From 1960 to 1963, Olsen was vice chairperson of *Peqatigît Kalâtdlit* (the Greenlanders' Association) in Copenhagen, and in 1965 he was a cofounder of *Kalâdtlit Inûsugtut Ataqatigît* (The Young Greenlanders' Council) in Copenhagen, which he chaired from 1965 to 1968. In 1970–1971, he was among the founders of the cooperative store in Sisimiut, and from 1971 to 1973 he was a member of the Danish parliament. From 1975 to 1977, he was the coordinating leader of the Siumut (Forward) movement, and from 1978 he served as the Party's vice chairperson.

During Greenland's Home Rule, Olsen served as a member of Greenland's parliament (Inatsisartut) from 1979 until 1991. He was the vice president of the parliament and the government (Naalakkersuisut) and he was appointed Home Rule minister for Social Matters (1979–1973), for Economy and Taxes (1983–1986), for Fishing and Industry (1986–1988), and for Social Matters and Housing (1988–1991).

Since his withdrawal from politics in 1991, Olsen has worked as a political consultant for the Workers' Association of Greenland (SIK). From the contributions he has made to the public debate during recent years, it seems clear that he has amended his original, nationalist, and essentialist views on what constitutes a Greenlander, now claiming that non-Greenlandic-speaking persons living in Greenland can also be considered Greenlanders.

Apart from being one of the most influential politicians of the latter 40 years, Olsen is well known in Greenland as a poet and prose writer. He has published his work in the anthologies *Taigdlat* (1974), *Inuit* (1980), *Meeqqat* (1992), and in a collection of poems, *Anersaama pikialaarneri* (1998).

SØREN FORCHHAMMER

See also **Greenland; Greenland Home Rule Act; Johansen, Lars Emil; Motzfeldt, Jonathan; Olsen, Jørgen; Royal Greenland Trade Company (KGH); Siumut**

Further Reading

Lidegaard, Mads, "Olsen, Simon Johansínguaq Moses Valdemar." In *Dansk Biografisk Leksikon*, Copenhagen: Gyldendal, 1984

Lodberg, Torben (editor), *Grønlands grønne bog*, Copenhagen: Tusagassiivik, 2001

OPEN POLAR SEA

The notion that behind the icy barrier of Arctic ice there was a large body of open and navigable water—the "Polar Sea"—was one of the most persistent ideas within 19th-century exploration. The origins of this romantic belief are obscure, although they appear to date back at least to the 17th century, when the Royal Society in England debated reports from Dutch merchant ships that they had discovered a North West Passage across the pole. The existence of a Polar Sea faded from debate when neither scientists nor explorers could corroborate these reports, but the question resurfaced in 1817. That year, William Scoresby wrote a letter to Sir Joseph Banks detailing the highly unusual and complete breakup of the ice on the coast of Greenland he and others had observed that summer. Scoresby, a veteran whaling captain, did not give any credence to the idea of open water beyond the ice; he only suggested that the unusual conditions were propitious for the exploration of Arctic waters.

John Barrow, the second secretary of the Admiralty at the time, was a far more credulous and less cautious man. He appropriated and amplified Scoresby's observations to gain the endorsement of the Royal Society in his efforts to convince Lord Melville to launch two major Arctic exploratory voyages the following year. Despite the fact that both expeditions—David Buchan's to the north of Svalbard, and John Ross's to search the boundaries of Baffin Bay—eventually encountered impenetrable ice, Barrow remained convinced that they had encountered only a temporary "barrier." Throughout the 1820s, and culminating with Sir William Edward Parry's expedition by ship and sledge in 1827, Barrow sent out sorties in search of some opening in this barrier, but their failure only increased his resolve. When Sir John Franklin's expedition—the last sent on Barrow's watch—was dispatched, Barrow made certain that its orders included the option of a northerly turn in search of open water. Barrow died before the full understanding of Franklin's failure was realized and went to his grave believing in an Open Polar Sea.

The American explorer Elisha Kent Kane was only slightly less enthusiastic about the idea of an Open Polar Sea. On his second Arctic voyage in 1853–1855—the first under his own command—Kane deliberately sailed north of Baffin Bay with the idea that he might meet up with open water and find Franklin and his men by sailing through it. At the extreme end of his efforts, his steward William Morton, accompanied by the Danish-speaking West Greenlander Hans Hendrik, achieved the northern outlet of the "Kane Basin." They returned with an account of a vast open body of water to the north, surrounded by clouds of gulls. This report earned Morton the sobriquet "discoverer of the Open Polar Sea." Kane's surgeon Dr. Isaac Hayes returned a few years later with a similar report, although his observations were later discredited.

Nonetheless, a navigable Polar Sea was marked on many maps and charts of the day. Matthew Fontaine Maury, whose authoritative *Physical Geography of the Sea* (1883) was a standard reference in his day, devoted an entire chapter to the Open Polar Sea, describing it with almost poetic fervor:

> Seals were sporting and water-fowl feeding in this open sea of Dr. Kane's. Its waves came rolling in at his feet, and dashed with measured tread, like the majestic billows of old ocean, against the shore. Solitude, the cold and boundless expanse, and the mysterious heavings of its green waters, lent their charm to the scene. They suggested fancied myths, and kindled in the ardent imagination of the daring mariners many longings.

Other geographers concurred with Maury, although they offered differing explanations as to how the polar sea remained ice-free. Counterpoised to Kane and others who assumed that a deep Atlantic current similar to the Gulf Stream kept the sea free from ice, the preeminent German geographer August Petermann credited a warm-water current from the Pacific. He claimed that Kane could not in fact have seen his "Great Polar Sea." United States Naval officer Silas Bent, who accompanied William Perry on his mission to Japan in 1852, advanced a similar notion. Bent became convinced that warm-water currents north of Japan fed a body of warmer water in the Arctic. His theory achieved a fairly wide circulation and enjoyed particular credence in the United States.

It thus came as something of a shock when Charles Francis Hall, the first to actually sail north past the Kane Basin, encountered only a further barrier of ice. The British expedition under captain George S. Nares on the HMS *Discovery* (1875–1876), which used Hall's findings as the basis for sledging trips much further north, encountered nothing but immense fields of ancient and unyielding ice. The return of Nares's exhausted and scurvy-ridden men to their ships marked the bitter end of the British belief in an Open Polar Sea, and indeed of British interest in Arctic exploration altogether.

The Americans clung to the notion however. American Arctic explorer George Washington De Long's expedition on the *Jeannette* of 1879 was based in large part on Petermann's belief that the Bering Strait would lead to the "Great Polar Sea." The deaths of De Long and most of his men due to exposure and starvation put an end to the American credence in such notions. United States Naval officer and explorer Robert Peary's eventual progress still further north beyond Hall Basin also demonstrated the persistence and solidity of the polar ice cap, although seasonal warming and the action of currents and floes could frequently open up leads and small areas of open water.

The mystery of the Open Polar Sea exercised a substantial influence in the world of literature. The fictional Captain Walton in Mary Shelley's *Frankenstein* (1818) gives an energetic defense of the idea, and is on his way to discover it when he encounters Victor Frankenstein. Jules Verne, in his *The English at the Pole* (1875), pushed the dream one step further, placing an active volcano at the Pole, with its boiling lava flowing down into (and presumably keeping warm) a vast polar ocean.

RUSSELL A. POTTER

See also **Barrow, Sir John; De Long, George Washington; Hall, Charles F.; Hendrik, Hans (Suersaq); Kane, Elisha Kent; Peary, Robert E.; Petermann, August; Scoresby, William**

Further Reading

Barrow, Sir John, *Voyages of Discovery and Research Within the Arctic Regions, from the Year 1818 to the Present Time: Under the Command of the Several Naval Officers Employed by Sea and Land in Search of a North-West Passage from the Atlantic to the Pacific; with Two Attempts to Reach the North Pole. Abridged and arranged from the official narratives, with occasional remarks*, New York: Harper & Brothers, 1846

Bent, Silas, *Thermometric Gateway to the Pole*, St Louis: St Louis Historical Society, 1856

Hayes, Isaac Israel, *The Open Polar Sea: A Narrative of a Voyage of Discovery Towards the North Pole, in the Schooner "United States,"* New York: Hurd and Houghton, 1867

Kane, Elisha Kent, *Arctic Explorations: The Second Grinnell Expedition in Search of Sir John Franklin, 1853, '54, '55*, Philadelphia: Childs & Peterson, 1857

Maury, Matthew Fontaine, *Physical Geography of the Sea*, New York: University Publishing Company, 1883 (revised by Mytton Maury in 1885)

OROCHI

The Orochi are one of Russia's northern indigenous people living in the Khabarovsk Kray of southeast Siberia. According to the Soviet census of 1989, they numbered 915. They live mostly along rivers flowing into the Tatar Strait of the Pacific Ocean, mainly on the lower reaches of the River Tumnin and its tributaries, along the Khungary River flowing into the Amur River, along the Amur River proper, and at Lake Kizi. A small group live on Sakhalin Island.

The Orochi language belongs to the Tungusic-Manchurian group of the Altaic language family. Spoken use of Orochi is in decline: in the 1989 census, 17.8% of the Orochi considered Orochi to be their native tongue, the rest naming Russian as their native language. The Orochi people have no written language. Their self-designation is *Nani* (meaning "local inhabitants"), which is similar to that of the Ul'chi, Nanais, and Orok. The Orochi came under influence of the Russians during colonization of the Amur River basin in the mid-19th century. In the 1930s, the Russians designated this ethnic group as Orochi.

The Orochi ethnic group originated on the slopes of the Sikhote-Alin mountain range, within an area from De-Kastri Bay in the north to Botcha River in the south. The group developed in prehistoric times from interactions with both local (Nivkhi, Ainu) and incoming (Evenki) northern indigenous peoples. Five territorial groups were distinguished by the start of the 20th century: the Amurskaya, Khungariyskaya, Tumninskaya, Maritime (Khadinskaya) and Koppinskaya.

Major traditional occupations were hunting and fishing, and, to a lesser extent, sea-hunting. Men hunted furs from October to March while their families waited at the winter settlements. Elk, musk deer, Siberian stag, roe deer, wild boar, reindeer, and also bear were hunted all year round, with the adoption of firearms in the late 19th century. Carp, sturgeon, and taimen were fished all year round, and salmon during spring and summer spawning. In De-Kastri Bay, coastal fishing or fishing from boats by means of harpoons, and hunting of seals were common.

The traditional food was fish. Both salmon and red caviar (salmon roe) were dried in the sun, chopped chum salmon was often eaten raw, and all kinds of fish were cooked in soup or mixed with berries and dressed with seal fat. In the late 19th century, Orochi adopted fish smoking and pickling from the Russians. Dog meat was a ritual food. The heart and liver of elk and bear were delicacies, as was fresh bone marrow.

Bilberry, cranberry, black and red currants, and ramson were gathered, and dozens of edible herbs and roots were added to soups and meat. Delicacies were Siberian millet and runner beans bought from the Manchu and Chinese merchants. From the late 19th century, Orochi obtained grains, vegetables, potatoes, and goods such as sauerkraut, salted mushrooms, and jam from the Russians.

Culture

Orochi culture reveals Tungus and Amur-Sakhalin elements. Among the traditional crafts are woodworking, birch bark working (for boats and cookware), sewing, and manufacturing fishing nets from nettle fiber. Orochi blacksmiths were capable of forging iron arrowheads, harpoon heads, and knives from old iron implements and simple tools such as anvil, hammer, and forge bellows. They also created adornments of silver and gold.

Skis and dog sledges were major means of travel. In winter and spring, domesticated reindeer were used to pull sleds on skis. In summer, large and small log canoes were used for river transport, and big flat-boats and log canoes (*omorochka*) were used for sea transport. On deep water, oars and sails were used. Boats of birch bark were no longer in use by the time the Russians came.

Permanent settlements were located in the vicinity of the winter hunting grounds, on riverbanks. Some of these settlements have existed for dozens or even hundreds of years. The population of these settlements was usually small, with settlements of five or six dwellings located at distances of several dozen kilometers from each other. Winter dwellings were rectangular earth dugouts with a gable roof of poles covered by fir bark. Dry grass and snow were used to make such dugouts more habitable in winter. Two to three families usually inhabited such dwellings. There were also barns for storing dried fish and hunting equipment, awnings for drying fish and clothes, and log houses for bringing up bear cubs for the Bear Festival. In the late 19th to early 20th centuries, log dwellings of a Russian type began to be used.

Summer dwellings were above-ground constructions of poles with vertical walls, and a gable roof covered by fir bark. Blankets were made of dog skins. Clothes and fish were dried on the poles suspended inside. The autumn-summer dwelling was a construction made of poles, with a gable roof. Conical skin tents (*chum*) covered by fir or birch bark were temporary dwellings, such as those used by groups of hunters in winter. During migrations, wind barriers and span roof tents covered by fish skin were constructed.

The territorial commune of all dwellers in a settlement, often representatives of several ethnic groups, was a major form of social organization. The Orochi formed both big and small families, each family being an independent economic unit. Usually, members of a commune comprised families from various clans that were related by marriage. Mutual interchange with sisters and brothers was a common form of marriage. Until the early 20th century, the custom was that the youngest brother should marry the widow of the eldest brother. Friendly exogamic alliances were made between the families of some clans and sometimes with representatives of other ethnic groups (such as the closely related Nanais, Ulchis, Udeghes).

Clothing

A belted Japanese style kimono was the traditional dress. Plastrons, a thin metal breastplate, were decorated with iron pendants and other adornments. Women wore earrings, and both men and women wore silver bangles. Jackets of musk deer, reindeer, and elk leather and also fish-skin aprons were sewn for hunting and fishing. Men wore knives, amadou (tinder box), and a powder flask on their belts; women carried knives for cutting, and bone needle cases. Underclothes were short pants of cloth, fish skin, and chamois. Festival dress included chamois aprons for men and shoulder capes and round fur collars for women. Wealthy women had silk coats backed with fur.

In summer, women wore conical caps of birch bark, and in winter cotton wool or fur caps. Kerchiefs became popular from the second half of the 19th century. Hunters' caps were round and made from white reindeer fur. Necks were covered by neckerchiefs of squirrel brush. High fur boots (*porshni*) and short bootlegs of fish skin or suede were used for skiing. Women's *porshni* were made of fish skin and had blunt toe caps. *Porshni* of elk suede were barbed and designed for traveling on icy surfaces. Boots were made of elk *kamus* (skins from the elks' legs), with their upper edge decorated with fur. Fur stockings were tucked inside the boots.

Men braided their hair into one plait and women into two plaits. Women wove strings of beads and metallic shields into the plaits.

Beliefs

A system of religious faith and taboos, according to which the world is inhabited by both kind and evil spirits, regulated Orochi life and behavior in society and their environment. Animals, rivers, and seas all had their own spirit masters, and fables of these formed a considerable part of Orochi mythology. There were several fire-related taboos. It was prohibited to spit at fire, to throw anything into it, and to light up from fire. The Orochi sacrificed to animals and nature spirits. *Temu*, meaning master of waters, and cowfish—a sacred animal possessing power over the sea animals and fishes—were especially esteemed. The Universe was represented as upper, middle, and lower worlds. The god of the upper world is a supreme spirit (*Boa*) governing the Universe with numerous spirit-helpers. The god of the middle world was a cultural hero *Khadau*. Having created the Earth, he quarreled with his wife and subsequently they both turned into stone: *Khadau* became the sacred rock at the Keppi River and his wife a tall mountain in Sakhalin Island. According to folklore, the Earth is a great female elk with eight legs. Her backbone is a mountain ridge, her hair is the trees, fluff is grass and bushes, bugs are animals, and the insects flying around her are the birds.

The rare Siberian tiger was a sacred animal, and its spirit-master featured in many fables. *Duente*, meaning guardian spirit of bears, was also sacred. The Orochi, like other Amur nations, raised bear cubs for the Bear Festival. The ritual eating of the meat of the killed bear and various competitions took place during the festival (*see* **Bear Ceremonialism**).

Shamans, both men and women, were intermediaries between people and gods of the upper and lower worlds. Every shaman had his own spirit-patron and many spirit-helpers. Ritual dress and sacraments were a timbrel (a small hand drum) with a tampon (two-headed drumstick), a belt with clackers, and a skirt. The wings of an eagle or an other bird were attached to the back of his robe. Pictures of spirit-helpers (snakes, worms, frogs, lizards, birds, and fishes) were painted on the shaman's dress and on the timbrels and tampons. The shamans could be either kind or evil. It was believed that evil shamans ate the souls of people and animals. In the second half of the 19th century, the Orochi were converted to the Russian Orthodox church, but retained much of their shamanistic practices.

The Orochi's music is lyric, epic, and related to rituals such as the Bear Festival. Musical instruments are *dudumanku* (a one-string bow instrument), *pupan* (a whistle like flute of willow), *tenkere* (a reed instrument of cane), *muene* (an arched metallic Jew's harp), *kunkay* (a bamboo Jew's harp), *kanokto* (sleigh bell), *kaukharakta* (bell), and *achian* (metallic rattle boxes). Shamans performed ritual singing accompanied by the "magic" sound of a timbrel and a set of conical pendants worn on a special belt. The content of these songs is improvisation.

OLGA BYKOVA

See also **Northern Altaic Languages; Tungus**

Further Reading

Bytovoy, S.M., *Poyezd prishiel na Tumnin. Putevye ocherki* [The train comes to Tumnin. Travel notes], Leningrad, 1951

Larkin, V.G., *Orochi. Istoriko-etnograficheskiy ocherk s serediny XIX veka do nashikh dney* [Orochi. Historic-ethnographic legacy from the middle of the 19th century to our time], Moscow: Nauka, 1964

Smolyak, A.V., "Orochi." In *Narody Sibiri*, edited by M.G. Levin & L.P. Potapov, Moscow: Russian Academy of Sciences, 1956; as *The Peoples of Siberia*, Chicago: Chicago University Press, 1964

http://www.raipon.net/Web_Database/oroch.html

OROK

The Oroks are an indigenous people of Sakhalin Island, in Russia's Far East. Their self-designation is *Ul'ta, Uilta, Ul'cha,* or *Ol'cha* (reindeer people, from *ula* = reindeer). The name *Orok* was given to them by the Ainu people and was later adopted by others. In English, the Russian plural *oroki* is often used. Old Russian neighbours also called them *orochoni*, which led to confusion with the Orochi, a different ethnic group, or the Orochons, a subgroup of the Evenks. Japanese names for the Orok are *uiruta* and *orokko*.

According to the official Soviet census of 1989, there were 190 Oroks in the entire Soviet Union, 179 of them in the Russian Federation, and 129 living on Sakhalin Island; 15% lived in rural areas. Because of the confusion about the ethnic group names mentioned above, numbers are not certain, and they cannot uncritically be correlated with those of earlier censuses: 749 people in 1897; only 126 people in 1926 after a number of diseases and famine; and 450 people in 1979. Estimates range between 300 and 400 through most of the 20th century.

Ethnogeograsphy and Language

Some researchers claim that non-Nivkhi and non-Tungusic elements in the Orok language and culture point toward an autochthonous origin. The Orok oral tradition, however, points to a continental and common ethnic origin with the Ul'chi people. Migration of the group that became the Oroks, from the area of the Amgun River to Sakhalin, probably took place in the 17th century at the latest. On Sakhalin, the Oroks lived in close proximity to the Ainu, Nivkh, and later also the Evenki.

In the 1920s, the Oroks on northern Sakhalin were still divided into five groups, each with their own migratory zone. In the course of Soviet collectivization, in 1932, the northern Oroks joined the collective farm of Val, which specialized in reindeer breeding, together with smaller numbers of Nivkhi, Evenk, and Russians.

On southern Sakhalin, Oroks have lived in some villages in the Poronaisk District since the 19th century. After having given up reindeer herding for economic reasons, they settled on the coast and took to fishing. Until World War II, this part of Sakhalin Island belonged to Japan. Treated with suspicion on both sides, but risking being sent to labor camps by the Soviet authorities, some Oroks were evacuated to Hokkaido (Japan), when Sakhalin Island was handed over to the Soviet Union in 1945. A small Orok community of possibly 20 people still exists on Hokkaido near the city of Abashiri.

Language

The Orok language belongs to the Tungusic-Manchurian languages of the Altaic family. The closest related languages are Ul'chi and Nanais. There are distinct differences between the dialects in northern and southern Sakhalin.

According to the census of 1989, 47% of the Oroks spoke their native language (44.7% as their mother tongue). More recent sources suggest that there are no more than 60 speakers, most of them over 40 years old. The language can thus be considered as nearly extinct. A project aiming at teaching the language in elementary schools and creating a literary norm for Orok based on the Cyrillic alphabet has recently been proposed in cooperation with Japanese scholars. The Japanese syllabic alphabet, *katakana*, has earlier been used to transcribe Orok.

Lifestyle and Subsistence

When the Oroks first arrived on Sakhalin, they lived only in the northern part of the island. They took to nomadic reindeer breeding, with fishing and hunting as subsidiary activities. They thus differ significantly from their ethnically related neighbors, the Ul'chi, in regard to their economy. Reindeer were used for all purposes, including food, clothing, and transportation (riding and draught animals). During the summers, the Oroks stayed mostly at the eastern shore and were occupied with fishing and seal hunting. They lived in tents covered with tree bark and reindeer skins. Small huts were built to store fish and meat.

In the early or middle part of the 19th century, some of the Oroks moved southward to the Poronai River mouth and other places in southern Sakhalin, where they became sedentary, gave up reindeer breeding, and adopted the ways of the other indigenous groups there: the Ainu and Nivkhi (fishing, sea mammal and game hunting, and dog breeding). But they often kept one or a few reindeer for transportation purposes.

From the 1870s, Russian influences became significant. For the northern Oroks, vegetable farming and cattle breeding are gaining ground.

Today, the Oroks inhabit villages of standardized dwellings together with Nanais, Nivkhi, and Russians, in Russian-type log cabins. Only the herdsmen in the collective farm of Val (northern Sakhalin) lead a semi-nomadic life. The main occupation of the southern Oroks in the Poronaisk District is fishing, but there are also people employed in industry.

Only a few items, mainly clothing and fishing gear, have been preserved from the old culture. The cultural survival of the Oroks is particularly endangered because of their very low number.

Society and Social Structure

The Oroks lived in clans, of which there were eight prior to the October Revolution, but more than 15 in former times. Like those of their neighbors, the Nivkhi, the clan regulated the exogamic customs of intermarriage between clans, protected its members, and performed common rites. As opposed to the Nivkhs, however, the clans had no defined territory, and disagreements about land or water resources (or women) often led to skirmishes with other clans, or even with Ainu groups.

The family was the basic economic unit. Several families—possibly belonging to different clans—would join into groups that would share certain pastures or hunting grounds.

Religion

In the animistic belief of the Oroks, they had to make bloodless sacrifices to the spirits of nature—earth, water, heaven, and fire—to ensure good relations with their guardians. The spirit of the sea, *Teum*, held a special status, and food sacrifices were given to him from a certain, sacred bowl twice a year. Women were excluded from such rituals. The shamanistic practices of the Oroks were similar to those of the Ul'chi and Nanais.

Like many Arctic peoples, the Oroks held bear festivals, which lasted for several days; the climax was the killing of a 2–3-year-old cage-raised bear with a bow and arrow. Both the consumption of the meat as well as the burial of the bones were connected with certain taboos. Taboos also existed for the consumption of seal meat.

Myths account for a cosmogenic cycle; they include the creator of man and bear, earth, and heaven, *Khadau*, who also established the spiritual rituals.

The Oroks first came into closer contact with the Russian Orthodox Church during the second half of the 19th century. They adopted Russian customs and beliefs earlier than their neighbors, the Nivkhs, although Christian ideas only had a superficial influence on their spiritual lives.

Folklore

The Oroks have many legends about their arrival on Sakhalin and their encounter with the older aboriginal population. Graphic arts and ornaments have a lot in common with the other ethnic groups of the Russian Far East.

WINFRIED K. DALLMANN

See also **Nanai; Northern Altaic Languages; Sakhalin Island; Tungus; Ulchi**

Further Reading

Ivanov, S.V., A.V. Smoliak & M.G. Levin, "Oroki." In *Narody Sibiri*, edited by M.G. Levin, & L.P. Potapov, Moscow: Russian Academy of Sciences, 1956; as *The Peoples of Siberia*, Chicago: Chicago University Press, 1964

Kuznetsov, A.I. & L.I. Missonova, "Oroki Sakhalina: problemy sovremennogo razvitiia" [Sakhalin Oroks: Problems in contemporary development]. In *Issledovaniia po prikladnoi i neotlozhnoi etnografii IEA RAN* [Research in applied and urgent ethnography of the Institute of Ethnography and Anthropology of the Russian Academy of Science], Moscow, 1991

Majewicz, A., "The Oroks. Past and Present." In *The Development of Siberia: People and Resources*, edited by A. Wood & R.A. French, New York: St Martin Press and Basingstoke: Macmillan, 1989, pp. 124–145

Novikova, K.A., "Oroki i ikh ustnoe narodnoe tvorchestvo" [The Oroks and their oral folk art]. In *Uchenye zapiski Leningradskogo Pedinstituta Im. A.I. Gertsena* [Transactions of the Leningrad A.I. Herzen Pedagogical Institute], Volume 356, Leningrad, 1967

Petrova, T.I., *Yazyk orokov (Uil'ta)* [The Orok language (Uilta)], Leningrad: Nauka, 1967

Ron, T.P., "Traditsionnaia sistema olenevodstva ul'ta" [Traditional Ulta system of reindeer husbandry]. In *Kraevedchesky biulleten'* [Local History Bulletin], Volume 3, 1994

Shternberg, L.Ia, *Giliaki, orochi, gol'dy, negidal'tsy, ainy* [Gilyaks, Orochi, Golds, Negidals, Ainu], Khabarovsk: Dal'giz, 1933

Smoliak, A.V., "K voprosy o proiskhozhdenii orokov" [On the problem of the origin of the Oroks]. In *Kratkie soobshcheniia IE AN SSSR* [Short Reports of the Institute of Ethnography, Acad. Sci. of the USSR],Volume 23, 1953

Taksami, Ch.M., "Oroki Sakhalina" (Oroks of Sakhalin). In *Doklady vostochnoi komissii Geograficheskogo Obshchestva SSSR* [Reports of the Eastern Commission of the Geographic Society of the USSR], Issue 4, Leningrad, 1967

OWL

Owls encountered in Arctic areas include species that are able to cope with conditions prevailing in these northern latitudes, namely the availability of voles and lemmings as their staple dietary prey item, the permanent daylight in summer, the absence of trees as potential nest sites, and the long winter with extremely low temperatures and snow cover protecting voles from avian predators. These latter factors are responsible for the fact that no owl species became a truly permanent resident of the Arctic.

Among the whole order of Strigiformes, only representatives of so-called typical owls (Strigidae) have evolved to species adapted to these Arctic conditions. Only one species, the snowy owl (*Nyctea scandiaca*), can be considered as truly Arctic-specific, with circumpolar breeding range restricted to the tundra biome (Arctic Slope of Alaska, Arctic Canada up to north Labrador, northeast Greenland, Scandinavian Highlands and Lapland, Northern Siberia). The snowy owl's presence in Svalbard and other parts of Greenland concerns only transient birds, while occasional breeding has been reported for Iceland and Shetland Islands.

As this biome also includes vast open grasslands, moorland, and marshes, it offers habitat structures common to the short-eared owl (*Asio flammeus*), a Holarctic species exhibiting a large circumpolar range, with several subspecies within its American range. By and large, the distribution range in the North is mostly limited to the Low Arctic belt, being absent from Greenland, Svalbard, great parts of the Canadian Archipelago, as well as from most Siberian islands.

Owl species whose breeding habitats are closely linked to forested landscapes display distribution ranges that never extend off the forest tundra belt. Such species that therefore may be recorded at the southern limit of the Arctic mainly include species like the northern hawk owl (*Surnia ulula*) and the pygmy owl (*Glaucidium passerinum*).

In the Nearctic, owls that may be encountered in the forest tundra also encompass great horned owls (*Bubo virginianus*) as counterparts of the Eurasian eagle owl (*Bubo bubo*).

As the only tundra-specific species, the large snowy owl (up to 70 cm and 3 kg) displays some adaptations and strategies not shared with the other species. While similar to eagle owls (*Bubo*) osteologically and genetically, the most striking difference is provided by the white, exceptionally dense plumage, this extreme pale coloration being most developed in adult males, adult females and immatures being speckled and barred with dark brown. It provides camouflage during most of the time when habitat is covered with snow. Smaller appendages and a more compact body when compared to its counterparts in the south may also be regarded as an adjustment to life in the North. Unlike nocturnal relatives, snowy owls lack well-developed ear-tufts. Furthermore, the facial ruff and the facial disc that covers it are smaller and less well developed in snowy owls than in nocturnal species. A characteristic shared with other Arctic birds like ptarmigan is that they grow feathers on the legs as well as on their bodies as a protection, this toe and tarsal feathering being in accordance with Kelso's Rule: stating that these patterns are more pronounced in species that inhabit high latitudes. In their Arctic breeding grounds, both species have no option but to hunt in daytime, but in their winter ranges activity seems to concentrate more on crepuscular periods.

As in the case of most owls, female snowy owls are generally larger than males in structural characters and body mass, but reasons for this reversed sexual dimorphism remain unclear. For example, while sharing relatively similar foraging and migration strategies, snowy owls exhibit strikingly different dimorphism indices compared to the short-eared owl. Indeed, some other attributes displayed by the snowy owl do not apply to the smaller-sized (up to 500 g) short-eared owl, whose distribution range extends across many biomes up to neotropics. These include the brownish plumage coloration, its looser density, and the less pronounced toe and tarsi feathering.

Habitat use and movement patterns of the two species are largely governed by the availability of their staple prey: the microtines. Dependency on lemmings is probably more pronounced in snowy owl than in short-eared owl, whose breeding range also includes that of many vole species. The dramatic

Female snowy owl (*Nyctea scandiaca*), Canada. *Copyright Bryan and Cherry Alexander Photography*

changes displayed by most northern microtine populations prevent both species from establishing any permanent residency at a given site, even if there are reports of snowy owls still present in the Arctic during polar night. Snowy and short-eared owls leave Arctic breeding grounds once snowfall sets in, and they move southward in autumn, a feature that could be considered a migration. Their winter range then includes mainly open landscapes and grasslands of the Canadian Prairies or Eurasia, where their presence may denote irruptive character. Some authors consider these irruptions as resulting from a shortage of food, but arrival in great numbers in autumn may just reflect foregoing lemming and vole highs in the North. Patterns of these movements are rather nomadic. Communal roosting behavior noticed among other owl species was suggested for short-eared owls in winter, while communal groups of snowy owls are only known from Wrangel Island in September just before owls leave this remote island for winter quarters.

The densities of these two species in breeding grounds are closely related to microtine availability. In some regions, snowy owls may settle in spring only when certain threshold densities of lemmings are met, and they may be absent in the animal community for three years in continuation. Following population outbreaks of lemmings, densities may exceed 2 pairs per 10 km^2, with locally internest distances of less than 1 km. Likewise, short-eared owls also settle in a certain site when voles are abundant. Despite the relatively huge size that enables snowy owls to exploit a great diversity of prey types, the supply of such food items

as alternate prey (birds, Arctic hares, etc.) may not be sufficient to raise a family. In this connection, a particular aspect for both species is that clutch size varies annually in accordance with prey abundance. For example, as a response to a lemming high, up to ten or even more eggs were already reported for snowy owls.

While recent studies attribute a paramount role to predation in governing vole cycles, telemetry records of lemmings as well as round–the-clock observations on snowy owls have evidenced that this species may be involved in summer crashes following lemming peaks.

A single pair may predate up to one lemming per hour, a pressure that may contribute to a marked decline in prey. But as in the case of their movement patterns, there is still a crucial need for more in-depth surveys of the bond between this rodent specialist and its staple prey.

Unlike their relatives in temperate regions, these two owl species may not be considered as globally threatened within their Arctic range.

B. SITTLER

See also **Microtines (Lemmings, Voles)**

Further Reading

Bruemmer, Fred, *Arctic Animals*, Toronto: McClelland and Stewart, 1986
Pedersen, Alwin, *Polar Animals,* London: Harrap, 1962
Portenko, L., *Die Schnee-Eule - Nyctea scandiaca (The Snowy Owl),* Volume 454, Die Neue Brehm-Bücherei: Magdeburg, 1972
Snyder, L.L., *Arctic Birds of Canada*, Toronto: University of Toronto Press, 1957

Vaughan, Richard, *In Search of Arctic Birds*, London: Poyser, 1992

Watson, A., "The behaviour, breeding and food ecology of the Snowy Owl." *Ibis*, 99(1957): 419–462

OZONE DEPLETION

Ozone is a very important part of our atmosphere due to its strong ability to absorb solar ultraviolet radiation, especially the part of the solar spectrum that is particularly harmful to living organisms, namely UVB and UVC radiation. The major part of atmospheric ozone (90%) is concentrated in the stratosphere, about 15–30 km above the Earth's surface. This ozone layer varies naturally with seasons and latitude and is continuously formed and destroyed by the variability of the solar ultraviolet radiation itself. However, during the past 2–3 decades or more, anthropogenic emissions of chlorofluorocarbons (CFCs) and other ozone-depleting substances have significantly depleted this important natural sunglass above us, thus providing less UVB protection and increased stress on the human population and the biota in terrestrial and aquatic environments.

Although crucial for all life on the Earth's surface, the ozone layer contains a very small amount of ozone. Approximately 20% of the air is normal oxygen, and only 0.00003% is ozone. Ozone is a poisonous molecule with three oxygen atoms, while the normal oxygen that we depend on contains two. The total amount of ozone as measured from the Earth's surface to the outer space (column ozone) is normally measured in Dobson units (DU). Typical total ozone levels in the Arctic are between 300 and 400 DU, showing a large seasonal and daily variation. If this ozone were taken down to the much higher atmospheric pressure at ground level, the ozone would compress to a 3–4-mm-thick layer.

The potential stratospheric ozone depletion and the effects of CFCs on ozone were not given any attention before the late 1970s. Significant scientific evidence

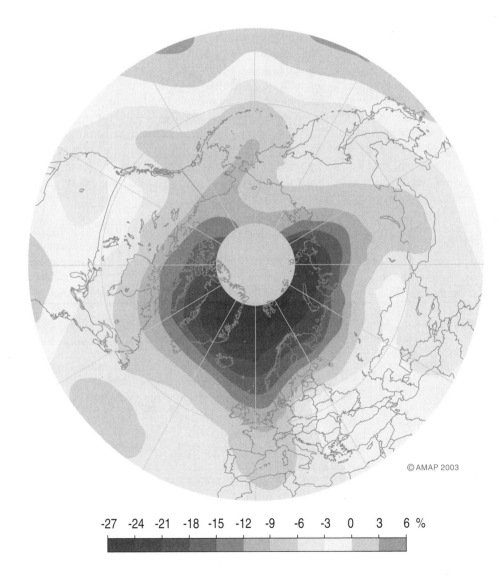

© AMAP 2003

-27 -24 -21 -18 -15 -12 -9 -6 -3 0 3 6 %

An example of an ozone anomaly, showing levels of ozone depletion relative to the long-term mean. From *AMAP Assessment Report: Arctic Pollution Issues*, Arctic Monitoring and Assessment Programme, 1998. Reproduced with permission.

now shows that the global mass of ozone is still being effectively depleted as a result of the increasing anthropogenic emissions of ozone-depleting substances from the 1950s to the late 1980s. The CFCs, which are very stable compounds and are not washed out of the lower troposphere by rain, are transported to the stratosphere by winds and convection over a long time period of the order of 10 years. There, the strong ultraviolet radiation is able to break them apart, releasing atomic chlorine. This atomic chlorine has a tremendous destructive effect on ozone, with the potential to destroy over 100,000 ozone molecules during its lifetime, and consequently accelerating the net destruction of ozone. The most well-known example of ozone depletion occurs each austral spring over Antarctica, where more than half of the total amount of ozone is depleted during September.

Whereas this most severe depletion event over Antarctica is referred to as the Ozone Hole, the northern midlatitudes have shown decreasing ozone by about 2–4% per decade during the past approximately three decades. Large ozone depletion events have also been observed over the Arctic in some recent years. During the winter of 1999/2000, the most severe Arctic ozone depletion event up till now was observed in a thin layer around 18 km altitude, with a reduction of up to 70%. The effect of such lower stratospheric ozone depletion events on the total column of ozone has not been dramatic, but analysis of the events shows the importance of heterogeneous chlorine chemistry occurring on the surface of polar stratospheric clouds, and thus a close link to stratospheric temperatures and climate change. Temperatures colder than normal stratospheric winter temperatures and a more stable and isolated stratospheric vortex have characterized those years with large seasonal ozone depletion during late Arctic winter/spring. An important factor for Arctic ozone depletion in the coming decade will therefore be the evolution of the anthropogenic climate change, since decreasing stratospheric temperatures are associated with a warming troposphere.

The 1987 Montreal Protocol, the international treaty that governs the protection of stratospheric ozone, has been successful in reducing the anthropogenic emissions of ozone-depleting substances. Chlorine is no longer increasing in the stratosphere, although some substances are still increasing. Given that the emissions and concentrations are still decreasing and that no new severe ozone-depleting substances are produced, it is estimated that the trends in stratospheric ozone will gradually reverse with full recovery of the ozone layer during the 21st century. However, the future consumption of ozone-depleting substances by developing countries and the anthropogenic warming of the global climate and its impact on the stratospheric temperatures and circulation still introduce significant uncertainties on the Arctic ozone layer and hence the surface UVB radiation. In the Arctic, the ice-covered polar ocean and the marginal ice zone are one of the most productive areas of the world in terms of biomass production. The increased levels of UVB radiation will still in several decades represent severe stress on the marine and terrestrial ecosystems, whose potential harmful effects are yet to be determined.

JON BØRRE ØRBÆK

See also **Polar Stratospheric Clouds; Ultraviolet-B radiation**

Further Reading

Bodeker, G.E., B.J. Connor, J.B. Liley & W.A. Matthews, "The global mass of ozone: 1978—1998." *Geophysical Research Letters,* 28(14) (2001): 2819–2822

Houghton, J.T. et al. (editor), *Climate Change 2001: The Scientific Basis*, Cambridge and New York: Cambridge University Press, 2001

Newman, Paul & John Pyle, 2003. "Polar Ozone: Past and Future." In *2002 UNEP/WMO Scientific Assessment of Ozone Depletion*, United Nations Environment Program and World Meteorological Organization, 2002

Schultz, A. et al., "Arctic ozone loss in threshold conditions: match observations in 1997/1998 and 1998/1999." *Journal of Geophysical Research*, 106(D7) (2001): 7495–7503

Solomon, Susan, "Stratospheric ozone depletion: a review of concepts and history." *Reviews of Geophysics*, 37(3) (1999): 275–316

Staehelin, J., N.R.P. Harris, C. Appenzeller & J. Eberhard, "Ozone trends: a review." *Reviews of Geophysics*, 39(2) (2001): 231–290

P

PALANA

Palana is the administrative center of Koryak Autonomous Okrug (district), Kamchatka Oblast' (province), in far eastern Russia, and one of the three largest towns in the okrug. The settlement is situated on the western coast of the Kamchatka Peninsula and lies along the Palana River, 8 km (5 miles) from its mouth on the Sea of Okhotsk. The place was on the route of native dog-team travelers when they crossed the axial Sredinny range of Kamchatka toward its western coast. The place is very picturesque, lying in a wide valley and surrounded by mountains. The population is now around 4000, mostly constituting Koryak (30%) and Evens (20%), with small numbers of Russians and Itel'men.

The settlement was founded in 1730, soon after Kamchatka became a part of Russia, as a small Russian stronghold against the threat from nomadic Koryaks to the North. After some time, the fortress was ruined, and as Stepan Krasheninnikov mentioned during his 1731 travel (Krasheninnikov, 1994), Palana was a settlement of only Koryaks and Itel'men. The Koryak name of the river Pilalianie, transformed to Palana by Cossacks, gave its name to the settlement. Fishing and dog training were the main occupations of local people. Later, Itel'men started livestock managing. When Karl Ditmar visited Palana in 1853 (Ditmar-von, 1901), there were 12 houses, four yurts, and a church. Houses were of a single room, a kitchen divided by a curtain. There was a population of 73 men and 70 women, with 14 horses and eight heads of cattle in their possession. The local priest and some settlers kept vegetable gardens. By the 1920s, Palana was just one of many tiny settlements spread throughout the Kamchatka north. The palana radio station connected all these islets of human activity. Thus when in 1924 the USSR was established and Koryak Autonomous Okrug was founded, Palana was nominated as its center.

For a long time, transportation to and from Palana was very poor. Landing at the airport was difficult in bad weather and there was no good harbor; thus, ships unloaded on frozen river ice and then loads were carried out by cars to the settlement. There are no good arable lands or industrial resources, and thus no industry except a fish-processing plant on the coast. Nevertheless, since 1962 Palana has been named an urban settlement and has served as an administrative center focused on the development of indigenous people. In addition to administrative institutions like a municipal hall, newspaper, court, hospital, and high school, there is also a college for reindeer herders with two-year courses in veterinary and husbandry. There is a museum of local history, and the Palana folk music group is well known throughout Russia and abroad. Today, transport communications in Palana have improved, a highway is under construction along the Sea of Okhotsk coast, the airport has been renovated, and the Internet connects Palana with the world.

LEONID M. BASKIN

See also **Kamchatka Peninsula; Koryak Autonomous Okrug**

Further Reading

Ditmar-von, Karl, *Poyezdki I prebyvaniye na Kamchatke v 1851–1855* [Travels and Stay at Kamchatka in 1851–1855], Volume 1, St Petersburg: Imperatorskaya Akademiya Nauk, 1901

Koyanto, V., *Severniye Zori* [Northern Downs], Moscow: Sovietskaya Rossiya, 1984

Krasheninnikov, Stepan, *Opisaniye zemli Kamchatskoi* [Records of the Kamchatka], St Petersburg: Nauka, 1994

Kuzakov, K., *Marshrutami schast'ya, Social'no-economicheskii ocherk* [By Paths of the Happiness, Social-Economic Essay], Petropavlovsk-Kamchatskii: Dal'nevostochnoye Knizhnoye Izdatel'stvo, 1980

Safronov, F., *Okhotsko-Kamchatskii kray* [Okhotsk-Kamchatka Region], Yakutsk: Yakutskoye knizhnoye izdatel'stvo, 1958

PANCAKE ICE

The formation of ice from the liquid phase, both in fresh water and in sea water, comprises a sequence of steps, which starts with the growth of new ice crystals and ends with the complete coverage of the water surface by a solid sheet of ice (Weeks and Ackley, 1982). Factors influencing the development of particular forms of ice include the ambient air temperature in comparison with the temperature of the near-surface water layer (i.e., the temperature gradient between the atmosphere and ocean), the salinity of the water, the presence or absence of near-surface wind and its speed, the dynamic state of the uppermost water layer (i.e., the presence or absence of turbulent flow, its magnitude and direction), and the presence or absence of earlier formed ice. The formation of pancake ice comprises a growth process that is typical for dynamic/turbulent conditions in the water column, both in fresh water and in saline waters.

Development of Pancake Ice

The development of pancake ice starts with the formation of frazil ice crystals (fine needles and platelets) in the uppermost surface layers of the water body. They form in supercooled water (i.e., water with temperatures slightly below the ambient- and salinity-dependent freezing point). Under quiet conditions, the frazil crystals will slowly float toward the water surface and will gradually form a thicker and thicker layer of suspended ice crystals, a so-called slush layer, which may also be called grease ice. The thickening of this layer by continued accumulation of frazil crystals and lifting of crystals above the level of the water surface will lead to the formation of a solid ice layer known as dark nilas.

However, in the presence of surface winds and/or enhanced turbulence in the near-surface water layer, for example, in rivers or streams or in the presence of surface waves in the open ocean, the suspended frazil crystals will be subjected to continued mutual collisions with each other (Figure 1). During each collision, an enhanced pressure will be exerted at the contact point, which will lead to a momentarily lowered melting point (i.e., punctual (partial) melting will take place at temperatures below 0°C for freshwater ice). This process is called regelation in glaciology (Hobbs, 1974), and also enables ice skaters to glide over a solid ice cover by forming temporarily a thin film of water at the metal-ice interface. A shift in the flow direction of the surface water (e.g., as part of a wave field) may lead to a divergent movement of the crystals that had collided a moment before. This causes the pressure at the contact point to be released again. Consequently, the freezing point returns to ambient conditions, the punctually formed meltwater refreezes, and leads to the "welding-together" (also called sintering in metallurgy) of the crystals (Figure 1). As this process continues, more and more crystals or crystal aggregates collide and are formed into increasingly bigger aggregates. This process eventually leads to aggregates or ice pads, which are partly raised above the level of the water surface (Figure 1). Further freezing due to cold air temperatures solidifies their tops, and collisions at random orientation with other such aggregates lead to raised rims, from plastic deformation of the slush near the edges of the pad and from splashing water (Figure 1). Due to continued collisions, the edges of these aggregates will start to thicken and will gradually form a ring-shaped outer confinement with thicknesses above the mean thickness of the ice pads. The resultant shapes of the aggregates resemble those of pancakes that are cooked in a pan, hence this somewhat strange name for an ice-growth form (Weeks and Ackley, 1982). A subsequent process often observed is the rafting of individual pancakes (i.e., the "stacking" of two or more pancakes on top of each other; Figure 1) and the formation of aggregate pancake ice, that is, the formation of entire ice-floes consisting of a number of individual and/or

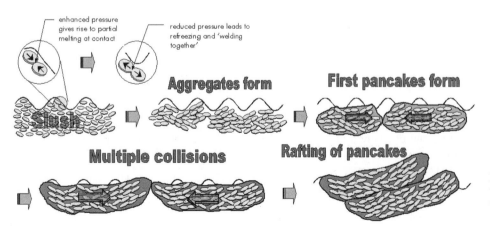

Figure 1: Schematic representation of pancake ice formation; frazil crystals simplified as disk shaped; not to scale.

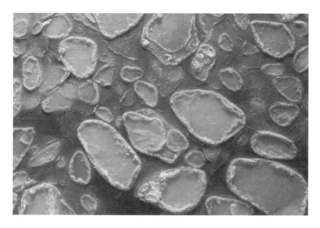

Figure 2: Pancake ice as seen in the Ross Sea, Antarctica (Photographer: Michael Van Woert; NOAA Photo Library).

rafted pancakes (Figure 2). As has been observed in Antarctica, this process, which forms a part of the so-called pancake cycle, represents a major mechanism for sea ice formation in Antarctic waters (Lange, 1990; Lange et al., 1989). Ice growth via the pancake cycle proceeds much more rapidly than any other growth process, particularly congelation growth, which is the dominant form of ice formation in the Arctic.

Basic Characteristics

Ice pancakes can reach diameters between a few centimeters and up to several tens of centimeters. Thicknesses range between a few centimeters and a few tens of centimeters. The shape of the pancakes depends on the place where they are formed. In open water, pancakes tend to be nearly circular, while along the coast, more elongated forms with the long axis paralleling the shoreline evolve. Pancakes essentially consist entirely of frazil crystals, occasionally substituted by small amounts of congelation ice at the bottom of rafted pancakes. Thus, the principal textural characteristic of pancake ice is that of granular ice (for an explanation of terms, see Eicken and Lange, 1989). Grain sizes range from submillimeter to several millimeters (Lange, 1988). Individual pancakes are still fairly unconsolidated, but usually do not break apart when lifted out of the water. Their mechanical integrity increases the larger the fraction of the pancake above sea level, which allows brine drainage from this part of the ice and consequently stronger bonds to be developed between grains. Depending on the stage of their formation, pancake ice may contain copious amounts of pore water.

Experiments and Modeling

The formation of pancake ice has been simulated, both in the laboratory and through numerical model studies.

Because of its rapid formation process, pancake ice is difficult to study in the field. Recent laboratory investigations include experiments in ice tanks aimed at separating dynamic growth processes from thermodynamic effects (Evers et al., 2002) and tests designed to determine the major processes controlling the size of pancakes (Ackley et al., 2002). Concurrently, numerical models are being developed and tested to gain a more comprehensive understanding of the principal formation processes of pancake ice (see, e.g., Hopkins and Shen, 2001; Leonard et al., 1999; Shen et al., 2001).

MANFRED A. LANGE

See also **River and Lake Ice; Sea Ice**

Further Reading

Ackley, S.F., H.H. Shen, M. Dai & Y. Yuan, "Wave-Ice Interaction During Ice Growth; The Formation of Pancake Ice." *In Proceedings of 16th IAHR International Symposium on Ice*, Dunedin, New Zealand, 2002, edited by V.A. Squire & P.J. Langhorne, Rotterdam: Balkema, 2002, pp. 158–164

Eicken, H. & M.A. Lange, "Development and properties of sea ice in the coastal regime of the southeastern Weddell Sea." *Journal of Geophysical Research*, 94 (1989): 8193–8206

Evers, K., H.H. Shen, M. Dai, Y. Yuan, T. Kolerski & J. Wilkinson, "A twin wave tank pancake ice growth experiment." In *Proceedings of 16th IAHR International Symposium on Ice*, Dunedin, New Zealand, 2002, edited by V.A. Squire & P.J. Langhorne, Rotterdam: Balkema, 2002, pp. 150–157

Hobbs, P.V., *Ice Physics*, Oxford: Clarendon Press, 1974

Hopkins, M.A. & H.H. Shen, "Simulation of pancake-ice dynamics in a wave field." *Annals of Glaciology*, 33 (2001): 355–360

Lange, M.A., "Basic properties of Antarctic sea ice as revealed by textural analysis of ice cores." *Annals of Glaciology*, 10 (1988): 95–101

———, "Properties of sea ice in the Weddell Sea, Antarctica." In *Proceedings of IAHR 10th International Symposium on Ice 1990*, Espoo, Finland, 1990, IAHR, 1990, pp. 289–299

Lange, M.A., S.F. Ackley, P. Wadhams, G.S. Dieckmann & H. Eicken, "Development of sea ice in the Weddell Sea, Antarctica." *Annals of Glaciology*, 12 (1989): 92–96

Leonard, G.H., H.T. Shen & S.F. Ackley, "Dynamic growth of a pancake ice cover." In *Proceedings of 14th IAHR International Symposium on Ice*, Potsdam, New York, USA, 1998, edited by H.T. Shen, Rotterdam: Balkema, 1999, pp. 891–896

Shen, H.H., S.F. Ackley & M.A. Hopkins, "A conceptual model for pancake-ice formation in a wave field." *Annals of Glaciology*, 33 (2001): 361–367

Weeks, W.F. & S.F. Ackley, *The Growth, Structure, and Properties of Sea Ice*, Hanover, New Hampshire: US Army Cold Regions Research and Engineering Laboratory (CRREL Monograph 82–1), 1982

PAPANIN, IVAN DMITRIEVICH

Ivan Papanin, a well-known Russian polar explorer, was leader of the world's first scientific expedition on a drifting station in the Arctic. Papanin made his first trip to the Arctic in 1931 on board the icebreaker

Malygin, which was sent to Franz Josef Land to exchange mail with the German dirigible *Graf Zeppelin.* A year later, he returned to the Franz Josef archipelago as chief of the polar radio station. Very soon, Papanin organized the world's northernmost geophysical observatory in Bukhta Tikhaya on Gukera (Hoover) Island, which was one of the most important events of the Second International Polar Year 1932–1933.

Papanin's next trip was to Cape Chelyuskin (the northernmost point of mainland Asia, on the Taymyr Peninsula), where he completely renovated the old meteorological station. Due to his excellent organization skills, Papanin was appointed as chief of the Russian expedition to the North Pole. The expedition was planned by academician Otto Shmidt, who had suggested setting up a research base camp on drifting ice close to the North Pole. Papanin was responsible for logistics and was involved in the construction of the station on Rudolf Island in the Franz Josef archipelago 800 km from the Pole. The station was supposed to serve as an intermediate base for the participants of the expedition, providing the link between the continent and the Pole.

On the morning of May 21, 1937, the four-engined aircraft piloted by Mikhail Vodop'yanov took off from Rudolf Island with six passengers on board, and 6 hours later landed on the 3 m thick and 4 km^2 large ice pack 36 km (20 miles) from the North Pole. The passengers on board the aircraft were academician Otto Shmidt, four members of the expedition, and the cameraman Yakov Khalip. Following this flight on May 25, 28, and June 5, three other planes delivered all the necessary equipment and supplies, totaling about 9 tons.

The ultimate goal of the expedition, which is now known as the North Pole 1 drifting station, was to study the meteorological, oceanographic, and atmospheric processes in the central Arctic. After the opening ceremony on June 6, the aircraft returned to the continent and left the four explorers on the drifting polar station. These were the chief of the expedition Ivan Papanin, oceanographer Pietr Shirshov, astronomer, geophysicist, and meteorologist Evgeniy Fedorov, and radio operator Ernst Krenkel. They spent nine months on the drifting ice station. During the first six months, the station drifted southward along the 0° meridian, but then shifted to eastern Greenland. It was planned that the expedition would spend about one year on the drifting ice and would reach the 81–83 parallel close to Spitsbergen or Franz Josef Land in the spring of 1938. However, in nine months the ice pack had drifted to the south of the 71 parallel, and on February 19, 1938 the icebreakers *Taymyr* and *Murman* picked up the participants of the expedition in the Greenland Sea.

The North Pole 1 station drifted more than 2500 km in 274 days. The researchers obtained valuable meteorological, bathymetric, gravitational, and magnetic data that were used to correct the local curvature of the Earth geoid, to calculate and map the magnetic declination. This information found direct and immediate implications in Arctic navigation and long-distance intercontinental transatlantic flights over the North Pole first performed in 1937 by Russian pilots Valerij Chkalov and Mikhail Gromov.

Data collected by the expeditions revealed intensive cyclonic activities over the North Pole. Meteorological observations allowed estimation of the amount of heat transported by air and water circulation from the Atlantic Ocean to the Arctic. Hydrological observations confirmed Nansen's conclusion that relatively warm Atlantic waters penetrate deep into the high latitudes. This stream of warm Atlantic waters was detected at the depth of several hundred meters and traced throughout the route of the drift. Data on the thickness, temperature, and velocity of this stream allowed evaluating the advective heat inflow to the Arctic Ocean. The expedition collected valuable data on the directions and velocities of the ice drift, and on the Arctic Ocean circulation. The results of the expedition completely changed the widespread opinion about the poor biodiversity and life forms in the Arctic. Birds, seals, and polar bears were found to the north of the 88 parallel. In summer ocean waters were rich in plankton, shellfish, and jellyfish. Plankton was found even in the probes taken from the 3 km deepwater layers.

The participants of the expedition were awarded the status of Hero of the Soviet Union and a Gold Medal. Despite the very simple instrumentation, the North Pole 1 results were tremendously important. The new scientific approach to the study of the Arctic Ocean proved to be effective, although living conditions on floating ice were extremely difficult. Since 1950, similar Russian and US floating stations have worked continuously in the Arctic.

In 1939, Papanin was appointed minister of the Northern Sea Routes administration (Glavsevmorput), and became responsible for all the scientific and logistical aspects of the exploration of the Russian Arctic. In 1940, he participated in rescuing the icebreaker *Sedov* and was given the second highest State Award. During World War II, he was a commissioner of the State Defence Committee responsible for the navigation over the northern sea routes. He constructed and renovated seaports in Severodvinsk, Arkhangel'sk, and Murmansk. In May 1943, he was conferred the rank of rear admiral.

Papanin was the chief of the Russian scientific fleet for more than 40 years. In 1951, he became the head of the expeditory department in the Russian Academy of Science. He organized the Institute of Biology of Inland Waters and headed it for 20 years. Since 1945, he was the chairperson of the Moscow branch of the Russian Geographical Society. In 1980, he received The Big Gold Medal of the Russian Geographic Society in recognition of his outstanding services in Soviet geography. His name can be found on the maps of the Arctic and Antarctic.

Biography

Ivan Dmitrievich Papanin was born into the family of a poor sailor in Sebastopol, Russia, on November 26, 1894. His grandfather was lost in the Crimean war at the time of Sevastopol defense in 1855. His father Dmitrii Nikolaevich was also a sailor and his mother Sekletinia Petrovna was a charwoman. There were nine children in the family, but only six of them survived. In 1903–1907, Ivan went to elementary school. When he was 12 years old, he started to work in the workshop in the harbor. During World War I, he served in the Navy on the Black Sea. In 1920, Papanin became a staff officer in the headquarters of the South-Western Army in the Ukraine; from 1922, he worked in Moscow as a commissioner in the Ministry of Sea Routes. In 1925, after graduation from the Higher Communication courses, he was sent to Aldan River in Yakutia as the deputy head of the expedition to construct the radio station. Papanin completed this task successfully and returned to Moscow to study at the Academy of Planning. He was married to Galina Kirillovna Papanina, and died in Moscow on January 31, 1986.

MARINA BELOLUTSKAIA

See also **Drifting Stations; North Pole Air Expedition, 1937; Shmidt, Otto Yul'evich**

Further Reading

Papanin, I.D., *Life on an Ice Floe: Diary of Ivan Papanin*, translated from Russian, New York: Messner, 1939
———, *Zhizn' na L'dine* [Life on Ice] (7th edition), Moscow: Mysl, 1977
———, *Led i Plamen'* [Ice and Fire] (4th edition), Moscow: Politizdat, 1988

PARRY, SIR WILLIAM EDWARD

Sir William Edward Parry personified British imperial expansion in the 19th century as "the beau ideal of an Arctic officer." Over the course of his four expeditions, Parry set the standard in the public's perception for the Arctic explorer. His name dominates polar exploration as the first European explorer to pierce the mysterious Arctic Archipelago.

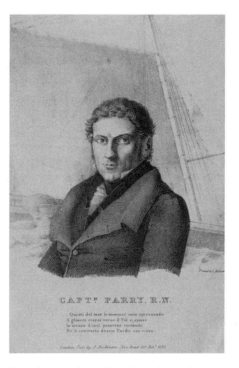

Portrait engraving of Arctic explorer "Captn. Parry, R.N." Originally published by J. Dickinson, London.
Copyright Bryan and Cherry Alexander Photography

After cultivating friendships in 1817 with Sir Joseph Banks, president of the Royal Geographical Society, and John Barrow, secretary of the Admiralty, Parry became one of the Royal Navy's most experienced polar navigators and explorers. Parry captured popular attention as well as the acclaim of his peers. Constantly concerned with the health and welfare of his men, he set up a strict work and exercise schedule, plays and musical concerts, and educational classes to combat the deadly boredom of the long Arctic winters.

Barrow appointed the young lieutenant Parry second-in-command on John Ross's 1818 Arctic expedition. Although the Ross expedition achieved the first survey of Baffin Bay in centuries and the Royal Navy's first encounter with the region's native Inuit, all paled beside an unfortunate decision. After heading up Lancaster Sound, Ross reported that the sound was merely a bay closed off by a range of mountains he called the Croker Mountains and inexplicably returned to England. No other officers, including Parry, confirmed the existence of the mountain range and this decision all but ruined Ross's career. An angry Barrow absolved Ross's junior officers, especially Parry, of blame. Afterwards, Barrow selected Parry to command the next Arctic expedition.

Parry's excursion into Lancaster Sound in 1819 proved to be the most successful of all 19th-century Arctic voyages. The Admiralty gave Parry—at 28 the oldest officer on the expedition—the *Hecla* and the *Griper*. He left England on May 11, 1819 and sailed north through heavy ice into Lancaster Sound, passing the imaginary Croker Mountains, entered Barrow Strait, and into unchartered waters. On September 17, stopped by ice, Parry retreated east to Melville Island, anchoring his ships in a cove he named Winter Harbor. This year-long sojourn was the first winter spent on the Arctic Ocean by British ships. On August 1, 1820, defeated by the Arctic weather, Parry sailed for home after pushing 600 miles west, further than any ship would sail through the Arctic for decades. Having opened the first leg of the North West Passage with minimal loss of life, Parry received a hero's welcome.

Parry spent the winter of 1820–1821 preparing for his second voyage to conquer the Passage. The quest had now taken on the characteristics of a race, with the British fearing that the Russians would beat them to the Passage. With two ships, the *Hecla* and its sister ship the *Fury*, Parry's second expedition began on May 8, 1821. Stopped by Somerset Island, Parry opted to go east toward Winter Island, where the ships froze in, just south of the Arctic Circle. On February 1, 1822, Parry's expedition met and developed a close relationship with 25 Inuit. Parry introduced them to pencil and paper, which they used to draw detailed maps of the region. Caught by the ice at Melville Peninsula and locked in for another ten months, Parry and his crew spent more time with the Inuit studying their culture. By August, still held by the ice, and with a crew sick and demoralized despite his best efforts, Parry admitted defeat and on October 10, 1823, he anchored off the Shetland Islands. Having discovered no route to the Passage by Hudson Bay, he was barely home before he began lobbying for a third expedition.

The Admiralty agreed and he recommissioned *Hecla* and *Fury*, and sailed on May 19, 1824. Entering Davis Strait in late June, Parry immediately encountered huge icebergs. On August 1, *Hecla* was almost lost in the crushing ice. In early July 1825, Parry and his men sawed channels through the ice and towed the ships into open water, but soon the ice moved back in, trapping the ships against Somerset Island. In August, the heavily laden *Fury* had to be beached, unloaded, and abandoned. *Hecla*, barely escaping the same fate, moved further south only to be stopped by the ice. Parry's third expedition retreated and reached Britain on October 16, 1825. Parry had not found the passage, had explored no more than a few miles of new land, and, more importantly, had lost a ship. He swore to never again seek the elusive passage.

By the winter of 1826, Parry reversed his decision to abandon the Arctic and fixed his attention on the North Pole. He developed an ingenious new invention, the "sledge boat," a flat-bottomed boat, 20 ft long and 7 ft wide, with two sledge runners mounted underneath. Parry's endeavor represented the first realistic attempt to reach the Pole and the first scientific expedition to the Arctic Ocean. His last Arctic voyage left London aboard the *Hecla* on March 25, 1827. Again, he was unlucky due to bad weather and the slow, painful progress of his sledge boats. On July 10, Parry became the first explorer in the world to reach 82°45′ N latitude, a new record that would stand for 50 years. His men, wet and exhausted, were subsisting on scant rations when Parry realized that due to the southward movement of the ice, they had actually traveled only 178 miles north of the anchored *Hecla* instead of the 978 miles clocked. Finally, on August 22, Parry, defeated and dispirited, left for England, arriving in London on October 6, 1827. Although Parry remained a hero to the public, his Arctic career was over; he settled into a sinecure as a naval hydrographer.

Biography

William Edward Parry was born in Bath, England, on December 19, 1790. His father, an eminent physician, was the governor of the Bath hospital and a member of the Royal Geographic Society. Raised in a cultured family and exposed to art, literature, and music, Parry attended grammar school in England before joining the navy at the age of 13 through the influence of Admiral Cornwallis. After serving in the last years of the Napoleonic Wars and in the Revolutionary War against the United States, Parry served in the West Indies until 1817. He made his first voyage to the Arctic in 1818 with Sir John Ross. He returned to the North in a highly successful expedition (1819–1820), and made two unsuccessful attempts to discover the North West Passage in 1821–1823 and 1824–1825. In 1827, Parry made an unsuccessful attempt to reach the North Pole by sledge. He described his travels in *Voyage for the Discovery of a North West Passage* (1821) and *Narrative of an Attempt to Reach the North Pole in Boats* (1828). In October 1826, he married Isabella Stanley. After her death, he married Catherine Hoare in 1841 and fathered 13 children. Knighted in 1829, he was promoted to rear admiral in 1853 and his last post was as lieutenant governor of the Greenwich Hospital for naval pensioners. Parry died near Coblenz, Germany on July 8, 1855.

JAMES YATES

See also **North West Passage, Exploration of; Ross, James**

Further Reading

Berton, Pierre, *The Arctic Grail: The Quest for the Northwest Passage and the North Pole: 1818–1909*, New York: Penguin, 1988

Delgado, James P., *Across the Top of the World: The Quest for the Northwest Passage*, New York: Checkmark Books, 1999
Holland, Clive, *Farthest North: Endurance and Adventure in the Quest for the North Pole*, New York: Carroll and Graf, 1999
Mirsk, Jeannette, *To the Arctic: The Story of Northern Exploration from Earliest Times*, Chicago: University of Chicago Press, 1970

PASTORALISM

For indigenous human societies to survive in the Arctic, gathering or growing plants as the central focus of household economies has never been an option. Animal protein, including land and sea mammals, sustained indigenous Arctic residents until the global economy of the Middle Ages brought agricultural trade goods to the north. Initially, strategies for acquiring animal protein involved some aspect of hunting or fishing, whether as individuals or in groups. Although the exact reasons for the transition are unknown, pastoralism, defined loosely as humans utilizing domesticated animals in their subsistence strategy, developed among indigenous Arctic societies in Eurasia, but not in North America. One of the central theoretical questions concerning Arctic pastoralism is why that difference evolved.

Following this loose definition, however, pastoralism existed in both Eurasia and North America for over a millennium. In North America, the ancestors of the Inuit used dogs for a variety of purposes, not the least of which was transportation. When Icelandic Norse led by Eirík the Red settled in Greenland around AD 1000, they brought domesticated cattle, sheep, goats, and perhaps horses to the North American continent. In the late 1800s, Sheldon Jackson imported Saami herding families and reindeer into Alaska to establish pastoralism among the Inuit. Today, several animal species are tended in the North American Arctic, including muskoxen in Canada, where they are exploited for a variety of purposes.

A narrower definition of pastoralism, using herd animals as the socioeconomic basis for a society, restricts indigenous Arctic pastoralism to Eurasia, and to a single animal species, reindeer (*Rangifer tarandus*). Initially, Arctic peoples such as the Evenk, Chukchi, and Nenet of Siberia probably used reindeer for three purposes that define pastoralism broadly: work, raw materials, and food. During the initial phase of Arctic pastoralism called intensive herding, herds were small and tame. Tame reindeer were excellent for transportation work (draft), especially in winter, either as pack animals or with sleds. Another job for tame reindeer was as a decoy for wild reindeer, and as a lead reindeer for migrating herds. Additionally, reindeer provided much of the raw material to make clothes, tents, tools (such as knives), and religious objects. Lastly, herders used their animals for food, especially milk and milk products such as yogurt from tame reindeer, since most of the meat probably still came from wild reindeer. Unlike later pastoralism, during intensive herding, most household products were probably derived from hunting and fishing. Intensive herding societies therefore looked very similar to hunting societies.

Pastoralism in the restricted sense of providing the basis for household subsistence required both economic and political changes involving how animals were utilized and how humans were organized to utilize them. Since many social scientists believe that Arctic herding societies evolved from reindeer hunting societies, moving from reindeer hunting to reindeer herding required three specific types of changes. These included changes in human-animal relationships, human social relationships, and economic production. These changes fundamentally transformed hunting societies' basic value systems, the foundations of their cultures.

The change in human-animal relationships as Arctic societies transformed from hunting to herding meant that humans no longer competed for reindeer as just another predator, although a more effective predator because of technology such as taming reindeer decoy. Pastoralists began to protect reindeer from other predators (including other humans) so that the herders could utilize the animals exclusively. Protecting reindeer from other predators such as wolves was a deeply ingrained value in Arctic herding societies. In modern times, this deeply held value has come into conflict with majority societies such as Sweden, where Saami herders have been prosecuted for violating that county's ban on hunting wolves, a protected species.

The second change in emergent Arctic pastoralists involved social relationships, as they transformed from egalitarian to stratified societies. Indigenous Arctic sea and land mammal hunting societies had a central value of sharing. Animals were often hunted in teams, such as Inuit whale hunting boats (umiaks), and these are supported by extended families or villages. The entire hunting sociey owned access to land and water and the animals that lived there. Although harvested meat was technically the property of the hunter who actually killed the animal, "ownership" meant the right to divide the meat among all members of the group. Since joint ownership and sharing in hunting societies meant that no individuals accumulated wealth in the form of land or animals, all members of the society were equal in economic terms.

Once a society transformed to pastoralism, land and water were still held in common, however, animals become the property of individuals (or families). This duality created an inherently unstable aspect of the herding economy called the "tragedy of the commons." Although pastoralist societies had access to common land, a central practice for individual herders was to acquire as many animals as possible for protection against herd loss. Since an individual herder competed with other herders in the society for pasturage, the common subsistence strategy broke down when herders accumulated more animals than their pastures could support. The only way individual herders could accumulate more animal wealth without damaging their own long-term ability to maintain large herds was if other herders dropped out. While families and unrelated members of the society helped each other out to a limited degree, it was in the individual's best interests for some herders to fail. Thus, Arctic pastoralists developed as incipient capitalists, who strove to maximize their own animal wealth at the expense of others.

The third change in Arctic societies as they adapted to pastoralism occurred when a new form of economic production developed, based upon the commercial slaughter and sale of reindeer meat. That type of pastoralism is called extensive herding or reindeer ranching, which characterizes the modern forms of Arctic pastoralism today. Individuals and families own large numbers of animals, very few of whom are tame (if any), and the goal is commercial meat production for profit. Although some traditional activities associated with intensive herding may still occur, such as fishing and hunting, households most often need a full-time wage earner for a steady income to support commercial enterprises. Today, reindeer ranching in the Arctic is fully mechanized, and herders utilize motorized vehicles such as snowmobiles, boats, aircraft, and automobiles for their work. The mechanization of herding disconnected women from pastoralism, since their associated skills and occupations like milking reindeer and supervising nomadic moves are no longer needed. Mechanization also resulted in a more sedentary lifestyle for formerly seminomadic herders, since tending free-ranging animals is a daily commute for the men who use modern transportation means. Finally, mechanization has increased stratification in herding societies as individuals and families require very large herds to successfully participate in the commercial reindeer industry, and these societies are today characterized by both wealthy and poor herders.

Social scientists have not satisfactorily answered the question of why reindeer pastoralism developed in the Eurasian but not the North American Arctic. The answer to this question may be that the indigenous Eurasian Arctic herding societies bordered state-level agricultural societies, while those in North America did not. Eurasian reindeer herders depended heavily upon supplementing hunting and fishing by trading with agricultural societies. To meet these needs, they practiced intensive herding with small herds. For example, until the early 1600s, many Saami families maintained small herds and acquired much of their products from fishing and hunting. At that time, the Swedish (which controlled much of Norway and Finland as well) and Russian Empires taxed and traded with the Saami in natural products like fur and fish to participate in the European commodities markets. The ability of state societies to impart their wills on indigenous Arctic herding societies probably also influenced the transition to extensive herding. Again, using Sweden as an example, Swedish tax and trade relationships changed around the mid-17th century, and the Crown began to tax in reindeer meat to feed their massive armies in the field throughout northern Europe. The taxation required more reindeer as it forced Saami herders to adopt a more extensive herding strategy.

ROBERT P. WHEELERSBURG

See also **Eirík the Red; Reindeer; Reindeer Pastoralism; Umiak**

Further Reading

Ingold, Tim, *Hunters, Pastoralists and Ranchers: Reindeer Economies and Their Transformations,* Cambridge Studies in Social Anthropology, Volume 28, Cambridge: Cambridge University Press, 1980

Krupnik, Igor, *Arctic Adaptations: Native Whalers and Reindeer Herders of Northern Eurasia Hanover:* University of New England Press, 1993

Pelto, Pertti J., *The Snowmobile Revolution: Technology and Social Change in the Arctic,* Ithaca: Waveland Press, 1973

PATTERNED AND POLYGONAL GROUND

The generic terms "patterned ground" and "polygonal ground" are often used interchangeably to describe the ubiquitous geometric patterns that decorate ground surfaces throughout the Arctic. In the *Glossary of Permafrost and Related Ground-Ice Terms* (1988), polygonal ground is cross-referenced with patterned ground, which is defined as "any ground surface exhibiting a discernibly ordered, more-or-less symmetrical, morphological pattern of ground and, where present, vegetation" (Permafrost Subcommittee, 1988: 61). In 1956, A.L. Washburn published a descriptive classification of patterned ground phenomena based on geometric form and the degree of sorting (Washburn, 1956, 1973). Washburn's classification, which is still in use today, distinguished between circles, polygons, nets, stripes, and steps as geometric categories, which were further classified as either sorted or nonsorted. Washburn identified 19 processes that contribute to the formation of patterned ground; however, not all are related to cold environments. He also concluded that a combination of several processes

Low- and high-center polygons. From *AMAP Assessment Report: Arctic Pollution Issues,* Arctic Monitoring and Assessment Programme, 1998. Reproduced with permission. Aerial view of patterned ground, Polar Bear Pass, Bathurst Island, Nunavut (photographed in 1970). *Copyright David R. Gray*

may contribute to a single patterned ground feature and that morphologically similar features may be formed by different combinations of processes.

On the basis of formational processes, patterned ground phenomena can be grouped into two basic categories of landforms. The first includes small-scale geometric patterns produced by cryoturbation. Cryoturbation is the vertical and horizontal displacement of sediments and mineral clasts within the active layer associated with the complex interaction of soil water and soil particles during repeated freezing and thawing. The genetic use of the term patterned ground is reserved for this category of landforms. Although widespread in the Arctic, this category of patterned ground also occurs in other periglacial settings. The second category includes macroscale geometric patterns produced by thermal contraction cracking of ground and the formation of networks of intersecting vertically oriented ice veins. Over time, this process creates large V-shaped bodies of ground ice called ice wedges. Networks of ice wedges are called ice-wedge

polygons or polygonal ground. Ice wedges and ice-wedge polygons occur only in areas underlain by permafrost and are most frequently associated with continuous permafrost.

Patterned ground associated with cryoturbation is best developed in regions of intensive frost action (both present and past) and occurs in both permafrost regions and areas of deep seasonal frost. Since it forms mainly within near-surface layers that seasonally freeze and thaw, it is therefore limited to the active layer in permafrost regions. Patterns include sorted and nonsorted circles, polygons, nets, stripes, and steps. In most cases, the shape of the pattern is defined either by bare soil with vegetated outlines or sorted arrangements of coarse and fine mineral clasts. Patterns may occur as single cells or as groups of cells. Cryoturbation involves several processes, including frost heaving and up-freezing, frost jacking, cryostatic pressure, and thaw settlement. Soil water and its redistribution during freezing and thawing, the formation of segregated ice lenses, and the tendency for different particle sizes to heave at different rates underly most of these processes. The presence of frost-susceptible soils (silt to fine sand-sized particles) plays an important role in the redistribution of soil moisture during freezing and segregated ice lens formation. Sorted and nonsorted circles, polygons, and nets occur predominantly on flat surfaces (<3° slope) and typically have diameters from 0.5 to 3.0 m. Cell shapes tend to become elongated at gradients between 2° and 7° (Washburn, 1956); thus, on progressively steeper slopes, patterns trend toward sorted and nonsorted steps and stripes. Frost hummocks and mud boils are forms of nonsorted circles. Several contemporary patterned ground models invoke a convection cell process as part of the formational process.

Polygonal ground (ice-wedge polygons) are the largest and most distinctive patterned ground phenomena. Ice–wedge formation involves repetition of two processes: first, thermal contraction cracking of the ground and, second, infiltration and freezing of meltwater resulting in the formation of an ice vein. Cold winter air temperatures cause intense cooling of the surface and near-surface sediments, which in turn results in differential thermal contraction of the ground. Thermal contraction generates tensile stresses sufficient for trigger cracking. Thermal contraction cracks 1–2 cm in width and ranging from a few meters up to 30–40 m in length propagate several meters downward into the permafrost (Lachenbruch, 1962). The resulting cracks remain open through the winter but at the onset of spring meltwater infiltrates into the crack and freezes, forming a vertically oriented vein of ice. Since thermal contraction cracking tends to occur in the same place year after year, the incremental addition of ice veins forms large vertically foliated V-shaped bodies of ground ice called ice wedges. Networks of thermal contraction cracks evolve to release tensile stresses for large areas. The spatial pattern in cracking reflects the three-dimensional pattern of ground temperatures and the corresponding stress field. Local factors such as snow cover, vegetation, surface water bodies, and soil type also affect the pattern and frequency of thermal contraction cracking. Since thermal contraction cracking does not occur every year, it may take several tens or even hundreds of years to produce a sizeable ice-wedge. Furthermore, there is a hierarchy of ice wedges that reflects the tendency for some ice wedges to crack more often than others. The result is the formation of a three-dimensional network of ice-wedges called ice-wedge polygons or polygonal ground. As an ice-wedge grows, it usually develops a surface trough over the long axis of the wedge bordered on each side by low ramparts. The trough marks the middle of the wedge and the ramparts reflect an upturning of sediments on either side of the wedge. Polygons normally have four or five sides and vary from 10 to 30 m in diameter. Ice-wedge polygons tend to be either high or low centered. Low-centered polygons develop shallow circular tundra ponds within inter-wedge depressions, while high centered polygons tend to channel runoff along the ice-wedge troughs and develop deep tundra ponds at ice-wedge junctions. Surface runoff will tend to follow ice-wedge troughs, causing thermal erosion that enhances polygon relief. Beaded drainage patterns readily develop in low-lying areas when a series of tundra ponds are connected by drainage along ice-wedge troughs.

WAYNE POLLARD

See also **Fossil Periglacial Phenomena; Frost and Frost Phenomena; Gelifluction Processes**

Further Reading

French, H.M., *The Periglacial Environment* (2nd edition), Harlow, England: Addison-Wesley, Longman Limited, 1996

Lachenbruch, A., "Mechanics of thermal contraction cracks and ice-wedge polygons." *Geological Society of America, Special Paper,* 70 (1962)

Permafrost Subcommittee, *The Glossary of Permafrost and Related Ground-Ice Terms. National Research Council Technical Memorandum 142,* Ottawa, Canada, 1988

Washburn, A.L., "Classification of patterned ground and review of suggested origins." *Bulletin, Geological Society of America,* 67 (1956): 823–865

———, *Periglacial Processes and Environments,* London: Edward Arnold Press, 1973

PAYER, JULIUS

In 1866, the mountaineer Julius Payer was already well known for exploring and mapping unknown regions of the Austrian Alps when August Petermann invited him to participate in the Second German North Polar Expedition as a topographer and leader of the sled journeys. The ships *Germania* under Karl Koldewey and *Hansa* under Captain Paul Hegemann finally left Bremerhaven on June 15, 1869. The aim of the journey was the exploration of the region north of 74°, at the eastern coast of Greenland.

The ships were separated on July 20 at 74°4′ N 12°52′ W in foggy weather by a misleading signal. They never met again. On September 14, 1869, the *Hansa* was beset at 73°25.7′ N and, drifting south, was heavily damaged by ice pressures. The ship sank on October 21, 10 km off the east coast of Greenland at 70°52′ N 21° W. The crew of 14 escaped onto an ice-floe and spent the polar winter on it. After a southward drift of about 2000 km over 237 days, the crew finally reached the missionary station, Friedrichsthal (now Narsaq Kujalleq) in southern Greenland, on June 13, 1870 and thus was rescued.

Meanwhile, the *Germania* reached its northernmost point at 75°30′ N 17°30′ W and finally wintered in a bay of Sabine Island, from where Payer made four sled trips. Together with Koldewey, he reached the northernmost point of the land journeys on April 15, 1870 at 77°1′ N 18°50′ W at the east coast of Greenland. The *Germania* continued sailing on July 22 and going south, Payer discovered and named the *Kaiser Franz Josef-Fjord* (August 3, 1870). He ascended the 2200 m high (later so called) *Payer Spitze* and mapped the area. The *Germania* was back at Bremerhaven on September 11, 1870. As the ship could not reach a higher latitude, the only geographical success was Payer's sled journeys.

Back in Vienna, Payer was awarded the Order of the Iron Crown by the Austrian Emperor Franz Josef, for his scientific achievements during the Second German North Polar Expedition, on November 29, 1870. This honor brought him to the attention of the Austrian ship-of-the-line lieutenant Karl Weyprecht, the future promoter of a global polar research and initiator of the First International Polar Year in 1882.

Sponsored by Count Johann Wilczek and supported by August Petermann, Payer and Weyprecht initiated a preliminary expedition during the summer of 1871. They successfully examined the ice conditions between Spitsbergen and Novaya Zemlya, and increased the chances for a future advance, further to the north, having reached their highest latitude at 78°37′ N on September 1, and their easternmost point at 77°30′ N 59° E some days later.

Thus, the way was paved for the Austro-Hungarian North Pole Expedition. In Payer's words: "the ideal aim of the journey had been the northeastern passage, its actual purpose was the exploration of parts of sea or land northeast of Nowaja Semlja." According to Weyprecht, the North Pole has not been a primary target. The result of the expedition was the discovery of Franz Josef Land.

The ship, the *Admiral Tegetthoff*, was a three-mast schooner of 220 tons, 38.34 m length, and an auxiliary steam engine of 100 hp. It was built in Bremerhaven and carried 130 tons of coal and food provisions for up to three years.The crew consisted of Karl Weyprecht (commander of the ship), Julius Payer (leader of the land journeys), the officers Gustav Brosch, Eduard Orel, and Dr. Julius Kepes, the ice pilot Elling "Olaf" Carlsen (from Tromsø), and 18 sailors (including two glacier guides from Tyrol).

The *Tegetthoff* left Bremerhaven on June 13, 1872, checked its provisions and equipment in Tromsø, and sailed north. By August 21, the ship was trapped in ice at 76°22′ N 62°3′ E. The *Tegetthoff* started drifting north with the ice and remained beset by ice throughout the winter.

On August 30, 1873, land was sighted at 79°42.5′ N 59°34.1′ E, and named Kaiser Franz Josef Land. By the end of September, the drifting *Tegetthoff* had reached its northernmost position at 79°58′ N, but the crew was unable to make a visit to the land until November 1. Then, preparations for a second winter in the Arctic had to be made.

On April 12, 1874, during his second sled journey north to Kronprinz Rudolf Land, Payer reached Cape Fligely, the northernmost point of the journey, at 82°5′ N (located today at 81°52′ N 59°12′ E). At the Cape, Payer raised the Austrian flag and left a document.

Meanwhile, the situation of the *Tegetthoff* had become hopeless. The crew realized that the ship would never be able to free itself from the ice, and there was not enough food left to get them through a third winter. On May 20, 1874, the *Tegetthoff* was abandoned and the journey back south was started with three sledges. On August 18, the crew reached Novaya Zemlya. Five days later, they were rescued by the Russian schooner *Nikolaj* and finally, 453 days after they left, the crew arrived back in Vienna on September 25, 1874.

Although he received many honors and awards upon his return, Payer took his leave from the army, primarily because several officers were of the opinion that there was no Franz Josef Land, and the reports about his sled journeys were pure fiction.

Payer was invited by the Royal Geographic Society to London, where he was awarded the Gold Medal and was introduced to Lady Jane Franklin (wife of the explorer Sir John Franklin). He received an inheritable knighthood on October 24, 1876 (and thereafter was called Julius von Payer). He decided to make use of his other talent and became a painter.

But 20 years later—still attracted by the Arctic—he joined a meeting of the German Commission for the South Polar Exploration in Berlin and pleaded for a southerly expedition, which he offered to join. For the summer of 1896, he planned a trip to eastern Greenland, primarily for painting studies. Both plans were never carried out.

To his great satisfaction, Fridtjof Nansen confirmed his research at Franz Josef Land and restored his reputation during a meeting of the Vienna Geographical Society on May 6, 1898.

Biography

Julius Payer was born on September 2, 1841 in Schönau near Teplitz, Bohemia (now Teplice, Czech Republic), the son of a cavalry captain. From 1851 to 1857, he attended the K.K. cadet school in Lobzowa (near Krakow), followed by the Theresian Military Academy at Wiener Neustadt (near Vienna) from 1857 to 1859. Then, he was ordered to Northern Italy. In 1859, he was decorated in the battle of Solferino and again in 1866 in the battle of Custozza. Between 1860 and 1862, he was stationed at the garrison of Verona. Between 1864 and 1868, he explored and mapped the Adamello- and Presanella-group and the Ortler-Alps, where he made 60 summit- and 30 first ascents. At this time, he was already in contact with the German geographer August *Petermann,* who finally directed his attention to polar exploration.

After three successful Arctic expeditions, he married a wealthy woman (Fanny) in 1877 and went to Frankfurt and Munich, where he received a professional artistic education (until 1882). Between 1884 and 1890, he worked and lived with his family as a painter in Paris. The couple had two children: Jules and Alice.

In 1890, he divorced his wife and returned alone to Vienna, where he founded a painting school for women. Two years later, he painted by order of Emperor Franz Josef his largest and most famous picture, *Nie zurück.*

Julius Payer died in Veldes, Oberkrain (today Bled in Slovenia) on August 29, 1915.

HERMANN F. KOERBEL

See also **Franklin, Lady Jane; Franklin, Sir John; Franz Josef Land; Nansen, Fridtjof**

Further Reading

Benesch, Kurt, *Nie zurück! Die Entdeckung des Franz-Josefs-Landes*, Wien, 1967

Haller, Johann, *Erinnerungen eines Tiroler Teilnehmers an Julius v. Payer's Nordpol-Expedition 1872–1874* (published by his son Ferdinand Haller), Innsbruck, 1959

Krisch, Otto, *Tagebuch des Nordpolfahrers Otto Krisch, Maschinist und Offizier der zweiten österr.-ungar. Nordpol-Expedition* (published by his brother Anton Krisch), Wien, 1875

Linke, Karl, *Die Österreichische Nordpolfahrt von Payer und Weyprecht in den Jahren 1872 bis 1874*, Wien, 1924

Müller, Martin, *Julius von Payer ein Bahnbrecher der Alpen- und Polarforschung und Maler der Polarwelt* [Julius von Payer a pioneer of alpine- and polar-research and painter of the polar world], Stuttgart: Wissenschaftliche Verlagsgesellschaft, 1956

Payer, Julius, "Das Innere Grönlands" [The interior of Greenland]. *Annual of the Austrian Alpine Club*, 1871

Payer, Julius, *Die Österreich-Ungarische Nordpol Expedition in den Jahren 1869–1874* [The Austro-Hungarian North Pole Expedition], Wien, 1876

———, *New lands Within the Arctic Circle. Narrative of the Discoveries of the Austrian Ship "Tegetthoff" in the Years 1872–1874*, London, 1876

Straub, Heinz, *Die Entdeckung des Franz-Joseph Landes. K.u.K. Offiziere als Polarforscher*, Graz: Styria, 1990

PEARY, ROBERT E.

American Robert Edwin Peary (1856–1920) was among the world's most famous and controversial explorers. Believed by many to have been the first person to reach the North Pole, Peary's claim was also disputed by others in his own era and since. Despite the contested historical claims, his personal prowess in planning and carrying out Arctic expeditions as well as his dogged determination clearly exemplified Peary's polar endeavors.

In 1886, inspired as a child by Elisha Kent Kane's *Arctic Explorations*, Peary sought leave from the US Navy to lead a three-month expedition to Disko Bay, Greenland. In 1891, he staged his first major expedition to the High Arctic and traversed Greenland's vast ice cap from McCormick Bay to Independence Bay in the far north of the island (today known as Independence Fjord). Peary returned to northern Greenland in 1893–1895 and conducted summer voyages in 1896 and 1897 to carry off the famous Cape York meteorites, which the Inughuit had used to fashion their tools. These were later sold to the American Museum of Natural History, New York city, and the cash was used to finance future assaults on the Pole.

In 1898, on extended leave from the Navy, Peary commenced the first of three expeditions with the straightforward objective of attaining the North Pole. For the next four years, Peary established bases of operations at Etah, north Greenland, as well as Cape D'Urville and Fort Conger on Ellesmere Island, and Payer Harbour on Bedford Pim Island. He experimented with establishing a network of caches and temporary shelters, and organized dog-sledge trains to move men and material to the far North. During the 1898 expedition, Peary made two attempts to strike out across the polar ice pack toward the Pole, but was stopped by difficult ice and snow conditions. In April 1902, he believed he reached 84°17′27″, a new farthest north for the Western Hemisphere, before turning back.

For his next expedition in 1905–1906, Peary determined the need to establish wintering quarters much farther north, on the northern coast of Ellesmere Island, so that his sledging parties would be based nearer to the intended target. Requiring a ship capable of both navigating the channel and providing wintering quarters, he commissioned the building of the USS *Roosevelt*, a round-hulled, reinforced steam vessel designed to negotiate the treacherous ice conditions of Nares Strait. His party established winter quarters at Cape Sheridan at the northern end of Ellesmere Island and hunted muskoxen and caribou to stockpile provisions during the fall and winter. In the late winter, they sledged provisions across the northern coast of Ellesmere Island to Cape Hecla, then on to Cape Moss, in preparation for the foray over the polar ice pack. Striking out in several divisions during February and March, his party was moved significantly off course by the moving ice, but managed to reach 87°6′ N, according to Peary's notes, 51 km beyond the then-current farthest north record.

Thwarted in his second major attempt on the North Pole, Peary returned to the United States determined to stage one last effort to reach his goal. Backed by businessman Morris K. Jesup, who had funded several Arctic expeditions but died in 1907 before Peary left, and the Peary Arctic Club, he left New York on July 6, 1908 and again established wintering quarters at Cape Sheridan. As in 1905–1906, intensive hunting and other preparations were followed by the transhipment of supplies to Cape Columbia. Peary worked out the logistics of the planned advance in minute detail. He divided the group into seven divisions of four men and worked out a minimal allocation of fuel for each party. Each division advanced supplies to advanced staging points, before returning to move successive loads to these camps. In the final stage, Peary, his long-time assistant Matthew Henson, and the Inughuit men Uutaaq, Iggiannguaq, Ooqueah, and Sigluk pressed on toward their goal. By April 6, 1909, Peary reckoned that they had reached 89°57′11″ N, and his party celebrated the attainment of the North Pole.

Peary returned to the United States in late September to discover that his rival Frederick A. Cook had already claimed to have reached the Pole on April 21, 1908, making his claim public on September 1, 1909. The issue of who first attained the North Pole continues to animate polar writers today. Most observers credit Peary with coming much closer to the goal than Cook, but some have doubted that he actually reached 90° N latitude, asserting a lack of verifiable evidence.

Of perhaps greater consequence were Peary's achievements in the application of High Arctic survival techniques, based largely on Aboriginal knowledge and precedent. He learned to live off the land through the employment of Inughuit. He depended on their knowledge and methods of sledge travel, clothing, provisioning, hunting, and shelter. Sustained contact introduced the Inughuit to a cash economy and Western technology, but also brought infectious disease epidemics and the diversion of their productive efforts to support Peary's exploration goals. In terms of European exploration, Peary influenced several subsequent expeditions to Greenland and Ellesmere Island, many of which followed his practices.

Viewed historically, Peary's skills in fund-raising, organization, and leadership in staging his expeditions were remarkable. He was one of the first major figures to understand the potential of the popular press to advance a cause, and he shrewdly used the media to promote his polar objectives, through Herbert Bridgman, secretary of the Peary Arctic Club.

Following his disputed polar triumph, Peary became preoccupied with defending his achievement before a Congressional committee and in the media. He nevertheless was celebrated by American presidents and European monarchs, and elevated by the general public to the status of a national icon. To many Americans, the iconic Peary embodied the image that the United States wished to present to the world, as supremely confident, self-reliant, expansionist, and conquering. His presumed polar triumph played a pivotal role in the development of his country's self-image as a world power.

Biography

The son of a long-established New England family, Robert Edwin Peary was born on May 6, 1856 at Cresson, Pennsylvania. Graduating from Bowdoin College in Brunswick, Maine, in 1877, he worked for several years for the Coast and Geodetic Survey before joining the Civil Engineer Corps of the United States Navy in 1881. In 1888, he married Josephine Diebitsch, who assisted him on his expeditions in the 1890s and raised money for his North Polar voyages. They had two children: a daughter (Marie) and a son (Robert). Between 1884–1885 and 1887–1888, he was subchief for the Inter-Ocean Canal Survey, charged with charting sections of the route of the Panama Canal. His principal Arctic expeditions comprised his excursion to traverse the ice cap of northern Greenland in 1891–1892, another extended expedition to Greenland in 1893–1895, and his North Polar excursions in 1898–1902, 1905–1906, and 1908–1909. He died on February 20, 1920 in Washington, District of Columbia, and was buried at Arlington National Cemetery. Peary's principal publications include his expedition accounts *Northward over the Great Ice* (1898), *Nearest the Pole* (1907), *The North Pole* (1910), as well as *Secrets of Polar Travel* (1916), a monograph on his methods of polar exploration.

LYLE DICK

See also **Cook, Frederick A.; Exploration of the Arctic; Henson, Matthew; Kane, Elisha Kent; Race to the North Pole**

Further Reading

Dick, Lyle, *Muskox Land: Ellesmere Island in the Age of Contact*, Calgary, Alberta: University of Calgary Press, 2001
Goodsell, John W., *On Polar Trails: The Peary Expedition to the North Pole, 1908–1909,* edited by Donald W. Whisenhunt, Austin, Texas: Eakin Press, 1983
Green, Fitzhugh, *Peary, the Man who Refused to Fail*, New York and London: G.P. Putnam's Sons, 1926
Hayes, J. Gordon, *Robert Edwin Peary: A Record of His Explorations, 1886–1909*, London: Grant Richards and Humphrey Toulmin, 1929
Herbert, Wally, *The Noose of Laurels: The Discovery of the North Pole*, London and Toronto: Hodder and Stoughton, 1989
Peary, Robert E., *The North Pole: Its Discovery in 1909 Under the Auspices of the Peary Arctic Club*, New York: Stokes, 1910
Rawlins, Dennis, *Peary at the North Pole: Fact or Fiction?*, Washington/New York: Luce, 1973
Weems, John Edward, *Peary: The Explorer and the Man*, Boston: Houghton Mifflin, 1967

PEATLANDS AND BOGS

Peatlands are wetland ecosystems characterized by the accumulation of organic matter. The amount of organic matter that accumulates in any soil type is dependent on the balance between the inputs from the biota and the losses occurring through decomposition. In peat-forming wetland ecosystems, organic material may build up to a depth of several meters, as decomposition is inhibited by waterlogging, low temperatures, and the recalcitrant nature of the deposited litter. Water inundation inhibits oxygen diffusion into the soil, which leads to depletion of oxygen in the deep peat layers and a reduction of available alternative electron acceptors. Under these environmental conditions, decomposition proceeds at very low rates and the organic carbon that is not oxidized accumulates as peat.

In the Arctic, the occurrence of permafrost prevents complete drainage of the unfrozen top soil during the summer seasons, and decay of plant material is impeded by water inundation and low temperatures. The thickness of the seasonally unfrozen layer represents a physical limit to much of the biological activity in the soil, and although microbial activity may take place at temperatures below 0°C, it is greatly reduced compared to unfrozen conditions. Accumulation of organic material in peat-forming ecosystems is therefore a common feature in the Arctic landscape, and in spite of comparably low vegetative production, low decomposition rates may give rise to a considerable storage of soil carbon. Arctic tundra regions contain approximately 12–14% of the total global soil carbon pool, and carbon stocks in boreal and Subarctic peatlands have been estimated to amount to about 30% of the global total (Gorham, 1991). Peatlands cover over 50% of the land area in western Siberia, much of central Canada (e.g., the Hudson Bay Lowlands), southeastern Alaska, and significant areas of Subarctic Finland and Scandinavia.

Peat-forming ecosystems may be classified and termed depending on, for example, shape, pH, nutrient conditions, and plant community associations. Different terminologies are often used in different parts of the world, but one common distinction is the one separating bogs from fens. Bogs are by definition ombrotrophic, that is, they depend on precipitation alone for their supply of water and nutrients, while fens are minerotrophic since part of the water in the ecosystem has flowed through or over mineral soil (Clymo, 1987; *see* **Fens**).

Many boreal peatlands display a very characteristic surface microtopography formed by a continuous pattern of features that are more or less elevated above the groundwater level. On so-called hummocks, where the watertable is below the surface, the vascular vegetation is often dominated by dwarf shrubs with a shallow growth pattern, for example, *Calluna vulgaris* and *Empetrum* spp. *Eriophorum vaginatum*, a graminoid species with deeply penetrating roots, is also commonly found on hummocks and is a typical tussock-forming plant in Arctic tundra wetlands (*see* **Wet Tundra**). The most characteristic components of the field layer in so-called lawns (watertable at or just below the surface) are clonal graminoids or herbs with well-developed rhizomes, for example, *Eriophorum angustifolium* and *Carex* spp. The wettest depressions (so-called hollows, with the watertable at or above the surface) are characterized by an often sparse cover of various graminoid species with deep root systems that are rich in aerenchyma. The distribution of various moss species, for example, *Sphagnum* spp., follows a moisture gradient that corresponds to the variation in microtopography (Malmer et al., 1994).

Because of the large storage of organic matter in the soil, peatlands are in general considered to be sinks for atmospheric carbon (CO_2). The accumulation of carbon makes the peat-forming ecosystems important components of the global carbon cycle since the sequestration of CO_2 from the atmosphere leads to a dampening of the natural greenhouse effect (*see* **Carbon Cycling**). However, the impact of peatlands on the global climate is not that straightforward, because peatlands are also significant sources of another important greenhouse gas, namely methane (CH_4). On a global scale, wetlands are the largest single source of atmospheric CH_4 (estimated at 110 Tg CH_4 per year), and between one-third and half of these emissions are from northern wetlands (defined here as all nontidal wetlands north of 50° N). On a molecule-to-molecule basis, the spectral and

chemical properties of CH_4 make it approximately 25 times as efficient as a greenhouse gas compared to CO_2 (over a time horizon of 100 years) (IPPC, 2001). The waterlogged conditions in peat soils favor anaerobic decomposition and provide an ideal environment for microbial CH_4 production (methanogenesis). However, CH_4 efflux from peatlands to the atmosphere depends not only on the rate of production but also on the degree of CH_4 consumption (methanotrophy) that may occur in oxic surface layers and in the close vicinity of plant roots where oxygen is available. In this process, CH_4 is oxidized to CO_2 and the resultant rate of CH_4 emission that can be measured at the surface is the net result of the two counteracting processes of methanogenesis and methanotrophy.

The strength of peatlands as sources or sinks of (carbon-) greenhouse gases not only has the capacity to influence the climate but is also strongly controlled by it. Temperature is one of the central environmental constraints on both CO_2 and CH_4 fluxes because it directly affects the microbial activity and also indirectly influences decomposition rates by regulating the water content of the soil. The turnover rate of organic material is further coupled to the overall nutrient status of the soil, which in turn affects the carbon exchange between the ecosystem and the atmosphere.

Apart from being important components of the present-day climate system, peatlands also serve as records of past ecological conditions. Different peat layers represent successive stages of the participating plant communities, but paleoclimatic information can also be extracted from well-preserved pollen grains and spores that have fallen onto the surface in the past. Age determination by radiocarbon dating techniques is, in this context, a valuable tool for accurate reconstructions of the vegetation history. Moreover, the organic archive held in peat can not only provide information of the peatland's own vegetational history but can also be used to portray the evolution of the surrounding vegetation. Pollen and spores may be transported by the wind over long distances and eventually be deposited in areas far away from the original source. The open surfaces of peatlands thus serve as catchment areas representing the vegetation "fingerprint" from the surrounding landscape.

ANNA EKBERG

See also **Carbon Cycling; Fens; Soil Respiration; Wet Tundra**

Further Reading

Clymo, R.S., "The ecology of peatlands." *Science Progress, Oxford,* **71**(1987): 593–614

Gorham, E., "Northern peatlands: role in the carbon cycle and probable responses to climatic warming." *Ecological Applications,* **1(2)** (1991): 182–195

IPCC, *Climate Change 2001: The Scientific Basis. Contribution of Working Group I to the Third Assessment Report of the Intergovernmental Panel on Climate Change*, edited by J.T. Houghton, Y. Ding, D.J. Griggs, M. Nouger, P.J. van der Linden, X. Dai, K. Maskell & C.A. Johnson, Cambridge and New York: Cambridge University Press

Malmer, N., B.M. Svensson & B. Wallén "Interactions between *Sphagnum* mosses and field layer vascular plants in the development of peat-forming systems." *Folia Geobotanica et Phytotaxonomica*, **29** (1994): 483–496

PECHORA BASIN

The Pechora Basin is located almost exclusively in the Komi Republic and Nenets Autonomous Area (Okrug) of the Russian Federation, between 61°20′ and 68°20′ N and 48°20′ and 66°20′ E. The Pechora Basin is shaped like a triangle stretching from the south to the northeast and northwest. Its eastern border is confined by the Ural Mountains and its western border is bound by the Timan mountain range. The basin derives its name from the Pechora River.

Geologically, the Pechora Basin is largely congruent with the Pechora syncline. This basin and the adjacent mountain ranges provide large reserves of mineral resources (see below), and the region is therefore known as the Timan-Pechora Oil and Gas Province.

The mean air temperatures vary between −21°C (northeast) and −16°C (west) in January, and between 11°C (northeast) and 16°C (south) in July. In the south there are, on average, 180 days per year with an air temperature above 0°C; the same figure is 120 for the extreme northeast. Accordingly, the number of days with snow cover varies between 190 and *c.*250. The eastern part has the highest average snow cover in European Russia (between 90 and 140 cm in the Urals and its foothills). The annual precipitation amounts to *c.*−450 mm in the northernmost area and *c.*−1050 mm in the higher parts of the Urals. Discontinuous and continuous permafrost prevail north of the Arctic Circle and in the Urals.

Most of the Pechora Basin is situated in the taiga zone (with spruce as predominant species), but the part beyond the Arctic Circle falls largely under the tundra zone and there is mountain tundra in the Northern and Polar Urals. Owing to the lowland character in many parts of the basin, the taiga and tundra are interspersed with numerous peatbogs and wetlands. Large areas of the Urals are under natural protection or are part of the Yugyd-Va National Park.

The abundance of fur animals, fish, and timber provided the basis for the regional economy in the Pechora Basin, although hunting lost its importance when the most valuable species became rare. Reindeer herding, fishing, and cattle breeding represent the main activities of the rural population, consisting of

Komi, Nenets, and Russian "Old Believers." The latter settled mainly in and around Ust'-Tsil'ma; they arrived c. 500 years ago. At the same time, a Russian fortress—Pustozersk, today known as Naryan-Mar—was constructed near the Pechora Delta. Contacts between the Komi, Nenets, and the Russians had developed even earlier, and since AD1100 Russian traders traveled in the area. The Komi, too, acted as traders and guides.

Scientific exploration in the Pechora Basin was undertaken by Lepekhin (1768–1772), Schrenk (1837), Latkin (1825–1843), Krusenstern (1843–1876), and others. F.N. Chernyshev and A.A. Chernov conducted geological research that led to the later development of the oil, gas, and coal fields of the Pechora Basin. Large-scale development began in the 1930s, when forced labor was used to open and work the coalfield of Vorkuta and build a railway connection with the south. After 1955, large numbers of Russians, Ukrainians, Tatars, and others came in, attracted by higher wages. The region's role in the economy of Russia is considerable: oil and gas extraction and production are increasing again after a period of crisis in the early 1990s. Coal mining is, however, still in decline.

Principal settlements include Ukhta (population 98,000), Vorkuta (population 90,000, without suburbs), Pechora (population 58,000), Inta (population 55,000), and Usinsk (population 48,000). Vorkuta and Inta are dependent on coal mining, and Usinsk is the regional center of oil production. Ukhta and Pechora are characterized by a more diversified economy. The administrative center of the Nenets Autonomous Okrug is Naryan-Mar (population 19,000; all population figures as of January 1, 2000 and according to the regional official statistics).

JOACHIM OTTO HABECK

See also **Komi Republic; Nenets Autonomous Okrug; Pechora River; Russian "Old Settlers"; Vorkuta**

Further Reading

Kuhry, Peter & Päivi Soppela, *Sustainable Development of the Pechora Region in a Changing Environment and Society (SPICE);* http://www.ulapland.fi/home/arktinen/spice/spice.htm

Lausala, Tero & Leila Valkonen (editors), *Economic Geography and Structure of the Russian Territories of the Barents Region*, Rovaniemi: Arctic Centre (University of Lapland), 1999

Respublika Komi: Entsiklopediia [Republic of Komi: Encyclopedia], Volumes 1–3, Syktyvkar: Komi knizhnoe izdatel'stvo, 1997–2000

Savel'eva, E.A. (compiler), *Istoriko-kul'turnyi atlas Respubliki Komi* [Historico-cultural atlas of the Komi Republic], Moskva: Izdatel'skii dom "Drofa" and Izdatel'stvo "DiK", 1997

PECHORA DELTA

The Pechora River forms an extended delta and bay at the opening into the southeastern Barents Sea, at Naryan-Mar in Nenets Autonomous Okrug. Starting with two major arms, the delta branches into 20 channels along its course, reaching nearly 65 km in width. Most arms and channels are shallow, with the main arm Bolshaya Pechora being up to 4.5 m in depth. The delta is an important summer breeding habitat for migrating aquatic or water birds.

The entire delta is located beyond the Arctic Circle. The mean annual air temperature ranges from −3.2°C to −5.6°C, with the lowest recorded temperature being −44°C. The climate varies from maritime to inland, being more continental in the upper delta. Air temperature averages +9°C in July to August at the mouth area, reaching +13°C at the top of the delta; the observed maximum exceeds +30°C. In winter, cold offshore winds prevail, while northerly winds are typical in summer. The annual precipitation averages 450 mm; an excess moisture regime is characteristic. The snow cover period lasts from early October until early June. Freeze-up commences in early October and averages 190–210 days.

Annual water level fluctuations are significant. Highest levels (8m above the winter minimum) are recorded during the spring flood (May to July) when most of the delta islands are submerged. Strong northerly winds result in surge phenomena when saline sea water can penetrate 5–7 km upstream into the Bolshaya Pechora.

The delta is surrounded by a vast tundra plain with relatively low shores. The area is located within the permafrost zone, but there are taliks (local areas of unfrozen ground within permafrost) under the riverbed. Delta islands are sandy and clay/sandy with tundra alluvial soils. The vegetation along the mainland delta banks changes from shrub tundra in the north to forested tundra in the south. Floodplain riverine plant communities on the delta islands are represented by dense willow and alder bushes, grassy meadows, and sedge marshes.

The Pechora estuary is famous as a highly productive ecosystem supporting rich biological resources. The delta with its developed lake-river systems provides a perfect environment for the year-round habitation of various whitefishes, and is an important migrating junction for both fishes and birds. The Pechora stock of Atlantic salmon, which is still the largest spawning population in Russia, passes through the delta. The delta is a key stopover for diverse migrating waterfowl, which also breed here in great numbers. Pechora Delta is of utmost importance to Bewick's swans, supporting as much as 20% of the autumn migratory population. Over 20 species of mammals can be found in the delta, which is a meeting point for Arctic and marine species like Arctic fox, polar bear, beluga whale, and ringed seal, and boreal and terrestrial animals like the red fox, brown bear, and elk. The most valuable (or important) habitats of the Pechora Delta are protected areas, including Nenetskiy zakaznik (also known as Pechorskij zakaznik; established in 1985, its present area is 300,000 ha) and Nizhnepechorskiy zakazink (since 1998, its area is 106,000 ha), both IUCN Management Category IV. Part of the delta is within Nenetskiy zapovednik (established in 1999, its total area is 313,400 ha, but the delta proportion is unknown), IUCN Category Ia—strict nature reserve.

The Pechora River mouth has served as an important transport junction for a long time. In 1499, a large settlement—Pustozersk—was established in the delta (today its former area of 2 ha is protected as a natural-historical site/monument). Nowadays, about half of the inhabitants of the sparsely populated Nenets Autonomous Okrug live in Naryan-Mar, which is the major port in the upper delta. An agricultural population, both Russian and Nenets live in small villages along the delta banks. Their main occupations are hunting, fishing, and reindeer herding. The development of the petroleum industry in the Low Pechora area presents a major threat to the delta ecosystems.

Maria Gavrilo

See also **Barents Sea; Naryan-Mar; Nenets Autonomous Okrug; Pechora River**

Further Reading

Bryzgalo, V.A. & V.V. Ivanov, "Hydrochemical regime of Pechora River under conditions of anthropogenic influence." *Ecological Chemistry*, 8(2) (1999) (in Russian)

Eerden van, M.R. (editor), *Pechora Delta: Structure and Dynamics of the Pechora Delta Ecosystems (1995–1999)*, Lelystad: Institute for Inland Water Management and Waste Water Treatment RIZA, 2000 (RIZA report 2000.037)

Ivanov, V.V., "River Water Inflow to the Arctic Seas." In *Proceedings of the ACSYS Conference on the Dynamics of the Arctic Climate System*, World Climate Research Programme, 1996 (WCRP-94, WMO/TD No. 760)

Korepanova, L.Yu. (editor in chief), *Nenetskiy avtonomny okrug. Entsiklopedicheskiy slovar* [Nenets Autonomous Okrug. Encyclopedia], Moscow: Avanta+ Publishing House, 2001 (in Russian)

Krasnov, Yu., Yu. Goryaev, N. Nikolaeva, A. Shavykin, M. Gavrilo & V. Chernook, *Atlas morskikh ptits Pechorskogo moray* [The Atlas of marine birds of the Pechora Sea], Apatity: Kola Scientific Center Russian Academy of Science, 2002 (in Russian)

Lukin, Anatoliy A., V.A. Dauvalter & V.P. Novoselov, *Ekosistemy Pechory v sovremennykh usloviyakh* [Pechora ecosystems under modern conditions], Apatity: Kola Scientific Center Russian Academy of Science, 2000 (in Russian)

Mineyev, Yu.N., *Vodoplavayushchie ptitsy Bolshezemelskpy tundry* [Waterfowl of Bol'shezemel'skaya tundra], Leningrad: Nauka, 1987 (in Russian)

Potanin, V.A. (editor in chief), *Ekosistemy, bioloresursy i antropogennoezagryaznenie Pechorskogo morya* [Ecosystems, biological resources and anthropogenic contamination of the Pechora Sea], Apaptity: Kola Scientific Center RAS, 1996 (in Russian)

PECHORA RIVER

The Pechora is the largest river of the North European part of Russia. It rises at the northern end of the Urals and flows north through the territory of Komi Republic and Nenets Autonomous Okrug into Pechora Bay, an inlet of the Barents Sea above the Arctic Circle. The river's main right tributaries are the Ilych and the Shchugor; its main left tributaries are the Lemyu, the Kozhva, the Izhma, and the Sula. On its way, the river crosses taiga, tundra, and forest-tundra zones, changing its direction several times. The river's total length is 1809 km, and the area of the basin is over 320,000 km^2.

According to the differing character of river valley and water conditions, the river can be divided into three parts: the Upper Pechora, the Middle Pechora, and the Lower Pechora. The Upper Pechora is a mountain river: winding, shallow, and full of rapids. Regular navigation is only possible below Troitsko-Pechorsk, and the ice-free period is on average 165 days. The Middle Pechora rises in the town of Vuktyl. Salmon come to spawn in the clear waters of the Shchugor tributary, which is why this river has been declared a reserve over its entire length. Navigation in this section of the Pechora usually starts ten days later than in the Upper Pechora, and the interval between the beginning and the end of ice drifting is more than two weeks. In spring, the level of water in the Pechora at Ust-Usa rises by up to 11–12 m. Floods often exceed 10 km^2 in area. The Lower Pechora begins below Usa. The riverbed processes are very dynamic here, which makes navigation expensive and difficult.

As the Pechora River approaches the sea (188 km from the coast), it divides into two large channels: eastern (the Bolshaya Pechora) and western (the Malaya Pechora). The width of the delta reaches 45 km, and the length of some islands reaches 15–30 km. Tidal currents in the delta are rather small; the tidal amplitude near Naryan-Mar is only 20 cm.

The water conditions of the Pechora are characterized by high spring floods (water rises 4–8 m) and low winter levels. Freeze-up begins in mountain tributaries from October 5 to 10 and in the river itself from October 15 to 30. Ice is usually thickest in March and April, about 140–160 cm thick. The average freeze-up period is from 160–170 to 190–200 days. The process of breaking up ice in the river lasts 1–1.5 months.

The Pechora is rich in fish—salmon and white salmon, omul sig, chir, and pelyad (all whitefish species) are of the greatest value.

The Pechora is of great importance for transportation, because it flows within territory that has an underdeveloped railway and highway network. A large amount of timber, oil, coal, and building materials are carried by vessels and ships. The most important ports and piers are Pechora, Naryan-Mar, Vuktyl, and Troitsko-Pechorsk.

IGOR SERGEYEV

See also **Naryan-Mar; Pechora Delta**

Further Reading

Ilyina, L.L. & A.N. Grahov, *Reki Severa* [Rivers of the Russian North], Leningrad: Gidrometeoizdat, 1987

PECK, EDMUND JAMES

In 1875, Bishop John Horden wrote from Moose Factory to the Church Missionary Society (CMS) in England asking them to send a missionary to Canada to work with the Inuit of Hudson Bay. Edmund James Peck, an unordained seaman, accepted the challenge, underwent brief training, and left for Hudson Bay in June 1876.

His mission was at Little Whale River, where he ministered to both Cree and Inuit. Peck set himself an arduous program for learning the languages of both, believing that "the first work of every missionary is to acquire the language of the people as well as gain their confidence." He concentrated, however, on Inuktitut and claimed to have collected between 80 and 100 words per day. Part of his mandate from the CMS was to produce written religious material, and he approached this task eagerly, using the Syllabic system of writing created by James Evans in 1840 for the Cree and modified for Inuktitut by CMS missionaries John Horden and Rev. E.A. Watkins. Peck was the first missionary in the Hudson and James bays to work almost exclusively with Inuit. He promoted the use of the Syllabic script, transcribed material into it, and taught reading and writing skills to the Inuit. His first Inuktitut publication, *Portions of the Holy Scripture, for the Use of the Esquimaux on the Northern and Eastern Shores of Hudson's Bay*, was printed in the Syllabic orthography by the Society for the Promotion of Christian Knowledge (SPCK) in 1878.

Peck took furlough in England in 1884 after eight uninterrupted years in the field. He returned with a bride the following year, and the next year relocated his mission 200 miles south to Fort George. The Pecks had three children there, but Mrs. Peck was often sick and depressed, and in 1892 the family returned to England. In 1894, the SPCK published Peck's second major work in Inuktitut, *Portions of the Book of Common Prayer, Together with Hymns, Addresses, etc., for the Use of the Eskimo of Hudson's Bay*.

PECK, EDMUND JAMES

In England, Peck immediately began making plans to establish a mission to the Inuit of Baffin Island. He reasoned that his wife's health was sufficiently poor that she would never be able to accompany him again to the Arctic, and therefore he should leave already-established missions to other married men and go instead to isolated and undeveloped areas where he felt no woman should go.

In 1894, he established a mission at Blacklead Island in Cumberland Sound, off the coast of Baffin Island, beside a Scottish whaling station. The whalers provided Peck and his assistant, J.C. Parker, spartan living quarters in a two-room shack, each room 10 ft square. The Inuit to whom Peck would minister lived nearby in a camp of skin tents and wooden shacks. Their population numbered 171. Peck found little difference between the dialect that he had mastered in Hudson Bay and that of Cumberland Sound, and he immediately began to preach the gospel and teach the children. He maintained a disciplined routine of teaching, studying, and preaching. Peck faced opposition to his ministry from the Inuit shamans, whom he regarded as sly tricksters against whom he spoke out openly and strongly. He persevered and eventually all the Inuit of Cumberland Sound were converted to at least a nominal acceptance of Christianity. His first Inuk convert, a woman named Atanngaujaq, was baptized on May 7, 1901.

Peck spent four periods of two years each at Blacklead Island. On each of his one-year furloughs to England, he continued working to oversee the publication of church literature in Syllabics, lecture publicly about the importance of his mission to the Inuit, and lobby the mission society for the mission's continuance. Other missionaries, whose terms generally overlapped Peck's, maintained the mission during his absences. Their names are well known in the history of northern missions: Charles Sampson, Julian Bilby, and E.W.T. Greenshield.

Peck left Blacklead Island permanently in 1905. The following year, with the departure of Greenshield, the mission was left with no resident nonnative minister. But Peck and his colleagues had trained a number of Inuit catechists, the most well known being Luke Kidlapik and Peter Tooloogakjuaq. When Greenshield returned on a summer voyage in 1909, on which he was shipwrecked and forced to spend the winter, he discovered that these native catechists had faithfully continued the work of the mission.

Peck moved his family to Ottawa, Canada, where he became Superintendent of Arctic Missions for the Diocese of Moosonee. Occasionally, he traveled north on supply vessels in the summer, usually to Hudson Bay. His eyesight failed and, almost blind, he retired in 1919.

Although Peck is often credited with adapting Evans's Cree Syllabics to Inuktitut, that innovation had already been made by Horden and Watkins. Peck's great accomplishment was proselytizing among the Inuit, promoting the use of the Syllabic orthography, and translating and publishing scripture material in Inuktitut. He promoted literacy in Syllabics. Following his lead, all Anglicans who followed him in the eastern Arctic used the Syllabic orthography, as did Roman Catholic missionaries. The Syllabic orthography is still used today in Arctic Québec and all but a few western communities of Nunavut. Occasionally, debate occurs about its continued efficacy in promoting Inuktitut literacy in an increasingly bilingual population, but such debates are usually short-lived; the Syllabics that Peck promoted are viewed by now as being the traditional Inuit way of writing in the eastern Canadian Arctic.

Peck's contributions to the study of the Inuktitut language are contained in two works: his *Eskimo Grammar*, published by the Geographic Board of Canada in 1919, and subsequently reprinted four times, and his *Eskimo-English Dictionary*, published posthumously in 1925.

Inuit remember Peck, whose Inuktitut name, Uqammak, means "the one who speaks well," as a dogmatic and tenacious man, at once stubborn yet caring, stern yet friendly. Nonnative history remembers him as "The Apostle to the North." In 1877, one year after Peck's arrival in Canada, Bishop John Horden wrote to the Church Missionary Society about Peck, "I thank the Committee for *a* man; I thank them doubly for *the* man; a better selection could not have been made."

Biography

Born on April 15, 1850 in Rusholme, England, Edmund James Peck was raised from the age of seven in Ireland. Orphaned at 13, he spent eight years in the British Navy. In 1875, the Church Missionary Society recruited him as a missionary to the Inuit. Between 1876 and 1892, he served two terms as missionary to Little Whale River and Fort George, and between 1894 and 1905 four two-year terms as missionary at Blacklead Island, Cumberland Sound. He moved to Ottawa, Canada where he served as Superintendent of Arctic Missions for the Diocese of Moosonee. Peck married a Miss Coleman (first name unknown) during a furlough in 1884–1885; they had three children. He is the author of *Eskimo Grammar* (1919) and *Eskimo-English Dictionary* (1925) and translator of a large body of church literature into Inuktitut. He died in Ottawa on September 10, 1924.

KENN HARPER

Further Reading

Boon, Thomas, *These Men Went Out,* Toronto: Ryerson Press, n.d.

Fleming, A.L., *Perils of the Polar Pack,* Toronto: Missionary Society of the Church of England in Canada, 1932

Gould, S., *Inasmuch: Sketches of the Beginnings of the Church of England in Canada in Relation to the Indian and Eskimo Races,* Toronto, 1917

Harper, Kenn, "Writing systems and translations." *Inuktitut* (53) (September 1983)

———, "The early development of Inuktitut Syllabic orthography." *Etudes Inuit Studies,* 9(1) (1985): 141–162

———, "Missionary to the Inuit." *Above & Beyond,* 4(4) (fall 1992): 41–44

———, "The Blacklead Mission...one hundred years." *The Arctic News* (fall 1994): 7, 10

Lewis, Arthur, *The Life and Work of the Rev. E.J. Peck Among the Eskimos,* London: Hodder & Stoughton, 1904

Peck, E.J., *The Eskimo. Our Brethren of the Arctic (With Note by Canon Bertal Heeney),* Toronto: The MSCC, 1922

PENNY, WILLIAM

During his seafaring career (1821–1868), the Scottish whaler William Penny made about 40 Arctic whaling voyages, five of them extending over a winter. After serving his apprenticeship under his father's command at the Greenland whale fishery (between Spitsbergen and Greenland) from 1821 to 1827, he concentrated on the Davis Strait fishery (between Greenland and Baffin Island) during the next third of a century, and made one voyage into Hudson Bay.

Between 1600 and 1915, whalers from Europe and North America exploited five discrete stocks of Greenland (bowhead) whales (*Balaena mysticetus*) extending from Spitsbergen halfway round the world westward to the Sea of Okhotsk. In the Atlantic sector alone (Spitsbergen to Hudson Bay), they made upward of 30,000 voyages. Their first-hand knowledge of the Arctic and its native peoples was substantial, although much of it remained within the whaling fraternity and was communicated orally. Some captains, however, brought their geographical discoveries to the attention of the government and the public, and William Penny was one of these.

Penny made two outstanding contributions to European geographical knowledge. In 1840, following up Inuit reports of an area called "Tenudiackbeek," he found, explored, and charted a large inlet on Baffin Island south of Davis Strait. It turned out to be Cumberland Sound, which had last been visited by John Davis two and a half centuries before. Penny's rediscovery of the gulf led to a significant expansion of the Davis Strait whale fishery, and in the remaining three-quarters of a century of commercial whaling, this region attracted more wintering voyages than any other. A decade later, while commanding an Admiralty expedition in search of Sir John Franklin, he and his men,

hauling sledges of camping gear and food over the snow and ice, traced for the first time both shores of Wellington Channel, the north coast of Cornwallis Island, and part of the south coast of Grinnell Peninsula (on Devon Island). After discovering a large expanse of open water (today Queen's Channel) and exploring it by open boat for a month, Penny suggested that Franklin had passed through it into an ice-free polar sea. Although there was no real evidence that this was so, the idea caught the imagination and had the effect of turning the search for Franklin in the wrong direction.

Penny strove constantly to improve whaling. In 1852, he proposed an ambitious scheme. Under the auspices of a Royal Arctic Company, he would establish a year-round colony in Cumberland Sound. Its residents, in cooperation with local Inuit, would pursue whales, process them, and send the whalebone (baleen) and oil to Britain each summer on a supply ship. But his application to the Colonial Office and Board of Trade for a large grant of land and exclusive privileges of hunting, fishing, and mining was strongly opposed by other whaling interests, and at the last minute a change of government doomed the project. After failing to obtain the grants, he took his two ships to Cumberland Sound anyway, wintered there in 1853–1854, and secured an impressive number of whales, most of them killed in the productive floe edge whaling of spring. In 1857, he established two whaling stations in the gulf, the first year-round European bases in the Arctic islands.

Inevitably, wintering ships and permanent stations affected Inuit settlement patterns, population, economy, and culture. Penny was aware that the behavior of sailors ashore was causing social problems, so on his wintering voyage of 1857–1858 he took a Moravian missionary with him to assess the feasibility of opening a permanent mission in Cumberland Sound. Brother Warmow was the first missionary to preach Christianity among the Inuit north of Labrador. The church, however, decided not to set up a mission.

In thinking of better ways to exploit the whale resources of the Arctic, Penny's imagination and enthusiasm sometimes outstripped good sense. He suggested a circumpolar approach to whaling that would involve steam auxiliary ships operating throughout a vast region stretching from Novaya Zemlya in the east to Baffin Bay in the west, and even extending their operations across the supposedly ice-free Arctic Ocean.

Penny achieved an unusual degree of success in whaling, frequently bringing back more blubber and whalebone than most other ships, and capturing more than 160 whales during his career. He had a reputation for bold navigation, skillfully dodging ice-floes and icebergs with all sail set, and often forcing his ship into narrow leads when others hesitated, yet he never lost a ship. Many of the innovations that occurred in

Arctic whaling during the 19th century (wintering; rendering oil ashore; employing Inuit to help in whaling and hunting; establishing shore stations) came as a result—at least in part—of his imagination, energy, and determination.

Although the exploits of most whaling captains were largely unknown beyond the whaling ports, Penny became a well-known figure in Britain. He first received public attention in 1839 when he brought a young Inuk, Eenoolooapik, to Aberdeen for the winter. He attracted more notice in the following season when, with Eenoo's help, he expanded the frontier of whaling into Cumberland Sound. The efforts he made to find evidence of Franklin during whaling voyages in 1847 and 1849 received favorable comment, and he was widely admired when he secured command (with the help of Lady Franklin) of an official search expedition in 1850. After the return of the search expeditions in 1851, the acrimonious dispute between him and Captain Horatio Austin, R.N. was widely reported in the press. Narratives of three of his voyages were published by his surgeons—Dr. M'Donald (on the *Bon Accord* in 1841), Dr. Goodsir (on the *Advice* in 1849), and Dr. Sutherland (on the *Lady Franklin* in 1850–1851)—all of whom praised Penny's resourcefulness and skill. In letters to influential people, prominent newspapers, and the Royal Geographical Society, Penny expressed his own ideas on Arctic exploration and the Franklin search. Like Vilhjalmur Stafansson more than half a century later, Penny perceived the Arctic as a hospitable place where Europeans could safely and comfortably reside.

Biography

According to handwritten parish records, William Penny was baptized in Peterhead, Scotland, on July 24, 1808. (Other sources indicate his birth year as 1809.) He was one of nine children (possibly ten) born to William Penny and Janet (née Robertson). Following his father's vocation, he embarked on a whaling career in 1821, obtained his first command in 1835, secured a "Master's Certificate of Service" in 1853, and made his last sea voyage in 1868. In addition to several letters published in newspapers, Penny wrote *Letter to the Lords Commissioners of the Admiralty* (1852). He married Margaret Irvine in 1840 and they had five children—William Kennedy, Helen Eliza, William, Janet Robertson, and Margaret Irvine. On two of his wintering voyages, he was accompanied by his wife (probably the first European woman to winter among the Inuit), and on one he took his 12-year-old son. Predeceased by his wife, Penny died in Aberdeen on February 1, 1892.

W. GILLIES ROSS

See also **Davis, John; Eenoolooapik; Franklin, Lady Jane; Franklin, Sir John**

Further Reading

Goodsir, Robert Anstruther, *An Arctic voyage to Baffin's Bay and Lancaster Sound, in search of friends with Sir John Franklin*, London: Van Voorst, 1850

Holland, Clive A., "William Penny, 1809–1992: Arctic whaling master." *Polar Record*, 15(94) (1970): 25–43

———, "The Arctic Committee of 1851: a background study." *Polar Record*, 20(124) (1980): 3–17; and 20(125) (1980): 105–118

M'Donald, Alexander, *A narrative of some passages in the history of Eenoolooapik, a young Esquimaux, who was brought to Britain in 1839, in the ship "Neptune" of Aberdeen.* Edinburgh: Fraser and Hogg, 1841

Penny, William, *Letter to the Lords Commissioners of the Admiralty*, London: Chapman & Hall, 1852

Ross, W. Gillies, "Whaling, Inuit, and the Arctic Islands." In *A century of Canada's Arctic Islands 1880–1980*, edited by Morris Zaslow, Ottawa: Royal Society of Canada, 1981, pp. 33–50

———, "William Penny (1809–1892)." *Arctic*, 36(4) (1983): 380–381 (Reprinted in *Lobsticks and Stone Cairns: Human Landmarks in the Arctic*, edited by Richard C. Davis, Calgary: University of Calgary Press, 1996, pp. 210–212)

———, *This distant and unsurveyed country: a woman's winter at Baffin Island, 1857–58*, Montreal: McGill-Queen's University Press, 1997

Sutherland, Peter C., *Journal of a voyage to Baffin's Bay and Barrow Straits, in the years 1850–1851, performed by H.M. Ships "Lady Franklin" and "Sophia," under the command of Mr. William Penny, in search of the missing crews of H.M. Ships Erebus and Terror*, London: Longman, Green, and Longmans, 1852

Woodward, F.J., "William Penny, 1809–1892." *Polar Record*, 6 (46) (1953): 809–811

PENZHINA RIVER

The Penzhina River in Koryak Autonomous Okrug of northeast Siberia (upper reaches 64°08′ N 133°05′ E, mouth 62°01′ N 133°02′ E) drains into the Penzhina Gulf of the Sea of Okhotsk. The river is navigable for much of its length (713 km), and its basin (73,000 sq km) is an extensive lowland.

The Penzhina River basin is bordered by the Koryak Plateau to the east and by Kolyma Uplands to the west. The headwaters of the Penzhina rise in the low mountains (600–700 m) of the Kolyma Uplands and the river then flows east in a narrow forested canyon. Farther on, the valley becomes wider (3–4 km) and smooth, the riverbed width increases to 50–120 m at a distance of 140–150 km, and water depth decreases. The riverbank at the settlement of Penzhino is low (3.5 m), so the settlement occasionally floods in spring. At that distance, Penzhina takes ten tributaries, the most significant being the Chernaya River. The Penzhina then makes wide meanders, and near the confluence with its largest tributary, the Oklan River, the Penzhina turns sharply to the southwest and flows between steep-sided 100 m walls for about 50 km. At the end of this distance, there is a confluence of Penzhina with the River Belaya. The tides of the shallow Sea of Okhotsk may reach the confluence. Within 1.5 km of the bay, the Penzhina is 110–180 m wide, and its depth is between 50 cm and 2.5 m, with a sandy, pebbled riverbed. Near the mouth, there is a spit at the left bank as long as 1 km known by its shifting sands. At the tide, water "boils" due to discharge of air bubbles from the ground. Water debit in the mouth is 680 m^3 s^{-1}.

The climate of the Penzhina basin is severe. The average annual temperature is +6.5°C; the coldest month is January with a median temperature of –24.1°C and an absolute minimum of –56°C. The median temperature of the warmest month, July, is +13°C. Strong winds are frequent, from north and northeast in winter, and from west and southwest in summer. Snowstorms are typical. Precipitation occurs up to 200 mm per year, mostly as summer rains. Snow depth occurs up to 80 cm. Snow cover remains from October to the end of April, although the first snow appears at the end of September and the last snow disappears at the beginning of June.

Permafrost melts in the riverbed to 1 m, in the surrounding tundra to 25–40 cm, and on mountain slopes to 50–70 cm. Ice covers the river from November to May or the beginning of June.

Vegetation of the Penzhina Basin is predominantly tundra, both mountain and plain, covered with cottongrass and sedges. Mountain slopes are covered with dwarf pine shrubs. There are forests in the upper and middle reaches of Penzhina, along the riverbed. The dominant species are poplar and *Chosenia*. Good birch forests in Oklan Basin are of economic value. Many species of fish inhabit the river, including some endemic species. There are five species of salmon, which constitute a significant part of the local people's diet. The coastal waters are an important stop for southward migrating birds.

There are a few settlements on the river: Penzhino, Kamenskoye (district center), Slavutnoye, Oklan at Penzhina River and its tributaries banks. The population mainly constitutes Russians; one-third of the residents are indigenous people such as Koryak, Even, and Chukchi. Most people are involved with reindeer husbandry, fishing, hunting, and timber floating.

LEONID M. BASKIN

Further Reading

Gurvich, Ilia & Kuzakov Kuz'ma, *Koryaksii natsional'nyi okrug* [Koryak National Okrug], Moscow: Izdatel'stvo Akademii nauk, 1960

Sergeev, M., *Koryaksii natsional'nyi okrug* [Koryak National Okrug], Leningrad: Institut narodov Severa, 1934

Slunin, N., *Okhotsko-Kamchatskii krai* [Okhotsk - Kamchatka regions], 2 volumes, St Petersburg: Ministerstvo finansov, 1900

Solov'ev, A., "Penzhina River" [Penzhina River]. *Zemlevedenie*, 38(1) (1936): 82–105

PERIGLACIAL ENVIRONMENTS

The term periglacial refers to the conditions, processes, and landforms produced by cold but non-glacial climates. Periglacial geomorphology is the study of physical and chemical geomorphic processes, and landforms characteristic of cold non-glacial environments. Periglacial environments are currently defined by two criteria: intense frost action and/or the presence of permafrost. Periglacial environments are therefore areas where landforms and geomorphic processes reflect the cumulative effects of cold conditions, freezing, and thawing. Today, periglacial conditions affect 25–35% of the Earth's land surface, mostly in the Northern Hemisphere.

In 1909, a Polish geologist, Walery von Lozinski, proposed the term "periglacial" to describe the weathering processes responsible for the production of shattered rock surfaces in the Carpathian Mountains. The concept of a "periglacial zone" was introduced by Lozinski in 1910 to describe climatic and geomorphic regimes peripheral to the Pleistocene ice sheets. Since its introduction, the periglacial concept has gone through a series of contextual changes. In its original context, the periglacial concept was firmly rooted in climatic geomorphology and was constrained to locations near glaciers and ice sheets. Climatic geomorphology is a geomorphic approach that was popular in the 1930s and 1940s. It equates landscapes with climate and is predicated on the hypothesis that the climatic regime controls the geomorphic process, which in turn controls landforms. Even though climate remains a defining variable, the current focus of periglacial geomorphology is on the mechanics of heat flow, ice formation, the properties of ice, freezing and thawing, and the dynamic interaction between these processes and various distinctive landforms. Thorn (1992) proposed linking the term periglacial specifically to ground ice processes and landforms; however, this shift in emphasis failed to gather much support. Accordingly, the periglacial environment remains synonymous with areas characterized by frost action and/or permafrost (French, 1996). Even though there is considerable overlap between the terms permafrost and geocryology (both are defined in terms of frozen earth materials), the term periglacial is used more broadly and is applicable to areas with and without permafrost as long as the climate and landforms reflect an environment in which frost action is significant.

Frost action is the collective term for processes that result from freezing and thawing. An essential component of frost action is the change in phase of soil water between liquid and ice and the corresponding 9% increase in volume as water turns to ice. Frost action occurs in any area that experiences subfreezing soil temperatures. The effects of frost action range from the formation of needle ice in areas that experience freezing only at the surface to frost heave in areas of deep-seated freezing and permafrost. In areas characterized by seasonal frost, it occurs mainly in the fall and late spring. But in areas of permafrost, frost action can occur anytime during the summer. Practically all soils undergo some frost action; however, the magnitude is dependent upon the local climate, availability of water, and soil texture. Frost action is divided into two phases: freezing the soil water and thawing the soil water. In periglacial environments, frost action becomes critical when either the freezing phase is accompanied by noticeable heaving of the ground surface or the thawing phase is accompanied by a noticeable softening of the ground. Three conditions must be fulfilled before "frost heave" can occur: (i) the climate must be sufficiently cold to allow freezing temperatures to penetrate below the ground surface; (ii) there needs to be an adequate supply of water; and (iii) there must be soil material that is frost susceptible and lying within the freezing zone. The heaving is caused by the formation of ice lenses in the soil and below large rock fragments and the 9% expansion in volume as water freezes to ice. The size of an ice lens depends upon the quantity of free water available within the soil as it freezes. Once started, ice lenses continue to grow as long as a source of free water is available. Free water migrates through the soil to a forming ice lens by capillary action. Water may migrate as far as 20 ft for certain frost-susceptible soils. Some soils are more susceptible to the formation of ice lenses than others. Silts or silty clay soils are considered among the most frost susceptible. Because of the extremely small size of its particles, silt permits and spurs the flow of water by capillary action through its pores. Consequently, silts supply the water necessary to promote the formation of ice lenses in the freezing zone. Other soils considered to be frost-susceptible include fine sands, clayey gravel, and rock flour. Moderately frost-susceptible soils include dirty sands and gravels and glacial tills.

Frost wedging is a form of mechanical weathering (i.e., weathering that involves physical rather than chemical change). Frost wedging is caused by the repeated freeze-thaw cycle of water in extreme climates. Most rocks have small cracks in them, called joints (or tectonic joints). When it rains, water seeps into these joints. As the day cools and temperatures at night drop below freezing, water inside the joints freezes. As water freezes, it expands and the expanding ice puts pressure on the joints in the rock. Finally, when the pressure exceeds the rock strength, the joint expands. In some cases, the rock will split, although this usually occurs after repeated freeze and thaw. As new water is added during the warmer days, more ice is created at night, wedging the joints further apart.

Frost-jacking is another heave-based frost process. When heaving occurs as described above, a structure embedded in the ground that is not properly anchored will be forced upward along with the ground surface. In most cases, the structure does not return to its original position when the active layer thaws during the following summer. The net upward movement is called "jacking." This phenomenon can occur whenever there is seasonal freezing and thawing of the active layer, and is not limited to permafrost areas.

Thaw settlement is a frost action process that occurs during the thawing phase of the cycle. Objects or structures built on "thaw-unstable" permafrost will settle if excess ice in permafrost is melted (see **Thermokarst**). Melting is typically caused by heat from the structure itself (e.g., the flow of warm oil in a pipeline) or changes to the natural thermal conditions.

A final frost action process is frost cracking. It was once thought that the freezing and thawing of solid rock could produce a mechanical weathering process called frost shatter. The extensive rock rubble surfaces of many periglacial regions were deemed as evidence of such a process. Experimental evidence has subsequently indicated that pure frost shatter is probably rare and that hydration shatter is possibly more common. However, rapid cooling of the ground may cause thermal contraction stresses that may result in frost cracking (thermal contraction cracking) of frozen ground. Repeated thermal contraction cracking in permafrost areas is the mechanism responsible for the formation of ice wedges and ice-wedge polygons (see **Patterned and Polygonal Ground**).

Permafrost is the second defining criterion for periglacial environments. Permafrost is "ground that remains at or below 0°C for at least 2 years" (Permafrost Subcommittee, 1988: 63). It reflects a thermodynamic balance between ground surface temperature and geothermal gradient. The spatial distribution and depth of permafrost are closely related to climate. Locally, the nature of the ground surface defines the boundary layer conditions that determine the degree to which air temperatures influence ground thermal regimes. Geologic, tectonic, and subsurface hydrologic conditions further influence permafrost. Permafrost underlies approximately 26% of the Earth's land surface (Williams and Smith, 1989) and occurs extensively in Arctic and Subarctic regions, affecting up to 80% of Alaska and 50% of Canada and Russia. In North America, permafrost is divided into continuous and discontinuous zones defined on the basis of the location and areal extent of cryotic ground. Permafrost depths range from >1000m (1450m in Siberia) to only a few meters near its southern limit. During the summer, ground surface temperatures rise above 0°C and produce thaw of a thin layer above permafrost called the active layer. Active layer depths range from a few decimeters in the High Arctic to more than 2 m in parts of the discontinuous permafrost zone. The seasonal freezing and thawing of the active layer and the seasonal pattern of temperature change in the upper part of permafrost produce a number of very distinctive features unique to Arctic tundra, like patterned ground, gelifluction lobes, active layer detachments, seasonal frost mounds, frost cracks, and tundra tussocks.

WAYNE POLLARD

See also **Fossil Periglacial Phenomena; Frost and Frost Phenomena; Ground Ice; Permafrost**

Further Reading

Dixon, J.C. & A.D. Abrahams (editors), *Periglacial Geomorphology,* Chichester: Wiley, 1992
French, H.M., *The Periglacial Environment* (2nd edition), Harlow, Essex: Addison-Wesley, Longman, 1996
———, "Does Lozinski's periglacial realm exist today? A discussion relevant to modern usage of the term periglacial." *Permafrost and Periglacial Processes,* 11 (2000): 35–42
Permafrost Subcommittee, *Glossary of Permafrost and Related Ground-Ice Terms,* Associate Committee on Geotechnical Research, National Research Council of Canada, Ottawa, 1988
Thorn, C.E., "Periglacial Geomorphology: What, Where, When?." In *Periglacial Geomorphology,* edited by J.C. Dixon & A.D. Abrahams, *Proceedings of the 22nd Annual Symposium in Geomorphology,* Chichester: Wiley, 1992, pp. 1–30
Washburn, A.L., *Periglacial Processes and Environments,* London: Edward Arnold, 1973
Williams, P.J. & M.W. Smith, *The Frozen Earth: Fundamentals of Geocryology,* Cambridge and New York: Cambridge University Press, 1989

PERMAFROST

The term permafrost (perennially frozen ground) refers to any sub-surface materials (soils, gravel, or rock) that remain below 0°C throughout two or more consecutive years. Unlike other components of the cryosphere, permafrost is not necessarily associated with frozen water, although most ground materials in permafrost regions contain ice. Permafrost underlies nearly one-fourth of the Earth's land areas, of which about 16.7 million km^2 is located in northeastern Eurasia and 10.2 million km^2 in North America. Most of the islands in the Arctic Ocean are underlain by permafrost, which also extends offshore beneath the shallow polar seabed. In the Southern Hemisphere, permafrost is present in ice-free areas in Antarctica and on some Subantarctic islands. Alpine permafrost can be found at high elevations in many mountain ranges and plateaus of the world.

Permafrost may be continuous, or separated by areas of seasonally frozen ground. The continuity of permafrost is governed by many factors, including climate, the presence of large water bodies, snow cover, vegetation, soil conditions, and topography. Depending on areal extent, permafrost is divided into continuous, discontinuous, and sporadic zones, which are defined as having more than 90%, 50–90%, and less than 50% of the terrain underlain by frozen ground, respectively. Permafrost thickness varies from as much as 1500 m at selected locations in Siberia and 740 m in northern Alaska to a few meters in the southern zone, and is typically between 100 and 800 m, 25 and 100 m, and 10 and 50 m thick in continuous, discontinuous, and sporadic zones, respectively. A complex interplay of the surface temperature, thermal conductivity of ground material, and the geothermal flux transporting heat from the interior of the Earth governs the thickness of permafrost, which may thus be quite variable even under similar climatic conditions.

Annual variations in the surface ground temperature become attenuated in the uppermost 10–12 m. Permafrost temperature below these depths remains constant throughout the year and is typically between −8°C and −13°C in the northernmost zone of continuous permafrost, between −3° and −7°C in the discontinuous zone, and between 0 and −2°C in the southern marginal zone. Indigenous peoples following traditional lifestyles use this unique permafrost feature to serve their needs. They dig deep cold caves to store frozen meat, fish, berries, and mushrooms long before modern refrigerators were available.

The areal extent and position of permafrost boundaries depend largely on climate. Although vegetation, snow, and surface layer of organic matter mitigate climatic influences, modern permafrost is clearly a product of past cold climates that caused it to develop from the ground surface downward. Permafrost areal extent and thickness increased progressively during the cold epochs of the Earth's geological history and retreated during warmer intervals. In the last glacial period, 18,000 years before present, permafrost expanded from the Arctic region down to 47–50° latitude in Eurasia and to 40° latitude in North America. The subsequent retreat of permafrost continued until it reached a minimum extent 3000–6000 years ago. At that time, the permafrost boundary was shifted several hundred kilometers from the present-day location to the north in North America, and northeast in Eurasia. Contemporary distribution of

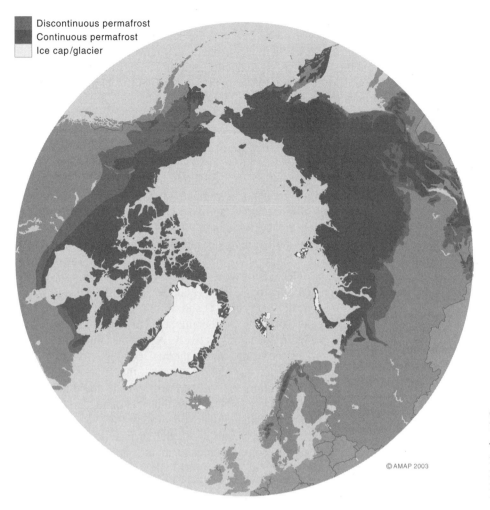

Discontinuous permafrost
Continuous permafrost
Ice cap/glacier

© AMAP 2003

Circumpolar permafrost distribution. From *AMAP Assessment Report: Arctic Pollution Issues*, Arctic Monitoring and Assessment Programme, 1998. Reproduced with permission.

permafrost is crudely conformable with climate zones and thus may be predicted using climatic data. At the end of the 19th century, the Russian climatologist G. Vild suggested corresponding the southern permafrost boundary with the −2°C annual mean air temperature isotherm. A more elaborate classification by Albert Washburn suggested that permafrost is likely to occur in areas having air temperatures below freezing point for three-quarters of the year, less than 10°C for half a year, and very rarely above 20°C, with precipitation below 100 mm in winter and less than 300 mm in summer. Mathematical models of different complexity developed more recently allow calculation of the position of permafrost boundaries from climatic data available from weather stations with relatively high accuracy.

The uppermost layer of terrestrial permafrost is subject to seasonal summer thaw even under the most severe climate conditions. This seasonally thawed layer, termed the active layer, varies in thickness from several centimeters on the Arctic coast to a few meters. The active layer thickness is governed largely by the air temperature; however, the snow cover, vegetation, and layer of organic matter on top of the permafrost moderate the fluxes of heat between the atmosphere and frozen ground. Snow cover prevents excessive cooling of frozen ground in winter, and ultimately increases the depth of summer thawing. The active layer is shallower in the presence of organic materials and vegetation, particularly mosses, as they have very low thermal conductivity and reduce the heat flux to the thawing ground. Seasonal thawing penetrates deeper into gravel and sandy soils than into finer-grained silt or clay, and the thaw depth increases with soil moisture content in all types of soil due to the difference in soil thermal conductivity.

The active layer plays a key role in specific forms of mass movement in permafrost terrain, such as ground settlement, frost heave, solifluction (soil flowage), detachment slides, and retrogressive thaw slumps on the slopes. It is an important regulator of many biological processes associated with the accumulation and decomposition of organic material, and emission and absorption of gases (carbon dioxide and methane). Active layer thickness has a direct effect on the water storage, runoff, and ultimately Arctic hydrology.

Global anthropogenic climate change is a serious concern in permafrost regions. Many studies predict that climatic warming will be more intensive at high latitudes than in other parts of the world, and significant impacts on permafrost are expected. By the middle of the 21st century, permafrost may shrink by 12–16%. The depth of seasonal thawing is projected to increase on average by 15–30%, and by 50% and more in the northernmost locations. Such changes are detrimental to structures built upon permafrost, as they eventually decrease the bearing capacity of pile foundations, which may exceed the safety factor incorporated in their design. Where permafrost is ice-rich, such changes may cause uneven ground settlement and severe damage to buildings, pipelines, roads, airfields, bridges, and other elements of human infrastructure.

OLEG ANISIMOV

See also **Global Change Effects; Permafrost Hydrology; Thermokarst**

Further Reading

Baulin, V.V. & N.S. Danilova, "Dynamics of Late Quaternary Permafrost in Siberia." In *Late Quaternary Environments of the Soviet Union*, edited by A.A. Velichko, Minneapolis: University of Minnesota Press, 1984, pp. 69–77

Black, R.F., "Permafrost." In *Applied Sedimentation*, edited by P.D. Trask, New York: Wiley, 1950, pp. 247–275

Brown, J., "Disturbance and Recovery of Permafrost Terrain." In *Disturbance and Recovery in Arctic Lands: An Ecological Perspective*, edited by R.M.M. Crawford, Dordrecht: Kluwer, 1996, pp. 167–178

Ives, J.D., "Permafrost." In *Arctic and Alpine Environments*, edited by J.D. Ives & R.G. Barry, London: Methuen, 1974, pp. 159–194

Koster, E.A. & M.E. Nieuwenhuijzen, "Permafrost Response to Climatic Change." In *Greenhouse-Impact on Cold-Climate Ecosystems and Landscapes. Catena Supplement 22*, edited by M.M. Boer & E.A. Koster, Cremlingen-Destedt, Germany: Catena Verlag, 1992, pp. 37–58

Nelson, F.E., O.A. Anisimov & N.I. Shiklomanov, "Subsidence risk from thawing permafrost." *Nature* (410) (2001): 889–890

Washburn, A.L., "Periglacial Problems." In *Field and Theory: Lectures in Geocryology*, edited by M. Church & O. Slaymaker, Vancouver: University of British Columbia Press, 1985, pp. 166–202

PERMAFROST HYDROLOGY

Permafrost hydrology studies the distribution, movement, and storage of water as is directly or indirectly influenced by the presence of perennially frozen ground (*see* **Permafrost**). Since permafrost is a temperature-related phenomenon and not synonymous with perennially frozen ground, moisture in permafrost materials may not always be frozen into a solid state. The freezing point of water is depressed by pressure and by the presence of impurities. Furthermore, water in soil pores and water that forms a film around soil grains usually freezes at temperatures below 0°C.

Figure 1 shows a schematic ground temperature profile in the permafrost zone. At the top of the profile, the summer maximum and the winter minimum temperature curves bracket the temperature ranges found at various depths. Where the annual maximum temperature (represented by the summer curve) falls below the 0°C boundary, cryotic ground (defined as soil or rock at temperatures ≤0°C) exists. At the bottom of the profile, geothermal heat warms the ground and the temperature rises above 0°C to mark the lower limit of the perennially cryotic zone. Permafrost corresponds with the perennially cryotic section of the profile. The frozen condition occurs only when most of the soil water changes into ice. The amount of unfrozen water present in the permafrost depends on the ground temperature, the moisture content, the soil particle size, the salinity of the soil water, and the pressure exerted on the fluid.

In permafrost areas, summer warming of the near-surface zone causes thawing. The ground layer that undergoes annual freezing and thawing in a permafrost environment is known as the active layer. Unfrozen ground in a permafrost area is known as a talik (a term of Russian origin), which may occur within or below the permafrost, or may lie above the permafrost as is frequently found beneath deep Arctic lakes. Fast hydrological processes such as daily freeze-thaw and water flow take place mostly within the active layer; the taliks usually have a slower movement of groundwater and moisture migration.

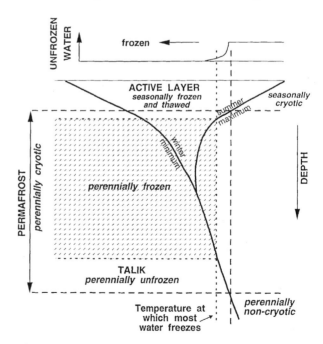

Figure 1: Schematic ground temperature profile defining the active layer, cryotic (<0°C), and frozen (most of the water in the ground is changed to ice) zones in permafrost materials.

Hydrological Processes

Permafrost hydrology is closely linked to thermal considerations and to the prolonged presence of snow and ice. Persistent and extreme cold conditions increase the significance of several processes unique to the cold environment, including ground freeze-thaw, moisture migration in frozen soil, snowmelt, and the formation and decay of ice and icing.

Snow Hydrology

Snow usually represents the major form of precipitation in the permafrost region and the snow can remain for over six months with little melting due to the persistent cold. Typically, the snow cover is (1) intensely cold, with snow temperatures often below −10°C prior to spring melt, superimposed on frozen soils that are also cold; (2) stratified into layers due to differential snowfall deposition events and the frequent development of cup-shaped hoar frost at the base; and (3) unevenly distributed caused by snow drifting across the open tundra or by the shielding presence of trees.

Snow exerts strong influences on permafrost hydrology because a substantial amount of meltwater is released within a short melt season, often lasting only several weeks. The duration of melt is extended if the terrain traverses a range of elevations so that snowmelt advances gradually from the low to the high elevations. Spatial variations in solar radiation receipt due to slope aspect, shadiness, and cloud coverage can exaggerate differential melting of the snow cover, leading to patchy snow cover as melt progresses. The bare spots are heated up to temperatures above 0°C, and the advection of warm air over the adjacent snow patches will accelerate the melt.

When meltwater percolates the subfreezing snowpack, it may refreeze as ice lenses along the boundaries between the snow layers, flow along macrofissures to form vertical flow fingers, or descend behind a broad front. Upon reaching the base of the snowpack, the meltwater may freeze to form a layer of basal ice if the ground remains very cold. The wetting of the cold, dry snow and the refreezing of the meltwater cause a time lag between snowmelt and runoff generation, at least by several days.

Freeze-Thaw and Ground Ice Processes

Freezing, thawing, and related ice formation-decay in the soil are affected by moisture availability and fluxes. These processes in turn modify the storage, distribution, and movement of water.

Ground freezing is often accompanied by the formation of ground ice. Several types of ground ice may be distinguished (*see* **Ground Ice**). Ground ice in the soil pores or lenses of segregated ice hinder water movement. The permeability of ice-rich frozen materials decreases substantially, regardless of their intrinsic perviousness in the thawed state. Even if the cold ground started off being relatively ice-free, it has high propensity to freeze the water that percolates the soil to render the soil much less pervious. Thus, frozen soils usually have hydraulic conductivities that are several orders of magnitude lower than their thawed counterparts (Burt and Williams, 1976). Water transfer in frozen soils is limited, thereby focusing most hydrological activities in the thawed active layer or the taliks.

The amount of ground ice in the active layer strongly affects the rate at which ground thaw proceeds. Studies have shown that active layer thaw is related not only to heat flux entering the soil, the thermal properties of the soil, but also to the ground ice content, which affects the amount of latent heat required for ice melt. In the course of a summer, soils with large ice content may have limited thaw depth because a large amount of latent heat is needed to melt its ice (Woo and Xia, 1996).

In the freeze-back period, both the ground surface and the permafrost table are colder than the middle portion of the active layer. The active layer is subject to freezing from two sides, favoring moisture migration to the top and the bottom zones. The resulting moisture redistribution in the soil profile often leads to desiccation of the mid-section of the active layer. In addition, a large temperature gradient may exist in the winter between the snow and the soil. This induces a vapor pressure gradient that causes the soil ice to sublimate and then flux upward from the soil to the overlying snow cover (Santeford, 1978; Smith and Burn, 1987).

Infiltration

As noted above, the permeability of frozen ground is considerably reduced. Infiltration of snow meltwater or rainfall into the frozen ground is thus strongly dependent on the amount of ice in the soil pores, and the ability of the soil to freeze the infiltrated water. For most soils other than coarse sand, the infiltration rate is one or more orders of magnitude lower than those for the same materials in a thawed state (Kane and Stein, 1983), meaning that for most soils, infiltration represents a small portion (about 5–20%) of total snowmelt. In discontinuous permafrost areas with an organic top layer, meltwater infiltrates along soil cracks and through the lichen and moss cover to be stored in the organic mat. The infiltrated water may freeze in the interstitial space in the soil to decrease the soil perviousness.

Groundwater Flow

The imperviousness of most frozen materials confines the storage and movement of groundwater largely to the thawed zones. Based on the location of groundwater occurrence with respect to the permafrost, Tolstikin and Tolstikin (1976) distinguished between (1) suprapermafrost groundwater, which, together with soil moisture, lies above the permafrost and mostly within the active layer, (2) intrapermafrost groundwater, which occupies the taliks within the permafrost, and (3) subpermafrost groundwater, which is found below the permafrost (Figure 2).

Suprapermafrost groundwater is often restricted to the thawed zone above the frost table, and therefore its storage capacity varies during the thaw season as the active layer thaws and freezes. Groundwater is recharged by snowmelt and rainfall infiltration, and by lateral runoff from upslope. This source of groundwater supports evaporation and drainage to the lower slopes, while in discontinuous permafrost areas it also provides the conduit that permits meteoric water to recharge the intrapermafrost or subpermafrost groundwater reservoirs. The recharge and discharge of the deep groundwater are limited to the discontinuous permafrost region, with the taliks providing the passage for the flow. The occurrence of fault zones or solution conduits (such as in the carbonate karst) facilitates groundwater movement. Unlike seepage from suprapermafrost groundwater, which usually ceases in the freezing season, the deep-seated water source maintains perennial flows.

Groundwater also occurs in isolated taliks confined entirely by the permafrost. Regardless of confinement or otherwise, intrapermafrost and subpermafrost groundwaters are highly mineralized and therefore have a depressed freezing point. Since such waters do not freeze at 0°C, they can occupy those parts of the permafrost peripheral to the taliks as well as within the taliks. The water usually flows under pressure, carrying heat and a high mineral content to keep the talik unfrozen.

During freeze-up, groundwater collected from lateral drainage may freeze as an ice core (Figure 2), sometimes lifting the seasonally frozen ground to create a frost blister. If the water ruptures through the frozen cap, it will be chilled by the winter coldness. Repeated discharge and freezing of this water produces an icing (naleds in Russian and aufeis in German), which is a sheetlike mass of layered ice formed above ground. Carey (1973) distinguished icings into ground, spring, and river icings, depending on their location. The growth of icing terminates when the groundwater supply from the active layer is exhausted, but the discharge of groundwater from a deeper source can support icing growth throughout the winter. The result is an extensive and thick icing covering a large part of the valleys (Sokolov, 1991).

Evaporation

Evaporation often reaches the highest values in the spring because of ample water supply from snowmelt

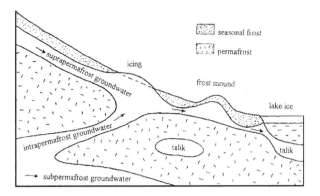

Figure 2: Occurrence of groundwater in permafrost area, formation of frost mound, and icing.

and a large amount of radiation energy available. Later, evaporation declines as the ground becomes drier and as radiation input is reduced. Evaporation is restricted when the winter snow arrives. The length of the evaporation season decreases poleward because of a long snow-covered period, although sublimation from the snow can be notable in a dry atmospheric environment (*see* **Sublimation**). Poleward reduction in evaporation rates is also attributed to lower radiation. Permafrost areas of the low latitudes but at high elevations (such as the Tibetan Plateau) may receive large radiation input, and the evaporation rates can be high. This offers a large potential for evaporation, although actual evaporation is limited by moisture supply.

Runoff Generation

The active layer remains mostly frozen during the snowmelt period and, despite limited infiltration, much of the meltwater fills up ground surface depressions or is held in the snowpack until its retention capacity is exceeded. Lateral flow begins when the snow cover is saturated. Drainage within the snow frequently occurs at the bottom of the snowpack but on top of the basal ice layer. Sometimes, meltwater carves channels in the snow, particularly where the snow is thick and saturated. Meltwater may also mix with the snow to produce slush flow. The initial stage appears to be the collection of meltwater and rainwater in a zone of low gradient, leading to saturation of the snowpack in the channel. This is followed by a steepening of the water table (thus increasing the hydraulic gradient of the saturated zone) in the snow. A sudden release of the snow and water mixture gives rise to slush flow (Gude and Scherer, 1995).

Ground thaw begins immediately after snowmelt. At this time, groundwater storage capacity in the active layer is limited by the depth of thaw, and the ground is usually saturated by a large influx of meltwater. Later in the year, the loss of water to evaporation and a lowering of the frost table lead to a drop in the water table and drying of the ground. Summer snowfall usually melts within hours or days and so both rainfall and summer snowmelt raise the water table, sometimes saturating the thawed zone and rejuvenating surface flow. Melting of ground ice adds unfrozen water to the thawing zone but does not represent a net water gain to the active layer. Similarly, melting of extensive icings can augment water supply to the slopes and to the streams (Williams and van Everdingen, 1973), and this represents the delayed yield from groundwater discharged during the winter.

Slope Hydrology

Runoff

Surface flow and subsurface (suprapermafrost groundwater) flow in the active layer are the major modes of slope runoff in continuous permafrost areas, while in discontinuous permafrost zones lateral flow is augmented by discharge of intrapermafrost and subpermafrost groundwater. The general pattern includes a high flow period during the spring when abundant snow meltwater is released to the frozen soil that has low infiltration capacity. The water table is close to the ground surface, and widespread surface flow is generated. Runoff declines as the frost table drops and as meltwater is depleted, leading to a decline in the water table and the cessation of surface flow unless summer precipitation (rainfall or snowfall) replenishes the soil moisture. Slope runoff ceases in the winter, except in some discontinuous permafrost areas where subpermafrost groundwater discharge builds up icings.

On slopes underlain by continuous permafrost, widespread surface flow occurs during and immediately after the snowmelt season, with prominent diurnal cycles that reflect the daily snowmelt pattern. After snowmelt, the water table drops below ground as the frost table deepens, and surface flow declines. For the rest of the summer, surface flow is rare, but exceptions are found at local sites below late-lying snowbanks, and slope concavities or depressions where groundwater seeps to the surface. Subsurface flow is limited by the thickness of the thawed zone and by the amount of water in the active layer. Lewkowicz and French (1982) found that subsurface flow is more significant during the snowmelt season than in the postmelt period, but the flow is spatially highly variable.

In the discontinuous permafrost areas, some slopes have only seasonal frost but not permafrost. For such slopes (e.g., some south-facing slopes), the paucity of ground ice permits meltwater and rainwater to infiltrate and then percolate deeply, depriving them of the opportunity to generate runoff (Carey and Woo, 1999). Slopes underlain by permafrost (e.g., north-facing slopes) are often covered by a highly porous peat and living moss-lichen layer. In the snowmelt season, meltwater can infiltrate the porous organic layer even when the ground temperature is below 0°C, but this water may not percolate easily into the frozen and ice-rich mineral soil with hydraulic conductivities that are orders of magnitude lower than the organic. Consequently, the organic layer is saturated, followed by surface flow and rapid lateral drainage in the organic soils. The slope area contributing to direct runoff is usually variable, depending on the local and upslope supply of meltwater and the pattern of slope drainage. It is during this time of the year that most of the slope runoff occurs. In the summer, a gradual downward thawing of the frozen soil allows percolation to occur. Surface flow ceases unless revived by heavy rainfall events. Subsurface flow may continue, although often at very low rates due to the low hydraulic conductivity of the mineral soil. Unless replenished by rainfall, the flow declines gradually as water continues to be lost to lateral discharge and in support of evapotranspiration. In some parts of the Subarctic, subpermafrost groundwater may be connected to the ground surface via taliks to emerge as mineral springs, or supply water to streambeds. In the fall, downslope drainage can create frost blisters or the extrusion of groundwater can form icings on the slope (Figure 2).

Flow Paths

Surface flow on slopes takes several forms. One mode commonly found on the barren slopes of the Arctic is overland flow in which water moves as a thin sheet. In the Low Arctic, runoff may concentrate along some topographically indistinct but hydrologically efficient linear pathways called water tracks, which follow the maximum gradients of the local slopes (Kane et al., 1992). While water tracks are marked merely by more lush vegetation growth than their surrounding tundra, well-defined gullies provide distinct paths for running water, which may enlarge these ephemeral flow channels. Where a highly porous organic layer overlies a mineral soil substrate of considerably lower hydraulic conductivities, soil pipes may be formed at the organic-mineral interface. These soil pipes may be linked with small rills to form a network that concentrates fast flow on slopes.

Subsurface flow rates are curtailed by reduced hydraulic conductivities in frozen silt and sand soils. Where the interstitial space in gravels is occupied by ice, subsurface flow is also hindered. In alpine permafrost areas, many slopes are underlain by boulders and other coarse materials that are not cemented by ice in the winter. Infiltration of snow meltwater and rapid subsurface flow can occur in the spring to deliver water downslope (Woo et al., 1994). Flow in the highly porous organic layer, soil pipes, and surface rills constitute fast flow. When the water table recedes into the underlying mineral soil with much lower hydraulic conductivity, slow flow in the mineral layer yields considerably less runoff to the downslope. Fast flow recurs when rainstorms raise the water table into the organic layer.

Wetland Hydrology

Permafrost, being largely impervious, provides a substrate that inhibits water losses to deep percolation, and if water supply is ample and reliable, the active layer becomes saturated to enable the formation of a wetland. Favorable locations include sites with a steady water supply such as late-lying snowbanks or adjacent to lakes, riparian zones or groundwater seepage, or sites with low gradients to retard lateral outflow.

The conventional perception that a wetland is a regulator of flow (i.e., stores high flows and releases the water gradually during the low flow period) does not apply generally to the wetlands in permafrost areas mainly because the frozen active layer has limited storage capacity to absorb the rapid release of snowmelt or intense rainfall. At the end of winter, uneven distribution of snow and ice blocks the flow path of meltwater across the wetlands. The substantial meltwater supply, the low infiltration capacity of the frozen soil, together with flow blockage, lead to filling of the surface depressions followed by the flooding of extensive areas, sometimes irrespective of the indistinct water divides in the flat terrain (Rovansek et al., 1996; Woo and Winter, 1993). At this time, the wetland acts as a pathway along which meltwater is delivered out of the catchment (Roulet and Woo, 1988). Riparian wetlands are further subject to overbank flow of the rivers, sometimes accompanied by a spectacular breakup of the river ice cover.

Lake Hydrology

Many lakes occupy the permafrost region. Some lakes are very large (e.g., Great Bear Lake, Lake Baikal), but their hydrological interactions with permafrost are poorly known. The occurrence of smaller lakes may be related to nonpermafrost considerations such as preferential clustering along belts of structural weaknesses (e.g., many lakes in the Canadian shield) or the migration of river channels. However, permafrost degradation or aggradation can be a major factor in the formation of many lakes. The melting of permafrost followed by land subsidence favors the infilling of the depressions to create thermokarst lakes (e.g., the frequent presence of lakes in the "alas" thermokarst terrain in Siberia). The aggradation of permafrost in newly deposited sediments can interrupt lateral drainage to create lakes in some low gradient areas. Myriads of small lakes in the Mackenzie Delta are sealed from seepage loss and they are hydrologically connected to the distributary channels only through lateral flooding during the spring freshets (Marsh and Hey, 1989).

Lake morphology may be modified by permafrost melt; for example, shoreline erosion could be accelerated due to permafrost degradation. The oriented lakes found along the Alaskan Arctic coastal plain and in west-central Baffin Island, Canada, with their long axes perpendicular to the prevailing wind, are attributed to morphological change induced by wind, wave, and permafrost interactions.

Although most small lakes are sealed from seepage loss by the underlying permafrost, they also have a talik at the lake bottom but lying directly above the permafrost, kept unfrozen by the lake water. When such a lake is drained, the talik that used to be buffered by the lake water against the low air temperatures then undergoes freezing from all sides. The freezing of the pore water in the soil and the expulsion of intrapermafrost groundwater, subsequently freezing with the shrinking talik, favor the growth of thick bodies of segregated ice and sheets of intrusive ice.

Lakes in permafrost areas have a winter ice cover, with the duration and thickness of ice increasing with latitude and with altitude. The ice cover of some lakes is 2.5 m thick and lasts more than 11 months in the northern extremities of Arctic Canada or Greenland. The presence of an ice cover for a protracted period each year limits evaporation loss from the lakes.

In the open water period (ice-free or partial ice cover), lake evaporation is usually larger than from the surrounding land areas. The lakes receive rainfall and lateral inflows in the form of overland flow, channel runoff, or subsurface flow. Many lakes in the discontinuous permafrost region are probably connected to a subpermafrost groundwater reservoir through the taliks (Kane and Slaughter, 1973), permitting significant exchanges between the surface and groundwater sources. In a carbonate area of Subarctic Canada, for example, Brook (1983) observed the flooding of karst depressions during the snowmelt season. However, when the ice blocking the drainage routes melted in the autumn, these large temporary ponds, measuring over 100 m in length, disappeared quickly as the water drained through the talik. If a lake is not connected to a groundwater system below the permafrost, the subsurface flow is small relative to the other modes of inflow, such as overland flow or stream input. In most cases, lakes of the permafrost region depend upon their catchment rather than on direct precipitation alone for water supply.

Like the lakes elsewhere, lakes in permafrost areas serve a flow regulation function, whereby sudden influxes of water are stored and the water is then released downstream gradually. This storage effect significantly modifies the pattern of streamflow downstream of lakes. A special situation is the accumulation of drifted snow that blocks the outlet channels of small lakes. In the spring, meltwater runoff is collected in the lake, but the drift acts as a temporary dam that impounds the lake, against outflows. Eventually, when this snow barrier is breached, rapid draining of the impounded water releases a torrent downstream to generate the largest flood of each year.

Streamflow

Permafrost regions are drained by rivers that originate within the permafrost area and by rivers that traverse several natural regions, including nonpermafrost areas, so that their flow is not entirely governed by permafrost hydrology (e.g., Mackenzie, Ob', Lena, and Yenisey). Only rivers with large parts of their catchments underlain by permafrost exhibit characteristics that reflect the influence of permafrost (Slaughter et al., 1983).

The presence of permafrost accentuates runoff peaks while reducing the base flow. Newbury (1974) concluded that permafrost basins behave like impermeable catchments in terms of their rainfall-runoff relationship. One consequence is the rapid streamflow response to rainfall and snowmelt events. For small basins (e.g., McMaster River, Cornwallis Island, Canada, area 33 km^2) in the barren High Arctic, a thin active layer offers little storage capacity, and streamflow response to rainstorms is within several hours. For large, vegetated basins (e.g., Kuparuk River, Alaska, area 8140 km^2), the storm hydrograph typically shows fast initial response as a network of water tracks on the hillslopes quickly conveys runoff to the stream channels, but there is a long lag time between the centroids of the rainfall and of the storm flow as water is released slowly from the organic soil and the tundra vegetation. The ratio of runoff to precipitation is high, indicating that most of the storm water goes to streamflow.

Nival Regime

A streamflow regime is defined by the average seasonal pattern of runoff variations. The most common seasonal rhythm of streamflow in the permafrost region is the nival regime, so termed by Church (1974) to signify the dominance of snowmelt in runoff production. Under this regime, high flows prevail in the spring, often including the annual maximum. Diurnal streamflow fluctuations are prominent, reflecting the daily cycles of snowmelt rates. The presence of snow jams and/or ice jams in the channels accentuates the floods.

Flow patterns can be further subdivided into Arctic and Subarctic nival regimes. The Subarctic regime is distinguished from the Arctic counterpart by a longer streamflow season and more prominent summer peaks generated by heavy rainfall events. Taliks in the discontinuous permafrost allow low winter flows to be sustained by the discharge of subpermafrost and intrapermafrost groundwater.

Modifications of the Nival Regime

Nival regime is modified where additional sources of water supply or changes in the storage regimen alter the streamflow pattern. The influences of glaciers, the emergence of springs, and the presence of lakes and wetlands are notable.

Rivers issued from glaciers exhibit a proglacial regime (Church, 1974) in which the snowmelt runoff is prolonged or even superseded by glacier melt contribution. Summer water yield is controlled largely by the energy available for ice melt. During periods of overcast or cold conditions, melt runoff is reduced. However, on warm days with abundant radiation, runoff increases in response to more intense snow and glacier melt. Where the glaciers impound ice-dammed lakes, their bursting at irregular intervals produces exceptionally large floods known by their Icelandic term jökulhlaups (see **Jökulhlaups**).

Lake storage has a pronounced effect upon the streamflow pattern by reducing the peak inflows while enhancing the low flow discharges. Consequently, compared with the nival regime, a lake-modified or prolacustrine regime moderates the inflow to produce lower peaks and higher base flows. The timing of peak flow in response to rainfall or snowmelt is also delayed. Wetland storage is far less effective than the lakes in regulating runoff. Streams with a wetland regime are fed by poorly drained areas, which when thawed have some capacity to attenuate high flows. However, this does not occur in the spring if the wetland is frozen. Spring high flows are often generated similar in magnitude to those of the nival regime rivers. Only when summer thaw enlarges the water storage capacity will a wetland reduce rainfall-generated floods and sustain moderate recession flow.

Streams fed by subpermafrost groundwater, notably in carbonate terrain, exhibit a spring-fed regime (Craig and McCart, 1975). These streams have relatively stable discharges maintained by deep-seated groundwater. The springs do not cease to flow in winter, but snowmelt and heavy rainfall in the thawed season superimpose discharge peaks upon the steady baseflow.

Basin Water Balance

There is inadequate information to compute accurately the long-term water balance of permafrost areas. However, several studies carried out over short periods permit the evaluation of annual water balance of small drainage basins, to characterize various parts of the permafrost region.

Many water balance studies include the partitioning of precipitation into three major components of evaporation, runoff, and change in storage. Precipitation in permafrost areas is generally low, being less than 500 mm per year, but 200–400 mm is more common for the North American Arctic, northern Russia, and the high plateaus.

Evaporation is restricted by the short snow-free season and by the low energy supply. Kane et al. (1990) compared the evaporation amounts reported for several small basins in permafrost areas. The thawed season values range from 40 mm in the polar deserts to over 200 mm in the Mackenzie Delta. The presence of vegetation and wetlands increases the evaporation rate. In the High Arctic, for instance, the polar oases (zones within the polar desert where the local vegetation density and biodiversity are enhanced by a milder microclimate) of Truelove Lowland, Devon Island, Arctic Canada, had 65–110 mm a^{-1} of evaporation, consuming about 40% of the annual precipitation (Rydén, 1977). However, the largely barren McMaster Basin, Cornwallis Island, yielded 30–50 mm, even when both areas had a similar mean annual precipitation of about 190 mm. In the vegetated Low Arctic, evaporation is also larger than the High Arctic. Increased evaporation occurs at the expense of basin runoff.

Quick and flashy responses of runoff to snowmelt and rainfall events allow the shedding of a large portion of the precipitation to streamflow. Thus, the runoff ratio, being the ratio of runoff to precipitation, is generally quite high for the permafrost areas. Typical values range from 0.7–0.8 in the polar deserts to 0.35–0.65 in the polar oases of the Arctic (Rydén, 1977) and 0.4–0.6 in the tundra-clad Low Arctic because of higher evaporation (Kane et al., 1992; Lilly et al., 1998).

The annual change in basin storage is the smallest of all the water balance components, but can be significant in certain years. At the end of a warm and dry summer, basin storage can be reduced by a depletion of the residual snowbanks and of the soil moisture, while a cold, wet summer can rebuild the semipermanent snow cover and saturate the suprapermafrost groundwater storage before the freeze-up.

All components of the water balance vary considerably from year to year, as does the duration of the thawed season. To determine the water balances representative of various parts of the permafrost region, a wide coverage of accurate measurements taken over a period of decades is required.

MING-KO WOO

See also **Geomorphology**

Further Reading

Brook, G.A., "Hydrology of the Nahanni, a Highly Karsted Carbonate Terrain with Discontinuous Permafrost." *Proceedings, Fourth International Conference on Permafrost*, Fairbanks, Alaska, 1983, pp. 86–90

Burt, T.P. & P.J. Williams, "Hydraulic conductivity in frozen soils." *Earth Surface Processes*, 1 (1976): 349–360

Carey, K., "Icings developed from surface water and ground water." US Army, *CRREL Monograph III-D3*, Hanover, New Hampshire, 1973

Carey, S.K. & M.K. Woo, "Hydrology of two slopes in subarctic Yukon, Canada." *Hydrological Processes*, 13 (1999): 2549–2562

Church, M., "Hydrology and permafrost with reference to northern North America." *Proceedings, Workshop Seminar on Permafrost Hydrology*, Ottawa: Canadian National Committee, IHD, pp. 7–20

Craig, P.C. & P.J. McCart, "Classification of stream types in Beaufort Sea drainages between Prudhoe Bay, Alaska, and the Mackenzie delta, NWT, Canada." *Arctic and Alpine Research*, 7 (1975): 183–198

Gude, M. & D. Scherer, "Snowmelt and slush torrents—preliminary report from a field campaign in Kärkevagge, Swedish Lappland." *Geografiska Annaler*, 77A (1995): 199–206

Kane, D.L. & C.W. Slaughter, "Recharge of a Central Alaska Lake by Subpermafrost Groundwater." *The North American Contribution to the Second International Conference on Permafrost, Yakutsk*, Washington, District of Columbia: National Academy of Sciences, 1973, pp. 458–462

Kane, D.L. & J. Stein, "Water movement into seasonally frozen soils." *Water Resources Research*, 19 (1983): 1547–1557

Kane, D.L., R.E. Gieck & L.D. Hinzman, "Evapotranspiration from a small Alaskan Arctic watershed." *Nordic Hydrology*, 21 (1990): 253–272

Kane, D.L., L.D. Hinzman, M.K. Woo & K.R. Everett, "Arctic Hydrology and Climate Change." In *Arctic Ecosystems in a Changing Climate: An Ecophysical Perspective*, edited by F.S. Chapin, R.L. Jefferies, J.F. Reynolds, G.R. Shavers & J. Svoboda, San Diego, California: Academic Press, 1992, pp. 35–57

Lewkowicz, A.G. & H.M. French, "Downslope water movement and solute concentration within the active layer, Banks Island, NWT." *Proceedings of the Fourth Canadian Permafrost Conference*, Calgary, Alberta: National Research Council of Canada, 1982, pp. 163–172

Lilly, E.K., D.L. Kane, L.D. Hinzman & R.E. Gieck, "Annual water balance for three nested watersheds on the North Slope of Alaska." *Proceedings, Seventh International Conference on Permafrost*, Yellowknife, 1998, pp. 669–674

Marsh, P. & M. Hey, "The flooding hydrology of Mackenzie Delta Lakes near Inuvik, NWT, Canada." *Arctic*, 42 (1989): 41–49

Newbury, R.W., "River hydrology in permafrost areas." *Proceedings, Workshop Seminar on Permafrost Hydrology*, Ottawa: Canadian National Committee, IHD, 1974, pp. 31–37

Roulet, N.T. & M.K. Woo, "Runoff generation in a Low Arctic drainage basin." *Journal of Hydrology*, 101 (1988): 213–226

Rovansek, R.J., L.D. Hinzman & D.L. Kane, "Hydrology of a tundra wetland complex on th Alaskan Arctic Coastal Plain." *Arctic and Alpine Research*, 28 (1996): 311–317

Rydén, B.E., "Hydrology of Truelove Lowland." In *Truelove Lowland, Devon Island, Canada: A High Arctic Ecosystem*, edited by L.C. Bliss, Edmonton: University of Alberta Press, 1977, pp. 107–136

SIMMS LIBRARY
ALBUQUERQUE ACADEMY

Santeford, H.S., "Snow Soil Interactions in Interior Alaska." In *Modeling of Snow Cover Runoff*. edited by S.C. Colbeck & M. Ray, Hanover, New Hampshire: US Army CRREL, 1978, pp. 311–318

Slaughter, C.W., J.W. Hilgert & E.H. Culp, "Summer streamflow and sediment yield from discontinuous-permafrost headwaters catchments." *Proceedings, Fourth International Conference on Permafrost*, Fairbanks, Alaska, 1983, pp. 1172–1177

Smith, M.W. & C.R. Burn, "Outward flux of vapour from frozen soils at Mayo, Yukon, Canada: results and interpretation." *Cold Regions Science and Technology*, 13 (1987): 143–152

Solokov, B.L., "Regime of naleds." *The USSR Contribution to the Second International Conference on Permafrost*, Yakutsk, Washington, District of Columbia: National Academy of Sciences, 1978, pp. 408–411

Sokolov, B.L., "Hydrology of rivers of the cryolithic zone in the USSR." *Nordic Hydrology*, 22 (1991): 211–226

Tolstikhin, N.I. & O.N. Tolstikhin, "Groundwater and surface water in the permafrost region (translation)." *Inland Waters Directorate Technical Bulletin No. 97*, Ottawa, 1976

Williams, J.R. & R.O. van Everdingen, "Groundwater investigations in permafrost regions of North America: a review." *The North American Contribution to the Second International Conference on Permafrost*, Yakutsk, Washington, District of Columbia: National Academy of Sciences, 1973, pp. 435–446

Woo, M.K., "Permafrost hydrology in North America." *Atmosphere-Ocean*, 24 (1986): 201–234

Woo, M.K. & T.C. Winter, "The role of permafrost and seasonal frost in the hydrology of northern wetlands in North America." *Journal of Hydrology*, 141 (1993): 5–31

Woo, M.K. & Z.J. Xia, "Effects of hydrology on the thermal conditions of the active layer." *Nordic Hydrology*, 27 (1996): 129–142

Woo, M.K., P. Marsh & P. Steer, "Basin water balance in a continuous permafrost environment." *Proceedings, Fourth International Conference on Permafrost*, Fairbanks, Alaska, Washington, District of Columbia: National Academy Press, 1983, pp. 1407–1411

Woo, M.K., Z.N. Yang, X.J. Xia & D.Q. Yang, "Streamflow processes in an alpine permafrost catchment, Tianshan, China." *Permafrost and Periglacial Processes*, 5 (1994): 71–85

PERMAFROST RETREAT

Permafrost is defined as "ground (soil or rock and included ice and organic material) that remains at or below 0°C for at least two consecutive years." As such, it is a thermal phenomenon and its extent, distribution, and thickness are controlled by atmospheric climate, as modified by the geothermal heat flow. As a consequence, the extent of permafrost changes as the climate changes, although with time lags of years to millennia, as a result of the thermal properties of the ground. The absolute value of the geothermal heat flow and any changes in it are orders of magnitude less than the heat exchange between the ground and the atmosphere and so, for the purposes of this discussion, the geothermal heat flow may be regarded as effectively constant. Changes in the extent of permafrost are considered on two time scales: geological time scales, or millennia, and the decadal to annual time scales of human experience.

On the geological time scale, the areal extent of Arctic permafrost has varied widely. During the major glaciations of the Pleistocene Epoch, Arctic climatic conditions prevailed over the middle latitudes of the Northern Hemisphere and permafrost developed in what is now the northern USA, southern Canada, and across much of central Europe and southern Russia. Three lines of evidence, coupled with climate modeling, support this interpretation.

First, numerous ice-wedge casts, pingo remnants, and other periglacial soil features, such as involutions, are found in the middle latitudes. Of these, ice-wedge casts and pingo remnants are the most diagnostic of the former presence of permafrost.

Second, in central West Siberia, there exists an extensive body of deep permafrost, overlain in part by thawed ground, which is believed to be relict permafrost dating from the period of the last glacial maximum. This deep permafrost, which ranges in thickness from a few meters to more than 400 m, is overlain by over 200 m of thawed ground at its southern limit, at approximately 60°N. This relict permafrost is not in thermal equilibrium with the present climate and so is continuing to degrade. Similar bodies of relict, glacial-age permafrost are known to underlie the continental shelves of the Arctic Ocean—areas where the seafloor was exposed to ice age climatic conditions during periods of low sea levels induced by the development of the great ice sheets during the last glaciation. Given sufficient time, all these masses of relict permafrost will degrade completely.

Finally, ground temperature profiles measured in deep boreholes in several permafrost regions show fluctuations in gradient that are interpreted as remnant signals from earlier periods of colder (or warmer) climatic conditions.

In the period since the last great ice age, conventionally dated at 10 ka, climate has undergone a series of changes between warmer and cooler and between wetter and dryer conditions. While these must have affected the extent and distribution of permafrost, little is known of the details. Certainly, there is evidence that during the period from about 8 to 6 ka, a period known as the climatic optimum, Holocene warm period or Hypsithermal, the mean annual air temperature may have been as much as 5°C warmer than during the 20th century. This is shown by data from pollen recovered from peat cores in west central Canada, which show a pattern of floristic changes consistent with a significantly warmer climate and with permafrost zonal boundaries some 300–500 km to the north of their present position. These data also show that permafrost began to form and aggrade in peat bogs in the southern part of the region about 4 ka, indicating a cooling of the climate and an expansion of the permafrost region. This expansion likely continued, with minor changes at the

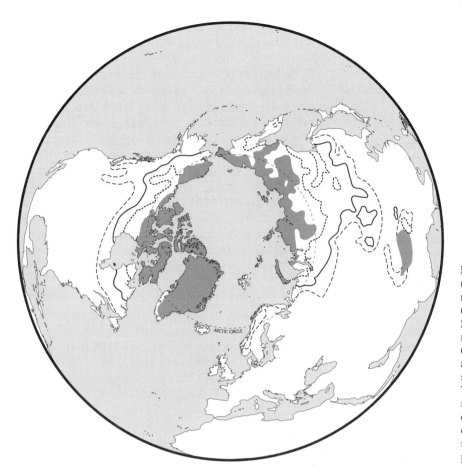

Predicted permafrost distribution under a 2°C climate warming scenario. After Anisimov and Nelson (1996) and Brown et al. (1997). Shaded areas indicate the approximate extent of continuous permafrost (>90%). The dotted line indicates the approximate southern limit of extensive, discontinuous permafrost (50%). The solid line indicates the approximate southern limit of sporadic discontinuous permafrost (<10%). The dashed line indicates the approximate southern limit of contemporaneous permafrost (c.2000).

margins, until the so-called Little Ice Age of the 17th and 18th centuries, when permafrost apparently reached its maximum extent of recent time.

In the 150 years since the Little Ice Age, natural climate warming has resulted in the thaw of many localized occurrences of permafrost near the southern margin, as shown by the presence of numerous and widespread collapse scars in peat plateaus. Isolated patches of permafrost found in areas of organic terrain along the southern fringe of discontinuous permafrost zone may well be remnants of the Little Ice Age extent of permafrost. Since the mid-20th century, other indications of climate change and permafrost retreat have been detected, including changes in air and ground temperatures, thickening of the active layer, changes in the distribution of ice wedges, changes in sea-ice regimes, plant growth patterns, and glacier extent. The result has been a general northward movement of the southern limit of permafrost; in west central Canada, for example, this has averaged about 40 km, but in places has been as much as 200 km. All these changes have significant implications for the Arctic environment and for human development in the permafrost regions.

Today, the permafrost region occupies about 23×10^6 km^2 or about 25% of the exposed land area of the Northern Hemisphere. The temperature of the permafrost is warmer than −2°C beneath about half of this area and is thus susceptible to thaw under even fairly moderate climate warming scenarios. Various computer models of permafrost distribution have been constructed, based on climate statistics and global climate circulation models. Following validation, by comparisons with present-day maps based on geological field data and with maps of interpreted environmental conditions at selected times in the geological past, these have been used to predict the future distribution of permafrost. For a −2°C warming scenario, the models all show a similar pattern of response—continued permafrost retreat, with all the permafrost zones displaced several hundred kilometers to the north and northeast of their contemporary positions in both North America and Eurasia. In this scenario, the overall extent of the permafrost region of the Northern Hemisphere is likely to diminish by about one-quarter, when equilibrium conditions have developed. The rates of these changes will be far from uniform and there will be significant lag times involved.

Permafrost is also forming today in the northern parts of the region, in areas where land, such as drained lake beds, expanding mudflats, or coastal regions where uplift is ongoing, is newly exposed to the Arctic winter climate, and this is likely to continue. At its southern limit, however, permafrost is thawing and disappearing in response to the present period of warming climate, and this trend is anticipated to continue throughout the century.

J.A. HEGINBOTTOM

See also **Climate Change; Global Change Effects; Global Warming; Impacts of Climate Change; Permafrost; Thermokarst**

Further Reading

Anisimov, O.A. & F.E. Nelson, "Permafrost distribution in the Northern Hemisphere under scenarios of climatic change." *Global and Planetary Change*, 14, (1996): 59–72

Brown, J., O.J. Ferrians Jr., J.A. Heginbottom & E.S. Melnikov, *Circum-Arctic Map of Permafrost and Ground Ice Conditions*, Washington, District of Columbia: US Geological Survey, for the International Permafrost Association, USGS Circum-Pacific Map Series, Map CP-45. Scale 1:10,000,000, 1997

French, H.M., *The Periglacial Environment* (2nd edition), New York: Longman Group Ltd., 1996

Nelson, F.E., O.A. Anisimov & N.I. Shiklomanov, "Climate change and hazard zonation in the circum-Arctic permafrost regions." *Natural Hazards*, 26(3) (2002): 203–225

van Everdingen, Robert O. (compiler and editor), *Multi-Language Glossary of Permafrost and Ground-Ice Terms*, International Permafrost Association, 1998 (available from The Arctic Institute of North America, The University of Calgary, Calgary, Alberta, Canada, T2N 1N4)

Washburn, A.L., *Geocryology*, London: Edward Arnold, 1979 and New York: Wiley, 1980

Yershov, E.D., *General Geocryology*, Cambridge: Cambridge University Press. 1998

Zoltai, S.C., "Permafrost distribution in peatlands on west-central Canada during the Holocene warm period 6000 years BP." *Géographie physique et Quaternaire*, 49(1) (1995): 45–54

PERSISTENT ORGANIC POLLUTANTS (POPs)

The United Nations Environmental Programme (UNEP) considers persistent organic pollutants (POPs) as a subgroup of persistent toxic substances (PTSs) and describes POPs as "chemical substances that persist in the environment, bioaccumulate through the food web, and pose a risk of causing adverse effects to human health and the environment." The global extent of POP pollution first became apparent with their detection in areas such as the Arctic and Antarctic, at levels posing risks to both wildlife and humans. Usually, POPs are not produced and used in Arctic regions; thus, citizens of Arctic regions do not benefit from the economic advantages associated with the chemical production of these compounds. However, some POPs are prone to long-range atmospheric transport and subsequent deposition in remote regions, and certain Arctic indigenous people are contaminated with the highest known POP exposure reported so far. POPs tend to accumulate in fat-rich tissue and, thus, high concentrations are found in the blubber of, for example, marine mammals, polar foxes, glaucous gulls, and polar bears. Indigenous people in the Arctic are particularly exposed to high POP contamination due to their traditional diets. Traditional hunting is often an important social part of the cultural identity and is, in addition, an important source of nourishment since no other food sources exist.

POPs containing chlorine in the molecular structures are usually named organochlorines in the scientific literature: this covers dioxins, the insecticide DDT, and polychlorinated biphenyls (PCBs). POPs include a wide range of compounds and can be roughly separated into three major subgroups:

(1) Compounds that are produced for industrial applications and released into the environment during production, which include PCBs (*see* **Polychlorinated Biphenyls (PCBs)**), chlorinated naphthalenes, short-chain chlorinated paraffins (SCCPs), pentachlorophenol (PCP), brominated flame retardants like polybrominated biphenyls (PBBs), polybrominated diphenylethers (PBDEs) and tetrabromo-bisphenyl-A, and fluorinated organic compounds (FOCs) like perfluorooctane sulfonate (PFOS).

(2) Compounds produced as unwanted by-products during large-scale chemical production processes, especially processes that use, produce, or dispose of chlorine or chlorine-derived chemicals. Such compounds are released into the environment during incineration processes or in wastewater, and include polychlorinated-p-dioxins and furans (PCDD/Fs), hexachlorobenzene (HCB), and polycyclic aromatic hydrocarbons (PAHs).

(3) Chemicals used in agricultural applications are the third POP subgroup. Pesticides, insecticides, fungicides, piscicides, rodenticides, etc., designed to have toxic effects on specific target organisms are included in this category. Compounds like hexachlorocyclohexane isomers (HCHs), p,p'-DDT (dichlorodiphenyl-trichloroethane) and its transformation products, cyclodiene-insecticides like *trans-, cis*-chlordane, *trans-, cis*-nonachlor, heptachlor, dieldrin, and chlorobornanes (e.g., compounds of the technical Toxaphene®) belong to this POP subgroup.

Some POPs reach the remote Arctic regions due to long-range transport and deposition of volatile particles.

In addition, owing to increasing activities related to the exploration and production of oil and gas, especially in the Russian and the Norwegian Arctic, PAHs are considered as a potential local source of POP pollution. Few local POP sources within the Arctic are known; besides fossil fuel burning and house heating in the sparse settlements, several military installations and "early warning sites" are known as local POP sources (e.g., PCBs) in the Arctic. Industrial installations like smelters and industrial waste disposal units release POPs like PCDD/Fs and PAHs into the Arctic environment. However, to date the total inventory of POP release from local sources into the Arctic environment is not exactly known, but is considered as minor compared to long-range transport.

Due to the low average annual temperature and the special seasonal daylight conditions in polar regions, suitable conditions for the deposition of persistent pollutants are present. Thus, high deposition levels, prolonged half-life times in addition to effective biomagnification and bioaccumulation in the polar food web lead to high concentrations of the long-range transported POPs in the higher trophic levels of the Arctic ecosystem, including indigenous people. High concentration levels have been detected for compounds like PCBs and Toxaphene® as well as DDT and its metabolites. The following environmental conditions are considered as important factors for the understanding of the processes leading to favorable deposition and accumulation conditions for anthropogenic POPs in the Arctic.

Daylight Conditions

The polar night at 80° N latitude lasts from October until March and changes within a few weeks into the midnight sun. This has a tremendous effect on the photochemical degradation of some persistent pollutants. Due to the lack of photochemical degradation processes, the long-range transport of certain highly volatile organic compounds is only observed during the winter. Photochemical processes during the summer usually rapidly degrade chemicals like short-chain alkanes and alkenes (ethane, propane, ethene, etc.). Therefore, only low concentration levels are usually observed in Arctic air. In winter, on the other hand, concentrations of this type of compound are usually elevated by one or two orders of magnitudes. Indications for a seasonally dependent photochemical degradation were also found for the persistent pesticide *trans*-chlordane.

Temperature Conditions

The low annual average temperature of the polar regions is the main reason why microbiological degradation processes of organic material slow down to a minimum. Microbiological metabolization of persistent pollutants in the Arctic is practically nonexistent. This extends the half-life time of these compounds exponentially during their stay in the Arctic. Compounds that are degraded in temperate regions within weeks or months have a much higher persistency in the Arctic regions. Thus, half-life times up to a year are possible for this type of compounds.

Deposition

Most POPs have very low freezing points, which is the main reason why they are transported far into polar regions before condensation. Due to the low annual average temperature, snow is the dominant form of precipitation in polar regions. The snow crystal possesses a large surface and adsorbs particles and contaminants to its crystalline surface more effectively than a water droplet can. Therefore, snow precipitation can transport contaminants better to the surface (soil, water surface) just as a rain droplet can. In contrast to rain, snow crystals change the surface properties during aging on the surface. The surface of a snow crystal is reduced drastically after a short time on the ground due to the overall pressure of the surrounding snow crystals and also weather and climate conditions. Thus, due to surface reduction, the adsorbed contaminant is either released into the soil/ground, stays absorbed to the snow crystal, or is reevaporated into the atmosphere again. These three possibilities are totally dependent on the vapor pressure of the respective contaminant and the ambient climatic conditions. Therefore, high POP levels can often be found in upper layers containing new snow surface, whereas in aged snow, situated near the ground, the contaminants are already released into the soil. Further bioaccumulation takes place from soil microorganisms into high trophic-level organisms.

Biological Effects

POPs do not easily dissolve in water, but are easily soluble in fats and oils. This is why effects in the Arctic were first noticed in the blubber of ringed seals. POPs also accumulate in the breast milk of humans and other mammals. The most significant effect is on reproductive systems, since POPs are hormone disrupters. The thinning of egg shells affecting the reproduction of birds of prey is one of the most well-known toxic effects of DDT. Fewer young, and complete failure to reproduce have been exhibited in marine mammals. The immune system is also very sensitive, and reduced immunological responses in polar bears and northern fur seals have been shown to lead to increased susceptibility to infection. POP effects on

TABLE 1. Toxaphene biomagnification in Arctic Canada

Compartment	Concentration ppb (wet weight)
Air[1]	0.0007
Snow[1]	0.0009–0.002
Sea water[1]	0.0003
Zooplankton[1]	3.6
Arctic cod muscle[2]	14–46
Arctic char whole body[2]	44–157
Ringed seal blubber[2]	130–480
Beluga blubber[2]	1380–5780
Narwhal blubber[2]	2440–9160

[1]From Bidleman et al. (1989).
[2]From Hargrave et al. (1993).

humans are yet to be demonstrated, but the high POP levels in indigenous peoples are a cause for alarm.

Table 1 provides an overview of the levels of the pesticide toxaphene in different Arctic environments and in animals. A similar picture is generally seen for other POPs. The table clearly illustrates the effect of biomagnification in the food chain, and the importance of fat in the accumulation of POPs.

ROLAND KALLENBORN

See also **Arctic Environmental Protection Strategy; Bioconcentration; Environmental Problems; Local and Transboundary Pollutants; Polychlorinated Biphenyls (PCBs)**

Further Reading

AMAP, *The AMAP Assessment Report: Arctic Pollution Issues,* Oslo, Norway: Arctic Monitoring and Assessment Program (AMAP), 1998

Bidleman, T.F., G.W. Patton, M.D. Walla, B.T. Hargrave, W.P. Vass, P. Erickson, B. Fowler, V. Scott & D.J. Gregor, "Toxaphene and other organochlorines in Arctic Ocean fauna: evidence for atmospheric delivery." *Arctic,* 42 (1989): 307–313

Hargrave, B.T., D.C.G. Muir & T.F. Bidleman, "Toxaphene in amphipodes and zooplankton from the Arctic Ocean." *Chemosphere,* 27 (1993): 1949–1963

Harrad, Stuart (editor), *Persistent Organic Pollutants, Environmental Behaviour and Pathways for Human Exposure,* Dordrehct: Kluwer, 2001

Jensen, J., K. Adare & R. Shearer (editors), *Canadian Arctic Contaminants Assessment Report,* Minister of Indian Affairs and Northern Development, 1997

Swedish Environmental Protection Agency, *Persistent Organic Pollutants, a Swedish View of an International Problem,* Monitor 16, Stockholm, Sweden: Swedish Environmental Protection Agency, 1998

Useful Internet Addresses

United Nations Environmental Program (UNEP) chemicals website: http://www.chem.unep.ch/pops/

Environment Canada website: http://www.ec.gc.ca/pops/index_e.htm

US-EPA Office of Pesticide Program website: http://www.epa.gov/oppfead1/international/lrtap2pg.htm

Swedish EPA website: http://www.environ.se:8083/sweionet/issues/pop/pop.html

PETERMANN, AUGUST

August Petermann, a German geographer and expedition sponsor of the 19th century, wrote over 600 articles on the development of polar exploration and was regarded as the father of German polar exploration. Like US Navy oceanographic researcher Matthew Fontaine Maury, Petermann was both an expert in the study of ocean currents in the 19th century, and an indefatigable theorist on the causes and effects of such currents, especially in the Arctic. Through his founding of the geographical research journal *Mitteilungen aus Justus Perthes' Geographischer Anstalt über wichtige neue Erforschungen auf dem Gesammtgebiete der Geographie* (Reports from Justus Perthes's Geographical Institution upon Important New Investigations in the Whole Subject of Geography) — known ultimately and more popularly as *Petermann's Geographische Mitteilungen* — Petermann is credited with advancing polar research not only in Germany but in Russia, Sweden, Norway, America, and France. His reputation in his later years and after his death suffered as it became clear that his support of such ultimate Arctic chimeras as an "Open Polar Sea" was mistaken.

After training as a cartographer in Germany, Petermann worked as a mapmaker in Edinburgh from 1845 to 1848, coincidentally the three disastrous three years of the Franklin expedition in search of a North West Passage. The search for Franklin became the touchstone for many of Petermann's ideas and hypotheses about the Arctic. He then worked as an independent cartographer in London for six years.

His *Historical Summary of the Search for Sir John Franklin* (1853) typifies Petermann's collation of vast amounts of data in an apparently neutral essay, which he then diverts in support of Arctic expeditions designed to test his hypotheses. The summary is nominally a history of all the attempts to find Franklin between 1848 and 1853. But it moves at length from the primary object of these relief expeditions to a discussion of the immediate geographic and future expeditionary benefits of the search. These are defined as the location and character of newly discovered coastlines and Arctic ocean currents, and the survival of relatively small overwintering vessels like the American ships *Advance* and *Rescue*, as opposed to the mounting evidence that Franklin's much larger ships had been destroyed.

Petermann eventually concluded that the North Pole would not be reached from the American side of the Arctic, where the highest latitude reached by any of the Franklin searchers was Inglefield's 78°35′. He proposed instead a route to the pole from the European High Arctic. There, north of Svalbard, Parry had already achieved a latitude of 82°45′ decades earlier. Petermann also suggested that the search for Franklin be extended west from Canada to the north coast of Siberia, a suggestion tabled by the British Admiralty.

Petermann returned to Germany in 1854 to become director of Perthes Geographical Institution in Gotha. A year later, he founded the *Mitteilungen*. His views of polar geography, in particular of a warm ocean current flowing into the Arctic Ocean from the Gulf Stream and his notion of a far northern extension of Greenland, were published on his map *Karte der arktischen und antarktischen Regionen zur Übersicht des geographischen Standpunktes in J. 1865, der Meere strömungen* (Map of the Arctic and Antarctic Regions Reflecting the Geographical Points of View in 1865, [and] the Sea Currents).

Petermann's belief in an Open Polar Sea derived from more than his study of ocean currents. Early 19th-century expeditions such as those of the Russian Hedenström and the Baltic-German Wrangell had discovered areas of open water, polynya, in the Arctic Ocean north of Siberia. Elisha Kent Kane's account of the Second Grinnell Expedition in search of Franklin describes how one of Kane's men stood at Cape Constitution at 81°22′ N latitude and heard "dashing waves … and a surf." Petermann did not believe in an Arctic Ocean completely free of ice, as did Kane, but suggested instead that explorers would find a sea partially filled with navigable ice broken by wind, storms, currents, rain, fog, and especially the continuous summer light.

Petermann divided his polar sea into two roughly equal sectors. He created isothermal maps, traced the drift of glass bottles around the polar basin, and followed the reported presence of animals on various islands to hypothesize a far northern extension of Greenland. This extension, which he thought might exist as either an undersea ridge or as a land bridge into the central Arctic, created, in effect, two polar oceans: one north of Canada and eastern Siberia, and the other north of Svalbard, Franz Josef Land, and western Siberia. The barrier of ice discovered by expeditions searching north from Baffin Bay Petermann ascribed to the former, which he named the "Pack-Ice Sea," and the route to the pole, he thought, would be found through the latter, which he thought of as the "Floating-Ice Sea."

To investigate these hypotheses, Petermann personally sponsored a German geographic expedition to the Arctic led by Karl Koldewey in 1868 aboard the *Grönland*. Koldewey returned to lead a second German polar expedition a year later, on board the specially constructed research vessel *Germania*. The same ice Petermann thought might loosen to allow a passage to the north pinned *Germania* to East Greenland for ten months in 1869–1870.

Petermann extended his dual-sea theory to anthropology, arguing that the East Greenland Eskimos must have migrated out of Asia westward, not eastward. In his later years, Petermann came to question many of his own conclusions, yet he clung to the idea that Greenland and Franz Josef Land converged near the North Pole. As if to immortalize his doubts, a landmass once thought to exist north of Franz Josef Land—and named after Petermann—eventually proved nonexistent.

Biography

August Heinrich Petermann was born on April 18, 1822 in the small Prussian town of Bleichrode am Eichsfelde, the second child of an actuary named August Rudolph Petermann. From the age of six to 14, Petermann attended the local public school, before transferring to the Gymnasium at Nordhausen to fulfill his mother's desire that he attend a theological seminary. He attended the Royal Geographic Art School in Potsdam from 1839 to 1844, after which he worked for the atlas publisher Keith Johnston in Edinburgh from 1845 to 1848, and as an independent cartographer in London from 1848 to 1854. He returned to Germany in 1854 to direct Justus Perthes's Geographic Institute in Gotha, and the following year founded *Petermann's Geographische Mitteilungen*. He died at Gotha, a suicide, on September 25, 1878. Among geographical features named after August Petermann are a *breen* (glacier) in Svalbard—which flows into another glacier named for the Italian geographer Negri—along with a kapp (cape) and a fjell (mountain) in Widjefjorden in Svalbard, as well as a fjord in Greenland.

P.J. CAPELOTTI

See also **Koldewey, Karl; Open Polar Sea**

Further Reading

Goetzmann, William H., *New Lands, New Men*, New York: Viking Penguin, 1986

Kane, Elisha Kent, *Arctic Explorations: The Second Grinnell Expedition in Search of Sir John Franklin, 1853, '54, '55*, 2 volumes. Philadelphia: Childs & Peterson, 1856

Orheim, Olar (editor), *The Placenames of Svalbard*, Oslo: Norsk Polarinstitutt (Skrifter Nr. 80 and 112; Ny-Trykk), 1991

Petermann, August, *The Search for Franklin: A Suggestion Submitted to the British Public*, London: Longmans, 1852

———, "Sir John Franklin, the Sea of Spitzbergen, and whale-fisheries in the Arctic Regions." *Journal of the Royal Geographical Society*, 23 (1853): 129–136

———, *Historical Summary of the Search for Sir John Franklin* (reprinted from Seemann's Narrative of the Voyage of HMS Herald) [Printed for private circulation], London, *c*.1853

————, "On the proposed expedition to the North Pole." *Proceedings of the Royal Geographic Society,* 9 (1864–1865): 90–99

————, *Spitzbergen und die arktische central-region,* Gotha: J. Perthes, 1865

Petermann, August & Thomas Milner, *The Library Atlas of Physical and Political Geography,* London: W.S. Orr & Co., 1855

Tammiksaar, E., N.G. Sukhova & I.R. Stone, "Hypothesis versus fact: August Petermann and Polar research." *Arctic,* 52(3) (1999): 237–244

Weller, Hugo Ewald, *August Petermann,* Leipzig: O. Wigand, 1911

Wright, John K., "The Open Polar Sea." *Geographical Review,* 43 (1953): 338–365

PETERSEN, ROBERT

Robert Petersen is a native Greenlandic scholar known for his numerous publications in anthropology and linguistics, as well as for his contributions to the academic development of his country. He was the founder and first rector of Ilisimatusarfik, the University of Greenland.

Robert graduated from Ilinniarfissuaq in 1948, and then moved to Denmark to complete his teacher training. He received his Danish teaching license in 1953 and moved back to Nuuk, where he taught at Ilinniarfissuaq from 1954 to 1956.

Petersen later commented that during these teaching years, he was struck by the fact that a majority of his students had problems writing Greenlandic without mistakes, because the official orthography in use, devised in the second half of the 19th century, did not correspond any more to the current pronunciation of the language. To further his training in order to help resolve this problem, he went back to Denmark to study anthropology and linguistics at the University of Copenhagen.

Petersen completed his master's degree in 1967 under the supervision of Professor Erik Holtved. Two years later, University of Copenhagen's newly established Institute of Eskimology hired him as lecturer. In 1975, he became full professor at the Institute. During this period, he also sat on a committee that planned an orthographic reform for the Greenlandic language. The committee proposed a new orthography better adapted to present-day pronunciation, which became official in 1973. Petersen thus attained his original goal.

He continued to teach, conduct research, and publish. Now that the reformed orthography had been adopted, Petersen and the committee set themselves to the task of compiling a new Greenlandic-Danish dictionary. A first version was published in 1977 and a second, much enlarged one in 1990.

Greenland had acceded to Home Rule in 1979, and it was decided that it should have its own institution of higher learning. In 1983, Petersen was invited to return to Nuuk to chair a newly created "Inuit Institute" that would award degrees in Greenlandic and pan-Inuit culture, language, society, and history. This institute was transformed into a fully fledged university (Ilisimatusarfik—University of Greenland) in 1987, and Petersen became its first rector (president). Right from the beginning, Petersen insisted that the quality of teaching at Ilisimatusarfik should be equal to that found in Danish institutions.

When Petersen retired from Ilisimatusarfik in 1995, the University of Greenland had developed undergraduate, master's, and Ph.D. programs in four disciplines: language and literature; culture, society, and history; theology; and administration. Petersen moved back to Denmark and settled in Odense. A Professor Emeritus as of this writing, Petersen remains active publishing, lecturing, and consulting on various committees.

Petersen is widely recognized as the foremost Greenlandic intellectual in the fields of social sciences and linguistics, and as a world-class Arctic scholar. He has published some 419 books, articles, and reports written in Greenlandic, Danish, and English between 1944 and 1995: about, among other topics, Greenlandic and pan-Inuit traditional culture and society; dialectology and phonology; Inuit prehistory; mythology; and present-day social problems. His writings are completed by the numerous lectures he gave at national or international scientific conferences.

Robert Petersen has always been eager to participate actively in the academic, scientific, and political developments of his time. He has belonged to a large number of boards and committees for various universities, scholarly journals, scientific associations, and governmental organizations, in Greenland as well as in Denmark and abroad. He participated in various work groups for the Greenlandic Home Rule, the Inuit Circumpolar Conference, and the Nordic Council. Between 1973 and 1976, he acted as consultant for the Canadian Inuit Language Commission, which proposed a standard orthography for Inuktitut, and from 1995 to 1998 he was vice-president of the International Arctic Social Sciences Association. Petersen also finds it important to disseminate knowledge among the general population; accordingly, he has given many talks on Greenlandic and Danish radio, and has published a large number of newspaper articles.

These accomplishments were publicly recognized. Through the years, Petersen was awarded the following honors: the Prize for Scientific Vulgarization of the Danish Authors' Association (1977); membership in the Swedish Gustav Adolf Academy (1985); an honorary doctorate from Université Laval, in Québec City (1992); the Cultural Award of the Greenlandic Home Rule (1993); and the Nersornaat Medal of Merit for

Greenland (1996). In 1988, a *Festschrift* was published in Denmark by *Folk*, the Danish ethnographical journal, on the occasion of his 60th birthday, and another in Greenland in 1996, when he retired from Ilisimatusarfik.

Biography

Robert Petersen was born on April 18, 1928 in Maniitsoq on the central west coast of Greenland, to Ole Petersen, an office clerk, and Jakobine Rosing. After having completed his initial schooling in Maniitsoq (where he learned Danish as second language), he was admitted to Ilinniarfissuaq (Seminarium), Greenland's teacher-training school in Nuuk (Godthåb), following in the steps of his older brother Hans Christian Petersen (who was later to become a noted professor and specialist of Greenlandic folklore). In 1957, he married Inge Hansen, a Danish nurse originally from the Odense area. After having received teacher training in Nuuk and in Denmark, he studied anthropology and linguistics at the University of Copenhagen, where he was granted a *Magister Artium* in 1967. He taught at that university's Institute of Eskimology from 1969 to 1983, and then moved back to his native country to establish Ilisimatusarfik, the University of Greenland. Robert Petersen headed Ilisimatusarfik until his retirement in 1995. His numerous publications include "Burial-Forms and Death Cult among the Eskimos" (*Folk*, 1967); "On the West Greenlandic Cultural Imperialism in East Greenland" (in *Cultural Imperialism and Cultural Identity*, 1977); *Nunatta oqaluttuassartaanit* (Nuuk, Pilersuiffik, 1987); *Oqaatsit Kalaallisuumiit Qallunaatuumut—Grønlandsk Dansk Ordbog* (with Chr. Berthelsen et al., Nuuk, Atuakkiorfik, 1990); and "On ethnic identity in Greenland" (*Études/Inuit/Studies*, 2001).

LOUIS-JACQUES DORAIS

Further Reading

Andreasen, Claus, "Robert Petersen, Professor Emeritus, Dr. H.C." In *Cultural and Social Research in Greenland 95/96. Essays in Honour of Robert Petersen*, edited by Birgitte Jacobsen, Nuuk: Ilisimatusarfik/Atuakkiorfik, 1996

Anonymous, "Petersen, Robert Karl Frederik." In *Grønlands Grønne Bog* [Greenland's Green Book], edited by Torben Lodberg, Nuuk: Grønlands Hjemmestyres Informationskontor, 1998

Hansen, Klaus Georg, "Robert Petersen. Bibliography 1944–1995." In *Cultural and Social Research in Greenland 95/96. Essays in Honour of Robert Petersen*, edited by Birgitte Jacobsen, Nuuk: Ilisimatusarfik/Atuakkiorfik, 1996

Petersen, Robert, *Nunatta oqaluttuassartaanit* [From the Stories of Our Land], Nuuk: Pilersuiffik, 1987

PETITOT, FATHER ÉMILE

Father Émile Petitot was a French Catholic Oblate missionary who worked in the Northwest Territories of Canada between 1862 and 1878. He had a first-hand knowledge of several Athapaskan Indian nations: the Yellowknife: and the Dogrib, the Slave, the Hare, and the Kutchin (today's Gwich'in) from the Peel and Porcupine rivers. He visited the Tchiglit Inuit, living on the Beaufort Sea coast between the Mackenzie River and the Anderson River to the East, five times.

Émile Petitot's scientific contribution to the Arctic and the Subarctic lies in three main fields of study: ethnography and cultural anthropology; linguistics; and geography and geology. The ethnographic records he kept are among the first that were made in a near professional manner. His work on the Tchiglit Inuit approaches topics as diverse as human ecology (area occupied, territorial limits, trails, settlements, population figures), material culture (raw materials, knives, axes, harpoons, bows and arrows, sledges, umiaks and kayaks, various types of dwellings and their construction techniques, types of clothing, garments and ornaments, hunting and fishing techniques), social organization (political organization, family structures, life cycles, games), religion and worldview, and interethnic relations. Donat Savoie has synthesized this information in his *The Amerindians of the Canadian Northwest in the 19th Century, as Seen by Émile Petitot, Volume 1: The Tchiglit Eskimos* (1970). Even though Petitot's work is far from exhaustive, the data it provides are the only information we now have on the Tchiglit Inuit, who became nearly extinct in the decades following their regular contact with Euro-Canadians.

Petitot's ethnographic fieldwork with the Athapaskan Indians is even more impressive. As for his research on the Tchiglits, it covers several subfields, but here his work bears on four different nations, which, taken together, subdivide into a few dozen independent bands. This part of his work is particularly notable for the collection of myths in indigenous language he amassed, accompanied by a French translation. Volume two of Donat Savoie's work (1970) (*The Loucheux Indians, Preceded by General Observations on the Déné-Dindjié Indians*, 1970) offers a synopsis of the data collected by Petitot and published in French in a variety of books and articles.

In linguistics, Petitot's main achievement was his French, Chipewyan, Hare, and Gwich'in quadrilingual dictionary. While he received initial support from his fellow missionaries, he conducted much of the linguistic interviews necessary for this endeavor himself. His dictionary was accompanied by grammar and synoptic tables of verb conjugations. His other main linguistic contribution was his French-Inuit dictionary.

For the majority of his missionary life, Father Petitot did not shun exploring the uncharted areas that surrounded him. Some of the many field trips he undertook (snowshoeing, dog teams, canoeing, or simply walking) lasted from three to six months. Although he had no adequate instrument to calculate geographical positions, he managed—with the help of a simple compass, a watch, and the general positioning of the Mackenzie River given by earlier explorers—to precisely chart several unknown territories. His knowledge of minerals allowed him to give adequate information on the geological formations he located, and thus make it easier for us today to verify the accuracy of his geographical positioning. Finally, in the course of his travels, he systematically located and recorded some 1500 indigenous place-names in native languages, which have now become crucial in land claim negotiations. This part of his work is synthesized and discussed in Donat Savoie's *Land Occupancy by the Amerindians of the Canadian Northwest in the 19th Century, as Reported by Émile Petitot: Toponymic Inventory, Data Analyses, Legal Implications* (2001).

Father Petitot developed an interest in the life of the French Canadians who had first explored the Northwest Territories. He met with the *Métis* descendants of Laurent Leroux, who in 1784 had explored part of what would later become known as the Mackenzie River, before Alexander Mackenzie's own "discovery voyage" of 1789. Petitot also met with the descendants of some of the 14 French Canadian traders who had settled around Great Slave Lake prior to 1786.

In addition to his missionary activities and scholarly research, Petitot drew and painted. His 1861 murals in the Fort Good Hope church are still visible. He also produced numerous scenes of Athapaskan and Inuit daily life, as well as detailed drawings of their encampments, means of transportation, houses, equipments, body ornamentations, and trading forts.

Émile Petitot's research was awarded important prizes in both Paris (the Palmes académiques in 1875) and London (the Admiral Back Award in 1883). Yet from a contemporary viewpoint, some aspects of his work are obsolete. He rightly held that the Inuit and Athapaskan languages came from Asia, but his theory that ultimately they were of Semitic origin is untrue. Similarly, his theory that early man was "perfect," and that civilization represented degeneration from that state, is today regarded as misconstrued.

Petitot does not seem to have been a very dogmatic Catholic. The Anglican Church Missionary Society Archives contains a copy of a letter referring to his request to join the Society because of problems with the Catholic hierarchy.

Petitot has been the subject of a documentary produced by SCN Broadcast Network (Saskatchewan, Canada), which was aired on Canadian television by the Canadian Broadcasting Corporation.

Biography

Émile Petitot was born in 1838 in western France to a watchmaker's family. He was ordained a priest in Marseille in 1862 and left for Canada two days later. His first mission was in the Great Slave Lake area. Twelve years later, exhausted by too many different missions and expeditions, he returned to France. He used his time there to arrange for the publication of much of his field material. He returned to the North in 1876, but unable to stay, he moved to southern Canada in 1878, where he conducted research with the Blackfoot. Finally, he returned to France in 1883, where he became a regular priest while maintaining his scientific interests until his death in 1917.

DOMINIQUE LEGROS

See also **Athapaskan; Inuit; Missionary Activity**

Further Reading

Petitot, Émile, *Dictionnaire de la langue déné-dindjiè* [*Dictionary of the Déné-Dindjiè Language*], Paris: F. Leroux éditeur (et San Francisco, A.L. Bancroft and Co.), 1876

———, *Vocabulaire français-esquimau* [*French-Eskimo Vocabulary*]. Bibliothèque de linguistique et d'ethnographie américaines publiées par A.L. Pinart, Volume III, Paris: L. Leroux éditeur (et San Francisco, A.L. Bancroft and Co.), 1876

———, *Monographie des Dènè-Dindjié,* Paris: E. Leroux, 1876

———, "Monograph of the Esquimaux Tchiglit of the Mackenzie and of the Anderson." *New Dominion Monthly* (October 1878): 403–417; (November 1878): 513–525

———, *Traditions indiennes du Canada Nord-Ouest* [*Indian Traditions of Northwest Canada*]. Littératures populaires, Volume XXIII, Paris: Maisonneuve Frères et Ch. Leclerc, 1886

———, *Les Grands-Esquimaux,* Paris: E. Plon, Nourrit & Cie, 1887, illus., map

———, "Traditions indiennes du Canada Nord-Ouest." [Indian Traditions of Northwest Canada]. *Transactions de la société philologique,* 16–17 (1887): 169–614

———, *Quinze ans sous le cercle polaire* [*Fifteen Years Beneath the Polar Circle*], *Volume 1. Mackenzie, Anderson et Youkon,* Paris: E. Dentu, 1889, illus., map

———, *Among the Chiglit Eskimos,* translated by E.O. Hohn, Edmonton: Boreal Institute for Northern Studies, 1981

———, *Around Great Slave Lake (1891) and Explorations in the Region of Great Bear Lake (1893),* edited by Paul Laverdure & John Moir, Toronto: Champlain Society, 2004

Savoie, Donat (editor), *The Amerindians of the Canadian Northwest in the 19th Century, as seen by Émile Petitot, Volume 1: The Tchiglit Eskimos, Volume 2: The Loucheux Indians, Preceded by General Observations on the Déné-Dindjié Indians,* Ottawa: Northern Science Research Group, Indian Affairs and Northern Development, Mackenzie Delta Research Project (MRP), 1970, pp. 9–10

———, "Bibliographie d'Émile Petitot, missionnaire dans le Nord-Ouest Canadien." [Bibliography of Émile Petitot,

Missionary in Northwest Canada]. *Anthropologica*, 13(1–2) (1971): 159–168

———, (editor); Rachelle Castonguay, Geoffrey S. Lester (contributors), *Land Occupancy by the Amerindians of the Canadian Northwest in the 19th Century, as Reported by Émile Petitot: Toponymic Inventory, Data Analyses, Legal Implications,* Occasional Publication No. 49, Canadian Circumpolar Institute, Edmonton: Canadian Circumpolar Institute Press, 2001

PETROPAVLOVSK-KAMCHATSKY

The city of Petropavlovsk-Kamchatsky nestles in the sheltered harbor of Avacha Bay, on the eastern, Pacific shore of the southern Kamchatka Peninsula in Russia. The city has been the main administrative settlement of Kamchatka Peninsula since 1812. The current population is 201,900; almost half of the population of the Kamchatka Oblast' is predominantly Russians, Ukrainians, and other natives of the former Soviet Union.

Petropavlovsk-Kamchatsky's geopolitical position as a port and military base in the Russian Arctic was enhanced by the natural resources, in particular, rich fishing grounds and volcanic thermal water. Snow-covered peaks of active volcanoes including Koriaka (3456 m/11,348 ft), Avacha (2741 m/8992 ft), and others adorn the surrounding landscape. The climate is wet (the annual precipitation is 1335 mm) and moderately cold; the average temperature is –8.5°C in January and 13.7°C in August. The harbor is ice-free for seven months of the year.

The first use of the harbor as a port was in 1740 when Vitus Bering's expedition to Avacha Bay arrived on October 17, 1740, the date that marks the founding date of Petropavlovsk. Bering used the harbor as overwintering headquarters of his Second Kamchatka Expedition, and the town is named after his two boats, *St Peter* and *St Paul.* In 1779, British ships of James Cook's expedition (led by Charles Clark after Cook's earlier death) visited the Bay, as later in 1787 did ships of Jean-Francois de Galaup de Laperouse. Monuments stand to Bering, Clark, and Laperouse in Petropavlovsk-Kamchatsky. Laperouse found only 100 residents in 1787, while in 1804 explorer Ivan Krusenshtern recorded two brick and 50 timber houses, with 180 inhabitants in the settlement. At the beginning of the 19th century, the Russian-American Company began business in Petropavlovsk, sending supplies to the Russian colonies in Alaska and receiving furs to send overland back to Russia. In 1822, Petropavlovsk registered as a town with nearly 1000 inhabitants. The first lighthouse—the only one on the entire Russian Pacific coast at that time—was constructed in Petropavlovsk in 1850; the main Russian military marine base was located in the harbor. With the start of the so-called Crimean War in 1854, joint French-British forces attacked the town; their commander, Admiral David Powell Price, committed suicide on the eve of the attack. Following a ten-day siege, the British and French offensive was forced to retreat. Nevertheless, the Russian fleet and army had evacuated to Nikolaev-on-Amur, leaving Petropavlovsk-Kamchatsky attacked and destroyed. All military and trade activity ceased. By 1890, the inhabitants numbered only 338. Within a decade, the Japanese had shelled Petropavlovsk during the Russo-Japanese war in 1905.

In 1916, Petropavlovsk became the administrative capital of Kamchatskaya Oblast', a town with a population of 1200 and with one car (imported for the Kamchatka governor). As the center of military, trade, and fishing fleets in the Russian Pacific, Petropavlovsk developed rapidly. Shipyards and a seaport were constructed, as well as fish-processing, can-making, net-making, and ship-repairing factories. The town established a scientific marine station in 1932, which later became the Pacific Scientific Institute of Fishery and Oceanography. The Kamchatka Volcano Station, opened in 1936, developed into the world-renowned Institute of Volcanology, administered by the Russian Academy of Sciences.

The population of the city increased rapidly, numbering 1700 in 1926, 35,000 in 1939, 85,000 in 1959, and 153,000 in 1970. The first uniform ship connections with Vladivostok port began in 1930; in 1936, the first airdrome was constructed to serve locations within Kamchatka. Before 1936, it took several months to reach Kamchatka from Moscow. With construction of the Elisovo modern airport, Petropavlovsk was linked with the mainland via Khabarovsk, Vladivostok, and Moscow. During the Cold War, Petropavlovsk emerged as a location with immense strategic significance and the town remains home to Russia's Pacific nuclear submarine fleet and early warning radar sites.

Since 1991, the city rapidly declined; periodic shortages in electricity supply and hot water forced many inhabitants to leave. Today, the future of the city seems promising, with new factories opening, ore deposits being explored, and infrastructures for tourism and the marine industry developing. Petropavlovsk remains the center of a large province and the base of military, fishing, and trade fleets. In 2003, more than 700 industrial enterprises were based in the city, providing employment for 30,000 engineers and technicians, as well as 14 scientific and educational institutes, and local publishing houses that issue several newspapers and magazines.

LEONID M. BASKIN

See also **Kamchatka Peninsula; Kamchatskaya Oblast'; Krasheninnikov, Stepan; Russian American Company**

Further Reading

Krasheninnikov, S., *Opisanie zemli Kamchatki* [Description of Kamchatka Land], 2 vols, St Petersburg: Nauka, 1994 (originally published 1786); as *The History of Kamtschatka and the Kurilski Islands, with the Countries Adjacent*, Chicago: Quadrangle Books, 1962

Martynenko, V. & S. Stepanov, *Pamyatniki Petropavloska-Kamchatskogo* [Monuments of Petropavlovsk-Kamchatskii], Petropavlovsk-Kamchatskii: Dal'nevostochnoe knizhnoe izdatel'stvo, 1989

Piragis, A., *Petropavlovsk-Kamchatskii. Ulitsy goroda rasskazyvayut* [Petropavlovsk-Kamchatskii. Town Streets Tell], Petropavlovsk-Kamchatskii: Dal'nevostochnoe knizhnoe izdatel'stvo, 1986

Sergeev, V., *Stranitsy istorii Kamchatki dorevolutsionnyi period* [Pages of Kamchatka History: Period before the Revolution], Petropavlovsk-Kamchatskii: Dal'nevostochnoe knizhnoe izdatel'stvo, 1992

Voyt, V., *Kamchatka I ee obitateli s vidom goroda Petropavlovska, planom goroda I opisaniem srazheniya* [Kamchatka and its Inhabitants, with View of Petropavlovsk town, map and description of the battle], St Petersburg, 1855

http://www.petropavlovsk.ru

PEVEK

The city of Pevek (a settlement until 1967) is a major port in Chaun Bay on the East Siberian Sea, and the easternmost port on the Northern Sea Route. It is the administrative center of the Chaunsky region of Chukotka Autonomous Okrug in the Magadan province of the Russian Federation. The city arose and grew in the Soviet Arctic in the 1930s and the first half of the 1940s as a result of mining, especially due to the exploitation of nonferrous industrial metals (gold, tin, and nickel). In 1935–1936, a vast deposit of tin was discovered on Cape Val'kumej ("Raven precipice"), and the settlement of Pevek flourished on the coast some 15 km away. Since tin mining began here in 1941, mining has been the basis of Chukotka's economy. The population of Pevek, once numbering 40,000, is now less than 6000, and decreasing further as the mines close.

The management of large-scale tin extraction in Chaunsky region was initially under Dal'stroi (the General Industrial and Highway Construction Company, which operated mostly by forced labor) during World War II. Val'kumej mine began tin extraction on April 12, 1941, but production was accelerated later when a road was laid between Pevek and Val'kumej. The road was built by the inhabitants of Pevek under extremely difficult conditions, literally cutting down into frozen ground. World War II increased the demand for tin, and in 1941 the first heavyweight machinery for Val'kumej and a new large group of workers arrived in Pevek via the Northern Sea Route, bringing mining equipment, vehicles, and building timber. The Val'kumej processing factory produced the first tin within one year. New mines were soon opened at Pirkikaj near Pevek and Iultin, a tin and tungsten mine. Further roads connecting Pevek to the Krasnoarmeysky tin mine and gold field settlements were constructed.

The Northern Sea Route promoted the development of large industrial centers in the Russian North such as Pevek. When Glavsevmorput (the Chief Office for the Northern Route) was established, sea operations (ice monitoring, forecasting, icebreaker management) and the conduct of industrial materials were combined under one ministry. In 1952, a Glavsevmorput staff was based in Pevek, which is now the Marine Operational Headquarters for the eastern region of the route.

The icebreaker *Krasin*, which accompanied Arctic convoys during World War II, was used as a hydrometeorological research station in the Pevek and East Siberian Sea area. Seagoing research was conducted with the ship *Revolutionary* during voyages from Arkhangel'sk to Pevek. Today, there is an established network of polar stations on the eastern sector of the Northern Sea Route, including a polar station constructed in Pevek in 1934–1935 (Chaun Bay).

In 1942, the Soviet government sent ten ships on voyages from west to east, carrying asbestos and timber to Pevek. By 1944, the volume of cargo on vessels in the eastern Northern Sea Route constituted 88.3% of all cargo carried in the Soviet Arctic. At the end of the 20th century, Pevek remains one of the key ports along the Route and the major Arctic port for the Russian Far East.

VALERY MIT'KO

Further Reading

Belov, M., *Nauchnoe i khoziaistvennoe osvoenie Sovetskogo Severa, 1933–1945 gg* [History of Opneing and Developemnt of the Northern Sea Route, 1933–1945], Leningrad: Gidrometeorologicheskoe, 1969

Granberg, A.G., "Using of the Northern Sea Route: tendencies and perspectives." *Russian Economical Journal*, 5–6 (1997)

Pinkhenson, D.M., *Istoriya otkrytiya i osvoeniya Severnogo morskogo puti* [*History of Discovery and Assimilating of the Northern Sea Route*] Volume 2, Moscow: Morskoi transport, 1969

PHIPPS, CONSTANTINE

Constantine John Phipps was a British naval commander and member of parliament who, in 1773, was selected to lead the first British attempt since 1615 to reach the North Pole. He joined the naval service at a young age, under the sponsorship of his uncle Augustus John. Also at a young age, he became a member of parliament for Lincoln and was reputed to be an able parliamentary speaker. "Besides being an officer of the Royal Navy, Capt. Phipps's other assets were memberships in both the Royal Society and the Society of Antiquaries. He had served his country in the Seven Years war and had been at the capture of Havana. Phipps's ability to form a friendly comradeship with his men would stand him in good stead on the [Arctic] voyage" (Buchmann, 1997).

Phipps's Arctic expedition consisted of two specially strengthened bomb (for shore bombardment) vessels, the *Carcass*, commanded by Skeffington Lutwidge, and the *Racehorse*, a former French privateer captured by the British in 1757 and commanded by Phipps. *Carcass* carried 80 officers and men, and *Racehorse* carried 90. Phipps's instructions were to follow open water between Greenland and northwest Svalbard to reach as far north as possible.

The expedition originated in the advocacy of an Englishman, Daines Barrington. For decades, the logbooks of whalers operating around Svalbard had recorded the changing nature of the polar ice in those northern waters. The line of ice would shift in different summers, at some years crushing down upon the islands of northwest Spitsbergen, and in others moving offshore and leaving an ice-free passage trending northeast from the whaling stations of Amsterdam and Danes islands all the way to the Seven Islands. Despite such occasional open waters, pack ice near 81° N always remained as an impassable barrier to the North Pole.

Yet, these seasonal variations were used by Barrington in 1773 to argue that one need only push a bit further north before an ice-free corridor was located that would allow ships to sail directly to the Pole. Barrington convinced the Council of the Royal Society to ask the British Admiralty to mount a polar expedition north from Svalbard. Disregarding a century and a half of whaler logbooks that showed nothing but a wall of ice north of Spitsbergen, the Admiralty agreed.

Phipps's expedition left England in May 1773, and by the end of June encountered largely ice-free waters along the north coast of Svalbard, but no ice-free passage to the pole itself. The two vessels reached the Dutch roadstead at Vogelsang Island in mid-July and anchored in 11 fathoms. Phipps went ashore and saw a uniform field of ice extending to the northeast. Prevented from sailing north, Phipps turned east along Reinsdyrflya, and then north again when he encountered loose ice north of Woodfjorden. On July 27, the expedition attained a new furthest north of 80°48′ N, where the vessels were blocked by a line of ice extending nearly east to west. This record held for more than three decades, until Scoresby gained it in 1806.

Phipps continued to force his vessels northeastward, occasionally entering openings in the ice wall that extended a few miles north. But each time, the leads closed, and forced Phipps to retreat. On August 3, the ships reached the Seven Islands (Sjuøyane), the northernmost islands in the Svalbard archipelago, farther north and east than any exploring expedition before them. They were also beset by ice, which rose at some places higher than the mainmasts of the ships themselves. The pressure of the ice forced Phipps to contemplate abandoning the vessels.

With northward progress halted, Phipps nevertheless continued a program of scientific research, using such instruments as a thermometer designed by Lord Cavendish for measuring water temperature, and an apparatus invented by Dr. Irving for distilling fresh water from saltwater. Phipps's account of the voyage contains considerable data on Svalbard, and describes an incident between a large polar bear and a midshipman on board the *Carcass*, 14-year-old Horatio Nelson, who was almost killed in a failed attempt to secure the bear's skin for his father.

For a week, Phipps combined his attempt to free the ships from the ice with an effort to haul the ship's boats over the ice in case the ships became trapped and the boats became the only method of escape. By August 9, the ships had overtaken the boats, and the next day, with all sails set, the *Racehorse* and *Carcass* smashed through to open sea. Failing to locate any other openings in the ice to the north, Phipps left the waters around Svalbard on August 22. On September 7, the expedition reached the Shetlands, and then fought through a succession of gales until they regained the Thames on September 24.

The Phipps expedition demonstrated conclusively that no direct open sea route to the North Pole could be had from the waters between Svalbard and Greenland, nor from the waters directly north of Svalbard.

Biography

Constantine John Phipps was born in 1744. His father, Constantine Phipps, a captain in the Royal Navy and a descendant of the Anglesey family, was made Baron Mulgrave in Ireland in 1767. Constantine John Phipps married Eliza Anne Cholmley, the daughter of Nathaniel Cholmley, Esq., and they had one daughter. On the death of his father, Phipps became the second Baron Mulgrave. In 1790, Phipps was made a peer of Great Britain, becoming Lord Mulgrave. When Constantine John Phipps died in 1792 without a male heir, his English title became extinct, although it was brought back two years later for his brother Henry, who became an earl in 1812. Phipps published his *A Voyage Towards the North Pole Undertaken by His Majesty's Command 1773* in 1774. At his death, he reportedly left behind one of the best naval science libraries in

England, one that included many unpublished charts and notes of soundings from his expeditions.

P.J. CAPELOTTI

Further Reading

Buchmann, Jane, "The Arctic Voyage—1773" (see: http://www.cronab.demon.co.uk/jane3.htm)

Langdale, Thomas, *A Topographical Dictionary of Yorkshire for the Year 1822* (see: http://www.genuki.org.uk/big/eng/YKS/yrksdict/north/index.html)

Phipps, Constantine John, *A Voyage Towards the North Pole Undertaken by His Majesty's Command 1773*, London: Printed by W. Bowyer & J. Nichols for J. Nourse, 1774

The English Peerage or, a View of the Ancient and Present State of the English Nobility, London, 1790 (see: http://www.genuki.org.uk/big/eng/History/Barons/index.html)

PHYSICAL ANTHROPOLOGY OF THE ARCTIC

Physical or biological anthropologists study how and why individuals and groups of people differ physically and genetically, both in the past and the present. Biological variation in humans is usually broken down into more specific categories, including demography, health and disease, and adaptation. Sources of this variation fall into the areas of genetic differences and consequences of the interaction between the environment and genetic potential. Physical anthropologists also examine human origins and the evolutionary path that humans have followed to get where they are today, which also encompasses studies of nonhuman primate anatomy and behavior. Other areas of research include dental anthropology, forensic anthropology, and studies of growth and development.

Physical anthropologists study questions with both long time depth, such as when examining human origins, and problems on a much shorter generation-to-generation scale, such as with secular trends for increased stature within a population. They must incorporate into their research the work of geneticists, biochemists, and other scientific disciplines while at the same time remembering that there is another set of conditions that must always be considered: culture.

The study of physical anthropology in the Arctic is very important in light of the fact that the northern circumpolar region was populated very late with respect to human history in general. Most areas of the Arctic were peopled as late as 15,000–25,000 years ago. The only population from prior to 25,000 years ago that might be considered an Arctic group is the Neanderthals. Neanderthals occupied areas of Europe between 30,000 and 100,000 years ago and may be considered to be an Arctic population from the standpoint of climate rather

than latitude. However, for the purposes of this discussion, examples will be limited to the anatomically modern populations who have inhabited the Arctic beginning in the late Pleistocene and into the Holocene.

Physical anthropology research in the Arctic focuses on two main problems: population history and human adaptation. Population history includes population movements as well as the study of genetic affinities between populations. Human adaptation focuses on the ways in which people react to outside stressors. These reactions can be behavioral, physiological, or even genetic. There are a number of stresses acting upon human populations in the Arctic. The major ones are (1) extreme cold, (2) inconsistent diet, usually comprising high protein and fat and low carbohydrate content, (3) high levels of physical activity, especially during seasonal hunting pursuits, (4) variable levels of sunlight associated with high latitudes, and (5) diseases, both local and introduced.

Population History

Physical Characteristics

Although the discipline of physical anthropology did not emerge until the late 19th century following Charles Darwin's publication of *On the Origin of Species* (published in 1859), several researchers were already examining Arctic populations. One of the earliest examples is an anthropological description of an Inuit skull from Greenland by Jacob B. Winslow in 1722. Continued examination of the Inuit of Greenland in 1782 led David Crantz to the early postulations that the Inuit had some close biological ties to populations in northern Asia. Several 18th-century scholars noted similarities of appearance between the north Asian groups and populations in North America and Greenland, which included skin, hair, and eye color. These early researchers agreed, for the most part, that American Indians and Inuit most likely had an Asian origin. However, they also recognized the fact that these groups were clearly differentiated from one another, suggesting separate migrations into North America. In 1795, Johann Friedrich Blumenbach categorized American Indians and Inuit as separate racial groups, placing the Inuit with his Mongolian subdivision including most of east and north Asia. Contemporaries of Blumenbach who shared his view of the origin of the Inuit included William Lawrence, Samuel Morton, G.W. Steller, and Baron Ferdinand Von Wrangell.

In the late 19th century and into the early 20th century, the focus of research changed from the degeneration from pure racial stocks, as proposed by Blumenbach, to the biological adaptation of humans to differing geographical regions. Two of the main researchers discussing Inuit origins at this time were Hinrich Rink and Franz Boas. Rink supported the view that Alaska was the place of origin for Inuit, but that they were derived from the American Indians already inhabiting the more southerly areas of North America. Many contemporaries of Rink also supported this same position. Most notably, R. Brown, Alexander Chamberlain, and Rudolf Virchow all agreed that the Inuit were part of a wave of Native Americans who had migrated to the north from more temperate climates.

Boas supported a similar yet slightly different viewpoint. Between 1897 and 1903, Boas ran the Jesup North Pacific Expedition. The main goal of this expedition was to investigate the relationship between the different groups of the North Pacific, including the United States, Canada, and Asia. Anthropometric measurements were taken, and physical characteristics were observed in each village encountered during the expedition. Archaeological investigations were also conducted; however, there are no reports of human remains being collected. Boas pointed out the similarities of facial features and cultural practices between the native groups inhabiting northeastern Siberia and northwestern North America. He believed that these groups were related and most likely formed a single cultural group in the past. Furthermore, he considered the Arctic groups of Alaska and Canada to be the stock from which nearly all other Native American groups arose. He also believed that the native populations inhabiting Siberia were split off from groups in North America, after having "migrated back to the Old World after the retreat of the Arctic Glaciers." Boas saw a great need for the study of both Canadian and Alaskan populations in order to help determine the relationships between the numerous native groups. His suggestions for study included linguistics, archaeology, and ethnographic investigations. However, Boas did not recognize the usefulness of studying the human skeleton for analyzing relationships between human groups.

At the beginning of the 20th century, a number of researchers were starting to realize the scientific value of observations of the Inuit skeleton. A large number of early publications focused primarily on cranial morphology of the Inuit. Several European researchers, including Marcelin Boule, William Boyd Dawkins, Gabriel de Mortillet, and Leo Testut, argued for a European origin of the Inuit based on apparent similarities between the archaeological assemblages of the Magdalenian tradition and the Inuit of North America. William J. Sollas attempted to corroborate this theory by showing parallels in skull morphology between the Chancelade skull from a French Aurignacian site and an Inuit skull. Unfortunately, results based on the comparison of one skull from each group would not hold up to the rigors of modern research.

Very early in the 20th century, another key player in the debate regarding the origins and relationships of the Inuit came onto the scene. Aleš Hrdlička of the US National Museum was a major proponent of the Asian origin for the Inuit as well as all other Native American groups. He organized and directed expeditions to Alaska, Canada, Greenland, and Siberia to collect human skeletal remains for the Smithsonian Institution's research collection. Hrdlička took numerous measurements of skeletal components; however, the vast majority of his work was concentrated on crania. He published catalogues of skull measurements from various geographic regions, including numerous Arctic populations. Hrdlicka then compared the measurements of different collections to try to address questions of biological affinity. He looked for differences in the measurements that he felt represented significant discontinuities and, based on these differences, he would try to determine the degree of relatedness between two samples.

One of the main drawbacks to the research methodology of both Boas and Hrdlička is that it was not problem oriented. The only statistics applied to the data by either researcher were simple descriptive statistics (means and ranges). This was a common theme among scientists studying anthropometric and osteometric data during this time period.

While the debate over the Inuit and American Indians origins was occurring, other Arctic populations were also causing considerable discussion. Researchers in Russia and Japan were debating the problem of the origins and relationships of the Ainu. Based on a number of physical characteristics, including body hair and the lack of an epicanthic eyefold, anthropologists reasoned that the Ainu were not Asian, but rather a residual group of Caucasians who had previously inhabited much of Europe and Asia. Another group in question was the Saami of northwestern Scandinavia. Early researchers had considered the Saami to be an offshoot of the Mongoloid race from eastern Asia. However, this attitude began to change during the beginning of the 20th century when work by C.H. Stratz and K.E. Schreiner suggested that the Saami were a remnant population who had phylogenetic roots beginning before the split of the Europeans and the Mongoloids.

Genetics

Not all researchers in the early part of the 20th century were concerned with simply measuring skeletal materials. Starting in the late 1920s, the foundations were laid for what would become the study of genetics in relation to population history. Early blood group genetic studies were limited to the ABO, MN, and Rh systems. By the 1940s, researchers were able to draw conclusions regarding the relationship of Arctic populations based on the frequencies of blood types. Researchers such as Victor E. Levine concluded that American Indians and Inuit were related to one another and were distinct from Asians based on their very low frequency of blood type B and high frequency of blood type M. All three of these groups did, however, share the trait of being nearly monomorphic for the positive Rh factor. Given the information from these three genetic loci, Levine concluded that the most likely hypothesis for the origin of the Inuit was that proposed by Rink and Boas, with the Inuit originating in North America.

In the mid-1940s, a major paradigm shift occurred with regard to the conceptualization of the theory of evolution. A merging of evolutionary theory with concepts of the population geneticists produced what has come to be known as the "modern evolutionary synthesis." With this change in thinking came a distinct change in the way in which research in physical anthropology was conducted and the questions that were being asked. Population genetics, along with evolutionary theory and the study of human biological adaptation, came to the forefront of analytical problems. That is not to say that craniometry and anthropometry were abandoned. With the increased usage of both statistics and computers, many more interpretations could be made regarding population differences in both living and extinct groups. However, given the early advances in genetics, many researchers were quick to conclude that taxonomic evaluations based on genetic variation would be more useful than the traditional skeletal measurements. Serological studies were conducted among northern groups beginning in the 1950s, but it was not until the 1970s that researchers began to realize the importance of genetic variation within groups when accounting for diversity in many populations. Also, in the 1970s, there was a distinct shift away from studies of blood groups and proteins toward the study of the genetics of heredity through the use of DNA.

During the same time that studies of genetic variability were becoming increasingly popular, research into nonmetric dental and cranial traits was also on the rise. Physical anthropologists such as Poul O. Pederson, Cornraad F.A. Moorrees, and Christy G. Turner II examined the dental morphology of Arctic populations to answer questions regarding the peopling of the Arctic, as well as microevolution and population variation within the Arctic.

With the change in research strategy came a change in the way in which the key problems of the Arctic were addressed by physical anthropologists. In North America, the questions regarding the peopling of the New World were: (1) How many migration events into the New World are required to explain the diversity among the different native populations currently living there? (2) When did these migration(s) occur?

(3) Where did the group(s) come from originally? (4) What is the exact genetic relationship of the differing native populations currently inhabiting North and South America?

Of these questions, the one regarding the number of migration events continues to be extremely contentious. Anthropologists have traditionally followed the multiple migration event hypothesis to explain the high degree of both cultural and biological diversity exhibited by the native populations of North and South America. However, it has been proposed by some geneticists that a single migration event, coupled with a long period of isolation, could account for the variation. Nevertheless, most anthropologists and geneticists believe that the differences between the native populations are too great to be explained by a single event. They do not agree on the exact number of migrations, however, with the speculation ranging from two to as many as six separate migrations. Traditional genetic research tends to suggest a three or four migration event scenario, whereas mitochondrial DNA (mtDNA) results are highly variable, with scenarios ranging from one to six migrations. In 1986, an article published by Greenburg, Turner, and Zegura utilized genetic, dental, and linguistic data as evidence in favor of a three-wave migration hypothesis beginning at least 12,000 years ago.

More recently, scientists have begun to focus on Y chromosome distribution in both Siberian and North American native groups in an attempt to trace ancestral populations and population movements in the past. The Y chromosome is passed paternally from father to son with no recombination with the X chromosome. Their research thus far has tended to focus on the geographic distribution of particular Y chromosome markers that occur in all Native American populations. Data compiled by researchers of the Y chromosome seem to contradict the three-wave hypothesis. Unfortunately, their data do not yet allow them to speculate on the exact number of migrations. Y chromosome markers have a great deal of potential for future research in questions of the peopling of the New World. However, as with most genetic studies, they do not answer the question of the timing of these migration events.

The major reason for much of the disagreement regarding the peopling of the New World rests with the problem of time depth. The archaeological record within North America is excellent; however, unlike in Europe, it does not have the same temporal depth. The genetic diversity of the native populations of North America is difficult to assess with regard to time, with the possible timing of migrations from as recently as 12,000 years ago to as far back as 40,000 years ago. This issue remains a very problematic topic in American archaeology.

Closely related to the question of the peopling of the New World is the issue of the peopling of Siberia. This too is a complex and contentious problem. It would appear that the first inhabitants of the area came in as early as 45,000 years ago. The major problems arise with the question of the origins of those people. Both mtDNA and Y chromosome markers are potentially very good research tools in helping to answer this question. There has been considerable population movement in the Siberian Arctic over the past 45,000 years with a great deal of cultural interaction interspersed with long periods of genetic isolation. Given the time depth and the extremely low population density over such a vast geographic region, it is no wonder that tracing the origins and movements of the different populations has proven to be difficult.

The genetic research into the origins of the Saami has also been inconclusive. It would appear from the ABO blood groups that they are of a clearly European origin; however, based on linguistics, dental patterns, and more recent genetic analysis, the Saami seem to fall between common European and Asian patterns. Based on these findings, it is still unclear whether the Saami are a remnant of an ancestral European population or rather a result of the merging of two distinct groups.

Human Adaptation

The Arctic climate poses some unique challenges to the humans that decide to live there. Not only do they have to deal with extremely low temperatures in the winter months, but also the limited and inconsistent nature of the diet and fluctuating sunlight associated with high latitudes. No stress in the Arctic has prompted an adaptive response among humans such as that seen in the sickle cell blood trait in areas where malaria is endemic. Nevertheless, this has not stopped researchers from searching for genetic adaptations to the climatic conditions unique to the Arctic. As far back as 1775, German philosopher Immanual Kant recognized that humans living in the Arctic expressed anatomical and physiological characteristics that were distinct from those of lower latitudes. However, research in the 18th and most of the 19th centuries was focused on population history rather than questions of adaptability.

The first half of the 20th century witnessed a great deal of change with regard to physical anthropology and the questions raised in the area of Arctic adaptability. Some of the major questions were: (1) Did the Inuit differ significantly in their basal metabolic rates (BMR) from other populations? (2) Is there any evidence for genetic polymorphisms that have adaptive significance in the Arctic? (3) How does the climate affect the growth and development of the Inuit?

Metabolism
Danish physiologists August and Marie Krogh were the first researchers to carefully measure dietary intake, oxygen consumption, and carbon dioxide production of Greenlandic Inuit in 1908. Looking at the basal metabolic rates (BMRs) of the Inuit, they found that the Greenlanders had a much higher BMR than that of Europeans. The Kroghs also noted that the Inuit consumed a diet that was very high in protein and fat and low in carbohydrates. Following the work of the Kroghs, many researchers continued analysis of the elevated BMR among Arctic populations. Higher BMRs were observed in native populations from Canada and Alaska.

Since these early findings of increased metabolic rates among Arctic populations were published, there has been a great deal of debate as to whether or not the increase in BMR observed is "real" or rather a result of the stresses involved in the testing procedure itself. It has also been speculated that the traditional diet of most Arctic populations, which is extremely high in animal proteins, may have a significant impact on metabolic rate. The exact mechanisms behind the observed instances of elevated BMR in Arctic populations remain unclear. Furthermore, since the 1970s, research efforts have shifted from BMR to the mechanisms of acclimatization of workers moving to the Arctic from more southerly latitudes.

Adaptation Versus Acclimatization
Associated with the idea of acclimatization is the problem of the distinction between genetic adaptation and developmental acclimatization. Acclimatization occurs when a human is moved from one environment to another with a different set of stressors. Usually, humans can physiologically adjust to these new conditions within a few days or weeks of exposure. However, these adjustments are only temporary and a person will return to their baseline physiological levels upon returning to their original climatic conditions. Developmental acclimatization differs in that it occurs when an individual is raised under those same stressful conditions. The physiological capabilities of those who are developmentally acclimatized are changed to better meet their needs of survival in that particular environment. These physiological changes are permanent in the individual, as the environmental conditions in which they are raised are their baseline conditions. Clearly, it would be relatively easy to distinguish between temporary acclimatization and genetic adaptation; however, it is much more difficult to distinguish between genetic adaptation and developmental acclimatization.

The question then arises as to whether or not northern populations have any physiological advantages to the cold stresses of the Arctic. As noted above, Inuit seem to exhibit a higher metabolic rate than populations from more southerly latitudes. As a result, in tests conducted comparing northern versus nonnorthern groups, groups from the Arctic are better able to withstand cold temperatures due to the increase in BMR. Inuit also show an increased ability to warm their extremities when exposed to a cold stress. In cold water immersion tests, Inuit have consistently shown an increase in blood flow to their extremities. This has the effect of keeping their extremities warmer when exposed to cold stress and reducing the chance of frostbite. Once again, it is still not clear whether these physiological differences are the result of genetic adaptation or simply developmental acclimatization.

Researchers of the 1950s revived the principles set forth by Bergmann and Allen regarding body size and geography, which state that animals inhabiting colder climates will have shorter extremities and a larger body mass to surface area ratio. They found that the wealth of skeletal measurement data from earlier in the century could be applied to questions of stature, extremity length, and other skeletal indicators relating to heat conservation. It was proposed by Carleton Coon and others that the suite of Mongoloid facial characteristics were in fact the result of adaptation to a cold climate. More recently, other researchers have contended that the craniofacial morphology of the Inuit is more likely associated with the actions of mastication. Inuit skulls show an increase in features associated with mastication such as sagittal keeling, pinched nasal bones, a thickening of the tympanic plates, large zygomaxillary tuberosities, and large tori of the palate and mandible.

Growth and Development

The body size and proportions of the Inuit may also play a key role in their ability to live in the Arctic. The overall statement that can be made regarding the growth of circumpolar native populations is that they are shorter than European control groups, nearly the same weight, and have a higher weight to height ratio without a higher proportion of body fat. They are also characterized by a longer trunk, in proportion to leg length, and a greater relative sitting height. It is still unclear as to the reasons behind these differences, but there is a great deal of speculation. The pattern of high weight for height is established at a very young age, within the first few months after birth, which suggests that this is not a direct function of diet. Higher relative sitting height appears to be the result of less leg growth rather than greater trunk growth during childhood and adolescence. It is possible that the high metabolic rates seen in many circumpolar populations play an important role in the fat patterning and body composition of these groups. Researchers also speculate that the overall body shape

and size of Arctic populations is a result of the genetic background of these groups (short Asiatic stock), coupled with the ecogeographical rules of Bergmann and Allen, resulting in a genetic adaptation to a cold climate and producing the physical type that is so common throughout circumpolar indigenous populations.

Related to this is the question of whether or not body size and proportions observed in these groups is a recent phenomenon among circumpolar populations. This is very difficult to say, but based on the earliest height and weight measurements available, it would appear that the high weight for height is a trait that most likely goes back a long way into the biological history of these populations. On the other hand, there is some suggestion of a secular trend toward an increase in height among many circumpolar populations. Among the Igloolik Inuit of Canada, evidence indicated that younger children were taller than their cohorts from 10 years earlier. However, recent data from the Igloolik suggest that there may even be a reversal of this trend in older adolescents and adults. Still, there is a question as to the amount of spinal trauma caused by the use of snowmobiles and all-terrain vehicles and the consequent effect on anthropometric measurements. Finnish Lapps have also had a major height increase during the period of 1912–1968; yet, given the lack of recent data collections, it is unknown whether this trend has continued.

However, there is evidence of a secular trend among both males and females in many populations toward an earlier onset of puberty, which would negatively affect stature. Associated with the onset of puberty is a hormone release that causes the fusion of several longbone epiphyses. The fusion of these longbones results in the cessation of growth and an earlier attainment of adult stature. The result is a shorter period of growth in a population that is already growing at a rate slower than most other populations.

Increased nutritional status, improved social conditions, and a greater availability of health care have all been pointed to as possible contributing factors to increased stature among these groups. These same factors are also involved in the secular trend toward earlier puberty. With the differing pressures of the many stresses being encountered, it may be impossible to separate out the role that each individual element plays in the growth potential of a person.

There is a clear research problem emerging in this particular area. With the increased admixture of nonindigenous genetic stock, a greater availability of health care, and a shift away from the native subsistence base in many circumpolar communities, the growth of these children will undoubtedly be affected. How this effect is manifested in their growth patterns becomes another interesting question altogether, and researchers have shown that there is a strong need for further study as all of these changes take place.

Recent Changes in the Direction of Physical Anthropology Research in the Arctic

In recent years, there has been a considerable decline in broad scope research efforts in the Arctic such as were put forth by the International Biological Program of the late 1960s and early 1970s. More recent investigations have tended to focus more narrowly on questions of population history that can be addressed using mtDNA or Y chromosome analysis.

There is also a push from cultural anthropologists and the medical community toward researching the health consequences of major cultural shifts in both diet and subsistence activities. There have been significant changes in the dietary patterns of many Arctic populations and a consequent change in subsistence patterns. Many native communities have switched from a pattern of seasonal subsistence hunting to seasonal wage labor. The effects of these types of changes are just beginning to be realized with the loss of many traditional lifeways and an increase in diseases associated with the change to a western diet, such as dental caries and diabetes mellitus.

Another major issue of recent years relates back to the Native American Graves Protection and Repatriation Act of 1990. This act assigns ownership of Native American human remains and funerary objects to Native Americans. Many of the skeletons collected from the early 1900s onward in the United States are subject to return if so requested by the Native American groups. This has led to the return of a large number of skeletal collections along with an intensive data collection effort prior to their reburial. It has also stimulated a great deal of debate regarding both cultural and biological continuity through time within a geographic area. This is of key importance as ownership and cultural affiliation of many skeletal collections come into question. The biological continuity of many Alaskan populations has been debated in recent years and it is still an ongoing debate between the Alaskan Natives and members of the anthropological community.

Hopefully, this debate will lead to better communication between Native groups and anthropologists in the future. Native populations have begun to be much more vocal on both the educational and political fronts with regard to their cultural heritage. By working together with the Native communities, both physical anthropologists and medical researchers can help them understand the past histories, present conditions, and future challenges of indigenous populations of the Arctic.

SCOTT S. LEGGE

See also **Boas, Franz**

Further Reading

Boas, Franz, "The Jesup North Pacific Expedition." *American Museum Journal*, 3 (1903): 73–119

Greenberg, Joseph H., Christy G. Turner II & Stephen L. Zegura, "The Settlement of the Americas: a comparison of the linguistic, dental, and genetic evidence." *Current Anthropology*, 24 (1986): 477–497

Hrdlicka, Ales, "Catalog of human crania in the United States National Museum collections: the Eskimo, Alaska and related Indians." *Proceedings of the US National Museum*, 63 (1924): 1–51

———, "Catalog of human crania in the United States National Museum collections: Eskimos in general." *Proceedings of the US National Museum*, 91 (1942): 169–429

———, "Catalog of human crania in the United States National Museum collections: non-Eskimo peoples of the Northwest Coast, Alaska and Siberia." *Proceedings of the US National Museum*, 94 (1944): 1–172

Jamison, Paul L., Stephen L. Zegura & Frederick A. Milan, *Eskimos of Northwestern Alaska: A Biological Perspective*, Pennsylvania: Dowden Hutchinson and Ross, 1978

Laughlin, William S. & Albert B. Harper, "Peopling of the Continents: Australia and America." In *Biological Aspects of Human Migration*, edited by C.G.N. Mascie-Taylor & G.W. Lasker, Cambridge: Cambridge University Press, 1988

Levin, M.G., *Ethnic Origins of the Peoples of Northeastern Asia*, Arctic Institute of North America, Anthropology of the North, Translations from Russian Sources/No. 3, Toronto: University of Toronto Press, 1963

Milan, Frederick A. (editor), *The Biology of Circumpolar Populations*, New York: Cambridge University Press, 1980

Schreiner, K.E., *Zur Osteologie der Lappen*, Oslo: Brøgger, 1935

Scott, G. Richard & Christy G. Turner II, *The Anthropology of Modern Human Teeth: Dental Morphology and its Variation in Recent Human Populations*, New York: Cambridge University Press, 1997

Scott, G. Richard, Scott S. Legge, Robert W. Lane, Susan L. Steen & Steven R. Street, "Physical Anthropology of the Arctic." In *The Arctic: Environment, People, Policy*, edited by Mark Nuttall & Terry V. Callaghan, Amsterdam: Harwood Academic Publishers, 2000

Shephard, Roy J. & Andris Rode, *The Health Consequences of "Modernization": Evidence from Circumpolar Peoples*, New York: Cambridge University Press, 1996

Szathmary, Emoke J.E., "Genetic markers in Siberian and northern North American populations." *Yearbook of Physical Anthropology*, 24 (1981): 37–73

———, "mtDNA and the peopling of the Americas." *American Journal of Human Genetics*, 53 (1993): 793–799

PILOT WHALE

Pilot whales (*Globicephala* spp.) are among the largest of the dolphins, second only to killer whales in size. The name "pilot whale" seems to have derived from the observation that a leader guides or "pilots" a pod of these animals, an observation that is not necessarily accurate. They are also commonly known as "blackfish" or "potheads," the latter name referring to the bulbous forehead bulge of the males. Pilot whales are almost all black, except for a light-colored anchor-shaped patch on the underside, reaching from the flippers to the anus. Males are larger, reaching a length of 20 ft (6.2 m) compared to a maximum of 17.7. ft (5.4 m) for females. A full-grown male can weigh 3 tons. In addition to the diagnostic bulbous forehead, males also have a thicker, wider-based dorsal fin that becomes more hooked as the animal matures, and more pronounced keels on the tail stock. The dorsal fin in males and females is set far forward. After a 16-month gestation period, a 6-ft-long calf is born. It nurses for 20 months, one of the longest periods for any cetacean. Newborn calves are not black, but brownish-gray that darkens with age.

There are two kinds of pilot whales, differentiated by the length of their sickle-shaped pectoral fins. The fin of the longfin (*Globicephala melaena*) is long and graceful, and may be as much as 27% of the animal's total length, while in the shortfin (*G. macrorhynchus*), it does not exceed 19%. The two species are virtually impossible to distinguish at sea, but one can guess that a temperate or colder-water sighting is likely to be the longfin and a tropical sighting is likely to be the shortfin. In the eastern North Atlantic, the long-finned species is found in the waters of Greenland, Iceland, and the Barents Sea, the Faroes, Shetlands, and Orkney Islands, and off Scotland, Ireland, and England. In the western North Atlantic, they can be seen from Davis Strait to the Canadian Maritimes, occasionally as far south as New Jersey. The shortfin is sometimes known as the Pacific pilot whale, although its range overlaps that of the longfin in many areas, including the North Atlantic. (Both species are also found in the Southern Hemisphere.)

In Arctic and Subarctic countries, pilot whales are known by a variety of names: in the Orkneys and in Shetland, they are known as caa'ing whales (which may be derived from the word "calling," or from caa'ing meaning to drive, referring to the practice of driving pilot whales into bays to kill them); *naiso-gota* and *gondo-kujira* in Japanese; *marsvín* and *grindhval-ur* in Iceland; *grindeval* in Danish; *grinde* in Norwegian; *Grindwal* in German; and *grindy* in Russian. (The word *grind* pronounced to rhyme with "pinned" is Old Norse and means "lattice" or "fence" and might refer to the appearance of a group of pilot whales swimming or resting at the surface.)

Pilot whales eat squid almost exclusively. Their upper and lower jaws are equipped with conical teeth, 9–12 pairs in each jaw, ideal for snagging the slippery cephalopods. Like most odontocetes (toothed whales), pilot whales are echolocators, and emit clicks and whistles that bounce off whatever is around them, reading the returning echoes to avoid obstacles, find food, or identify predators. From tests conducted on captive animals, it is known that pilot whales can dive to at least 1654 ft (504 m).

In the 19th century, a substantial fishery for "blackfish" was operated along the North Atlantic coasts of North America, relying upon the natural inclination of this species to strand, and also upon the fishers' ability to drive a school ashore to be slaughtered. Those whales that did not die after stranding were killed on the beach, and the blubber was peeled off to be tried out on the spot. Oil boiled down from the blubber was of the quality of ordinary whale oil, but the oil obtained from the melon was drained off and was used by watch and instrument makers. It was known as "blackfish melon-oil" or "porpoise-jaw oil." Whalers also hunted "blackfish" at sea, harpooning them from longboats as they did the larger whales.

Pilot whales are compulsively gregarious animals, always seen in groups of 15–200, and sometimes in loose aggregations that may number in the thousands. This gregariousness has its downside, because pilot whales are notorious group stranders, and have come ashore in groups of up to 200 in Newfoundland, Cape Cod, and the British Isles. Moreover, their gregarious inclinations have been exploited by whalers, who used to drive them into the shallows en masse and slaughter all of them. The pilot whale fishery in Newfoundland reached a peak of some 10,000 animals killed in 1956, but declined in the 1960s, and is no longer pursued. This technique was used in the past in Norway, Japan, Massachusetts, particularly Wellfleet and even New Jersey, but it is still being used today in the Faroe Islands, where the method of killing pilot whales has been employed at least since the 16th century. Nowadays, as many as 1500 pilot whales are killed annually in a ceremony known as a *grind*, after the Danish name for the pilot whale. After an offshore motorboat chase, islanders herd the whales into a bay, where the exhausted, panicked, and confused whales are driven into the shallows. Here, the islanders wade into the water and hammer heavy metal gaffs into the flesh of each whale until they can be held with iron hooks, whereupon they are stabbed to death with knives in a bay that soon runs red with blood. The Faroese claim the right to hunt pilot whales in their traditional fashion because they need the meat, and also because they do not appreciate interference from outsiders. Pilot whales are one of the small cetacean species that are not covered by the International Whaling Commission's ban on commercial hunting.

RICHARD ELLIS

See also **Dolphins and Porpoises**

Further Reading

Bernard, H.J. & S.B. Reilly, "Pilot Whales *Globicephala* Lesson, 1928." In *Handbook of Marine Mammals, Volume 6, The*

Second Book of Dolphins and Porpoises, edited by S. Ridgway & R. Harrison, London and San Diego: Academic Press, 1999

Clark, A.H., "The Blackfish and Porpoise Fisheries." In *The Fisheries and Fishery Industries of the United States, Section V, History and Methods of the Fisheries*, edited by G.B. Goode, Washington, District of Columbia: Government Printing Office, 1887, pp. 297–310

Ellis, R., *Dolphins and Porpoises*, New York: Knopf, 1982

Mowat, F., *Sea of Slaughter*, Boston: Atlantic Monthly Press, 1984

Olson, P.O., "Pilot Whales." In *Encyclopedia of Marine Mammals*, edited by W.F. Perrin, B. Wursig & J.G.M. Thewissen, London and San Diego: Academic Press, 2002

Sergeant, D.S., "The biology of the pilot or pothead whale *Globicephala melaena* (Traill) in Newfoundland waters." *Bulletin of the Fisheries Research Board of Canada*, 132 (1962): 1–84

PIŁSUDSKI, BRONISŁAW PIOTR

Bronisław Piłsudski was a Polish political activist who, as a consequence of his exile to Sakhalin Island, became an ethnographer and museum worker focusing on the Nivkhi and Ainu peoples. In 1887, Piłsudski was arrested in St Petersburg by the czarist police. He was accused of participating in an attempt to assassinate Czar Alexander III and was sentenced to 15 years of hard labor in Sakhalin. He arrived in Sakhalin the same year and was conscripted to hard labor at a forest clearing in the Tymovskii District. Later, he was employed as a schoolteacher. At that time, he began his first scientific observations in the area of meteorology. In 1891, he met with Lev Iakovlevich Shternberg, also an exile, who became a guide for Piłsudski in the area of ethnography. Piłsudski was permitted some freedom of movement on Sakhalin and began to collect ethnographic material among Nivkhi (Giliaks). From the beginning of his ethnographic career, he was interested in establishing a museum. In 1896 the museum in Aleksandrovsk was opened. In the same year, Piłsudski was sent to Ainu settlements to collect materials for the museum.

In 1899, Piłsudski obtained a post at the museum of the Society for the Study of the Amur Region in Vladivostok and stayed there until 1902. At the same time, he worked as the Vladivostok secretary for the Imperial Russian Geographical Society. In July 1902, he was officially appointed by the Imperial Academy of Sciences for the ethnographic expedition to Sakhalin to study the Ainu. In 1903, together with Wacław Sieroszewski, he went to Hokkaido to study the Ainu there. From there he returned to Sakhalin to the village Ai, where he lived with his Ainu wife Chuhsamma and their son Sukezo. In 1905, he made a short trip to the Lower Amur Region and conducted a survey among Ul'chi and Nanai people. The same year, after a short last visit to Sakhalin and his family, he left for Japan, and from there through North America and France he returned to Poland.

Piłsudski's work among the Nivkhi and Ainu encompassed a wide range of subjects. Particularly, he stressed the necessity to study the language and the importance of researching topics that have the most direct relevance for the welfare of the people. Hence, although among his published works there are articles on Shamanism and the bear festival on Sakhalin, the bulk of his work concerned the structure and vocabulary of the Ainu language and oral folklore, including a unique collection of recordings of Ainu tales.

He also published works on the economy, subsistence, and health conditions among the Ainu and Nivkhi. In two of his works, *Nuzhdy i potrebnosti sakhalinskikh giliakov* [Needs and necessities of the Giliaks of Sakhalin] and *Proekt pravil ob ustroistve upravleniia ainov o. Sakhalina* [Project of principles concerning the organization of the Ainu from Sakhalin], he addresses the situation of the Nivkhi and Ainu populations directly, making policy recommendations. Although he wrote in terms of the necessity to bring the indigenous population to a higher level of civilization, he also stressed many negative effects of Russian colonization. He especially underlined the exploitation of natural resources and a careless attitude toward the environment on the part of the Russian settlers. He advised that all the officials should have a good command of the local languages and that all the inhabitants should be equally treated in the courts. Still, ultimately Piłsudski recommended the introduction of the local people to a sedentary life and cattle breeding instead of fishing and hunting.

During his lifetime, Piłsudski managed to publish only a small part of his ethnographic material. New manuscripts have recently been found, especially owing to the work of the International Committee for the Restoration and Assessment of Bronisław Piłsudski's Work, which functioned between 1981 and 1986.

Biography

Bronisław Piłsudski was born in 1866 in Zułów (contemporary Lithuania) into the family of a Polish landowner, Józef Wincenty Piotr Piłsudski. In 1874, a disastrous fire destroyed the family estate in Zułów and the family moved to Vilnius, where Bronisław Piłsudski and his younger brother Józef (who later became a leader of independent Poland) attended high school. From September 1885, Bronisław studied law in St Petersburg. He was arrested in 1887 and exiled to Sakhalin, where he lived until 1905. He was married to an Ainu woman, Chuhsamma, and they had two children: a son (Sukezo) and a daughter (Kiyo). His descendants now live in Japan.

Piłsudski returned to Poland via Japan, North America, and France. In 1915, he moved to Switzerland and then to Paris, where he became involved in the work of the Polish National Committee, a Polish political organization abroad, headed by Roman Dmowski. Bronisław Piłsudski committed suicide in Paris on May 17, 1918.

AGNIESZKA HALEMBA

Further Reading

Kuczyński, Antoni, *Syberia: czterysta lat polskiej diaspory: antologia historyczno-kulturowa* [Siberia: four hundred years of Polish diaspora: historic-cultural anthology], Wrocław: Zakład Narodowy im. Ossolińskich, 1993

———, *Polskie opisanie świata* [Polish Description of the World], Wrocław: Wydawnictwo Uniwersytetu Wrocławskiego, 1994

Majewicz, Alfred F. (editor), *The Collected Works of Bronisław Piłsudski*, Berlin, New York: Mouton de Gruyter, 1998

Piłsudski, Bronisław, "Nuzhdy i potrebnosti sakhalinskikh giliakov" [Needs and necessities of the Giliaks of Sakhalin]. *Zapiski Priamurskogo otdela Imperatorskogo Russkogo geograficheskogo obshchestva*, 4(4) (1898), 1–38

———, "Kratkii ocherk ekonomicheskogo byta ainov na o. Sakhalin" [Short outline of economic life of the Ainu of Sakhalin]. *Zapiski Obshchestva izucheniia Amurskogo Kraia*, 10 (1907): 89–116

———, "Szamanizm u tubylców na Sachalinie" [Shamanism among the locals of Sakhalin]. *Lud*, 15(4) (1909): 261–274

———, *Materials for the Study of the Ainu Language and Folklore,* Kraków: Imperial Academy of Sciences, 1912

———, "Na medvezhim prazdnike ainov o. Sakhalina" [At the bear festival of the Sakhalin Ainu]. *Zhivaia starina*, 23(1–2) (1914): 67–162

———, *Materials for the Study of the Orok (Uilta) Language and Folklore,* Poznań: Institute of Linguistics, 1985

———, "Proekt pravil ob ustroistve upravleniia ainov o. Sakhalina" [Project of principles concerning the organisation of the Sakhalin Ainu]. In *Materialy k izucheniiu istorii i etnografii naseleniia Sakhalinskoi oblasti* [Materials for study of the history and ethnography of Sakhalin population], edited by V.M. Latyshev, Yuzhno-Sakhalinsk: Sakhalinskii oblastnoi kraevedcheskii muzei, 1986, pp. 131–147

B.O. Pilsudskii—issledovatel' narodov Sakhalina [B.O. Piłsudski—the researcher of the Sakhalin peoples], Yuzhno-Sakhalinsk: Sakhalinskii oblastnoi kraevedcheskii muzei, 1991

PINGO

A pingo is a perennial frost mound comprising a core of massive ice, produced principally by injection of water, and with a covering of soil and vegetation. Named after a local Inuktitut term used in the Mackenzie Delta region, northwest Canada, pingos are one of the most recognizable landforms associated with permafrost regions. The Russian term for pingo is *bulgunnyakh*, which is derived from a Yakut word. Pingos occur in both the continuous and discontinuous permafrost zones, and the scars of former

pingos, identified in midlatitudes, are evidence of the previous extent of permafrost. Two types are recognized: closed-system and open-system. For their development, both depend on water being injected into the soil under some pressure, in such a way that the pressure is relieved by heaving of the ground surface. Most pingos are domed to conical in shape, somewhat asymmetric, with a circular to oval base and a fissured top that may be cratered. The fissures and craters result from rupturing of the soil and vegetation cover during doming, due to progressive growth of the ice core. Snow and meltwater, entering the fissures and freezing therein, contribute to the process. While most pingos develop in unconsolidated sediments, a few are known to have formed in sedimentary bedrock.

Closed-system pingos are found most commonly in areas of low-lying, poorly drained terrain in regions of continuous permafrost. In these areas, bodies of unfrozen ground (taliks) exist beneath the larger water bodies such as lakes and rivers. When a lake drains, sediments of the lake floor cool, and permafrost begins to develop in this unfrozen soil. The freezing occurs both downward from the exposed ground surface and inward from the sides and bottom of the talik, eventually sealing off the remnant of unfrozen soil. Permafrost aggradation creates high pore water pressures within the unfrozen core, principally as a result of pore water being expelled from the freezing sediments.

The normal expansion of water as it freezes into ice makes only a modest contribution to the process. This high hydrostatic pressure is relieved by an upward movement of the ground surface, usually commencing at the site of a residual pond on the lake bed, where the cap of newly frozen ground is thinnest. As the heaving continues over time, a mound is formed, which continues to grow—the pingo. If the rate of water injection exceeds the rate of freezing, a subpingo water lens may develop; drilling into pingos has demonstrated the existence of such lenses. The surface cover of soil and vegetation over the pingo may rupture, either near the base, allowing the escape of water under pressure, or, more commonly, at the top, creating the fissures and craters so visible from the air. Pingo growth tends to be episodic, with the rate of growth governed by the stratigraphy and texture of the lake sediments. Several pingos may develop on site of residual ponds within a single drained lake basin.

The largest closed-system pingos known are about 50 m high, with side slopes as steep as 45° and basal diameters of several hundred meters. More typically, they are smaller than this figure suggests. Surveys of selected closed-system pingos in the Mackenzie Delta region, northwest Canada, have shown that in recent decades the growth rates of pingos have ranged from nil to as much as 34 cm per year, with most being in the range of 1–10 cm per year; the rate of growth is greatest during their middle years. Depending on the nature of the sediments involved and the relative rates of freezing, the ice core may consist of a planoconvex body of more or less clear ice, a series of ice lenses, or a combination of these. Ice wedges and ice formed in dilation cracks may comprise a significant proportion of the ice core. Geothermal analyses suggest that pingos range in age from a few decades to many thousand years.

Open-system pingos are found in hilly to mountainous regions, where they occur in valleys and at the base of slopes. The high water pressure necessary for their growth is artesian in nature, which accounts for their locations. Open-system pingos develop primarily in areas of discontinuous permafrost with ground temperatures close to 0°C, as a balance has to be maintained between the rate of water flow and the freezing rate. Too high a rate of water flow and injection will lead to rupture of the pingo; too high a rate of freezing will seal off the water flow and prevent continued pingo growth. A few open-system pingos are known in areas of continuous permafrost where taliks provide conduits for the artesian water supply. Overall, the mechanisms involved in their formation remain poorly understood. Open-system pingos tend to be smaller than closed-system pingos.

The world's greatest concentration of closed-system pingos is found in the Mackenzie Delta region of northwest Canada, where some 1450 are known. They are also found in northern Alaska, on the islands of the Canadian Arctic Archipelago, and in much lesser numbers elsewhere in northern Canada. In Asia, they occur along the north coastal regions of Russia, and are most common in the northern parts of West Siberia. Open-system pingos, first described from Svalbard, also occur in the ice-free areas of Greenland and the mountainous regions of northern Russia. In North America, they are most common in the Yukon-Tanana lowlands of central Alaska and in central Yukon; a few are known for other regions of northern Canada. In northwestern North America, the majority of pingos are found in areas that were unglaciated during the Wisconsinan glaciation.

Should the inflow of water cease, a pingo will stop growing. For a closed-system pingo, this will normally occur when the underlying talik is fully frozen and, at this point, the size of the pingo will be proportional to the original volume of the talik. Open-system pingos are vulnerable to changes in either the water flow rate or the freezing rate, and so may cease to grow even as a result of a minor change in climate affecting these rates; equally, however, growth may be resumed should the situation change.

All pingos, whether actively growing or not, are subject to the normal processes of weathering and erosion that affect all slopes in Arctic regions. Minor landslides can occur on the side slopes of rapidly growing pingos. Continued growth of a pingo will generally lead to rupture of the soil and vegetation cover across the summit. Should this expose the ice core, melting of the ice and thawing of the surrounding soil can lead to complete collapse of the pingo. Collapsed pingos are recognizable by their ringed shape; the resulting crater will often contain its own residual pond. Pingos near shorelines are also subject to erosion resulting from shoreline retreat and wave action.

As with all permafrost features, pingos are essentially thermal phenomena. As such, they are influenced by changes in climate. A warmer or wetter period may lead to the drainage of Arctic lakes and so initiate the development of new pingos. Such conditions may also contribute to the erosion and collapse of extant pingos. A cooler or dryer period is likely to have the opposite effect. The overall effects of long-term changes of climate on pingos are unpredictable in detail.

Pingolike features on the seabed of the Beaufort Sea continental shelf, once thought to be submarine pingos, have been determined to be the result of natural gas venting and are not related to true pingos, which are found only on land.

J.A. HEGINBOTTOM

See also **Ground Ice; Permafrost**

Further Reading

Brown, J., O.J. Ferrians Jr., J.A. Heginbottom & E.S. Melnikov, *Circum-Arctic Map of Permafrost and Ground Ice Conditions*, Washington, District of Columbia: US Geological Survey, for the International Permafrost Association, USGS Circum-Pacific Map Series, Map CP-45, scale 1:10,000,000, 1997

French, H.M., *The Periglacial Environment* (2nd edition), Harlow, Essex and New York: Longman

Mackay, J. Ross, "Pingos of the Tuktoyaktuk Peninsula Area, Northwest Territories." *Géographie physique et Quaternaire*, XXXIII (1) (1979): 3–61

———, "Pingo growth and collapse, Tuktoyaktuk Peninsula Area, Western Arctic Coast, Canada: A long-term field study." *Géographie physique et Quaternaire*, 52 (3) (1998): 271–323

van Everdingen, Robert O. (compiler and editor), *Multi-Language Glossary of Permafrost and Ground-Ice Terms*, International Permafrost Association, 1998 (available in 16 sections from The Arctic Institute of North America, The University of Calgary, Calgary, Alberta, Canada, T2N 1N4)

Washburn, A.L., *Geocryology*, London: Edward Arnold and New York: Wiley, 1979

Yershov, E.D., *General Geocryology*, Cambridge and New York: Cambridge University Press, 1998

PINKFOOTED GOOSE

The pinkfooted goose (*Anser brachyrhynchus*, or *Nerleq siggukitsoq* in Greenlandic) breeds in the Arctic region only in Iceland, East Greenland, and Svalbard. It is not divided in to subspecies, but is separated into two "flyway" populations according to the breeding areas in Iceland/Greenland and Svalbard. It is a medium-sized goose species of 60–75 cm from bill to tail and a weight of 2–3 kg. The goose has a brown and gray plumage, a compact dark brown head, and a short black and pink bill. The legs are pink. Young birds are grayish-brown with beige legs.

The breeding habitats in Iceland and Greenland are inland oasis areas, cliffs, riverbanks, lush meadows, and islands. In Svalbard, some geese breed on inland tundra, but most nest on islets off the coast, and high nest concentrations are found on cliffs beneath grassy slopes close to seabird colonies.

The pinkfooted goose migrates to wintering grounds in Scotland and England (Iceland/Greenland population), and Belgium, the Netherlands and Denmark (Svalbard population). The winter habitats are today grasslands, stubble fields, winter cereal fields, and root crops. In former days, the geese wintered on saltmarshes and seminatural grasslands. The geese roost in estuaries, reservoirs, and brackish ponds, but in Belgium they often stay on the feeding grounds at night.

The two flyway populations are increasing in number, and the total wintering population was estimated at about 290,000 birds in 1994–1997. The Iceland/Greenland population is by far the largest, with 250,000 birds.

In mild winters, pinkfooted geese leave the southern parts of their wintering grounds and build up concentrations in northern Britain and Denmark. These northward movements are probably a response to grass growth, since fresh grass has higher protein content and less fiber than older leaves. From mid-April, the geese migrate North to staging areas in either southern lowlands in Iceland or coastal sites in central and northern Norway. The geese stage at the stopover sites for two to three weeks, where they build up stores of fat and nutrients on grasslands, stubble fields, and saltmarshes. The breeding grounds are reached in mid- to late May and egg laying commences from late May to early June. The pinkfooted geese breeding in East Greenland and Svalbard migrate about 3000 km, whereas Iceland breeding birds migrate some 1500 km.

It was previously thought that most geese build up their condition only on the wintering grounds, but recent studies have shown that the geese must feed on or near the breeding grounds to be able to breed successfully. The female goose needs fat and especially protein to produce a full clutch of four to five eggs. The nest is a shallow depression lined with down, feathers, and grass. Here, the female alone incubates the clutch for 26–28 days. The pinkfooted goose breeds in either colonies, where nests are usually more then 50 m apart, or in solitary nesting. In colony-breeding geese, the female leaves the nest for on average 4% of her time on short feeding trips. These trips are not sufficient to maintain her body mass and the female might lose up to 40% of her body mass by the end of incubation. The male goose stays vigilant through most of the incubation period, but has some time to feed. When the goslings are hatched, the male has lost about 20% of his weight, but he continues to lose weight because he must stay vigilant to defend the goslings from predators. In eastern Iceland, tussock nesting is scarce and a high proportion of the nests are accessible to Arctic foxes (*Alopex lagopus*).

After hatching, families tend to aggregate into groups of several hundreds at the time when adults become flightless. In the first weeks after hatching, the goslings feed more on herbs and horsetail *Equisetum* than adults. Later, the geese feed almost exclusively on sedges and grasses. The goslings are able to fly when they are seven to eight weeks old.

Like other goose species, the pinkfooted geese have only one body molt every year, and the most conspicuous is the wing molt. The duration of the wing molt is three to four weeks, and the development of the flying feathers is more rapid than in many duck species, indicating an adaptation in Arctic breeding goose species to the short Arctic summer. Immature geese and failed breeding birds molt in July, breeding birds about two weeks later. In the Svalbard population, the geese aggregate to molt in flocks of several hundreds, both inside the breeding range and outside in eastern and northern parts of Svalbard. Many thousands of nonbreeding birds migrate from Iceland to molt in Northeast Greenland. They arrive in Greenland from late June, and molting flocks have recently been observed as far North as in Peary Land (83° N). In the southernmost part of the molting range (70° N), the pinkfooted goose competes successfully with the barnacle goose *Branta leucopsis* for the limited food resources. The molting sites contain refuge lakes or rivers, and abundant food resources. During molt, up to one-third of the total body protein content is shed. Despite this loss over a relatively short period, geese are able to meet their energy and protein demands by moderate feeding, and do not have to deplete their energy and nutrient reserves. During this period, proteins are degraded from the breast muscles and build into leg muscles. These changes are ascribed to disuse-use of the muscle groups.

The autumn migration from Greenland starts in late August toward Iceland to join the pinkfooted geese here. Probably the geese do not stay in Iceland for long and they arrive in Britain in late August and mid-September. The Svalbard geese pass through Norway from mid-September to mid-October, and some flocks stage in central Norway during the same period.

The pinkfooted goose is heavily hunted with annual goose bags of about 500 birds in Greenland, 10,000 in Iceland, and 20,000 in Britain. In Svalbard and Norway, about 1000 birds are shot annually, and about 2000 in Denmark. Hunting is banned in the Netherlands and Belgium. Local people in Iceland and Greenland gather some eggs. In Greenlandic myths, geese have the ability to give back sight to blinded people by squirting people's eyes with their feces.

CHRISTIAN M. GLAHDER

Further Reading

Batt, B.D.J., A.D. Afton, M.G. Anderson, C.D. Ankney, D.H. Johnson, J.A. Kadlec & G.L. Krapu (editors), *Ecology and Management of Breeding Waterfowl*, Minnesota: University of Minnesota Press, 1992

Cramp, Stanley & K.E.L. Simmons (editors), *Handbook of Birds of Europe, the Middle East, and North Africa: The Birds of the Western Palearctic*, Volume 1, Oxford: Oxford University Press, 1977

del Hoyo, Josep, Andrew Elliott & Jordi Sargatal (editors), *Handbook of the Birds of the World,* Volume 1, Barcelona: Lynx Edicions, 1992

Madsen, Jesper, Gill Craknell & Tony Fox (editors), *Goose Populations of the Western Palearctic: A Review of Status and Distribution*, Wageningen: Wetlands International; Denmark, Rönde: National Environmental Research Institute, 1999

Owen, Myrfyn, *Wild Geese of the World: Their Life History and Ecology*, London: Batsford, 1980

Rose, P.M. & D.A. Scott (compilers), *Waterfowl Population Estimates* (2nd edition), Wageningen: Wetlands International, 1997

Salomonsen, Finn, *Grønlands Fugle: The Birds of Greenland*, Copenhagen: Munksgaard, 1950

———, "The molt migration." *Wildfowl*, 19 (1968): 5–24

PITSEOLAK, PETER

Peter Pitseolak, a 20th-century Canadian Inuit photographer, artist, and writer, was widely known as Baffin Island's first indigenous photographer. His work reflects a lifelong dedication to cultural preservation, documenting the stories and practices of Inuit life, which were rapidly disappearing in his lifetime.

Pitseolak departed sharply from the view expressed by many Inuit and Qallunaat (non-Inuit) that respect for oral cultural traditions means maintaining them in preference to written texts. Like many Inuit in Greenland, Pitseolak stressed the importance of writing and literacy as companions (rather than alternatives) to oral storytelling and record keeping. Pitseolak expressed regret that the Inuit had not developed written texts to enable them to document and record their own lives and traditions earlier in their history.

Pitseolak conceived of himself as a social and cultural historian recording a rapidly changing way of life. He wrote in the syllabics that missionaries had developed for Inuit of this region (unlike the Roman orthography used in Greenland) and richly illustrated his work with drawings, carvings, and photographs. The 1975 book *People from Our Side* documents Pitseolak's early life experiences. Compiled and published (two years after his death) by Dorothy Harley Eber, a Montreal writer specializing in oral history, photography, and documentary reportage, it comprises Pitseolak's written narrative and an interview conducted by Eber. His narrative is one of the few records of early 20th-century Inuit life, and the only account that presents an Inuk's point of view—his story, situated firmly in the context of his community and his life.

Pitseolak spent his childhood in nomadic camps. As an adult, he observed and documented the experiences of Inuit who were hosting an increasing array of missionaries and fur traders from southern North America and Europe, Canadian government officials, educators, and other newcomers and visitors. Pitseolak's writing and photography portrayed the legal and administrative changes brought about by Canadian and Northwest Territories representatives and the negative and positive outcomes of the myriad incursions, shifts, and changes. He welcomed the arrival of schools and community education programs, but was distressed by the devastating effects on Inuit, including the alcohol so many visitors brought with them.

Pitseolak became fluent in the syllabic writing system that missionaries had adapted for Inuktitut, the Inuit language, from a system originally created for Cree people. He kept a diary; he began taking photographs only when a *Qallunaaq* visitor, afraid to get close enough to photograph a polar bear, asked for his help. Pitseolak's daughter, Kooyoo Ottochie, claimed that her father's interest in photographing his own people, the *Seekooseelakmiut*, may have been sparked by his early encounter with the filmmaker Robert Flaherty. Flaherty visited Baffin Island in 1913 and 1914 and took extensive still photographs. Pitseolak was about 12 at the time, and remembered what may well have been a formative experience. Certainly, his own photographic work and historical research provide an insider's alternative to Flaherty's visitor's-eye view of Inuit camp life.

After acquiring his own camera in the early 1940s, Pitseolak began photographing daily life in Inuit camps, a way of life he knew would be forever changed by the increasing movement of Inuit into settlements and the emergence of schools and of wage labor. Pitseolak and his wife Aggeok taught themselves to develop film at home, adapting darkroom techniques to the challenging requirements of the Arctic climate. Aggeok was an active partner who did a great deal of the developing and printing of negatives and was also at home with a camera. She took a famous image of Pitseolak around 1946 standing in the snow beside his beloved "122" camera. The designation "122" reflects his habit of naming cameras by the film they took rather than the brand name.

Pitseolak's work is attributed to the Late Historic Period of Inuit art. Although known primarily as a photographer, he merits broader recognition. Pitseolak began working in watercolor 20 years before James and Alma Houston arrived with art supplies in Cape Dorset, having purchased paints and supplies from a Hudson's Bay Company trader in 1939 (Hessel, 1998: 26). There was virtually no experimentation with paint in Cape Dorset until the establishment of the Cape Dorset cooperative in the 1970s. Even today, in the midst of increasing excellence in Inuit video and film (including Zacharias Kunuk's award-winning 2001 feature film, *Atanarjuat*), there are few Inuit still photographers. About 2000 of Pitseolak and Aggeok's negatives dating from the 1940s to the 1960s are housed in the Notman Archives of the McCord Museum at McGill University, Montreal.

Biography

Peter Pitseolak was born in November 1902 on Nottingham Island in the Canadian eastern Arctic, then part of the Northwest Territories (now Nunavut). His father was Inukjuarjuk and his mother was Kooyoo (the third of Inukjuarjuk's four wives). Peter Pitseolak was the youngest of Kooyoo and Inukjuarjuk's eight children: sisters Nee, Annie, and Pee, and brothers Echalook Joanasee, Paulasie, Pootoogook, and Eetoolook. He had nine half-siblings: sisters Eteriak, Atsutoongwa, Eleeshushee, and Shovegar, and brothers Petalosie, Tukiki, Kavavow, and a brother and sibling whose names are not known.

On July 15 1923, he married Annie in Lake Harbour. In 1941, after her death, he began living with Aggeok, who became his second wife and lifelong collaborator, developing and printing most of his photographs and taking many of her own. Pitseolak had six children: Udluriak and Rebecca Kooyoo, his daughters with Annie; a daughter, Mary, with Nyla of Lake Harbour; and with Aggeok, an adopted daughter, Annie, son, Mark Tapungai, and Ashevak, Aggeok's son from her first marriage. Peter Pitseolak died on September 30, 1973, having spent most of his life on south Baffin Island. Aggeok died in 1977.

VALERIE ALIA

See also **Images of Indigenous Peoples; Kenojuak**

Further Reading

Hessel, Ingo, *Inuit Art*, Vancouver and Toronto: Douglas and McIntyre, 1998

Petrone, Penny (editor), *Northern Voices: Inuit Writing in English*, Toronto, Buffalo, and London: University of Toronto Press, 1988

Pitseolak, Peter, *Peter Pitseolak's Escape from Death*, edited by Dorothy Eber, Toronto: McClelland and Stewart, 1977

Pitseolak, Peter & Dorothy Harley Eber, *People from Our Side: A Life Story with Photographs and Oral Biography*, translated by Ann Hanson, Edmonton: Hurtig Publishers, 1975 [Reprinted with a new preface by Dorothy Harley Eber, Montreal and Kingston: McGill-Queen's University Press, 1993]

PIUGAATTUK, NOAH

Noah Urunaaluk Piugaattuk was born around 1900 in a small, seasonal hunting camp at Sarvva, on the Melville Peninsula, some 55 km south of Igloolik Island. His early years were spent in isolated camps on the shores and islands of the northern Foxe Basin, where he mastered the skills that were to make him a prominent hunter and leader. He was about 12 years old when he first met a *qallunaaq* (the term applied by Inuit to describe white Europeans or North Americans), Alfred Tremblay—a prospector with Joseph Bernier's Northern Baffin Island gold-searching expedition—who reached Igloolik from the Pond Inlet area with his Inuit guides in 1913,

Noah Piugaattuk photographed in Nunavut, Canada.
Copyright Bryan and Cherry Alexander Photography

after a bitterly cold and difficult journey. Tremblay's bizarre expression of *qallunaaq* possessiveness made a lasting impression on the young Piugaattuk who, years later, recalled the prospector likening Igloolik Island to a wild animal, saying it was extremely difficult to catch.

Baptized in 1942 by John Turner, an Anglican priest at the missionary outpost of Moffet Inlet, situated between Igloolik and Arctic Bay, Piugaattuk became one of the region's staunchest Christians. He assisted Turner in his missionary work throughout the region and beyond, guiding him on many lengthy, often hazardous, dog team journeys, one as far west as King William Island in 1942, where they faced hostility from powerful Netsilik shamans. When Turner died in 1947 after accidentally shooting himself while seal hunting at Moffet Inlet, Piugaattuk strongly suspected the malevolent involvement of these same shamans bent on thwarting the spread of Christianity.

For many years, Piugaattuk lived on Jens Munk Island, at Kapuiviit, one of the largest Inuit habitations in the Igloolik area. Here, his abilities as a hunter, leader, and organizer ensured that his people and others in nearby camps were never seriously in want, even in times of scarcity. Throughout this period, he also served as the region's Anglican catechist until a permanent mission was established in Igloolik in 1959.

Moving to the government-administered settlement of Igloolik in the late 1960s, Piugaattuk gradually withdrew from active hunting. He became a tireless exponent and teacher of Inuit drum dancing, performing in various locations across the Arctic and in southern Canada. He was well known for his crafting of traditional Inuit instruments and tools, especially drums, and bows and arrows manufactured from caribou antler. Examples of his work are found in the Royal Ontario Museum (Toronto) and in the British Museum (London). Piugaattuk's knowledge of hunting techniques, animal migrations, and weather conditions was widely respected and frequently sought. He was especially instructive on how to survive polar bear attacks, having done so on a number of occasions in his younger years. He was also a familiar voice on Igloolik's community radio offering advice and comment on various topics ranging from hunting to social behavior.

Piugaattuk's acute sense of being one of the last living links to a vanished way of life—his early years predated the introduction of both the rifle and Christianity to the region—led him to communicate his vast experience and knowledge of the past. In particular, during the final decade of his life, he was a founding member and an active supporter of Igloolik's Inullariit Elders Society, which embarked on a major oral history project in 1986. Piugaattuk contributed almost 80 h of audiotaped interviews to the project, covering such diverse subjects as traditional Inuit law, religious ritual, games and recreation, Inuit music, stone and antler implement manufacture, kayak construction, weather prediction, and astronomy. His original interviews, together with their English translations, are in the archives of the Inullariit Society at the Igloolik Research Centre. The Prince of Wales Northern Heritage Centre in Yellowknife also accessioned copies of this material. Toward the end of his life, Piugaattuk appeared on Inuit television to audiences across Nunavut and Nunavik (Arctic Québec) through numerous video interviews he recorded on Inuit cultural themes for the Inuit Broadcasting Corporation and the regional service of the Canadian Broadcasting Corporation.

Piugaattuk assisted and encouraged many researchers seeking to record Inuit traditions and oral history. He believed passionately that Inuit knowledge should be recorded, translated, and disseminated as widely as possible to enhance the understanding and appreciation of Inuit culture. Through his wide-ranging interviews, he contributed to many studies, theses, and publications centered on Iglulingmiut society. These included,, for example, a legal-anthropological study by W.C.E. Rasing

(1994), Frédéric Laugrand's examination of *siqqi-tirniq*—a ritual formerly practiced by Inuit when converting from shamanism to Christianity—(1997), and John MacDonald's study of Inuit astronomy and navigation (1998).

The year before his death, Piugaattuk publicly voiced his opinion that bowhead whale numbers around Igloolik had increased to the point where one might be taken without threatening the recovery of the species. He longed to taste *maktaq* (the much-prized edible whale skin) again, regardless of the ban on bowhead hunting in effect since 1979. His request did not go unheeded. In September 1994, Piugaattuk's son-in-law and two grandsons killed a young bowhead whale they happened to encounter while seal hunting near Igloolik Island. The hunters were charged under the federal Fisheries Act, and roundly criticized by the Nunavut Wildlife Management Board, which at the time was in negotiation with the federal Department of Fisheries and Oceans for a permit for Inuit to legally hunt a bowhead. However, an outpouring of public sympathy and support for the hunters emerged from all across Nunavut. The charges against them were dropped in 1996—prosecution being considered not in the public interest—and in that same year, the territory's first legally sanctioned bowhead hunt took place at Repulse Bay. Piugaattuk's longing for a last taste of *maktaq* might have sparked a succession of events leading to, or at least hastening, the symbolic restoration of Inuit bowhead hunting rights in Nunavut.

Biography

Noah Urunaaluk Piugaattuk was born at Sarvva, on the northern Melville Peninsula, Nunavut, Canada, around 1900. He was raised by his parents, Inuaraq and Ilupaalik, and spent his formative years in seasonal hunting camps in the northern Foxe Basin. A renowned traveler and dog team driver, Piugaattuk guided the area's first Anglican Missionary on many lengthy journeys around Northern Baffin Island during the 1940s. He spent much of his adult life as leader of a major Inuit camp at Kapuiviit on Jens Munk Island, where he also served as the community's Anglican catechist. He was married to Elisabeth Tatiggat: they had two daughters, Pittaaluk and Uirnngut, and three sons, Maliki, Qaunnaq, and Palluq. He moved to Igloolik in the late1960s, where he became a tireless advocate for Inuit language and culture, and was especially well known as an exemplar of traditional music and drum dancing. As principal contributor to the Igloolik Oral History Project, he added considerably to the corpus of recorded Inuit traditional knowledge in the Canadian Eastern Arctic.

He also collaborated generously with many academic researchers, whose work was greatly enriched by his vast knowledge of Inuit traditions and history. Piugaattuk died in Igloolik on August 31, 1995.

JOHN MACDONALD

See also **Iglookik**

Further Reading

Damas, David, *Igluligmiut Kinship and Local Groupings: A Structural Approach*, Ottawa: National Museum of Canada (Bulletin 196), 1963
Flint, Maurice, S., *Operation Canon*, London: The Bible Churchmen's Missionary Society, 1949
Hay, Keith (editor), *Final Report of the Inuit Bowhead Knowledge Study*, Iqaluit: Nunavut Wildlife Management Board, 2000
Høgh, Helle, "Bowhead Whale Hunting in Nunavut: A Symbol of Self-Government." In *Nunavut, Inuit Regain Control of Their Lands and their Lives*, edited by Jens Dahl, Jack Hicks & Peter Jull, Copenhagen: International Work Group for Indigenous Affairs, 2000
Laugrand, Frédéric, "*Le siqqitiq*: renouvellement religieux et premier rituel de conversion chez les Inuit du nord de la Terre de Baffin." *Études Inuit*, 21 (1–2) (1997): 101–140
MacDonald, John, "Tauvijjuaq: the great darkness." *Inuit Art Quarterly*, 8(2) (1993) 18–35
———, *The Arctic Sky—Inuit Astronomy, Star Lore, and Legend*, Iqaluit and Toronto: Nunavut Research Institute and the Royal Ontario Museum, 1998
Malaurie, Jean, *The Last Kings of Thule*, New York: E.P. Dutton, 1982
Rowley, Graham W., *Cold Comfort—My Love Affair with the Arctic*, Montreal and Kingston: McGill-Queen's University Press, 1996
Tremblay, Alfred, *Cruise of the Minnie Maud—Arctic Seas and Hudson Bay 1910–1911 and 1912–1913*, Québec: The Arctic Exchange and Publishing Limited, 1921
Tungilik, Victor & Rachel Uyarasuk, *The Transition to Christianity, Volume 1, Inuit Perspectives on the 20th Century*, edited by Jarich Oosten & Frédéric Laugrand, Iqaluit: Nunavut Arctic College, Language and Culture Program, 1999

PLACE-NAMES

Place-names play an important role in shaping the sense of place and the representation of a land. The study of place-names is called toponymy, and is of particular interest to Arctic researchers. In the Arctic, several unconnected toponymic sets usually coexist: the toponymic set of the local indigenous peoples; that of the explorers, which has become the official one; and the toponymic sets of other people who came to the Arctic (whalers, trappers, and settlers).

Indigenous place-name sets are the most extensive. Ludger Müller-Wille shows that indigenous place-names are true toponymic systems—all names are related and connected and make a whole picture that can be of use in many ways (2000). Place-names are often presented as a key element of peoples' geographic knowledge because of their descriptive qualities. Related to land use and movements, place-names are seen as traveling helpers. However, Béatrice Collignon's research among Inuit has shown that although useful to the traveler, toponymy is not essential for that purpose (2004). Traveling knowledge relies mainly on other skills: orientation, spatial reconnaissance, and memorization. Yet, toponymy is always mentioned by elders when discussing cultural preservation. Place-names are crucial, not for movement and survival, but for building a sound relationship among the various elements—including humans beings—of the living environment of the past, present, and future, so that cultures may flourish. They ensure the continuation of a specific perception and understanding of spaces and places through names that are a commentary on the land. Descriptions concentrate on the physical qualities of a place (feature's definition, shape, color, etc., as with *Aqiarualuk* meaning "The shape of a big stomach") or on its human characteristics (daily camp-life, hunting activities, travels, such as *Havviurvik,* i.e., "The place to make knives"). Variations in place-names' densities reflect the importance of the various parts of the land in people's lives, usually indicating a wide use of complementary areas, inland and along the coastline. With other elements of the oral tradition, place-names function as the guardians of Arctic peoples' memory, the anchor points of their history, through anecdotal toponyms—fixing in memory an incident, a strong emotion, a name—as well as through those that recount the use of a place, or just describe it. Mark Nuttall writes of the "hidden meaning" of place-names and refers to named landscapes as "memoryscapes" (1991).

Explorers' toponymic sets do not reflect such a depth of meaning and seldom exhibit the distinctive descriptive character of indigenous place-name sets. They also reflect a narrower comprehension of the land, concentrating along the trails followed for exploration such as major valleys and coastlines. Here, place-names belong to three categories: usage names ("Anchor Bay," "Freshwater Bay"), commemorative names, and names that refer to emotions. The latter, with toponyms such as "Dismal Lakes" or "Repulse Bay," emphasize feelings related to the image of the Arctic as a harsh and dangerous environment: fear, desperation, coldness, solitude, starvation, rarely hope and never joy. However, most explorers' names are commemorative, given in honor of those who sponsored the expedition: kings, queens, and princes, as well as private societies such as the geographical societies that flourished in the 19th century (e.g., King

William Island). Expedition commanders in chief and lieutenants, vessel captains, cooks, etc., have also left their names to numerous features: bays, coves, capes, and points (e.g., Stefansson Island, Cape Krusenstein, Jago Bay). These toponymic sets reflect a mind frame in which the Arctic was a barren piece of land and waters waiting to be conquered and claimed by imperialist states. Such names are not meant to transmit knowledge about the place, but rather to recreate a sense of the Western world left behind, with its familiar hierarchies of kings, queens and princes, admirals, and captains. There is also a need to express to those who will read the map in the comfort of their reading rooms the difficulties endured by those explorers who ventured into this alien and frozen world. Place-names also reinforce a narrative about the Arctic from which further expeditions will be organized. Although this narrative appears quite negative, it must be replaced in the Romantic context of 19th-century Western (including Russian) culture that was fascinated with all feelings, and especially dark ones. A toponym such as "Desperation Cove" is to be considered against this specific cultural framework. In this toponymic narrative, the inhabitants of the Arctic are ignored. Although explorers valued indigenous peoples' mapping skills, most of them despised their place-names. They argued that indigenous place-names meant nothing in the West and so were difficult to remember, or that they were hard to pronounce, or too long to print on small maps. While never mentioned, geopolitics was of central concern: recognition of local toponymy would give recognition to the local peoples, something incompatible with the imperialist agenda and the spirit of discovery.

Whalers' toponymic sets demonstrate a restricted knowledge that is concentrated on sea channels and shores. Although whalers were active in place naming, a large part of their toponyms disappeared when they ceased to exploit Arctic waters. Very few were integrated into either the "official" toponymic system of the imperialist authority or that of the local peoples. Their place-names focused on petty things and reflected their ordinary world: names of whiskey brands were popular, as well as "coffee point" and so on, and those expressing feelings of suffering, fear, and homesickness. Trappers and settlers exhibited a deeper commitment to Arctic lands; for this reason, their toponymic systems are fairly close to those of the indigenous peoples. Yet, stemming from a cultural background alien to the Arctic, they express a different relationship with the land, a different understanding of it, and a different sense of place and identity.

Each toponymic set reflected the culture of the name givers, had its own use, and was called upon in its own cultural context. The existence of other sets (among indigenous peoples, explorers and their colonial powers, trappers, whalers, etc.) was either ignored or despised. However, there came a time (different in the various parts of the Arctic) when local people were confronted by the "official" alien toponymy and expected by foreigners to refer to it. The latter, often the dominant or colonial power, could enforce its own place-name system because it was written down. Realizing that maps of their own land bore strange names that did not make sense to them was a shock to the indigenous peoples and, in many parts of the Arctic, the request to see indigenous place-names officially recognized and to replace the foreign ones grew stronger from the early 1970s. In the following decades, local toponymic surveys multiplied. As indigenous peoples gain more control over their land, indigenous place-names slowly replace alien ones, inscribing a crucial part of the Arctic peoples' cultural heritage in the maps.

BÉATRICE COLLIGNON

See also **Naming**

Further Reading

Collignon, Béatrice, *Understanding Arctic Environment: The Inuinnait Knowledge of Their Land* (working title), Edmonton: CCI Press, University of Alberta, 2004 [translated from the French edition, Paris: L'Harmattan, 1996]

Müller-Wille, Ludger, *Inuttitut Nunait Atingitta Katirsutauningit Nunavimmi (Kupaimmi, Kanatami)/ Gazetteer of Inuit Place Names in Nunavik (Québec, Canada)/Répertoire toponymique Inuit du Nunavik (Québec, Canada)*, Inukjuak: Institut Culturel Avataq, 1987

———, "Nunavut Place Names and Self-determination: Some Reflections." In *Nunavut, Inuit Regain Control of their Lands and Their Lives*, edited by J. Dahl, J. Hicks & P. Jull, Copenhagen: IWGIA, 2000

Nuttall, Mark, "Memoryscape: a sense of locality in Northwest Greenland." *North Atlantic Studies*, 1(2) (1991): 39–51

Pitkänen, Liisa Ritva & Kaija Mallat (editors), *You Name it. Perspectives on Onomastic Research*, Helsinki: Finnish Literature Society (Studia Fennica, Linguistica 7), 1997

PLANKTON

Plankton includes all organisms suspended in the water body of the ocean and drifting with the currents. Many of these organisms have the ability to move, but motion is mainly restricted to the vertical axis. Traditionally, plankton is divided into the categories phytoplankton (unicellular algal plants) and zooplankton (microscopic drifting animals). The first description dates back to the early Arctic explorations during, for example, Fridtjof Nansen's *Fram* drift in 1893–1896. Since the 1970s, bacteria (bacterioplankton), fungi (mycoplankton), and most recently viruses (virioplankton) have been studied in the Arctic. Due to

practical reasons, many scientific studies use size classes, ranging from femto- to megaplankton (see Table 1), which are all represented in the Arctic. Besides the truly planktonic organisms (holoplankton), some inhabitants of the seafloor, for example, crustaceans and echinoderms, have pelagic juvenile stages for species distribution (meroplankton). Those temporary planktonic inhabitants are frequently found on the shallow Arctic shelves during the summer.

Arctic plankton is physiologically adapted to grow at cold water temperatures down to $-1.8°C$ and to the strong seasonality of light with several months of long dark winter. Algal cells are shade-adapted and thus able to photosynthesize at light levels about one order of magnitude below threshold intensities for taxa living in tropical seas. The major primary producers in Arctic waters are diatoms and flagellates. Cyanobacteria, which contribute large fractions of primary production in tropical and temperate waters, are nearly absent from the Arctic. While algal biomass (indicated by the pigment chlorophyll a) is very low in winter (less than 0.1 µg Chl a l^{-1}), high biomass of phytoplankton (more than 4 µg Chl a l^{-1}—called phytoplankton blooms—is found in spring and summer mainly at the marginal sea ice zone of the Arctic shelves. Biomass remains low in the central Arctic Ocean throughout the year due to the low light intensities below the permanent sea ice cover. Dominant taxa in Arctic blooms are chain-forming diatoms (e.g., *Thalassiosira* spp., *Chaetoceros* spp.) and the colony-forming haptophyte *Phaeocystis pouchetii*, and cell concentrations exceed 10^6 cells l^{-1}. The major primary consumers of phytoplankton in Arctic waters are herbivorous copepods, *Calanus* spp. being the major genus. The copepods overwinter at great water depths down to below 1000 m. In spring, they reproduce and both juveniles and adults return to the surface waters to feed on the phytoplankton blooms. The rich food resources during this time allow the copepods to accumulate high lipid concentrations in a lipid sac. This is used for overwintering and reproduction in the following spring. The lipid-rich zooplankton organisms are the major food source for whales (e.g., the bowhead whale *Balaena mysticetus*) and birds (e.g., auks like *Alle alle*), which migrate to Arctic waters to feed during the short polar summer. Recent studies revealed that nutrients (mainly nitrogen) can periodically limit diatom growth on the Arctic shelves in summer and autumn. Bacterial mineralization thus becomes an important factor determining the production of organic carbon during nutrient limitation. The bacterioplankton is consumed by heterotrophic flagellates and mixotrophic ciliates as important components of the microbial network.

ROLF GRADINGER

TABLE 1. Definition of size classes and important representatives in Arctic waters

Size category	Size range	Arctic representatives
Femtoplankton	0.02–0.2 µm	Viruses
Picoplankton	0.2–2 µm	Bacteria, picoalgae (mainly prasinophytes), heterotrophic flagellates
Nanoplankton	2–20 µm	Algae (single-celled diatoms, flagellates), fungi, heterotrophic flagellates
Microplankton	20–200 µm	Algae (large single-celled and chain-forming diatoms, flagellates), heterotrophic flagellates, heterotrophic and mixotrophic ciliates
Mesoplankton	0.2–20 mm	Algae (chain-forming diatoms, *Phaeocystis pouchetii*), ciliates, metazoa (mainly herbivorous copepods)
Macroplankton	2–20 cm	Metazoa (ctenophores, amphipods, euphausiids)
Megaplankton	20–200 cm	Metazoa (scyphozoa)

See also **Food Chains; Food Webs, Marine; Primary Production, Marine**

Further Reading

Gosselin, M., M. Levasseur, P.A. Wheeler, R.A. Horner & B.C. Booth, "New measurements of phytoplankton and ice algal production in the Arctic Ocean." *Deep-Sea Research*, 44 (1997): 1623–1644

Gradinger, R. & M. Spindler, "Coupled Ecosystems in the Ice-Covered Arctic Ocean." In *Operational Oceanography. The Challenge for European Co-operation*, edited by J.H. Stel, J.C. Borst, L.J. Droppert & J.V.D. Meulen, Amsterdam: Elsevier Science, 1997, pp. 385–390

Herman, Y., *The Arctic Seas. Climatology, Oceanography, Geology and Biology*, New York: Reinhold, 1989

Legendre, L., S.F. Ackley, G.S. Dieckmann, B. Gulliksen, R. Horner, T. Hoshiai, I.A. Melnikov, W.S. Reeburgh, M. Spindler & C.W. Sullivan, "Ecology of sea ice biota. 2. Global significance." *Polar Biology*, 12(1992): 429–444

Mumm, N., H. Auel, H. Hanssen, W. Hagen, C. Richter & H.J. Hirche, "Breaking the ice: Large-scale distribution of meso-zooplankton after a decade of Arctic and transpolar cruises." *Polar Biology*, 20 (1998): 189–197

Parsons, T.R., M. Takahashi & B. Hargrave, *Biological Oceanographic Processes*, Oxford: Pergamon Press, 1984

Smith Jr., W.O., *Polar Oceanography, Parts A and B*, San Diego: Academic Press, 1990

PLANT-ANIMAL INTERACTIONS

The group of vertebrate grazer (herbivore) species inhabiting Arctic tundra and polar desert habitats has a low diversity with just over 50 species, of which about 20 species are birds, particularly geese. Similarly, invertebrate herbivores are impoverished, but with probably just under 1000 species by far exceeds the number of vertebrate grazers. The invertebrates encompass a wide range of feeding modes, including species consuming aboveground plant parts (sap suckers, leaf chewers) as well as root feeders (particularly crane flies), but their collective impact on plants is poorly understood. Pollination by insects is likely to be of limited importance as plant reproduction is largely vegetative (*see* **Plant Pollination and Reproduction**).

Vertebrate herbivores occur at densities that vary greatly through time, both within years (due to seasonal migration and reproduction) and between years (cyclic populations of, for instance, lemming species). Herbivore densities also differ markedly between areas, with very high densities in some places (e.g., around goose colonies), whereas other parts of the Arctic are virtually free of grazing (e.g., isolated High Arctic islands).

The density of grazers is constrained by both summer and winter conditions. Most grazers, notably geese, overwinter in warmer climes, thereby avoiding long periods of food scarcity and low temperatures. Few species, including invertebrates, have developed specific physiological and behavioral adaptations to overcome the long and harsh winters. But even populations of well-adapted grazers such as muskox and reindeer/caribou suffer great losses in winters when unfavorable weather results in deep snow or thick ice layers that prevent access to the vegetation.

The relatively short and cool summer growing season offers nutritious food but in limited quantities, and consequently grazers, particularly early in the growing season, may be severely food limited. Food quality is high compared to lower latitude systems, but nevertheless strongly related to the phenological state (seasonal timing of plant growth) of the plants, with young growth produced directly after snowmelt often being most nutritious. Seeds provide a second flush of energetically valuable food items during late summer. In the rugged Arctic landscape, different patches of vegetation become snow free at different times of the season and brief pulses of high-quality forage become available at different times and places. This leads to a strong, predictable, and uneven spatial use by grazers over the summer, with only a few habitats being exploited at any given time.

There is considerable debate as to what extent grazers influence patterns and processes in Arctic vegetation. It is claimed that grazer impact is limited, particularly in systems with relatively low grazer densities. The detection of any grazer-related impact on Arctic systems, however, is greatly impeded by the patchiness of the vegetation at a small spatial scale, and the relatively slow response of plants to any imposed changes. Therefore, even in situations where grazing impact may, in the short term, be negligible, the long-term consequences can be substantial as has become apparent from exclosure studies throughout the Arctic. Because grazers do not use their environment uniformly, they may exert greater pressure on parts of a system than expected based on their average densities year after year, and in so doing greatly modify the vegetation.

Most vascular plants appear relatively resilient to defoliation, probably because of their substantial belowground reserves, which allow rapid recovery. However, lichens and mosses, which in contrast to temperate systems account for most of the Arctic plant species diversity, are more sensitive to grazing. Some of the erect species of lichens (notably *Cetraria* and *Cladonia* spp.), for instance, are strongly suppressed by reindeer/caribou throughout their range. This is perhaps most noticeable in northern Scandinavia, where reindeer husbandry led to the complete suppression of lichens over large areas, having consequences for local reindeer populations. The devastating impact of reindeer on lichens is also evident in natural grazing systems such as in Spitsbergen, where lush carpets of lichens dominate in areas where reindeer have not recovered yet from overhunting in the 19th century.

Grazers have the potential to greatly modify Arctic systems by increasing the rate of nutrient cycling. Feces and urine enhance the critically low levels of plant-available nitrogen and phosphorus, and stimulate belowground bacterial and soil faunal activity. These combined effects can lead to increased plant biomass and a shift in plant species composition toward grasses, sedges, and rushes, which are highly successful in capturing additional soil nutrients. However, nutrients derived from feces can also be intercepted by mosses, which readily take up nutrients with their leaves and stems. The relative success of mosses compared to vascular plants depends on the level of damage caused by grazers. Although mosses are not commonly grazed in temperate areas, a variety of Arctic grazers include these lower plants in their diet. Reindeer and several goose species consume a substantial amount of mosses, and it is a staple food for the widespread and often numerous lemmings. Moreover, mosses are sensitive to trampling, and therefore suffer from the presence of larger grazers. The moss layer acts like a thermal blanket and effectively keeps Arctic soils cool. A reduction in the depth of the moss layer due to grazing or trampling results in an increase in soil temperature from which vascular plants, in particular grasses, benefit. The combined effects of both feces and moss-mediated increase in soil temperature may explain why grasses are more abundant in grazed systems.

These positive feedback mechanisms based on high rates of nutrient turnover mean that grazers manipulate their own food supply, and effectively increase the number of grazers that a system can sustain. However, these mechanisms may be relatively unstable in the long run, and certainly can be disturbed by human interference, allowing whole ecosystems to collapse. This is exemplified by studies on snow geese breeding along the Hudson Bay coast in Canada. Here, geese have greatly benefited from agricultural intensification in the over-wintering areas, allowing a spectacular increase in population size, well beyond the carrying capacity of their traditional breeding areas in the Arctic. In early spring, breeding and staging birds break up the vegetation to grub for roots. This leads to enhanced evapotranspiration of the exposed topsoil during summer and results in hypersaline conditions and the destruction of large parts of the system. Due to the lack of food, the birds have to move on to different areas, which are subsequently also overgrazed causing large-scale destruction of Arctic coastal habitats. Whereas in the past populations of geese were regulated by winter conditions, the system is now heading toward regulation by the availability and condition of the summer habitat.

RENÉ VAN DER WAL

Further Reading

Bazely, D.R. & R.L. Jefferies, "Trophic Interactions in Arctic Ecosystems and the Occurrence of a Terrestrial Trophic Cascade." In *Ecology of Arctic Environments*, edited by S.J. Woodin & M. Marquiss, Oxford: Blackwell Science, 1997

Jefferies, R.L., J. Svoboda, G. Henry, M. Raillard & R. Ruess, "Tundra Grazing Systems and Climate Change." In *Arctic Ecosystems in a Changing Climate*, edited by F.S. Chapin, R.L. Jefferies, J.F. Reynolds, G.R. Shaver & J. Svoboda, San Diego: Academic Press, 1992

Jefferies, R.L., D.R. Klein & G.R. Shaver, "Vertebrate herbivores and northern plant communities: reciprocal influences and responses." *Oikos*, 71 (1994): 193–206

Jonasson, S., T.V. Callaghan, G.R. Shaver & L.A. Nielsen, "Arctic Terrestrial Ecosystems and Ecosystem Function." In *The Arctic: Environment, People, Policy*, edited by M. Nuttall & T.V. Callaghan, Amsterdam: Harwood Academic Publishers, 2000

Matveyeva, N. & Y. Chernov, "Biodiversity of Terrestrial Ecosystems." In *The Arctic: Environment, People, Policy*, edited by M. Nuttall & T.V. Callaghan, Amsterdam: Harwood Academic Publishers, 2000

Van der Wal, R & R. Brooker, Does soil temperature directly regulate the composition of high arctic plant communities? *Journal of Vegetation Science*, 14 (2003): 535–542

PLANT GATHERING

Plants play a vital role for subsistence life in the Arctic. Plants add important variety to the diets of Arctic peoples and are beneficial in producing medicine, insulation, and fuel. Researchers have generally recognized the significance of *gathering* as a vital contribution to the food supply in hunter-gatherer groups, yet, the Arctic has remained the exception to this, since people rely heavily upon a meat diet. Hunting is a vital part of life in many Arctic communities and consequently continues to be the dominant focus of many ethnographies. Thus, the role of gathering has often been overlooked or dismissed. Division of labor among Arctic peoples is commonly divided along gender lines; men usually hunt while women perform other tasks, including gathering. Plants were recognized for the essential role they played for animals, but direct human usage was often overshadowed.

The import of plants should be evaluated in terms of multiple uses and social significance rather than through an exclusive focus on nutritional analysis. The procurement of Arctic plants is a key part of knowing the land. The gathered materials enter into a complex sharing network that reflects peoples' relationships with the land and one another.

Plants were often the main ingredient for the medicinal remedies to heal wounds, treat burns and rashes, as well as cure internal problems such as bladder infections or stomach troubles. Traditional knowledge involving plant usage and preparation for medicines is extensive. Some uses for plants have been replaced by conventional medical practices, while others traditional uses remain commonly practiced.

Some plants were used for more than one purpose, such as for comfort, fuel, sanitation, shelter, and transportation. For example, mosses are an important component of the sod used to build shelters and to make sled runners. Mosses, heather, grasses, and Arctic cotton were particularly important in keeping both people and homes dry and warm. Plants were essential for absorption use in diapers and during menstruation. To ensure warmth, plants acted as an insulating layer between the layers of sealskin on tents. Plants have also been used as insulation by placing them under the skins on the sleeping platform of a snow house, thus keeping the area dry, warm, and comfortable. Mosses and grasses were also an important insulator in boots. Dried grass prevents feet from perspiring, which is important for keeping them warm and to prevent the formation of ice on the outside of the boots. The same plants gathered as insulation may have also been used to tinder a fire or to provide the material for the wick on a *qulliit* (seal oil lamp). In the Canadian Arctic, the practice of using plants as insulation has largely been replaced by wool, fleece, or other imported materials. Although ceremonially used, the seal oil lamps have been replaced with camping stoves. For use as fuel, mosses and heather are still collected to grill meat outdoors, enhancing the taste of the meat.

Some edible plants are eaten raw, while others are mixed with fat or boiled to make tea. Plants and roots do not contribute a significant amount of calories in a meat-dominated diet: however, they are indispensable in providing some essential nutrients, along with a welcomed variety. Purple saxifrage is one of the more common plants and its petals can be mixed with seal fat, or eaten raw.

Berries are a favorite and are readily available in late summer or early autumn. Some of the common berries in the Arctic include crowberries, blueberries, cranberries, bear berries (stone berry), moose berries (soapberry or buffalo berry), salmon berries, and cloud berries. Berries are mainly gathered by women and children, but occasionally by an entire family as an event. Berries that have been picked are often preserved for future use and occasions. In times of inadequate storage, people were known to shake the snow off branches and collect the frozen berries during the winter. To preserve berries, people would store them in oil; today people commonly freeze them in plastic bags.

Berries, like meat, are also a part of the Arctic people's culture of sharing and are an important part of kinship exchange. In locations where there are not many berries to be gathered, people may receive them as gifts from relatives, or they can be an important item of trade. Societies might celebrate a girl's first berry picking with a feast in much the same way that a boy's first catch is celebrated. Arctic peoples celebrate their children's good fortune and accomplishments of passing through these cultural markers. Bodenhorn remarks that, "Today no special occasion would be complete without *agutaq*, or Eskimo ice cream, which is made from whitefish, caribou fat, and salmon berries" (Bodenhorn, 2000: 134). Berries are often served at special family feasts and parties.

Although technically not a plant, mushrooms also provide an important supplement to some Arctic people's diet. Whether or not mushrooms are eaten depends upon the cultural perception of mushrooms as a food. Some groups in Siberia eat mushrooms, while others consider them unclean. Although mushrooms grow in many localities, they are not always considered food for humans.

Not all plants gathered are terrestrial; people also utilize different kinds of seaweed. Both bladder and thong seaweed were eaten, and it was believed among some Inuit that a woman could increase her fertility by eating seaweed (Graburn, 1969). Seaweed is sometimes boiled and added to certain dishes, or it can also be eaten raw and snacked upon while engaging in other activities, such as mussel picking.

Thus far, most of the focus has been on plant gathering in tundra climate. Some of the Arctic, however, is below the treeline and the plants gathered in northern forests have a greater variety, such as wild onions, horseradish, rhubarb, adder's-tongue, and lily-root. Additionally, tree sap was the essential ingredient in making a drink with soured milk for people in Siberia (Levin and Potapov, 1964). Also in Siberia, cedar (Siberian pine) nuts, gathered in large quantities, are a source of food.

Although we think in terms of "gathering" plants and berries, it is not uncommon to hear people say that they go out "hunting" for berries. Hunting and gathering, although different terms, are not necessarily entirely separate categories of how people view their own activities. Approaches to the hunting and gathering of plants are quite similar. There are times when plant gathering is conducted in a purposeful manner, meaning that people know where they might find the best berries and they go out in search of them. In this way, it is similar to hunting for something specific. At other times, berries, as well as plants, are collected as part of traveling and moving within the landscape, and people learn to seize opportunities. Any procurement from the environment, plant or animal, requires a person to have a combination of skills, knowledge, and luck.

KERRIE ANN SHANNON

See also **Food Use of Wild Species**

Further Reading

Andre, Alestine & Alan Fehr, *Gwich'in Ethnobotany: Plants used by the Gwich'in for Food, Medicine, Shelter and Tools*' Inuvik: Gwich'in Social and Cultural Institute and Aurora Research Institute, 2002

Bodenhorn, Barbara, "The Iñupiat of Alaska." In *Endangered Peoples of the Arctic*, edited by Milton M.R. Freeman, Westport: Greenwood Press, 2000

Farrow, Judy, "Flora." In *Nunavut Handbook*, Iqaluit: Nortex Multimedia, 1998

Freeman, Milton M.R. (editor), *Endangered Peoples of the Arctic: Struggles to Survive and Thrive*, Westport: Greenwood Press, 2000

Graburn, Nelson, *Eskimos Without Igloos: Social and Economic Development in Sugluk*, Boston: Little Brown, 1969

Inuuqatigiit: The Curriculum from the Inuit Perspective, Northwest Territories: Education, Culture and Employment, 1996

Levin, M.G. & L.P. Potapov, *The Peoples of Siberia*, Chicago: University of Chicago Press, 1964

Pielou, E.C., *A Naturalist's Guide to the Arctic*, Chicago: University of Chicago Press, 1994

Polunin, Nicholas, *Circumpolar Arctic Flora*, Oxford: Clarendon Press, 1959

"The Flora of Nunavik: edible plants." *Tumivut*, (3) (1992): 45–48

"The Flora of Nunavik: tea and fuel." *Tumivut*, (2) (1991): 45–48

PLANT REPRODUCTION AND POLLINATION

Plants must reproduce to maintain their populations and to spread into new areas. Reproductive strategies of plants fall into two broad categories: sexual and asexual. The division between the two is not always clear, and many Arctic plants combine both.

The most obvious kind of asexual reproduction is vegetative. In the Arctic, many plants reproduce this way. Some reproduce by subterranean runners or rhizomes (underground stems that differ from roots by having scalelike leaves, nodes, and buds). Some sedges and cottongrasses (*Carex* spp., *Eriophorum* spp. (Cyperaceae)) bind soil and other plants into tough, extensive mats. Some grasses (e.g., *Poa, Dupontia, Puccinellia, Festuca, Elymus* (Poaceae)) similarly form dense turf with stolons (mostly underground stems, but sometimes aboveground, that produce new plants at their tips). Some crowfoot plants (Ranunculaceae) (e.g., buttercups, *Ranunculus* spp.) are stoloniferous, and others are rhizomatous (e. g., goldthread, *Coptis*). Some plants, for example, some willows (*Salix* spp.) (Salicaceae) and heathers (Ericaceae), reproduce by rooting from their stems to produce surface mats that may become buried with age. The spider plant (*Saxifraga flagellaris* (Saxifragaceae)) produces exquisitely long, threadlike, naked stolons that radiate over the soil from the central, flowering rosette of leaves. Each stolon terminates in a tiny, rooting rosette.

Another type of obviously asexual reproduction is bulbil production. Bulbils are adventitious buds formed on the stem and in the leaf axils. They break off readily and roll or blow away from the parent plant. Bistort (*Polygonum viviparum* (Polygonaceae)), nodding saxifrage (*Saxigraga cernua* (Saxifragaceae)), and some fescues (*Festuca* spp. (Poaceae)) reproduce in this way.

Sexual reproduction involves flowers. Flowers, mostly by their corollas (petals and sepals), advertise and contain plants' sexual organs, the stamens (with filaments and pollen-producing anthers) and pistils (with pollen-receiving stigmata, styles, and ovaries containing egg cells or ova). Pollination is the movement of pollen from the anther to the stigma of the same (autogamy) or a different flower on the same (geitonogamy) (together called self-pollination) or a different plant (xenogamy) (called cross-pollination). Pollination can occur by physical means, mostly by wind (anemophily) or gravity, or through animal agents (zoophily), mostly insects (entomophily).

Sex, and sexual function, is distributed in plants in various ways in space and time. The distribution makes one kind of pollination more or less likely to occur. Willows (*Salix* spp.), birches (*Betula* spp.), and cloudberry (*Rubus chamaemorus* (Rosaceae)) are characteristically unisexual or dioecious, so pollen must move from the staminate flowers of male plants to the pistillate flowers of female plants. In moss-campion (*Silene acaulis* (Caryophyllaceae)), the sexual structure of populations can be complex with male,

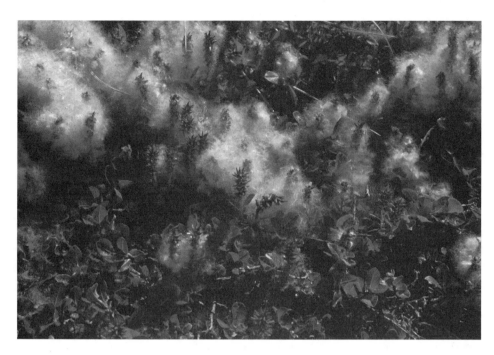

Exploded seed heads of Arctic willow (*Salix arctica masik*), Chukotka. *Copyright Bryan and Cherry Alexander Photography*

female, and hermaphrodite plants. In some sedges (*Carex* spp.), spikelets of inconspicuous, small flowers are unisexual and form on the same plant. This is particularly obvious in the very common *C. stans*. Most Arctic plants produce hermaphroditic flowers with both male and female parts. Nevertheless, cross-fertilization is encouraged by flowers that have differences in the timing (dichogamy) of pollen release, mostly earlier (protandry: the converse, protgyny relatively uncommon), and stigmatic receptivity, such as is easily seen in showy-flowered willow herbs (fire weeds) (*Chamaerion* spp. (Onagraceae)). Most Arctic plants, though, have flowers in which the sexual parts mature almost simultaneously (homogamy). In some of these, the sexual parts are separated from each other so that automatic self-pollination cannot occur (herkogamy). Showy-flowered *Chamaerion* show this well, combined with protandry, but most Arctic plants are only weakly herkogamous at best.

In the Arctic flora in general, mechanisms for promoting out-crossing seem weakly developed. It is often assumed that self-fertilization is secondarily important after vegetative reproduction. Self-fertilization following self-pollination can be thwarted by self-incompatibility, whereby the maternal tissue of the flower recognizes pollen from the same plant and prevents it from siring seeds. Few studies on pollination and seed-set have been conducted on the Arctic flora. Dioecious species may be pollinated by wind (anemophily) (e.g., birch), insects (entomophily) (e.g., cloudberry), or both (ambophily) (e.g., willows). In some of the most common plants, such as mountain avens (*Dryas integrifolia* (Rosaceae)) and purple saxifrage (*Saxifraga oppositi-*

folia), obligate out-crossing seems to operate in some places and self-fertilization in others. Automatic self-pollination or self-fertilization does not result in seed-set in at least some louseworts (*Pedicularis* spp. (Scrophulariaceae)) and legumes (e.g., *Astragalus* (Fabaceae)). Insect pollination is now recognized as common in Arctic flowers. The most common pollinators are flies (Diptera) that mostly seek nectar from flowers. Some also ingest pollen (e.g., hover flies: Syrphidae). Flies (especially of the families Muscidae, Anthomyiidae, and Syrphidae) mostly visit open, bowl- or bell-shaped flowers such as of Rosaceae (*Dryas*, *Potentilla*, *Saxifraga*), Ranunculaceae, Brassicaceae, and inflorescences of composites (Asteraceae) and willows (*Salix* spp.). Butterflies and moths (Lepidoptera) also visit the same suite of flowers while feeding on nectar. Judging by floral form and color, primroses (*Primula* spp. (Primulaceae)), with deep-tubed flowers and a corolla that forms a horizontal landing pad, may be well pollinated by butterflies. Plants with complex bilaterally symmetrical flowers, as of louseworts (*Pedicularis* spp.) and legumes (*Astragalus*, *Oxytropis*, *Lupinus*, etc.), are served in pollination by bumblebees (*Bombus* spp.: Apidea: Hymenoptera) that must learn how to operate the flowers to obtain nectar and pollen to provision their nests. Small wasps that are parasitoids of other insects seem to be drawn to white flowers of chickweeds (*Stellaria* spp. and *Cerastium* spp. (Caryophyllaceae)), but it is unlikely that they are pollinators.

Most flying insects require carbohydrate fuel for flight, and floral nectar is the primary source. Other insects, even lowly springtails (Collembola), may feed in flowers. Apart from nectar and pollen, Arctic flowers provide floral tissue to some caterpillars and warmth to baskers that rest in flowers. Some flowers turn to face the sun (diaheliotropism) for part or all of the 24-h day (e.g., *Papaver radicatum* (Papaveraceae), *D. integrifolia*, and *Senecio congestus* (Asteraceae)), a habit that is important in seed maturation.

The flowers of Arctic plants vary enormously in size, shape, and color. Larger, showier flowers are visited by more insects, either generally for flowers with easily accessible rewards used by the diversity of Arctic insects or those with specialist visitors to flowers with hidden rewards (e.g., louseworts and legumes visited by bumblebees). In the Arctic, there are more yellow and white flowers than in other zones. Some Arctic flowers reflect intensively in ultraviolet (e.g., *Arnica alpina* (Asteraceae) and *Saxifraga hirculus* (Saxifragaceae)), which human beings cannot see but insects can. Most Arctic flowers are slightly scented, but even in one family or genus (*Draba* spp., *Braya* spp. and relatives (Brassicacaea)), some seem almost scentless whereas a few are well scented. Thus, the depauperate Arctic flora seems to offer, relatively, as wide a range of floral attractants and rewards for flower visitors and pollinators as other floras.

Knowledge of breeding, mating, and general reproductive systems of Arctic plants remains rudimentary. The importance of insect pollination and of seeding to the Arctic flora is debatable and seems variable. Some of the most common and showy flowers are often visited by pollen-vectoring insects, but cross-pollination may not be required for seed to set. The insects' relative importance in cross-pollination (obligate in cloudberry) and in self-pollination depends on species and locality. Many species of Arctic plants produce seed asexually: the ova mature to form seeds without the union of sperm from the pollen. This form of seed production, called agamospermy, reaches its zenith in Arctic dandelions (*Taraxacum* spp. (Asteraceae)), which do not even produce pollen. Agamospermy is associated with high numbers of chromosomes in plants (polyploidy), which is commonly represented in Arctic species.

Pollination and seeds are probably more important to Arctic plant reproduction, long-distance dispersal, and colonization than is commonly thought. Almost all Arctic plants are perennial and so have chances, if conditions are favorable, to produce seed each year. Most have set periodic patterns of growth dictated by the seasons, but a few can stop and start growth at various stages. *Braya humilis* (Brassiccaeae) is notably aperiodic because it can overwinter with its inflorescence at any stage of development. There are few annuals in the Arctic flora (e.g., *Androsace septenrionalis* (Primulaceae)), but it may be that some louseworts are monocarpic in growing vegetatively for a number of years before flowering, setting seed, and dying. Clearly, seeding is vital to the continued existence of such plants. Vegetative reproduction is important within sites where clonal stands prevail, and in a few plants that produce easily dispersed propagules (e.g., bulbils) probably has the same role as seeding.

PETER G. KEVAN

See also **Flora of the Tundra**

Further Reading

Billings, D.W., "Constraints to plant growth, reproduction, and establishment in Arctic environments." *Arctic and Alpine Research*, 19 (1987): 357–365

Erikson, B., U. Molau & M. Svensson, "Reproductive strategies in two Arctic *Pedicularis* species." Ecography, 16 (1993): 154–166

Gabrielsen, T.M. & C. Brochman, "Sex after all: high level of diversity detected in the Arctic clonal plant *Saxifraga cernua* using RAPD markers." *Molecular Ecology*, 7 (1998): 1701–1708

Kevan, P.G., "Insect pollination of high Arctic flowers." *Journal of Ecology*, 60 (1972): 831–847

———, "Flowers, insects and pollination ecology in the Canadian High Arctic." *Polar Record*, 16 (1973): 667–674

Levesque, E. & J. Svoboda, "Germinable seed bank from soils of polar desert stands (Central Ellesmere Island, Canada) and survival of seedlings in controlled conditions." *Botanicheskii Zhurnal*, 82(2) (1977): 30–45

Molau, U., "Relationships between flowering phenology and life history strategies in tundra plants." *Arctic and Alpine Research*, 25 (1994): 391–402

Philipp, M., J. Böcher, O. Mattsson & S.R.J. Woodell, "A quantitative approach to the sexual reproductive biology and population structure in some Arctic flowering plants: *Dryas integrifolia*, *Silene acaulis* and *Ranunculus nivalis*." *Meddelelser on Grønland*, 34 (1990): 1–60

Proctor, M., P. Yeo & A. Lack, *The Natural History of Pollination*, London: Harper Collins, 1996

Richards, A.J., *Plant Breeding Systems,* London: Allen and Unwin, 1986

PLEISTOCENE MEGAFAUNA

These large ice age (Pleistocene—about 2 million to 10,000 years ago) mammals were among the most spectacular and interesting animals to have lived in circumpolar regions from what is now the British Isles in the west to the Atlantic coast of North America in the east.

Although the definition of megafauna varies, a land mammal with an adult body weight estimated to be 40 kg (wolf size) or more is nominally used here. The focus here is also on the Late Pleistocene megafauna of northern Eurasia and North America rather than on that of more southerly areas or different continents. The appearance of many of these species is well recorded in carcasses from frozen ground in Siberia, as well as in European Paleolithic cave art. Comments on a few of the more significant or unusual species follow.

Mammoths and mastodons were the largest members of the group. Mammoths were derived from Eurasia, entering North America by the Bering Isthmus (sometimes called the Bering Land Bridge), a broad grassy plain connecting northeastern Siberia with Alaska, exposed during periods of heavy glaciation when sea level lowered up to 100 m in the Bering Strait area because so much water became locked up on the continents as glacial ice (*see* **Beringia; Land Bridges and the Arctic Continental Shelf**).

Woolly mammoths, characterized by thick dark brown pelts, were first recorded in Eurasia perhaps 150,000 years ago and grew to the size of Asiatic elephants—their closest living relatives. Adults stood between 2.7 and 3.4 m at the shoulder and weighed up to 6 tons. Several excellent carcasses have been found in permafrost in Siberia, including the famed Dima, a baby recovered from frozen ground on a tributary of the Kolyma River near Magadan in northeastern Siberia and radiocarbon dated to 400,000 years. Parts of the fur, skin, and flesh were preserved, but the DNA is incomplete and fragmented.

Mastodons were widely distributed in North America, reaching northwestern North America (Alaska, Yukon, Northwest Territories) from the south in the Late Pleistocene. They were squatter (2–3 m in shoulder height), longer (about 4.5 m), and had straighter tusks than most woolly mammoths. Whereas woolly mammoths were adapted to grazing, American mastodons browsed mainly in open spruce forests.

Perhaps one of the most interesting members of the megafauna was the giant beaver—the largest rodent in North America during the ice age. It reached a length of nearly 2.5 m (the size of a black bear) and may have weighed as much as 200 kg compared to a modern beaver 1 m long and weighing about 30 kg. It ranged from Florida to the Yukon and from New Brunswick to Nebraska.

Small, sturdy horses, perhaps related most closely to Przewalskii's horse, dominated the Late Pleistocene steppelike grasslands of northern Eurasia and northwestern North America. One of the best preserved is the Selerikan horse carcass, discovered in permafrost by drift gold miners in Siberia in 1968. Another well-preserved carcass from Last Chance Creek in the Klondike, Yukon, is that of a horse that died about 26,000 years ago.

Woolly rhinos were among the most spectacular members of the Eurasian megafauna, and two well-known carcasses have been preserved: one from Starunia, Poland, that was trapped in an oil seep, and the other from frozen ground near Churapcha, Siberia. They were widespread grazers that ranged from Spain and the British Isles to Siberia. They never reached the New World.

Large cats such as the ubiquitous lion and the rarer scimitar cat also characterized the Holarctic faunas. Probably the Eurasian cave lion and American lion are only different at the subspecific level. From about 300,000 to 10,000 years ago, cave lions lived in steppelike and parkland regions of Eurasia from as far west as England and at least as far east as the Kolyma River in Siberia—some 1400 km west of the nearest known specimen of the "American" lion (Kaolak River, Alaska). Cave lions probably entered Alaska by the Bering Isthmus some 150,000 years ago giving rise to the American stock. American lions reached an enormous size—nearly 25% larger than modern lions. Males would have weighed about 235 kg. They may have been best adapted to killing bison. In fact, the frozen carcass of a steppe bison (named Blue Babe) found at a gold-mining site near Fairbanks, Alaska, in 1979 showed signs of having been killed by lions in early winter some 36,000 years ago. Toward the end of the last glaciation, American lions ranged as far south as Florida, Mexico, and California.

Scimitar cats were slender-limbed (with relatively long forelimbs and short, powerful hindlimbs) and short-tailed, with upper fangs like curving steak knives. Although much rarer than sabertooths and American lions, this species ranged broadly throughout North America (Yukon and Alaska, south to California and west to Florida). Evidently, it preyed mainly on young tough-skinned animals such as juvenile mammoths.

Giant short-faced bears (*Arctodus simus*) were the largest land carnivores in North America during the ice age. They were unusually lanky, highly carnivorous, and may have weighed up to 700 kg. These "Bulldog Bears" ranged from Alaska and Yukon to Mexico, and from Pacific to Atlantic coasts. They were capable of bursts of speed when necessary and could cover large areas for prey or for scavenging. Likely *Plionarctos*, of Pliocene age from Texas, gave rise to both the short-faced bear and the modern spectacled bear of South America.

Perhaps the strangest member of the North American megafauna is Jefferson's ground sloth. This long-haired, ox-sized mammal with peglike teeth and hooked claws was one of several (including the American mastodon, giant short-faced bear, and flat-headed peccary) to enter Yukon and Alaska from southern North America. However, the main mammalian invasion of North America came from Eurasia via the Bering Isthmus. This ground sloth stemmed from Wheatley's ground sloth probably more than 150,000 years ago. In southern North America, fossils are known from Atlantic to Pacific coasts.

Nevertheless, there is a noteworthy uniformity in the Late Pleistocene Holarctic megafauna dominated by bison, horses, mammoths, and caribou/reindeer, because of its mainly central and northern Asian origin (implying remarkable cold adaptation) and the fact that it was well adapted to the "Mammoth Steppe" or polar steppe—a vast northern belt of steppelike grassland with no modern analog. Russians call it the "mammoth fauna," and another Eurasian term is the "*Mammuthus—Coelodonta* (woolly mammoth—woolly rhino) faunal complex." The Mammoth Steppe biome broke down due to unusually rapid climatic change toward the end of the last glaciation about 10,000 years ago, greatly stressing the large herbivores and their specialized large carnivores (e.g., lions, scimitar cats, and giant short-faced and cave bears). Nearly three-quarters of the North American megafauna became extinct. In some cases, humans may have exacerbated the extinctions by overhunting.

As northern steppelike grasslands gave way to tundra and boreal forest, most of the megafauna became more confined and isolated, finally reaching extinction toward the close of the Pleistocene. However, some dwarfed woolly mammoths were able to survive on Wrangel Island off the coast of northeastern Siberia until about 3700 years ago.

C.R. HARINGTON

See also **Beringia; Fossils: Animal Species; Mammoth; Polar Steppe**

Further Reading

Harington, C.R., "Jefferson's Ground Sloth (No. 1, 1995), Woolly Mammoth (No. 2, 1996), American Mastodon (No. 3, 1996), North American Short-Faced Bears (No. 4, 1996), American Lion (No. 5, 1996), Giant Beaver (No. 6, 1996), American scimitar cat (No. 7, 1996)." *Beringian Research Notes,* Whitehorse: Yukon Beringia Interpretive Centre

Kahlke, R.-D., *The History of the Origin, Evolution and Dispersal of the Late Pleistocene Mammuthus—Coelodonta Faunal Complex in Eurasia (Large Mammals)*, Rapid City: Fenske Companies, 1999

Kurtén, B. & E. Anderson, *Pleistocene Mammals of North America*, New York: Columbia University Press, 1980

Lister, A. & P. Bahn, *Mammoths*, New York: Macmillan, 1994

Martin, P.S. & R.G. Klein (editors), *Quaternary Extinctions: A Prehistoric Revolution* Tucson, Arizona: University of Arizona Press, 1984

Stuart, A.J., *Life in the Ice Age*, Aylesbury, Buckinghamshire: Shire, 1988

Vereshchagin, N.K. & G.F. Baryshnikov, "Paleoecology of the Mammoth Fauna in the Eurasian Arctic." In *Paleoecology of Beringia,* edited by D.M. Hopkins, J.V. Matthews Jr., C.E. Schweger & S.B. Young, New York and London: Academic Press, 1982

POLAR BEAR

The polar bear (*Ursus maritimus*, or maritime bear) is a large member of the bear family (Ursidae) that is restricted in range to the circumpolar Arctic (coast and surrounding sea of Greenland, Canadian Arctic islands, Svalbard, Novaya Zemlya, Severnaya Zemlya, and the coastal Russian Arctic). The distribution of polar bears is tied to that of sea ice. While extremely strong swimmers, capable of swimming over 60 km, polar bears spend most of their time on sea ice. Extending as far north as the North Pole, polar bears also range as far south as the Gulf of St Lawrence and James Bay in Québec, the same latitude as London. Bears either move onto land when the ice melts in summer or retreat northward to the permanent multiyear ice. Polar bears have highly variable home ranges ($c.500–300,000$ km^2) as the availability of sea ice changes, and show long-term fidelity to these ranges, suggesting a well-developed sense of navigation. The global population of polar bears numbers about 20–30,000 divided into about 20 relatively discrete populations.

Polar bears evolved from a brown/grizzly bear ancestor within the last 200–300,000 years and, in contrast to most other carnivores worldwide, still occupy most of their historic range. No subspecies exist. In captivity, polar bears and brown/grizzly bears can interbreed and produce fertile young. Polar bears have a longer neck and narrower head than other bears. In addition, their claws are much shorter and more curved and their teeth are sharper than brown/grizzly bears, reflecting their use for predation and consumption of meat. Polar bear fur varies from white to pale yellow, depending on season and light conditions, and does not provide any fiber-optic transmission of ultraviolet light despite speculation in this area. The skin is black, and can be seen on their nose and paw pads. Adult females become sexually mature at 4–5 years of age, usually give birth to their first litter at 5–6 years of age, and can live up to 30 years. Adult males mature at 6–8 years of age and normally do not exceed 24 years of age. Adult females weigh from 200 to 400 kg, depending on season and reproductive status, and adult males weigh from 300 to 600 kg with rare individuals reaching 800 kg. The length of females is about 200 cm from the nose to the tail tip, with males about 40 cm longer.

Polar bears, unlike other bears, are almost entirely carnivorous. The prey varies geographically, but consists largely of ringed seals, bearded seals, and harp seals. In some areas, walrus, white whales, narwhal, seabirds, carrion, and even reindeer form part of the diet. A keen sense of smell and good vision assist in finding prey. Polar bears consume most of their food in the spring and early summer when seal pups are born. Most prey is taken by "still hunting," which involves waiting for seals to appear at a breathing hole, stalking, or crashing into birth lairs. The blubber of seals is preferentially stripped from the carcass to maximize energy

Polar bear (*Ursus maritimus*), Churchill, Manitoba, Canada. *Copyright Paul Nicklen/National Geographic Image Collection*

intake. A single meal can comprise over 10% of a bear's body mass and in one case the meal weighed 70 kg. Polar bears can store huge fat deposits up to 10 cm thick, which are used to sustain the animal through extended fasts when prey are unavailable. Their specialized physiology allows bone mass and muscle mass to be maintained during fasting. Pregnant females can easily fast for 6–8 months using up to 1 kg of fat per day to sustain themselves and rear their cubs.

Polar bears live a solitary life (typically about one bear per 30–150 km^2) and are only found in groups as mothers with cubs, briefly as pairs during the breeding season on sea ice in March-June, or in all-male aggregations during ice-free periods. Competition between males can be intense for access to females in estrus. Large wounds, sprained limbs, and broken teeth are common fight injuries and reduce the survival rate of males. Following mating, the fertilized egg is not implanted in the uterus until September, when pregnant females enter dens and remain dormant until the young are born.

Only pregnant females enter dens for extended periods (at least 90 days) over winter. Other age and sex groups sometimes enter dens temporarily for periods of days to months during inclement weather or food shortage; there is no true hibernation. Most maternity dens occur on land, except in Alaska where sea ice dens are common. Land den concentrations occur on Wrangel Island, Russia, near Cape Churchill in western Hudson Bay, and on Kong Karls Land, Svalbard. Most dens are within 5 km of the coast, but in Hudson Bay some females den over 50 km inland. Dens are either single or multichambered with a long entrance tunnel and are dug into snow deposits along areas with some relief (e.g., riverbanks and cliffs).

Litters are of 1–3 cubs (less than 10% have triplets), born around the end of December. As the mother does not eat while pregnant, the cubs are born very small (400–700 g or 16–24 oz). By the time of den emergence in March to early May, cubs would have grown to about 10 kg. Offspring remain with the mother for 2.5 years; however, weaning at 1.5 years of age occurs regularly in Hudson Bay. Cub survival in the first year ranges between 20% and 80%, depending upon hunting and sea ice conditions. Adult survival rates exceed 94% in populations not harvested by hunting. Population growth rates rarely exceed 5% and are often much lower due to the long mother-offspring rearing period.

Diseases and their effects on polar bears are poorly documented. Exposure to the parasitic worm *Trichinella* spp. is widespread, and trichinosis can be transferred to humans by consuming under-cooked meat. The level of vitamin A in polar bear liver is toxic to humans as discovered by early polar explorers.

Polar bears are not an endangered or threatened species, but most jurisdictions consider that they warrant special management consideration. The major threats to polar bears are from climate change, toxic chemicals from industrial waste, oil resources development, tourism, and over-harvest. Climate change can affect the distribution of sea ice and the prey of polar bears. If sufficient changes occur, polar bears may become locally extinct in parts of their current range. Toxic chemicals, particularly persistent organic pollutants such as polychlorinated biphenyls and pesticides, are known to affect hormone regulation, immune system, and development in the most polluted populations from East Greenland to western Russia. Most populations are well managed to sustain a harvest and about 500–900 bears are harvested each year, mostly in subsistence hunts by indigenous peoples, with some sport hunting. The international Agreement on Conservation of Polar Bears provides guidelines for management and research throughout the Arctic and has been instrumental in regulating harvest. Polar bears are culturally important to indigenous peoples throughout the Arctic for clothing and food. Canadian Inuit harvest the most bears followed by Greenland, Alaska, and eastern Russia. Trade in polar bear parts is regulated by the Convention on International Trade in Endangered Species (CITES).

ANDREW E. DEROCHER

See also **Agreement on the Conservation of Polar Bears; Bears; Convention on International Trade in Endangered Species (CITES); Persistent Organic Pollutants (POPs)**

Further Reading

Amstrup, S.C., "Polar bear, *Ursus maritimus*." In *Wild Mammals of North America: Biology, Management, and Conservation,* edited by G.A. Feldhamer, B.C. Thompson & J.A. Chapman, Baltimore: Johns Hopkins University Press, 2003

Amstrup, S.C. & G.M. Durner, "Survival rates of radio-collared female polar bears and their dependent young." *Canadian Journal of Zoology,* 73 (1995): 1312–1322

Derocher, A.E. & I. Stirling, "Maternal investment and factors affecting offspring size in polar bears (*Ursus maritimus*)." *Journal of Zoology (London),* 245 (1998): 253–260

Polar Bear Specialist Group, In *Polar Bears: Proceedings of the 12th Working Meeting of the IUCN Polar Bear Specialist Group,* edited by A.E. Derocher, G.W. Garner, N.J. Lunn & Ø. Wiig, Gland, Switzerland and Cambridge: IUCN, 1998

Ramsay, M.A. & I. Stirling, "Reproductive biology and ecology of female polar bears (*Ursus maritimus*)." *Journal of Zoology (London),* 214 (1988): 601–634

Stirling, I., "Midsummer observations on the behavior of wild polar bears." *Canadian Journal of Zoology,* 52 (1974): 1191–1198

———, *Polar Bears,* Ann Arbor: University of Michigan Press, 1998

Stirling, I. & W.R. Archibald, "Aspects of predation of seals by polar bears." *Journal of the Fisheries Research Board of Canada,* 34 (1977): 1126–1129

Stirling, I. & A.E. Derocher, "Possible impacts of climatic warming on polar bears." *Arctic,* 46 (1993): 240–245

POLAR CONTINENTAL SHELF PROJECT (PCSP)

The Polar Continental Shelf Project (PCSP) is an organization approved by the Government of Canada on May 22, 1958, as a direct consequence of Prime Minister John Diefenbaker's "Northern Vision," with an initial mandate to conduct multidisciplinary scientific investigations of the continental shelf to the north and west of the Queen Elizabeth Islands, Canadian High Arctic.

The foundation of PCSP was recommended in March 1958 by a Technical Sub-Committee of the Advisory Committee on Northern Development, comprising representatives of various Canadian government agencies and presided over by W.E. van Steenburgh. The Canadian Arctic Archipelago had become of immense geopolitical importance following the development of intercontinental ballistic missile systems and the Soviet launch of Sputnik (1957). Consequently, the paucity of Canadian research in the region came to national attention. Moreover, the Law of the Sea Conference (1958) had concluded that maritime states should have control over the resources on their continental shelves. It was therefore deemed expedient to initiate a program of hydrographic, oceanographic, geophysical, and biological studies of the continental shelf, as a direct means of asserting Canadian sovereignty in the High Arctic. Under its first coordinator E.F. Roots, a PCSP field party began work to establish a navigation system in 1959, and the first full-scale field season commenced the following year based out of the Joint Arctic Weather Station at Isachsen, Ellef Ringnes Island.

PCSP was to be an autonomous organization, separate from the requirements of other established agencies conducting Arctic research such as the Geological Survey of Canada (GSC). Following completion of the study of the continental shelf area, PCSP's research focus grew to encompass the entire Canadian High Arctic. At its peak, PCSP had 26 scientists on staff. Most of these returned to their originating Canadian government agencies in the late 1960s. Maintaining bases at Resolute and Tuktoyaktuk from 1968, PCSP increasingly undertook a logistical role, supporting other Canadian and foreign agencies as well as facilitating the growth of research by Canadian universities in the High Arctic. As an exclusively logistical organization since 1986 when the remaining staff scientists were transferred to the GSC, PCSP's client base has diversified significantly as other federal agencies have intensified reliance upon PCSP services, as territorial government agencies and comanagement boards have developed their own research agendas, and as non-Canadian programs have increased.

Despite its complicated institutional history involving a number of Federal departments, PCSP has maintained an outstanding international reputation as a research facilitator over the past four decades. Among its many achievements, PCSP has supported the Dominion Observatory Polar Gravity Expedition (1967), the international AIDJEX (Arctic Ice Dynamics Joint Experiment) (1975), the LOREX multi-disciplinary project to study the nature and origins of Lomonosov Ridge (1979), and CESAR (Canadian Expedition to Study the Alpha Ridge)

(1983). Moreover, PCSP has been a leader in encouraging consultation between natural scientists and local indigenous communities in the Canadian Arctic since the early 1970s, and has recently pioneered the Canadian Arctic-Antarctic Exchange Program.

PCSP presently maintains its base at Resolute, the Tuktoyaktuk facilities having been dormant since 1998.

RICHARD C. POWELL

See also **Resolute Base**

Further Reading

England, J.H., A.S. Dyke & G.H.R. Henry, "Canada's crisis in Arctic science: the urgent need for an Arctic science and technology policy; or, 'Why work in the Arctic? No One lives there'." *Arctic*, 51, (1998): 183–190

Foster, Michael & Carol Marino, *The Polar Shelf: The Saga of Canada's Arctic Scientists*, Toronto: NC Press, 1986

Hobson, George, "Polar Continental Shelf Project." In *Canada's Missing Dimension: Science and History in the Canadian Arctic Islands,* Volume I, edited by C.R. Harington, Ottawa: Canadian Museum of Nature, 1990

Polar Continental Shelf Project, *Islands in the Midnight Sun: The Story of the Polar Continental Shelf Project*, Ottawa: Information Canada, 1974

———, *Islands in the Midnight* Sun, Ottawa: Supply and Services Canada, 1979

POLAR DESERT

The term desert, derived from the Latin word *desertis* meaning "barren" or "deserted," is used to describe regions of the Earth that are capable of supporting only a few forms of life. The term is used most frequently to describe areas barren of life due to dryness; however, even the ice-covered expanses of Antarctica and central Greenland are included as true deserts since moisture is locked up in ground ice and unavailable as liquid water. There is indeed low precipitation in polar climates due to the dry, cold, sinking air, but also seasonal water released as the surface layer above the permafrost (the active layer) thaws leading to water-saturated soils in spring.

In typical desert classification systems where the amount of precipitation is the defining factor, extremely arid lands have at least 12 consecutive months without rainfall, arid lands have less than 250 mm of annual rainfall, and semiarid lands have a mean annual precipitation of between 250 and 500 mm. In this classification, arid and extremely arid lands are considered to be deserts, and semiarid grasslands are generally referred to as steppes. Arid lands found at high latitudes would thus be considered polar deserts.

In one of the most widely used climate classification systems, the Köppen Climate Classification System distinguishes two desert climates, dry climates (denoted by "B") and polar climates ("E"), among its five main categories. The most important feature of Köppen "B" climates is that potential evaporation and transpiration exceed precipitation. Polar climates (E) are identified separately under the Köppen Classification as either tundra (ET) or polar desert or ice climates (EF). Polar desert climates are located in the high latitudes over continental areas like Greenland and Antarctica. For half of the year, no solar radiation is received. During the summer months, available insolation is fairly high because of long days and a relatively transparent atmosphere. However, the high albedo of snow-covered surfaces results in up to 90% of the insolation being reflected back to space. Average monthly temperatures are all generally below 0°C.

Polar deserts cover nearly 5 million square kilometers on Earth and dominate the landscape throughout much of the circumpolar High Arctic. The land surface consists mostly of exposed bedrock, frost shattered rock, rubble, gravel plains, and bare mineral soil with sparse vascular plant cover (usually <5%). In polar deserts, sand dunes occur only sporadically, but snow dunes are common features in areas where precipitation is adequate. Occasionally, composite dunes composed of interbedded snow and sand occur. Temperature changes in polar deserts frequently cross the freezing point of water. If the underlying permafrost is dry, then above-freezing temperatures have little impact. But if the permafrost is wet, the seasonal "freeze-thaw" alternation produces various features and patterned textures on the ground surface, including ice-wedge polygons (formed when ice-filled cracks meet in a geometric pattern to enclose a low or high central area), and sorted and nonsorted stone polygons. The seasonal thawing of the ground may release considerable moisture from ground ice. Thus, despite the lack of precipitation, polar deserts may display wet tundra and surface bodies of water and tundra ponds. High evaporation of water released from permafrost leaves a salty efflorescence on the ground surface.

Areas of polar desert in the Arctic correspond well with regions referred to as the High Arctic. In northern Eurasia, polar desert ecosystems are spread over the Arctic Ocean islands and archipelagos (Novaya Zemlya, Franz Josef Land, etc.); Greenland, central Iceland, and other ice caps; Svalbard; and Wrangel and Gerald islands in the Russian Far East. In North America, polar desert zones include ice caps such as on Ellesmere Island, and ice-free but mainly unvegetated areas such as Devon Island, Nunavut.

In polar desert regions, short growing seasons and availability of liquid water to a brief summer season limit the annual net primary production to only 5–30 g m^{-2}. Vegetation classification systems have in the past differed in their definition of polar desert biomes. In much of the North American literature, "Polar Desert"

Polar desert showing sparse summer tundra in the north of Ellesmere Island, Northwest Territories, Canada. *Copyright Bryan and Cherry Alexander Photography*

refers to areas of scant vegetation cover in a range of climatic zones. These barren areas result from a variety of influences, including climate, moisture, soil texture, and substrate chemistry. In the Russian and European zonation schemes, polar desert refers to the climatic zone north of the limit of woody plants. The Circumpolar Arctic Vegetation Map (CAVM) classification encourages a common terminology, based on distributions of plant species and functional types as controlled by climate: CAVM vegetation type 1 (cushion-forb barrens) corresponds most closely to polar desert. The vegetation cover in polar deserts is sparse (usually <5%), widely spaced, and mainly horizontal with a very low vertical structure (generally <2 cm tall). Spore plants dominate —algae, lichens, liverworts (*Hepaticaei*), and mosses (*Bryophytes*), together with soil algae, cushion flowering plants such as *Saxifraga* spp., *Puccinelia* spp., Arctic poppy (*Papaver lapponicum*), moss campion (*Silene acaulis*), and grasses such as *Poa* spp. The total number of species excluding lichen, mosses, and liverworts is typically less than 50. Fell-field habitats (a mottled, mosaiclike patterning of rock, plant, and soil) are typical of polar desert landscapes, and vegetation types associated with Arctic fell-fields (mat and cushion alpine plants, lichens, mosses) may also characterize polar deserts. In polar semideserts, tundra plant species such as mats of *Dryas* spp. along with *Draba* spp., *Salix arctica,* and *Carex* spp. may also be found alongside bryophytes.

WAYNE POLLARD

See also **Fell-Fields; High Arctic; Vegetation Distribution**

Further Reading

Aleksandrova, V.D., *Vegetation of the Soviet Polar Deserts*, Cambridge and New York: Cambridge University Press, 1988

Bliss, L. "Arctic Tundra and Polar Desert Biome." In *North American Terrestrial Vegetation*, edited by M. Barbour and D. Billings, Cambridge & New York: Cambridge University Press, 1988

———, "Arctic Ecosystems of North America." In *Polar and Alpine Tundra*, edited by F.E. Wielgolaski, Amsterdam: Elsevier, 1997

Bliss, L.C., J. Svoboda & D.I. Bliss, "Polar deserts, their plant cover and plant production in the Canadian High Arctic." *Holarctic Ecology*, 7 (1984): 305–324

Bliss, L.C., G.H.R. Henry, J. Svoboda & D.I. Bliss, "Patterns of plant distribution within two polar desert regions." *Arctic and Alpine Research*, 26 (1994): 46–55

Péwé, T.L. "Geomorphic processes in polar deserts." *Polar Deserts and Modern Man*, edited by T. Smiley & J.H. Zumberge, Tucson, Arizona, University of Arizona, 1974

Priscu, J.C. (editor), *Ecosystem Dynamics in a Polar Desert*, Washington District of Columbia: American Geophysical Union, 1998

Smiley T.L. & J.H. Zumberge (editors), *Polar Deserts and Modern Man,* Tucson, Arizona: University of Arizona Press, 1971

POLAR FRONTS

A polar front is a semipermanent weather front at the surface separating Arctic and polar air masses from tropical air masses. The polar air mass to the north is usually less moist than the warmer tropical air mass to the south. The frontal surface slopes vertically to the north so that warm air lies over the cooler air. The theory of fronts was developed by Jacob Bjerknes and other Scandinavian meteorologists from 1919 to 1922 to explain the formation and movement of cyclonic (rotating low-pressure) storms that formed along polar lines, which they identified as fronts between colliding air masses. The energy that drives the cyclone is derived from the temperature contrast across the front. The Polar Front Theory of Cyclones is now an effective tool in weather forecasting.

Bjerknes and Solberg (1921, 1922) pointed out that the polar front should not be considered a global phenomenon in that it appears as an air-mass boundary around the whole hemisphere because then a meridional air-mass exchange and the necessary air mass conversions would be prohibited.

Because fronts are marked by a concentration of isotherms and packing of isotherms is a measure of the intensity of the front, frontal intensity is related to season. The temperature contrast across the front is greater during winter than in summer. Thus, the polar front experiences strong frontogenetical processes during winter but only weak such processes during summer. Polar fronts migrate poleward during summer reaching 70° latitude and equatorward during winter to as low as 20° latitude. The westerly jet stream associated with a polar front also plays an important role in frontal development since it is a reflection of the integrated effect of the temperature contrasts at lower levels. Developments in the low levels are reflected by developments at the jet stream level and vice versa.

It is well known that air masses from the polar latitudes have thermodynamic characteristics distinct from those originating from the tropics. Recently, Gultepe and Isaac (2002) have presented data indicating that air masses from the Pacific and Arctic Oceans have distinct microphysical characteristics as well.

General Characteristics

The polar frontal cyclones experience characteristic life cycles. For example, according to Godske et al. (1957), frontal cyclones form as a low-pressure center along a stationary front. During the development of the frontal cyclone, warm air moves northward to the east of the center while cold air moves southward to the west. Usually, the cold front overtakes the warm front by a process known as occlusion. The synoptic system is at its peak during the occlusion stage, with clouds and precipitation covering a wide area.

Petterssen et al. (1963) investigated the cloud structure of several winter and spring cyclones over the United States Midwest. Special observations of clouds gathered by aerial observers were utilized. Fronts were quite distinct at the surface, but did not extend beyond 700 mb (3000 m) in one cyclone. Extensive cirrostratus covered east of the cyclone with breaks in the west. The center was recognized as a wave. Further details of this cyclone and other cyclones may be seen in Petterssen et al. (1963) or in Palmen and Newton (1969).

In some circumstances, separating a polar front from an Arctic front is difficult because the frontogenetical processes are similar. Reed and Kunkel (1960) stated that Arctic frontal zones could be viewed as further extensions of the midlatitude polar fronts. Intense Arctic frontal activity is observed along the northern shores of Alaska, eastern Canada, and the northern shores of Siberia. Strong differential heating between ocean (~0°C) and land surfaces (−15°C to −20°C) generates coastal baroclinic zones. These baroclinic zones in turn are associated with significant latent and sensible heat fluxes (Gultepe et al., 2002). Rao (1966) had shown that the differential latent heat fluxes promote further frontogenesis. Serreze et al. (2001) studied Arctic fronts using model-derived data. They suggested that high-latitude frontal activity occurred along 100° E longitude during July. According to them, topography has an influence on frontal zones. The location of polar fronts depends on the interaction of isotherms with large-scale synoptic patterns. The contribution of surface fluxes toward frontal development is mostly over shorelines during transition and summer seasons.

In the final stage, a warm front cannot be located easily, and topographical features can modify existing fronts. The jet stream associated with the polar front shows strong fluctuations with time and space longitudinally.

Polar lows (*see* **Polar Lows**) are being studied increasingly. These occur over the ocean to the rear of the cold front. In general, they form close to places where strong temperature gradients exist. They can become very intense, generating lines of convective activity. Atlantic polar lows tend to form in a northerly or northwesterly air stream with a strong low-level baroclinicity (Businger and Reed, 1989). Atlantic polar lows cannot be related to midlatitude frontal activity; on the other hand, the Pacific polar lows are often related to frontal activity and cover a much larger area compared to the Atlantic ones. According to Reed (1979), when a polar low interacts with a polar front, an "instant occlusion" forms, with the polar low providing energy to the low center and the occluded portion of the polar front. He furthermore questioned whether the conventional description of the occlusion process always occurs. While agreeing that the occurrence of occlusion is indisputable, he admitted that no simple explanation exists on the precise behavior of fronts, lows, and troughs in the occlusion.

Polar Front and Related Clouds

Clouds related to polar fronts occur in different parts of the system. The classical cloud locations related to a polar front were shown in Palmen and Newton (1969) and Musk (1988). In their work, convective clouds were observed along the cold front boundary and stratiform clouds were observed along the warm front boundary. Reed (1979) described a polar low with a comma cloud that develops typically in a baroclinic region within the upper level flow poleward but close to the polar front. Small synoptic-scale distur-

bances often occur in the polar air stream behind or poleward of the polar front (Mullen, 1982). An analysis of polar lows and comma cloud formation was given in Businger and Reed (1989). They stated that when a comma cloud and its accompanying region of positive vorticity advection approach a polar front, a wave often occurs on the front. If the wave is away from the comma cloud, it develops into a midlatitude cyclone. If the wave is close to the comma cloud, the comma cloud merges with the wave, resulting in the formation of cold and warm fronts (by "instant occlusion"). Figure 2 shows a typical comma cloud and its location with respect to the polar occluded front. A rapid cyclogenesis may occur when there is an interaction between comma clouds and polar frontal cloud bands (Mullen, 1982; Businger and Walter, 1988).

Because of the mixing that occurs between warm and cold air parcels, microphysical and dynamical characteristics of polar frontal clouds can be very different compared to those of Arctic and tropical cloud systems. The mixed phase cloud having both water and ice particles occur frequently. These mixed phased clouds are an important part of the polar frontal systems. The Alliance Icing Research Study (AIRS) took place over Ottawa, Ontario and Mirabel, Québec regions during the winter of 1999–2000 (Isaac et al., 2001), mixed phase clouds occurring at ~35% of the time (Cober et al., 2001). They noted that winter polar fronts could be very important for aircraft icing studies.

Climatic Effects of Polar Frontal Positions

The polar fronts are strongly related to cloud formation that occurs in convective and stratiform zones. Their occurrence can easily affect local weather and climate. When the polar front is located further north than usual, precipitation is below normal from central western Europe toward the east and northeast. Weather conditions in central west Europe are characterized by severe droughts when the polar front is located further north. Moene (1986) showed that significant northern location of the polar frontal zone resulted in frequent severe droughts in central western Europe during the 1970s. In the 1960s, the polar front was located in southern latitudes causing local floods. Moene's results showed that polar fronts associated with or without polar lows play a significant role in the local climate and weather of North America and Europe.

The Polar Front Theory developed by the Norwegian school of meteorologists still provides a useful model to describe weather systems in the mid- and polar latitudes. The characteristics and intensities of fronts affect the storms and their characteristics that occur in these regions. The climate of a region is strongly related to the mean positions of the polar front.

I. GULTEPE, G.V. RAO AND P. KING

See also **Climate; Polar Lows; Polar Vortex; Weather**

Further Reading

Bjerknes, J. & H. Solberg, "Meteorological conditions for the formation of rain." *Geofysiske Publikasjoner*, 2(3) (1921): 1–60

——— "Life cycle of cyclones and the polar front theory of atmospheric circulation." *Geofysiske Publikasjoner*, 3(1) (1922): 1–18

Businger, S. & R.J. Reed, "Polar Lows." In *Polar and Arctic Lows*, edited by P.F. Twitchell, E.A. Rasmussen, & K.L. Davidson, Hampton, Virginia: A. Deepak Publishing, 1989, pp. 3–45

Businger, S. & B. Walter, "Comma cloud development and associated rapid cyclogenesis over the Gulf of Alaska: a case study using aircraft and operational data." *Monthly Weather Review*, 116 (1988) 1103–1123

Cober, S.G., G.A. Isaac, A.V. Korolev & J.W. Strapp, "Assessing cloud-phase conditions." *Journal of Applied Meteorology*, 40 (2001) 1967–1983

Godske, C.L., T. Bergeron, J. Bjerknes & R.C. Bundgaard, *Dynamic Meteorology and Weather Forecasting*, Boston: American Meteorological Society, 1957

Gultepe, I. & G.A. Isaac, "The effects of air-mass origin on Arctic cloud microphysical parameters during FIRE.ACE." *Journal of Geophysical Research—Ocean*, 107(C10) (2002): SHE 4-1–4-12

Gultepe, I., G. Isaac, A. Williams, D. Marcotte, & K. Strawbridge, "Turbulent heat fluxes over leads and polynyas and their effect on Arctic clouds during FIRE-ACE: Aircraft observations for April 1998." *Atmosphere and Ocean*, 41(1) (2002): 15–34

Isaac, G.A., S.G. Cober, J.W. Strapp, A.V. Korolev, A. Tremblay & D.L. Marcotte, "Recent Canadian research on aircraft in-flight icing." *Canadian Aeronautics and Space Journal*, 47 (2001): 213–221

Moene, A., "Associations between North Atlantic sea surface temperature anomalies, latitude of the polar front zone, and precipitation over Northwest Europe." *Monthly Weather Review*, 114 (1986): 636–643

Mullen, S.L., "Cyclone development in polar air streams over the wintertime continent." *Monthly Weather Review*, 110 (1982): 1664–1676

Musk, L.F., *Weather Systems*, Cambridge and New York: Cambridge University Press, 1988

Palmen, E. & C.W. Newton, *Atmospheric Circulation Systems*, New York and London: Academic Press, 1969

Petterssen, S., D.L. Bradbury, E.P. McClain, Y. Omoto, G. V. Rao, E.R. Ternes, & G.F. Watson, "An investigation of the structure of cloud and weather systems associated with cyclones in the United States." *Final Report*, Contr. AF 19 (604)-7230, Article H, Dept. of Geophys. Sci. Univ. Chicago, 1963

Rao, G.V., "On the influences of fields of motion, baroclinicity latent heat source on frontogenesis." *Journal of Applied Meteorology*, 5 (1966): 377–387

Reed, R.J., "Cyclogenesis in polar air streams." *Monthly Weather Review*, 107 (1979): 38–52

Reed, R.J. & B.A. Kunkel, "The Arctic circulation in summer." *Journal of Meteorology*, 17 (1960): 489–506

Serreze, M.C., A.H. Lynch & M.P. Clark, "The Arctic frontal zone as seen in the NCEP-NCAR reanalysis." *Journal of Climate*, 14 (2001): 1550–1567

POLAR LOWS

Polar lows are small, short-lived (lifetime usually less than one day) atmospheric low-pressure systems that occur poleward of the main polar front in both hemispheres. Because of their small horizontal scale and short lifetime, they can often pass undetected between conventional meteorological reporting stations and are usually identified via satellite imagery. The more vigorous lows occur mainly over the ice-free ocean areas during the winter months and dissipate rapidly once they make landfall. Although these systems are small, they can have a major impact on maritime operations and coastal communities since the more vigorous lows can have winds of gale or even storm force.

One problem that has been encountered by those investigating polar lows is the wide range of terms used to describe the phenomenon. In addition to polar low, terms used in the literature have included mesocyclone, polar mesoscale vortex, comma cloud, Arctic hurricane, Arctic low, and cold air depression. However, all these terms refer to the same type of weather system, but with the different names often indicating the strength of the lows. The term polar low is usually reserved for systems that have surface wind speeds of greater than gale force (51 km h^{-1}).

Satellite imagery has shown that polar lows can have a wide range of cloud signatures and that these can often provide information on the mechanisms behind the formation and development of the vortices. A limited number of polar lows have the appearance of small depressions, with warm, cold, and occluded frontal bands. Such systems are thought to develop through baroclinic instability—the main mechanism behind the development of midlatitude frontal depressions. At the other extreme, some polar lows have the appearance of tropical cyclones in satellite imagery, with deep thunderstorm clouds surrounding a cloud-free "eye," which has given rise to the use of the term Arctic hurricane to describe some of the more vigorous systems. There is still considerable debate regarding the role that conditional instability of the second kind (the mechanism behind the development and maintenance of tropical cyclones) plays in the development of polar lows. It is clear that both polar lows and hurricanes exist in air masses that are unstable through deep layers of the atmosphere, with relatively very warm air near the surface and very cold air aloft. In the polar regions, such conditions are often found near the edge of the sea ice when very cold air flows off the ice and encounters warm waters carried poleward by the ocean currents. Such conditions result in very large fluxes of heat and moisture from the ocean into the lowest layers of the atmosphere and, if the atmosphere becomes unstable through a deep layer, perhaps because of the presence of a cold upper trough, then cumulonimbus clouds can develop in association with the polar lows.

Analysis of satellite imagery has shown that there is in fact a spectrum of polar lows with, at the extremes, purely baroclinic systems and deeply convective polar lows. In between, there are a wide range of systems that change their nature during their brief lifetimes. Many polar lows develop initially through baroclinic instability, but can develop more convective characteristics later in their life cycle.

Although polar lows can be found in all parts of the polar regions, they are much more common over the ice-free ocean areas than in regions covered by land- or sea-ice. Some systems are found close to the midlatitude polar front, and are often referred to as comma clouds. These systems are usually associated with minor troughs in the polar airstreams to the west of large depressions and can interact with the polar front, forming new weather systems. The most active polar lows are found in regions where the air-sea temperatures differences are largest and include the Norwegian and Barents seas area of the North Atlantic, the Gulf of Alaska, the Sea of Japan, and the Labrador Sea. Here, air masses with temperatures well below freezing cross waters that have surface temperatures as high as 10°C, thus inducing strong air-sea interactions that are extremely important in the development of the polar lows. One area where large air-sea temperature differences exist is close to the sea ice edge, and many of the documented cases of very active polar lows have been concerned with lows in such areas.

Since many polar lows are associated with winds of gale force or stronger, it is very important to be able to forecast much systems and issue warnings to those involved in maritime operations or living in coastal communities. However, since the lows are very small, they are not well handled by the current generation of weather forecasting models. So, at present, the forecasting of such systems is carried out using a nowcasting approach. This involves the use of satellite imagery to detect and follow the movement of the lows, and to monitor the evolution of the systems via their cloud signatures. The intensity of the surface winds associated with the lows can be determined via radar instruments on the polar orbiting satellite. Such a nowcasting approach allows forecasts to be made for up to about 12 h ahead.

A great deal has been learnt about polar lows since they were first identified as an important meteorological feature of the Arctic in the middle of the 20th century. However, there are still a number of questions to be resolved regarding the mechanisms involved in their formation and development, and how we can better forecast these systems. The answers to these questions will probably come through experiments with high-resolution atmospheric models that are already being used within research studies and will find increasing use operationally during the coming decades.

JOHN TURNER

See also **Polar Fronts**

Further Reading

Carleton, A.M., "Satellite climatological aspects of cold air mesocyclones in the Arctic and Antarctic." *Global Atmospheric Ocean Systems,* 5 (1996): 1–42

Lystad, M., *Polar Lows in the Norwegian, Greenland and Barents Seas. Final Report, Polar Lows Project,* Oslo, Norway: Norwegian Meteorological Institute, 1986

Rasmussen, E.A. & J. Turner, *Polar Lows: Mesoscale Weather Systems in the Polar Regions,* Cambridge and New York: Cambridge University Press, 2003

Shapiro, M.A., L.S. Fedor & T. Hampel, "Research aircraft measurements of a polar low over the Norwegian Sea." *Tellus,* 39A (1987): 272–306

Turner, J., T. Lachlan-Cope & E.A. Rasmussen, "Polar lows." *Weather* 46 (1991): 107–114

Turner, J.,T. A. Lachlan-Cope & J.P. Thomas, "A comparison of Arctic and Antarctic mesoscale vortices." *Journal of Geophysical Research,* 98 D7 (1993): 13019–13034

Twitchell, P.F., E.A. Rasmussen, & K.L. Davidson, *Polar and Arctic Lows,* Hampton, Virginia: Deepak, 1989

POLAR STEPPE

Based upon a number of studies of fossil pollen and plant-macrofossil assemblages and vertebrate fauna across the region of Beringia, extending from eastern Siberia to Alaska and northwestern Canada, it has been proposed that a major late Pleistocene biome, the so-called polar or Arctic steppe-tundra, is now extinct. This former biome is defined by tundra vegetation dominated by species of grass (*Agropyron, Calamagrostis*), forbs, sedges (*Carex*), and sage (*Artemisia*) that supported a diverse herbivore fauna primarily composed of hoofed grazing animals such as bison and horses.

Steppes are broadly defined as open, semi-arid grasslands and range from the prairies of North America to Mongolia and as far south as Patagonia in South America and the Tibetan Plateau in Asia. The polar steppe of Beringia differs because it exists today only in small, fragmented relics, if at all. The hypothesized presence of large regions of steppe-tundra across Alaska and Siberia during the Pleistocene glacial epochs has led to a search for modern analogs. However, it is generally recognized that steppe-tundra was an ecosystem complex with a mosaic of landscapes and associated vegetation rather than a few simple community types.

An ecological definition of steppe incorporates such factors as physiognomy, floristics, soils, and climate.

Insect fauna can also be important. For example, the pill beetle (*Morychus viridis*) is common in the cold steppes of northeast Asia. Its regular co-occurrence there with the dominant dry ground sedge (*Carex argunensis*) and its fodder plant, the moss *Polytrichum piliferum*, in both fossil and contemporary assemblages, has led Russian scientists to consider modern hemicryophytic steppes as one of the possible analogues of the Pleistocene steppes.

Beringia remained largely ice-free during the Pleistocene glaciations and was likely a major northern refugium for plants escaping the advancing ice. As an environment, Beringia would have been more continental than today, having significantly drier and colder winters but with warmer summers that allowed deeper seasonal thawing of the permafrost. American biologist Steve Young notes that although there were probably no forests, there would have been coppices of cottonwood (*Populus*) and thick dwarf woodlands of scrub willow (*Salix*) and perhaps alder (*Alnus*). Windblown deposits of silt (loess) provided a fresh, unweathered source of nutrients that were continually replenished to the soil and that were made available to the vegetation during the growing season because of the thawing permafrost that deepened the active layer.

Great differences exist in the composition and functional groups of Arctic vertebrates between the late Pleistocene and today. For example, the Pleistocene steppe fauna of Alaska contained up to 95% grazing animals such as bison, horse, and megafauna (e.g., mammoth) in a region today characterized by tundra vegetation. Large mammals found in the fossil assemblages that still coexist in Alaska include moose, caribou, muskoxen, and sheep. The high species richness of the ungulate animal community of the late Pleistocene steppe-tundra has been explained as the result of a more fine-grained and complex mosaic of plant communities than today. A greater diversity of plant communities, and higher net primary productivity made possible by longer, warmer growing seasons and increased nutrient availability, together with a selection of grassland (especially graminoid) species that were more palatable than the tussock tundra sedges such as cottongrass (*Eriophorum*) that predominate over extensive areas today, would have reduced competition among large herbivores and allowed them to coexist.

Unfortunately, paleoecological data do not permit a definitive characterization of Pleistocene steppe vegetation, as has been stressed by some scientists, including Russian botanist Yuri Kozhevnikov. Nonetheless, it is now generally accepted that major habitat types included: (1) flood plains and lower river terraces with tall shrub communities dominated by species of willow, with an understory rich in herbs and grasses in openings (habitat representing 5% of the total area);

(2) poorly drained lowlands supporting sedge-moss meadows (10% of the total area); (3) well-drained, nutrient-rich, rolling uplands covered with a mosaic of upland sedges, grasses, and *Artemisia* (65% of the total area); and (4) wind-exposed, relatively dry mountain slopes supporting tundra cushion plants including *Dryas*, *Saxifraga*, and *Draba*, along with dry-ground sedges and lichens (20% of the total area).

Russian botanist Boris Yurtsev contends that a complete transition exists from the true steppes of interior Asia to the tundra-steppes of the Arctic coast, with the most extreme tundra steppes found on Wrangel Island. Steppe-tundra areas in Siberia have been described primarily from calcareous substrates. In North America, relatively isolated and well-circumscribed examples of transitional steppe or steppe analog communities have been reported from steep, dry south-facing slopes and river bluffs in interior Alaska and Yukon Territory, pingos on the North Slope of Alaska, and the west coast of Greenland. Although they differ in important respects, the Yukon and Alaska grasslands are more similar to each other than either is to the prairie grasslands of the American Great Plains.

It is often assumed that changes in climate at the end of the Pleistocene resulted in destabilization of the Arctic steppe-tundra biome and altered the efficiency of energy transfer from one trophic level to the next. According to this view, disassembly of the Arctic steppe-tundra biome at the beginning of the Holocene interglacial interval was probably a major factor in the widespread extinction of many species of large herbivores. An alternative view, the "Pleistocene overkill hypothesis," holds that advances in hunting technology *c.*10,000—15,000 years BP allowed a mobile and growing human population to hunt the steppe megafauna to the point of extinction. Some scientists, including Russian Sergei Zimov and colleagues, contend that the grazing megafauna played a major role in maintaining steppe conditions during the Pleistocene and that its disappearance, which coincided with increased human hunting, contributed greatly to the transition from steppe to tundra at the end of the Pleistocene.

Clearly, the appearance, composition, and even the existence of the polar steppe or steppe-tundra remain open to conjecture. We do know that a number of animals unlike any other extant today existed in Beringia because of the fossil evidence. At the same time, we suspect that a different climate and widespread vegetation types prevailed because of the palynological evidence. It is to be hoped that in the future we can learn more about this intriguing chapter of the Arctic's past.

BRUCE FORBES

See also **Beringia; Environmental History of the Arctic; Pleistocene Megafauna; Tussock Tundra**

Further Reading

Berman, Danil I., A.V. Alfimov, G.G. Mazhitova, I.B. Grishkan & Boris A. Yurtsev, *Cold Steppes of North-East Asia*, Madagan: IBPN FEB RAS, 2001 (in Russian)

Bliss, Lawrence C., "Arctic Ecosystems of North America." In *Ecosystems of the World, Volume 3, Polar and Alpine Tundra*, edited by Frans-Emil Wielgolaski, Amsterdam: Elsevier Science, 1977, pp. 551–683

Cwynar, Leslie C. & James C. Ritchie, "Arctic steppe-tundra: a Yukon perspective." *Science*, 208 (1980): 1375–1377

Delcourt, Hazel R. Paul A. Delcourt, *Quaternary Ecology: A Paleoecological Perspective*, New York: Chapman & Hall, 1991

Edwards, Mary E. W. Scott Armbruster, "A tundra-steppe transition on Kathul Mountain, Alaska, USA." *Arctic and Alpine Research*, 21 (1989): 296–304

Elias, Scott A. & Julie Brigham-Grette (editors), "Beringian Paleoenvironments: Festschrift in Honour of D.M. Hopkins." *Quaternary Science Reviews*, 20 (2001): 1–574

Hopkins, David M., John V. Matthews Jr., Charles E. Schweger & Steven B. Young (editors), *The Paleoecology of Beringia*, New York: Academic Press, 1982

Kozhevnikov, Yuri P. & V.V. Ukraintseva, "Arguments for and against a pleistocene tundra-steppe." *Polar Geography*, 21 (1997): 51–69

Martin, Paul & Richard G. Klein (editors), *Quaternary Extinctions: A Prehistoric Revolution*, Tucson: University of Arizona Press, 1984

Vetter, Mary A., "Grasslands of the Aishihik-Sekulmun Lakes area, Yukon Territory, Canada." *Arctic*, 53 (2000): 165–173

Walker, Marilyn D., Donald A. Walker, Kaye R. Everett & Susan K. Short, "Steppe vegetation on south-facing slopes of pingos, central Arctic coastal plain, Alaska, USA." *Arctic and Alpine Research*, 23 (1991): 170–188

Young, Steven B., "Is Steppe Tundra Alive and Well in Alaska?" In *Abstracts of the Fourth Biennial Meeting of the American Quaternary Association*, Tempe: Arizona State University, 1976, pp. 84–88

——, "Beringia: An Ice-Age View." In *Crossroads of Continents: Cultures of Siberia and Alaska*, edited by William W. Fitzhugh & Aron Crowell, Washington, District of Columbia: Smithsonian Institution, 1988, pp. 106–110

Zimov, Sergei A., V.I. Chuprynin, A.P. Oreshko, F. Stuart Chapin III, James R. Reynolds & Melissa C. Chapin, "Steppe-tundra transition: a herbivore-driven biome shift at the end of the Pleistocene." *American Naturalist*, 146 (1995): 765–794

POLAR STRATOSPHERIC CLOUDS

Polar stratospheric clouds (PSCs) are thin clouds of condensed matter, droplets, or particles that can form in the high-latitude lower stratosphere during polar winter. PSCs are nearly translucent, but they can sometimes be seen from the ground, particularly when the sun is a few degrees below the horizon but still illuminates the PSCs at approximately 20 km altitude. The appearance of PSCs ranges from a patchy faint opalescent veil to an intense display of iridescent colors in the dark sky of the polar night. Based on their appearance, PSCs are also called mother-of-pearl clouds. The colorful appearance of PSCs is due to the fact that the individual PSC particles or droplets are very small, and the particle size distribution is smaller than or overlaps the wavelength range of visible light. Therefore, the spatial distribution of light scattered by PSC particles is a function of wavelength, and in a given direction the stray light is colored. In the Northern Hemisphere, PSC occurrence is usually limited to the region north of approximately $60°$ N, but on rare occasions, they have also been observed as far south as $50°$N. Polar ozone depletion is linked to the presence of PSCs in the polar stratosphere.

The stratosphere is a very dry environment and the existence of clouds in the stratosphere is limited to areas of extremely low temperatures. The frost point, the temperature at which water ice particles can form, is approximately $-85°$C at 20 km altitude and even lower at higher altitudes. Temperatures below the frost point are regularly attained in the Antarctic stratosphere in winter, but are rare in the Arctic. However, different mixtures of sulfuric acid (H_2SO_4), nitric acid (HNO_3), and water (H_2O) can form stable liquid or solid particles in the temperature range of up to about $10°$C above the frost point. The following stable phases have been suggested to be present in different types of PSCs: liquid droplets of varying fractions of H_2O, H_2SO_4, and HNO_3 (supercooled ternary solutions, STS), crystals of one part HNO_3 to three parts H_2O (nitric acid trihydrate, NAT), crystals of one part HNO_3 to two parts H_2O (nitric acid dihydrate, NAD), and crystals of one part H_2SO_4 to four parts H_2O (sulfuric acid tetrahydrate, SAT). The formation of SAT and NAD under stratospheric conditions is under debate, but the existence of STS and NAT in the stratosphere has been confirmed. PSC formation usually occurs within the polar vortex, either in large-scale areas of low temperature with horizontal scales of several hundreds or thousands of kilometers (synoptic PSCs) or in smaller patches of low temperatures over mountain ridges (mountain wave PSCs or lee wave PSCs). These patches have horizontal scales of some ten to a couple of hundred kilometers and are caused by the presence of vertically propagating atmospheric waves (gravity waves) that are exited in the troposphere by a fast flow of air over mountain ridges.

Based on the properties of the cloud particles, PSCs are often classified into different categories. PSCs that exist above the ice frost point and consist of particles other than water ice crystals are often termed PSC type I, with the distinction of type Ia for clouds of solid, non-spherical particles and type Ib for clouds of liquid, spherical droplets. PSCs, which consist primarily of water ice, are referred to as PSC type II. Due to the limited abundance of nitric acid and sulfuric acid in the stratosphere, PSC type I particles are either very small (smaller than a couple of micrometers in diameter) or exist at a very low concentration, in the order of only a few particles per liter of air. PSC type II particles can grow to sizes of tens of micrometers with considerable particle concentrations in the PSC.

PSCs have a major impact on the stratospheric chemistry in polar winter/spring. It is the presence of PSCs in the wintertime polar stratosphere that enables anthropogenic halogen compounds to effectively destroy ozone, causing the ozone hole above the Antarctic and substantial ozone destruction above the Arctic (ozone depletion). In PSC-free parts of the stratosphere, the ozone-depleting potential of anthropogenic halogen compounds is much smaller. The effect of PSCs on the stratospheric composition is twofold. First, heterogeneous chemical reactions take place on the surface of the PSC particles. These heterogeneous reactions initiate a chain of reactions that convert the stratospheric reservoir of passive chlorine compounds into very reactive radical species. The passive compounds do not react with ozone, but the reactive radical species effectively destroy ozone in a catalytical process when sunlight is present. Second, PSC particles fall with appreciable velocities when they grow larger than a few micrometers. The subsidence of PSC particles irreversibly removes nitric acid and water vapor from the stratospheric layer where they form, a process that is referred to as denitrification and dehydration. Nitric acid plays an important role in the chemical mechanism that eventually converts the reactive chlorine radical species back into passive compounds. This deactivation process normally terminates the ozone loss event in polar spring, but is slowed down or completely prohibited in severely denitrified air masses, causing a larger overall ozone loss in these air masses, or the complete loss of ozone in a broad altitude range in the Antarctic.

MARKUS REX

See also **Ozone Depletion; Polar Vortex; Upper Atmosphere Physics and Chemistry**

Further Reading

Carslaw, K.S., T. Peter S.L. Clegg, "Modeling the composition of liquid stratospheric aerosols." *Reviews of Geophysics*, 35 (1997): 125–154

Godin, S., L.R. Poole, S. Bekki, T. Deshler, N. Larsen, T. Peter, "Global Distributions and Changes in Stratospheric Particles." In *Scientific Assessment of Ozone Depletion: 1998*, WMO (World Meteorological Organization), Global Ozone Research and Monitoring Project—Report No. 44, Geneva, 1999

Solomon, S., "Stratospheric ozone depletion: a review of concepts and history." *Reviews of Geophysics*, 37 (1999): 275–316

Tabazadeh, A., E.J. Jensen, O.B. Toon, K. Drdla & M.R. Schoeberl, "Role of the stratospheric polar freezing belt in denitrification." *Science*, 291 (2001): 2591–2594

POLAR VORTEX

The polar vortex is a stable low-pressure system in the middle atmosphere, which is present at high latitudes of both hemispheres during the respective winter season. The lowest pressure is usually located close to the pole. Air masses within the Arctic polar vortex circulate anticlockwise (cyclonically) due to the Coriolis effect, causing a westerly circulation that covers most of the Arctic region. The absolute wind velocity and even the angular velocity maximize at the edge of the polar vortex, leading to a strong west wind jet located usually at about 60°–70° N—the polar night jet. Vertically, the circulation system extends from approximately 15 to 80 km altitude, although the term polar vortex is often only used for the lower part of it, up to about 30 km altitude. The zonally averaged wind velocity in the Arctic polar night jet varies between approximately 10 ms^{-1} at 15 km and 80 ms^{-1} at 60 km altitude, with considerable short-term and year-to-year variability. The Arctic polar vortex forms around September/October each year and often persists into early spring. However, the date of the final breakup of the Arctic polar vortex is very variable from year to year and may occur as early as January or as late as May. In the Arctic, the polar vortex is quite variable, is often displaced from the pole by hundreds or thousands of kilometers, and is often distorted by planetary scale waves. Sometimes, parts of the polar vortex are pushed as far south as 30° N for a few days.

The polar night jet effectively inhibits the transport of air masses across the edge of the vortex, particularly in the vertical region between approximately 18 and 30 km altitude. This results in a high degree of isolation of air masses inside the vortex from extravortex air at these altitudes. At higher levels, a slow average poleward motion of air prevails. The air masses within the polar vortex descend slowly, with average vertical velocities between a few hundred meters per month at the lowest levels and a few kilometers per month at higher levels. The temperatures inside the polar vortex are determined by a balance between radiative cooling and dynamic heating. Dynamic heating is caused by continuous adiabatic compression of the subsiding air masses as they reach increasing pressure levels. In the vertical region around 20 km, altitude temperatures can drop to very low values. The interannual variability of the temperatures inside the Arctic polar vortex is pronounced and minimum temperatures usually range between −65°C and −85°C. In cold Arctic winters, polar stratospheric clouds can form inside the polar vortex. Heterogeneous chemistry on the surface of the cloud particles initiates the chemical mechanism that eventually destroys ozone, when the sunlight returns to the Arctic region in late winter/spring (ozone depletion).

The Arctic polar vortex is less stable and warmer than its Antarctic counterpart. The differences mainly arise from large differences in the activity of atmospheric waves in both hemispheres. The poleward and downward motion of air at high latitudes is driven by a zonal forcing, which is exerted from dissipating waves. Strong wave activity is connected with larger zonal forcing, faster poleward transport, faster subsidence, larger dynamical heating, and higher temperatures in the polar vortex. The Arctic geography is characterized by the asymmetric distribution of continents and oceans and by high mountain ridges in north/south orientation, which are both a source of atmospheric waves. Hence, the level of wave activity at northern latitudes is larger than in the Antarctic, and the Arctic polar vortex is warmer and less stable than the Antarctic polar vortex. In the Antarctic temperatures regularly drop below −85°C in winter and the formation of polar stratospheric clouds is widespread each winter. The stable Antarctic polar vortex persists longer into spring than the Arctic vortex. These differences in the properties of the polar vortices eventually result in largely different degrees of polar ozone depletion in both hemispheres.

The barrier inhibiting the exchange of air from the polar vertex edge with midlatitudes is not perfect, as the edge is constantly disturbed by planetary scale waves. During "Rossby wave breaking" events, the sharp vortex edge becomes eroded into a sea of filaments. This shedding of filaments, shown by high-resolution measurements of trace gases, provides a one-way transport mechanism out of the polar vortex.

MARKUS REX

See also **Ozone Depletion; Polar Stratospheric Clouds**

Further Reading

Brasseur, G. P. (editor), *The Stratosphere and its Role in the Climate System*, NATO ASI Series, Series I: Global Environmental Change, Volume 54, Berlin, Heidelberg: Springer, 1997

McIntyre, M.E. "The Stratospheric Polar Vortex and Sub Vortex: Fluid Dynamics and Midlatitude Ozone Loss." In *The Arctic and Environmental Change*, edited by P. Wadhams, J.A. Dowdeswell & A.N. Schofield, Royal Society, London, 1996

Salby, M.L., *Fundamentals of Atmospheric Physics*, San Diego: Academic Press, 1996

WMO (World Meteorological Organization), *Scientific Assessment of Ozone Depletion: 1998*, Global Ozone Research and Monitoring Project—Report No. 44, Geneva, 1999

POLITICAL ISSUES IN RESOURCE MANAGEMENT

Some of the most contentious issues in the Arctic arise from decision-making over contested resources—resources in which more than one actor has a stake in or right to the decision-making forum. Here "politics" and "political issues" are defined as the process involved in the making of decisions. In the Arctic, the most controversial political issues arising from resource decision-making can boil down to three general spheres of conflict: ownership, management scheme, and equity in the distribution of costs and benefits.

Positive trends in the North have included a cultural and political resurgence of indigenous peoples, innovative approaches to sustainable development, and devolution of decision-making to northern peoples. At the same time, a majority of decision-making powers remain with national governments for most regions, and extractive companies have considerable influence over decision-making about key lucrative resources.

Ownership

The Arctic is a land of political contrasts. Concurrent with a surge of national interests in the exploitation of northern resources, Arctic peoples in all Arctic nations have gained political savvy and strength in pushing devolution of power from colonial national government agencies to locally controlled bodies. The resolution of ownership issues in the North often provides a basis for more equitable exploitation of resources and the establishment of self-government for aboriginal peoples. The two most striking examples include the 1979 establishment of a Greenlandic Home Rule government (Kalaallit Nunaat-Grønland) and the 1999 creation of the territory of Nunavut in Canada as a result of a 28-year drive for self-government for Inuit people in Canada's eastern Arctic. Because they form the basic framework of power sharing and mutual recognition, land rights and claims resolutions clarify decision-making authority and often build a strong foundation for self-government.

At the same time, because both Greenland and Nunavut rely on significant transfer payments from their respective colonial governments, a certain level of decision-making is reserved by most national governments and tied to ongoing national interests including foreign relations, military installations, and migratory wildlife. For instance, the Nunavut Land Claims Agreement Act, which is the framework for the Inuit/Canadian mutual recognition of rights and claims to Inuit land, recognizes Inuit ownership of 350,000 square kilometers of land, but only includes subsurface rights on 10% of that land. In exchange for concessions such as this, Nunavut receives up to 95% of its operating budget from the Government of Canada. Greenland and its colonial power Denmark share jurisdiction over subsurface rights but the Greenland Home Rule Act grants Denmark sole power over foreign affairs.

The Defense Agreement of 1951 between Denmark and the United States granted American military installations in Greenland in exchange for defending Greenland in the event of a military attack. Without consultation with the indigenous population (Inughuit), Denmark evacuated the Thule Inuit from the rich trapping grounds in northwest Greenland to clear the site for the construction of the US Thule Air Base in the village of Uummannaq (Dundas). They were forced to relocate to Qaanaaq, about 140 km (90 miles) to the north. The surviving relocates and their descendants first sought compensation for their lost lands and then demanded the right to return. In response to a landmark court case in 1999, Denmark's Eastern Circuit High Court ruled in favor of the Inughuit trappers, awarding them a lump settlement as compensation for lost livelihoods (a collective indemnity of 500,000 Danish kroner in addition to 17,000 Danish kroner for each individual), but the Greenlanders have since appealed that decision to the Danish Supreme Court, asking for 234 million Danish kroner in damages. The Supreme Court, however, rejected the claims in late 2003 and held the 1999 verdict. In February 2003, the United States returned jurisdiction over contested hunting grounds on the Pituffik (Dundas) Peninsula to Greenland.

In December 2002, Greenland received a request concerning the deployment of the Thule radar in the US National Missile Defense program, an internationally controversial weapons program. According to terms of the 1951 Defense Agreement, the United States is allowed to deploy the program without consent from Greenland or Denmark, but has entered into formal negotiations over the program. In exchange, Greenland is keen to renegotiate the terms of the 1951 agreement, as the majority of Greenlanders do not approve of any escalation of American military activities in Greenland.

Where ownership is contested, decisions of resource management become contentious and much time, energy, and money is tied up in lobbying or campaigning in the public sphere or clarifying land rights and interests in the court system. One case in point involves Saami reindeer herders in northern Sweden struggling to maintain their reindeer herds in sufficient numbers to create a viable business and maintain vital cultural practices. The Saami community of Tåssåsen in the Swedish mountains was sued by a group of 50 private landowners in 1990 for resource damage to their forestlands, which are contested winter grazing grounds for Saami reindeer herds. In addition, Tåssåsen is affected by another larger legal process in which four Saami communities have been sued by 700 private landowners in the nearby county of Härjedalen. The two lawsuits affect 75% of the available winter grazing grounds for the community. The key points of contention are that the forest owners demand to be compensated for resource damage to their forestlands due to grazing and demand that the Swedish court invalidate Saami land rights to grazing grounds on private property that the Saami herders maintain encompass their traditional winter grazing grounds.

As of February 2003, the Saami had lost in a Court of Appeals and vowed to take the case to the Supreme Court. In its decision, the lower Court acknowledged that it was the Swedish State's responsibility to ensure that Saami reindeer herding be maintained. In the wake of the Court's decision, a coalition of 32 environmental and indigenous rights organizations from 14 countries wrote a joint letter to the Swedish Prime Minister Göran Persson demanding that the Swedish State move to secure the future of Saami herding lands and rights.

Management Scheme

The Arctic is seen by most national governments as a resource-rich area as well as an interconnected ecosystem to be shared across jurisdictions. Most national governments actively maintain their stake in the vast natural resources as well as numerous northern defense outposts. In addition, many transnational indigenous government bodies such as the Saami Council or the Inuit Circumpolar Conference as well as international and national environmental groups, religious associations, and international government bodies have a stake in resource decision-making. Because there are so many actors with claims and rights to resource decisions in the Arctic, balancing the interests of these various agents becomes fraught with politics, nowhere more so than on state-controlled "public" lands.

Many management decisions on public or disputed lands bring up contested issues because of the multiple functions that public lands serve, such as subsistence animal and plant harvests, recreation, tourism, and ecosystem services as well as industrial exploitation of resources. In order to promote multiple-use management approaches and reduce disputes through fostering participation by potential critics, many public land management agencies are moving toward multistakeholder management advisory processes. In these "roundtables" or advisory processes, dialogue among interest groups—rather than litigation and campaigning—informs and shapes management planning in making determinations.

In Russia, a proposal to conserve the lands and traditional cultures of indigenous peoples has resulted in the establishment of several small, defined territories of traditional economies, called ethnoecological territories. These special status territories, under unified administration and management, are set aside with the goal of preserving a particular cultural formation and the environment on which its traditional land uses depend. As a new category of protected territory under

Russia's conservation legislation, ethnoecological territories would benefit from the historically rigorous conservation legislation and enjoy its popular support. Activity on the land would be limited only to "traditional" activities; industrial development would be excluded from such territories. According to scholars and Khanty communities in Western Siberia that have chosen to establish these territories, problems exist with the implementation of these territories, as their opportunities for economic development are limited. Moreover, the concept implies that "culture" is a static entity that should be conserved, rather than evolve through self-government, and the territories have often been set aside as compensation for highly damaging industrial oil and gas development without adequate enforcement of environmental protection, integrated regional development, or public participation in wider land-use planning.

Distribution of Costs and Benefits

Along with devolution of ownership and decision-making has come greater scrutiny of the costs and benefits of resource management. Both the Mackenzie Valley Pipeline in the Northwest Territories and the opening up of the Prudhoe Bay Oil Fields in Alaska were postponed until the resolution of land claims. The 1971 Alaska Native Claims Settlement Act (ANCSA) responded to pressure from indigenous peoples in Alaska to greater equity in resource development and the resolution of land claims following the discovery of the Prudhoe Bay Oil Field. The bill provided Alaska Natives $962.5 million and 44 million acres of land and required the establishment of 12 regional corporations to be set up to administer the settlement. Later, a 13th corporation was established for Alaska Natives who lived outside the state.

In 1976, a Thomas Berger, a British Columbia Supreme Court Justice, was selected to chair a Royal Commission to investigate the development of an Arctic gas pipeline through the Mackenzie Valley in the Northwest Territories. After the Berger inquiry heard from First Nations throughout the Mackenzie Valley, Northwest Territories, most of whom opposed the plan, the plan was shelved until the resolution of land claims. Since then, two of the major First Nations in the Valley, the Gwich'in and the Sahtu, have settled land claims and now have their own regulatory regimes for development on their lands. The battleground has shifted to bilateral relations between the United States and Canada, as well as competing corporate oil and gas giants. There are two major gas pipelines proposed to transport gas from the Arctic Ocean to the continental United States. On the Canadian side, authorities and the many aboriginal governments in the Mackenzie Delta region are proposing a jointly owned and operated gas pipeline that would maximize economic benefits to the aboriginal governments whose land the gas pipeline would travel through. On the American side, revenue would most likely accrue to the state of Alaska and corporations involved in the pipeline, including Native Corporations.

Another dominant trend toward resource sharing is in the development of Impact and Benefit Agreements (IBAs). IBAs vary in their efficacy and legal status, from negotiated provisions in land claims settlements to Memoranda of Understanding (MOUs) between adjacent communities or aboriginal nations and a particular company or government entity. Requirements of IBAs depend on the legal status of the land, a regulatory regime for extraction, and public perception of the project. For lands not under legal requirements to negotiate social benefits, public perception or pressure as well as conditions tied to government or multilateral financing can have a bearing on agreements and their strength. Early IBAs focused on employment and training opportunities, but with devolution of decision-making and a rise in self-governments across the North, more sophisticated IBAs have included provisions for revenue-sharing, environmental protections including reclamation procedures, cross-cultural training, economic diversification planning, and dispute resolution.

The Ulu project with Echo Bay Mines Ltd. is an underground gold deposit located on Kitikmeot Inuit lands in Nunavut. The Kitikmeot Inuit Association owned the lands on which the gold deposit was, and under the terms of the Nunavut Land Claim Agreement, the development of the subsurface deposit required the negotiation of an IBA. The agreement included the creation of Inuit-owned business and industry, the development of a formula to ensure that contracts went to Inuit and locally owned businesses, a social and educational program, and establishment of an implementation panel.

CHANDA L. MEEK

See also **Alaska Native Claims Settlement Act (ANCSA); Common Property Management; Conservation; Ecology and Environment; Greenland Inuit; Inuit Circumpolar Conference (ICC); Land Claims; Mackenzie Valley Pipeline; Prudhoe Bay; Relocation; Saami; Saami Council; Self-Determination; Self-Government; Sustainable Development; Thule Air Base**

Further Reading

Arctic Council, *Taking Wing: First Arctic Council Conference on Gender Equality and Women in the Arctic*, Saariselkä, Finland, August 3–6, 2002

Minority Rights Group (editor), *Polar Peoples: Self-Determination and Development*, London: Minority Rights Publications, 1994

O'Reilly, Kevin & Erin Eacott, *Aboriginal Peoples and Impact and Benefit Agreement: Summary of the Report of a National Workshop*, Yellowknife: Canadian Arctic Resources Committee, 1998

Smith, Eric A. & Joan McCarther (editors), *Contested Arctic: Indigenous Peoples, Industrial States and the Circumpolar Environment*, Seattle: University of Washington Press, 1997

Wiget, Andrew & Olga Balalaeva, "Siberian Perspectives on Protected Use Areas as a Strategy for Conserving Traditional Indigenous Cultures in the Context of Industrial Development (I): Ethnoecological Territories and Territories of Mixed Economy." In *Proceedings from the Symposium Development in the Arctic*, Slettestrand, Denmark, January 9–11, 1998, Danish Polar Center Publication No. 5

Young, Oran R. & Gail Osherenko (editors), *Polar Politics: Creating International Environmental Regimes*, Ithaca: Cornell University Press, 1993

POLLOCK

Pollock (also known as saithe) or *Pollachius virens* is a fish of the cod family (Gadidae). Pollock are distributed in the North Atlantic from Labrador to Cape Cod (sometimes southward to South Carolina), off southwest and south Greenland, Iceland, and along European coasts from West Spitsbergen and western shores of Novaya Zemlya to the Gulf of Biscay off Spain, including the White (in warmest years), North, and Baltic (westernmost part) seas. The species *Theragra chalcogramma* (also a gadid) is known as Alaska or walleye pollock, and although commercially important within Alaska, is not considered within this entry.

The maximum body length is 115–130 cm, the weight is 16–32 kg, and the maximum age is 20–25 years. The upper part of the body is dark, olive, or black-green, the lower part is light, silvery-gray, and the lateral line is whitish. Pollock have three dorsal and two anal fins; the caudal fin is forked. A small barbel (whisker) is found at the tip of the lower jaw.

Pollock is a gregarious pelagic fish, forming large schools. It inhabits midwater over the continental shelves and near bottom to depths of 200–250 m. Pollock is a very agile fish, undertaking long-distance migrations. It matures at the age of 6–7 years in northern and at 4–5 years in southern parts of its range; common maturation is at 8–10 years. It spawns in all parts of its range except in the Barents, White, and Baltic seas. Spawning occurs in winter and early spring, usually from January-February to March-April, except in American coasts where it reproduces from fall to early spring. It occurs in Atlantic waters over depths of approximately 100–200 m, at temperature of usually 6–9°C. Eggs are pelagic, with an average diameter of 1.15 mm, and are dispersed with currents. Fecundity varies, according to female size, from 0.2–4 million eggs to 6.5 million eggs in large females. The larvae hatch, depending on temperature, on the 6–12th day and are 3–4 mm in length. At the age of 7–8 days, larvae start feeding on external food sources, and on reaching 30 mm in length (about 3 months) they transform to juveniles. At that time, young pollocks migrate in masses from the sea to the gulfs and fjords, including nearshore waters of Norway and the western Murman coast. There, it spends its first and second years of life, moving very close to the coast, sometimes entering river mouths. During winter, part of the young pollock stock returns to sea, while the other part remains in the gulfs during the entire winter season. During its third year of life, young pollock migrate to the sea and usually never return to the gulfs.

Growth is rapid, particularly when the fish are young: at the age of 1, 2, 3, 5, and 10 years, pollock reach the size of ~20, 35, 50, 60–65, and about 95 cm, respectively. Young pollock feed on plankton (copepods, euphausiids, amphipods, etc.) and also consume fish fry. Large specimens are active predators, feeding on capelin, sand eels, herring, blue whiting, young codfish, and also crustaceans, jellyfish, etc.

Pollock migrate from Norwegian coasts to the north, to Spitsbergen and in the Barents Sea, and to the south, into the North Sea, to Faroes, Shetlands, and Iceland. Migrations of young fish are connected to feeding, and those of adults to feeding and spawning. The migration range varies strongly from year to year, depending on generation strength, age, and size composition of the stock and water temperature (because the stock is enhanced in warmer periods). In the Barents Sea, pollock inhabit warm Atlantic currents with temperatures of 3–4°C. In this area, pollock appear in May, after spawning off northwestern Norway. During June-July, they inhabit the most southwestern part of the sea. During August-September, they reach the northern and eastern areas, but are usually concentrated in the central and southern areas. June-August and early September are the usual time for commercial fishery for the pollock in the Barents Sea. At the beginning of November, adult fishes migrate back to the Norwegian waters. During feeding time, pollock undergo diurnal vertical migrations, rising at night in pursuit of plankton into the upper water layers, commonly to the very surface, and descending to the bottom during daytime. Its migrations from the sea to the bays and back are also connected with feeding.

Commercial fishing for pollock exists in all parts of its range, but usually in the Norwegian and North seas, off Scotland, Iceland, and Nova Scotia. In the northeastern Atlantic it is fished during the entire year, and in the northwestern Atlantic mostly in the fall (October–December). The main fishing gear is the bottom trawl. Fish older than 3 years are caught, with length of 30–110 cm, usually 50–80 cm. Usually, pollock is not the main target species but is caught as a bycatch to cod and haddock. Besides the bottom trawl, it is caught by the longlines, set nets, and purse nets. The annual catch, according to FAO fishery statistics, is about 300–400,000 tons (in 1987, it reached 484,000 tons). For the most part, it is caught off Norway and Iceland, but it is also caught by fishermen of France, Canada, Germany, Faroe Islands, Great Britain, Ireland, and Denmark. In the Barents Sea, the average catch is about 20,000 tons (including up to 5000 tons for Russia). The pollock stock in the European area is not threatened, and the admissible catch in 2000–2001 was estimated approximately at 750–800,000 tons.

Pollock meat is very good. Particularly delicious is canned pollock imitating salmon ("sea salmon") in refined and fragrant oil, which gives an otherwise somewhat dry meat a rose-orange color and fatty flavor. A large part of the pollock catch is sold frozen and as fillets, but smoked fish is also good. Smaller fish are made into klipfisk (dried-salted). It is also used salted and baked.

K.N. NESIS

Further Reading

Bigelow, H.B. & W.C. Schroeder, *Fishes of the Gulf of Maine*, Washington: Government Printing Office, 1953 (Fishery Bulletin, US, Volume 53; also available online at http://www.gma.org/fogm/)
Cohen, D.M., T. Inada, T. Iwamoto & N. Scialabba, "Gadiform fishes of the World (Order Gadiformes). *An Annotated and Illustrated Catalogue of Cods, Hakes, Grenadiers and Other Gadiform Fishes Known to Date*, Rome: Food and Agriculture Organization of the United Nations, 1990 (FAO Species Catalogue, 25, Volume 10)
Konstantinov, K.G. (editor), *Fisheries Biological Resources of the North Atlantic and Adjacent Parts of the Arctic Ocean*, 2 volumes, Moscow: Pishchevaya Promyshlennost' Publishing House, 1977 (in Russian)
Matishov, G.G. (editor), *Ichthyofauna and Conditions of its Existence in the Barents Sea*, Apatity: Murman Marine Biological Institution of the USSR Academy of Sciences, 1986 (in Russian)
Müller, H., *Fische Europas*, Leipzig: Neumann, 1983
Wheeler, A., *The Fishes of the British Isles and North-West Europe*, London: Macmillan, 1969

POLLUTION: ENVIRONMENTAL INITIATIVES

Most circum-Arctic countries have developed and maintain environmental initiatives where Arctic issues are included without mentioning the Arctic specifically. Many new national and international initiatives are under negotiation and some of the current environmental initiatives will be finalized or strongly reduced in the years to come. The situation presented here will probably, therefore, be totally changed within a short time after this encyclopedia is published. This entry therefore represents an extract of the situation within the year 2003.

Multinational Initiatives

The United Nations Environmental Program (UNEP) recognizes that although in comparison with most other areas of the world, the Arctic remains a clean environment, for some pollutants, combinations of different factors give rise to concern in certain ecosystems and for some human populations.

To monitor and assess the impact of environmental pollution on the Arctic environment, the ministers for the environment from the eight Arctic rim countries decided to establish the Arctic Environmental Protection Strategy (AEPS; *see* **Declaration on the Protection of the Arctic Environment**) in Rovaniemi in 1991. The objectives of this initiative were:

- to protect the Arctic ecosystems, including humans;
- to provide for the protection, enhancement, and restoration of environmental quality and sustainable utilization of natural resources, including their use by local populations and indigenous peoples in the Arctic;
- to recognize and, to the extent possible, seek to accommodate the traditional and cultural needs, values, and practices of indigenous peoples as determined by themselves, related to the protection of the Arctic environment;
- to review regularly the state of the Arctic environment; and
- to identify, reduce, and, as a final goal, eliminate pollution.

AEPS also formally recognized the importance of the active participation in the process of groups representing the indigenous peoples of the North.

Under the auspice of the AEPS initiative, the Arctic Monitoring and Assessment Program (AMAP) was established in 1991 in order to implement important components of the AEPS into pollution control and assessment. In total, five general AEPS programs were installed in parallel.

(1) Arctic Monitoring and Assessment Program (AMAP) with responsibilities to monitor the levels of, and assess the effects of, anthropogenic pollutants in all compartments of the Arctic environment, including humans.
(2) Conservation of Arctic Flora and Fauna (CAFF) with responsibilities to facilitate the

exchange of information and coordination of research on species and habitats of Arctic flora and fauna.

(3) Emergency Prevention, Preparedness and Response (EPPR) with responsibilities to provide a framework for future cooperation in responding to the threat of Arctic environmental emergencies.

(4) Protection of the Arctic Marine Environment (PAME) with responsibilities to take preventative and other measures, directly or through competent international organizations, regarding marine pollution in the Arctic, irrespective of origin.

(5) Sustainable Development and Utilization (SDU) with responsibilities to propose steps governments should take to meet their commitment to sustainable development of the Arctic, including the sustainable use of renewable resources by indigenous peoples.

In 1998, the Arctic Council ministers instructed senior Arctic officials (SAO) to develop an overall plan identifying actions to address the pollution sources identified through AMAP. The ministers requested that the resulting Arctic Council Action Plan to eliminate Pollution of the Arctic (ACAP) should:

• complement existing arrangements; this should include existing legal arrangements, and existing structures and mechanisms under the Arctic Council, such as the Regional Plan of Action for the Protection of the Arctic Marine Environment from Land-based Activities;

• allow for actions on a wide scope of pollution prevention issues and corresponding remediation measures; and

• include the identification of cooperative activities for implementation. ACAP will act as a strengthening and supporting mechanism to encourage national actions to reduce emissions and other releases of pollutants.

These cooperative actions are intended to make an important and significant contribution to the overall international effort to reduce environmental damage on a global level, not only the Arctic environment.

ACAP consists of two major parts: an overall strategy designed to provide a framework for cooperation and an accompanying "Action Plan," which can evolve dynamically on a shorter time frame in response to identified priorities reflecting specific projects and activities. The overall strategy is designed to cover all pollution issues of concern under the Arctic Council. The Action Plan will give priority to actions that are complementary to existing action plans and actions

both under the Arctic Council and in other fora. The implementation of ACAP will be consistent with the responsibilities, capacities, and work plans of the existing Arctic Council working groups as they pertain to pollution prevention.

In 1998, the Arctic Council also adopted the Regional Program of Action for the Protection of the Arctic Marine Environment from Land-Based activities (RPA). Some of the key considerations for the RPA are:

• that 80% of marine pollution is land-based and it is important to recall that certain Arctic populations are among the most exposed populations in the world to certain environmental contaminants;

• to address several global and regional commitments such as the United Nations Environmental Program (UNEP) Global Program of Action on the Protection of the Marine Environment from Land-based Activities (GPA), UNECE LRTAP and UNEP negotiations on persistent organic pollutants (POPs);

• to strengthen regional cooperation and capacity building, particularly in relation to NPA-Arctic addressing regional priority pollution sources found in the Russian Federation.

The Russian Federations' National Program of Action (NPA-Arctic) is an important component of RPA. The initial phase of RPA focuses on POPs and heavy metals, which present a major pollution threat to the Arctic marine environment. In subsequent phases, the RPA will be expanded to address other contaminants and activities that destroy or degrade the Arctic marine and coastal environment.

In addition to circum-Arctic governmental initiatives, exclusively scientific activities are coordinated by the International Arctic Science Committee (IASC). IASC is a nongovernmental organization whose aim is to encourage and facilitate cooperation in all aspects of Arctic research, in all countries engaged in Arctic research and in all areas of the Arctic region. Several initiatives concerning research on pollution control and monitoring are performed under the official auspice of IASC.

In order to coordinate research activities on environmental issues, the Arctic Environmental Data Directory (ADD) was initiated by the member countries of the Arctic Council as a network cooperation between major Arctic environmental data holders. This cooperation shall make Arctic data and information available to circum-Arctic users.

The 5th framework for European Research has established an institutional network for multidisciplinary environmental research in alpine and Arctic areas (ENVINET). ENVINET is a network of 17 research infrastructures in northern Europe. It focuses on multi-disciplinary environmental research, primarily within atmospheric physics and chemistry, marine and terrestrial biology, including studies on the fate of anthropogenic pollution in the Arctic and Alpine environments. Atmospheric pollution monitoring data from Arctic stations like Alert (Canada), Pt Barrow (Alaska), and Ny-Ålesund (Svalbard) are important information for the Global Atmospheric Watch (GAW) network.

National and Binational Initiatives

In the early 1990s, radioactive waste-management practices of the former Soviet Union came under increased international discussion. Russian scientists disclosed several dumped-nuclear-waste sites in the Kara and Barents seas that contravened the London convention ban on radioactive waste disposal at sea. Therefore, the United States funded the Office of Naval Research Arctic Nuclear Waste Assessment Program (ANWAP) in order to quantify the types, amounts, and rates of release of radionuclides from marine disposal sites in Russian sources.

Due to the obvious need for suitable research locations in the Arctic, a network of circum-Arctic national research stations like Alert (Canada), Pt Barrow (Alaska), Ny-Ålesund (Svalbard), Station North (Greenland), Summit (Greenland), and Zackenberg (Greenland) has been established where research and monitoring on pollution in the Arctic is performed. As an additional part of the international circum-Arctic efforts to evaluate and assess the impact of anthropogenic pollution in the Arctic environment, several Arctic rim-countries have initiated national initiatives as frames for coordinated research on pollution issues in the northern regions.

The joint Norwegian-Russian Commission for Environmental Cooperation was established in 1992, with protection of the marine environment in northern areas as one of the main priorities of the commission. A working group on the marine environment of the Barents region (WGMEBR) was initiated with the task of establishing and supplementing the scientific basis for sustainable utilization of the living and nonliving resources in the Barents region through joint scientific efforts. Investigations on the fate of anthropogenic pollutants were also initiated as a part of the scientific work. As an effort to strengthen scientific research in the Norwegian Arctic, in 1991 the Norwegian parliament decided to establish the Polar Environmental Center in Tromsø, where all national institutions with significant scientific research activities and interests in the Norwegian Arctic should be present. Today, the Polar Environmental Center houses all important national Norwegian institutions for Arctic research and covers scientific issues including research topics related to environmental and pollution aspects as one of the top priorities of the scientific work performed at the Polar Environmental Center.

In Norway, a national Arctic monitoring initiative was established to introduce a comprehensive surveillance system for the environment around Svalbard and Jan Mayen (MOSJ: "Miljøovervåkingssystem for Svalbard and Jan Mayen"). The surveillance system is designed as a first step toward a comprehensive monitoring system of environmental parameters like biological diversity, including effects of environmental pollution and cultural heritage. As an additional national surveillance initiative for radioactivity and other pollution in northern oceans (MONRA: "Miljøovervåkingssystem for radioaktivitet og andre miljøgifter i de nordlige havområder"), a new environmental initiative was started in 1999 exclusively for marine monitoring purposes.

Health Canada's Northern and Arctic Contaminant Health Initiative is a component of the Federal Arctic Environment Strategy. Its goal is to provide advice on public consultation, health risks, and health research activities related to contaminant issues in the North. The initiative aims to:

(1) provide timely and up-to-date information and advice to the governments of the Northwest Territories on multimedia exposure trends, toxicological research, epidemiology studies, human biomarkers, tissue sampling/storage, and consultation strategies;

(2) ensure that international Arctic initiatives adequately address human health issues and are informed of current human impacts associated with exposure to environmental contaminants; and

(3) ensure a well-coordinated "health" initiative under the federal Arctic Environmental Strategy (AES) and the Health Canada Action Plan for Health and Environment Arctic Health Initiative.

Since a strong circum-Arctic international network of various environmental initiatives is already established through AEPS and IASC, all member countries of the Arctic Council intend to focus their work on strengthening international efforts to develop suitable countermeasures against the permanent inflow of long-range transported pollution and on the documentation of local sources for man-made pollution, including POPs, trace metals, and radioactive substances through AEPS.

ROLAND KALLENBORN

See also **Arctic Council; Contaminants; DANCEA (Danish Cooperation for Environment in the Arctic); Declaration on the Protection of the Arctic Environment; Environmental Problems; Persistent Organic Pollutants (POPs)**

Further Reading

AMAP, *The AMAP Assessment Report: Arctic Pollution Issues*, Oslo: Arctic Monitoring and Assessment Program (AMAP), 1998

Jensen J., K. Adare & R. Shearer (editors), *Canadian Arctic Contaminants Assessment Report*, Minister of Indian Affairs and Northern Development, 1997

Layton, David, Robert Edson, Marilyn Varela & Bruce Napier (editors), *Radionuclides in the Arctic Seas from the Former Soviet Union: Potential Health and Ecological Risks*, Arctic Nuclear Waste Assessment Program (ANWAP), Office of Naval Research (ONR), 1997

Tikhonov, Sergey, Konstantin Sjevljagin, Harald Loeng, Geir Wing Gabrielsen, Salve Dahle, Ole Jørgen Lønne & Roald Sætre (editors), *Status Report on the Marine Environment of the Barents Region,* The Joint Norwegian-Russian Commission on Environmental Cooperation, The Working Group on the Marine Environment of the Barents Region, 1997

AMAP website: http://www.amap.no

IASC website: http://www.iasc.no

MOSJ website: http://miljo.npolar.no/mosj/

UNEP website: http://www.unep.net/arctic/

European Network for Arctic-Alpine Multidisciplinary Research (ENVINET) website: http://www.npolar.no/envinet

Arctic Council Action Plan to Eliminate Pollution of the Arctic (ACAP) website: http://www.arctic-council.org/f2000-acap.html

POLLUTION: RESEARCH PROGRAMS

Most circum-Arctic countries include research activities on Arctic issues in their national funding programs without specifically mentioning the Arctic as funding criteria. Since new national and international programs are under negotiation and some of the present research programs will be completed in the years to come, the situation for funding of research projects described here must be viewed as a summary for 2003.

International Research Programs

Several international research programs have been launched in the past to ensure comprehensive method development and data evaluation of scientific aspects related to man-made pollution in Arctic environments (*see*, e.g., ENVINET, in **Pollution: Environmental Initiatives; Intergovernmental Panel on Climate Change (IPCC)**). The Nordic Council of Ministers (NMR) initiated a new Nordic Arctic Research Program (NARP) in 1999 with the goal of enhancing Nordic competence by building scientific cooperation within selected subject areas network building, training and mobility of researchers, workshops, and pilot studies. The research program covers three main topics: natural processes, biological diversity and environmental threats, and living conditions of the inhabitants of the Arctic. In addition, several regional cooperations were initiated to cover and provide funding for region-specific aspects of Arctic research cooperation, including scientific investigations on hazardous compounds.

National Programs

Research on issues related to environmental pollution in the Arctic are often implemented in the environmental research programs of the national funding bodies and not especially dedicated to the Arctic environment. However, several funding agencies have developed research programs restricted to financial support of research in the Arctic.

The US National Science Foundation (NSF) has established an Arctic research program where research on environmental pollutants is also supported. Arctic research is coordinated at NSF by the Office of Polar Programs (OPP). However, NSF is just one of 12 Federal US agencies that sponsor or conduct Arctic science, engineering, and related activities. Thus, federal interagency research is coordinated through the Interagency Arctic Research Policy Committee, chaired by NSF.

The Canadian National Polar Commission was established in 1991 as the lead national agency in the area of polar research. The Canadian Polar Commission has responsibility for monitoring, promoting, and disseminating knowledge of the polar regions; contributing to public awareness of the importance of polar science to Canada; enhancing Canada's international profile as a circumpolar nation; and recommending polar science policy direction to government. The Northern Contaminants Program (NCP) was established in response to studies that showed the presence of contaminants in the Arctic ecosystem. The three main contaminant groups of concern are persistent organic pollutants (POPs), heavy metals, and radionuclides. The NCP is managed by the Department of Indian Affairs and Northern Development of Canada in partnership with other federal Canadian departments (Health, Environment, Fisheries, and Oceans), the three territorial government departments, Aboriginal organizations (Council of Yukon First Nations, Dene Nation, Inuit Tapiriit Kanatami, Inuit Circumpolar Conference, and Métis Nation-Northwest Territories), and university researchers. The aim of the NCP is to work toward reducing and eliminating contaminants in traditionally harvested foods, while providing information that assists informed decision-making by individuals and communities in their food use.

The Danish Cooperation for Environment in the Arctic (DANCEA) was established in 1994, as part of Denmark's environmental assistance to the Arctic. Research activities and strategies covered by DANCEA are supposed to be a part of the national support to

AEPS and AMAP. DANCEA programs are divided into four subprograms: AEPS/AMAP, Arctic Environment Program-Knowledge Building, Arctic Environment Program-Concrete Measures, and Indigenous Peoples. Activities are administered by the Danish Environmental Protection Agency and initiated by the Ministry of Environment and Energy in agreement with the Greenland Home Rule and environmental organizations in Greenland, with the overall objective of improving and preserving the local environment and increasing environmental awareness. Projects are often pilot or demonstration projects relating to concrete plants, information activities, and administrative tools. Research activities related to projects at Greenland and the Faroe Islands are also coordinated via the Danish Environmental Protection Agency in cooperation with the respective local governments.

The Swedish Polar Research Secretariat is a government authority under the Ministry of Education and Science and has the task of promoting and coordinating Swedish Polar research. This means, for example, to follow and plan research and development and to organize and lead expeditions to the Arctic and Antarctic regions. Research on Arctic issues, including the fate of pollutants in the Arctic, is an implemented part of the Swedish Research program.

Polar research is defined as one of the central key areas for the Research Council of Norway in the forthcoming years. This also includes studies on the fate of environmental pollution in Arctic regions. Therefore, the Norwegian National Committee on Polar Research has been appointed by the Research Council of Norway to promote and coordinate the planning of research and the use of resources and logistics in Norwegian polar research. The Norwegian National Committee on Polar Research evaluates research projects for the Research Council of Norway covering all aspects of Arctic and Antarctic research including environmental pollution.

Finland's Arctic research strategy comprises a comprehensive research program covering various environmental aspects including pollution control and research. Research on Arctic scientific topics is an implemented part in Finland's National Research program.

Research on pollution aspects in the Arctic in Russia is channeled through the Russian Academy of Sciences and the Russian hydrometeorological service (RosHydromet). Several bilateral and multilateral cooperation programs for Arctic Research, including investigations of pollution, are currently ongoing. A Russian-Norwegian cooperation program was initiated, which includes investigations of sea ice formation and destruction and the energy-mass exchange responsible for the redistribution of pollutants. One important motivation for this work is to investigate the fate of contaminants in the region, including studies for different climate scenarios and possible origins of contaminants. In 2000, a successful long-term cooperation between German research institutions and Russian partners on Arctic environmental issues resulted in the establishment of a joint laboratory for Arctic environmental research. The Otto Shmidt Laboratory for Polar and Marine Sciences (OSL) was inaugurated in St Petersburg. Today, this joint project is part of a comprehensive cooperative agreement on polar and marine research between the Russian and German Ministries of Science and Technology. This agreement intends to promote the progress of science and closer collaboration between scientists and engineers of Russia and Germany as well as to support young Russian scientists in polar and marine research, including environmental investigations.

Several non-Arctic countries have their own Arctic research activities with considerable funding opportunities. The international research facilities at Ny-Ålesund (Svalbard) are host to various research projects related to Arctic environmental issues, including the Global Atmospheric Watch (GAW) network of the World Meteorological Organization. The Zeppelin mountain atmospheric research station, which is host to many international collaborations, takes measurements of atmospheric chemistry such as SO_2, CFCs, and persistent organic pollutants, and stratospheric ozone. Within the frame of the human potential program, the European Union has recognized the international research facilities at Ny-Ålesund (Svalbard, Norway) as a European Large-Scale Facility (LSF) and grants access for European researchers to the research infrastructure at the site for environmental studies, including research on anthropogenic pollution. In general, the 5th framework of the European-funded research program has recognized the need for Arctic research on environmental issues as an important scenario to understand global environmental processes, including long-range transport of pollutants, and is therefore currently funding several large international projects on this topic in the European Arctic, including Russia.

ROLAND KALLENBORN

See also **Arctic Council; Arctic Research Consortium of the United States (ARCUS); Contaminants; DANCEA (Danish Cooperation for Environment in the Arctic) ; Environmental Problems; International Arctic Science Committee (IASC); Office of Polar Programs, National Science Foundation; Persistent Organic Pollutants (POPs)**

Further Reading

AMAP, *The AMAP Assessment Report: Arctic Pollution Issues*, Oslo: Arctic Monitoring and Assessment Program (AMAP), 1998

Useful websites

AMAP website: http://www.amap.no

Canadian Polar Commission website: http:// www.polarcom.gc.ca/cpin/resources.htm

Danish Polar Center website: http://www.dpc.dk/

Finnish Arctic Centre website: http://www.arcticcentre.org/

IASC website: http://www.iasc.no

LSF-Ny-Ålesund website: http://www.npolar.no/nyaa-lsf/

National Science foundation (NSF), Arctic program (USA) website: http://www.nsf.gov/od/opp/arctic/start.htm

Nordic Arctic Research Programme website: http:// thule.oulu.fi/narp/

Norwegian National Committee on Polar Research website: http://www.program.forskningsradet.no/polarkomiteen/en/index.html

Russian Arctic and Antarctic Research Institute (AARI) website: http://www.aari.nw.ru/

Scott Polar Research Institute website: http://www.spri.cam.ac.uk/

POLYCHLORINATED BIPHENYLS (PCBS)

Polychlorinated biphenyls (PCBs) are chlorinated organic compounds, chemically similar to dioxins, that do not occur naturally, but have been used since the 1930s. PCBs do not easily dissolve in water, but do so easily in fats and oils, and can adsorb to sediment particles. There are up to 209 possible compounds. The different PCB compounds contain the same biphenyl basic molecular structure, but differ in number and substitution pattern of the chlorine substituents. Up to ten chlorine atoms on the biphenyl ring system are possible (PCB 209). The single PCB compound is called PCB congener in scientific reports. Between 50 and 100 PCB congeners can be found in the environment depending on sample type and environmental compartment investigated. The technical PCB mixture is primarily used as coolants, flame retardants in paintings, additives for insulation purposes, and dielectric fluids as, for example, in electric transformers and capacitors. PCBs were normally applied in closed systems until the ban in the early 1970s for the majority of the western world, including Europe, the United States, and Canada. In general, technical PCB is released into the environment during waste treatment and in the destruction of phased-out transformers, capacitors, refrigerators, etc. as well as painting residues. To date, more than 1,000,000 tons of various PCB mixtures are reportedly produced on a global basis. However, unlike agrochemicals, not all technical PCB produced has yet been released into the environment. It is therefore assumed that till today PCB residues are continuously being released from former waste disposals and treatment plants as well as during the destruction of defect electrical installations into the environment. PCBs belong to the large chemical group of persistent organic pollutants (POPs). Thus, they may persist in the environment for a long period and accumulate in the food webs in high concentration levels often found in top predators. Due to different production methods for technical PCB mixtures, the PCB patterns are different. Technical PCB was sold under various brand names (e.g., Arochlor®, Chlophen®, Chlorextol®, Cylophen®, Dykanol®, Fenclor®, Kanechlor®, Montar®, Noflamol®, Pyralene®, Pyranol®, Santotherm®, Sovol, etc.). Thus, technical PCB from Russia (e.g., Sovol®) is characterized by a different PCB composition than technical PCB from Europe or USA. Due to atmospheric and waterborne long-range transport, PCBs can be found in remote regions, far from potential sources. Therefore, characteristic pattern differences are often used to find indications for possible source regions for PCB patterns found in environmental samples. Through a process called cold condensation or global distillation, airborne PCBs are deposited in the colder regions of our globe, such as those of the northern lakes and seas and the polar and subpolar regions. Global distillation contributes significantly to the unexpectedly high concentrations of PCBs that have been observed in the air, sea water, precipitation, plankton, wild animals, and people of the Arctic region.

The most commonly observed health effects in people exposed to large amounts of PCBs are skin conditions such as acne and rashes. Studies in exposed workers have shown changes in the blood and urine that may indicate liver damage. PCB exposures in the general population are not likely to result in skin and liver effects. Most of the studies of the health effects of PCBs in the general population examined the children of mothers who were exposed to PCBs. Animals that ingested food containing large amounts of PCBs for short periods had developed mild liver damage. Animals that ingested smaller amounts of PCBs in food over several weeks or months developed various kinds of health effects, including anemia, acnelike skin conditions, and liver, stomach, and thyroid gland injuries. Other effects of PCBs in animals include changes in the immune system, behavioral alterations, and impaired reproduction. PCBs are not known to cause birth defects. Today, some PCB congeners are also considered as artificial hormones mimicking biochemical responses of the natural endocrine system (endocrine disruptors). In general, the persistence of PCBs increases with an increase in the degree of chlorination. Mono-, di-, and trichlorinated congeners biodegrade relatively fast, tetrachlorinated biphenyls biodegrade slowly, and higher chlorinated biphenyls are usually very resistant toward biodegradation. PCBs have been shown to bioconcentrate significantly in aquatic organisms. Average log BCFs (bioconcentration factors) of 3–5, reported for various congeners in aquatic organisms, show increasing accumulation with the more highly chlorinated congeners.

The major PCB exposure routes to humans are through food and drinking water, and by inhalation of contaminated air. PCBs are POP compounds that are known to effectively bioaccumulate in the Arctic food webs. The polar bear (*Ursus maritimus*) is a top predator in the Arctic and to be considered at the top of the marine Arctic food web. It is therefore exposed to elevated levels of persistent, fat-soluble POP compounds and especially PCBs. The diet of polar bears almost exclusively consists of seal blubber. The PCB levels measured nowadays in polar bears at the Svalbard archipelago (Norway) are considerably higher than those measured in Canada and Alaska. It is still uncertain as to how elevated POP levels affect polar bears in Svalbard, but ongoing studies provide reason to believe that PCBs impair the immune system, hormone regulation, development, reproduction, and possibly survival of the cubs. New scientific investigations have found indications that the significantly increased occurrence of hermaphrodite polar bear cubs at Svalbard is directly correlated with the elevated PCB levels in the animals. The highest PCB levels in Arctic birds have been found in the great black-backed gull, glaucous gull, and great skua. Concentrations in these species are 5–10 times higher than those found for other seabird species from the same area belonging to lower trophic levels (e.g., common eider, puffin, kittiwake, etc.). Already in the early 1980s, elevated PCB levels were found in the blood and milk of Canadian Inuit women. Especially Inuit living the traditional way are exposed to high levels of PCB due to the high consumption of fat-rich food usually originating from marine mammals and fish. A recent comparison confirmed that relatively high PCB levels are present in Canadian and Greenland Inuit as well as in some part of the Russian Arctic population.

ROLAND KALLENBORN

See also **Arctic Environmental Protection Strategies; Bioconcentration; Contaminants; Environmental Problems; Persistent Organic Pollutants (POPs)**

Further Reading

AMAP, *The AMAP Assessment Report: Arctic Pollution Issues,*Oslo, Norway: Arctic Monitoring and Assessment Program (AMAP), 1998

Dewailly, É. *et al.*, "High levels of PCBs in breast milk of Inuit women from Arctic Québec." *Bulletin of Environmental Contamination and Toxicology*, 43 (1989): 641–646

Jensen, J., K. Adare & R. Shearer (editors), *Canadian Arctic Contaminants Assessment Report,* Minister of Indian Affairs and Northern Development, 1997

Pereg, D., É. Dewailly, G.G. Poirier & P. Ayotte, "Environmental exposure to polychlorinated biphenyls and placental CYP1A1 activity in Inuit women from northern Québec." *Environmental Health Perspectives*, 100(6) (2002): 607

Waid, John, *PCBs and the Environment*, Boca Raton, Florida: CRC Press, 1987

Useful Internet Addresses

Agency for Toxic Substances and Disease register (ATSDR) website: http://www.atsdr.cdc.gov/tfacts17.html
AMAP website: http://www.amap.no
Environment Canada website: http://www.ec.gc.ca/pcb/eng/index_e.htm
US-EPA website: http://yosemite.epa.gov/r10/owcm.nsf/pcb/pcb

POLYGONS—*See* PATTERNED AND POLYGONAL GROUND

POLYNYAS

The word *polynya* (pl. polynyas or polynyi) is a derivative of the Russian word *polyn'ya* for a "glade or meadow." A polynya is defined as the name for open water in sea ice. It is a relatively persistent extensive area of open water and/or thin ice amidst more thick and compacted sea ice cover, or between that ice cover and ice at the coast (fast ice).

Polynyas appear at recurrent locations through the polar regions in winter when air temperature is well below the freezing point of sea water, climatic conditions under which one would expect a continuous ice cover.

Hundreds of miles of open unfrozen water under severe temperatures make a great impression, even for experienced researchers. It is not surprising that during the 16th through the 19th centuries, observations of open water in the winter during polar expeditions were used as a basis for the hypothesis of an "Open Polar Sea" in the central Arctic Ocean. The idea of an Open Polar Sea attracted many people to the North at the cost of numerous lives. Only by the end of the 19th century did it become clear that vast areas of open water and thin ice are not an open polar sea, but polynyas.

In a purely geographical sense, the age of exploration is over. However, in polar areas of both hemispheres, scientists continue exploration of polynyas, trying to understand and predict changes in their development and their ecosystems.

Polynyas are a significant feature of sea ice distribution in the winter, during the period of ice growth. Polynyas in polar regions can appear everywhere near the coastline or islands. Polynyas can be classified according to their location:

- shore polynya between coast or ice barrier and drifting ice;
- flaw polynya between motionless fast ice and drifting ice;

Large, late winter polynya in Barrow Strait, Nunavut, May 1973.
Copyright David R. Gray

- oceanic (open sea) polynya amidst drifting ice;
- near-delta polynya formed in spring between the river mouth or delta and ice cover. A further polynya classification is based on their stability;
- recurring polynyas existing more than 75% of the time;
- stable polynyas observed for 50–75% of the time; and
- unstable polynyas existing less than 50% of the time.

Polynyas are formed under the influence of dynamical factors, mostly wind action. Thus, predominant winds blowing offshore from the coast cause a drift of ice away from the coast and expose sea water to cold air. A combination of wind direction and speed with thermal conditions determines ice growth and explains the variable size and configuration of polynyas that can reach widths of hundreds of kilometers.

Both thermodynamic and dynamic processes form sea ice in polynyas. Ice motion leads to the appearance of ice-free areas. Low winter temperatures cause freezing of open water and subsequent ice growth. A mixture of open water and ice of different ages can be observed in polynyas, but ice thickness and concentration in polynyas are always lower than in surrounding ice cover.

Polynyas extending over extensive parts of the polar regions are a phenomenon that influences both the underlying ocean and the overlying atmosphere. First, polynyas exert a significant influence on the exchange of heat and moisture between the ocean and atmosphere. The exposed warm water results in a large heat flux from ocean to air and in the rapid formation of new ice. The rate of ice growth at open water areas and the thickness increase of thin (newly frozen over) ice are significantly larger than for thicker ice, which is insulated from the colder atmosphere. Newly formed ice continuously moves downwind like a conveyor belt and is replaced by new ice. Therefore, polynyas are a significant source of ice formation in the winter.

Polynyas also play an important role in ice melting. Open water and thin ice in polynyas have a lower surface reflectance (albedo), absorb a greater proportion of incoming solar radiation than surrounding ice, and accumulate heat. Thus, polynyas lead to further accelerated melting of the surrounding ice cover. In summer, the processes of ice melting increase the stability of the vertical water structure.

During ice formation in polynyas, the salt from sea water that freezes is released from the ice lattice into the water below the polynyas. Seawater salinity in polynyas increases and water becomes denser than in surrounding regions. The difference in water salinity could cause modification of large-scale current systems such as the thermohaline circulation.

The formation of polynyas is accompanied by upwelling of deep waters and formation of water convection influencing vertical salt exchange. The sinking denser water contributes to the formation and maintenance of the halocline, a layer separating and insulating the cold surface layer from warmer deeper waters.

The influence of polynyas is not limited to physical processes since these processes directly affect ecosystems and the carbon cycle. In winter, convection improves the nutritional properties of ocean water. In spring, open water or thin ice allows the penetration of sunlight in to surface water layers and triggers early algae blooming. Thus, polynyas are considered as the most productive ecosystems in high latitudes. Increased algal biomass cascades to lower levels of the food chain, making a polynya a polar oasis of life. Birds, fish, and animals adjust their life to local conditions. Highly productive polynya waters serve as feeding, mating, spawning, and overwintering grounds for populations of birds and mammals.

The availability of polynyas is a favorable factor in ice navigation and oil exploration. In particular, polynyas are often used as the easiest routes in ice-bound waters for vessels during autumn, winter, and spring. Knowledge of the polynya regime can also be used to great advantage in climatic and synoptic studies. In the context of current global change, polynyas have received increased attention as possible early indicators of the effect of warming in polar areas. Many recent international interdisciplinary projects have been devoted to studies of polynyas near St Lawrence Island in the Bering Sea, between the Canadian islands and Greenland, on the northeast Greenland shelf, in the Laptev Sea, and the Ross and Weddell seas in Antarctica. An unprecedented data set has been collected that allows critical links between meteorology, ocean physics and chemistry, geological processes, and ecosystems in polynyas to be examined.

IGOR APPEL

See also **Leads; Open Polar Sea; Sea Ice**

Further Reading

Cavalieri, D.J. & S. Martin, "The contribution of Alaskan, Siberian, and Canadian coastal polynyas to the cold Halocline layer of the Arctic Ocean." *Journal of Geophysical Research*, 99 (1994): 18343–18362

France, R. & M. Sharp. "Polynyas as centers of organization for structuring the integrity of Arctic Maine communities." *Conservation Biology*, 6(3) (1992): 442

Gordon, A.L. & J.C. Comiso, "Polynyas in the Southern Ocean." *Scientific American*, 256 (1988): 90–97

Maykut, G.A., "An Introduction to Ice in the Polar Oceans." *Technical Report* APL-UW 8510, Applied Physics Laboratory, University of Washington, 1985, p. 177

Smith, S.D., R.D. Muench & C.H. Pease, "Polynyas and leads: an overview of physical processes and environment." *Journal of Geophysical Research*, 95 (1990): 9461–9479

POMOR

The Pomors are a Russian ethnic group living on the White and Barents Sea coasts in the territories of Arkhangel'sk Oblast' and Murmansk Oblast' of the Russian Federation, and are the descendants of the first Russian migrants to the northern coast. Pomor settlements presently range from the river Mezen in the southeastern White Sea to the river Ponoi on the southeast coast of the Kola Peninsula. The name Pomors means "coast dwellers," and the area of their dwelling is known as *Pomoriye*. Seven regions along the coast of the White Sea are traditionally Pomor areas: Zimniy, Letniy, Onezhskiy, Pomorskiy, Karelskiy, Kandalakshskiy, and Terskiy. The main settlements on the Zimniy coast are the town of Mezen and the village of Zimniaya Zolotitsa. Villages on the Letniy coast include Una and Nionoksa; settlements on the Onezhskiy coast include the town of Onega and the village of Pushlakhta. The town of Belomorsk (Soroka) and the village of Sumskoy Posad are located on the Pomorskiy coast; the town of Kem and the village of Keret are on the Karelskiy coast. The town of Kandalaksha and the village of Kniazhaya Guba are found on the Kandalakshskiy coast, and the villages of Umba, Varzuga, and Ponoi are located on the Terskiy coast.

History

The Pomors were formed gradually by the interaction of several nationalities, primarily the Eastern Slavs. Settlement of the White Sea coast occurred during the process of Slavic colonization of the East European Plain. The first records of the Eastern Slavs reaching the White Sea date back to the early 11th century; permanent Slavic settlements in this area were established at the close of the 13th century. The Eastern Slavs penetrated into Pomoriye (the White Sea coast areas) in the 13th to 15th centuries by two migrant flows: from Novgorod and from the Upper Volga. The first flow originated in the area subject to Velikiy Novgorod and progressed to the western areas of Pomoriye (Karelskiy, Pomorskiy, and the western part of the Letniy coast). This flow also involved Finno-Ugric and Baltic people. The second flow included people from the Russian princedoms situated in the Upper Volga, and moved mostly to the Eastern Pomoriye (Terskiy, and the eastern part of the Letniy coast). The Upper-Volga migrant flow included even more non-Slavic people than that of Novgorod, for example, Finno-Ugric nationalities of the Volga-Oka Interfluve, and of the farther southern areas, such as Vod, Izhora, Meria, and Ves tribes. At the settlements, the newcomers inevitably encountered the aboriginal (pre-Slavic) people such as Chud, Karelian, Saami, and Nenets tribes.

In the 15th to 17th centuries, the migrants continued to the White Sea region, and separate ethnic groups (Karelians and Saami) migrated within Pomoriye proper, due to a number of different factors of military, political, economic, social, and religious nature.

At the close of the 17th century, the migrant movement toward Pomoriye began to decline and the ethnocultural mixing stabilized, which resulted in cultural and domestic stability of the Pomor people, isolation of the Pomor ethnic group, and preservation of their local features, that is, their separation from the northern Russian population as a whole. Neither sporadic inflows from the neighboring areas nor internal migrations of the local people changed this situation significantly until the first third of the 20th century.

Since the 1930s, a mass inflow of Russians from the inland territories of Russia, and of other nationalities such as Ukrainians, Belorussians, and Tatars has taken place. For this reason, and due to the development of modern communications, and the growth of such towns as Mezen, Onega, Belomorsk, Kem, and Kandalaksha with industrial influence on the Pomor way of life, the traditional economic structure has changed, and the differences among Pomor and non-Pomor people of the White Sea region have been disappearing. In the past, these differences were largely caused by the actions of the central Soviet government following the policy of consolidation of Russian people, and elimination of differences between their regional groups. In conducting national censuses and registration of the population, the term *Pomors* remains fluid and not fixed in terms of defining ethnicity; thus, no accurate calculation of the number of Pomors is possible at present.

Since the early 1990s, researchers have observed rising interest in traditional Pomor culture and the revival of self-consciousness in Pomoriye, particularly among the local intelligentsia. In 1991, the Arkhangel'sk Pedagogical Institute became the Pomor State University in Arkhangel'sk, Russia. Moreover, folk-music ensembles, restaurants, hotels, and private companies use the word Pomor in their names. Attempts to revive traditional Pomor trades have been made, but they are sporadic and aimed primarily at attracting tourists.

Language and Religion

Pomors speak Russian (various local northern Russian dialects) and use a variant of the Cyrillic alphabet. Most of the believers are Orthodox. Both the local and central monasteries historically played a central role in maintaining religiousness among Pomors, but after the Russian Orthodox Church Reform carried out by the Patriarch Nikon (1605–1681) in 1654, Pomoriye emerged as one of the centers of the Old Believer movement. Since the 17th century, one of the largest Old Believer communities, *Vygoretskoe Obshchezhitelstvo* [Vyg-River Communal Life], has been situated on the river Vyg.

Occupations and Economy

The basis of the traditional Pomor economy was fishing and marine mammal hunting. Among the various Pomor trades, salmon fishing remains the oldest and one of the prime components of the Pomor economy. Historically once a new settlement appeared somewhere in Pomoriye, salmon fishing, as a coastal trade, began. As a valuable commodity with high demand in inland Russia, the salmon trade emerged as one of the most essential activities on the White Sea coast in the 13th to 15th centuries. At the early stages of Pomoriye development, lake fishing and coastal marine mammal hunting (seals and white whales) spread as well.

As Russians colonized the White Sea region and increased their numbers, utilization of the sea resources of the White and Barents seas intensified. In the early 16th century, Pomors began to develop cod fishing (cod, haddock, and halibut) at the northern coast of the Kola Peninsula—the so-called Murman Fishery. In the same period, Pomors initiated industrial development of remote territories of the Arctic Ocean, for example, walrus and seal hunting near Novaya Zemlya and, probably, Spitsbergen. In the 18th century, large-scale herring fishing commenced, and in the late 19th century, Pomors began fishing navaga.

Agriculture and cattle breeding in various areas of Pomoriye developed to a different extent, but in general those branches of economy remained secondary due to unfavorable geographical conditions. In addition, forest hunting, salt making, pearl fishing, mica extraction, boatbuilding, and various seasonal works were occupations of the Pomors.

In the early 18th and again in the early 20th centuries, another important element of the Pomor economy materialized, that is, illegal trade with the people of northern Norway. Outlawed by the Russian and Norwegian-Danish authorities, Pomor trade with Norway continued, and by the mid-18th century the authorities of both countries realized that the trade relations were profitable and began to encourage them. The trading began as barter: Pomors imported grain, timber, and hemp into Norway at ports such as Hammerfest and Vardø and exchanged them for fish; from the mid-19th century, bartering ceded to monetary relations. Trade relations between Pomors and northern Norwegians existed until the 1920s, but were suspended following the Russian Revolution of 1917; finally when Soviet government monopoly for foreign trade was established, they were banned completely. Since then, the traditional Pomor economy has changed significantly under the influence of industrialization, losing many of its traditional practices in the process.

ALEXEI YURCHENKO

See also **Arkhangel'sk Oblast'; Kola Peninsula; Murmanskaya Oblast'; Svalbard**

Further Reading

Bernshtam, Tatjana, *Pomory: formirovanie gruppy i sistema hozjaistva* [Pomor: forming the group and the system of household], Leningrad: Nauka, 1978

———, *Russkaja narodnaja kultura Pomorya v kontze 19 nachale 20 veka* [Russian folk culture of Pomorye at the end of 19th to beginning of 20th century], Leningrad: Nauka, 1983

Ostrovskiy, Dmitriy, *Ocherk torgovoi i promishlennoi dejatelnosti russkih na pribrezie Severnogo okeana* [Essay of trade activities of Russians on the Arctic Ocean coast], St Petersburg, 1910

Schrader, Tatjana, "Pomor trade with Norway." *Acta Borealia*, 5(1–2) (1988): 111–118

Ushakov, Ivan, *Kolskaja zemlja* [Kola land], Murmansk: Murmanskoe knizhnoe izd-vo, 1972

Yurchenko, Alexei, "The colonization of the Russian Barents Sea coast (mid-19th to early 20th century): two approaches to the economic development of the area." *Acta Borealia*, 1 (2002): 5–25

POND INLET

Pond Inlet (Mittimatalik) lies on the southern shores of Eclipse Sound at 72° 42′ N 77° 59′ W, northeastern Baffin Island, Nunavut, Canada. It is situated on a loamy sand terrace surrounded by tundra and sheltered by high mountains.

The many Dorset and Thule archaeological sites along this coast show that the area has been inhabited by Inuit for about 4000 years. The present settlement has a population of 1154—1085 (94%) Inuit and 69 (6%) nonnative—with a high proportion of young people (Statistics Canada Census, 1996). With the establishment of Nunuvut, Pond Inlet became a regional center for some government departments.

In 1818, the British explorer John Ross named the area Ponds Bay, after the astronomer John Ponds. The previous year, whalers came in search of the bowhead whale, and in 1854 the whaler John Gray named Eclipse Sound after his ship. In 1903, James Mutch established the first shore whaling station at Albert Harbour, a few miles from the present settlement. Captain Joseph-Elzéar Bernier utilized the whaling station in 1906–1907 on the first of his three Canadian government expeditions to the area. With the decline in whaling, traders settled in the area, exchanging items for skins and ivory. During the 1920s, the Hudson's Bay Company, the Royal Canadian Mounted Police, and various missionaries established posts within the community. During the 1960s, a federal school was established, and many families left their camps to live in the settlement.

Pond Inlet is an example of an Inuit society that has adapted to modern life without abandoning its indigenous culture. A modern wage economy exists alongside the traditional skills of hunting, trapping, fishing, and carving. A satellite dish links the community to the rest of the world, and Internet and e-mail links further enhance communications and opportunities. First Air operates regular flights from Iqaluit to Pond Inlet, with further plans to extend the runway. Canada's most northerly theater group, Tunnooniq, was founded in Pond Inlet in 1986, and performs throughout Canada and Europe. The Nattinak Centre in Pond Inlet chronicles the history of the region and houses the Rebecca Idlout Library, which has books in English and Inuktitut, videos as well as a local history photographic collection. Adjacent to the library is an Elders Centre where traditional activities take place. During the spring, traditional games, dog team races, and igloo building contests are held on the ice of Eclipse Sound.

The land and waters surrounding Pond Inlet are rich in natural resources, including caribou, seals, and narwhal, which provide sustenance for the community and economic strength. The Toonoonik Sahoonit Cooperative and Northern Store provide employment in retail and construction and tourism. The growing number of people visiting Pond Inlet, including cruise ships, provide seasonal opportunities for work, and the cooperative runs a small hotel. The government remains the major employer, providing jobs in areas of education, health, the local Hamlet, and the Royal Canadian Mounted Police (RCMP). In 1999, Pond Inlet opened Nasivvik High School, whose facilities include a fully equipped science and computer lab, a day care center, career instruction, and technology studies classes.

With the establishment of Nunavut in 1999, a number of government jobs were to be transferred to Pond Inlet, establishing the area as a regional center providing a local political voice for the community. In August 1999, the federal government and the Qikiqtani Inuit Association signed an agreement to establish a National Park in the area. The Government of Nunavut will use this as a model for future agreements between the government and aboriginal peoples, resulting in the local people managing their local environment.

SHIRLEY SAWTELL

See also **Baffin Island**

Further Reading

Anaviapik, Simon, "Early days in Mittimatalik." *Inuktitut*, 72 (1990): 47–58

Hamilton, W. Richard (editor), *The Baffin handbook: Travelling in Canada's Eastern Arctic*, Iqaluit, Northwest Territories: Nortext Publishing Corporation, 1993

Mott, Gordon & Georgie Stone, "New northern theatre." *Uphere*, 8(1) (1992): 22–24

Myers, Heather & Scott Forrest, "Making change: economic development in Pond Inlet, 1987 to 1997." *Arctic*, 53(2) (2000): 134–145

Pelly, David F., "Pond Inlet: an Inuit community caught between two worlds." *Canadian Geographic*, 111(1) (1991): 46–52

Soubliere, Marion (editor), *Nunavut Handbook*, Iqaluit, Northwest Territories: Nortext Multimedia Inc., 1997

Weissling, Lee E., "Inuit life in the eastern Canadian Arctic, 1922–1942: change as recorded by the RCMP." *Canadian Geographer*, 35(1) (1991): 59–69

POPOV, ANDREI

While working as a teacher in his native ulus in the village of Batulintzi in 1922–1924, Andrei Popov wrote down folklore materials, collected information on the worldview of the Yakuts, and made drawings of the artifacts. He spoke the Yakut language and knew the local culture; this made it possible for him to collect valuable ethnographic data without special ethnographic training.

In 1925, he joined the ethnographic department of Leningrad University. His teachers were such famous Russian ethnographers and linguists as Lev Sternberg, Vladimir Bogoraz, Sergei Malov, and others. During his university years, Popov participated in the work of the Siberian department of the Museum for Anthropology and Ethnography (MAE) and he was a researcher of the commission for studying the Yakut ASSR in the Academy of Sciences. A year after his graduation, Popov was sent to Taymyr peninsula, where he collected materials on the ethnography of the Dolgans and Nganasans from May 1930 until August 1931. He made his second long trip to Taymyr as a participant of the Tavguiy ethnographic expedition in 1936–1938. There he learned the Nganasan and Dolgan languages .

In 1931, Popov started working at the Institute for Ethnography of the Academy of Sciences of the USSR. He worked there in the department of Siberia until the end of his life. Popov was also a teacher: in 1936, he taught the Yakut language to the postgraduates of the Institute of the Peoples of the North, and from 1940 to 1952 he lectured in the Department for Ethnography in Leningrad University, teaching ethnography of the Yakuts and Dolgans, history of the primitive economy, technique, and field ethnography.

All published and unpublished research works by Popov were devoted to several topics: worldview, folklore, economy and material culture, social organization, and fine arts of the peoples of Siberia; most of all he was interested in shamanism. His publications were based on the field notes he made among the Yakuts, Dolgans, Nganasans, and Nenets of the Yenisey, and Russian Old Believers (so-called "zatundrenskiye krest'ane"); he also used literature and museum materials about many other peoples of Siberia. During his life, more than 40 works were published, including his translations from the languages of the peoples of Siberia into Russian; he also worked as executive editor of some publications. His scientific heritage is represented by the materials, translations, descriptions, essays, commentaries, and monographic works based on the comparison of materials on the different Siberian peoples.

The subject of shamanism was one of his main scientific interests. When he was only a student, he published an article "Materials on shamanhood. Cult of the yakut goddess Ayihit" (1928). The reference book "Materials for the bibliography of the Russian literature on the study of shamanhood of the north—asiatic peoples" (Leningrad: Institute of the Peoples of the North, 1932: 117 + XVpp.), compiled by Popov, was published in 1932 and became one of the most complete not only in the Soviet but also in the world of ethnography for many decades. Later, Popov continued working on the materials on shamanism accumulated by him and his predecessors. His publications "Receiving the "shamanic gift" by the vilyui yakut" (1947) and "Materials on the yakut history of religion in the former Vilyui okrug" (1949) are widely known. Popov seems to be the first researcher of Yakutiya who refused to study and describe "the Yakuts in general" and instead concentrated totally on the materials of the Yakuts of only one ulus (former Udyugeiskiy ulus) of the Vilyui Okrug —this focus has become an undoubted merit of his work.

"Materials on the yakut history of religion ..." was planned by Popov as a series of publications. Descriptions of cosmogonical and theogonical views, festivals, family rites, interpretations of dreams, and fortune telling were included in this part. The largest part of "Materials...," which is unique both in its idea and execution, remained unpublished. It consisted of descriptions of 30 kamlanies of the Vilyui shamans with the complete notes of the texts with translation into Russian (the size of the manuscript is 18 printer's sheets). Popov also worked on publishing Nganasan and Dolgan materials on religion, but he could not publish the greatest part of what he had planned. His main works are in the archive of MAE as manuscripts.

Popov worked on translating folklore texts. One of his first works is "The yakut folklore" (Leningrad: "Sovetskiy pisatel," 320pp.). Two epic songs-olonkhos, fairy tales, stories, legends about shamans, songs, conjurations, and works of the small genres of folklore were included in the book. This book was in fact the result of the collective work. Popov was translating word-for-word the works that he had written down himself (only part of them were written down by the other collectors) and was reading them in the Yakut language many times to E.M. Tager, who was processing the literature of the texts. After consultations with the academician E.K. Pekarskiy, the prepared translations were given to the ethnographer and literature critic M.N. Sergeev for the final editing. For the first time in the practice of Soviet translations, the authors made an adequate and at the same time literary translation of Yakut folklore into the Russian language. The book had commentaries and indexes. In a year, the same team of authors prepared and published a second similar book—"The dolgan folklore" (Leningrad: "Sovetskiy folklore," 1937: 256 pp.). Several Dolgan, Nganasan, and Yakut fairy tales translated by Popov were published in the collected stories "Fairy tales of the peoples of the North" (Moscow, Leningrad, 1951: 109–119, 237–279, 607–626; Moscow, Leningrad, 1959: 131–132, 136–140, 251–252). Popov edited two volumes of "Historical legends and stories of the Yakuts," which were prepared by the Yakut folklorist G.U. Ergis (Moscow, Leningrad: publishing house of the USSR AS,1960).Popov spent six years, from 1949 till 1954, on the translation of one of the most interesting Yakut olonkhos, "Obstinate Kulun Kullustuur" (with a size of more than 27 printer's sheets), into the Russian language. The work was published before by E.K.Pekarskiy only in the language of the original. In the archives of the researcher in MAE, materials on the folklore of the Nganasans, linguistic materials on the Nganasan language of more than 4000 words, and information on morphology and syntax are still unpublished.

Works devoted to the description and classification of the economy and the material culture of the peoples of Siberia occupy a special place in the scientific heritage of Popov. His first works were limited by the frames of one ethnic tradition (the articles: "The dolgan deer-raising," 1935; "The dolgan hunting and fishing," 1937; "The dolgan technique," 1937; "The ancient yakut birch bark yurta," 1949; "Nomad life and types of the dolgan dwellings," 1952; "Collections of the material culture of the dolgans in the Museum for anthropology and ethnography," 1958; and the monograph "The nganasans, Volume 1, The material culture," Moscow, Leningrad, 1948: 116pp.).

In 1950, in connection with the development of several important subjects for "Historical and ethnographic atlas of the peoples of Siberia" (Moscow, Leningrad, 1961), Popov wrote outstanding works that demonstrated he was an expert on the materials of all ethnic groups of the aboriginal population of Siberia, and he displayed his analytical abilities by giving the initial classification of this huge amount of factual data. In his research, Popov came very close to clarifying the ethnogeny and cultural contacts of the peoples of Siberia. Three works were written: "Wicker-work and weaving among the peoples of Siberia in the XIX and in the first quarter of the XX century" (published as a separate article in 1955), "Dwelling" (published in the above-mentioned "Atlas" in 1961), and "Tools for hunting used by the peoples of Siberia in the XIX and in the first quarter

of the XX century" (13,500 printer's sheets and more than 600 drawings kept in the archive of MAE). Popov himself made the following statement about the last-mentioned work, which was planned to become one of the chapters in "Historical and ethnographic atlas…": "It is not interesting, I have not found any ethnic specifics" (reported by prof. L.P. Potapov in conversation, 1990). This evaluation of the work was the reason for not including this chapter in "Atlas."

However, the description and study of the dwellings of Siberian peoples became one of the works by Popov most demanded by the next generations of Soviet ethnographers. All research of the types of habitations based on the data of specific ethnic traditions by all means correlated with the classification carried out by Popov. A new classification of the dwellings of Siberian peoples was given 40 years later (Sokolova, Z.P., Zhilishe narodov Sibiri (Dwellings of the [peoples of Siberia] Moscow, 1998: 284pp.).

G.N.Gracheva was preparing the publication of the unpublished archive heritage of Popov in 1980 and at the beginning of 1990. In 1984, due to her efforts, the second part of the work by Popov about the social organization and folk beliefs of the nganasans was published ("Nganasany: Socialnoye ustroystvo i verovaniya,"/edited by G.N. Gracheva & Ch.M. Taksami, Leningrad: "Nauka", 1984: 150 pp.). The researcher was unable to bring the fundamental work by Popov, "The religion of the dolgans" (533 typed pages), to publication (she perished during an expedition in the summer of 1992).

In all his scientific works, Popov revealed himself as an expert on specific ethnographic material. His knowledge of the languages of the peoples with whom he lived and conducted his field researches helped him to obtain unique information and reflect it precisely in his publications. He was a wonderful field ethnographer and a master of ethnographic descriptions and classifications that were of great value for Soviet ethnographic science. Popov made an important contribution to the folklore study of Siberia with his translations and publications of unique field notes. Practically everything that he wrote down, processed, published, and translated was a "first" in the field, and this makes him an outstanding ethnographer.

Biography

Andrei Aleksandrovich Popov was born on November 8, 1902 in the village of Ugulyatzi, Vilyui Okrug of Yakut province in the Russian Empire. His father was a village priest. Popov could speak both the Yakut and the Russian languages from his childhood. He completed the school at the 2nd level in the city of Yakutsk.

He received his Candidate Degree in 1935; his work was based on the tavguiy (nganasan) materials. In spite of his vast experience in fieldwork, knowledge of the yakut, dolgan, and nganasan languages, and fundamental scientific ethnographic and folklore publications, Popov did not receive a doctorate degree. Popov died in Leningrad at the age of 57 on March 2, 1960.

DMITRIY FUNK

Further Reading

Bogoraz, V.G., "Introduction." In *The Collected Articles of the Museum of Anthropology and Ethnography of the USSR AS*, Volume XI, 1949, pp. 255–257 (in Russian)

Ergis, G.U., "Andrei Alexandrovich Popov." In *The Collected Articles and Materials on the Ethnography of the Peoples of Yakutiya*, edited by S.I. Nikolayev, Yakutsk: The Yakut Publishing House, 1961, pp. 98–106 (in Russian)

Group of co-workers, "To the memory of Andrei Alexandrovich Popov." *Soviet Ethnography* (2) (1961): 137–140 (in Russian)

PORPOISES—*See* DOLPHINS AND PORPOISES

PRECIPITATION AND MOISTURE

When one thinks of Arctic climate, images arise of a dark, cold forbidding place, covered with ice and snow. What is less well known is that the Arctic is a dry polar desert. However, latitude, local variations in climate produced by topography, and the presence of bodies of water, among other factors, create significant differences in precipitation and moisture regimes from one part of the Arctic to another.

Water in the Air

Water vapor is an essential component of the atmosphere, and is an essential element of weather. Humidity is a measure of the amount of water vapor in the atmosphere, and temperature and pressure govern the amount of water vapor held by a body of air. Absolute humidity is the amount of water vapor in a unit mass of air, usually measured in grams per cubic meter.

Relative humidity is the ratio between the actual amount of moisture in the air and the amount that would be present if the air were saturated at the same temperature. Specific humidity is the ratio of the weight of water vapor in a parcel of air to the total weight of the air, measured in grams of water vapor per kilogram of air. The amount of water that the air can hold increases when the air becomes warmer. When air is holding the maximum amount of water vapor that it can hold, it is said to have reached its saturation point or dew point.

As you move toward the pole, Arctic climates become drier and more desertlike, since low temperatures limit atmospheric water content. Air masses cool when traveling over ice and snow, reducing the water-holding capacity of the air. Although precipitation decreases with increasing latitude, the humidity increases, making abundant moisture available. The specific humidity of very cold dry air is low; however, the relative humidity of the air above the Arctic Ocean in the winter is always close to 100%. Relative humidity reaches a maximum in midwinter and a minimum in June over ice and August over water.

Rain and Snow

Precipitation, is defined as the deposition of moisture on the surface of the Earth from atmospheric sources, and is classified according to its form when it reaches the ground, including dew, hail, rain, sleet, and snow.

When air has reached its saturation point, water vapor in the air will begin to condense or form a liquid. If condensation occurs at ground level, water molecules will cling to surfaces, forming small droplets called dew. At temperatures below freezing, water vapor sublimates into ice crystals called frost. Condensation in the atmosphere requires minute airborne particles for water vapor to condense onto, including materials such as salt, dust, and suspended pollutants.

Annual precipitation in the Arctic ranges from 70 mm inland to 200 mm in coastal regions, most of it falling as snowfall. Mountainous regions, such as Baffin Island, southern Greenland, and northern Scandinavia, receive more precipitation (up to 600 mm). Precipitation is largely related to the passage of cyclones (a system of winds circulating anticlockwise round a center of low barometric pressure) over open water, and as large areas of open water are uncommon, the occasional open water areas in winter become important heat and moisture sources.

The coldness of Arctic air causes precipitation to take the characteristic form of small, dry, and hard snow particles that are easily redistributed by wind to produce blowing-snow storms. Blowing snow makes the accurate measurement of precipitation very difficult. The heaviest snowfalls usually occur in October, after which the air becomes so cold that it can carry only negligible amounts of moisture.

Hoarfrost, a white deposit of ice with a crystalline appearance formed directly from the cooling of water vapor on surfaces with a temperature below that of the dew point, is formed only when the relative humidity is greater than 100% and temperatures are below freezing. Generally, the smallest amount of hoarfrost formation occurs in April and the greatest in September.

Clouds and Fog

Condensation that takes place just above the ground forms fog, and when it occurs at higher levels, clouds form. Clouds over the Arctic Ocean are least in winter and spring and greatest in summer. The cloud maximum in summer is unique to the Arctic and is contrary to cloud patterns in midlatitudes. In winter, the combination of frozen ground and ocean and the absence of sufficient incoming radiation for evaporation create a limited supply of moisture to the atmosphere.

Low cloud and fog are especially characteristic of coastal areas and broken pack ice in summer. Melting of pack ice in summer leads to the formation of persistent fog and low cloud. During the winter, small patches of fog form over open water leads in the pack ice. This phenomenon, sometimes referred to as Arctic sea smoke, develops when cold air flows over open water and moisture and heat are rapidly released into the air. Ice fog often forms during the Arctic spring. Ice fog is a mist of tiny ice crystals floating in the air.

Changing Precipitation Patterns

The Arctic is entering a period of unprecedented change. Emissions of greenhouse gases due to human activities are altering the atmosphere and are expected to change global climate in ways that may be detrimental to our environmental, social, and economic systems. The warming of the Arctic since the 1960s has been accompanied by increases in precipitation in most Arctic regions since at least the 1950s. The percentage precipitation increase in the Arctic has been greater than any other latitudinal zone. General circulation models project substantial increases over the 21st century, ranging from 10 to 20% over land and 2% to 25% over the Arctic Ocean in summer, and 5% to 80% over land and 2% to 45% over the Arctic Ocean in winter. Model estimates vary widely, and are complicated by many factors such as cloud cover. Combined changes in temperature and precipitation will alter many aspects of the Arctic environment, including snow and ice distribution, hydrology, surface water budgets, wetlands, sea ice, ice sheets, glaciers, and the distribution of flora and fauna. A significant increase in precipitation leading to increased freshwater flow into the Arctic Ocean could also affect deep ocean circulation.

AYNSLIE OGDEN

See also **Polar Desert; Snow; Sublimation; Weather**

Further Reading

Aagard, K. & E.C. Carmack, "The Arctic Ocean and Climate: A Perspective." In *The Polar Oceans and Their Role in Shaping the Global Environment*, edited by O.M. Johannessen, R.D. Muench, J.E. Overland, Washington, District of Columbia: American Geophysical Union, 1994

Ahrens, D., *Meteorology Today: An Introduction to Weather, Climate, and the Environment*, Pacific Grove, California: Brooks/Cole, 2000

Barry, R.G. & M.C. Serreze, "Atmospheric Components of the Arctic Ocean Freshwater Balance and their Interannual Variability." In T*he Freshwater Budget of the Arctic Ocean*, edited by E.L. Lewis, Dordrecht: Kluwer, 2000

Houghton, J.T., Y. Ding, D.J. Griggs, M. Noguer, P. J. van der Linden & D. Xiaosu, *Climate Change 2001: The Scientific Basis, Contribution of Working Group I to the Third Assessment Report of the Intergovernmental Panel on Climate Change (IPCC),* Cambridge and New York: Cambridge University Press, 2001

Pielou, E.C., *A Naturalist's Guide to the Arctic*, Chicago: University of Chicago Press, 1994

Walsh, J.E., V. Kattsov, D. Portis & V. Meleshko, "Arctic precipitation and evaporation: model results and observational Estimates." *Journal of Climate*, 11 (1998): 72–87

Yang, D., "An improved precipitation climatology for the Arctic Ocean." *Geophysical Research Letters*, 26(11) (1999): 1625–1628

PRE-DORSET CULTURE

There are two different definitions for the term Pre-Dorset. The first one, initially employed by Collins (1954), refers, in a broader way, to the culture preceding the Dorset. Later, Meldgaard, by comparison with the Saqqaq complex of Greenland, proposed to name Saqqaq the preceding Dorset culture of Igloolik (Meldgaard, 1960). However, the term Pre-Dorset associated to a new definition will replace it. This second definition, more common today, gives a regional meaning to Pre-Dorset, identifying the preceding Dorset culture mainly in the Core Area. Thus, more or less contemporary cultures are Denbigh in the western Arctic, Independence I in the High Arctic, and northeastern Greenland and Saqqaq in southwestern Greenland. Also, the increase in research outside the Core Area has seen the use of the term Pre-Dorset extended to include peripheral regions, further modifying the accepted definition. Consequently, there is still ambiguity surrounding the use of this term since it is also called Early Paleo-Eskimo, particularly when avoiding its chronospatial meaning. Pre-Dorset culture remains classified as part of the Arctic Small Tool Tradition.

The problem of radiocarbon dating has taken an important place in the debate on the origin and contemporaneity of Pre-Dorset and its High Arctic counterpart, Independence I. McGhee and Tuck (1976) proposed that High Arctic was colonized before Low Arctic, but the review of chronology by Arundale (1981) indicates forward contemporaneity. Most archaeologists now accept an Alaskan origin for Pre-Dorset as being developed from the Denbigh Flint Complex or from another unknown western origin. According to this thesis, the Pre-Dorset hunter-gatherers spread from west to east broadly around 4000–4500 BP and will persist to a period between 2900 and 2600 BP before the Dorset culture (Maxwell, 1985: 77). Taylor (1968) and others, based on their research, established that Pre-Dorset was in continuity with the Dorset culture, while others define this key period as a transition. For example, Nagy (2000) interpreted this period or transition as a shift from Pre-Dorset forager's strategy to Dorset collector's strategy. The question of the transition to Dorset culture is still subject to debate. Some archaeologists argue that Early Dorset is in fact the final Pre-Dorset and that Middle Dorset is the beginning of Dorset culture (Gendron and Pinard, 2000; Ramsden and Tuck, 2001).

Pre-Dorset technology yielded diversified sets of stone tools such as microblades, a variety of knives, end scrapers, bifaces, projectile points, partially polished adzes, rubbed slate tools, etc., among which the spalled burin is the most characteristic compared to subsequent periods. Soapstone was also used mostly to produce round or oval-shaped lamps. Wood, bone, and ivory were also part of the raw materials used to produce weapons and tools such as harpoon, bows and arrows, lances, throwing spears, bipointed needles with small drilled eyes, etc. Little is known about transportation technology because of the preservation problem of Pre-Dorset organic material. There is no evidence of sledges even if the presence of dogs is attested (see, e.g., Harp, 1978; Knuth, 1967; Grønnow, 1994). Also, little is known about the use of boats, except for a kayaklike vessel piece found at the Qeqertasussuk site in West Greenland (Grønnow, 1994). It is generally assumed that there was no sea mammal hunting from boats during the Pre-Dorset (Maxwell, 1985: 84).

Evidence of arts is limited compared to Dorset, but schematic carving, animal carving, and maskettes are reported (Maxwell, 1985: 95–96). We must quote the maskette face portrait interpreted as an old tattooed Inuit woman, supporting the possible use of tattoos by Pre-Dorset people (Helmer, 1986).

The Pre-Dorset demonstrated a great capacity for adaptation by occupying different territories from the boreal forest edge to the High Arctic and by hunting a large variety of animals with different behaviors (Maxwell, 1985: 81). Depending on their locality, Pre-Dorset hunted muskox, caribou, polar bear, hare, fox, migratory birds as well as sea mammals: seal, walrus, beluga, and narwhal. There are also artifacts identified as fishing gear, like some barbed spear points, and some exceptional preserved fish remains (Maxwell, 1985: 90; Grønnow, 1994: 218).

According to McGhee (1976), one aspect of Pre-Dorset settlement is the clustered structure patterns while the settlement of Independence I exhibits a more linear arrangement of structures. He based this

suggestion on Pre-Dorset and Independence I sites from the Port Refuge settlement; both are oriented toward sea mammal hunting. The validity of this model was rapidly reconsidered (Mary-Rousselière, 1976: 53). There are probably no specific and exclusive characteristics for Pre-Dorset dwellings. The surface structure may or may not have axial features, box hearths in the center, and elliptical, round, or bilobate shape. There are also semi-subterranean dwellings either square or rectangular, and in some regions they may be recognized by depressions in boulder fields (Maxwell, 1985: 96–97; Gendron and Pinard, 2000: 131–133).

Two skeletal remains of Early Paleo-Eskimo people have been found in the eastern Arctic. The first came from North Devon Island in the High Arctic. Dated to 3800 BP, these remains are of a premature infant, thus limiting paleoanthropological studies and comparisons with subsequent population remains. The body of the infant was abandoned without any visible trace of ritual. The lack of evidence is not conclusive compared to the scarcity of burial practice in Late Paleo-Eskimo people (Helmer and Kennedy, 1986). The second remains come from West Greenland; it was found in layers dated between 3900 and 3700 BP. Spots of red ochre were found on the tibia, hair tufts associated with bone needle (Grønnow, 1994).

Climatic variations have surely influenced their evolution since the first Pre-Dorsets were developed during a postglacial period in a cooler environment, but warmer than today, 4000 years ago. This cooling may be responsible for the abandonment of the High Arctic around 1700 BP. The progressive isostasy rebound of the continent, after the last glaciations, resulted in the fact that in the eastern Arctic, Pre-Dorset sites are usually higher above sea level than subsequent period sites. However, in the eastern limit of the Canadian Arctic (southeastern Baffin and northern Labrador), early sites appear to be much lower and even underwater.

PIERRE M. DESROSIERS

See also **Archaeology of the Arctic: Canada and Greenland; Arctic Small Tool Tradition; Collins, Henry B.; Denbigh Flint Culture; Dorset Culture; Independence Culture; Knuth, Eigil; Migration, Prehistory; Saqqaq Culture; Mary-Rousseliere, Father Guy; Thule Culture**

Further Reading

Arundale, Wendy Hanford, "Radiocarbon dating in eastern Arctic arcaeology: a flexible approach." *American Antiquity*, 46 (1981): 244–271

Collins, Henry B., "Archaeological research in the North American Arctic." *Arctic*, 7 (1954): 296–306

Gendron, Daniel & Claude Pinard, "Early Palaeo-Eskimo Occupations in Nunavik: A Re-Appraisal." In *Identities and*

Cultural Contacts in the Arctic, edited by Martin Appelt, Joel Berglund & Hans Christian Gullov, Copenhagen: Danish National Museum and Danish Polar Center, Danish Polar Center Publication 8, 2000, pp. 129–142

Grønnow, Bjarne, "Qeqertasussuk—The Archaeology of a Frozen Saqqaq Site in Disko Bugt, West Greenland." In *Threads of Arctic Prehistory: Papers in Honour of William E. Taylor Jr.,* edited by David Morrison & Jean-Luc Pilon, Hull: Canadian Museum of Civilization, Mercury Series 149, 1994, pp. 197–238

Harp, Elmer Jr., "Pioneer cultures of the Sub-Arctic and Arctic." In *Ancient Native American*, edited by Jesse D. Jennings, New York: W.H. Freeman, 1978, pp. 94–129

Helmer, James W., "A face from the past: an early Pre-Dorset ivory maskette from Devon Island, NWT." *Études Inuit Studies*, 10 (1986): 179–202

Helmer, James W. & Brenda V. Kennedy, "Early Palaeo-Eskimo skeletal remains from North Devon Island, High Arctic Canada." *Canadian Journal of Archaeology*, 10 (1986): 127–143

Knuth, Eigil, "Archaeology of the musk-ox way." *Contributions du Centre d'Études Arctiques et Finno Scadinaves*, 5 (1967): 1–78

Mary-Rousselière, Guy, "The Paleoeskimo in Northern Baffinland." In *Eastern Arctic Prehistory: Palaeoeskimo Problems*, edited by Moreau S. Maxwell, *Memoirs of the Society for American Archaeology*, 31 (1976): 40–57

Maxwell, Moreau S., *Prehistory of the Eastern Arctic*, New York: Academic Press, 1985

McGhee, Robert, "Paleoeskimo Occupations of Central and High Arctic Canada." In *Eastern Arctic Prehistory: Palaeoeskimo Problems*, edited by Moreau S. Maxwell, *Memoirs of the Society for American Archaeology*, 31 (1976): 15–39

McGhee, Robert & James A. Tuck, "Un-Dating the Canadian Arctic." In *Eastern Arctic Prehistory: Palaeoeskimo Problems*, edited by Moreau S. Maxwell, *Memoirs of the Society for American Archaeology*, 31 (1976): 6–14

Meldgaard, Jörgen, "Origin and evolution of Eskimo cultures in Eastern Arctic." *Canadian Geographical Journal*, 60(2) (1960): 64–75

Nagy, Murielle Ida, "Palaeoeskimo cultural transition: a case study from Ivujivik, Eastern Arctic." *Nunavik Archaeology Monograph Series*, 1 (2000)

Ramsden, Peter & James A. Tuck, "A comment on the Pre-Dorset/Dorset transition in the Eastern Arctic." *Anthropological Papers of the University of Alaska*, 1(1) (2001): 7–12

Taylor, William E., "The Arnapik and Tyara Sites, An Archaeological Study of Dorset Culture Origins." *Memoirs of the Society for American Archaeology*, 22, Salt Lake City: University of Utah, American Antiquity, 33(4) (1968)

PRIBILOF ISLANDS

The Pribilof Islands, the fabled seal islands of the Bering Sea, are located in the south-central Bering Sea, about 482 km (300 miles) west of the Alaska mainland and 386 km (240 miles) north of the Aleutian Islands (*see* **Map in Alaska entry**). The archipelago is comprised of St Paul, with an area of 103.6 sq km (40 sq miles), St George, 70 sq km (27 sq miles), and islets Otter Island, Sea Lion Rock, and Walrus Island.

The Pribilofs were formed as a result of eruptions of basaltic lavas onto the southern edge of the Bering Sea shelf. The eruptions that formed St George Island began about 2.2 million years before the present and lasted until about 1.6 million years before the present. St Paul Island was formed about one million years after St George. The pulse of volcanism that formed St Paul Island may not be over, as a new radiocarbon date of 3230 ± 30 years has been obtained on the Fox Hill lava flow on southwestern St Paul Island. The young date of this lava flow indicates that future eruptions may be expected on St Paul Island. St George Island, a faulted block of layered basaltic lava flows, has precipitous sea cliffs, reaching a maximum elevation of 308 m (1012 ft). Glaciers smoothed the surface of St George and its former cinder cones are now rounded hills. St Paul, which has never been glaciated, has fewer coastal cliffs, more beaches, and numerous cinder cones that retain their steep slopes and sharp crater rims. Rush Hill, at 202 m (665 ft), is St Paul's highest elevation. Scattered remains of mammoths have been found on the islands, and fossil shells range in age from Pleistocene to Recent.

The islands are treeless and covered with lush grasses, dwarf willows, lichens, mosses, and numerous varieties of flowering plants. There are no natural harbors on the islands and only a few freshwater streams on St George.

The climate is Arctic Maritime, with a range of mean temperatures of $-7°C$ to $-11°C$ (19–52°F), an average precipitation of 558 mm (22 inches), and average snowfall of 1422 mm (56 inches). Heavy fog prevails during summer months. Coastal waters are open year round, and pack ice occasionally reaches the islands in winter.

Marine currents stir the shallow, nutrient-rich waters around the Pribilof Islands, accounting for the exceptional biodiversity of the region. Almost 70% of the world's population of northern fur seals—approximately 800,700 animals—migrate each year to breed on the rocky shores of the Pribilofs. Vast colonies of seabirds (an estimated 2.8 million) nest on the islands, including thick-billed murres, common murres, least auklets, parakeet auklets, horned puffins, tufted puffins, black-legged kittiwakes, and most of the world's population of red-legged kittiwakes. In 1984, the global importance of the seabird nesting sites earned them inclusion in the Alaska Maritime National Wildlife Refuge. Over 220 species of birds have been sighted on the islands, migrating from as far away as Siberia and Argentina.

The Pribilof region is also home to Steller's sea lions, harbor seals, whales, and many species of fish and shell fish. Terrestrial species include Arctic fox, the endemic Pribilof Island shrew, and reindeer (introduced in 1911 from Unalkaleet, Alaska).

Fur-seal rookery on a beach, St. Paul Island, Pribilof Islands, Alaska. Photo by Rear Admiral Harley D. Nygren, NOAA Corps.
Courtesy National Oceanic and Atmospheric Administration, Central Library

The Pribilof Islands were discovered in 1786 by Russian navigator Gavriil Pribilof, ending a three-year search by Siberian merchants for the breeding site of the valuable fur seals. The roaring of seals drew Pribilof's boat through the summer fog to St George Island. The following year, Pribilof discovered St Paul Island, 75 km (47 miles) to the north. The islands were uninhabited at the time of discovery, although Aleut oral history knew them as *Amiq*, a rich hunting ground visited by an Aleut chief lost in a storm.

The discovery of the islands extended the Russian-American fur trade for another 80 years. Sea otters had been hunted nearly to extinction, and the discovery of the fur seals' breeding rookeries brought a new source of wealth to Siberian traders. Aleuts were forcibly taken from the Aleutian Islands as seasonal laborers in the fur seal harvest, and by the 1820s permanent settlements were created on both islands. Seals were ruthlessly killed until the Russian crown approved the Russian America Company as a licensed fur seal monopoly in 1799. By 1847, Russians had adopted conservation methods in harvesting seals, taking three- to five-year-old nonbreeding males and prohibiting the killing of female seals.

After the 1867 sale of Russian-American territories to the United States, a series of monopolies continued sealing, often on an uncontrolled basis. Pelagic (high-seas) sealing further depleted the seal herds, and by 1910 the herd had been reduced to 250,000 animals. In 1911, the North Pacific Fur Seal Convention was signed by the United States, Japan, Russia, and Great Britain (for Canada), prohibiting the killing of seals at sea. Under the treaty, the herd gradually increased, until it peaked at about 2 million animals by 1950.

Pribilof sealing generated large revenues for the United States Treasury after the government assumed responsibility for the seal industry in 1910. Total receipts from fur seal pelts surpassed the purchase price of the Alaska territories after only a few years. The Aleuts, however, did not thrive under government rule. They were treated as wards of the government, paid in kind for their work in the seal harvest, and experienced repression and discrimination by government agents. In 1942, the Aleuts were evacuated and interned in dilapidated fish canneries in southeastern Alaska until the end of World War II, losing 10% of their population to poor living conditions, disease, and malnutrition.

Exposure to the outside world led Pribilof leaders to sue the US government for fair wages and individual freedoms, granted under the 1966 Fur Seal Act. The Aleuts gained more political and economic control with the 1971 passage of the Alaska Native Claims Settlement Act (ANCSA). Village corporations were established on St George and St Paul, and local governance grew to include city councils, school board, and tribal councils (established under the Indian Reorganization Act).

Animal protection organizations pressured the US government to withdraw from the fur seal industry. In

1984, the government failed to ratify the international fur seal convention and commercial harvesting of seals ceased on St Paul Island (sealing had ended on St George in 1973). The Aleuts are allowed to take approximately 2000 seals every year for subsistence food. The Pribilofs adapted to the loss of the seal industry by entering the flourishing Bering Sea bottom sea fishery, attracting government and industry capital to develop harbors, processing facilities, and vessel supply operations. The Aleuts achieved a rapid, successful transition to a day-boat halibut fishery. However, decades of intensive fishing in the Bering Sea, combined with climatic changes, have led to population declines in over 17 species of marine mammals, fish, and seabirds. Fur seals are listed as a depleted species under the Marine Mammal Protection Act. A crash in the Opilio crab population has brought economic crisis to the Pribilof villages, and in 2000 the Pribilofs were declared part of a federal disaster area. The bankruptcy of the airline servicing the Pribilof Islands has also made a small ecotourism industry much more vulnerable.

Today, the Pribilofs are home to the largest Aleut communities left in the world, with 800 of the total population of 3200 Aleuts. The Pribilof Aleuts have survived many challenges over two centuries: forcible relocation, influence and culture of two colonial nations, loss of aboriginal subsistence skills to a wage-based industry, and suppression of their language, religion, political structures, and human rights. A local cultural movement is successfully connecting young Pribilovians to the fur seals that so defined their island culture. Community leaders are working to diversify their economy so that future generations of Aleuts will continue to call these islands home.

HELEN D. CORBETT AND G.S. WINER

See also **Aleut; Bering Sea; Northern fur seal; North Pacific Fur Seal Convention**

Further Reading

Committee on the Bering Sea Ecosystem, National Research Council, *The Bering Sea Ecosystem*, Washington: National Academy Press, 1996

Corbett, Helen D. & Susanne M. Swibold, "The Aleuts of the Pribilof Islands, Alaska." In *Endangered Peoples of the Arctic: Struggles to Survive and Thrive*, edited by M.R. Milton, Freeman, Westport, Connecticut: Greenwood Press, 2000

Jones, Dorothy Knee, *A Century of Servitude: Pribilof Aleuts under US Rule*, Lanham, Maryland: University Press of America, 1980

Scheffer, Victor B., *The Year of the Seal*, New York: Charles Scribner and Sons, 1970

Torrey, Barbara Boyle, *Slaves of the Harvest: The Story of the Pribilof Aleuts*, St Paul, Alaska: Tanadgusix Corporation, 1978

PRIMARY PRODUCTION

Primary production and primary productivity refer to the quantity of organic matter fixed by autotrophs—photosynthesizing plants, or algae, phytoplankton, and cyanobacteria in aquatic or marine contexts—in a given area over a known time period. Production is generally expressed as a rate of weight increase per day or year. Gross primary production is the total amount of organic matter fixed including respiration, while net primary production is the increase in dry mass of a plant from the onset of the measured period (e.g., spring) to the end of the growing season, which allows for the respiratory energy required by the plant itself. The net primary production of a plant community or an ecosystem may be expressed as the change of the total plant dry mass over a time period, usually a year (net annual production).

The Arctic tundra and polar deserts (the climatically extreme confines of the tundra biome) have some of the lowest primary production rates of the world terrestrial biomes (net annual production rates of 1 g m^{-2} in the polar desert of the High Arctic to <1000 g m^{-2} for shrubs and tussock and sedge-dwarf shrub in the Low Arctic). The significance of the Arctic, nevertheless, results from the very large area the Arctic occupies on a global scale (5.6 million km^2 or 3.8% of ice-free land). Additionally, in comparison with other large ecosystems, Arctic tundra has for most of the Quaternary (and certainly in the last 10,000 years) been a net carbon dioxide sink, accumulating organic matter in the soil and building up thick peat deposits. It is estimated that Arctic ecosystems hold about 60 Gt of carbon, compared to approximately 750 Gt of carbon currently in the atmosphere as CO_2. Nearly the entire area covered by Arctic tundra is underlain by permafrost. The active layer (the unfrozen topsoil layer that develops seasonally) remains near freezing at its base. At such low temperatures roots grow slowly but live longer, and dead roots decompose poorly, especially under insulating moss and sphagnum carpets. Thus, over a long time period, there has been a slow but steady accumulation of belowground, and in dry habitats also of aboveground, biomass.

Highly productive ecosystems at lower latitudes such as tall grass prairies and tropical forests exhibit high peaks of annual production. These gains, however, are usually offset by losses of comparable size due to decomposition. More recently, however, due to climate warming and high atmospheric CO_2 concentration, North American and Eurasian forests have shown net carbon gains and their overall biomass is increasing (Myneni et al., 2001). The Arctic tundra has also recently shown a steady rise in plant cover and production along the entire latitudinal gradient (Fung, 1997; Myneni et al., 1997). However, in areas where the historically stored dead organic matter in permafrost (roots, peat, soil litter, and standing dead wood) now decomposes at greater rates due to recent warming, the generation of new biomass does not match the total carbon loss from respiration of CO_2 by plants and soil microorganisms. Although recent results have suggested that Arctic tundra can become carbon sinks in summertime, the result is still a net annual CO_2 loss (Oechel et al., 2000).

In contrast, polar deserts function as a net carbon sink (Jones et al., 2000). There is little or no dead residual biomass stored in the soil, which would now decompose and cause significant CO_2 yield. While these systems produce little biomass in absolute amounts, a significant percentage of annual production remains undecomposed, resulting in a net annual surplus in primary production.

Ecologically, and to a large degree climatically, the Arctic realm is determined by the extent of tundra biome, which encompasses a large portion of the circumpolar lands north of the treeline. With the increasing climate severity along the south-north gradient, the diversity, standing biomass (standing crop), and productivity of tundra vegetation diminish. The Low Arctic tundra, with distinguishable subzones such as tall shrub-, low shrub-, and open contagious tundra, is manifested prevalently on the continental mainland. It is composed of a relatively diverse (>400 vascular species), dense, and productive vegetation. In moist habitats, lush graminoid (rush, sedge, grass) communities with a notable shrub component predominate, while in well-drained drier habitats, lichen-heath thickets and carpets are more common. Along the extensive coastal margins, productive saltmarshes develop.

In contrast, for the terrestrial High Arctic, a discontinuous plant cover is more typical. With minor exceptions, a mosaic of scanty vegetation complexes is present on islands positioned within the Arctic Circle. Uplands of the Canadian Arctic Archipelago support meager growth classified as polar semidesert (<50% ground cover) and polar deserts (<10% cover) with extremely low productivity per unit area (Aleksandrova, 1988; Bliss, 1997). Here, vascular diversity is made of a mere handful of species. Cushion plants, scattered prostrate shrubs, and tiny herbs predominate. Old deglaciated landscapes are covered with a dark cryptogamic crust, made of lichens, green algae, liverworts, and mosses, which are important primary producers in these otherwise barren areas. The crust's total biomass is relatively high but its live standing crop and production rates are mostly unknown (Bliss and Matveyeva, 1992; Bliss and Gold, 1999). Recently deglaciated landscapes are bare, entirely void of non-vascular and flowering plants, yet highly productive algal assemblages establish here quickly (Elster et al., 1999).

Due to postglacial isostatic recovery, numerous flat lowlands have emerged along the islands' margins. Some of them maintain favorable climate in summer. In such sheltered and, by meltwater, irrigated environments, green oases have developed with high diversity (100+ vascular species) and productivity (Svoboda and Freedman, 1994). A variable mosaic of herb, lichen-cushion plant, heath-dwarf shrub, and sedge meadow communities can be identified in these enclaves, with primary productivity increasing from herb fields to meadow stands (Muc et al. 1994). Although these widely scattered ecosystems represent only a minute percentage of the terrestrial High Arctic, they support most of the wildlife, especially large herbivores such as muskoxen.

Less apparent is the west-east vegetation and primary productivity gradient. The warm Gulf Stream current, which ameliorates the climate of northern Scandinavia, is felt up to islands of Novaya Zemlya. East of this geographic hurdle, the climate becomes progressively colder and drier. Consequently, tundra along the northern Eurasian coast and on the islands is poorer and less productive. In the North American Arctic, the west-east climate-vegetation-productivity gradient is even more pronounced, especially across the Canadian Arctic Archipelago. While the low-elevation western islands are known for their productive meadow complexes, the mountainous eastern islands are prominent with polar deserts and some are still glaciated.

JOSEF SVOBODA AND ESTHER LÉVESQUE

See also **Carbon Cycling; Lichen; Microbial Mats; Polar Desert; Primary Production, Marine; Trophic Levels**

Further Reading

Aleksandrova, V.D., *Vegetation of the Soviet Polar Desert*, Studies in Polar Research, Cambridge: Cambridge University Press, 1988

Bliss, L.C., "Arctic Ecosystems in North America." In: *Polar and Alpine Tundra. Ecosystems of the World*, Volume 3, edited by F.E. Wielgolaski, Amsterdam: Elsevier, 1997, pp. 551–683

Bliss, L.C. & W.G. Gold, "Vascular plant reproduction, establishment, and growth and effects of cryptogamic crust within a polar desert ecosystem, Devon Island, NWT, Canada." *Canadian Journal of Botany*, 77 (1993): 623–636

Bliss, L.C. & N.M. Matveyeva, "Circumpolar Arctic Vegetation." In *Arctic Ecosystems in a Changing Climate. An Ecophysiological Perspective*, edited by F.S. Chapin III, R.L. Jefferies, J.F. Reynolds, G.R. Shaver and J. Svoboda, New York: Academic Press, 1992, pp. 59–89

Elster, J., A. Lukešová, J. Svoboda, J. Kopecký & H. Kanda, "Diversity and abundance of soil algae in the polar desert, Sverdrup Pass, central Ellesmere Island." *Polar Record*, 35(194) (1999): 231–254

Fung, I., "A greener North." *Nature*, 186 (1997): 659–660

Jones, M.H., J.T. Fahnestock, P.D. Stahl & J.M. Welker, "A note on summer CO_2 flux, soil organic matter, and microbial biomass from different High Arctic ecosystem types in Northwestern Greenland." *Arctic, Antarctic and Alpine Research,* 32 (2000): 104–106

Muc, M., B. Freedman & J. Svoboda, "Vascular Plant Communities of a Polar Oasis at Alexandra Fiord, Ellesmere Island." In *Ecology of a Polar Oasis Alexandra Fiord, Ellesmere Island, Canada,* edited by Josef Svoboda and Bill Freedman, Toronto: Captus University Publication, 1994, pp. 53–64

Myneni, R.B., C.D. Keeling, C.J. Tucker, G. Asrar & R.R. Nemani, "Increased plant growth in the northern high latitudes from 1981 to 1991." *Nature,* 386 (1997): 698–702

Myneni, R.B., J. Dong, C.J. Tucker, R.K. Kaufmann, P.E. Kauppi, J. Liski, L. Zhou, V. Alexeyev & M.K. Hughes, "A large carbon sink in the woody biomass of Northern forests." *Proceedings of the National Academy of Science USA,* 98(26) (2001): 14784–14789

Oechel, W.C., G.L. Vourlitis, S.J. Hastings, R.C. Zulueta, L. Hinzman & D. Kane, "Acclimation of ecosystem CO_2 exchange in the Alaskan Arctic in response to decadal climate warming." *Nature,* 406 (2000): 978–981

Rodin, L.E., N.I. Basilevich & N.N. Rozov, "Productivity of the world's main ecosystems." In *Productivity of World Ecosystems,* edited by David E. Reichle, F. Franklin Jerry & David W. Goodall, Washington: National Academy of Sciences, 1975, pp. 13–27

Svoboda, J. & B. Freedman (editors), *Ecology of a Polar Oasis: Alexandra Fiord, Ellesmere Island, Canada,* Toronto: Captus University Publication, 1994

PRIMARY PRODUCTION, MARINE

The central Arctic Ocean is covered by sea ice up to 2 m thick even in summer, while the marginal seas have seasonal snow and ice cover limiting the penetration of light to the water below.

Despite the low temperatures and low light intensities, productivity in Arctic seas is not as low as once thought. Shelf areas of the Arctic Ocean are now thought to be among the world's most productive marine areas. Productivity is greatest in open seas over continental shelves, where nutrients transported from freshwater inputs are greatest. Typical primary production rates are about 60 g carbon per square meter per year (60 g $m^{-2} a^{-1}$) over the Arctic continental shelves and may reach 400 $m^{-2} a^{-1}$ in the Chukchi Sea. There is a pronounced seasonal peak in productivity in spring when light becomes available, accelerated by snow and ice melt. The timing of the peak has an important influence on marine food webs as a whole: in the Bering Sea large marine ecosystem, the primary productivity explosion in spring results in increased secondary production and draws migrating seabirds and other animals such as gray whales to feed on the phytoplankton, zooplankton, and fish.

Primary producers are within the ice (ice algae), floating (pelagic) phytoplankton, and deep-sea (benthic) algae, including kelp. Summer melt ponds in the upper surface of ice also harbor communities of freshwater algal species, transported into the Arctic Ocean by lakes and rivers.

Ice Algae

Several hundred microscopic unicellular plant species, such as diatoms (phytoplankton with cell walls composed of silica) and other algae, live within a network of briny cracks from micrometers to several centimeters thick within sea ice. Strands of algae such as *Melosira arctica* may also attach to the bottom of the ice-floes. The sympagic (ice associated) community also includes bacteria and protozoans (unicellular organisms such as foraminifera, ciliates, and flagellates), and small crustaceans and nematodes (roundworms), which graze on the algae within the ice or on the underside of the ice pack.

Although the ice algae face total darkness for up to six months, experiments have shown that they can survive the long dark winter with large lipid (fat) reserves, and begin growth within days of increased light intensity. The contribution of ice algal primary production to total primary production in seasonally ice-covered Arctic waters is poorly known, but may be up to 25%. This fraction may increase in perennially ice-covered waters where reduced radiation penetration limits phytoplankton primary production in deeper waters.

First-year ice has the highest light penetration and highest biomass production, and the continental shelves with seasonal ice also benefit from increased nutrient flow from rivers.

Phytoplankton

The major primary producers in Arctic waters are protists in the form of algae, diatoms, and flagellates (although not all flagellates are photosynthetic). Cyanobacteria, which contribute large fractions of primary production in tropical and temperate waters, are nearly absent from the Arctic. Maximum phytoplankton biomass is in surface waters along the ice edge of the Arctic shelves, although production occurs even beneath the ice cover. Some species of diatoms simply float in the water currents near the surface. Others attach themselves to larger floating objects or to the seafloor. The development period is very short, with rapid growth—called phytoplankton blooms—in spring and summer when solar radiation increases and nutrients, accumulated during winter, are released by ice breakup and river melt. Dominant taxa in Arctic blooms are chain-forming diatoms (e.g., *Thalassiosira* spp., *Chaetoceros* spp.) and pelagic microflagellates (e.g., *Phaeocystis pouchetii* and *Protoperidinium* spp.).

Benthic Microalgae and Macroalgae

Ocean bottom (benthic) microalgae, primarily elongated diatoms, contribute only a small fraction of the total marine primary productivity. They bloom when light reaches the sediment surface, and are mostly found beneath first-year ice where light penetration is greatest and nutrient supply higher. In outer fjords and nearshore environments, primary production by benthic macroalgae (primarily brown algae rather than green algae, of the orders Laminariales (kelps), Fucales (rockweeds)) may meet or exceed that of local phytoplankton. Most brown algae are intertidal or upper subtidal, except for the giant kelps, which are found down to 15–40 m. In the High Arctic, intertidal areas have no shoreline flora due to ice scour, but species that are normally intertidal are displaced to the subtidal.

Kelp is a very efficient primary producer, and occurs in cold, nutrient-rich shallow coastal waters of northwestern Europe, Iceland, Greenland, Canada, and sheltered lagoons in the Bering-Beaufort-Chukchi seas. Kelp of the family Laminariales is harvested from wild stands in these areas as a food source, and is dried and exported in Iceland.

Protected bays may harbor extensive eelgrass (*Zostera marina*) meadows in the subtidal zone, but it is not abundant in the Arctic.

Global Change

Most models predict greatest warming in the polar regions, which would substantially decrease the thickness and area of sea ice cover and could severely affect the polar food web if it continues. Increases in ultraviolet radiation caused by stratospheric ozone depletion are known to inhibit phytoplankton productivity in the Southern Ocean, and are being studied for phytoplankton and kelp in the Arctic. Since different species may vary in their sensitivity to ultraviolet exposure, this may cause changes in biodiversity, and decrease primary productivity. Any decrease in productivity or population would likely affect higher species and trophic levels, although since the ozone hole was observed, no such effects have yet occurred.

GILLIAN LINDSEY

See also **Food Webs, Marine; Large Marine Ecosystems; Marine Biology; Microbial Mats; Plankton; Trophic Levels**

Further Reading

Gosselin, M., M. Levasseur, P. A. Wheeler, R. A. Horner & B. C. Booth, "New measurements of phytoplankton and ice algal production in the Arctic Ocean." *Deep-Sea Research*, 44 (1997): 1623–1644

Horner, R.A., "Ice-Associated Ecosystems." In *Polar Marine Diatoms*, edited by L.K. Medlin & J. Priddle, Cambridge: British Antarctic Survey, 1990

Horner, R., S.F. Ackley, G.S. Dieckmann, B. Gulliksen, T. Hoshiai, L. Legendre, I.A. Melnikov, W.S. Reeburgh, M. Spindler & C.W. Sullivan, "Ecology of sea ice biota. 1. Habitat, terminology, and methodology." *Polar Biology*, 12 (1992): 417–427

Pomeroy, L.R, "Primary production in the Arctic Ocean estimated from dissolved oxygen." *Journal of Marine Systems*, 10(1997):1–8

Thomas, D.N., "Primary Production in Sea Ice." In *Sea Ice: An Introduction to its Physics, Chemistry, Biology and Geology*, edited by D.N. Thomas & G.S. Dieckmann, Oxford: Blackwell, 2003

PRINCE CHARLES ISLAND

Prince Charles Island (67°30′ N, 76°00′ W) is located in Foxe Basin, Nunavut, immediately south of central Baffin Island. It is the largest (nearly 10,000 km^2) uninhabited island south of the Canadian Arctic Archipelago. Little used by Inuit and not even known to non-Inuit until the late 1940s, Prince Charles is a haven for large populations of birds and polar bears.

The most striking feature of the island's physiography is its flatness. Prince Charles Island is a relatively young landform; before the last ice age, the island was entirely submerged beneath the prehistoric Tyrell Sea. The center portion of the island is composed of flat expanses of unvegetated broken shale and contains a number of large lakes. This inner core is ringed by extensive and productive wetlands and ponded tundra that have emerged more recently from the sea. Finally, there is a broad saltmarsh and mudflat interface between the wetlands and the surrounding waters of Foxe Basin. As uplift continues, the barren center of the island will expand outward and new areas of wetland will form. The island is morphologically similar to the adjacent Air Force Island and to the Great Plains of the Koukdjuak on the west coast of Baffin Island.

Climate on Prince Charles is greatly influenced by the waters of Foxe Basin. The basin is relatively shallow, and the ice pack remains in motion throughout the winter. Along most of the island's coast, shorefast ice persists until sometime in July, and Foxe Basin as a whole is not usually navigable until late August or September. However, along the northern side of Prince Charles Island, a polynya forms around January, and a persistent lead opens southeast of the island in March. Summer ice in Foxe Basin keeps coastal areas significantly cooler than inland sites. Summer temperatures on the island are generally comparable to those recorded approximately 80 km northeast at Longstaff Bluff, Baffin Island. Snowmelt occurs in the last half of June. Temperatures are above freezing on most days in the latter part of June, July, and the first half of August.

Vascular plant collections were made on the northern and southern tips of the island in 1949, and at numerous locations in 1996 and 1997. Fifty-four species were identified. This compares to a total of 73 species on the Great Plains of the Koukdjuak, western Baffin Island, and 64 at Igloolik Island, northern Foxe Basin. It is likely that further effort would add a few more species to the Prince Charles Island list; however, its known flora is similar to the flora of the Great Plains of the Koukdjuak.

A habitat classification for Prince Charles was developed from satellite imagery and ground checks. Generally, there are three types of habitat (excluding water) on the island: graminoid, tundra, and barren. Graminoid habitats, which include grasslands, sedge and mossy marshes, and saltmarshes, account for roughly half of all habitat. The island contains some of the most extensive tracts of productive wetlands in Nunavut. Sparsely vegetated and unvegetated habitats cover 40% of the land area and are concentrated near the center of the island. Dwarf-shrub tundra is relatively uncommon and covers 10% of the total land area. An interesting feature of this island is the network of beach ridge complexes (alternating beach ridges and wetland areas) that run the length of the western coast. The coastal beach ridge complexes and the wet graminoid habitats are the most important habitats from a wildlife perspective.

The composition of the bird community on Prince Charles is typical of areas at similar latitude in Nunavut. Researchers recorded 41 species on the island in 1996–1997; research confirmed breeding for 24 of these species. What distinguishes the island, however, is the large numbers of particular species that breed there. Prince Charles has nationally significant numbers of breeding Sabine's gull, Atlantic brant, red phalarope, white-rumped sandpiper, and ruddy turnstone. The Ross's gull, which has only one other known breeding location in Nunavut, was recorded on Prince Charles in 1997.

The island's lesser snow goose breeding population has increased over the past 20 years. However, the population has not yet increased to the point where the habitat is in danger of destruction, as has happened at some other colonies in the Foxe Basin and Hudson Bay regions.

The importance of Prince Charles Island to birds is underscored by its selection as a site under the Important Bird Areas (Canada) program. The Canadian Wildlife Service also recommends legislative protection of Prince Charles, Air Force, and Foley Islands as part of the South Baffin Land Use Plan that is currently under development.

Prince Charles is a significant winter denning area for polar bears. Snow and earth dens are found on eskers throughout the island with a concentration in the southwest portion. In late summer and autumn, the island serves as a retreat for bears awaiting the freeze

of Foxe Basin. In any given year, between 200 and 350 bears probably use the island.

Caribou live on the island, and their numbers appear to fluctuate from year to year as they move between Prince Charles and adjacent islands, including Baffin Island. Arctic foxes are quite numerous, particularly in years of lemming cycle highs. Both collared and brown lemmings are present. Researchers have recorded no other mammals from the island.

Use of the island by prehistoric peoples seems to have been minimal. Oral history studies show that Prince Charles did not figure largely in the life of pre- or postcontact Foxe Basin Inuit. The island does not have a specific name in Inuktitut. There was little or no resource harvesting or occupation in the past, most likely due to the difficulty of access. Prince Charles was not selected by Inuit to be Inuit-owned private land as part of the Nunavut Land Claims Agreement.

The island was first charted on maps in 1948 by the Royal Canadian Air Force aircraft. The island was named after the then-infant Prince Charles of Great Britain. Since then, the island has been given scarce attention by non-Inuit. The island's polar bear and bird populations, however, have been studied and continue to be of interest to scientists and other scholars. There has been no activity in the area by industry, and tourism has been limited to occasional transits through Foxe Basin by a cruise ship. The annual community resupply vessels enter Foxe Basin, but route through the deeper eastern side of the basin.

VICKY JOHNSTON

See also **Baffin Island; Nunavut**

Further Reading

Baldwin, W.K.W., "List of plants collected on Prince Charles and Air Force
Islands in Foxe Basin, NWT." *Bulletin No. 128*, National Museum of Canada, Ottawa: Queen's Printer, 1953
Béchet, A., J.-L. Martin, P. Meister & C. Rabaouam, "A second breeding site for Ross's gull (*Rhodostethia rosea*) in Nunavut, Canada." *Arctic*, 53 (2000): 234–236
Gaston, A.J., R. Decker, F.G. Cooch & A. Reed, "The distribution of larger species of birds breeding on the coasts of Foxe Basin and northern Hudson Bay, Canada." *Arctic*, 39 (1986): 285–296
Martini, I.P., (editior), *Canadian Inland Seas*, Amsterdam and New York: Elsevier, 1986
Morrison, R.I.G., "The use of remote sensing to evaluate shorebird habitats and populations on Prince Charles Island, Foxe Basin." *Arctic*, 50 (1997): 55–75

PRINCE OF WALES ISLAND

Prince of Wales Island (71°20′–74°05′ N 96°10′–102°50′ W) is part of Nunavut in the central Canadian Arctic Archipelago. Located to the west of Somerset

Island and across M'Clintock Channel from Victoria Island, it is a roughly oval-shaped island with several large bays, including Ommanney Bay in the west and Browne Bay in the east.

The area of the island measures around 31,000 km^2 and the north-south extent is roughly 300 km. Several smaller islands—notably Russell to the north and Prescott and Pandora islands to the east—are located just offshore. No permanent villages exist on Prince of Wales Island, although it is used for fishing and hunting by Inuit from neighboring islands, and there are some land claim areas defined on the island. The island is relatively inaccessible due to persistent ice in M'Clintock Channel, Peel Sound, Franklin Strait, and Victoria Strait. The coasts and parts of the northern interior of the island were explored in 1851 and 1852 by expeditions searching for the missing Sir John Franklin expedition. Several studies by the Geological Survey of Canada since the 1960s have increased our knowledge of Prince of Wales Island.

The southwestern part of the island is flat and low-lying. Many small and large lakes are found here, including the largest, Crooked Lake, in the central part of the island. The highest lands are located in the northern and eastern part of the island, where dissected plateaux with elevations from 100 to 200 m are found. The highest land is a belt of dissected uplands along the eastern side of the island, decreasing from over 400 m in the north to 200 m in the south. There are fewer lakes in the north and east.

Most of Prince of Wales Island is comprised of Paleozoic limestone or dolomite, but a north-south trending band of sandstone exists to the east. Along the eastern coast of southern Prince of Wales and Prescott and Pandora islands is a small band of Precambrian metasediments and intrusive rocks.

No climate data exist from Prince of Wales Island, except for scattered measurements made by geological field parties since the 1950s. The climate is probably similar to that of Somerset Island or northern Victoria Island. The transition between the High-Arctic and mid-Arctic vegetation zones cuts through the island and trends northwest-southeast between Ommanney Bay and Browne Bay. Vegetation density is greater in the east and south. Vegetation density and diversity in the Arctic depends not only on temperature and moisture but also significantly on bedrock type, as nutrients are frequently limited. The Precambrian bedrock and sandstones on the eastern portion of the island support a more dense vegetation. There are caribou and muskoxen herds.

The island was entirely covered by ice during the last glaciation and there is till over most of the island. Deglaciation began around 11,000 BP in the northwestern past, and proceeded generally from north to south. The southeastern portion was entirely submerged after the last glaciation, as were low-lying lands across the entire island. Only uplands in the north and east remained above sea level. Little is known of the environmental history of the postglacial period on Prince of Wales. Maximum warmth probably occurred between 7000 and 4000 BP, but few data do not permit a more detailed interpretation.

K. GAJEWSKI

See also **Holocene; Victoria Island**

Further Reading

Canadian Hydrographic Service, *Pilot of Arctic Canada,* Volume 1, Ottawa: Queen's Printer, 1959

Dyke, A.S., T.F. Morris, D.E.C. Green & J. England, *Quaternary Geology of Prince of Wales Island, Arctic Canada*, Ottawa: Geological Survey of Canada Memoir 433, 1992

Woo, V. & S.C. Zoltai, *Reconnaissance of the Soils and Vegetation of Somerset and Prince of Wales Islands, NWT,* Edmonton: Northern Forestry Research Centre Information Report NOR-X-186, 1977

PRINCE PATRICK ISLAND

This island of the High Arctic is part of the Queen Elizabeth Islands in the Northwest Territories of Canada. It was named after Prince Arthur William Patrick, Queen Victoria's third son. It is located in the western Arctic, northeast of Mackenzie King Island, southeast of Melville Island, Kellet and Fitzwilliam Strait, and south of the M'Clure Strait and Banks Island. The area of the island is 15,848 sq km (6119 sq mi). The relief is mostly flat with the exception of cliffs, on the southeastern coast, sandstone bluffs, escarpments, and deep sinuous channels developed by rivers. Lakes are rare on the island, but there are numerous small water bodies caused by permafrost, which limit subsurface drainage. There are also many pingos, or icy mounds, covered by soil. The surrounding seas are permanently frozen, making it impossible to reach the island by icebreakers. The island remains accessible by plane. The ice barrier allows a constant connection with Melville and Mackenzie King islands. A dry and cold climate prevails on the island's surface, typical of the High Arctic zone. According to the Mould Bay weather station, the average temperature in July varies between 1°C and 7°C and between −31°C and −38C°C for the month of February; the annual precipitation average is only 105 mm (Mould Bay, Environment Canada).

The vegetation is tundra composed of sedges, mosses, and grasses alternating with polar desert conditions in some places. Peary caribou visit the island every summer. Stoat, polar bear, Arctic fox, wolf, collared lemming, Arctic hare, and ringed seal live on the island. There was a herd of muskox present in the past, but the herd mysteriously disappeared during the 1950s. The High Arctic brant goose is abundant on the island, especially in the important bird area on the eastern coast; this site was recognized as a key terrestrial habitat for migratory birds in the 1990s.

The extent of the last ice age on the island occasions many controversies among specialists, but the distribution of erratic boulders seems to attest that continental ice once covered at least part of the island. There has been no prehistoric or contemporary presence of Inuit groups known on the island. The first Europeans arrived on Prince Patrick Island during Sir Edward Belcher's expedition (1852–1854). With the help of his knowledge of the art of sledding, acquired during the Franklin search expedition of 1850–1851, Sir Francis Leopold McClintock explored and mapped most of the island.

In 1948, an airport and a weather station were built at Mould Bay during a cooperation program between Canada and the United States. At the beginning of the 1960s, a magnetic and seismic observatory was established in Mould Bay to allow surveys by the Polar Continental Shelf Project and the Dominion Observatory. In 1970, the Americans stopped contributing and the weather station became entirely administered by the Canadian government. By the end of the 1990s, an automatic system was installed and replaced the permanent presence of people in the station (Natural Resources Canada, 1998). Today, the island is still occasionally visited by Rangers of the Canadian Forces (Nunatsiaq News, 26/01/2001).

PIERRE DESROSIERS

See also **Mackenzie King Island; McClintock, Francis Leopold; Melville Island; Queen Elizabeth Islands**

Further Reading

Andrews, J.T., "Quaternary Geology of the Northeastern Canadian Shield." In *Quaternary Geology of Canada and Greenland*, edited by R.J. Fulton, Ottawa: Canadian Government Publishing Center, 1989

Berton, Pierre, *The Arctic Grail: The Quest for the North West Passage and the North Pole, 1818–1909*, Toronto: Anchor Canada, 2001

Hodgson, D.A., "Quaternary Geology of the Queen Elizabeth Islands." In *Quaternary Geology of Canada and Greenland*, edited by R.F. Fulton, Ottawa: Canadian Government Publishing Center, 1989

McClintock, Francis Leopold, *In the Arctic Seas: A Narrative of the Discovery of the Fate of Sir John Franklin and his Companions*, Philadelphia: Porter & Coates, 1859

Pissart, A., *The Pingos of Prince Patrick Island*, Ottawa: National Research Council of Canada, 1970

Taylor, R.B. & D.A. Hodgson, *Coastal Studies in the Canadian Arctic Archipelago, Brock, Devon, Prince Patrick and the Polynia Islands, NWT*, Ottawa: Geological Survey of Canada, 1991

PROJECT CHARIOT

The Plowshare Program was established in 1958 by the US Atomic Energy Commission (AEC) to "investigate and develop peaceful uses for nuclear explosives." One of the first projects from this program was located at the mouth of Ogotoruk Creek near Cape Thompson, Alaska. It was to be called Project Chariot. Edward Teller, often referred to as the "Father of the H-Bomb," toured the territory of Alaska in the 1958 in the hopes of realizing a vision of geographic engineering, in which one could reshape the earth through the use of nuclear explosions. Ogotoruk Creek was chosen as the site of an experimental harbor excavation, in which a massive atomic device, said to be 100 times more powerful than the one in Hiroshima, was scheduled to be detonated in 1962. In 1958, the AEC applied to the Bureau of Land Management to segregate these lands in order to conduct the experiment. By June 1, 1959, the permit was given, and construction began at the site.

Ogotoruk Creek is located at latitude 68° 06′ N and longitude 165° 46′ W. It is about 100 miles north of the Arctic Circle, and despite AEC's assertion that the site of Project Chariot was far in the wilderness, and far from human habitation, the Iñupiat village of Kotzebue was only approximately 125 miles northwest.

Although Ogotoruk Valley has never been a permanent residence of Iñupiat people, it has been a seasonal place of occupancy for thousands of years, and remains a strategic point for the hunting of whales, as well as caribou hunting and other subsistence gathering activities.

By 1960, support for the Project was divided publicly, and both scientists and Iñupiat were strongly opposed to the detonation of nuclear bombs at the site. This led to the AEC discontinuing the program in favor of testing in the Nevada Desert. This marked an important historical point in the environmentalist movement in Alaska, as well as internationally. Those who spoke out against Project Chariot had achieved the first successful opposition to the American nuclear establishment.

However, since the AEC could not proceed with the detonation, tracer experiments were conducted by placing fresh radioactive fallout in small selected plots in the Ogotoruk Creek basin. At the time, it was decided that these plots did not pose any health risk, and were not posted until 1992 by the US Fish and Wildlife Service.

With the passing of the Alaska National Interest Land Claims Act in 1980, the Ogotoruk Valley became included in the Cape Thompson Subunit of the Chukchi Sea Unit of the Alaska Maritime National Wildlife Refuge, and much of the area of the Project Chariot site then fell under the jurisdiction of the US Fish and Wildlife Service. A native allotment for the site was granted to Mr. Wilfred Lane in 1987.

However, it was not until 1992, when researcher Dan O'Neill obtained declassified documents detailing the tracer experiments and the plots of radioactive materials buried in the Project Chariot site, that the presence of these materials became known. Due to increasing concern of the environment, and the radioactive waste disposal in the Arctic, the site of Project Chariot once again became contentious. The Department of Energy cleaned the site of its radioactive material in 1993.

The legacy of Project Chariot not only reflects the historical views of the environment in the postwar nuclear era but also continues to reflect ongoing concerns for the Arctic environment and its future.

RACHEL OLSON

See also **Environmentalism; Iñupiat; Radioactivity**

Further Reading

Coate, Peter, "*Project Chariot: Alaskan roots of environmentalism.*" Alaska History Magazine, (2) (fall 1989)

O'Neill, Dan, *Project Chariot: A Collection of Oral Histories* Alaska Humanities Forum, 2 Volums., 1989

———, *The Firecracker Boys*, New York: St. Martin's Press, 1994.

Vandegraft, Douglas L, "*Project Chariot: Nuclear Legacy of Cape Thompson.*" Presented at the *Workshop on Arctic Contamination*, Anchorage, Alaska, May 6, 1993

Vanstone, James W., Point Hope: An Eskimo Village in Transition, Washington: University of Washington Press, 1962

PROTECTED AREAS

The establishment and management of protected areas is an important tool in the long-term protection of wildlife diversity, wetlands and other ecologically significant wildlife habitats, marine environment, natural landmarks, and culturally significant or sacred sites in the Arctic. Many indigenous peoples and local rural populations depend on the consumption of Arctic flora and fauna, and many land areas have historical, cultural, and spiritual significance for indigenous peoples. Protected areas also provide excellent opportunities for environmental education, outdoor recreation, tourism, and scientific research, providing a benchmark against which to assess (and hence mitigate) the cumulative and long-term impacts of industrial and infrastructure development, and long-range persistent pollutants and climate change.

Arctic wildlife and habitats will benefit from the global conventions that focus on biodiversity and endangered species; however, there is also a need to protect habitats in order to maintain biodiversity. Action is needed on a circumpolar level, since many Arctic birds and mammals are migratory and their range in one habitat during feeding or breeding cycles may cross national jurisdictions.

While polar desert and lowland Arctic tundra areas are the best-represented protected biomes (27% and 13%, respectively, as a percentage of their total Arctic territory that is protected), many marine areas and the northernmost boreal forests remain relatively unprotected. Furthermore, while a total area of 2.5 million km^2, roughly 17% of the land area as defined by CAFF (*CAFF, 2000: 77*), is currently protected, nearly half of this area falls within one site, the Northeast Greenland National Park (area = 972,000 km^2).

Categories of Protected Areas

National or provincial legislation can classify many categories of protected areas, such as national parks, nature reserves, national preserves, wilderness, wildlife refuges, and natural monuments. In Russia, the terms *zapovedniki* (nature reserves) and *zakazniks* (state nature reserves) are the most common designations. A recent Russian federal law (2001) established a new category, territories of traditional nature use, to protect sacred sites and land for traditional aboriginal activities, such as reindeer herding. In Canada, strategies for protected areas and Special Management Areas often result from land claim agreements, with provisions for subsistence activities, namely, hunting, fishing, trapping, and gathering. Sacred, cultural, or historical sites may be protected as national monuments under antiquities laws (e.g., Sitka National Monument in Alaska, Þingvellir National Park in Iceland) or by international recognition as World Heritage Sites.

The International Union for Conservation of Nature and Natural Resources (IUCN) has devised six protected areas management categories (IUCN, 1994), which establish an international standard for classifying protected areas (both land and marine). Category 1a (strict nature reserve) is a protected area managed mainly for science; category 1b is a wilderness area managed mainly for wilderness protection; category 2 is a national park managed for ecosystem protection and recreation; category 3 is a natural monument; category 4 is a Habitat/Species Management Area; category 5 is a Protected Landscape/Seascape; and category 6 is a Managed Resource Protected Area. Categories are determined at the international level, although depending mainly on information provided by national governments. The United Nations List of Protected Areas is compiled by the United Nations Environment Programme (UNEP) World Conservation Monitoring Centre (WCMC) working in close collaboration with the IUCN World Commission on Protected Areas (WCPA).

Other international initiatives that designate protected areas include the UNESCO Man and Biosphere

(MAB) reserves, Ramsar sites (wetlands of international importance), World Heritage Sites, and WWF Global 200 ecoregions.

Several initiatives specific to the Arctic have built on the work of the Arctic Environmental Protection Strategy (AEPS, adopted by ministerial declaration of the eight Arctic countries held in 1991 in Rovaniemi, Finland) and the Arctic Council. In 1996, the Conservation of Arctic Flora and Fauna (CAFF) working group of the Arctic Council established the Circumpolar Protected Areas Network (CPAN). Following early reports on the status of established and proposed protected areas, CPAN published a Strategy and Action Plan describing actions to be taken nationally and internationally to achieve "an adequate and well-managed network of protected areas that has a high probability of maintaining the dynamic biodiversity of the Arctic in perpetuity." A permanent CPAN working group was established in 1999 and is chaired by the United States.

Marine protected areas (MPAs) are recognized internationally by the IUCN, and at the national level by the United States. MPAs are of many types, including national marine sanctuaries, fishery management zones (such as the nearshore Bristol Bay fishery closure area off Alaska that protects king crab aggregations and their habitat), national parks and preserves (such as Glacier Bay National Park and Perserve), habitat conservation zones (such as the Pribilof Islands Area Habitat Conservation Zone), and national wildlife refuges with marine components. Some of the Canadian and Russian land national parks also protect the offshore waters; for example,

Ellesmere Island National Park has a relatively large marine component and the nature reserve on Wrangel Island has a 5 km buffer zone. Melville Bay (Greenland) is protected as an IUCN category I marine area.

GILLIAN LINDSEY

See also **Conservation; National Parks and Protected Areas; Russian Federal Law on Territories of Traditional Nature Use; Wilderness**

Further Reading

Chape, S., S. Blyth, L. Fish, P. Fox & M. Spalding, *United Nations List of Protected Areas*, Gland, Switzerland and Cambridge: IUCN and Cambridge: UNEP World Conservation Monitoring Centre, 2003

Conservation of Arctic Flora and Fauna (CAFF), "The State of Protected Areas in the Circumpolar Arctic 1994." *CAFF Habitat Conservation Report No. 1*, Trondheim: CAFF, Directorate for Nature Management, 1994

———, "Circumpolar Protected Areas Network (CPAN) Strategy and Action Plan. *CAFF Habitat Conservation Report No. 6*, Trondheim: Directorate for Nature Management, 1996

Haruchi, Sergei, S., Sohlberg & P. Sulyandziga, *The Conservation Value of Sacred Sites of Indigenous Peoples of the Arctic: A Case Study in Northern Russia*, Moscow; RAIPON, 2002

International Union for Conservation of Nature and Natural Resources (IUCN), *Guidelines for Protected Areas Management Categories*, Gland, Switzerland and Cambridge: IUCN, 1994

PROVIDENIYA

Provideniya ("providence" in English) is a city and port, and the administrative center of the Providencheskogo

Provideniya, the nearest Siberian seaport to the Bering Strait, Chukotka. *Copyright Bryan and Cherry Alexander Photography*

region of Chukchi Autonomous Okrug (Chukotka) of the Russian Federation. The port is situated at 64°24′ N 173°12′ W on the coast of Provideniya Bay, located in the Gulf of Anadyr on the Bering Sea, at the southeast coast of the Chukotka Peninsula about 200 miles due west of Nome (Alaska). The bay was discovered by K. Ivanova's Russian expedition in 1660, and named by Captain Thomas Moore in commemoration of the "happy foresight" that allowed his ship HMS *Plover* to overwinter in this bay in 1848–1849, on its way to search for Sir John Franklin's lost expedition. The Russian government established an administrative center in Provideniya in 1888.

The bay is long and narrow, about 50 km long with an entrance width of about 9 km. The surrounding land is high (up to 600–800 m) and rises steeply from the bay. Tidal range is low—up to 1 m. Provideniya's climate is relatively mild for Chukotka, and the port is ice-free in full or in part from May until October. The history of the port is connected with the development of navigation on the Northern Sea Route. Provideniya is situated at the easternmost end of the Northern Sea Route, and the port played an important role in the development of Arctic navigation. Before 1917, only American whaling ships used Provideniya Bay. Since the second half of the 1930s, its deep and sheltered anchorage, and strategic position at the exit of Bering Strait to the Pacific Ocean made it the main port of northeastern Siberia. The distance from Murmansk to Providence Bay is 5970 km (3706 miles), a journey of several weeks in favorable navigation conditions for the icebreakers that supply ports along the Russian Arctic coast.

In 1934 a polar weather station was opened in Provideniya Bay and there was also a trading station organized by the Committee of the North. Geological and surveying investigations for the port's construction began in 1934–1935. Coal discovered locally aided in power supply for the developing port, and the construction of moorings, warehouses, workshops, and apartment houses. By 1941, the port held second place in Arctic regions for the turnover of goods.

During the Cold War, Provideniya was also a significant military center. The city's population is steadily declining today, from a high of 5000 inhabitants in 1990 to about 2000 as of 2003. Declining shipping traffic and cutbacks on military forces stationed in Provideniya have resulted in many non-natives returning to Russia. Indigenous people (Chukchi and Yupik) comprise about half the population. The chief economy of the region today is reindeer husbandry, fur trapping, marine mammal hunting, and fishing. The city has a plant handling reindeer products (skins and processing of meat and milk).

Transportation in Provideniya is limited to sea and air, with only one road leading to Novo Chaplino, a coastal village 18 miles from Provideniya that was built in 1959, resettling Yupik from Old Chaplino (*Ungazik*). Provideniya's airport is located in the settlement of Ureliki, on the far shore of the bay from the community of Provideniya, with air links to Nome (Alaska) and Anadyr.

VALERY MIT'KO

See also **Anadyr; Bering Sea; Chukchi Autonomous Okrug (Chukotka); Committee of the North; Northern Sea Route**

Further Reading

Belov, M.I., *Nauchnoe i khoziaistvennoe osvoenie Sovetskogo Severa, 1933–1945* [Scientific and economic development of the Soviet north 1933–1945], *Istoriia otkrytiia I osvoeniia severnogo morskogo puti* [History of opening and development of the Northern sea route], Volume 4, Leningrad: Hydrometeoizdat, 1969

PRUDHOE BAY

Prudhoe Bay is a small inlet of the Beaufort Sea along the Alaskan Arctic Coastal Plain, located at the mouth of the Sagavanirktok River. The Arctic Coastal Plain in this region comprises a tundra environment underlain with permafrost up to 605 m deep; the average active layer thickness is 46 m near the coast.

Prudhoe Bay is synonymous with the largest oil and gas field in North America. Discovered by Atlantic Richfield and Humble Oil companies on February 1, 1968, the 103,600 hectare (400 square mile) Prudhoe Bay reserve was estimated at five to ten billion barrels of oil (Rutledge, 1998). A plan was soon developed to transport Prudhoe Bay oil to the Port of Valdez, Alaska, via the 1,287 km Trans-Alaska Pipeline System, completed in 1977. The pipeline would facilitate oil transportation in marine tankers to the west coast of the United States of America for market distribution.

Oil recovery did not begin in Prudhoe Bay until June 20, 1977, after nine years of feasibility and environmental impact studies, and the resolution of legal challenges made by various native and environmental groups. Construction of the Trans-Alaska Pipeline (1974–1977), a haul road from Fairbanks, Alaska, to Prudhoe Bay (Dalton Highway), and an oil terminal at Valdez were required before drilling could begin. Up through 2001, over 14 billion barrels of oil had passed through the Trans-Alaska Pipeline, amounting to about one-quarter trillion US dollars (State of Alaska Dept. of Revenue, 2001).

Historical Development

Prior to the discovery of oil at Prudhoe Bay, the small native settlements of Oliktok and Nuiqsut were the

Insulated ducting carrying power and water to buildings with the headquarters of BP Exploration in the background, Prudhoe Bay oil fields, Alaska.
Copyright Bryan and Cherry Alexander Photography

only communities in the area. Other native villages within 300 km of Prudhoe Bay included Kaktovik (on Barter Island), Anaktuvik Pass, Umiat, Atqasuk, and Barrow. Deadhorse, Alaska, developed as the industrial center of North Slope oil and gas exploration in the 1970s, is located approximately 13 km inland from the Prudhoe Bay inlet. Situated at the north end of the haul road on Lake Colleen and at the southeast boundary of the Prudhoe Bay oil field, the North Slope Borough established Service Area 10 at Deadhorse in 1975. Service Area 10 provided utility services to industrial users in the area.

Industrial users at Deadhorse include oil and gas service contractors and suppliers, with infrastructure built on man-made gravel pads and connected by gravel roads on the tundra. An airport was also built on aboveground gravel foundations. From Deadhorse, a network of gravel roads and supported aboveground pipelines span east, west, and north to exploration pads and oil company facilities. During the 35 years since oil discovery at Prudhoe Bay, 18 additional oil and gas fields have been developed in the region.

Socioeconomic Effects

The recovery of Prudhoe Bay oil has had a profound economic impact on Alaska and the United States since 1977. Oil revenue profits have heavily contributed to Alaska's annual operating budget over the last 25 years. Today, the petroleum industry directly or indirectly employs nearly one-fifth of the state's workforce, profits numerous vendors and native corporations, and benefits every Alaskan citizen through an annual dividend from oil and gas royalties.

At the national level, the economic health of the United States is reflected to some extent by its stock market performance. In the 20 years preceding 1977, the Dow Jones Industrial Average (DJIA) increased by a factor of 1.83. This same index increased by a factor of 8.43 between 1977 and 1997 (Rutledge, 1998). Although the degree to which Prudhoe Bay oil influenced the US stock market cannot be accurately measured, economists generally recognize its significant influence.

In 1971, the Alaska Native Claims Settlement Act (ANCSA) resulted in the division of 17.8 million hectares (44 million acres) of land between 12 regional native corporations. Prudhoe Bay and its neighboring oil fields, including the National Petroleum Reserve-Alaska (NPR-A) and Arctic National Wildlife Refuge (ANWR), exist within the boundaries of the Arctic Slope Regional Corporation (ASRC). ASRC comprises eight native village corporations, several of which have formed for profit subsidiaries and joint venture companies that support North Slope oil and gas development.

The success of ASRC was marginal through the mid-1980s, namely because the North Slope Borough (the largest Iñupiat Eskimo employer) offered favorable jobs, oil industry jobs required specific skills the Iñupiat did not have, and the Iñupiat did not like the working conditions and schedules offered by the oil companies. Subsequent to changes in state and federal hiring practices, improved management has made the ASRC more profitable. For example, in the fiscal year 1996, ASRC earned $530 million US dollars gross revenue and $22.9 million U.S. dollars profit (Rutledge, 1998).

The socioeconomic effects of Prudhoe Bay oil and gas development have not all been positive for North Slope Iñupiat people. Development has linked a cash economy with their traditional subsistence lifestyle, affording modern amenities while compromising cultural heritage. Some researchers have suggested that control of oil exploration by nonnatives demeans Iñupiat self-esteem, and that development has lead to increased crime rates and substance abuse and a weakened traditional social fabric (Ganapathy, 1996).

Of great concern for the future are the socioeconomic effects of depleting oil and gas reserves on native populations and the Alaskan economy. Alaska, ASCR, and other regional native corporations recognize the inevitable and are beginning to encourage other business development and diversification of existing corporate structures.

Environmentalism

Prudhoe Bay oil and gas recovery catalyzed an environmental movement within Alaska. Environmentalist grassroots groups—typically affiliated with national and international organizations (e.g., National Audubon Society, Sierra Club, National Wildlife Federation, The Wilderness Society, Greenpeace, and World Wildlife Fund)—rally against oil and gas development in Alaska. The majority of citizens and political sentiment in Alaska support oil and gas development. The Iñupiat in ASRC are generally supportive. However, other native groups oppose North Slope oil and gas development. Environmental activists from outside Alaska lobby politicians in Washington DC as well as the general public in the continental US. Historical records of spills related to North Slope oil development and incidents of poor environmental practices support the arguments of the environmentalists. Interest in reserves east and west of Prudhoe Bay (NPR-A and ANWR) also invigorates environmental concerns.

Environmental opposition played a major role in delaying oil and gas recovery at Prudhoe Bay between 1970 and 1974. Conflicts within the Middle East and the US 1973 oil embargo influenced momentum with government approvals for construction of the necessary infrastructure to support Alaska oil development. Environmentalism and congressional action blocked further exploration in ANWR in the late 1980s. In 1998, federal support for a management plan for oil and gas leasing on about 87% of NPR-A prompted lawsuits from eight environmental groups to halt oil exploration. This plan set aside nearly one-quarter of the 1.9 million hectare (4.6 million acre) NPR-A region for wildlife conservation; oil and gas lease sales for developable portions began in 1999.

The battle lines would appear to be drawn for 21st-century development of the next great oil and gas reserve in North America. Environmental opposition remains strong despite technological advances in exploration and oil drilling, whereby oil recovery would be concentrated within the northwest corner on 0.07% of the 7.7 million hectares (19 million acres) that is ANWR. Historically, industry has failed to demonstrate that it can successfully integrate profit with environmental protection of Arctic wilderness.

DENNIS M. FILLER

See also **Alaska Native Claims Settlement Act (ANCSA); Arctic Slope Regional Corporation (ASRC); North Slope; Oil Exploration; Trans-Alaska Pipeline**

Further Reading

Alaska Consultants, Inc., *North Slope Borough Background for Planning, Service Area 10*. Barrow: Alaska Consultants Inc., 1983

———, "Barrow Arch Socioeconomic and Sociocultural Description." *Technical Report 101*, Social and Economic Studies Program, Anchorage: Minerals Management Service and Alaska Outer Continental Shelf Office, 1984

Anders, G., "The role of Alaska native corporations in the development of Alaska." *Development and Change*, 14 1983: 555–575

Berger, Lewis et al., "Social Indicators for OCS Monitoring," 3 volumes. *Technical Report 77*, Alaska OCS Socioeconomic Studies Program, Anchorage: MMS, Alaska OCS Office, 1983

Braund, D.R. et al., "North Slope Subsistence Study, Barrow 1987." *Technical Report 133*, Institute of Social and Economic Research, University of Alaska, Anchorage: US Department of Interior, MMS, Alaska OCS Office, 1988

Clough, N.K., P.C. Patton & A.C. Christiansen (editors), *Arctic National Wildlife Refuge, Alaska, Coastal Plain Resource Assessment—Report and Recommendation to the Congress of the United States and Final Legislative Environmental Impact Statement*, Washington, District of Columbia: US Fish and Wildlife Service, US Geological Survey, Bureau of Land Management, 1987

Coates, Peter A., *The Trans-Alaska Pipeline Controversy: Technology, Conservation, and the Frontier*, Bethlehem, Pennsylvania: Lehigh University Press, 1991

Cole, Dermot, *Amazing Pipeline Stories*, Kenmore: Epicenter Press, 1997

Dryzek, J.S., *Conflict and Choice in Resource Management: The Case of Alaska*, Boulder, Colorado: Westview Press, 1983

Ganapathy, Uma, *Interactions Between Wage Employment and Subsistence Lifestyle: Oil Development on the North Slope, Alaska*, Ann Arbor: UMI Dissertation Services, 1996

Institute of Social and Economic Research, University of Alaska, "Beaufort Sea Petroleum Development Scenarios: Economic and Demographic Impacts." *Technical Report 18*, Alaska OCS Socioeconomic Studies Program, Anchorage: Bureau of Land Management, Alaska OCS Office, 1978

Klausner, S.Z. & E.F. Foulks, *Eskimo Capitalists: Oil, Alcohol, and Politics*, Montclair: Allanheld and Schram, 1982

Rutledge, Gene, *Prudhoe Bay ... Discovery to Recovery!* Anchorage: Wolfe Business Services, 1998

State of Alaska Department of Revenue, Oil and Gas Audit, Juneau 2001

Worl, R. & C.W. Smythe, "Barrow: A Decade of Modernisation." *Technical Report 12*, Alaska OCS Social and Economic Studies Program, Anchorage: MMS and Alaska OCS Region, 1986

PRYDE, DUNCAN MCLEAN

Duncan Pryde, a furtrader, polyglot, legislator, writer, and storyteller, was a lifelong student of the Inuit language. Pryde was born in Scotland in 1937 and raised in orphanages. He went to sea at the age of 15. In 1955 he responded to a newspaper advertisement placed by the Hudson's Bay Company: "Fur traders wanted for the far north." The ad asked for single, ambitious, self-reliant young men, and promised a life of isolation, hardship, and adventure, all for $135.00 per month. Pryde was accepted and spent his first three years in Canada in northern Ontario and Manitoba, where he learned the Cree language. In 1958, he moved to the Arctic, serving first at Baker Lake. From there he was posted to increasingly isolated locations: Spence Bay, then Perry River in 1961, and finally Bathurst Inlet in 1965.

Pryde immersed himself in the language of the Inuit. With an enormous talent for Inuit dialects, Pryde's ambition included the compilation of a definitive dictionary of the Inuit language as spoken in the Central Arctic. Furthermore, Pryde mastered the art of dog-team travel; he traveled extensively throughout the region, visiting Inuit, hunting, and trapping.

In 1966, Pryde was elected to the Territorial Council of the Northwest Territories, the law-making body that is the present-day Legislative Assembly. This was the first time that representatives from the Inuit area of the Northwest Territories, an area almost contiguous with present-day Nunavut, had been elected. The area was divided into three ridings; Simonee Michael of Iqaluit (the first Inuk elected to the Territorial Council) and Robert Williamson of Rankin Inlet represented the other two areas and served one-year terms. In 1967, Pryde was reelected to the Territorial Council for a three-year term. Pryde devoted his attention to the Inuit whom he represented and issues that concerned them, namely hunting and gaming laws. He proposed the sports hunting of polar bears as a way of bringing monies into Inuit communities.

In 1969 Pryde married Gina Blondin, a Dene, in Yellowknife. They had one daughter, Fiona. Two years later, Duncan's fame transcended the north and Canada when he published his autobiography, *Nunaga—My Land, My Country*. A compelling albeit mythic portrayal of the life of a trader at the end of an era when Arctic posts were truly isolated, the book sold extremely well and was subsequently translated into a number of languages. The controversial text turned Pryde's fame into notoriety in the Canadian North for his frank recounting of sexual exploits among the Inuit. Pryde's marriage ended a few years later, and he hastily left for Alaska where he taught Inuit languages at the fledgling Iñupiat college in Pt Barrow, an institution established with Alaskan land claims money. Although conflicts with the administration resulted in him being fired from the teaching post, he stayed on as janitor so that he could remain in an academic environment. A few years later, Pryde suddenly left Alaska.

Friends recognized Pryde, despite his notoriety, as a person with tremendous linguistic talents to contribute to the study of the North. With only a sixth-grade education, Pryde had, nonetheless, privately studied the principles of linguistics as a science, and learned a number of languages. In addition to many dialects of the Inuit languages, Cree, and some Slavey and Dogrib, Pryde spoke Gaelic, Italian, and German, and a smattering of other languages.

John MacDonald of Igloolik, who had first met Pryde in Baker Lake in 1959, eventually tracked the recluse down. Pryde had been living (remarried) in Cowes on the Isle of Wight as a yachtsman. The man who had billed himself as "the Pryde of the Arctic" now ran a small news agency called "Pryde of Cowes." MacDonald and this author also tracked down a trunk full of Pryde's memorabilia and language notes, which had presumably been discarded after the breakup of his marriage. The trunk was found in a garage in Yellowknife; copies of his papers were given to the Prince of Wales Heritage Centre in Yellowknife for the invaluable study of Central Arctic dialects.

Around 1994, after a diagnosis of cancer and chemotherapy treatment, Pryde began work on his Inuit dictionary project. Arctic College (today Nunavut Arctic College) provided financial support for the first volume (the letter "A"). Pryde completed it in early 1997; a multidialectal comparison with examples of usage, the first volume ran in excess of 280 pages. The remainder of the project was unfortunately aborted due to the recurrence of Pryde's cancer.

Perhaps because of a lack of formal education, Pryde deeply appreciated recognition for his accomplishments, especially in the field of Inuit linguistics. In 1997, Michael Fortescue, one of the foremost linguists specializing in Eskimo languages at the Institute for Eskimology, University of Copenhagen, sent Pryde a letter of congratulations on the completion of the first volume of the Inuit dictionary.

At the end of his autobiography, Pryde wrote, "There will never be a job such as the one which enticed me as a dreamy-eyed young man all the way from Scotland with romantic notions in my otherwise empty head. There will never be another fur trader in the old tradition, just as there will never again be an Eskimo in the old image."

Biography

Born in 1937, in Glasgow, Scotland, Duncan Pryde left school at the age of 15 to join the merchant marines. After joining the Hudson's Bay Company in 1957, he served in northern Ontario and Manitoba and the Inuit communities of Baker Lake, Spence Bay, Perry River, and Bathurst Inlet, all in the Northwest Territories (today Nunavut). Pryde served for four years in the Territorial Council of the Northwest Territories (1966–1970). He published his autobiography, *Nunaga: My Land, My Country,* in 1971. Pryde moved to Alaska in the 1970s, and from there to England, settling at Cowes in the Isle of Wight. Pryde married twice, to Gina Blondin (deceased), with whom he had a daughter, Fiona, and to Dawn (maiden name unknown). He died of cancer at Cowes on November 15, 1997 at the age of 60.

KENN HARPER

Further Reading

Anderson, Sarah, "Duncan Pryde." *Independent*, December 30, 1997, p. 17

Harper, Kenn, "Obituary." *Nunatsiaq News*, November 21. 1997, pp. 16–17

McPhee, John, *Coming Into the Country*, New York: Farrar, Straus and Giroux, 1977

Pryde, Duncan, "The Breath of Arctic Men." *North*, XIV(2) (March-April 1967)

———, *Nunaga: My Land, My Country*, Edmonton: Hurtig, 1970

PTARMIGAN AND GROUSE

Rock (*Lagopus mutus*) and willow (*L. lagopus*) ptarmigan are the most Arctic of birds, living year round in the tundra and taiga habitats of Arctic, Subarctic and boreal North America, Europe, and Asia. They are members of the Phasianidae, a large (*c.*180 species) family of gallinaceous birds that includes grouse, quail, and pheasants, as well as domestic chickens (which ptarmigan superficially resemble). Ptarmigan are exceptionally well camouflaged for most of the year, white in winter and brown in summer, the evolutionary result of attention from a variety of predators, including humans, who find that they make an excellent meal. Willow ptarmigan are called red grouse or willow grouse in Europe.

Research on Arctic ptarmigan has contributed much to our understanding of animal life histories, population dynamics, evolution, and behaviour. It was on recognized early that ptarmigan population sizes fluctuated dramatically (tenfold or more) on a roughly ten-year cycle. Detailed studies of these cycles helped scientists appreciate both the importance of predator-prey and host-parasite interactions in population regulation, and the ways in which an animal's life history (fecundity, survival, mating) becomes adapted to its environment. Research on red grouse in Scotland led to the development (in the 1960s) of a general theory of group selection to explain evolutionary change. Although this idea no longer has wide support, it did rekindle interest in Darwinian natural selection and thus a better understanding of the nature of adaptations. More recently, molecular techniques have revealed the historic relations among ptarmigan populations and species, how and when populations

Arctic ptarmigan.
Copyright Paul Nicklen/ National Geographic Image Collection

dispersed from glacial refugia, and the relation between kinship and population cycles.

In winter, Arctic ptarmigan have feathered feet and horny sheaths on their toenails that help them walk on snow, and are almost entirely white except for black tail feathers. In summer, both sexes have an exceptionally cryptic mottled brown plumage. After snow melts from the tundra in spring, white male ptarmigan become one of the most conspicuous of birds while they court females and defend their territories, even though they are well-camouflaged the rest of the year. Males of both species also have a fleshy red comb above the eye, which is raised by engorging with blood when courting females and fighting other males. In spring, males also give loud, raucous calls and flight song displays when defending their territories. In the breeding season, males are usually monogamous although some will have two to three females settle on their territories.

Females lay a clutch of 3–14 eggs in a shallow grassy nest that they build on dry, well-vegetated tundra. Ptarmigan eggs are unusual in that the surface pigment stays wet for a few minutes after they are laid. Females incubate the eggs almost continuously for c.21 days, leaving the nest only to feed a few times each day. The chicks leave the nest within a few hours of hatching and accompany the female for the next 10–12 weeks as she protects them from predators and inclement weather. In all seasons, ptarmigan feed mainly on the buds, twigs, seeds, and flowers of shrubs (especially willow, birch and heather) and herbs (e.g., saxifrages and Arctic avens).

Both species are heavily preyed upon by humans and a variety of mammals (fox, wolf) and raptors (gyrfalcon, peregrine, snowy owl). Ptarmigan still form an important part of the diet of indigenous peoples, especially during the summer, and consequently few ptarmigan are found close to human settlements. Wherever they are hunted, ptarmigan are wary, but elsewhere they are quite tame and easily observed.

Rock ptarmigan are the smaller (400–600 g) and more northern of the Arctic ptarmigan, breeding to the northern extent of tundra worldwide and retreating only to the southern edge of their breeding range (about latitude 55° N) in winter, where temperatures can still dip to −40°C and the landscape is snow-covered for 6 months or more. They are well adapted to Arctic life with uniquely structured feathers that have microscopic air pockets and an extra downy shaft (the "afterfeather") that aid in insulation. Following Pleistocene glaciations, rock ptarmigan dispersed throughout the circumpolar Arctic, establishing populations on all of Alaska's Aleutian Islands, and in high alpine tundra as far south as Japan, Newfoundland, and the Pyrenees. Many of these populations are morphologically and genetically distinct and have been given subspecies status. Breeding densities vary from 1 to 32 pairs km^2 depending upon the stage of population cycle and local conditions. Male rock ptarmigan do not participate at all in the care of their brood.

Willow ptarmigan are somewhat larger (500–800 g) and have a more southerly breeding distribution in the Subarctic and boreal forest biomes, being particularly common in shrubby (willow) habitats. In spring, males first moult their head and neck plumage to a rich rufous, unlike rock ptarmigan males who remain completely white while courting and defending territories. Male willow ptarmigan also assist their mate with brood care, the only grouse to do so. This species has been studied extensively in Scotland, where it is an important game bird, making its ecology and behaviour one of the best known of any bird species. Fifteen subspecies are recognized worldwide mainly due to variation in body size and plumage coloration. The Scottish subspecies (L. l. scoticus) is distinctive enough that some consider it to be a separate species.

Probably because of their importance as food to indigenous peoples, there are many Iñupiaq (Nighaktuk, Aqiggiq, Atajulik, Ungawik, Niksaktongik, Akudagin) and Yu'pik (Atikatoohach, Aghadeghahh) names for rock ptarmigan. Both species are often seen in Inuit art.

Both ptarmigan species have large, healthy populations worldwide, despite heavy hunting pressure in some areas (particularly Scotland). The worldwide population of rock ptarmigan, for example, varies between 5 and 15 million birds depending in part upon the stage of the population cycle in different areas. Distinctive subspecies of rock ptarmigan on Newfoundland and the Aleutian Islands are small and threatened by human activities and introduced predators (mainly foxes). A long-term population decline of red grouse in the UK is attributed to loss and degradation of moorland and increased predation from corvids and foxes.

ROBERT MONTGOMERIE

Further Reading

Bergerud, A.T. & M.W. Gratson (editors), *Adaptive strategies and population ecology of northern grouse*, Minneapolis: University of Minnesota Press, 1988

Cramp, Stanley & Christopher M. Perrins (editors), *The Birds of the Western Palearctic*, Volume II, Oxford: Oxford University Press, 1980

Hannon, Susan J., Perri K. Eason & Kathy Martin, "Willow Ptarmigan (*Lagopus lagopus*)." In *The Birds of North America, No. 369*, edited by Alan Poole & Frank Gill, Philadelphia: Academy of Natural Sciences, 1998

Holder, Karen R. & Robert Montgomerie, "Rock Ptarmigan (*Lagopus mutus*)." In *The Birds of North America, No. 51*, edited by Alan Poole & Frank Gill, Philadelphia: Academy of Natural Sciences, 1993

Hudson, Peter J., *The Red Grouse: The Biology and Management of a Wild Gamebird*, Fordingbridge: Game Conservancy, 1986

Tufted puffin (*Fratercula cirrhata*), Farallon Islands National Wildlife Refuge, Farallon Islands, California. *Copyright Bates Littlehales/ National Geographic Image Collection*

Johnsgard, Paul, *The Grouse of the World*, Lincoln: University of Nebraska Press, 1983

Kuz'mina, M.A., *Tetraonidae and Phasianidae of the USSR: Ecology and Morphology*, Washington: Smithsonian Institution Libraries, 1992

Wynne-Edwards, Vero C., *Evolution Through Group Selection*, Oxford: Blackwell Scientific Publications, 1986

PUFFINS

Puffins are seabirds of the Alcidae (auk) family, distinguished by their large, laterally compressed, brightly colored bills and distinctively marked white faces; indeed, the Atlantic puffin is known in Newfoundland, Canada, as the "sea parrot." Both males and females share the gaudy bill coloration during the breeding season. Along with the rhinoceros auklet (*Cerorhinca monocerata*), the Atlantic puffin (*Fratercula arctica*), tufted puffin (*Fratercula cirrhata*), and horned puffin (*Fratercula corniculata*) comprise the tribe *Fraterculini*.

Compared to other Alcids, puffins are relatively large, ranging from the Atlantic puffin (length = 35 cm) to the tufted puffin (length = 40 cm). Within the Atlantic and horned puffins, individuals from southern populations are smaller than those from northern regions. For all species, males are slightly heavier than females (6–8%).

Horned and tufted puffins share similar ranges in the north Pacific. However, horned puffins range somewhat farther north into the Bering Sea and Sea of Okhotsk, whereas tufted puffins tend to be found somewhat closer to the coast, at least in the southern extent of their range. Atlantic puffins range widely throughout the North Atlantic, from New England and North Africa north to Iceland, Baffin Bay, Svalbard, and Novaya Zemlya. Summer ranges extend farther north than winter ranges for all three species, but are generally more coastal, focused about breeding colonies.

Puffins are among the most colonial of the Alcids, with horned and tufted puffin colonies typically numbering in the thousands and Atlantic puffin colonies often supporting tens to hundreds of thousands. Colonies are located on islands where terrestrial predators are absent. Indeed, introduced species such as rats, raccoons, and foxes have decimated puffin colonies on some islands. However, their habit of nesting in burrows does allow for some degree of successful reproduction, relative to other Alcids, when predators are present.

Like other seabirds, puffins come ashore only to raise their young. A month or so prior to egg laying, breeders and nonbreeders (age of first breeding is three or older) arrive at the colony where courtship and territorial behaviors occur in the vicinity of burrows. Depending on weather and other factors, the numbers of birds at the colony fluctuate greatly over the course of several days. Younger nonbreeders may be forming pair bonds and scouting potential burrow sites.

Puffins, like other Alcids, are monogamous and usually retain their mate from year to year. The lack of sexual dimorphism in facial and bill features, small degree of size dimorphism, relatively small testes size compared to other Alcids, and low frequency of extrapair copulation (at least in the Atlantic puffin) suggest strong selection for mate quality by both males and females.

Their habitat of gathering in large, social groups at sea, where copulation occurs, may foster mate choice.

Although both male and female puffins possess a double brood patch, only one, relatively large egg is typically laid in a nest chamber lined with grass, leaves, or feathers at the end of a 1–2-m-long burrow excavated or usurped from another species (i.e., rabbits). Horned puffins are more likely to nest under boulders or in rock crevices, although all three species will nest in a similar habitat if good burrowing soil is absent or if digging predators are present.

Incubation is done by both parents (although more by females), with switchover occurring typically at night. Hatching occurs after about 39–45 days, and soonest in Atlantic puffins and latest in tufted puffins. Hatchlings are just under 10% of the parents' body weight. For the next 5–6 weeks, the chicks will increase in weight to about 75% of adult weight. During this period, chicks are typically fed small fish (≈70 mm) of schooling species, with sandlance and capelin among the most important. The fish are taken at sea, often many miles from the colony, at depths up to 60 m (although typically much less). Adults hold the fish behind the head in their bills; they possess a special hinge mechanism and backward-pointing spines that allow them to hold onto fish already caught while pursuing others. Up to 60 fish might be carried in one trip, although the average provisioning load is smaller. From as few as two or three to as many as 24 provisioning trips may occur per day. Kleptoparasitism, in which other species (i.e., gulls, corvids) harass and steal fish from returning adults, is common at some colonies. As the locations of fish schools are unpredictable, the habit of nesting in colonies may have evolved to allow adults to exploit information on school location provided by successful foragers returning to the colony.

During their final week in the nest, chicks lose about 10–20% of their maximum weight. This weight recession is likely a consequence of their slow growth rate, which in turn is apparently an adaptation to the unpredictable nature of their food resources. Excess intake of food over that used for growth is converted to fat, which then fuels the last week or so of development, when provisioning by parents drops off sharply. The nestling period ends some 42–50 days after hatching, when the chicks scramble, flutter, or fly to the ocean. To avoid avian predators such as eagles and falcons, they leave the colony at night so that by morning they are far out to sea.

The fledglings undertake a general seaward and southward migration, unaided by the parents. At the same time, the adults abandon the colony, the gaudier features of the bill are shed, and molting occurs.

The diet of young and adults away from the colony, particularly during the winter, is not well known. Fish continue to figure in the diet, but both squid and various zooplankton become more important.

Estimates of species populations (c.1998) were 5–10 million for the Atlantic puffin, 1–2 million for the horned puffin, and 2.5–5 million for the tufted puffin. Trends in populations are not easy to determine. Populations that breed at colonies in more accessible (to humans) areas have generally been more vulnerable, suffering reductions due to the collection of eggs (now largely banned), introduction of predators, fouling in oil, drowning in gill nets set for fish, and reduction of prey species due to human overfishing in waters near colonies.

Puffins have traditionally been harvested for food by Alaskans and also in Iceland and the Faroe Islands. Aleuts also used the puffin skin, feather side inward, to make parkas. Hunting has not had a drastic effect on large populations in the Arctic, as it did in Maine in the late 19th century, and today in Iceland, where hunting is still permitted, the hunters take care to take only nonbreeding animals.

FRED HARRINGTON

See also **Auk; Seabirds**

Further Reading

Ainley, David G. & Robert J. Boekelheide, *Seabirds of the Farallon Islands*, Stanford, California: Stanford University Press, 1990

Boag, David & Mike Alexander, *The Atlantic Puffin*, Poole, Dorset: Blandford Press, 1986

Flint, Vladimir E. & A.N. Golovkin, *Birds of the USSR: Auks (Alcidae)*, Moscow: Nauka, 1990

Gaston, Anthony J. & Ian L. Jones, *The Auks*, Oxford: Oxford University Press, 1998

Haley, Delphine, *Seabirds of Eastern North Pacific and Arctic Waters*, Seattle: Pacific Search Press, 1984

Harris, Michael P., *The Puffin*, London: T. and A.D. Poyser, 1984

Lockley, Ronald M., *Puffins*, London: J.M. Dent and Son, 1953

Nettleship, David N. & Tim R. Birkhead, *The Atlantic Alcidae*, London: Academic Press, 1985

Taylor, Kenny, *Puffins*, London: Whittet Books, 1993

Vermeer, Kees, Kenneth T. Briggs, Kenneth H. Morgan & Douglas Siegel-Causey, *The Status, Ecology and Conservation of Marine Birds of the North Pacific*, Ottawa: Canadian Wildlife Service, 1993

PULLAR, GORDON

Gordon L. Pullar is a Kodiak Island Alutiiq, a Native leader, and an advocate for revitalizing cultural heritage. Pullar has spoken internationally and published many articles on his work related to regaining ethnic identity and cultural pride, repatriation of Native remains and artifacts, and development of higher education, leadership, and skills in Native communities.

Pullar was named director of the Department of Alaska Native and Rural Development at the University of Alaska Fairbanks (UAF) in 1996 and became assistant professor in 1998. He first went to UAF in 1992 as director of the Alaska Native Human Resource Development Program. Pullar teaches development strategies, research techniques, planning, and grant writing as they apply to Alaskan Native communities. His students have also benefited from his expertise in the Alaska Native claims process, federal Indian law in the Alaska context, and Alaska Native politics. Pullar's vision for the Department of Alaska Native and Rural Development is to provide technical and leadership skills to Native people in remote communities for whom undergraduate and graduate training has been unavailable or impractical in the past. Using a combination of distance learning, intensive seminars, and international field trips, the innovative program prepares students to be effective leaders not only through course work, but by connections with Natives in other settings and exposure to indigenous issues on a circumpolar scale. Pullar feels that both the master's degree program (added in 2000) and the undergraduate curriculum can provide the tools that Native people need to exercise self-determination in their communities.

As president and CEO of Kodiak Area Native Association (KANA, Kodiak Natives' not-for-profit association) from 1983 to 1989, Pullar moved to make cultural revitalization a priority for Alutiiq Natives. He tenaciously led a campaign for the construction of an Alutiiq museum and cultural center, which was finally realized when the Alutiiq Museum and Archaeological Repository opened in 1995. The museum is a small but state-of-the-art facility hosting both locally and nationally curated exhibits highlighting Native culture and art. Pullar was also instrumental in the return of Native remains from the Smithsonian to Kodiak Island. Over 50 years after archaeologist Ales Hrdlicka removed over 800 skeletons from a burial site in Larsen Bay, Pullar encouraged village residents to ask that the remains be returned, and guided the repatriation process through eight years of political and legal struggles.

At the beginning of his tenure at KANA, Alaska Natives were just beginning to see connections between self-destructive behaviors and the need to heal the wounds of culture loss. In a 1992 *Arctic Anthropology* article, Pullar described the categories of trauma that have damaged Alutiiq and other indigenous cultures: epidemics; institutionalization of children in boarding schools, orphanages, and missions; children being educated in schools that taught that Native people were inferior; introduction and use of alcohol; natural disasters; and disasters such as the Exxon Valdez oil spill, caused by humans. Pullar felt that regaining a more spiritual connection with aboriginal heritage was a key for Natives to heal from these traumas, the legacy of which interfered with success in claiming aboriginal rights. The first step

was to teach Alutiiq people their own history. Leading the Native organization in that direction, Pullar insisted on equal partnerships with archaeologists and other researchers who collaborated with KANA. Researchers were encouraged to include community participation and training of youth in their projects and to present their findings in the Native villages. Alutiit began to contribute more directly to research and to learn from archaeologists and others, who in the past had often departed with artifacts or human remains and given back little or nothing to local people. Alutiit from Kodiak's remote villages were also supported to participate in international conferences held in Kodiak that highlighted their culture. Educational initiatives in Kodiak Island schools had youth carving masks and other objects inspired by artifacts they had seen. Oral history projects with elders, archive development, formation of a traditional dance group, and activities focused on healing from alcoholism and social trauma all had significant impacts on the perception Alutiit of Kodiak had of themselves, and spread to adjoining Alutiiq populations. Many of these programs initiated during Pullar's time at KANA continue.

While at KANA, Pullar also served on the board of directors of the Alaska Federation of Natives (AFN), and worked to pass the "1991 Amendments" to the Alaska Native Claims Settlement Act (ANCSA) as a member of the AFN Legislative Committee. He spent two years as a Program Director developing cultural programs for the Chugachmiut Regional Corporation (a neighboring Alutiiq group) before moving to the University of Alaska.

Pullar sits on many boards, including the Alaska Native Advisory Board to the Indian Law Resource Center (an international nongovernmental organization), the Steering Committee of the Arctic Studies Center at the Smithsonian Institution, and the Leisnoi Village (Woody Island) Tribal Council, of which he is president. Beginning in 1996, Pullar has served on the advisory board of *Dig Afognak*, a program of the Afognak Native Corporation that combines archaeological research, ecological and heritage tourism with a site used for spirit camps and cultural education for Alutiit. Since 1994, he has been on the board of directors of the Koniag Education Foundation, and in the position of president since 1997. He also served as president of the board of the National Keepers of the Treasures: Cultural Council of American Indians, Alaska Natives, and Native Hawaiians from 1991 to 1997 and was on the board of the Alaska Keepers of the Treasures between 1992 and 1996. Internationally, Pullar serves on the governing council of the International Arctic Social Sciences Association (IASSA), the editorial boards of the *Fourth World Journal* and *Ethnicity and Health*

Journal, and has advised projects of the International Work Group for Indigenous Affairs.

Biography

Gordon Lee Pullar was born on January 22, 1944 in Bellingham, Washington. He graduated from Bellingham High School (1962) and received a B.A. in Anthropology and Sociology from Western Washington University (1973) while working as a machine operator for the Georgia Pacific paper company. Between 1979 and 1981, Pullar worked for indigenous organizations in Washington State, editing *The Indian Voice* and *Nations Magazine*. He completed a master's degree in Public Administration at the University of Washington in 1983 with a focus on Tribal Administration and Natural Resources and Energy Policy. That year, Pullar moved to Alaska at the urging of his uncle, Karl Armstrong Jr., who had long been involved in Kodiak Native organizations and land claims issues. Pullar earned his Ph.D. from the Union Institute in Organizational Anthropology and International Studies in 1997. He has three children, Greg (born 1960), Tracy (born 1963), and Gordon Jr. (born 1985), and lives in Anchorage.

Among Pullar's publications are discussions of identity in: "Two Centuries of Changing Identity: The Case of the Tangirnarmiut," a chapter in the upcoming *Jesup Volume* from the American Museum of Natural History in New York; and *Looking Both Ways: Heritage and Identity of the Alutiiq People*, coedited with Aron Crowell and Amy Steffian for University of Alaska Press (2001). In Ethnic identity, cultural pride, and generations of baggage: a personal experience," which appeared in *Arctic Anthropology* (Vol. 29, No.

2, 1992), Pullar told how his own family background and experience fit a pattern that led to cultural confusion. "The Qikertarmiut and the Scientist: Fifty Years of Clashing World View" describes the repatriation of human remains from the Smithsonian to a village on Kodiak Island. The article appeared in *Reckoning with the Dead: The Larsen Bay Repatriation and the Smithsonian Institution* (T. Bray and T. Killion, editors, Washington, District of Columbia: Smithsonian Institution Press, 1994) and was reprinted in the British Columbia Law Review in 1995.

DEBORAH B. ROBINSON

Further Reading

Crowell, Aron, Gordon L. Pullar & Amy Steffian (editors), *Looking Both Ways: Heritage and Identity of the Alutiiq People*, Fairbanks: University of Alaska Press, 2001

Pullar, Gordon L., "Ethnic identity, cultural pride, and generations of baggage: a personal experience." *Arctic Anthropology*, 29(2) (1992): 182–191

———, "The Qikertarmiut and the Scientist: Fifty Years of Clashing World Views." In *Reckoning with the Dead: The Larsen Bay Repatriation and the Smithsonian Institution*, edited by T. Bray & T. Killion, Washington, District of Columbia: Smithsonian Institution Press, 1994

———, "Two Centuries of Changing Identity: The Case of the Tangirnarmiut." In *Jesup Volume*, New York: American Museum of Natural History (in press)

Pullar, Gordon L. & Richard A. Knecht, "Alutiiq." In *Crossroads Alaska: Native Cultures of Alaska and Siberia*, Washington, District of Columbia: Arctic Studies Center, Smithsonian Institution Press, 1995

Pullar, Gordon L., T.J. Ferguson & Joe Watkins, "Native Americans and Archaeologists: Commentary and Personal Perspectives." In *Native Americans and Archaeologists: Stepping Stones to Common Ground*, edited by N. Swidler, K.E. Dongoske, R. Anyon & A. Downer, Walnut Creek, California: Alta Mira Press, 1997

Q

QAANAAQ

The coastal town of Qaanaaq (Qânâq) is the administrative center of the Greenlandic municipality of Avanersuaq, the district that is home to the Inughuit (Polar Eskimos) and the northernmost district in Greenland. The town's name, loosely translated, means "the place where one first sees the sun rise." Qaanaaq was built in 1953–1954 on a grassy foothill facing southwest near Cape Ackland on Redcliff Peninsula. An old settlement for hunters, Qaanaaq has been inhabited since the late 1800s. Greenlandic explorer and ethnographer Knud Rasmussen (known for his seven Thule expeditions between 1912 and 1933) wanted to establish a trading post in Qaanaaq. However, due to ice conditions in 1910, he settled at North Star Bay where the Thule trading post was subsequently built.

The town of Qaanaaq was created in 1953 as a result of forced relocation by the Government of Denmark. Under the terms of the 1951 Defense Agreement between Denmark and the United States, the latter was granted rights to build military installations in Greenland in the event of a military attack. One of the most important bases was the Thule Air Base, constructed in 1951–1955 during the Cold War in the Inughuit village of Uummannaq (Dundas). The local population was required to move from the small Uummannaq settlement (not to be confused with the municipality and town of Uummannaq) when the air base planned to expand its boundaries. Most of the displaced hunting families wished to settle at Qaanaaq, where houses had been built for them. They adopted the name Thule; for a time, the town was called New Thule (Qaanaaq) and Old Thule (Uummannaq) near the Thule Air Base.

Adjacent to the town is a natural reef in the Greenland Sea, the top of which can be seen above sea level at low tide. The reef protects boats against floating icebergs near the shore. Only from mid-July to mid-September is the area ice-free, allowing large ships to travel to Qaanaaq with supplies for the remaining part of the year.

Qaanaaq faces the Inglefield Fjord, which is excellent hunting ground. Seals and walrus are hunted year-round. From June to September, narwhal and beluga can be hunted in the fjord. The large numbers of hunters in Qaanaaq have resulted in the further migration of game; consequently, hunting trips have grown longer over the years.

In 2000, 864 Inughuit resided in the Qaanaaq municipality (the former Thule District): 665 resided in the town proper and 199 resided in nearby settlements. Of these 864 inhabitants, 47 were born outside Greenland. This does not, however, mean that the 817 are Inughuit. In the southern part of the area, many West Greenlanders have settled, and the government does not differentiate between Inughuit and West Greenlanders, even though they are two different ethnic groups.

The town of Qaanaaq has a hospital, post office, old people's home, boarding school, supermarket, church, hotel, and museum. Drinking water comes from freshwater ice from the ice cap. Trucks pick up the ice from trapped icebergs and transport it back to Qaanaaq, where it is melted and piped into homes. East of the town is a cemetery and a small airstrip. Qaanaaq was used as the base for various polar expeditions, including Knud Rasmussen's Thule expeditions and Robert Peary's North Pole expedition. In recent years, Qaanaaq has become popular as a tourism destination, particularly as an overnight stop for tourists traveling to the North Pole.

The layout of Qaanaaq town differs from other towns in Greenland. A power station, providing electricity, was built at the town's inception in 1953. The wooden homes of most of the locals are located around the center of the town. Due to permafrost, all wooden houses are built on stilts. The houses are heated by coal or oil. As there is no wood in Greenland, all material for building houses is · imported from Denmark or Europe. During the dark season (late October to late February), street lights keep the town lit, albeit isolated.

ROLF GILBERG

See also **Rasmussen, Knud; Peary, Robert E.; Relocation; Thule Air Base**

Further Reading

Statistics Greenland, *Greenland 2000–2001. Statistical Yearbook,* Nuuk: Statistics Greenland, 2001
http://www.turistqaanaaq.gl/

QAQORTOQ

Qaqortoq is a town and municipality in South Greenland, centrally located in the Julianehåb Bay. The area of the municipality is 8500 sq km, of which 2500 sq km constitutes land free of ice. Qaqortoq is located north of the municipality of Nanortalik, and is adjacent to Paamiut in the north. The municipality of Narsaq bisects it from east to west, with the larger parts of the municipality south of Narsaq while a small area is situated northwest of Narsaq.

The name of the town—Qaqortoq—means "the white" in Greenlandic. The Danes named the town Julianehåb after King Frederik V's Queen Juliane Marie. Qaqortoq was founded in 1775 by the Norwegian merchant Anders Olsen as a center of trade and missionary work in southern Greenland. At that time, the district was one of Greenland's most populated due to the variety of sea mammals available for hunting and harvesting in the area. However, the population was geographically scattered most of the year along the open waters of the outer coastal line.

One of the reasons for the high productivity of renewable resources in the region is the arrival of ice masses during late spring and the first part of summer, passing from the east coast south of Kap Farvel (Uummannarsuaq) up along the southern part of the west coast. Along with the ice come a substantial number of seals, including, among others, the large hooded seal. These mammals provide meat, blubber, and skin for subsistence as well as for commercial use. The commercial importance of the seal hunt declined, however, with the vanishing markets for blubber and skin at the beginning of the 20th century. With the warming of the seas during the 1920s and the 1930s, a remarkable increase in the cod stock created a new

basis of the livelihood in the region, supplanting seal hunting as the primary resource for both formal economy and subsistence production.

The ice conditions of Qaqortoq not only contribute positively to the renewable resource base but also create severe problems for other business development. The blocking of the harbors by large ice masses severely limits communication and transportation during summer months, preventing the yearly access of both small and large boats from Denmark.

Of the total population of the municipality (3416 according to data from 2000), over 90% of Qaqortoq's inhabitants live in the main town of Qaqortoq (3112), while the rest reside in one of the three settlements—Saarloq (65), Equalugaarsuit (141), and Qassimiut (62)—and in the 13 clusters and individually situated sheep farms.

Commercial fisheries developed and became firmly rooted in the region, and fisheries and agriculture continue to play a vital role, with around 20% of the workforce employed in fisheries, the fishing industry, and agriculture. Qaqortoq has, in periods, been pioneering in relation to advances in the fishing industry, for instance, refining products from the fishing industry such as canned products and recently in the production of fantail shrimp, just as agriculture has played an important role. In 1915, a research station for sheep farming was established in Qaqortoq, where it functioned until the establishment of the Upernaviarsuk research station in 1966. In addition to farming, the Upernaviarsuk station also conducts research in the planting of trees in sheltered places in South Greenland.

In connection with renewable resources, the tannery in Qaqortoq is the only place for the professional preparation of skin in Greenland, and the dressmaker's workroom produces skin products both for the home market and for export. In addition, there is a small shipyard that maintains the local fishing fleet and builds high-quality boats for the area's fisheries. A little more than 20% of the workforce is involved in the hunting, fishing, and agriculture industries. Outside this, approximately 30% of the workforce is involved in the building sector, while the majority of the population is involved in the service sector. Although Qaqortoq generates the primary source of tourism in South Greenland (the ruined Norse church at Hvalsey is a major historical attraction), education and educational institutions chiefly dominate cultural life in Qaqortoq. In addition to a primary school and a vocational training school, one of the three grammar schools (gymnasium) in Greenland as well as a business college adds to the variety of education opportunities in the region. In addition, a folk high school (Sulisartut Højskoliat), originally established as a training center for members of the trade union SIK (Sulinermik Inuutissarsiuteqartut Katuffiat), presently serves as a training center for both public and private organizations.

In many ways, Qaqortoq has functioned as the cultural center for South Greenland. For many years, the sheep farmer's organization SPS (Savaatillit Peqatigiit Suleqatigiissut) has held its annual meetings in Qaqortoq, just as the town has been in focus in connection with a large number of cultural activities such as exhibits and theater performances. In addition, the folk high school has functioned as a forum for workshops and seminars, attracting international artists.

Within the town there are several buildings from the 1920s and the 1930s designed and built by Pavia Høegh, a local constructor and architect, in which local building materials such as the colorful Igaliku sandstone are used to reflect an unusual architectural style. One of Høegh's remarkable works is the beautiful village hall Katersortarfik, a structure built on local initiative; it was paid for by local funds and opened in 1937. Among his work is also the so-called Mindebrønd ("Memory Well" in Danish) in the town square (from 1927), a well and fountain based on the amalgamation of European fountain building traditions with local symbols.

RASMUS OLE RASMUSSEN

See also **Greenland**

Further Reading

Berthelsen, Christian, Inger H. Mortensen & Ebbe Mortensen (editors), *Kalaallit Nunaat Atlas, Greenland*, Nuuk: Atuakkiorfik, 1992
Nielsen, Nielsen, Peter Skautrup & Christian Vibe (editors), *J.P. Trap Danmark, bind XIV, Grønland*, Copenhagen: Gads Forlag, 1970
Rasmussen, Rasmus Ole, "Formal economy, renewable resources and structural changes in West Greenland." *Études/Inuit/Studies*, 24(1) (2000): 48–78
Statistics Greenland, *Greenland 2000–2001. Statistical Yearbook*, Nuuk: Statistics Greenland, 2001
http://iserit.greennet.gl/qaqortoq
http://www.qaqortoq.gl

QEQERTARSUAQ

Qeqertarsuaq is the Greenlandic name for both Disko Island and for its major settlement, situated close to the southern point of the island. Its Danish name was Godhavn ("Good Harbor"), a feature that doubtless attracted settlers throughout its history. Although traces of Inuit settlement date from Paleo-Eskimo and Dorset cultures (6000 and 2000 BP, respectively), the present settlement only came to prominence in the 17th and 18th centuries through whaling activity along the west coast. Godhavn was established in 1773 to regulate Dutch, German, and English whaling activities in the area. At this, the most northerly outpost of Danish rule, ships arrived in autumn to overwinter in Godhavn or nearby Fortuna Bay in preparation for the spring hunt. Trading opportunities also drew Greenlanders from the sparse population scattered throughout the island, such that by 1801, the colony was trading 350 barrels of blubber, 14,000 baleens, and large quantities of skins and pelts. The Napoleonic Wars broke trading links with Europe and, without the means to hunt whales, the colony fell into decline. In 1862, new local administration laws established Godhavn as an administrative center, and the six-man local council (including three Greenlandic representatives) began a program of social reform, which embraced support for the elderly, orphaned children, and others in need; the establishment of a local court; a kayak school for boys; and a sewing school for girls. From these humble roots of self-improvement, the settlement again began to thrive, and in 1906 the botanist Morten Petersen Porsild was impressed enough to found the Arctic Station 1 km east of the town. His idea to establish an Arctic research facility in Greenland was supported by famous explorers of the time such as Knud Rasmussen and Fridtjof Nansen, as well as a grant from the Danish government. Porsild remained the scientific leader of the station for almost 40 years and ownership passed to the University of Copenhagen in 1953. In latter years, the station has embraced other disciplines, including zoology, geography, and geology, and the station remains highly popular with students and a focus for research activity in West Greenland.

In May 1940, when Germany occupied Denmark, Greenland was again cut off from Europe, and the two Councils that administered the two halves of the country (the northern half from Qeqertarsuaq) gathered in Godhavn to discuss the country's future. The resulting "Godhavn Declaration" confirmed the interdependence of Denmark and Greenland, but also established the right to conduct independent foreign policy, which involved forging strong links with the United States to secure the interests of Greenland during the war. One consequence that shaped subsequent world events was the establishment of American bases and personnel on Greenlandic soil. However, another outcome was the acknowledgement that, with Greenlandic administration so concentrated in Godthåb (present-day Nuuk), the role of Godhavn as a governmental seat over the settlements of the north was no longer appropriate and 1950 saw the establishment of The National Council of Greenland in the new southern capital. Godhavn, the first town in Greenland to establish direct medium-wave radio transmissions with Denmark in 1925, gradually lost its claim to prominence, but settled to a new and successful period as a local trading center, with a population in 2001 of just over 1000 inhabitants (90% Greenland-born). Qeqertarsuaq now enjoys a sound economy based on traditional seal trapping, whaling, and fishing (based on its fishing fleet of 17 vessels), more recently supplemented by a thriving tourist trade servicing folk eager to witness the spectacular delights of Disko Island. Its coat of arms (featuring a whale under the spread rays of the aurora borealis) celebrates its founding past, but symbolizes its involvement in a bright future: the Danish Meteorological Institute recently celebrated 75 years of geomagnetic observations in the town, which have demonstrated the influence of the Earth's magnetic field on the solar wind and northern lights.

TONY FOX

See also **Disko Island**

Further Reading

Caulfield, R.A., "Aboriginal subsistence whaling in Greenland: the case of Qeqertarsuaq municipality in West Greenland." *Arctic,* 46 (1992): 144–155

Fisker, J., *Godhavn*, Umanak, Greenland: Nordiske Landes Bogforlag, 1984

Statistics Greenland, *Greenland 2000–2001 Kalaallit Nunaat—Statistical Yearbook*, Nuuk, Greenland: Atuagkat, 2001

QILAKITSOQ MUMMIES

The eight mummies of Qilakitsoq are the oldest and best preserved find of human remains and Inuit clothing not only in Greenland but also in the entire Arctic.

Qilakitsoq, which literally means "the sky is low" (Hansen et al., 1991), is located on the mainland of Greenland's northwest coast, 450 km north of the Arctic Circle. The abandoned settlement is situated on the steep northern side of the Nuussuaq Peninsula opposite the town and island of Uummannaq. Qilakitsoq's sandy beach offered a suitable landing place for boats and, on the small grassy area at the foot of a 250 m high mountain, seven different settlement structures together with more than 30 graves and grave-like structures have been found. These finds testify to the long-lasting habitation of the area before its abandonment.

About 200 m west of the main settlement area runs a stone-filled ravine, which cuts into the side of the mountain. On October 9, 1972, Hans and Jokum Grønvold, two brothers from the nearby town of Uummannaq, accidentally discovered the untouched graves while grouse hunting. Beneath a protruding rock, two graves with eight naturally mummified corpses were uncovered. The burial sites, which

appeared to have been haphazardly constructed, were covered with flat stones from the immediate vicinity. The eight astonishingly well-preserved mummies were fully dressed, and loose skins and garments, either wrapped around the mummies or used as padding, were also discovered in the graves. In total, archaeologists found 78 items of apparel, made from either sealskin, caribou fur, or bird skin: 24 inner and outer *anoraqs*, 12 pairs of inner and outer trousers, 19 boots, 21 stockings, two sleeves, and numerous extra loose skins to cover sleeping platforms or tents. A sole amulet was also found, which may have once ensured its wearer warm boots when traveling.

Until the scientific investigation began, the Grønvold brothers voluntarily took care of the site. In 1978, the mummies were delivered to the National Museum in Nuuk, Greenland's capital. After a short exhibition period, the entire find was sent on to the Department of Conservation at the National Museum in Copenhagen, where an ambitious investigation program, together with cleaning and conserving methods, began. The scientific results were published in an illustrated book in 1991 (see Hansen et al., 1991). In 1982, the entire find was returned to the National Museum in Greenland, where much of the material, including four of the mummies, has since been on permanent display. Today, the local museum in Uummannaq owns an accurate copy of one of the women's costumes, sewn by Karen Pedersen, who was born and raised near Qilakitsoq.

The mummies (six women and two children) have been radiocarbon dated to around the year 1475, about 250 years before Hans Egede began his missionary work in Greenland. The graves were probably filled gradually by several burials. Due to low ground temperature and the constant dry air, the corpses dried out slowly and remained well preserved with little decay for over 500 years. The graves were also naturally drained, aired, and protected from direct sunlight, rain, and snow by overhanging rock.

Detailed X-rays of the mummies provided information on their sex, age, and health. In more than one case, the cause of death could not be determined. Grave I contained five mummies: a six-month-old baby, whose sex was not examined; a four-year-old boy, whose skeletal deformations suggested Down's syndrome; and three women aged about 25, 30, and 45 years. While the youngest of the women may have died from a kidney stone or from swallowing a small bone fragment, the 30-year-old woman had had a remarkably distended abdomen (she may have had a water cyst stemming from her ovary, but the exact cause of death could not be determined). Grave II contained three female mummies: two had died at the approximate age of 50 years and one woman was aged

Archaeological site of the Qilakitsoq mummies, Uummannaq, West Greenland.
Copyright Bryan and Cherry Alexander Photography

between 18 and 22 years. One of the older women may have died from late-stage cancer of the nasopharynx. Her skull was damaged from the tumor.

X-ray examinations illustrated that several mummies had periods of arrested growth in childhood due to illness or malnutrition. Tissue type evaluation of the mummies indicated that in each grave, one family was buried. Grave I seemingly contained a grandmother, with her two daughters and two grandchildren, while grave II contained two sisters and a young woman who was the daughter of one of the sisters, who were also probably sisters of the oldest woman in grave I.

The average height of the adults was approximately 150 cm. Some mummies had nails with slightly pronounced transverse grooves on their upper side probably caused by eczema or nail infection. The older women had lost some teeth during their lifetime, and their teeth's crowns showed extreme attrition due to the use of teeth as a tool. No carious lesions were found, but some may have had chronic inflammation of the gums (gingivitis).

After cleaning the mummies, tattooing became visible on five of the six adult women's faces, but no tattoos were found on the torsos or limbs, and the youngest woman had no tattooing at all. With a special photographic technique using infrared light, researchers could clearly distinguish different tattoo patterns of elegantly formed lines, drawn on their foreheads, cheeks, and chins.

All the mummies were infested with remarkably well-preserved mummified head lice, with lice eggs still attached to the head hair. No body lice or crab lice were found. Scientists found no evidence of trichinosis infec-

tion, but one mummy's intestinal content showed many pinworm eggs (*Oxyuris vermicularis*), which may have caused some itching around the anal opening.

Together with the mummies, several insects (winter gnats, swamp flies, Borboridae, and blowflies) and a number of plants (lyme grass, alpine foxtail, alkali grass, Arctic bell-heather, willow, crowberry, Arctic blueberry, mountain avens, and seeds of crowberry and alpine chickweed) were found. Some of the insects likely appeared the first year after burial. The plant material was used to line the soles of stockings, as an insulating layer between the stocking and the boot, or as bedding on which the dead were placed.

The hair of the skins and the hair of the mummies were examined for contamination by heavy metals and compared with samples from the present-day Uummannaq district. Scientists undertook this investigation using two methods: X-ray fluorescence in the United States and atomic absorption spectrophotometry in Denmark. Both methods showed that the mummies had much lower levels of lead, mercury, and copper than present-day humans and animals. Only the cadmium contamination was similar to present-day levels. The mummies also had higher selenium intakes than present-day Greenlanders, while the selenium in animal hair was the same as today.

The Qilakitsoq mummies are representatives of the so-called Thule culture, which reached the Qilakitsoq area about AD 1200, and offered invaluable ethnographic data on the precolonial Greenlandic Inuit. The facial tattoos enabled a close study of a custom that was abandoned during Greenland's colonization. The well-preserved garments clearly demonstrated the clothing styles of children and adult women in the 15th century. The women's garments substantially contributed to the study of Greenlandic clothing traditions. The women's outer *anoraqs* made of sealskin clearly showed the same use of skins and the same distinct cuts, with the typical narrowing, pointed tails in the front and at the back, and the distinct, tall, narrow hoods with a dark middle rim of fur as seen on artists' depictions of kidnapped Inuit in the 16th and 17th centuries. Clothing styles changed substantially during Greenland's colonial time.

VERENA TRAEGER

See also **Egede, Hans; Tattooing; Uummannaq**

Further Reading

Hansen, Hart, Jens Peder & Hans Christian Gulløv (editors), "The mummies from Qilakitsoq: eskimos in the 15th century." In *Meddelelser om Grønland, Man & Society*, Volume 12, Copenhagen: Nyt Nordisk Forlag, 1989

Hansen, Hart, Jens Peder, Jørgen Meldgaard & Jørgen Nordqvist (editors), *The Greenland Mummies*, Washington, District of Columbia: Smithsonian Institution Press and London: British Museum Publications, 1991 (first published in Danish and Greenlandic in 1985)

QILLARSUAQ

The Inughuit, known to history and anthropology as the Polar Eskimos, live in northwestern Greenland farther north than any other civilian population on earth. In the mid-19th century, their world was a narrow strip of coastline bounded on three sides by glaciers and on the fourth by the sea. For reasons unknown, they had lost much of the material culture on which other groups of Inuit traditionally relied—the qajaq (kayak) and the larger so-called woman's boat, the umiaq, as well as the bird spear, fish leister (a forklike antler or bone fishing harpoon), and bow and arrow. The loss of sea transportation confined them to land during summer, where they survived on food cached during the long, sun-filled spring. The absence of the bow and arrow prevented the hunting of caribou. Consequently, the Polar Eskimos were primarily sea mammal hunters. They had adapted to their technological losses, but survival was difficult and the population was in decline. A fortuitous immigration of Inuit from Baffin Island in the 1860s alleviated their harsh conditions by reintroducing the technology that they had lost.

The migration was led by a shaman Qillaq, more commonly known by his Greenlandic name Qillarsuaq (also spelled Qitdlarssuaq), and it led from northern Baffin Island to northwestern Greenland. Qillarsuaq, however, was not a native of northern Baffin Island, but an Uqqumiutaq, a person from southeastern Baffin Island. He may once have lived at Cumberland Sound,

and his son, Ittukusuk, was born at Cape Searle. Research by Michael Hauser, a Danish ethnomusicologist, indicates that Qillarsuaq's roots may go farther back, southwest to the Cape Dorset region. Qillarsuaq's murder of a fellow Uqqumiutaq, probably between 1830 and 1835, precipitated his sudden departure to the Pond Inlet area with his accomplice Uqi, and their families and followers. Some years later, near Pond Inlet, a party of their enemies attacked them in a memorable battle, which Qillarsuaq and his group survived after having taken refuge on an iceberg. They fled the district, first heading in the direction of Igloolik but eventually crossing Lancaster Sound to Devon Island.

There in the summer of 1853, near Dundas Harbor, Captain Edward Inglefield of the *Phoenix* met a group of 25 Inuit men, women, and children, led by Qillaq. He may well have remained on Devon Island were it not for the chance meeting with Inglefield. Although Inuit legend tells of spirit flights in which Qillarsuaq discovered that there were Inuit living far to the northeast, he likely learned this from Inglefield and his Greenlandic interpreter and a perusal of the explorer's charts. Nevertheless, he was in no hurry to leave the south coast of Devon Island, an area rich in game, and five years later the British naval officer Francis McClintock met him at Cape Horsburg, only 50 miles from Dundas Harbor.

It was probably in the spring of 1859 that Qillarsuaq began his great journey from Devon Island in search of the new land and the people that he knew to be farther north. Accounts vary, but he probably led a group of 50–60 people, which included Uqi and his followers. Qillarsuaq was already old. McClintock noted that he was bald, unusual among Inuit, and that his few remaining hairs were white. But he was a born leader, remembered as someone to be "feared and obeyed."

At the island of Ingersarvik, at the mouth of Talbot Inlet off the east coast of Ellesmere Island, Uqi had misgivings about the wisdom of this trip. He questioned Qillarsuaq's leadership and turned back, with at least 25 people, probably in 1861 or 1862. Qillarsuaq continued north, leading the remainder of the party, eventually crossing from Pim Island to Anorituq, Greenland, where they found abandoned habitations but no people. Hunting and moving southward, they established themselves temporarily at Taserartalik near Etah. It was there, probably in 1863, that they finally encountered a Polar Eskimo, Arrutak, and at his behest they moved their camp south to Pitorarvik, where a large group of Inuit were encamped for spring hunting.

Qillarsuaq's quest was over; he had finally reached a land where he had no enemies. For the Polar

Eskimos, a time of desperation was also at an end. They had also met new people, speaking a language similar to their own, who were, in the words of Father Guy Mary-Roussilière, who documented this migration, "bringing with them knowledge which would help them in their battle for survival." American explorers with some knowledge of the Polar Eskimos had already predicted the extinction of the tribe, whose population numbered no more than 140. The newcomers brought new blood and new hunting technology, as well as their stories and folklore.

But Qillarsuaq, who had left both the Cumberland Sound area and later northern Baffin Island to distance himself from his enemies, was destined not to find peace. He had a falling out with a powerful sorcerer who had befriended him shortly after his arrival in Greenland. Believing that the man, Avatannguaq, was plotting against him, Qillarsuaq and two accomplices murdered his former friend. Soon after, Qillarsuaq's health began to fail and he was overcome with a strong urge to see his homeland again before he died. He and his followers had been in Greenland for six years when Qillarsuaq left again, traveling westward toward Ellesmere Island from where he would continue south to Baffin Island. Twenty or so people accompanied him. But the journey had only begun when Qillarsuaq died on the ice off Cape Herschel, 20 km south of Cape Sabine. His followers buried his body at Cape Herschel, a point that the Polar Eskimos have known since as Qillaqarvik.

The rest of the party traveled on to Makinson Inlet, where game and fish were scarce. Starvation, murder, and cannibalism ensued. With their leader dead, two brothers concluded that there was no point continuing southward with the remainder of the treacherous party. Merqusaaq and Qumangaapik along with three relatives returned instead to the safety of Greenland, reaching Etah probably in 1873. They remained, and many of the families of northwestern Greenland today claim descent from the "allarsuit"—the "Canadian" migrants.

The story of Qillarsuaq and the migration that he led from Baffin Island to Greenland may be representative of countless undocumented migrations by which Inuit from the Bering Sea gradually populated the North American Arctic. Unlike the relocations of later days, in which whalers, traders, and government moved Inuit from location to location to satisfy their own commercial and administrative purposes, Qillarsuaq's story is unique in that his motives were his own. However, his brief encounters with non-Inuit explorers and the sparse tracks he left in the historical record enable a rich picture of his and his followers' exploits to be fashioned from non-Inuit history and Inuit oral accounts.

Biography

Qillarsuaq (Qitdlarssuaq, Qitdlaq, Qillaq), an Inuk leader and shaman, was born in southern Baffin Island, perhaps in the area of Cape Dorset, in the early 1800s. He lived for a time in the Cumberland Sound area and in northern Baffin Island before leading a migration of Inuit to Greenland in the 1860s. While returning to his homeland, he died off Cape Herschel, Ellesmere Island, around 1870. His descendants live in northwestern Greenland.

KENN HARPER

See also **Greenland Inuit**

Further Reading

Gilberg, Rolf, "Changes in the life of the Polar Eskimos resulting from a Canadian immigration to the Thule District, North Greenland, in the 1860's." *Folk*, 16–17 (1974–1975): 159–170

Holtved, Erik, "Contributions to Polar Eskimo ethnography." *Meddelelser on Grønland*, 182(2) (1967)

Mary-Rousselière Guy, *Qitdlarssuaq: The Story of a Polar Migration*, Winnipeg: Wuerz Publishing Ltd., 1991

Petersen, Robert, "The last migration to Greenland." *Folk*, 4 (1962): 95–110

Rasmussen, Knud, *The People of the Polar North*, London: Trubner & Co., 1908

———, *Greenland by the Polar Sea*, London: W. Heinemann, 1921

Savelle, J.M., "The nature of nineteenth century Inuit occupations of the High Arctic Islands of Canada." *Etudes/Inuit/Studies*, 5(2) (1981): 109–123

Ulloriaq, Inuutersuaq, *Beretningen om Qillarsuaq of hans lange rejse fra Canada til Nordgrønland i 1860erne*, Copenhagen: Det Grønlandske Selskab, 1985

Uvdloriaᴋ, Inûterssuaᴋ, *K'itdlarssuákúnik Oᴋalualâk*, Nuuk: Det Grønlandske Forlag, 1976

QIMMUSSERIARSUAQ—*See* MELVILLE BAY

QUATERNARY PALEOCLIMATOLOGY

The Earth experienced considerable climate and environmental changes during the Quaternary. Many of these climate changes are only now being worked out, as new data are constantly changing our view of past climates.

One of the most important sources of information about the climate of the Arctic during the Quaternary comes from the various cores collected from the Greenland Ice Cap. Other ice cores have been collected from other ice caps in Canada and Eurasia (*see* **Ice Core Record**). Information about climate changes can also be extracted from marine sediment cores, by analyzing the fossils of plankton buried in the sediment or characteristics of the sediment matrix. On land, information can be obtained by studying landscape features caused by glaciers or ice sheets, such as moraines or eskers. Using this information, the extent of the ice sheets can be determined, and the climate changes that caused their development and decay can be interpreted. Fossil pollen or other organisms from sediment cores collected from lakes and bogs provide information of past climates on land in areas away from ice sheets.

During the Tertiary, the Geological Era before the Quaternary, the Earth was generally warmer than at present, and the Arctic in particular was very different than today. Subtropical to temperate forests grew on Greenland and the Canadian Arctic, through time giving way to boreal forests and tundra conditions, in response to a long-term cooling. First evidence of the development of ice sheets dates to 2.75 million years ago.

The most striking characteristic of the Quaternary is the alternation of glacial and interglacial conditions. Although the ice sheets were located toward the poles, the climate changes associated with the development of these ice sheets were felt across the entire Earth's surface. Between 2.75 and 0.9 million years ago, there was an alternation of buildup and decay of ice sheets, with a period of roughly 41,000 years. This occurred perhaps up to 50 times, although the ice sheets may not have been too extensive. For the past 0.9 million years, the ice sheets persisted for longer time periods. Glacial periods lasted over 100,000 years, while the interglacials that separate these tend to last only around 10,000 years. We are presently in an Interglacial, the Holocene.

The last of these glacial-interglacial cycles is known in the most detail. There is little information about previous interglacials on land, as subsequent ice sheet advances destroyed much of the evidence. Most of the information of previous times must therefore be obtained from ocean sediments. However, for the previous interglacial—called Isotope Stage 5e, the Eemian or the Sangamon—there is a considerable amount of information known, pieced together from fragmentary sources. In general, the data suggest that the Eemian interglacial was warmer than the present Holocene interglacial across the Arctic. Rough estimates suggest temperature differences up to 4–5°C compared to the present, with a displacement of vegetation zones compared to today of at least several hundred kilometers.

Beginning around 120,000 years ago, ice sheets began to form, reaching maximum volumes around 21,000 years ago. Ice volumes were relatively small for the first 40,000 years, increasing during the later portions of the Glacial Period. In addition to the expansion of Greenland and Antarctica ice, four major ice sheets (Laurentide and Cordilleran in North America, Scandinavian and Barents in Eurasia) developed. As a result, during the full-glacial, North America and Europe were mostly covered by ice, except for small ice-free refugia. The Scandinavian and Barents ice sheets extended eastward through present-day Russia, but the eastern Siberian Arctic, which apparently did not contain an ice sheet, was cold enough such that the region north of 60° N supported a tundra ecosystem. The presence of these large barriers caused major changes in the global atmospheric and ocean circulation, with repercussions on the surface climate around the world. For example, the North Atlantic was much colder than today and tundra vegetation grew across much of Europe.

In North America, the southern limit of ice sheets during the late glacial period—the Wisconsinan—has been known for some time. The extent of ice and nature of the ice sheet in the Canadian Arctic has been controversial. It is now felt that a large ice cap, called the Innuitian Ice Sheet, covered the Queen Elizabeth Islands. This abutted to the Laurentide Ice Sheet to the south, which covered much of present-day Canada and parts of the United States, including the southern islands from Baffin to Banks Island. Some parts of the Canadian Arctic, for example, the northwestern islands, much of Alaska, and parts of the Yukon, were not glaciated at all during the Wisconsinan, although they probably maintained a severe climate.

The melting and final collapse of the ice sheets was relatively rapid, occurring between 14,000 and 6000 years ago for the Laurentide Ice Sheet and several thousand years earlier for the Scandinavian. Deglaciation occurred irregularly, with periods of rapid retreat causing pulses of meltwater discharge affecting large areas of the North Atlantic. These are recorded as millennial-scale oscillations in oxygen isotope records and also as periods of extensive rafting of icebergs, which left records in sediments of the North Atlantic. The causes of these are not certain. The final collapse of ice over the region that is now Hudson's Bay released huge amounts of water into the ocean relatively rapidly. This would have cooled a large volume of the ocean, and the climate change caused by this was felt across North America and probably elsewhere.

The weight of the ice sheets depressed the Earth's surface. As the ice sheets melted, the land rebounded. At the same time, water, which had been locked in the ice, now filled the oceans and the sea level rose. These two effects combined to change the paleogeography of the continents, especially in areas such as the Canadian Arctic and Scandinavia, which were centers of the ice sheets (*see* **Quaternary Paleogeography**).

One area of particular interest is the "Beringia" region. During the glacial period, with much water locked in ice sheets, the sea level was lower, and North America and Asia were connected across the Bering Strait. This provided an area for the plants and animals of Asia and North America to mix. Although the Alaska and Brooks ranges supported local ice caps, much of the central part of Alaska was unglaciated, although the climate during this time is controversial. Large deposits of mammal bones suggest relatively rich steppe vegetation, whereas fossil pollen suggests less productive tundra climates. Although located in the north and surrounded by ice sea and land ice, the circulation around the Laurentide Ice Sheet may have caused southerly winds, raising the temperatures of central Alaska.

K. GAJEWSKI

See also **Environmental History of the Arctic; Holocene; Ice Core Record; Quaternary Period**

Further Reading

Bradley, R.S., *Paleoclimatology: Reconstructing Climate of the Quaternary* (2nd edition), San Diego: Academic Press, 1999

Fulton, R.J., *Quaternary Geology of Canada and Greenland*, Ottawa: Geological Survey of Canada, 1989

LIGA members, "Report of 1st discussion group: the last interglacial in high latitudes of the northern hemisphere: terrestrial evidence." *Quaternary International*, 10–12 (1991): 9–28

Nesje, A. & S.O. Dahl, *Glaciers and Environmental Change*, London: Arnold, 2000

Ruddiman, W.F., *Earth's Climate Past and Future*, New York: Freeman, 2001

Wilson, R.C.L., S.A. Drury & J.L. Chapman, *The Great Ice Age*, London and New York: Routledge, 2000

QUATERNARY PALEOGEOGRAPHY

Paleogeography deals with the reconstruction of the physical geography of past geological times, where the focus is on physical features such as the shifting locations of shorelines, rivers, and drainage systems, tectonics and mountain building, paleolatitude and continental drift, and location in time and space of continental shelf areas and other sedimentary basins. The field of Quaternary paleogeography broadly includes all aspects of paleo-map reconstructions through the Quaternary Period; ice sheet and sea-level fluctuations in time and space; the delineation of past topographic or bathymetric contours; and the compilation of biologic, morphologic, or lithostratigraphic data that can be presented on time slices, such as paleovegetation maps or distribution of loess basins and fossil permafrost. A Quaternary paleogeographic data set will cover a number of time intervals, showing, for example, deviations from the present-day values of the winter, summer, and annual mean temperatures, and annual precipitation for the time slices; values of albedo, sea surface temperatures; sea-ice distribution; zones of permafrost, mountain glaciation, and inland ice; geomorphic processes; and loess formation, natural vegetation, and landscape types for the different time intervals. Paleogeographical maps and reconstructions are used as base information for studies of past fossil distributions, past climatic changes, evolution of vegetational or oceanographic patterns, and for computer modeling studies.

The frame for major global environmental changes is set by large-scale tectonics and the position and configuration of the continental landmasses. These affect the paths of ocean currents and air masses and in turn decide the global energy distribution. The steady northward drift of Europe, Asia, and North America through the Tertiary Period, 65–2 Ma (million years) BP (before present), caused the gradual tectonic closing of the connection between the Pacific Ocean and the Arctic Ocean and reduced the previously efficient ocean heat transport from equatorial regions toward the North Pole. The Northern Hemisphere thereby experienced increased cooling. The ice sheet in Greenland presumably first formed about 7 Ma BP in response to this cooling. The buildup of huge mountain chains (the Himalayas, the Alps, the Rocky Mountains, and the Andes) as well as the closing of equatorial ocean pathways also greatly affected global circulation patterns. The onset of glaciation in Antarctica can be traced back to late Eocene times, 35–40 Ma BP, reflecting the drift of Antarctica over the South Pole and the establishment of the circum-Antarctic pattern of oceanic and atmospheric circulation that inhibits energy transfer to high Southern Hemisphere latitudes. There is strong evidence of large ice sheets in Antarctica during the Miocene, after $c.$24 Ma BP, and since then Antarctica has functioned as a heat sink in the global climate system and strongly influenced the global energy budget and climate.

Most Quaternary paleogeographic reconstructions focus on time slices through the past $c.$130 ka (kiloyears). This is because there is ample geological and biological evidence preserved in the geological record with a resolution high enough to allow for reasonably detailed reconstructions, whereas evidences of earlier large-scale Quaternary environmental changes are usually fragmentary. During the past 130 ka, the climate has changed from interglacial to glacial and then back to the present-day interglacial, that is, it has fluctuated between end members in the climate-environmental system. It is assumed that environmental changes through the last interglacial-glacial cycle have occurred repeatedly through earlier glacial cycles. The climate-environmental system is an interactive system consisting of five major components: the atmosphere, the hydrosphere, the cryosphere, the land surface, and the biosphere, forced or influenced by various external forcing mechanisms, the most important of which is the sun. There is a general consensus among Quaternary scientists that changes in the Earth's orbital parameters that influence the amount and distribution of energy from the sun (the tilt of the Earth's rotational axis, the eccentricity of the Earth's orbit about the sun, and season of perihelion) are very important for explaining the fundamental timing of interglacial and glacial events. However, the phasing and the amplitude of the climate response to orbital changes are nonlinear and involve atmosphere, ocean, ice sheet, land, and vegetation feedbacks. It is the purpose of paleogeographic reconstructions to highlight spatial and temporal differences in these physical parameters as expressed in the geological archives, for better understanding the underlying processes and dynamics.

The following reconstructions will focus on paleoenvironments in Eurasia and Beringia, with brief references to Arctic Canada, Greenland, and Svalbard during the Pliocene and three widely defined time periods through the last 130 ka: (a) the last interglacial, the Eemian/Sangamon/marine oxygen isotope stage (MIS) 5e, 130–115 ka BP; (b) the Early-Middle Weichselian/Wisconsin/MIS 5d-4, c.115–50 ka BP; and (c) the last glacial maximum (LGM)/MIS 2, 20–18 ka BP. The reconstructions are based on a range of proxy data, from terrestrial macrofossil and pollen data to marine and ice-core data.

Paleogeographic Reconstruction of the Pliocene (5.4–1.8 Ma) in the Arctic

The Arctic is not a uniform environment today. Different geological histories, large differences in topography and proximity to the Arctic Ocean between regions, as well as varying weather patterns bring diversity to the present Arctic environment and has done so through time. Climatically, the Arctic today is often defined as the area north of the 10°C July isotherm, that is, north of a line or region that has a mean July temperature of 10°C. In some areas, the treeline roughly coincides with the 10°C July isotherm and defines the southern boundary of the Arctic. The treeline defines a transition zone where continuous forest gives way to tundra with sporadic stands of trees and finally to treeless tundra. The Arctic is thus by definition primarily a treeless area with low summer temperatures. But it has not always been so.

Generally, the Pliocene world was warmer than at present. The ancient distribution of warm-climate ocean plankton, and of animal and plant fossils on land, shows that globally the greatest warming relative to the present situation was in the Arctic and cool-temperate latitudes of the Northern Hemisphere. There, summer and annual mean temperatures were often warm enough to allow species of animals and plants to exist hundreds of kilometers north of the ranges of their nearest present-day relatives. In the Arctic, boreal-type forests dominated all the way to the present Arctic Ocean where tundra exists today. This has been verified by finds of fossil wood at a number of sites in northern Greenland and Arctic Canada. Fossil wood logs that have been identified include *Larix*, *Pinus*, and *Picea*. Fossil mammalian remains include the extinct rabbit *Hypolagus*, and fossil insects and marine molluscs from a number of sites around the Arctic confirm with a considerably warmer-than-present environment prior to the onset of Pleistocene cooling and expanding Arctic glaciers. Paleogeographical reconstructions for the Pliocene in the Arctic suggest that summer sea surface temperatures in the Arctic Ocean were at least 1–3°C higher than today, and sea-ice cover was considerably reduced or even absent during long periods of time. There was considerably more rainfall over the Arctic, originating over the warmer Arctic Ocean, and permafrost was probably restricted to higher terrain. Because there were less ice volumes at high latitudes, the global sea level may have been as much as 30 m higher than at present during the warmest intervals. The peak phases of warmth during the Pliocene were mostly during the interval 3–4 Ma (the mid-Pliocene), although almost all of the Pliocene was warmer than today's world.

The Pliocene warmth in the Arctic has been enigmatic for our understanding of what controls the Quaternary development of climate and glaciations, since the present continental configuration was largely in place in Pliocene. The Arctic then, as now, experienced a polar night north of the Arctic Circle. The causes of the generally warmer climate of the Pliocene are something of a mystery. The warmth may have been related to changes in ocean and atmospheric circulation patterns, perhaps combined with higher-than-present concentrations of greenhouse gases in the atmosphere. Temperature estimates derived from paleoenvironmental data reveal that when the global temperature warms, changes at higher latitudes, and in the polar regions in particular, are systematically larger than those nearer the equator. In general, climate models do a better job of estimating global temperature changes through time than regional changes. This is because the energy budget of the entire planet is affected. Regional changes reflect the response of the atmosphere and ocean circulation to changes in the total energy budget, and, as a result, are more difficult to model and understand. One of the challenges for Pliocene paleogeographical reconstructions in the Arctic is to provide an understanding, in the perspective of the geologic record, of possible environmental responses to a future greenhouse situation.

The Eemian/Sangamon Interglacial, 130–115 ka BP

The beginning of the last interglacial is reflected in the marine records by an abrupt shift to lighter isotope values. The preceding Saalian/Illinoian glaciation was extremely extensive at both high and middle latitudes, and the onset of the Eemian/Sangamon interglacial is marked at many Arctic locations by marine transgression across isostatically depressed coastal areas. Deposits from this marine transgression are particularly pronounced along the northern Russian and Siberian coastal lowlands. A range of proxy data suggests that the Eemian/Sangamon climate optimum summer temperatures were considerably (2–4°C) warmer than that of the present day, and that vegetation zones on the continents migrated northward. Regional sea surface temperature zones also migrated, and subtropical warm water was pushed northward in the North Atlantic. Estimates of sea surface temperatures suggest considerably warmer waters than present in coastal Arctic waters, and even the Arctic Ocean may have been ice-free some summers. Glacier extent throughout the Arctic was probably significantly more restricted than present during the Eemian/Sangamon interglacial, with the Greenland inland ice considerably reduced. The global eustatic sea level was 4–6 m higher than the present as a result of extensive melting of glaciers on the continents and thermal expansion of ocean water.

In northern Russia and western to central Siberia, Eemian marine and estuarine sediments are widely exposed in river sections from the Kola Peninsula in the west to the Taymyr Peninsula in the east. Their fossil content of warm boreal benthic faunas, in areas that today have Arctic waters lacking boreal species, easily identifies them. Fennoscandia was an island, with water passage between the North Sea and the White Sea across the Baltic Sea and Finland. Finds of fossil marine mammals, such as narwhals, in marine sediments on the Siberian High Arctic islands suggest at least seasonally reduced sea-ice cover compared to the present. The warm Eemian climate in the Eurasian north is also evidenced by more northerly treeline limits than present, with boreal forests spreading all the way to the Arctic Ocean in northern Russia. Summer temperature estimates suggest 2–8°C warmer temperatures than present in the Eurasian north, depending on site and proximity to the Arctic Ocean.

Studies of marine and terrestrial deposits of the last interglacial in Beringia suggest that it was warmer than present conditions. There is evidence for warmer-than-present marine conditions offshore Alaska during the Eemian/Sangamon interglacial, and the winter sea-ice limit in the Bering Strait was at least 800 km further to the north than present. At the same time, the treeline was more than 600 km further north in places, displacing the tundra. A compilation of last interglacial localities indicates that boreal forest was much extended beyond its present range in Alaska and Yukon Territory and probably extended to higher elevation sites now occupied by tundra in the interior. The treeline on Chukotka Peninsula, easternmost Siberia, was more than 600 km further north than today and displacing the tundra all the way to the Arctic Ocean. Summer temperature reconstructions for Beringia vary considerably, from showing values similar to modern to considerably warmer summers. Studies of fossil beetle assemblages estimate that Eemian/Sangamon interglacial July temperatures at certain sites in Beringia may have been about 5°C warmer than modern.

Investigations on East Greenland have revealed that during the Eemian/Sangamon interglacial, dwarf-shrub heaths with a diverse insect fauna and tree birch and alder growing in sheltered localities dominated the terrestrial environment in areas around 70° N, which today are polar deserts. This suggests that summer temperatures were at least 3–4°C warmer than present. To the contrary, fossil molluscs from proposed Eemian deposits on Svalbard suggest sea surface temperatures similar to modern, but not as warm as during the Holocene climate optimum (see below). There are numerous collections of fossil shells and some of terrestrial plant materials from Arctic northwest Canada that are thought to correlate to the Eemian/Sangamon interglacial. Most fossil mollusc species are representative of Arctic conditions, but few finds of Subarctic species suggest that the marine climate may have been somewhat warmer than present.

The Early-Middle Weichselian/Wisconsin, 115–50 ka BP

In a Northern Hemisphere and global perspective, this time interval represents a transition from interglacial to glacial conditions, with successively falling global sea level as continental ice volumes increased. Recent research has, however, increasingly shown that ice sheets in the High Arctic probably reached their maximum extent and volume during the early stages of ice buildup, during the Early-Middle Weichselian/Wisconsin.

In the Eurasian north, west of the Taymyr Peninsula, the limits of the Eurasian ice sheets have been reconstructed for two Early-Middle Weichselian/Wisconsin glaciations. The Late Quaternary glacial maximum in the Eurasian Arctic occurred around 90 ka BP, in strong contrast to the ice sheets over Scandinavia and North America, which at that time were much smaller than during the LGM. During the 90 ka BP glaciation, an ice sheet centered in the Barents Sea-Kara Sea area expanded far onto the Russian continent and blocked the northbound drainage of rivers toward the Arctic Ocean (Figure 1). A regrowth of the ice sheet occurred at 60–50 ka BP. The Barents-Kara ice sheet expanded well onto the continent in northern Russia and covered the northwestern rim of the Taymyr Peninsula, also leading to the blockage of rivers draining to the north and the formation of huge, ice-dammed lakes. Siberia, east of Taymyr Peninsula, was ice-free throughout the last interglacial-glacial cycle, and constituted an enormous steppe environment. It has been called "the mammoth steppe" because of the characteristic presence of mammoths in its ecosystem, but supported a diverse herbivorous fauna including mammoths, caribou, muskox, bison, and horses. It differed from the modern tundra environment in having a higher biomass, much higher productivity, and a reduced snow cover in winter. The floral composition of the mammoth steppe (or polar steppe) may have its closest modern analogue with the Central Asian grass steppe, where grasses form the base of the nutritional chain, although brushes and trees have occurred in sheltered and wet locations.

There is evidence from both Svalbard and East Greenland of two Early-Middle Weichselian/ Wisconsin glaciations, with ice extent and volumes similar to or smaller than the LGM glaciation. In Beringia, glacial mapping, soil/loess profiles, and chronological data suggest that during Early-Middle Weichselian/ Wisconsin, Alaskan glaciers were considerably expanded. In southwestern Alaska, glaciers broadly extended beyond the present coast, while further north the glacial expansion was more limited. This was probably due to differences in proximity to moisture sources. Early-Middle Weichselian/ Wisconsin glaciers in Alaska defined a considerably more extensive glaciation than the following LGM glaciation. The glacial record on Chukotka Peninsula likewise suggests that Early-Middle Weichselian/ Wisconsin glaciers were more extensive than during the very limited LGM glaciation there. Because much of Beringia was not glaciated throughout the last glacial cycle, vast areas remained open to active eolian deposition, with resultant loess/yeodoma dune fields and blanketing of the landscape.

The Last Glacial Maximum (LGM), MIS 2, 20–18 ka BP

LGM is defined as the maximum global ice volume as seen in marine oxygen isotope records from foraminifera in sediment cores, and coinciding with the maximum extension of middle latitude Northern Hemisphere ice sheets during the last glacial cycle. It

is generally thought to have occurred around 20–18 ka BP, but it is, however, acknowledged that the timing, duration, and extent of ice cover at LGM differed considerably in different regions of the Arctic.

Recent interpretations of the northern Eurasian glacial record suggest that most of the mainland of northern Russia and Siberia remained ice-free during the LGM. A huge LGM ice sheet built up in the Barents Sea area and extended over Svalbard and Franz Josef Land. It probably coalesced with an ice sheet over Novaya Zemlya as well as with the Scandinavian inland ice sheet.

The Greenland inland ice expanded considerably, filling many outer shelf basins and extending out on the shelf areas. Major ice streams probably developed in many Greenland fjords, feeding extensive ice shelves fringing the ice sheet. The LGM ice cover over northern Greenland was thin and probably cold-based, except in the fjords where fast-moving outlet glaciers and ice streams terminated or fed ice shelves. In northwestern Greenland, the ice coalesced with the Innuitian ice sheet over Ellesmere Island. The Innuitian ice sheet probably covered most of the islands in the northeastern Canadian Arctic during LGM. With the exception of a few nunataks on Ellesmere Island, the margin of the Innuitian ice sheet at LGM lay offshore. West of the Innuitian ice sheet and north of the Laurentide ice sheet, some islands (e.g., Banks Island, Prince Patrick Island, and Melville Island) experienced limited glaciation or were ice-free at LGM. Baffin Island was heavily glaciated and partly overrun by ice of the Laurentide ice sheet advancing from the Foxe Basin to the west. The ice drained through ice streams developing in the major fjord systems on southeastern and eastern Baffin Island. It has been suggested that some coastal nunataks on eastern Baffin Island remained ice-free during the LGM.

Climatic conditions in Beringia during the LGM are generally believed to have been cold and dry. Glaciers grew in regional mountain ranges, but reached the lowlands only south of the Alaska Range. The environment was largely a mosaic of steppe-tundra landscapes. The lowest parts of the Bering land bridge were covered with shrub tundra. The Bering land bridge was flooded by the sea about 11 ka BP, and closed migration routes for plants and animals between North America and Asia.

ÓLAFUR INGÓLFSSON

See also **Beringia; Holocene; Ice Core Record; Quaternary Period**

Further Reading

Andersen, B.G. & H.W. Borns Jr., *The Ice Age World*, Oslo: Scandinavian University Press, 1994

Clark, P.U. & A. Mix (editors), "Ice sheets and sea level of the last glacial maximum." *Quaternary Science Reviews,* 21(1–3) (2002)

Elias, S.A. & J. Brigham-Grette (editors), "Beringian paleoenvironments. Festschrift in honour of D.M. Hopkins." *Quaternary Science Reviews,* 20(1–3) (2001)

Elverhøi, A. (editor), "Glacial and oceanic history of the Polar North Atlantic margins." *Quaternary Science Reviews,* 17(1–3) (1998)

Frenzel, B., M. Pécsi & A.A. Velichko (editors), *Atlas of Paleoclimates and Paleoenvironments of the Northern Hemisphere: Late Pleistocene-Holocene,* Budapest: Geographical Research Institute, Hungarian Academy of Science, 1992

Manley, W.F., *Postglacial Flooding of the Bering Land Bridge: A Geospatial Animation,* Volume 1, INSTAAR, University of Colorado, 2002; http://instaar.colorado.edu/QGISL/bering_land_bridge

Manley, W.F. & D.S. Kaufman, *Alaska PaleoGlacier Atlas,* Institute of Arctic and Alpine Research (INSTAAR), University of Colorado, 2002; http://instaar.colorado.edu/QGISL/ak_paleoglacier_atlas, v.1

Thiede, J. & H.A. Bauch (editors), "The Late Quaternary stratigraphy and environments of Northern Eurasia and the adjacent Arctic Seas—new contributions from QUEEN." *Global and Planetary Change,* 31(1–4) (2001)

QUATERNARY PERIOD

The Quaternary is the most recent geological period of time in Earth's history, spanning the last two million years and extending up to the present day. The Quaternary Period is subdivided into the Pleistocene ("Ice Age") and the Holocene (present warm interval) epochs, with the Pleistocene spanning most of the Quaternary and the Holocene covering the past 10,000 years. The Quaternary Period is characterized by a series of large-scale environmental changes that have profoundly affected and shaped both landscapes and life on Earth. One of the most distinctive features of the Quaternary has been the periodic buildup of major continental ice sheets and mountain ice caps in many parts of the world during long-lasting glacial stages, divided by warm episodes (interglacials) of shorter duration, when temperatures were similar to or higher than today. During long periods of these climatic cycles, perhaps eight-tenths of the total time, temperatures were cool or cold. The number of Quaternary interglacial-glacial cycles is probably in the order of 30–50.

There have been shifts in the frequency of climate oscillations and amplitude of temperatures and glaciations through the Quaternary. At the onset of the Quaternary, many Arctic areas were comparatively warm, with trees and bushes growing far north of the present treeline. Prior to about 800,000 years ago, each interglacial-glacial cycle lasted for about 40,000 years, but after that the periodicity shifted to a prevailing rhythm of about 100,000 years. Prior to this shift in frequency, there was a repeated buildup of relatively small-to-moderate-sized ice sheets at high northern latitudes. After c.800,000 years ago, there occurred a major intensification of glaciations, with repeated growth of continental-scale ice sheets reaching midlatitudes and with ice volumes much larger than during the earlier Quaternary glaciations. There have occurred 8–10 major glaciations during the past 800,000 years. Two of the largest Northern Hemisphere glaciations are the last one (called the Weichselian/Wisconsin glaciation, at its maximum about 20,000 years ago) and the one occurring prior to the last interglacial (called the Saalian/Illinoian glaciation, occurring prior to c.130,000 years ago). During the peak of both glaciations, ice sheets covered extensive areas north of 40–50° N in both Eurasia and North America. The Saalian glaciation was particularly extensive in the high Eurasian north, covering vast areas of northern Russia, the coastal Arctic Ocean, and Siberia.

The effects of the Quaternary climate oscillations were not only repeated expansion of glaciers at mid- and high latitudes, but midlatitude areas were repeatedly subject to cold climate and permafrost, forcing plant and animal populations to migrate or adapt to changed environmental conditions—or become extinct. At lower latitudes, forested areas, deserts, and savannahs shifted through several degrees of latitude as climate zones responded to higher-latitude cooling. Global patterns of wind and energy transfer by ocean currents changed, causing large-scale shifts in the pattern of aridity and precipitation around the world. Rates of weathering and erosion changed globally in response to changes in temperature and precipitation, and river regimes fluctuated considerably. During peak glaciations in the Eurasian north, the large rivers of northern Russia and Siberia entering the Arctic Ocean were dammed by the huge ice sheets and forced to flow southward. When huge volumes of water were trapped in ice sheets during peak glaciations, the global sea level fell up to 150 m. This caused vast continental shelf areas to become dry land, particularly the shallow shelf areas bordering the Arctic Ocean. Land bridges formed across sounds and between islands, in turn affecting ocean surface currents, shallow-sea life, and productivity and opening and closing routes of migration for plants and animals. The Bering land bridge, existing due to the lowering of sea level during the last glaciation, made possible the spread of humans from Asia to North America.

The frequent and rapid Quaternary environmental changes stimulated rapid evolution and the rise of large mammals, or megafauna. The Pleistocene megafauna included woolly rhinoceros, woolly mammoths, and large wolves that were well adapted to cold climates. The major type of ecosystem covering the European, Asian, and North American continents south of the ice sheets was a type of grass steppe that has been called the "mammoth steppe." It differed from the modern tundra environment in having a higher biomass, a much higher productivity, and a reduced snow cover in winter. The changing precipitation patterns at the end of the last glaciation probably caused the collapse of the mammoth steppe. Since many animals were dependent on the grass steppe, they became highly vulnerable to extinction when the ecosystem collapsed. This, together with hunting by humans, has probably been the root cause of many of the megafaunal extinctions at the end of the Pleistocene. The last mammoths, lingering on the Siberian islands, became extinct 4000 years ago. Other mammals that evolved during the Pleistocene, like the caribou, the muskox, and the polar bear, continue to be an important part of the Arctic fauna. It is also during the Pleistocene that humans evolved and developed the use of technology, language, art, and religion. Earliest signs of human occupation in the Russian Arctic are 30,000–40,000 years old. Much of the Arctic flora and fauna, including native peoples of the Arctic, have, however, migrated from lower latitudes to the Arctic latitudes during the past 10,000–15,000 years.

The repeated Northern Hemisphere Quaternary glaciations have left a complex of landforms, sediments, and landscapes that set the frame for mid-high latitude life and human activities. Human societies rely on natural resources that are products of the Pleistocene glaciations, such as sand and gravel deposits for construction activities, groundwater aquifers in ancient fluvial deltas, and fertile glacial till and outwash planes for forestry and agriculture. Large and rapid environmental changes define the Quaternary Period—most Quaternary scientists adopt the view that the present (Holocene) interval of relatively warm and stable climate at mid- and high Northern Hemisphere latitudes is, like previous interglacial periods, an exception in the overall cool to cold Quaternary climate—and there is every reason to expect the future to hold major environmental shifts in store.

ÓLAFUR INGÓLFSSON

See also **Beringia; Climate Change; Holocene; Ice Ages; Pleistocene Megafauna; Quaternary Paleogeography**

Further Reading

Dawson, A., *Ice Age Earth*, London and New York: Routledge, 1992

Lowe, J.J. & M.J.C. Walker, *Reconstructing Quaternary Environments* (2nd edition), Harlow: Addison Wesley Longman, 1997

Nilsson, T., *The Pleistocene*, Dordrecht and Boston: Reidel, 1983

Pavlov, P., J.I. Svendsen & S. Indrelid, "Human presence in the European Arctic nearly 40,000 years ago." *Nature*, 413 (2001): 64–67

Ward, P., *The Call of Distant Mammoths: Why the Ice Age Mammals Disappeared*, New York: Springer, 1997

Williams, M., D. Dunkerley, P. Decker, P. Kershaw & J. Chappell, *Quaternary Environments*, London: Arnold, 1998

Wilson, R.C.L., S.A. Drury & J.L. Chapman, *The Great Ice Age: Climate Change and Life*, London and New York: Routledge, 1999

QUÉBEC

Québec is the second largest province in Canada with a territory that represents 15.5% of the country's total area, which corresponds to 1.5 million km^2. Although the province of Québec is located outside of the Arctic Circle, its northern area Nunavik, inhabited by Inuit, is considered a part of the Arctic due to its *nordicity* as defined by Hamelin (1978, 2000). Hamelin introduced the concept of nordicity in order to best reflect the diversity of Nordic milieus. As Hamelin contends, nordicity is not only a question of latitude but can be best understood when applying a multidisciplinary perspective that includes climate as well as civilization and population facts. Following Hamelin, it can be said that several northern communities of Québec have a high Nordic index because of their isolation or because of the nature of the territory occupancy.

The majority of Québec's population live in the Saint Laurent (St Lawrence) valley, which runs in the southern part of the province, from the Great Lakes to the Gulf of St Laurent (Gulf of St Lawrence). Montreal, the largest city in Québec (comprised of over 3 million inhabitants when including the suburbs), is located in the southern region of the province not far from the United States Border. The city of Québec, founded by Champlain in 1608, is the capital of the province and is well renowned for its French architecture and way of life. French is the official language of the province and is spoken by a large majority of Québeckers. However, Montreal is also home to an important English community as well as many settled immigrants that give this city a cosmopolitan flavor, which contrasts French-Catholic rural Québec. There are also 11 Aboriginal Nations that also contribute to the ethnic and linguistic diversity of the province.

North of the St Laurent Valley lies the Laurentian Mountains and Canadian Shield. These areas are sparsely occupied and it is the forest, one of the province's most important natural resources, that mainly covers this large territory. North of the 55th parallel lies Nunavik, the Arctic area of Québec. Taiga and tundra mainly comprise its landscape. The Arctic tundra zone encompasses the territory from the 56th

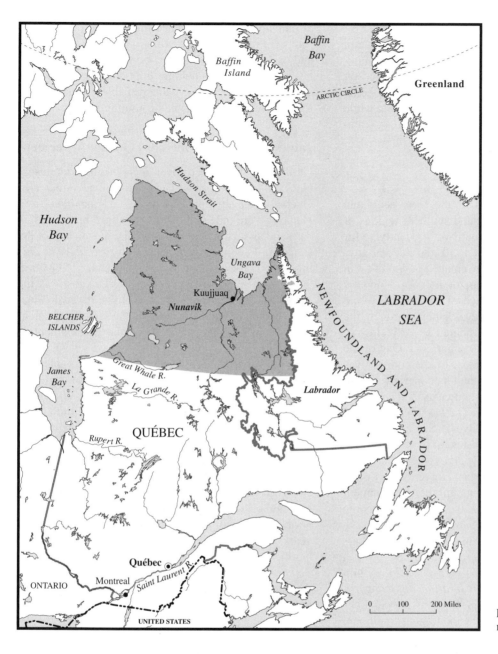

Province of Québec and its main towns and rivers.

parallel up to the northern region of the province. The area is mainly comprised of nonforested landscape: lichens and mosses mainly cover the ground. The taiga zone borders the southern limit of Nunavik. It is characterized by a lack of forest covering, although some vegetation such as spruce, fir, and dwarf shrub grow in some areas of the region. The Nunavik territory covers over 563,000[2], approximately the area of France or one-third the area of Québec (Québec, 1984: 151). It is the natural habitat of the polar bear, fox, Arctic hare, and caribou. Three herds of caribou inhabit Québec's Arctic. The George River herd is one of the largest herd of caribou in the world with 680,000 heads.

Historically, three Inuit groups inhabited Northern Québec: the Tarramiut (located in the northern area),

the Itvimiut (who occupied the Belcher Islands and coastal area of Hudson Bay), and the Siqinirmiut (located in the Ungava Bay area). These three groups were hunter-gatherer family clans. It was only in the 19th century that Europeans (mainly traders of the Hudson's Bay Company followed by missionaries) established significant relations with the First Peoples of Nunavik. Up until the 1950s, the primary governing agency in the region was the Canadian Federal government. Although the provincial boundaries were extended northward to include the Nunavik region as a result of the 1912 Québec Boundaries Extension Act, it was not until the 1960s that the Québec provincial government made its presence known by providing its own health and education services to Nunavik residents.

As of today, approximately 9000 Inuit are distributed among 14 villages along the coastline (Hamelin 2000). Kuujjuarapik, Umiujaq, Inukjuak, Povungnituk, and Akulivik are located on the East Coast of Hudson Bay. The southern shore of the Hudson Strait is home to Ivujivik, Salluit, Kangiqsujuaq, and Quaqtaq, while Kangirsuk, Aupaluk, Tasiujaq, Kuujjuaq, and Kangiqsualujjuaq lie in the area along the Ungava Bay.

Northern Economy

Due to the distinct isolation of the area, economic exchanges between the north and southern regions of the province were restricted, until very recently, to fur trade activities. At the end of 1950, the Federal government encouraged Inuit to create cooperatives in order to make the Inuit a part of modern economic activities. Inuit took advantage of this initiative and organized their economic development through the cooperatives, which they considered as very close to their tradition of sharing and cooperation. One of the major factors in the development of the cooperatives came in 1967, when the first Inuit's cooperatives were incorporated into a federation known as the *Federation des cooperatives du Nouveau Québec* (Federation of Northern Québec's Cooperatives). Since that time, cooperatives have been established in most Inuit communities, and the cooperative movement has been credited as the most important force in terms of involving the local inhabitants in the development of their communities. In 1967, the total gross income of the *Fédération des coopératives du Nouveau-Québec* was 1 million Canadian dollars. Twenty years later (1987), that total increased to 20 million Canadian dollars and eventually reached 31 million Canadian dollars in 1998 (*Fédération des coopératives du Nouveau-Québec*, 1999). The cooperatives secured their development by encouraging traditional activities such as carving and other craft activities. Since 1980, these cooperatives have begun to diversify their activities and have thus encouraged the development of new industries such as tourism. In 1998–1999, Inuit from Nunavik received over 7.5 million Canadian dollars from these cooperatives in wages, returns, and purchases of crafts.

It is estimated that about 85–90% of the total Nunavik economy is directly dependent on government programs (Simmard et al., 1996). Despite the influx of money from the state, the monetary revenues of the Inuit are still below the national average. In 1991, the per capita income for Nunavik's Inuit was $15,765, whereas in the same year the per capita income for southern residents was approximately $21,511 (Robichaud et al., 1998). Nevertheless, Inuit still gain some nonmonetary revenues stemming from traditional pursuits. In 1983, Québec implemented the Hunter Support Program, whose primary focus was to support and sustain the traditional economy. This program has been instrumental in helping Inuit communities secure a supply of game that is made available, free of charge, to all members of Nunavik's communities.

James Bay and the Northern Québec Agreement

Until 1970, the Québec government had little interest in Nunavik and its citizens. The provincial government of Québec even attempted to prove that the Inuit from Nunavik were indeed Indians (as defined by the Indian Act) and as such would fall under the jurisdiction of the Canadian Federal government. However, in 1970 during the oil crisis, Robert Bourassa, premier of Québec, launched a major hydroelectric project known as the James Bay project that sought to utilize the hydroelectric potential of the major rivers of the James Bay catchment basin. The project included the development of three different complexes composed of several dams and reservoirs. The construction of the first complex, La Grande, on the river bearing the same name started in 1971 without any consultation with the aboriginal groups of the area, namely the Cree, Inuit, and Naskapis. However, following the announcement of the hydroelectric project, the native people stated a legal claim to the territorial rights of the land. On November 19, 1973, the Québec Supreme Court confirmed the existence of native rights to the land, thus forcing political authorities to negotiate with the inhabitants of northern Québec. On November 11, 1975, after two years of intense negotiations, the James Bay and Northern Québec Agreement (JBNQA) was signed.

The JBNQA defines the land regime applicable to the Cree and the Inuit and also recognizes their rights in matters such as resource management, economic development, policing and the administration of justice, health and social services, and environmental protection. The agreement covers an area of 410,000 square miles. The terms of the agreement specify that 1% of the area is the sole property of native peoples, 12% of the area is public property but is reserved for native people's traditional activities such as hunting, fishing, and trapping, and 87% of the area is public property and is open for economic development. The agreement essentially structured the area of Arctic Québec by setting up a series of new public institutions such as the Makivik Corporation, which was created with the mandate of preserving the integrity of the agreement, maintaining the implementation of the agreement, and managing the 90 million Canadian dollars allocated to the Inuit in exchange for their rights to the land. The JBNQA also created the Kativik Regional Government, which is a supramunicipal government.

With the JBNQA, the Inuit never truly did obtain their own regional government. Nevertheless, based on the JBNQA, Québec and Ottawa have transferred most of the administration of public institutions to the Inuit such as health education and police.

Since Québec is interested in the development of the northern natural resources, its relationship with the Inuit population has greatly evolved. Presently, Québec is no longer reluctant to provide services to aboriginal people living in Nunavik and is currently offering a wide variety of services to the Inuit. However, the Federal government remains fairly involved in the area and thus still maintains some administrative presence. In fact, this has led to competition between the two levels of government (Duhaime, 1985) that, as a result, has contributed to the creation of several employment opportunities for the Inuit. Also, in an attempt to create bridges between the northern aboriginal communities that speak English (although Inuktitut is still the first language of the majority of the Inuit) and the French-speaking population of the South, Québec now offers two school curriculums—one in French and one in English—and students choose to be enrolled in the program they prefer. Nevertheless, the Inuit population as well as the majority of the Aboriginal Nations of Québec remain very concerned with the possibility of Québec's sovereignty, as they wish to remain in Canada in the event that Québec decides to become an independent state.

Toward a Governmental Autonomy

The idea of having political and administrative autonomy for the Inuit of Nunavik was first formulated by the leaders of the cooperative movement. However, their quest for autonomy was in fact interrupted by the implementation of the JBNQA. Notwithstanding, in 1983 the leaders of the new institutions and political bodies created by the JBNQA resumed the quest for autonomy for the people of Nunavik. In 1996, following the Royal Commission of Aboriginal People (Canada, 1996), the Canadian government recognized the governmental autonomy rights of Aboriginal people, and in 1999 the Nunavik commission was created with the purpose of proposing a structure for Nunavik's government. The recommendations of the commission were published in March 2001 and proposed an agenda for the implementation of the forthcoming Nunavik's government. It is anticipated that the transfer of appropriate powers from Québec and Ottawa will begin in 2003.

THIBAULT MARTIN

See also **Canada; James Bay and the Northern Québec Agreement; Nunavik**

Further Reading

Canada Royal Commission on Aboriginal Peoples, *Report of the Royal Commission on Aboriginal Peoples*, Ottawa: Communication Group Publishing, 1996

Dorais, Louis-Jacques, *Quaqtaq. Modernity and Identity in an Inuit Community*, Toronto: University of Toronto Press, 1997

Duhaime, Gérard, *De l'igloo au H.L.M. Les Inuit sédentaires et l'État providence*, Québec: Centre d'Études Nordiques, Collection Nordicana, Université Laval, 1985

———, (editor), *Atlas Historique du Québec. Le Nord: habitants et mutations*, Québec: Presses de l'Université Laval, 2000

Fédérations des Coopératives du Nouveau-Québec, *Growing with Co-ops*, Baie d'Urfé, Fédérations des coopératives du Nouveau-Québec, 1999

Hamelin, Louis-Edmond, *Canadian Nordicity: It's Your North Too*, translated by William Barr, Montréal: Harvest House, 1978

———, *Le Québec par des mots*, Québec: Centre international de recherche en aménagement linguistique, 2000

Jacquoud, Mylène, *Justice Blanche au Nunavik*, Montréal: Éditions du Méridien, 1995

Québec, *La Convention de la Baie James et du Nord québécois*, Québec: Éditeur officiel du Québec, 1976

———, *Le Nord du Québec. Profil régional*, Québec: Direction générale des publications gouvernementales du ministère des Communications et Service des communications de l'office de planification et de développement du Québec, 1984

Robichaud, Véronique, Pierre Fréchette & Gérard Duhaime, *The 1991 Social Accounting Matrix for the Nunavik Regional Economy*, Québec: GÉTIC (Université Laval), 1998

Saladin d'Anglure, Bernard, "Contemporary Inuit of Québec." In *Handbook of North American Indians, Volume 5, Arctic*, edited by D. Damas, Washington: Smithsonian Institute, 1984, pp. 683–688

Simard, Jean-Jacques, "La coopération au Nouveau-Québec Inuit: Alternative au contre-développement." In *L'avenir du Nord québécois/The Future of Northern Québec*, edited by L.-E. Hamelin & M. Potvin, Québec: Les Presses de l'Université du Québec, 1989, pp. 122–123

Simmard, Jean-Jacques et al., *Tendances nordiques. Les changements sociaux 1970–1990 chez les Cris et les Inuit du Québec. Une enquête statistique exploratoire*, Québec: GÉTIC (Université Laval), 1996

The Canadian Encyclopedia, *The Canadian Encyclopedia Year 2000 Edition*, Toronto: McClelland and Stewart Inc., The Canadian Publishers, 2000

QUEEN ELIZABETH ISLANDS

The Queen Elizabeth Islands in Nunavut, Canada, comprise a triangular archipelago north of Lancaster Sound, west of Greenland, and washed by the Beaufort Sea in the west. The main islands include Ellesmere at the northern apex, and Devon, Cornwallis, Bathurst, Melville, and Prince Patrick Islands across the base. Within the archipelago, the smaller islands of the Svedrup group in the north and the Parry Islands to the southwest are found. The total area of the archipelago is about 425,000 km², of which one-fifth is ice covered.

Geologically, the islands are mostly composed of Cambrian to Upper Devonian rocks that are highly folded. Much of the topography of the eastern islands is mountainous, with land rising to 2000 m. Spectacular cliffs are located around Devon, Ellesmere, and Axel Heiberg Islands. To the west, the landscape is flatter and rolling peneplain, characterized by horizontally bedded sedimentary rocks. Interesting fossil forests of Eocene age (45 million years) have been found on Axel Heiberg and Ellesmere Islands and other fossil beds.

Exploration of the Queen Elizabeth Islands has been recent, although William Baffin may have sighted them as early as 1616. John Ross and William Parry confirmed the island's existence in the early 19th century. Many famous expeditions in search of the North West Passage and the North Pole ventured into the region. Nevertheless, Vilhjalmur Stefansson discovered the last of the islands only in 1916–1917. After World War II, meteorological and radar stations were established for purposes of North American defense and Canadian sovereignty. Since then, mineral exploration and mining has taken place, and tourism started with the establishment of Quttinirpaaq National Park Preserve, based at Tanquary Fjord on northern Ellesmere Island, in 1988.

The vegetation on Queen Elizabeth Islands is depauperate and characteristically a polar desert flora, with meadow oases along watercourses, around ponds and lakes, and in flat, poorly drained areas. Precipitation is at most a few centimeters per year, mostly as snow. The summer climate varies from relatively warm and sunny (50–60 frost-free days) in a band from Pearyland in Greenland, across the Lake Hazen area of Ellesmere Island, southwest to southern Axel Heiberg Island to the harshest in the Arctic in the western part of the Svedrup group (the bleakest barren lands).

Peary's caribou and muskoxen comprise small populations of large herbivores. Arctic hares and lemmings have periodically abundant populations. Mammalian predators on the islands include Arctic wolves, foxes, and least weasels. The avifauna comprises several passerines and shore birds, but populations of seabirds, as of marine mammals, are high in some places. Gyre falcons and snowy owls are the main raptors. Ptarmigan may be abundant from time to time. The insect fauna is scant, but two species of bumblebee (*Bombus* spp.) range to the northernmost land.

Human settlement dates back about 4000 years, with periodic human occupation by Dorset and Thule cultures to about AD 1350. The islands were uninhabited thereafter until recently, with the establishment of the Inuit communities at Grise Fjord (1953) and Resolute (1955), apart from joint Canadian-US weather and radar stations and teams of explorers. The Queen Elizabeth Islands were named in 1953.

PETER G. KEVAN

See also **Axel Heiberg Island; Bathurst Island; Beaufort Sea; Cornwall Island; Cornwallis Island; Devon Island; Ellesmere Island; Lancaster Sound; Melville Island; Nunavut; Prince Patrick Island**

Further Reading

Harington, C. Richard (editor), *Canada's Missing Dimension: Science and History in the Canadian Arctic Islands*, Ottawa: Canadian Museum of Nature, 1990

Hodgson, D.A., "Quaternary Geology of the Queen Elizabeth Islands." In *Quaternary Geology of Canada and Greenland*, edited by R.F. Fulton, Ottawa: Canadian Government Publishing Center, 1989

Taylor, Andrew, *Geographical Discovery and Exploration in the Queen Elizabeth Islands*, Ottawa: Department of Mines and Technical Surveys, 1955

QUMAQ, TAAMUSI

Taamusi Qumaq was a prominent figure among 20th-century Arctic Québec Inuit, having played a crucial role in the social, political, and cultural development of the region. Born in 1914 at Natsiturlik ("Place with many seals"), an island north of Inukjuak, on the east coast of Hudson Bay, Qumaq was immediately adopted by his paternal grandparents, according to Inuit custom. When both grandparents died at a short interval a few years later, Qumaq went back to live with his biological parents. He soon started following his father to the hunting grounds, thus learning the first rudiments of traditional subsistence techniques. His mother taught him to read and write Inuktitut in the syllabic characters that had been introduced by missionaries to the Canadian eastern Arctic, some 45 years earlier. One of Qumaq's first recollections was when his mother played the part of Nanook's wife in Robert Flaherty's movie *Nanook of the North*, which was shot near Inukjuak in 1920.

Qumaq's father drowned when he was 13, leaving his mother with five young children and no support, because Qumaq was not old enough to act as provider for the family. He was permitted, though, to follow his campmates on hunting expeditions, thus completing his learning experience the hard way, bringing home whatever food hunters were willing to share with him and his family. This may partly explain why Qumaq, although later able to support a family of his own through hunting and trapping (he got married in 1937 and fathered or adopted seven children), was never considered an *angusuqtuq*, a great hunter. To supplement his income, he did some soapstone carving and took odd jobs with the Hudson's Bay Company—transporting mail by dog team, stocking the store shelves—whenever the occasion arose. He and his family settled in Puvirnituq (formerly Povungnituk), on the Québec (eastern) coast of Hudson Bay, in the early 1950s.

Qumaq never went to school, because none existed in his time. He only spoke Inuktitut, although he understood some English, learned through his contacts with Hudson's Bay Company personnel. This did not prevent him from becoming actively involved in the development of modern Inuit organizations. When the Puvirnituq hunters, trappers, and carvers cooperative was established in 1959, he left the Hudson's Bay Company to become one of its cofounders, sitting for several years on its board of directors. Qumaq was also active in the establishment of the Federation of Arctic Québec Co-operatives, the community council of Puvirnituq (which he chaired for some time), and the Saputik Museum of Puvirnituq. Politically conscious, he deemed that Inuit should enjoy the highest possible degree of economic and political autonomy if they wanted to be masters on their own land. Accordingly, he fought for Inuit rights and had a part to play in the discussions leading to the James Bay and Northern Québec Agreement (1975), and to its rejection by the Puvirnituq and Ivujivik Inuit (on the ground that land cannot be alienated). Qumaq served on the board of Inuit Tunngavingat Nunaminiit (ITN), the organization opposed to the Agreement, and, later, on Nunavik's Inuit Justice Task Force and Avataq Elders Conference.

Rather late in life, Qumaq realized that he should do something concrete for the survival of Inuit language and culture, which he perceived as rapidly eroding among younger generations. In 1976–1977, he wrote an encyclopedia of traditional Inuit life, which was published in 1988 (in Inuktitut syllabic characters) under the title *Sivulitta Piusituqangit* ("The long-standing customs of our ancestors"). In 1978, he set himself the task of compiling an Inuktitut dictionary of definitions, something that had never been done before. Writing down, by hand, every word he knew, he devised for each of them a short definition in Inuktitut. This took him about seven years—during which he received financial support from the government. He ended up with a monumental manuscript of some 30,000 entries (including many derivatives of the same word-bases), classified in the syllabic order. The dictionary, titled *Inuit Uqausillaringit* ("The real Inuit words"), appeared in early 1991. Both of Qumaq's books are widely used in Nunavik (Arctic Québec) schools.

Besides these major works, Qumaq authored several articles on various aspects of traditional life (e.g., survival skills, animal anatomy), which appeared in *Tumivut*, the cultural magazine of the Nunavik Inuit. He also wrote on the political and cultural future of the Inuit. Most of these texts have been translated into English and French. On his death, in Puvirnituq on July 13, 1993, Qumaq left two manuscripts: an autobiography (excerpts of which were later published in *Tumivut*) and an exhaustive compilation of body parts terminology in Inuktitut.

Taamusi Qumaq was concerned with the dual necessity of preserving his native language—for several years, he had a program on Canadian Broadcasting Corporation's Arctic Québec radio network, where he discussed rarely used traditional Inuktitut words—and explaining to non-Inuit that cultural and linguistic survival is essential to aboriginal peoples. His achievements were publicly recognized when he was awarded the Order of Québec (1989), Canada's Award for Northern Research (1991), the Order of Canada (1993), and an Honourable Citation from Université du Québec (1993).

Taamusi Qumaq has had, and continues to have, a strong influence on Nunavik students, intellectuals, and cultural activists. His books and articles are frequently used, and he is often cited as a person with a well-defined vision about the economic, political, and cultural future of the Inuit. He serves as an example for other elderly and middle-aged Inuit from Nunavik and Nunavut, who have already completed, or are still working on, encyclopedic or lexicographical compilations dealing with their aboriginal culture and language. Qumaq also serves as an example of a monolingual self-taught person who always had a keen interest in learning about what was going on in the rest of the world, listening religiously to radio news broadcasts, trying, with his very limited passive knowledge of English, to understand what was happening elsewhere on earth. Finally, he left professional anthropologists and linguists with an important corpus of "naive" (i.e., produced by an unschooled native speaker) Inuit texts, and his people are indebted to him for these precious tools toward cultural and linguistic survival.

Biography

Taamusi Qumaq was born in January 1914 on the island of Nunaturlik, in eastern Hudson Bay, off the coast of Arctic Québec near Inukjuak. He was the son of Juusua Nuvalinngaq and Aalasi Qingalik. In 1937, he married Maina Milurtuq, with whom he raised seven children. Never formally schooled, Qumaq learned to hunt and trap with his father and campmates, and was taught by his mother to read and write Inuktitut in syllabic characters. After having settled in Puvirnituq, Nunavik (Arctic Québec), in the early 1950s, he became actively involved in the cooperative movement, as well as in various political, social, and cultural organizations. From the mid-1970s, Qumaq started to write extensively—in Inuktitut—on Inuit culture and language, publishing an encyclopedia (*Inuit Piusituqangit*, 1988), a dictionary of definitions (*Inuit Uqausillaringit*, 1991), and several articles on culture and society, some of them published posthumously. He died in Puvirnituq on July 13, 1993.

LOUIS-JACQUES DORAIS

Further Reading

Avataq Cultural Institute, "Taamusi Aulajiniq. In Memory of Taamusi. À la mémoire de Taamusi." *Tumivut*, 5 (1994): 12

Dorais, Louis-Jacques, "Taamusi Qumaq (1914–1993)." *Études/Inuit/Studies*, 17(1) (1993): 137–138

Qumaq, Taamusi, *Sivulitta Piusituqangit*, Québec: Association Inuksiutiit Katimajiit (Inuksiutiit Allaniagait 5), 1988

———, *Inuit Uqausillaringit*, Québec: Association Inuksiutiit Katimajiit and Montreal: Avataq Cultural Institute, 1991

———, "Taamusi Qumaup Inuusirisimajangata Unikkaangit. The Autobiography of Taamusi Qumaq. L'autobiographie de Taamusi Qumaq." *Tumivut*, 6 (1995): 35–52; 7 (1995): 53–73; 8 (1996): 62–79; 9 (1997): 61–78; 10 (1998): 43–59

———, "The Future of Inuktitut." In *Québec's Aboriginal Languages. History, Planning, Development*, edited by Jacques Maurais, Clevedon: Multilingual Matters, 1996

Therrien, Michèle, "Corps sain, corps malade chez les Inuit, une tension entre l'intérieur et l'extérieur, entretiens avec Taamusi Qumaq." *Recherches amérindiennes au Québec*, 25(1) (1995): 71–84

R

RACE TO THE NORTH POLE

Few episodes of discovery have so captivated explorers and armchair travelers alike as the Race to the North Pole. While it eventually came to be characterized as a "race," the search for the North Pole developed fitfully over several centuries, during which it periodically attracted the attention of various interests, whether commercial, national, or individual. For 19th-century exploring nations such as Great Britain or the United States, North Polar expeditions played an important role in forging support for their leaders' expansionist policies. The heyday of High Arctic exploration also coincided with the great expansion of the popular press in the 19th century and its capacity to generate enormous public interest and support for polar excursions. By 1900, the race assumed the character of an athletic contest, as competitors pitted themselves against the Arctic wilderness in a contest for rewards and honors.

Initially, the polar quest emerged out of another long-standing preoccupation of European commercial interests, the search for a North West Passage to the Orient. In 1527, the Bristol merchant Robert Thorne proposed a northern route to Asia via the North Pole. In the 1590s, the Dutch mariner Willem Barents made two attempts to reach the Pole via the Barents Sea north of Russia, attaining a farthest north of 79°49′ N. In the late 16th and early 17th centuries, a series of British explorers, most notably Martin Frobisher (1576), John Davis (1585), and William Baffin and Robert Bylot (1615, 1616), staged voyages in search of the North West Passage via Davis Strait. On their second voyage in 1616, Baffin and Bylot reached the northern parts of Baffin Bay to 78° N, as they sailed to the entrance to Smith Sound.

Interest in the North Pole waned for almost two centuries. However, in the 1770s, the Englishman Daines Barrington advanced the theory of an "open polar sea" around the Pole, which presumed clear sailing beyond a presumed barrier of pack ice around 80° N. He persuaded the Council of the Royal Society to sponsor an expedition to determine the feasibility of sailing to the North Pole via Svalbard (Spitsbergen). Accordingly, in 1773, Captain John Phipps of the British Royal Navy led an expedition of two ships toward the Pole, but was stopped by the ice around 80°37′ N.

Following the Napoleonic Wars, Britain emerged as the preeminent naval and commercial power in the world. Unleashed British expansionism contributed to a renewed focus on the search for a North West Passage via the North Pole to markets in Asia. Led by Sir John Barrow, First Secretary of the Admiralty after 1804, the Royal Navy embarked on an ambitious program of exploration in the Arctic Archipelago, beginning with the voyage of John Ross in 1818.

By mid-century, a major competitor emerged in the United States, whose aggressive expansion across the North American continent was already well under way. By then, the focus of Arctic exploration had shifted from the North West Passage to a straightforward competition to be the first to reach the North Pole. For the United States, the quest for the Pole offered an opportunity to continue its own imperial expansion; specifically, it also hoped to find new whaling grounds.

The race began in earnest in the 1850s with a voyage led by British Commander Edward Inglefield in the *Isabel* to northern Baffin Bay. Inglefield demonstrated both the existence of a saltwater channel beyond Smith Sound and the possibility of navigating through the ice congestion in southern Kane Basin. He reached a north latitude of 78°28′21″, surpassing by 210 km the farthest north attained by previous sailings to Baffin Bay.

In 1853, alarmed that the British might return and reach the presumed open polar sea, American Elisha Kent Kane sailed to northern Greenland to try to get there first. He sent two sledge parties to the north in the spring of 1854. On the first excursion, Dr. Isaac Israel Hayes and William Godfrey crossed the pack ice of Smith Sound and traveled along Ellesmere Island's eastern coast to 79°42′9″ N. On the other notable sledge journey, William Morton, West Greenlander Hans Hendrik, and two other Americans sledged up the Greenland coast as far as Cape Constitution.

Kane's stirring narratives inspired a generation of American explorers and fueled public support in the United States for continuing the polar quest. In 1860, Isaac Israel Hayes, who had served with Kane, organized his own private expedition to continue the search for the presumed open polar sea and the North Pole. Setting up wintering quarters in northern Greenland, he undertook a sledging excursion along the Greenland coast in April 1861, before crossing the pack ice to Ellesmere Island and proceeding up the coast, probably only to 81°35′ N.

By the 1860s, the revival of American expansionist sentiment after the Civil War provided a favorable ideological climate for continued Arctic exploration. In 1871, with the support of President Grant and the Congress, Charles Francis Hall sailed north in the *Polaris* with instructions from the US Navy to reach the North Pole. He arrived at the Lincoln Sea on the edge of the Arctic Ocean by August 30, attaining 81°35′ N before being stopped by the pack ice. Forced to establish wintering quarters in northern Greenland, Hall died within two months. Part of his party subsequently survived a dramatic drift to the south while marooned on an ice-floe.

In response to Hall's foray, the British Admiralty promoted staging one further Arctic expedition by the mid-1870s. Concerned about the extension of American influence in the region, the British government instructed Captain George S. Nares to lead a naval party to be the first to reach the North Pole. In 1875, the expedition's two ships, HMS *Alert* and HMS *Discovery*, set up wintering quarters at Lady Franklin Bay and at Floeberg Beach on the Arctic Ocean. In the spring of 1876, Nares sent man-hauling sledging parties out from both ships. The party under Commander Albert Markham struck out across the polar ice pack toward the North Pole. Although they set a new farthest north at 83°20′26″ N, Markham's crew and the members of the other sledging parties developed scurvy, precipitating the premature return of the expedition to England.

In 1881, the Signal Office of the United States Army sent its own military expedition to northern Ellesmere Island, officially for science but with under-

lying motives of taking away the prize of the North Pole. This party of 23 Army members and two West Greenlanders established their headquarters at Fort Conger, northern Ellesmere Island off Lady Franklin Bay in August 1881. In April 1882, Lieutenant James Lockwood and ten others sledged to northern Greenland and reached 83°23′8″ N. Lieutenant Adolphus Greely's party remained at Fort Conger until August 1883, when, owing to the failure of resupply vessels to reach northern Ellesmere Island, he ordered a general retreat. Most members of the party died of starvation, exposure, or frostbite while stranded at Camp Clay on Bedford Pim Island in Smith Sound.

North Polar exploration ceased for a decade after the Greely disaster, but was renewed through a developing rivalry between Norway and the United States. In 1893–1896, the Norwegian explorer Fridtjof Nansen drifted in his vessel *Fram* in an attempt to reach the North Pole. The Norwegian government then sent Otto Sverdup to the North American High Arctic, unofficially, to claim the North Pole. In 1898, Sverdup attempted to sail along Ellesmere Island's east coast before being stopped by pack ice off Cape Sabine, just north of Smith Sound. Around the same time, the Swedish engineer Salomon August Andrée and two colleagues undertook a dangerous flight toward the Pole via hydrogen balloon. These adventurers disappeared over the pack ice north of Svalbard, Norway. Their remains were eventually discovered on a remote island in 1930.

The Race to the Pole via surface travel culminated in a series of expeditions by Robert E. Peary (1898–1902, 1905–1906, and 1908–1909) and Frederick Cook (1907–1908). The first of Peary's North Pole expeditions was hastened by the announcement of plans for Sverdup's voyage. Peary spent the next four years developing a base of operations on Ellesmere Island and northern Greenland and in perfecting his method of "living off the country." In the spring of 1902, he made an attempt on the North Pole, reaching 84°17′27″.

For his next expeditions, in 1905–1906 and 1908–1909, Peary commissioned the design of a steam ship, the *Roosevelt*, to deliver his party to the edge of the Arctic Ocean. Peary relied on Inughuit from northwestern Greenland for the lion's share of labor on these expeditions. From base camps on the northern coast of Ellesmere Island, he used relay teams to advance men and materiel across the polar ice cap, a practice he later perfected on his last expedition in 1908–1909. In 1906, Peary was obliged to turn back at 87°6′ N, but on his last expedition, in April 1909, he claimed to have reached 89°57′, that is, the North Pole. For his part, Cook claimed to have reached the Pole a year earlier by traveling from northern Greenland, across Ellesmere Island, along Eureka Sound to northern Axel Heiberg Island, and thence across the pack ice toward the Pole. The exploration community was soon consumed by a protracted debate between supporters of Peary and Cook, a public relations battle in which Peary emerged the victor, after which interest in the North Pole as a geographical milestone began to wane.

In the same year as Peary's final surface attempt, Walter Wellman, an American journalist, attempted to reach the North Pole in a hydrogen-filled dirigible. Wellman was forced back after flying 50 km over the polar ice pack, but his and Andrée's failed attempts at polar aviation initiated what would become a major preoccupation in the future. By the 1920s, further advances in the technology of fixed wing aircraft set the stage for renewed efforts to reach the Pole by air. In 1925, the American Richard Byrd attempted to fly to the North Pole, using Etah, northern Greenland as a base. The following year, learning of the Norwegian Roald Amundsen's impending flight in a dirigible, Byrd again flew toward the North Pole on May 9, 1926, although some have doubted that he reached his destination. Then, between May 11 and 13, 1926, Amundsen and Lincoln Ellsworth flew in their airship from Svalbard to Alaska via the North Pole. In 1928, the British aviator George Hubert Wilkins completed the first flight across the Arctic Ocean via the Pole, traveling between Alaska and Svalbard.

The major national and individual goals of polar exploration having been achieved, continued activity in the area around the North Pole was largely driven by scientific and, later, military imperatives. In 1937–1938, a Soviet party led by Ivan Papanin wintered on an ice-floe near the North Pole and drifted with the current for 274 days, during which they collected hydrological, meteorological, and magnetic data. In 1958, the *Nautilus*, an atomic-powered submarine of the US Navy, became the first vessel to reach the North Pole under water, and its counterpart the *Skate* succeeded in surfacing at the Pole in 1960. In 1977, the Soviet nuclear icebreaker *Arktika* became the first surface ship to reach the North Pole. Submarine activity by the nuclear superpowers continued in this area at least until the end of the Cold War, c.1990.

Since the 1960s, a large number of adventurers caught the polar fever and staged attempts to be the first to reach the North Pole by distinctive techniques, with varying degrees of success. Among the more notable explorers were Ralph Plaisted, who traveled to the Pole by snowmobile in 1968, Wally Herbert of Great Britain, who used dogs with air support to traverse the Arctic Ocean via the Pole in 1968–1969, and the Americans Will Steger and Paul Schurke, who traveled to the Pole by dogsled without resupply in

1986. Although the North Pole no longer holds geopolitical or strategic significance, a spirit of adventure and pitting oneself against great physical odds is still at play.

LYLE DICK

See also **Cook, Frederick A.; Exploration of the Arctic; North Pole; Peary, Robert E.**

Further Reading

Dick, Lyle, *Muskox Land: Ellesmere Island in the Age of Contact*, Calgary, Alberta: University of Calgary Press, 2001

Fogelson, Nancy, *Arctic Exploration and International Relations, 1900–1932*, Fairbanks: University of Alaska Press, 1992

Great Britain, Admiralty, *Journals and Proceedings of the Arctic Expedition, 1875–6, Under the Command of Captain Sir George S. Nares*, Parliamentary Paper C-1636, London: Harrison & Sons, Queen's Printer, 1877

Hayes, J. Gordon, *The Conquest of the North Pole: Recent Arctic Exploration*, London: Thornton Butterworth Ltd., 1934

Herbert, Wally, *The Noose of Laurels: The Discovery of the North Pole*, London, Sydney, Aukland, and Toronto: Hodder and Stoughton, 1989

Holland, Clive, *Arctic Exploration and Development, c. 500 BC to 1915*, New York and London: Garland Publishing Inc., 1994

Kane, Elisha Kent, *Arctic Explorations: The Second Grinnell Expedition in Search of Sir John Franklin, 1853, '54, '55*, Volumes I and II, Philadelphia: Childs and Peterson, 1856

MacMillan, Donald B., *How Peary Reached the Pole: The Personal Story of His Assistant*, Boston and New York: Houghton Mifflin, 1934

Markham, Clements, *The Lands of Silence: A History of Arctic and Antarctic Exploration*, Cambridge, England: Cambridge University Press, 1921

Maxtone-Graham, John, *Safe Return Doubtful: The Heroic Age of Polar Exploration*, New York: Charles Scribner's Sons, 1988

Peary, Robert E., *Secrets of Polar Travel*, New York: The Century Company, 1917

Rawlins, Dennis, *Peary at the North Pole: Fact or Fiction?*, Washington/New York: Robert B. Luce Inc., 1973

Vaughan, Richard, *The Arctic: A History*, Dover, New Hampshire: Alan Sutton Publishing, 1994

Weems, John Edward, *Race for the Pole*, New York: Henry Holt and Company, 1960

RADIO GREENLAND (KNR)

Radio Greenland (*Kalaallit Nunaata Radioa*, or KNR) is Greenland's primary media outlet. Its headquarters are in the capital city of Nuuk, and it maintains news departments in Nuuk, North Greenland, South Greenland, and Copenhagen. KNR transmits daily broadcasts throughout Greenland and produces a daily radio newscast for Greenlanders living in Denmark, transmitted from a station in Copenhagen. Its television service is linked to Danmarks Radio (DR)—Danish public radio—which distributes its newscasts throughout Greenland via satellite.

An independent public body administered by the Government of Greenland, KNR is financed by both private and public sources—primarily by advertisers and sponsors in the first instance and, in the second, by government contributions from the national treasury. It employs approximately 120 people, headed by a seven-person board of directors and a management committee that oversees daily programming and administration. KNR-TV produces about 300 h of Greenlandic and about 2000 h of Danish programming a year.

In 1980, KNR became one of the first institutions to come under the control of Greenland Home Rule jurisdiction. The station emerged in the midst of a cultural revival that included much of the music broadcast on its radio outlet. Greenland's singer-songwriters were among the first to write and record in their own language and have since influenced indigenous musicians worldwide. Of the approximately 5400 h of annual broadcasting, some 2200 h are devoted to music, supported by Greenland's strong and rapidly expanding music recording industry. In addition to music broadcasts, KNR's radio and television outlets feature a wide range of regional, national, and international entertainment, news, public affairs, and cultural and youth programming.

In its early days, Greenlandic broadcasting was dominated by Danish programming and people. Starting in the 1950s, radio programs became available in both Greenlandic and Danish, and Greenlandic voices featured increasingly on the broadcasts. As Hans Lynge has noted, radio broadcasts soon became "as necessary a part of life as food" (Alia, 1999: 94). In 1978—a year before the official inauguration of Greenland Home Rule and the same year Canada launched Project Inukshuk, sending satellite-delivered, Inuit-produced television and radio broadcasts to communities in the Canadian eastern Arctic— *Kalaallit Nunaata Radioa* (KNR) became an associate member of the European Broadcasting Union. One of the outcomes was to legitimize indigenous Greenlandic radio and television in the eyes of European broadcasters. KNR moved quickly to extend its international ties, establishing exchange programs with Faroe Islands Radio, Radio Iceland, and Canadian Broadcasting Corporation (CBC) Northern Service.

With a goal of eventually producing virtually all of its programming in Greenlandic, the number of Greenlandic-language radio and television programs is steadily increasing. Although KNR is Greenland's primary broadcaster, Greenland also has several privately owned radio and television stations. KNR's managing director, Peter Frederik Rosing, is one of the two Greenlandic representatives to the Inuit Circumpolar Conference (ICC) Communications Commission, established in 1998 to represent Inuit communications internationally.

VALERIE ALIA

See also **Greenland Home Rule Act; Media**

Further Reading

Alia, Valerie, *Un/Covering the North: News, Media, and Aboriginal People*, Vancouver: UBC Press, 1999
KNR-website: http://www.knr.gl/English.htm
Stenbaek, Marianne, "The politics of cultural survival: towards a model of indigenous television." *American Review of Canadian Studies*, 18 (autumn 1988): 331–340
Stenbaek-Lafon, Marianne, "Kalaallit-Nunaata Radioa: to be master of one's own media is to be master of one's own fate." *Etudes/Inuit/Studies*, 6(1) (1982): 39–48

RADIOACTIVITY

In 1896, Henri Becquerel discovered the emission of penetrating rays from uranium compounds. This process was coined "radioactivity" by Marie and Pierre Curie in 1898. In 1899, Ernest Rutherford distinguished differing types of penetrating radiation: alpha and beta radiation. In 1900, the most penetrating type of radiation, gamma radiation, was identified by Paul Villard. In 1934, the Curies (Frederic and Irene Joliot-Curie) discovered the first example of artificial radiation.

Radioactivity is the spontaneous decay of the nuclei of particular radioactive atoms (radioisotopes). Nuclei exhibiting radioactivity are unstable and in a continual process of gradual breakdown (i.e., disintegration), which is referred to as radioactive decay. The effect of radioactivity is to produce a more stable state. The decay is most commonly of three main types, alpha, beta, and gamma radiation, accompanied by the emission of ionizing radiation in the form of high-energy particles or rays. As alpha, beta, and gamma radiation penetrate matter, they bump electrons out of atoms or molecules, thus ionizing them. The rate of breakdown or decay is calculated by the half-life, or the time it takes for a given number of atoms to decay by half, which can range from milliseconds for short-lived isotopes to billions of years. The amount of radioactivity exhibited is measured by the number of disintegrations per second (dps); 1 becquerel (Bq) = 1 dps, and 1 curie (Ci) = 3.7×10^{10} dps = 3.7×10^{10} Bq.

Alpha, Beta, and Gamma Radiation

Alpha particles are positively charged, high-energy particles emitted from the nuclei of radioactive atoms.

They are the largest in mass and the slowest traveling at less than one-tenth the speed of light. Alpha particles are produced following the decay of radioisotopes of heavy nuclei such as radium, plutonium, uranium, and radon. The process of alpha decay transforms one element into a different element. The new element has a lighter nucleus than the original radioisotope because of the emission of an alpha particle, which consists of two protons and two neutrons. The total energy (including the masses of the new element and the alpha particle) is the same as before, but some of the nuclear binding energy is converted into kinetic energy of the alpha particle.

Beta particles are electrons emitted from the spontaneous decay of unstable nuclei when one of its neutrons turns into a proton and emits an electron and an electron antineutrino. Tritium, carbon-14, phosphorus-32, and strontium-90 all decay by beta emission. Beta particles travel at a high velocity, which can be as high as 98% of the speed of light. Beta particles are electrons and thus have only about 1/2000th the mass of a proton or neutron; their emission does not affect the mass number, and no new element is created.

Gamma rays are produced following spontaneous decay of radioactive material, such as cobalt-60 and cesium-137. A gamma ray is an electromagnetic wave that is similar to ordinary visible light, but differs in its wavelength. Gamma rays have a wavelength that is far shorter than visible light, and thus higher in energy, greater than 100 keV. Gamma decay generally occurs simultaneously with alpha or beta decays it does not affect the atomic number or the mass number of a nucleus, and no new element is created.

Alpha, beta, and gamma radiation each produce differing amounts of ionization. Alpha particles produce the most ionization because they are heavy, slow moving, and carry two positive charges. Gamma rays produce the least because they are photons that carry no charge, while beta particles have an ionizing potential in between alpha and gamma rays. The ionizing potential of alpha and beta particles and gamma radiation causes damage on contact or proximity with living cells and can result in radiation sickness.

Each of the particles has a differing penetration ability, which is based on the energy they carry. Alpha particles can only travel a few centimeters in air since their large mass and slow speed mean that they lose energy quickly by many collisions with air molecules. A single sheet of paper can stop an alpha particle. Beta particles can travel different distances, depending on the kinetic energy of the particle, but they have a slightly higher penetration ability than alpha particles and can be stopped by 2–3 mm of aluminum. However, gamma rays, which are high-energy electromagnetic waves, interact with atoms with a probability much smaller than either alpha or beta particles, and thus penetrate matter more easily. Gamma ray producers such as cobalt-60 are used for medical and research purposes, including radiocarbon dating, measuring chemical reactions, dating rocks, X-rays, and cancer therapy.

Pathways

There are three basic pathways for the introduction of radioactivity into the human body: external exposure, inhalation, and ingestion. Each of these pathways result in different parts of the body being exposed, and the degree of exposure a human receives is moderated by the differing penetration ability of the radioactive particles. Injuries resulting from external exposure to radioactive contaminates vary. For instance, due to the limited mobility and penetration capability of alpha particles, direct exposure will generally not penetrate the outer layer of skin, unless an individual has an open wound. Beta particles can cause reddening of the skin and, less frequently, damage to the eyes. Gamma rays are the most detrimental to human health, because they can penetrate through the whole body, thus exposing every organ. The degree of damage from gamma rays is dependent upon strength and proximity to the source.

If radioactive contaminated dust, smoke, or gaseous radionuclides (e.g., radon gas) are inhaled into the lungs, the radioactive particles, especially alpha and beta emitters, remain in the lungs. This exposes the individual to continual radiation until all the particles decay and/or are processed through the body. An individual who ingests either radioactive contaminated food or water exposes the entire digestive system to elevated levels of radioactivity. The radionuclides not passed through the digestive system remain in the body, releasing a varied amount of energy directly into the body's tissues. This, in turn, damages major organs (i.e., kidneys), DNA, and bones. Acute doses of radiation can result in reddening of the skin (i.e., radiation burn), lowered white blood cells, and/or disruption of the gastrointestinal tract, while chronic dosage results in an elevated risk for cancer.

Radioactivity in the Arctic

Radioactivity can occur naturally or be artificially produced. Naturally occurring radioactive material (sometimes referred to as NORM) occurs from primarily two sources: terrestrial (e.g., the Earth's surface and atmosphere) and cosmic radiation. The background level of natural radiation varies regionally and is dependent on the particular rock formations. The uranium parent (U-238) is present in small amounts in all rocks and soil on the Earth's surface, and decays in a long sequence of alpha, beta, and gamma decays until ultimately radon gas is produced. Radon gas is the most common NORM that humans encounter, since it can accumulate in enclosed spaces and be inhaled. Radon gas is radioactive with a half-life of 3.825 days and itself decays via a series of decays to other radioactive substances, including polonium-218, 214, and 210, lead-214, 210, and 206, and bismuth-214 and 210, which can be deposited in the lungs and cause damage by alpha and beta particles and gamma ray emission. Other natural sources of radiation are potassium-40 and thorium-223 from rocks and soils, and carbon-14, which is produced from the interaction between cosmic rays and the atmosphere. At present, an individual's average yearly external exposure to natural radiation (global average) is about 0.85 millisievert. There is considerable geographic variation, and living in the Arctic environment increases an individual's lifetime dose, on average, by approximately 0.6 millisievert per year, due to a combination of artificial (former weapons tests, dump sites, and Chernobyl) and natural radiation sources (radon, cosmic rays, and terrestrial). However, locally high concentrations of natural sources (e.g., high concentrations of natural uranium) in the Arctic can further increase an individual's radiation dose by up to 10 millisieverts per year.

Artificial radiation was introduced into the Arctic environment (atmosphere, ocean, and land) by nuclear weapon detonations beginning in the 1950s, dumping/storage of nuclear waste and spent fuel in Arctic waters from 1960 to 1991, as well as nuclear accidents (e.g., Chernobyl in 1989, and the nuclear-powered satellite Cosmos 954 that crashed in Canada in 1978 spreading debris across 1000 km). Radionuclide emissions from aboveground atomic blasts peaked in the circumpolar region in the early 1960s, remained stable until 1980, and are presently believed to be in gradual decline.

Nuclear Detonations and Weapons

A number of atomic weapons have been detonated in the Arctic. At Novaya Zemlya, Russia, 130 nuclear tests were conducted from 1955 to 1990. Of these atomic tests, 88 were detonated in the atmosphere, 39 were underground, and three were underwater atomic tests in 1955, 1957, and 1961 in Chernaya Bay, on the southern tip of Novaya Zemlya.

In 1969, 1970, and 1971, three underground atomic tests were conducted on Amchitka Island, part of the Rat Islands in the western Aleutian Islands.

Since the mid-1950s, nuclear weapons have been placed in the Arctic, accidentally or purposefully. In 1968, a US B52 bomber carrying four nuclear weapons crashed near Thule Airbase in Greenland, releasing approximately one pound of plutonium into the atmosphere. The US military also housed nuclear surface-to-air and other tactical warheads at Thule Airbase, which was in violation of the Greenland Danish agreement prohibiting nuclear weapons on the island. Assorted tactical nuclear weapons are assumed to be located in the Arctic region, in secret locations.

Nuclear Plants and the Dumping/Storage of Nuclear Waste

In the Russian Arctic, there are two nuclear plants (Kola and Bilibino plants) and three fuel reprocessing plants (Mayak, Krasnoyarsk, and Tomsk). The effluents of Mayak and Tomsk are released into the Ob' River and those from Krasnoyarsk flow into the Yenisey River. From 1962 to 1973, an experimental SM-1A nuclear reactor at Fort Greely, 100 miles southeast of Fairbanks in Alaska, was used to test a nuclear reactor's ability to operate in adverse climatic conditions. There are also several nuclear power plants near the Arctic region in Finland, Russia, and Sweden.

Disposing of the radioactive waste of nuclear plants and storage practices have resulted in dramatic exposure levels in certain communities in Russia. For example, due to the excessive dumping of highly radioactive waste into the Techa River, from 1949 to 1956, citizens received doses ranging from 350 to 3500 millisieverts. From 1950 to 1951, the citizens of Muslimova, 20 miles downriver from the Mayak Chemical Combine, received doses of 240 millisieverts. Nuclear waste was also dumped west and east of Novaya Zemlya, from 1960 to 1991, in the Barents Sea and Kara Sea, respectively.

The British Nuclear Fuels Limited reprocessing plant in Sellafield, England (formerly Windscale), is one of the chief sources of radionuclide emission into the Arctic marine environment, due to the magnitude of discharges. Ocean currents around Sellafield carry the contaminants, mostly cesium-137, north into the Barents Sea, and subsequently into the Kara Sea, Laptev Sea, and central Arctic Ocean (*see* Figure 2 in **Local and Transboundary Pollutants**). Almost all of the plutonium and americium discharged from Sellafield are retained in the sediments of the northeast Irish Sea.

Accidents and Human Experiments

The Chernobyl accident is another main source of radioactivity and radiation in the Arctic. The fallout from the Chernobyl nuclear accident resulted in the contamination of fish and berries in Saamiland (i.e., the ancestral home of the Saami presently referred to as the northern parts of Norway, Sweden, Finland, and Russia). The various Saami herders had to destroy over 70,000 reindeer, which resulted in pervasive cultural disruption and impoverishment in Saamiland. The promises of compensation from the government, shortly after the accident, were forgotten by the respective governments. In 1997, the Saami community living in Mala, Sweden, opposed a referendum that would have established a nuclear repository in the community.

There have been human experiments involving radioactive materials in the Arctic. In Alaska in the late 1950s, the US military fed approximately 100 Iñupiat and other Alaskan Natives radioactive iodine-131, without their knowledge, to evaluate the effects on their thyroid glands. In addition, the US military performed tracer experiments (dispersal of particles) by setting up soil plots filled with radioactive materials (e.g., strontium-85 and cesium-137) from the Nevada test sites in the Ogotoruk Creek basin, southeast of Cape Thompson, Alaska. These projects were part of the program called "Project Chariot."

Military and Commercial Use of Nuclear Power

On the Kola Peninsula in Russia, there are three nuclear submarine naval facilities (Murmansk, Gremikha (Yokanga), and Severodvinsk (Sevmash), and a cache of spent fuel rods and spent fuel, of which a sizeable amount is highly enriched uranium and plutonium. There are two storage facilities on the Kola Peninsula—Andreeva Bay and Gremikha—as well as 90 decommissioned nuclear submarines. The Pacific Fleet also has 75 decommissioned nuclear submarines stranded in harbors in the Russian Far East.

The US, UK, France, and China all have nuclear-powered military vessels that travel in Arctic waters. The Russian Murmansk Shipping Company has eight nuclear-powered ships used as icebreakers in the tourist trade and for scientific research. Under normal conditions, all of these vessels do not pose an increased risk, but do introduce nuclear products to the Arctic and, in the event of an accident, the outcome could be highly destructive to the fragile Arctic ecosystems.

Effect on People, Flora, and Fauna of the Arctic

The effect of radioactivity and radiation on the flora and fauna is of serious concern in the Arctic, because the ecosystems are especially ineffective at natural dissipation. The slow growing season and a limited soil heat result in slower decomposition rates. Freshwater ecosystems of the Arctic are poorly buffered and thus incapable of withstanding pollutants. The frozen ground of the Arctic prevents foreign substances from seeping in and results in material, such as radioactive waste, traveling vast distances. Further, should an accident occur with radioactive waste, the effect on the freshwater fisheries would be drastic.

Radioactive materials are distributed in various ways. For example, radionuclides from natural and artificial sources are captured by raindrops and snowflakes and redistributed to vegetation and soil. Radioactive isotopes from the atmospheric nuclear tests of the 1950s and 1990s still persist in lichens and moss, which are particularly effective at gathering radionuclides from the air via precipitation. Radioactive materials are also distributed by biomagnification or the process by which radionuclides are amplified as additional organisms are consumed up the food chain.

The introduction of radioactive contaminants into the Arctic ecosystem has affected the people, flora, and fauna. As an illustration of how the ecosystem is connected, lichens and moss are a staple food for reindeer, and the reindeer, in turn, are a main food source for many Arctic indigenous people, and thus a significant source of cesium-137. The same process of bioaccumulation occurs in marine animals, starting with plankton and then moving up the food chain to larger mammals such as seals, otters, and whales, which in turn are consumed by humans. However, the concentration of radionuclides is diluted in the ocean.

Radioactivity sources and pathways are still being investigated in the Arctic and new knowledge is being acquired through national and international research programs and initiatives, such as the Arctic Monitoring and Assessment Program (AMAP), European Environment Agency (EEA), and the United Nations Environmental Program Global Resource Information Database (UNEP-GRID). Further studies are needed to determine the levels of radioactivity and radiation effects on human populations, especially those communities downwind and/or downriver from the nuclear plants, waste sites, and weapons tests/accidents. Knowledge of how the ecosystem interacts with radiation contamination needs to be researched more fully.

ANDREW HUND

See also **Bilibino Nuclear Power Plant; Contaminants; Local and Transboundary Pollution; Nuclear Testing; Ocean Dumping; Pollution: Environmental Initiatives; Project Chariot; Thule Air Base**

Further Reading

Aarkrog, A., "Doses from the Chernobyl accident to the Nordic populations via diet intake, Nordic radioecology: the transfer of radionuclides through Nordic ecosystems to man." *Studies in Environmental Science*, 62 (1994): 433–456

AMAP (Arctic Monitoring and Assessment Program), *Arctic Pollution Issues: A State of the Arctic Environmental Report*, Oslo, 1998; available online at http://www.amap.no/amap.htm

Hägg, C., "Consequences from Sweden of the Chernobyl accident." *SSI-rapport 90-07*, Sweden, 1990

Jaffe, D., A. Mahura & R. Andres, "Atmospheric transport pathways to Alaska from potential radionuclide sites in the former Soviet Union." *Research Report, UAF-ADEC Joint Project 96-001*, 71, 1997

Jensen, J., J. Adare & R. Shearer (editors), *Canadian Arctic Contaminants Assessment Report Northern Contaminants Programme*, Indian and Northern Affairs Canada, Minister of Public Works and Government Services, Ottawa, Canada, 1997

O'Neill, Dan, *Project Chariot: A Collection of Oral Histories*, 2 volumes, Anchorage, Alaska: Alaska Humanities Forum, 1989

———, *The Firecracker Boys*, New York: St Martin's Press, 1994

Sjöblom, K. & G. Linsley, "Radiological assessment: waste disposal in the Arctic Seas." *IAEA Bulletin*, 39(1) (1997)

RAE, JOHN

John Rae spent 22 years in British North America and accurately mapped more miles of hitherto unexplored territory than any other explorer. Rae's background was aptly suited for his extraordinary feats. He spent his first 14 years in the bleak surroundings of the Orkney Islands, described by him as a "paradise for boys." He was an independent, outdoors-type reveling in pitting himself against rugged surroundings and bad weather. He was not, however, lacking in scholarly ability, and at the age of 16 went to Edinburgh to study medicine, qualifying as a surgeon at the Royal College of Surgeons in 1833, and joining the Hudson's Bay Company as surgeon on HSS *Prince of Wales* in the same year. On his first duty at sea, the ship was forced to winter on Charleston Island in St James Bay. When supplies of fresh food became exhausted, the crew developed scurvy, and Rae successfully treated them with cranberries and sprouts of wild peas.

The next five years of Rae's life were spent in the vicinity of Moose Fort on James Bay. During this period, he distinguished himself by his ability to travel rapidly across great distances, usually by foot and in the worst weather. He spared no effort to treat the ill. On one occasion, he walked 105 miles in two days to reach an ill patient. Rae made good use of the practices and knowledge of native peoples, traveling light and in small groups, and living off the land as much as possible. This was in sharp contrast to the British tradition, which practiced polar travel in accordance with regulations that were poorly suited to the harsh environment.

In June 1846, Rae and 11 men successfully explored the Melville Peninsula, which forms the northwest tip of Hudson Bay, and in 8 days, successfully portaged the approximately 40 miles of the peninsula's southern isthmus (which now bears his name). Rae successfully wintered above the treeline without the benefits of a ship to house the party. This was a monumental feat, especially in view of the −47°F temperatures they encountered.

In 1848, Rae joined Dr. John Richardson in his search for Franklin; the contrast between the two physicians was striking. The 60-year-old Richardson had slowed down after 14 years of relative inactivity, whereas Rae was at the peak of his activity. Both physicians had a mutually healthy respect for each other, but there is little doubt that Rae felt somewhat hampered by Richardson's deliberateness and conservatism. In his autobiography, however, Rae is generous in his praise for Richardson (see Dafoe, 1993). The search covered the area between the MacKenzie and Coppermine rivers, but yielded no relevant information concerning Franklin.

For 8 months in 1851, Rae led another party in search of Franklin, traveling about 5300 miles, including 700 miles of the southern coast of Victoria Island, unaware that Franklin's ships had been entrapped in the ice only 50 miles to the east. His search uncovered two pieces of wood thought to be part of one of Franklin's ships.

In 1853–1854, Rae again set out for the Canadian Arctic to complete the exploration of the remaining Canadian northern continental coastline. While at Repulse Bay, the Inuit brought him artifacts of the Franklin expedition consisting of silver plate and silverware. They reported that "a party of white men had perished from starvation at some distance to the west" and that they had been seen dragging sledges down the coast of King William Island to the south. They also reported having found bodies on the Canadian mainland that showed evidence of cannibalism. In support of the Inuit reports, Rae purchased monogrammed silver forks and spoons and Franklin's Hanoverian Medal of Merit from them. Rae then proceeded westward to King William Land and demonstrated its insularity.

Rae returned to England and presented his report and the Franklin relics to the Admiralty in October 1854. He also related the Inuit account of evidence of cannibalism. Despite the strenuous and indignant objections of Lady Jane Franklin (Franklin's widow) to the report of cannibalism, Rae and his men received a reward of £10,000 for discovering the fate of Franklin. On hearing Rae's report, Lady Franklin petitioned the British Admiralty to support an expedition to King William Island in the hope that survivors might still be living among the Inuit. Nine years had elapsed, however, and the Admiralty, now heavily involved in the Crimean War, considered the matter closed.

In later years Rae returned to England, but remained active. He did telegraph surveying in the Faroe Islands, Iceland, and Greenland, and in Canada, he explored the Carlton Trail, the Yellowhead Pass, and the Fraser River. He also served as a guide for a private hunting party in Saskatchewan. Following two years in the Orkney Islands, Rae moved to London, devoting his later years to writing. He was a consultant in many matters related to Arctic exploration. He was particularly critical of Sir George Nares and the conduct of the Nares expedition of 1875–1876, in which, among other things, there were many casualties due to scurvy. In this regard, Rae made the following prophetic remarks:

> I consider scurvy a blood disease caused by a lack of something it gets from vegetables and that when you have no vegetables or bread there is something that the system wants which is in very small quantities in animal food and therefore you have to eat a very great deal more than you want in order to get the quantity from meat. (Richards, 1985)

This is a remarkably accurate statement considering that it was made before the discovery of vitamins and over 50 years before the discovery of ascorbic acid, the antiscorbutic vitamin C.

Biography

Born on September 13, 1813 near Stromness, Orkney Islands, Scotland, John Rae was the son of a well-to-do tenant farmer. At the age of 16 Rae was sent to Edinburgh for formal training, where he qualified as a surgeon at the Royal College of Surgery in 1833. He satisfied his dual love of the outdoors and medicine by joining the Hudson's Bay Company in Canada, where he initially served with distinction as a ship's surgeon. His exploratory skills were recognized and he subsequently became involved in a series of expeditions which took him to many of Canada's previously unexplored areas. His feats of long-distance walking became legendary and he was known as the Great Pedestrian. His success in the capacity was in large measure due to his adoption of Inuit and other native exploratory techniques, methodologies often resented by other more traditional English explorers. In 1857, he established a practice of medicine in Hamilton, Ontario, and in 1860, at the age of 47, he married Kate Thompson in Toronto; the marriage was childless. He devoted his last years to writing, composing a book, 20 journal articles, and 45 letters to the editor of *Nature*. He received an honorary

LL.D. degree at Edinburgh in 1866. He died in London on July 22, 1893 at the age of 79.

RALPH M. MYERSON

See also **Franklin, Sir John**

Further Reading

Dafoe, C., "The great pedestrian." *The Beaver,* 73(5) (October–November 1993): 2–3
Richards, R.L., *Dr. John Rae*, Whitby, North Yorkshire: Caedmon, 1985, p. 158

RAGLAND MINING PROJECT

The Ragland mining project is located in the barren part of the Ungava Peninsula toward the northernmost sector of Nunavik, Québec, Canada. The site lies approximately 60 km west of the Inuit village of Kangiqsujuaq and 100 km southeast of the Inuit village of Salluit. The mine is a wholly owned subsidiary of Falconbridge Limited, a company that locates, develops, mines, and processes metals and minerals ranging from nickel and ferronickel to copper, zinc, cobalt, and precious metals.

The Ragland mine is the site of one of the world's finest undeveloped sulfide nickel deposits. It contains more than 20 million tons of proven and probable ore reserves grading 3.17% nickel and 0.88% copper. The $500 million mining and concentration facility will produce 20,000 tons of nickel per year when it is fully operational. The site consists of a 2400 ton per day concentration open pit and underground mining operation designed to produce 130,000 tons of nickel-copper concentrate per year. The mining complex includes housing accommodations for 300 people, including provisions for sleeping, eating, recreational, and administrative activities. There is a 24 MW diesel power generation plant that is required to supply the site with energy, and an elaborate network of water supply, waste disposal, and other service infrastructures required to establish a largely self-sufficient mining complex in the North.

In the middle of the 1930s, surface sulfide showings were discovered in the Cap Smith-Wakeham Bay region of the Ungava Peninsula, and 20 years later exploration started in the region. By the mid-1960s, extensive exploration was completed and the construction of 60 km of road and a number of campsites had been completed. By the 1980s, prospects for developing the mining project were significantly advanced through positive changes in the worldwide price of metals on the one hand and the signing of the James Bay and Northern Québec Agreement on the other. In addition, other important factors contributed to the positive prospect of a major mining operation in the

North. Cost-effective Arctic and Subarctic mining had been proved in Greenland and the Northwest Territories of Canada, specifically at the Nanisivik mine site, and icebreakers had successfully doubled the marine shipping season in Arctic waters from 4 to 8 months. The Asbestos Corporation, caught in a worldwide boycott of its product, ceased operations in the immediate area of the projected mine, freeing up port and road facilities of direct benefit to the mining operation. The reliability of air service to the site had increased and a system of cost-effective modular buildings required to support the resident mining population became available.

Almost concurrently, the James Bay and Northern Québec Agreement established many of the ground rules for development of the resources in the North, and provided a framework for negotiations between the Inuit residents of Nunavik and a wide range of promoters, including Falconbridge, interested in the potential of northern development. Insofar as the proposed mining complex is situated in the heart of Nunavik, relatively close, in Arctic terms, to two Inuit villages, Falconbridge initiated early and ongoing discussions with the leadership of the villages, the Kativik Regional Government, and with Makivik Corporation in order to assure that the project would be mutually beneficial to all concerned.

Ongoing negotiations between the Inuit and Falconbridge resulted in the signing of an extensive agreement between Makivik Corporation, acting on behalf of the Inuit, and the Société Minère Ragland de Québec ltée, representing Falconbridge, that addressed, among many other issues, the three major concerns of the Inuit. These focused on the need to:

- provide job training and employment opportunities for the resident Inuit population,
- establish priority entrepreneurial business relationships with Ragland such that there would be some Inuit economic participation in the project, and
- monitor and address potential local and regional social and environmental impacts of the Ragland mine over the 20–50-year life span that is projected for its operation and ultimate closure.

The Memorandum of Understanding Regarding Negotiation of an Agreement in Respect of the Mining Project near Deception River was signed in March 1993. The agreement included a guaranteed contribution of more than $60 million in operating profits over 18 years to be distributed through Makivik Corporation to the residents of Salluit, Kangiqsujuaq, and Nunavik. Joint measures, in conjunction with the Kativik Regional Government, were undertaken to provide a variety of job training opportunities in the use of heavy equipment, and a number of avenues were developed that led to maintenance and supply contracts being provided to the site by Inuit entrepreneurs. Throughout the exploration and development process, extensive environmental baseline data were required to respond to engineering requirements and eventually to furnish answers to environmental and social impact directives.

Environmental studies furnished by the Proponent to the Kativik Environmental Quality Commission, the body responsible for environmental and social impact review in Nunavik, included extensive data on climate, plant life, archaeology, land-use patterns including hunting and fishing practices, and the habitats of marine and terrestrial wildlife in the region. These were subject to rigorous review and to a public hearing process that was held in the two villages most directly affected by the project, as well as in Kuujjuaq, where the Head Offices of the Kativik Regional Government and the Makivik Corporation are located.

Effluent runoff and windborne pollutants from the mining and tailing sites was of particular concern to the residents of the region. It is of interest to note that a current proposal to establish a provincial park in the area of Pingualuit, a 1.4 million-year-old crater and potentially a world-class ecotourist site in the vicinity of the mine, led to considerable discussion with respect to airborne pollutants that could significantly affect the quality of water contained in the crater, water that is among the three most pure sites in the world.

The Ragland mining operation is projected to last for at least 20 years based on current proven and probable ore deposits, and its life may well be extended through the discovery of other viable deposits in the immediate vicinity of the site. Thus, the Ragland Committee was formed with representatives of the Makivik Corporation, Falconbridge, and the local Inuit villages to monitor and assure that the environmental and social requirements associated with the environmental review process are fully respected, to discuss project process, and address local issues and those that might arise on the basis of the Memorandum of Understanding.

PETER JACOBS

See also **Makivik Corporation**

Further Reading

Sustainable Development at Falconbridge, Toronto, Ontario: Falconbridge Limited; http://www.sjross.com/falconbridge.html

RAINEY, FROELICH

Froelich Rainey, one of the central figures in the development of Arctic archaeology, made important discoveries on four continents during a career that spanned half a century; yet it was his early work in Alaska that Rainey regarded as his most significant research.

Rainey grew up in eastern Montana as a working cowhand on the *R-lazy-B*, the Rainey Brothers Ranch. At the University of Chicago, Ralph Linton ignited his curiosity about the world in an anthropology course, and in 1929, Rainey shipped out on a tramp freighter bound for Shanghai, China. That year he received a cable from his father informing him of the stock market collapse; his family would not be able to support him financially.

Rainey had planned to travel to inner Mongolia, but suddenly finding himself on short rations, shipped out again, and after fighting off pirates in Formosa Straits, he jumped ship and found a job teaching English in Luzon in the Philippines, an experience that opened his eyes to the difficulty of communicating culturally laden abstractions among different ethnic groups.

A year later, Rainey returned to the United States intent on joining the Army Flying Corps, but shortly before he signed up, Cornelius Osgood, of the Peabody Museum at Yale University in New Haven, Connecticut, convinced him to enter graduate school there. Rainey conducted pioneering fieldwork in the Caribbean and Puerto Rico before accepting an offer from the American Museum of Natural History in New York to collaborate in Alaska with Otto Geist, a German naturalist who had excavated on St Lawrence Island, near the Bering Strait. While in Alaska, Rainey developed a regular pattern of research: in the early summer he hunted for Athapaskan sites in the interior; in late summer he worked on the tundra with Eskimos.

This work prepared him for his seminal work at Pt Hope, Alaska. In 1938, at an international congress in Denmark, Rainey met Danish archaeologist Helge Larsen who proposed, on Knud Rasmussen's suggestion, joint excavations in the middens of Pt Hope. The following year, on the beaches east of the middens, Larsen, Rainey, and J. Louis Giddings discovered an Ipiutak site and defined the Ipiutak archaeological culture. Their findings have proven to be one of the Arctic's most enigmatic, both because of the Ipiutak's lithic relationship with American Eskimo traditions and because of the culture's complex ivory carvings that bear a strong resemblance to the artistic traditions of northeastern and central Asia.

Rainey, with his wife and daughter, returned to Pt Hope in January 1940 where he could better interpret the Ipiutak materials. There he joined a whaling crew and simultaneously carried out ethnographical research. The success of these investigations led Rainey henceforth to emphasize the interrelatedness and combined usefulness of ethnographical and archaeological research, and the Eskimos of Pt Hope themselves quickly understood the value of these investigations for the preservation of their own history.

With the American entry into World War II, Rainey put his competence and adaptability to use as the director of the US Quinine Mission in Ecuador. Shortly thereafter, Rainey found himself at 15,000 ft in the Andes, running a band of *vaqueros* and hijacking German mule trains of cinchona bark, which he shipped to the United States for processing into quinine and reshipment to the South Pacific, where more soldiers were dying of malaria than bullet wounds.

By 1944, Rainey had joined the Foreign Service and was assigned to the planned Allied Control Commission for Occupied Germany. He advanced across Western Europe with the troops and was one of the first Americans to reach Vienna. Seated in the turret of a B-25 bomber, he watched for flak bursts from Soviet antiaircraft guns on the approach into the city.

With the war's end, Rainey was appointed as the US Commissioner for the Rhine and began working to rebuild the Ruhr coal industry in the face of a brutal winter in Germany. Viewing the utter destruction among European nations, Rainey was among the first US officials to call for massive American aid, an initiative that ultimately became the Marshall Plan.

In 1947, Rainey assumed the directorship of the University Museum of the University of Pennsylvania, where his efforts launched the museum as one of the leading archaeological research institutions in the world. His work produced seed money for hundreds of University museum expeditions throughout the world, as well as for founding the Museum Applied Science Center for Archaeology, where the latest techniques and technologies are applied to the study of excavated materials.

Rainey remains well known for introducing archaeology and anthropology to the medium of television. In 1949, he developed a small show called *What in the World*, wherein several experts tried to guess the provenance of obscure artifacts. The program ran in various venues for 15 years, gaining a huge audience and becoming a CBS Television prime-time feature. The televised program helped to launch many young people on careers in anthropology and archaeology. Moreover, Rainey used the medium to stress the fundamental importance of conducting research into all aspects of humankind history and development, while at the same time humanizing these arcane pursuits.

Biography

Froelich Gladstone Rainey was born on June 18, 1907 in Black River, Wisconsin. However, his parents moved the family to eastern Montana, where Rainey grew up on a ranch. He received a Bachelor of Arts degree in English from the University of Chicago in 1929 and a Ph.D. in anthropology from Yale University in 1935. Although he carried out archaeological work on four continents, Rainey made his most important discoveries in Arctic Alaska. From 1947 to 1976, Rainey was director of the Museum of Anthropology and Archaeology at the University of Pennsylvania in Philadelphia. His publications include *Archaeological Excavations at Kukulik, St Lawrence Island, Alaska* (1937), *The Whale Hunters of Tigara* (1947), and *Ipiutak and the Arctic Whale Hunting Culture* (with Helge Larsen, 1948). His first marriage, to Penelope Lewis, was dissolved in 1973. They had two daughters, one of whom, Penelope Rainey, survives. In 1976, he married Marina Cippico and moved to Launceston, Cornwall, UK, where Rainey lived for the remainder of his life. He died on October 11, 1992 in St Austell, Cornwall.

JOHN R. BOCKSTOCE

See also **Ipiutak Culture; Larsen, Helge**

Further Reading

Giddings, J. Louis, *Ancient Men of the Arctic*, New York: Knopf, 1967

Larsen, Helge & Froelich Rainey, "Ipiutak and the Arctic Whale Hunting Culture." *Anthropological Papers of the American Museum of Natural History*, 42 (1948): 1–276

Lipton, Barbara (editor), *Survival: Life and Art of the Alaskan Eskimo* (exhib. cat.), introduction by Froelich Rainey, and annotated bibliography by Allan Chapman, Newark, New Jersey: Newark Museum, 1977

Rainey, Froelich G., *Archaeological Excavations at Kukulik, St. Lawrence Island, Alaska,* Washington, District of Columbia: Government Printing Office, 1937

———, "The Whale Hunters of Tigara." *Anthropological Papers of the American Museum of Natural History*, 41 (Part 2) (1947): 231–283

———, *Reflections of a Digger: Fifty Years of World Archaeology*, Philadelphia: University Museum of Archaeology and Anthropology, University of Pennsylvania, 1992

RAPTORS

Arctic regions are probably among the poorest areas in terms of raptor diversity. Among the 307 species of raptors that have been described in the world, less than ten breed in the Arctic. The circumpolar gyrfalcon (*Falco rusticolus*) is the northernmost species, breeding as far north as Peary Land in Greenland and Ellesmere Island in Canada. Peregrine falcon (*Falco peregrinus*) and rough-legged buzzard (*Buteo lagopus*) are also two circumpolar tundra breeders, but these are only found in the Low Arctic, missing in most of the High Arctic islands. The second exclusively breeds in

Peregrine falcon (*Falco peregrinus*).
Photo by Craig Koppie, courtesy US Fish and Wildlife Service

the tundra and northern taiga compared to the peregrine falcon, which is not a true Arctic species since different subspecies are found all over the world. Four other species breed in the taiga zone and locally in the southern tundra. The hen harrier (*Circus cyaneus*), the golden eagle (*Aquila chrysaetos*), and the merlin (*Falco columbarius*) breed both in Eurasia and North America. The white-tailed sea eagle (*Haliaeetus albicilla*) is only found in Eurasia, Iceland, and southwestern Greenland.

The gyrfalcon (syn. Gyr, Jerfalcon) is the largest falcon in the world. The female, larger than its male (also called tiercel) like in most falcons, can weigh more than 2 kg and has a wingspan of 135 cm. It is generally the first species that starts breeding in the Arctic, laying its eggs as early as in April-May to have enough time to incubate (5 weeks) and rear the brood (7 weeks). The coloration of this raptor varies considerably and several subspecies have been differentiated according to this criterion. The High Arctic birds (subspecies *candicans*) breeding in Canada and Greenland are white with only a few dark marks. Southern forms are darker. The gyrfalcon eats birds and mammals generally captured on ground or water, but the diet varies considerably. When available and abundant enough, ptarmigans and other grouses are preferred but seabirds, ground squirrels, hares, or even lemmings form the bulk of the prey in some other regions. The species is not a long-range migrant, some birds even being sedentary, but some movements do occur in winter as attested, for example, by the white gyrfalcons recorded in Iceland where only gray birds breed. The world population is estimated between 5000 and 17,000 pairs and is still threatened by bird's-nesters since it is one of the most valuable raptors in falconry, a reputation it has acquired since the Middle Ages.

The peregrine falcon is a smaller (maximum 1500 g and 120 cm wingspan) and more slender species than the gyrfalcon. Specialized to take prey generally on the wing, its body is designed for rapid pursuit and nosedives. Speeds of more than 200 km^{-1}h have been recorded for this falcon, the fastest animal on earth. Another difference with the gyrfalcon is that Arctic breeding peregrine falcons are long-distance migrants. From their breeding grounds in northern Canada and Greenland, they can fly over the entire United States and the Amazonian forest to go to their winter quarters in South America. The population of peregrine falcon drastically declined in the 1960s and 1970s as a result of PCB contamination, but is now recovering since these chemicals have been banned.

The merlin is the third falcon species that can be found in the Arctic. Much smaller than the two previous species (maximum 250 g and a wingspan of 50–70 cm), it only feeds on small prey, especially small birds. After having raised two to six young, generally in an old corvid nest, most merlins migrate south from the taiga to the temperate region, some even reaching the equator in South America.

Only breeding at high latitudes, rough-legged buzzards (700–1600 g; 120–150 cm wingspan) have a dense cover of small feathers on their tarsus and toes to protect them from the harsh climate. This characteristic, shared with other Arctic birds (ptarmigan, snowy owl), is at the origin of its name. Like the weasels, snowy owl, and some jaeger species, the rough-legged buzzard (or rough-legged hawk) is one of many Arctic predators, whose numbers fluctuate highly with lemming cycles. Although they can eat other prey (young birds, hares, or ground squirrels), rodents form the basis of this buzzard's diet. When these small herbivores reach the low phase of their 3–5-year cycle, buzzards are rare breeders and their clutch size is smaller. In winter, all rough-legged buzzards migrate south to the boreal and temperate regions: United States, Europe, and southern Russia. With a world population of several hundred thousand of individuals, this species is probably the most common raptor in the Arctic.

The hen harrier (350–530 g; 100–120 cm wingspan) has similar but slightly more southern breeding and wintering grounds than the merlin. Also feeding on small prey, it prefers rodents to birds. Living in open landscapes (southern and alpine tundra, moorland, and regenerating forests in the taiga), the male is gray and the female is brown. However, both sexes have a typical white rump and a V-shaped silhouette, which are obvious criteria when they slowly fly close to the ground to locate their prey by sound.

The golden eagle (3–6 kg; 200 cm wingspan) and the white-tailed sea eagle (4–6 kg; 200–250 cm wingspan) are the two largest Arctic raptors. Both breed on cliffs or trees and prefer open areas to hunt. The golden eagle feeds on a large number of medium-sized vertebrates (hares, grouses, ground squirrels) while the white-tailed sea eagle specializes more on fishes, seabirds, and wildfowl. The latter is also more often seen feeding on carrions, including domestic animals, a behavior that has led to many mistakes and to the killing of many birds, for example, in southwest Greenland, where there is an isolated population of about 100 pairs. Today, the white-tailed sea eagle is the only endangered Arctic raptor. Considered vulnerable by the International Union for the Conservation of Nature and Natural Resources (IUCN), it seems to be slowly recovering from the drastic decline that took place in the 19th century.

The north American bald eagle (*Haliaeetus leucocephalus*), the far eastern Steller's sea eagle (*Haliaeetus pelagicus*), and the osprey (*Pandion haliaetus*) are three other raptors depending on fish and waterbirds that locally reach the southern border of the Arctic.

OLIVIER GILG

Further Reading

Cramp, Stanley & K.E.L. Simmons, *Handbook of the Birds of Europe, the Middle East and North Africa,* Volume 2, Oxford: Oxford University Press, 1980

Del Hoyo, Joseph, Andrew Elliot & Jordi Sargatal, *Handbook of the Birds of the World*, Volume 2, Barcelona: Lynx Edicions, 1994

Sage, Brian, *The Arctic and its Wildlife*, New York: Facts on Files, 1986

Vaugan, Richard, *In Search of Arctic Birds*, London: Poyser, 1992

RASMUSSEN, HENRIETTE

Henriette Rasmussen, a radio journalist and among Greenland's leading political and cultural leaders, was born Henriette Ellen Kathrine Vilhelmine Jeremiassen in Qasigiannguit in the northern part of West Greenland in 1950. At the age of 13, Rasmussen left her parents' home to attend a boarding school in Nuuk, the capital city of Greenland. Like many Greenlanders of her generation, she had to move to Denmark in order to obtain advanced education.

Rasmussen historically has been politically ambitious and sensitive to social issues. In the early 1970s, she, among many other Greenlandic politicians, musicians, artists, and poets, joined *Kalaallit Inuusuttut Ataqatigiit* (KIA, The Young Greenlander's Council), a politically active group of Greenlanders living in Denmark. The 1970s witnessed a growing political and cultural awareness among young people with an eye toward replacing traditional colonial patterns in Greenland's society. KIA sought to inform and educate Danes and Greenlanders living in Denmark about Greenland affairs. From 1970 to 1975, Rasmussen served as KIA's accountant and wrote several articles for their newsletter *Avataq* (Hunting Bladder). Further, Rasmussen actively worked for *Kilut* (Stitches), a Greenlandic women's organization of which she was a member, from 1976 to 1982, serving as editor of the organization's eponymous newsletter.

Politically, Rasmussen has been affiliated with *Inuit Ataqatigiit* (IA, Inuit Brotherhood), Greenland's left-wing socialist party. Over the years, she played a vital role within the party and became one of its vital opinion makers. In 1983, Rasmussen was elected as IA's sole member to the municipal council in Nuuk, a position she held until 1991. From 1983 to 1987, she served as member of the Commission on Scientific Research in Greenland. Concurrently, Rasmussen was a board member of IA's local organization in Nuuk and for some years she also served as a board member of the party's national organization. From 1987 to 1989, Rasmussen edited *Aningaaq* (the Moon), the party's newsletter.

Between 1984 and 1995, Rasmussen was elected several times to Greenland's Parliament. In 1991, when *Siumut* (Forward), Greenland's social democrats, and IA formed a coalition, Rasmussen was appointed as minister for social affairs in the Greenland Home Rule government. During a full four-year term (1991–1995), she led many important negotiations. For example, during 1994–1995, Rasmussen negotiated with the Danish government on the settlement of the Judicial Commission on Greenland. During her tenure as a minister, she liberated alcohol regulations in Greenland, and also proposed a United Nations Permanent Forum for Indigenous Peoples at the UN meeting in Vienna in 1993. Throughout her political career, Rasmussen worked in line with her party's political visions for Greenland's political and economic independence and sovereignty.

In 1996, Rasmussen left Greenland to enter the field of international politics. Greenland's Home Rule government appointed her to the United Nations High Commission on Human Rights based in Geneva, Switzerland. Until 2000, she acted as the chief technical advisor at ILO (the International Labor Office) under the auspices of the UN. In this capacity, Rasmussen managed ILO projects designed to promote policies on indigenous and tribal peoples. She raised awareness for ILO standards and encouraged dialogue between governments and indigenous and tribal peoples. On behalf of the ILO, Rasmussen led important negotiations in Africa and South East Asia. Here, she negotiated with the South African government on the living conditions of the San people and with the governments of the Central African Republic and Cameroon on its indigenous peoples situation. With her international work at ILO, Rasmussen substantially contributed to world politics concerning indigenous peoples' rights and working conditions.

Biography

Henriette Rasmussen was born Henriette Ellen Kathrine Vilhelmine Jeremiassen in Qasigiannguit in the northern part of West Greenland on June 8, 1950. She is the eldest of three sisters and four brothers. Raised in a working class family, she experienced Greenland's transition from a hunting society to a worker's society within her own family. Both Rasmussen's paternal and maternal grandparents subsisted on hunting, while her parents belonged to Greenland's new working class. Her father, Axel Jeremiassen, was a skipper; her mother, Margrethe J.F. Møller, was a factory worker.

At the age of 13, Rasmussen left her parents' home to attend boarding school in Nuuk, Greenland's capital. After earning her baccalaureate at *Nykøbing Falster Katedralskole* in 1970, Rasmussen attended the *N. Zahlesí Seminarium*, a teacher's training college in Copenhagen, where she graduated as a teacher of English and Danish in 1975. After several teaching jobs at the Knud Rasmussen's Folk High School in Sisimiut, the elementary school in Sisimiut, and the high school in Nuuk, she went to Alaska where she taught at Barrow High School for the next three years. From 1979, Rasmussen worked for three years as a radio reporter for *Kalaallit Nunaata Radioa*, the national Greenlandic radio corporation. During the period from 1982 to 1985, she studied journalism at *Niuernermik Ilinniarfik* in Nuuk. She subsequently acted as head of department of radio education, video, and film at *Pilersuiffik*, a publisher of school textbooks in Greenland.

Rasmussen was an active member of *Inuit Ataqatigiit* (IA, Inuit Brotherhood) as well as the Commission on Scientific Research in Greenland. Rasmussen was elected several times to Greenland's Parliament between 1984 and 1995. In 1991, she was appointed as minister for social affairs in the Greenland Home Rule government; she filled a four-year term from 1991 to 1995.

VERENA TRAEGER

See also **Greenland Home Rule Act**

Further Reading

"Henriette fights for the cause of indigenous peoples." *Nomadic News* (2000/2001): 54–55, Nairobi: Indigenous Information Network

Informationsafdelingen, Grønlands Hjemmestyres Danmarkskontor (editor), *Grønlands Grønne Bog*, Nuuk: Attuakkiorfik, 1996

RASMUSSEN, KNUD

Growing up in Greenland gave Knud Johann Victor Rasmussen a unique advantage over many ethnographers and explorers of his generation; he was fluent in Greenlandic and learned to drive a dog team before his tenth birthday (Cruwys, 1990). Even as a child, Inuit culture and folktales fascinated Rasmussen, particularly the stories about a fabled people in the north of the island (Freuchen, 1958; Rasmussen, 1927).

The family remained in Greenland until 1896, after which they relocated to Lynge in Denmark, where Rasmussen completed his schooling. He was invited to join the Danish Literary Expedition led by Danish writer and explorer Ludwig Mylius-Erichsen in 1902–1904. The four-person team included artist Count Harald Moltke and medic Alfred Bertelsen. The expedition left Denmark in June 1902, strongly opposed by some members of the Danish government (Freuchen, 1958) who believed that contact with the western world would have a deleterious impact on Inuit culture and should be limited to the activities of official research expeditions and missionaries (Cruwys, 1990).

The party traveled north across Melville Bay on Greenland's west coast, in search of the Polar Inuit (Inughuit) who were living near Cape York. Rasmussen and the others arrived exhausted and near starvation to find a deserted settlement; the inhabitants had already left. Undaunted and determined to meet the mysterious people whose existence had fascinated him since childhood, Rasmussen set off in pursuit of the Inughuit and found them within 20 h. He chronicled the meeting in his *People of the Polar North: A Record* (see Rasmussen, 1908). Rasmussen and his fellow expedition members spent several months with those they called the "People of the Polar North," and these engagements spurred Rasmussen's skills and talent for ethnography. After a grueling return journey, the expedition arrived safely in Denmark in the spring of 1904, where Rasmussen embarked on a vigorous and enthusiastic round of writing and lecturing. He followed this success with the Ethnographic Expedition of 1906–1908 to northeast Greenland, a trip that solidified Rasmussen's goals.

In the early years of the 20th century, Denmark's rule over Greenland was not yet complete, particularly

Portrait of Knud Rasmussen.
Licensed with permission of the Scott Polar Research Institute, University of Cambridge, UK

in the north, and the founding of a sealing station by the Norwegian Otto Sverdrup in 1910 made Rasmussen aware that Denmark's claim for sovereignty might be challenged. Rasmussen hastened north with Freuchen and established a trading station at a location they called "Thule" on the coast of northwest Greenland. From here, Rasmussen undertook a number of hunting and trading expeditions, traveling hundreds of kilometers in search of game and furs. Eventually, the little station began to show a profit, some of which was used to finance a hospital and a church for the local village, and later to fund other expeditions.

The first of the Thule Expeditions occurred in 1912, when Rasmussen decided to test Robert E. Peary's claim that a channel divided Peary Land from Greenland. If this were the case, and Peary Land comprised a separate island, then Denmark would have no sovereignty over it (Rasmussen, 1913–1914, 1915). Rasmussen, Freuchen, and two Inuit companions (Uvdluriark and Inukitsork) sledged 1000 km across the inland ice to Danmark Fjord, discovering that nearby Independence Fjord was not a channel but "in unbroken connection to Peary Land" (Rasmussen, 1915). By September, after a determined round journey of nearly 2000 km, the party arrived home in Thule. Sir Clements Markham, one-time president of the Royal Geographical Society in London and a staunch promoter of British polar exploration, described the journey as "the finest ever performed by dogs" (Markham, 1921).

The second Thule Expedition was a much more ambitious project, and members included geologist and cartographer Lauge Koch, botanist Thorild Wulff, and a hunter named Hendrik Olsen. The aim was to chart Greenland's northern coast, and its members gathered a mass of biological, geological, and archaeological information, although the second Thule Expedition is chiefly remembered for its fatalities. The expedition members began the 2300-km journey across Melville Bay from Godthåb (present-day Nuuk) on April 18, 1916 and wintered at Thule. On April 6 the following year, they left for De Long Fjord on the northern coast, but appalling weather, wretched traveling conditions, and severe game shortages made for a miserable journey plagued by sickness and near-starvation. The morale of the party plummeted when Olsen failed to return from a hunting foray; no trace of him was ever found, and he was assumed to have been eaten by wolves (Cruwys, 1990; Rasmussen, 1921). Meanwhile, Wulff's health and state of mind deteriorated quickly, and, at his own request, he was left behind to die. The surviving members of the expedition returned to Thule on October 22, 1917 to face recriminations and questions about the deaths of Olsen and Wulff.

Rasmussen was not involved in the third Thule Expedition (a depot-laying exercise to support Roald Amundsen's drift in *Maud*), but he led the fourth, which traveled in 1919 to Ammassalik in East Greenland to collect ethnographic data. However, the massive Fifth Thule Expedition is generally regarded as Rasmussen's finest achievement. The 1921 expedition involved some of Denmark's foremost scientists (including archaeologist Therkel Mathiassen, ethnographer Kaj Birket-Smith, and writer Helge Bangsted), and began on June 18. Soon, however, the ship *Bela* foundered off Danish Island (west of Baffin Island) with the loss of valuable equipment, and many of the Inuit members of the team became ill with influenza. However, despite this inauspicious beginning, the group conducted a number of sledging trips from the base on Danish Island and made contact with Inuit and Indian groups as far as Repulse Bay and Southampton Island. These journeys resulted in the collection of a wide range of ethnographic and archaeological data.

On April 11, 1923, Rasmussen left Danish Island with Qavigarssuaq and Arnarulunguaq (probably the first woman to take part in a research expedition of this magnitude) and two 12-dog sledges. They carried only essential supplies because, as on his previous expeditions, Rasmussen intended to procure fresh game along the way. The party traveled across Repulse Bay and the Boothia Isthmus to Rae Strait, collecting information on the Netsilingmiut. On June 13, they arrived at King William Island, where they spent the summer,

the hunters making food caches and Rasmussen assembling ethnographic data that he gathered from the local people. In the spring, the expedition continued its journey west, crossing into Alaska on May 5, 1924. Their 6000 km sledge journey ended at Icy Cape on June 30, where they traveled by boat to Kotzebue and then Nome. Rasmussen had intended to cross the Bering Strait and continue sledging in Siberia, but the relevant paperwork was not forthcoming and he was obliged to return to Denmark instead, arriving there to a warm welcome in October 1924. The ethnographic data collected by the Fifth Thule Expedition included a wide variety of artifacts and interviews, and remain a valuable record of Inuit culture and oral history. Rasmussen published a popular account of the expedition in *Across Arctic America* (Rasmussen, 1927) as well as a (mostly) posthumous ten-volume report (Rasmussen, 1927–1952).

The Sixth Thule Expedition comprised a voyage along Greenland's east coast from Julianehåb to Aapilattoq to confirm Denmark's claim to East Greenland, following a Norwegian counterclaim in 1931 (Rasmussen, 1932). The expedition collected cartographic and magnetic data, and this work continued in the Seventh Thule Expedition of 1933. On this final journey, Rasmussen contracted pneumonia following food poisoning and was forced to return to Denmark, where he died on December 21 in the same year.

From his first expedition in 1902, Rasmussen devoted himself to the study of the Inuit people, language, culture, and history. His writings are still regarded as some of the best sources of ethnographic information on the Arctic.

Biography

Knud Rasmussen, of Danish descent, was born on June 7, 1879 in Jacobshavn (now Ilulissat), Greenland. He claimed to have Inuit blood on his mother's side. As a child, Inuit culture and folktales fascinated Rasmussen, particularly the stories about a fabled people in the north of the island. He intended to become an opera singer, but his career took a different direction when he was invited to join the Danish Literary Expedition led by Danish writer and explorer Ludwig Mylius-Erichsen. In 1908, Rasmussen married Dagmar Andersen, daughter of a wealthy Danish businessman, and shortly afterward met Danish journalist, writer, and explorer Peter Freuchen, who became a lifelong friend, traveling companion, and business partner. Rasmussen is best known for his seven Thule expeditions (between 1912 and 1933), which established him as one of Denmark's foremost polar ethnographers. Perhaps most famous was the Fifth Thule Expedition of 1921–1924, during which he traveled by sledge from Greenland to the Bering Strait. He married Dagmar Andersen in 1908. He was superbly suited to Arctic fieldwork, not only because he had spoken the language from childhood and was familiar with Inuit modes of travel, but because he held a deep esteem and respect for the traditions and lifestyles of the people he met. Rasmussen died in Denmark on December 21, 1933.

LIZ CRUWYS

See also **Fifth Thule Expedition; Freuchen, Peter; Greenland Inuit; Mylius-Erichsen, Ludvig**

Further Reading

Cruwys, E., "Profile: Knud Rasmussen." *Polar Record,* 26(156) (1990): 27–33

Freuchen, Peter, *I Sailed with Rasmussen*, New York: Julian Messner, 1958

Markham, Clements, *The Lands of Silence: A History of Arctic and Antarctic Exploration*, Cambridge and New York: Cambridge University Press, 1921

Rasmussen, Knud, *People of the Polar North: A Record,* London: Kegan, Paul, Trench, Truber & Co., 1908

———, "Foreløbig beretning om 'Den Første Thule-Ekspedition' 1912–1913." *Geografisk Tidsskrift,* 22(5) (1913–1914): 183–198

———, "Report on the First Thule Expedition 1912." *Meddelelser om Grønland,* 51(8) (1915): 283–340

———, *Greenland by the Polar Sea: The Story of the Thule Expedition from Melville Bay to Cape Morris Jesup*, London: William Heinemann, 1921

———, *Across Arctic America: Narrative of the Fifth Thule Expedition*, New York: G.P. Putnam and Sons, 1927

———, "Report of the II. Thule Expedition for the exploration of Greenland from Melville Bay to de Long Fjord 1916–1918." *Meddelelser om Grønland,* 65(1928): 1–180

———, "South East Greenland. The Sixth Thule Expedition, 1931, from Cape Farewell to Ammassalik." *Geografisk Tidsskrift,* 25(1932): 169–197

———, *Report of the Fifth Thule Expedition 1921–1924. The Danish Expedition to Arctic North America in Charge of Knud Rasmussen, Ph.D.,* Volumes, 1–10, Copenhagen: Gyldendalske Boghandel, Nordisk Forlag, 1927–1952

RAVEN

The common raven—*Corvus corax, Suor* in Yakut, *Oli* in Evenk, *Olindya* in Even, *Tulukaruk* in Yupik Eskimo, and *tulugaq* in Inuktitut—is widespread in the Northern Hemisphere and is also a central figure in the mythology of all indigenous peoples of the Arctic. In northern Russia and Siberia, it inhabits the taiga and partially the tundra area. Birds dispersing from their overwintering grounds may also reach the coastal tundra and some of the islands in the northern seas. In Alaska, northern Canada, northern Scandinavia, and Greenland, the raven is a year-round resident, when most other birds migrate south for winter, and is found from coastal meadow to Arctic

Raven (*Corvus corax*).
Copyright Tom Murphy/National Geographic Image Collection

tundra. It may also congregate near human habitations, particularly in winter.

Ravens are large birds, reaching more than 24 inches (60 cm) long. They have black feathers with an iridescent sheen. They are members of the Corvidae family, which includes jays, magpies, and crows. They can be distinguished from crows by their wedge-shaped tail, larger bill, and larger size.

The raven is considered to live longer than other birds (up to 30 years). While its fertility and level of reproduction are relatively high, its numbers are not large. The high rate of bird mortality in the winter period and migration to other regions with a mild winter climate largely account for such low populations.

During autumn and winter, the raven lives singly (rarely in pairs) in groups or in flocks of 10–30 only in areas where they can sustain themselves. Ravens begin courtship behavior in January, with plays by the male in the air becoming more frequent and prolonged in the second half of February. Throughout the breeding season, ravens usually live in pairs, and may remain paired for life. Ravens can use the same nest several times. When starting to build the nests, ravens are territorial and actively banish their relatives and other birds of prey from the nest area. Nests are situated at least 3–5 m from each other, and are usually built on cliff ledges or in tall trees. Along the coast, ravens often live near seabird colonies where they prey on eggs and nestlings.

The nest frame, which may be 51–80 cm (2–4 ft) in diameter, is constructed of twigs and branches and the bedding comprises two layers. The nest bottom consists of ground dry manure, moss, soft willow inner bark, thin roots, and twigs. The upper layer of the nest is lined with fur of different animals such as cows, horses, deer, elk, or hares along with feathers and other materials.

Eggs are laid from mid-February to late May, depending on latitude: in central Yakutia, egg laying takes place from March 20 to April 5 under winter conditions (a solid layer of snow, often blizzards, snowfall and frost when the temperature is 25–35ºC below zero at nights). Usually, there are three to seven eggs in a single laying, although up to three periods of laying may occur. Eggs are on average 49 × 33 mm, with an average mass of 25 g. The incubation period is 19–24 days per egg. The female incubates the eggs alone, with the male feeding her from time to time. Usually, the male remains 50–100 m from the nest and emits a signal in case of danger.

The nestlings increase weight rapidly, from 17–21 g at hatching to 990 g when they fledge from the nest about 6 weeks after hatching. In the nest, the young are fed by both parents until their first flight from the nest. The female probably keeps nestlings warm during the day until the babies are 8–10 days old; the mother raven sleeps with them in the nest until they are about 20 days old. They remain with their parents during the summer months in the location of the nest. Disintegration of the brood takes place at the end of August to the beginning of September.

Ravens are omnivorous, and will eat almost everything. The composition of its diet changes, depending on the seasons. In snowless periods of the year, ravens feed on rodents, other birds' eggs, insects, worms, green parts of grass, berries, fruits, and seeds. In winter, when food is scarce, ravens are primarily scavengers, feeding on carrion—corpses of wild ungulates, horned cattle, hare, ptarmigan, and heath-cocks, and wild reindeer in the tundra region. Another important food source in winter comes from garbage from human homes, waste products from slaughter houses, and carrion from hunting and trapping. The losses caused by ravens to the hunting industry are considerable. They destroy the valuable furs of animals caught in traps, and eat and carry away meat of ungulates and hares caught by hunters. For example, in Central Yakutia, 40–60% of trapped hares are eaten and carried away by ravens. For these reasons, ravens are often exterminated by hunters.

Ravens may disperse south in autumn and return north to breed in spring. Mainly, the migration is connected with separating the younger ones from their parents, since ravens' feeding habits are adapted to survive harsh winters when food is scarce, by scavenging on carrion. According to visual observations, a raven's winter hunting range in Central Yakutia is no less than 500–1000 sq km. It is one of the rare species that locates food by flying around vast areas.

The raven is one of the rare birds often mentioned in folk tales and myths from the indigenous peoples of northwestern America and the Bering Sea area (Tlingit, Athapaskan, Yup'ik, and Alutiiq). However, the attitude toward the raven in these myths is contradictory. In some of them, for instance to the Yup'ik, the raven is a beloved son (sometimes a relation) of Ulu Toyon who lives in the third heaven—one of the creators of the human soul, the supreme judge, punishing people's sins. In these myths, the raven can either speak or its feathers are bright red and flame-like. At the same time, it is prohibited to scold, tease, or kill a raven for no reason. Ulu Toyon may get angry and punish the sinner. In an Evenki myth, the raven is also the creator's assistant, and the Tlingit, Tutchone, Haida, Tsimshian, and Alutiiq all view the raven as a deity, the creator of the world and bringer of daylight. The raven is also important in the creation of myths by the Eskimo. However, in another Yakut myth, the raven is related to underground spirits—*abaasy*. In one of the epics, the raven embodies the spirit of the road, which leads to the underground world, and the result of its curse in the epic is that the hero falls asleep (Mordosov, 1999). Images of ravens are also important in Siberian shaman rites. Among the elders, the belief exists that one is not allowed to hunt and kill the raven because doing so can curse the offender and make him unhappy for the rest of his life. In the Canadian and Alaskan Arctic and Subarctic, the raven is also a trickster, because of his intelligence, bravery, and sense of humor.

In general, these myths and superstitions reflect the fact that the raven is one of the most crucial elements of the environment, playing a significant role in the life of people and other living beings and doubtlessly having the right to exist.

BORIS IGNATIEVICH SIDOROV

See also **Mythology of the Inuit**

Further Reading

King, Alexander D., "Raven Tales from Kamchatka." In *Voices from the Four Directions*, edited by Brian Swann, Lincoln: University of Nebraska Press, 2003

Krechmar, A.B., A.V. Andreyev & A.Y. Kondratyev, *Birds of the Northern Plains*, Leningrad: Nauka, 1991 (in Russian)

Larionov G.P., N.I. Germogenov & B.I. Sidorov, "Fauna and Ecology of Winter Birds of Leno-Viluy Basin." In *Fauna and Ecology of the Overland Vertebrates of the Taiga of Yakutia*, Yakutsk: Yakutsk State University Publishing House, 1980, pp. 85–141 (in Russian)

Melzack, Ronald, (editor), *Raven: Creator of the World*, Boston: Little, Brown, 1970

Mordosov, I.I., *Fur-Bearing Animals of Yakutia*, Yakutsk: Yakutsk University Publishing House, 1999 (in Russian)

Vorobyev, K.A., *Birds of Yakutia*, Moscow: USSR Academy of Sciences Publishing House, 1963 (in Russian)

RAZORBILL

The razorbill (*Alca torda*) is among the larger members of the Alcidae family of marine seabirds. They are more closely related to the common (*Uria aalge*) and thick-billed (*Uria lomvia*) murres than the smaller dovekie (*Alle alle*), which comprise the other living members of the auk tribe Alcini. The recently (*c.*1860) extinct great auk (*Pinguinus impennis*) was also a member of the Alcini, and some taxonomists believe that the great auk may have shared the genus *Alca* with the razorbill.

Although shorter, lighter, and thicker-bodied than murres, razorbills have a longer tail, which gives them a slightly overall length advantage (42 cm versus 40 cm). Razorbills of the subspecies *A. t. islandica*, found in Iceland, the Faroes, and the British Isles, are smaller (620 g versus 720 g) than those in the subspecies *A. t. torda* found elsewhere. All razorbills are similar in color pattern to the murres. They have a black head, neck, and back, contrasting with a white chest and belly. Razorbills are most distinguished from murres by their deeper, more robust black bills marked with a vertical white stripe.

Like murres, razorbills are well adapted in body and wing morphology for diving and swimming underwater in pursuit of their prey, typically mid-water schooling fish found in coastal waters of the continental shelf. Their primary prey include capelin, sandlance, herring, and sprat. Razorbills are capable of diving to depths of 120 m in pursuit of these fish, but the majority of their dives are shallower (25–40 m). In shallow water (less than 25 m deep), their dives average about half a minute in duration. Swimming speed may be on the order of 1.5 ms^{-1}. Razorbills probably use vision to locate their prey, and may have several adaptations about the eyes to aid the flow of water and resist pressure deformation when diving at depth.

Razorbills are found only in the North Atlantic. Their range is most similar to that of the common murre, although murres are also found in the North Pacific, where razorbills are absent. Razorbills winter farther south than the other auks. In North America, razorbills are most often found in winter from Nova Scotia (particularly Georges Bank) to Cape Cod and in Europe from southern Scandinavia to the Mediterranean and North Africa. They migrate north to breed on islands or coastal cliffs from Newfoundland and the Gulf of St Lawrence north to Baffin Island and Greenland in the west and from northern France to northern Norway in the east. The majority (96%) of birds breed in Europe, with Iceland hosting 70% of the breeders and the British Isles another 20%. One immense colony in Iceland (Látrabjarg) may host half the world's population of razorbills. (It is also home to about one million pairs of murres, which is much more than the entire world population of razorbills!) Only about 2% of the razorbill population breeds in North America (chiefly in Canada).

Razorbills are highly colonial seabirds, nesting in colonies typically numbering in the thousands. Breeders and nonbreeding birds alike return to the nesting colony a month or more prior to egg laying. Colony attendance varies on a 4–6-day cycle during this period, with very few birds present some days to large numbers a few days later. Breeders typically return to the same mate and nest site each year. Nonbreeders apparently spend their time at the colony prospecting for both mates and nesting sites. About a third of these birds begin breeding at four years of age and most are breeding by five years. Social activity takes place either in large "rafts" of birds on the water, near the nest site (typically in a crevice or among boulders), and in "arenas" where both male and female breeders may engage in "extrapair copulations" with individuals other than their mates. Copulation takes place on land, with mated pairs copulating frequently (on average 80 times) prior to egg laying. Extrapair copulations account for about 2.4% of all copulations; evidence suggests that females seek these "extramarital" copulations as fertility insurance.

A single egg, averaging 13% of the female's weight, is laid in mid-May to early June. If the first egg is lost, a second, smaller egg may be laid. Both parents incubate the egg, trading duties several times a day. The chick hatches after about five weeks and weighs about 60 g, relatively low among the other auks. Parents feed it 3–4 times per day, mostly in the early morning, bringing relatively small loads of 1–11 fish that are carried crosswise in the parent's bill. In about two to three weeks, the chick reaches its maximum nestling weight of about 200 g. At this time, around dusk, it leaves the colony for the sea. The male parent accompanies it at sea for another month or so, where it continues to develop. Chicks that are not accompanied by an adult during this period have a lower chance of survival. About two months after hatching, the chick is able to fly.

Breeding birds are successful in fledging young in about 70% of their breeding attempts, with the failure of eggs to hatch and avian predators accounting for most of the losses. Little is known of chick survival after they fledge. The annual survival of breeding adults is about 90%.

The worldwide population of razorbills is estimated to range between 500,000 and 700,000 breeders. These numbers are significantly lower than those for both murre species (estimated at 27–35 million breeders combined) and for the dovekie (7–15 million). Razorbills have perhaps never been as numerous as the other auks, but have likely faced the same population threats they have. The species appears to have increased in some portions of its range on both sides of the Atlantic in recent decades. However, its small total population and the location of both its breeding and winter distributions near human activities does put it at risk to such threats as drowning in gill nets, oil fouling and other forms of pollution (i.e., PCBs), and loss of prey base due to human overfishing. In Newfoundland, Canada, some razorbills are killed during the legal hunting of murres as well.

FRED HARRINGTON

See also **Auk; Seabirds**

Further Reading

Birkhead, Tim R. & Anders P. Møller, *Sperm Competition in Birds*, London: Academic Press, 1992

Chapdelaine, Gilles, Anthony W. Diamond, Richard D. Elliot & Gregory J. Robertson, *Status and Population Trends of the Razorbill in Eastern North America*, Ottawa: Canadian Wildlife Service, 2001

Croxall, John P., Peter GH Evans & Ralph W. Schreiber, *Status and Conservation of the World's Seabirds*, Cambridge: International Council for Bird Preservation, 1984

Gaston, Anthony J. & Ian L. Jones, *The Auks*, Oxford: Oxford University Press, 1998

Lloyd, Clare S., Mark L. Tasker & Ken Partridge, *The Status of Seabirds in Britain and Ireland*, London: T. and A.D. Poyser, 1991

Montevecchi, William A., *Studies of High Latitude Seabirds 4*, Ottawa: Canadian Wildlife Service, 1996

Montevecchi, William A. & Anthony J. Gaston, *Studies of High Latitude Seabirds 1*, Ottawa: Canadian Wildlife Service, 1991

Nettleship, David N. & Tim R. Birkhead, *The Atlantic Alcidae*, London: Academic Press, 1985

Petersen, A., *Icelandic Birds*, Reykjavik: Rit Landvernander 8, 1982

Wagner, Richard H., "Behavioural and breeding habitat related aspects of sperm competition in razorbills." *Behaviour*, 123(1992): 1–26

RED DOG MINE

Pilots and geologists discovered Red Dog's mining potential in 1953 when they noticed mineral staining in the area while flying overhead. In 1980, the Red Dog Mine was formally co-opted by the Northwest Alaska Native Association (NANA), a corporation that represents the interests of Iñupiat natives of northwest Alaska. Two years later, NANA signed an agreement with Teck Cominco, a Canadian mineral resources group, to exploit the deposits at Red Dog. The company currently holds 150,000 hectares of mineral rights in the region. The site consists of the mining camp and a port located 52 miles away. The two sites are linked by a haul road, which passes through Cape Krusenstern National Monument and National Forest lands.

Since it first began operation in 1989, Red Dog Mine has become the largest and richest operating zinc mine in the world. In total, the mine contains 17% of the known reserves in the Western world. Located in the fragile Arctic environment of the DeLong Mountains of Alaska's Brooks Range, Red Dog is approximately 55 miles from the Chukchi Sea. The nearest town is Kotzebue (population 3000), located some 90 miles away.

The mine is prolific and, in 2000, Red Dog milled 3 million tons of ore. Most of the ore is shipped to smelters in British Columbia, Europe, Korea, Japan, and Australia. In fact, Red Dog's exports are divided evenly among Asia, Europe, and Canada. In 2000, Teck Cominco discovered natural gas and coal deposits in the area. In the near future, the company plans to use the natural gas reserves to power the mine, thereby reducing its reliance on more expensive diesel fuel.

The boom in production at Red Dog has come at an environmental cost. Spills along the haul road between the mine and port are a relatively common occurrence and this has caused alarm in local communities. In 1997, the company paid a US$4.7 million settlement to the United States Department of Justice for committing hundreds of Clean Water Act violations. In May 2001, the United States Forest Service published a study of heavy metals in mosses and soils along the haul road. The study found levels of contamination that equaled or exceeded levels found in samples, "from the most severely polluted regions of Central European countries."

A health assessment was conducted by the Alaska Public Health Department on the impact of the spills on Alaska natives living near the mine. In October 2001, the Health Department took blood samples of residents and found that contamination does not currently pose a public health threat. Native residents of Kivalina remain deeply concerned that the mine may be polluting the local ecosystem. They believe that the haul road and shipping activities associated with the port have disrupted the migration of wildlife in the region. According to Colleen Koenig, Tribal Administrator of the Native Village of Kivalina, treated wastewater is dumped into the Wulik River, which Iñupiat natives use for subsistence fishing, the Iñupiat community still depends on subsistence foods like caribou, fish, and seal.

Alaska state and federal agencies are evaluating Teck Cominco's plan to dredge its port on the Chukchi Sea and to extend its loading dock in order to accommodate larger shipping vessels. The company is also expanding its operations and improving the efficiency of its mill. The mine will soon produce 1.1 million tons per year of 56% zinc concentrate. This project will cost an estimated US$90 million. Teck Cominco believes that the region still holds substantial undiscovered zinc reserves and will continue to explore the area for high-grade deposits. Recent discoveries at the site will ensure that it will continue to be highly productive into the next decade. But the pace of production will likely depend on the rise and fall of zinc prices, which have shown a steady decline since 1996. This decline has been offset by a concomitant increase in demand for zinc, however.

Early in the 21st century, the Red Dog Mine is of enormous economic importance to the region and is the financial lifeblood of the nearby Inupiaq Eskimo community of Kivalina (population 383). It employs 443 workers, 60% of whom are Alaska natives. In 2000, wages exceeded US$15 million.

KOREY CAPOZZA

Further Reading

Alaska Department of Environmental Conservation, Red Dog Mine Contamination Project, website: http:// www.state.ak.us/ local/akpages/ENV.CONSERV/press/reddog/index.htm

Ford, Jesse & Linda Hasselback, "Heavy metals in mosses and soils on six transects along the Red Dog Mine haul road Alaska." *National Park Service Study*, May 2001

Horswill, Doug, Deidre Riley & David Parker, "Zinc and sustainable development: the case of Red Dog Mine." Published online by the International Zinc Association: http://www.iza.com/zwo_org/Environment/040107.htm#up

O'Brien, Michael, "Alaska natives and environmentalists battle injustice at Red Dog." *Vermont Journal of the Environment*, November 13, 2001

Skok, Mark, "Alaska's Red Dog Mine: beating the odds." Online publication of the Interagency Minerals Coordinating Group, Department of the Interior, State of Alaska and the US Forest Service, http://imcg.wr.usgs.gov/usbmak/mt1.html

St John, Jeff, "Red Dog truck spills tons of zinc." *Anchorage Daily News*, July 21, 2001

REDFISH

"Redfish" is a common name for four closely related fish belonging to the genus *Sebastes* (family Scorpaenidae, order Scorpaeniformes, class Osteichthyes) that inhabit the north Atlantic and adjacent Arctic regions: golden redfish (*Sebastes marinus*), deepwater redfish (*S. mentella*), small redfish (*S. viviparous*), and rosefish (*S. fasciatus*). The other species of this genus, numbering more than a hundred, inhabit subtropical and temperate waters of the Pacific Ocean.

Redfishes are important food resources. In the region of the Barents Sea, about 3.4 million ton of redfish were caught between 1955 and 1999, which is about 16–17% of the total fish catch in the area. In the eastern North Atlantic, *S. mentella* comprises about 69.5% of the total annual catch of redfish, *S. marinus* about 30%, and *S. viviparus* less than 0.5%. At present, all populations of redfish are in decline.

All species of the genus are viviparous: insemination takes place internally, but females carry the sperm and fertilization may take place a few months later. Live young are hatched after about two months. Adults are benthopelagic (living and feeding near the bottom as well as in midwaters or near the surface), and make daily vertical migrations: downward by day, upward by night. Redfish grow very slowly: larvae and young are morphologically very similar, and thus age determination is difficult.

The golden redfish *S. marinus* is distributed from Kattegat and the North Sea northward to Spitsbergen and the Barents Sea and eastward to Novaya Zemlya, and rarely in the White Sea. It is also common around Iceland and along the southern part of Greenland, and along the North American coast southward to Flemish Cape, Grand Banks, and Gulf of St Lawrence. *S. marinus* differs from the deepwater redfish and rosefish in having the tip of the lower (fifth) preopercular spine directed usually downward and slightly backward versus mostly obliquely forward and downward. Its color is bright red with a dusky area on the posterior part of the opercle (the largest thin bone forming the gill cover in bony fishes). Body length can be up to 100 cm, usually 35–55 cm. The juveniles live in the fjords, bays, and inshore waters. The adults are found off the coast in waters at 100–1000 m depth. Adults feed on krill (euphausiids) and small fish such as herrings and capelin, and ctenophores (comb jellies). Insemination of females takes place in August-September in the Barents Sea, and from October to January off Iceland and Greenland. Fertilization of the ripe oocytes takes place during February and March, with the release of larvae from April to June or even to August. On hatching, the larvae are about 6–8 mm long. Females of size 43–45 cm long usually spawn 87–311,000 eggs, while those up to 51 cm long spawn 255–288,000 eggs.

The deepwater redfish *S. mentella* (also known as ocean perch) is distributed in the Norwegian Sea from the Lofoten Islands northward to Svalbard, and in the southern part of the Barents Seas, rarely to 35° E. *S. mentella* also occurs on the Iceland-Faroes Ridge, around Iceland, along the coast of Greenland, and from the southeastern coast of Baffin Island, southward to the latitude of Long Island. Its color is bright red, and its length can be up to 55 cm, usually up to 40 cm. The fish may reach an age of 27 years. Males become mature at 11–15 years of age, at a length of 33–38 cm; females mature at 12–17 years of age, at a length of 35–42 cm. The deepwater redfish has both benthic and bathypelagic stocks, mostly offshore, found between 300 and 910 m depth. *S. mentella* feeds on euphausiids, hyperiids, cephalopods, chaetognaths, and small fishes. Insemination of the females takes place in August-September in the Barents Sea or from

September to mid-December off Iceland. Fertilization of the oocytes occurs during January-February in the Barents Sea or in March off Iceland, and larvae are released in April-May or June. The length of larvae at hatching is about 7–9 mm. Females may lay from 10,500 to 124,900 eggs.

The rosefish or *S. fasciatus* is distributed from the southeastern coast of Labrador southward to Long Island, also southwest off Iceland, and rarely off western Greenland. In shallow waters at Eastport, Maine, a subspecies *S. f. kellyi* occurs. Its color is bright grayish-red with a dusky zone on the upper and posterior part of the opercle. Its size is up to 42 cm (usually to 30 cm). It is most abundant on the banks off the Atlantic coast of North America at 70–500 m depth, and feeds on euphausiids, decapods, mysids, small molluscs, and fishes. Insemination of the females occurs from June to August or even November. The ripe oocytes are fertilized from November to February and the larvae are released from June to August or even to October.

The small redfish *S. viviparus* occurs along the Norwegian coast from Kattegat northward to Tanafjord in Finmark, rarely off the coast of Bear Island, also in the northern part of the North Sea, around Shetland Islands, the coast of Scotland, northern England, Wales, and Ireland, rarely in the English Channel, and westward on the Rockall bank, common around the Faroes and Iceland (rare along the northern coast and absent on the eastern coast). It is found sporadically off East Greenland. *S. viviparus* differs from other redfish in having less than 55 oblique scale rows below the lateral line (versus more than 55 rows); the tip of the lower (fifth) preopercular spine is also directed backward or obliquely backward or downward. Its color is bright red, with several large dark bands on the sides, and it reaches a length of up to 35 cm (usually to 25 cm). It is a benthic species found on rocky bottoms, close to the shore, usually between 10 and 150 m, but also recorded at 760 m. It is gregarious, but to a far smaller degree than the other *Sebastes*. The insemination period and fertilization of the oocytes are unknown, but larvae are released from May to August. The length of larvae on hatching is about 4–5 mm. The fish attain sexual maturity at 12 cm length and at 12 or more years of age. Females produce between 12 and 29,000 eggs.

NATALIA CHERNOVA

Further Reading

Barsukov, Vladimir V., Lubov' V. Shestova & Nina V. Mukhina, "Redfishes of the Genus Sebastes." In *Ikhtyofauna i usloviya ee suschestvovaniya v Barentsevom more*, edited by Gennady G. Matishov, Apatity: Kol'sky Filial AN SSSR, 1986, pp. 48–55 (in Russian)

Boehlert, George W. & Mary M. Yoklavich, "Reproduction, embryonic energetics, and the maternal-fetal relationship in the viviparous genus Sebastes (Pisces: Scorpaenidae)." *Biological Bulletin*, 167(2) (1984): 354–370

Litvinenko, Nikolay I., "Sebastes fasciatus kellyi Litvinenko 1974 (Scorpaenidae) from coastal waters off Eastport (Maine, USA)." *Voprosi Ikhtiologii*, 19(3) (1979): 387–401 (in Russian)

Whitehead, P.J., M.-L. Bauchot, J.-C. Hureau, J. Nielsen & E. Tortonese (editors), *Fishes of the North-Eastern Atlantic and the Mediterranean*, Volume I, Paris: UNESCO, 1984

REINDEER

The reindeer (*Rangifer tarandus*) is a ruminant of the deer family Cervidae with a circumpolar distribution, and is known as caribou in the New World. Reindeer are well suited to life in cold regions, with specially adapted hooves for mobility on snow or soft, swampy ground and fur comprised of hollow guard hairs that efficiently conserve body heat by retaining warm air near the skin surface. Both males and females have antlers.

Wild reindeer certainly developed by the early Pleistocene (2 million years ago), perhaps even earlier, in the forests of North America, where they were widely distributed. Researchers believe the animals entered Eurasia via Beringia. At present, reindeer number more than 5 million, most of them in the Old World. Of these, some 2.5 million semidomestic and 1 million wild reindeer are found in Russia, with over half of the latter in the Taymyr Peninsula population. Much smaller wild populations persist in places like south Finland and Karelia (*R. t. fennicus*) and southern Norway (*R. t. tarandus*). Together, these populations of wild and semidomestic animals are highly valued by aboriginal and nonnative peoples for spiritual beliefs and many subsistence purposes, including nutrition, clothing, and shelter. Commercial products include meat, but also skins, handicrafts, and even antler velvet for the market in Southeast Asia.

Estimates for the origins of reindeer domestication range widely from 1000 to 3000 years ago. For example, although uncertain, it is believed that Nenets of the Yamal-Nenets Autonomous Okrug arrived in that region *c.*2500–3000 years ago and they were already herding reindeer. Others suggest that reindeer husbandry, as we know it today, started about 1000 years ago. It has been suggested that Saami of Fennoscandia and adjoining Kola Peninsula learned reindeer herding and breeding from the Nenets prior to migration into their present homeland and later adapted the practice to their own socioeconomic and environmental conditions. However, writings from as early as the 9th century describe the Saami engaging in regular reindeer husbandry, based on the systematic utilization of the land, and it is possible that they developed husbandry independently of the Nenets.

In recent centuries, more intensive modes of husbandry evolved, although still based on human and animal labor and traditional materials. A high-tech system involving motor vehicles (snowmobiles, motorcycles, and helicopters) developed in the 1970s. This modern system is characterized by an emphasis on meat production via autumn slaughtering of calves. Supplemental feeding of animals in late winter has become increasingly common as a strategy for buffering against mortality and malnutrition. Thus, agricultural norms and regulations prevail, often at the expense of sociocultural traditions and knowledge involving reindeer management.

The Svalbard reindeer (*R. t. platyrhynchus*) occurs in four areas within the Spitsbergen Archipelago. The origin of these populations is unknown, but dated fossil feces suggest that they arrived there between 6700 and 5000 years ago. While this taxon is closely related to the Peary caribou of the Canadian High Arctic (*R. t. pearyi*), recent genetic evidence indicates that they had a Eurasian origin and migrated to Svalbard from Novaya Zemlya via Franz Josef Land. In the Russian Arctic, the largest remaining populations of wild reindeer (*R. t. tarandus*) inhabit the western Taymyr Peninsula, while small populations of the subspecies *R. t. pearsoni* survive on Novaya Zemlya and the Novosibirsk Islands.

The fact that reindeer populations fluctuate is well known and has been extensively documented. Among the known factors responsible for population changes include predation, human exploitation, natural mortality, climate, range condition, and immigration-emigration. For example, during the winter of 1975–1976 on Edgeøya, Svalbard, an estimated 23% of the reindeer population starved to death. The surviving animals seemed to recover rapidly, which indicated that there was no food shortage, but that adverse snow and ice conditions made it inaccessible. Similar crashes have been documented in the Canadian Arctic Archipelago. Predators of reindeer include wolf, wolverine, bear, eagle, and lynx, except on Svalbard where humans are the only predators.

Mating takes place mainly in the first half of October, after which male antlers are shed. Although the timing varies somewhat geographically, calves are born beginning in late April, peaking in mid-May, after which female antlers are shed. Several individual herds of reindeer carry out distinct annual migrations that appear to have restricted calving areas as their focal point. In the Russian Arctic, the calving grounds of the Taymyr Peninsula herd are on the tundra in the north of the peninsula and the wintering grounds lie astride the Arctic Circle in the boreal forest to the south, thus

requiring a twice-yearly movement of some 965 km. Semidomestic herds on neighboring Yamal Peninsula undergo a similar migration pattern, albeit with somewhat shorter distances of up to 800 km.

The seasonal movements of reindeer are partially controlled by the availability and quality of their food resources. Throughout the winter and early spring, when forage is often in short supply, reindeer feed extensively on lichens. The primary value of lichens lies in their high carbohydrate content that is needed to meet the animals' high energy requirements. Reindeer have the highest metabolic demands in spring and early summer, when plant growth is most rapid, and the nutritive quality of the forage is highest. Peak forage nitrogen and phosphorus concentrations in tundra forage species are high compared to most temperate and tropical forages. Free-ranging reindeer have the opportunity to maximize forage nutrient quality during spring and summer by migrating north into the tundra as the seasonal timing of plant growth progresses, and also by selecting among plant species—graminoids, willows, and herbs—and among local feeding sites. However, feeding time must be balanced against avoidance of periodically intense harassment by insects and predators. Persistent heavy grazing has frequently reduced or eliminated deciduous shrubs and preferred lichen species, through the effects of both actual grazing and incidental trampling when lichens are dry and brittle. Repeated grazing on summer ranges may lead to loss of shrubs and poorly trample-resistant lichens and replacement by highly productive lawnlike sedge/grass communities.

Human-related threats to reindeer populations range in scale from local harassment of individual feeding animals by motor vehicles to climate change. The most widespread and immediate problems facing wild and semidomestic populations are habitat degradation from resource extraction enterprises. Some examples include the following: (1) large-scale forestry, which eliminates both arboreal and ground lichens; (2) mining, oil and gas, hydroelectric power and tourism developments, which can seriously fragment or even destroy critical habitats; (3) air pollution, such as sulfur dioxide and radioactive cesium, which affects lichens, in particular, in places like Noril'sk on Taymyr Peninsula; and (4) poaching, which has become a major problem throughout the Russian Arctic and affects annually up to 10–20% or more of certain herds, for example, on Kola Peninsula. Anthropogenic disturbances to pastures are often relatively small or patchy individually, but collectively they comprise a regional concern since many occur over extensive areas and their effects can persist indefinitely. For example, in Purovsky and Nadym in northwest Siberia alone, some 60,000 km² of pastures have been destroyed due to uncontrolled off-road vehicle traffic and fires attributed to human agency.

BRUCE FORBES

See also **Caribou; Lichen; Reindeer Pastoralism**

Further Reading

Baskin, Leonid, "Reindeer Husbandry in the Soviet Union." In *Wildlife Production: Conservation and Sustainable Development*, edited by Lyle A. Renecker & R.J. Hudson, University of Alaska, Fairbanks: Agriculture and Forestry Experiment Station, 1991, pp. 218–226

Forbes, Bruce C., "Reindeer herding and petroleum development on Poluostrov Yamal: sustainable or mutually incompatible uses?." *Polar Record*, 35 (1999): 317–322

Forbes, Bruce C. & Gary Kofinas (editors), "The human role in reindeer and caribou grazing systems." *Polar Research*, 19(1) (2000): 1–142

Gunn, Anne & Terje Skogland, "Responses of Caribou and Reindeer to Global Warming." In *Global Change and Arctic Terrestrial Ecosystems*, edited by Walter C. Oechel et al., Berlin: Springer-Verlag, (1997), pp. 189–200

Karlsson, Ann-Marie & Tord Constenius, *Reindeer Husbandry in Sweden*, Jönköping: The Swedish Board of Agriculture, 2000

Klein, David R., "The role of climate and insularity in establishment and persistence of *Rangifer tarandus* populations in the High Arctic." *Ecological Bulletins*, 47 (1999): 96–104

Klein, David R. & Tatiana J. Vlasova, "Lichens, a unique forage resource threatened by air pollution." *Rangifer*, 12 (1992): 21–27

Kojola, Ilpo, Timo Helle & Pekka Aikio, "Productivity of semidomesticated reindeer in Finland." *Rangifer*, 11 (1991): 53–63

Krupnik, Igor, *Arctic Adaptations: Native Whalers and Reindeer Herders of Northern Eurasia*, Hanover: University Press of New England, 1993

Lent, Peter C. & David R. Klein, "Tundra Vegetation as a Rangeland Resource." In *Vegetation Science Applications for Rangeland Analysis and Management*, edited by P.T. Tueller, Dordrecht: Kluwer Academic, 1988, pp. 307–337

Podkoritov, F.M., *Reindeer Herding on Yamal*, Sosnovyi Bor: Leningrad Atomic Electrical Station, 1995

Riseth, Jan Åge, "*Sámi Reindeer Management Under Technological Change 1960–1990: Implications for Common-Pool Resource Use Under Various Natural and Institutional Conditions*," Ph.D. thesis, Ås: Agricultural University of Norway, 2000

Staaland, Hans, J.O. Scheie, F.A. Grøndahl, E. Persen, A.B. Leifseth & Ø. Holand, "The introduction of reindeer to Brøggerhalvøya, Svalbard: grazing preference and effect on vegetation." *Rangifer*, 13 (1993): 15–19

Syroechkovskii, Evgenii E., *Wild Reindeer*, New Delhi: Amerind Publishing Co., 1995

Torp, Eivind, "Reindeer herding and the call for sustainabilty in the Swedish mountain region." *Acta Borealia*, 1 (1999): 83–95

REINDEER PASTORALISM

The keeping of domestic reindeer is one of the primary traditional, economic, ecological, and spiritual activities of the indigenous peoples of northern Eurasia. Until after World War II, reindeer provided the most common form of transport in northern Eurasia. For traditional nomadic herding societies (Saami, Evenki, or Nenets), the reindeer is the focus for folklore, songs, traditional crafts, and rituals. The activity of keeping reindeer is often referred to as "herding," "ranching," or "husbandry." The term *reindeer pastoralism* captures the ecology nature of how people control the reindeer's use of land and teach the animals to recognize certain pastures as home.

If dog husbandry is associated primarily with Inuit of the North American Arctic, reindeer husbandry is the most common form of domestication in Arctic Eurasia. However, herders in western Eurasia also use trained dogs to keep the herds, and in some rare instances domesticated moose and Yakut horses were also used for transport. Reindeer husbandry is not confined to Arctic Eurasia. In the late 19th and early 20th centuries, the American and Canadian governments introduced reindeer to Alaska and to Canada's Mackenzie River delta. Isolated herds also exist in Scotland, Greenland, and northern China and Mongolia. The Saian mountains of southern Siberia are considered by many to be the source of reindeer pastoralism, up to 3000 years ago.

All domestic reindeer are classified as *Rangifer tarandus* and, unlike wild *Rangifer* (or caribou), have no scientifically recognized subspecific designations. However, local reindeer herdsmen often make regional distinctions of biological type based on appearance (typically stature and pelage) and behavior (typically, the animals' tolerance of people and fidelity to their home pastures). These differences are attributed to local breeding traditions extending over several hundred years. The most widely recognized difference among the species is between short tundra reindeer and taller forest reindeer. Technically, no biological difference exists between domestic and wild *Rangifer*, and both populations can and do interbreed. However, researchers have found significant differences in behavior, which may have a genetic basis, although this remains unestablished.

The seasonal breeding cycle of domestic reindeer is offset by several weeks by that of their wild cousins, the caribou. Further, domestic reindeer tend to follow "leaders" along established trails, made by herders with skis or snow machines. Wild reindeer, by contrast, strike out over open terrain. Although reindeer herders have often captured or conducted controlled interbreeding between wild and domesticated *Rangifer*, all insist that the progeny remain "wild" for up to three generations.

Herding practices vary between different circumpolar peoples. While herders in western Eurasia kept

Saami reindeer herders take hay to their reindeer on winter pastures, Sapmi, Norway.
Copyright Bryan and Cherry Alexander Photography

large stocks of reindeer for several centuries, in most areas large-scale reindeer ranching was introduced only during the Soviet period (1917–1991). European Saami use unique riblike saddles and boatlike sleds when using reindeer for transport. Saami husbandry is closest to ranching in that the status of the herder is dependent on reindeer numbers. Saami herders mark reindeer ownership by cuts into the ears of reindeer using hereditary patterns. Although individual and extended family (*siida*) ownership of herds is well-marked, the numeric size of herds is a closely guarded secret. Saami pastoralism has suffered from the division of their herds, pastures, and their herdsmen across four nations (Norway, Sweden, Finland, and Russia).

In Siberia, Nenets, Komi, and Chukchi husbandry is also characterized by keeping large herds of several thousand head of small tundra reindeer. On the whole, these diverse peoples keep reindeer without the assistance of dogs. These large-scale herders do not ride reindeer, but instead use wooden sleds with thick runners that can be used over snow as well as over spring and summer grasses. Nenets, Komi, and Chukchi herders, partly due to the size of their herds, travel extremely vast distances to the Arctic Ocean during the hot summers and then south toward the treeline in the winter. Nenets herding is often singled out as unique due to the robustness of the herding tradition and the important role the reindeer plays in almost every part of social life. It is among Nenets people that one often finds cases of living exclusively with reindeer, without speaking Russian, and in some cases never having been registered by Russian authorities.

By contrast, the Evenki, Even, Dolgan, Khanty, Enets, and Ket people, to name just a few, have traditionally kept smaller groups of reindeer (around one hundred head) primarily for transport in order to support a nomadic way of life and an economy that relied upon hunting, fishing, and long-distance trade. Of these mixed-economy pastoralists, Evenkis are the most well known. Evenkis combine the use of wide saddles for transport and, in northern regions, the use of high sleds. Unlike western Siberian people, Evenki herdsmen control their reindeer from the right-hand side. Evenki healers often used the reindeer and its product in healing rituals, armed with the conviction that the reindeer could "absorb" illness or ill fortune in their human masters.

North American reindeer husbandry was founded upon stock imported from Chukotka using techniques transferred by hired Saami herders. In the early part of the 20th century, herdsmen lived and followed their herds in a traditional Eurasian manner. In the postwar period, reindeer were kept by means of mechanized transport. Alaska is the only place where the movement of herders is confined to specific pastures that are held in individual ownership, and the majority of reindeer keepers are not indigenous people.

Reindeer products enjoy a solid but specialized market. Reindeer milk (one of the richest mammalian milks) can be harvested in the spring. Pastoralists traditionally boil reindeer meat, although they eat some parts raw. Reindeer meat is most commonly sold frozen. Smoked reindeer products are becoming increasingly popular. Reindeer fur provides one of the warmest materials for winter clothing and is used in both traditional and modern crafts.

Reindeer husbandry throughout the world was radically transformed by forms of nation-state administrative intervention. In Soviet Siberia, reindeer ranching (*olenevodstvo*) was identified as one of the primary branches of the national economy, such that indigenous traditions of small-scale husbandry were forcibly replaced with large-scale herding systems. In the Soviet period, the budget of entire northern villages often depended upon the number of head or reindeer reported. The loss of a single reindeer could carry severe legal sanctions. In Scandinavia, the government allocation of pastures, combined with a complex subsidy system on reindeer products, has restricted the ability of herders to regulate the relationship of reindeer to pastures, and has led to a situation where pastures are overgrazed. In Norway, the keeping of reindeer forms part of the legal rights assigned to the Saami ethnicity. In Alaska and Canada, reindeer husbandry was a government-designed project at its onset. The challenge of the 21st century lies in negotiating a relationship between herders and indigenous governments.

Since the end of the Cold War, the interest of nation-states in reindeer economies has radically subsided. In Russia, state support to reindeer pastoralism has collapsed, creating a dramatic decline in numbers from several million to less than one hundred thousand in the space of ten years. In the Yamal-Nenets Autonomous Okrug, over half of the 500,000 strong herd was privatized between 1991 and 1998. Impoverished Siberian herders have let their herds go wild, have been forced to eat their herds, or have lost stock to exploding wolf populations since state-subsidized wolf hunts ended in the early 1990s. In present-day Siberia, many aboriginal communities and several entire nations exist for the first time in history without reindeer. In Scandinavia, the post-Cold War division of Saami territory contributed to a land shortage. In Alaska, the changing migration routes of wild caribou combined with a strict property-rights regime led to the loss of herds due to unexpected incursions of wild caribou. Reindeer herding has increasingly come to the attention of international ecological nongovernmental organizations. Although reindeer husbandry in northwestern Russia is relatively stable ecologically, in the Yamal region there are too many animals relative to pasture losses from the petroleum industry; and Yakutia, Chukotka, and Kamchatka face ecological threats to pastures from forestry, mining, air pollution, fires, and off-road vehicle traffic.

DAVID G. ANDERSON

See also **Association of World Reindeer Herders; Caribou; Caribou Hunting; Chukchi; Clothing; Evenki; Lichen; Nenets; Reindeer; Saami; Saami Council**

Further Reading

Anderson, David G., *Identity and Ecology in Arctic Siberia: The Number One Reindeer Brigade*, Oxford and New York: Oxford University Press, 2000

Bogoras-Tan, Vladimir Germanovich, *The Chukchee*, New York: Johnson Reprint Corporation, 1966
Golovnev, A.V. & Gail Osherenko, *Siberian Survival: The Nenets and Their Story*, Ithaca, New York: Cornell University Press, 1999
Jerstad, Jan & Ivar Bjorklund, *Living with Reindeer: A Story about Sami Reindeer-Herding Through the Eight Seasons of the Year*, Video Recording (43 minutes), Tromsø Museum, 1990
Lappalainen, Heimio, *The Skills You Passed On*, Video Recording (50 minutes), Taiga Nomads: A Documentary Series About the Evenki of Siberia, Helsinki: Illume Ltd., 1992
Olson, Dean Francis, *Alaska Reindeer Herdsmen: A Study of Native Management in Transition*, SEG Report. College: Institute of Social, Economic and Government Research, University of Alaska, 1969
Paine, Robert, *Herds of the Tundra: A Portrait of Saami Reindeer Pastoralism*, Washington: Smithsonian Institution Press, 1994
Popov, A.A., *The Nganasan: The Material Culture of the Tavgi Samoyeds*, The Hague: Mouton, 1966
Vasilevich, Grafira Makar'evna & Maksim G. Levin, "Tipy olenevodstva i ikh proiskhozhdenie." [Types of Reindeer Pastoralism and their Origins]. *Sovetskaia Etnografiia* [Soviet Ethnography] (1)(1951): 63–87

RELIGION—*See* **CHURCHES IN GREENLAND AND THE NORTH AMERICAN ARCTIC, ESTABLISHMENT OF; CHURCHES IN ICELAND AND THE SCANDINAVIAN ARCTIC, ESTABLISHMENT OF; CHURCHES IN RUSSIAN ARCTIC, ESTABLISHMENT OF; MISSIONARY ACTIVITY**

RELOCATION

Contact between indigenous and nonindigenous societies has led to the displacement and dispossession of indigenous peoples wherever this contact has occurred. Relocation is one example of such displacement. In this context, relocation is defined as the resettlement of people without their prior informed consent. The practice of relocation was official government policy and occurred in many places around the circumpolar world and affected people in Russia, Canada, Greenland, and the Aleutian Islands.

While most of the Arctic relocations took place in the mid-20th century, the policy, as it applies to indigenous populations, dates from much earlier. The United States began relocating practices, for example, in the early 1800s.

Relocation in the Arctic has occurred for two main reasons. Firstly, indigenous populations considered in the way of development or settlement plans of the dominant society—including hydrodam construction and resource extraction—were removed. Secondly, various governments have utilized relocation for administrative reasons.

At times, governments initiated "administrative relocation" in order to centralize populations or to facilitate the delivery of services or programs. At other times, governments relocated in order to disperse populations or to return indigenous peoples to what government officials considered to be their "natural state." This usually entailed moving indigenous peoples away from the corrupting influence of nonindigenous settlements or trading posts. Governmental action often relied upon erroneous assumptions about indigenous peoples, their quality of life, and their prospects for survival. Under the auspices of such misinformation, officials deduced problems that afflicted indigenous peoples and applied their own solutions, usually with little or no consultation and almost invariably without consent.

In North America and what was the Soviet Union, administrative relocations were based in ideology. Despite the fact that the United States and the Soviet Union espoused different political and economic philosophies, both countries considered their indigenous populations to be backward and in need of civilizing forces, either in the image of a productive member of industrial society (which was the focus in the Soviet Union and, in a number of cases, in Canada) or in the romantic image of the "noble savage" who only needed to be returned to the land (but preferably not land that was needed for other purposes).

The Royal Commission on Aboriginal Peoples, established in August 1991 to investigate the relationship between Aboriginal peoples and the Government of Canada, where relocation practices were widespread throughout the 20th century, stated:

Governments saw relocation as providing an apparent solution for a number of specific problems.... Government administrators saw Aboriginal people as unsophisticated, poor, outside modern society, and generally incapable of making the right choices. Confronted with the enormous task of adapting to "modern" society, they faced numerous problems that government believed could solve only with government assistance. If they appeared to be starving, they could be moved to where game was more plentiful. If they were sick, they could be placed in new communities where health service and amenities such as sewers, water, and electricity were available. If they were thought to be "indolent," the new communities would provide education and training facilities, which would lead to integration into the wage economy. If they were in the way of expanding agricultural frontiers or happened to occupy land needed for urban settlements, they could be moved "for their own protection." And if their traditional lands contained natural resources—minerals to be exploited, forests to be cut, rivers to be dammed—could be relo-

cated "in the national interest." (Royal Commission on Aboriginal Peoples, 1996: 412–413)

In a report on the relocation of Inuit from northern Québec to the High Arctic in 1953, the Royal Commission stated that such resettlement policies must be seen as part of a "broader process of dispossession and displacement." No matter what the reason for removal, research indicates that the removal of indigenous peoples from their lands results in a number of predictable and negative consequences. These include severing ties to the land, a decline in economic self-sufficiency, and, in many cases, a concomitant increase in dependency on government welfare. Health standards also deteriorate with relocation. Changes in the social and political relations of the populations similarly occur (Royal Commission on Aboriginal Peoples, 1996: 415). Numerous international studies corroborate these effects.

The human rights implications of population transfer, especially its effects upon indigenous peoples, are being increasingly acknowledged. The International Labour Office (ILO) Convention No. 169 deals with the rights of indigenous peoples to their land. Article 10 of the United Nations Draft Declaration on the Rights of Indigenous Peoples states explicitly that indigenous peoples

...shall not be forcibly removed from their lands or territories. No relocation shall take place without the free and informed consent of the indigenous peoples concerned and after agreement on just and fair compensation and, where possible, with the option of return. (United Nations Draft Declaration on the Rights of Indigenous Peoples E/CN.4/SUB.2/1994/2/Add.1, 1994)

Canada

The most famous example of relocation in Canada was the resettlement of Inuit from northern Québec (Nunavik) to the High Arctic in 1953. Following years of lobbying, numerous studies and inquiries, and a three-volume report in 1994 by the Royal Commission, the Government of Canada apologized and offered $10 million in compensation to the survivors and descendants of the transplanted Inuit.

Numerous other relocations occurred in the Canadian North in the 1950s and 1960s. Among these included the Inuit of Hebron, Labrador, who were moved south to other communities; the Inuit of Baffin Island moved to Devon Island; and the Inuit of the Kivalliq (Keewatin) moved to several different locations over a number of years. Various First Nations were relocated in the Yukon and the Sayisi Dene of northern Manitoba were centralized at Churchill.

In light of the pervasiveness of the policy and the effects it had on numerous populations, the Royal

Commission recommended, among other things, that a special tribunal be created under the Canadian Human Rights Act to hear relocation complaints. The recommendation is yet to be implemented.

Relocation policies diminished by the early 1970s, although in late 2002 the federal government began to relocate the Innu of Davis Inlet, Labrador. This resettlement from Iluikoyak Island, where the Innu were moved by the government in the 1960s back to the mainland, came after years of discussion and pressure from the community. The Innu had lived without running water or other basic services available to other Canadian citizens and felt strongly that a new community would help deal with the social problems and other ills, many of which they said were caused by the first relocation.

Russia

In the 1950s and 1960s, a large-scale campaign was conducted to lead people into a "modern socialist civilization" in the Soviet Union. Policies for northern peoples were guided by decrees of the Central Committee of the Communist Party of the Soviet Union announced in 1957 and 1980. The plan was to further the economic and social development of indigenous peoples of the North, to improve village production, increase specialization, and equalize the standard of living between rural and urban areas. Nomadism was declared a primitive lifestyle and not suitable for a modern socialist society.

What followed in the Soviet Union was the forced resettlement into planned communities of indigenous populations previously reliant on land-based activities such as reindeer herding. According to historian Aleksandr Pika, "Territories rich in productive resources were abandoned and traditional natural resource use—reindeer herding, hunting and fishing—lost its complex character as a result of the 'increasing specialization'" (Pika, 1999: 124). The same author refers to the resettlement scheme as an "experiment," echoing terms applied to the move of the Inuit to the Canadian High Arctic. Relocation failed as a tool of economic change in northern Russia. People generally fared better and were more productive in old communities where they had lived for many generations.

As in other relocations, decisions about how and where people should live were made by distant bureaucracies with little consideration of local conditions or needs, and at best limited consultation. Relocation also exacerbated social problems because people found themselves in new, anonymous settlements without the social structures that had supported them. In Russia, enforcement consisted of depriving rural areas of the support of hospitals, schools, and shops.

Greenland (Kalaallit Nunaat)

In 1953, the Danish government relocated Inuit from Ummannaq (Thule) at the request of the United States government, which wanted to expand antiaircraft batteries at its Thule Air Base. The base was part of a Cold War defense system and, while there had been discussions for a number of years about expansion, the Inuit were told nothing. In May 1953, government officials informed the people that they would have to move and those who resisted would not be given replacement houses. The Inuit complied but did not consent.

For years, the relocatees argued that their rights had been violated. In 1996, the survivors and their descendants launched a court case. In 1999, a Danish court ruled in their favor, ordered a financial payment of DKK 1.7 million (228,500 euro), but rejected the Inuit demand to be returned to Thule. The Danish government apologized for the move.

In the meantime, with the assistance of the Inuit Circumpolar Conference, the Inuit appealed. They argued, among other things, that in 1953 Denmark had already ratified the European Convention on Human Rights and was bound by other international human rights agreements, all of which it failed to live up to. A final decision on the case came down in late November 2003. The Danish Supreme Court upheld the 1999 ruling and stated that the trappers and their families were not eligible for any additional compensation. Their claim to return to their ancestral lands around the current Thule Air Base was also denied.

JOHN CRUMP

See also **Collectivization; Grise Fjord; ILO Convention No. 169; Nomadism; Qaanaaq; Thule Air Base**

Further Reading

Al-Khasawneh, A.S. & R. Hatano, *The Human Rights Dimensions of Population Transfer, Including the Implantation of Settlers*, New York: United Nations Economic and Social Council, Commission on Human Rights, Sub-Commission on the Prevention of Discrimination and Protection of Minorities, 1993

Brøsted, Jens & Mads Fægteborg, *Thule—fangerfolk og militaeranlaeg* [Thule, Hunting People and Military Bases], Denmark: Jurist-og okonomforbundets Forlag, 1985

Goebel, Christopher M., "A unified concept of population transfer." *Denver Journal of International Law and Policy*, 21(1) (1993): 20–53

Lynge, Aqqaluk, *The Right to Return: Fifty Years of Struggle by Relocated Inughuit in Greenland*, Nuuk, Greenland: Forlaget Atuagkat, 2002

Marcus, Alan, *Relocating Eden: The Image and Politics of Inuit Exile in the Canadian Arctic*, Dartmouth, New Hampshire: University Press of New England, 1995

McRae, Donald M., *Report on the Complaints of the Innu of Labrador to the Canadian Human Rights Commission*, Ottawa, Canada, 1993

Pika, Aleksandr, *Neotraditionalism in the Russian North: Indigenous Peoples and the Legacy of Perestroika*, Edmonton: Canadian Circumpolar Institute, 1999

Royal Commission on Aboriginal Peoples, *The High Arctic Relocation: A Report on the 1953–55 High Arctic Relocation*, Ottawa: Supply and Services, 1994

———, *Report of the Royal Commission on Aboriginal Peoples, Volume I, Looking Forward, Looking Back. Chapter 11: Relocation,* Ottawa: Minister of Supply and Services Canada, 1996

REPATRIATION

Repatriation refers to a body of legislation, the Native American Graves Protection and Repatriation Act (NAGPRA), that mandates the return of human remains, funerary objects, sacred objects, and cultural patrimony by United States federal agencies and certain museums, educational and other institutions, and state and local governments to recognized Native American Indian tribes, bands, nations, or other organized groups or communities, including Native Hawaiians and Alaska Native villages (as defined in, or established pursuant to, the Alaska Native Claims Settlement Act), that are indigenous to the United States. Enacted by the United States Congress on November 16, 1990, NAGPRA establishes a framework within which the lineal descendants and members of a specific indigenous group have the legal right to control the disposition of identified objects that are culturally affiliated to them. NAGPRA also provides penalties for individuals convicted of trafficking in human remains.

NAGPRA is based, in part, on the 1989 National Museum of the American Indian Act (NMAIA) that established culturally sensitive processes for the conservation, management, and repatriation of particular objects. Although the NMAIA covered only the repatriation of human remains and funerary objects, subsequently adopted policies provided that Native applicants could request the repatriation of sacred or ceremonial materials essential to the contemporary religious and ceremonial life of the community. However, the NMAIA, which also authorized the founding of the Smithsonian Institution's National Museum of the American Indian (NMAI), is unique in that it provides for the repatriation of indigenous cultural materials—housed at the NMAI—outside of the United States.

NAGPRA requires museums and federal agencies to inventory their collection holdings of human remains and associated funerary objects, including information on the geographical origin and cultural affiliation, manner of acquisition, and to then notify the culturally affiliated tribe. Furthermore, each museum or federal agency that has possession or control over collections of unassociated funerary objects, sacred objects, or patrimonial objects shall provide the requesting party with a written summary of such materials based upon available records. These documentary processes are to be completed in consultation with the proper culturally affiliated indigenous community because they decide whether to make a claim for repatriation.

Because repatriation involves an array of complex, and sometimes competing, social interests, it should embody the highest values and ethics of the community that it is intended to serve. Indigenous communities must have broad access to and use of information pertaining to museum collections to ensure that informed decisions can be made regarding the traditional care and ultimate disposition of these objects, especially since many objects eligible for repatriation were treated with pesticides and other chemicals to ensure their preservation in the museum environment.

The use of pesticides on museum collections began more than 200 years ago. Dusting, spraying, and sometimes shoveling chemical solutions of arsenic and mercuric chloride onto artifact mounts discouraged insect infestations. Other chemicals such as DDT and even mothballs were used and left behind hazardous residues. Under NAGPRA, museums must inform the recipients of repatriated objects about any known treatments. However, there is no legal obligation to remove pesticides, and museums are not legally responsible for health risks. The statute defines "sacred objects" as "specific ceremonial objects needed by traditional Native American religious leaders for the practice of these traditional religions by their present day adherents." By definition, NAGPRA requires such objects to be actively used in the contemporary practice of traditional Native religions. Thus, active use of contaminated objects poses a significant risk to human health. "Objects of cultural patrimony" are defined under NAGPRA as those having "ongoing historical, traditional, or cultural importance central to the Native American groups or culture itself." These objects exemplify group identity and are of vital importance to each generation. Although the level of human contact may vary with such objects, it seems plausible that the nature of each requires members of the group to have continuing access to them.

Today, through the process of consultation with Native peoples and communities, protocols for the conservation of contaminated objects targeted for repatriation are being developed and implemented. Tribes and individuals need to be aware of the problems and how to protect themselves. Because museum records associated with repatriated objects do not always indicate that chemical treatments actually occurred, and despite the fact that there are sometimes no visual indications of chemical residues on objects, museums do conduct surface sampling for arsenic and mercuric chloride, the chemicals most commonly used historically in the museum environment. The presence of these compounds would cause adverse health effects.

It is advised that skin protection (barrier gloves and/or frequent skin washing) be used when handling contaminated objects. Additional protective measures may be warranted, depending on intended use by those acquiring the object. If repatriated objects are funerary in nature and are intended for reinterment, safety precautions should be observed during any pre-reinterment handling. When sacred, ceremonial, or patrimonial objects are intended for ceremonial use in the community or family, direct skin contact with the object by children, the elderly, or other persons with compromised immune systems may be inappropriate. It may likewise be inappropriate to store such objects next to eating utensils, food supplies, and in certain parts of the home. Anyone handling or using the object should promptly wash exposed skin with hot soapy water after use.

For assistance with remediation such as cleaning and storage of repatriated objects, or for additional pesticide testing information, it is recommended that Native communities contact a local university or the conservation department at a local museum.

Repatriation offers a solution to the common legacy and historical roots of those communities separated by decades, and in some cases centuries, of artificial isolation from their past. Although each museum or federal agency follows its own set of repatriation guidelines under NAGPRA, it is the responsibility of these institutions to maintain constructive relationships with indigenous communities at various levels of communication. Given the culturally sensitive issues, repatriation is critical to support the continuation of ceremonial and ritual life among Native peoples, to foster and support the study by Native peoples of their own traditions, and to forge consensus among the museum community and Native communities while accounting for and balancing the interest of each.

LARS KRUTAK

Further Reading

Goldberg, Lisa, "A history of pest control measures in anthropology collections." *Journal of the American Institute for Conservation of Historic and Artistic Works*, 35 (1996): 23–42

Hawkes, Cathy A. & Stephen L. Williams, "Arsenic in natural history collections." *Leather Conservation News*, 2(2) (1986): 1–4

Meister, Barbara (editor), *Mending the Circle: A Native American Repatriation Guide: Understanding and Implementing NAGPRA and the Official Smithsonian and Other Repatriation Policies*, New York: American Indian Ritual Objects Repatriation Foundation, 1996

Mihesuah, Devon A. (editor), *Repatriation Reader: Who Owns American Indian Remains?*, Lincoln: University of Nebraska Press, 2000

National Museum of the American Indian, *Pesticide Testing Disclosure Statement*, 2001, pp. 1–2

REPTILES

Reptiles (Reptilia) is the class of poikilothermic (also known as cold-blooded) terrestrial vertebrates whose ontogenesis occurs without the stages of aquatic eggs and larvae. The majority of reptiles live in tropical and subtropical areas, deserts, and semideserts, from where species richness decreases northward and southward. Few reptile species cross the Arctic Circle, since cold-blooded reptiles cannot generate and regulate their internal temperatures, but rely on ambient temperatures and absorption of heat from solar radiation. Reptiles cannot be considered as true Arctic species, because the main part of their distributions covers Subarctic or temperate zones. Reptiles in the Arctic may be subdivided into two groups: sea turtles, which appear in the Arctic waters as singular migrating individuals, and some lizards and snakes that form real populations above the Arctic Circle. These populations are often stable, but usually neither dense nor numerous.

The common lizard, *Lacerta vivipara* (Squamata: Lacertidae), is found over much of central and northern Europe. It is a small lizard, up to *c.*210 mm in total length, and the tail is about two times longer than the body. Coloration on the dorsal surface is brown, or yellowish-brown, with a typical pattern consisting of dark and light longitudinal stripes and spots. Sometimes the dorsal pattern is not developed. Some individuals are very dark, almost black, especially in northern populations. The black coloration allows lizards better heating under sunrays. The belly is from light yellow to orange. The common lizard has the widest range of any species of the genus. It is distributed from northwestern Spain through Europe and Siberia to Mongolia and eastward to Sakhalin Island in the Pacific. The northern margin is extended over the coast of the Norwegian and the Barents seas in Scandinavia (the northernmost localities are Karesuando, Sweden: 68°30′ N; and Varangerfjord, Norway: 70° N) and the Kola Peninsula (Murmanskaya Province of Russia), then eastward through the coast of the White and the Barentz seas in Arkhangelskaya Province, and then to Komi Republic (the northernmost Arctic records are the middle current of the Rogovaya River and Vorkuta City: 67°29′ N, 64° E). The margin is extended eastward to the Polar Urals (Tyumenskaya Province, Yamalo-Nenets

Autonomous Okrug, lower current of the Sob River: 67°36′ N 65°30′ E; and Krasnyi Kamen Station: 66°46′ N 65°51′ E) and then eastward above the Arctic Circle to the lower reaches of the Yenisey River near the mouth of the Khantaika River (c.69°20′ N); next the margin crosses the Arctic Circle and runs southeastward to the Far East. The common lizard lives mainly in the forest zone, where it inhabits relatively wet but open and well-illuminated habitats. It penetrates in the tundra with forests, where it occurs on elevated, dry, and well-illuminated sites. Sometimes the lizard occurs on hummocks surrounded by water in tundra swamps. The species is rather rare in the Arctic. Hibernation in the Arctic lasts up to nine months, from late August/early September to early June. The viviparous or live-bearing reproductive mode promotes the existence of this lizard in Arctic areas because it makes the embryos less dependent on warm substrates, where oviparous reptiles deposit their eggs. The ecology of Arctic populations of this species is poorly known.

Adder, *Vipera berus* (Squamata: Viperidae), is a medium-sized (total length to c.90 cm) venomous snake. The head is large, well delimited from the body by the neck. Dorsal coloration is from brownish to entirely black in melanistic individuals; in nonblack snakes, there is a longitudinal zigzag line on the back and an X-shaped pattern on the head. The adder is one of the most widespread venomous snakes of Eurasia. The distribution range extends from France through Europe and the western part of the former Soviet Union eastward to the continental Far East, the Sakhalin Island, and southward to Mongolia. The northern margin of the range exceeds the Arctic Circle in northern Sweden, Norway (Varangerfjord: 70° N), and Kola Peninsula (Murmanskaya Province of Russia). Then the margin extends near the White Sea coast above the Arctic Circle in Arkhangelskaya Province, and runs southward from the Arctic Circle eastward from Komi Republic. The northern populations of the adder inhabit forested areas in the tundra and forest tundra zones, where the snake stays in open, dry, and well-illuminated habitats. Probably, the penetration into these areas is promoted by viviparous habits of the northern populations of this viper.

Other than these two reptiles, few species have no populations in the Arctic regions. Old northernmost records of the grass snake, *Natrix natrix* (Squamata: Colubridae), were known from near Sømna, Sweden, as far as 67° N. Marine turtles are widespread in the tropics and are famous in their distant migrations. Sometimes, they also visit Arctic waters. The loggerhead turtle, *Caretta caretta* (Testudines: Cheloniidae), was recorded from the coast of Norway, as well as from near the Kola Peninsula (Murmansk Bay: 68°59′ N

33°07′ E). Another species, leatherback turtle, *Dermochelys coriacea* (Testudines: Dermochelyidae), has been recorded from the cold waters of Alaska, Labrador, Chukotka, and Iceland. This species has some morpho-physiological peculiarities allowing it to visit cold waters more often than do other marine turtle species. Evidently, marine turtles may visit the Arctic seas only with warm sea currents and only during the summer season. If they do not migrate southward for winter, they would die in cold water.

SERGIUS L. KUZMIN

See also **Amphibians**

Further Reading

Ananjeva, N.B., L.Ya. Borkin, I.S. Darevsky & N.L. Orlov, *Entsiklopediya Prirody Rossii: Zemnovodnye i Presmykayushchiesya* [Encyclopedia of Nature of Russia: Amphibians and Reptiles], Moscow: ABF Publ., 1998 (in Russian)

Anufriev, V.M. & A.B. Bobretsov, *Fauna Evropeiskogo Severo-Vostoka Rossii 4. Amfibii i Reptilii* [Fauna of the European North-East of Russia 4. Amphibians and Reptiles], St Petersburg: Nauka, 1996 (in Russian)

Gasc, J.-P., A. Cabela, J. Crnobrnja-Isajlovic, D. Dolmen, K. Grossenbacher, P. Haffner, J. Lescure, H. Martens, J.P. Martinez-Rica, H. Maurin, M.E. Oliveira, T.S. Sofianidou, M. Veith & A. Zuiderwijk (editors), *Atlas of Amphibians and Reptiles in Europe*, Paris: SHE and NMNH Publ., 1997

Gislen, T. & H. Kauri, *Zoogeography of the Swedish Amphibians and Reptiles with Notes on Their Growth and Ecology*, Stockholm: Almquist and Wiksell Publ., 1959

Kuzmin, S.L., *The Turtles of Russia and Other Ex-Soviet Republics (Former Soviet Union)*, Frankfurt am Main: Edition Chimaira, 2002

Shvarts, S.S. & V.G. Ishchenko, *Puti Prisposobleniya Nazemnykh Pozvonochnykh Zhivotnykh k Usloviyam Sushchestvovaniya v Subarktike 3 Zemnovodnye* [The Ways of Adaptation of Terrestrial Vertebrate Animals to the Subarctic Conditions 3 Amphibians], Sverdlovsk: Inst. Plant and Anim. Ecol. Uralian Sci. Center of USSR Acad. Sci. Publ., 1971 (in Russian)

Storey, K.B. & J.M. Storey, "Natural freezing survival in animals." *Annual Review of Ecological Systems,* 27 (1996): 365–386

Voituron, Y., J.M. Storey, C. Grenot & K.B. Storey, "Freezing survival, body ice content and blood composition of the freeze-tolerant European common lizard, *Lacerta vivipara.*" *Journal of Comparative Physiology*, 172 (2000): 71–76

RESEARCH STATIONS

Scientific research in the Arctic plays a leading role in the policies of Arctic nations. Its importance as a strategic area during the Cold War and for air and sea routes resulted in bases that also had weather stations. Today, the greatest portion of Arctic research programs constitutes projects exploring the role of the Arctic in climate change, global oceanic and atmospheric circulation, and geophysical phenomena such as the aurora.

Much consideration has been focused on investigations of ice conditions, ice drift character, impacts of continuous permafrost on ecosystems, development of materials, constructions and technologies for cold regions, and human adaptation. Stations may be permanent and manned, temporarily or seasonally manned on sea ice or land, drifting on sea ice. Today, many government meteorological stations in the Arctic are automated, and can send data by satellite.

Permanent and drifting ice stations to conduct research were first established in the 1930s. The greatest number of drifting ice stations was built on the territory of the former Soviet Union; the first, named North Pole-1, was set up on June 6, 1937 (*see* **Drifting Stations**). Stations with differing purposes were located practically on all islands and along the entire Soviet Arctic shore area. The operations of most stations were managed by the Arctic and Antarctic Research Institute of St Petersburg. Presently, the majority of the stations have been closed down temporarily due to a lack of funding. Research works are conducted mostly at the stations in zapovedniks (nature reserves), national parks, and at Rosgidromet (the Russian hydrometeorological service) stations. Thanks to WWF support, two international biological stations were established in 1995: William Barents Station in the Great Arctic (Bol'shoy Arktichesky) *zapovednik* (nature reserve), Taymyr Peninsula, and Lena-Nordenskiold Station, *zapovednik* in the mouth of the Lena Delta, Sakha Republic. There are currently 11 stations carrying out ionospheric research, located from Spitsbergen to Chukotka and the Northeastern Research Station, Far East Division, Russian Academy of Sciences in the Kolyma mouth.

The main Arctic research center in Northern Europe is Tromsø, where the Roald Amundsen Arctic Research Center is located. The Norwegian Polar Institute coordinates the ENVINET (European Network for Arctic-Alpine Multidisciplinary Environmental Research) that joins 17 stations from the European Alp's to the Arctic. The network includes Sverdrup Research Station and Zeppelin Air Monitoring Station, Norway; Harland Arctic Station, England; Koldewey Station at Ny-Ålesund, operated by Germany; the dirigible *Italia*, positioned in Ny-Ålesund and operated by Italy, Abisko Scientific Research Station and Kiruna Observatory, Sweden; and Zackenberg Field Station in Greenland.

The main research centers for US Arctic science are located at Fairbanks and Pt Barrow, Alaska. Small scientific outposts for static observations—mainly of weather—are established at US military facilities throughout Alaska and at Distant Early Warning (DEW) stations from Alaska to Greenland. The United States operated an average of one drifting ice station per year between 1951 and 1985 and established a few temporary drift camps.

Canada's Arctic research is conducted by several ministries and universities from a network of permanent research stations and field research camps, including Alert on Ellesmere Island, Bylot Island Field Station, Devon Island Research Station, McGill Arctic Research Station, and Walker Bay Research Station, all in Nunavut. The Canadian Department of Energy, Mines and Resources coordinates much of the Arctic research through its Polar Continental Shelf Project at Resolute Base, which was started in 1959 to study the continental shelf, the waters, and the Arctic islands. Research coordination and information exchange are also performed by the Institute of Ocean Science, British Columbia. Canada has also carried out some unilateral work at temporary ice stations in the nearshore zone.

Ny-Ålesund on Svalbard has been developed as an international research station. Many non-Arctic nations with polar research programs have permanent research bases here, such as the United Kingdom, Germany, France, Italy, Japan, and Norway, while a number of other countries have permanent observation programs there, and Korea and China plan to set up stations.

Denmark operates several stations on Greenland under the Danish Polar Center and the Danish Defence Command, while Greenland Home Rule operates the Greenland Institute of Natural Resources in Nuuk and the US National Science Foundation runs stations at Thule Air Base and Summit.

Specialized vessels of icebreaker class have been commissioned for research cruises to the Arctic since the late 1980s; for example, *Academician Fedorov* and *Mikhail Somov* from Russia, *Polarstern* from Germany, *Oden* and *Polar Star* from the United States, and *Louis Saint-Laurent* and *Polar Sis* from Canada have regularly been used for Arctic research.

VLADIMIR VASILIEV

See also **Drifting Stations; Meteorological Stations; Research Stations**

RESOLUTE BASE

Following the postwar geopolitical reconfiguration, an agreement between Canada and the United States was reached to establish five Joint Arctic Weather Stations (JAWS) in the Canadian High Arctic (February 1947). The central supply station was to be located at Winter Harbour, Melville Island, with the other bases at Isachsen, Mould Bay, Eureka, and Alert. However, during the seaborne mission to construct the base at Winter Harbour in the summer of 1947, the icebreaker

USS *Edisto* damaged its propellers in heavy ice, resulting in the selection of an alternate site at Resolute Bay, Cornwallis Island. Due to the necessarily hasty adoption of Resolute, the harbor was less than ideal with only a seven-week ice-free season, shallow landing beaches, and complications resulting from drifting sea ice. Although the harbor is still used for the annual sealift, it was the construction of an airstrip by the Royal Canadian Air Force (RCAF) in 1949 that consolidated the emergence of Resolute as the communications hub of the High Arctic.

The weather station was moved 4 km inland to the airport, as the airstrip had the great advantage that aircraft could taxi directly to the base complex. Various government agencies utilized this Main Camp as a staging post for activities over the following decades, such as the Geological Survey of Canada (GSC) and the Polar Continental Shelf Project (PCSP). The Defence Research Board (DRB) and the Department of Fisheries and Oceans (DFO) maintained facilities at South Camp, the original weather station site on the south coast of the island. The RCAF also operated an Arctic Survival School at South Camp. The military managed the airport until control was transferred to Transport Canada in 1964. During the massive expansion of natural resource exploration in the 1960s, Resolute served as a logistical center and saw the growth of various commercial operations. When the US withdrew support for JAWS in 1970, the meteorological station at Resolute was maintained as a solely Canadian High Arctic Weather Station (HAWS).

An Inuit community is located 8 km from Main Camp, at Resolute Bay. In the summer of 1953, three Inuit families from Inukjuak (Port Harrison), Québec, together with a family from Pond Inlet, were resettled at Resolute on the recommendation of the Department of Northern Affairs and National Resources. This was part of a Canadian expression of sovereignty over the High Arctic, and was seen as a reasonable way to create a seasonal labor force for South Camp and Main Camp. A Royal Canadian Mounted Police (RCMP) detachment administered the relocated families, and facilitated a social-spatial separation of the hamlet from the bases. With further Inuit migration into the community, the town site expanded directly under the airstrip approach. The community was thus transferred to its present site in 1975. The Royal Commission on Aboriginal Peoples awarded CDN$10 million compensation to the survivors of the original resettlement from Québec in 1996.

Resolute presently remains the transport center for mining, tourism, and scientific research in the High Arctic, with scheduled jet services to Yellowknife, Ottawa, and Iqaluit. The activity of Federal agencies in Resolute has declined over the past decade, although the PCSP and DFO remain a significant seasonal presence and Environment Canada maintains a small staff at the weather station.

RICHARD C. POWELL

See also **Resolute Bay**

Further Reading

Bissett, Don, *Resolute: An Area Economic Survey*, Ottawa: Industrial Division, Department of Indian Affairs and Northern Development, Government of Canada, 1967

Environmental-Social Program, Northern Pipelines, *General Development Plan, Resolute Bay, NWT*, Ottawa: Environmental-Social Program, Northern Pipelines, Government of Canada, 1980

Foster, Michael & Carol Marino, *The Polar Shelf: The Saga of Canada's Arctic Scientists*, Toronto: NC Press, 1986

Gajda, R.T., *Radstock Bay, NWT, Compared with Resolute Bay, NWT, as a Potential Airbase and Harbor*, Ottawa: Geographical Branch, Department of Mines and Technical Surveys, Government of Canada, 1964

Jesudason, Terry, "Resolute." In *The Nunavut Handbook*, edited by Marion Soublière, Iqaluit: Nortext Multimedia, 1998

Kemp, W.B., G. Wenzel, N. Jensen & E. Val, *The Communities of Resolute and Kuvinaluk: A Social and Economic Baseline Study*, Montreal: McGill University, Office of Industrial Research, 1977

Tester, Frank James & Peter Kulchyski, *Tammarniit (Mistakes): Inuit Relocation in the Eastern Arctic 1939–63*, Vancouver: University of British Columbia Press, 1994

RESOLUTE BAY

Resolute Bay was named after the HMS *Resolute*, a ship in the British H.T. Austin expedition of 1850–1851, searching for the lost Sir John Franklin. The ship was abandoned in the summer of 1854 and drifted into Davis Strait, where it was picked up by an American whaler, the *George Henry*, in September 1855. After repairs, the HMS *Resolute* was returned to the British as a token of goodwill. Cornwallis Island, on which Resolute Bay is located, was first visited by Edward Parry in 1819, searching for a North West Passage. He named the area after British Admiral, Sir William Cornwallis (1744–1819).

Originally a weather station with no native population, Resolute Bay (*Qausuittuq* in Inuktitut) is a small settlement on Cornwallis Island, Northwest Territories. No Inuit were living on Cornwallis Island when a jointly operated Canadian/American weather and ionospheric station was established there in 1947. The choice of Resolute was an accident. The United States icebreaker *Edisto,* escorting a cargo ship the *Wyandot*, was attempting to establish a weather station at Winter Harbour, Melville Island, and was blocked by heavy ice. Resolute was chosen as an alternative. The station was established in anticipation of a surge in trans-Atlantic flights between Europe and North America after World War II.

Resolute's importance as a weather station soon paled in comparison to its strategic importance as a Cold War outpost, with the Soviet Union lying just over the horizon. By 1949, a large $1.5 million airstrip had been constructed. By the mid-1950s, the Distant Early Warning (DEW) line and missile defense systems reduced Resolute's importance as an Arctic air base.

Resolute Bay is the site of Thule Culture encampments at least 300 years old. These were extensively examined, commencing in 1949, by the National Museum of Canada and the Smithsonian Institution in Washington, District of Columbia. The excavations revealed articles over 1000 years old from the Dorset Culture.

In 1953, Resolute became the site of a relocation. The Canadian government transported 22 Inuit, 11 of whom were children, from Inukjuak (Port Harrison), Arctic Québec, to a gravel beach 1920 km north, away from family, friends, and relatives to a landscape unknown not only by its geography, but by its historical, spiritual, and practical content. The relocation was badly planned. Inuit were anything but "volunteers" heading north, as the government claimed. For years, women were confined to the community because the Royal Canadian Mounted Police (RCMP) was wary of relationships that might otherwise develop between the female Inuit and armed forces personnel at the base to the north. Impoverished children and adults reportedly scavenged through the dump at the military base, retrieving anything that appeared useful, including discarded food.

There were no facilities at Qausuittuq when the Inukjuak "colonists" arrived. The Canadian administration built a store for supplies run by the RCMP constable, Ross Gibson, and financed by the Eskimo Loan Fund, created in 1953. Money borrowed from the fund paid for supplies, with the fund being reimbursed as Inuit purchased goods from the store. The store was converted into an Inuit-run co-op in November 1960.

By 1958, there were 20 school-age children in the settlement—and no school. Government plans for a school at Clyde River, Baffin Island, were canceled and the building materials, which had been loaded on the *C.D. Howe* at Churchill Manitoba, unloaded at Resolute. The following year, a federal day school was opened.

By 1961, Resolute had 14 homes combining government "matchbox" houses and scrap material, housing 78 Inuit. In 1975, the community was rebuilt at the head of Resolute Bay.

In the 1960s and 1970s, Resolute became a base for High Arctic mineral and oil and gas exploration. The opening of the Polaris Mine on nearby Little Cornwallis Island established Resolute as a significant center for the transhipment of supplies. In the early 1970s, the International Biological Program opened a research center where the original weather station had been located.

In 1982, the Makivik Corporation sought compensation for Inuit who, in the late 1970s, had returned to Inukjuak at their own expense. The corporation asked for an apology on behalf of the Inuit and the creation of a $10 million trust fund. The Canadian government granted compensation, but did not issue an apology.

Since the early 1990s, Resolute has become a point of departure for adventurers from all over the world attempting to reach the North Pole on everything from skis to motorcycles. It has seen a cast of colorful characters trooping through what some still regard as one of the most formidable landscapes for human habitation in the world. Today Resolute Bay has a population of about 215. Sixty-eight percent of residents are Inuit, and 32% are nonnative.

FRANK JAMES TESTER

See also **Dorset Culture; Relocation; Resolute Base; Thule Culture**

Further Reading

Grant, Sheila, "Their Garden of Eden' sovereignty and suffering in Canada's High Arctic." *Northern Perspectives*, 19 (1) (spring 1991): 2–29

Haygood, Wil, "The Lie at the Top of the World." *Boston Globe Magazine* (August 9, 1992): 13–42

Jesudason, Terry, "Resolute." In *Nunavut Handbook*, Iqaluit: Nortext Multimedia Inc., 1998, pp. 265–269

Marcus, Alan, *Relocating Eden: The Image and Politics of Inuit Exile in the Canadian Arctic*, Hanover, New Hampshire: University Press of New England, 1995

Nungak, Zebedee, "Exiles in the High Arctic." *Arctic Circle* (September/October 1990): 36–43

Tester, Frank James & Peter Kulchyski, *Tammarniit (Mistakes): Inuit Relocation in the Eastern Arctic, 1939–63*, Vancouver: University of British Columbia Press, 1994

REYKJAVÍK

Reykjavík is the capital of the Republic of Iceland. It is located at the southeastern shores of Faxaflói in southwestern Iceland, at 64°09′ N and 21°56′ W, which makes it the most northerly capital in the world. A large part of the city occupies a small peninsula with low, wooded hills, a small lake, and a few geothermal fields. A small river, Elliðaár, flows through the eastern part. The bedrock is mostly made of ice-scoured, old lavas. The city is not located within an active volcanic area, but earthquakes are commonly felt. It is heated by geothermal means. The average temperature (1998) is –0.6°C in January to March and 10.8°C in June to August; the highest temperature on record is 24.3°C. The average annual precipitation is about 900 mm and sunny periods are frequent but often short.

Reykjavík covers 280 sq km (108 sq mi), of which about one-fifth is densely populated. The city covers large recreational areas to the east and is itself rather spread out, with a few high-rise buildings and extensive green areas and parks. The population was 112,490 in 2002. The designated Greater Reykjavík Area includes the neighboring towns of Kjalarnes, Kópavogur, Garðabær, and Hafnarfjörður. With about 180,000 inhabitants, it is by far the most densely populated part of Iceland (total population of 288,201 in 2002).

The early settlers in Reykjavík (*reykur*, smoke or steam, and *vík*, cove; thus "Cove of Steam," referring to the steam rising from local hot springs) were people in the first wave of farmers and Vikings who came mainly from Norway and the northern British Isles. History relates that the chieftain Ingólfur Arnarson was among the settlers. Archaeological findings date back to the 10th century and include farms by the present town lake. Small-scale farmers and fishermen lived in Reykjavík for centuries and no urban development occurred until the 18th century. The first attempt to industrialize the wool production led to a small village forming around the middle of the century. Only a few hundred residents were in Reykjavík when it achieved market town rights in 1786. It became a separate jurisdiction with a town magistrate in 1803. Rapid changes characterize the period from 1820 to 1920. Reykjavík developed as an educational, cultural, and political center in the 19th century, and soon industry and fishing became important social factors along with commerce and services. In 1901, 6700 people lived in Reykjavík, which was already by then the largest Icelandic town. When Iceland received home rule from Denmark in 1904, the government offices and the minister's residence were located in Reykjavík, establishing the town as the future capital of Iceland. The rapid change from a rural society to an urban society led to a rapid growth of Reykjavík in the 20th century. The population was 56,250 in 1950 and 108,362 in 1998.

Reykjavík has seven geothermal swimming pools, 27 museums and libraries, six theaters, and one opera house. The museums include the National Art Gallery, the National Museum, and the Árbær Municipal Museum of Reykjavík. There are also 18 professional drama and dance groups operating in the city and, along with, for example, 7 cinemas and 220 restaurants, pubs, and entertainment facilities, they provide ample opportunities to spend one's leisure time.

ARI TRAUSTI GUDMUNDSSON

See also **Iceland**

Further Reading

Gudmundsson, A.T. & R. Th. Sigurdsson, *Reykjavík: Into a New Millennium*, Reykjavík: Arctic Books, 1999
Líndal, P., *The Story of a Capital: 200th Anniversary of Reykjavík*, Reykjavík: Hagall, 1986

RIBBON SEAL

Probably the most strikingly colored of all pinnipeds (seals and walrus), the ribbon seal (*Phoca fasciata*) is also one of the least known. Adults are brown, with a wide band (hence *fasciata*) around the neck, another that encircles the flippers, and another around the hips. They are found only on the pack ice-floes of the Arctic North Pacific, from Alaska to Northern Japan, in the Bering, Chukchi, and Okhotsk seas. Ribbon seals are common near the northern coast of Hokkaido, where they often gather on the winter pack ice. They hardly ever haul out on shore-fast ice, and seem disinclined to come ashore. In 1962, an adult male was captured on the beach at Morro Bay, California, about midway between San Francisco and Los Angeles. In the Sea of Okhotsk, they feed on walleye pollock, Pacific cod, herring, cephalopods, and shrimp. They are primarily creatures of the ice, and show a remarkable indifference to the approach of predators, including Arctic foxes and humans. They live south of the range of polar bears, but in the water they are preyed on by killer whales and Greenland sharks. There is no reliable population estimate, but a total estimate of 240,000 was made in the mid-1970s.

One of the smaller phocids, this species attains a total length of 5.5 ft (1.65 m) and a weight of 220 pounds (100 kg). Ribbon seals are born white, but after a couple of weeks the white coat known as the *lanugo* is shed. Pups are suckled for three or four weeks, and triple their birth weight of 23 pounds (10.5 kg) in this period. The "ribbons" that characterize the adults do not appear until they are between two and four years old. Males are dark brown in color, while females are grayish-yellow; hence, the pale yellow ribbons are much more conspicuous in males. Some females become mature at two years of age, some at three, and almost all by four. They may live as long as 30 years. Like crabeater seals of the Antarctic, ribbon seals move over the ice by extending their foreflippers alternately, with their hindflippers held together off the ice. Over short distances, they can move surprisingly fast.

Although providing less meat and carrying less prestige than the whale or walrus, seals have always been an important subsistence item of the Iñupiat people; it is their staple winter food and most valuable resource. It provides them with dog food, clothing, and materials for making boats, tents, and harpoon lines, as well as fuel for both light and heat. A wide array of Inuit names describe the various age classes, sex, and condition of seals. The generic word for seal is *natsiq*, but yearlings are called *netsiavinerk*, and breeding males are *tiggak*. During the winter, when the sea is completely frozen over, seals maintain a series of breathing holes through the ice, where a hunter waits patiently until the seal surfaces. Traditionally, harpoons were devised specially so that the head could be detached from the valuable shaft. On sighting a seal, the hunter would thrust the harpoon down through the narrow opening at the surface of the ice and into the seal's neck or head. As the animal pulled away, the shaft worked loose from the ivory harpoon head. Laying the shaft aside, the hunter then took hold of the line attached to the harpoon head and pulled the seal to the surface, where it was then killed.

During the late spring and summer months when seals lay on top of the ice, surface stalking was undertaken. At this time, the Iñupiat ranged over a wide territory, frequently obtaining large numbers of seals in a short period of time. Prior to the introduction of the rifle, a throwing harpoon was used. But since its effective range was seldom more than 25 ft, great skill was needed in stalking. A hunter could approach to within 300 yards of the seal without taking special precautions. Still, he might wear light clothing to camouflage himself against the ice and cloud background, or he might wear dark clothing and try to imitate another seal by moving closer at a much slower pace. By mimicking the animal's movements and timing his advance to accord with the seal's short "naps," a capable hunter could approach to within a few feet of the seal. As soon as it was introduced, the harpoon was replaced by the rifle whenever possible. Not only did it kill the seal more quickly, but the animal did not seem to be apprehensive at the crack of a rifle shot. Thus, the hunter could take several seals from the same location. Seals that were shot would often sink, however, making retrieval of the carcass difficult or even impossible.

Today, Alaskan and Russian Inuit hunt ribbon seals on the ice, and the strongly marked skin is still highly prized. They are hunted by Chukchi on St Lawrence Island and Little Diomede. Around 1961, Soviet sealers began harvesting ribbon seals in the Bering Sea for skins, oil, fertilizer, and as food for Siberian mink and fox farms. From 1961 through 1967, some 13,000 ribbon seals were killed annually. The world population has been estimated at about 200,000 animals, but because there is no more commercial hunting in the ribbon seals' remote habitat, the actual number is unknown.

RICHARD ELLIS

Further Reading

Bruemmer, F., *Encounters with Arctic Animals*, New York: American Heritage, 1972

Burns, J.J., "Ribbon seal—*Phoca fasciata* Zimmerman, 1783." In *Handbook of Marine Mammals, Volume 2, Seals*, edited by S.H. Ridgway & R.J. Harrison, San Diego: Academic Press, 1981, pp. 89–109

Fedoseev, G., "Ribbon seal. Whales." In *Encyclopedia of Marine Mammals*, edited by W.F. Perrin, B. Wursig & J.G.M. Thewissen, London and San Diego: Academic Press, 2002

King, J.E., *Seals of the World*, Ithaca, New York: Cornell University Press, 1983

Nelson, R.K., *Hunters of the Northern Ice*, Chicago: University of Chicago Press, 1969

Reeves, R.R., B.S. Stewart & S. Leatherwood, *The Sierra Club Handbook of Seals and Sirenians*, San Francisco: Sierra Club Books, 1992

Riedman, M., *The Pinnipeds: Seals, Sea Lions, and Walruses*, Berkeley: University of California Press, 1990

RICHARDSON, SIR JOHN

In 1818 and 1819, England launched a two-pronged attack on the Arctic: an attempt to find the North West Passage by sea; and an overland expedition to explore the northwestern area of Canada and its Arctic coastline. Commander John Ross was selected to command the sea party and Lieutenant John Franklin, 33 years old at the time, was selected to command the party to explore the northern Canadian land territories. Franklin selected his friend, Dr. John Richardson, as surgeon and naturalist; two midshipmen, George Back and Robert Hood; and a seaman, John Hepburn.

Richardson was 33 years old, a graduate of the University of Edinburgh School of Medicine, and had a wide range of interests including botany, natural history, and geology. His abilities enabled him to assume an increasing leadership role as the expedition progressed. Physically, Richardson was well suited to the hardships of Arctic exploration, being large in stature and having considerable strength and stamina.

After lengthy preparations, the party, numbering 20 members, set out from their winter headquarters at Fort Enterprise in June 1821 to begin the major component of the expedition—the trip to the mouth of the Coppermine River and the polar sea. The weather was favorable; game, supplied by Indian hunters in the party, was plentiful; and the trip was uneventful. However, as the party turned eastward along the northern coast of Canada, hoping to reach as far east as Hudson Bay, the weather and water conditions made it impossible to navigate further. Accordingly, the party turned inland at Bathurst Inlet to complete a triangular route back to Fort Enterprise. The return trip was beset with disaster, with the party facing extreme cold, starvation, and fatigue. Midshipman Back hurried forward to seek assistance, while Franklin and seven others followed at a slower pace. The remainder, under the leadership of Dr. Richardson and including Hepburn and the severely ill midshipman, Hood, proceeded even more slowly.

Four of Franklin's group turned back to rejoin Richardson. Only one, an Indian named Michel, returned; the other three were never found. Michel's behavior became increasingly suspicious and one day, while Richardson and Hepburn were foraging, a shot was heard and Hood was found dead, a bullet wound in the back of his head. Michel had been observed leaving the scene and there was no doubt in the minds of Richardson and Hepburn that Michel had been the perpetrator of the crime, and that he constituted a threat to the remainder of the party. This led Richardson to shoot Michel, ending his life. At a subsequent board of inquiry held in England, Richardson was exonerated from any wrongdoing.

When the Franklin and Richardson groups were united at Fort Enterprise, the entire party had been reduced to four survivors—Franklin, Richardson, Hepburn, and Adam, an Indian. Fortunately, Back arrived with life-saving supplies to rescue the party. The survivors gradually recovered and made their way to a settlement and eventually to England. Their journey had covered 5500 miles of previously uncharted terrain at the cost of much physical and mental suffering and loss of life.

The British Admiralty and Parliament were undaunted by this, and Franklin was commissioned to lead a second expedition to the same region. On this occasion, he was to ascend the Mackenzie River to its estuary. At this point, the party would split into two. One group, headed by Franklin, proceeded westerly toward Alaska, and the second group, headed by Richardson, proceeded in an easterly direction and explored the Beaufort Sea coastline between the estuaries of the Mackenzie and Coppermine rivers.

This expedition lacked the dramatic events of the first. The descent of the Mackenzie, previously made by Alexander Mackenzie in 1779, was uneventful. Franklin's group proceeded westward reaching the Alaskan coastline, but was prevented by the weather from proceeding further. Richardson's group successfully reached the mouth of the Coppermine, thus charting the previously unexplored coastline between the estuaries of the two rivers.

Both parties rendezvoused successfully and returned to a heroes' reception in England in 1827. Both men were knighted by a grateful queen. Lengthy accounts of this expedition were written by both Richardson and Franklin. Although unsuccessful in achieving their main objective, the North West Passage, they had successfully surveyed thousands of miles of the Arctic shoreline and Canadian interior previously unknown to English mariners. Richardson returned to private practice, but was retained by the British Admiralty as a consultant on their Arctic Council.

In 1847, the British Admiralty commissioned three expeditions to relieve the expedition of Franklin and his crew of 129, missing since 1845 in their search for the North West Passage. Richardson, now 60 years of age, was placed in command of one of the three expeditions, and charged with exploring the Mackenzie River to its estuary and then pursuing a course eastward to the mouth of the Coppermine River. Richardson chose Dr. John Rae as his second in command and physician The Richardson search for Franklin, his last Arctic experience, yielded no information, nor did those of the other two parties led by Henry Kellett and James Ross Clark.

Biography

The oldest of 12 children of a wealthy brewer, Richardson was born in Dumfries, Scotland, on November 5, 1787. His aptitude as a scholar was recognized early and he was educated in Edinburgh, obtaining his license from the Royal College of Surgeons in 1807 and his medical degree in 1816. He served seven years in the Royal Navy, participating in the Napoleonic Wars and serving in Canada. He began medical practice in 1816 in Leith, but his ability as a naturalist and medical practitioner gained him an appointment with John Franklin's expedition. After his last expedition, he was knighted by Queen Victoria and served with distinction in the practice of medicine as chief medical officer at Haslar Hospital, Gosport, at that time the largest hospital in the world. Richardson's name is associated with numerous plants, fish, birds, and mammals as well as some geographical features. He died near Grasmere in the Lake District on June 5, 1865, and is buried near William Wordsworth.

RALPH M. MYERSON

See also **Franklin, Sir John; Rae, John**

Further Reading

Berton, P., *The Arctic Grail*, New York: Penguin Books, 1988
Franklin, J., *Journey to the Polar Sea*, Köln: Konemann Verlags Gesellschaft, 1998
———, *Journey to the Polar Sea; Dr. Richardson's Narrative*, Köln: Konemann Verlags Gesellschaft, 1998

RINGED SEAL

Ringed seals (*Phoca hispida*) are small members of the Phocidae family, and also known as *natseq* (Greenlandic) and *ringsel, snadd* (Norwegian). The seals are silver-gray through to brown in color. Their

Young ringed seal (*Phoca hispida)* on sea ice, Greenland.
Copyright Bryan and Cherry Alexander Photography

bellies are light silver in color, while their backs are darker and bear a conspicuous pattern of small rings that gives them their common name. Adult animals reach lengths of 1.1–1.6 m and weights of 50–90 kg. Like all of the northern seals, their body mass varies markedly on a seasonal basis. Ringed seals are fattest in the fall and thinnest in the late spring following the breeding period. Males are slightly larger than females, and in the spring, male's faces appear to be much darker than those of females because of an oily secretion from glands in the facial region. At other times of the year, the sexes are difficult to distinguish. When ringed seals are born, pups are about 60 cm in length and weigh about 4.5 kg. They bear a white, wooly "lanugo" coat at birth that is shed when they are about 2 months old. Their juvenile coat is silver on the belly and dark gray on the back. They acquire their patterned pelt gradually as they age.

Ringed seals occur throughout the Arctic, north to the pole. They are in many respects the "classic" Arctic ice-seal in that their unique ability to maintain breathing holes in thick sea-ice enables them to occupy areas far away from ice edges, which other seal species are unable to reach. Ringed seals use sea ice exclusively as their breeding, molting, and resting (haul-out) habitat; rarely (if ever) do they come onto land. They create or maintain their holes in the ice using both their teeth and their very well-developed front claws. Ringed seals disperse quite broadly following the breeding season and young animals can be

found far outside the typical species range. Adults tend to return to the same areas to breed year after year and so have an annual range that is modestly fixed. Most ringed seals are found in association with land-fast ice in fjords, but following the molt ringed seals become much more dispersed. Some live pelagically (in the open sea), while others move north to the southern limits of the permanent ice edge. Through the summer and fall, ringed seals are found in ice-filled waters of virtually any depth. In some regions, including Baffin Bay and the Barents Sea, ringed seals occupy free-floating pack ice areas, even during the breeding season. Ringed seals also occupy the ice in the Baltic Sea and subspecies *Phoca hispida ladogensis* and *P. h. saimensis* live in Lake Ladoga and Saimaa (Finland), respectively.

Ringed seals give birth in the early spring to a single pup. Peak birthing occurs in most locals in early April. The pups are born in lairs (small caves, accessed from the water via a hole) in the snow on top of sea ice, which serve as shelters against inclement weather. Ringed seal pups are nursed and cared for by their mothers for approximately 6 weeks, which is a relatively long period of maternal care among the ice-living seals. During the time that they are with their mothers, pups increase their body mass approximately 4 or 5 times over, to a mass of about 20 kg. Ringed seal pups are extremely active swimmers and divers, spending about 50% of their time in the water during the nursing period. Pups only a few weeks old are capable of remaining underwater for more than 10 min and dive to the bottom of the fjords where studies of their aquatic abilities have been performed (90 m). They start feeding on small crustaceans and other invertebrates that are available under the ice while they are still drinking milk. Toward the end of lactation, mating takes place. The embryo then remains dormant for about 4 months before implanting in the wall of the uterus (delayed implantation, similar to polar bears) and starting to grow actively. Populations appear to be structured such that immature animals and young adults are restricted to suboptimal habitats during the spring birthing and mating season, when breeding adults hold territories in the most stable ice. Following the breeding season, ringed seals generally remain in fjords and land-fast ice areas until they have completed their annual molt in June or July. Ringed seals are the most abundant northern seal and, although no accurate estimate is available, the species is thought to number at least a few million animals globally. Although their density varies considerably according to ice conditions from region to region, they can be described as abundant throughout most of the Arctic.

Ice-associated crustaceans and fish constitute much of the ringed seals' diet, although they also eat a wide variety of pelagic and benthic fishes and invertebrates. Ringed seals are the favorite food of polar bears. In addition, Arctic foxes prey heavily on pups. In years with poor snow cover, birds such as glaucous gulls can also be the source of significant pup mortality. In addition, some seal-eating walruses take ringed seals as do Greenland sharks. Although ringed seals are rather small phocids, they survive the thermal challenges posed by the Arctic winter by having a very thick blubber layer, and by using their snow lairs (see above) for both birthing and resting during the winter and early spring. Their lairs also afford them some protection against predators; each seal builds several lairs so that they can escape if a predator attacks one of their structures. Outside the breeding and molting periods, ringed seals are solitary. Despite their small size, they are capable of diving to 500 m for periods up to 20 min. Ringed seals are a long-lived species that can be as old as 45 years of age.

Humans have hunted ringed seals in the Arctic since the arrival of people to the region millennia ago. They are a fundamental subsistence food item for most coastally dwelling northern people. Their hides have been an important item for making clothing and other household items and have, at various times, been an important source of cash income for people in the Far North. The species has never been the subject of large-scale commercial hunting because of their dispersed distribution and inaccessibility to hunters, but are an extremely important commodity to Arctic coastal indigenous peoples.

KIT KOVACS

See also **Marine Mammal Hunting**

Further Reading

Gjertz, I., K.M. Kovacs, C. Lydersen & C. ØWiig, "Movements and diving of adult ringed seals (*Phoca hispida*) in Svalbard." *Polar Biology*, 23(9) (2000): 651–656

Hammill, M.O., C. Lydersen, M. Ryg & T.G. Smith, "Lactation in the ringed seal (*Phoca hispia*)." *Canadian Journal of Fisheries and Aquatic Sciences*, 48(12) (1991): 2471–2476

Heide-Jørgensen, M.P. & C. Lydersen (editors), *Ringed Seals in the North Atlantic*, Tromsø: The North Atlantic Marine Mammal Commission, 1998

Lydersen, C. & H.O. Hammill, "Diving in ringed seals (*Phoca hispida*) pups during the nursing period." *Canadian Journal of Zoology*, 71(5) (1993): 991–996

Lydersen, C. & K.M. Kovacs, "Behaviour and energetics of ice-breeding, North Atlantic phocid seals during the lactation period." *Marine Ecology Progress Series*, 187 (1999): 265–281

Simpkins, M.A., B.P. Kelly & D. Wartzok, "Three-dimensional analysis of search behaviour by ringed seals." *Animal Behaviour*, 62 (2001): 67–72

Smith, T.G., "Ecology of the ringed seal, *Phoca hispida*, in its fast ice breeding habitat." *Canadian Journal of Zoology*, 59(6) (1981): 966–981

———, "The ringed seal, *Phoca hispida*, of the Canadian Western Arctic, Ottawa, Department of Fisheries and Oceans, Canada." *Canadian Bulletin of Fisheries and Aquatic Sciences*, 216 (1987)

Smith, T.G., M.O. Hammill, & B. Taugbol, "A review of the developmental, behavioural and physiological adaptations of the ringed seal, *Phoca hispida*, to lie in the arctic winter." *Arctic*, 44(2) (1991): 124–131

RINK, HINRICH JOHANNES

The 19th-century Danish scientist Hinrich Johannes Rink first came to Greenland in 1848, where he lived on and off until 1871. Formally trained as a geologist, Rink became known for his photographs and drawings, and for collecting and recording mythological tales from Greenland. In 1857, he started the first publishing house in Greenland and in 1861 the first newspaper.

Rink's career as a scientist began in 1845–1846, when he participated in the first Galathea expedition as a geologist, visiting the Far East, the Pacific Ocean, and Latin America. His observations were published in 1847 as *Die Nikobarischen Inseln* (The Islands of the Nicobars).

In 1848–1851, he researched the graphite layers in northwest Greenland, and in 1853 he published an article on the movements of the inland ice cap. "Om Isens udbredelse og Bevægelse over Nordgrønlands Fastland" became a turning point in the study of glaciology and geology. Rink nurtured a special interest in all topics related to Greenlandic society, but particularly related to governmental and administrative issues.

In 1853, he was appointed colony manager and inspector of the Royal Greenland Trading Company (Kongelige Grønlandske Handel, or KGH) in the Qaqortoq district, and in 1855 Rink moved to Nuuk to become inspector for the whole southern part of Greenland from 1857. His achievements as a civil servant in Greenland were remarkable. Rink is counted as one of the three reformers to suggest the introduction of local native councils in order to involve Greenlanders in the administration of local affairs. In concordance with the prevailing mood in Denmark (absolutism superseded by democracy in 1849) of giving the people a voice in the running of public affairs, the reformers argued that Greenlanders would be more self-reliant and more productive if given political influence. The suggestion was accepted in Denmark and the first Guardian Councils (what were called *forstanderskaber* in 19th-century Denmark) was established on a district basis in 1857. The Greenlanders elected the Greenlandic members of these heretofore Danish-dominated councils. The councils distributed poor relief and served as the court of first instance in criminal and civil cases involving Greenlanders. As an inspector in Greenland, Rink was in the best position to make these councils successful. Council members remained in office until 1911 when a new round of reforms took place and superseded the Guardian Councils with two Country Councils and a sequence of municipality councils.

In addition to his administrative duties, Rink took genuine interest in promoting knowledge and awareness of Greenlandic society. In 1857, he established a printing office in Nuuk to publish educational and ethnographic booklets in Greenlandic. In 1861, he began publishing a news magazine, *Atuagagdliutit*, which he distributed free of charge among the Greenlanders. It was the only mass media in Greenland until broadcasting became possible in the 1920s. *Atuagagdliutit* is still in print, and since 1952 has been published as a bilingual newspaper in Greenlandic and Danish.

Rink's concern for Greenland's cultural heritage led him to collect and document its various narratives and publish them as a matter of historical record. Aron from Kangeq—a gifted illustrator—contributed illustrative drawings to accompany Rink's published texts. Many of these articles and books on Greenland were printed in English, including *Tales and Traditions of the Eskimo* (1875). *Danish Greenland: Its People and its Products* (1877 is a geographical and statistical description, while *The Eskimo Tribes, Their Distribution and Characteristics, Especially in Regard to Language I–II, 1887–91* is a highly regarded contribution to the study of the Greenlandic language.

In 1868, Rink left his beloved Greenland due to ill health, and became director of the Royal Greenland Trade Company (KGH) from 1871 to 1882 in Copenhagen. In this capacity, in 1879 he established Grønlænderhjemmet (Greenlanders Home), an educational institution for Greenlanders living in Denmark.

Rink died in 1893 in Oslo, Norway, where he had spent his retirement. In 1919, a memorial was erected in Nuuk with the inscription "Kalatdlit Ilisimavai Isumagai Asavai" (he knew the Greenlanders, he guarded them, he loved them).

Biography

Hinrich Johannes Rink was born on August 26, 1819 in Copenhagen to the merchant Johannes Rink and his wife Agnese Margaretha Hedde. Both his parents came from the German-speaking duchy of Holstein. On April 28, 1853, Rink married Nathalia Sophia Nielsine Caroline Møller, who was born in Greenland.

Rink passed his general certificate of education at The Academy of Sorø in 1838. From 1840 onward, he studied physics and chemistry at the Polytechnic High School, and was employed as amanuensis at the chemistry laboratory. It is not known if Rink ever graduated, although his gold medal essay in chemistry from 1843 was awarded the title of Doctor of Philosophy in Kiel in 1844. Thereafter, Rink attended lectures in medicine in Berlin, but ended his studies in order to participate as a geologist in the Galathea expedition of 1845. However, he was forced to return prematurely to Denmark in 1846 due to a serious infection, probably malaria, which nagged him for the rest of his life. Rink died on December 15, 1893 in Oslo, Norway.

AXEL KJÆR SØRENSEN

See also **Literature, Greenlandic; Royal Greenland Trade Company (KGH)**

Further Reading

Oldendow, Knud, *Grønlændervennen Hinrich Rink* [Hinrich Rink: The Friend of the Greenlanders], Copenhagen, 1955

Rink, H.J., *Die Nikobarischen Inseln*, Kopenhagen: H.C. Klein, 1847

———, *Tales and Traditions of the Eskimo*, London: Hurst, 1875 (originally published in Danish); reprinted Montreal: McGill-Queen's University Press, 1974, and New York: AMS Press, 1975

———, *Danish Greenland; Its People and its Products*, London: Henry King, 1877 (originally published in Danish); reprinted Montreal: McGill-Queen's University Press, 1974, and New York: AMS Press, 1975

———, *The Eskimo Tribes, Their Distribution and Characteristics, Especially in Regard to Language I–II, 1887–91*, Copenhagen: C.A. Reitzel, 1891

———, *Dansk Biografisk Leksikon*, Copenhagen: Gyldendal, 1982

RIVER AND LAKE ICE

The solid phase of water ranges in form from microscopic ice crystals and snowflakes to the large, thick ice sheets of Antarctica and Greenland. Between these two extremes are the relatively thin water surface forms of sea, lake, and river ice. Although these forms have many characteristics in common, they differ mainly in that sea ice is formed from sea water, and river and lake ice are the solid form of fresh water. River and lake ice, nearly all of which is ephemeral (freezing over every winter, but melting in spring), represent only a small percentage of the total ice on earth. Nonetheless, these are the types of ice that most directly affect humans because they are land based and occur in populated areas, especially in the Northern Hemisphere.

When the surface of a calm body of water cools to a temperature of 0°C (or slightly below), freezing sets in. Small spicules, or needles, and crystals of ice form on the water's surface and eventually merge to establish a thin surface cover known as primary ice or skim ice. This cover sets the stage for the downward freezing of the water body and the production of a layer of large columnar crystals (secondary or black ice, up to 3 m thick). Whereas in lakes ice tends to form in place, in rivers (and in lakes that might be wind-stressed) freezing is more complicated. Lake ice formation and decay are mainly a function of air temperature; river ice formation, on the other hand, is affected by river flow and channel morphology as well as temperature.

Although the freezing of lake or river water usually forms the bulk of an ice column, a layer of snow ice (slush or white ice) may form on the top when the snow cover is flooded by water from below and refreezes.

Since this new layer of ice contains a high concentration of air bubbles, it has a granular appearance and looks white under natural light. Generally, the higher the latitude the thinner this snow-ice layer because of a decreased thickness of snow cover and an increased rate of ice growth with latitude. The timing and thickness of snow cover, which insulates the ice below, affects the growth of the season's ice layer. It also adds weight to the ice and, when thick, depresses it.

Portions of many high-latitude streams and rivers are subject to the formation of aufeis (German for ice on top; also known as naleds or icings) when there is overflow from the river below, from tributaries, or from springs. Such formations are common in Alaska, Canada, and Russia, and at some locations may last throughout the summer. Some aufeis deposits are large; one on the Indigirka River in Siberia was 25 km long, 8 km wide, and 4 m thick.

Lakes, ponds, rivers, and streams are numerous in the high latitudes of the Northern Hemisphere, where temperatures remain below zero for long periods of time. For example, more than 10% of the surface of Canada is fresh water, most of which is in the frozen state for varying lengths of time during the year. A similar situation exists in Alaska, northern Scandinavia, and Siberia.

The lakes of the Arctic and Subarctic range in size from small (less than 100 m² in area), as in the case of the low-centered ice-wedge polygonal lakes of northern Alaska and Siberia, to some of the largest on earth, such as Great Bear Lake (31,000 km²) and Great Slave Lake (28,400 km²) in Canada. They are equally varied in depth. Most high-latitude lakes are shallow, especially those on the coastal plains bordering the Arctic

Ice crusts a river in the Arctic National Wildlife Refuge, Alaska. *Copyright Annie Griffiths Belt/National Geographic Image Collection*

Ocean. Many of these shallow lakes are less than 2 m deep and usually freeze to the bottom. Deeper lakes, many of which are found in the high-relief areas of the Arctic, freeze to depths that seldom exceed 2 m.

Just as high-latitude lakes vary greatly in area and depth, Arctic rivers are highly variable in length, volume of water carried, and in freeze-up and breakup characteristics. An idea of number and length might be gathered from the fact that more than 300 rivers and streams drain into Lake Baikal, which supports an ice cover that averages 1 m in thickness for 4–5 months, and only one (the Angara that is part of the 4130 km long Yenisey River) drains it.

In addition to the rivers that flow into the numerous lakes of the Arctic, there are those that drain directly into the Arctic Ocean. Included are four of the ten longest rivers in the world, namely the Mackenzie in Canada and the Lena, Ob', and Yenisey in Russia. These four rivers, along with some of the other longer rivers, originate outside the zone of permafrost and flow throughout the year, much of the time under an ice cover. In contrast, there are other Arctic rivers such as the Kolyma and Indigirka in Russia and the Colville in Alaska that originate within the zone of continuous permafrost and have very restricted flow during the winter season when all surface water in lakes and rivers and all groundwater in the active layer are frozen.

Although snowmelt on the lake ice surface creates pools and reduces albedo, it is along the edges of the lake where lake-ice melt is most rapid. The ice is thinner there and snowmelt water along with a warming shoreline speeds melting and leads to the creation of a moat around lakes. The thick ice in the center of a lake may last for weeks after the melt season begins and can often be used by ski planes even after a moat develops. With increased radiation, melting occurs between the crystals (candles) of ice and leads to breakup. Breakup is aided by wind and any lake currents that may develop. These agents also lead to ice drift and the piling up of lake ice along the shoreline.

The decay of river ice is similar to that of lake ice; however, breakup, because of river flow, is more complex. In the Arctic, prior to breakup, river ice is generally more than 1.5 m thick, bottom-fast along the shallow portions of the river, and floating on the slow-moving or stationary water in deeper channels. Once the melt season begins, water accumulates on the top of river ice and begins to move downstream. Because of buoyancy, fracturing of the ice, especially along the shoreline and the boundary with bottom-fast ice, occurs. Water also flows beneath the ice, which then fluctuates up and down with stage. Sediment carried by floodwaters is deposited on top of the bottom-fast ice as well as along the shore and on flats and bars. Rising stage and increasing velocity combine with a

weakening of the ice cover to initiate breakup. Breakup along any one cross section is usually a matter of hours or days. It may occur on a rising stage, during which an increasing river cross section can often accommodate the floating ice with few jams and the sound level is relatively low, or it may occur on a falling stage, which not only tends to be noisy but also leads to more frequent ice jams and the stranding of ice-floes on channel bars. Stranded ice-floes may last for weeks before candling to destruction.

For most Arctic rivers, which generally drain in a northerly direction, breakup progresses from upstream to downstream so that the shortest ice-free periods are near the mouths of the river channels. In Russia, rivers west of the Taymyr Peninsula have an average of 120 ice-free days, whereas to the east the average is less than 90 days.

Networks of ice observing stations have operated in Alaska and Canada for nearly 50 years. The stations are scattered across the landscape and range as far north as Alert in Ellesmere Island (82°30′ N) in Canada and Pt Barrow (71°20′ N) in Alaska. Standard measurements include ice thickness and the dates of freeze-up and breakup. Similar statistics have been gathered in Russia.

Lake and river ice in the Arctic are important physically and biologically and impact heavily on human activities. Some scientists have asserted that the greatest importance of river, lake, and sea ice is biological because, along with its snow cover, it forms a cap over the water bodies that protect those plants and animals that live beneath it. Geologically, ice, especially river ice, is an important erosional, transportational, and depositional agent and hydrologically it greatly affects the discharge characteristics of Arctic rivers.

Because much of human activity in the Arctic is adjacent to rivers and lakes as well as the sea, ice is of critical importance. Although river ice limits boat navigation to only a few months, it provides a relatively smooth surface for winter transport, and, along with lake ice, for aircraft landings. Although freshwater ice has been used as a water supply, it is the fresh water beneath the ice cover, especially in lakes, that is the main source for many communities. Possibly, the most important effect of river ice in the Arctic occurs with the ice jams and flooding that accompany breakup. River floodplains and deltas, and therefore the villages located on them, are especially affected.

Any change in the climate of the Arctic, as has been predicted as likely to occur, will have a major impact on river and lake ice and therefore on human activities. Some of these impacts may be positive. For example, increased snowfall and a less intense freeze-up period would lead to thinner ice covers and possibly less intense but earlier ice jams. A longer ice-free season would benefit shipping and other river- and delta-based activities such as fishing.

H. JESSE WALKER

See also **Ice Jams; Sea Ice; Snow**

Further Reading

Adams, W.P., "Snow and Ice on Lakes." In *Handbook of Snow*, edited by D.M. Gray & D.H. Male, Oxford: Pergamon Press, 1981, pp. 437–474

"Arctic deltas." *Journal of Coastal Research*, 14(3): 718–738

Ashton, G.D. "River ice." *American Scientist*, 67(1) (1979): 38-45

Michel, B. & R. Ramseier, *Classification of River and Lake Ice Based on its Genesis, Structure and Texture*, Québec: Universite Laval, 1969

Morris, K., M.O. Jeffries & W.F. Weeks, "Ice processes and growth history on Arctic and Subarctic lakes using ERS-ISAR data." *Polar Record*, 31 (1995): 115–128

Pounder, E.R., *The Physics of Ice*, Oxford: Pergamon Press, 1965

Walker, H.J., "Landforms and Development in an Arctic Delta: The Role of Snow, Ice and Permafrost." In *Landscapes of Transition: Landscape Assemblages and Transitions in Cold Regions*, edited by K. Hewitt, M. Byrne, M. English & G. Young, Dordrecht and Boston: Kluwer, 2002, pp. 159–183

Weeks, W.F. & R.L. Brown, "Snow and Ice." In *Centennial Special Volume 3*, Geological Society of America, 1991, pp. 333–350

Welch, H., "Comparisons between lakes and seas during the Arctic winter." *Arctic and Alpine Research*, 23 (1) (1991): 11–23

ROCK GLACIERS

Rock glaciers are characteristic and widespread large-scale flow features of frozen material in cold-climate high-relief regions. They are located at the foot of rock faces with a high supply of talus (weathered rock fragments) and, when active, typically take the form of 20–100 m thick tongue- or lobe-shaped bodies with cascading frontal slopes standing at the angle of repose. Their length may be as much as several kilometers, but their typical length is 200–800 m measured along the flow direction. The longest rock glacier recorded on Earth is about 5.5 km in length, in West Greenland. The surface of rock glaciers is typically covered by coarse (0.2–5 m) and angular rock fragments, and displays a curving transverse furrow-and-ridge topography 1–5 m high. Active rock glaciers typically flow downslope 0.1–1 m per year, that is, they are more sluggish than normal glaciers, but are nevertheless highly efficient as coarse debris transport agents due to their sheer size.

Internal Structure

The interior structure of rock glaciers is still incompletely known. The landforms are generally inaccessible, and although research efforts have intensified during recent years, the period during which intensive rock glacier research has been carried out is relatively short. The available knowledge suggests that active rock glaciers possess a characteristic three-layer structure: a 1–3 m thick top layer consisting of large rock fragments (essentially representing the active layer), covering a deforming ice-rich permanently frozen core that creeps downslope on top of the third and lowermost unit, which consists of rock fragments deposited in an apron at the terminus of the active rock glacier and is subsequently overrun by the uppermost two units. This general three-layer stratigraphy is supported by deformation rates measured in a borehole drilled into a rock glacier in the Alps. Many researchers would agree to this overall model, but opinion diverges regarding the origin and characteristics of the deforming ice-rich second unit. A number of researchers are of the opinion that the deforming core consists of glacier ice for some rock glaciers, while other scientists reject this model in favor of a nonglacial (periglacial) origin of ice within the creeping unit.

Meteorological Conditions

Very few examples of active rock glaciers occur for a mean annual air temperature above about –2°C, and the majority of active rock glaciers occur at sites with a mean annual air temperature below –6°C, that is, the typical rock glacier site is located within the zone of continuous permafrost.

Available meteorological data suggest that there is no significant regional climatic difference between sites occupied by normal glaciers and rock glaciers, and that the typical rock glacier site is only slightly drier compared to the typical site of a normal glacier. Active rock glaciers, however, appear to be restricted to comparatively dry areas with a regional annual precipitation not exceeding about 1700 mm water equivalent and a mean summer air temperature not exceeding 5–6°C. The typical regional rock glacier site is therefore not exactly continental as has often been argued; it is rather a dry to moderate humid climate with cool summers. In regions with warm summers, wind-induced, forced ventilation of the rock glacier top layer (the active layer) would rapidly lead to degradation of the permanently frozen rock glacier core.

The main environmental difference between sites with active rock glaciers and normal glaciers should presumably be sought in local differences in topoclimatic conditions, with normal glaciers located at sites with a high accumulation of snow in relation to the input of talus, glacier-derived rock glaciers located at sites with less snow accumulation in relation to the input of talus, and talus-derived rock glaciers located at sites with low snow accumulation in relation to the input of talus. The role of wind in removing snow should therefore not be overlooked for the initiation and growth of rock glaciers. Both rock glaciers and normal glaciers with conspicuous moraines containing little subglacially derived sediment signal extraordinary high weathering rates on the rock faces above, and it is the site-specific net accumulation of snow at the foot of the headwall that controls the type of debris transport agent developed at this place. The typical rock glacier site is at the foot of a rock face, providing both rock debris and shade (in contrast to ice caps exposed to wind deflation and solar radiation), and not prone to high snow accumulation due to snowblow (in contrast to cirque glacier sites). Due to the delicate balance between net snow accumulation and the rate of talus production, respectively, a climatic change toward more humid winter conditions may produce glaciers at former rock glacier sites, and vice versa.

Climatic Significance

From a purely scientific point of view, rock glaciers are important, as they represent a landform indicating a limiting situation between the glacial and the periglacial environment. Because the accumulation and survival of ice bodies in rock glaciers, whatever the precise origin, must be a complex function of responses to air temperature, insolation, wind, and seasonal precipitation over a considerable period of time (50–200 years), the topographic and altitudinal distribution of rock glaciers must contain unique climatic information, much the same as normal glaciers do. As knowledge on the typical rock glacier climate (regional and local) is extended and improved, the occurrence of relict rock glaciers will therefore represent an important object in future paleoenvironmental reconstructions.

Geomorphic Significance

The presence of active rock glaciers signals exceptional high rock face retreat rates; weathering rates of 1–5 mm per year appear to be quite typical for sites with active rock glaciers. Rock glaciers also represent one of the most effective transport agents of weathered debris in cold-climate high-relief regions. Rock glaciers are, however, not directly responsible for the retreat of their headwalls, but are a landform derived from rapid rock weathering processes in a permafrost environment. Acting as transport agents, however, rock glaciers presumably exercise some indirect control on long-term headwall retreat, by counteracting the tendency toward progressing burial of the free face in weathering products that would otherwise tend to inhibit further weathering.

Although rock glaciers are thus suggested to represent diagnostic forms for exceptional high headwall retreat rates, their sedimentological role is somewhat particular. While normal glaciers act as temporary storage units for new sediment, which is soon released and at least partly transferred further downvalley by meltwater streams, this is not the case for rock glaciers. Water draining from rock glaciers tends to lack much sediment (ignoring solutes), and most of the debris produced from the headwall above tends to remain within the rock glacier body for an extended period, as much as several thousands of years, even though the rock glacier on a local scale is highly efficient in transporting new talus away from the headwall. In general, debris is stored in rock glaciers during interglacials, and is presumably transferred significantly further downvalley only during glacial periods, in connection with the evolution of large valley glaciers. This may have implications for the interpretation of interglacial and interstadial marine sedimentology along coasts with numerous rock glaciers in the hinterland.

OLE HUMLUM

Further Reading

Barsch, D., *Rockglaciers. Indicators for the Present and Former Geoecology in High Mountain Environments*, Berlin: Springer, 1996

Haeberli, W. & D. Vonder Mühll, "On the characteristics and possible origins of ice in rock glacier permafrost." *Zeitschrift für Geomorphologie*, NF., Suppl.-Band, 104(1996): 43–57

Humlum, O., "Rock glacier appearance level and rock glacier initiation line altitude: a methodological approach to the study of rock glaciers." *Arctic and Alpine Research*, 20(2) (1988): 160–178

———, "Origin of rock glaciers: observations from Mellemfjord, Disko Island, central West Greenland." *Permafrost and Periglacial Processes*, 7(1996): 361–380

———, "Active layer thermal regime at three rock glaciers in Greenland." *Permafrost and Periglacial Processes*, 8(1998): 383–408

———, "The climatic significance of rock glaciers." *Permafrost and Periglacial Processes*, 9(4) (1999): 375–395

———, "The geomorphic significance of rock glaciers: estimates of rock glacier debris volumes and headwall recession rates in W Greenland." *Geomorphology*, 35(2000): 41–67

Kerschner, H., "Palaeoclimatic inferences from late Würm rock glaciers, Eastern Central Alps, Western Tyrol, Austria." *Arctic and Alpine Research*, 10(1978): 635–644

Whalley, W.B. & H.E. Martin "Rock glaciers: II models and mechanisms." *Progress in Physical Geography*, 16(1992): 127–186

ROSING, HANS-PAVIA

Hans-Pavia Rosing held various leading posts in several organizations dealing with Greenlanders in Denmark. When he returned to Greenland in 1975, he worked for an adult education organization. Upon his return, his political involvement began to focus on indigenous peoples as such, and he was a cofounder of the World Council of Indigenous Peoples (WCIP) in 1975, and member of the board from 1977 till 1980. In 1980, Rosing became director of the Information Department of the Home Rule.

In 1977, when the Inuit from Alaska, Canada, and Greenland met in Barrow (Alaska) at the First Inuit Circumpolar Pre-Conference, Rosing participated. Representatives from the three countries brought home ideas to discuss them thoroughly before the next conference that took place in Nuuk in 1980. Rosing was elected the first president for a period of three years. During this period, Rosing succeeded in making Inuit Circumpolar Conference (ICC) gain acceptance as an NGO with consultative status at the United Nations Economic and Social Council (ECOSOC). At the 1983 General Assembly in Iqaluit, Canada, Rosing was reelected as president for another three-year period, but when he was appointed Minister of Economic Affairs in 1986, Mary Simon from Canada succeeded him. He held the ministerial position for one year, and then decided to run for the Danish parliament (*Folketinget*). Rosing was a previous member of the Greenlandic parliament (*Landstinget*) in 1983–1984. He represented the Siumut party, except for a period in the Danish parliament (1994–1998), where he represented an alliance between Siumut and Inuit Ataqatigiit, called Siumut Ataqatigiit. Rosing stayed in the Danish parliament until 2001, when he decided not to run again. In 2002, he ran for the Greenlandic parliament, but did not succeed.

Biography

Hans-Pavia Rosing was born in 1948 and grew up in Nuuk and Denmark. After school, he was educated as translator in Danish/English languages in 1969, and in 1970 he supplemented this with a computer education. Rosing was one of the international figures in Greenlandic politics. Today, he has withdrawn from political work, and has taken up photography. Another passion of his is radio making; over the years he has a number of productions for both Greenlandic and Danish radio to his credit. He was also a coauthor of a political television drama "Den blåøjede satan," in which he played the leading role.

MADS FÆGTEBORG

See also **Greenland Home Rule Act; Inuit Circumpolar Conference (ICC); Simon, Mary; Siumut**

Further Reading

Fægteborg, Mads, *Grønland i dag: en introduktion år 2000*, Copenhagen: Arctic Information, 2000, p. 190
Lodberg, Torben (editor), *Grønlands Grønne Bog*, Nuuk: Tusagassiivik, 1998

ROSS, SIR JAMES

Serving under his uncle, John Ross, James Clark Ross saw active service on the *Actaeon* in the Baltic, the White Sea, and the English Channel during the final years of the Napoleonic wars. He also served on board the *Driver* off the west coast of Scotland. In 1817, the British Admiralty appointed John Ross to command an expedition in search of the North West Passage. In the summer of 1818, John Ross, commanding the *Isabella,* with Lieutenant William Edward Parry commanding the *Alexandra*, sailed for the west coast of Greenland. After crossing and naming Melville Bay, they made the first recorded Western contact with the Inughuit off Cape York. The expedition headed westward toward Ellesmere Island, and then set a southerly course passing Jones Sound and briefly entering Sir James Lancaster Sound. A relatively short distance into the Sound, John Ross announced further passage blocked by what he called the Croker mountains. Upon returning to England, this pronouncement was hotly contested, particularly by the scientific officer, Edward Sabine, and the commander of the *Alexandra*, William Parry.

In 1819, the Admiralty placed William Parry in command of an Arctic expedition to investigate Lancaster Sound. James Ross joined as midshipman. Having shown great aptitude for scientific work on the 1818 expedition, Ross was given the opportunity to carry out magnetic and lunar observations. He also developed a keen interest in natural history. One of many plants he collected, *Geum rossii*, was named after him. Luck and good seamanship enabled Parry to bring his ships, *Hecla* and *Griper*, successfully through Lancaster Sound and Barrow Strait. On September 5, they crossed the 110° meridian and became entitled to a reward of 5000 pounds. After reaching 112°51′ W, Parry retraced his route back to Winter Harbour on the south coast of Melville Island, where he spent the winter on board his ships before returning to England. James Ross served with Parry on three more voyages; the first was the 1821–1823 expedition to Foxe Basin in the *Fury* and *Hecla*. Two midshipmen serving on this expedition, Francis Rawdon Moira Crozier and Edward Bird, became his lifelong friends. In July 1823, he shot a bird not seen before and which in due course was named after him—Ross's gull (now called *Rhodostethia rosea*). When he returned to England, he was promoted to lieutenant and was elected a Fellow of the Linnean Society.

In 1824, James Ross joined Parry's third Arctic expedition as second lieutenant. In the ships *Hecla* and *Fury*, the expedition encountered severe ice conditions. After spending a winter at Port Bowen, they pushed south along the east coast of Somerset Island. In August 1825, the *Fury* was wrecked. Stores were landed on Fury Beach and both crews returned on board the *Hecla*. The zoological appendix to Parry's expedition report was written by James Ross.

James Ross was second in command during the fourth voyage under Parry in 1827. The objective was to reach the North Pole from Spitsbergen. From the *Endeavour* and the *Hecla*, the expedition headed northward using small boats fitted with runners to cross the ice. The attempt was abandoned at 82°43′ N. The farthest North record stood for 50 years. Ross was honored by having an island, Ross Islet, named after him.

James Ross was promoted commander in 1827. In 1828, he was elected Fellow of the Royal Society, yet there was little prospect of active service. Since 1818, John Ross had been unemployed and on half-pay. In 1829, he obtained financial support from Felix Booth (Booth's gin) and organized a private expedition in search of the North West Passage with James Ross as second-in-command.

The expedition left England in May 1829 on the *Victory*, a converted paddle steamer, the first steamer used in Arctic exploration. Not until 1833 were the survivors of the expedition rescued in Lancaster Sound. During the expedition, James Ross collected ethnographic information about the Inuit living in the "Boothia Felix" region and sledded across Boothia Peninsula to King William Island. Here he erected a stone cairn, which was later found by the members of Franklin's ill-fated expedition. James Ross also reached the magnetic North Pole on the western shore of the Peninsula.

In 1835, James Ross was offered a knighthood for his attempted rescue of trapped whalers in the Arctic. He declined the honor. Between 1837 and 1839, he conducted magnetic surveys in Great Britain.

In 1839, James Ross sailed for the Antarctic in the *Erebus* and *Terror*. He entered what is now known as the Ross Sea, providing the foundation for future Antarctic explorations. Upon his return to England in 1843, he retired, and declined when the Admiralty urged him to lead Britain's next attempt to penetrate the North West Passage. John Franklin was chosen to lead the 1845 expedition; James Ross convinced the admiralty to place his close friend and trusted second-in-command in Antarctica, Crozier, as second-in-command to Franklin.

In 1848, James Ross entered Arctic waters once again, this time in search of the missing Franklin Expedition. He wintered his ships, *Enterprise* and *Investigator*, near Port Leopold and, together with his second lieutenant, Francis Leopold McClintock, he searched the west coast of Somerset Island, but failed to reach Franklin's ice-bound ships. Not until ten years later did McClintock reach King William Island, where he discovered the fate of the Franklin Expedition. James C. Ross never returned to the Arctic.

Biography

James Clark Ross was born on April 15, 1800, at Finsbury Square in England. James was the third of five surviving children born to George Ross and Christian Clark. His father was a merchant and entrepreneur, whose brother John would play a crucial role in James's naval career. John Ross entered the Royal Navy at the age of nine in 1786, and his nephew, James, served under his tutelage as a first-class volunteer starting at the age of 12. James Ross married Anne Coulman and they had four children: James, Anne, Thomas, and Andrew. James Clark Ross was knighted following his return from the Antarctic in 1843. He died on April 3, 1862.

PETER SCHLEDERMANN

See also **Ross, John**

Further Reading

Parry, W.E., *Journal of a Voyage for the Discovery of a North-West Passage from the Atlantic to the Pacific, Performed in the Years 1819–20, in His Majesty's Ships Hecla and Griper*, London: John Murray, 1821

Ross, J.C., *A Voyage of Discovery and Research in the Southern and Antarctic Regions During the Years 1839–43*, London: John Murray, 1847

Ross, M.J., *Ross in the Antarctic*, Caedmon of Whitby, England, 1982

———, *Polar Pioneers: John Ross and James Clark Ross*, Montreal-Kingston: McGill-Queen's University Press, 1994

Ross, M.J., & J.M. Savelle, "Retreat from Boothia: the original diary of James Clark Ross, May to October 1832." *Arctic*, 45(2) (1992): 179–194

ROSS, SIR JOHN

Sir John Ross's association with Arctic exploration began in 1818 when, on the recommendation of his mentor Sir George Hope, he was offered the command of an expedition to ascertain the extent of Baffin's Bay (thought by many at the time to be little more than a rumor) and to attempt a North West Passage.

Ross, on board the *Isabella*, with William Edward Parry commanding the smaller *Alexander*, did indeed succeed in reaching Baffin's Bay, confirming the accuracy of Baffin's original observations. Ross successfully navigated almost the entire coastline, sailing further north than any previous explorer, and became the first European to visit the home of the Polar Eskimos in Etah, northwest Greenland. John Sackhouse (Sacheuse), a West Greenlander who traveled with Ross, was able to serve as interpreter despite large differences in dialect, and the Inughuit (Polar Eskimos)—whom Ross dubbed "Arctic Highlanders"—spoke in amazement of Ross's ships and sails. Ross probed further north, but was arrested by ice at the entrance to

Vintage print illustrating "Capt. Ross's Interview with the Eskimos," published by Thomas C. Jack, Edinburgh.
Copyright Bryan and Cherry Alexander Photography

Smith Sound, reaching his furthest north at around 76° of latitude; he also attempted several western waterways in search of a navigable passage. At Lancaster Sound, Ross sailed through clear water some miles inland, and might well have discovered what would later be known as Barrow's straits. However, deceived by a mirage that he took to be mountains blocking the way west, he turned around and sailed home, much to the frustration of Parry, who along with other officers wished to press on. Parry returned the next year, earning the Parliamentary prize by finding a navigable passage as far west as Melville Island.

Despite the successes of Ross's voyage, he was widely blamed for not having pursued the potential passage further and was criticized for bringing home little more than polar-bear skins and some "red snow." (Ross sampled this snow, which he observed off the western coast of Greenland, unaware that its color was due to a tiny microorganism). He was retired on half-pay, and never again commanded a naval expedition. John Barrow savaged him in the press, and even his old friends kept their distance. Ross had plenty of time to meditate on his error, but pronounced himself quite ready to go to the Arctic again if asked—he was not. He remained at home, took up an interest in steam engines, wrote furious letters, and practiced phrenology.

In the meantime, his nephew James Clark Ross, who had sailed with his uncle in 1818 and had accompanied

Parry on all his expeditions, advanced rapidly in the Navy. An unusual opportunity to combine their interests developed in 1829, when London gin magnate and Lord Mayor Sir Felix Booth offered to fund a private expedition to the Arctic. Scholars are uncertain as to exactly who was Booth's first choice as commander—in the end, both Rosses went, although they differed afterward about just who was in command. Their ship, christened the *Victory*, was powered by a new side-wheel steam engine which, despite Sir John Ross's advocacy of similar machinery, he later condemned as "infernal" and had removed from the ship. Aboard the *Victory*, the Rosses discovered a previously uncharted body of water to the south of Barrow's straits, which they dubbed the "Prince Regent Inlet," giving the name "Boothia" to the land to its west. Near the southern limit of this gulf, they made the ship fast in an inlet Ross dubbed "Lord Mayor Bay." There they wintered, and despite numerous attempts, they were never able to pilot the *Victory* more than a few miles from its first harbor—three winters were to pass before they again reached the entrance to the Prince Regent Inlet. The Rosses might well have perished, had it not been for the fortuitous appearance of a winter village of Netsilingmiut on the hills above their harbor, whose assistance in hunting, and the supply of fresh meat that resulted, saved the party from both starvation and scurvy.

On a sledge expedition late in the first winter, James Clark Ross discovered the then location of the North Magnetic Pole, giving the expedition a unique geographical claim. The following two winters witnessed the eventual abandonment of the *Victory* and a difficult northward retreat, with a final winter camp near "Fury Beach," where supplies from Parry's ship of that name were cached. Against all hope, the Rosses and their crew were able to take to the water in boats and were spotted by a passing whaler, John Ross's old ship of command, the *Isabella*, now of Hull. Their rescue and return in 1833 after having long been presumed dead, along with their discovery of the Magnetic Pole, earned the Rosses tremendous fame, and almost entirely erased the past embarrassment of Sir John's error in Lancaster Sound. Parliament voted a bounty to Ross, and paid Booth's expenses and the crew's wages, and Sir John Ross retired again amidst a shower of laurels.

Surprisingly, it was not the elder Ross's final Arctic voyage. In 1845 when, the Admiralty appointed Sir John Franklin to lead a new expedition in search of the North West Passage, Ross was astonished to find that no preparations had been made for the possibility of failure. He promised to search for his old friend should he become lost, and honored the promise by sailing, aboard a refurbished schooner he dubbed the *Felix*, to Beechey Island in 1851. Ross was thus among the first to find the graves of three Franklin crewmen found on that island, and although he was unable to bring aid to Franklin, this voyage made a fitting close to 33 years of Arctic service.

Biography

Born in Inch (Dumfries and Galloway) on June 24, 1777, John Ross entered the Royal Navy as a first-class volunteer on November 11, 1786 at the age of nine, and served on HMS *Pearl* from 1786 to 1789. On the advice of a friend, he spent the years 1790–1794 serving as an apprentice seaman in the merchant marine; from 1794 to 1797, he worked for the East India Company. Ross rejoined the Navy in 1799 as a midshipman, and in 1803 when war broke out, he served aboard HMS *Grampus*, the flagship of Admiral Sir James Saumarez, whom he followed on several subsequent commands, including the *Victory*, where he was Saumarez's first lieutenant for five years. Ross commanded the Admiralty expedition to Baffin's Bay in 1818, and was co-commander of the private Arctic expedition sent by Sir Felix Booth (1829–1833), which discovered Prince Regent Inlet and the Boothia Peninsula, as well as surveying the North Magnetic Pole. Ross returned to the Arctic in 1851 to aid in the search for Sir John Franklin, and on his return was promoted to rear-admiral on the retired list. He died on August 30, 1856, and was interred at Kensal Green Cemetery.

RUSSELL A. POTTER

See also **North West Passage, Exploration of; Sabine, Edward; Sacheuse, John**

Further Reading

Dodge, Ernest S., *The Polar Rosses: John and James Clark Ross and Their Explorations*, London: Faber & Faber, 1973

ROUSSELL, AAGE

In 1924, Aage Roussell, an architect and employee at the Cryolite Mine in Ivittuut in South Greenland, contacted the historian Poul Nørlund of the National Museum of Denmark who had initiated archaeological research in Norse Greenland in 1921. Roussell became Nørlund's assistant on his following two expeditions to the Eastern Settlement and Western Settlement, respectively (1926 and 1930). On the latter, he, in Igaliku, joined Nørlund in excavating the important site at *Gardar*, the Bishop's See of Medieval Norse Greenland. They published the results jointly in the monograph *Norse Ruins at Gardar* (1929). Nørlund, in his attempts to collect comparanda for the archaeo-

logical material of Norse Greenland, in 1931 arranged for Roussell to take a study tour to the Scottish Isles to record what might have survived of Scandinavian elements in the vernacular architecture there. Roussell subsequently published the results of this journey in the book *Norse Building Customs in the Scottish Isles* (1934). In the book, which seems originally to have been intended as his doctor of philosophy thesis, Roussell presented a chronologically based classification of the farmsteads in the Western and Northern Isles of Scotland, in which the architecture of the Hebrides represents the earliest stage, followed by the Shetland farm, and with the Orkney farm representing the most complex and developed stage. He later applied this simple typology to the material from Norse Greenland.

Roussell gradually, and from 1932 completely, took over Nørlund's engagement in Greenland and became director of four expeditions to Greenland in 1932, 1934, 1935, and 1937, respectively. The results of these investigations were presented in the monographs *Sandnes and its Neighbouring Farms* (1936) and *Farms and Churches in the Mediaeval Norse Settlements of Greenland* (1941). The latter provided a survey of the research so far done in Norse Greenland and also presented a classification of the architecture of the Norse farmsteads. Roussell's established typology, based on the works of earlier scholars and on his own experiences from the Scottish Isles and Greenland, contains three chronologically based categories and stages: longhouse, passage-house, and centralized farm. This work, despite the fact that he was formally not an academic, was accepted as his doctor of philosophy thesis by the University of Copenhagen.

In 1939, Roussell was the Danish representative in the Pan-Scandinavian archaeological expedition to fijórsárdalur in Iceland. Roussell's assistant in this project, which was orchestrated by Nørlund, was Kristjárn Eldjárn (1916–1982), an Icelandic student of archaeology. Eldjárn, who had already been with Roussell in Greenland in 1937, later became State Antiquary and president of Iceland. Roussell, already the leading authority in the field, arrived in Iceland completely updated, because on his way he had visited the ongoing excavations of Viking Age farmsteads in Orkney and Shetland. The results of the project in Iceland were published in the monograph *Forntida Gårdar i Island* (1943), to which Roussell contributed with presentations of his own excavations as well as with an important comparative chapter on the architecture of the Scandinavian buildings in the North Atlantic.

Roussell's approach to the archaeology of the Viking Age and medieval settlements of the North

Atlantic was mainly that of the architecture and morphology of buildings. It has been stated that Roussell, to a certain degree, represented a change from Nørlund's allegedly more historical approach to the archaeology of Norse Greenland. However, Roussell and his contribution should rather be seen in the line of and as valuable products of Nørlund's visions and strategies for research into the Norse in Greenland. Roussell's contribution to the archaeology of the North Atlantic, and Greenland in particular, is substantial, and the fact that he published his results extensively, quickly, and in English in the monograph series *Meddelelser om Grønland* added greatly to its importance for future research.

Roussell was involved when Scandinavian buildings were found at l'Anse aux Meadows in Newfoundland in 1961 and for a while he caused repercussions of the old Danish-Norwegian dispute about sovereignty in Greenland.

Biography

Aage Roussell was born in Copenhagen on October 27, 1901. He was the son of Rudolf Christian Roussell (1859–1933), a merchant, and Sidse Hansine Nielsen (1868–1941). On July 21, 1931, he married Elisabeth Mathilde Velschou (1898–1985). He became a student in 1919. The following year, he took filosofikum (an obligatory exam in philosophy taken at the end of the first university year) at the University of Copenhagen. The same year, he was accepted at the School of Architecture under the Academy of Arts in Copenhagen, from which he graduated in 1922. After engagements at various drawing offices, he was employed at the Chryolite Quarry at Iviituut in Greenland in 1924–1926, and was its manager in 1925–1926.

In 1937, he was appointed curator at the Second Department (medieval) of the National Museum of Denmark, and became the head of the department in 1949. He was active in the Danish resistance movement during World War II. It was therefore not a surprise when he was appointed director of the newly established Museum for the Danish Resistance in 1957. For a number of years, he was a conservative councillor at Frederiksberg (Copenhagen). In 1953, he was decorated with the Icelandic "Order of the Falcon" for his contribution to Icelandic archaeology in 1939. Roussell retired in 1971, but cancer had already doomed him and he died the following year. He was buried at Frederiksberg (Copenhagen).

STEFFEN STUMMANN HANSEN

Further Reading

Guldager, Ole, Steffen Stummann Hansen & Simon Gleie, *Medieval Farmsteads in Greenland. The Brattahlid Region 1999–2000*, Copenhagen: Danish Polar Center Publications 9, 2002

Stummann Hansen, Steffen, "Steep hills, strong winds and wealthy sportsmen. Aage Roussell and his journey to the Scottish Isles in 1931." *Review of Scottish Culture,* 11 (1997–1998): 116–134

———, "How to get at a man in Greenland I don't know." Aage Roussell og hans Orkney forbindelse. *Grønland,* 1, (2000): 5–20

ROVANIEMI

Rovaniemi, the largest city of Finnish Lapland, has been the capital of the province (lääni) of Lappi since 1939, when the new province was created as a new administrative unit. It is situated above the Arctic Circle at the junction of the Kemi and Ounas rivers, and covers an area of some 93 sq km. Initially a settlement to which the railway had arrived from the Gulf of Bothnia coast in 1909, Rovaniemi was finally incorporated as a city in 1929 after the extension of roads in the region had drawn a considerable number of settlers, and in 1934 the railway was extended to Kemijärvi, the Finnish railway's most northerly point. The city was almost totally destroyed in the autumn of 1944, toward the end of World War II, by retreating German troops, fearful that Rovaniemi would be used as an Allied base. A striking new town, however, rose up from the ruins, designed by the most famous Finnish architect of the 20th century, Alvar Aalto (1898–1976).

Already at the end of 1944 and into 1945, Aalto designed a master plan for the rebuilding and redevelopment of the city, which, between 1950 and 1955, came to include an architectural plan for the whole of Lapland. Individual projects included the Korkalovaara housing development of 1957–1961, an office and apartment block in 1961–1962, a housing development and urban improvement scheme in 1962–1963, and the Rovaniemi Library, designed in 1963. Later works in Rovaniemi included single-family houses, as well as the Lappia Theatre and Radio Building built between 1969 and 1975. Whereas earlier designs often incorporated a fan motif, his later ones tended to fall back upon a cellular model, which could be reinterpreted in a variety of situations.

There is a notable church by Bertel Liljeqvist (1885–1954), with monumental frescoes by Lennart Segerstråle (1892–1975). The University of Lapland, founded in 1979, has also assumed international importance. Especially noteworthy in this regard is its

Arctic Centre, founded by the Finnish government in 1989, in which various aspects of cultural and scientific interest are taught and researched.

Rovaniemi is an important seat of the Finnish timber industry and reindeer herding, carried out by Saami people. Fur trading is also a significant economic activity, as is the service industry, while tourism, especially in winter, has grown hugely in recent years. The Ounasvaara Winter Games, held in March when snow still covers the ground to a considerable depth but temperatures have begun to rise, are especially of note in this regard.

Aside from a plethora of bus connections, there are important rail links to Russia, as well as elsewhere in Finland, and air travel is especially important, because of the considerable distance of Rovaniemi from Helsinki and other major southern Finnish cities. With a population of 14,219 in 1951, it had risen to around 35,000 by 1998, almost all of whom are Finnish speaking.

NEIL KENT

See also **Lappin Lääni**

Further Reading

Kent, Neil, *The Soul of the North. A Social, Architectural and Cultural History of the Nordic Countries. 1700–1940*, London, Reaktion, 2001
Quantrill, Malcolm, *Alvar Aalto. A Critical Study*, Helsinki, 1983

ROWLEY, GRAHAM

Graham Westbrook Rowley was an English-born explorer, archaeologist, public servant, and educator. After graduating from Cambridge University in Natural Sciences, Rowley spent two years studying archaeology and anthropology. In 1935, Tom Manning, explorer and zoologist, invited him to be an archaeologist on the scientific expedition that Manning intended to lead to the Eastern Canadian Arctic. Other members would be ornithologist Reynold Bray, geologist Patrick Baird, and surveyor Peter Bennett.

The 1936 British Canadian Arctic Expedition was planned to conduct research and exploration in Hudson Bay and the Foxe Basin coast of Baffin Island. It was mounted with limited private donations and contributions from the members. It represented the end of an era in which southerners in the north adapted to Inuit ways, rather than expecting the contrary, which became common later. The members tried to learn the language because few Inuit spoke any English, they wore caribou skin clothing in winter, copied Inuit methods of traveling, and ate local food. This was the last exploratory expedition in the Canadian Arctic to rely on traditional means of transport: in winter, they traveled over ice- and snow-covered tundra by dog sledge and on foot, and in summer by small boat.

In the summer of 1936, the members of the expedition helped to complete building their 30-ft whaleboat in Churchill and then sailed north to Repulse Bay, carrying out scientific work wherever possible, especially on Southampton Island. In the winter of 1937, Graham Rowley and Reynold Bray sledged to Igloolik from Repulse Bay, building snow houses to sleep in each night. They lived in Igloolik with the Amitturmiut Inuit leader Ittuksarjuat and his wife Ataguttaaluk, both of whom were highly respected in the Eastern Arctic. These two introduced and instructed Rowley and Bray in the Inuit ways of living. Following local custom at the time, Rowley was given an Inuit name: Makotenak, or young man (*makkuktunnaaq*).

The peace of mind that Rowley found living with the Inuit influenced profoundly both his journeys and the course of his later life. He enjoyed traveling with Inuit, who, although expert travelers, would avoid hardships and preferred comfort. With Inuit companions Kutjek and Mino, Rowley and Bray sledged across Foxe Basin to map the last uncharted part of the Foxe Basin coast of Baffin Island. In doing this, they completed the coastline begun by Martin Frobisher on the eastern side nearly 500 years earlier.

In the spring of 1939, with his old traveling companions Kutjek and Mino, Rowley rediscovered a long-discontinued route across the unexplored interior of northwestern Baffin Island and managed to descend through the mountains to the east coast. Later in the spring, they returned to the start of the crossing to make some more observations and, on the way back, sighted two large islands not shown then on the map of Canada.

Before leaving for the Arctic, Rowley had asked the eminent anthropologist and scholar Diamond Jenness, chief anthropologist at the National Museum of Canada, for advice as to what archaeological work would be most useful. Jenness had defined the Dorset Culture as the predecessor to the Thule Culture, a theory not fully accepted by Danish archaeologists of the Fifth Thule Expedition, who maintained that Dorset and Thule were essentially the same people. Finding a site containing only Dorset artifacts, said Jenness, would prove the existence of a separate Dorset people.

In the summer of 1939, Rowley was able to excavate a site near Igloolik, from which he had seen a collection of objects given by the Inuit to one of the priests. The site proved to contain only Dorset artifacts, establishing beyond doubt that the Dorset Culture was distinct from the later Thule, a major Canadian achievement in Arctic archaeology.

In late summer, the annual mission ship *Thérèse* brought news of the outbreak of war. Rowley traveled south on the *Thérèse*, and was commissioned into the Canadian Army. Throughout the war, he served with the Canadian Army in the United Kingdom, France,

Belgium, and the Netherlands, and was a member of the D-Day planning staff. After the war, he returned to Canada to take part in Exercise Musk-Ox, a 5000 km motorized Arctic patrol, designed to demonstrate the peacetime applications of Arctic knowledge and equipment developed, some in secret, by the Services during the war. He retired with the rank of lieutenant colonel.

Although the British Canadian Arctic Expedition represented the end of an era, it also represented the beginning of a new one. World War II caused a series of developments that changed northern life profoundly. Among these was the expansion of air travel, which removed the isolation of northern settlements whose only contact with the south had been the annual ship. Rowley's maps and topographical information from the Foxe Basin area were incorporated into maps prepared for the US air force during the war.

In 1946, he joined the Defence Research Board, where he was responsible for Arctic research and its application to the northern needs of the armed forces. For a time, he was seconded to organize and be the first director of the Joint Intelligence Bureau. In 1951, he was assigned to the Department of Northern Affairs and National Resources as secretary and coordinator of the Advisory Committee on Northern Development, which had been formed to advise the cabinet on Arctic policies and to coordinate government activities there. In 1968–1969 he was a visiting fellow at Clare Hall, Cambridge. On his return, he became scientific adviser to the Department of Indian Affairs and Northern Development.

In 1981, he joined Carleton University as a research professor and started their program of Northern and Native Studies. Students benefited from his enthusiasm, his encyclopedic knowledge of the Arctic, and his extensive network of contacts during the next five years. He enlivened classes by frequently inviting guest lecturers, thereby exposing students to a wide array of aboriginal leaders, politicians, public servants, and researchers.

Graham Rowley was appointed a Member of the Order of Canada in 1980. He is a fellow of the Arctic Institute of North America, on which he served as chairperson of the Board of Governors, the Royal Geographical Society, and the Royal Canadian Geographical Society. He is an honorary Member of the American Polar Society. He was awarded the Massey Medal of the Royal Canadian Geographical Society, the Centenary Medal for Northern Science, and the US Arctic and Antarctic Service Medal, and holds honorary doctorates from the University of Saskatchewan and Carleton University. The Canadian Permanent Committee on Geographical Names named Rowley Island in Foxe Basin and the Rowley River on Baffin Island after him.

He is an active supporter of the Inuit community in Ottawa and served on the board of Tungasuvvingat Inuit, the Ottawa Inuit community center.

Biography

Graham Westbrook Rowley was born on October 31, 1912, in Manchester, to Stamford Harry Rowley and Emma Mary Rowley. He attended Giggleswick School (1926–1931), Clare College at Cambridge University (B.A. 1934, M.A. 1936), Staff College Camberley (1941), and National Defence College Kingston (1961–1962). He served with the Canadian Army overseas from 1939, retiring as lieutenant colonel in 1946. From 1946 to 1951, he conducted research for the Defence Research Board, and worked in the Canadian public service until 1974. He was a visiting fellow at Clare Hall, Cambridge, in 1968–1969. From 1981 to 1986, he was a research professor at Carleton University. He married Diana Crowfoot in 1944. Their children are Anne, Susan, and Jane. His publications include *Cold Comfort* (1998) and *The Circumpolar North* (1978) as well as many scientific papers, reviews, and chapters in general Arctic books. Rowley traveled widely in Siberia, Alaska, Greenland, and Scandinavia and visited the South Pole and other stations in Antarctica. Graham Rowley died on January 1, 2004, aged 92.

JOHN BENNETT

Further Reading

Hughes, Graham, "Christmas among the Inuit." *Ottawa Citizen,* December 26, 2000, p. A5

Kenney, Gerard, "Last of the old-time explorers." *Ottawa Citizen,* April 19, 1998, p. B3

Labreche, Juliane, "The Rowleys: husband and wife are both arctic authorities." *Canadian Geographical Journal* (February–March 1981): 70–75

Rowley, Graham, *Cold Comfort,* Montreal: McGill-Queens University Press, 1998

Smith, Dan "The explorer Rowley: a long and passionate love affair with the north." *Toronto Star,* October 12, 1986, pp. D1–2

ROYAL CANADIAN MOUNTED POLICE (RCMP)

The Royal Canadian Mounted Police is Canada's national police force. The image of the Mountie in the dress uniform of scarlet tunic and Stetson hat is one of Canada's most widely known symbols internationally. The Government of Canada formed the force in 1873 as the Northwest Mounted Police (NWMP). The NWMP's initial purpose was to establish and maintain law and order in the Northwestern Territory and

Rupert's Land, two vast and sparsely populated regions Canada bought from the Hudson's Bay Company in 1870. In 1904, King Edward VII conferred the prefix *Royal* to the force's name. In 1920, the RNWMP merged with the Dominion Police, took over federal law enforcement, and was renamed the Royal Canadian Mounted Police (RCMP).

From its beginning, the NWMP was no ordinary police force. In 1885, it helped the Canadian militia put down the Northwest Rebellion in central Saskatchewan. This was not the last time the force took on a military role. Over 250 members served in Canadian military units in the Boer War, and the force worked in conjunction with Canadian armed forces in the two world wars. Since the 1990s, RCMP officers have provided international policing, sometimes as part of United Nations peacekeeping missions, in Namibia, Yugoslavia, Haiti, Kosovo, Bosnia/Herzegovina, East Timor, Guatemala, Croatia, and the Western Sahara.

The force's military history is consistent with its role as a defender of Canadian sovereignty. This is clearly illustrated by the role the force has played in Canada's North. In 1895, the NWMP was sent to the Yukon to keep order among the small, but growing, influx of miners and trappers. The following year, gold was discovered at Rabbit (later, Bonanza) Creek near present-day Dawson City and the Klondike Gold Rush was on. The Gold Rush brought tens of thousands of gold-seekers, many American, to the territory. The fact that the force preceded the gold-seekers led to a degree of order unfamiliar to those accustomed to the wild west of the United States. Of more import is that the force established effective control of the territory at a time when the border between Alaska and Canada had yet to be fixed and some feared American annexation of the gold fields.

In the 1920s, the RCMP established detachments in Canada's Arctic explicitly as a sign of Canadian sovereignty in those areas. As part of this mission, an RCMP supply vessel, the *St Roch,* made a historic voyage through the North West Passage from 1940 to 1942.

Today, the RCMP numbers almost 21,000 officers, public servants, and civilian members in 15 divisions across Canada, plus a headquarters in Ottawa. The RCMP enforces provincial and territorial law in all provinces and territories, except Ontario and Québec. The force also provides policing to almost 200 municipalities. In addition to conventional policing duties, the RCMP is responsible for airport policing, VIP security, drug enforcement, and commercial crime. In 1984, its intelligence-gathering role was transferred to a separate entity, the Canadian Security and Intelligence Service (CSIS).

FLOYD MCCORMICK

Further Reading

Kelly, Terrance Frederick, *Comptroller Fred White and the Arctic Presence of the RNWMP 1903–1911*, Edmonton: University of Alberta, 1985
Larsen, Henry, *The North-West Passage, 1940–1942 and 1944: The Famous Voyages of the Royal Canadian Mounted Police Schooner St Roch*, Ottawa: Queen's Printer, 1969
Morrison, William R., *Showing the flag: The Mounted Police and Canadian Sovereignty in the North, 1894–1925*, Vancouver: University of British Columbia Press, 1985
North, Dick, *The Lost Patrol: The Mounties' Yukon Tragedy*, Vancouver: Raincoast Books, 1994
Royal Canadian Mounted Police website: http://www.rcmp-grc.gc.ca/
Ward, Robert D.S., *Policing in Canada's Northland*, Wetaskiwin, Alberta: Books by Bob, 2000

ROYAL GEOGRAPHICAL SOCIETY

The Royal Geographical Society (RGS) was formed in 1830 with roots in the Raleigh Travellers' (or Dining) Club, a dinner club for those interested in travel. The Society principally intended to contribute to and further exploration and then disseminate research and information regarding geography. The founders and original members of the RGS included prominent men of position with connections to the British government and the ability to influence government decisions. One of the leading RGS members was Sir John Barrow, a founding fellow and the society's third president. He also held the position of second secretary of the British Admiralty. Barrow took active part in RGS proceedings and, as second secretary of the Admiralty, was an enthusiastic advocate for the promotion of Arctic discovery toward both the North Pole and the North West Passage. Other original members included figures such as admirals Edward Belcher and Frederick William Beechey.

From its inception, the RGS advocated for, and made direct financial grants to, explorers whose efforts could lead to vital discoveries in geography. In 1832, the RGS supported the private subscriptions then being sought for an expedition to be led by Sir George Back for the relief of Sir John Ross, who had then been absent for three years in the Arctic in search of a North West Passage. Upon Back's return in 1835, the RGS awarded him its Royal Premium, a monetary award of 50 guineas, for his findings on that expedition. Back received the first RGS medal for his efforts. As a consequence of Back's discoveries and the still unsolved question of the geography of Arctic North America, in 1836 the RGS appointed a committee to examine proposals for the completion of a survey of the Arctic coast of North America. The RGS Committee received proposals from various Arctic experts, including Sir John Barrow, Sir John Franklin, Sir John Richardson, and Sir John Ross. The RGS

Committee presented these proposals to the British government and supported its intention that one of these plans be put into effect. As a consequence of the RGS actions, the British government supported this expedition and appointed Back as its commander.

The RGS contributed to Arctic discovery by the publication and dissemination of the results of Arctic exploration in its *Journal of the Royal Geographical Society*, which included in these early years, among other items, the report of the important discoveries of Peter Dease and Thomas Simpson on the Northern Coast of America (Simpson also received the RGS Founder's medal). During its nascent years, the RGS also became an important repository of geographical works and began to establish its large and important map collection.

By 1848, British interest in the Arctic centered on the search for Sir John Franklin, an original RGS member. The Society, and in particular its president, Sir Roderick Murchison, actively engaged in advocating the continued search and relief of Franklin in the Arctic by both Admiralty action and by private subscription. The Franklin search contributed greatly to the mapping of large portions of the Canadian Arctic, and the RGS published reports and maps of the returning search parties. Dr. John Rae, who returned to England with the first knowledge of the fate of the Franklin expedition, was awarded the RGS Founder's Medal in 1852. RGS medals were awarded to other explorers during the Franklin search for geographical discoveries, including Admiral Robert McClure (for discovery of the North West Passage), Admiral E.A. Inglefield, Admiral Richard R. Collinson, and an American, Dr. Elisha Kent Kane. In addition, Murchison personally lobbied for a monument in Greenwich in honor of Lt. J.R. Bellot, a Frenchman lost during the search for Franklin.

By 1860, the British Admiralty had closed its search for Franklin and, as a result of that long, costly, and frustrating Arctic campaign, lacked interest in sponsoring further exploration solely for scientific and geographical purposes. Concerned with growing American and European activity in Svalbard, Greenland, and the European Arctic during the late 1860s and early 1870s, the RGS approached other learned societies and the British Admiralty for a renewal of Arctic efforts, including an attempt at the North Pole as well as advancements in different scientific fields. A reluctant British Admiralty declined to support Murchison's efforts in 1865. However, the RGS persevered, and in 1874 following a series of lectures by Arctic veterans, including Captain Sherard Osborne, lobbying by its president, General Sir Henry Rawlinson, and its Secretary Sir Clements Markham, the new British Prime Minister, Benjamin Disraeli, was convinced to organize a new Arctic expedition, the British Arctic Expedition of 1875–1876, under the command of Admiral Sir George S. Nares. The efforts of the RGS and the Royal Society of the UK, working together through a joint Arctic Committee, were directly responsible for the British Arctic Expedition. In order to provide instruction for the scientific work of the expedition, the RGS prepared a document on Arctic geography and ethnology and the Royal Society published a manual of scientific instruction. Although the British Arctic Expedition of 1875–1876 failed in its attempt to reach the North Pole, its participants did succeed in making important scientific and geographical contributions.

Following the British Arctic Expedition, the RGS would never again advocate or financially support an Arctic enterprise on the scale of this 120-plus member Arctic expedition. The RGS did, however, direct its attention to the Antarctic, largely through its President Sir Clements Markham, and forcefully promoted and supported the National Antarctic Expedition under the command of Captain Robert Falcon Scott. As for the Arctic, smaller financial contributions were granted to expeditions such as Sir W. Martin Conway's Spitsbergen expedition of 1895–1896, Ejnar Mikkelsen's Greenland expedition, and Roald Amundsen's voyage to study the region near the Magnetic North Pole. The RGS continued its practice of supporting Arctic relief expeditions (which had began with its support of Back's first expedition of 1832), when it contributed 1000 GBP to mounting a relief expedition to search for the overdue Benjamin Leigh Smith in Franz Josef Land.

Rather than a direct promoter and sponsor of Arctic exploration, the role of the RGS in the 20th century evolved into one of dissemination of the activities and results of research expeditions to the Arctic. The Society published results of American and European efforts in the *Geographical Journal*, among other publications, and bestowed awards of recognition upon explorers with distinguished achievements. The RGS also provided public lectures and classes for explorers, scientists, and the would-be travelers and explorers. All of these activities kept the public apprised of Arctic activities. The work of the RGS—which has recently merged with the Institute of British Geographers (IBG)—continues today, and it remains an important source of financial, technical, and educational support for both individual researchers and expedition teams.

DOUG WAMSLEY

See also **Amundsen, Roald; Back, Sir George; Barrow, Sir John; Beechey, Frederick; Belcher, Sir Edward; British Arctic Expedition, 1875–1876; Franklin, Sir John; Markham, Sir Clements R.; McClure, Sir Robert; Ross, Sir John; Simpson, Thomas**

Further Reading

Arctic Geography and Ethnology. A Selection of Papers on Arctic Geography and Ethnology. Reprinted, and Presented to the Arctic Expedition of 1875, by the President, Council, and Fellows of the Royal Geographical Society, London: John Murray, 1875

Back, Captain George, "An account of the route and appearances of the country through which the Arctic Land Expedition passed, from Great Slave Lake to the Polar Sea" (communicated by Capt. Back, R.N. Read 23rd November, 1835). *Journal of the Royal Geographical Society*, VI (1836): 1–11

David, Robert G., *The Arctic in the British Imagination 1818–1914*, Manchester and New York: Manchester University Press, 2000

Dease, Peter W. & Thomas Simpson, "An account of recent Arctic discoveries by Messrs. Dease and T. Simpson" (communicated by J.H. Pelly, Esq., Governor of the Hudson's Bay Company). *Journal of the Royal Geographical Society*, VIII (1838): 213–225

Frere, Sir H. Bartle, "Address to the Royal Geographical Society. Delivered at the Anniversary Meeting on the 22nd June, 1874." *Journal of the Royal Geographical Society*, 44(1874): clxix–clxxii

Hints to Travellers. Edited by a Committee of Council of the Royal Geographical Society, Consisting of Admiral Sir G. Back, F.R.S., Admiral Richard R. Collinson, K.C.B., and Francis Galton, Esq., F.R.S., London: Published for the Royal Geographical Society, 1878

Manual of the Natural History, Geology, and Physics of Greenland and the Neighbouring Regions; Prepared for the Use of the Arctic Expedition of 1875, Under the Direction of the Arctic Committee of the Royal Society, and edited by T. Rupert Jones, F.R.S., F.G.S., Together with Instructions Suggested by the Arctic Committee of the Royal Society for the Use of the Expedition, London: Printed for Her Majesty's Stationery Office, 1875

Markham, C.R., *Proceedings of the Royal Geographical Society, on the Best Route for North Polar Exploration*, Volume IX, Session 1864–1865, pp. 138–163

Mill, Hugh Robert, *The Record of the Royal Geographical Society 1830–1930*, London: The Royal Geographical Society, 1930

Osborne, Captain Sherard, *Proceedings of the Royal Geographical Society, on the Exploration of the North Polar Region*, Volume IX, Session 1864–1865, pp. 42–70

Osborne, Captain Sherard, *Proceedings of the Royal Geographical Society, on the Exploration of the North Polar Region*, Volume XII, Session 1867–1868, pp. 92–112

Osborne, Sherard, *Proceedings of the Royal Geographical Society, on the Exploration of the North Polar Basin, with a Resume of Recent Swedish, German and Austrian Attempts to reach the Polar Circle from the Atlantic Ocean*, Volume XVI, Session 1871–1872, pp. 227–240

Petermann, Dr. Augustus, *Proceedings of the Royal Geographical Society, on the Proposed Expedition to the North Pole* (A Letter Addressed to Sir Roderick I. Murchison, K.C.B.) Volume IX, Session 1864–1865, pp. 90–103

Rawlinson, General Sir H.C. Bartle, "Address to the Royal Geographical Society, Delivered at the Anniversary Meeting on the 24th May, 1875." *Journal of the Royal Geographical Society*, 45(1875): clxv–clxxiii

"Report of the Royal Geographical Society." *Journal of the Royal Geographical Society*, VI(1836): 3–6

ROYAL GREENLAND

Royal Greenland is the world's largest producer of cold-water shrimp and a market leader in a wide range of seafood products. It is also by far the largest production company in Greenland. The present company is in principle based on the Danish trade monopoly established in 1774 and organized through the Royal Greenland Trade Company (KGH—Kongelige Grønlandske Handel) established in 1776. During colonial times, KGH was the sole buyer of products such as skin and blubber, and from 1902 also fish, just as it was the only supplier of amenities to the Greenland population.

By abandoning colonial relations and including Greenland as a county in Denmark in 1953, the principle of monopoly in trade was in principle erased. But because attempts to attract private business to Greenland were not successful and the government still wanted to maintain a firm grip on the economic situation, KGH as a company owned by the Danish State continued to dominate both trade and supply activities, and continued to maintain the crucial position as the main buyer and processor of fish and wildlife products, as well as the central agent in the introduction of offshore trawlers.

With the creation of Home Rule, KGH and all its activities and responsibilities were transferred to the new Home Rule government. The new government decided to split the company into different divisions, one for trade and transportation (KNI), one for fishing (The Trawler Division), one for production and processing (KTU), and one for export and international trade (Royal Greenland), all supervised by the government. During the 1990s, however, all activities related to marine resources—that is, part of fisheries, production and processing of products from fishing and hunting with production facilities in most settlements in Greenland, as well as export and international trade—have been reunited as a stock company under the auspices of Royal Greenland, with the Greenlandic government as the sole shareholder. In the late 1990s, the activities in the larger settlements were maintained by Royal Greenland, while another Home Rule-owned company, Nuka A/S, is responsible for the production facilities in two towns and 26 villages.

The company presently operates a fleet of 20 factory trawlers, of which six are owned by Royal Greenland and 14 are contracted. On shore, the company currently runs 20 processing factories for the production of shrimp, fish, and oven-ready seafood dishes, of which 16 are in Greenland. Besides the facilities in Greenland, the company possesses four processing facilities in Denmark, as well as facilities in China—both aimed at the Japanese and American markets—and a large plant in Ludwigshafen, Germany, which, among other products, produces ready-made meals for the European market. The production volume of this plant is at the same level as on all plants in Greenland together. The most important products are unprocessed, cooked, and shelled shrimp, which constitutes approximately 50% of the total production. In addition, halibut production accounts for 20% while battered products and ready-made meals constitute approximately 15%. In addition, there is production of cod, seawolf, scallops, and snowcrab.

Because the resources in Greenland are dwindling and fisheries therefore are exposed to cuts in shrimp quotas in Greenlandic territorial waters, Royal Greenland Overseas has tried to ensure a constant supply of raw materials and seafood products for the market by means of cooperative contracts, joint ventures, and strategic alliances with companies outside Greenland (Iceland, Faroe Islands, Alaska, Russia).

During the last ten years, the company's turnover has increased from 450 million to 3.5 billion Danish kroner (450 million US$) in 2001/2002, with total assets of 527 million Danish kroner (70 million US$). Royal Greenland A/S sales subsidiaries have been established on the most important markets in Denmark, France, Germany, Italy, Japan, Sweden, the UK, and USA, with Royal Greenland Export, Royal Greenland Overseas, and Royal Greenland Development as the main international divisions. The Export Division sells about 65,000 tons of high-quality products from an expanding product range to 40 main markets all over the world, and the group employs approximately 2500 full-time workers. In order to compete on the world market, all production is in accordance with the Royal Greenland quality control system (HACCP) with strict laboratory control of raw materials and finished products. In addition, as a part of its policy, the company markets to specific retail chains by producing their own brands as private labels.

The company argues that lower costs and higher efficiency are needed in Greenland in order to compete on the world market. This means an increase of efficiency with the fleet and in the land-based processing plants through ongoing improvements and investments. This, however, has led to further concentration and centralization of the production, with closure of production facilities that used to be the central economic activity for many settlements. Consequently, this has led to the company being considered by many to be unfriendly to the everyday life of most towns and villages, and to more openness to private initiatives such as the expansion of activities by private companies like Polar Seafood A/S and others.

RASMUS OLE RASMUSSEN

See also **Denmark Strait: Fisheries (Commercial); Greenland Hunters and Fishers Association**

(KNAPK); Greenland Seafishery and Export Association; International Whaling Commission (IWC); Royal Greenland Trade Company (KGH)

Further Reading

APK, *Bestyrelsens beretning til APKs ordinære generalforsamling*, Nuuk: APK, 1993, 1994, 1995, 1996

Poole, Graham, *The Development of Greenland's Shrimp Fishing and Processing Industry Since 1979: A Study of Applied Economics*, Institut for Nationaløkonomi, København: Handelshøjskolen i København, 1990

Rasmussen, Rasmus Ole, *Resource Management in Greenland*, Publications from Institute of Geography and International Development, Roskilde: Roskilde University 2001

Royal Greenland, *Annual Report*, Nuuk: Greenland, 1989, 1990,…,2000

Statistics Greenland, *Greenland 2000–2001—Kalaallit Nunaat. Statistical Yearbook*, Nuuk: Grønlands Statistik, 2001

Skydsbjerg, Henrik, *Grønland 20 år med hjemmestyre—en samtidshistorie om Grønlands udvikling under hjemmestyret*, Greenland, Forlaget Atuagkat, 1999

ROYAL GREENLAND TRADE COMPANY (KGH)

From 1721, trade in Greenland was in the hands of a private company—*Bergenskompag niet*—that was supported by the Danish crown and given a monopoly in return for upholding a missionary station. In 1726, this company went bankrupt and the Danish government took responsibility for the project. From 1734 to 1749, a merchant named Jacob Severin ran the business. The trade and mission in Greenland were then taken over by another trading company, *Det Almindelige Handelskompagni*, which also traded in Iceland, the Faroese Islands, and Finnmark in Norway. In 1774, this company folded, and the king was forced again to finance Greenlandic trade until 1776, when the Royal Greenland Trade Company, or *Den Kongelige Grønlandske Handelskompagni* (KGH), was created. The company received the usual privileges: a monopoly on trade and financial support to sustain the missionary station. This state of affairs continued until 1950.

KGH's prime task was to buy, process, and export Greenlandic trade products (mainly sealskins, seal oil, and whale blubber), and to take European (preferably Danish) merchandise to Greenland in exchange. In its early years, the company attempted to make whaling the prime business, but this effort was unsuccessful and suffered poor results. Whaling from Denmark to Greenland ended in 1789.

Taking the native people under its tutelage, the state issued guidelines for the company in 1782 (*The Instruction of 19 April 1782*), and in 1781 placed two inspectors in Greenland to survey the company. The guidelines of 1782 required KGH's merchants to treat the native population civilly, and to assist them in making as much produce as possible, but not to buy more from them than they needed for subsistence. KGH was charged to refrain from interfering with native society unless the Greenlanders offended the trade and its servants. However, as the Danish presence became more widespread, KGH was drawn into the civil administration of Greenlandic society, first in jurisdiction and later in education and health care.

The economic policy established equal prices for Greenlandic produce all along the coast as well as for imported merchandise regardless of internal costs. In principle, the prices on imported goods should cover the cost of acquisition in Europe with an overhead to cover the transportation to Greenland, but in fact goods that were considered vital for production, such as rifles, ammunition, iron, and steel, bore an especially low overhead. Also, the prices on Greenlandic produce were to a degree unrelated to market prices. For instance, hides from polar bears and Arctic foxes were paid well beneath their worth in Europe. In the case of misfortune in hunting or other calamities for the Greenlanders, the company was obliged to support them with imported foodstuffs, a directive that had the potential to economically devastate the company.

After a reconstruction in 1789, KGH continued with the utmost frugality and managed to reasonably balance budgets until the war with Britain from 1807 to 1814, which was most disastrous. Trade with Greenland was almost interrupted, and the company fell into heavy debt that the government finally covered. A new policy of expanding the number of trading posts was established in order to collect more of the surplus from the Greenlanders' seal catches. The first post was in Arsuk in 1805, and by 1850 approximately 35 such outposts were dispersed along the west coast, most of which were maintained until the 1950s. Each outpost was linked to one of the greater settlements, a named colony, from which it received its goods and to whom it delivered its produce.

After 1825, the endeavors succeeded. KGH freed itself of debt in 1830 and ran a surplus for many years until the 1880s, with the exception of a few lean years in the 1860s. Fortunately, royalties from the cryolite mine at Ivigtut in 1856 stabilized the total Greenland budget, but KGH could not fend off the permanent deficit from the 1880s and onward. The decline resulted primarily from falling prices of Greenlandic animal oil caused by the competition from mineral and vegetable oil.

The accumulated Greenland budget maintained a surplus from 1850 until 1909. Commercial fishery boosted the account from the mid-1920s as did the rising prices and expanded production of cryolite in the late 1930s. The accumulated account held a surplus of 9 million Danish kroner just before World War II.

The position of KGH became overwhelming in Greenland during the 19th century. By law it managed all export and import, and by being in charge of processing Greenlandic produce, the company also created a monopoly on everything connected therewith, such as all handicrafts and transportation. Early on, KGH hired a local labor force, which grew from 22 employees in 1834 to 377 in 1930, numbers that constituted 5–10% of the Greenlandic labor force. In 1908, the company was relieved of its duty to administer the civil society in Greenland. A Greenland administration was set up in Copenhagen (*Styrelsen for kolonierne i Grønland*), of which trade was only a part.

From the very beginning, KGH held a monopoly on Greenlandic trade, sealing the country off from all other economic prospects. On several occasions during the 19th century, there was discussion concerning a lift of the monopoly. Politically and philosophically speaking, many liberal Greenlanders were uneasy with the country's economic reality. But with each of these discussions, the monopoly survived the challenges. The core reason stemmed from the Greenlanders' ability to manage in a liberal economy. It was believed that the risk to the treasury—if free enterprise ruined parts or the whole of Greenland—was too great. Nonetheless, in 1950 free trade was introduced, and access to the country opened. KGH continued its business, now only with an obligation to deliver the imported goods and to buy, process, and export Greenlandic produce.

The company still dominated much of Greenlandic society after 1950. Competing private local stores and enterprises were slow to develop alongside KGH, which was the only wholesale agent.

The Home Rule Authorities took over KGH in 1985 and renamed it Kalaallit Niuerfiat (KNI or Greenland Trading). The business has since been divided into several companies, the largest of which is Royal Greenland (established in 1990) in charge of fishery, fish processing, and the exportation of fish products.

AXEL KJÆR SØRENSEN

See also **Rink, Hinrich Johannes; Royal Greenland**

Further Reading

Bobé, Louis, *Den Grønlandske Handels og Kolonisations Historie indtil 1870* [The History of the Greenlandic Trade and Colonization until 1870], Copenhagen, 1936

Christiansen, H.C., "Den kongelige grønlandske handel." In *Danmark*, Volume XIV, edited by J.P. Trap, Copenhagen, 1970, pp. 134–153

Gad, Finn, *The History of Greenland, Volume II, 1700–1782*, London: Hurst, 1973

———, *The History of Greenland, Volume. III, 1782–1808*, Copenhagen: Busck, 1982

————, "History of Colonial Greenland." In *Handbook of North American Indians, Volume 5, Arctic*, edited by William Sturtevant, Washington, District of Columbia: Smithsonian Institution, 1984, pp. 556–576

Sveistrup, P.P., *Economic Principles of the Greenland Administration Before 1947*, Copenhagen: Meddelelser Om Grønland, 1949

Sørensen, Axel Kjær, *Danmark-Grønland i det 20. århundrede* [Denmark-Greenland in the 20th Century], Copenhagen: Nyt Nordisk, 1983

RUDENKO, SERGEI

In 1904, Sergei Rudenko became a student at St Petersburg University and developed an interest in physical anthropology. As a student, he participated in expeditions to the Finno-Ugric peoples of the Volga region. In 1909–1910, on an expedition in the north of Western Siberia, he collected rich ethnographic material and also large collections of household items of the Mansi, Khanty, and Nenets. Engaged in physical anthropology, he conducted a series of anthropometric measurements. These materials were the basis of his publications. For one of them, "Anthropometric studies of native people of northwest of Siberia," Tomsk University awarded him the Kuznetsov prize (1910).

After finishing university in 1910, Rudenko became a scientific employee of the Academy of Sciences. He continued to study the Finno-Ugric peoples, engaging in ethnology, archaeology, and physical anthropology. In December 1917, Moscow University awarded him a degree of the magister for "Bashkirs. Experience of the ethnological monography." In 1919–1921, Rudenko lived in Tomsk, where he was a professor of geography and anthropology of Tomsk University. In 1921, he returned to Petrograd, where he became a professor of anthropology of Petrograd University, and simultaneously headed an ethnographic department of the Russian museum (now the independent Russian Ethnographic Museum). He also renewed work at the Academy of Sciences as the scientific secretary of a Commission to study the tribal composition of the population of Russia. He led Kazakh's, Tuva's, and other expeditions of the Academy of Sciences. In the 1920s, Rudenko became one of the leaders of ethnological science in Russia. At the same time, he had significant experience with archaeological studies. During one of the Tuva expeditions, Rudenko opened the now world-famous Pazyryk tumulus on Altai. In 1929, he managed archaeological excavations on Pazyryk. The finds, made in permafrost, were sensational and opened a new page in the study of Skiphian time.

Rudenko was arrested on August 5, 1930 on a false charge. While in custody, he renewed his physics knowledge and worked as an engineer. In March 1934, Rudenko was released, but stayed on, working as a hydrologist. He returned to Leningrad on the eve of World War II.

In 1942, he began to work at the Institute of the History of Material Culture (now Archaeological Institute of the Russian Academy of Sciences). In 1944, the degree of doctor of engineering science was awarded to Sergei Rudenko for hydrological works published in the 1930s. However, his primary activity at this time was archaeology. In 1945, Rudenko worked at excavations on Chukotka, and in 1947–1954 continued archaeological studies on Mountain Altai. In the last years of his life, he headed the radiocarbon laboratory in the Leningrad branch of the Archaeological Institute. He also headed the department of ethnography of the Geographic Society of the USSR.

As a scientist, Rudenko was an excellent systematizer and utilized the comparative method. One of the major directions of his studies was the ethnography and physical anthropology of the Khanty and Nenets. Practically all his life, Rudenko worked on the generalizing monograph about Ob'-Ugric and Nenets. This monograph under the title "Die Ugrien und Nenzen am Unteren Ob" (1972) was published after his death in Hungary. His major works "Anthropological studies of the native people of northwest Siberia" (1914), "Native people of Low Ob (Ethnographic essay)" (1914), and "Folk art of Ostyak and Vogul" (1929) are devoted to the same problem. He systematized all known data about the Khanty and Nenets of Low Ob'. Also, he paid attention to tribal marks (tamga) and the semantics of tattoos of the Khanty and Mansi. Rudenko's works in this field are used by modern scientists as a rich source of ethnographical materials. As a result of archaeological studies on Chukotka, he published the book "Ancient culture of the Bering sea and Eskimo problem" (1947), in which he attempted to demonstrate the Asian derivation of the population of Northern America. The archaeology of Altai occupied a very large place in Rudenko's studies. He described and systematized finds from Pazyryk tumulus; on the basis of finds of bronze casting, he constructed the schema of progress of bronze manufacture of Skiphian time; and he defined the level of cultural progress of the population of southern Siberia. His studies in this field are still used by archaeologists and form the basis for dating monuments to this time. Among the basic works, it is possible to name "Second Pazyryk tumulus" (1948), "Art of Skiphians of Altai" (1949), and "Culture of the population of Central Altai in Skiphian time" (1960). Because Rudenko was very scrupulous with respect to scientific materials, he avoided sensational theories and strictly followed the received sources. Therefore, his works are not controversial.

Nevertheless, his role in furthering the archaeology and ethnology of the North is great: he has constructed a base for further scientific study.

Biography

Rudenko Sergei Ivanovich was born on January 16, 1885 in Kharkov (Russia) of noble lineage. Soon after his birth, the family moved to the city of Perm. Here, he studied in a classic grammar school. In Perm and around it, there were numerous Finno-Ugric peoples. Rudenko became interested in their culture and began to collect his own ethnographic materials during his school years. Simultaneously, he was involved with natural sciences, in particular, physics and medicine. Rudenko Sergei Ivanovich died on July 16, 1969 in Leningrad.

ALEXEY ZEN'KO

Further Reading

Masson, Vladimir, "To the 80 anniversary of Sergei Ivanovich Rudenko." *Soviet Archaeology*, 4 (1965) (in Russian)

RUSSIA

Russia, also called the Russian Federation, occupies the northern part of Eurasia. It is the world's largest country covering 17,075,400 sq km. Present-day Russia, with Moscow as its capital, is the successor state of the Russian Soviet Federative Socialist Republic of the USSR (1917–1991), which was preceded by the Russian Empire. Under the present constitution, Russia is a "democratic federative state with the republican form of government." The population of Russia in November 2002 (census) was estimated to be 145,287,400, of which less than 10% live in the Far North, although more than one-third of Russia's territory lies north of the 60th parallel. The indigenous peoples of the Far North, from over 30 ethnic groups, number about 200,000.

Russia is made up of 89 administrative-territorial units having the status of a republic, kray (region), oblast' (province), city under direct federal administration, autonomous oblast', or autonomous okrug (district). In theory, all autonomous okrugs, except Chukotka, are subordinated to a parent oblast' or kray, although in practice they have differing amounts of independence. Those administrative territories falling within the Arctic or Subarctic have their own entries in this Encyclopedia.

For the convenience of administration, the country's territory is divided into 11 economic regions: North, Northwest, Central, Volga-Vyatka, Central Black Earth, North Caucasus, Volga, Ural, West Siberia, East Siberia, and the Far East. A 2000 presidential decree divided the country into seven federal okrugs (districts), each encompassing a number of respective economic regions.

Physical Geography

Russia occupies a major part of eastern Europe and northern Asia. It stretches 2500–4000 km from north to south and 9000 km from west to east. The westernmost point of the country lies at its border with Poland (19°38′ E), easternmost on Ratmanov Island (Bering Strait) (169°02′ W), southernmost at the border with Azerbaijan (41°10′ N), and northernmost on the islands of Franz Josef Land (81°51′ N).

Extensive plains occupy nearly 70% of Russia's territory. The East European Plain in the west consists of a series of low rolling uplands up to 350–400 m high (Valdaiskaya, Srednerusskaya, Privolzhskaya) alternating with lowlands (Oksko-Donskaya and Prikaspiyskaya Nizmennost'). The Ural Mountains (800–1200 m) running from north to south form the eastern limit of the East European Plain. Their highest summit, Mt Narodnaya, reaches 1895 m. East of the Urals lies the West Siberian Plain, which is exceedingly flat and featureless compared with the Eastern European Plain. Its lowest portions, the waterlogged and swampy Kondinskaya, Sredneobskaya, and Barabinskaya lowlands, are in the central part of the Plain surrounded by elevated terrains of up to 120–150 m.

The raised Central Siberian Plateau is situated between the Yenisey and Lena rivers. Its gently rolling surface is broken by a dense network of deep river valleys. Here and there, occasional tablelands occur, such as the Putorana Plateau (up to 1701 m) and the Yenisey Ridge (1104 m). On its eastern side, the Plateau gives way to the Central Yakut Lowland with river valleys lying 100–120 m above sea level.

Mountain areas having rugged relief of variable elevation predominate in the eastern part of the country and in some areas of its southern part. In European Russia, they include a series of ranges on the northern slopes of the Great Caucasus with the principal peak of Mt Elbrus (5642 m), the highest point in Russia and in Europe.

A chain of mountain ranges running along Russia's frontier in southern Siberia includes the Altai Mountains with a maximum height of 4506 m (Mt Belukha), Kuznetsky Alatau, Western Sayan and Eastern Sayan Mountains extending to the territory of Tyva, the mountain systems west and east of Lake Baikal, and the Stanovoy Range. Northeastern Siberia and the Russian Far East are the territory of largely mid-altitude mountain ranges (1500–2000 m). They include the Verkhoyansk Range, Chersky Mountains (highest point Mountain Pobeda, 3147 m), Kolyma

Administrative regions, and main cities, towns, and rivers in northern Russia.

Mountains, Chukchi and Koryak Mountains, Dzhugdzhur and Bureya Ranges, and the Sikhote-Alin. A line of mountains running along the Pacific coasts comprises mountain systems of the Kamchatka-Kuril region (Klyuchevskaya Sopka, 4750 m and Alaid, 2339 m, respectively) with numerous volcanic peaks.

Inland Waters

There are almost 120,000 rivers in excess of 10 km in Russia with a total length of 2.3 million km. Their overall catchment area of 12.8 million sq km largely constitutes the drainage basin of the marginal seas of the Arctic Ocean. The greatest rivers are Severnaya Dvina, Pechora, Ob' with Irtysh, Yenisey, Lena, Indigirka, and Kolyma. Highlands and lowlands of the Far East are drained by rivers flowing to the seas of the Pacific Ocean (Amur, Anadyr, Penzhina, etc.). Inland seas of the Atlantic Ocean receive waters of the greatest rivers of European Russia. The famous Volga River flowing into the Caspian Sea and its tributaries form a huge inland basin. The total annual average flow of all Russian rivers reaches 4000 km^3.

Most of the rivers are fed by rains and melting snow. Floods are highest in spring and early summer excepting southern areas of the Far East where they occur in late summer. From 65% to 100% of the annual flow falls in the warm season. Ice cover persists from 1–2 months in the rivers of Krasnoyarsk Kray to 8 months in northern Siberia.

Rivers are navigable and fit for floating timber along 400,000 km of their total length. They are a major source of water supply for cities and industries. In the south, they are extensively used for irrigation. The hydroelectric potential of Russian rivers is estimated at 320 million kW. Great Siberian rivers (Yenisey, Angara, Lena, Ob') and also Amur and Volga have the highest potential for hydroelectric power.

There are nearly 2 million freshwater and salt lakes in Russia. The largest are Caspian Sea, and lakes Baikal, Ladoga, Onega, and Taymyr. Some rivers dammed for hydroelectric power form huge reservoirs, such as Rybinskoye, Kuibyshevskoye, Volgogradskoye, Kamskoye, Krasnoyarskoye, Irkutskoye, Bratskoye, etc.

Climate

A major part of Russia is situated in the low temperate climatic zone. Islands of the Arctic Ocean and mainland areas in the Far North lie in the Arctic and Subarctic regions. Subtropical climate occurs in a

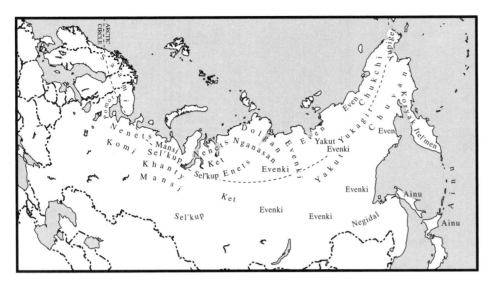

Indigenous peoples of northern Russia.

small area at the Black Sea coast of the Caucasus. A continental climate dominates most of Russia with minor exceptions. The degree of continentality markedly increases from west to east as effects of the Atlantic Ocean become weaker. East Siberia has a severely continental climate, with the difference between the mean July and January temperatures reaching 50–65°C. In summertime, the southern areas of the Far East experience the influence of the marginal seas of the Pacific Ocean, while in winter they are under the influence of the inland Siberian anticyclone. The monsoonal climate of the Pacific region brings cold, relatively snowless winters and moderately hot rainy summers. During wintertime, high atmospheric pressure is very frequent, accounting for cold weather in most of the Russian territory. The average temperature in January ranges from 0°C to –5°C in the west of European Russia and Caucasia and from –40°C to –50°C in the east of Yakutia, where it may fall as low as –65°C to –75°C. In summer, a relatively low atmospheric pressure predominates over most of the country's territory. Therefore, the season is generally warm (excepting Far North areas) and even hot in the south. The average July temperature is 1°C in the north of Siberia and 24–25°C on the Prikaspiyskaya Nizmennost in the East European Plain.

The duration of the frostless period varies considerably. It is highly variable in the Far North and islands in the Arctic Ocean and lasts for 110–120 days in the steppes of western Siberia and 180–200 days in the North Caucasus.

Most precipitation comes from the west, with air masses originating over the Atlantic. In the Far East, these are derived from the circulation over the marginal seas of the Pacific Ocean. Precipitation is especially high in the Caucasus and Altai Mountains (up to 1500–200 mm annually), the forest zone of the East European Plain (600–700 mm), and in the southern part of the Russian Far East (as much as 1000 mm). Much less precipitation falls in the tundra and steppe zones and in the taiga zone of Yakutia. Precipitation is lowest in the semidesert areas of the Prikaspiyskaya Nizmennost (120–150 mm), where intense summer evaporation accounts for acute seasonal water deficit.

The duration of snow cover is 60–80 days in the south and 260–280 days in the Far North. It varies from 70 to 100 cm depth in western Siberia and Kamchatka.

The especially severe continental climate of Siberia and the Far East is responsible for perennially frozen ground in these regions. In Russia, permafrost (sometimes highly saturated with ground ice) occurs over an area in excess of 10 million sq km. Not infrequently, it reaches a depth of 200–500 m in the north (1500 m in the Markha River (tributary of Vilyuy) basin).

Ice sheets are common in high-mountain and polar regions. Their total area on the Arctic Ocean islands (Novaya Zemlya, Severnaya Zemlya, Franz Josef Land) exceeds 56,000 sq km. In the mountain ranges of the North Caucasus, Altai, Sayans, Kamchatka, and northeastern Siberia glaciers cover about 3500 sq km.

Russia occupies a territory with the most unfavorable natural and climatic conditions, long winters, low temperatures, and a poor supply of moisture over vast areas. Such a physiographic situation predetermines a highly power-consuming national economy, difficult and unprofitable farming (the agroclimatic potential of the United States is 2.5 times that of Russia), and high costs of labor supply.

Vegetation

Plainland soil and vegetation distribution corresponds to consecutive zones changing one another from north to south. The polar desert zone on the islands of the Arctic Ocean and the coastal strip of the Taymyr Peninsula has shallow primitive Arctic soils. Its poor vegetation largely consists of various lichens, mosses, and relatively few perennial flowering plants, which form a sparse ground cover. Large patches of bare ground are a common feature in this zone. South of it lies the tundra zone dominated by acidic gley tundra soils. Its vegetation is composed of widespread low-growing (dwarf birch and low birch, willows) and berry-producing (cowberry, blueberry) shrubs, besides mosses and fruticose lichens (*Cladonia, Cetraria*). Herbaceous plants (sedges, cottongrass) become much more abundant. The transition forest-tundra zone features an alternation of treeless tracts of tundra vegetation (lichens, mosses, low shrubs) and patches of sparse tree growth consisting of birch, spruce, and (in Siberia) larch. Tundra, peaty-gley, weak podzolic, and cryogenic gley-taiga soils predominate.

Nearly 65% of the territory of Russia lies in the forest zone, which is occasionally (east of the Yenisey River) as wide as 2000 km. Its northern part, boreal subzone, is dominated by podzolic soils, which support dark coniferous taiga of spruce and fir in the east of European Russia, Siberian cedar east of the Urals, and pine everywhere. The territory east of the Yenisey river is occupied by light coniferous taiga of Siberian and Dahurian larch on cryogenic taiga soils. The forest vegetation in the Far East is dominated by Ayan larch and Khingan fir. Large stretches of mires, usually raised bogs, are very common in the taiga subzone, especially in western Siberia.

Swampy forests form a characteristic feature of boreal vegetation. In the south of the East European Plain, the taiga joins the subzone of mixed forests. Their turf-podzolic soils support coniferous forests intermixed with birch, aspen, oak, maple, linden, and other broad-leaved trees. Mixed forests of this subzone in the south of the Russian Far East are composed of Korean pine, needle fir, Mongolian oak, hornbeam, elm, maple, Amur cork-tree, and many other tree species. The southernmost areas of the forest zone in European Russia are occupied by broad-leaved stands, largely of oak and linden.

To the south, the forest-steppe zone features small oak groves in the west and isolated patches of birch and aspen in the east of the country on gray forest soils. They alternate with herb meadow steppes on leached or typical chernozems. Poorly drained soil underlies swampy meadows and marshes. The steppe zone in the southern parts of the East European and West Siberian Plains gives rise to highly productive chernozems with a thick humus horizon (humus content 4–10%) and dark chestnut soils. They are occupied by herb-grass and grass steppes dominated by feather-grass, fescue, and other turf grasses. Virtually all steppes are turned to extensively cultivated arable land. Steppe areas also occur in eastern Siberia, where they are largely found in intermontane basins (Minusinskaya, Tuvinskaya, etc.). Further south, Prikaspiyskaya Nizmennost harbors semidesert areas on light chestnut and brown soils with solonchaks formed by the evaporation of subsoil water. Very sparse semidesert vegetation consists of sages, saltworts, and arid-adapted narrow-leaved grasses.

Highly varied soils and vegetation are found in mountain areas of different altitude. Their diversity is best represented in the Caucasus, where herb-grass black earth steppes of foothill areas give way first to oak and beach forests on mountain-forest soils (600–800 m) and then to coniferous stands. Above the timberline (2000–2000 m), the predominant type of vegetation is subalpine and alpine meadows on mountain-meadow soils. The highest ridges, with their bare rock outcrops, glaciers, and accumulations of rock debris, are practically devoid of vegetation.

The mountains of Siberia and the Far East exhibit much simpler vertical stratification patterns. Most of them are covered with mountain boreal forests on stony skeletal and shallow mountain-podzolic and brown mountain-forest soils.

Only the highest ridges and virtually barren summits above the timberline support mountain-tundra vegetation.

Fauna

The entire territory of Russia belongs to the Palearctic zoogeographic region. The distribution of animals closely correlates with geographic zones. Typical representatives of polar deserts and tundra zone are Arctic fox, lemming, reindeer, polar bear, snowy owl, ptarmigan, and numerous migratory waterfowl species. Many large seabird colonies are found on the islands and coastal cliffs of the Arctic and Pacific Oceans. The forest zone, especially its boreal subzone, is of paramount importance for commercial hunting and fur trapping. It is inhabited by the elk, brown bear, lynx, sable, red fox, squirrel, chipmunk, and varying (snowshoe) hare. In addition, red deer, musk deer, and Siberian weasel occur in the eastern Siberian taiga and black bear, goral, Siberian tiger, yellow-throated marten, raccoon dog, and wild boar in the south of the Far East. Typical forest birds include capercaillie, hazel grouse, black grouse, and woodpeckers.

Forest-steppe and steppe faunas are dominated by small rodents (voles, jerboas, ground squirrels, marmots, hamsters) and such birds as houbara bustard, little bustard, and eagles. The seas surrounding Russia, especially the Barents Sea and marginal seas of the Pacific Ocean, are important sources of high biological production and biodiversity. Many aquatic animals, including salmonid fishes, herring, cod and other gadids, flatfishes, mackerel, crabs, and squids, as well as marine mammals (whales, walruses, seals, etc.) are of great commercial importance. Inland waterbodies and rivers are fished for sturgeon, salmon, and a variety of small fish.

Nature Conservation

Russia has a well-developed system of strictly protected natural areas designed to conserve the country's biological and landscape diversity. The core of the system is a unique network of state nature reserves (category I by the IUCN classification) whose organization was initiated by Russian scientists in the early 20th century. The very first protected territory of this kind (Barguzinsky Nature Reserve) was organized to protect the habitat of the Barguzin sable in 1916. A few national parks have been organized since 1983, starting from Losiny Ostrov (Moscow and an adjoining area) and Sochinsky (Krasnodar Kray). As of the beginning of 2001, Russia had 100 zapovedniks (nature reserves), including 22 biosphere reserves and 35 national parks covering a total area of 27 and 7 million ha, respectively. Other protected areas are federal (67) and regional (nearly 400) zakazniks (sanctuaries) (77.4 million ha), federal (18) and regional (about 8500) natural monuments (roughly 2.5 million ha), 30 natural (regional) parks, over 80 botanical gardens, health resorts, and some other territories, most of which are protected by regional or local legislation. Seven natural features at the territory of Russia were designated as UNESCO's World Heritage Sites. These are Komi Virgin Forests, Lake Baikal, Kamchatka Volcanoes, Altai Golden Mountains, West Caucasus, and Central Sikhote-Alin and Uvs Nuur Basin (shared with Mongolia) (*see* **National Parks and Protected Areas: Russia**).

Population

According to the 1897 general census, the population within the frontiers of present-day Russia was 67.5 million of the 124.6 million in the entire Russian Empire. Demographic crises occurred during World War I and Civil War, which resulted in epidemics, famine, and large-scale emigration. The next demographic crisis was provoked by forced collectivization involving repression and expulsion of hundreds of thousands of peasant families to Siberia and the Far East, with the inevitable recession in agriculture. However, the greatest loss of the population was experienced by the country during the Great Patriotic War of 1941–1945. The victory over Nazi Germany, militaristic Japan, and their satellites cost Russia at least 18 million lives. A concomitant decline in the birth rate brought the cumulative loss to a total of 27 million. The overall depletion of the population in Russia throughout the 20th century is estimated at more than 120 millions. Such was the price the country paid for wars and social upheavals. The situation has further deteriorated since the early 1990s when the mortality rate started to consistently exceed the lowering birth rate. In 1999, the difference amounted to 926,600 and the natural population loss index was 6.4 per 1000 or 4.2 times that in 1992. One cause was the secondary "demographic echo of the war," but by far more important were the consequences of the economic crisis that followed the collapse of the Soviet Union. Despite a significant gain through immigration, the total population declined by more than 2.1 million and in 2000 was only 98.6% of its size in 1990. It is expected that depopulation will persist for many years to come. The State Statistical Committee of Russia predicts a decrease of 11.5 million in the country's population between 1999 and 2016, with a concurrent fall in the average life expectancy to 69.6 years. Since the early 1990s, there has been a deterioration in the qualitative parameters of the population such as its educational and health (morbidity) status. According to experts, these trends may have an overall negative effect on the country's future.

Severe natural and climatic conditions at a larger part of Russia's territory are responsible for the low mean population density (9 persons per sq km), one of the world's lowest. Moreover, it varies considerably between different regions of the country, from 330 persons per sq km in the Moscow region to 0.03 persons per sq km in the Evenk Autonomous Okrug. In terms of population density, the territory of Russia is divided into two large parts. One part (densely populated) comprises European Russia and areas in southern Siberia and the Far East along the Trans-Siberian Railroad, and the other encompasses northern regions accounting for two-thirds of the country's territory and less than 10% of its population.

People of old Russia saw their country as a land of cities. Old Russian chronicles mention as many as 150 such cities. The oldest ones, Novgorog Veliky, Smolensk, Murom, Rostov Veliky, and Beloozero, arose in the 9th century. The number of cities greatly increased since the late 18th century. A decree of Catherine II divided the country into 42 *guberniyas* (provinces), which were in turn divided into *uyezds* (districts), each to have a city as its administrative center. As a result, 165 settlements were raised to city status in a short span of time in addition to the 232 existing ones. By the end of the 19th century, there were 430 cities within the limits of present-day Russia, two of them with a population over 1,000,000. In spite of this, Russia remained a rural country, with 90% of the population living in agricultural areas. It came to be a highly urban one in the 20th century. Today, 74% of the population live in cities compared with 10% at the turn of the century. The highest urbanization rates are recorded in metropolitan areas (Moscow and Leningrad oblasts, 91%), in the Far North (Murmansk and Magadan oblasts, 92% and 90%, respectively), and in industrial regions (Sverdlovsk and Kemerovo oblasts, 88% and 87%). The rural population still predominates in Koryak, Evenk, and Komi-Permyak Autonomous Okrugs (75%, 71%, and 70%, respectively).

The most characteristic feature of Russia's population is its high ethnic diversity. Over 100 ethnic groups are scattered over the country's territory. According to the latest national census (1989), an overwhelming majority of the population are virtually ubiquitous Russians. Most people speak Slavic languages of the Indo-European family. These are Russians, Ukrainians (3%), and Belorusians (0.8%). The second most important language family in Russia is Altaic. These languages are in the first place spoken by Turkic peoples. Tatars are the most numerous of them and the second largest ethnos in Russia (3.8%), followed by Chuvash (1.2%) and Bashkirs (0.9%). Less numerous are peoples speaking Uralic (Mordvins, Udmurt, Mari, etc.) and North Caucasian (ethnic minorities of Dagestan, Chechen, Kabardin, Ingush, etc.) languages. Each of the two groups number over 3 million people.

North Caucasus inherited the most complicated ethnic structure. Besides Russians and Ukrainians, the region is inhabited by peoples speaking the language of the Iranian (Ossetes), Turkic (Karachay, Balkar, Kumyk, Noghay), and two groups of North Caucasian (Abkhazo-Adyghian and Nakho-Dagestanian) families.

Northern quarters of European Russia are inhabited by Karelians, Veps, Izhora, Saami, Komi, and Komi-Permyaks belonging to the Finno-Ugric branch of the Uralic language family. This area is also home of the Pomor, an ethnic group of Russians. Minor indigenous peoples of Siberia and the Far East are scattered over vast territories, which are not infrequently bigger than large European countries. The Yakut, Dolgan, Khakass, Altai, Shor, and Tuvans speak Turkic languages; the Buryat a Mongolian tongue; the Khanty and Mansi speak Finno-Ugric; the Nenets, Nganasan, and Sel'kup speak Samoyedic; the Evenk, Even, Nanais, Ul'chi,

Orochi, Udege, and Negidals speak Tungusic-Manchurian languages; the Eskimo and Aleut peoples speak Eskimo-Aleut languages; and the Chukchi, Koryak, and Itelmen speak Chukotko-Kamchatkan languages of the Paleo-Asiatic family. The Nivkh, Yukagir, and Ket speak genetically isolated Paleo-Siberian languages (see **Chukchi-Kamchadal Languages**; **Eskimo-Aleut Languages**; **Northern Altaic Languages**; **Northern Uralic Languages**; on the peoples, see **Chukchi; Chuvan; Dolgan; Enets; Even; Evenki; Itel'men; Ket; Khanty; Komi; Koryak; Mansi; Nanais; Negidal; Nenets; Nganasan; Nivkhi; Orochi; Orok; Pomor; Saami; Sel'kup; Tungus; Yakut; Yukagir; Udege; Ul'chi**).

Russian is the official state language and is also used throughout the country as a medium of everyday transactions. It is spoken by 98% of the population, of which 82% are ethnic Russians, 5% are representatives of other nations who consider Russian as their mother tongue, and 11% speak Russian as a fluent second language. Russian is one of the world's main languages, the fifth most important in terms of the number of speakers, and is one of the six official languages of the United Nations.

The ethnic diversity of Russia's population is reflected in the diversity of creeds and confessions. The church has been formally separated from the state since 1917. Therefore, the number of believers is not reported in official statistics; it is estimated to be less than 20% of the total population. Nevertheless, even practical atheists objectively belong to a certain cultural and religious tradition, which accounts for a still important role of religion in contemporary Russian society. The overwhelming majority of believers in Russia are members of the Orthodox Church, eastern branch of Christianity. Orthodox Christianity was officially introduced into the country over 1000 years ago. It was adopted not only by Slav peoples, that is, Russians, Ukrainians, and Belorusians, but also by Finno-Ugric peoples living in the North and along the Volga River, some Turkic peoples (Chuvash, Yakut), indigenous minorities of Siberia and the Far East, Armenians, Georgians, Moldavians, etc. Large groups of the population represent two other principal world religions: Islam and Buddhism. Such large nations as Tatars and Bashkirs along with most North Caucasian peoples are predominantly Muslims while three other ethnic groups, the Buryats, Tuvans, and Kalmyks, are mostly Buddhists. A part of the population in northern Siberia and the Far East (Chukchi, Koryak, Khanty, Yupik Eskimo, a fraction of Nenets, and some others) hold traditional religious beliefs centerd on natural phenomena and everyday life (see **Shamanism**). Relics of paganism continue to exert influences on cult practices and culture at large of many other peoples.

History

The oldest artifacts yet found that may be called the beginning of man's presence at the territory of Russia come from the North Caucasus and date to about 700,000 years ago. Evidence of human habitation in the Middle Paleolithic Period (100,000–35,000 years ago) is given by the finding of early settlements of the Neanderthals in the lower Volga region and Central Ural. In the Upper Paleolithic Period (35,000–10,000), people crossed the Arctic Circle and initiated colonization of Siberia.

New tribes made their appearance during the Neolithic Age and gave rise to a long and complicated process of the development of ethnic groups, progenitors of modern nations in European and Asiatic Russia. The transition from food gathering to food producing, that is, ancient forms of land cultivation and animal domestication, occurred around the 5th–6th millennium BC. It prepared the ground for different rates of development of individual tribes. The Bronze and Iron Ages witnessed an even more conspicuous social and economic differentiation. During the 1st millennium BC, Scythian and then Sarmatian tribes began to be absorbed into larger communities. Numerous Greek slave-holding city-states sprang up on the north coast of the Black Sea and along the Sea of Azov. A period of great migrations in the 1st millennium AD was marked by the invasion of the East European Plain by the Goths and Huns, merging of the Alani tribes, and constitution of a powerful seminomadic confederation ruled by the Avars. In parallel, the Khazar Kaganate and Bulgar kingdoms, around the confluence of the Volga and Kama rivers, were established to become the first antecedents of future states in what is now Russia.

The old Russian nation came into existence in Kievan Rus (9–12 centuries) and gave rise to the Russians, Ukrainians, and Belorusians in the 13th–15th centuries. Vladimir-Suzdal Knyazhestvo (Principality) and the Novgorod Feudal Republic arose in the 12th century and played an important role in the history of Russia. In the 13th century, the country repelled Swedish and German aggression but was conquered by the Mongols (Tatars). It took Russians almost 250 years to liberate the country from the Mongol yoke. During the 14th–16th centuries, the Princes of Moscow consolidated the surrounding independent principalities of northeastern and northwestern Russia into a centralized state. It was made multinational by annexing vast territories along the Volga River, in the Urals and Siberia during the 16th–17th centuries. In the early 17th century, Russia had to resist Polish-Lithuanian and Swedish intervention.

A series of reforms undertaken by Peter I greatly promoted the socioeconomic and cultural development of Russia. As a result of the victorious Northern War of 1700–1721, Russia gained strategically important access to the Baltic. In the early 19th century, Russia successfully repelled the Napoleonic invasion. The social reform of 1861 abolished serfdom and accelerated capitalistic development of the country. The bourgeois revolution in February 1917 overthrew the czarist regime. Nicholas II, the last Russian emperor of the Romanov dynasty, abdicated the throne. In October 1917, the socialist revolution occurred in Petrograd and brought to power the Bolshevik government headed by Vladimir Lenin. It proclaimed the creation of the Russian Soviet Federative Socialist Republic, which became the core of the expanding Soviet Union and played a leading role in the economic and social development of the new country. Also, Russia bore the greatest burden of the war against Nazi Germany in 1941–1945.

For more than 70 years, the country was ruled by the Communist party headed, after Lenin's death, by Joseph Stalin (until 1953) and thereafter by Nikita Khrushchov, Leonid Brezhnev, and other leaders. In 1985, Mikhail Gorbachev came to be at the head of the party and state.

The democratic reforms he undertook eventually brought about the dissolution of the USSR into a few independent states, including Russia. Its constitution was adopted in 1993. Boris N. Yeltsin, the first president of Russia, was replaced by Vladimir Putin in 1999.

Economy

Russia is a developed industrial country with modern mechanized agriculture. Its GDP in 2001 was 6277.8 billion Russian rubles (US$224.2 billion) or 62,457 Russian rubles (US$2231) per capita. The country's economic independence is supported by the unique potential of natural resources sufficient to satisfy all basic requirements of the population and economy in terms of food, fuel, and raw materials. Another important prerequisite for the successful economic development is a generally high educational level of the population, which guarantees the necessary number and quality of skilled workers and personnel for all branches of national economy, including technologically sophisticated ones. Rapid progress in its industrialization drive in the 1930s made Russia a world leader in oil and gas extraction, coal mining, the timber industry, the production of electric power and mineral fertilizers, steelmaking, nonferrous metallurgy, tractor construction, and other areas of mechanical engineering. The achievements of Russia in such highly technological fields as space exploration, atomic energy, and in the production of modern armaments are universally recognized. Russia is the world's largest exporter of oil, gas, timber, and products of ferrous and nonferrous metallurgy.

Throughout a major period of its modern history, Russia ensured the onward march of its economy. In certain periods, the rates of GDP growth exceeded 10%. However, during the 1960s and the following years, the development rates gradually declined and economic depression reached crisis proportions as a result of bureaucratization of administration, the lack of competition, militarization, and other negative trends. This situation was aggravated by the concomitant social and political turmoil at the turn of the 1990s, which brought Russia on the verge of collapse. The deep and prolonged recession in the last decade of the 20th century resulted in a 2.5-fold decrease in industrial production and a decline in agriculture by almost one-third. Catastrophic inflation amounted to almost 200% per year in 1995 and 80% in 1999. The country experienced unemployment, markedly reduced living standards, and impaired social security. Russia's open economy is exposed to world economic cataclysms such as the 1998 "Asian" crisis. The country bears a heavy burden of external debt in excess of US$130 billion.

From 2000, the economic situation started improving. High rates of economic growth were recorded for the first time after the beginning of the crisis, the government's budget revenues exceeded expenses, inflation decreased, and per capita incomes increased. The government negotiated no new external loans and was able to pay off the old ones. However, stabilization of the macroeconomic situation is believed to be due to favorable world oil market conditions rather than to an increase in economic efficiency.

Industry

Russia shows a very high concentration of industrial activity both at the regional and local levels and at the level of individual enterprises. Ten largest regions of Russia produce 45% of all industrial goods. Almost 20% of the total comes from Tyumen and Sverdlovsk oblasts and the city of Moscow. Bashkortostan, Samara, and Chelyabinsk oblasts yield 4–5.5% each. Other major producers are Kemerovo, Nizhegorod and Moscow oblasts, and Krasnoyarsk Kray.

Not only the industrial but also the socioeconomic potential of Russia is based on its fuel and power resources. Being the world's coldest country, Russia needs at least 500 million tons of conventional fuel to survive the winter, the equivalent of approximately US$40 billion. It annually produces almost 600 million m^3 of natural gas, 300 million tons of oil, and 300 million tons of coal. Producing fossil fuel fields are concentrated within a few territories, of which Yamal-

Nenets and Khanty-Mansi Autonomous Okrugs, both of Tyumen Oblast', deliver 70% of Russian gas and 90% of oil. The remaining largely comes from the Urals and Volga region. Small-scale gas and oil extraction is practiced in the Republic of Komi, North Caucasus, Central Yakutia, Sakhalin, and Kaliningrad Oblast'. The largest coalfields are in Kuzbass. They bring 40% of the total national production (and two-thirds of it collectively with the neighboring Kansk-Achinsk Basin). Other areas of extensive coal mining are the Pechora Basin (Komi Republic), Donbass (Rostov Oblast'), Mosbass (Tula Oblast'), South Yakut Basin, and minor fields in the Urals, Siberia, and the Far East.

Fossil fuels extracted in Russia are mostly used to produce electric power. Its total output amounts to 850 million kWh. The major single producer is the Central Economic Region (20% of the total) followed by East Siberia and the Urals. The Ural Region is also the main power user, the second and third most important being the Central Economic Region and West Siberia. Coal, gas, and mazut-firing (heavy oil) stations generate two-thirds of the electricity consumed in Russia; hydroelectric stations account for about one-fifth and atomic stations for 15% of the total power production. There are nine nuclear power stations in Russia, including two beyond the Arctic Circle (Kola and Bilibino).

Metallurgy is a traditionally important branch of industry in Russia, and the country has a number of very large smelters. Large metallic ore resources make metal industry production competitive on world markets. Over one half of the produced ferrous metals are exported. Nonferrous metals also account for a high percent of mining exports. Many nonferrous works are in the Arctic (such as the cities of Noril'sk, Monchegorsk, and Nikel). The most serious problem encountered by the metal industry in Russia is the excessive wear and tear of basic equipment, which has environmental implications should waste leak to the external environment.

Machine building is one of the most important branches of industry.

The economic crisis of the 1990s affected it to a large extent. Only the automotive industry avoided recession. The largest automobile plants are situated in Tolyatti (about 80% of the total production), Moscow, Nizhny Novgorod, Ulyanovsk, Miass, and Izhevsk.

Agriculture

Agriculture in Russia is severely restricted by its highly unfavorable geographical situation and environmental conditions. Principal crops have to be cultivated in the so-called high-risk zone, and low productive reindeer pastures on the tundra are the main type of natural forage areas available for domestic livestock. Long and cold winter seasons make it difficult to grow perennial crops and exclude plantation agriculture. Nevertheless, Russia is a major grain producer by virtue of the enormous size of its territory. The annual grain yield is about 80 million tons (world's fourth largest harvest). The production of potato amounts to 40 million tons, meat to almost 10 million, and milk over 40 million. Agriculture is centered on the cultivation of cereal crops (wheat, barley, rye, oats, millet, buckwheat, rice, and corn). The principal industrial crops are sunflower, sugar beet, flax, soybean, and hemp. Potato ("second bread" in Russia), vegetables, and forage crops are grown throughout the country.

Transportation

The transportation system of Russia comprises all modern means of conveyance and plays an important role in the development of national economy. Pipelines account for 52% of the country's freight turnover. They are followed by railways (33%), sea routes (8%), motor roads (4.3%), and inland waterways (2.5%). However, the motorized transport carries the bulk of good (77%) and passenger (nearly 90%) traffic. Railway transport is most efficient under Russian conditions for wholesale goods being transported long and middle distances and for the middle-distance and local passage of passengers. The density of the railway networks is highest in European Russia. There are practically no railroads in the vast territories of Siberia and the Far East. Automobiles and trucks are most extensively used to facilitate suburban, intra- and intercity good and passenger traffic. The total length of hard-surfaced roads amounts to one million km. Their density varies regionally, the difference between the highest and lowest figures approximating two orders of magnitude. Maritime transport plays a vital role in foreign trade. The Russian merchant fleet ranks seventh in the world in terms of tonnage, but most ships suffer from a high degree of physical wear. The Far East (Pacific) accounts for about half of the total sea freight turnover. The next most important ones are the Black Sea and Sea of Azov Basin, Arctic Ocean Basin, and Baltic Basin. The chief ports are St Petersburg (general), Novorossiysk (oil), Vladivostok, Nakhodka, Murmansk, Arkhangel'sk, Tuapse, and Kaliningrad. River traffic is traditionally of importance for communication and carrying goods in the northern and eastern parts of Russia: the rivers Lena and Amur and their tributaries in the Far East; the Ob'-Irtysh in Western Siberia; the Yenisey, Angara, and Lena in eastern Siberia; and the Severnaya Dvina, Pechora, and Volga rivers in European Russia. The Arctic Ocean ports are only ice-free for short periods each summer.

Recreation and Tourism

Russia has numerous holiday and health resorts and recreation sites. The resorts have been under state patronage since the early 19th century. Resort towns, such as Sochi and Anapa, Kislovodsk, and Yessentuki, are important features of the Black Sea coast and North Caucasus region. Various forms of tourism have become increasingly popular, including cultural tourism (visits to the cities of the "Golden Ring" of Russia, St Petersburg, Novgorod Velikiy, Pskov, Smolensk; nature reserve museums, etc.), ecotourism (Siberian rivers, Lake Baikal, Kamchatka, Russian Arctic), active sports (such as trekking, ski mountaineering, and rafting), and other leisure activities.

Culture and Cultural Heritage

The cultural revolution in Russia and other republics of the former USSR provided a basis for the creation of economic and political power of the country in the 1930s and subsequent years. In contrast, inadequate cultural policy of the 1980s resulted in the breach of cultural traditions and moral principles, which inevitably led (coupled with some other factors) to a deep and prolonged crisis that affected the country. The current trends of the Russian society dictate the necessity to give more attention to culture as an instrument for the promotion of national economic and political development and involve cultural phenomena in federal and regional policies.

Of primary importance among the immovable objects of Russian cultural heritage are historical and cultural monuments. In early 2001, as many as 86,220 such monuments were protected in Russia, including 24,888 of federal and 59,965 of local importance. The most valuable of these were included in UNESCO's World Heritage List. As of the end of 2002, the List contained 11 objects in the territory of Russia, viz. the Moscow Kremlin and Red Square, the historical center of St Petersburg and palace-and-park settings of its outer region, the Kizhi Island with examples of wooden architecture (Karelia), historical monuments of Novgorod Velikiy and its surroundings, the complex of historical and cultural objects on Solovetski Islands (Arkhange'sk Oblast'), white-stone monuments of Vladimir and Suzdal, Troitse-Sergiyeva Lavra (Trinity-St Sergius Monastery) in Sergiyev Posad near Moscow, Voznesenie (Ascension) Church in Kolomeskoye (Moscow), Kazan Kremlin, Ferapontov Monastery (Vologda Oblast'), Kurskaya Kosa (Courland Spit), and the ancient city of Derbent.

Activities of museums are crucial for the cultural development of the nation. Russia has more than 2900 museums, including almost 1000 public ones. A specific type of museum is the open-air museum based on nature reserves, a major form of strictly protected historical and cultural sites in Russia. The first attempts to set up such museums date to the 1920s–1930s. A government decree designated as specialized museums a number of historically and culturally most valuable landlord's estates, former monasteries, and palace-and-park ensembles nationalized after the revolution. Today, there are more than 90 such museum sites in Russia. Some of them hold a high rank on the List of cultural heritage of the Russian Federation kept since 1992. These are Alexander Pushkin memorial museum "Mikhailovskoye," house museums of Leo Tolstoy in Yasnaya Polyana and Mikhail Lermontov in Tarkhany, Peterhof and Tsarskoye Selo near St Petersburg, etc.

Almost 50,000 books and booklets with a total circulation of 450 million are annually published in Russia. Libraries are paramount for maintaining cultural traditions. A total of more than 52,000 libraries in Russia contain 1,053,000 books and other printed materials.

YURI MAZOUROV

See also **Arkhangel'skaya Oblast'; Buryat Republic (Buryatiya); Chukchi Autonomous Okrug (Chukotka); Evenki Autonomous Okrug; Kamchatskaya Oblast'; Karelia; Khanty-Mansi Autonomous Okrug; Komi Republic; Koryak Autonomous Okrug; Krasnoyarsk Kray; Magadanskaya Oblast'; Murmanskaya Oblast'; Nenets Autonomous Okrug; Sakha Republic (Yakutia); Taymyr (Dolgan-Nenets) Autonomous Okrug; Tyumen Oblast'; Yamal-Nenets Autonomous Okrug**

Further Reading

Arktica na Poroge Tret'ego Tysyacheletiya: Resursnui Potentsial i Problemy Ecologii [The Arctic on the Threshold of the Third Millenium: Resources Potential and Ecological Problems], St Petersburg: Nauka, 2000

Bradshaw, Michael, J., "The Russian North in transition: general introduction." *Post-Soviet Geography*, 36(4) (1995): 195–203

Ebbinge, B.S. et al. (editors.), *Heritage of the Russian Arctic: Research, Conservation and International Co-operation*, Moscow: Ecopros Publishers, 2000

Environmental Performance Reviews, Russian Federation, Paris: OECD, 1999

Fondahl, A., "The status of indigenous people in the Russian North." *Post-Soviet Geography*, 36 (4) (1995): 215–224

Forsyth, J., *A History of the Peoples of Siberia*, Cambridge and New York: Cambridge University Press, 1992

Gosudarstvennyi Doklad "O Sostoyanii i ob Okhrane Okrushayusschei Prirodnoy Sredy Rossiiskoi Federatsii v 2002 godu" [State Report "State of Environment and Conservation in the Russian Federation in 2002"], Moscow: MPR, 2003

Khruscheva, A.T. (editor), *Economicheskaya I Sotsial'naya Geographiya Rossii: Uchebnik dlya Vuzov [Economic and Social Geography of Russia]*, Moscow: Drofa, 2001

Kotkin, Stephen & David Wolff (editors), *Rediscovering Russia in Asia: Siberia and the Russian Far East*, New York: M.E. Sharpe, 1995

Kotlyakov V.M. & V.E. Sokolov (editors), *Arctic Research: Advances and Prospects. Proceedings of the Conference of Arctic and Nordic Countries on Coordination of Research in the Arctic*, Parts 1 and 2, Moscow: Nauka, 1990

Poiseev, I.I., *Ustoichivoye Razvitiye Severa: Ecologo-Economicheskii Aspekt* [Sustainable Development of the North: Ecological and Economic Aspects], Novosibirsk: Nauka, 1999

Promyshlennost' Rossii: Statisticheskii Sbornik [Industry of Russia: Statistical Handbook], Moscow: Goscomstat of Russia, 2002

Regiony Rossii: Statisticheskii Sbornik [Regions of Russia: Statistical Handbook, 2 volumes], Moscow: Goscomstat of Russia, 2002

Russia 2002: Statistical Handbook, Moscow: Goscomstat of Russia, 2003

Sel'skoye khozyaistvo Rossii: Statisticheskii Sbornik [Agriculture of Russia: Statistical Handbook], Moscow: Goscomstat of Russia, 2001

Stephan, John, J., *The Russian Far East: A History, Stanford*, California: Stanford University Press, 1994

The Demographic Yearbook of Russia: Statistical Handbook, Moscow: Goscomstat of Russia, 2002

Vaté, V., "Siberian Indigenous Peoples." *In Encyclopedia of the World's Minorities*, edited by C. Skutsch, New York and London: Routledge, 2004

Yablokov A.V. (editor), *Rossiiskaya Arctika na Poroge katastrofy [Russian Arctic: On the Edge of Catastrophe]*, Moscow: Tsentr Ecologitcheskoi Politiki Rossii, 1996

RUSSIAN "OLD SETTLERS"

The term Russian "Old Settlers" (*starozhily*—literally "long-time residents") does not refer to a self-identified ethnic or social group, but is a broad label applied to a variety of groups of Russian descent who have lived in various parts of the former Russian Empire outside of European Russia (e.g., Caucasus, Central Asia, Russian Far East, Siberia) since at least the 19th century. The qualifier "Russian" is often omitted since the term Old Settlers is rarely ever applied to groups other than eastern Slavs (Byelorussians, Russians, and Ukrainians). This points to the fact that the existence of Old Settler groups is intricately tied to the process of Russian colonization of North Asia.

The origin of Old Settler groups in Siberia and the Russian Far East can be generally traced back to the early stages of the Russian expansion east of the Ural Mountains, which hit western Siberia in the late 16th century, reached the Pacific Ocean by the mid-17th century, and was basically completed with the annexation of

Kamchatka in the early 18th century. Among the Old Settlers of North Asia are several communities of "Old Believers" (*staroobriadtsy* or *starovertsy*). There is no causal connection, however, between the two similar-sounding terms: neither are all groups of Old Settlers Old Believers nor are Old Believers necessarily Old Settlers. The majority of Old Believers who are also considered Old Settlers inhabit the southern parts of Siberia, such as the Altai area or the region east of Lake Baikal. In general, Old Settler communities in the southern parts of Siberia and the Russian Far East, whether Old Believers or not, settled along the tributaries of large rivers and combined agriculture and cattle breeding with hunting, fishing, and, rarely, reindeer herding.

The Old Settler communities of the Russian Arctic and Subarctic maintained a lifestyle of sedentary fishing, trapping, and hunting, necessitated by the environmental conditions of taiga and tundra. Most of these groups are to be found in the deltas of the large Siberian rivers draining into the Arctic Ocean (from west to east: Ob', Yenisey, Anabar, Olenek, Lena, Yana, Indigirka, Kolyma), on the Taymyr Peninsula, and in a few areas along the Pacific Ocean (middle course of the Anadyr River, Kamchatka Peninsula, deltas of the Gizhiga, Okhota, Yana (near Magadan) rivers). These communities have always been small enclaves in a natural environment unsuited for agriculture and outnumbered by a variety of indigenous Siberian groups.

Despite significant local and regional variation, numerous cultural similarities can be detected. Most groups continue to use Russian (or antiquated forms thereof) as their native language, consider themselves as belonging to the Russian Orthodox Church, and, if pressed to define themselves as either "Russian" or "Native," more or less reluctantly choose the first label. The fact that the first settlers were almost exclusively males who took indigenous women as wives resulted, however, in considerable biological admixture. Similarly, religious, economic, and social practices are interspersed with elements adopted from neighboring indigenous groups. Previously, it was customary to distinguish Old Settlers from groups of mixed population (*smeshannoe naselenie*), that is, groups of Old Settlers who switched to a non-Russian language or native groups who became Russianized. If there is a unifying trait of all Old Settler groups in the Russian North, however, it is their mixed nature.

The ethnographic study of Old Settlers in the Russian North started considerably later than of the groups native to Siberia, which can be traced back to at least the 18th century. Vladimir Bogoraz, during his long exile along the Kolyma River in the 1890s, was among the first to pay close attention to the cultural specifics of the Russian-speaking population of the area. Apart from a number of other political exiles (e.g.,

Zenzinov, 1921, 1931), the anthropologist Georgiy S. Vinogradov was among the few who studied Russian culture in Siberia during the first decades of the 20th century (Sirina, 1993). It was only after World War II that Russian groups inside and outside of Russia received more and more scholarly attention in the anthropological literature. Since the 1960s, the study of Russian groups in (southern) Siberia has grown steadily (e.g., Aleksandrov, 1964; Bunak and Zolotareva, 1973; Lipinskaia, 1996; Liutsidarskaia, 1992; Maslova and Suburova, 1969; Russkie Sibiri, 1998). Old Settler communities in the North, which for a long time had primarily attracted students of Russian folklore (e.g., Azbelev and Meshcherskii, 1986), only belatedly received anthropological attention (e.g., Chikachev, 1993; Murashko, 1985; Kamenetskaia, 1986). Studies of Old Settler groups in non-Russian languages have been extremely rare and were primarily conducted by historians such as Sunderland.

The 1996 article by Sunderland addresses a peculiar rise of state interest in the fates of Old Settler communities in the North. After they had been literally forgotten for about 200 years, state emissaries tasked with inventorying the social and ethnic groups of the Empire showed up in northern Siberia during the second part of the 19th century. Equipped with notions of social and cultural evolution, the officials were troubled by the levels of cultural assimilation they encountered in northern Siberia. Instead of what some of them saw as the civilizing duty of Russian colonization, namely "Russianizing the Natives," they encountered "Nativized Russians."

Soviet nationality policies had little room for the Old Settlers. They neither fit the category of the "small peoples of the North" (i.e., indigenous peoples), who, at least on paper, received special attention during the decades following the Russian Revolution, nor were they considered "real Russians." Still, at least two Old Settler groups joined the ranks of indigenous peoples during Soviet years: the Chuvans and the Kamchadals. In both cases, Old Settlers had gradually taken over indigenous ethnonyms that had been vacated—either by the group's disappearance (Chuvans) or because of renaming by state authorities (Kamchadals, who came to be known as Itel'mens).

The contemporary situation of Old Settler groups in the Russian North is still characterized by the fact that they are generally not recognized as an ethnic category distinct from Russians. In recent years, however, certain groups have been successful in achieving aboriginal status vis-à-vis the federal Russian government. Still, "Old Settler" continues to be a descriptive term without particular rights assigned to it and without an interregional association representing Old Settler individuals and communities. Only the future can tell whether "Old Settler" will ever become a federally recognized umbrella label, distinguishing the groups it encompasses from both Russians and Natives, comparable to the Canadian ethnonym, Metís.

PETER P. SCHWEITZER

Further Reading

Aleksandrov, Vadim A., *Russkoe naselenie Sibiri XVII—nachala XVIII v. (Eniseiskii krai)* [The Russian Population of Siberia in the Eighteenth and Early Nineteenth Centuries (Yenisei *krai*)], Moscow: Nauka, 1964

Azbelev, S.N. & N.A. Meshcherskii (editors), *Fol'klor Russkogo Ust'ia* [The Folklore of Russkoe Ust'e], Leningrad: Nauka, 1986

Bunak, V.V. & I.M. Zolotareva (editors), *Russkie starozhily Sibiri. Istoriko-antropologicheskii ocherk* [The Russian Old Settlers of Siberia: A Historical and (Physical) Anthropological Essay], Moscow: Nauka, 1973

Chikachev, Aleksei G., *Pokhodsk. Starinnoe russkoe selo na Kolyme* [Pokhodsk: An Ancient Russian Village on the Kolyma River], Irkutsk: Papirus, 1993

Kamenetskaia, R.V., "Russkie starozhily poliarnogo areala" [Russian Old Settlers of the Polar Region]. In *Russkii Sever. Problemy etnokul'turnoi istorii, etnografii, fol'kloristiki,* edited by T.A. Bernshtam & K.V. Chistov, Leningrad: Nauka, 1986

Lipinskaia, Viktoriia A., *Starozhily i pereselentsy: Russkie na Altae. XVIII—nachalo XX veka* [Old Settlers and Migrants: Russians in the Altai Region, Eighteenth to Early Twentieth Centuries], Moscow: Nauka, 1996

Liutsidarskaia, Anna A., *Starozhily Sibiri: Istoriko-etnograficheskie ocherki. XVII–nachalo XVIII v* [Old Settlers of Siberia: Historical and Ethnographic Essays, Seventeenth to Early Eighteenth Centuries], Novosibirsk: Nauka, 1992

Maslova, G.S. & L.M. Suburova (editors), *Etnografiia russkogo naseleniia Sibiri i Srednei Azii* [The Ethnography of the Russian Population of Siberia and Middle Asia], Moscow: Nauka, 1969

Murashko, Ol'ga A., "Starozhily Kamchatki v istoriko-demograficheskoi i sotsial'noi-ekonomicheskoi perspektive" [The Old Settlers of Kamchatka in Historical-Demographic and Socio-Economic Perspective. In *Mezhetnicheskie kontakty i razvitie natsional'nykh kul'tur. Sbornik statei,* edited by I.I. Krupnik, Moscow, 1985

Russkie Sibiri: kul'tura, obychai, obriady [The Russians of Siberia: Culture, Customs, Rituals], Novosibirsk: Institut arkheologii i etnografii SO RAN, 1998

Sirina, Anna A., "Vydaiushchiisia etnograf i fol'klorist G.S. Vinogradov (1887–1945)" [The eminent ethnographer and folklorist G.S. Vinogradov (1887–1945)]. *Etnograficheskoe obozrenie,* 1 (1993): 115–128

Sunderland, Willard, "Russians into Iakuts? 'Going Native' and problems of Russian National identity in the Siberian North, 1870s–1914." *Slavic Review,* 55(4) (1996): 806–825

Zenzinov, Vladimir, *Russkoe Ust'e* [Russkoe Ust'e], Berlin: Russkoe Universal'noe Izdatel'stvo, 1921

———, *The Road to Oblivion*, New York: Robert M. McBride, 1931

RUSSIAN AMERICAN COMPANY

In the second half of the 18th century, Russia colonized large territories in Alaska and along the Pacific coast of North America. The Russian American Company (*Rossiiysko-Amerikanskaia Kompaniia*) was organized as the trading monopoly under the patronage of the Russian government to carry on the fur trade and to confront foreign activity in the North American colonies. The company was established largely due to the efforts of Grigorii Shelikhov (1747–1795), a merchant from the Russian city of Rulsk. In 1781, Shelikhov organized with Ivan Golikov the Northeastern Company, whose primary goal was to oversee the fur trade in Alaska. Three years later, in 1784, Shelikhov established the first Russian settlement in Kikhtak (today Kodiak Island) in Three Saints Harbor. In addition to the traditional fur trade, Shelikhov planned to raise agricultural crops, build ships, and establish trade relations with other countries that had interests in the new Russian lands. He even thought of contributing to geographical knowledge by exploring the North American coasts, finding new sea routes in the Arctic Ocean, and producing geographical maps.

Shelikhov wrote a report in which he emphasized the key role of the trade monopoly in the economic development of Alaska. The report was published in St Petersburg in 1791; however, only after Shelikhov's death did several trade groups merge to form the United American Company. In 1799, the nascent organization was granted a 20-year charter and was renamed the Russian American Company. Russian Czar Pavel I gave the company exclusive rights to manage territories in North America to the north of 550 latitude, as well as the islands in the Pacific Ocean between Kamchatka and Alaska on the North and Japan on the South. The company was granted a mandate to explore the natural resources, including fossil, to colonize new lands to the South of 550 latitude, and to develop trade with neighboring countries. The Russian American Company established its headquarters in the Siberian city of Irkutsk, but eventually moved to St Petersburg, while the company's outpost was located in Fort Ross (today in California). In 1821, Czar Alexander I prescribed foreign ships to stay away from the 10-mile zone along the coasts of Russian colonies in North America, despite their amorphous boundaries. Treaties with the United States (1824) and Great Britain (1825) officially recognized the boundaries of the Russian possessions over the territory north of 54° 40′.

In the early years of the 19th century, the government lobbied vigorously for the Russian American Company. Its formidable stockholders included Czar Alexander I, dowager Empress Maria Fedorovna, State Chancellor N. Rumiantcev, and Navy Minister Admiral N. Mordvinov. The largest stockholder was Shelikhov's son-in-law, M. Buldakov (also the director of the Company), who owned 370 of 1724 stocks.

The first chief manager of the Company was Aleksandr Baranov, who operated the concern from Kodiak Island until 1804, when he moved his office to the new founded city of Novo-Arhangel'sk (New Archangel, today Sitka). Baranov organized the ship factory in Novo-Archangel'sk and built more than 25 sailing vessels and steamships. Remarkably, all ships were constructed using local materials and resources. The fur trade was the primary source of income, and the ships of the Russian American Company sailed to China, Hawaii, and America. During 1797–1821 the colonies exported 17,298 sables, 40,596 blue and white foxes, 72,894 sea beavers, 34,546 European beavers, 59,530 beaver tails, 66,482 red and black foxes, 14,969 otters, 1,232,374 fur seals and other furs, 25 tons of walrus teeth, and 20 tons of whalebones.

At the beginning of the 19th century, the number of Russian colonists in North America was only 600. State Chancellor Rumiantcev and Nikolai Petrovich Rezanov (1764–1807) prepared, in 1803 and 1806 respectively, two projects that attempted to establish new Russian settlements and develop local industry and trade in Alaska. Although neither of these projects was implemented, Baranov was intensively developing Alaska's infrastructure. Under his management, the Russian American Company built churches, hospitals, schools, factories, and a library. Baranov organized sawmills and tanning works, and he built mines extracting iron ore, copper, mica, and coal. Since 1804, the company has sent 13 sea expeditions to the Arctic and around the world, plotted maps of the northwestern coast of America, and published a geographical atlas.

The Russian American Company's charter was renewed twice, in 1824 and 1844; however, by the middle of the 19th century, demand for fur in China as well as the fur resources in Alaska declined. Several attempts were made to increase the revenues from the colonies. From 1840 to 1850, the Hudson's Bay Company leased the Russian lands between the southern border and 58° 40′ latitude. In 1841, the Russian southernmost settlement of Fort Ross, which was founded in the North San Francisco Bay in 1812, was ceded to the United States. After the discovery of gold in California and its annexation, the Russian American Company received several contracts to supply furs, fish, and ice from the North. Since 1852, the company has transported about 3000 tons of ice to California each year. This arrangement was short-lived as the company's profits waned. In 1860, in response to the company's request, the Russian government informed the administration that the charter could be renewed; however, the company must discontinue practicing forced labor of the native people, which was widely exploited in order to keep labor expenses low. The company rejected these reforms, and the charter was not renewed.

After Russia lost the Crimean War (1853–1856), the Russian American Company's difficulties increased, and the governing board decided to sell its holdings in North America. Great Britain and the United States shared in the geopolitical and commercial interests of the Russian colonies. Both countries had a stake in the territorial expansion along the Pacific Ocean coast, in fur trade, and in the construction of the telegraph line across North America by the Western Union Telegraph Company. Since there were political and commercial rivalries with Great Britain, Russian colonies in North America were sold to the United States in 1867.

M. BELOLUTSKAIA

See also **Fur Trade, History in Russia**

Further Reading

Andrews, Clarence Leroy, *Sitka, The Chief Factory of Russian American Company,* Cadwell, Idaho: The Caxton Printers, 1945

Barratt, Glynn, *Russia in Pacific Waters, 1715–1825: A Survey of the Origins of Russia's Naval Presence in the North and South Pacific,* Vancouver: University of British Columbia Press, 1981

Essig, E.O., Adele Ogden & Clarence John DuFour, *Fort Ross: California Outpost of Russian Alaska 1812–1841,* edited by Richard A. Pierce, Kingston, Ontario: Fairbanks, Alaska: Limestone Press, 1991

Gibson, J., "Russia in California, 1883: Report of Governor Wrangel." *Pacific Historical Review,* 60(4) (1969)

Ivashintsov, Nikolai A., *Russkie krugosvetnye puteshestviia* [Russian round-the-world voyages, 1803–1849: with a summary of later voyages to 1867], translated by Glynn Barrat, edited by Richard A. Pierce, Kingston, Ontario: Limestone Press, 1980

Iverson, E., "Nicolai Rezanov and Concepcion Arguello: the tale of Old California." *California Historian,* 42(4) (1996)

Okun, Semen Bentsionovich, *The Russian-American Company,* edited with an introduction by B.D. Grekov, translated by Carl Ginsburg, Cambridge, Massachusetts: Harvard University Press, 1951

Pierce, Richard A., *The Russian Governors: Builders of Alaska, 1818–1867,* Kingston, Ontario: Limestone Press, 1986

Shelikhov, Grigorii I., *Puteshestviie v Ameriky* [Voyage to America 1783–1786], translated by Marina Ramsay and edited by Richard A. Pierce, Kingston, Ontario: Limestone Press, 1981

Tikhmenev, Petr A., *Istoria Rossisko-Amerikanskoi Kompanii* [A History of the Russian-American Company], translated from the Russian edition of 1861–1863 and edited by Richard A. Pierce & Alton S. Donnelly, Seattle: University of Washington Press, 1977

RUSSIAN ASSOCIATION OF INDIGENOUS PEOPLES OF THE NORTH (RAIPON)

The Russian Association of Indigenous Peoples of the North (RAIPON) is currently the most important non-governmental indigenous rights organization in the

Russian Federation. RAIPON's main office is in Moscow, with approximately 32 regional and local chapters throughout Russia, representing 39 different ethnic and indigenous groups and a total of approximately 200,000 persons. The constituency of these chapters is geographic (the Khanty-Mansi Association comprises two distinct cultural groups in one locality), singularly cultural (the Kola Saami Association), or thematic (the Association of Elderly Indigenous Professionals).

With perestroika and glasnost, a growing awareness among indigenous peoples led to the establishment of the Association of the Indigenous Minorities of the Far North, Siberia, and the Far East in March 1990. RAIPON adopted its current name at its Second Congress in November 1993. In March 1994, RAIPON was incorporated as a public organization within the Russian Ministry of Justice. The Association is a permanent member of the Arctic Council, and was incorporated into UN Rolls of Honors in 1995. These are impressive achievements and a testimony to RAIPON's success in raising awareness about the problems of Russia's indigenous peoples in both national and international arenas. Yet in the mid-1990s, with increasing socioeconomic and political problems throughout Russia, success in terms of new federal legislation abated. For indigenous peoples, the transition from the Soviet system into the Russian Federation had the particularly negative effect of reducing the number of indigenous representatives in the regional and federal legislative bodies—a problem continually addressed by RAIPON.

RAIPON's president, who represents the association on the national and international level and directs the association's day-to-day operations, is elected by a vote at the Congress of Indigenous Peoples of the North, Siberia, and the Far East, which is held every four years. Between these congresses, the Coordination Council—comprising the Association's president, vice-presidents (culture, health, and so on), and the presidents of the regional and territorial associations—assumes administrative duties. The Coordination Council convenes at least twice a year to discuss matters of common interest and concern, and to coordinate joint activities.

RAIPON and its regional and ethnic organizations work with federal and legal government bodies and municipalities on issues related to development and fulfillment of legal and social programs. The groups are also working with the Federal Assembly and the Government of the Russian Federation preparing legislation toward guaranteeing the rights of indigenous peoples.

The Association's Charter was adopted in the early 1990s. Its main purpose is to protect the interests and lawful rights of the peoples it represents, and its main objectives are as follows: promote the unification of indigenous peoples in Russia; defend their rights and interests, with particular emphasis on issues such as land rights, the environment, and self-government; and help solve issues relating the sociocultural and economic development and northern regions. In this function, together with other organizations, RAIPON also provides workshops and seminars in cultural development and education, promotes international exchange and cooperation, and organizes humanitarian aid.

PETRA RETHMANN

RAIPON website: http://www.raipon.org

RUSSIAN CIVIL WAR

The Russian Civil War was a bloody series of battles fought between V.I. Lenin's Bolsheviks and uncoordinated and scattered forces of anti-Bolsheviks between 1918 and 1920. Following the abdication of Czar Nicholas II during the February Revolution of 1917, a provisional government consisting of industrialists and lawyers was unable or unwilling to end Russia's disastrous involvement in World War I, participation that had led to more than one million Russian soldiers being killed in action.

The provisional government itself was ousted between September and November by armed workers known as Red Guards, along with other revolutionary groups, under the leadership of Lenin's vanguard. Lenin then announced a new socialist order in Russia, one that was immediately beset by czarist and capitalist opponents on all sides. In the words of Richard Luckett, the civil war that followed was fought "amongst, and with, the military and political debris of a world war" (Luckett, 1971: 5).

With Lenin in Moscow in early 1918, anti-Bolshevik, so-called White resistance groups began to coalesce around former czarist generals Lavr G. Kornilov and Mikhail V. Alekseev. A still-formidable German army in the east advanced on the Russian Arctic ports of Arkhangel'sk and Murmansk, and the two million tons of Allied military supplies there. Ostensibly to guard these supplies, the British and French sent marines to Murmansk on March 9, 1918, where they quickly became involved on the side of the anti-Bolsheviks in the spreading civil war. British warships used in these Arctic operations included the pre-dreadnought *Glory* and the armored cruiser *Cochrane*. A Royal Navy base was established and named HMS *Glory III*. In August, the United States dispatched 4000 troops to Murmansk to help maintain order. Once there, the British diverted these forces into combat, and 96 Americans died while fighting the Bolsheviks.

In the White Sea region of northern Russia, General Yevgeny Miller, with the support of US and British troops, closed off Bolshevik access to the Arctic shore. Miller occupied Murmansk and Arkhangel'sk in August 1918, and harassed the Reds as far as the approaches to Petrograd. On the western front on November 11, 1918, the Germans agreed to an armistice, leading to their eventual withdrawal from Russian territory. But the departure of the Germans did not bring peace to Russia.

In the spring of 1919, White resistance in Siberia under Admiral Alexander Kolchak advanced rapidly toward the Volga, placing vast areas of Russia under White control. Seven thousand American and 72,000 Japanese forces landed in southeastern Siberia, occupying Vladivostok and the Maritime Province and policing the Trans-Siberian Railway. From the west, a small army under General Nikolai Yudenich also advanced on Petrograd, while in south Russia, General Anton Denikin began a march toward Moscow. Poland occupied parts of Lithuania, eastern Galicia, and Ruthenia, before moving into the western Ukraine. There, Nestor Makhno, an anarchist brigand with a following of disaffected peasants, harassed and killed both Red and White troops alike.

Then, almost as suddenly as they had advanced— and nearly simultaneously—the various White resistance factions were beaten back. Leon Trotsky's Red Army took advantage of interior lines of supply and communications and concentrated forces where the fighting was most intense. Yudenitch was forced back to the Baltic states, where his army wandered about for a time before disbanding. Kolchak's overextended forces were defeated before reaching the Volga, and began a tortuous retreat to Siberia, at the rear of a million refugees. Kolchak himself was captured and executed. Denikin's forces in the south were defeated at Orel and forced to surrender Kharkov to the Bolsheviks on December 13, 1919.

Under pressure to get their troops home, the British and the Americans withdrew from Russia's Arctic shore, leaving Miller's army to its fate. A final White advance from the south was defeated in the summer and fall of 1920. Combined with the Japanese withdrawal from Vladivostok in 1922, this brought the conflict to an effective end and allowed the Bolsheviks to create a Soviet republic.

Victory allowed the Soviets to bring the Russian Arctic under their control, beginning with the Trans-Siberian Railway, the cities along it, and the rivers that flowed from it to the Arctic Ocean. The reconquest of the northwestern Russian Arctic ports of Arkhangel'sk and Murmansk soon followed. This consolidation enabled the Soviets to use the Arctic to partially relieve the great 1920–1922 famine in the Volga and Ukraine regions. Large quantities of supplies were floated north on the Ob' River first to the Arctic Ocean, and then to Arkhangel'sk via the Kara Sea. As John McCannon writes, "in the context of developing the North, the Bread Expedition was the direct precursor to the famous Kara Expeditions and can be considered the USSR's first major operation in the Arctic" (McCannon, 1998: 21). The Kara Expeditions, begun in 1921, initiated foreign trade in the Kara Sea between the Soviet Union and Norway, Germany, and Britain. By exchanging raw materials shipped from the interior, the Soviets received manufactured goods from the West and valuable experience for their sailors in the conditions that prevailed in the Arctic.

A broader approach to development in the North, however, one that included relations with native Siberians, was swamped amid a new collection of unwieldy bureaucracies. Such failure was made manifest in the ultimate use of large parts of the Soviet Arctic, such as Novaya Zemlya, as nuclear test grounds and radioactive waste dumps.

Yet there were many successes as well. In scientific research, the Soviets began oceanographic surveys of the polar basin in 1921 on board a specially fitted research vessel, the *Persei*, in an initial attempt to study the complex geography and oceanography of the Arctic. Throughout the 1920s, pioneering aeronautical explorations led to the first airfields in the Russian Arctic, to the Aeroarctic Graf Zeppelin flight to Franz Josef Land in 1931, and to record-breaking Soviet flights over the pole itself later in the 1930s.

P.J. CAPELOTTI

See also **Kolchak, Alexander**

Further Reading

Armstrong, T.E., *The Russians in the Arctic*, London: Methuen, 1958

Griffiths, Franklyn, *Arctic and North in the Russian Identity*, Toronto: University of Toronto Press, 1990

Lincoln, W. Bruce, *The Conquest of a Continent: Siberia and the Russians*, New York: Random House, 1993

Luckett, Richard, *The White Generals: An Account of the White Movement and the Russian Civil War*, New York: Viking, 1971

McCannon, John, *Red Arctic: Polar Exploration and the Myth of the North in the Soviet Union, 1932–1939*, New York: Oxford University Press, 1998

Pipes, Richard, *The Russian Revolution*, New York: Vintage Books, 1991

———, *Communism: A History*, New York: Modern Library, 2001

RUSSIAN FEDERAL LAW GUARANTEEING THE RIGHTS OF NATIVE SPARSE PEOPLES OF THE RUSSIAN FEDERATION

Signed into action on April 30, 1999, the Law "On Guarantees of the Rights of Indigenous Numerically

Small Peoples of the Russian Federation" is lauded as the first Russian federal law creating a legal basis for the rights of aboriginal peoples in Russia. This federal law guarantees the distinct socioeconomic and cultural development of Russia's aboriginal peoples, the protection of their natural habitat and traditional way of life, and of their economic activities and occupations. It applies to those aboriginal persons who live in "traditional places of habitation," adhere to a traditional way of life, and engage in occupations that are traditional for that given people. In essence, it is intended to guarantee aboriginal peoples equal right and opportunities with other Russian citizens to develop their cultures. The law provides a framework for guaranteeing such rights. It anticipates the passage of more concrete governmental acts at the federal and subfederal level to address the specifics of implementation of the rights it safeguards.

The subjects of the law, the "indigenous numerically small" (aboriginal) peoples include those peoples who live within the territory that was traditionally occupied by their ancestors, maintain a traditional way of life, number less than 50,000 in the Russian Federation, and recognize themselves as distinct peoples (§1.1). The law specifies that the state will maintain an official list of such peoples. Eleven months after the law was adopted, the Russian government confirmed such a list, of 44 peoples (Yediniy, 2000). Most of these peoples live in the Russian North. The law also covers numerically small peoples living in other parts of the Russian Federation, mainly in the Caucasus. The law does not stipulate how individuals establish membership within such groups.

Although several laws dealing with rights and privileges of aboriginal peoples were adopted during the early Soviet period, after the war the state's approach shifted to passing legal acts that assigned special rights and privileges to the areas in which aboriginal peoples lived. These laws mainly benefited the nonnative population. Only at the end of the Soviet period did the need for laws protecting native rights receive renewed recognition. After the United Nations adopted the International Labour Organization Convention 169, "Indigenous and Tribal Peoples Convention" (1989), aboriginal leaders began to pressure for Russia to ratify the convention. The Russian government conceded the need at least to develop a federal level law on the rights of indigenous peoples living within the Russian Soviet Federated Socialist Republic (later the Russian Federation), and formally called for this in March 1991 (Gosudarstvennaya, 1991). The drafting of such a law had already begun the previous fall.

The development of this law endured a rough ride. For the next eight years, the draft law proceeded through numerous versions, and various attempts at adoption. Representatives from various state commit-

tees worked on drafts, along with invited experts from the Russian Association of Indigenous Peoples of the North (RAIPON) and the Institute of Ethnology and Anthropology. The parliament adopted the law three times, only to have the president veto it, and return it for redrafting, due to its inclusion of articles that purportedly contravened constitutional articles. President Yeltsin rejected the law for a final time in early April 1999; however, this time the veto was overturned by the parliament. By the time it was passed, the law had been whittled down from 64 to 16 articles.

Under the law, the federal and regional governments must defend the rights of aboriginal peoples to pursue distinct forms of socioeconomic and cultural development. Their lands and traditional ways of life must be protected. The law authorizes federal and regional governments to adopt laws and programs to these ends. The law calls for boundaries of lands of traditional nature use to be established, and regimes of native use established within these. It recognizes the rights of aboriginal peoples to possess and use lands in the areas they have traditionally inhabited, in order to pursue traditional activities. They also have the right to financial support from the different levels of government to pursue their traditional way of life and protect their environment. They can participate in decisions made by different governmental levels that impact their lands and way of life, and in environmental analysis of state projects that might impact them. They also have the right to compensation for losses caused by damage of the environment on their traditional lands. These rights are enjoyed collectively and individually.

Native individuals enjoy free social services, free medical care, and free travel for annual checkups. Those persons involved in traditional activities may substitute alternative civil service for the otherwise mandatory armed forces service required of all young men. The law recognizes the rights of aboriginal peoples to maintain and develop their languages, to observe their traditions and religious customs, and to encourage communication among native individuals across the Russian state and beyond its boundaries. Aboriginal peoples can establish organs of territorial self-government according to the law. They may set up communes or *obshchinas*. Native enterprises and individuals receive priority rights to property and resources when forming enterprises based on traditional activities. Native peoples enjoy not only the right to protection of their rights via the court system, but courts are directed to consider aboriginal customs and traditions in their deliberations.

Issues

The law suffers from several problems. One involves definition of terms. Although the law depends heavily on the concept of traditional activities, "tradition" itself is not defined, nor are "traditional economic activities and trades." The law also establishes rights for those peoples living on "the territory of traditional occupation of their ancestors"—a problematic term, given the high mobility and historic iterative displacements of aboriginals over the last five centuries.

Another issue is the lack of agreement with other laws. For example, a provision allowing regional governments to establish quotas for aboriginal representation appears to contradict federal election laws. Such disagreements will need to be addressed through further legal acts.

Implementation is incapacitated by the lack of financial means to support the protections that the law guarantees. Nevertheless, the Law on Guarantees of Rights is seen as a critical first step toward recognizing aboriginal rights in the Russian Federation. It provides a set of guidelines for regional governments to use in crafting more concrete laws, or in revising their laws to accord with federal standards, a process that has begun. The consequences of the law's approach regarding differentiating rights between those who pursue "traditional" activities and those who do not, rather than basing rights on a purely ethnic' basis, will merit attention.

GAIL FONDAHL

Further Reading

Anonymous, "Parlamentskie slushaniya 'O realizatsii Federal'nogo zakona "O garantiyakh prav korennykh malochislennykh narodov Rossiyskoy Federatsii"' [Parliamentary hearing 'On the realization of the Federal Law "On Guaranteeing the rights of indigenous numerically small peoples of the Russian Federation"']. *Mir Korennykh Narodov/ Zhivaya Arktika*, 3(2000): 24–26

Fondahl, G., *Gaining Ground? Evenkis, Land and Reform in Southeastern Siberia*, Wilton, Connecticut: Allyn and Bacon, 1998

Gosudarstvennaya, "Gosudarstvennaya programma razvitiya ekonomiki i kul'tury malochislennykh narodov Severa 1991–1995 godakh" [State program of development of the economy and culture of numerically small peoples of the North]. Confirmed by Decree No. 145 of the Council of Ministers of the RSFSR, March 11, 1991

Korolev, S.N., "Problemy zakonodatel'stva o korennykh malochislennykh narodakh Severa" [Problems of legislation on the indigenous numerically sjall peoples of the North]. *Gosudarstvo i Pravo*, 7(1996): 19–23

Kryazhkov, Vladimir A. (compiler), *Status malochislennykh narodov Rossii. Pravovye Akty i Dokumenty* [The Status of Numerically Small Peoples of Russia: Legal Acts and Documents], Moscow: Yuridicheskaya Literatura, 1994

——, "Korennye malochislennye narody i mezhdunarodnoe pravo" [Indigenous numerically small peoples and international law]. *Gosudarstvo i Pravo*, 4(1999): 95–102

——, (compiler), *Status malochislennykh narodov Rossii. Pravovye Akty* [The Status of Numerically Small Peoples of Russia. Legal Acts], Moscow: Izdanie g-na Tikhomirova M. Yu, 1999

"O garantiyakh prav korennykh malochislennykh narodov Rossiyskoy Federatsii" [On guarantees of the rights of the indigenous numerically small peoples of the Russian Federation]. *Russian Federal Law* N°. 82-F3, April 30, 1999

Pika, Aleksandr, *Neotraditionalism in the Russian North. Indigenous Peoples and the Legacy of Perestroika*, Edmonton: Canadian Circumpolar Institute and Seattle: University of Washington Press, 1999

Sokolova, Z.P., N.I. Novikova & N.V. Ssorin-Chaikov, "Enografy pishut zakon: Kontekst i problema" [Etnographers write the law: the context and the problem]. *Etnograficheskoe obozreniye*, 1(1995)

Vakhtin, Nikolay B., "Indigenous people of the Russian Far North: land rights and the environment." *Polar Geography*, 22(2) (1998): 79–104

"Yedinyy perechen' korennykh malochislennykh narodov Rossiyskoy Federatsii" [Unified list of indigenous numerically small peoples of the Russian Federation]. Confirmed by Decree N°. 255 of the Russian Government, March 24, 2000

RUSSIAN FEDERAL LAW ON CLAN COMMUNES (OBSHCHINAS)

Many (although not all) Russian ethnographers characterize aboriginal socioeconomic and political organization as having evolved from clan lines to a more territorially based structure of family-clan communes or *obshchinas* at the end of the 19th century. These obshchinas were "relatively stable, economic and demographic collectives, oriented to self-sufficiency and reproduction, which were able to exert real control over their territory…" (Pika, 1999: 67).

Aboriginal leaders have charged that the social malaise experienced by aboriginal peoples of the Russian North, as witnessed in low life expectancy, high homicide and suicide rates, and other indicators, is due in part to aboriginal people's loss of control over their lives and lands. Extreme dependency on the state, exacerbated by forced settlement and relocation, produced debilitating circumstances. When, in the late 20th century, aboriginal leaders and academics sought means to reinvest aboriginal groups with more power over their lives, they considered recreating pre-Soviet aboriginal structures as a way to encourage cultural persistence and economic self-sufficiency (ibid.). These individuals successfully convinced the government of the desirability of institutionalizing the obshchina in law.

In March 1992, a federal government decree called for the development and passage of a law on "clan, obshchina and family lands" which would govern the establishment of obshchinas and the transfer of land to these collectives (Ob uporyadochenii, 1992). Soon after this, the then President Boris Yeltsin issued an edict ordering the transfer of lands important to traditional activities "to clan obshchinas and families of the numerically small peoples of the North" who pursued traditional activities "for life long possession... or lease" (O neotlozhnykh, 1992). This edict was to serve as an interim measure, allowing aboriginals to receive land until a federal law was drafted.

The federal law on obshchinas was finally adopted eight years later, on July 20, 2000. Prior to this, a number of the Russian Federation's constituent units had adopted their own laws (Sakha Republic (Yakutia), Khabarovsk Territory) or temporary regulations (Sakhalin Province). Using these legal acts, or the presidential edict, aboriginal peoples across Russia established and registered hundreds of obshchinas before the passage of the federal law.

The Law on Obshchinas

The federal law defines obshchinas as "forms of self-organization of persons belonging to numerically small peoples and joined by blood-clan (family, clan) and (or) territorial-neighbor indication, created in order to defend their ancestral environment, and to maintain and develop traditional ways of life, economy, trades and culture" (§1). Thus, obshchinas are vested with goals of cultural protection and environmental preservation.

The obshchina is legally authorized to be a non-commercial economic and potentially self-governing unit. It controls its internal affairs, which may be governed by customary law. It may also be invested with specific authorities held usually by the local government in which it is located. The law on obshchinas establishes general procedures for establishing, reorganizing, and liquidating obshchinas. It provides general membership rules: neither foreign nor nonaboriginal persons can found obshchinas, nor can foreign persons be members. The law lays out what the government or council of the obshchina is responsible for, and what issues are handled at general assemblies. Obshchinas are entitled to join in unions or associations, to facilitate pursuit of their goals.

Obshchina members are given the right to access faunal, plant, common mineral, and other resources in the course of their traditional activities. Perhaps amazingly, the law on obshchinas says nothing specific on land (although it requires the obshchina to have a physical location). This contrasts notably with the Sakha Republic's law on obshchinas, the first and most comprehensive of such laws, which dedicated eight of its 25 articles to describing the structure of land relations (O kochevoy, 1992). The federal law does invoke the provisions of previous laws dealing with aboriginal rights, most notably the Russian Federation Law on Guaranteeing the Rights of Indigenous Numerically Small Peoples of the Russian Federation, adopted the previous year, which speaks in a limited way about rights to land (*see* **Russian Federal Law Guaranteeing the Rights of Native Sparse Peoples of the Russian Federation**).

Obshchinas also enjoy the right to establish schooling for members' children, based on traditions and customs. The law authorizes regional governments and the federal government to establish tax breaks for obshchinas, and to budget monies for their operations in regional and local development programs.

Effects of the Law

Although hundreds of obshchinas were formed prior to the federal law's passage, its adoption provided new ammunition to aboriginals living in areas where regional governments and local administrations hesitated to register obshchinas and allocate land. Some had justified their refusal to register obshchinas precisely on the basis of the absence of a federal law.

The law's definition of the obshchina as a potential self-governing unit also legally expands the rights of many extant obshchinas. For instance, in the Sakha Republic, where over 200 obshchinas were registered by 1999, the republican law stipulates the obshchina as an economic unit, but not as a possible locus of self-government. Aboriginal leaders fought hard for a self-government clause, but eventually forfeited this designation in order to ensure the law's passage. In that President Putin has demanded that regional laws be brought into accordance with federal laws, the federal construal of obshchinas as political-administrative as well as economic units may have far-reaching consequences in some of Russia's regions.

Yet, the issue of bringing local laws in accordance with federal laws poses other interesting challenges for extant obshchinas. Again, if we take the example of the Sakha law, it allowed nonaboriginal persons pursuing occupations and ways of life traditional for aboriginal peoples to also form obshchinas. This move circumvented potential ethnic tensions arising from providing special rights or provisions for members of some ethnic groups, and not for members of others, who live in the same communities and practice the same activities. Bringing the local law into accordance with the federal law in this instance may exacerbate carefully avoided ethnic antagonisms.

GAIL FONDAHL

See also **Collectivization; Relocation**

Further Reading

Fondahl, Gail, Olga Lazebnik & Greg Poelzer, "Aboriginal territorial rights and the sovereignty of the Sakha Republic."

Post-Soviet Geography and Economics, 41(6) (2000): 401–417

Kryazhkov, Vladimir A. (compiler), *Status malochislennykh narodov Rossii. Pravovye Akty i Dokumenty* [The Status of Numerically Small Peoples of Russia. Legal Acts and Documents], Moscow: Yuridicheskaya Literatura, 1994

———, (compiler), *Status malochislennykh narodov Rossii. Pravovye Akty* [The Status of Numerically Small Peoples of Russia. Legal Acts], Moscow: Izdanie g-na Tikhomirova M. Yu, 1999

———, "Land rights of the numerically small peoples in Russian Federation legislation." *Polar Geography,* 20(2) (1996): 85–98

Novikova, Natalya I. "'Rovodye ugodya': perspektivy pravovogo plyuralizma (predstavleniya predstavitely korennykh narodov i zakonodateley) ['Clan lands': prospects for legal pluralism (representations of representatives of indigenous peoples and law makers]." *Gosudarstvo i Pravo*, 6(2000): 102–107

"Ob obshchikh printsipakh organizatsii obshchin korennykh malochislennykh narodov Severa, Sibiri i Dal'nego Vostoka Rossiyskoy Federatsii [On general principals of organization of obshchinas of the indigenous numerically small peoples of the North, Siberia and the Far East of the Russian Federation]." *Russian Federal Law* N°. 104-F3, July 20, 2000

"Ob uporyadochenii polzovaniya zemelnykh uchastkami, zanyatami pod rodovye, obshchinnye i semeynye ugodya malochislennykh narodov Severa [On regulation of the use of land occupied by clan, obshchina and family lands of the numerically small peoples of the North]." *Resolution N°. 2612-3 of the Presidium of the Supreme Soviet of the Russian Federation*, March 30, 1992

"O garantiyakh prav korennykh malochislennykh narodov Rossiyskoy Federatsii [On guarantees of the rights of the indigenous numerically small peoples of the Russian Federation]." *Russian Federal Law* N°. 82-F3, April 30, 1999

"O kochevoy rodovoy obshchine malochislennykh narodov Severa [On the nomadic clan obshchina of the numerically small peoples of the North]." *Law of Republic of Sakha (Yakutia)* N°. 1278-XII, December 23, 1992

"O neotlozhnykh merakh po zashchite mest prozhivaniya i khozyaystvennoy deyatel'nosti malochiselennykh narodov Severa [On urgent measures to defend the places of habitation and economic activities of the numerically small peoples of the North]." *Edict N°. 397 of the President of the Russian Federation*, April 22, 1992

Pika, A. (editor), *Neotraditionalism in the Russian North. Indigenous Peoples and the Legacy of Perestroika*, Edmonton: Canadian Circumpolar Institute and Seattle: University of Washington Press, 1999

Sirina, Anna, "Rodovye obshchiny v Respublike Sakha (Yakutiya): shag k samoopredeleniyu? [Clan obshchinas in the Republic of Sakha (Yakutia): a step toward self-determination?]." *Issledovaniya po prikladnoy i neotlozhnoy etnologii*, 126(1999)

Vakhtin, Nikolay B. "Indigenous people of the Russian Far North: land rights and the environment." *Polar Geography* 22(2) (1998): 79–104

RUSSIAN FEDERAL LAW ON TERRITORIES OF TRADITIONAL NATURE USE

The Russian federal law on Territories of Traditional Nature Use (TTPs) is third in a suite of laws directing aboriginal-state relations (*see* **Russian Federal Law Guaranteeing the Rights of Native Sparse Peoples of the Russian Federation; Russian Federal Law on Clan Communes (Obshchinas)**). It governs the designation of tracts of land as "territories of traditional nature use" of aboriginal peoples, in order to protect and maintain these lands as a base for traditional aboriginal activities, such as reindeer herding and hunting. Although aboriginal groups can form clan communes (*obshchinas*) and then petition for possession of lands on which to pursue traditional activities, this results in archipelagos of "native lands." Meanwhile, aboriginal leaders also lobbied for the designation of more spatially extensive TTPs off limits to resource development, in order to provide ample space for the continuance of traditional fields.

Other potential resource users, including foreign investors, are interested in knowing what lands will fall under protected status. Native peoples have extensively used much of the 11.2 million sq km of Russia's North (64% of the country). A federal law to establish the limits of TTPs was first called for in 1991 (O dopol'nitelnykh, 1991). It was finally signed into action on May 7, 2001.

The federal law succeeds several regional laws (Irkustk Province 1997, Koryak Autonomous Province 1997) and lesser legal acts (Khanty-Mansiisk District 1990, Koryak Autonomous District 1992, Primorsk Territory 1993) (see Kryazhkov, 1994, 1999). It establishes as its goals the protection of the environment on which traditional aboriginal ways of life depend, and, in turn, the preservation and development of aboriginal cultures and the preservation of biological diversity. Like the two other major laws regarding aboriginal rights that preceded it, the federal law on TTPs is general and declarative in nature. It provides the framework for establishing TTPs, and the basis for regional governments to adopt more specific legislation on the creation of, and legal regime governing the operation of, such territories.

Aboriginal persons or obshchinas initiate applications for the creation of such territories at the federal, regional, or local level. They also participate in the drafting of the regulations that govern a TTP's operation. The federal law indicates what other bodies must participate in their formation, depending on level, and notes that the general population must be informed of their creation.

The size of a TTP is determined by the spatial extent necessary to ensure the maintenance of biological diversity of the territory's fauna and flora. It must also provide for the continuity of historical, social, and cultural ties among aboriginal persons, and preserve the inviolability of any cultural or historical objects.

The TTP is not a highly exclusive or protective designation. Aboriginal persons and obshchinas have the right to use natural resources for the pursuance of traditional activities, and can possess obshchina lands within the boundaries of a TTP. Nonaboriginal residents also may use resources for personal needs in accordance with the TTP's regulations. These regulations can permit the use of nonrenewable as well as renewable resources, for entrepreneurial as well as subsistence needs.

Land can be alienated from TTPs for state and municipal needs. Alienation requires that land of equal value be given to aboriginal obshchinas or individuals, and that they receive compensation for losses incurred by alienation.

The Russian Association of Indigenous Peoples of the North is considering establishing several model TTPs, in order to work out the mechanisms for establishing and operationalizing such territories.

GAIL FONDAHL

Further Reading

Fondahl, Gail, "Freezing the frontier: territories of traditional nature use in northern Russia." *Progress in Planning,* 47(4), (1997): 307–319

Kryazhkov, V. A. (editor),. *Status Malochislennykh Narodov Rossii. Pravovye Akty i Dokumenty [The Status of the Numerically Small Peoples of Russia. Legal Acts and Documents]*, Moscow: Juridical Literature, 1994

———, "Land rights of the numerically small peoples in Russian Federation legislation." *Polar Geography,* 20(2) (1996): 85–98

———, (compiler), *Status malochislennykh narodov Rossii. Pravovye Akty*, Moscow: Izdanie g-na Tikhomirova M. Yu, 1999

———, (compiler), *Status malochislennykh narodov Rossii. Pravovye Akty*, Moscow: Izdanie g-na Tikhomirova M. Yu, 1999

Murashko, Olga A., "Etnoekologicheskie refugium: kontseptsiya sokhraneniya traditsionnoy kul'tury i sredy obitaniya korennykh narodov Severa." *Etnograficheskoe obozreniye,* 5 (1998): 83–94

"O dopolnitelnykh merakh po ulushcheniyu sotsial'no-ekonomicheskikh usloviyakh zhizni malochislennykh narodov Severa na 1991–1995 gody" [On additional measures to improve the social-economic conditions of the life of the numerically small peoples of the North]. *Resolution of the Cabinet of Ministers of the USSR and the Soviet of the RSFSR* No. 84, March 11, 1991

Osherenko, Gail, "Indigenous rights in Russia: is title to land essential for cultural survival?." *The Georgetown International Environmental Law Review,* XIII(3) (2001): 695–734

Turaev, Mikhail, "Territorial'nyy podkhod k resheniyu etnicheskikh problem na rossiyskom Dal'nem Vostoke." In *Quest for Models of Coexistence. National and Ethnic Dimensions of Changes in the Slavic Eurasian World*, edited by K. Inoue & T. Uyama, Sapporo: Slavic Research Center, Hokkaido University, 1998, pp. 289–316

Yamskov, Anatoly N., "Traditsionnoe prirodopol'zovanie: problemy opredeleniya i pravovogo regulirovaniya." In *Yuridicheskaya Antropologiya. Zakon i Zhizn'*, edited by N.I. Novikova & V.A. Tishkov, Moscow: Strateigiya, 2000, pp. 172–185

RUSSIAN GEOGRAPHICAL SOCIETY

In October 1845, the Russian Geographical Society (*Russkoe geograficheskoe obshchestvo* or RGO) held its first general meeting in the building of the Academy of Sciences in St Petersburg. The society and its successor organizations subsequently played a tremendous role in the exploration and scientific study of the Russian Arctic and lay the institutional foundations for the emergence of ethnography (anthropology) within a Russian context.

While the establishment of geographical societies had become a general trend in European learned circles during the second quarter of the 19th century, recent advances in the accumulation of geographical knowledge in and about Russia, as well as administrative needs of the Russian state, acted as local triggers for the emergence of the RGO. The founding members of the RGO were either from the ranks of the Academy of Sciences, from the army or navy, or from the state administration. The main preparatory work was conducted by the academician Karl von Baer and by the naval officers Fedor P. Litke and Ferdinand P. Wrangell. In 1849, the RGO adopted its permanent charter and was granted the right to bear the title "Imperial" (thus making it the IRGO).

Initially, the society encompassed four departments: General Geography, Geography of Russia, Ethnography, and Statistics. The embryologist Karl von Baer, of German-Baltic descent, became the first president of the department of ethnography. His vision of ethnography was that of a comparative and empirical science, which had its intellectual roots in the 18th century. Von Baer's successor at the department, the Russian seminarian Nikolai Ivanovich Nadezhdin, on the other hand, was influenced by German idealist philosophers and by romantic nationalism. While Baer had been primarily interested in the non-Russian peoples of the Russian Empire, Nadezhdin shifted the emphasis to the study of Russians. He initiated a huge ethnographic survey of the Russian Empire, which was conducted by sending 7000 questionnaires to local correspondents throughout the country.

The society actively began sponsoring publication activities and editing journals. In addition to a variety of more short-lived journals in the fields of geography, ethnography, and statistics, the society has been publishing its flagship journal, *Izvestiia Russkogo geograficheskogo obshchestva* [News of the Russian Geographical Society], from 1865 until the present day.

The work of the IRGO was conducted not only from its headquarters in St Petersburg but also through local branch offices. For our purposes, the establishment of a Siberian branch of the IRGO in Irkutsk in 1851 is most relevant. Additional northern branch offices were opened later in Omsk, Khabarovsk, Vladivostok, and Yakutsk. Among the prerevolutionary expeditions sponsored by the IRGO and its branch offices, the following are most notable: the mathematical-geographical expedition to eastern Siberia (1854–1859) with the participation of the naturalist Gustav Radde, the Viliui Expedition (1854–1855) under Richard K. Maak, the Olekminsk-Vitim Expedition (1866) with the participation of the young Petr Kropotkin, and the Chukchi Expedition (1868–1870) under the command of Gerhard Gustav Ludwig von Maydell.

The two largest expeditions of those years were named after their sponsors and organized by the IRGO. The Sibiryakov Expedition (1895–1897) studied the indigenous peoples of the contemporary Sakha Republic (Yakutia). The Riabushinskii Expedition (1908–1910) covered not only Russian territories (Kamchatka and the Commander and Kuril islands) but also the Aleutian Islands in the United States. Vladimir G. Bogoraz and Vladimir I. Iokhel'son took part in the Sibiryakov Expedition, and Iokhel'son was in charge of the ethnological party of the Riabushinskii Expedition. A particular characteristic of the work of the IRGO in the 19th century was that they made extensive use of political exiles to Siberia. For example, 15 political exiles were among the 26 participants of the Sibiryakov Expedition.

The Russian Revolution of 1917 resulted in dropping the adjective "Imperial" from the name of the society, and in 1926 it become the State Geographical Society. Arctic exploration and research figured prominently during the 1920s and 1930s: it included the work of the famous drifting station "Severnyi polius" (North Pole-1), as well as ethnographic expeditions to the Saami and the Yupiget (Siberian Yupik). In 1938, the society was incorporated into the Academy of Sciences and renamed the All-Soviet Geographical Society. Since World War II, the network of branch offices in the North has expanded significantly and extends all the way from Arkhangel'sk to Petropavlovsk-Kamchatskii. In 1993, after the disintegration of the Soviet Union, the society reverted back to its initial name, Russian Geographical Society. During the more than 150 years of its existence, the society has conducted approximately 600 expeditions.

PETER P. SCHWEITZER

See also **Baer, Karl von;. Iokhel'son, Vladimir I.; Kropotkin, Petr; Litke, Fedor; Maak, Rikhard Karlovich; Wrangell, Baron Ferdinand Petrovich von**

Further Reading

Berg, L.S., *Vsesoiuznoe Geograficheskoe obshchestvo za sto let* [The All-Soviet Geographical Society During 100 Years], Moscow: Izdatel'stvo Akademii nauk SSSR, 1946

Knight, Nathaniel, "Science, Empire, and Nationality: Ethnography in the Russian Geographical Society, 1845–1855." In *Imperial Russia: New Histories for the Empire*, edited by J. Burbank & D.L. Ransel, Bloomington: Indiana University, 1998

Matveeva, T.P. & E.V. Soboleva, "Die Russische Geographische Gesellschaft" [The Russian Geographical Society]. In *Sibirien: Kolonie—Region*, edited by L. Thomas, Berlin: Akademie Verlag, 1996

Oglezneva, Tat'iana N., *Russkoe geograficheskoe obshchestvo: izuchenie narodov severo-vostoka Azii 1845–1917 gg* [The Russian Geographical Society: The Study of the Peoples of Northeast Asia 1845–1917]. Novosibirsk: Nauka, 1994

Sokolova, Z.P., "On the Role of the Russian Geographical Society and its Department of Anthropology as well as of the Academy of Sciences of Russia in the Development of Studies in the Peoples Kindred to the Finns." In *Pioneers: The History of Finnish Ethnology*, edited by M. Räsänen, Tampere: Finnish National Board of Antiquities, 1992

Solovei, T.D., "Nikolai Ivanovich Nadezhdin. U istokov otechestvennoi etnologicheskoi nauki" [Nikolai Ivanovich Nadezhdin: the beginnings of Russian ethnological science]. *Etnograficheskoe obozrenie*, 1 (1994): 103–107

Stepanov, N.N., "Russkoe geograficheskoe obshchestvo i etnografiia (1845–1861)" [The Russian Geographical Society and Ethnography (1845–1861). *Sovetskaia etnografiia*, 4 (1946): 187–206

RUSSIAN POLAR EXPEDITION, 1900–1902

In April to November 1898 during sessions of the Imperial Russian Geographical Society and Mineralogical Society, the Russian geologist Edward von Toll, known for his expeditions to northern Yakutia (1893) and to the Novosibirsky (New Siberian) Islands (1886), suggested organizing a polar expedition for scientific exploration of northern Russia and to search for the hypothetical Sannikov's Land. This mysterious island was observed for the first time by professional hunter Yakov Sannikov during his inspection of the northern shore of Kotel'ny Island (in the Novosibirsky Islands) in 1811, and had been seen by von Toll in August 1886. All eyewitnesses described this land in the same way: four mountains surrounded by lowland. However, nobody could reach it, its location was indefinite on the map, and it became known as Sannikov's Land.

Von Toll's proposal was supported both by Russian and foreign scientists (Fedor B. Schmidt, Alexander P. Karpinsky, Feodosiy N. Chernyshov, Fridtjof Nansen, Adolf Erik Nordenskiöld, and others) and by the Russian Government: 180,000 rubles were assigned for this expedition after a presentation made by the President of the Academy of Science, Grand Prince

Konstantin Konstantinovich. The whaling schooner *Zarya* (built in 1873 in Norway, formerly named *Harald Harfager*) was bought especially for this expedition and was supplied in abundance with provisions, equipment, and scientific instruments. Naval officers Nikolay N. Kolomeytsev (captain of the schooner), Fyodor A. Matisen, and Alexander V. Kolchak, zoologist Alexey A. Byalynitsky-Birulya, astronomer Friedrikh G. Zeeberg, and doctor German E. Valter took part in the expedition. Nikifor A. Begichev—the future famous explorer of Taymyr Peninsula—was the boatswain's mate of *Zarya*. The crew consisted of six sailors, two technicians, three stokers, and a cook. All were volunteers from the Russian Navy.

On June 8, 1900, *Zarya* left the port of St Petersburg. The ship additionally loaded in Kronstadt, Bergen, and Tromsø. Sixty sled dogs from eastern and western Siberia were loaded in the port Alexandrovsk-upon-Murman (Kola Peninsula). On July 25, *Zarya* passed through the channel Yugorsky Shar, where it was supposed to load coal. But the freight ship did not come, and *Zarya* continued on its way with only its own supply. This lack of fuel played a negative role in the expedition's fortune.

On August 5, the schooner left the port on Dixon Island, and later stopped for its first wintering after a very hard passage among small unknown islands in the Nordenskiold Archipelago in the strait between the mainland and Bonevy Island—now called Zarya's Road.

During overwintering from 1900 to 1901, numerous sledge and pedestrian journeys were undertaken by members of the expedition. A topographical survey of part of Middendorf Bay, the southern part of Taymyr Bay, and Zarya's Road was carried out. A food depot was organized in Knipovich Bay on the Depo Cape. (This was found by Dmitry I. Shparo's expedition in 1973.) In March 1901, Matisen reached the last southern extremity of Russky Island. Von Toll made a collection of rocks. Here, for the first time he reached a conclusion about the glaciation of Taymyr Peninsula, and about the peninsula's uplift in modern time. The Russian Polar Expedition also discovered the islands of Pilot Alexeev and Taimyr.

During the wintering, a conflict developed between von Toll and captain N.N. Kolomeytsev, the consequence of which was the discharge of the latter from the command of the ship. He was sent to the Gol'chikha settlement (800 km) for the organization of coal depots on Dixon and Kotel'ny Islands. Lieutenant Matisen was appointed as the captain of *Zarya*.

On August 12, 1901, *Zarya* was freed from the ice with the help of dynamite and had already passed by Cape Chelyuskin on August 19, where Begichev with his sailors had made a stone pyramid. For the first time, sailing in the Laptev Sea was in free water, but then heavy ice was encountered. Constant deep fog prevented searching for the mysterious Sannikov's Land. Bennett Island was also surrounded by ice, and von Toll made a decision to organize a second wintering in Nerpalakh Lagoon (Kotel'ny Island). During the wintering of 1901–1902, extensive investigations were made, the members of the expedition crossing Kotel'ny Island in different directions. Alexander Kolchak climbed the highest point of the Novosibirsky Islands (374 m).

In the spring of 1902, von Toll with astronomer F.G. Zeeberg and two guides N. Protod'yakonov and Vasily Gorohov went to Bennett Island on dogsleds. The group led by zoologist A.A. Byalynitsky-Birulya went to Novaya Sibir' Island. In summer, *Zarya* came to take both groups away, but ice conditions prevented captain Matisen from reaching Bennett Island. In the middle of July, he left the Nerpalakh Lagoon, made several attempts to reach the island, but had to leave due to heavy ice and a catastrophic fuel shortage. According to von Toll's instruction, he went to the Lower Lena. The ship could not enter the river and was left in Tiksi Bay. The crew came to Yakutsk on the ship *Lena* and then returned to St Petersburg. In December 1902, the group of Byalynitsky-Birulya also successfully returned.

The fate of Baron von Toll worried the general public, and during the winter, organization of a rescue expedition was discussed. The expedition's hydrographer Alexander Kolchak was appointed as the head of the rescue party, which consisted of Pavel V. Olenin, boatswain's mate Begichev, two sailors from *Zarya*, and four professional hunters from Mezen' (Province of Arkhangel'sk).

In the spring of 1903, the whaleboat from *Zarya* was delivered to Kotel'ny Island with incredible difficulties. In late July to August after the opening of the sea, the rescue party reached Bennett Island. There, evidence of von Toll's stay was immediately found. From their note, it was deduced that von Toll and his companions had left the island in November 1902 and went southward. A careful analysis of documents, buildings, and the various objects found on the island allowed one to suppose that there had been a serious conflict in the party between the scientists and guides. Kolchak's rescue party removed all documents and part of the rock collection, and returned successfully.

The other rescue party led by Mikhail I. Brusnev inspected the shores of Kotel'ny, Fadeev, and Novaya Sibir' Islands, but found nothing. The Russian Academy of Science announced that a prize would be awarded to anybody who could find von Toll and his companions, but no news came. Therefore, on November 22, 1904, the Commission of Academy of

Science concluded that Baron von Toll, astronomer F.G. Zeeberg, and two guides Nikolai Protod'yakonov and Vasily Gorokhov had perished, apparently drowned in the sea on the way from Bennett Island to Novaya Sibir' Island.

The scientific results of the Russian Polar Expedition touched mainly on the cartography, meteorology, geology, and zoology of the northern shore of Taymyr Peninsula and Novosibirskiye Islands, and on the hydrology and biology of the Kara and Laptev seas. Only in 1930–1950 was it proved for certain that the mysterious Sannikov's Land, so attractive to von Toll, does not exist today. But the issue of its existence in the past still remains open.

FEDOR ROMANENKO

See also **Kolchak, Alexander; Toll, Baron Edward von**

Further Reading

Chaykovsky, Yu.V., "Pochemu pogib Eduard Toll?" [Why was Edward Toll lost?]. *Voprosy istorii estestvoznaniya i tekhniki* [Problems of natural science and technical history], 1(1991): 3–14

"Russkaya polyarnaya expeditsiya na yakhte 'Zarya' pod nachal'stvom E.V. Tollya (1900–1903)" [Russian Polar Expedition on the Yacht "Zarya" headed by E.V. Toll (1900–1903)]. In *Istoriya otkrytiya i osvoeniya Severnogo Morskogo Puti* [History of Discovery and Development of the Northern Sea Route], Chapter 14, edited by Ya.Ya. Gakkel' & M.B. Chernenko, Volume II, Leningrad, 1962

Shparo, D.I. & A.V. Shumilov, *Tri zagadki Arktiki* [Three mysteries of the Arctic], Moscow, 1982

Toll, E.V., *Die Russische Polarfahrt der "Sarja" 1900–1902. Aus den hinterlassenen Tagebuchern*, Berlin, 1909

———, *Plavanie na yakhte "Zarya"* [Yacht "Zarya" Navigation], Moscow, 1959

Vittenburg, P.V., *Zhizn' i nauchnaya deyatel'nost' E.V. Tollya* [The life and scientific activities of E.V. Toll], Moscow, 1960

RYTKHEU, YURI

Yuri Sergeevich Rytkheu is the first and the most famous Chukchi writer. His books were first written in the Chukchi language and translated into Russian by A. Smolian; however, since the 1958 publication of the book *Vremia taianiia snegov* [When the Snow Melts], Rytkheu began to write in Russian. If he was sometimes reproached for relinquishing his native language, which is today endangered, Rytkheu decided to write in Russian in order to be accessible to a wider public. Rytkheu expressed his intentions in his collection of short stories *Chukotskaia Saga* (Chukchi Saga, 1957): "I write for you, my nativeland of Chukotka, but if my voice happens to be not too weak, I will tell about you to the big reader of all Soviet land..." (Rytkheu, 1957: 125, author's translation).

Rytkheu can be presented as a kind of symbol of Soviet achievement. Born to a family of hunters and heir to a rich oral tradition, he became the first Chukchi writer, thanks to the policy of developing of alphabets for native languages. Indeed, his first books brought only the positive aspects of the Revolution and the Sovietization to the fore.

Rytkheu's oeuvre can be divided into three epochs or trends. First, he depicted Soviet implantation. Pre-Soviet Chukchi way of life is presented without nostalgia. On the contrary, considering that according to the prevailing Soviet ideology the past had to be overcome, Rytkheu aimed at showing—sometimes through an approach that seems naive for the contemporary reader informed of the reality of brutal Stalinism—how his people enthusiastically adapted to change. However, naive presentations of indigenes' fortunate life under Soviet government ran parallel to allusions to some major problems. With deft subtlety, Rytkheu managed to evoke cynical incomers traveling to Chukotka only to receive higher salaries, alcoholism, and Russian contempt for indigenes.

Second, the publication of *Samye krasivye korabli* [The nicest vessels] in 1967 ushered in a new moment in Rytkheu's work. At this juncture, he realized that he was losing his Chukchi identity and that he would never really belong to the dominant Russian culture. Further to this awareness, in his writings, Rytkheu turned his attention to the values brought by traditional life and culture and became interested in the individual and collective past.

Finally, in his later works, Rytkheu offered a critical point of view on Soviet life: what he presented before as progress (for instance, how residents in settlements gave up *iarangas*—the traditional nomadic Chukchi tent covered with reindeer skins) is considered here as another form of oppression. The true face of the "new life" is now shown through his unflinching lens: young Chukchis sent to boarding schools were separated from their families and their origins (*Unna*); at the time of collectivization, herders were forced to give their reindeers to the *kolkhoze* (collective farms) under the threat of being arrested or killed (*L'étrangère aux yeux bleus* [The foreign girl with blue eyes]); and indigenes unwillingly abandoned their Chukchi way of life to assimilate with the dominant Russian culture. Rytkheu demonstrates how the "dictatorship of the party" in everyday Soviet life, through its desire to shape people according to its ideology, can lead to the destruction of individuals' destiny. It is the fate, for instance, of the main character of the novel *Unna*. Here, the young Chukchi girl is forced to choose between her private life or her political career in the communist party and, having visibly made the wrong choice, she ends up being desperate, lonely, and alcoholic.

Rytkheu can be considered as a writer of cultural mutual confrontation between two worlds either in its positive or negative aspects, according to the moment he writes: confrontation of the indigenous people with the Soviet life or with American traders (e.g., in *Chukotskaia Saga, Unna, La Bible tchouktche* [The Chukchi Bible]) and confrontation of the isolated "white man" adopting the traditional Chukchi life (*Son v nachale tumana* [A dream at the outset of fog] and *L'étrangère aux yeux bleus*).

Rytkheu published more than 50 books, some of which have been translated into nearly 30 foreign languages. In Anadyr, a literature prize named after Yuri Rytkheu was founded in 1998, first awarded to the Russian local poet Andrei Gazha, and then to the Chukchi novelist Valentina Veqet, also from Uelen.

Biography

Yuri Rytkheu was born on March 8, 1930 in Uelen, a marine mammal hunting village located in the extreme northeast part of Chukotka, on the Bering Strait. His Chukchi name "Rytkheu" means "the unknown one." As the Chukchi did not use surnames, he borrowed "Yuri Sergeevich" from the name of a man who took part in a geological expedition where Rytkheu was working in the region of Providenia. Rytkheu's parents, his mother Tuar and stepfather Givea, worked for the *kolkhoze*. His father died when Rytkheu was very young. As a child, he spent a great deal of time in the *iaranga* of his uncle Kmolia, a sea mammal hunter, where his grandmother also lived.

In 1939, Rytkheu registered in the Uelen school, where he spent seven years and learned to speak Russian and develop a taste for reading. He lived for a year in the boarding school from 1945. The following year, he went to Leningrad for further studies. Rytkheu next went to Anadyr, the capital of Chukotka, where he spent two years in the Pedagogical Institute (*Anadyrskoe peduchilishche*). In the meantime, he started writing for the local newspaper *Sovetskaia Chukotka*, where he published his first verses in 1946.

After an extended trip, he arrived in Leningrad in November 1948, where he studied at the Faculty of Northern Peoples until 1954. There, he translated the works of Russian authors such as Alexander Pushkin, Leo Tolstoy, and Maksim Gor'kij into the Chukchi language.

Rytkheu published his first short stories in 1951–1952 in reviews such as *Molodaia Gvardiia, Ogonëk, Dal'nii Vostok,* and *Novyi Mir.* His first book, *Liudi nashego berega* [People of our coast], a collection of short stories, was published in 1953 when he was just 23. He became a member of the Union of USSR writers in 1954. In 1958, he published his first novel *Vremia taianiia snegov,* a work that has been considered autobiographical, and one that has made him famous in Russia and abroad. Rytkheu lives in Petersburg.

VIRGINIE VATÉ

See also **Chukchi; Literature, Russian**

Further Reading

Barker, Adele, "The Divided Self: Yuri Rytkheu and Contemporary Chukchi literature." In *Between Heaven and Hell: The Myth of Siberia in Russian Culture,* edited by Yuri Slezkine & Galya Diment, New York: Saint Martin's Press, 1993

Otke, O.P., E.F. Rozhkov & T.N. Lukina, *Pisateli Chukotki* [Writers of Chukotka], Anadyr, Russia: Anadyrskaia tipografiia, 1993

Rytkheu, Yuri, *Liudi nashego berega* [People of our coast], translated by A. Smolian, Moscow: Molodaia Gvardiia, 1953

———, *Chukotskaia Saga* [Chukchi Saga], translated by A. Smolian, Leningrad: Gosudartsvennoe Izdatel'stvo Detskoi Literatury, Ministerstva Prosveshcheniia RSFSR, 1957

———, *Vremia taianiia snegov* [When the snow melts], Leningrad: Sovetskii Pisatel', 1958

———, *Samye krasivye korabli* [The nicest vessels], Moscow: Sovetskaia Rossiia, 1968

———, *Son v nachale tumana* [A dream at the outset of fog], Moscow: Sovetskaia Rossiia, 1970

———, *Belye snega* [White snows], Moscow: Sovremennik, 1975

———, *Reborn To A Full Life,* Moscow: Novosti Press Agency Publishing, 1977

———, *Sovremennye legendy* [Contemporary legends], Moscow: Sovetskii Pisatel', 1980

———, *Puteshestvie v molodost' ili vremia krasnoi moroshki* [A trip in the youth or the moment of the red cloudberry], Moscow: Sovremennik, 1991

———, *Unna,* translated into French by Yves Gauthier, Paris: Actes Sud, 2000

———, *L'étrangère aux yeux bleus* [Skitaniia Annoj Odintsovoj, The foreign girl with blue eyes], translated into French by Yves Gauthier, Paris: Actes Sud, Paris, 2001

———, *La Bible tchouktche ou le dernier chaman d'Ouelen* [The Chukchi Bible or The last Shaman of Uelen], translated into French by Yves Gauthier, Paris: Actes Sud, 2003

Salzmann, Monique, *Iouri Rytkheou, traducteur de son peuple* [Yuri Rytkheu, translator of his people], thèse de 3ᵉ cycle, supervised by Léon Robel, Paris: Institut National des Langues Orientales (INALCO), 1981

S

SAAMI

The Saami are an indigenous population inhabiting a large geographic area in northern Fennoscandia and the Kola Peninsula.

Land and Resources

The Saami land area stretches from the east coast of the Kola Peninsula in Russia, through northern Finland, Norway, and Sweden, and down along the Norwegian coast and interior to Hedmark and the interior of Sweden to Dalarna in the south. To the Saami, this large area is known as *Sápmi*, and covers approximately 600,000 sq km (231,660 sq mi). Earlier in history, the Saami population inhabited an even larger area, especially in Sweden and Finland, but was most probably pushed back by the majority populations or assimilated into them. The nature of Sápmi contains a great variety and can be divided into four different zones: a coastal area that enjoys open water all year round, a mountain region, a treeless mountain plateau in the inland, and finally large boreal forests. The area is intersected by numerous rivers, streams, and lakes of varying sizes. The Saami have populated all these zones, adapting to the varying circumstances.

Sápmi contains a large wealth of natural resources, such as minerals, timber, and hydropower. The industrial exploitation of the area gained speed in the late 19th century, when mining and the timber industry became established in the area. During the second half of the 20th century, hydropower development expanded in Sápmi. The industrial exploitation of the area, in combination with the development of communications and the use of the land for tourism and recreation, has had a major impact on the living conditions of the Saami and not least on the reindeer herding traditionally practiced by the Saami. The ownership of the land in Sápmi is claimed by the states, a notion the Saami have challenged with increasing strength since World War II, demanding control over the management of the land they regard as theirs.

Population

The first mention of the Saami people is in Tacitus' *Germania* from AD 98, where people called the *Fenni* are described, who most likely were the ancestors of the Saami. The Saami were, until after World War II, officially called Lapps or Finns, the names given them by the neighboring peoples. These exonyms were considered pejorative and have successively been replaced with the ethnonym Saami. The origins of the Saami people have been debated for a long period. At the beginning of the 20th century the dominating theory was that the Saami were of Mongolian ancestry, and had migrated to the area from the northeast. Today, it is considered most likely that the Saami as a distinct ethnic group originated within Sápmi, and they were the dominating group within this area up until the Middle Ages.

The Saami population is small and unequally distributed between the four countries partitioning Sápmi. Because ethnic affiliation is not recorded in the censuses, there are no exact numbers for how large the group is. Generally, the total number of Saami is considered to be approximately 60,000–100,000 persons, and most estimates lie closer to the lower count, placing the Saami population in Norway at 40,000–45,000, in Sweden at 17,000–20,000, in Finland at 5000–6000, and in Russia at approximately 2000 (Eriksson 1997: 78). The Saami are a small minority in all four countries when looking at the situation from a national perspective, but still form a majority in six local municipalities: five in northern

Norway, and one in northern Finland. Despite their few numbers, the Saami are a heterogeneous group consisting of several distinct cultural areas, with different traditions and cultural expressions.

After World War II, the general trend has been a decreasing population in the northern parts of these countries, and the Saami have been a part of this development and have spread from Sápmi. Even though the area still is the Saami homeland, relatively large Saami populations are found outside Sápmi. For example, there are more Saami in the Swedish and Norwegian capitals of Stockholm and Oslo than in any comparable area.

Language

The Saami language belongs to the Finno-Ugric language group, and is most closely related to Finnish. The language consists of several dialects, generally separated into three dialect groups: the South Saami dialects South and Ume Saami; the Central Saami dialects Pite, Lule, and North Saami; and the East Saami dialects Inari, Skolt, Kildin, and Ter Saami. Within the different dialects, there are also regional variations. The differences among the dialects are great, and increase with distance. Only speakers of neighboring dialects can understand each other, whereas others are mutually unintelligible. These differences are so profound that many today speak of Saami languages rather than dialects.

During the 17th century, the first books in the Saami language were published, and the missionary activities in the effort to Christianize the Saami played an important role in the development of written Saami. A major problem for the different Saami dialects has been that the national borders cut through many of the dialect areas. One effect has been that separate orthographies for the same dialect have been created in different countries. However, standardized orthographies have been developed in the 20th century, and today there are orthographies for six of the Saami dialects. The Saami language is rich in expressions concerning people's relationship with nature and the animals, which displays the Saami adaptation to the natural environment. However, many aspects of and concepts in modern society have been lacking, and during the 20th century, Saami words for these were created.

There are no exact numbers on how many Saami speakers there are today, but it is clear that the percentage of the Saami population who speak Saami decreased rapidly during the 20th century. A fairly large number of the Saami population still understand Saami, but fewer can speak the language and fewer still read and write Saami. North Saami is the dialect that holds the strongest position, with a majority of the

Saami belonging to this dialect. The awareness of the threatened position of the language increased after World War II, and greater importance is now given to these questions. Saami is today used in literature, the Saami media, and radio and television, and this has had a positive effect on the health of the language. Because of legislation in Norway, Sweden, and Finland, it is today possible for a Saami to use his or her native language in contacts with authorities in some areas in the northern parts of these countries. The smaller Saami dialects do, however, face a precarious future.

Social Organization

Traditionally, the Saami society was organized in *siidas*, organizational units consisting of a number of families and in control of a specified territory. Sápmi was partitioned among a large number of siidas, each of which had its own separate area. The siida had the responsibility for community affairs and distributed the use of the territory among the families within the group. This social structure was based on a clear concept of division of the territory among different groups and within these groups. The siida system seems to have started evolving during the 9th century, and was still functioning in the 20th century in some areas. The siida system had a different structure in different Saami areas, but some basic similarities existed. The siida system was so firmly established that the Swedish courts acknowledged the right of the siidas to manage their own territories at least until the middle of the 18th century. The siidas were based on kinship relations, and the Saami kinship system was an extended system based on social affinity that stretched beyond biological relationships. In a sense, it was a system based more on social relationships than on kinship; it was a determinant of the social relations between individuals.

Economy

The specific and sometimes harsh climate of Sápmi forced the Saami to use a wide variety of resources for their subsistence, such as hunting, fishing, and reindeer herding. The resources available were used in an effective way. Later, agriculture also came to play an important role among different Saami groups. The reindeer has been an important element in the Saami economy, first through the hunting of wild reindeer, and later as a domesticated animal. The domestication of the reindeer by the Saami is an early historical phenomenon; in the first millennium CE, there were already signs of domesticated reindeer. However, these were few in number and were mainly used for transport and as decoys in the hunt. Reindeer herding as a developed

Saami herder, Kautokeino, N. Norway.
Copyright Bryan and Cherry Alexander Photography

monocultural economy is a relatively modern phenomenon, which developed in the 16th and 17th centuries.

Reindeer herding is the industry most predominantly associated with the Saami. The traditional image of something genuinely Saami most often includes reindeer. In Sweden, reindeer herding is open to Saami alone; even if Swedes in some instances are allowed to own reindeer, only Saami are allowed to be herders. The situation in Norway is similar to that in Sweden, but Norwegians are allowed to herd reindeer in southern Norway. In Finland, anyone living in what is termed "the reindeer herding area" in northern Finland is allowed to herd reindeer, and in Russia the Saami are one of several groups involved in reindeer herding. Today, less than 10% of the Saami are involved in the industry. Reindeer herding has also been, and in many ways still is, the focus of the Saami policies of Norway and Sweden, because this industry has been considered the most important aspect of Saami culture. Other forms of traditional Saami livelihood such as fishing have been overshadowed by reindeer herding, despite the fact that many Saami, above all the Sea Saami, have relied primarily on fishing for their subsistence.

Traditional Religion

The pre-Christian Saami religion was based on the relationship that the Saami had with nature. All aspects of nature were seen as living entities with a spirit, and humans had to interact with these entities. There were both gods and spirits in the Saami cosmology, but the latter were seen as more important because they could help and give advice to humans. The deceased ancestors also played a central role in the Saami religion, and it was important to honor them. There were different male and female aspects of the Saami religion, where the male was concerned with the economy and the weather, and the female focused on the home and the family. The Saami shaman, the *noaidi*, functioned as a mediator between the human society and the supernatural world. He used a shaman drum to reach a state of trance, where he could communicate with other worlds.

Systematic missionary activities aimed at Christianizing the Saami did not begin until modern times and varied in time among the different states. In Russia, the missionary zeal of the Orthodox Church commenced in the 16th century, the missionary activities of the Nordic Lutheran Churches began in Sweden and Finland in the 17th century, and in Norway it began in the 18th century. Despite this late process of Christianization, Christian worldviews had begun to affect the Saami religion at an early stage through trade and other forms of contacts. The process of Christianization was completed in the 18th century, even though some forms of private practice of certain aspects of the traditional religion continued into the 20th century.

Culture

Many aspects of traditional Saami culture have survived, even though they developed and were given partly new meanings during the last century. Today, they are important ethnic markers signaling a Saami identity. The *yoik* can be described as a form of Saami literature and music in combination, a musical poetry with a long tradition in Saami culture. In a sense, yoik is an art of remembrance, where a place, a person, or an animal can be remembered or even in a sense recreated by the performer. The yoik tradition exists in all of Sápmi, even though it was suppressed after the Christianization of the Saami. After World War II, the yoik was revived and is today a popular form of cultural expression among the Saami population. Saami handicraft, or *duodji*, is also a distinct and important factor of Saami culture. Up until the beginning of the 20th century, the products of the duodji were utility goods, but the demand for these developed the handicraft tradition into an art form. The materials used are mostly from the surrounding environment and from the reindeer. The traditional Saami clothing is also a distinct feature of Saami culture. Today, these clothes are mostly used on certain more festive occasions. Only in the northern parts of Sápmi are they worn as everyday clothing. A common feature of the yoik, the *duodji*, and the Saami clothing is that they all have specific regional characteristics that distinguish them and clearly show from which Saami area they originate.

Political Organization

Contacts between the Saami and the neighboring peoples probably began in the form of trade. Slowly, these relationships changed as the surrounding societies gained in strength, and the Saami became more subordinate, but still relatively independent. When the states began to lay claims to the Saami area, this had more direct effects for the Saami who were forced to pay taxes, in some areas to more than one state. Despite this, the Saami could still retain some of their former independence, but when the borders between the four states partitioning Sápmi began to be fixed from the 18th century and onward, this changed. Several Saami groups had traditionally migrated in areas now partitioned by borders, a migration that has almost completely ceased due to the closing of several of these borders. Today, only reindeer-herding Saami in some areas of Norway and Sweden are allowed to cross the borders between these two states annually to use specified grazing lands in the neighboring country during limited periods of time. Apart from the Christianization, which was carried out with some force, the treatment of the Saami had generally been relatively positive in a comparative perspective. To a large extent, they had been left to themselves and had not been deeply touched by the state bureaucracies. From the 19th century onward this changed, and the Saami now felt the power of the authorities more and more in their everyday life. The state policies became aimed at assimilating the Saami, with the exception of the Swedish policy, which aimed at segregating the reindeer-herding Saami to preserve them.

The more direct influence of the state policies on the Saami made them slowly awaken and react to their situation. Being split among four different nation states also meant that the Saami had to approach different forms of state bureaucracies and were subject to four separate legal systems. The political mobilization along ethnic lines among the Saami began in earnest at the beginning of the 20th century, a development that took place separately in each nation, even though there were some contacts between the Saami movements in Norway and Sweden. However, more permanent Saami organizations were not established until after World War II. In Norway, the most important organizations have been the *National Union of Norwegian Reindeer Herding Saami* (Norske Reindriftssamers Landsforbund, NRL) founded in 1948, and the

National Union of Norwegian Saami (Norske Samers Riksförbund, NSR) founded in 1968. In 1979, NSR was split and those leaving the organization formed the *Saami National Union* (Samernes Landsförbund, SLF). In Sweden, the *National Union of Swedish Saami* (Svenska Samernas Riksförbund, SSR) was founded in 1950 and the *Swedish Saami National Union* (Landsförbundet Svenska Samer, LSS) was founded in 1980. In Finland, the *Saami Association* (Saami Liitto, SL) was founded in 1945. The first Russian Saami organization, the *Kola Saami Association*, was established in 1989. Organizations aiming at preserving Saami culture were established earlier by so-called friends of the Saami within the Nordic majority populations in cooperation with the Saami, organizations that later on have developed into genuinely Saami organizations.

The main demands of the Saami were to receive an equal treatment with the rest of the population, and that the Saami should have a say in matters concerning them. The development was slow, however, and real progress had not been made until the last few decades. During this period, the situation of the Saami was being strengthened, especially in the Nordic countries where they have achieved a form of cultural autonomy. To implement this, special institutions have been established: the Saami parliaments. Today, there are national Saami parliaments in all three Nordic countries, established in 1973 in Finland, in 1989 in Norway, and in 1993 in Sweden. However, these parliaments lack formal political powers. In Russia, there are ongoing but so far fruitless discussions concerning the establishment of a Saami parliament.

The Saami have also organized on a trans-national level. Saami contacts across the national borders have always been common, not least because the traditional Saami cultural areas cross these borders. During the first half of the 20th century, there were sporadic contacts between the Saami activists in Sweden and Norway, but nothing came of these. After World War II, the contacts among the Saami in the three Nordic countries intensified, and in 1956 this resulted in establishment of the *Nordic Saami Council*. In 1992, the Russian Saami joined the organization, and the name was changed to the *Saami Council*. The Saami have also been active in the international political scene. The Nordic Saami Council was one of the founding members of the World Council of Indigenous Peoples (WCIP) in 1975, and the Saami have been active in bringing the issues of indigenous peoples onto the agenda of the UN. Common national Saami symbols have also been created during the last few decades, such as a Saami flag, a Saami national day, and a Saami national anthem.

PATRIK LANTTO

See also **Finland; Lapland; Northern Uralic languages; Norway; Reindeer Pastoralism; Saami Council; Sweden**

Further Reading

Eriksson, Johan, *Partition and Redemption: A Machiavellian Analysis of Sami and Basque Patriotism*, Umeå: Department of Political Science, Umeå University, 1997

Karppi, Kristiina & Johan Eriksson (editors), *Conflict and Cooperation in the North*, Umeå: Kulturgräns norr, 2002

Pentikäinen, Juha (editor), *Sami Folkloristics*, Turku: NNF, 2000

Ruong, Israel, *Samerna i historien och nutiden* [The Saami in history and today], Stockholm: BonnierFakta, 1982

Rydving, Håkan, *The End of Drum-Time: Religious Change among the Lule Saami 1670s–1740s* (2nd revised edition), Uppsala: Uppsala University, 1995

Salvesen, Helge, "Sami Ædnan: Four States-One Nation? Nordic Minority Policy and the History of the Sami." In *Ethnicity and Nation Building in the Nordic World*, edited by Sven Tägil, London: Hurst & Company, 1995

Svanberg, Ingvar & Håkan Tunón (editors), *Samisk etnobiologi: Människor, djur och växter i norr* [Saami ethno-biology: man, animals and plants in the north], Nora: Nya Doxa, 2000

SAAMI COUNCIL

The Saami Council (*Sámirai* in Saami) is a pan-Saami institution that gathers the Saami from all four countries in which they reside: Norway, Sweden, Finland, and Russia.

The Saami Council was established in order to safeguard and promote the economic, social, cultural, and educational interests of the Saami. It also aims to strengthen the mutual understanding of the different groups of Saami, to provide information to others about the Saami, to promote the recognition of the Saami as a single people spread across four nation-states, and to defend Saami property rights.

Until 1992, the Saami Council was called the Nordic Saami Council. The Nordic Saami Council was founded at the second Nordic Saami Conference, held in Karasjok, Norway in 1956. At that time, the Nordic Saami Council was the world's first international Arctic indigenous organization. The quadrennial (previously sometimes triennial) Nordic Saami Conferences have continued to be the most important driving force both in Saami Council policy and in pan-Saami affairs. Among other important events that have occurred at the Nordic Saami Conferences are the proposal to establish the Nordic Saami Institute in 1971, the approbation of the (red, blue, green, and yellow) Saami flag in 1986, and the establishment of the Saami national day (February 6) in 1992.

The subject organizations of the Saami Council in Norway, Sweden, and Finland, appoint 20 delegates each to the Saami Conferences, while the Russian Saami appoint five delegates. The resulting 65 delegates subsequently elect 15 delegates to the Saami Council among themselves, five from Norway, four from Sweden, four from Finland, and two from Russia. The delegates from each country constitute their respective country sections, and elect their own country section head. The heads of the four country sections constitute the Saami Council's Working Committee. The Working Committee prepares cases for the Council and makes decisions on internal matters. In addition, the Saami Council has a Secretariat, which is currently located in Utsjoki in Finland. It has been suggested to move the Secretariat to one of the Nordic capitals. Such suggestions have met fierce resistance, and Tromsø in Norway and Kiruna in Sweden have been suggested as alternatives. The Secretariat is financed by the Nordic Council of Ministers.

In some limited respects, the Nordic Saami Council strove to function as a pan-Saami proto-government. The Russian Saami first achieved observer status in the Nordic Saami Council during Soviet perestroika, and then became full members in 1992, causing "Nordic" to be dropped from the name of the Council.

Among the Nordic Saami Council's original objectives were the publishing of extensive reports from conferences and meetings, the setting up of a joint Nordic body on reindeer herding, and the inclusion of Saami issues onto the agenda of the Nordic Council of Ministers. Originally, there were many non-Saami in the Nordic Saami Council, but from the late 1960s the Saami gradually took over the entire organization, resulting in its increased politicization. In this respect, the program written by Israel Ruong and adopted by the Nordic Saami Conference in Gällevare, Sweden, in 1971 marked a shift in the political orientation of the Council. In that program the following statement was included: "we are a people with its own area of habitation, its own language, and its own cultural and social structure." This formulation subsequently became one of the main ideological pillars of the Saami ethno-political movement.

As the national Saami organizations grew in strength during the 1970s and increasingly filled the national arenas, the Nordic Saami Council focused increasingly on specifically international issues. In 1975, the Nordic Saami Council became a member of the World Council of Indigenous Peoples. It has also had the status of Permanent Participant in the Arctic Council since it was established in 1996; consultative status in the United Nations Economic and Social Council and the International Labour Organization; and is recognized by and cooperates with the European Union.

In 1997, the Presidents of the Norwegian, Swedish, and Finnish Saami parliaments signed an agreement to establish a pan-Saami Parliamentary Assembly, with its headquarters in Kautokeino, Norway. Until then, the Saami Council had been functioning as the main channel for the interparliamentary cooperation. The status of the Saami parliaments as part of the respective nation-state apparatuses made it necessary to establish such an alternative institution for interparliamentary cooperation. If not, the gradual strengthening of the Saami parliaments and their cooperation through the Saami Council might have caused the Council to be considered a governmental organ, thus depriving it of its consultative status as an NGO in the United Nations Economic and Social Council. Thus, the Saami now have two universal pan-Saami organizations.

The Saami Council has a special committee on indigenous affairs and human rights, and another on culture. The latter, among other things, distributes Nordic funds for cultural purposes. Five of the committee members are proposed by various Saami cultural organizations, while two represent the Saami Council itself.

The Saami Council has, among other things, engaged itself in the issues surrounding the fishing rights of the coastal Saami, who lost out when quota restrictions were introduced in 1990.

INDRA OVERLAND

See also **Arctic Council; Indigenous Peoples' Organizations and Arctic Environmental Politics; Nordic Council of Ministers; Saami Parliaments**

Further Reading

Henriksen, John, "Strengthening Sami cross boundary institutions and relations." *Indigenous Affairs*, 3 (1998): 34–39
Minde, Henry, "The International Movement of Indigenous Peoples: an Historical Perspective." In *Becoming Visible: Indigenous Politics and Self-Government*, edited by Terje Brantenberg, Janne Hansen & Henry Minde, Tromsø: University of Tromsø

SAAMI PARLIAMENTS

A unique development in the creation of institutions of aboriginal self-determination has been the establishment of Saami assemblies—special representative institutions created by legislation and elected by the Saami themselves—in Finland (1973), Norway (1987), and Sweden (1992). The objective of these assemblies is to enable the Saami to present a collective view to the public authorities on issues that directly concern them. These Saami assemblies are popularly referred to as "Saami Parliaments."

The first Saami parliament was established by a Cabinet Decree signed by the President of Finland in November 1973. This assembly, officially named *Saamelaisvaltuuskunta* or Saami Delegation, had been a recommendation in a 1973 report published by the Finnish State Commission on Saami Affairs. This assembly was elected every four years by the Saami enumerated in a census. Under the provisions of the Cabinet Decree, the Saami Parliament served primarily as an advisory body to the Finnish state, overseeing the rights of the Saami population and making recommendations on a wide range of matters. The Saami Parliament soon began to take its own initiative on many issues by adopting resolutions that recommended new policies. Politically, the influence of the Saami Parliament came to be far greater than enunciated in the Cabinet decree, where legally, this institution only enjoyed the legal status of a committee. In 1995, Finland's *Eduskunta* enacted legislation to provide a statutory basis for the Saami Parliament (renaming it *Saamelaiskäräjät* or Saami assembly) and establishing revised criteria for registration. The President of Finland, Martti Ahtisaari, inaugurated the first Saami parliament established under this legislation in a ceremony held in Inari in the fall of 1995.

The first Saami assembly to be established under an act of Parliament took place in Norway, where in 1987 the Norwegian *Storting* enacted the *Saami Act*, establishing a Saami Assembly (*Samediggi* in Saami; *Sameting* in Norwegian): "to make it possible for the Saami people in Norway to safeguard and develop their language, culture, and way of life." Among the terms of reference outlined in this legislation is the all-encompassing provision: "The business of the Saami Assembly is any matter which in the view of the Assembly particularly affects the Saami people." This assembly had been a recommendation of a royal commission appointed by the Norwegian government.

The legislation provided for a Saami Electoral Register to include all persons who provide a declaration to the effect that they consider themselves to be Saami and who either: (a) have Saami as the language of the home; or (b) have, or have had, a parent or grandparent with Saami as the language spoken at home. Enrolment on the Saami electoral register is voluntary. Elections are held on same day as national elections for the Norwegian Parliament. The first Saami parliament was officially inaugurated in Karasjok in October 1989 by King Olav V after the national elections of that year. The King of Norway has inaugurated each new Saami assembly elected under this legislation.

In December 1992, Sweden's *Riksdag* approved legislation to establish a representative assembly (Swedish: *Sameting*) for its Saami minority—one of the main recommendations contained in the report of a government-appointed commission. A person of Saami origin is defined as one who can verify that he/she speaks or has spoken Saami at home or can verify that at least one of his/her grandparents has spoken

Saami at home, or has one grandparent who is, or has been, included on the voter's list for the Saami Assembly. The mandate of the Saami assembly is to initiate activities and propose actions to preserve Saami culture, on such matters as the distribution of state funding, the appointment of a Saami school board under the *Education Act*, Saami language development, community planning, and Saami living conditions. The first elected Saami Parliament was inaugurated by the King of Sweden at a ceremony in Kiruna in August 1993.

Political divisions within these Saami parliaments vary with each country. In Finland, representatives are elected individually with no declared political identification. A leading figure since its inception in 1973 has been Pekka Aikio. The Saami parliament in Norway is a hybrid of representatives from national political parties and from various Saami organizations. The Norwegian Saami Association (known popularly by its Saami initials, NSR) had majority representation in the first three Saami parliaments. However, many Saami in Norway have voted for representatives of national parties, most notably Labour and Centre party candidates. The 2001 election resulted in a close split between NSR and Labour with negotiations among smaller groups for a coalition.

The Saami parliament in Sweden consists of 31 members elected by proportional representation over a single nationwide constituency. All of the competing political groups are based on divisions within the Saami population. Proportional representation has led to the election of several small groups, often of just one or two members. This may be one reason why it has been difficult to devise coalitions that can develop effective long-range strategic policies. The Saami assembly in Sweden has had internal divisions within its leadership, hampering efforts at expanding the Saami position into some form of decision-making function. After the Saami assembly election of 1997, for example, the King of Sweden did not inaugurate the newly elected assembly. Questions have been raised as to the efficacy of this representative institution.

By establishing a Saami agenda on a wide range of issues, representatives of these assemblies have became increasingly adept at developing direct channels to decision-makers at both the national and local levels and at achieving a consensus dialogue between a state and its minority. While enjoying only consultative powers at first, these assemblies have sought to gain control of those issues having a definitive impact on the Saami people. These assemblies appoint or nominate Saami representatives to serve on various administrative bodies. Although most Saami inhabit the northern regions of each country, the legislation related to these Saami parliaments is not restricted to one region of a country, but rather espouses a national perspective to ensure that all Saami within the state can have a role in the decision-making process on matters related to their culture. The success of these Saami parliaments as effective representative bodies able to reflect the collective wishes of the Saami ultimately depends on the agenda that they are able to assert and the willingness of state authorities to engage in a constructive dialogue.

LENNARD SILLANPÄÄ

See also **Norwegian Saami Parliament**

Further Reading

Aikio, Pekka, "Experiences drawn from the Finnish Sami Parliament." In *Self-Determination and Indigenous Peoples*, IWGIA Document No. 58, 1987, pp. 91–102
Brantenberg, Odd Terje, "Norway: Constructing Indigenous Self-Government in a Nation-State." In *The Challenges of Northern Regions*, edited by P. Jull & S. Roberts, Darwin, Australia: Australian National University, Northern Australian Research Unit, 1991
Korsmo, Fae, "Claiming territory: the Saami assemblies as ethno-political institutions." *Polar Geography,* 20(3) (1996): 163–179
Sillanpää, Lennard, *Political and Administrative Responses to Sami Self-Determination*, Helsinki: Societas Scientiarum Fennica, Commentationes Scientiarum Socialium No. 48, 1994

SABINE, EDWARD

Edward Sabine was an early Arctic geophysicist and natural historian of the late 18th and 19th centuries. He was an Army officer but spent virtually all of his time on scientific work, both practical and analytical applications that led to considerable prominence within the scientific community.

Sabine commenced his work on astronomy, terrestrial magnetism, and ornithology, in 1816, guided by relatives and friends, notably Henry Browne F.R.S., his brother-in-law. The same year witnessed the start of his Arctic career. Sabine was appointed on the Royal Society's recommendation as a proper person to conduct the experiments on board one of the vessels, to a North West Passage expedition under Commander John Ross. This expedition is well known, particularly in terms of Ross's premature decision to return. However, Sabine achieved satisfying results from his studies including, among others, observations regarding "the variation and inclination of the magnetic needle, intensity of magnetic force, refraction, aurora borealis, and figure of the earth as determined by observation on the pendulum."

Sabine discovered a new gull that he sent to his brother, the naturalist Joseph Sabine, who described and named it after its original discoverer (as was customary), *Larus sabini.* On return from the North West Passage, Sabine himself wrote a paper published by the Linnean Society in 1819 describing 24 species of Greenland birds that he had been able to examine. That same year, he published a paper titled "An account of the Esquimaux, who inhabit the West Coast of Greenland." in the *Quarterly Journal of Science.* A description of the life of peoples encountered by the expedition, the volume of information that he was able to acquire indicates Sabine's diligent account. He observes that "amongst the various speculations which have been set forth of late, from which the probability of a N.W. passage has been inferred, it has surprised me that so little notice has been taken of the very remarkable fact, that the same people are found on the shores of Behring's Strait, and of those of Baffin's and Hudson's Bays" (Sabine, *Quarterly Journal of Science,* 1819).

Sabine publicly criticized Ross's account of the expedition. He noted that "observations which I was sent to make are therein published as having been made by others, and various information copied from my papers is given as his own, whilst I am principally introduced as having held an appointment (that of Naturalist) the duties of which I am represented as not having fulfilled, but which duties formed no part of my official engagement." A further reason for the discord originated in discrepancies between the two men's accounts; as Sabine claimed, in Ross's account of his actions in Lancaster Sound, "my name is twice introduced, and obviously for the purpose of supporting the propriety of his conduct in not prosecuting the examination of the Inlet."

Ross published a trenchant refutation in which he denied Sabine's right to the observations and implied that Sabine held an inflated idea of his position. Sabine was appointed to serve in a similar capacity on the 1819–1820 expedition commanded by Lieutenant Commander William Edward Parry. Sabine, who was regarded as among the most successful magnetic observers of his day, successfully conducted many experiments. While the expedition was wintering at Melville Island, the instruments were stored in a hut ashore. This work suffered a setback on February 24, 1820 when the hut burned to the ground. Sabine's servant, John Smith, saved the dipping needle at the cost of seven of his fingers. Sabine was also able to make collections, discovering a new grass, that botanist Robert Brown named *Pleuropogon sabinii.* His most noted activity was the edition of a weekly newspaper, the *North Georgia Gazette and Winter Chronicle,* intended for the amusement of the officers. Parry, who named a peninsula and a bay on Melville Island after Sabine, acknowledged the part he played in this successful expedition. The award of the Royal Society's Copley Medal recognized Sabine's scientific work.

Why Sabine did not take part in Parry's later expeditions is unclear. Most likely, he was more interested in scientific work and less in exploration. He did, however, take part in two further expeditions dispatched by the British government between 1821 and 1823. Commissioned at the request of the Royal Society, these involved a series of pendulum experiments at widely spaced localities to determine the relative and absolute acceleration of gravity, and hence the shape of the earth.

The first expedition occupied stations in the Atlantic and Caribbean, the second at Hammerfest and Trondheim (Norway), Spitsbergen (Norway), and on the east coast of Greenland. The team was instructed to ascend the Greenland coast to the northward, as far as might be compatible with a return to England in the same year. The station was established on one of the appropriately named Pendulum Islands. While Sabine recorded his observations, the vessel, HMS *Griper,* under Captain Clavering, came into contact with the most northerly community of Inuit on that coast.

The resulting publication—"An account of experiments to determine the figure of the earth, by means of the pendulum vibrating seconds in different latitudes..."—is considered Sabine's most famous work. In addition to details of the experiments that had given him "conclusive" results on the object of the expeditions, it also contained "geographical" and "atmospherical notices," which indicate that he used his time profitably between stations. In recognition of his accomplishments, he was awarded the Lalande Gold Medal of the Institute of France in 1826. Sabine also continued his work in natural history, for example, discovering two new West African birds, a spinetail and a puffback, both of which now bear his name.

In 1828, by this time a council member of the Royal Society, Sabine was appointed one of three scientific advisers to the Admiralty. That the appointments were confined to council members, and that Sabine was one, was criticized by Charles Babbage, a Lucasian Professor at Cambridge, in a work entitled "Reflections on the Decline of Science in England … ." Babbage printed a savage attack on Sabine's pendulum experiments, alleging that his observational techniques were faulty and his calculations were inaccurate.

Although Babbage's attack was libelous, Sabine did not take legal action. Instead, he published a dignified response: he stated that he *had* recomputed and republished his results on learning of the error, which was due to incorrect information from the manufacturer of the instrument, but concluded that the effects of the error were immaterial. Sabine noted difficulties caused by the lack of an assistant, and that Clavering had supplied him "with help from the ship's marines. However, after five had died he determined "to do the best I could alone, rather than obtain assistance at such fearful risk to others." Clearly, even scientific expeditions had their hazards.

After 1830, Sabine became prominent in the study of terrestrial magnetism. He was largely responsible for the first systematic magnetic survey of the British Isles. He was also influential in inducing the government to send an expedition to study the earth's magnetism in the Antarctic, the famous 1839–1843 expedition under Captain James Clark Ross. This was part of a worldwide research program under Sabine's supervision. Ross made clear the vital part played by Sabine and, indeed, the first sentence of the introduction to his account of the expedition drew attention to Sabine's call, at the May 1838 meeting of the British Association, for recognition of the importance of "that great practical branch of science called Terrestrial Magnetism." Ross recognized his indebtedness to Sabine by naming a mountain in Victoria Land after him.

Sabine was fortunate in that his wife was accomplished in science herself and was an excellent linguist. She actively assisted him in his work and translated a number of important texts, including Baron Ferdinand Petrovich von Wrangell's account of his expedition to Siberia and the Arctic Ocean in 1820–1823.

Biography

Edward Sabine was born on October 14, 1788 in Dublin, Ireland. He entered the Royal Military Academy, Woolwich in 1803, where he demonstrated a keen interest in mathematics and physics. He was commissioned into the Royal Artillery the same year. Sabine fulfilled garrison duty at home and in Gibraltar, 1803–1812. He was posted to the army in Canada in 1813. His transport surrendered to an American privateer after a 20-h action but was recaptured and he duly reached his destination. Sabine also participated in the Siege of Fort Erie, 1814, and was twice mentioned in dispatches. This was his only active service. In 1814–1816, Sabine was on garrison or staff duty. Returning home, he remained in the army but had very little regimental duty given that he was usually on expeditions, undertaking official and unofficial scientific work, or on general leave. Sabine advanced steadily through the ranks of the army as well as in the scientific establishment. He was elected F.R.S. in 1818, General Secretary of the British Association from 1839 to 1851 and 1853 to 1859, and was elected President in 1852. Sabine married Elizabeth Juliana Leeves in 1826. Sabine served as President of the Royal Society from 1861 to 1871, and was knighted in 1869. He earned the rank of General in 1870. Sabine retired from the army in 1877 after 74 years of service. He died on May 26, 1883.

IAN R. STONE

Further Reading

Levere, T.H., *Science and the Canadian Arctic: A century of Exploration 1818–1918,* Cambridge and New York: Cambridge University Press, 1993

Levere, T.H., "Edward Sabine, 1788–1883." In *Lobsticks and Stone Cairns; Human Landmarks in the Arctic,* edited by R. C. Davis, Calgary: University of Calgary Press, 1996

Ross, J., *An Explanation of Captain Sabine's Remarks on the Late Voyage of Discovery to Baffin's Bay,* London: J. Murray, 1819

Sabine, J., "An account of a new species of gull lately discovered on the west coast of Greenland." *Transactions of the Linnean Society of London,* 12 (1818): 520–523

———, *Remarks on the Account of the Late Voyage of Discovery to Baffin's Bay, Published by Captain J. Ross,* London: J. Booth, 1819

———, "A memoir of the birds of Greenland; with descriptions and notes on the species observed in the late voyage of discovery in Davis's straits and Baffin's Bay." *Transactions of the Linnean Society of London,* 12 (1819): 525–559

———, "An account of the Esquimaux, who inhabit the West Coast of Greenland, above the latitude 76 (degrees)." *Quarterly Journal of Science,* 8 (1819): 72–94

———, "Notices occasioned by the perusal of a late publication by Mr. Babbage." *Philosophical Magazine and Annals,* 8 (1830): 44–50

Stone, I.R., "Profile: Edward Sabine, polar scientist." *Polar Record,* 22 (1984): 305–309

Stone, I.R. and E. Tammiksaar, "Correspondence concerning the publication of Wrangell's *Narrative of an expedition to the polar sea, in the years 1820, 1821, 1822 & 1823." Polar Record,* 36 (2000): 155–156

SACHEUSE, JOHN

The Greenlandic Inuit Hans Zakaeus (Sakæus, Zaccheus, Sackhouse) was called Jack or John Sacheuse by the English explorer John Ross. In May 1816, Sacheuse concealed himself on board the whaling ship *Thomas and Ann* commanded by Captain Newton, offshore of Greenland. When the captain discovered the stowaway, Sacheuse earnestly entreated to be permitted to remain on board and travel to England. Ross wrote, "Sacheuse related many adventures and narrow escapes he had experienced in his canoe [kayak], in one of which he stated himself to have been carried to sea in a storm with five others, all of whom perished, and that he was miraculously saved by an English ship (Ross, 1819: xxxi)." Sacheuse had been converted to Christianity through the Danish missionaries in his native Greenland, and his religious desires provided the impetus for him to leave his home to see more of the Christian world.

Other sources indicate that Sacheuse was picked up at sea in his kayak, having been blown off the coast of Greenland in a storm (*Journal of a Voyage of Discovery, to the Arctic Regions . . .,* 1819). Sacheuse claimed a disappointing love affair as motives for his erratic behavior. He had quarrelled with the mother of his intended spouse and failed in obtaining the woman's consent to marry her daughter. The unhappy affair prompted Sacheuse to become a *qivittoq*—a person who withdraws from society to survive alone. Greenlandic people believed that the *qivittoq* often turned into unfriendly spirits upon death. Perhaps Sacheuse chose this path on the day he kayaked far offshore.

Newton took an interest in the young Greenlander and taught him to speak, read, and write English. Sacheuse returned to Greenland with the same ship in 1817, and, on his arrival at home, found that his only near relation had died in his absence. The loss of his kin prompted Sacheuse to stay on board the ship, returning to Leith in Scotland later that year.

Sacheuse completed a course in drawing during the winter of 1817–1818 with an artist, Mr. Nasmyth, who also introduced him to Sir James Hall. Sacheuse also met Sir John Ross during this time and told the explorer that he wanted to accompany the Ross Expedition north. Ross hired Sacheuse in 1818 as an interpreter and mentioned in his writings that Sacheuse "returned, like the rest of the crew, in perfect health, during the passage home; often repeating that, when he had got more instructions on religion, he would return to the 'wild people,' and endeavour to convert them to Christianity (Ross, 1819: xxxii)." By "wild people," Sacheuse presumably meant the Inughuit (the Polar Eskimos) or the "Arctic Highlanders" as Ross named them. Researchers believe that Sacheuse intended to return to Greenland where he had first received his religious conversion.

Seeking to further his education in order to teach Christianity to the Inughuit, Sacheuse returned again with Ross to England. He was sent to a school in Edinburgh, but during his stay at the school, he fell ill with typhoid fever and died shortly afterward in February 1819. About a hundred years passed before Christianity was brought to the Inughuit.

Other explorers, including Edward Parry (1819), documented travels with Sacheuse: "He is with us in the capacity of an interpreter, but does not confine himself to that alone, as he works with the rest of the seamen; and, from what I can learn, is not much inferior to any of them as a useful and willing man on every occasion. His excursions on the Thames, in his canoe [kayak], excited a good deal of noise."

Sacheuse's influence allowed John Ross in 1818 to return to Greenland with knowledge about the Inughuit, who, prior to Ross's August arrival, presumably existed in complete isolation. The two British ships, the *Isabella* and the *Alexander,* remained in the Cape York area for a few days, but Ross met Inughuit on five separate occasions.

The first contact took place on August 8, 1818. Ross thought the men he saw on the ice were shipwrecked whalers, but they were in actuality four natives on three dog sleds. Two days later, eight sleds approached from land out to the sea ice and stopped a few kilometers from the ships. Sacheuse, bearing no weapons, went out on the sea ice with gifts. He met four of the natives near the site where he had left the gifts, and separated from them by a large lead in the ice, spoke to them (despite differences in their dialect) to reassure them and explain that the ships were neither from the sun nor from the moon.

On August 13 and 14, Inughuit arrived at the flagpole where Sacheuse left his gifts and examined the contents without taking anything. Sacheuse was sent to invite them on board. Ross asked one of the Inughuit, Majaq, to bring some of the local iron to him. Majaq promised to get it but indicated it was far away, such that he would have to sleep at least twice before he would be back (i.e., two days and nights).

At the fifth meeting, on August 15, many men showed up on the ice in front of the ships. Because the Inughuit came without the meteoric iron that Ross had requested, they were not allowed on board. They became restless, and the British scared them away with a flourish of trumpets.

Biography

John Sacheuse was born in the Disko Bay area in West Greenland. Little is known of his early life. He was converted to Christianity by Danish missionaries while he was a young man, and in May 1816, hid as a stowaway on Captain Newton's whaling ship *Thomas and Ann*. In 1817–1818, Sacheuse met English explorer Sir John Ross and was hired as an interpreter on the Ross Expedition of that same year. He died of typhoid fever in Edinburgh, Scotland on February 14, 1819.

ROLF GILBERG

See also **Ross, Sir John**

Further Reading

"Account of the Expedition to Baffin's Bay, under Captain Ross and Lieutenant Perry. Drawn up from Captain Ross's account of the Voyage, and other sources of information." *Edinburgh Philosophical Journal*, 1(1819): 150–159

Gilberg, Rolf, "When the 'Moon Beings' visited The Only People in the World. The first ethnographical notes on the Inughuit, a North Greenland Inuit people." *Cultural and Social Research in Greenland 95/96. Grønlandsk kultur- og samfundsforskning. Essays in Honour of Robert Petersen*, red: Birgitte Jacobsen, Nuuk: Ilisimatusarfik/Atuakkiorfik, 1996, 332pp

Journal of a Voyage of Discovery, to the Arctic Regions, performed between the 4th of April and the 18th of November 1818, in His Majesty's Ships Alexander, Wm. Edw. Parry, Esq. Lieutenant and Commander, London: Richard Phillips Printer, 1819

Ross, John, *A Voyage of Discovery, Made Under Orders of the Admiralty, in His Majesty's Ships Isabella and Alexander, for the Purpose of Exploring Baffin's Bay, and Inquiring into the Probability of a North-West Passage,* London: John Murray, 1819

SACHS HARBOUR

Located on the southwestern shore of Banks Island, Sachs Harbour is the most northerly community in the new (post-Nunavut) Northwest Territories. Members of the Canadian Arctic Expedition of 1913–1918 who briefly anchored the expedition schooner *Mary Sachs* behind the sandspit in August 1914 first described the harbor. At that time, there were no people living year-round on the island, although archaeological sites along the coast dating to the Thule period demonstrated that the area was occupied some 500 years ago. The traditional name *Ikaahuk* ("where you go across") refers to both the movements of people from Victoria Island to Banks Island to hunt, and the later seasonal use of the island for fox trapping.

After the departure of the Canadian Arctic Expedition in 1917, the fox-trapping activity on Banks Island increased and people from the Mackenzie Delta and Victoria Island established several seasonal camps along the coasts. During a time known as "the Schooner Days," Sachs Harbour provided a place where schooners could be hauled up safely with the protection of the large sandspit at the mouth of the Sachs River.

Inuvialuit trappers first wintered at Sachs Harbour in 1932, and by the spring of 1941 seven families lived in the camp at the harbor. A Royal Canadian Mounted Police (RCMP) post was established in 1953. When a series of weather stations were planned for the Arctic islands in the late 1940s, the harbor was considered for the site of a joint US-Canadian station. However, the weather station was not completed as planned, and its construction was delayed until 1955.

The 1960s brought major changes to community life in Sachs Harbour. The last schooner trip to the harbor occurred in 1961. In 1966, under the Northwest Territories Wildlife Ordinance, the whole of Banks Island was registered as a group trapping area in which only members of the Sachs Harbour Hunters' and Trappers' Association earned the right to trap. A historic first meeting between representatives of the Sachs Harbour community and representatives of the federal government was held in Inuvik in 1966. Two years later, the first community school opened. In 1967, as part of a centennial project, a cairn incorporating several parts of the engines of the schooner *Mary Sachs* was constructed on the hillside above the town, commemorating the founding of Sachs Harbour.

By the early 1970s, the muskox population of Banks Island had increased dramatically, leading to the initiation of a quota system for hunting muskoxen in 1971. By 1981, the commercial hunting of muskoxen and the accompanying development of a local meat industry contributed to Sachs Harbour's economy. Although people no longer overwinter at the outcamps, the camps have been extensively used as part of the local trapping and hunting lifestyle. The current population numbers approximately 150, most of whom are Inuvialuit.

Sachs Harbour's economy is primarily based on hunting and trapping, although tourism is increasing in importance. The establishment of Aulavik National

Engine block from the Canadian Arctic Expedition ship *Mary Sachs* abandoned on Banks Island, Northwest Territories, in 1917. Photograph taken in June 1966.
Copyright David R. Gray

Park on northern Banks Island has been an important development for tourism. Local businesses include retail and food sales.

DAVID GRAY

See also **Banks Island; Inuvialuit Settlement Region**

Further Reading

Dunbar, Moira & Keith R. Greenaway, *Arctic Canada From the Air,* Ottawa: Defence Research Board, 1956

Grayhound Information Services, *Vuntut National Park: Resource Description and Analysis*, Ottawa: Parks Canada, 2000

Usher, Peter J., *The Bankslanders: Economy and Ecology of a Frontier Trapping Community,* Ottawa: Department of Indian Affairs and Northern Development, 1970

SAHTU LAND CLAIMS AGREEMENT

The Sahtu Dene and Métis Comprehensive Land Claim Agreement, also known as the Sahtu Treaty, was negotiated between the federal crown (Her Majesty in Right of Canada) and the Sahtu Tribal Council in 1993. The Sahtu Tribal Council represented Dene of Colville Lake, Deline (formerly known as Fort Franklin), Fort Good Hope and Fort Norman (today known as Tulit'a), and Métis of Fort Good Hope, Tulit'a, and Norman Wells.

The Sahtu Land Claim covers an area of 280,238 square kilometers, located to the west of Great Bear Lake, known to Dene as *Sahtu* (from *sah* or "bear," and *tu* or "lake"), for which the region is named. The claim area borders on the Gwich'in Final Agreement to the north on the Mackenzie River, the unceded territories of the DehCho Tribal Council to the south on the Mackenzie, and the Dogrib lands to the south and east, between Sahtu and Tucho ("big water" or better known as Great Slave Lake).

Under the Canadian constitution, the Canada Act of 1982, comprehensive land claims are considered to be treaties and are constitutionally protected. According to Section 35, "existing Aboriginal and Treaty rights of the Aboriginal peoples of Canada are hereby recognized and affirmed." The Sahtu Treaty therefore enjoys constitutional protection and cannot be altered without invoking a constitutional amendment.

The Sahtu region was the second region to settle a land claim based largely on the original comprehensive Dene/Métis Agreement in Principle. An agreement was negotiated in 1992. In July 1993, a ratification vote was held in each of the communities. After a ratification vote of 85% and approval by federal cabinet, the final agreement was signed in Tulit'a on September 6, 1993.

Approximately 2400 Sahtu Dene and Métis (who are also Canadian citizens) benefit from the agreement. The Sahtu Treaty provides for an enrollment process over an initial enrollment period of five years (cf. Article 4).

The financial value of the agreement was 75 million 1990 Canadian dollars to be paid over 15 years (cf. Article 8). The Dene and Métis costs of negotiating were borne by Dene and Métis, who are to pay $10,813,185.67 over 15 years, including interest. Dene and Métis were also entitled to a share of resource royalties on economic development in the area, in the amount of 7.5% of the first two million dollars and 1.5% of any additional royalties (Article 10). This latter clause represents a significant breakthrough in land claims negotiations; the federal government had refused for more than a decade to negotiate provisions of this sort.

Dene and Métis received titles to 39,624 square kilometers of land, but do not have rights to subsurface minerals or oil and gas for these settlement lands. In addition, they received a fee simple title that includes subsurface rights to 1813 square kilometers of land. As compared to other land claims, the Sahtu Treaty involved a larger proportion of surface title, implying a greater reliance on subsistence activities than on non-renewable resource activities in the regional economy.

Limited provisions respecting Aboriginal self-government were also included in the Sahtu Treaty. Negotiations may be held pursuant to the settlement of the agreement on a variety of areas respecting Aboriginal self-government. Similar to such provisions in other comprehensive land claims, Article 5 of the Sahtu Treaty contained a clause (5.1.6) that excludes it from the constitutional protections associated with the rest of the land claim.

The Treaty provided for the establishment of joint management boards or Dene and Métis participation on decision-making bodies in areas of renewable resources, environmental impact assessment and review, the land and water board, surface rights board, and land-use planning board.

In exchange for these benefits, Dene and Métis agreed to a series of provisions characterized by the federal government as "certainty" provisions and known more widely as the "extinguishments clause." The core clause (3.1.11) states that "the Sahtu Dene and Métis cede, release and surrender to Her Majesty in Right of Canada all their aboriginal claims, rights, titles and interests, if any, in and to lands and waters anywhere within Canada." An additional clause, 3.1.12, specifies surrender of rights to causes of action, which may have arisen due to nonfulfillment of obligations associated with Treaty 11.

The agreement was quite controversial between Sahtu Dene and Métis. One community, Colville Lake, asked for the possibility of separate ratification, on a community-by-community basis, but this request was rejected. Another specific group of Dene, the mountain

Dene of the Keele River area (Begade Shutagot'ine), presented the minister on arrival in Tulit'a for the final signing ceremony with a petition asking to be excluded from the Treaty. These were ignored. One of their elders, Gabe Etchinelle, narrator of a well-known National Film Board of Canada film called "The Last Mooseskin Boat," wryly noted in a 1997 conversation at traditional hunting grounds in the Mackenzie Mountains known as caribou flats that "any one of these mountains was worth more than seventy five million dollars," a sentiment widely echoed in the region. Begade Shutagot'ine leaders continue to assert with some justification that they have not surrendered their aboriginal title to traditional territories in the Sahtu region, an assertion that poignantly points to the continuing weaknesses of the current comprehensive land claims policies and processes.

Such views have made implementation of the Sahtu Treaty fraught with difficulties. Each of the communities maintains a degree of autonomy from the others and there have been divisions over, for example, where regional drug and alcohol land-based treatment centers (healing camps) should be situated, and whether financial benefits should be used in the form of cash payments to beneficiaries rather than longer-term investments. Nevertheless, a variety of initiatives by the Sahtu Land Board and other local management vehicles have provided strong support for cultural activities and mitigated against the frittering away of financial resources in cash payouts. Whether the Sahtu Treaty will serve as the basis for a renewed distinctively Dene and Métis presence on their traditional lands or as the latest expression of colonial assimilation remains to be determined.

PETER KULCHYSKI

See also **Dene; Gwich'in Comprehensive Land Claims Agreement; Land Claims; Sahtu Renewable Resources Board; Sahtu Settlement Area**

Further Reading

Abel, Kerry, *Drum Songs*, Montreal: McGill Queen's University Press, 1993

Blondin, George, *When the World was New*, Yellowknife: Outcrop, 1990

Dickerson, Mark O., *Whose North*, Vancouver: UBC Press, 1992

Fumoleau, Rene, *As Long As This Land Shall Last*, Toronto: McClelland and Stewart

Watkins, Mel (editor), *Dene Nation*, Toronto: University of Toronto Press, 1977

SAHTU RENEWABLE RESOURCES BOARD

The Sahtu Renewable Resources Board (SRRB) is a co-management board established in 1994, pursuant to section 13.8 of the Sahtu Dene and Métis Comprehensive Land Claim Agreement (SCLCA). The powers and responsibilities of the SRRB are detailed in Chapters 13, 14, and 15 of the SCLCA. The SRRB acts in the public interest to manage renewable resources in the Sahtu Settlement Area (SSA).

The Sahtu Settlement Area, covering approximately 280,238 square kilometers, is sparsely populated by about 3000 people located within the communities of Fort Good Hope, Tulita, Norman Wells, Deline, and Colville Lake. The Sahtu People still depend heavily on the renewable resources of the area such as caribou, moose, wolverine, and fish to maintain their lifestyle and their ties with the land.

The SRRB is the main instrument of wildlife and forestry management in the region. Its mandate is dedicated to protecting, conserving, and managing all renewable resources in the SSA. The Board creates policies and rules for harvesting wildlife and trees and gives advice and recommendations to the Minister responsible for wildlife and forestry.

The SRRB conducts research on renewable resources to make effective management decisions regarding the land and wildlife resources in the Sahtu Region. The Sahtu Settlement Harvest Study is the most important research project currently being conducted by the SRRB. This is a study of Sahtu Dene and Métis hunters, trappers, and fishers. The purpose of the study is to count the number of animals, fish, and birds harvested by the Sahtu People throughout a five-year period (1998–2003) in order to determine the number of animals required to feed all Sahtu households each year.

The SRRB is a regional public institution. The Governments of Canada and of the Northwest Territories jointly appoint three board members to the SRRB; three more board members are appointed by the Sahtu Secretariat Inc. The chairperson, the seventh member of the Board, is nominated unanimously by the six members of the Board and must be a resident of the SSA.

The Board meets about five times per year. Meeting locations rotate between the five communities. The SRRB staff (five to eight employees) provide support to the Board. The SRRB office is located in Tulita. The Government of Canada is the main funding source of the Board.

The SRRB works with two other forms of local renewable resources institutions. Each community has a Renewable Resources Council (RRC), which acts as a liaison organization between the SRRB and the local hunters and trappers. The five RRCs were created in 1994 pursuant to section 13.9 of the SCLCA. They are the local voices for renewable resource issues in the SSA. They promote local involvement in harvest studies, research, and wildlife management.

The Great Bear Lake Advisory Group (GBLAG) was established in 1994 pursuant to section 13.8.42 of the SCLCA. The Group represents the interests of the community of Deline. The GBLAG reports and provides advice to the SRRB regarding issues related to the health of the Great Bear Lake fish population.

ANDRÉ LÉGARÉ

See also **Sahtu Settlement Area**

Further Reading

Government of Canada, *Sahtu Dene and Métis Comprehensive Land Claim*
Agreement, Ottawa: Indian and Northern Affairs, 1994
———, Sahtu Dene and Métis Comprehensive Land Claim
Agreement: 1999–2000 Annual Report of the Implementation Committee, Ottawa: Indian and Northern Affairs, 2000

SAHTU SETTLEMENT AREA

The Sahtu Settlement Area (SSA) arose from the settlement of the Sahtu Dene and Métis Comprehensive Land Claim Agreement (SCLCA) in 1994. The Settlement Area is entirely located within the Subarctic zone of the Northwest Territories and covers an area of 280,238 sq km. The eastern part of the SSA encompasses the whole of the Great Bear Lake, the eighth largest lake in the world; the central part is dominated by a low-lying plain through which flows the Mackenzie River. To the west, along the border with the Yukon Territory, is the home of the Mackenzie alpine mountain range. The SSA is bordered by the Inuvialuit Settlement Area to the north, the Gwich'in Settlement Area to the northwest, the Yukon Territory to the southwest, the Nunavut Territory to the east, and the Deh cho Region and the North Slave Region to the south.

There are approximately 3000 people living in the SSA, most of whom are Sahtu People (2400). Most of the Sahtu People are Dene Indians (2100), although some are Métis (300). They live in five communities: Fort Good Hope, Tulita, Norman Wells, Deline, and Colville Lake. The SSA also constitute three administrative districts that reflect the three traditional cultural Dene subgroups in the region: the Mountain People, Tulita District; and the Hare People, K'ahsho Got'ine District; and the Bear People, Deline District. They all came together during the fur trade to form a distinct group: "Sahtu Dene," which means "the People of the Bear Lake."

The economy of the SSA includes the "traditional economy" based on the harvesting of plants and animals (caribou, fish, birds) and the "wage economy" based on full-time employment. The "wage economy" is dominated by government, Sahtu land claim-related employment and the oil and gas industry (Norman Wells).

Location of the Sahtu Settlement Area and main towns.

The Comprehensive Land Claim Process

The Comprehensive Land Claim Process is aimed at achieving negotiated settlements between the Government of Canada and Aboriginal Peoples in Canada, which clarify rights regarding land and resources. In Canada, Aboriginal land rights are rooted in Aboriginal title. This title is recognized in the historical British document known as *The Royal Proclamation of 1763.* According to British law, Aboriginal title arises from long and continuous use and occupancy of land by Aboriginal peoples prior to the arrival of European colonial powers in North America.

An Aboriginal group who negotiates through the Comprehensive Land Claim Process will obtain control and ownership of some lands and resources over a specific geographical area known as a "Settlement Area." In exchange, the claimant group will surrender its Aboriginal title. In sum, the process brings certainty to ownership and use of land and resources in order to facilitate the development of nonrenewable resource initiatives (oil, gas, and mining).

The Sahtu Land Claim

The Sahtu Land Claim began as an integral part of the Dene/Métis Comprehensive Land Claim Process involving the whole western part of the Northwest Territories south of the Inuvialuit Settlement Area.

In 1921, representatives of the Dene Indians living in the Mackenzie Valley signed the Canadian Government Treaty 11. In 1974, the Dene Nation brought the Canadian Government to court (*Paulette Case*). The Dene claimed that Treaty 11 did not represent a surrender of Aboriginal title and that Canada had not fulfilled the provisions of the Treaty. In 1976, Canada agreed to negotiate a Comprehensive Land Claim Agreement with the Dene Nation and Métis Association of the Northwest Territories. Negotiations began in 1981 and led to the initialing of a Dene/Métis final agreement in April 1990.

However, in July 1990 a majority of the delegates at the Dene/Métis Annual General Assembly rejected the initialed Dene/Métis Final Land Claim Agreement. The delegates felt that they should not have to surrender their Aboriginal title in exchange for the rights defined in the agreement. The Sahtu Dene/Métis opposed this position and requested (August 1990) that the Canadian government negotiate a regional land claim for the Sahtu Dene/Métis.

For the Sahtu, oil and gas development were of immediate concern in their region. Without a land claim, they had little control over oil development (Norman Wells) and could not benefit from it. In October 1991, Ottawa accepted the proposal from the Sahtu Tribal Council (STC). The STC comprised all Dene Chiefs and Métis local presidents representing the interest of the Sahtu Dene/Métis. Negotiations started, based on the provisions of the defunct Dene/Métis Land Claim Agreement, between representatives from the Government of Canada and representatives of the STC.

Negotiations between all parties went smoothly and on September 6, 1993, negotiators signed the SCLCA. The agreement was largely similar to the Gwich'in Comprehensive Land Claim Agreement, which had been signed the previous year. On June 3, 1994, the SCLCA came into effect. On the same day, the Sahtu Secretariat Inc. (SSI) succeeded the Sahtu Tribal Council as the Dene/Métis Institution responsible for implementing the Agreement.

The agreement provides certainty of land ownership and resources in the SSA. It gives the SSI ownership of 41,437 sq km of land (approximately 12% of the SSA), which includes 1813 sq km where the SSI owns mineral rights (subsurface/surface). The remaining land is mostly owned by the Government of Canada. In addition, SSI also received a financial compensation of 75 million Canadian dollars as well as annual royalties from resource development in the region, including a share in Norman Wells oil and gas royalties, (7.5% of the first 2 million Canadian dollars and 1.5% of any additional royalties). Finally, SSI has guaranteed participation in the management of renewable resources, land, and water throughout the SSA through the establishment of co-management Boards (see Table 1). Comanagement Boards are funded by the Canadian government, they have advisory power to the Minister responsible for land, water, and resources, and act in the public interest to manage land, water, and renewable resources within the SSA. Board members are equally composed of SSI and government representatives. In exchange for obtaining these defined rights, protected through the Canadian Constitution (*Section 35*), the Sahtu Dene/Métis have agreed to surrender their Aboriginal title over all of the lands in Canada.

Conclusion

The SCLCA has improved the general economic conditions of the Sahtu Dene/Métis. The SSI has used its money to stimulate regional economic growth and it is now involved in numerous activities (construction, trucking, oil drilling, and tourism), where Sahtu people find employment. However, the SCLCA did not meet all the needs of the Sahtu People.

First, the Government of Canada is often reluctant to properly fund the comanagement boards. Indeed, nothing in the SCLCA forces the government to provide for a determined amount of money, and funding is subject to yearly negotiations between all the parties (SSI, Government of Canada, Government of the Northwest Territories).

Second, the SCLCA has created numerous administrative structures in five communities throughout the three districts. This creates a very cumbersome process for any decisions regarding land development.

Third, the agreement does not address the issue of Sahtu self-government or the need to train Dene/Métis People so that they may access wage-economy employment. When the SCLCA was signed, the Government of Canada had no policy with regard to Aboriginal self-government and so the issue was post-

TABLE 1. Boards established under the SCLCA

Objectives of the Co-Management Boards	
Sahtu Land Use Planning Board	Responsible for developing and implementing the Sahtu Land Use Plan
Sahtu Renewable Resources Board	Responsible for the management of wildlife, fish, and forest
Sahtu Land and Water Board	Responsible for the management of land and water and the deposit of waste into water

Source: **Government of Canada, SCLCA (1994).**

poned to a later date. In 1995, Ottawa put forward its Aboriginal Inherent Right of Self-government Policy. In October 1998, the Government of Canada started negotiating self-government in the Sahtu Region based on a community approach. Thus, each of the five communities will eventually have self-government arrangements. Currently, only Deline has started negotiations. Residents of Deline are looking for decision-making powers in the areas of health, education, language, housing, social assistance, and justice.

ANDRÉ LÉGARÉ

See also **Dene; Norman Wells; Sahtu Land Claims Agreement**

Further Reading

Government of Canada, *Sahtu Dene and Métis Comprehensive Land Claim*
Agreement, Ottawa: Indian and Northern Affairs, 1994
———, *Sahtu Dene and Métis Comprehensive Land Claim Agreement: 1999–2000 Annual Report of the Implementation Committee*
Ottawa: Indian and Northern Affairs, 2000

SAKHA REPUBLIC (YAKUTIA)

The Republic of Sakha, previously known as Autonomous Yakutia, is situated in the northeast of Siberia, and is bordered by the Laptev Sea and the East Siberian Sea of the Arctic Ocean to the north. The interior covers the basins of five great rivers, the Olenyok, the Lena, the Yana, the Indigirka, and the Kolyma.

The Republic of Sakha stretches for about 2000 km from north to south and from west to east and has a total area of 3,103,200 km^2 and is the largest republic within Russia, comprising about one-fifth of the Russian Federation. The Yakut form the vast majority of its indigenous population, although immigrant Russians make up about half the population, and there are also Evens, Evenki, Yukagirs, and Chukchi. The total population of the republic is 985, 9000 (1.01.01), of whom about two-thirds live in urban areas. The population density is one of the lowest in the world (about 0.3 inhabitants km^{-2}). Yakutsk is the capital; other cities are Mirny, Neryungri, Aldan, Lensk, and Olyokminsk. The Arctic Ocean port of Tiksi on the Lena provides a summer route for transportation of goods inland by river and the Kolyma Highway links Yakutsk to the eastern port of Magadan, but rail and road infrastructure is generally poor and long-distance cargo is by air.

Over 40% of the republic lies above the Arctic Circle, and permafrost is found over nearly 95% of the land surface. The climate is severe continental: temperatures may reach −60°C in winter, +40°C in summer (in Yakutsk, the average summer temperature in July changes from +5°C to +13°C), and the average annual precipitation is low (150–200 mm in central Yakutia, and 500–700 mm on the slopes of the Verkhoyansk Range of eastern Yakutia). The northern area is polar desert and tundra, which grades into taiga, dominated by larch. The republic plays an important role in the economy of the Russian Federation due to the mining of rich deposits of gold and diamonds, other minerals, and its huge potential for oil and gas.

Political History

Since the 1620s, Russian settlers had imposed the fur tribute or yasak on the nomadic indigenous peoples, and Yakutia was considered to be more or less incorporated as part of Russia. The Yakut Autonomous Soviet Socialist Republic (YASSR) was founded as a member of the Russian Federation (then the Russian Soviet Federated Socialist Republic) on April 27, 1922. The current name of Republic of Sakha (Yakutia) was adopted in 1990 after declaring sovereignty within the Russian Federation.

The period 1922–1937 was a time of struggle but also the beginning of spiritual and economic revival. The young leaders (M.K. Ammosov, P.A. Oyunski, and I.N. Barakhov) who had achieved nominal autonomous status for the republic following Lenin's national policy during formation of the Soviet Union, undertook to gain further sovereign rights and autonomous authority for the republic, and liberation of the native peoples of Yakutia from social, civil, and national oppression.

The Soviets of Yakutia (nine of which were held from 1922 to 1937), being the only government body, drew up the laws of the republic in addition to listening to reports on the development of just developing economics, industry, finance, agriculture, and transport of a social sphere; on the congresses, it decided the problems of public health services, redemption of consequences of a national oppression, and protection of civil and political rights. At all nine congresses of Soviets of the republic, a process toward acceptance of a fundamental law of the Constitution was made, and two congresses were dedicated to the statement of statehood of the republic (September 26–30, 1936, March 3–9, 1937). The first article of the Constitution of YASSR, adopted by the IX Extraordinary Congress of the Soviets of Yakutia, stated: "the Yakut Autonomous Soviet Socialist Republic is the socialistic state of workers and peasants."

During these years, M.K. Ammosov, P.A. Oyunski, I.N. Barakhov, and other representatives of Yakut intelligencia led activity directed at the strengthening of statehood of the republic. It is known that by the decree of the Central Committee Party in 1928, several of these leaders were discharged from the management of the republic; then, in 1937–1938 they were called enemies of the people, which was a severe blow to the formation of sovereignty of the republic.

From the second half of the 1930s, totalitarianism was exhibited in a tragic way. Although Stalin's Constitution of 1936 included V.I. Lenin's principles of the right to self-determination for the national republics in the USSR, under Stalin they were implemented in a distorted way: human rights, freedom of nations, ways of establishing socialism, and fundamentals of state authority were disturbed. The authority from top to bottom was subordinated to a diktat of the Communist party, totalitarian socialist mode, and personal will of the leader of the dictators. The construction of socialism in USSR was turned into a system of communist dictatorship.

In the end, the Soviets, according to the Constitution being the political fundamentals of the USSR, and in Lenin's opinion "a driving belt from the party to masses," were replaced by autocracy of the Communist party, the domination of one philosophy, and a personality cult. For the national republics included in the Union, the right to self-determination, foreseen by Lenin, were limited by Stalin's Constitution and the constitution made it impossible for the autonomous republics to secede from the union.

The totalitarian political mode in USSR, although the personality cult of Stalin had been sharply criticized, continued to exist, and became stronger under other general secretaries (N.S. Khrushyov, L.I. Brezhnev). Thus, the Sakha republic actually lost sovereign territorial and thus economic rights. The republic's mineral riches became the property of central allied departments, and only 4% of industrial firms were in management of the republic. The territorial integrity and borders of the republic, approved in 1924 by an all-Yakut congress of Soviets, in the Constitution of the YASSR, were being disturbed. In the 1950s, the central authorities, having carved out from Yakutia the richest gold fields, split off Magadan Oblast' with a half million population, thus depriving the republic of an exit to eastern warm seas. The Regional Committee party and the Supreme Soviet of the republic agreed on this confirmation without any resistance; the people were not even asked. During many years, the regional committee of party of the republic conducted a policy of silent conciliation to violation of the sovereign rights of the Supreme Soviet of the republic.

In 1980–1990s, when the process of reconstruction began in the USSR under M.S. Gorbachev, the totalitarian mode failed and the ideological diktat stopped. When the autocracy of the communist party finished and the unitary Soviet state of the republic Sakha (Yakutia) was broken down, the republic elected to follow the path of a democratic state.

The Declaration on State Sovereignty of the Republic of Sakha (Yakutia) was adopted on September 27, 1990. It proclaimed the republic a sovereign state according to the principle of self-determination on the basis of free will of its citizens (article 1 of the Declaration). The people consisting of the citizens of republic (of all ethnic groups) were considered to be the bearers of sovereignty. The republic's right to direct implementation of a state authority was also consolidated.

Practically all provisions of a declaration subsequently are controlled by the laws. In particular, the Law of Yakut—Sakha SSR "About the state status of Yakut—Sakha Soviet Socialist Republic" on February 26, 1991 officially fixed the new status of the republic. A further stage in strengthening of statehood of the republic was the acceptance on April 4, 1992 of the Constitution of the Sakha Republic (Yakutia), which came into force on April 27, 1992. The Constitution proclaimed the republic a sovereign, democratic, and lawful state, founded on the right of the people to self-determination (article 1).

According to the Constitution, the people, being the source of authority and directly executing the authority, nevertheless form definite bodies for implementation of a state authority. The Constitution precisely determines the principles of implementation of the authority by these bodies: firstly, they are the competent representatives of the people and express their will. Secondly, the state authority implements come into effect according to a principle of separation of the legislative, executive, and judicial authorities. In accordance with this principle, the bodies of state power operate independently from the people. In this case, a danger that bodies of state power will be out of touch with the people is observed.

State authority in the Sakha Republic (Yakutia) according to the Constitution is executed by State Assembly of the parliament of the republic, the President and government of the republic, and Constitutional and Supreme Courts of the republic. The election in spring of 1990 to the Supreme Soviet of the 12th convocation commenced in establishing this system of the supreme bodies of a state authority. It was the first election in the history of the republic conducted on an alternate basis.

The Supreme Soviet of the 12th convocation operated till October 1993. About two hundred laws were accepted during that period, which became the legal fundamentals for implementation of the first steps on strengthening of the status of the republic, for the transition to a market economy, and for updating and creation of new state-legal institutions. So, according to the law of the Sakha Soviet Socialist Republic on

Location of Sakha Republic (Yakutia) and main cities and rivers.

October 16, 1991, the position of the President of the Sakha Republic (Yakutia) was established. During elections on December 20, 1991, the first president of the Sakha Republic (Yakutia), M.E. Nikolaev, was elected. Nikolaev, a Yakut, was also a member of the Executive Committee of the Northern Forum. Since January 2002, the president Vyacheslav Shtyrov is a head of the Republic, and also took a position in the Northern Forum. In connection with changes in the Constitution, the Government of the Sakha Republic (Yakutia) became a supreme executive body.

The coordination of activity of the Administration of the President, the control behind the implementation of the rights of the citizens, is executed by the vice-president of the Sakha Republic (Yakutia). The ministries are the central organs of the government. As a result of retrofit of a state authority in a republic, the new state body was allotted by imperious authorities, namely a Constitutional Court. By 1993, the system of

the supreme bodies of a state authority in republic was basically formed. But after the publication of Decree 1400 of the President of the Russian Federation and in connection with events that occurred in the Russian Federation, the management of the republic came to the conclusion that the system of the Soviet representative bodies had become obsolete, that it did not respond the modern requirements of the population, and consequently should be reformed. According to article 1 of the Order of the Supreme Body of the Sakha Republic (Yakutia) from October 12, 1993 "About reforming bodies (organs) of the representative authority in Sakha Republic (Yakutia)," Supreme Soviets of the republic was ceased.

Immediately after the termination of the Soviets, the formation of a new parliament began. A two-chamber parliament, the Lower House, which represents the interests of the population of the republic, and Upper, which is concerned with issues of the regions of the republic, were formed. Since 2003, the State Assembly became a single body having one chamber.

District and the city assemblies are obliged to abide by the laws of the republic and have the power to initiate legislation. They receive the statutory acts relating their competence. The district and city assemblies nevertheless are not subordinated directly to State Assembly (Il Tumen), and urban (except Yakutsk, Neruongry and Mirny), village, and small-village assemblies are the institutions of local administration.

In March 31, 1992 the Federation Treaty was signed by 18 of the 20 autonomous republics—a document guaranteeing the integrity of the Russian state, and an agreement on relationships between governments of Russian Federation and Sakha Republic (Yakutia) on economic problems was concluded. The republic achieved an admission of economic rights and authorities. According to the agreement on demarcation of state ownership between Russia and Yakutia, the republic gained control of 95% of all state-owned property built and located in its territory. On the basis of this agreement, the republic and state share ownership of the gold and diamonds procured in Yakutia. Together with the federal Government, the joint-stock company Almazy Rossi-Sakha (Diamonds of Russia and Sakha, ALROSA) was formed, and profits are shared between the Sakha Republic and Russian Federation and other local organizations.

The largest contribution to the development of constitutional and contractual relations between the Russian Federation and Sakha Republic (Yakutia) was the signing of the treaty about demarcation of the terms of reference and authorities between bodies of state power of the Russian Federation and bodies of state power of Sakha Republic (Yakutia) on June 29, 1995. In separate subjects of joint management, 15 Agreements between the government of the Russian Federation and the government of Sakha Republic were concluded. The agreements encompass all major aspects of economical and political life of the Sakha Republic. The concrete legal basis for broad cooperation of bodies of state power of Russia and Yakutia has been built. On September 26, 2002, an agreement on differentiation of powers between federal body and bodies of powers of the Sakha Republic (Yakutia) was reconcluded. Courts of the Republic, except the Constitutional one, directly submit to Federal bodies.

The process of national revival of all peoples inhabiting the Republic began. A law about languages supplied conditions for free development of languages of the indigenous peoples not to the detriment of Russian. National revival recognized not only form but also contents of culture. Spiritual heritage is being revived. There is a large body on research on the conventional world outlook and philosophy of the peoples of Yakutia. Customs and traditions that had been forgotten are now being revived. The state guarantees a liberty of conscience. The state financially supports the development of literature and art. Complete freedom for public cultural and educational organizations, national associations, communities, and national groups is ensured. The *ysyakh* (a Yakut summer festival) became a public holiday.

Today, there are complex processes in Russia, bound up with reduction of the republican constitutions pursuant to the federal constitution. As is well known, the Constitutional Court of the Russian Federation on June 27, 2000 ruled that the declaration of state sovereignty of the republics within the Russian Federation was nonconstitutional, and that their status as subjects of international law, and their proprietorship of natural resources within their own territories were illegal. The articles of the Constitution of Sakha Republic are still being discussed in the State Assembly. Actually, the Declaration of sovereignty did not attempt to usurp the political unity, territorial integrity, or spiritual solidity of Russia. The republic simply does not wish to be a raw material appendage of Russia. The joint ownership of natural resources in the territory of Sakha Republic (Yakutia) is a reasonable solution.

In Russia today, there are political forces calling for a return to unitary and even for liquidation of the national republics. When we speak about a federative state, we should not forget about its multinational nature. The so-called "sovereignty" was necessary for implementation of national self-expression. The experience in Yakutia demonstrates that the strengthening of federation in Russia should continue as a constitutional and agreed relationship between the executive branches of a central authority and the subjects of federation, and to not accede to efforts of those political forces of Russia which fight for cancellation of the bilateral agreements.

The president of the Russian Federation, Vladimir Putin, has spoken about strengthening of the vertical authority of the Russian Federation. He has described strengthening the legislative base, that is, creation of unified legal space, on the basis of which one economic space with the same common political and spiritual potential will be constructed.

Unconditionally, for the Sakha Republic (Yakutia), sovereignty is not a goal, wherefore there are problems of a global nature falling outside the regional limits, when many countries adjust their activity for the benefit and interest of transnational corporations. For the population of the republic to enter into the world community, it is necessary to resolve a twofold problem: material self-maintenance and ethnic self-preservation. Also, the future of Yakutia is connected with transnational corporations. The global issues of our time must be addressed by international cooperation. Such help from the world community has been felt by the people during a severe flood on the Lena River in the spring of 2001.

Despite advances in the field of environmental protection throughout the Arctic region, there are severe unsolved problems of the Russian Arctic as a whole, such as the problem of trans-boundary pollution. Practically all countries of the European quadrant of the Arctic region suffer from precipitation of airborne lead and acid particulates from industrial regions of Western Europe. In Arctic locales of northeast Asia, a declining trend in the auk population is observed. It is clear that transnational ecological problems of the Arctic cannot be solved without international cooperation. A well-timed scientific solution will create conditions for the transition to sustainable development not only in Yakutia but also in the Arctic region as a whole.

ANATOLY NOVIKOV

See also **Lena River; Yakuts; Yakutsk; Yukagir**

Further Reading

Balzer, M., "A State Within a State: The Sakha Republic (Yakutia)." In edited by S. Kotkin & D. Wolff, *Rediscovering Russia and Asia: Siberia and the Russian Far East*, London: Sharpe, 1991

Balzer, M. & U. Vinokurova, "Nationalism, interethnic relations and federalism: the case of the Sakha Republic (Yakutia)." *Europe-Asia Studies*, 48(1) (1996): 101–120

Borzhov, S.E., In "*Development Strategy of the Republic is Strong for Being on Demand*," edited by A.G. Novikov (scientific advisor and editor-in-chief), Yakutsk: Bichik, 2001 (in Russian)

Kempton, D.R., "The Republic of Sakha (Yakutia): the evolution of centre–periphery relations in the Russian Federation." *Europe-Asia Studies*, 48(4) (1996): 587–613

Nikolaev, M.E. "Period of historical revival and great prospects." Report of Mikhail Nikolaev, President of the Sakha Republic (Yakutia) during the solemn session devoted to the 10th anniversary of adoption of the Declaration on State sovereignty in September 27, 2000. Yakutsk, 2000

Okladnikov, A.P., In *Yakutia Before its Incorporation into the Russian State*, edited by Henry N. Michael, Montreal: McGill-Queen's University Press, 1970

Petrov, Y.D., "State Policy on Preserving the Small-Numbered Peoples of the North: New Methodological Approach." In *North: Problems and Prospects*, edited by P.L. Kazaryan, (editor-in-chief) Yakutsk, 2001, #1, pp. 23–26 (in Russian)

Tichotsky, J. *The Sakha Republic: Russian's Diamond Colony* Amsterdam: Harmood Academic Publishers, 2000

SAKHALIN ISLAND

Sakhalin is a large island (76,400 km^2) located in the Sea of Okhotsk and the Sea of Japan off the coast of southeastern Siberia in the Russian Far East. Sakhalin is long (948 km from the northernmost to the southernmost point) and quite narrow; its east-west dimensions vary from 30 km at its narrowest part to 160 km at its widest. Over two-thirds of the Sakhalin territory are covered with mountain ranges running along the south-north axis of the island. The highest point, Lopatin Mountain, rises 1609 m above sea level. The northern part of the island is predominantly a swampy plain.

More than 60,000 rivers and streams are found on Sakhalin Island. The two largest rivers are the Tym and the Poronai. The island has more than 16,000 lakes, the largest being Tunaicha and Nevskoye at approximately 170 km^2 each. Climate is moderate to monsoon in the south, where winter lasts from November to April, and colder in the north, where winter lasts from October to May. The average temperature in January is −6°C in the south and −24°C in the north. The average August temperature is +19°C in the South and +10°C in the North. Precipitation is 600–1200 mm a year.

The central and southern parts of the island are covered with taiga consisting mostly of conifers (spruce, fir, and pine) and birch. The Kuril bamboo constitutes much of the undergrowth, particularly in the south. Forest wildlife includes bear, wolverine, marten, sable, squirrel, and musk deer. Reindeer thrive in the northern part of the island, where taiga is gradually giving way to shrubs. Marine life in the seas around Sakhalin includes numerous species of sea mammals (seals, whales, and dolphins), fish (salmon, flounder, halibut, etc.), crab, shrimp, and clams.

As of January 1, 1999, the island population numbered 608,000, a decrease of 105,000 from 1990. Outmigration, high mortality, and low birth rates throughout the decade accounted for the decline. Sakhalin's population can be divided into two unequal ethnic groups: the indigenous peoples, and the relative newcomers who migrated to the island within the last 150 years. Indigenous groups include the Nivkh (Gilyak), who live mostly in rural communities throughout the island and account for 0.3% (about 2000) of its total population. The Ainu, an indigenous people who lived on the island when the first Japanese and Russian explorers arrived, are no longer present. Newcomers are mostly Russians (87.5% of the total population), Ukrainians (6.5%), Koreans (4.9%), Belarusians (1.6%), and Tatars

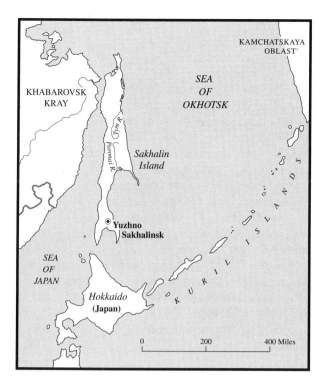

(1.5%). Between 1906 and 1945, when the southern portion of the island was under Japanese control, Sakhalin included a number of ethnic Japanese. However, they were relocated to Japan shortly after World War II. Approximately 87% of the population live in cities and towns. The largest city, Yuzhno-Sakhalinsk, has a population of 179,200.

The island of Sakhalin is a part of Sakhalin Province (Oblast'), an administrative unit within the Russian Federation. Apart from Sakhalin, the province includes the Kuril Islands. The governor of the province as well as the 27 deputies of the provincial legislature are elected by popular vote.

Japanese and Russian explorers visited Sakhalin in the late 18th and early 19th centuries. A Russian naval expedition claimed the island a Russian possession in 1806. The Japanese, however, disputed this claim. Extensive exploration of the island coastline and surrounding seas by the Russians continued for several decades, a process concluded in 1855 by the Russo-Japanese treaty, which recognized Russia's control over the island.

From its beginning in the mid-19th century, the Russian government led the development of Sakhalin, while private business played little or no role. In 1869, Russia established a penal colony on the island. Prisoners who finished their term were settled on the island after their release, thus contributing to the increase in population. In 1881, prisoners and internal exiles accounted for more than 16,000 out of a total population of 28,000. Coal mining, which started at the turn of the 20th century, attracted Korean and Chinese workers.

According to the Portsmouth Treaty of 1905, which ended the Russo-Japanese war, Russia ceded to Japan the southern part of Sakhalin (south of the 50th parallel). Japanese rule extended to the northern part of the island in 1920–1925 in response to the temporary power vacuum that followed the Russian civil war. The Japanese built the first railroad on the island and undertook considerable construction projects, particularly in Toyohara (currently Yuzhno-Sakhalinsk). In 1925, the Soviet government gave the Japanese companies concessions for oil drilling and coal mining in the northern part of Sakhalin (the concessions were revoked in 1944). Shortly after the Soviet Union entered the war against Japan in August 1945, the Soviet army ejected the Japanese forces from the southern part of the island, thus putting the whole of Sakhalin under Soviet administration. According to the San Francisco Treaty of 1951, Japan renounced all claims to the territories on the island of Sakhalin. Postwar development of the newly created Sakhalin province (Oblast') resulted in a rapid influx from the mainland Soviet Union. In 1945–1947, more than 200,000 people settled on Sakhalin Island.

Oilfields in the north and coal deposits in the central part of the island became major centers of industrial development. The fishing industry that was started by the Japanese expanded rapidly under Soviet rule when several fish-processing plants were built. Although the Sakhalin economy developed through the postwar period as a base for primary industries (oil, coal, timber, and fishing), it is currently suffering from depletion of many natural resources and difficulties of integration in the global market, many of which are endemic in the post-Soviet economy. Deteriorating quality of life in the years between 1990 and 1999 resulted in decreased life expectancies of men and women (58 and 70 years, respectively, in 1999, and 62 years for men and 72 years for women in 1990). Cross-border trade with Japan is facilitated by a ferry linking the port of Korsakov on the southern tip of Sakhalin and Wakkanai on the Japanese island of Hokkaido. Japanese companies continue to invest in exploration and drilling off the northern shore of Sakhalin.

ANDREW SAVCHENKO

See also **Ainu; Nivkhi; Okhotsk, Sea of**

Further Reading

Grant, Bruce, *In the Soviet House of Culture: A Century of Perestroikas,* Princeton: Princeton University Press, 1995
Sakhalin Oblast' Investment and Business Guide, USA: International Business Publications, 2000

Shternberg, Lev, *The Social Organization of the Gilyak*, New York: American Museum of Natural History, 1999

Vysokov, M.S., *A Brief History of Sakhalin and the Kurils*, Yuzhno-Sakhalinsk: Sakhalin Book Publishing House, 1996

———, *Sakhalin Region*, Yuzhno-Sakhalinsk: Sakhalin Book Publishing House, 1998

SALEKHARD

Salekhard (known before 1933 as Obdorsk) is the administrative center of the Yamal-Nenets Autonomous Okrug in western Siberia. The city was founded in 1595 as a Cossack fortress named Obdorsk, and is located on the bank of the Polui River, a tributary of the Ob' River, at the latitude of the Arctic Circle. Civil dwellers appeared in the settlement in 1635.

In 1731, the Russian empress Anna Ioannovna established by decree the Obdorsk emblem—a fox holding an arrow in its teeth. In 1930, Obdorsk became the center of the Yamal-Nenets Autonomous Okrug. In 1933, it was renamed as Salekhard, which in Nenets means "cape town." In 1938, the settlement obtained the status of a city. The population in Salekhard numbered 33,000 in 2003.

The climate is severe; winter lasts eight months and the mean air temperature in January varies from −22°C to −26°C. Summer is short and cool. The mean air temperatures in July are +4+14°C, although sometimes the temperature may reach +30°C. In mid-winter, daylight lasts only about four hours a day. Sharp seasonal and daily temperature fluctuations are typical for the area.

The historical part of Salekhard is near the riverboat station, originally the residence of a Khanty prince. Russian Cossacks destroyed it in the 1600s and built a small church. Archaeological sites such as the so-called Salekhard site of the Bronze Age (second half of the second millennium BC) have been excavated in Salekhard as well.

From the 18th century, the process of tribute levying (which occurred every year in January) gradually turned into the famous Obdorsk trade fair, which hosted merchants from Tobolsk, Omsk, Arkhangelsk, Irbit, and other Russian towns, mainly trading furs, mammoth tusks, and fish products. Obdorsk developed into an important trade center, and in 1897 residents numbered 500, with 30 houses, 150 shops, and a school for the children of the tundra people. By 1904, the town had 116 houses, a riverboat station, two churches, 19 shops, a prison of the Justice of the Peace, a post office, and residents of the Khanty and Nenets boards.

For a long time, architecture in Salekhard remained mostly wooden one- and two-story buildings, although exceptions included the stone Cathedral of Peter and Paul built on permafrost soils in 1894. The Obdorsk Christian mission managed the cathedral as well as the local orphanage. One hundred years later in the 1990s, centralized house building began. Today, five- and nine-story residences are being built in new districts, although additions to the historic old town include two- and three-story cottages.

Salekhard, along with Labytnangi (a settlement located 20 km to the west, across the Ob' River), is an important transport nodal point providing freight flow to the Arctic areas of Russia. Salekhard is home to a modern airport and landing strip and riverboat station; Labytnangi has a railway station. The oldest and largest enterprise of the city is the Salekhard fish cannery.

Salekhard hosts the main governmental bodies of the Yamal-Nenets Autonomous Okrug, the Okrug administration headed by the governor and the Yamal-Nenets Duma. Educational institutions in Salekhard include the Teachers' College, Veterinary College, and Medicinal and Trading Schools. Young people of the indigenous nationalities form a considerable part of the students. Several branches of higher education, including the Tyumen University branch, are located in the city.

OLGA BYKOVA

See also **Ob' River; Yamal-Nenets Autonomous Okrug**

Further Reading

Lappo, G.M. (editor), "Salekhard," entry in *Encyclopedia Goroda Rossii* [Encyclopedia: Towns of Russia], Moscow: Bolshaya rossiyskaya enciklopedia, 1994

Omel'chuk, A.K., *Salekhard*, Sverdlovsk: Sredne-Uralskoe, 1978 (in Russian)

SALINITY ANOMALIES

During the second half of the 20th century, three decadal-scale bursts of low-salinity, low-temperature water have been observed in the northern North Atlantic Ocean (Belkin et al., 1998). These waters feed into the global ocean circulation system. Since these events were better defined in the salinity field, they have become known as "salinity anomalies." The first well-documented salinity anomaly was recorded north of Iceland in 1968, when a vast volume of fresh, cold water and sea ice blocked Iceland's northern coast, causing a collapse of the important Icelandic fishery. This anomaly propagated around the Subarctic Gyre in the early 1970s, apparently being transported by the East Greenland Current, West Greenland Current, Baffin Current, Labrador Current, and the North Atlantic Current. By 1976, it had reached the Faroe-Shetland Channel, where its magnitude was found to exceed anything observed since the beginning of the 20th century. Deservingly, this anomaly was termed the "Great Salinity Anomaly" or GSA (Dickson et al., 1988). After passing through the Faroe-Shetland Channel, the 1970s GSA traversed the Norwegian Sea and entered the Barents Sea in 1978–1979. The 1970s GSA has also been noticed in the West Spitsbergen Current in 1979 and off northeast Greenland in 1981–1982, thus completing its journey around the Subarctic Gyre. The 1970s GSA was apparently boosted remotely, by a freshwater/sea ice pulse from the Arctic Ocean via Fram Strait, and consequently was accompanied by a large sea ice extent anomaly in the Greenland-Iceland Seas, propagated into the Labrador Sea.

On the contrary, the next GSA, of the 1980s, was likely formed locally, in the Labrador Sea-Baffin Bay area, largely because of the extremely severe winters of the early 1980s, with a possible contribution of the Arctic freshwater outflow via the Canadian Archipelago (likely facilitated by strong northerly winds), which would have enhanced stability and ice formation. The 1980s GSA has been tracked around the northern North Atlantic along the same route as the preceding GSA (Belkin et al., 1998). Like the 1970s GSA, the 1980s GSA was also associated with a positive sea ice extent anomaly in the Labrador Sea/Baffin Bay, which, however, unlike the GSA '1970s, had no upstream precursor in the Greenland Sea. Thus, the GSAs are not necessarily caused solely by an increased export of fresh water and sea ice from the Arctic Ocean via Fram Strait.

In the early 1990s, a new fresh, cold anomaly was formed in the Labrador Sea accompanied by a large positive sea ice extent anomaly. The harsh winters of the early 1990s that apparently caused the 1990s GSA were, however, confined to the Labrador Sea-Baffin Bay area, while the atmospheric and oceanic conditions in the Greenland, Iceland, and Irminger seas were normal. The Labrador Sea-Baffin Bay area therefore appears to play a key role in the formation of GSAs as well as in the propagation of the GSAs formed upstream. A likely contribution of the enhanced Canadian Archipelago freshwater outflow to the GSA formation also seems to be significant. Two major modes of the GSA origin are thus identified: *remote* (generated by an enhanced Arctic Ocean freshwater export via either Fram Strait or the Canadian Archipelago) and *local* (resulting from severe winters in the Labrador Sea-Baffin Bay area).

The magnitude of salinity anomalies decreases downstream as they interact with ambient water masses. Initially, the salinity anomaly magnitude is between 0.5 and 1.0 ppt as observed in the West Greenland Current over Fylla Bank. The corresponding temperature anomaly is between 0.5°C and 1.0°C. The most intense transformation of GSAs occurs where the Labrador Current meets the North Atlantic Current east of the Grand Banks of Newfoundland. Downstream from this confluence, the salinity anomaly magnitude drops down to 0.1–0.2 ppt

and remains approximately the same during the rest of its journey around the North Atlantic, through the Barents Sea (Belkin et al., 1998). Interesting enough, the temperature anomalies associated with the GSAs retain approximately the same magnitude, 0.5–1.0°C, all the way around the Subarctic Gyre.

The 1970s and 1980s GSAs extended vertically down to at least 500 m depth. Their horizontal dimensions have never been precisely determined since none of these GSAs has been mapped. With the planned advent of spaceborne sea surface salinity sensors under the Aquarius project (satellite launch expected in 2006–2008), such mapping would be possible.

The GSAs can influence deepwater formation in the northern North Atlantic. The upper layer freshening associated with the GSAs increases the upper layer stability, which inhibits deep vertical mixing by wintertime convection. The freshening-induced stability enhancement associated with the 1970s GSA led to the complete shutdown of wintertime convection in the Labrador Sea in the 1970s (Dickson et al., 1988) and has inhibited deep convection in the early 1980s (Belkin et al., 1998). The cessation of deep convection led to a gradual change in the Labrador Sea Water (LSW), which has become warmer and saltier. Both reinitiations of deep convection (1972 and 1985) resulted in dramatic decreases in the LSW temperature and salinity as the surface lid of fresh an cold water was convectively mixed into the LSW (Curry and McCartney, 2001).

The 1970s GSA has been shown to adversely affect the spawning success of many stocks of fish, whose breeding grounds were traversed by the anomaly, which also affected recruitment and was felt even in the semienclosed North Sea, where the entire ecosystem has changed abruptly following the anomaly's entrance [Belkin et al., 1998].

The 1970s GSA traveled from West Greenland to the Barents Sea for 9 years (1969–1978), whereas the 1980s GSA took just 6 years (1982–1988) to cover the same distance. Since the propagation speed of the GSAs could be used as a proxy of the circulation intensity, the Subarctic Gyre circulation was more vigorous in the 1980s compared with the 1970s.

IGOR BELKIN

See also **Freshwater Hydrology; North Atlantic Drift**

Further Reading

Belkin, I.M., S. Levitus, J.I. Antonov & S.A. Malmberg, "'Great salinity anomalies' in the North Atlantic." *Progress in Oceanography*, 41(1) (1998): 1–68

Curry, R.G. & M.S. McCartney, "Ocean gyre circulation changes associated with the North Atlantic Oscillation." *Journal of Physical Oceanography*, 31(12) (2001): 3374–3400

Cushing, D.H., "The Northerly Wind." In *Toward a Theory on Biological-Physical Interactions in the World Ocean*, edited by B.J. Rothschild, Dordrecht: Kluwer, 1988, pp. 235–244

Dickson, R.R., J. Meincke, S.A. Malmberg & A.J. Lee, "The 'Great Salinity Anomaly' in the northern North Atlantic, 1968–1982." *Progress in Oceanography*, 20(2) (1988): 103–151

SALMON

The common name *salmon* refers to several fish species within the Salmonidae family. The Salmonidae encompass three subfamilies with Arctic distributions: Coregoninae (whitefish, ciscoes), Thymallinae (grayling), and the Salmoninae (salmon, trout, and char). Within the Salmoninae, there are seven genera, although there is disagreement among taxonomists regarding the members of these subgroups. The genera *Salmo* (Atlantic salmon and trouts) and *Oncorhynchus* (Pacific salmon and trouts) include several species that are called salmon. Additionally, Arctic grayling (*Thymallus arcticus*) and Arctic char (*Salvelinus alpinus*) are often grouped with salmon because they share many traits.

Salmon are either exclusively freshwater or anadromous (spawning in fresh water but living much of their life in marine waters). They occur in the Northern Hemisphere, but because they are easily propagated in hatcheries, salmon are now also found in the cold, fresh waters of the Southern Hemisphere as well.

The Atlantic salmon *Salmo salar* spawns on both sides of the North Atlantic basin and migrates along the coasts of northern Canada, Greenland, Iceland, Europe, and the Kola Peninsula of Russia, into the Barents, Norwegian, North, and Greenland seas. They are called Atlantic salmon in English, CeMra in Russian, *kapisilik* in Greenlandic, *iqalukpik* in Inuktitut, (*iqaluk* in the North Baffin Island dialect), *laks* in Danish and Norwegian, *lax* in Icelandic, and *saumon* in French and French Canadian. The Saami people have a highly differentiated vocabulary for salmon, which reveals their thorough understanding of the complexities of the salmon's life cycle. In Saami, *diddi* are small male salmon; *lindor* are those male salmon larger than *diddi*; *goadjin* are the largest male salmon; *duovvi* are roe salmon; *Čuonžá* the fatty and sexually immature salmon that return in the fall; *vuorru* the salmon that overwinter in the river; and *šoaran* are *vuorru* that go to marine waters in the spring and return again to the river in the fall.

The genus *Oncorhynchus* comprises two groups, the Pacific trouts (e.g., {ADDIN ENRfu} rainbow trout or steelhead and cutthroat trout), and seven species of Pacific salmon. Five species of Pacific salmon spawn on both the Asian and North American sides of the North Pacific basin. Of these, the first, *O. kisutch*, are called coho or silver salmon in English, *qakiiyaq* in Alutiiq. *O. tshawytscha* salmon are king or chinook salmon in English, *lluq'akaaq* in Alutiiq, and *taryaqvak* in Yup'ik. *O. keta* are chum or dog salmon in English, *alimaq* in Alutiiq, and *iqalluk* in Yup'ik. The fourth species, *O. gorbuscha*, are pink or humpy salmon in English, *amartuq* in Alutiiq, and *amaqaayak* in Yup'ik; finally, *O. nerka* are sockeye or red salmon in English, *niklliq* in Alutiiq, and *sayak* in Yup'ik (the entirely freshwater form of *O. nerka* are called kokanee). Two species are found only in Asia: *O. masou* are called masou or cherry salmon, sakuramasu, yamane, or yamabe, and *O. rhodurus* are amago salmon. Pacific salmon are found along the coasts of Korea, Japan, and Siberia north to the Arctic Ocean, and in North America, from California north along the coast to Alaska and Arctic Canada. They migrate within the North Pacific, Gulf of Alaska, Okhotsk, and Bering seas.

A salmon's appearance changes dramatically as it passes through the various developmental stages of its life, with significant differences emerging as it moves into the freshwater and marine phases of its life cycle. Similarly, food and habitat preferences, predators, and competitors also change throughout the salmon's lifespan.

Life begins for the salmon in a freshwater stream, river, or lake as they emerge from the fertilized eggs that were deposited in the streambed gravel by the female salmon several months previously. The newly hatched salmon, called an *alevin*, has a large yolk sac attached, which it uses as an energy source. These alevin generally remain in the gravel of the redd (nest) until the yolk sac is absorbed. Upon emerging from the gravel, the salmon, now called fry, eat small zooplankton such as copepods and larval insects. As they grow larger, they develop "parr marks" (dark bars) on the sides of their bodies and disperse along the streambed. Juvenile salmon (called parrs) remain in fresh water from several weeks to years depending upon the species. Pink and chum salmon spend the least amount of time in fresh water. Many larger fish (such as burbot, trout, salmon, and sculpin) and birds (such as ducks, gulls, and terns) are predators in the freshwater environment.

Most salmon species undergo smoltification, a process in which they transform physically (changing coloration and becoming silvery) and physiologically, prior to migrating to marine waters in order to adapt to the rigors of saltwater. Salmon remain in coastal or estuarine waters consuming juvenile fish (including smaller salmon) and crustaceans prior to commencing their ocean migrations. As adults, they consume a variety of adult fish species (e.g., herring, anchovies, and sand lance) as well as squid and crustaceans (such as larval crab and euphausiids). Various birds, fish, and

Red salmon, also known as sockeye salmon (*O. nerka*), mating in Adams River, British Columbia, Canada.
Copyright Paul Nicklen/National Geographic Image Collection

marine mammals, including sea lions, seals, and toothed whales such as beluga and orca, prey upon salmon. In their ocean phase, salmon are silvery, streamlined, and possess forked tails and adipose fins. Chinooks are the largest salmon, weighing up to 57 kg and measuring up to 1.5 m (although most are smaller), while pinks are the smallest, weighing approximately 1.5 kg and measuring 0.76 m.

Salmon remain in the ocean for up to six years (pinks remain only one), and then return to their natal stream to spawn. This homing sense has led to the evolution of discrete populations or stocks. Once in fresh water, salmon transform markedly. Their bodies contort (their backs become "humped" and their upper jaws/noses become hooked) and change markedly in color to various combinations of red and green, taking on gender- and species-specific spawning forms. Females build redds (nests) in which they lay 500–5000 eggs, fertilized by the male at the time of deposition. Pacific salmon die after spawning once; however, Atlantic salmon (termed kelts after spawning) may survive, migrate to marine waters, and return to spawn again. Salmon carcasses are eaten by birds (e.g., eagles) and terrestrial animals such as bears, and provide nutrients to the surrounding aquatic and upland ecosystems.

Salmonids are the dominant fish in cold, freshwater systems of North America and Eurasia. The abundance of salmon stocks range from several hundred individuals in smaller streams to large runs numbering in the hundreds of thousands. Historically, salmon spawned in every country with rivers flowing into the North Pacific, North Atlantic, or Baltic Sea. However, during the 20th century, the spawning range was diminished due to the imposition of many in-river impediments of anthropogenic origin (such as dams and pollution) to upstream migration. During their long migrations, salmon are vulnerable to a multitude of geographically dispersed fisheries. Due to a combination of freshwater habitat destruction, overfishing, and other natural and anthropogenic factors, some wild stocks of both Atlantic and Pacific salmon are extinct and some are listed endangered or threatened; others remain healthy. Farmed and ocean ranched salmon may negatively affect wild salmon populations through the genetic impacts of interbreeding, the transmission of diseases and parasites, and through elevated harvest rates in mixed stock fisheries.

Salmon form the basis of large subsistence, commercial, and recreational fisheries in North America, Europe, and Asia. They are an important food resource for many Arctic peoples (including many Eskimo/Inuit groups, Aleut, Athapaskan Indians, Koryak, Saami, Ul'chi, and Itel'men), who have also used them as a source of oil and their skins, which are waterproof, as a material from which to fashion various items. Because of their relatively high oil content, prepared salmon can be stored for long periods of time, making it an extremely important winter food.

The worldview of Arctic peoples holds that the natural world is spiritually endowed. Their belief system dictates respect and prescribes appropriate and inappropriate behaviors toward individual animals, including the salmon. Salmon are an important component of many ceremonies and potlatches, considered essential but not necessarily the focal point, except in the case of the "First Salmon Ceremonies" performed by some Native groups in the Pacific Northwest. Salmon are eaten at feasts held to celebrate significant events such as deaths, birthdays, weddings, the first salmon of the season, and the first salmon caught by a child.

SYMA ALEXI EBBIN

See also **Fish**

Further Reading

Crisp, D.T., *Trout and Salmon Ecology, Conservation and Rehabilitation*, Oxford and Cambridge, Massachusetts: Blackwell, 2000
Fienup-Riordan, Ann, *The Nelson Island Eskimo Social Structure and Ritual Distribution*, Anchorage: Alaska Pacific University Press, 1983
Fitzhugh, William and Susan Kaplan, *Inua Spirit World of the Bering Sea Eskimo*, Washington DC: Smithsonian Institution Press, 1982
Groot, C. and L. Margolis, *Pacific Salmon Life Histories*, Vancouver: UBC Press, 1991
Jernsletten, Nils, "Sami Traditional Terminology: Professional Terms Concerning Salmon, Reindeer and Snow" in *Sami Culture in a New Era The Norwegian Sami Experience*, edited by H. Gaski, Davvi Girji, 1997
Mills, Derek, *Ecology and Management of Atlantic Salmon*, London: Chapman and Hall, 1989
Netboy, Anthony, *The Salmon Their Fight for Survival*, Boston: Houghton Mifflin, 1974
Roche, Judith and Meg McHutchison, *First Fish First People Salmon Tales of the North Pacific Rim*, Seattle: University of Washington Press, 1998
Smith, Gerald R. and Ralph F. Stearley, "The Classification and Scientific Names of Rainbow and Cutthroat Trouts" in *Fisheries*, 14, 1, 1989, 4–10
Stearley, R.F. and G.R. Smith, "Phylogeny of the Pacific Trouts and Salmon (*Oncorhynchus*) and Genera of the Family Salmonidae" in *Transactions of the American Fisheries Society*, 122, 1, 1993, 1–33
Stouder, Deanna, Peter Bisson and Robert Naiman, *Pacific Salmon and their Ecosystens Status and Future Options*, New York: Chapman and Hall, 1997

SANGI, VLADIMIR

Vladimir Sangi expressed himself as a talented personality in the spheres of political and cultural life. He is most famous as a writer and a poet. To characterize his literary work, critics usually call him "the first Nivkhi writer." Interest in the history and culture of his people, which Sangi felt since his childhood, later grew into scientific work. In 1959–1962, Sangi visited almost all nivkhi villages looking for people who knew folklore and ancient rituals. He collected a great number of folklore and ethnographic materials; the most numerous and interesting materials were written down by him from the epic singer Ker-Ker in Lunvo

nomad camp (e.g., about a bear festival that the Nivkhi still preserved in Soviet times).

During his postgraduate study, Sangi tried to disprove the opinion of A.N. Veselovski that the nivkhi epic folklore does not exist. In 1974, Sangi was the first in the history of the nivkhi folklore who managed to write down the epic song about Ikhmyth Man. He has not finished this research work.

Sangi's scientific, educational, and political work proceeded simultaneously for a long time. In 1959, Sangi worked out an alphabet for the Nivkhi language, which did not have a written language. This instantly and for a long time stuck a label of "the Nivkhi nationalist" on him. It was an unofficial accusation of nationalism, which was one of the reasons why he left Sakhalin in 1963 and in 1973. Yet, by the end of the 1970s, it was due to Sangi's persistence that the resolution of the Russian Government was adopted to include the languages of the Northern peoples into school programs. Sangi's work in the Russian Government had enabled him to influence the language policy of the Republic.

Sangi accused another Nivkhi, Ch.M. Taksami (Doctor of History, director of MAE Research Institute, S.P.), of plagiarism, poor knowledge of the Nivkhi language, and ignorance of the language teaching methods used by Sangi. Sangi was not able to bar Taksami from publishing textbooks, but a compromise was found. They prepared not a single textbook for Nivkhi children, but two different textbooks based on two dialects: the Amur by Taksami and the East Sakhalin by Sangi.

In the 1970–1980s, Sangi, together with the linguists G.A. Otaina and L.B. Gashilova and a teacher T.I. Paklina, wrote a number of textbooks and teaching aids on the Nivkhi (Sakhalin dialect) language for elementary school. They were published several times from 1981 till 1993. Due to the lack of professional staff for teaching the Nivkhi language at present it is taught in Sakhalin only by enthusiasts and only in the Nekrasovka and Nogliki village schools. It is an optional subject: the Nivkhi language is not a part of the curriculum.

During the period of perestroika, Sangi was interested in politics. He lost an election to the State in 1989, and then in 1990 to the Republic Parliaments. In the spring of 1990, Sangi was elected the President of the Association of small Northern peoples at the first congress of the peoples of the North, and the same year was elected a member of the Central Committee of the Communist Party of the RSFSR. In 1993, he nominated himself for the post of the President of the Association of small indigenous peoples of the North, but he was not reelected. In the same year, he was appointed secretary of the International Union of the writers' societies.

Literature devoted to Sangi as a political figure and, to a much larger extent, as a cultural worker is numerous. Such publications include no less than 20 interviews, two monographs about him, 50 articles devoted to the general characteristics and some specific aspects of his life and creative work, and also no less than 50 articles in which his novels and collected works are analyzed as literary works. These materials range from complimentary reviews on some books by Sangi and dithyrambs to the first Nivkhi writer to a very negative evaluation of his creative work and some stages of his literary path and accusations of plagiarism, plundering of the State's money, and political adventurism.

His most well-known novels are "False heat" (1965; translated into the Polish (1968) and the Lithuanian (1971) languages) and "Kevongs marriage" (1975; in 1978–1986, the novel was published in the Slovak, Ukrainian, Lettish, Polish, Uzbek, and Yakut languages). In the first novel, the author makes an attempt to create a literary character of a hereditary northerner who is testing his human resources during sable hunting. The author compared his protagonist to the characters popular in Soviet literature during the first half of the 1960s—young city men, "who are conquering the North." The second work is on a larger scale in its ideas and realization; it depicts the life of the traditional nivkhi society in colorful detail. Reviews called this book "the first novel about Nivkhi" (B. Nevskaya, 1976). His small book of folklore "Sevenfeathered bird: short stories and legends," first published in 1964, was republished in Russian many times and was translated into several languages of the peoples of the USSR.

Having started his creative work with the publication of folklore texts ("Nivkhi legends" 1961), Sangi addressed folklore not just in "Sevenfeathered bird"; in practically all his works, he used folklore motifs. "Ikhmyth Man: Epic poem on the motives of the folk epic songs"(1986, trans. into Russian by Natalya Grudinina) can be considered the most successful literary work containing Nivkhi folklore.

During Sangi's tenure as the President of the Russian Association of small Peoples of the North, the organizational structure of the Association took shape, relationships with the governmental and nongovernmental organizations of the country were established, and contacts with the leading nongovernmental organizations of the world began. Yet in 1990, Sangi proclaimed the idea of passing the Northern peoples to "family or kin tribe commune self-government." He made this proposal at the first session of the Association Council (autumn of 1992), but only three persons out of thirty supported him. The line about "commune self-government" was incorporated into the Russian legislation much later and without the direct participation of Sangi. One of the negative results of

Sangi's presidency of the Association was that he could not give a financial report to the delegates of the second congress and explain how millions of rubles from The State Committee for the North and other organizations were spent. For some time, Sangi refused to pass over the documents and seals to the new leader, claiming creation of a new organization by them (beginning from the second congress of the Northern Peoples, a new word, "aboriginal," was introduced).

In the 1990s, Sangi was an author of the unfulfilled projects of creating some autonomous republics such as Khantiyskaya, Mansiyskaya, Nivskhaya, and Nanayskaya; signing the treaty between Russia and the Nivkhi; and introducing passports for the members of "Ket nivgun tribe."

In 1993, Sangi managed to unite part of the Nivkhi (by the end of October of 1999, according to Sangi's expression "ten clans") of the Noglik region into the "Ket nivgun tribe" in order to make joint decisions in important spheres: creating territories of traditional use of nature, rebirth of the abandoned Nivkhi settlements ("to return the Nivkhi to the traditional environment"), language, and culture. Meetings of the tribe elders are being held, and joint decisions on economic life are being made. The plans of creating several bases, trading stations, a National park, and other projects are under development.

Biography

Vladimir Mikhailovich Sangi was born in a small village on the east coast of Sakhalin in 1935, a descendant of the Nivkhi Kevongun family. Sangi's father died when he was three years old. In the winter of 1944, he was sent to a boarding school that provided him not only with secondary education, but allowed him to survive since most men, providers, were being sent to the front.

From 1954 till 1959, Sangi studied in Gertsen Leningrad Pedagogical Institute and after graduating he came back to Sakhalin. He taught at Aleksandrovsk Pedagogical College. In 1960, Vladimir Sangi became an inspector on the Executive Committee of the East Sakhalin region responsible for the Northern peoples. In 1963, Sangi moved to Moscow to complete his education. From 1963 till 1965, he studied at the Advanced Courses in Literature, and in 1973 he entered the postgraduate course at the A.M. Gorky Institute of World Literature with the intention of continuing his research in folklore and ethnic studies. In 1974, his postgraduate program was interrupted by an invitation to work in the Council of Ministers of the Russian Federation, where he was concerned with the literature and education of the peoples of the North until the end of the 1980s. In 1988, Sangi won the

Russian State Prize in literature for the book of selected works "Journey to Lonvo nomad camp" (1985). In 1993, Sangi returned to Sakhalin. At present, he lives in the village of Nogliki.

DMITRIY FUNK

Further Reading

"The Earth and we on it's edge" (conversation between V.M. Sangi and A.S. Pik). In *Severnie prostori*, September 1991, pp. 7–9

Khanbekov, V., Open Heart of People: Essay on V. Sangi's Literary Work, Vladivostok: The Far East publishing House, 1978, 120pp

Ogrizko, V. (editor), "Vladimir Mikhailovich Sangi." In *Writers and Literary Men of the Small Peoples of The North and The Far East. Bibliography Guide*, Part 2, Moscow: Concern "Literary Russia," 1999, pp194–215

Panteleimonov, N., "Writer and people." *Education in the Far North*, 22 (1985): 140–156

Sobolkov., M., " The founder of the Nivkhi literature." *Polyarnaya Zvezda*, 3 (1985): 83–88

Vukolov, L., "Vladimir Sangi," Moscow: Sovetskaya Rossiya, 1990, 160p

SAQQAQ CULTURE

Saqqaq culture is the archaeological term for one of the oldest Paleo-Eskimo cultures in Greenland, dating roughly from 3900 BP (before present) to 2700 BP. It is preceded by, and partly contemporaneous with, Independence I culture, and followed by Independence II. There is some debate over the position of the Saqqaq culture in Eastern Arctic prehistory, and its relationship with Independence I culture, but it is generally agreed to be a Pre-Dorset variant of the Arctic Small Tool tradition (ASTt), centered in Greenland.

The term was first applied by the Danish archaeologist Jørgen Meldgaard, who in 1952 had hypothesized the existence of a "West Greenland Paleo-Eskimo culture," based on material excavated by Hans Mosegaard four years earlier from the site of Saqqaq in northern Disko Bay. By 1953, after excavations at Sermermiut, Meldgaard was able to define the Saqqaq culture as an entity, and had identified a number of diagnostic artifact types, including burins, burin spalls, tools with transverse edges, and triangular harpoon blades.

The main site concentrations seem to have been in the Disko Bay, Sisimuit, and Nuuk areas of West Greenland; however, while these are resource-rich areas, this distribution may also reflect greater archaeological concentration in these locales. In recent years, Saqqaq culture sites have also been found in southeast Greenland (Ammassalik), in East Greenland (Scoresbysund), and on Ellesmere Island, in northeast Canada. This has prompted lively debate concerning the exact distribution of the culture, and indeed its definition and distinction from other east Arctic Pre-Dorset cultures.

Principal sites include Saqqaq itself, Sermermiut, and Itivnera. The excellently preserved sites of Qajaa and Qeqertasussuk, discovered in 1981 and 1983, respectively, prompted a reawakening of research into the earliest cultures of Greenland. Settlement at Qeqertasussuk, a site composed of a series of raised beaches forming a promontory at the southern point of Disko Island, spans two-thirds of the Saqqaq culture period, from 3900 BP to 3100 BP, and can be divided into five chronological units through well-defined stratigraphy. In contrast to many Saqqaq sites, where only lithic materials remain, there was a wealth of organic material preserved in the permafrost, enabling new light to be shed on technology, subsistence, climate, and culture.

The basic Saqqaq hunting kit comprises toggling harpoons with a tanged, open-socketed head, for hunting on the ice, light throwing harpoons for open water, lances, atlatls, light throwing spears, bird spears, and bows and arrows. Hand tools include a variety of knives, more than five different types of sidescrapers, burins, adzes, awls, saws, grinding stones, hammers, wedges, flint flakers, and needles. Blades are bifacial, and microblades are also found. Snares, or perhaps nets, are suggested at one site by fragments of knotted baleen strings. Among the household inventory are trays and bowls carved of driftwood, of which there seems to have been an abundant supply since it was also burned as firewood, and spoons and ladles, elegantly made from whale bone, ivory, antler, or driftwood. Frame and oar fragments of kayaklike craft represent the earliest boats known in the Arctic. The general craftsmanship is of a high level, and perhaps even more advanced than that of the later cultures in the area. Although Saqqaq material culture has been noted for its complexity, there seems to be variation in the rate of both stylistic and metric change between sites. At Qeqertsussuk, for example, there seems to have been a remarkable conservatism over a 1000-year period, while the Sisimuit material shows greater diversity over time, particularly in raw material usage.

The dominant lithic material used by people of the Saqqaq culture is silicified slate, alternatively known in Arctic literature as *angmak* or *killiaq*. Huge extraction sources have been found in the Disko Bay and Nuusuaq areas of West Greenland, and there is evidence that trade and exchange networks operated to supply *killiaq* to other Saqqaq territories. Other exotic materials such as chalcedony, agate, and quartzite were also used for tools, and these differ in importance over time and by region.

House remains also show great variation, from relatively elaborate mid-passage dwellings some 6 m long and 3–4m wide, typically with a box hearth, to smaller paved areas or tent rings with hearths. In some particularly resource-rich areas, there are dozens of structures, probably contemporaneous, which may suggest group gatherings. This may have been a social pattern contrasting to that of other Paleo-Eskimo cultures, who seem to have used larger structures such as longhouses for this purpose. It has also been proposed that the original, possibly smaller, units of the Saqqaq culture eventually developed into regional groups, each operating within their own well-defined hunting territories.

As indicated by their specialized and complex hunting tool kit, Saqqaq subsistence practices were rich and varied. Studies on a rare find of human bones at Qeqertasussuk show that their diet was primarily based on marine resources. Faunal remains from the site, although comprising 50% seal bones, and 45% bird bones, represent 45 different mammal, bird, and fish species overall, along with molluscs, and traces of plant resources such as berries. In comparison, faunal remains from the late Saqqaq site of Nipisat I in the Sisimiut district of West Greenland show that caribou was the most important game mammal there.

Saqqaq origins, and indeed the origins of the Paleo-Eskimos, are not yet clear. Most Arctic prehistorians probably accept their broader relationship with ASTt, and a migration from Alaska, and even the hypothesis that these people were initially derived from Northeast Asian cultures, but further research into this question is required. Closer to Greenland itself, evidence so far suggests that Saqqaq peoples arrived in a population movement from eastern and central Canada into Greenland via Smith Sound, and this may have been either parallel to, or following the arrival of the Independence I culture. The descendants of the successful, seemingly prosperous, Saqqaq people were presumably a development into Independence II culture, although the possibility of new immigration into the area is also debated.

JENNIFER I. M. NEWTON

See also **Arctic Small Tool Tradition; Independence Culture; Pre-Dorset Culture**

Further Reading

Appelt, Martin, "The Construction of an Archaeological 'Culture': Similarities and Differences in Early Paleo-Eskimo Cultures of Greenland." In *Fifty Years of Arctic Research: Anthropological Studies from Greenland to Siberia*, edited by R. Gilberg & H.C. Gulløv, Copenhagen: Publications of the National Museum Ethnological Series, Volume 18, Department of Ethnography, National Museum of Denmark, 1997

Grønnow, Bjarne (editor), *The Paleo-Eskimo Cultures of Greenland: New Perspectives in Greenland Archaeology*, Copenhagen: Danish Polar Center, 1996

Larsen, Helge & Jørgen Meldgaard, "Paleo-Eskimo cultures in Disko Bugt, West Greenland." *Meddelelser Om Grønland*, 161(2) (1958)

Meldgaard, Jørgen, "A Paleo-Eskimo culture in West Greenland." *American Antiquity*, 17(3) (1952): 222–230

Møbjerg, Tinna, "New Aspects of the Saqqaq Culture in West Greenland." In *Fifty Years of Arctic Research: Anthropological Studies from Greenland to Siberia*, edited by R. Gilberg & H.C. Gulløv, Copenhagen: Publications of the National Museum Ethnological Series, Volume 18, Department of Ethnography, National Museum of Denmark, 1997

Schledermann, Peter, *Crossroads to Greenland*, Calgary: Arctic Institute of North America, 1990

SATELLITE REMOTE SENSING

Remote sensing, or Earth observation, is the collection of information about the Earth's surface or atmosphere from airborne or space instruments using a more or less downward-looking instrument that detects some form of electromagnetic radiation—ultraviolet, visible, infrared, or microwave. It is thus an extension of the idea of aerial photography. As an approach to mapping and monitoring the Earth's surface and atmosphere, it offers a number of advantages when compared with in situ measurement, including the fact that data can be collected from large areas or volumes in a short period of time, allowing a virtually instantaneous "snapshot" to be obtained. This is especially true of satellite remote sensing, in which the sensor is carried on board a (normally unmanned) spacecraft in orbit around the Earth. Satellite-based systems also offer the possibility of obtaining data from areas that would otherwise be difficult to reach. Within the atmosphere, these variables include the temperature, humidity, precipitation, wind velocity, and the spatial distribution of clouds, aerosol particles, and various molecular species. Over land surfaces, it is possible to measure the albedo, temperature, surface topography, and geomorphology, and to infer a wide range of land-cover classes such as the type of vegetation and its state of health and position in the phenological cycle (seasonal timing of plant growth), soil moisture content, rock type in the case of exposed surfaces, and the presence of various artificial structures such as settlements and roads. Over water, surface temperature, topography (from which surface currents, wave fields and tides, and even ocean bathymetry, can be inferred), wind velocity, and water color (which is related to sediment concentrations or biological productivity) can all be measured. The spatial extent and depth of snow cover, the spatial extent of glaciers, ice caps, ice sheets and ice shelves, the presence and size distribution of icebergs, the concentration and type of sea ice, and the surface facies of glaciers and other ice masses can all also, at least to some extent, be determined.

Two main types of orbit are used for satellite remote sensing. A satellite in a geostationary orbit is located approximately 36,000 km above the equator, and its orbital period is synchronized with the Earth's rotation so that its position is fixed with respect to the Earth's surface. This gives a fixed view of about a quarter of the Earth's surface, and is mainly used for operational meteorological observations since data from the same location can be acquired at short intervals, typically of the order of one hour. The disadvantage of such orbits is their large distance from the Earth, which means that it is difficult to obtain high spatial resolution, and in practice instruments carried in geostationary orbits cannot resolve details finer than a few kilometers. The other main type of orbit is the LEO, or low-Earth orbit, in which the satellite is typically between 500 and 2000 km above the Earth's surface. This can give greatly improved spatial resolution and versatility, but at the expense of a reduced swath width. A satellite in LEO takes approximately 100 min to orbit the Earth, thus making about 14 orbits per day and moving at a speed of about 7 km s^{-1} with respect to the surface. Data rates, in terms of square kilometers per second, acquired by instruments in LEO can thus be exceptionally high.

Although spaceborne photography continues to find some use (and archives of space photographs from the 1960s onward have proved to be exceptionally valuable), the most common, and most familiar, type of remote-sensing instrument is the imaging radiometer or multispectral imager (there is no generally agreed terminology). These are essentially spaceborne digital cameras, although they usually record radiation intensity in a number of wavebands extending from the blue or green part of the visible spectrum (0.4 or 0.5 μm) to the near-infrared (2 μm) or thermal infrared (10 μm). The calibrated digital output of these instruments is suitable for computer-based quantitative analysis. Within this general definition, there is a wide variety of specializations, from instruments offering exceptionally fine spatial resolution, down to 1 m or even less but at the cost of narrow spatial coverage and infrequent opportunities to revisit a particular location on the Earth's surface (an example of this type is the Ikonos sensor), to wide-swath, coarse-resolution instruments that provide frequent opportunities for observation (e.g., the Advanced Very High Resolution Radiometer, or AVHRR). An example of an instrument that is intermediate between these extremes is the Landsat Enhanced Thematic Mapper Plus (ETM+). This observes in six wavebands between 0.45 and 2.35 μm, each of which has a spatial resolution of 30 m, together with a panchromatic band with a 15-m resolution and a thermal infrared band with a resolution of 60 m. A single image covers an area of 185 km × 185 km, and a given location can be reimaged at intervals of 16 days. Some instruments are optimized to measure surface temperatures using observations in the thermal infrared region, some are optimized to measure ocean color, and so on.

One of the main disadvantages of optical and infrared instruments for viewing the Earth's surface is their inability to penetrate cloud cover or, except in the case of thermal infrared observations, to function at night. Both of these are significant limitations to observations of the polar regions, and both are addressed by the use of microwave instruments. The propagation of microwave radiation, with wavelengths between 1 mm and 1 m, is largely unaffected by absorption in cloud or precipitation. There are two principal types of microwave instruments. The first of these is the passive microwave radiometer (PMR). This detects naturally occurring, thermally generated radiation, and the signal detected by a PMR is contributed to by the temperature of the object in view, by a physical property of the object called its emissivity, which describes its efficiency compared with a theoretically perfect radiator termed a black body, and by a usually small contribution from the atmosphere. Assuming that the atmospheric effects can be corrected, the detected signal can thus be used to deduce the surface temperature if the emissivity is known (this mode is used, e.g., for determining the sea surface temperature), or to deduce the emissivity if the temperature is known or can be deduced. This latter mode of operation is particularly important for monitoring the distribution and type of sea ice, since ice and open water have substantially different emissivities. The chief disadvantage of PMRs is their coarse spatial resolution—a typical spaceborne instrument will have a resolution of the order of 10 km. They are thus more suited to global and regional synoptic studies than to local investigations.

The second main class of microwave instrument is the synthetic aperture radar, or SAR. Unlike the PMR, this is an active instrument, illuminating the Earth's surface with extremely short pulses of microwave radiation and analyzing the signal that is returned in order to build up a map of the surface's radar reflectivity. Sophisticated signal processing allows spatial resolutions as fine as 10 m or better to be obtained, although as with the optical imaging instruments, there is a trade-off between spatial resolution and spatial coverage, and the swath width of a fine-resolution SAR is generally limited to about 100 km. Unlike the optical instruments, SARs respond to variables for which the user is likely to have little intuitive feel—the fine-scale surface roughness, three-dimensional geometric structure, and the dielectric constant of the target material. This can inhibit nonexpert analysis of SAR images, but expert, usually computer-assisted, analysis can be applied to many fields, for example, for monitoring ocean waves, oil slicks, ship wakes, forest distribution, soil moisture, sea ice, snow, ice sheets, and glaciers. Two suitable SAR images can be combined, using a technique called SAR interferometry, to measure surface topography and bulk motion with accuracies of 1 m or less.

GARETH REES

See also **Albedo**

Further Reading

Campbell, J.B., *Introduction to Remote Sensing* (2nd edition), London: Taylor and Francis, 1996

Gurney, R.J., J. Foster & C. Parkinson, (editors), *Atlas of Satellite Observations Related to Global Change*, Cambridge and New York: Cambridge University Press, 1993

Kramer, H.J., *Observation of the Earth and its Environment* (3rd edition), Berlin and New York: Springer, 1996

Rees, W.G., *The Remote Sensing Data Book*, Cambridge and New York: Cambridge University Press, 1999

———, *Physical Principles of Remote Sensing* (2nd edition), Cambridge and New York: Cambridge University Press, 2001

SCANDINAVIAN LANGUAGES

The Scandinavian or North Germanic languages can be divided in two groups. These include the closely related and mutually intelligible Mainland Scandinavian languages: Swedish, Danish, and Norwegian; and the insular languages: Icelandic and Faroese. Swedish is spoken in Sweden and parts of southern and western Finland by approximately nine million people. Danish is spoken in Denmark by more than five million people. In Norway, Norwegian is spoken by 4.5 million people, and Icelandic is spoken in Iceland by approximately 250,000 people. Faroese is the language in the Faroe Islands, spoken by around 45,000 people.

The North Germanic languages are closely related to the West Germanic ones, the present German, Dutch, Frisian, and English languages. Scholars had commonly believed that the Germanic branch of the Indo-European phylum originated in Southern Scandinavia during the last millennium BC and from there spread southward, but little archaeological or other nonlinguistic evidence exists to substantiate this claim.

The North Germanic languages derive from a common "proto-Nordic," which was spoken during the first millennium AD and toward the end of that millennium began to divide into the varieties today known as Swedish, Danish, and Norwegian. It is customary at the early stage to group the North Germanic languages into West Nordic (also called "Old Norse," i.e., Norwegian and its derivates Icelandic and Faroese) and East Nordic (Swedish and Danish). Danish, however, soon began to develop special characteristics, which set it apart from the Norwegian and Swedish. Icelandic and Faroese derive from Western Norwegian dialects of the 9th and 10th centuries, when Iceland and the Faroe Islands were populated from that part of Norway. During the late Middle Ages, the Mainland Scandinavian languages were transformed both structurally, changing from a synthetic type of language (with an elaborate declension system) to an analytic type (with a simple morphology), and lexically, with a heavy influx of loanwords from Low German. Icelandic did not participate in these changes and Faroese only to a lesser extent, so that the main difference from that point came to be between the mainland and the insular languages.

Icelandic

Icelandic derives from Southwestern dialects of Old Norwegian. The language seems to have soon developed into a separate variety, but remained close to Old Norwegian, and thus mutually intelligible with the other Scandinavian languages throughout the Middle Ages. In the period 1400–1600, this intelligibility was lost as a result of the changes in the mainland Scandinavian languages aforementioned. Phonetically, Icelandic also changed, but in a direction quite different from the others. Since 1600, the Icelandic language has been quite stable and conservative. Icelandic was used extensively in writing, and a spelling reminiscent of the medieval written language was developed. The strong drive toward purity, to avoid and expel Danish and other foreign words and replace them with traditional Icelandic words or, often, to construct neologisms, started in the 19th century and was intensified in the 20th century. Today, Icelandic is characterized by a complicated inflection system and a vocabulary with only a modest degree of foreign influence as far as the form of words is concerned.

Norwegian

The Norwegian language developed significant dialect differences during the Middle Ages, when it was extensively used as a written language. In the late Middle Ages, the written language yielded to Danish as the political independence of the kingdom was undermined and finally extinguished. From the 16th century onward, the written language was Danish, while the dialects had reached their modern, analytic stage. After semi-independence was attained in a union with Sweden (1814–1905), a movement toward a separate written language commenced, leading to two different varieties: Nynorsk, which was codified by Ivar Aasen (1813–1896) in the 1850s and 1860s on the basis of a systematic comparison between the dialects, although its main base lay in the west; and Bokmål, which was based on a Norwegian-influenced pronunciation of Danish used by the urban elite and gradually was adapted to Southeastern Norwegian speech. Successive spelling reforms after 1900 brought the languages closer, although they still exist as separate varieties with a formally equal position. Bokmål is used by 85–90% of the population, and Nynorsk is used by 10–15%, mainly in the west. The dialects still fall into distinct groups, the primary ones including Eastern, Western, Trøndelag, and Northern. Bokmål, Nynorsk, and the dialects are mutually intelligible, and the dialects are more freely used even in formal contexts than in comparable countries.

Swedish

Swedish comprised, like Danish, originally a number of dialects within the Eastern Nordic group. Like the other Mainland Scandinavian languages, Swedish went through a simplification of the morphology during the late Middle Ages, combined with a strong lexical influence from Low German. A consolidation of a common Swedish written norm was part of the Swedish nation building process during the 16th and 17th centuries. The language received loanwords with regularity, but accepted relatively more from French than the other Scandinavian languages did. Swedish was the object of more intense official language cultivation than the other Scandinavian languages. Its standard pronunciation—originally formed among the educated classes in Stockholm during the 19th and especially during the 20th century—spread throughout the entire population and put the dialects under increasing pressure as modernization, urbanization, and geographical and social mobility set in. In addition to the dichotomy standard-dialects, a system with gliding transitions between a national standard (based on Central Swedish, above all Stockholm, speech) and regional standards developed. The most important regional standards are the southern ones, centered in the formerly (until 1658) Danish landscape of Skåne, the western one centered in Göteborg, and a northern one. The so-called East Swedish dialects in southern and western Finland developed a separate Finland-Swedish norm that differed from Sweden-Swedish in pronunciation. The East Swedish, in particular, lacked the two tonemes of Sweden-Swedish, as well as some words and idioms, but otherwise followed the Sweden-Swedish standard closely.

Danish

Danish developed a separate identity early in the Middle Ages when the three features, which still prominently distinguish this language, began to develop: namely the blurring of unstressed vowels into one (i.e., a *schwa*), the voicing of unvoiced plosives in postvocalic position, and the development of the glottal stop as a prosodic feature with a function partly reminiscent of the tonemes in Norwegian and Swedish. A codification and consolidation of a standard norm of Danish developed gradually over the period from 1500 to 1800. The basis of the standard was upper-class Zealandic, particularly Copenhagen, speech. From the 19th century onward, this standard began to suppress the dialects, and this development accelerated in the 20th century. Only in parts of Jutland in the west and in Bornholm in the east do the traditional dialects of Danish persist today, mostly among older speakers. However, regional accents of the standard have developed, and one particular speech variety—informal Copenhagen speech—has spread rapidly among youth all over Denmark. In this way, pronunciation changes rapidly, and the gap between speech and writing is larger in Denmark than anywhere else in Scandinavia.

Faroese

Faroese existed for several centuries as a Southwestern (Old) Norwegian dialect, and was commonly regarded as such as late as the 18th century, at which time the mutual intelligibility with Norwegian was probably long lost since. Remarkable phonetic changes took place here, too, although the changes were quite different from those of the Icelandic language. Morphologically, Faroese was partly simplified, and thus came to occupy a position between Icelandic and Scandinavian. Faroese was not used in writing until the 19th century, when the clergyman, linguist, and folklorist V. U. Hammershaimb constructed a spelling that was closely adapted to Old Norse and Icelandic. In the 20th century, Faroese was cultivated and gradually assumed the leading position in the Faroese community, which up until then the Danish had occupied. Today, Faroese and Danish are both official languages, although Faroese dominates. The Faroese have tried a puristic language cultivation, but less consistently than the Icelanders, and Danish words are today common in Faroese speech, but often shunned in writing.

Structural features of North Germanic

In the remainder of this entry, some of the basic characteristics of the North Germanic languages will be sketched against a historical background. Due to space constraints, only the standard varieties of the modern languages will be treated, unless otherwise indicated.

Phonology. The vowel systems of the Scandinavian languages have evolved from a five-vowel system:

a - e - i - o - u (as pronounced with their continental European values). Already in Proto-Nordic times, three new vowel phonemes arose: *y* (like German *ü*) - *ø* (like German *ö*) - *æ* (like English *a* in *man*). They proved lasting in most of the languages. All vowels could be short or long. In late medieval times, a great shift took place in all the languages, implying that where vowel and consonant quantity had at the outset been independent features that could be freely combined (as in present-day Finnish), the possibilities were now restricted so that long vowels could only occur in stressed syllables before single short consonants. This led to a restructuring of the system where the old quantity distinctions developed into quality distinctions. This change occurred in different ways across the different languages. In most of Mainland Scandinavian, several mergers led to simplification again.

Three diphthongs characterized Old Nordic: *ei, au,* and *øy* (something like Modern German *ei, au,* and *äu*). These were, however, monophthongized in Danish and Swedish already around AD 1000, to *e* and *ø*. Thus, where Old Norse had *bein,* "bone," *braut,* "broke," *høy,* "hay," Danish and Swedish became *ben, brøt,* and *hø.* In Norwegian, the diphthongs have remained until the present day. Also, the diphthongs remained in Faroese and Icelandic, although they changed in quality and partly merged. In these languages, new diphthongs arose from former long vowels. Danish also acquired many new diphthongs due to defricativization of postvocalic *v* and *g:* the words *tegn,* "sign" and *navn,* "name," are now pronounced as English "tine" and "noun."

The Old Nordic consonant system included the usual European inventory. The articulation places were lips, tongue-ridge, and velum, and the three articulation types of voiced and unvoiced plosives and nasals were present in all positions: *b, p, m; t, d, n; k, g, ng.* Voiced and unvoiced labial fricatives included *f, v,* dental: *þ, ð* (like English *th* in *thing* and *that,* respectively); alveolar *s* (with no voiced counterpart), and the velar *gh* (like a voiced German "ach-Laut") and uvular *h.* The lateral *l,* the vibrant *r,* and the semivowel *j* (like English *y* in *young*) also existed. This system has undergone a number of changes and differentiations. The dental and velar fricatives (of which only *þ* was phonemic) have disappeared or have been replaced by stops except in Icelandic (all three) and Danish (the voiced ones). For instance, Old Nordic and modern Icelandic *þing* "assembly; thing" has become *ting* in all the other Scandinavian languages. The *k* and *g* before *j* and front vowels have assumed a palatal pronunciation in Norwegian and Swedish (like German "ich-Laut" and English *y* in *young*), while in Faroese they sound like English *ch* and *j,* respectively. The clusters *sj, skj* (in Norwegian and Swedish), and (before front vowels) *sk* have become retroflex (like

English *sh*). In (Eastern) Norwegian and Swedish, the sequences *r* or + dental consonant have given rise to a series of retroflex consonants. The *r,* on the other hand, in Danish and in the southernmost Norwegian and Swedish changed from dental to uvular (as in French and German). In Danish, the voiceless stops in postvocalic position became voiced and later fricative quite early (e.g., *mat* "food" in most of Scandinavian, which in Danish is now written *mad* and pronounced "*mað*"). Danish has even developed a glottal stop that the other languages do not have, but that functions more as a prosodeme than a phoneme.

Prosodic Features. Norwegian and Swedish have developed an accent system with two tonemes, an unmarked toneme (called toneme 1), and a marked one (toneme 2). In most varieties, the toneme distinction occurs only in sequences with a stressed syllable followed by at least one unstressed one. In the northernmost part of Norway, this distinction has been lost, and this is also the case in other peripheral areas: Finland-Swedish, Danish, Faroese, and Icelandic. Stress is important in Scandinavian, which is mainly characterized by (word- or morpheme-) initial stress, but with regular exceptions in borrowed words with unstressed prefixes or with a Latin stress type later in the word.

Morphology. The morphological structure of the Scandinavian languages varies from the synthetic (inflectional) Icelandic to the much more analytic Mainland Scandinavian. The most important open word classes here include nouns, adjectives, and verbs. All inflection in the Scandinavian languages is done by adding suffixes to the word stems, except in a few cases where vowel changes within the stem are used with or without adding a suffix (as in the case of strong verbs).

Nouns are inflected by number and definiteness in all the languages. In addition, Icelandic features an elaborate system of four cases: nominative, accusative, dative, and genitive. Faroese retains nominative, accusative, and dative; genitive is used in the written language, but not in speech. Central Scandinavian also has a genitive case, invariably marked by an *-s* added to any other form. The definiteness inflection by a system of suffixes is peculiar to the North Germanic languages (within the Germanic group), for example, *stol,* "chair"; *stolen,* "the chair"; *stolar,* "chairs"; *stolarna,* "the chairs" (Swedish). The nouns are divided into classes called genders: three in Icelandic, Faroese, and Nynorsk (masculine, feminine, neuter), and two in Swedish and Danish ("common gender," derived from the old masculine, and neuter). Bokmål displays an internal variation, wherein feminine declension forms are widely used, although more in an informal than in a formal style.

Adjectives are given an indefinite and a definite declension in all the Scandinavian languages.

Adjectives are inflected by gender (two in Mainland Scandinavian, three in insular Nordic), number, and, in Icelandic and Faroese, case. While the latter two languages have full declensions, Mainland Scandinavian has undergone radical simplifications so that generally only three forms remain: a base form without ending (indefinite, common gender, singular); a form with the suffix -t (indefinite, neuter, singular, also used as an adverbial suffix corresponding to English -ly); and a form with the suffixed -e (Danish and Norwegian) or -a (Swedish) (indefinite plural—where there are no gender distinctions—and definite—without any further distinctions at all). In addition, there are three degrees of comparison: basic form, comparative, and superlative, for example, in Swedish: *ljus,* "bright"; *ljusare,* "brighter"; *ljusast,* "brightest." Longer or compounded adjectives are normally compared by using words denoting "more" and "most" as in English.

In the case of verbs, the base forms in all the languages end in a vowel: -a (Icelandic, Faroese, Swedish, facultatively in Nynorsk), or -e (Danish, Bokmål, facultatively in Nynorsk). Two morphological tenses (present and past) exist. In Mainland Scandinavian, each tense is marked by only one form. In Icelandic, the tenses are conjugated by persons (three), numbers (two), and moods (two, indicative and subjunctive), giving a full range of 24 forms. Faroese has reduced the number by abolishing subjunctive and merging the plural forms in each tense, mostly second- and third-person singular, providing for only six regular forms. Furthermore, all the languages have an imperative. Icelandic and Faroese have a separate form for plural, and Mainland Scandinavian has only one form. In addition to the morphological tenses, there are, as in English, a number of periphrastic tenses, using the verbs meaning "to have" and "to be" with the past participle. Peculiar to the North Germanic is the so-called -s-form, which may denote the passivity, reflexivity, and reciprocity. In Icelandic, Faroese, and Nynorsk the form is -st, in the others -s, such as this example from Swedish: *något måste göras* (passive: "something must be done"), and *du måste göra något* (active: "You must do something"). These s-forms are common in Swedish and Icelandic both in the present and past tense, while they are mostly used in the present tense in Danish and Bokmål, and used even more restrictively in Nynorsk (mostly in infinitive after modal auxiliaries). The verbs have two adjectival forms: a present participle ending in -ende (Danish, Bokmål), -ande (Swedish, Nynorsk), or -andi (Icelandic, Faroese), and a past participle that is declinable more or less like adjectives.

The verbs in all Scandinavian languages are divided into several conjugations. The main grouping is between weak verbs (characterized by suffixing in all forms), and strong verbs (characterized by vowel alternations), particularly in the past and the past participle, and the lack of suffixes in Mainland Scandinavian. (In Insular Nordic strong verbs, suffixes are also lacking in the first-and third-person singular indicative, although other forms are suffixed.) Consider this example from Swedish: *räkna,* "count"; *räknade,* "counted"; *skriva,* "write"; and *skrev,* "wrote."

Numerals are formed in characteristically different ways in Scandinavia, although the basic patterns are similar to the English system. Danish is the exception: the round numbers from 50 to 90 are formed by shorter expressions reflecting an old vigesimal system, for instance, 50 is *halvtreds,* formerly *halvtredsindstyve* or "half three times twenty," that is, two-and-a-half times twenty. The units (one, two, three, etc.) are, from 21 upward, regularly placed before the digits, indicating "number of tens" (i.e., twenty, thirty twenties, thirties, and so on), as in German and Dutch: 5 is *fem,* 55 is *fem og halvtreds.* Faroese has adopted the Danish system, while Swedish and Icelandic use a system similar to English. Consider this example in Swedish: *femti(o)fem,* or "fifty-five"; in Icelandic, *fimmtíu og fimm,* or "fifty and five." Norwegian traditionally also used the Danish system, although without the vigesimal numbers, so that 55 was *fem og femti,* or "five and fifty." However, Norway's Parliament decreed a new system similar to Swedish and English in 1951; hence, *femtifem,* or "fifty-five." Today, Norwegians use both systems extensively, often in conjunction with each other: the older in informal contexts, the new in formal situations (as when citing telephone numbers, etc.) Numerals above 1 are indeclinable in Mainland Scandinavian, while in Icelandic, the numbers 1 to 4 are inflected in a manner similarl to adjectives, and numbers from 5 onward are indeclinable. In Faroese, the numbers 1 to 3 are inflected, but not the higher ones.

Syntax. The syntax of the Scandinavian languages is quite similar to English and other Western languages. In principle, the case system of Icelandic and Faroese should allow for a less fixed word order than the others require, but in reality the differences are minor. The basic (neutral) sentence pattern is subject - verb - object - adverbials. In questions and in sentences introduced by the object or adverbial, the order between subject and verb is normally inverted. Consider this Norwegian example: *I februar fullførte han artikkelen* (the literal translation is "In February finished he the article," although it is understood to mean "In February he finished the article").

Nominal phrases normally place the nuclear element at the end with determiners and descriptors proceeding (as in English), for example, in Swedish: *tre stora hus* or "three large houses." When it comes to determiners denoting definiteness, however, there are some characteristic differences among the languages. Norwegian and Swedish feature an extensive use of the so-called "double definiteness," which means that determiners are combined with the definite form of the noun, for example, in Swedish: *det stora huset* or "the large house." Danish lacks this feature (e.g., *det store hus*). In this instance, Icelandic appears more flexible than the other Scandinavian languages: it may drop either the determiner (*stóra húsið*) or the definiteness suffix (*hið stóra hús*), or keep both (*hið stóra húsið*)—the differences being mainly stylistic.

LARS S. VIKØR

See also **Alphabets and Writing, Scandinavia and Iceland**

Further Reading

Braunmüller, Kurt, *Die Skandinavischen Sprachen im Überblick,* Tübingen: Francke Verlag, 1999
Haugen, Einar, *The Scandinavian Languages, An Introduction to their History,* London: Faber and Faber Ltd., 1976
Vikør, Lars S., *The Nordic Languages, Their Status and Interrelations,* Oslo: Novus forlag, 2001

SCHNEIDER, LUCIEN

In September 1938, Father Lucien Schneider's hopes of conducting missionary work among the Inuit became a reality: Schneider received a posting for the Oblate missions in Hudson's Bay. On February 3, 1939, he arrived in Halifax and traveled via Montreal, Winnipeg, and Churchill to Eskimo Point (Arviat). From 1941 to 1945, he spent most of his time in Mistake Bay (Tavani), a mission that had been opened temporarily near the community of Whale Cove (Tikiraqjuaq). During this period, Schneider also made several short visits to other Catholic missions around Hudson's Bay: in August 1940 and July 1943, he traveled as far as Wakeham Bay (Maricourt), today known as Kangirsuqjuaq.

When Bishop Lacroix closed the Tavani mission, Schneider entered into the service of Lionel Scheffer, Bishop of the newly formed Labrador apostolic curacy. From June 1946 to 1974, Schneider spent the rest of his missionary career in the vast Arctic region of Northen Québec (Nunavik), with two long stays in Hudson's Strait and Ungava Bay: the first in Wakeham Bay (Kangirsujuaq) from 1946 to 1958, and the second in Fort Chimo (Kuujuaq) from 1958 to 1974.

Over these years, Schneider dedicated himself to the in-depth study of Inuktitut. Nicknamed Ataatasiaq ("the grandfather") or Ijautilialuk ("the big man with glasses") by the Inuit, he authored several books on the Inuit language. In addition to reworking Bishop's Turquetil's grammar, he also wrote *Grammaire en esquimau* (1954) and a *Dictionnaire esquimau du dialecte de l'Ungava*

(1954) during his stay in Hudson's Strait. After translating and transcribing the *Livre de prières en Esquimau* used by the Inuit of the Labrador curacy (1959) and a book of Apologetic Catholic Doctrine (*Bambo*, 1961) into Inuit Syllabics, he undertook the task of publishing his grammar and several dictionaries. Schneider's contribution to linguistics has proved to be considerable. Among his other contributions on the level of morphology, he is attributed with the law of double consonants or law of alliteration. According to this law, in the Nunavik and Labrador dialects, no consonant group may be immediately followed by another consonant group. When two consonant groups are separated by a single or double vowel, the first consonant of the second group is systematically dropped (*natsik+mik* does not yield *natsikmik* as in other dialects, but *natsimik*). Schneider supplied other Oblate missionaries and numerous academic researchers who worked in Nunavik with equally remarkable didactic material. After the publication of *Grammaire esquimaude du sous-dialecte de l'Ungava* by the Presses du Gouvernement provincial (DGNQ) in 1967, a *Dictionnaire des Infixes du dialecte de l'Ungava* in 1968, the Presses de l'Université Laval and the Centre d'Études Nordiques published the first edition of his *Dictionnaire alphabético-syllabique du langage esquimau de l'Ungava et contrées limitrophes* in December 1966. Compiled with the help of two Inuit Elders, Christine Nutaraaluk and Salumi Mitiarjuk Nappaaluk, this high-caliber work has been added to and reedited several times since its first publication. In 1970, it was renamed *Dictionnaire esquimau-français du parler de l'Ungava et contrées limitrophes*. In 1985, this Inuit-French dictionary was translated into English (*Ulirnaisigutiit*) by the linguist Dermot R.F. Collis, who considered the work as "the largest piece of published lexicological scholarship on any Canadian Inuktitut dialect."

On a holiday in Paris in 1973, Lucien Schneider was honored with Chevalier de l'Ordre National du Mérite, a prestigious medal from the French government, for his missionary work, and for the great quality of his linguistic work. In August 1974, due to fatigue and illness, Schneider left the Northern Canadian missions to live in Paris. When he returned to his family, he spent his time by giving conferences and pursuing his work in linguistics.

Biography

Lucien Schneider was born in Paris on June 16, 1907. Schneider was the son of Albert Schneider, an accountant, and Louise Sallot. He studied Theology and obtained a Bachelor's Degree in Latin, Greek Studies, and Philosophy from La Sorbonne. After completing supplementary instruction in Theology and Morals at the Issy-les Moulineaux Seminary, and a year of military service in Tunisia, Schneider entered as an initiate into the order of the Oblates Missionaries of Mary Immaculate. On March 18, 1934, he was ordained into priesthood by Bishop Arsène Turquetil, then the apostolic vicar of Hudson's Bay. He died in Paris on June 6, 1978, after 36 years in the North.

FRÉDÉRIC LAUGRAND

Further Reading

Schneider, Lucien, *Grammaire esquimaude du sous-dialecte de l'Ungava*, Québec: Ministère des Richesses Naturelles, Direction Générale du Nouveau-Québec, 1967
———, *Dictionnaire des infixes de la langue esquimaude*, Québec: Ministère des Richesses Naturelles, Direction Générale du Nouveau-Québec, 1968
———, *Dictionnaire français-esquimau du parler de l'Ungava*, Québec: Presses de l'Université Laval, Travaux et documents du centre d'études nordiques, 5, 1970
———, *Ulirnaisigutiit. An Inuktitut-English Dictionary of Northern Québec, Labrador and Eastern Arctic Dialects (with an English-Inuktitut Index)*. Translated from the French and transliterated by Dermot Roman F. Collis, Québec: Presses de l'Université Laval, 1985

SCHULTZ, ED

Ed Schultz was elected Grand Chief of the Council of Yukon First Nations (CYFN) in February 2000, succeeding Shirley Adamson, and was elected to a second three-year term in July 2003. At the time of his election, Schultz, a member of the Little Salmon-Carmacks First Nation, was a senior administrator with CYFN.

Schultz's first foray into politics came in 1991 when he became the first Yukon aboriginal elected to Whitehorse city council. He served a three-year term. In 1993, Schultz unsuccessfully contested the Liberal nomination for the federal general election.

As Grand Chief, Schultz has identified, and acted upon, several priorities. Perhaps the most important is the unification of all Yukon First Nations (YFNs) under a single umbrella organization. Presently, the CYFN represents 11 of the Yukon's 14 First Nations. The other three—the Kwanlin Dun First Nation, the Liard First Nation, and the Ross River Dena Council—were members of the Council for Yukon Indians (CYI). However, when the CYI was reconstituted in 1995, these three First Nations refused to join the new organization. The CYFN constitution commits all YFNs to live by the letter of the Umbrella Final Agreement (UFA), the framework agreement for all land claims and self-government agreements in the Yukon. These three YFNs have problems with the UFA. Schultz is overseeing a process to rewrite the CYFN constitution without reference to the UFA. This, it is hoped, would be one step in bringing these three YFNs into the CYFN. In fact, Schultz has talked about bringing three other First Nations—the Taku River Tlingit and the two Kaska First Nations of Lower Post and Good Hope Lake—into a new umbrella organization. These First Nations are located in the province of British Columbia but are closely related to YFNs. They are also a part of the Yukon region as defined by Canada's federal Department of Indian and Northern Affairs.

Another important priority is completing the land claims process. Schultz calls the Yukon agreements "the best land claim and self-government agreements in the world." However, after almost 30 years of negotiations, only seven YFNs have completed land claims agreements. In addition to accelerating the process, Schultz has expressed concerns that the federal government is not living up to its obligations under those agreements. In his keynote address to the 2000 CYFN Annual General Assembly, Schultz assured delegates that his administration would be "dedicated to the task of achieving full implementation of the settlement agreements with the spirit and intent upon which they were conceived."

As a former First Nations civil servant, Schultz has identified capacity building within that civil service as another priority. First Nations administrations suffer a high rate of turnover. Schultz's goal is to make the first nations civil service as stable, skilled, and well compensated as those that serve the federal and territorial governments. This program also requires modern technology to deliver the benefits contained in the agreements to first nations citizens.

In 1997, the Little Salmon-Carmacks First Nation hired Schultz as executive director to oversee the implementation of its land claims and self-government agreements. While there, he saw the need to separate the political and corporate bodies created by claims agreements and to develop strategies to secure economic opportunities for YFNs. YFNs got few lasting economic benefits out of the Klondike Gold Rush and the building of the Alaska Highway. Since Schultz's election, the CYFN has organized two summits to bring together first nations representatives, the federal and Yukon governments, and companies planning to build natural gas pipelines in the north. At its 2001 conference, Schultz told the Association of Yukon Communities "(o)ur game plan is to position ourselves in such a way that we get maximum benefit (in oil and gas) for the next 30 or 40 or 50 years." This statement reveals Schultz's general desire to see YFNs take a more active part in the market economy.

Another of Schultz's priorities is better relations with other governments. Given the continuing claims negotiations, relations with the federal government are the most important and the most volatile. Conflicts have arisen over, among other things, the repayment of money that YFNs borrowed from the federal government to negotiate claims agreements, and certain tax provisions of the UFA. Although the Government of Canada has not changed its positions, it has made other concessions. As a result, the leadership of an eighth YFN, the Ta'an Kwach'an, signed its land claims and self-government agreements in August 2001. The agreement has yet to be ratified by Ta'an Kwach'an citizens.

YFN-Yukon relations took a step forward in February 2001 when the Yukon government, the CYFN, and all YFNs signed an agreement to establish regular meetings among themselves and create a secretariat to deal with intergovernmental issues other than land claims issues. The Yukon government has also supported YFNs in disputes with the federal government. There are still points of friction, however. Although YFNs are negotiating claims agreements with the Government of Canada, negotiations are continuing to devolve certain federal powers to the territorial government. Schultz has called the relative speed of the devolution negotiations unjustified, compared to the lengthy and difficult claims negotiations.

Schultz has also emphasized good intergovernmental relations at the local level. He has encouraged municipal leaders to engage first nations in their community and focused on the common interests that first nations governments and municipal governments have in natural resource development, and transportation and telecommunications infrastructure.

Schultz is also concerned about the preservation of First Nations cultures and languages. It was not until well into adulthood, through his involvement in the claims process, that Schultz says he came to understand himself and his people. One result of this is Schultz's focus on the Yukon's education system and the need to make first nations languages, cultures, and history a more integral part of the curriculum. Barring this, Schultz has said YFNs may opt to set up their own schools, which they are entitled to do under their claims agreements.

Biography

Ed Schultz is of Northern Tutchone ancestry, a member of the Little Salmon/Carmacks First Nation and belongs to the Wolf Clan. He has four children with his partner Yvonne Jack. He is also chair of the Arctic Athabascan Council.

FLOYD MCCORMICK

See also **Council of Yukon First Nations (CYFN); Council for Yukon Indians Umbrella Final Agreement**

Further Reading

Cameron, Kirk & Graham White, *Northern Governments in Transition: Political and Constitutional Development in the Yukon, Nunavut and the Western Northwest Territories.* Montreal: Institute for Research on Public Policy, 1995
Canada, The Government of the Council for Yukon Indians, The Government of Yukon, the *Council for Yukon Indians Umbrella Final Agreement*, Ottawa: Minister of Supply and Services Canada, 1993 (available on the CYFN website: http://www.cyfn.ca/. Other land claims and self-government agreements are also available at this site)
Council for Yukon Indians, *Together Today For Our Children Tomorrow*, Brampton, Ontario: Charters, 1977 (available on the CYFN website: http://www.cyfn.ca/)
McCormick, Floyd, "Still Frontier, Always Homeland: Yukon Politics in the Year 2000." In *The Provincial State in Canada: Politics in the Provinces and Territories*, edited by Keith Brownsey & Michael Howlett, Peterborough, Ontario: Broadview, 2001
Pedersen, Nadine, "From janitor to grand chief." *The Yukon News*, Whitehorse: Media North Limited, February 25, 2000, pp. 16–17
———, "FN support for devolution wanes." *The Yukon News*, Whitehorse: Media North Limited, March 3, 2000, p. 5
———, "Wayward nations may soon return to fold." *The Yukon News*, Whitehorse: Media North Limited, March 31, 2000, p. 3
———, "CYFN will be reborn." *The Yukon News*, Whitehorse: Media North Limited, May 29, 2000, p. 2
Small, Jason, "End 30 years' uncertainty, chief urges." *The Whitehorse Star*, Whitehorse: Whitehorse Star Ltd., January 11, 2001, p. 4 (website: http://www.whitehorsestar.com/)
Tobin, Chuck, "Ex-city councilor becomes grand chief." *The Whitehorse Star*, Whitehorse: Whitehorse Star Ltd., February 21, 2000, p. 5 (website: http://www.whitehorsestar.com/)
———, "Council considers a new constitution." *The Whitehorse Star*, Whitehorse: Whitehorse Star Ltd., March 31, 2000, p. 6 (website: http://www.whitehorsestar.com/)

SCHWATKA, FREDERICK

By the time he first became involved in the Arctic, Frederick Schwatka already had opportunities in three different careers opening up before him—the army, law, and medicine. He had seen action against the Sioux in the campaigns of 1872 and 1876, had been admitted to the Nebraska bar in 1875, and received a degree from Bellevue Medical College in New York in 1876. Yet, by the time of his early death, his fame was rather as an American Arctic explorer, lecturer, and writer. The turning point of his life came in 1878, when he heard that the American Geographical Society was planning an expedition to the eastern Arctic to follow up reports by a whaler, Captain Thomas Barry, that an

Inuit contact of his had found documents from John Franklin's last expedition (1845–1848) and had deposited them in a cairn. Schwatka, who had long harbored a fascination with Franklin, immediately volunteered for the expedition, and after an interview was appointed its leader, on transfer from the army.

The small expedition (other personnel included William Henry Gilder, Henry Klutschak, Frank Melms, and Joseph Ebierbing) left New York in the *Eothen* on June 19, 1878, and set up their base, Camp Daly, at Whitney Gulf on the northwestern shore of Hudson Bay on August 8. After wintering there, they set off overland to the northwest on April 1, 1879, coming upon a major river that matched their course before turning sharply southwest. They named it the Hayes, after President Rutherford B. Hayes, and it led them to the Back River near its mouth in Chantrey Inlet toward the end of May. Here, they found Inuit settlements and made contact with Nutargeark, who identified himself as the son of Barry's informant. They had no luck locating the cairn, however, and further interviews with local people (translated by Joseph Ebierbing, himself an Inuit) convinced them that no journals or other Franklin documents had survived. Nevertheless, Schwatka decided to push on across the ice of Simpson Strait to King William Island, where they knew Leopold McClintock had located Franklin relics. They retrieved and brought back with them the remains of the boat found by McClintock, some medals, and the body of John Irving, third officer of Franklin's ship the *Terror*, which they found in a grave in Collinson Inlet. They began their return journey on November 1, 1879 by following the Back River for some 80 km (50 mi), then striking out overland to the southeast, reaching Camp Daly in March 1880 after an absence of 11 months, 23 days, during which they had traveled 5231 km (3251 mi) by sledge—a non-Inuit record at that time.

Returning to active service, and stationed at Fort Vancouver in the state of Washington, Schwatka's next Arctic expedition was for the army itself. The US government was concerned at reports of violence in Alaska between native peoples and fur traders, and wanted to know what "feeling…exists among them [the native peoples] towards the present government," and what military commitment would be needed to pacify any disturbance, should that be necessary. Schwatka's experience recommended him as the leader of such a reconnaissance. Setting out from Portland, Oregon on May 22, 1883, he and his subordinates, including the surgeon George Wilson and topography assistant Charles Homan, sailed north up the inside passage to Chilkat (near present-day Haines), toward the head of the Lynn Canal. From there, they proceeded over the Chilkoot Pass (which

Schwatka named Perrier Pass, after Colonel J. Perrier of the French Geographical Society), along Lake Bennett (which he named after the newspaper magnate James Gordon Bennett) and down the Yukon by raft and canoe to its mouth, which they reached on August 30.

Although the published results of the Franklin search had been the work of journalist Gilder (Schwatka's second-in-command), the expedition leader began his own publishing career in describing his descent of the Yukon. His *Report of a Military Reconnaissance in Alaska* (1885), although it included a meticulous route survey in 20 detailed maps, makes odd reading today, with its sober discussion of the number and size of howitzers that would be required to subdue each village, and the need for steam launches "swift enough to run down [any hostile] canoes and large enough to carry a combating force equal to any village." The trip also found happier expression in his popular account, *Along Alaska's Great River* (1885), in which he emphasized the solid surveying achievement that had made the expedition successful "in a geographical sense."

In the same year that these books were published, Schwatka resigned his commission and from then on earned his living as a lecturer, writer, and expedition leader. In 1886, he led an abortive expedition financed by the *New York Times* to climb Mt St Elias, Alaska; they turned back at a low altitude when Schwatka collapsed with fever and pleuritic pain. He was chronically overweight, a problem that, along with the heavy drinking that others had noted from an early age, was beginning to take its toll. In 1887, he likewise suffered a breakdown of health during an expedition sponsored by the *New York World* to cross Yellowstone National Park in winter, although he successfully completed an expedition sponsored by the Chicago *America* to the Sierra Madre Mountains of Mexico in 1889.

In 1891, he made his last trip to the Arctic, leading an expedition to British Columbia, Yukon Territory, and Alaska sponsored by the *New York Ledger* (other personnel included the geologist Charles Willard Hayes and the prospector Mark Russell). Starting from Juneau on May 25, 1891, the party ascended the Taku River (south of his 1883 route), crossed Ptarmigan Pass, and then descended the Teslin and Yukon rivers as far as Fort Selkirk. From there, they struck out overland to the southwest, passing the headwaters of the White River and crossing Skolai Pass to reach the Nizina, Chitina, and Copper rivers. From the mouth of the Copper (east of Prince William Sound), they crossed to Hinchinbrook Island, which they reached on August 24. About 1130 km (700 mi) of the route, mainly between Fort Selkirk and the Skolai Pass, was mapped for the first time on this journey.

Schwatka's accomplishments as an explorer appeared more important at the time than they have generally been judged since, and his tireless lecturing schedule and swiftly published, easily approachable writings are perhaps largely responsible for the elevated profile he enjoyed during his lifetime. His 1878–1880 expedition, by being linked to the name of John Franklin, the most famous (if not the most accomplished) Arctic explorer of the 19th century, and by discovering something of Franklin's fate, shot Schwatka from the relatively closed social world of his army milieu to international fame in the geographical societies of Europe. He bolstered those connections during his 1883 expedition by naming many features after prominent geographers or explorers, the eminence of the dedicatees helping to ensure the reluctance of later mapmakers to change or ignore Schwatka's designations.

The Franklin search expedition was also hailed at the time as being the first example of non-Inuit successfully overwintering in the Arctic using only Inuit methods of survival in housing, clothing, and diet. Yet, this overlooks the fact that John Rae and Charles Francis Hall had both accomplished much the same over the previous three decades and had each done so for several winters. Schwatka's later Arctic journeys were each completed during a single summer season; one winter in the Arctic had, apparently, been enough. In the longer historical view, however, his first expedition's contribution to eliciting and preserving Inuit testimony about the fate of the Franklin survivors has provided a crucial source of information for Woodman's seminal work on the subject.

Schwatka's decision to abandon his military career to finance his travels by writing and lecturing about them marks him as a transitional figure on the road to the modern species of professional adventurer. Yet, at the time, his books and lectures played a crucial role in developing the American public's sense of their then-recently acquired territory of Alaska, defining the images of its people and places in the popular imagination.

Biography

Born on September 29, 1849 in Galena, Illinois, Frederick Schwatka was the seventh child of Frederick G. Schwatka of Maryland and Amelia Hukill of West Virginia. His family moved to Salem, Oregon in 1859. After briefly studying at Willamette University, he enrolled at West Point Military Academy in 1867, graduating as a second lieutenant in 1871. His principal expeditions (as leader) were: 1878–1880, American Geographical Society expedition to the eastern Arctic; 1883, US Army expedition to descend the Yukon River; and 1891, *New York Ledger* expedition to Alaska, British Columbia, and Yukon Territory. His books include *Report of a Military Reconnaissance in Alaska, Made in 1883* (1885), *Along Alaska's Great River* (1885), *Nimrod in the North* (1885), *Wonderland* (1886), and *Children of the North* (1886). He married Ada Brackett of Rock Island, Illinois, in 1882. Battling alcoholism and digestive problems for many years, he died from a laudanum overdose in Portland, Oregon, on November 2, 1892.

JONATHAN DORE

See also **Bennett, James Gordon Jr.; Ebierbing, Hannah (Tookoollito) and Joe; Franklin, Sir John; Gilder, William Henry; Hall, Charles F.; King William Island; Klutschak, Henry Wenzel; McClintock, Francis Leopold; North West Passage, Exploration of; Rae, John; Yukon River**

Further Reading

Gilder, William H., *Schwatka's Search: Sledging in the Arctic in Quest of the Franklin Records*, New York: Scribner, 1881, and London: Sampson Low, 1882; reprinted New York: Abercrombie and Fitch, 1966

Johnson, Robert E. et al., *Schwatka: The Life of Frederick Schwatka (1849–1892), M.D., Arctic Explorer, Cavalry Officer—A Précis*, Montpelier, Vermont: Horn of the Moon, 1984

Klutschak, Heinrich, In *Overland to Starvation Cove: With the Inuit in Search of Franklin, 1878–1880*, translated and edited by William Barr, Toronto: University of Toronto Press, 1987

Nourse, Joseph Everett, *American Explorations in the Ice Zones*, Boston: Lothrop, and London: Trübner, 1884

Schwatka, Frederick, *Nimrod in the North; or, Hunting and Fishing Adventures in the Arctic Regions*, New York: Cassell, 1885

———, *Report of a Military Reconnaissance in Alaska, Made in 1883*, Washington, District of Columbia: Government Printing Office, 1885

———, *Stories of Danger and Adventure*, Boston: Lothrop, 1886

———, *Wonderland: or, Alaska and the Inland Passage*, Chicago: Rand McNally, 1886

———, In *The Long Arctic Search: The Narrative of Lieutenant Frederick Schwatka, USA, 1878–1880, Seeking the Records of the Lost Franklin Expedition*, edited by Edouard A. Stackpole, Mystic, Connecticut: Marine Historical Association, 1965 [first publication of Schwatka's journal of the 1878–1880 expedition]

———, *Children of the Cold*, New York: Cassell, 1886; reprinted, New York: AMS Press, 1975

———, *Along Alaska's Great River*, New York: Cassell, 1885; reprinted, Anchorage: Alaska Northwest, 1983

Schwatka, Frederick & Charles Willard Hayes, In *Schwatka's Last Search: The New York Ledger Expedition Through Unknown Alaska and British America, including the Journal of Charles Willard Hayes*, edited by Arland S. Harris, Fairbanks: University of Alaska Press, 1996 [first publication in book form of Schwatka's journal of the 1891 expedition]

Woodman, David C., *Unravelling the Franklin Mystery: Inuit Testimony*, Montreal and Kingston: McGill-Queens University Press, 1991

————, *Strangers Among Us*, Montreal and Kingston: McGill-Queens University Press, 1995

SCORESBY, WILLIAM

The Royal Navy of England, having finally defeated Napoleon in 1815, decided to use its suddenly idle officers for Arctic exploration by 1818. Although many researchers have attributed England's nascent priority to the leadership of Sir John Barrow, the second secretary of the Admiralty, other researchers claim that the work of naturalist William Scoresby Jr. inspired the impetus.

Scoresby, the son of a whaler, had begun his life whaling out of Whitby, an English port, and made many journeys to the whale fishery off Spitsbergen and the western coast of Greenland. But Scoresby's interest in scientific observation led him to the University of Edinburgh. As a university student, his scientific work on Arctic ice patterns drew the attention of the influential President of the Royal Society, Sir Joseph Banks. Banks sent Scoresby's work on the Arctic to the British Admiralty, who used his information in support of once again attempting the North West Passage and the North Pole.

The data primarily concerned the phenomena unique to Arctic travel. For example, in 1820 and for the first time, Scoresby accurately drew snow crystals. He also surmised that even in daylight the aurora borealis would still be present, even if not visible, and studied polar mirages as a result of the refraction of light rays off ice. In 1814, Scoresby presented a paper to the Wernerian Society of Scotland in which he surmised that the pole was of ice, and he therefore suggested methods of traversing the distance. For example, not only did he suggest traveling by dogsled but also with what he called the sailing sledge, a contraption he had drawn 30 years before its use in the search for the John Franklin expedition, with both skates and a sail to take advantage of the prevalent wind and ice.

Scoresby's scientific works comprised some of the most relevant studies of the Arctic during his time and proved to be of great use to the Admiralty's growing program of polar exploration. Scoresby also hoped his research would contribute to the momentum of his career, and accordingly he sought leadership of an expedition from the Admiralty. The combination of Arctic expert, navigator, artist, and naturalist made Scoresby a promising candidate for the Royal Navy. However, the choice was up to John Barrow to select such a leader; despite the influence of Scoresby's former teacher Joseph Banks, Barrow denied Scoresby the opportunity. Historians have attributed Barrow's decision, on the one hand, to the Navy's convention of employing only officers to lead expeditions and, on the other, to differences in scientific opinion. Where Barrow believed in an open polar sea (and hence the ability for expeditions to navigate the North Pole), Scoresby contended that the pole was enveloped by ice. Barrow, a founding member of the Royal Geographic Society, believed his expertise threatened, and this perhaps influenced his decision to pass over Scoresby as leader of a polar expedition.

In 1820, however, Scoresby published his first book (*An Account of the Arctic Regions with a History and Description of the Northern Whale-Fishery*) to acclaim in scientific circles, if not to glowing reviews in literary circles. Two years later, Scoresby surveyed and mapped the Greenland coast between 69° and 75°, the first time since Henry Hudson in 1607. A whaling voyage in search of a plentiful fishery, away from Spitsbergen to the north toward Greenland, Scoresby named his findings "Scoresbysund" (today Ittoqqortoormiit) for his father, and he named Kater's Bay and Davy's Sound for other supporters. Scoresby then published his map the following winter in *Voyage to the Northern Whale-Fishery* (1823). However, the Royal Navy appointed an expedition the following season to make its own survey, and not until 1926 was Scoresby's work recognized on an official chart.

Scoresby's last voyage to Greenland was in the summer of 1823, at the age of 33. In 1848, Lady Jane Franklin consulted the expert Scoresby when her husband's famed expedition did not return from its 1845 departure. Scoresby's analysis of the situation resulted in his 1850 publication, *The Franklin Expedition*, in which he discussed the context of polar exploration, the party's possible fates, a brief history of the rescue attempts to date, and recommendations for further searches. He also devoted an entire chapter to "the middle ice" in Baffin Bay, describing the patterns of freeze and thaw, and the quality of ice-floes and bergs. Ever the naturalist, Scoresby divided the types of ice he encountered into categories, which would then be used to designate particular qualities. In 1851, the Admiralty requested Scoresby's advice on possible directions that the Franklin expedition might have taken within the Canadian Archipelago, prompting yet another rescue expedition.

By this time, Scoresby had achieved his doctorate and had become an ordained minister; throughout his life, he published over 90 works, not only on science but also in theology and literature. Scoresby died in March 1857.

Biography

William Scoresby Jr., was born in 1789 in Yorkshire, England, the third child and only son of Mary and William Scoresby Sr., a whaler. While apprenticed to a whaler out of Whitby, Scoresby sailed many seasons to the whale fishery off Spitsbergen; by the age of 21, Scoresby had command of his own ship. He attended the University of Edinburgh in Scotland where his scientific research flourished. He presented his first paper in 1809, which secured his admittance to the Wernerian Society. In 1814, he wrote another paper for the Wernerian Society on polar sea ice; by 1824, he was elected a Fellow of the Royal Society of London, and was a founding member of the British Association in 1831. Recognition came from the publication of two books: *An Account of the Arctic Regions with a History and Description of the Northern Whale-Fishery* (1820), and *Voyage to the Northern Whale-Fishery* (1823). In the meantime, Scoresby married Mary Eliza Lockwood in September 1811; a year later, their son William was born, followed in 1819 by their second son, Frederick. His wife died in early 1823, before Scoresby's last voyage to Greenland. After a lecturing tour, he enrolled in Queen's College, Cambridge; he became ordained in July 1825, becoming chaplain of the Floating Church for seamen in Liverpool, England, in 1827. He married Elizabeth Fitzgerald in June 1828, and four years later was appointed to lead Bedford Chapel, in Exeter. He finished his bachelor of divinity at Queens' College in 1834 and his doctorate in 1839, whereupon he became the Vicar of Bradford. His son, Frederick, died in 1835, followed in 1837 by his elder son. In 1848, his second wife died, and he married Georgiana Ker the following year. In 1855, the Scoresbys set out on an expedition to Australia, giving him much lecture material upon his return in addition to his lectures on the Arctic. Scoresby died on March 21, 1857.

ANNETTE WATSON

See also **Franklin, Sir John; Ittoqqortoormiit (Scoresbysund); North West Passage, Exploration of**

Further Reading

Martin, Constance, "William Scoresby, Jr. (1789–1857) and the Open Polar Sea—myth and reality," *Arctic,* 4(1) (1988): 39–47

McConnell, A., "The scientific life of William Scoresby, Jr., with a catalogue of his instruments and apparatus in the Whitby Museum." *Annals of Science,* 43 (1986): 257–286

Scoresby, William, *The Franklin Expedition: or Considerations on Measures for the Discovery and Relief of our Absent Adventurers in the Arctic Regions,* London: Longman, Brown, Green, and Longmans, 1850

———, *An Account of the Arctic Regions with a History and Description of the Northern Whale-Fishery,* 2 volumes, New York: Augustus M. Kelley, 1969 (reprint of 1820)

———, *Journal of a Voyage to the Northern Whale-Fishery: Including Researches and Discoveries of the Eastern Coast of West Greenland, Made in the Summer of 1822, in the Ship Baffin of Liverpool,* Whitby: Caedmon of Whitby, 1980 (reprint of 1823)

Stamp, Tom, & Cordelia Stamp, *William Scoresby, Arctic Scientist,* Great Britain: Caedmon of Whitby Press, 1975

SCORESBYSUND—*See* ITTOQQORTOORMIIT (SCORESBYSUND)

SCRIMSHAW

Scrimshaw, a word of disputed origins and diverse spelling, is the name given in the 19th century to the variety of objects made as a pastime by people involved with the whaling industries of Northern Europe and North America. In the days of sail and hand-held harpoons, whalers crafted thousands of useful and decorative items, many as presents. They included seamen's tools and ships' fittings; rolling pins, pastry cutters, cutlery, and napkin rings; toys and games; walking sticks and canes; jewelry, needle cases, and crochet hooks; birdcages, watch stands, boxes, and baskets; and a wide variety of ornaments.

The most common materials were sea mammal products: bone from the mandibles of large whales (jaw bone or pan bone); baleen (whalebone) from the mouths of baleen whales (the *Mysticeti*); the large ivory teeth of sperm whales (whale ivory) and walrus tusks. Other materials used as support for scrimshaw included wood, horn, shell, metal, and occasionally narwhal and other ivories. Although carvings and inlays were used, scrimshaw is characteristically decorated with pictures and designs resembling engravings, cut (or sometimes pricked) into polished surfaces with a fine blade or point and accentuated by color. Black was usually used on bone and ivory, but occasionally other colors (polychrome), especially red and Prussian blue, were used. Sperm whale teeth, walrus tusks, and bone plaques thus decorated remain the most popular scrimshaw. The softer baleen could take a very fine engraving, producing lighter lines or marks, the contrast improved by chalk and oil.

Whether naive or fine, the iconographic motifs give scrimshaw much of its appeal and help to indicate its origins and date. The images were legion, some copied or pricked out from popular illustrations of the time, such as women in fashionable clothes. Images drawn freehand included ships and whaling scenes, sailors, soldiers, naval battles, children and domestic scenes, theatrical and religious figures, buildings, patriotic emblems, animals and plants, valentines, the fantastic and the allegorical, often with trailing vines, hearts and flowers, and geometrical infill. Arctic scenes and fauna are surprisingly rare, but right whales with their rounded shape and two blowholes are occasionally shown among icebergs. Inscriptions with names, dates, and localities are rare, but can, as with provenances, confirm the scrimshaw as Arctic. Scrimshaw emerged during 17th-century Arctic whaling (in the Atlantic or Eastern Arctic) by

Scrimshaw carving on a sperm whale tooth that depicts an Inuk in a kayak hunting walrus.
Copyright Bryan and Cherry Alexander Photography

vessels from northern Europe hunting the Bowhead, Arctic Right whale, or Greenland whale, *Balaena mysticetus*. However, most scrimshaw is associated with American vessels hunting sperm whales on long voyages in the warm oceans of the world between 1830 and 1870, and decorated sperm whale teeth were among the most common form. However, as sperm whales declined, some ships also worked into the north Pacific (Western Arctic), where the first bowhead whale was caught in 1843. Thereafter, many whalers, even from Australia, worked north of the Bering Straits. In the 1880s, some vessels left New England ports for San Francisco. A plaque in the Hull Maritime Museum depicts an Arctic whaling scene, but the ship lacks a crow's nest, a barrel-shaped shelter near the main top- or topgallant-mast cap to protect the lookouts. It was used from the early 19th century by English and later Scottish Arctic whalers. Thus, the ship may have been a sperm whaler, in the Western Arctic. Most walrus tusks originated there too, so Western Arctic scrimshaw post-dates 1843 and earlier dates are fraudulent. Scrimshaw mirrored the rise and fall of old-style whaling (at times combined with sealing), which lingered into the early 20th century in both Arctic regions. It had a minor revival during modern mechanized (primarily Antarctic) whaling in the 20th century, but with sculpted forms predominating.

The most obvious materials used for Arctic scrimshaw are walrus and narwhal tusks and baleen. Walrus tusks can be 60–100 cm, are slightly curved, and angular in section with an irregular plug in the pulp cavity. They were decorated whole, usually engraved with many small motifs. Among the finest were those done by ex-whaleman Nathaniel S. Finney of San Francisco c.1860–70. Other tusks were cut up and used for tools or the staves for little tubs, and the like. Mature tusks have a layer of cementum surrounding a cortex of dentine. Unique to walrus is an inner core of marbled or crystalline secondary dentine.

Narwhal tusks reach 3 m and have obvious spiral ridges. They are primarily made of dentine with a layer of cementum around the root and the pulp cavity extends almost to the tip. Shortened, they made walking sticks, capped with ivory or silver. One was presented to Capt. Sir John Ross by Capt. Humphreys of the Hull whaler *Isabella*, which rescued him in 1833. They also made supports for bed canopies and companion rails on a luxury yacht.

The earliest datable scrimshaw is from the Arctic, a box of wood and baleen c.1631, engraved with Dutch whaling vessels and now at the Kendall Whaling Museum, Sharon, Massachusetts. The Dutch then dominated the whaling industry there. From 17th-century northern Germany and Friesland came mangle boards (linen presses) of wood or baleen, their upper surfaces usually deeply carved or relief cut.

Baleen is a form of keratin, a tough fibrous protein forming tightly packed horn tubes that grow from the roof of the mouth in thin, roughly triangular, tapering plates. Densely packed and with bristle fringes, they strain small crustaceans or fish from the sea. When intact, baleen from the twelve species of Mysticeti has a characteristic shape, size, and color but small pieces may be hard to identify. Baleen from the bowhead (Arctic right or Greenland whale), *Balaena mysticetus* grows the longest, up to 3 m, 30 cm wide and 2 cm thick at the base. However, without DNA analysis it would be difficult to tell pieces of it from that of the other right whales, *Eubaleana glacialis* (atlantic right or nordcaper) and *E. australis* (southern or black right), of a similar shape and black or dark brown when fresh.

As scrimshaw, baleen is most common as staybusks (corset stays), a rulerlike stiffening used in a pocket at the front of a bodice. Many finely engraved examples from the 19th century and some from the 18th have survived. Baleen can be heated and bonded together and was made into walking canes, switches, and riding whips. It was bent and molded into boxes, spoons, and ladles. When finely split, it could be braided and knotted and was more durable than rope: weighted with lead it made a cosh (a weighted weapon). As a dark contrast to bone or ivory, baleen was commonly used as edgings and inlays and is often mistaken for wood (although the dark rings on bone or ivory walking sticks are usually wood or horn).

A new type of art resembling scrimshaw developed after contact between Western whalemen and the Native people of Greenland, Canada, and Siberia, but especially of Alaska. Some turned to carving and engraving artifacts for Western taste, using mainly walrus tusks but also sperm whale teeth, mammoth ivory, bone, and baleen. Many, especially Angokwazhuk (Happy Jack *c.*1870–1918) of Little Diomede Island, are now famous. But although larger pieces may be distinctive, it can be impossible to distinguish their small objects from whalemen's work, although most native decorative art whether carvings, sculptures, or engravings is distinct from scrimshaw.

Since the revival of interest in scrimshaw in the United States during the mid-20th century and with high prices paid, especially for old pieces (19th century or earlier), the art form has been widely adopted by artists and craftsmen unconnected with whaling and the market has been flooded with modern scrimshaw, mostly decorated sperm whale teeth. Some is genuinely good modern art, occasionally signed and dated, but much is faking the old styles. Another large category of modern scrimshaw, mostly of small engraved or sculpted pieces and purporting to be done by Arctic native people on traditional materials, is sold in tourist and airport shops. In addition, the recent popularity of scrimshaw has stimulated the manufacture of plastic fakes, especially of walrus tusks and sperm whale teeth, decorated in the old styles.

JANET WEST

See also Bowhead (Greenland Right) Whale; Ivory Carving; Sperm Whale

Further Reading

Frank, S. M., *Dictionary of scrimshaw artists*, CT: Mystic Seaport Museum, 1991
———, *Fakeshaw: a checklist of plastic 'Scrimshaw'*, Sharon, Massachusetts.: Kendall Whaling Museum, 1993
Hellman, N. & N. Brouwer, *A Mariner's Fancy: The Whaleman's Art of Scrimshaw*, New York: Mystic Seaport Museum, 1992
Lawrence, M., *Scrimshaw, The whaler's legacy*, Pennsylvania: Schiffer, 1993
Malley, R., *Graven by the Fishermen Themselves*, Connecticut.: Mystic Seaport Museum, 1983
Ray, D.J., *Artists of The Tundra & The Sea*, Washington: University of Washington, 1980
West, J., "Scrimshaw in Australia with special reference to the nineteenth century." *The Great Circle (Journal of the Australian Association for Maritime History)*, Part 1: 8(2) (1986): 82–95; Part 11: 9(1) (1987): 26–39
———, "Scrimshaw and the identification of sea mammal products." *Journal of Museum Ethnography*, 2(1991): 39–79
West, J. & A.G. Credland, *Scrimshaw, the Art of the Whaler*, Hull: Hull City Museums & Hutton Press, 1995

SCULPIN

The sculpins are a diverse group of bottom-dwelling (benthic) fish comprising the family Cottidae (Order *Scorpaeniformes*, Class *Osteichthyes*). Of over 300 known species, a subset occupy Arctic waters throughout the north, where they are referred to as sea-scorpions by indigenous groups. Although indigenous peoples in some areas specifically recognize several species, the entire family is generally grouped under a single term. Within the Inuit and Yup'ik peoples of Arctic North America, as well as western Greenland, sculpins are generally known as *kanajuq* or *kanagjut*, a name that recognizes their similar body form to whales, despite their small size. In addition to *kanajuq*, sculpins are also known as *kajuqupak, kanijuraq*, and *kaauit* (i.e., "the one who puts himself in under the stones") by different dialects in Alaska. Additionally, the group is known as *nagssugtoq* or *nerokisilik* by groups in Eastern Greenland. Species inhabiting shallow coastal areas were traditionally captured by Inuit children either by hand or with a hook. It is said that these would be taken back to elders in the group, who considered them to be a delicacy (having a taste similar to cod).

Sculpins can most easily be recognized by their large, blunt heads (which can be over one-quarter of their body length), as well as posteriorly tapering bodies. Members of this family generally have few scales, but are often protected by plates or spines and possess further spines or bony knobs throughout the head region. The mouth and eyes are generally large, along with large pectoral fins. Spines are also often found on one of the two dorsal fin sections, as well as on the pelvic fins. Caudal, anal, and secondary dorsal fin

Arctic sculpin (*Myoxocephalus scorpioides*), Resolute Bay, Nunavut.
Copyright David R. Gray

portions are all generally soft-rayed. Species of the family Cottidae are bottom dwellers that lack swim bladders as adults, and are found ranging from shallow tide pools to great depths. As bottom feeders, they tend to be generalists, feeding on a variety of vertebrate and invertebrate prey.

Although sculpins are fairly diverse within Arctic waters, little is generally known about their biology and feeding habits, except for those that are abundant, or have had human uses. Examples of several species are given below.

The Arctic sculpin (*Myoxocephalus scorpioides*), also known by Canadian Inuit as *nagjulik*, is found from the East Siberian Sea westward across Northern Canada to the Bering Sea. This small species (generally less than 20 cm) is mostly found in shallow benthic or intertidal habitats, where it feeds mostly on crustaceans (particularly amphipods). Juveniles will often occupy shallow waters near stream inflows, which allows for facilitated human capture. Although little is known about the biology of this species in general, it is known to possess anti-freeze proteins that protect it against blood ice crystals to −2°C. Spawning takes place in the fall, with demersal (sinking to or deposited near the sea bottom) eggs.

The fourhorn sculpin (*Myoxocephalus quadricornis*) is an Arctic and Subarctic species with a wide circumpolar distribution, from the North American Arctic across to Greenland and Northern Eurasia. This common species is small (less than 25 cm), and easily identified by a dorsoventrally compressed head with four bony masses (that resemble horns) on top of the head, two between the eyes, and two further back. The fourhorn sculpin was occasionally used as food

by Inuit, who refer to it as *kanajurjuaq*. A likely reason for its traditional use was its ease of capture, as they inhabit shallow waters (generally less than 20 m), and periodically move into freshwater estuaries. This species is a generalist feeder, making use of crustaceans, molluscs, and small fish, as well as predating on eggs of its own or other species of fish. Reproduction generally occurs in the late fall, where adhesive eggs are laid in small clusters and are guarded by the male. Several relict populations of this species are also known to inhabit saline inland lakes in the Canadian Arctic, although these populations are said to be small and vulnerable to human influence.

The Arctic hookear sculpin (*Artediellus atlanticus*), also known as the snowflake hookear or the smooth hook-eared sculpin was traditionally known to the Inuit as *kanajuraq*. The range of this small species (less than 10 cm total length) extends northward along the Atlantic coast of North America to southern Baffin Island, and further east to Greenland (and may in fact be circumpolar). There has been considerable confusion about the actual range of this species, as it can be confused with similar species beyond Greenland such as the Atlantic hookear (*Artediellus atlanticus*=*Artediellus europaeus*). This and related species of sculpins can be easily distinguished by their hooked preopercular spines that are directed dorsally. Although little is known about the feeding habits of this species specifically, it is assumed to be a generalist on small bottom invertebrates within its 13–350 m range of bottom depth. Spawning takes place in late summer, where upward of 100 eggs are deposited in clumps.

The shorthorn or Greenland sculpin (*Myoxocephalus scorpius*) is well known to the Inuit as *kiivalik* or *kanajurjuaq*. It can be found throughout the Northern Atlantic Ocean and throughout the North American Arctic. Its range also extends past Greenland, Iceland, and Siberia. Reaching 90 cm in length, this is a much larger species that is distinguished in part by having upper preopercular spines that form straight points, and a large flat head with one short spine before the eyes. This sculpin occupies the benthos up to depths of 145 m (or deeper in warmer water), where it feeds on large crustaceans, sea urchins, molluscs, various fish species, and other prey that may be available. Well known to fishermen, the shorthorn sculpin was used as bait in lobster traps and angled around wharves for consumption. It also has a place in biological research, being used in pollution research. Spawning takes place in late fall, where adhesive eggs are laid in shallowwater (6–11 m deep) crevices, and guarded by the males until hatching.

Further Arctic-dwelling species in the family Cottidae include Arctic staghorn sculpin (*Gymnocanthus tricuspis*), armorhead sculpin (*Gymnocanthus galeatus*), Atlantic hookear sculpin (*Artediellus atlanticus*), bigeye sculpin (*Triglops nybelini*), bigmouth sculpin (*Hemitripterus bolini*), coastrange sculpin (*Cottus aleuticus*), leister sculpin (*Enophrys lucasi*), mottled sculpin (*Cottus bairdi*), moustache sculpin (*Triglops murrayi*), northern sculpin (*Icelinus borealis*), polar sculpin (*Cottunculus microps*), ribbed sculpin (*Triglops pingeli*), rough hookear sculpin (*Artediellus scaber*), slimy sculpin (*Cottus cognatus*), spatulate sculpin (*Icelus spatula*), spoonhead sculpin (*Cottus ricei*), and twohorn sculpin (*Icelus bicornis*).

CHRISTOPHER JASTREBSKI

See also **Fish**

Further Reading

Coad, Brian W., *Encyclopedia of Canadian Fishes*, Ottawa: Canadian Museum of Nature and Canadian Sportfishing Productions, 1995

Dickman, Mike, "An isolated population of fourhorn sculpins (*Myoxocephalus quadricornis*, Family Cottidae) in a hypersaline high Arctic Canadian lake." *Hydrobiologia*, 312 (1995): 27–35

Houston, J., "Status of the fourhorn sculpin, *Myoxocephalus quadricornis*, in Canada."*Canadian Field Naturalist*, 104 (1990): 7–13

Scott, W.B., & M.G. Scott, *Atlantic Fishes of Canada*, Toronto: University of Toronto Press, 1988

Smith, R.L., W.E. Barber, M. Vallarino, J. Gillispie & A. Ritchie, "Population biology of the Arctic staghorn sculpin in the Northeastern Chukchi Sea." *American Fisheries Society Symposium*, 19 (1997): 133–139

Walters, Vladimir, "Fishes of Western Arctic America and Eastern Arctic Siberia: taxonomy and zoogeography." *Bulletin of the American Museum of Natural History*, 106 (1955): 255–368

SEA ICE

The most dramatic feature of the Arctic is its ice-covered seas and ocean. Sea ice forms from the freezing of sea water during winter, and extends to cover most of the Arctic Ocean and its neighboring seas. Arctic sea ice covers an area of about 15 million km^2 at its wintertime peak. During the summer melt season, almost half this area melts, but sea ice persists through the summer over the central Arctic Ocean forming what is called the perennial ice pack. The area covered by sea ice only during winter is called the marginal ice zone. Sea ice also forms around the Antarctic continent, covering an area of about 19 million km^2. In contrast to the Arctic, most of the Antarctic sea ice is seasonal and only a quarter survives the summer melt. At any given time, about 25 million km^2 of sea ice covers the Earth, which is about the same area as the North American continent.

River ice and icebergs are often found at sea. Sea ice can be differentiated from these since river ice and glacier ice form from fresh water and are not salty like sea ice, and icebergs, produced by calving (breaking) off from land glaciers, are generally much larger than both sea and river ice.

Sea Ice Growth and Classification

The freezing point of sea water is typically about-1.8°C. Before freezing can begin at the sea surface, however, the entire uppermost (100–150 m) layer of sea water must be cooled to this temperature since cooling and sinking of surface sea water result in convection in this upper layer.

Sea ice is classified by its stage of development. The different stages are: new, nilas, pancake, young, first-year, and old (multi-year) ice. As sea ice grows, the prevailing atmospheric and ocean conditions affect how the sea ice forms.

There are four different types of new ice: frazil, grease, slush, and shuga. Frazil ice is composed of fine needles (or spicules) and platelets suspended in sea water. Under calm conditions, these needles and platelets grow and merge to form a thin sheet of ice at the water's surface. Under windy conditions, they are stirred up to form a soupy layer of coagulated frazil ice called grease ice, since this resembles a layer of grease on the surface of the water. Slush ice is formed when snow mixes with sea water, and shuga is a slightly more advanced stage of new ice composed of spongy white lumps that are a few centimeters across.

Nilas is a thin elastic crust of ice up to 10 cm thick (all thicknesses include both the above-water and below-water heights) that bends slightly with the waves. Pancake ice is composed of small, round, or polygonal pieces of ice that resemble pancakes, and often have raised edges that are produced when the

Sheets of nilas sea ice overlap each other with interlocking fingers, blown by the wind, Alaska. *Copyright Bryan and Cherry Alexander Photography*

pieces of ice rub against each other due to wind or wave action. Pancake ice can be up to 10 cm thick, with the individual pieces varying from 30 cm to 3 m in diameter. Young ice is in transition from nilas to first-year ice, and is composed of ice that is 10–30 cm thick. Thinner young ice is also called gray ice due to the visibility of the dark ocean beneath it, and the thicker young ice is called gray-white ice, the "whiteness" of the ice becoming more apparent. First-year ice, which also appears white, is 30 cm to 2 m thick, and can bear a man's weight. Helicopters can also land on thicker first-year ice. Old, or multiyear ice has survived at least one melting season, and has grown as ice is added to the underside. This ice is generally harder than first-year ice and is usually about 2–4 m thick.

Two other forms are fast and dirty ice. Fast ice is "fast" or anchored to the shore or to the seafloor and can usually be found over shallow ocean shelves at continental margins. Dirty ice contains sediments that may have been stirred up by waves and entrained in the ice while it was growing, or the ice may have formed on the seafloor and lifted sediments to the surface when it broke free.

Sea Ice Motion

Sea ice drifts over the ocean driven by winds and ocean currents. Over the Arctic Ocean, velocities are typically about 0.1 km h^{-1}, but may reach as high as 2 km h^{-1} during a storm. In Fram Strait and the Greenland Sea where ocean currents are faster, these velocities are typically about 0.5 km h^{-1}. Over the Arctic Ocean, most of the ice flows in a clockwise pattern known as the Beaufort Gyre, and exits the ocean through Fram Strait.

The average length of time for ice to drift from the central Arctic out through Fram Strait is about 5 years, but typically, ice at the North Pole will accelerate in the Transpolar Drift towards Fram Strait and only take a year to travel this distance (*see* **Transpolar Drift**).

The stresses imparted on sea ice by winds and ocean currents produce narrow cracks of open water, called leads (*see* **Leads**). It is in leads where most of the new ice forms during winter. Given that new cracks can form in areas of old ice, and that old ice may drift into areas of open water during summer, any given area of sea ice may have ice of a variety of ages.

Impacts of Sea Ice

Sea ice plays an integral part in the global climate system because it has a high albedo (reflectivity), it insulates the atmosphere from the ocean, and it transports fresh water (in the form of ice) across the Arctic Ocean. Most of the Sun's heat is absorbed in the Earth's warmer lower latitudes, but the atmosphere and ocean transport this heat to the poles where it is radiated back out to space. Sea ice plays an important role in maintaining the heat balance of the Earth because of its high albedo (reflecting most of the sunlight that shines on it), thus reducing the amount of heat absorbed by the Earth. If the area of sea ice increases, the average albedo of the Earth would increase. Conversely, sea ice acts like a blanket over the warm ocean, trapping the ocean's heat, insulating the cold atmosphere from the ocean below. This reduces the amount of heat that is radiated out to space. Most of the heat that does escape does so through the leads that expose areas of warmer sea water. As sea water freezes, heat is released to the atmosphere and

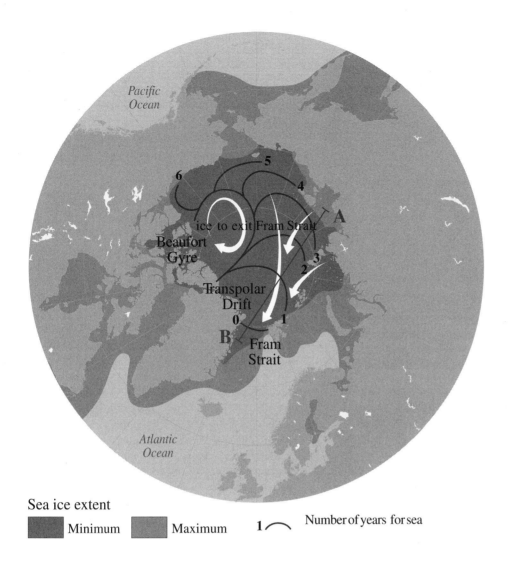

Sea ice extent

Minimum   Maximum   1 ⌒ Number of years for sea

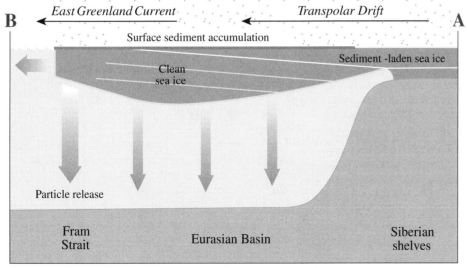

Average annual maximum and minimum sea ice extent. The numbered lines show the expected time in years for the ice at that location to exit the Arctic Ocean through the Fram Strait, based on drifting buoy data during 1979–1990. The lower panel shows a schematic representation of ice growth, surface melting, and sediment accumulation during drift of a hypothetical ice-floe.

Reproduced with permission from *AMAP Assessment Report: Arctic Pollution Issues*, Arctic Monitoring and Assessment Programme, 1998 some salt is expelled from the ice lattice, making older sea ice less salty. As sea ice drifts and eventually melts, it transports relatively fresher water from one region of the Arctic to another. Most of this ice is exported through Fram Strait into the convective regions of the Greenland and Labrador seas, where its melting may affect the global thermohaline circulation by lowering surface densities and preventing sinking of cold surface water. Sea ice may also provide a significant pathway for transboundary contaminant transport.

Sea ice provides a platform from which people and polar bears, seals, and walruses may hunt. Cracks in the sea ice also provide holes through which marine mammals, including whales, may breathe. Four species of seal also breed on Arctic sea ice.

Although sea ice accounts for roughly two-thirds of the Earth's ice cover by area, it only accounts for about 0.1% by volume. Thus, slight changes in climate greatly affect this thin veneer, and global warming will have a most pronounced effect in the polar regions. In fact, large decreases in sea ice extent and thickness have been noted in recent decades in the Arctic. This may be the first sign of global warming and climate change, which could ultimately lead to the Arctic Ocean becoming ice-free in summer. Changes in sea ice associated with changes in global climate may adversely affect polar bears, seals, and walruses, which depend entirely on sea ice for food and habitat. While sea ice presents a hazard to shipping, in a warmer climate, less ice may open the Northern Sea Route earlier and longer.

IGNATIUS G. RIGOR

See also **Arctic Ocean; Floe Edge; Ice Islands; Ice Shelves; Icebergs; Leads; Pancake Ice; Polynyas; Sikussak; Transpolar Drift**

Further Reading

Maykut, Gary A., *An Introduction to Ice in the Polar Oceans*, APL-UW 8510, Washington: Applied Physics Laboratory, University of Washington, 1985

Parkinson, C.L., *Sea Ice in the Polar Regions,* (CD-ROM) Consortium for International Earth Science Information Network (CIESIN), University Center, Michigan, 1996 (can be obtained from http://www.usra.edu/esse/learnmod.html.)

Parkinson, C.L., D.J. Cavalieri, P. Gloersen, H.J. Zwally, J.C. Comiso, "Arctic sea ice extents, areas, and trends, 1978–1996." *Journal of Geophysical Research*, 104(C9) (1999): 20837–20856

Pfirman, S.L., H. Eicken, D. Bauch & W.F. Weeks, "Potential transport of pollutants by Arctic sea ice." *Science of the Total Environment*, 159 (1995): 129–146

Rothrock, D.A. Y. Yu & G.A. Maykut, "Thinning of the Arctic sea-ice cover." *Geophysical Research Letters*, 26(23) (1999): 3469–3472

Smith, Orson P., *Observers' Guide to Sea Ice*, United States Department of Commerce, NOAA National Ocean Service, 2000 (can be obtained from http://www.engr.uaa.alaska.edu/ice/ice_guide/Ice_Guide.)

Wadhams, P., *Ice in The Oceans*, Amsterdam and Newark, New Jersey: Gordon and Breach, 2000

Wadhams, P. & N.R. Davis, "Further evidence of ice thinning in the Arctic Ocean." *Geophysical Research Letters*, 27(24) (2000): 3973–3975

Winsor, P., "Arctic sea ice thickness remained constant during the 1990s." *Geophysical Research Letters*, 28 (2001): 1039–1041

SEA OTTER

In 1741, the Russian ship *St Peter*, with Vitus Bering commanding and naturalist Georg Wilhelm Steller aboard, was wrecked on an uninhabited island off the shore of the Kamchatka Peninsula. Bering, who was 60 years old, died there of scurvy, but Steller and the other survivors managed to get back to the Siberian mainland, with descriptions of sea lions, gigantic "sea cows," and bundles of sea otter skins. Because it is the most luxurious fur on earth, the dense pelt of the sea otter sparked the invasion of the Aleutians by Russian fur hunters, which was perhaps the primary motivating factor for the colonization of "Russian America" (Alaska). The Aleuts knew the sea otter as *kalan*, and hunted them with spears from kayaks known as *baidarkas*. The early Russians forced the Aleuts (by holding their women hostage) to hunt otters for them because the Aleuts were better hunters and could better handle the *baidarkas*. The Russians called adult male otters *bobri morski* ("sea beaver"), the females *matka*, and the babies *medviedki*. An estimated 500,000–900,000 otters were killed between 1742, when the commercial harvest began, and 1910, when the unsuccessful final hunt was held.

The smallest of all marine mammals, sea otters (*Enhydra lutris*) do not exceed five feet in length, including the tail, and weigh no more than 75 pounds. They are almost totally aquatic, feeding, mating, and sleeping in the water, but, depending on conditions, giving birth in or out of the water. Males are larger than females, and can also be identified by their more massive head, neck, and shoulders, which become whiter with age. They have no blubber layer, but are insulated by tiny bubbles of air trapped in their two-layer fur coat. The color ranges from almost black through dark brown to reddish-brown, and it is darker when wet, which is almost always. The pelage consists of guard hairs that are about an inch-and-a-half long, and dense underfur that is about a quarter of an inch shorter. Each guard hair is surrounded by approximately 70 underfur hairs, and this makes the pelage of the otter about twice as dense as that of the fur seals. The coat of the average sea otter has close to a billion fur fibers. Sea otters spend a great deal of time floating on their backs, feeding and grooming themselves. They prefer to rest in kelp beds and often wrap themselves in kelp fronds to remain stationary. Sea otters

Pair of sea otters, Amchitka, Alaska.
Copyright Robert F. Sisson/National Geographic Image Collection

usually dive for their food in water that is less than 20 fathoms deep, but they can dive to 55 fathoms to forage for invertebrates such as sea urchins, abalone, clams, snails, and crabs. An average dive is about 90 seconds, but there have been recorded dives that lasted more than four minutes. They are among the few tool-using mammals, breaking open shellfish with rocks that they hold in their front paws. Their forefeet consist of manipulative "hands" with retractile claws, while their webbed hind feet have the longest toes on the outside, a unique arrangement in mammals. Their life expectancy, judging from a captive specimen, is around 17 years.

Once believed to be almost extinct, the sea otter has made a remarkable comeback. In the past, it was hunted for its fur, from northern Japan all around the islands of the north Pacific, and as far south as Baja California. By 1938, it was considered commercially extinct, that is, hunting was no longer worthwhile. After it was fully protected, "seed populations" were discovered in Alaskan and Russian waters, and the animal was reintroduced into its former range where it is now fully protected. There may be as many as 200,000 sea otters alive today. Most of them live in Alaskan, Aleutian, and Kamchatkan waters, but the somewhat smaller California sea otter, the subspecies known as *Enhydra lutris nereis*, has been reintroduced to the waters of northern California, where it is having an impact on the sea urchin population.

With no blubber layer, sea otters depend almost exclusively on their dense fur for insulation, and if the fur becomes matted by oil, they become dangerously vulnerable and subject to chilling in icy waters. On March 24, 1989, the 987-foot-long supertanker *Exxon Valdez* ran aground, dumping 11 million gallons of crude oil into Alaska's Prince William Sound, the largest oil spill ever to occur in the United States. Winds and shifting tides spread the oil over 10,000 square miles along the Alaska Peninsula, qualifying it as one of the worst ecological disasters in history. When the oil began to penetrate the fur of sea otters, the fur's insulating capacity was destroyed, and the otters may have groomed obsessively, increasing their ingestion of oil. Almost a thousand sea otter carcasses were picked up in the weeks following the spill, but the number that died may have been three or four times as high. Some 350 otters were captured for rehabilitation; of these, 114 died. In 1990, more than 1,000 sea otter carcasses were recovered, and for two more years, higherthan expected numbers of prime-age adult sea otters were found dead in western Prince William Sound.

RICHARD ELLIS

See also **Exxon Valdez; Fur Trade**

Further Reading

Brody, A.J., K. Ralls, & D.B. Siniff, "Potential impact of oil spills on California sea otters: implications of the *Exxon Valdez* spill in Alaska." *Marine Mammal Science,* 12(1) (1996): 38–53
Elliot, H.W., "The Sea Otter and Its Hunting." *A Report upon the Condition of Affairs in the Territory of Alaska.* House Executive Document 83, 44th Congress, 1st Session, Washington, 1875, pp. 54–62

————, "The Sea-Otter Fishery." *In The Fisheries and Fishery Industries of the United States*, edited by G.B. Goode, Section 5, Volume 2, General Printing Office, 1887, pp. 483–491

Estes, J.A., "*Enhydra lutris*. Mammalian species." *American Society of Mammalogists*, 133 (1980): 1–8

Garrott, R.A., L.L. Eberhart & D.M. Burn, "Mortality of sea otters following the *Exxon Valdez* spill." *Marine Mammal Science*, 9(4) (1993): 343–371

Gibson, J.R., *Otter Skins, Boston Ships, and China Goods*, Seattle: University of Washington Press, 1992

Kenyon, K.W., *The Sea Otter in the Eastern Pacific Ocean*, Washington: Bureau of Sport Fisheries and Wildlife, 1969

————, "Sea otter." In *Marine Mammals of Eastern North Pacific and Arctic Waters*, edited by D. Haley, Seattle: Pacific Search Press, 1978, pp. 226–235

————, "Sea otter—*Enhydra lutris* (Linnaeus, 1758)." In *Handbook of Marine Mammals, Volume 1: The Walrus, Sea Lions, Fur Seals and Sea Otter*, edited by S.H. Ridgway R.J. Harrison, San Diego: Academic Press, 1981, pp. 209–223

SEABIRDS

Seabirds are species that can live and feed offshore. Typical seabirds are pelagic and only come on land to breed. Others, more coastal seabirds, like divers, grebes, and ducks, also often occur on fresh water and are not described here (*see* **Brent Geese; Divers or Loons; Eider; Grebe; King Eider; Waders**). Typical seabirds breeding in the Arctic include the northern fulmar (*Fulmarus glacialis*), the great and pelagic cormorants (*Phalacrocorax carbo* and *P. pelagicus*), four skuas (*Stercoraius spp.*), 11 gulls, the Arctic tern (*Sterna paradisaea*), and 13 alcids. A few other species like the short-tailed and great shearwater (*Puffinus tenuirostris* and *P. gravis*), breeding in the Southern Hemisphere, also occur in Arctic waters during the summer season.

The only Arctic flightless seabird, the great auk (*Pinguinus impennis*), disappeared in 1844 when the two last birds were killed in southern Iceland for collectors (*see* **Auks**).

Arctic seabirds are particularly adapted to the harsh environment of polar seas. The round shape and short neck of alcids limit heat losses, as does the poor vascularization of many seabirds' feet. With the exception of cormorants, outer feathers are protected by an oil layer to avoid direct contact of the body with cold water.

If the tundra is generally poor in terms of productivity, Arctic marine ecosystems can be very rich, and even richer in biomass than many warm seas. Deepwater upwelling favors the development of phytoplankton, a basic component of a food web that includes animal plankton, small fishes, and finally seabirds. Also, upwelling (*see* **Polynyas**) is frequent in Arctic seas: close to the ice edge, where heavy winds mix and carry superficial waters away, where cold currents run along lands or encounter islands and more generally where waters differing in temperature and salinity meet (as, e.g., at the face of glaciers). It is therefore not surprising to find huge seabird colonies in the Arctic, sometimes holding several hundreds of thousands of pairs. The Bering Strait area (including Wrangel Island) is particularly well known for its endemic murrelets and auklets. In the northern Atlantic Ocean, largest colonies are found in Iceland, Svalbard, Bear Island, Norway, Jan Mayen, Iceland and West Greenland. Novaya Zemlya (Siberia), east of the Barents Sea, and the Lancaster Sound (Canada), west of the Baffin Sea, are also two major breeding areas for seabirds. In the central Canadian Arctic, East Greenland, and Siberian Islands (Franz Josef and New Siberian Islands), where seas remain frozen for most of the breeding season, black guillemot (*Cepphus grylle*) and ivory gull (*Pagophila eburnea*) are the most typical species, being particularly adapted to feed on the ice-associated fauna of the High Arctic.

Fulmar, alcids, and kittiwakes (*Rissa tridactyla*) form the largest colonies, some of the little auk (*Alle alle*) colonies holding several millions of birds. They breed in coastal cliffs (sometimes inland for fulmar), burrows (common puffin: *Fratercula arctica*), or scree slopes (little auk, auklets). Nesting in large colonies is sometimes necessary due to the lake of alternative breeding sites, but it is probably also advantageous to locate resources (if following successful feeders) and reduce predation risk, which is very high in the Arctic (by locating predators, mobbing them, and synchronizing emancipation of young). Arctic terns breed in small to medium colonies (rarely more than a hundred pairs) on fox-free island and are sometimes associated with Sabine's gull (*Xema sabini*). Isolated nests are occasionally found on gravely shores. Of special interest are the ivory and Ross's gull (*Rhodostethia rosea*). The first is found on High Arctic unvegetated islands, plateaus, or nunatak, sometimes several kilometers from the sea, while the second breeds in the central Siberian tundra and even in some wetland below the treeline, which is unexpected for a seabird that spends most of the year in the Arctic Ocean pack ice. Because they partly feed on birds and small mammals, skuas breed in the tundra or in seabird cliffs (great skuas). The long-tailed skua breeds as far north as Peary Land and northern Ellesmere Island and is therefore the northernmost seabird on Earth.

Excluding skuas, whose numbers vary annually (see below), population sizes of Arctic seabirds can be summarized as follows.

Alaska is one of the richest region in terms of seabirds. It holds 40 million birds (individuals), a quarter of them being guillemots. Other major species are northern fulmar (2 million), storm petrels (9 million), kittiwake (2.5 million), crested auklet (*Aethia cristatella*; 2 million), parakeet auklet (*Cyclorrhynchus psittacula*; 6 million), horned puffin (*Fratercula corniculata*; 1.5 million), and tufted puffin (*Fratercula cirrhata*; 4 million).

The former Soviet Union is poorer with only 6.5 million pairs (including about 1 million northern fulmar, 1.8 million Brünnich's guillemot, 0.6 million kittiwake, and more than half a million of auklets), the richest areas being Novaya Zemlya (west coast) and the Bering Strait (at least 3.3 million individuals).

Canadian censuses give a minimum figure of 4 million pairs with 1.3 million Brünnich's guillemot, 568,000 common guillemot (*Uria aalge*), 360,000 northern fulmar, 333 000 Atlantic puffin, and 204,000 kittiwake.

In Greenland, only 20 seabird species occur, but the total number of pairs is between nine and 27 millions. This inaccuracy is due to poor estimates of little auk (8–25 millions) and kittiwakes populations (140,000 to 1.15 million). Other major species are northern fulmar (about 200.000 pairs) and Brünnich's guillemot (200–250.000 pairs).

Similarly, Svalbard estimates give only 2.6–3.5 million pairs, but could increase if the minimum figure of 1 million little auks was clarified. Important populations of northern fulmar (100,000 to 1 million pairs), kittiwakes (270.000 pairs), Brünnich's guillemot (1.3 million individuals), and common guillemot (406,000 individuals) also breed on this archipelago.

According to some estimates, little auks could be the most abundant bird species in the Northern Hemisphere with more than 80 million individuals. On the other hand, some species have only small, and sometimes restricted, populations. Seventy percent of the 30–130,000 Kittlitz's murrelets, the rarest of all the alcids, breed in Alaska. Among gulls, Ross's and the ivory gulls have only a few tens of thousand pairs each, while the great skua is the rarest Arctic representative of its family with 13,600 pairs.

With the exception of some gulls and skuas, the seabirds mentioned above take all their food from the sea. Fish, molluscs, and crustaceans are the main prey types. Razorbill (*Alca torda*) and Brünnich's guillemot (*Uria lomvia*) are very specialized on fish while black guillemot, Arctic tern, and glaucous gull (*Larus hyperboreus*) also take significant numbers of molluscs when available. Pelagic crustaceans are the main prey of the little auk and are also highly sought after by northern fulmar, black guillemot, and Arctic tern. Many gulls have a more eclectic diet, including food collected on land (eggs, birds, lemmings, and berries), on shore (dead animals), or on the ice (ivory gull is famous for feeding on sea mammal carcasses and polar bear leftovers). During the summer season, great and Arctic skua (*Stercoracrius skua* and *S. parasiticus*) eat a significant number of birds (mainly young), but Pomarine and long-tailed skua (*Stercorarius pomarinus* and *S. longicaudus*) are highly specialized on brown (*Lemmus lemmus*) and collared lemmings (*Dicrostonyx groenlandicus*). Because these rodents undergo cyclic fluctuations (*see* **Microtines**), the breeding success of skuas greatly varies from year to year. This is totally original for seabirds spending the rest of the year in pelagic waters.

Wintering grounds of most Arctic seabirds are within the Northern Hemisphere, north of the Tropic of Cancer. Some species stay very far north, close to the ice edge, and even in polynyas. Ivory, Ross's gull, little auk, and, to a lesser extent Brünnich's guillemot belong to this group. A few, however, like skuas and Sabine's gull, migrate further south and can be found in the Southern Hemisphere during wintertime. The Arctic tern is a particular case since it spends winter in the Antarctic waters and summer in the Arctic, performing the longest migration of any animal on Earth, some 30–50,000 km a year for the round-trip.

Migration routes are generally coastal or pelagic for fulmar, skuas, and auks that are only accidentally encountered inland but some species, especially gulls, have continental flyways. The Tayer's gull (*Larus thayeri*), breeding in the Canadian Arctic archipelago and in the Thule region (Greenland), has an inland migration of several thousand kilometers through North America to join its wintering ground of the west coast, from British Columbia to Baja California.

Although all alcids have decreased (both in population size and in breeding range) during the last century, none of the Arctic seabirds is currently threatened with extinction. But some have small populations, and the threats are numerous.

Human exploitation for food by aboriginal people is no longer significant in Alaska, where seabirds suffer more from introduced foxes and rats on their breeding islands. In Canada and Greenland, where nowadays seabird hunting is more for recreation than for subsistence, this threat is still serious for guillemots (several hundred thousands killed annually in Canada). Oil pollution is the most serious threat in many regions and especially in Alaska where seabirds are numerous and nearly half of the US oil stock is located. This was illustrated by the 35,000 tons of oil released by the *Exxon Valdez*, which killed about half a million birds compared with only 4500 birds killed by the 250,000 tonn released by the *Amoco Cadiz* in France. It is believed that one major spill could kill several million birds in Alaska. Commercial fishing is another important threat for guillemots, puffins, and migrating shearwaters, with several hundred thousands of birds killed annually in nets, only in Alaska. Indirectly, fisheries also reduce numbers of breeding seabirds through reduction of their preys. On Bear Island in the Barents Sea, the common guillemots' population decreased from 245,000 to 36.000 pairs within one year following the collapse of the capelin (*Mallotus villosus*) stock, its main prey.

Persistent organic pollutants, heavy metals, and radioactivity are other worrying threats that do not spare Arctic seabirds. Atmospheric and oceanic currents transport pollutants through the entire Arctic. Most exposed are top predators of the marine food web. Organochlorine levels are five to ten times higher in Canadian glaucous gull than in other seabirds. For many Canadian and Norwegian species, PCB (polychlorinated biphenyls) levels exceed critical values that are known to affect reproduction.

Among the Arctic seabirds, some species were crucial for the subsistence of some aboriginal populations. Gulls were only occasionally hunted since large colonies are rare, except for the kittiwake. Terns were highly sought after for their eggs. But the most important seabirds for Arctic peoples are unquestionably the alcids. In Novaya Zemlya, where several million Brünnich's guillemots occur, villagers have used eggs, meat (for humans, dogs, and to bait foxes), feathers, down, and skins for several centuries and they even exported some produces to other Russian regions. These produces were of high value (guillemot eggs being heavier and richer in some vitamins and carotenoids than hen eggs) and represented up to 35% of the island exports in 1933. At the beginning of the 20th century, foreign traders also joined to collect eggs for the soap industry.

Seabirds were even more important in some Inuit settlements that could not hunt seal in summer after the ice had gone. In such places, peoples would not have survived without feeding on little auks. This was the case in Greenland, where auks and Brünnich's guillemots have always been a major food source, even in the southern Norse colonies of the Middle Ages. Hence, settlements were often located close to auk colonies. Birds were eaten raw (fresh or frozen), boiled, and also after being stored for several months under piles of stones.

Cormorants, auklets, little auk, and guillemot skins were also used to make clothes, rugs, and bags, especially in northern Greenland and Alaska, where auklet feather sheaths were used as ornaments.

Nowadays, seabird hunting and egging have become recreational activities rather than subsistence ones. But due to population increase, the use of rifles, and easy access to colonies by motorboats, the number of seabirds taken annually in some region has increased during the last decades. This is especially true in West Greenland, where many initiatives (including regulation and also information and education) have been developed to increase public awareness of this issue.

Whalers and explorers have also used seabird colonies for several hundred years. Although all species of birds were hunted and eaten, they were also looking for some edible plants. The rich and tall vegetation that is found beneath the colonies is due to the eutrophication (high levels of nutrients: potassium, phosphors, calcium, nitrogen, and others) of the tundra through accumulation of bird droppings and dead animals (including young birds and lost preys). Also, in northwest Svalbard, where whaling was important, scurvy grass (*Cochlearia officinalis*) is far lusher beneath kittiwake and Brünnich's guillemot colonies than anywhere else.

OLIVIER GILG

See also **Auks; Brent Geese; Divers or Loons; Eider; Fulmar; Grebe; Guillemot; Gulls; King Eider; Kittiwake; Puffins; Razorbill; Skuas and Jaegers; Tern; Waders**

Further Reading

AMAP (Arctic Monitoring and Assessment Programme), *Arctic Pollution Issues: A State of the Arctic Environment Report*, Oslo: AMAP, 1997

Brown, R.G.B. & N.D. Nettleship, "The seabirds of northeastern North America : their present status and conservation requirements." *ICBP Technical Publication, 2* (1984): 85–100

Del Hoyo, Joseph, Andrew Elliot & Jordi Sargatal, *Handbook of the Birds of the World*, Volume 3, Barcelona: Lynx Edicions, 1996

Evans, P.G.H., "The seabirds of Greenland : their status and conservation," *ICBP Technical Publication, 2* (1984):49–84

Golovkin, Alexandre N., "Seabirds nesting in the USSR : their status and protection of populations," *ICBP Technical Publication, 2* (1984): 473–486

Harrison, Peter, *Seabirds*, London: Christopher Holm, 1983

Konyukhov, Nikolai B., Ludmila S. Bogoslovskaya, Boris M. Zvonov & Thomas I. Van Pelt, "Seabirds of the Chukotka Peninsula, Russia." *Arctic*, 51(4) (1998): 315–329

Lensink, Calvin J., "The status and conservation of seabirds in Alaska," *ICBP Technical Publication*, 2 (1984): 13–27

Mehlum, Fridtjof & Vidar Bakken, "Seabirds in Svalbard (Norway): status, recent changes and management." *BirdLife Conservation Series*, 1 (1994): 155–171

Nettleship, David N. & Tim R. Birkhead, The Atlantic Alcidae, London: Academic Press, 1985

Sage, Brian, The Arctic and its Wildlife, New York: Facts on Files, 1986

Tuck, Gerald S. & Hermann Heinzel, *A Field Guide to the Seabirds of Britain and the World*, London: Collins, 1978

Vaugan, Richard, In Search of Arctic Birds, London: Poyser, 1992

SEAL SKIN DIRECTIVE

In 1983, the Council of Ministers for the European Economic Community approved Directive 83/129/EEC, banning importation of skins of harp and hooded seal pups for two years. This was renewed in 1985 and amended in 1989 (Com 89/198/final). It was the culmination of the first Animal Rights/antiharvest campaign, and was a harbinger of more campaigns to follow. Focused on the industrial seal hunt for harp and hooded seal pups off Newfoundland, it had profound corollary impacts on peoples around the circumpolar Arctic, and harvests of other kinds of seals.

Public attention was focused on the hunt in the 1950s, based on concerns about cruelty and ecological damage caused by the size of the hunt. Canada brought the hunt under strict and detailed regulatory supervision by 1961, and by the 1970s the survival of the population was ensured. At that time, several conservation organizations withdrew from the antisealing campaign. Greenpeace, however, claimed in 1977 that unless the seal quotas were reduced, seals would be extinct in five years. When it was proven that there was no population threat, and the management system was effective, Greenpeace moved to an animal rights position that seals should not be hunted at all.

The International Fund for Animal Welfare and Greenpeace took the campaign to Europe and the United States, where there was a long history of wildlife loss, and a public sympathetic to animals. Tactics included gruesome films of the seal hunt (later proven to have been staged), pictures of blood-stained pups, performances of blood-spattered sealers clubbing "baby" seals in Trafalgar Square in London and other European centers, and direct mailings to households containing pictures of the hunt. Against this, scientists' models showing the strength of seal populations, and veterinarians' proofs that clubbing was indeed the most humane and effective way to kill seal pups, were powerless. Indeed, they failed to deal with the foundation of the campaign, which was actually the acceptability of killing animals.

The campaign was most effective; within a few years, the European Parliament and the European Community decided to ban imports of seal pup pelts, thus ending an industry that had been an important part of the Newfoundland economy for 150 years. Because of the Danish concern about the effects of the EC Directive on Greenland's sealing, the ban explicitly allowed for Inuit sealing and other harvesting, but only as "traditionally practiced" and if it formed "an important part of the traditional way of life and economy."

The Inuit, at first, thought that the campaign had nothing to do with them; they did not normally hunt seal pups, and some had concerns themselves about the nature of the industrial hunt in Newfoundland. After a few years, it became obvious that consumers did not discern between different kinds of sealskins, and the adult seal pelts sold by Inuit were equally affected. The thriving Inuit economy, based on seal hunting for food and skins, had also been destroyed.

The seal hunt revenues of $13 million per year in 1981 (roughly split between 2000 Inuit hunting adult seals and 3000 Newfoundlanders hunting pups) declined to less than $3 million in 1983. In the Northwest Territories and northern Québec, seal pelt sales declined from 44,268 in 1980/1981 to 7699 in 1983/1984; the value of pelts sold declined from $952,590 to $76,681 in the same period. Eighteen out of 20 Inuit villages in the Northwest Territories were estimated to have lost 60% of their total annual community income. Food security and economic independence were undermined. Self-supporting communities were reduced to welfare dependency, with a staggering suicide rate, as people seriously questioned themselves and their culture in the face of condemnation by a modern, dominant, and more powerful society in southern North America and Europe.

The Inuit continue to feel embittered by the campaign and its results. They feel misrepresented, and undermined by the persistent ignorance of Inuit lifestyles and economies, including the relevance of subsistence and cash-economy activities. Further threats exist from some activists who question whether modern Inuit seal-hunting is "traditional" and "an important part of the economy."

Greenland continues to actively support hunters in their production of sealskins, and the Nunavut government is developing a Sealskin Strategy, aimed at enhancing the potential uses of sealskins. Seal hunting is recognized as a key part of Inuit identity and nutrition. Fuller use of sealskins would complement the continued food hunt of seals and create some much-needed economic opportunities. Whether markets outside the North can be educated about the sustainability of this kind of use of seals remains to be seen.

HEATHER MYERS

See also **Animal-Rights Movements and Renewable Resources; Fur Trade; Trapping**

Further Reading

Allen, Jeremiah, "Anti-sealing as an industry." *Journal of Political Science,* 87(2) (1979): 423–428

Bonner, Nigel, *Seals and man: a study of interactions,* Seattle: University of Washington Press, 1982

Davies, Brian, *Savage luxury: the slaughter of the baby seal,* London: Souvenir Press

Lynge, Finn, *Arctic Wars: animal rights, endangered peoples,* Hanover: University Press of New England, 1970

Malouf, Albert (Chair), *Seals and sealing in Canada: Report of the Royal Commission,* 3 volumes, Ottawa: Supply and Services Canada, 1986

Wenzel, George, *Animal rights, human rights: ecology, economy and ideology in the Canadian Arctic,* London: Belhaven, 1991

SECOND KAMCHATKA EXPEDITION

The Second Kamchatka Expedition of 1733–43 (also known as the Great Northern Expedition) was perhaps one of the largest scientific expeditions ever organized and the most ambitious in scope, and resulted in comprehensive exploration, mapping, and scientific investigation of the Russian-Siberian coast and the west coast of North America. Proposed by Captain-Commander Vitus Bering to the Russian Admiralty College after his return in 1730 from the First Kamchatka Expedition, the expedition was officially organized on April 17, 1732 following a decree issued to the Senate by the Empress Anna Ioannovna, niece of Peter I (note: all dates are old Russian style or Julian Calendar: add 11 days for the modern equivalent). Bering, head of the First Kamchatka Expedition, was appointed as the leader of the new expedition. Captain of second rank Alexey Chirikov was appointed as his second-in-command. The goal of the second expedition was to prove a question that had not been completely resolved by the First Kamchatka Expedition, that is, to discover whether Asia and North America were separated by sea (thus enabling a North East Passage to India and China), and also to chart the northern coasts of Siberia and the Far East, and locate and map the American coastline. On the order of the Senate to the Admiralty of May 2, 1732, and later on the instructions of the Admiralty of October 16, 1732 and February 28, 1733, it was recommended to Bering to build two packetboats in Kamchatka and to start an expedition with the purpose of exploring the coasts and seas of the northern part of the Pacific Ocean. Bering and Chirikov were to initiate trade with the inhabitants of the newly discovered territories, and to include them, under favorable circumstances, in the Russian Empire as its subjects. Simultaneously, Bering was to observe maximum caution when contacting Europeans in America, and not to inform them, by any means, of the sea routes to Kamchatka: strict secrecy was the tradition of all Russian government expeditions to the Pacific Ocean during the 18th century. A detachment headed by Captain Martin Spanberg was set apart within the Second Kamchatka Expedition with the special aim of further exploration of the Kuril Islands (1738–1742). A further semiindependent group consisting of members and students of the St Petersburg Academy of Science, the so-called Academic Expedition, was an overland expedition led by Gerhard Friedrich Müller and Johann Georg Gmelin and included Stepan Petrovich Krasheninnikov.

Preparations for Bering's expedition to America lasted for several years. The two packetboats were built in Okhotsk. Each ship had a dead weight of more than 360 tons and each had 14 cannon and three falconets (short cannon). The *St Peter* was designated as a flagship; it carried 77 men, including Commander Bering. The second ship, the *St Paul*, under the command of Captain Chirikov, had a crew of 75. On June 4, 1741, the two ships sailed from Avacha Bay in Kamchatka, after having wintered in Petropavlovsk. For over a week, the vessels made their way southeast in search of the mythical Juan da Gama Land, said to lie in the North Pacific. Not finding any signs of land in the ocean, they turned east, toward the American continent. On June 20, in storm and fog, the ships lost each other and eventually reached the American shore separately.

Chirikov's packetboat approached the American coast first on July 15, (55°20′ N). This was in the vicinity of the Alexander Archipelago, populated by Tlingit Indians. After sailing along the coast to the north, Chirikov reached latitude 58°N and on July 8 decided to renew the ship's supply of fresh water. He sent a well-armed boat, with ten men headed by naval master A. Dement'ev, to the coast. The boat disappeared near the wooded shore and never returned. After five days spent near the place of the assumed debarkation of Dement'ev, the crew of the *St Paul* noticed fire and smoke on the shore. Chirikov decided that it was a distress signal, and on July 24, sent out his last boat, with three seamen headed by boatswain S. Savel'ev. That boat also disappeared. In vain, Chirikov maneuvered near the coast, from time to time firing the ship's cannon to give his men a signal to return. The fire on the shore seemed to burn more brightly after each cannon shot, but Savel'ev's boat was not seen again. The day after its loss, two Indian canoes carrying several Tlingit appeared from the bay. They did not approach the ship, but called out and made gestures inviting the *St Paul* crew to follow them to the coast. Having waited for another couple of days, Chirikov, together with his officers, made the difficult decision to return to Kamchatka without the men who had gone ashore. The shortage of fresh water on the vessel and the approach of autumn made it necessary to hurry. Lack of food and water on the return journey led to extreme weakness among the crew; six people died of scurvy. Although the *St Paul* on its way to Kamchatka noticed and passed the Kenai Peninsula on August 1, Kodiak Island on August 3, and a group of the Aleutian Islands (Umnak Island on September 5, Adak Island on September 9, and the Near Islands on September 22), the crew was unable to renew the ship's supply of water and provisions, in spite of occasional contacts with the Aleut near Adak Island. Finally, on October 12, 1741, the *St Paul* cast anchor in Petropavlovsk.

The fate of Chirikov's men who disappeared on the American shore remains mysterious. Chirikov himself (as well as the majority of contemporary researchers) assumed that they had been killed or captured by natives. Some researchers prefer to believe that the men perished in the dangerous whirlpools on the coast. However, the version that survived in local legend appears more convincing: the Russians who landed on Kruzof Island in search of fresh water simply chose not to return to the ship because of the severe discipline aboard. The deserters were welcomed by the local Tlingit and eventually married native women. But fearing that sooner or later the Russian ship would come to collect them, and they would have to undergo punishment as deserters, they, together with their families, went south and settled on Prince of Wales Island. Thirty-five years later, members of a similar Spanish expedition saw several Russian objects on Prince of Wales Island, and even in the early 20th century the head of the Tlingit settlement Klawock on that island was a Native Alaskan whose name and appearance clearly betrayed his Russian origin.

The voyage of the *St Peter* under the command of Bering was no less dramatic. His vessel approached the coast of America on July 17, in the Kayak Island area at latitude 58°14′ N. The crew, and the naturalist Georg W. Steller, landed on the island several times, but failed to establish contact with the natives. On the mainland shore, they discovered one of the highest mountains of Alaska, Mt St Elias (5 488 m). After several days near Kayak Island, Bering took his vessel northwest. On their way back to Kamchatka, the crew saw the shores of the large Kodiak Island. Subsequently, they discovered Chirikov Island and the Shumagin Islands, where on September 5, the first contact with the Aleut took place. The ship then went along the Aleutian island chain. The Andreianov Islands were passed on September 25, Kiska Island of the Rat Islands on October 23, and the Near Islands on October 28. Finally, after a stormy passage, on November 6, the *St Peter* approached an uninhabited island and cast anchor. On November 28, the vessel was wrecked on the coast of that island, later named in honor of Bering who died here on December 8. Many seamen also died of scurvy during the severe winter of 1741–1742. In August 1742, 46 surviving men built a small vessel from the remainders of their ship and sailed to Kamchatka. On August 26, they reached Petropavlovsk, bringing with them several hundred valuable sea otter and Arctic fox skins—the product of their winter hunting on Bering Island.

While the surviving members of the crew of the *St Peter* prepared to return to Kamchatka, on May 25, 1742, Captain Chirikov left for a new voyage on the *St Paul* to the east of Kamchatka. On June 9, the ship approached Attu Island (the Near Islands). After ascertaining that this was indeed an island and not part of a continent, Chirikov decided to turn back. On June 17, the *St Paul* passed Bering Island and on July 2 Chirikov brought his ship into the Petropavlovsk har-

bor, where about two months later the surviving crew members of the *St Peter* also arrived. Thus, the Second Kamchatka Expedition was completed. Officially, it ended according to the edict of the Senate on September 25, 1743.

On the whole, the Russian government was dissatisfied with the results of the expedition. It had yielded only very fragmentary geographical information, the discovered territories had not been fully explored, and their inhabitants had not been turned into Russian subjects. Moreover, it had cost an enormous sum of money (more than 360,660 roubles) to organize and supply the Second Kamchatka expedition. Losses increased further through the wreck of one of the vessels. Fifty-two men, a third of all participants in the expedition, including its head, never returned home. For a long time, the government showed no interest in the organization of new research voyages to the Pacific Ocean. The initiative in this matter was switched to private individuals—the enterprising Siberian merchants and *promyshlenniks*, who started hunting and trading valuable furs in the islands to the east of Kamchatka, discovered by the Bering-Chirikov expedition. In contrast to the czarist government, the results of the Second Kamchatka Expedition were very highly appreciated later by seafarers and scientists; many features in the Pacific Ocean were mapped and named by its participants. Thanks to the efforts of the expedition's members, the city of Petropavlovsk was founded; the infrastructure of East Siberia was improved; the southeastern coasts of Alaska with the adjacent islands and the Aleutian chain were discovered; and a scientific study of the land, flora, and fauna of Kamchatka and Alaska was initiated. The fact that a Russian, Captain Chirikov, first reached the American coast at 55° N in 1741 gave Russia grounds to pretend to have discovered all American territories north of this point. This was the political value of the Second Kamchatka Expedition. But its most important results were without doubt the beginning of the Russian colonization of the Komandorsky (Commander) Islands, the Aleutian Islands, and Alaska. A group of Russian colonies, the so-called "Russian America," was formed there toward the end of the 18th century.

A.V. GRINEV

See also **Bering, Vitus; Chelyuskin, Semyon; Chirikov, Alexei; Krasheninnikov, Stepan; Laptev, Dmitriy; Laptev, Khariton; Steller, Georg**

Further Reading

Alekseeva, A.I., A.L. Narochnitskogo, I.N. Solov'eva & T.S. Fedorovoi (editors), Russkie ekspeditsii po izucheniu severnoi chasti Tikhogo okeana v pervoi polovine XVIII v. Sbornik dokumentov. [Russian Expeditions for the Study of the North Pacific Ocean in the First Half of the 18th century. A Collection of Documents], Moskva: Nauka, 1984

Divina, V.A. (editor), Russkaia tikhookeanskaia epopeia [Russian epoch of the Pacific Ocean. A collection of Documents], Khabarovsk: Khavarovskoe knizhnoe izdatel'stvo, 1979

Ekspeditsia Beringa. Sbornik documentov. Podgotovil k pechati A. Pokrovskii [Bering's Expedition. A Collection of Documents. Prepared for print by A. Pokrovskii], Moskva: Glavnoe arkhivnoe upravlenie NKVD SSSR, 1941

Fisher, Raymond H. Bering's Voyages, Whither and Why, Seattle: University of Washington Press, 1977

Frost, A.W. (editor), Bering and Chirikov: The American Voyages and Their Impact, Anchorage, Alaska: Alaska Historical Society, 1992

Golder, Frank A., Bering's Voyages: An Account of the Efforts of the Russians to Determine the Relation of Asia and America. Volume 2 New York: American Geographical Society, 1925

Jacobs, Jr., Mark, In Early Encounters between the Tlingit and Russians Russia in North America. Proceedings of the Second International Conference on Russian America (Sitka, Alaska, August 19–22, 1987), edited by R.A. Pierce, Kingston, Ontario: Fairbanks, Alaska: Limestone Press, 1990, pp.1–6

Lebedev, Dmitrii M. Plavanie A.I.Chirikova na paketbote "Sv.Pavel" k poberezhiam Ameriki. S prilozheniem sudovogo zhurnala 1741 g [The Voyage of A.I. Chirikov in the packetboat St. Paul to the shores of America, together with the ship's log-book of 1741], Moskva: AN SSSR, 1951

Salisbury, Oliver M., The Customs and Legends of the Tlingit Indians of Alaska, New York: Bonanza Books, 1962

Steller, Georg Wilhelm, In Journal of a Voyage with Bering, 1741–1742, edited by O.W. Frost, Stanford, California: Stanford University Press, 1988

SECONDARY PRODUCTION

Secondary production is the increase in mass of species that are not primary producers, beginning with herbivores that feed on plants or algae (the primary producers) at the base of the food web and extending through to carnivores like bears and wolves. Rates of Arctic photosynthesis (see **Primary Production**) are relatively low, and therefore secondary production is also low. Arctic consumers are thus adapted to sparse and/or periodic food supplies. For example, most arctic animals also store large amounts of fat during or after the summer season, metabolizing it later in winter and spring.

On land, food chains are short, typically with three trophic levels, such as plants → caribou and muskox → wolves; or plants → lemmings → owls and Arctic foxes. Lemming populations tend to be cyclic along with their predators. Good lemming years result in high survival of young predators, which then overpower the herbivores in the following years, perpetuating the abundance and decline cycle. Although most terrestrial Arctic mammals are nonmigratory, many caribou herds move north and south with the seasons, their wolf predators following. Caribou production is critical to most

wolf populations, and is also very important to humans, who use the meat for food and the skins for clothing. Muskox production is also high in some areas, especially Canada's Arctic islands.

In freshwater ecosystems, food chains are also short, for example, plants and algae → aquatic insects such as caddis fly larvae → birds or fish.

In the sea, food chains are remarkably long, with five trophic levels in the Arctic Ocean despite the low rates of photosynthesis per unit area (see **Primary Production, Marine**). Depending upon latitude, the return of sunlight in February or March allows algae living in the bottom of the sea ice to grow. With the disappearance of snow cover in June comes the beginning of the phytoplankton bloom, accelerated when the ice breaks up sometime in July. The bloom wanes in September as the polar night again approaches.

Thus, marine consumers are dependent upon a brief pulse of primary production. Those species exploiting ice algae, predominantly amphipods, copepods, and nematodes, get a head start in early spring. But most herbivores depend upon two months or so of phytoplankton production in summer, storing large quantities of lipids to tide them over the lean winter. These fat herbivores are then eaten by predators, and as the energy is transferred up the food web the seasonal pulse of growth and lipid deposition comes later in the year, becoming less pronounced in top carnivores.

In the Arctic seas, algae and phytoplankton consumers (herbivores) include the microscopic zooplankton carried passively by ocean currents (crustaceans like the amphipods, copepod *Calanus hyperboreus*, mysids); planktonic larvae of barnacles, crabs, clams, and worms; and larger crustaceans, such as the benthic bivalve *Mya truncata*. Many small invertebrates in the zooplankton, including the euphausiids such as *Euphausia pacifica*, are carnivores feeding on other plant-eating crustaceans. Note that while the Antarctic krill, *Euphausia superba*, is the dominant zooplankton species in the Antarctic, there is no dominant Arctic zooplankton species. At the third trophic level, Arctic cod (*Boreogadus saida*) are the most abundant and are a keystone secondary producer species. Occurring both singly and in schools of many million individual fish, they convert microscopic zooplankton into packets of energy large enough to sustain narwhal, beluga, ringed and harp seals, and the seabirds northern fulmar, thick-billed murre, and black-legged kittiwake, all at the fourth trophic level. At the apex of the pyramid is the polar bear, which preys primarily on ringed seal throughout the Arctic.

Marine species tend to be long-lived and grow slowly. Thus, in Lancaster Sound (Canada), the clam *Mya truncata* maintains a high biomass of 115 g dry biomass per square meter (115 g m^{-2}), but its annual growth (production) is only 3% as much. Other examples are seabird colonies where, despite the hundreds of thousands of breeding birds, the annual production is low because the birds do not become mature for up to five years (depending upon the species), and even then, fledging success for one or two chicks is also low. This maintenance of high biomass with relatively low growth is typical of Arctic animals and explains why, despite there apparently being a large harvestable biomass in a population, the sustained yield is only a few percent of that biomass.

How much secondary production is there in polar waters? Typical primary production rates are about 60 g carbon per square meter per year ($60 \text{ g m}^{-2}\text{a}^{-1}$), or 150 g dry biomass, over the Arctic continental shelves. This productivity rate is reduced by about 90% at each subsequent trophic level. For the polar bear at the fifth trophic level, for example, this leaves on the order of $0.001 \text{ g m}^{-2}\text{a}^{-1}$ for polar bear production. To grow a 400 kg bear requires production from $4 \times 10^8 \text{ m}^2$ or 40 square kilometers of ocean surface, and over the deep Arctic Ocean the productivity is even less — hence the scarcity of polar bears.

Arctic lakes are even less productive per unit area, as low as $10 \text{ g m}^{-2}\text{a}^{-1}$. Food webs are simple and short, dominated by one or two species of herbivorous copepods and numerous dipteran species belonging to the family Chironomidae. Chironomid larvae live on the lake bottoms and emerge as adults after ice disappears, quickly laying their eggs to begin another one-, two-, or three-year generation. Throughout most of the Arctic, the Arctic char (*Salvelinus alpinus*) is the common fish species, with additions of lake trout (*S. namaycush*), sticklebacks, and coregonids. These fish depend mostly on chironomid larvae for early growth. Char and especially lake trout become fish-eaters as they grow larger, and in lakes with only one or two species, develop a "cannibal" fourth trophic level.

Many Arctic char populations are landlocked, but in those lakes and large rivers with access to (and from) the sea, they become anadromous. At several years of age and 15–20 cm length, the smolts go to sea in late June, feed heavily, and return in late August to overwinter in fresh water. While overwintering, they feed little or not at all, living on stored fat. Anadromous char runs are impressive, often with many thousand fish returning simultaneously, and they traditionally supported Inuit in fall and early winter, when the fat fish were speared with the *kakivak* (leister) and stored in rock caches. Despite the obviously high biomass, though, only a few percent of that biomass can be harvested as annual production without decimating the stock, as human consumers have learned the hard way.

HAROLD WELCH

See also **Food Chains; Food Webs, Marine; Primary Production; Trophic Levels**

Further Reading

Bliss, L.C. (editor), *Truelove Lowland, Devon Island, Canada: A High Arctic Ecosystem*, Edmonton, Alberta: The University of Alberta Press, 1977

Bliss, L.C., O.W. Heal & J.J. Moore (editors), *Tundra Ecosystems: A Comparative Analysis*, Cambridge: Cambridge University Press, 1981

Fridriksson, S., "Factors Affecting Production and Stability of Northern Ecosystems." In *Grazing Research at Northern Latitudes*, edited by O. Gudmundsson, New York: Plenum Press, 1986, pp. 27–35

Murray, J.L., "Ecological Characteristics of the Arctic." In *Arctic Monitoring and Assessment Programme: Arctic Pollution Issues*, Oslo: AMAP Secretariat, 1998 (references practically all other important Arctic productivity studies as well as reviews, and has several appropriate food web diagrams)

Rigler, F.H., "The Char Lake Project." In *Energy Flow—Its Biological Dimensions: A Summary of the IBP in Canada, 1964–1974*, edited by W.W.M. Cameron W. Billingsley, Ottawa: Royal Society of Canada, 1975, pp. 171–198

Sakshaug, E., C.C.E. Hopkins & N.A. Øritsland (editors), "Proceedings of the Pro Mare Symposium on polar marine ecology, Trondheim, 12–16 May 1990." *Polar Research*, 10(1) (1990)

Welch, H.E., M.A. Bergmann, T.D. Siferd, K.A. Martin, M.F. Curtis, R.E. Crawford, R.J. Conover & H. Hop, "Energy flow through the marine ecosystem of the Lancaster Sound region, Arctic Canada." *Arctic*, 45(1992): 343–357. (includes practically all the Arctic marine productivity references up to 1992)

SEDGE MEADOWS

Sedge meadows are among the most distinctive and characteristic of tundra plant communities, appearing in imperfectly drained lowlands as dense green swards or lawns dominated by a variety of grasslike sedges and cottongrasses. Sedge meadows are wetlands related structurally, functionally, and botanically to the open peatlands or mires of the northern boreal forest. Although they occur across some 40° of latitude, and are circumpolar in distribution, sedge meadows and their associated soils become considerably less extensive as one moves from the Low Arctic to the High Arctic. For example, sedge-dominated wetlands are restricted to less than about 3–5% of all the lands north of the treeline in Canada. They tend to be floristically impoverished habitats with only a few species of mosses, sedges, and dwarf shrubs providing the bulk of the primary production above and below ground. The total standing crop ($1400–3700 \text{ g m}^{-2}$) and net production ($100 \text{ to} > 300 \text{ g m}^{-2}$) are similar between High and Low Arctic meadows and tend to vary little among years.

The nomenclature for mires and wetlands differs somewhat between North America and Eurasia and can seem complex to the nonexpert. However, mires

Sedges, willow, and cotton-grass on summer tundra, Yamal, Siberia.
Copyright Bryan and Cherry Alexander Photography

are generally divided into homogeneous and polygonal types. Homogeneous mires are mostly situated in valleys, near lakes, pools, and along river banks. Ice-wedge polygons may have low- or high-center morphologies, which correspond to different stages of development of the polygons. (Ice-wedge polygons formed from contraction and expansion of permafrost begin with ridges either side of the ice-filled crack containing a central pool- low-center polygons—but as vegetation fills the central pool, the center becomes higher and open water becomes restricted to a narrow channel around each polygon.) Polygonal mires form only where the mean annual temperature is below $-1°$ C. Frost action in the surface layer of these mires forces coarse-grained soil to the edge of the polygon, while fine-grained soil remains in the center. Technically, low-center lowland polygons are considered fens, whereas high-center lowland polygons are classified as bogs. In either case, the majority of sedges, in terms of both species and individuals, are derived from two genera: *Carex* and *Eriophorum*. Each genus is rich in species, even though local diversity within a given sedge meadow is generally restricted to a half-dozen or less different taxa.

Arctic wetlands, by definition waterlogged throughout the year, are associated with peatlands, but can also occur on wet mineral soils. The so-called peat mosses, *Sphagnum* spp., are important components of Low Arctic sedge meadows but are replaced by other semiaquatic bryophytes (mosses and liverworts) in the High Arctic. Peat is defined as organic matter that originated as a result of incomplete decomposition of plant material under conditions of high moisture. Peat accumulation results from the abundant growth of sedges and mosses. Mineral matter is generally a minor component, and the soils are usually acid (pH of 4.5–6.0). Where peats are thin (15–40 cm) and overlie mineral soils, these are frequently termed half-bog soils. Where peats are thicker (>40 cm), bog soils occur. These two soil types are typical of the circumpolar Low Arctic. Soil classification schemes vary widely and there are three classification systems for Arctic soils in North America alone (*see* **Soils**).

It is common to divide mire or peatland plants into ecological groups according to trophic conditions (eutrophic, mesotrophic, and oligotrophic). However, the ecological characteristics of mire plants can be established only as a result of regional studies of ecological ranges in various zones. For example, for Russian scientists working in northwest Siberia, oligotrophic *Sphagnum* species are subdivided into "wet" (e.g., *Sphagnum balticum, S. cuspidatum, S. lindbergii, and S. majus*) and "mesic" (e.g., *S. angustifolium, S. capillifolium and S. fallax*).

The zone of Arctic mires stretches in a wide belt across northern North America and northern Eurasia and includes both homogeneous and polygonal mires. The wet portions (hollows and cracks) are dominated by non tussock-forming sedges (*Carex stans, C. rotundata, C. rariflora, Luzula*), cottongrasses (especially *Eriophorum angustifolium*, but also *E. brachyantherum, E. scheuchzeri, E. russoleum*), grasses (*Arctophila fulva, Dupontia fisheri*), and both *Sphagnum* and hypnoid mosses (*Drepanocladus*,

Mnium, etc.). The drier portions (ridges of low-center polygons and the centers of high-center polygons) are characterized by abundant dwarf shrubs (*Betula*, *Dryas*, *Empetrum* , *Ledum*, *Salix*, *Vaccinium*) and herbs (especially cloudberry, *Rubus chamaemorus*).

Tussock tundra is a special type of sedge meadow derived from caespitose clumps (dense clusters) of the cottongrass *Eriophorum vaginatum*. Tussocks are long-lived, ranging in age from 122 to 187 years. The individual tussocks are densely packed with dead culms (stems), leaf bases, and other detritus and are flammable enough to allow the spread of wildfire. In dry summers, thousands of acres can burn actively or smoulder for weeks. The fires generally kill many dwarf shrubs but burn only the outer layers of the tussocks, rejuvenating them by removing dead tissue and releasing nutrients into the soil for uptake into the plants. Tussock tundra thus has an ecology and surface hydrology very different from sedge meadows where *E. vaginatum* is absent or only a minor component.

Sedge meadows serve as important forage habitat for a number of terrestrial herbivores, most conspicuously caribou and reindeer (*Rangifer tarandus*) and muskoxen (*Ovibos moschatus*), but also a number of smaller animals such as microtine rodents (lemmings and voles) and Arctic hare. In addition to their significance for plants and terrestrial herbivores, mires constitute an excellent habitat for insects and, consequently, for nesting birds such as waders and geese. Grazing intensity is important in determining the structure of Arctic sedge meadows, mainly through increasing the cover of bryophytes and the availability of nitrogen. Of all the meadow plant species, rhizomatous graminoids are especially well adapted to moderate to heavy grazing (e.g., the sedges *Carex stans*, *Eriophorum angustifolium*, and *E. scheuchzeri* and the grasses *Alopecurus alpinus* and *Dupontia fisheri*). With the majority of their biomass held belowground, these species undergo compensatory regrowth after defoliation during the growing season. Evidence indicates that moderate grazing can thus stimulate shoot turnover and productivity relative to ungrazed sedge meadows. Under very heavy grazing, dwarf shrubs tend to disappear, while ruderal mosses and nitrophilous grasses (i.e., *A. alpinus*) increase in abundance.

Human impact is an important factor in sedge meadows because they: (i) comprise critical habitat for sedentary and migratory herbivores within any given region, particularly in the High Arctic; and (ii) are easily degraded by a variety of anthropogenic disturbances. Substantial habitat loss within Arctic wetlands is well documented in North America and Russia in conjunction with petroleum development, mining, and atmospheric pollution. Significant impacts range from off-road vehicle traffic in spring and summer to airborne road dust and smelter pollutants year-round. Moist tundra generally resists mechanical disturbance better than wet tundra, but it is less resilient once disturbed.

BRUCE FORBES

See also **Peatlands and Bogs; Tussock Tundra; Wet Tundra**

Further Reading

Botch, Marina S. & V.V. Masing, "Mire Ecosystems of the USSR." In *Ecosystems of the World 4B. Mires: Swamp, Bog, Fen and Moor*, edited by A.J.P. Gore, Amsterdam: Elsevier Scientific, 1983, pp. 95–152

Callaghan, Terry V., Alistair D. Headley & John A. Lee, "Root Function Related to the Morphology, Life History and Ecology of Tundra Plants." In *Plant Root Growth: An Ecological Perspective*, edited by D. Atkinson, Oxford: Blackwell, 1991, pp. 311–340

Gorham, Eville, "Northern Peatlands: Role in the Carbon Cycle and Probable Responses to Global Warming." *Ecological Applications*, 1, (1991): 181–195

Henry, Gregory H.R., *Ecology of Sedge Meadow Communities of a Polar Desert Oasis: Alexandra Fiord, Ellesmere Island, Canada*, Ph.D. thesis, Toronto: University of Toronto, 1987

———, "Environmental Influences on the Structure of Sedge Meadows in the Canadian High Arctic." *Plant Ecology*, 134, (1998): 119–129

Kershaw, Kenneth A., "Studies on lichen-dominated systems. X. The Sedge Meadows of the Coastal Raised Beaches." *Canadian Journal of Botany*, 52, (1974): 1947–1972

Muc, Michael, "Ecology and Primary Production of the Truelove Lowland Sedge-Moss Meadow Communities." In *Truelove Lowland, Devon Island, Canada—A High Arctic Ecosystem*, edited by Lawrence C. Bliss, Edmonton: University of Alberta Press, 1977, pp. 157–184

Ovenden, Lynn & Guy R. Brassard, "Wetland vegetation near Old Crow, Northern Yukon." *Canadian Journal of Botany*, 67, (1989): 954–960

Roulet, Nigel & Ming-Ko Woo, "Hydrology of a Wetland in the Continuous Permafrost Region." *Journal of Hydrology*, 89, (1986): 73–91

Tarnocai, Charles & Stephen C. Zoltai, "Wetlands of Arctic Canada." in *Wetlands of Canada*, edited by C.D.A. Rubec, Montreal: Polyscience, 1988, pp. 27–53

Thannheiser, Dietbert, "Beach and Bog Vegetation of the Western Canadian Arctic Archipelago and Spitsbergen." *Polarforschung*, 46 (1976): 62–71

SEDNA: THE SEA GODDESS

Within Inuit tradition, there is a legend of a female spirit, sometimes referred to as *Sedna*, who dwells at the bottom of the ocean. For generations, pan-Arctic oratory related how this woman came to be the mistress of the sea creatures as well as the details of her influence on Inuit society. Despite variations in her name and her background, the Sea Goddess myth extended in one form or another from East Greenland across the Canadian North, west into Alaska and

Siberia. This legend, which initially was fostered through oral tradition, has continued to be a part of Inuit culture into the 21st century, where it has been perpetuated in literary, performing, and visual arts.

Traditional Inuit oratory was transcribed by anthropologists from the South into literary narratives in the 18th, 19th, and early 20th centuries. Scandinavian missionary Hans Egede lived among the Greenlandic people for 25 years beginning in 1721. In his *A Description of Greenland* that appeared in English in 1818, Egede refers to Greenlanders' belief in a good spirit named *Torngarsuk* who dwells beneath the sea. With him, lives his nameless daughter referred to as a "ghastly woman," who has dominion over all the fish and sea mammals. Another European missionary, David Crantz, documented his experiences in Greenland during the 1760s and published a volume in 1767. Crantz's *History of Greenland* (Historia om Grönland) described the *angekoks* (his spelling of angakkut) or shamans who traveled between the physical and the spiritual worlds. Crantz also described a female spirit without name, who purportedly lived under the ocean where she controlled the sea creatures. When there was a scarcity of seals and fish, an angekok would journey to her undersea home to precipitate the release of food sources for the people on the land. In 1824, Captain George Francis Lyon published his private journal (*The Private Journal of Captain G.F. Lyon, Of H.M.S. Hecla, During the Recent Voyage of Discovery Under Captain Parry*), which recounted tales of the Igloolik Inuit from what is today known as the Canadian Arctic. The shaman or wizard would chant in order to contact the female spirit of the sea (*Aywilliayoo* or *Nooliayoo*). In this version, the *annatko* or shaman cut off the hands of the sea goddess to release her grip on the sustenance she has been withholding from Inuit on land. Captain Charles Francis Hall published his *Life with the Esquimaux; the narrative of Captain Charles Francis Hall of the whaling barque "George Henry" from the 29th May, 1860, to the 13th September, 1862* in 1864. In this, Hall related his experiences among Inuit of Frobisher Bay on Baffin Island between 1860 and 1862. *Anguta* is considered the Supreme Being of the people, but the writer also referred to a secondary divinity, a woman, the daughter of *Anguta*, who was called *Sid-ne*. According to legend, *Sid-ne* supposedly created all things having life. Once each year the *angeko* (shaman) led a gathering of people in a ceremony to honor *Sid-ne*. In Hall's account of travels to Repulse Bay area in 1864 and 1865—*Narrative of the Second Arctic Expedition* (1879)—he identified a "Spirit Below" as "Sidney."

Europeans throughout the Arctic of the late 19th and early 20th centuries documented diverse legends of an underwater goddess who controlled the creatures of the sea, and thus the hunting success of Inuit. Hinrich J. Rink's *Tales and Traditions of the Eskimo* was published in 1875 and described a sea spirit called *Arnarkuagsak* or "old woman." Rink's perception was that this and other traditional Inuit narratives were an integral part of the daily lives of the Greenlandic people he encountered. Ernest William Hawkes posited that belief in *Sedna,* prominent among people of Baffin Island, was not unknown in Northern Labrador as well. In Alaska, as early as 1894, anthropologists Harlan Smith and Franz Boas also substantiated the existence of a sea goddess. In Boas's *The Central Eskimo* (1888), the anthropologist discussed at considerable length different versions of the Sea Goddess legend, including those documented by Crantz, Lyon, Hall, and Rink.

In 1909, Vladimir Bogoraz documented the legend of Maritime Chukchi people of what is today Siberia, who believed in a powerful old woman who dominated all sea-game and lived at the bottom of the sea. Inuit of Indian Point in Siberia gave sacrifices to an "old woman of the sea" named *Nulirah*. Thus, versions of a sea goddess who ruled the creatures of the sea have been documented in Greenland, Labrador, the Central Arctic, Alaska, and Siberia.

How the sea goddess came into being and her role within the watery realms is the subject of many different myths; yet, at their core remains a *Sedna* character. Boas, in his *Notes on the Eskimo of Port Clarence, Alaska* published in 1894, discussed a myth of how a girl was thrown overboard from a boat by her father. As she clung to the gunwale of the boat, her father cut off her hands and fingers. According to myth, the first joints were transformed into salmon, the second into seals, the third into walrus, and her metacarpal bones into whales. This creation story of a woman having the digits of her fingers cut off as she clung to a boat for life was fairly widespread throughout the Arctic. Greenlandic legend, Smith Sound Inuit tradition, Central Inuit oratory, the Iglulik of Melville Island, and the Chukchi people of Siberia all portray the father as the one who severed the fingers. Other Inuit traditions, such as that of Cumberland Sound, relate how the father also punctured his daughter's eye. For the Polar Inuit of Greenland observed by Knud Rasmussen in 1903–1904, it was the girl's grandfather who severed her entire hand. Peter Freuchen and Rasmussen described how for other Inuit, the myth is that of an orphan girl who is abandoned by her community; when she attempted to swim to the community's boat to go with them, the crew cut off her fingers. In most versions, the violence enacted upon the girl resulted in the creation of the undersea world of fish and sea mammals. The mythology of Sedna's

the ship ran aground; in a rising gale it was severely battered by drifting ice-floes. It finally slid into deeper water but was beset in the wind-packed floes. An enforced wintering on Novaya Zemlya was now inevitable.

Sedov and his men were not idle; meteorological observations were taken throughout the winter. In the spring of 1913, two major sledging trips were made; geographer Vladimir Vize and geologist M.A. Pavlov made a crossing of the northern island over the ice cap that rises here to over 900m. Meanwhile, Sedov sledged north along the coast to Zelenyy Mys (the northernmost tip of the island) and beyond it to Mys Flissingskii, a distance of over 700 km. On the basis of these trips, he produced a remarkably accurate map of the northwest coast of Novaya Zemlya. Several other maps of areas around the wintering site were also produced.

Although reserves of food and fuel had been seriously depleted, Sedov was still determined to mount an attempt to reach the Pole in 1913. To try to improve the fuel situation, bears and seals were hunted and their blubber was stowed in barrels, while driftwood was hauled to the ship from over a wide area. On September 11, the other expedition members advised Sedov to abandon his plans for the Pole, but he refused.

The ice did not break up, freeing the ship, until September 16. After only two days steaming, it ran into heavy ice; when the last of the coal was exhausted the stokers were reduced to firing the boilers with blubber, driftwood, ropes, and old sails. On September 26, *Sv. Foka* reached Mys Flora, the expedition base of British explorer Frederick Jackson (1894–1897). Here, they found some coal and also dismantled some buildings for fuel. But as it pushed north along Britanskii Kanal, the ship ran into increasingly heavy ice and finally, all fuel exhausted, it was brought to a halt. On October 1, 1913, Sedov was forced to put his ship into winter quarters at Tikhaia Bukhta on Ostrov Gukera.

It was a tough winter; the ship was minimally heated with blubber and with dismantled partitions from between the cabins. The diet was both monotonous and nutritionally inadequate; all but three members of the expedition developed scurvy. By early January 1914, Sedov himself was seriously ill, yet still insisted on making a last-ditch attempt at the Pole. He set off on February 15, 1914 with three sledges and 24 dogs, accompanied by two sailors. Their supplies were sufficient only to get to the Pole; admittedly, Sedov was hoping to salvage some of the supplies left by the Duke of Abruzzi and Anthony Fiala at Bukhta Teplitsa on Ostrov Rudol'fa.

Temperatures dipped to –40°C. After a week, Sedov could no longer walk and was riding on his sledge; later he lapsed into unconsciousness and his dogs simply followed the other sledges. On March 3, the party was halted by a blizzard at a camp on the sea ice of Proliv Neumeiera, about 3 km south of Ostrov Rudol'fa. Sedov died there at 2.40 a.m. on March 5. The two sailors buried him under a low mound of rocks at Mys Auka on Ostrov Rudol'fa and erected a cross made from Sedov's skis. After a hard journey, the two sailors returned to base on March 19.

Dr. P.G. Kushakov, the medical officer, then assumed command of the expedition. *Sv. Foka* got under way, heading south, on July 30, 1914. Having again ransacked Jackson's base at Mys Flora for fuel materials, the ship cleared the pack ice before the fuel was again totally exhausted. *Sv. Foka* reached the Murman coast under sail, and having coaled there, reached Arkhangel'sk on September 6, 1914.

Biography

Georgiy Yakovlevich Sedov (Georgii Iakovlevich Sedov) was born in 1877 on Krivaia Kosa, at the extreme eastern limit of present-day Ukraine. As a young lad, Sedov assisted his fisherman father and so first attended school at the age of 14. At 18, he ran away from home to Rostov where he enrolled in navigation courses, which he financed by working on steamers on the Black Sea in summer. In 1898, he gained his deep-sea navigation officer's ticket. He soon became first mate, and then captain of a small freighter plying between Novorossiysk and Batumi, but continued to study navigation in his spare time.

In 1900, he took the exam for the rank of ensign in the Imperial Russian Navy. Then he traveled to St. Petersburg, entering the Naval College, which normally accepted only the sons of aristocrats, senior civil servants, and church dignitaries. A year later, Sedov made a brilliant showing in his final exams and with the rank of Lieutenant was seconded by the Admiralty to the Chief Hydrographic Directorate. His first posting took him to the Arctic as a member of the Arctic Ocean Hydrographic Expedition on board *Pakhtusov*, commanded by Captain A.I. Varnek. During that summer and the following summer, when Sedov was again involved, the expedition focused on surveying and sounding the mouth of the White Sea and the southeastern shores of the Barents Sea.

During the Russo-Japanese War, Sedov served in the Far East, where he commanded a torpedo boat in the Amur flotilla. Then, from late 1906 until the end of 1907, he was in charge of establishing navigation beacons in Far Eastern waters.

In 1908, Sedov was posted to the Caspian Sea to establish navigation aids in connection with the increasing amount of shipping associated with the burgeoning oil industry in the Baku area. Then followed his first independent Arctic postings, to the mouth of the Kolyma in 1909 and to Novaya Zemlya in 1910. In the summer of 1911, he was back in the Caspian, in charge of surveys of the waters around Apsheronskii Polusotrov. Finally, from the spring of 1912 onward, he was occupied with plans and preparations for his North Pole expedition—from which he was not fated to return. Sedov died on March 5, 1914.

WILLIAM BARR

Further Reading

Barr, William, "Sedov's expedition to the North Pole 1912–1914." *Canadian Slavonic Papers*, 15(4) (1973): 499–524

Kucherov, I.P., "Gidroraficheskie issledovaniia G. Ia. Sedova v Arktike." In: *Russkie arkticheskie ekspeditsii XVII-XX vv* [Russian arctic expeditions of the 17th–20th centuries], edited by M.I. Belov, Leningrad: Gidrometeorologicheskoe Izdatel'stvo, 1964, pp. 118–123

Laktionov, A.F., "Liudi velikogo muzhestva." In *Russkie arkticheskie ekspeditsii XVII-XX vv* [Russian arctic expeditions of the 17th-20th centuries], edited by M.I. Belov, Leningrad: Gidrometeorologicheskoe Izdatel'stvo, 1964, pp. 93–105

Pinegin, N.V., *Georgii Sedov*, Moscow/Leningrad: Izdatel'stvo Glavsevmorputi, 1948

———, *Zapiski polyarnika* [A polyarnik's memoirs], Moscow, 1952

Pinkhenson, D.M., *Problema Severnogo morskogo puti v epokhu kapitalizma. Istoriia otkrytiia i osvoeniia Severnogo morskogo puti, II* [The problem of the Northern Sea Route in the capitalist era. The history of the discovery and exploitation of the Northern Sea Route, II], Leningrad: Izdatel'stvo "Morskoi Transport," 1962

Vize, V. Iu, "Georgii Iakovlevich Sedov." In: *Russkie moreplavateli* [Russian seafarers], edited by V.S. Lupach, Moscow, 1953

SEI WHALE

The name comes from the Norwegian *seje* (pronounced "say"), the pollock or saithe that appeared off the coast of Norway every spring, at the same time these whales did. At a maximum length of 60+ feet and a weight of 30 tons, the sei whale (*Balaenoptera borealis*, Balaenopteridae family) is among the largest of the rorquals, exceeded only by the blue and fin whales. As with all balaenopterids, females are larger than males. Sei whales are fast and graceful swimmers, able to achieve speeds up to 24 mph. They can be easily differentiated from blue whales by their dark gray or brownish coloration, and from fin whales because they lack the white coloration on the right lower jaw. The underside of the sei's flippers and flukes is dark. The sei whale has a slightly arched upper jaw, giving it something of a "roman-nosed" profile. Adults are almost always seen with a random pattern of oval white spots that were originally believed to be the whale's normal coloration, but are now thought to be scars left by lampreys, parasitic worms, or the cookie-cutter shark, all of which attack the whales in warmer waters. The dorsal fin is prominent and strongly falcate, and the rostrum has a single median ridge. (Bryde's whale, with which the sei whale can be easily confused, has three ridges on the rostrum.) After a gestation period of 12 months, a single 15-foot-long calf is born, which is nursed by it mother for six to nine months. When it is weaned, a sei whale calf is about 8 m (26 ft) long. The normal life span for a sei whale has been estimated at 70 years, but 20th-century commercial whalers did not allow many to die of old age.

The baleen plates number between 300 and 380 per side, and are dark in color. While other rorquals such as the blue and fin whales take in mouthfuls of small organisms and then expel the water through the fringes of the baleen plates, the sei whale is a "skimmer," and swims through schools of krill with its mouth open, allowing the food items to become trapped in its silky baleen fringes. They also eat small crustaceans such as *Calanus* spp., and sand lances, herring, cod, pollock, sauries, and sardines. (The Japanese name for this species is *iwashi-kujira*, which means "sardine whale.") Unlike blue and fin whales, sei whales do not raise their flukes above the surface when diving, but sink innocuously below the surface, leaving only swirls to indicate where they have been.

Sei whales are normally seen as singletons or in pairs, but they may congregate in larger numbers when on their feeding grounds. Seis in the eastern North Pacific spend the summer off the coasts of North America, from central California to the Gulf of Alaska, and winter off Baja California and the Revillagigedo Islands. In the west, they are common off Japan and Korea. Two separate stocks are recognized in the North Atlantic; one that lives over the Nova Scotian Shelf, and the other in the Labrador Sea. The seis of the eastern North Atlantic winter off Spain, Portugal, and northwest Africa, and migrate in the summer to northern Norway, Bear Island, Spitsbergen, and Novaya Zemlya.

Although they occasionally come close enough to shore, sei whales were too fast and too powerful to have been hunted by aboriginal whalers. When they were sighted or stranded, Inuit identified sei whales as *komvoghak*, and the Aleut as *agalagitakg*. As long as blue and fin whales were available, the sei whale was ignored by the early Norwegian whalers; by the 1880s, as blues were being thinned out off Finnmark, the catch of fin whales rose, but when these whales also became scarce, the whalers turned to the next largest species, the sei whale. In 1885, Norwegian whalers killed 771 sei whales. This species was also hunted by

Scottish whalers from land stations in the Outer Hebrides and the Shetland. Sei whales are found in both hemispheres, and after the Antarctic whalers had practically wiped out their larger relatives, they aimed their harpoon cannons at the sei whales. What may have been a pre-exploitation population of 300,000 around the world has been reduced to perhaps 75,000.

RICHARD ELLIS

See also **Whaling, Historical**

Further Reading

Andrews, R.C., "The sei whale." *Memoirs of the American Museum of Natural History*, 1(4) (1916): 291–388

Ellis, R., The Book of Whales, New York: Knopf, 1980

Gambell, R., "Sei Whale *Balaenoptera borealis* Lesson, 1828." In *Handbook of Marine Mammals, Volume 3: The Sirenians and Baleen Whales*, edited by S.H. Ridgway and R. Harrison, New York: Academic Press, 1985, pp. 155–170

Hershkovitz, P., "Catalog of living whales." *United States National Museum Bulletin*, 246 (1966): 1–259

Horwood, J., "Sei Whale." In *Encyclopedia of Marine Mammals*, edited by W.F. Perrin, B. Wursig & J.G.M. Thewissen, London and San Diego: Academic Press, 2002

International Whaling Commission, "Report of the special meeting of the Scientific Committee on sei and Bryde's whales." *Reports of the International Whaling Commission* (Special Issue 1), 1977, pp. 1–150

Jonsgård, Å. & K. Darling, "On the biology of the eastern North Atlantic sei whale." *Reports of the International Whaling Commission* (Special Issue 1), 1977, pp. 124–129

Tønnesen, J.N. & A.O. Johnsen, *The History of Modern Whaling*, London: C. Hurst & Company and Canberra: Australian National University Press, 1982

SEL'KUP

The Sel'kup, an indigenous people of Siberia, live in the Tomsk and Tyumen oblasts (Yamalo-Nenets and Khanty-Mansi Autonomous Okrugs) and in Krasnoyarsk Kray. According to the Soviet population census of 1989, their population numbered 3564.

There are two geographically isolated groups: the northern Sel'kups (whose self-designation is Sol'kups or Shol'kups) and the southern Sel'kups (whose self-name is Chulym-Kup, "people of earth," "taiga dwellers"). The separate population of northern Sel'kups originated in the 17th century by migration of part of the southern population from the Middle Ob' River to the upper courses of the Taz and Turukhan rivers.

The Sel'kup language belongs to the Samodian group of the Uralic language family, and has a written language based on the Cyrillic script. The Russian language is, however, widely spoken, and about 50% of Sel'kups regard Russian as their native language.

By the time Siberia was annexed to Russia, Sel'kups inhabited areas along the Middle Ob' River and its tributaries from Tym in the north to the lower course of the Chulym in the south. Strong resistance to Cossack troops was shown by the Sel'kup tribal unit "Pegaya Orda" headed by the local prince Vonya, who was in alliance with the Siberian Tatar, Khan Kuchum. Final conquest of the area and laying of the Sel'kups under tribute (yasak) occurred in the late 16th and early 17th centuries when Russians, moving upstream along the Ob' River, founded Narym Burg (1596), Keta Burg (1602), and the town of Tomsk (1604). In the early 17th century, the population of Sel'kups in the four Siberian districts that paid tribute was about 2700.

Russian colonization brought significant changes to the spatial distribution of the Sel'kups. A number of southern Sel'kups that had already experienced demographic pressure from the neighboring Turkic people migrated to the north. The rest of the southern Sel'kups were assimilated into Russian ways of life, becoming settled into villages, living in houses, and adopting Russian culture. The process of assimilation was accelerated by the baptism of Sel'kups living in Tomsk in the beginning of the 18th century. The Sel'kups from the Surgut District (mainly from the Tym River basin) who had migrated to the north first penetrated the Taz River basin in the mid-17th century, to areas that were primarily populated by forest-dwelling Enets. In the 18th century, a rather numerous and active group of the northern Sel'kups was formed in the area. They migrated further to the northeast (to the Turukhan River basin and other Yenisey tributaries) and assimilated the remainder of the Enets population and some families of the eastern Khanty. By the end of the 19th century, the population of Sel'kups within the territory of the modern Tomsk Oblast, in spite of the losses in assimilation and migration, was about 4000. The population of the northern Sel'kups by the end of the 19th century was about 800.

Hunting and fishing are the Sel'kups' main traditional occupations. Squirrel is the main animal hunted for fur, while sable and Arctic fox are hunted in the north by means of wooden traps. Elk and wild boar are hunted as game. Waterfowl (geese and ducks), formerly hunted by bow, are today hunted by gun. Molting geese (in the summertime geese cast their feathers and cannot fly) were herded into nets that partitioned outlets of lakes and bays. Taiga game birds were hunted by various wooden traps. Partridge was bagged by clap-nets made of horsehair.

Traditional methods of fishing were traps made of willow, strips of broad-leaved trees, and cedar bark. Fishing with a spear (at night by the light of torches) and with a bow also existed, mainly for pike fishing. Reindeer breeding occurs only in the territory of the northern Sel'kups. The number of reindeers in herds is comparatively small (about 1000–1200 head), and the routes of seasonal migrations are rather short. Unlike the Nenets, Sel'kups do not use dogs for reindeer herding, but did use reindeer to pull sledges.

In the winter, skis made of fir-tree or cedar and lined with reindeer or otter skin were the main method of transport. A canoe gouged from an unbroken cedar or aspen trunk with a single oar blade was commonly used for water transport.

Traditional Sel'kups' dwellings were square or rectangular caves (local name *karamo*) that were dug out in steep river terraces. The fireplace was located near the entrance. A narrow corridor led from the river to the living area. People reached the entrance from the side of the river by canoe. Sel'kups' *karamo* settlements had the local name *yurt*. However, in the 19th century, *karamo* settlements were already rather uncommon. Most commonly dwellings were earthhouses or semi-subterranean houses with a timber frame, and a roof covered by turf. Some Sel'kups lived in more usual timber houses. In the summer, the most common dwellings were huts with birch-bark roofs. Cooking was usually done on a campfire near the hut. The winter dwelling of the northern Sel'kups was a timber frame installed over a rectangular pit. The roof was covered by turf; only one window was "glazed" by a piece of ice. At present, many Sel'kups live in settlements in modern houses of the Russian type. Sel'kups who live in tundra and forest-tundra use *chums* (tents) similar to the Nenets' ones. In winter, the *chum* is covered by reindeer skins. In summer, traditionally *chums* were covered by pieces of birch bark that were boiled down and sewed into a big sheet. At present they often use tarpaulin.

Male and female winter clothes of the northern Sel'kups consisted of an unfastened coat made of reindeer skins with fur turned outside and with a hood (local name *parka*). Under the parka, men wore textile shirts (textile was usually bought) and trousers sewed of dressed reindeer chamois—local name *rovdugi*. Women wore a shirt or *sokui* beneath their parka. Winter shoes for men and women (*pimy*) were made of skin from reindeer or elk legs. Summer shoes were made of sturgeon skin.

The head-dress was designed in the form of a hood and sewed from the skins of young reindeers, and Arctic fox or squirrel feet. In the summer, both women and men wore kerchiefs tied round the head or as a turban. In former times, the clothes and utensils were decorated with traditional ornament.

In former times, fish was the Sel'kups' most common food. Fish was boiled, dried in the air, fermented in pits along with berries, and made into fish flour. Other common foods were game birds and reindeer meat. Wild onion, nuts, and wood berries were also gathered. Tea was made from juniper. By the 19th century, bought produce included flour, sugar, tea, butter, and cereals.

Sel'kup folklore includes heroic songs, fairy tales, legends, puzzles, and sayings. Musical instruments including the *vargan*—a Jew's harp made of reindeer antler— and the *swan*—a seven-stringed harp are common among southern Sel'kups. Of the northern Sel'kups only the shaman's tambourine is known.

Sel'kups had an animist conception of the world. When somebody fell sick, Sel'kups appealed to the shaman for help, and the shaman's spirit fought against evil spirits; if the shaman won, the person recovered. Shaman also took an active part in the funeral rites of Sel'kups. Coffins were made of tree trunks or canoes. Children were buried on high trees, commonly cedars. When graves were used, a small timber frame was put on top of the grave, since permafrost prevented burial in the ground. The dead person's belongings, having first been broken, were placed with the grave. Sel'kups believed that in the other world, all things would become whole and serve their owner.

OLGA BYKOVA

See also **Northern Uralic languages**

Further Reading

Tishkov, V.A. (editor), *Narody Rossii, entsyklopediia* [The Peoples of Russia], Moskva: Bol'shaia Rossiiskaia Entsyklopediia, 1994
http://www.indigenous.ru/russian/people/r_slkoop.htm
http://www.raipon.org/Web_Database/selku.html

SELF-DETERMINATION

Self-determination, as a political concept, defines a social actor's capacity vis-à-vis its cultural value-system to control its political environment in such a way that it is able to determine its own being in a sovereign fashion. Taken as a concept in and by itself, self-determination is an ultimate, absolute category about sovereign power. However, as with many other categories such as "pure reason" or "true love," it is an ideal, which only exists in the real social world to some degree of approximation. Hence, no one has ever been the absolute sovereign in any social system be it Hitler, Stalin, the American President, or the Emperor of China. In the real world, political self-determination is a matter of degree. By logic implication, this is also true for the concept of "dependency." As F.W.J. Schelling has noted: "But dependence does not exclude autonomy or even freedom." In other words, neither self-determination nor dependency is a matter of a zero-sum game.

Generally, the Arctic is characterized by a broad variety of stages of political self-government, from explicit sovereign states like Iceland, Norway, and Finland, to the federal provinces of Canada, to the various republics and autonomous region of the former Soviet Union, to the special home-rule arrangement of Greenland. What determines the actual political self-determination of these actors is not the legal character or constitutional order of their system but an organic complex of factors. Of these factors, the most important are the social system's objective position in the developing division of labor in the world, on the one hand, and the developmental potential invested in its the social and cultural institution, on the other. The latter can be summed up as the vitality of a culture. Today, each region in the Arctic has attempted with various success to conduct its own foreign policy and become a factor in the world. Not only society itself but also its political life is marked by the process of "institutionalized individualization," which is a major aspect of the forces of globalization. The result has been an increase in the relative importance of regional players and regional politics. Hence, various players like Iceland, Greenland, and the Khanty-Mansiisk Autonomous Okrug, although shaped by different levels of legal sovereignty, have politically utilized the diverse options that the worldwide process of societal differentiation is establishing.

One important aspect of the history of political self-determination in the Arctic is presented in the history of the indigenous people's attempt to reach various degrees of self-determination. Generally, as in other marginalized areas in the world, actors outside their own rim have politically controlled communities in the Arctic. Since World War II, indigenous people within the Arctic area have struggled for increased political self-determination. The result of this struggle has taken different forms in various places. Particularly, in the 1970s, various indigenous groups formed political parties and front organizations. In 1971, the Inuit Tapirisat of Canada (ITC) was founded in Ottawa, and the Inuit Circumpolar Conference (ICC) was formed in Alaska in 1977. Also, in Greenland, various political parties were formed during the 1970s. In Alaska, a crucial point of political impact was when the United States Congress passed the Alaska Native Claims Settlement Act (ANCSA) in 1971, in effect giving indigenous groups administrative control over one-ninth of Alaska's territory. The modern history of Arctic Canada is marked by a series of land-claim settlements between the Queen's government and various indigenous groups beginning with the 1984 settlement with the Inuvialuit. Another important settlement occurred when the Québec government signed a land claim agreement with the Inuit of northern Québec in 1975, an agreement that arose out of the controversy surrounding the establishment of a hydroelectric power plant in James Bay. The most famous settlement was the 1992 agreement between the Canadian government and the Tungavik Federation of Nunavut, leading to the establishment of Nunavut as an independent providence in April 1999. In Greenland, the quest for a higher degree of self-rule resulted in the establishment of a Home Rule government in 1979. After years of Soviet repression, enhanced political influence for the indigenous people in the Russian North became a real possibility with the collapse of the Soviet Union (1985–1991). It resulted in the creation of the Russian Association of Indigenous Peoples of the North (RAIPON). However, indigenous people in Russia are handicapped by the fact that they have been a declining minority in almost all regions in Russia.

The struggle for various degree of self-determination among indigenous people in the Arctic has so far nowhere led to the establishment of an independent nation-state in the full and classic meaning of the term. The creation of Nunavut was not the creation of an independent state but a territory of Canada and the land claim agreement acknowledged and thereby legitimized that the great majority of the land of Nunavut is Crown land. The same was the case in the Alaska Native Claims Settlement Act of 1971. The Greenlandic case is quite special. Although it is formally an integral part of the Danish Commonwealth, "the Rigsfællesskabet," the Greenland Home Rule government has actually expanded its active involvement in regional and international politics in cooperation with the Danish government. In reality, however, the Greenland government is very far from any real independence because Greenland is neither economically nor societally sustainable, at the current level of social reproduction.

In reality, the communities of the Arctic World cannot attain a higher degree of political self-determination beyond a certain point before they radically enhance the sustainability of their economic and societal base. Political power does not stand alone in the social system. Its capacity to come to life is conditioned on the matrix of other social factors. Social actors who do not have sufficient capacity to control or reproduce their own economic system will have great difficulties in exercising a high degree of political power. Their power base becomes artificial. In reality, political self-determination and sustainability is closed linked together.

JENS KAALHAUGE NIELSEN

See also **Indigenous Rights; Self-government**

Further Reading

Bartmann, Barry, "Footprints in the Snow: Nunavut, Self-Determination and the Inuit Quest for Dignity." In *Management, Technology and Human Resources in the Arctic*, edited by Lise Lyck & V.I. Boyko, Dordrecht: Kluwer, 1996, pp. 149–164
Canada, Indian Affairs and Northern Development, and Tungavik Federation of Nunavut, *Agreement between the*

Inuit of the Nunavut Settlement Area and Her Majesty the Queen in right of Canada, 1993

Chaturvedi, Sanjay, "Arctic Geopolitics Then and Now." In *The Arctic: Environment, People, Policy,* edited by Mark Nuttall & Terry V. Callaghan, New York: Harwood, 2000

Dahl, Jens, "Indigenous People of the Arctic." In *Arctic Challenges. Report from the Nordic Council's Parliamentary Conference,* Reykjavik, August 16–17, 1993

Ernerk, Peter et al., "Nunavut: Vision or Illusion?" *Canadian Parliamentary Review,* Spring 1990, pp. 6–10

Espiritu, A., "Aboriginal Nations: Natives in Northwest Siberia and Northern Alberta." In *Contested Arctic,* edited by E. A. Smith & J. McCarter, Seattle: University of Washington Press, 1997

Heurlin, Bertel, *Global, Regional and National Security,* Copenhagen Danish Institute of International Affairs, 2001

Kaalhauge Nielsen, Jens, "Greenland's Geopolitical Reality and its Political–Economic Consequence." In *Danish Foreign Policy Yearbook 2001,* edited by Bertel Heurlin & Hans Mouritzen, Copenhagen Danish Institute of International Affairs, 2001

Kristinsson, Gunnar Helgi, "From Home Rule to Sovereignty: The Case of Iceland." In *Lessons from the Political Economy of Small Islands,* edited by Godfrey Baldacchino & David Milne, New York: Macmillian Press, St Martin Press & University of Prince Edward Island, 2000

Nuttall, Mark, "Nation-building and Local Identity in Greenland: Resources and the Environment in a Changing North." In *Arctic Ecology and Identity,* edited by S.A. Mousalimas, Budapest and Los Angeles: Hungarian Academy of Science and ISTOR, 1997

———, "Indigenous Peoples, Self-Determination and the Arctic Environment." In *The Arctic: Environment, People, Policy,* edited by Mark Nuttall & Terry V. Callaghan, New York: Harwood, 2000

SELF-GOVERNMENT

Colonization, oppression, dispossession, disease, and assimilation of indigenous peoples by settlers and nation states around the world have wrought devastating consequences. Negative impacts of contact and assertion of sovereignty over indigenous peoples and their lands in circumpolar areas by nations states began to be addressed in the 1960s. Positive changes are a direct result of indigenous peoples' political organization and activism, and national and international legal and political recognition of indigenous peoples' rights. Among these rights is the right of "self-determination," the ability of a people to determine its own governance and destiny. Nation-states claiming indigenous peoples' traditional territories have largely forgone the term self-determination and its associated internationally recognized legal implications in favor of the term "self-government." self-government is interpreted as a right conforming to and exercised within the institutional and constitutional arrangements of nation-states. Evolving understandings and implementation of the right of self government vary according to internal legal, social, political, and economic regimes and interests of nation-states,

against a backdrop of increasing international support for the recognition of indigenous peoples' rights.

Key to social, cultural, spiritual, and economic revitalization is indigenous peoples' control over the material and cultural foundations of their existence. "Self-government" is a term encompassing a wide variety of forms of increased control in various areas including land, resources, culture, and economy. Forms of self-government evolving throughout the circumpolar world range from state agencies with limited advisory powers in Fennoscandia to constitutionally recognized public governments with law-making authority in Canada.

Alaska: History

Indigenous peoples within Alaska include Inuit, First Nation, and Aleut peoples, known also as Alaska Natives. Recent history of indigenous peoples in Alaska has been shaped by missionaries, traders, and settlers from both Russia and America, and since the late 1800s by American national and state governments. Since the 1800s, self-government policies in the United States alternatively promoted assimilation and dispossession, or limited self-administration. Court cases of the 18th century established tribal sovereignty limited geographically and substantively, yet based in preexisting and inherent aboriginal rights. After Alaska was sold to the United States of America by Russia in 1867, the status of the rights and land ownership of indigenous peoples in Alaska remained unresolved. In1966, the Alaska Federation of Natives called for a moratorium on development until indigenous peoples' land rights were resolved. The discovery of oil reserves at Prudhoe Bay in 1968 played a major role in motivating a land and rights settlement. The Federation subsequently negotiated a massive land and resource rights agreement on behalf of Alaska Natives, which came into effect through the Alaska Native Claims Settlement Act (ANCSA), 1971 (*see* **Alaska Native Claims Settlement Act (ANCSA); Native Corporations**)

Legal Basis

The state intended ANCSA to assimilate the Natives of Alaska into the institutions of Alaska; the corporate structure of the settlement served to create divisions within Native communities and alienate lands from them. ANCSA's provisions included one-ninth of the state's land plus $962.5 million in compensation to Alaska Natives in exchange for the extinguishment of their claims to Alaska lands. The relationship between the 80,000 Alaska Natives and the land was completely transformed. No longer was ownership directly linked to Native government. Land title went to the 12 regional corporations and approximately 200 local village ones; traditional or "tribal" governments were bypassed—ANCSA made no specific provisions for internal self-government or tribal government development.

Institutional Basis

ANCSA was a way to attain economic self-sufficiency, a key aspect of self-determination. Village and regional corporations are set up as for-profit, corporate entities, answering to individual shareholders. However, in some areas such as the North Slope Borough, wealthy corporations and a strong economy based on resource royalties have resulted in effective and far-reaching measures strengthening local control over the regional and local government. The North Slope Borough government was established in 1972 under state laws, and is an example of innovative approaches to effecting self-government by promoting and investing in cultural, educational, and social initiatives.

Canada: History

Patterns of contact with First Nations and Inuit in Northern Canada are similar to those of indigenous peoples throughout the, circumpolar world. Missionaries, fur traders, explorers, resource development, and the significance of Northern regions for sovereignty and national defense are factors, that continue to shape the lives and futures of indigenous peoples. Generally, missionization and government administration required indigenous peoples to abandon nomadic for sedentary lifestyles. This, coupled with disease epidemics, ongoing colonization and assimilation policies, and disenfranchisement from Canadian economic and political life, wrought catastrophic change for indigenous peoples. Political organization and advocacy among First Nations and Inuit beginning in the 1960s resulted in land-claim and self-government negotiation processes that continue today. In these processes, which may last for many years, indigenous peoples negotiate rights over land, resources, and governance with federal, provincial, and territorial governments. In 1975, the James Bay and Northern Québec Agreement was the first land claim in Canada containing provisions for limited self-government. In the Northwest Territories, most indigenous peoples have entered into self-government negotiations. The Nunavut Territory, created in April 1999 (*see* **Nunavut Final Agreement**), implements Inuit self-government through a territorial public government system. Yukon First Nations may negotiate self-government based on a framework agreement signed in 1995 between Canada and the Council of Yukon First Nations.

Legal Basis

Canada views self-government as a right of indigenous peoples that must be exercised within the Canadian Constitutional framework. In contrast, it has been recognized that treaties signed with First Nations were ones of peace and friendship affirming mutual respect, recognition, and coexistence of indigenous peoples and newcomers. Treaties have since been reinterpreted by Canada as agreements of extinguishment and surrender of indigenous peoples rights. Administration of treaties and the relations between the Crown and First Nations, and the administration of the internal affairs of First Nations were regulated under section 91(24) of the Canadian Constitution and its associated legislation, the Indian Act. In many respects, Inuit were deemed to be Indians for the purposes of government administration.

Section 35 of the Constitution, added in 1982, recognizes Aboriginal rights. In 1995, Canada issued a formal policy recognizing self-government as a section 35 right. Canada's policy is to build on the original intent of treaties and establish new relationships by negotiating First Nation and Inuit control of specific subject matters such as health and education. For First Nations and Inuit, self-government is an opportunity to begin to restore recognition and the means necessary to regain control of their own communities and lives.

Yukon: History and Legal Basis

In 1970, the Council of Yukon Indians (CYI), representing 14 Indian Bands (First Nations) of the Yukon, organized to negotiate a land claim and self-government toward establishing their rights to land, resources, and the protection of their cultures and way of life. Discussions on negotiations began in 1973. In 1993, Canada, the Yukon, and the CYI signed an Umbrella Final Agreement (UFA; *see* **Council for Yukon Indians Umbrella Final Agreement**) and final agreements with four Yukon First Nations. The UFA is the basis for negotiating individual settlements with each of the 14 First Nations. It also provides for the negotiation of self-government agreements with them. Self-government agreements with four First Nations came into effect in February 1995, after Canada passed the Yukon First Nations Self Government Act 1994. In August 1995, the CYI adopted a new name—the Council of Yukon First Nations (CYFN).

Institutional Organization

Self-government agreements recognize First Nations' local control over decisions and replace Indian Act band councils. First Nations have their own constitutions, membership codes, and organizational policies and procedures. First Nations have law-making authority on their lands over land use and control, hunting, trapping and fishing, licensing, and business regulation. They have the power to make laws for their people in the Yukon outside settlement lands relating to language, culture, and spiritual beliefs; health services; social and welfare services; training programs; adoption, guardianship, and child welfare; education and training; estates; resolving disputes outside the courts; and licenses to raise revenue.

Northwest Territories: History and Legal Basis

In 1970, the Council For Original Peoples Entitlement (COPE) was established to pursue the rights of Dene and Inuvialuit. This was soon followed by the establishment of the Indian Brotherhood of the Northwest Territories (now the Dene Nation), and the Metis Association of the Northwest Territories. COPE pursued recognition of Inuvialuit rights, while the Dene and Métis embarked on a long struggle for rights recognition. The year 1977 was a watershed in the struggle for all groups, as the results of an extensive public enquiry over the establishment of an oil pipeline down the Mackenzie Valley called for a moratorium on development until land claims were settled. This led to negotiations over land and resources between indigenous peoples and governments, which continue to the present. Until the 1995 self-government policy, self-government could not be negotiated alongside land claims. The Inuvialuit Final Agreement (1984), Gwich'in Comprehensive Land Claim Agreement (1992), and Sahtu Dene and Métis Comprehensive Land Claim Agreement (1994) are land-claim agreements obligating the government to negotiate self-government provisions; these are currently being negotiated.

Institutional Organization

The federal self-government policy states that in the Northwest Territories, agreements will be implemented primarily through public government. This means that community and regional governments will have powers in areas similar to those of Yukon First Nations, such as increased law-making powers and authority over areas such as education, health, and housing. The new public governments will be created through self-government agreements, not territorial legislation. With the exception of Yellowknife, the majority of residents in the Northwest Territories's 36 communities are indigenous peoples. Residents have the opportunity to shape new governments according to their cultural values and traditions.

Nunavut Territory: History and Legal Basis

In 1976, the Inuit Tapirisat of Canada began talks with Canada on an Inuit land claim and self-government

agreement. In 1993, after 17 years of negotiations, the Inuit and Canada reached a land-claim and self-government agreement. Inuit self-government was established by the federal *Nunavut Act* in 1999, creating the new territory of Nunavut. Its territory geographically approximates Inuit traditional territory, covering approximately 2 million km^2. With a population 85% Inuit, the intention is to shape the public government according to Inuit values and culture.

Institutional Organization

The Nunavut government serves its 28 communities through decentralized services. There are 19 members elected to the Nunavut Legislative Assembly every 4 years; all Nunavut residents may vote, be elected, and participate. There are no political parties; the legislature operates on a consensus basis, consistent with Inuit political custom. The assembly has a premier and cabinet elected by Members of the legislature, and an independent judiciary. Its powers are similar to the Yukon and Northwest Territories governments. Inuit as indigenous peoples continue to have their indigenous rights represented and land claim administered by the Nunavut Tunngavik Incorporated.

Nunavik: History and Legal Basis

A massive hydroelectric development on James Bay prompted the negotiation and settlement of a land claim with Cree, Naskapi, and Inuit of Québec in the early 1970's. The James Bay and Northern Québec Agreement (1975; *see* **James Bay and Northern Québec Agreement**) established a limited form of self-government for the Inuit of Northern Québec.

The Kativik Act established Inuit villages as municipalities under provincial legislation. In the late 1990s, the federal and Québec governments began negotiating with Makivik Corporation to further self-government powers beyond those originally contained in the 1975 Agreement.

Institutional Organization

Local councils have a structure similar to municipalities in Québec; the 13 communities cooperate under the umbrella of the Kativik Regional Government. The Kativik Regional Government has municipal powers over lands that are not part of municipal corporations, and regional powers within Nunavik including municipalities (*see* **Kativik Regional Government**). Governments in Nunavik are public—all residents may vote, be elected, and participate. More than 90% of the population is Inuit. Their rights as indigenous people are represented by Makivik Corporation, set up to administer Inuit land-claim rights (*see* **Makivik Corporation**).

Greenland: History and Legal Basis

Inuit are the indigenous people of Greenland. Between 1380 and 1953, Greenland was a colony of Denmark, following a familiar pattern whereby missionaries and traders had a profound impact on the lives of Inuit. The year 1953 initiated a period of increasing autonomy for Greenland with a Danish Constitutional Amendment providing for Greenland's representation by two members in the Danish Parliament, the *Folketing*. Greenlanders were recognized as Danish citizens. Internally, Greenland's affairs were administered by Denmark under the advice of an elected National Council, which took on increasing responsibility until 1979. In 1979, Greenlanders' increased control over their affairs was formally mandated with the establishment of "home rule." Its legislative basis is the Danish Parliament's Home Rule Act (*see* **Greenland Home Rule Act**). It came into force in May 1979 following its acceptance by a popular referendum in Greenland. According to the Act, Greenland is designated as a special cultural community in the Kingdom of Denmark. Approximately 48,000 of Greenland's 56,000 residents are Inuit—the vast majority—and home rule was gained in the context of indigenous self-determination. However, like Nunavut, home rule is a form of self-government that allows for all Greenlanders to participate in a representative and responsible public government. Unlike Nunavut, home rule was not accompanied by a separate Land Claim Agreement, recognizing the rights of Inuit as indigenous peoples.

Institutional Organization

The Greenland Home Rule Parliament, the *Landesting*, has 31 members. Members are directly elected by Greenlanders every four years by secret ballot. *Landesting* members elect a *Landsstyre*, or Executive Council, from among themselves, headed by the prime minister. Currently, five political parties are represented. Home rule includes two types of control over internal affairs: the law-making authority known as Parliamentary Acts, and authority delegated to Greenland by Denmark, known as Parliamentary Orders. Authority is exercised in areas such as local government, taxation, renewable resource management, conservation and environmental protection, commerce and business licensing, social welfare, health services, education, culture, economic development, and housing. Continuing Danish sovereignty over Greenland is reinforced by Danish control of foreign affairs, defense, the judiciary, and currency.

Norway, Sweden, and Finland: History and Legal Basis

Formerly known as Lapps, Saami are indigenous to the area of northern Fennoscandia, called Sápmi (or Lapland), which runs from Femunden in Norway's Hedmark county to Idre, in Dalarne, Sweden; from the Kola Peninsula in northern Russia, it extends southeast to Finland. The estimated population of 65,000 Saami includes 40,000 in Norway; 17,000 in Sweden; 5700 in Finland; and 2000 in Russia. Saami culture has its spiritual and material basis in the land and its resources, including hunting, fishing, farming, and reindeer herding. Saami culture, land use, and control of internal affairs have been affected greatly by differing activities, laws, and policies of the nation-states claiming Sápmi within their borders. While Norway, Sweden, and Finland recognize Saami distinctiveness and rights through elected bodies of Saami representatives, the power and autonomy of these bodies and their effective involvement in law and policy making vary. In all three countries, Saami identity, rights, and self-governance were shaped by competing policies of cultural preservation and assimilation; laws affecting rights, economic activities, and land use; and various agreements and border treaties dividing Sápmi between the nation-states. Up to the 16th century, Saami were largely able to pursue a nomadic way of life. The *Treaty of Teusina (1595)* established borders in *Sápmi* between Russia and Sweden-Finland, and the *Stromstad Treaty (1751)*, establishing borders in Sápmi between Denmark, Norway, and Sweden, contained the *Lappekodicillen* or *Lapp Codicil of 1751*. These agreements profoundly shaped the future and rights of Saami. The *Lapp Codicil* is often referred to as the Saami *Magna Carta*. The *Codicil* was meant to guide the signatories' determination of Saami citizenship and movement across borders. It contains regulations providing Saami with a form of internal self-government, recognizing extant Saami rights, and their traditional form of socio-political organization. While in all three countries Saami rights were generally interpreted in a manner that afforded resource exploitation and settlement throughout Sápmi, the 1950s was a period of increasing Saami activism, and international recognition of indigenous peoples' rights. This resulted in the recognition of Saami rights, culture, and language in law and policy. Today, Sweden, Norway, and Finland have each established Saami Parliaments (*see* **Saami Parliaments**). Internationally, Saami collaborate through the Nordic Saami Council, established in 1956, becoming fully representative of all Saami since 1992 (*see* **Saami Council**).

Institutional Organization

Norway Increased activism since the 1950s culminated in the passage of the Saami Act in June 1987. In April 1988, Norway amended its *Constitution* with *Article 110a* setting out Saami Constitutional rights. The *Sameting*, or Saami Parliament, was established in 1989. Elected every 4 years, its 39 members represent 13 districts, supported by a modest secretariat. The *Sameting's* mandate is to act as an advisory body to the Norwegian Parliament, and specifically to protect and develop Saami culture, language, and way of life.

Sweden Saami language, educational, and political rights and recognition are based on Saami status as an ethnic minority in accordance with the Swedish *Constitution*. In 1991, the Saami Parliament, *Sametinget*, was established; the first election took place in 1993. It consists of 31 members representing ten political parties, with terms of office lasting up to 4 years. Elected by eligible Saami, it is an advisory body to the Swedish government, responsible for promoting, developing, and allocating state funding for Saami culture. It also appoints Saami school boards and advises Sweden on Saami affairs.

Finland The *Samedeggi*, or Saami Parliament, was established through an *Act of Sami Parliament* (1996), in accordance with section 51a of the Finnish *Constitution*. Its 21 members and four substitutes are elected every four years by the Saami community. The *Samedeggi* promotes Saami language, culture, and Saami rights. The Parliament determines funding allocations for Saami-focused initiatives; represents Saami nationally and internationally; and participates in and advising government on decision making affecting Saami. The Samedeggi is supported by a small secretariat located in the village of Inari.

Russian Federation

Historical Basis

There are over 40 indigenous peoples with a combined population of approximately 250,000 in the Russian North, an area of about 7 million km^2, or 40% of Russian territory, in five republics, ten administrative areas, and eight autonomous regions. They comprise 2% of the Russian Federation's Northern population.

Indigenous peoples in Russia's North have been subjected to both imperialist and communist colonization and assimilation policies, which eroded their cultural, spiritual, social, and economic traditions. Contact with missionaries, traders, and government transformed mainly nomadic subsistence patterns of life to sedentary ones increasingly vulnerable to colonial assimilation and its attendant social and economic ills. Under imperial rule, indigenous peoples communities were largely self-regulating and were seen as beneficial for economic stability and productivity. Under the Soviet regime, they were often indiscriminately amalgamated into *kolkhozes,* or collectives.

Legal Basis

Since 1989, *glasnost* has afforded opportunities for indigenous peoples to pursue increased control over land and resources, crucial to establishing a material basis for long-term, stable economic development, and cultural and social revitalization. While indigenous peoples' rights are recognized in the Russian constitution, increased local control over lands is not linked to preexisting Aboriginal rights. Rather, it has its basis in institutional and economic reforms occurring throughout the Russian federation. At the same time, laws providing for increased local control recognize indigenous peoples' traditional social and economic organization as the basis for new institutional units at the local level called *obschinas*; traditionality is a foundation for laws and rights, not necessarily aboriginality. *Obschina* members are indigenous peoples, related through kinship, or living in the same area, pursuing traditional ways of life.

In 1992, a federal decree called for the passage of a law governing the processes for the establishment of *obschinas* and transfer of land to them. As an interim measure, a Presidential edict ordered traditional lands transferred to *obschinas*. The federal law *Ob obshchikh* was passed in July 2000. The 1992 edict allowed for the passage of supporting *obschina* legislation in Northern regions, and the opportunity for indigenous peoples to establish *obschinas* and petition for land.

Institutional Organization

Obschina types and institutional structures vary, differences being based on the type of economic activity, amount and type of land, number of members, and other factors. Provisions of supporting legislation in regions may vary which may affect the organization, structure, and land use of obschinas.

Indigenous peoples in the Russian North are under represented in legislatures both regionally and nationally. However, they have developed various associations to represent their interests nationally and internationally, most notably through the umbrella organization RAIPON—Russian Association of Indigenous Peoples of the North, established in 1990.

STEPHANIE IRLBACHER FOX

See also **Colonization of the Arctic; Indigenous Rights; Land Claims; Self-determination**

Further Reading

Alfred, Taiaiake, *Peace, Power, Righteousness: An Indigenous Manifesto*, Toronto: Oxford, 2000

Berger, Thomas R., *Village Journey: The Report of the Alaska Native Review Commission*, New York: Hill & Wang, 1985

Cook, Cutis & Juan Lindau, *Aboriginal Rights and Self-Government*, Montreal: McGill-Queens, 2000

Petersen, Hanne & Birger Poppel (editors), *Dependency, Autonomy and Sustainability in the Arctic*, Aldershot: Ashgate, 2000

Sillanpää, Lennard, *The Development of Sami Assemblies in Fennoscandia: Towards Aboriginal Self-Government*, Ottawa: Indian and Northern Affairs Canada, 1992

Watkins, Mel, *Dene Nation: The Colony Within*, Toronto: University of Toronto Press, 1976

Greenland website: www.gh.gl
Nunavut website: www.gov.nu.ca

SERVICE, ROBERT

Robert William Service, a Scottish writer of popular verse and novels, was nicknamed "Canada's Kipling" and "the Bard of the Yukon." His reputation is almost entirely due to his ballads about the Canadian North and the Klondike Gold Rush, and he contributed significantly to mythologizing the Canadian Arctic.

Service lived in the Yukon for eight years (1904–1912) working as a bank clerk and writing. His most famous books come from this period: *Songs of a Sourdough* (1907) (also published as *The Spell of the Yukon*), *Ballads of a Cheechako* (1909), *Rhymes of a Rolling Stone* (1912), and a lesser-known novel *The Trail of Ninety-Eight* (1911). Service continued to write after leaving Canada in 1912, publishing 14 more books of ballads, five collections of verse, five novels, a two-volume autobiography (*Ploughman of the Moon* in 1945 and *Harper of Heaven* in 1948), a song book, and a fitness manual. His *Rhymes of a Red Cross Man* (1916), about his experiences as an ambulance driver in World War I, was well received. However, none of Service's later works approached the wide popularity of his books of northern verse, the royalties from which he was able to live on for the rest of his life after 1909.

Writing about the Klondike Gold Rush less than a decade after it occurred, Service was able to capitalize on an internationally popular happening. He defined both a time and a place by capturing the energy and excitement of the Gold Rush and articulating a mystique of the North. The North itself is the main character in Service's verse. He first presents his vision in *Songs of a Sourdough* through a number of hymns to the Yukon: "The Spell of the Yukon," "The Law of the Yukon," "The Call of the Wild," and "The Lure of Little Voices." He characterizes the land as cold, wild, vast, dark, savage, silent, and barren—but also captivating. It is at once harsh yet beautiful, dangerous yet alluring. Although the North represents riches waiting to be exploited, the enticement of gold is merely the initial attraction. In "The Spell of the Yukon," the narrator tries to account for his longing to return, despite the Yukon being "the cussedest land" that he knows and "a fine land to shun."

The North is also a site for the struggle of man against nature, a place where manly men test their mettle. As a testing ground of strength and character, the Yukon, as Service presents it, becomes a foil for modern civilized life. Despite its hardship, the North promises adventure and challenge unattainable in the safe, comfortable, and boring south.

The human characters in Service's poems tend to be folksy individuals—quirky misfits, rugged outdoor types, reckless goldseekers, and sundry scoundrels. His cast is "The Men that Don't Fit In," as one of his poems is titled, and he invented some of the most enduring characters in poetry. The titles of Service's ballads are a who's who of northern fictional characters: "The Shooting of Dan McGrew," "The Cremation of Sam McGee," "The Ballad of Pious Pete," "The Ballad of Blasphemous Bill," "Clancy of the Mounted," and "Athabasca Dick," of whom he drew brilliant caricatures.

The exotic locales, historical touchstones, and intriguing characters only partially explain Service's popular appeal. He wrote in the rhythmic, rhyming tradition of the English popular ballad that lent itself to reading aloud and memorizing. Although his verse includes colloquialisms and slang, the language itself is distinctly middle class and accessible. In addition, Service's ballads are melodramatic, narrative, anecdotal, and frequently humorous. He felt that vice was "a more vital subject for poetry than virtue," and his poetry was consciously created to appeal to common folk.

Service's great achievement was to bring together two popular movements of the late 19th and earlier 20th centuries, namely the English ballad tradition of Rudyard Kipling and the American tall tale tradition of Bret Harte, who had captured the spirit of the California goldfields, and Mark Twain of the Mississippi river boatmen. Service imitated and adapted Kipling's rollicking rhymes and rhythms and shared Kipling's themes of manly adventure on the frontiers of the world, rowdy establishments, rough characters, and love triangles. Service versified tall tales that stressed character, action, local color, irony, and surprise. Service's most famous ballads, "The Cremation of Sam McGee" and "The Shooting of Dan McGrew," most clearly illustrate this melding of traditions. Other influences on his early travels and his poetry were fellow Scotsman Robbie Burns's irreverent humor and simple style, Robert Louis Stevenson's notion of romantic vagabondage in *The Amateur Emigrant*, and Jack London's tales of the North.

Service himself has an enduring legacy. He has influenced Canadian popular musicians Stan Rogers and Stompin' Tom Connors. Yukon painter Ted Harrison has illustrated Service's ballads of Sam McGee and Dan McGrew. The novel *The Man from the Creeks* (1999) by Canadian Robert Kroetsch is based on "The Shooting of Dan McGrew." A Yukon literary magazine *Out of Service*, established in 2001, takes its title from a pun on the Yukon Bard's name. Service continues to pervade Yukon tourism and local life: Dawson City is home to Robert Service School; a main thoroughfare in Whitehorse is named Robert Service Way; each January around Service's birthday, his life and work are celebrated in Whitehorse; Yukon cabarets and winter festivals always feature some recitation or dramatization of Service's work; and in the summer, daily readings are performed at his cabin in Dawson City.

Although Service is clearly recognized as a popular poet, the style of his poetry as well as its content have not been conducive to academic study. For example, although Service presents the conflict of man in the North, he often focuses on action and humor, rather than exploring issues such as suffering or death. Service deserves more serious study as a popular cultural figure and as a contributor to the myth of the North. In his verse, Service created a genuine Canadian myth, and his depiction of the Yukon continues to be perpetuated in the Yukon and around the world.

Biography

Robert William Service was born on January 16, 1874 in Preston, England, to Scottish parents Robert Service and Sarah Emily (Parker). The family returned to Scotland when Service was five, and he was educated in Glasgow. At 15, he began working for the Commercial Bank of Scotland. He took night courses at the University of Glasgow, but soon gave up formal education. In 1896, he immigrated to Canada and spent several years working and traveling in the Canadian and American west. In 1903, he joined the Bank of Commerce in Vancouver, British Columbia. In 1904, he transferred to Whitehorse, Yukon and then to Dawson City in 1908. He left the Yukon in 1912, and in 1913 he married Parisian Germaine Bourgoin. In 1917, twin daughters Iris and Doris were born, but Doris died of scarlet fever in 1918. During World War I, Service was a war correspondent and an ambulance driver in France. After leaving Canada, Service lived most of his life in France, except for two periods in Hollywood, in the 1920s working on a movie version of *The Shooting of Dan McGrew* and in the 1940s, during World War II. He died on September 11, 1958 in Lancieux, France.

MAUREEN LONG

Further Reading

den Ouden, Pamela, "My Uttermost Valleys': patriarchal fear of the feminine in Robert Service's poetry and prose." *The Northern Review*, 19 (1998): 113–121

Johnson, Jay, "The age of brass: Drummond, Service, and Canadian 'Local Colour,'" *Canadian Poetry,* 23 (1988): 14–30

Lockhart, G. Wallace, *On the Trail of Robert Service*, Barr, Scotland: Luath Press, 1991

Klinck, Carl F., *Robert Service: A Biography*, Toronto: McGraw-Hill Ryerson, 1976

Mackay, James, *Vagabond of Verse: Robert Service: A Biography*, Edinburgh: Mainstream, 1995

———, "Bard of the Yukon: the Klondike in the poetry of Robert Service." *The Northern Review*, 18 (1998): 93–100

Mitham, Peter J., "*Dementia borealis: The Canadian North in the Verse of Robert W. Service*." MA thesis, Edmonton: University of Alberta, 1994

———, "Recalling the gold rush: autobiography, history, and Robert W. Service." *The Northern Review*, 1998, 101–112

———, *Robert W. Service: A Bibliography*, New Castle, Delaware: Oak Knoll, 2000

SETTLERS (LABRADOR)

The Settlers (or Native Settlers) of Labrador are a people of mixed background, part Inuit and part Euro-Canadian. However, their distinctiveness as a group did not derive from a dual ethnic ancestry alone because the family tree of nearly every person claiming Inuit identity in Labrador today features an Old World branch. Rather, the critical factor underscoring Settler distinctiveness has been a tendency to identify more closely with their *qallunaaq* (white) forebears, and, in turn, to be regarded as nonaboriginal by the legions of merchants, missionaries, and functionaries with whom they have had dealings over time. That said, important change in this historic pattern has been unfolding over the last quarter-century, a political response to developments on the national scene that have led to the constitutional entrenchment of the aboriginal rights of Canada's Indian First Nations, Inuit, and Métis, the last a generic reference to people of mixed heritage. As a consequence, the Settlers living in five villages of northern Labrador—Rigolet, Makkovik, Postville, Hopedale, and Nain—have now joined their Inuit kin in seeking settlement of land claims under the banner of the Labrador Inuit Association. Association documents refer to them as Kablunangajuk, "half-white." Those in the twenty or so communities scattered along the shoreline southward from the head of Hamilton Inlet to the Strait of Belle Isle, among them Happy Valley-Goose Bay, Cartwright, Black Tickle, Port Hope Simpson, and Lodge Bay, are pursuing similar goals. They have remade themselves as the Labrador Métis Nation for the purpose.

Settler origins date to the late 18th century, a period when Labrador, formerly a French possession, passed into British hands. Colonization was not among the new governors' plans. Yet it occurred anyway, albeit haphazardly, the first pioneers to settle the region's subarctic coasts being a hodgepodge of fortune hunters and freedom seekers—fishermen, sailors, indentured laborers, and the like—from England, Ireland, and Scotland, and from Britain's North American colonies. In later decades, their number was augmented by men who chose to remain behind after leaving the service of the mercantile firms that brought them to Labrador in the first place. Although a few tried their luck as itinerant traders, most quickly adopted a way of life similar to that of the Inuit: an existence predicated on subsistence hunting and fishing, and production of furs and other commodities for sale to local merchants. Practically all married into Inuit families, liaisons that produced more than the first generation of people of mixed ancestry. They also gave birth to a distinct cultural pattern, a blending of attributes derived from two different worlds: on the one hand, a solid foundation of centuries-old indigenous expertise in wresting a living from land and sea, and on the other, an overlay of western ethos, nominal Christianity, and retention of English (or French), rather than Inuttut, as their first language. Over time, these traits became definitive markers of the self-ascribed Labrador Settler identity.

These general points aside, the course of Settler history in Labrador's northern and southern precincts differed in one crucial respect. In the south, intermarriage eventually led to the complete absorption of what remained of the resident Inuit population there, a population that was already in decline in the late 1700s owing to disease and migration back to customary territory beyond Hamilton Inlet. By contrast, wholesale amalgamation did not occur in the north. This was largely due to the (partial) success of Moravian missionaries in thwarting the growth of relations between natives and newcomers. The latter were singled out as sources of moral corruption and economic competition, clearly deleterious to the mission work in converting the Inuit, settling them at permanent stations, and teaching them to be trustworthy, industrious clients of the mission's own trade branch. Waged until the mid-1800s when détente was finally reached, the Moravian campaign helped foster the development of a distinct Settler community on the margins of the mission sphere. The resultant Inuit-Settler ethnic boundary, although far from impermeable, persists as a conspicuous feature of social life in modern-day northern Labrador.

Traditional social and economic organization was based on the extended family, each associated with a territory in which its members routinely harvested wildlife and other resources. Residence shifted with the seasons, winter quarters generally being situated in sheltered bays, and summer ones on headlands or inner islands. Most Settlers relied on salmon and cod fishing and fur trapping as mainstays of their livelihood, some trappers operating trap lines running deep into the interior. Other common activities included hunting for seals, caribou, and smaller game, and where conditions allowed, keeping kitchen gardens. Wage labor, relatively rare before the 20th century, became increasingly common from the 1940s onward, the wartime construction of the Goose Bay airbase playing a singular role in exposing traditional society in northern and southern Labrador to the forces of modernization. Newfoundland and Labrador's political union with Canada in 1949 accelerated this process, government policies encouraging (or in some cases forcing) families to resettle in year-round villages where education, health, and other services could be provided more easily. Since then, Settlers, like their Inuit neighbors, have struggled to maintain a semblance of their former way of life in the face of outside competitors, market volatility, local ecological change, and environmentalist protest.

Under current conditions, most Settlers see the successful negotiation of land claims as their best hope for the future. A recent Labrador Métis Nation statement puts the matter this way: "Our goal in a land claim is to put our communities back in charge, and to stop the arbitrary rule over our lives that has been a constant threat since World War II first introduced us fully to Canada, and to Newfoundland" (nd, p. 10). Final resolution of the longstanding Inuit-Kablunangajuk claim in northern Labrador is now at hand. In the south, however, the process is likely to drag on for some time to come.

BARNETT RICHLING

Further Reading

Ben–Dor, Shmuel, *Makkovik: Eskimos and Settlers in a Labrador Community: A Contrastive Study in Adaptation*, St John's: Institute of Social and Economic Research, Memorial University of Newfoundland, 1966

Brody, Hugh, "Permanence and Change among the Inuit and Settlers of Labrador." In *Our Footprints Are Everywhere: Inuit Land Use and Occupancy in Labrador*, edited by Carol Brice & Bennett, Nain: Labrador Inuit Association, 1977

Goudie, Elizabeth, *Woman of Labrador*, Toronto: Peter Martin Associates, 1973

Kennedy, John C., *People of the Bays and Headlands: Anthropological History and the Fate of Communities in the Unknown Labrador*, Toronto: University of Toronto Press, 1995

———, "The changing significance of Labrador settler ethnicity." *Canadian Ethnic Studies*, 20 (1988): 94–111

Labrador Métis Nation, "In the Spirit of Our Ancestors," posted on Labrador Métis Nation website: http://www.labmetis.org

Plaice, Evelyn, *The Native Game: Settler Perceptions of Indian/Settler Relations in Central Labrador*, St John's: Institute of Social and Economic Research, Memorial University of Newfoundland, 1990

Zimmerly, David William, *Cain's Land Revisited: Culture Change in Central Labrador, 1775–1972,* St John's: Institute of Social and Economic Research, Memorial University of Newfoundland

SEVERNAYA DVINA

The Severnaya Dvina (Northern Dvina) is one of the largest rivers of the North European part of Russia, and is formed by the confluence of the Sukhona and the Yug rivers. Severnaya Dvina flows into Dvina Bay of the White Sea, just below Arkhangel'sk. The length of the river is about 744 km (465 miles), and the catchment area of the basin is 360,000 km^2. Severnaya Dvina has a mean annual discharge of 110 km^3. The average flow rate of water in the mouth is 3490 m^3 s^{-1}.

The drainage network of Severnaya Dvina includes about 600 rivers. The largest right tributaries are the Vychegda (1109 km) and the Pinega (657 km), and the largest left tributary is the Vaga.

The river goes by the name of the Malaya (Small) Severnaya Dvina in the first 74 km before the Vychegda River joins it. The Vychegda flows into the Malaya Northern Dvina near Kotlas and the water volume of the river increases more than two times, which is why the river is called the Bolshaya (Great) Northern Dvina downstream. The delta of Severnaya Dvina, a labyrinth of more than 150 arms and channels, is about 45 km wide and 37 km long.

The spring flood in Severnaya Dvina starts in the second half of April or at the beginning of May and finishes at the end of June or beginning of July. The water level sometimes rises to 8 m because of ice jams. The summer water level is lowest from July to September. Freeze-up begins in the middle of November, and breakup of ice in the river takes place during April and May. The average duration of ice drifting in this period is 6–8 days, although sometimes it lasts about 20 days.

There are over 30 species of fish in Severnaya Dvina, and many of them are of commercial fishing significance. The river is also a popular recreation place. The Severnaya Dvina river is of great transport importance, because it flows over a territory with an underdeveloped network of railways and highways. It was an important navigable and timber-rafting river up to the late 1980s. The most important ports are Arkhangel'sk, Kotlas, Novodvinsk, Bereznik, Verkhnyaya Toyma, and Krasnoborsk.

The Severnaya Dvina has ecological problems. An increase in pollutants such as iron, copper, and phenols has been noted in many sections of the river, and some sections near Arkhangel'sk contain methanol and formaldehyde. Severnaya Dvina is subject to the largest anthropogenic loading in the estuary section, where large pulp and paper enterprises are situated. A large number of pollutants enter the river from the Vologda region (the Sukhona River) and Komi Republic (the Vychegda River).

IGOR SERGEYEV

See also **Arkhangel'sk; Arkhangel'skaya Oblast'; White Sea**

Further Reading

Denisenko, L.N., "Socialno-ecologicheskiye problemy delty Severnoy Dviny." In *Socialno-ecologicheskiye problemy Europeyskogo Severa* [Social–ecological problems of the North Dvina delta. In Social–ecological problems of the European North], edited by M.N. Belogubovoy et al., Arkhangelsk: filial Geographicheskogo obshestva SSSR, 1991, pp. 95–108

Ilyina, L.L. & A.N. Grahov, *Reki Severa* [Rivers of the Russian North], Leningrad: Gidrometeoizdat, 1987

Inzhebeykin, U.I. & S.P. Glavatskih, "Raspredeleniye microelementov v basseyne Severnoy Dviny." In *Pomorye v Barents-regione na rubezhe vekov: ecologia, economica, kultura. Materialy Mezhdunarodnoy konferencii* [Location of microelements in North Dvina area. In Pomorye in Barents-region on the border of ages: ecology, economy, culture. Reports of International conference], Arkhangel'sk: IEPS UrO RAN, 2000, p. 96

Karpov, V., "Severnaya Dvina na vse subyekty Rossii odna" [North Dvina for all Russia], *Pravda Severa,* 8 July 1998, p. 3

Kuznetsov, V.S., I.V. Miskevitch & G.B. Zaytceva, *Gidrokhimicheskaya characteristica krupnykh rek basseyna Severnoy Dviny* [HydroChemical character of large rivers of North Dvina drainage-basin], Leningrad: Gidrometeoizdat, 1991

Miskevitch, I.V. & M.V. Dobroskok, "Uchet prostranstvennoy neodnorodnosty processov formirovaniya kachestva vod delty Severnoy Dviny pri planirovanii hoziaystvennoy deiyatelnosti na ee territorii." In *Sever: ecologia* [Account of spatial spottiness of forming processes a quality of water in North Dvina with planning of economic activity. In North: ecology], edited by F.N. Udakhin, Ekaterinburg: Izd-vo UrO RAN, 2000, pp. 109–117

SEVERNAYA ZEMLYA

The archipelago of Severnaya Zemlya (77°54′ to 81°16 N, 91°08′ to 107°46′ E) lies at the boundary of the Kara and Laptev seas off the Taymyr Peninsula of Krasnoyarsk Kray, Russia, and consists of five large islands and several smaller ones. The main islands are Bolshevik (11,572 km^2), October Revolution (13,992 km^2), Pioneer (1649 km^2), Komsomolets (9244) km^2, and Schmidt (500 km^2). The total land area is 36,800 km^2, of which 50% is ice covered. The ice-free land is dominated by sparsely vegetated upland plains. Periglacial lakes occur on many islands, and braided meltwater channels are common on Bolshevik Island and the northern part of Komsomolets Island.

Climatic conditions are governed largely by strong southwesterly winds. The mean annual temperature is −15°C, with a July maximum of +0.9°C to 1.9°C, and a February minimum of −29°C. The annual precipitation ranges from 94 mm to over 250 mm. Large ice caps dominate the landscape, lying on marine sedimentary rocks. There are four main ice caps, the largest of which is Academy of Sciences Ice Dome (5860 km²) on Komsomolets Island. The equilibrium line altitude ranges from around 200 m in the far northwest to 600 m in the far southeast. Few ice cap margins reach the sea, although iceberg calving fronts occur on Academy of Sciences, Rusanova, Karpinsky, and University ice caps. Some of the major ice caps feed floating ice shelves, including the 222 km² Matusevich Ice Shelf on October Revolution Island. The ice caps have a simple morphology. Large ice caps such as Academy of Sciences Ice Cap are stable, but small low-elevation ice caps such as Pioneer Ice Cap are decaying rapidly.

Flora and fauna become increasingly impoverished moving southeast to northwest. In the northwest (Komsomolets and Pioneer islands), dwarf shrub-lichen and grass-moss tundra cover 10–15% of the ice-free ground, with less than 30 vascular plant species recorded. Nesting conditions are generally unfavorable for marine birds, although black guillemot, little auk, kittiwake, and glaucous gull nest in small numbers. Seal and sea hare are common, but walrus and Greenlandic seal are rare. In the southeast (October Revolution and Bolshevik islands), dwarf shrub-lichen tundra covers 20–30% of ice-free ground, with over 60 species of vascular plants recorded. Thirty-two bird species have been noted. Eight species nest in significant numbers (Brent goose, purple sandpiper, glaucous gull, kittiwake, ivory gull, black guillemot, little auk, and snow bunting), and nine others nest in small numbers or infrequently (red-throated diver, king eider, sanderling, Arctic skua, long-tailed skua, herring gull, Arctic tern, snowy owl, and Lapland bunting). Arctic fox, collared lemmings, wolves, ermine, and Arctic hare all inhabit the region, and there is a small reindeer population on Bolshevik Island.

Severnaya Zemlya is uninhabited and was discovered in 1913 by the 1909–1915 Arctic Ocean Hydrographical Expedition, but was not fully mapped until the 1930–32 Ushakov expedition. During the periods 1962–1969 and 1974–1988, glaciological expeditions studied Severnaya Zemlya. Weather stations operated on Severnaya Zemlya from the 1950s to the mid-1990s, and there is a small military base on the island of Sredniy. Since the early 1990s, foreign scientists, polar expeditions, and Arctic tourists have been allowed limited access. On April 3, 1996, a nature reserve covering Severnaya Zemlya was created by the Russian Government.

MEREDITH WILLIAMS

See also **Arctic Ocean Hydrographical Expedition, 1909–1915; Kara Sea; Laptev Sea; Ushakov, Georgiy**

Further Reading

Barr, William, "Severnaya Zemlya, the last major discovery." *Geographical Journal*, 141(1) (1975): 59–71

Govorukha, L.S., "The study of contemporary glaciers in the Soviet Arctic." *Polar Geography and Geology*, 9(1) (1985): 29–37

Govorukha, L.S. et al., *Katalog lednikov SSSR. Tom 16. Angaro-Yeniseyskiy rayon. Vypusk 1. Yenisey. Chast' 1* (Catalogue of glaciers of the USSR. Tom 16. Angaro-Yeninsey region. Vypusk 1. Yenisey. Part 1. Severnaya Zemlya), Leningrad: Gidrometeoizdat, 1980

Korte, Jacobus de, Andrey Volkov & Maria, Gavrilo, "Bird observations in Severnaya Zemlya." *Arctic*, 48(3) (1995): 222–234

Semenov, I.V., "Natural districts of Severnaya Zemlya." In *Problems of Physiographic Zoning of Polar Lands*, edited by L.S. Govorukha & Yu.A. Kruchinin, Leningrad: Gidrometeorologicheskoe, 1971

Starokadomskiy, L.M., "Otkrytiye novykh zemel'v severnom ledivitom okeane" [Discovery of new lands in the Arctic Ocean]. *Morskoy Sbornik*, 386(1) (1915): 1–51

Urvantsev, N.N., *Severnaya Zemlya. Kratkiy ocherk issledovaniya* (Severnaya Zemlya. A short survey of exploration), Leningrad: Izdatel'stvo Vsesoyuznogo Arkticheskogo Instituta, 1933

———, *Na Severnoye Zemle* (In Severnaya Zemlya), Leningrad: Gidrometeiozdat Izdatel'stvo, 1969

Williams, Meredith & Julian Dowdeswell, "Historical fluctuations of the Matusevich Ice Shelf, Severnaya Zemlya, Russian High Arctic." *Arctic, Antarctic and Alpine Research*, 33(2) (2001): 211–222

SEWARD PENINSULA

The Seward Peninsula is located in northwestern Alaska in the United States. The area is bound to the north by Kotzebue Sound in the Chuckhi Sea and to the south by Norton Sound in the Bering Sea. Seward Peninsula stretches 320 km from the eastern mainland of Alaska to Cape Prince of Wales on the westernmost tip where it lies only 90 km from Siberia. The peninsula is 190 km north-south and its northernmost tip is Cape Espenberg, which lies just inside the Arctic Circle (66°30′ N). The total land area measures approximately 60,000 km². Nome is the largest town, located on the southern coast with a population of 3505 in 2001. Seward Peninsula is host to the wild and remote Bering Land Bridge National Preserve (27 million acres).

The major mountain range on Seward Peninsula is the Bendeleben range that runs centrally east-west and whose highest peak is Mt Bendeleben (1137 m). Other mountain ranges include the Kigluaiks, 25 miles north of Nome, which boasts the highest point on the peninsula, Mt Osborn (1437 m). These mountains feature the only permanent ice fields on the peninsula, surviving remnants from the Pleistocene. Permafrost underlies the entire landscape and is discernable at the surface by features such as pingos, ice-wedge polygons, thaw lakes, and solifluction lobes.

An Arctic river meanders with scrub growing on the floodplains, Seward Peninsula, Alaska. *Copyright Bryan and Cherry Alexander Photography*

The Imuruk Lava Plateau is located north of the Bendeleben Mountains. Composed of at least five different lava flows ranging in age from 5 million years to the 2000-year-old Lost Jim Flow, Imuruk Lava plateau is part of the Bering Land Bridge National Preserve. Imuruk Lake, Cloud Lake, and Lava Lake are prominent features in the Plateau. Imuruk Lake, the largest on the peninsula, has been nominated as an ecological reserve as it has a significant scientific value for plant ecology.

Further north along the coast is a 1.6 km wide coastal plain that is characterized by sea coast beaches, saltwater lagoons, and freshwater estuaries, as well as a dynamic barrier bar system. Several rivers flow out from the peninsula, including the Buckland in the northeast and the Kuzitrin and Niukluk in the south. These rivers are important spawning grounds for fish and transport routes for natives and settlers.

Seward Peninsula's geology comprises rocks that are mainly deformed sedimentary and volcanic rocks with granite intrusions. Surface deposits of loose materials cover the northern Peninsula. Upland soils are gravel to loamy, while the coastal plains are wet with thick peat and tundra cover. The petroleum potential is low, but there may be coal deposits of economic value. Geothermal activity in recently active volcanic areas has been noted at Serpentine Hot Springs. A large potential for precious mineral extraction, including gold and silver, exists on the peninsula.

The climate on Seward Peninsula is continental, with cool and windy summers that are often wet along the coast. Inland conditions are generally warmer and drier with average temperatures around 0–16°C with

extremes of 32°C. Winters are harsh with temperatures averaging –20°C to –30°C with extremes of –50°C. The average precipitation varies from roughly 250 mm in the north to 500 mm in the south, with the majority falling in summer. Snowfall varies from 1000 to 1500 mm, with 2500 mm on higher peaks.

The climate and topography of the peninsula support a variety of flora and fauna. Tundra is the dominant vegetation type on the Seward Peninsula and is found in areas with well-developed soils. According to the US Forest Service, the southern two-thirds of the Peninsula is classified as the Seward Peninsula tundra-meadow ecological subregion, while the northern one-third is Bering tundra (Northern) Province. The peninsula's tundra comprises moist (40%) and wet (24%) tundra communities at lower elevations and alpine (23%) tundra communities in the high mountains. Vegetation is primarily composed of sedge tussocks interspersed with scattered willows and birches, which is favored by the region's numerous moose. The Bering tundra vegetation along the wet coastal areas is chiefly sedge and cottongrass with woody plants growing on higher sites. Birch-willow-alder thickets are extensive between the beach and forest. The lower Yukon and Kuskokwim valleys are dominated by white spruce mixed with cottonwood and balsam poplar in tall, relatively dense stands, with a dense undergrowth of thinleaf alder, willow, rose, dogwood, and various species of berry bushes.

Seward Peninsula boasts a rich and diverse birdlife. More than 170 known species include seabirds such as gulls, murres, and kittiwakes; migrating and nesting waterfowl such as ducks, swans, and geese; birds of prey such as hawks, eagles, falcons, and owls; and many songbirds of tundra and uplands. At the crossroads of the Asiatic-North American flyway, this area offers rare opportunities to observe several Old World species. Mammals include muskox, grizzly bears, moose, reindeer, wolves, wolverines, foxes, and other smaller species. Muskoxen were eliminated by the early 1900s and reintroduced in 1970. Reindeer from Siberia were introduced here in 1891 as a meat source to replace native caribou that seem to have disappeared earlier in the century. Marine mammals include various seals, bowhead whales, walrus, and beluga whales, which have been important to Iñupiat Eskimos and remain so today. Polar bears visit the northern shores during winter and ride ice-floes from further north. Fish in the peninsula's rivers, streams, and lakes include several species of salmon, grayling, char, whitefish, and pike.

In terms of human activity on the peninsula, during the last glacial period (Wisconinan) a sea-level drop of around 100 m exposed a shallow continental shelf between Siberia and Alaska that formed the 90 km wide Bering land bridge. One common view of the habitation of the Americas purports that Paleo-Indians arrived from Asia over this land bridge around 12–15,000 years ago and rapidly established eastward and southward (the present-day north and south American Indians). Researchers believe that a second migration around the same time along the southern coast led to the present-day Eskimo and Aleut populations, who still lead subsistence lifestyles.

In the 18th century, Russian and English explorers mapped the Bering Strait. The Strait was named after Vitus Bering, a Danish explorer for the Russian Czar in the 18th century, who explored the waters between Russia and North America. In the early 19th century, European trade in goods increased and by mid-century whaling operations flourished but had a detrimental effect on native people. The gold rush to the Seward Peninsula in 1898–1899 accelerated change in the area with prospectors spread all over the peninsula. The gradual depletion of gold, a major influenza epidemic in 1918, and the Depression led to a decline in the non native population. Development again increased during World War II when the United States established military bases to serve as transfer points to the Soviet Union. Today, nonnatives continue to come to the area to support the nearby oil and gas developments and government extension services. Tourism is presently bringing more people to the area with events such as the Iditarod dogsled race.

Reindeer herding is an important industry with substantial subsistence benefits, including meat, craft, footwear, and accessories. The peninsula is covered by 16 leases covering 14.7 million acres and dominates almost all public land. Private land accounts for less than 1% of the total.

The population of the Seward Peninsula region, which includes the Nome and Northwest Arctic boroughs, numbered 16,404 as of 2002; 78% of these are native Alaskan. Most of these indigenous people are Iñupiaq Eskimos. Following the 1971 Alaska Native Lands Claim Settlement Act (ANCSA), 12 native corporations have been formed. The Seward Peninsula is home to two native corporations: the NANA and Bering Straits corporations.

JASON BERINGER

See also **Alaska Native Claims Settlement Act (ANCSA); Bering Sea; Beringia; Nome**

Further Reading

Alaska Department of Commerce and Economic Development, *Nome: An Alaska Community Profile*, Juneau: Alaska Department of Commerce and Economic Development, 1989

Alaska Geographic Society, *Alaska's Seward Peninsula*, Volume 14(3), Anchorage: Alaska Geographic Society, 1987

Anderson, D.D. & R.A. Henning, *The Kotzebue Basin*, Volume 8(3), Anchorage: Alaska Geographic Society, 1981

Cole, T., *Nome, City of the Golden Beaches*, Volume 11(1), Anchorage: Alaska Geographic Society, 1984

Joint Federal-State Land Use Planning Commission for Alaska, *Seward Peninsula: A Description*, Anchorage: Joint Federal-State Land Use Planning Commission for Alaska, 1973

Mattson, S., *Iditarod fact book: A Complete Guide to the Last Great Race*, (1st edition), Kenmore, Washignton: Epicenter Press, 2001

MvNab, W.H. & P.E. Avers, Ecological Subregions of the United States, Report number WO-WSA-5, prepared in cooperation with Regional Compilers and the ECOMAP Team of the Forest Service July 1994., US Forest Service, 1994

Ray, D.J., *Eskimos of Bering Strait, 1650–1898*, Washington: University of Washington Press, 1991

Schaaf, J. & T.H. Smith, *Ublasaun—First Light: Inupiaq Hunters and Herders in the Early Twentieth Century, Northern Seward Peninsula, Alaska*, Anchorage: National Park Service, Alaska System Support Office, 1996

Swanson, J.D., M. Schuman & P.C. Scorup, *Range Survey of the Seward Peninsula Reindeer Ranges, Alaska*, Anchorage: US Department of Agriculture, Soil Conservation Service, 1985

Till, A. & J. Dumoulin, Geology of the Seward Peninsula. In *The Geology of North America, Volume G-1, The Geology of Alaska*, Geological Society of America, 1994

US Census Bureau, *Census 2000 Redistricting Data (Public Law 94–171) Summary File, Matrices PL1 and PL2*, 2002

West, F.H. & D.M. Hopkins, *American Beginnings: The Prehistory and Palaeoecology of Beringia*, Chicago: University of Chicago Press, 1998

SHAMANISM

"Shaman" derives from words of similar pronunciation in the Tungus languages (Evenki and Even) that signify a person who experiences ecstasies in union with spirits more often than other people do, learns to control these experiences, and thus fulfills particular social roles. Assimilated into the Russian language through early contact, the word "shaman" came to be applied to persons with similar propensities or capacities in the Russian North and East. Correlatively, the verbal form "*shamanstvo*" developed in Russian to signify the shamans' ecstatic activities. Diffused into other European languages, the term "shaman" was extended across America and Greenland. "Shamanism" is a neologism from these roots.

Throughout the indigenous Arctic, the world was traditionally seen as imbued or animated by spirit or spirits, and the shamans assumed roles in relation to them. Typically, spirits would overpower the shaman-to-be without the latter soliciting the encounters. Even in societies where shamans came from certain lineages, the spirits would overwhelm the person among those eligible. Disorienting, these experiences constituted an initiation through which the person would interact with spirits, mediating with them and learning to control them. In some cases, the neophyte would receive training from an experienced shaman, but not always.

Emerging from these initial experiences, the shaman would obtain paraphernalia and rite techniques. Paraphernalia symbolized the presence and attributes of particular spirits with which a shaman was in contact. During rites, at the steady beating of a drum (tambourine) in most cases, and usually with chants, the shaman would induce trance states or levels of ecstasy. Variations existed in the results: the shaman would converse with spirits, or the spirits would speak through the shaman, or both would occur.

Through such rites, shamans assumed vital social roles, principally as healers, among the tribes. A shaman would identify the spirit that caused the malady, and then drive it away or persuade it to cease acting malevolently. Facilitating the hunt was another task frequently associated with shamans. Shamans would placate the spirits of the animals, thus attracting the game or locating food sources. Other tasks included foreseeing events, affecting the weather, identifying transgressors of tribal customs, and learning the fate or situation of missing people. In some societies, the shaman would also act as a psychopomp.

Shamans would astound and could entertain. They would seem to travel to the sky, the sea, or other realms, from which they would return with stories. Some would heighten the effect by disappearing and reappearing. Some might undergo an apparent metamorphosis, apparently turning into other forms of beings, such as wolves.

Shamans' stories, and tales about shamans, could serve as pedagogy, teaching about cosmology, and as means of social control, emphasizing conformity to social norms. These tales could be so vivid that they entered as elements into the great sagas and metaphorical philosophies of the Arctic, such as the Karelian *Kalevala* and the Sakha *Olonho*.

Manifesting the extraordinary, transcending common boundaries, even a benign shaman might be treated with caution, because a shaman could choose to turn such power to various purposes or because a shaman's spiritual power might become erratic. Distinctions were made between those who were stable and helpful on the one hand, and those who were inconsistent or ineffective on the other. In a society such as the Sakha, with tendencies toward dualism in cosmology, shamans were referred to as either "white" (good) or "black" (evil).

Contact with Christianity has been diverse. When Christian doctrines demand a radical severance from the past, the results tend to be the suppression of almost all things indigenous, particularly shamans' practices. Not all doctrines demand such a rupture. When Christian traditions embody an affirmative outlook, they tend to engage vital native characteristics and strengthen the use of native languages while being more tolerant. The results, then, can be a transformation, not a disjunction, within the indigenous context. Personalities also differ: someone who is formally attached to affirmative traditions might not reflect these in action. Careful studies identify the type of Christianity, consider its own presuppositions, and focus on individual personalities within the context.

In anthropological discourse, three meanings coincide in the use of the neologism, "shamanism." One is narrower, and more exact. It reflects the origins of this word by referring to the ecstasies, rites, and social functions of shamans. An even finer precision in meaning is gained when the term "shaman" is used to translate a specific word, or a specific set of interrelated words, in a local language.

The other meaning is wider, more diffuse. It developed to indicate a level above "animism" in some hypotheses about human social evolution. As hypotheses about human social evolution decreased through the 20th century, and cultural relativism increased, the use of the term "shamanism" no longer necessarily involved any rankings of cultural inferiority or superiority. It no longer conveyed a negative meaning categorically. Yet, it continued to designate a classification of whole cultures.

Correlatively, "shamanistic" came to refer to peoples' worldviews (cosmologies) as well as various types of legends, dances, songs, and other customs beyond those pertaining to shamans. "Shamanic" came to be applied to diverse forms of folk healing, regardless of distinctions in vocabulary in the local languages. Indigenous terms may be preferred instead. In the Sakha Republic (Yakutia), for example, the

Sakha (Yakut) term "*ayi yorehe*" is being used (not "shamanism") as a generalized reference in school textbooks for lessons about indigenous worldview and spiritual culture.

A third strand of meaning can also be recognized. "Shamanism" has been used as a reference for a type of religion. Although there is no consensus as to whether shamanism can be defined as religion (Shirokogorov, for one, states that it cannot), some academics have promoted "shamanism" as no less than "the indigenous religion." Extreme movements in this direction have resulted in the codification of beliefs and, in a few instances, the construction of temples for rites, in some regions of the former Soviet Union. This has occurred In Yakutsk, for example, where such a movement presses for a radical definition of the nation (*ethnos*), diverging from mainstream religious and political movements. Codification and construction of this sort are unprecedented; therefore, such movements may be referred to as "neo-shamanism."

International academic interest in the study of shamanism increased during the later 20th century. In July 1988, the first large-scale international gathering focusing on the study of shamanism was convened as a symposium in the 12th International Congress of Anthropologists and Ethnologists (ICAE). A number of key participants from the symposium joined other academics and scholars for a regional conference in Helsinki, in May 1990, convened by the International Association of the History of Religion (IAHR) to study "Northern Religions and Shamanism." Between these two events, the International Society for Shamanistic Research (ISSR) was organized. The ISSR held its first international conference in Seoul, Korea in July 1991, including a sizeable representation from Arctic regions. Subsequent international conferences were convened by the ISSR in Budapest, Yakutsk, Nara (Japan), Chantilly (France), and Ulaanbaatar (Mongolia), each including contributions from the Arctic. Reports can be found in the ISSR journal titled *Shaman*, published in Budapest.

Other international meetings have been convened under different auspices to study shamanism relevant to the Arctic, such as the "International Conference on Animism and Shamanism in the North," Sapporo (Japan), October 1995, and the "Symposium on Shamanic Culture" (Manchuria, China), August 2001. The latter concentrated particularly on the Manchu, which are related to the Tungusic peoples of the Arctic. The first international consultation ever convened to consider the relationships between "Christianity and Shamanism" was held with Arctic representation in Seoul, Korea, in June 2000.

S.A. MOUSALIMAS

Further Reading

Alekseev, N.A., *Shamanizm Tyurkoyazichnykh Narodov Sibiri* [Shamanism among the Turkic Peoples of Siberia], Novosibirsk: Nauka, 1964

Balzer, Marjorie Mandelstam, (editor), *Shamanic Worlds: Rituals and Lore of Siberia and Central Asia*, Armonk, New York: North Castle Books, 1997

Eliade, Mircea, *Shamanism: Archaic Techniques of Ecstasy* (revised edition), translated by Willard Trask, Bollingen Series, Princeton: Princeton University Press, 1972

Hoppál, Mihály & Keith Howard (editors), *Shamans and Cultures: Selected Papers of the First Conference of the International Society for Shamanistic Research*, Budapest and Los Angeles: Akadémiai Kiadó and ISTOR, 1993

Jakobsen, Merete Demant, *Shamanism: Traditional and Contemporary Approaches to the Mastery of Spirits and Healing*, Oxford: Berghahn Books, 1999

Ksenofontov, Gavriil Vasilyevich, *Shamanizm: izbrannyye trudy* (*Publikatsii 1928–1929 gg.*) [Shamanism: selected works (Publications from 1928 to 1929)], Yakutsk: Sever-Yug, 1992

MacCulloch, James, "Shamanism." In *Encyclopedia of Religions and Ethics*, Volume 11, Edinburgh: T. and T. Clark, 1920, pp. 441–446

Mousalimas, S.A. (editor), *Christianity and Shamanism: Proceedings of the First Seoul International Consultation*, available at http://www.OxfordU.net/seoul/, 2001

Pentikäinen, Juha (editor), *Shamanism and Northern Ecology*, Berlin and Hawthorne, New York: Mouton de Gruyter, 1996

Shirokogoroff, Sergey Mikhailovich, *Psychomental Complex of the Tungus*, London: Kegan Paul, Trench, Trubner and Co., 1935

Siikala, Anna-Leena, *The Rite Technique of the Siberian Shaman*, Folklore Fellows Communications 93, Helsinki: Finnish Academy of Science, 1987

Znamenski, Andrei A., *Shamanism and Christianity: Native Encounters with Russian Orthodox Missions in Siberia and Alaska, 1820–1917*, Westport, Connecticut: Greenwood Press, 1999

SHARING

Among the indigenous cultures of the Arctic and the world, no society is perceived as being so absolutely reliant on hunting for the whole of its well-being as are the Inuit. Although not strictly correct, Inuit is used here as a cultural referent in place of the more encompassing Eskimo, which includes within it all members (Iñupiaq Inuit, Yup'it, and Aleut) of the Eskaleut language family. However, because Inuit has perhaps become the better-known identifier of this culture group, here the Inuktitut term for "The People" indicates Eskimos and Aleut. The image of a solitary hunter stooped over a seal's winter breathing hole is all but the defining symbol of everything Inuktitut or authentically Inuit. Indeed, this is so much so that the action of hunting—with all its tools, techniques and strategies, traditional knowledge, and the wealth of the hunters' harvests—is often interpreted as being the whole of Inuit subsistence culture and economy.

Hunting (and fishing) was, and still is, the primary means of provisioning the traditional economy and *niqituinnaq* (real food) is its substance. However, as obvious as the centrality of hunting is, not least because almost all Inuit inhabit local environments that preclude reliance on plant foods, its drama has often masked the other important aspect of the traditional Inuit economy, sharing, which coupled with hunting forms the core of Inuit subsistence. Thus, hunting and the food it produces are, in fact, part of a larger social process through which those who are less well off—be they temporarily unsuccessful hunters and their families, widows and children or the aged and the infirm—are not forced to do without.

Inuit sharing has been portrayed as following one or the other of two models. The first is one of open sharing in which anyone desiring food can obtain a share without incurring any specific obligation to the giver to reciprocate other than (perhaps) at some time in the future. Such systematic generalized reciprocity fits a widely held perception of hunter-gatherers (see Sahlins, 1972) and is best, if somewhat inaccurately, exemplified for Inuit by North Alaskan Iñupiaq communitywide sharing of bowhead whale *maktaaq* and meat (see Worl, 1980).

The second Inuit model is the *pigatigiit-niqaturvigi-it* seal sharing systems of the Central Arctic Copper (Damas, 1972a) and Netsilik Eskimos (see Van de Velde, 1956). Unlike the open distribution of Iñupiaq bowhead sharing, *pigatigiit* sharing involves partnerships between individuals who consistently give each other the same part of the ringed seals captured by either. These partnerships are identified by the term for the seal part that a partnered pair shares, to which the suffix denoting connectedness is added; thus, hindquarter partners are *ukpatiqatigiik* (*ukpatiq* = hindquarters + *atigiik* = pair). Damas (1972a) has recorded Copper Eskimo hunters as having as many as 18 *pigatigiit* partners.

These two examples, although often presented as near-archetypes, are also virtual opposites. The open or general sharing of the Iñupiaq is seemly rooted in an ethos that requires neither rules of preference nor of reciprocity. Copper Eskimo practice, in contrast, is apparently precise with respect to who gives what to whom and what can be expected in return. Yet, although both are accurate to their particular situations, neither is the whole of Inuit sharing. Rather, Inuit sharing or *ningiqtuq*, like Inuit society, is more nuanced than can be represented in a single model.

In actuality, Inuit *ningiqtuq* encompasses the generalized pattern of Iñupiaq sharing, while, like all economies, focusing on the distribution of food and other resources within a normative framework that provides both for access and also sanction. (Properly, *ningiqtuq* is the term used by Inuit of the Central Canadian Arctic to describe the economy of food shar-

ing. See Fienup-Riordan (1982) and Bodenhorn (2000) for the related Yup'it and Iñupiaq terminologies.) The result is a system that is far more complex than notions of generalized reciprocity might indicate because sharing is intimately connected to the two central social institutions in Inuit society—kin group and community. These rules of right of access and of reciprocity are known to everyone and exclude no one.

Across the North American Arctic (see Bodenhorn, 2000; Damas 1972a, b; Fienup-Riordan, 1982), the core of Inuit life is framed by two central precepts: *naalaqtuq* (respect and obedience) and *ungayuq* (solidarity-generosity). Together, these structure and direct interpersonal behavior, with *naalaqtuq* ordering intergenerational relations and *ungayuq* emphasizing solidarity (Damas, 1963).

Naalaqtuq, meaning respect and obedience, defines authority relations as these are constructed through, most often, genealogical sub-superordinance but sometimes also age difference, and *ungayuq* mandates generational and group communality and, thus, moderates the sharp edge of *naalaqtuq*. Moreover, because kinship is the centripetal institution in Inuit culture, both of these precepts are most clearly expressed in the *ilagiit*, or multigenerational, male-focused consanguinal extended family. It is the focal social unit in Inuit society (Damas, 1972b) and the principal unit for the production, primary distribution, and, often, consumption of food. It is within the *ilagiit* that the behaviors of *piliriqatigiingniq* (cooperation) and *pijitsirniq* (responsibility) are most clearly and obviously lived.

The order that *naalaqtuq* and *ungayuq* provides to family-community social relations extends to virtually all other areas of Inuit sociality, including economy. Through *pijitsirniq* and *piliriqatigiingniq*, these two critical social structural elements organize and facilitate the flow of *niqituinnaq* to all levels of the Inuit social universe, from the individual to the *ilagiit* and from the *ilagiit* to the community.

For all its apparent underlying structural simplicity, *ningiqtuq* is operationally complex. In functional terms, sharing integrates hunter, family, and community and operates via a web of complementary communal and individual mechanisms. The result is a system considerably subtler than is suggested by either the Inupiaq or Copper Eskimo examples outlined earlier.

Overall, the most intensive and *naalaqtuq*-influenced sharing takes place within the social context of the extended family. It is almost invariable that *ilagiit* males hunt together and that extended family members are in a *niqiliriiq* (literally, "those who share food") relationship with each.

The most basic element of intra-*ilagiit* sharing is *tugagauyuk*. *Naalaqtuq*, as an effector of sharing within the extended family, is found most obviously in the *tugagaujuq* transfers. This aspect of *ningiqtuq* is best described as the upward movement of resources from genealogical subordinate extended family members to the *ilagiit* head of the social unit. In outline, upon returning from a hunt, the successful hunter deposits the greater part, if not all, of his harvest at the home of the extended family head or *isumataq*, usually the oldest male in the family but possibly a senior woman when there is no older experienced male. In practical terms, the output from the hunting activity of younger family members, once deposited with the *ilagiit* leader, becomes common property to all members of the extended family.

This *naalaqtuq*-directed upward flow from subordinate hunter to *isumataq* is complemented by *tigutuinnaq* (essentially "taking away") by which any member can freely draw at will from the leader's "store" according to household or individual need. *Tigutuinnaq*, in effect, reverses the flow of resources by virtue of the responsibility imposed upon a family leader by *naalaqtuq* to ensure the welfare of his/her *ilagiit*.

Two other *naalaqtuq* types of sharing, each involving the distribution of resources within non-kin-based task groups, bear mentioning. The first is *katujiyuk* or *taliktuq* and refers to the distribution of meat by the senior hunter-leader among unrelated hunters. Although relatively rare, *katujiyuk-taliktuq* appears to be a variation of the *ilagiit*-based sharing process adapted to the conditions of modern Inuit communities where hunters sometimes find kindred unavailable. The other form is *uummajusiutiit* in which the owner of a boat distributes the harvest among the crew. In this respect, *uummajusiutiit* bears a close resemblance to the primary-level distribution that takes place within Iñupiaq whaling crews (Worl, 1980; also see Dahl, 2000 regarding Greenland).

Whereas *tugagaujuk-tigutuinnaq* activities function almost wholly within the social context of the extended family, mechanisms for the more generalized distribution of food resources are also present. Chief among these is *nirriyaktuqtuq* commensalism, in which the head of an *ilagiit* hosts a communal meal. Such commensal activity may, when resources are scarce, be limited to the extended family, but more often includes a significant segment of the overall community.

There are two essential differences between restricted and open commensal meals. When a *nirriyaktuqtuq* is intended only for family, word is circulated directly to the expected participants. Open meals, which may involve upward of 100 participants and last for several hours, on the other hand, are preceded by general announcement throughout the community. The other difference between the two subtypes is in the disposition of surplus food. After a restricted *nirriyaktuqtuq*, any uneaten food is left for later consumption by the host and his household; food remaining from an open meal, which may be substantial if participation is low, is generally taken away by attendees or gifted to designated non-kin.

Niqiliriiq and *nirriyaktuqtuq* describe, respectively, the two basal mechanisms for distributing and redistributing food within extended families and across communities, although *nirriyaktuqtuq* also plays a role in inter-*ilagiit* transfers (at this level, commensalism is always in the form of a shared meal). There are, however, also a number of voluntary sharing practices in which individuals, as initiators and receptors, are focal. These are *akpallugiit* ("inviting-in"), *paiyuktuq* (gifting), and *niqitatianaq* (the division of game between hunting partners).

Akpallugiit, as its gloss might suggest, entails a prospective host inviting a specific person or persons to partake of a meal, often of an especially desirable food, at the host's dwelling. Typically, invitees are unrelated to the host. Rather, the bond between each may be long friendship, knowledge that the guest shares a fondness for the specialty to be eaten, or the mutual experience of long life. In any case, *ungayuq* underpins this practice.

Paiyuktuq is in some senses complementary to *akpallugiit*, but, unlike it, may be influenced by *naalaqtuq* or *ungayuq*. The gifting usually entails the sending of parcels of food to designated persons. These may, as in the case of *paiyuktuq*, be favorite non-kin, but such gifting is often directed to elders and widows who are without the support of hunting kinsmen. Although a *paiyuktuq* gift may be something especially favored by the receiver, when the gifting involves persons less well supplied, it almost always is of cooked meat.

The final voluntary practice is *niqitatianaq* or the division of game between two cooperating hunting partners. This form, in contrast to other types of *ningiqtuq*, only occurs away from the hunters' community close to the conclusion of the hunt. It is exclusive to partners who are unrelated and without formal obligation to be *niqiliriiq*. Superficially, this relationship appears similar to the Copper and Netsilik Eskimos *pigatigiit-niqaturvigiit* seal-sharing partnerships outlined earlier. However, these were much more formal and, once established, were guided by *naalaqtuq*, while *niqitatianaq* is an association that is essentially founded in friendship and *ungayuq*.

Ningiqtuq cannot simply be described as a system of open food distribution and generalized reciprocity. Nor is it one in which rules rigidly define and circumscribe economic relationships. Open and directed sharing are both present as evidenced by the generalized nature of communitywide *nirriyaktuqtuq* and by *ilagiit*-focused *tugagauyuq*. However, these two poles, one restrictive and the other open, are complemented by a variety of intermediate mechanisms that ensure that the principal social elements of Inuit society are economically integrated. In this regard, the system mirrors the structural complementarity of *naalaqtuq* and *ungayuq* and the organizational flexibility that characterizes Inuit society overall—the rules are clear, but they are neither exclusive nor rigid.

The result is an economy that, from Alaska to Greenland, optimizes social inclusiveness rather than the maximization of individual or family economic well-being. Rooted in individual-*ilagiit*-community dynamic of Inuit society, sharing joins each person as *niqiliriiq*.

GEORGE WENZEL

Further Reading

Bodenhorn, B., "It Is Good To Know Who Your Relatives Are But We Were Taught To Share With Everybody: Shares and Sharing Among Iñupiaq Households." In *The Social Economy of Sharing: Resource Allocation and Modern Hunter-Gatherers*, edited by G.W. Wenzel, G. Hovelsrud-Broda & N. Kishigami, Osaka: National Museum of Ethnology, 2000, pp. 27–60

Dahl, J., *Saqqaq: An Inuit Hunting Community in the Modern World*, Toronto: University of Toronto Press, 2000

Damas, D., *Igluligmiut Kinship and Local Groupings: A Structural Approach*, Bulletin 196, Ottawa: National Museum of Canada, 1963

——, "Central Eskimo systems of food sharing." *Ethnology*, XI(3) (1972a): 220–240

——, "The Structure of Central Eskimo Associations." In *Alliance in Eskimo Society*, edited by L. Guemple, Proceedings of the American Ethnology Society 1971, Supplement, Seattle: University of Washington Press, 1972b, pp. 40–55

Fienup-Riordan, A., *The Nelson Island Eskimo: Social Structure and Ritual Distribution*, Anchorage: Alaska Pacific University Press, 1982

Sahlins, M., *Stone Age Economics*, Chicago: Aldine, 1972

Van de Velde, F., "Rules for sharing the seals among the Arviligjuarmiut Eskimo." *Eskimo*, 41 (1956): 3–6

Worl, R., "The North Slope Iñupiat Whaling Complex." In *Alaska Native Culture and History*, edited by W. Workman & Y. Kotani, Osaka: National Museum of Ethnology, 1980, pp. 305–320

SHEEP

Sheep, genus *Ovis*, order *Artiodactyla*, include both wild and domesticated species. Wild sheep are slender, nicely built, with a short tail, long neck, high head with small ears, and long, slender legs with small hoofs. Some species are decorated with a large pendant of long hair on the neck and breast. Sheep horns are large, sometimes huge, heavy, and spiral. The horns of males are larger than those of females. The type of horn differs markedly and allows distinguishing among sheep species. Sheep survive temperatures from −60°C to +50°C because their wool serves as a remarkable thermal insulator. The color of sheep varies from yellowish white to reddish brown. The belly is mostly white. Spirally twirled horns, a lack of beard in males, as well as a tail covered with wool both on the top and bottom distinguish sheep from their relatives—goats (genus *Capra*). Sheep are ruminates; their stomach is four-chambered.

Sheep eat mostly herbs and grasses, and also branches and shoots of bushes and trees, consuming daily about 10 kg (22 lb) of fresh green plants in summer. Due to thin lips, sheep can graze on very low grass. These animals are good ground and snow diggers, although they avoid snow deeper than 25–30 cm (10–12 inch). Sheep graze in the daytime, interchanging periods of grazing and rest. They regularly drink water (in summer in the mornings and evenings) and make special trips from pastures to water springs. In desert mountains, they use small streams, groundwater seepage, and puddles with rainwater. They drink fresh water and in dry years saltwater with up to 20 g salt liter^{-1}. If necessary, they can live without water for some days.

The same home range including trails, latrine, and lying places is used for several years by many generations, in addition to shelters on rocks, which are usually used to escape from predators. Caverns in mountains and rooflike rocks are often used as shelters against the sun and winds or snowfall, and are also used during calving. Sheep populations include groups of females with newborn lambs and yearlings, groups of young (2–5 years) males, groups of males older than 5 years, and single males older than 11 years. In spring and summer, sheep live in groups of 2–20 animals, males and females separately. In places with plenty of forage, gatherings up to 50–90 sheep exist. Fierce combats between males take place at the beginning of rut and also before the rut. Hierarchy is settled by these fights and dominant rams mate with females first. The gestation period is from 150 to 180 days (varies by species and by wild or domestic animals). From April to the beginning of June, one, sometimes two, lambs are born.

Sheep are good runners. The maximum speed on the plains is 60 km (37 mi) per hour (when pursued by car). Sheep have endurance when running; dogs are not able to catch them. Leaders (usually old females and males, constant in a group) determine escape behavior, the direction, and way of escape. The maximum duration of sheep life is 18 years. The wolf as well as the leopard are important predators if and when sheep are weakened by starvation. Lambs are the prey of eagles and lammergeier. Ecologically, sheep keep to open hilly grassy spaces, which provide possibilities to escape predators by running and jumping from steep escarps.

The total numbers of wild sheep are declining, and many species are listed as endangered or extinct. Delicious meat, beautiful horns, and warm skin made wild sheep an important hunting goal. Nowadays, hunting is aimed mostly at horn trophies. Sheep were among the first domesticated animals (about 5000 BCE). Since that time, sheep became one of the main sources of meat, wool, and leather. There are now 1,068,669,000 domestic sheep, covering 200 breeds. The total harvest of sheep wool in 1999 was 2,363,000 tons, and 7,474,000 tons of meat. In 2000, there were 2,399,000 domestic sheep in Norway, 477,000 in Iceland, 128,000 in Finland, and 22,000 in Greenland. In Norway, 24,000 tons of mutton were harvested, and in Iceland 8000 tons (FAO, 2001).

In the genus, there are ten species, of which two inhabit North America (*O. Dalli* and *O. Canadensis)*, with others in Eurasia. Dall's sheep (*O. dalli*) are found in alpine environments of Alaska, the Yukon, the western Northwest Territories, and extreme northwestern British Columbia. Bighorn sheep (*O. canadensis*) are divided into two groups of subspecies, of which one is found in Arctic environments. These are the bighorns of the Rocky Mountains and California. They are some of the largest in the world; some males are as heavy as 135 kg (300 lb) (average weight is 102 kg (226 lb)). Horns are as long as 108 cm (42 inch) and more, 40 cm (15.7 inch) round at the widest. Bighorn prefer open spaces with a rich supply of cereals and woody species. About 30,000 bighorn inhabit the Rocky Mountains.

Snow sheep (*O. nivicola*) have heavy bodies (males weigh 70–100 kg (155–222 lb) and females weigh 40–70 kg (90–155 lb)) with thick, heavy horns of moderate length (rarely longer than 110 cm). Their range comprises two uneven parts: the larger one covers Yakutiya to the east of Lena River, Kolyma Plateau, mountains at the Okhotsk Sea shore, Kamchatka Peninsula. The smaller part covers Putorana Mountains at the South Taymyr. Snow sheep inhabit moderately high mountains and prefer open terrains, grassy slopes with sparse shrubs and trees, and mountain and maritime tundra of rough relief. Snow sheep use as forage not only grass, herbs, and sedges, but also branches, leaves of bushes and trees, coniferous needles, and lichens. The total number of snow sheep in North Asia is about 55,000. Snow sheep are an important hunting animal; about 5000 annually are harvested for meat and fur (for clothing).

Arkhar (*O. ammon*) inhabit the Pamir, Tien-Shan, Altai, and Sayany mountains. These are champions in horn sizes (males adorned by horns to 190 cm (6.2 ft) length, 160 cm (5.2 ft) in width, and as heavy as 35 kg (78 lb). The average weight of a male is 70–85 kg (155–190 lb) and that of a female is 40–55 kg (89–122 lb). *O. ammon* inhabit mountain levels from 2000 to 4000 m (6500 to 13,100 ft), mostly grasslands on mountain plains, usually avoiding rocky and stony places. Canyons, very steep valley slopes, or other forms of rugged terrain are important for shelter.

Urials (*O. vignei*) inhabit mountains of West Pamir and Kopet-Dag, in areas with temperatures from −30°C (in winter mountains) to +45°C (in shadow; summer, deserts), on levels higher than 2000–3000 m (6500–9800 ft) as well as on sea level at the desert plateau Ustyurt. They mostly keep to semidesert and desert grasslands with stony grounds, savannas on mountain slopes, and plateaus. The number of urials is constantly declining. Some subspecies are regarded as endangered. There are about 6000 urials at the Ustyurt and about 2000 in the Nuratinskii Nature Reserve, and less than 1000 in Tadjikistan.

LEONID M. BASKIN

See also **Dall's Sheep; Sheep Farming**

Further Reading

Alexandr, Fedosenko & Kapitonov Vladimir, "*Gornye barany*" (Mountain sheep) (*Ovis ammon* Linn. 1758). In *Mlekopitayushchie Kazakhstana* [Mammals of Kazakhstan], Volume 3(3), edited by Gvozdev Evgenii & Kapitonov Vladimir, Alma-Ata: Nauka, 1983

Baskin, Leonid Kjell Danell, *Ecology of Ungulates: A Handbook of Species in Eastern Europe and Northern and Central Asia*, Heidelberg: Springer, 2003

FAO Bulletin of Statistics, 1(2) (2001): 155–157

Geist, Valerius, *Mountain Sheep A study in Behavior and Evolution*, Chicago and London: The University of Chicago Press, 1971

Heptner, Vladimir, Nasimovich Andrey & Bannikov Andrey, *Mammals of the Soviet Union*, Volume 1, Leiden: Model Press Pvt. Ltd., 1989

Larin, Vladimir, *Snezhny baran plato Putorany* [Snow sheep (*Ovis nivicola borealis*) at the Putorany plateau], Thesis, Moscow: Vsesoyuznyi nauchno-issledovatel'skii institut okhrany prirody i zapovednogo dela, 1990

Leslie, David & Douglas Charles, "Desert bighorn sheep of the River Mountains, Nevada." *Wildlife Monographs*, 66 (1979)

Ponting, K., *Sheep of the World*, Poole Dorset: Blanford Press, 1980

Revin Yuriy, Sopin Leonid & Zhelesnov Nikolay, *Snezhnye barany* [Snow sheep], Novosibirsk: Nauka, 1988

Ross, C., *Sheep Production and Management*, Englewood Cliffs, New Jersey: Prentice-Hall, 1989

Sapozhnikov, Gennadii, *Gornye barany Tadjikistana* [Wild Mountain Sheep (*Ovis*) of the Tadzhikistan], Dushanbe: Donish, 1976

Zheleznov-Chukotsky, Nikolay, *Ekologiya Ovis nivicola v Severnoy Asii* [Ecology of *Ovis nivicola* in Northern Asia], Moscow: Nauka, 1994

SHEEP FARMING

Sheep farming in the Arctic is relatively marginal because the sheep's diet consists of primarily southerly species. However, in the Subarctic and boreal parts of the North, two wild species of sheep exist—the Dall's sheep (*Ovis dalli*) in Alaska and Canada, and the snow sheep (*Ovis nivicola*) in Russia. Neither

Dall's nor snow sheep, however, is suitable for domestication. Hunters prey upon both species, and trophy hunters can collect as much as $5000 per animal.

The development and spread of agriculture in the North in connection with colonization included the introduction of sheep. During the 18th and 19th centuries, sheep farming existed exclusively for the subsistence of the colonies, but with the growing need of alternative resources to ensure the necessary sustenance in the early the 20th century—and especially with the growing focus on monetary economies—farmers repeatedly attempted to increase sheep reproduction.

Despite these efforts, the introduction of sheep in Arctic Canada and Alaska has not succeeded, neither among the indigenous nor the nonindigenous newcomers, although sheep farming has remained significant to nonindigenous inhabitants in several of the Nordic countries and Russia. In the latter half of the 16th century, Nordic and Russian farmers travelled with the animals during their northward migrations, thereby establishing unique, northerly types of hunting, fisheries, field crops, and animal husbandry. In Norway, this resulted in the establishment of coastal communities distinguished by distinct "combination farming," that is, amalgamations of fisheries and farming, and in the northern regions, sheep farming. Today, combination farming in the northernmost countries includes a total sheep stock of approximately 200,000 animals.

Within the chief geographic areas of the North, sheep reproduction varies considerably. Sheep farming is minimal in both Sweden and Finland; Iceland, however, is known for its high-quality mutton, producing approximately half a million lambs each year. Iceland's economy depends upon lamb production, particularly in the remote regions of the country. Researchers believe that when Iceland was first settled in the 9th century, dense vegetation and trees covered over 60% of its land. Since then, unchecked sheep grazing and logging for fuel and building materials has led to a substantial loss of vegetation, resulting in massive land erosion. Today, the management of soil erosion and replanting of forests in Iceland is a concern of national importance, and to this end, the government has imposed quotas on sheep farming.

The name of the Faroe Islands (in Danish, the *Færøerne* or "Sheep Islands") suggests the importance of sheep farming within that culture. Until the advent of commercial fisheries in the late 19th century, the Faroe islanders' survival depended completely upon sheep rearing, and to this end, farmers in the Middle Ages developed a sophisticated system of regulation to prevent overgrazing. However, since World War II, fisheries have dominated the Faroe Islands economies, although a production of approximately 70,000 animals sustains the home market consumption.

Due to turmoil in Russia after the breakdown of the Soviet system in the early 1990s, precise data concerning sheep farming in Russia are unavailable, although present estimates indicate approximately half a million sheep. Sheep farming in the North was introduced by the Soviets in the 1930s, which emphasized large-scale production in *sovkhoz* (state owned farms) and *kolkhoz* (cooperatives). Despite the dismantling of the Soviet Union and some of its systemic policies, sheep farming in the North is still managed by the sovkhoz and kolkhoz structures.

The history of sheep farming in Greenland is noteworthy for two reasons: first, the farming system demonstrated how a hunting culture could be transformed into a sheep farming culture in a relatively short time period (three generations). Second, sheep farming has served as an excellent illustration of sustainable development in the Arctic. Local farmers in Greenland have ensured a stable meat production and a successful economy through the development of a distinct and flexible farming culture that is based on local resources, all without compromising the environment.

Depreciation of resources in Greenland during the late 19th century, in conjunction with the growing sedentary character of the population, led to the introduction of sheep farming to combat growing starvation and malnutrition. Reverend Jens Chemnitz of Frederiksdal, a settlement in South Greenland, initiated commercial agriculture in Greenland. During a stay in Copenhagen in 1905–1906, Chemnitz convinced the colonial authorities of the potential for sheep farming in South Greenland. Consequently, he went to the Faroe Islands to study sheep farming and eventually introduced flocks to Greenland.

In 1906, the first 11 sheep (nine mares and two rams) were transported from Faroe Islands to Julianehåb in Greenland, followed by an additional eight animals. After a few years, the initiative proved successful, and in 1914, Amos Egede started a farm in Igaliku with two emes and one ram. In addition to the sheep from Faroe Islands, Scotland and northern Iceland exported sheep in 1915. Greenlandic sheep stock appears to have developed as a mixture of these three strains, although the Icelandic genes dominate. In order to increase farming activity, farmers began lending mares and rams so that anybody willing to try breeding and farming could access a stock of sheep, grow a flock, and "repay" the initial lender in time. Sheep rearing remained an important but smaller supplement to fishing and hunting in Greenland during these years until 1924, when Otto Frederiksen settled in Qassiarsuk and created the first full-time commercial sheep farm in Greenland. He borrowed 145 sheep from the sheep-rearing station in Julianehåb/Qaqortoq in order to build his farm supply.

Up until 1935, a total of eight different settlements existed; Qassiarsuk and Igaliku were the largest, and secondary farms in places such as Igaliku Kujalleq developed as a result of large resources in the hinterland. During the next 10–15 years, sheep farming steadily increased, and a substantial portion of the potential usable locales for sheep rearing was exploited between 1935 and 1950. Animals were slaughtered at the sheep production station in Julianehåb/Qaqortoq. Some meat was distributed locally, but a substantial amount was transported to Copenhagen and sold.

During the 1930s, Greenland exported a substantial portion of its production to Denmark, even though Greenlandic consumption was increasing. Exports to Denmark accounted for approximately 80% of the value of production, and this was partly affected as a consequence of the outbreak of World War II. The war isolated Denmark, and its centralized colonial system, wherein much of country's decision-making occurred in Copenhagen, could potentially have suffered severe economic losses. However, sheep farming actually thrived during and after the war because time-consuming connections to Copenhagen were eliminated.

Post-World War II, modernization and its accompanying industrialization in the North influenced the sheep-farming business tremendously. The difficult winter temperatures, however, have consistently hampered production. In most years, farmers can maintain the sheep on the land during wintertime when the local Föhn winds keep the snow at a manageable level, enabling the sheep to access the vegetation below. Nonetheless, the accumulation of excess snow often necessitates supplementary feed. Slaughterhouses were built in Narssaq in conjunction with a new production facility for shrimp in 1949, when officials decided to make the factory adaptable for both species. Thus, production facilities were available for fish processing during most of the year, and transformed for slaughtering during a two-month period in September and October.

A key element in the development of sheep farming has been the question of access to land. All land in Greenland is common property; private ownership of land is impossible. According to a governmental ruling in 1929, access to land areas was distributed in conjunction with the right to conduct sheep farming. These rights included the right to manage a certain piece of land in connection with the establishment of a farmstead, what traditionally would be termed an "infield area." This right was transferable to sons and daughters as long as they wished to practice sheep farming and continued to care for the land by removing stones, building fencing, and creating watering and draining systems.

Traditional sheep farming, however, was expensive and complicated. During summer months, farmers let the sheep alone in the hills and mountains where the animals could find satisfying grazing areas. In the winter, the flock stayed close to the farm, although in cases of limited vegetation, commercial farmers suffered massive flock reductions. One remedy during the 1960s was the import of fodder from Denmark, although transportation was considered too expensive over time. Another problem connected to the farming in Greenland was the potential for overgrazing, particularly in the areas near the settlements.

The establishment of Greenland Home Rule in 1979 ushered in new policies that argued that Greenland's economy should be based on living resources and developed with respect to the traditional settlement pattern. Sheep farmers, headed by the director of the Sheep Farmers Organization, Kaj Egede, worked toward the development of a sustainable farming system in Greenland as a long-term goal.

The first step in this process entailed the analysis of the potential productivity of the vegetation resources to determine the sustainable basis for farming. Second, the Sheep Farmers Organization planned the new settlement structure in order to facilitate social interaction among farmers, including the sharing of machines and equipment, while at the same time preventing overgrazing of specific areas. They also sought ways to create suitable architecture, as maintaining the sheep in stables during winter was considered the best solution to prevent the overgrazing and flock reduction. The final step involved clearing the fields of winter fodder production in order to build new stables. Since the early 1980s, the number of sheep in Greenland has stabilized at a reasonably high level of approximately 20,000 ewes. Keeping the sheep in stables during the winter, and feeding them the locally produced rather than imported fodder have prevented fluctuation.

Due to these changes in the Greenland sheep-farming system, the situation today reflects an overall rise in total production, despite the lower number of ewes today than farmers had 30 years ago. A total cost-benefit analysis demonstrates that sheep-farming activity contributes positively to the Greenland economy. In addition to contributing to the national economy and creating better living conditions for the population in southern Greenland, sheep farming also created the basis for other forms of cultural development. A true example of sustainable development in the Arctic, sheep farming takes into account not only the environmental but also the economic, social, and cultural dimensions of this concept.

RASMUS OLE RASMUSSEN

See also **Dall's Sheep; Faroe Islands; Sheep**

Further Reading

Rasmussen, Rasmus Ole, "The Sheep-Farming Kujataamiut of South Greenland." In *Endangerede Peoples of The Arctic—Struggles to Survive and Thrive*, edited by Milton M.R. Freeman, Westport, Connecticut—London: The Greenwood Press, 2000
http://www.si.is/utgafa/ymis/PDF-skrar/Partners-for-Life/Agro-industry.pdf

SHIROKOGOROV, SERGEY MIKHAILOVICH

Providing detailed descriptions about the Tungus, Sergey Mikhailovich Shirokogorov also developed theories about "ethnos" and about "shamanism" that are relevant more widely. He also offered advice about methodology. He used the term "Tungus" to encompass the various Tungusic-speaking peoples, and he broadened his studies to include the Manchus.

In his first major work about the Tungus (1929), he concentrates on their social organization with reference directly to indigenous vocabulary and concepts. Identifying clans, social structures within them, and interactions between them, he achieves a depth and breadth in his descriptions that are rarely available for any group. He develops his theory of ethnos while indicating ways by which the Tungus maintain themselves as "ethnical units."

Ethnos is a dynamic process, not a static phenomenon, through which an ethnical unit is formed and is maintained or disintegrates through responses to primary (natural), secondary (cultural), and tertiary (interethnic) milieus. Originally published in Russian (1922, 1923) and English (1924), this theory derives from a concern that he held during his field research, 1912–1918: how to enable the Tungus and similar peoples to maintain themselves as ethnical units while being incorporated into a larger unit, Russia.

In his second major work about the Tungus (1935), he analyzes manifold aspects in their psychomental complex. By the term "psychomental complex," he means "those cultural elements which consist of psychic and mental reactions on milieu" (ibid., p. 1). This work is organized into three preliminary parts: positive knowledge, hypotheses, and practical methods resulting from hypotheses. He clearly differentiates between positive knowledge and hypotheses. He also differentiates between positive knowledge and folklore, and notes the errors that can occur when a cursory observer confuses these aspects.

Shirokogorov devoted himself to the study of "shamanism" as an aspect of the psychomental complex (ibid., pp. 241–402). Having studied the Tungus concepts about spirit (within the positive knowledge), delineating the various types of spirits (among the hypotheses) and the various methods of influencing or managing them (among the practical methods resulting from hypotheses), he differentiated between those spirits that are "dealt with" by shamans, those "dealt with" by other specialists, and those "managed" without shamans or other specialists. Thus, he was able to identify the scope of the shamans' type precisely. He then describes the shamans' roles and techniques with details from various locations.

He explains that a shaman cannot function among the Tungus without social approval, and how the Tungus distinguish between effective shamans and pretenders. Shirokogorov proves that an effective shaman must have "a healthy body, good nervous and normal psychic functions" for physical stamina and mental balance to maintain psychological control during ecstasies and to fulfill the shamans' "chief function." This is "a social function of regulating the psychomental complex of the social unit" (ibid., p. 350). This role becomes important particularly during episodes of mass psychic upset (which are not the same as individual instances of Arctic hysteria). Shirokogorov's depth of understanding is so unusual that it can be misinterpreted through hasty reading. He describes the effective shaman as a healthy and psychically balanced person within episodes of mass "psychosis" that sometimes afflict the "ethnical unit."

His conclusions about shamanism are relevant for the Arctic today. For instance, describing the "plasticity" of Tungus shamanism, he recognizes that a divergence, "maladjustment," occurs when it becomes a fixed system instead. Furthermore, he states, "Shamanism is well adapted to the existing complex, and it can hardly exist in a different complex, but it forms only one of the elements of the existing complex. On the other hand, the shamanism may exist in association with different complexes, and the Tungus complexes may include no shamanism at all" (ibid., p. 47).

Providing advice for field research, Shirokogorov emphasizes the essential importance of a researcher's "love" for the people (*Psychomental Complex*, 1935: 39–48). Nothing less than love is an essential quality in his experience. He furthermore explains that the researcher must abandon preconceptions in order to understand a mentality that is different from the researcher's own. He describes the difficulty in disallowing new impressions from proceeding along one's own predisposed channels of thought and being assimilated into one's own "psychomental complex." His brief but exact criticism of Lévy-Bruhl, a contemporary, is particularly meaningful in this regard. The first-hand insights that Shirokogorov obtains from these principles are remarkably free from social evolutionary theories, which he also criticizes, and from sorts of relativism that are a reaction to them.

His approach is holistic. Shirokogorov maintains that aspects, including language, social organization, material culture (physical objects), decorative art, and various customs, cannot be understood except in relation to other components in the "psychomental complex." Intent that the Tungus should be understood as their own "ethnoses," he dispels any theory that would abstract fragmentary evidence to subsume the Tungus under artificial categories, whether it be theories about primitive mentality that he criticizes consistently, or the Mongol race theory that he rejects through his work in physical anthropology ("Who Are the Northern Chinese?," 1924), or the Ural-Altaic theory that he dismisses through his expertise in linguistics (1931).

His linguistic research is extensive. A few transliterations and translations had been produced, yet the Tungus traditions remained oral. Unlike the Manchu, these languages did not contain traditions of literature while he was conducting his research. Later, during the 1920s and 1930s, literature increased for the purpose of communist party propaganda. Therefore, in response, in an essay that he wrote close to the time of his death (published posthumously in 1991), he states: "the Literary Tungus language has no scientific value, nor any future." It has no scientific value, he would say, because it does not convey Tungus indigenous ideas or aspirations. It has no future, because writing for such a purpose was designed to lead to the disintegration of the ethnical unit.

Shirokogorov's work remains a valuable source for discovery. His complete work has not yet come to the forefront in Russian language studies. A short article about him was printed toward the end of the Soviet era (Reshetov, 1989). Interest him surfaced in the CIS at the millennium. In 2000, a scientific seminar was convened in his honor in Vladivostok, jointly by the Far Eastern Branch of the Russian Academy of Sciences, Omsk State University, and the Siberian Department of the Russian Academy of Sciences. Also in 2000, the "first attempt to investigate his English papers" was published in *Vesti Natsiyanalnai Akademii Navuk Belarusi* (no. 3). He published his major works in English while he was an émigré in China. Foreign to the British and American establishments on the other hand, his work has never received the attention it deserves in English language studies. Attention has been given to his work, particularly in Japan and somewhat in China.

Biography

Sergey Mikhailovich Shirokogorov was born in Suzdal, Russia, on July 2, 1887 or possibly 1889. He received a broad education in Russia combining history, economics, sociology, physical anthropology, prehistory, and ethnography, as well as biology. Joining the Museum of Anthropology and Ethnography of the Imperial Academy of Sciences in St Petersburg in 1911, he embarked on field research, choosing the Tungus, among whom he then lived with some interruptions from 1912 to 1918. Returning to St Petersburg to consolidate his initial findings, in 1914, he supervised Afanassief, a Tungus researcher in linguistics, and he prepared Czaplicka for her expedition. When the Bolshevik Revolution broke out in 1917, he was briefly arrested on a train of the Amur Railway, accused of being a "helper of the old regime." He worked in the University of the Far East, Vladivostok, from 1918 to 1922. Migrating to China in 1922, he lectured in universities in Shanghai and Beijing. He died in Beijing on October 19, 1939.

S.A. MOUSALIMAS

See also **Shamanism; Tungus**

Further Reading

Koichi, Inoue, "Bibliography, in S.M. Shirokogoroff, 'Tungus Literary Language'." *Asian Folklore Studies*, 50(1) (1991): 35–66

Mironov, N.D. & S.M. Shirikogoroff, "Sramana-shaman: etymology of the word 'shaman'." *Journal of the North China Branch of the Royal Asiatic Society*, 55 (1924): 105–130

Reshetov, A.M., "S.M. Shirogokorov, ego zhizn i trudy" [S.M. Shirokogorov: his life and work]." In *Polevye issledovaniya Gosudarstvennogo Muzeya etnografii narodov SSSR 1985–1987 gg.*, edited by O.V. Lysenko, Leningrad [St Petersburg]: State Museum of the Ethnography of the Peoples of the USSR, 1989, pp. 25–27

Serebrennikov, I.I., "In memoriam (Professor S.M. Shirokogoroff)." *The China Journal*, 22(5) (1940): 205–209

Shirikogorov [Shirikogoroff], S.M., "Sound Recordings, Siberia 1912–1912." In *The Historical Collections (1899–1955) of the Phonogram Archive of the Institute of Russian Literature (Pushkinsky Dom)*, St Petersburg: Russian Academy of Sciences, pp. 1912–1913

———, "Obyt issledovaniya osnov shamanstva u tungusov" [Enquiry into the General Theory of Shamanism among the Tungus], *Uchenye zapiski istoriko-filologicheskogo fakul'teta Dal'nevostochnogo universiteta [vo Vladivostoke]*, Volume 1, Vladivostok: History and Philology Faculty, University of the Far East, 1919, pp. 3–20

———, *Mesto etnografii sredi nauki i klassifikatsiya etnosov* [The Place of Ethnography in the Science and Classification of Ethnoses], Vladivostok: University of the Far East, 1922

———, *Etnos. Issledovanie osnovnykh printsipov izmeneniya etnicheskikh i etnograficheskikh yavleniy* [Ethnos: a theory of the fundamental principles of variation in ethnical and ethnographical phenomena]. Izvestiy Vostochnogo fakul'teta Gosudarstvennogo dal'nevostochnogo universiteta, Volume 67, Vladivostok, 1922; reprinted Shanghai, 1923

———, "General theory of Shamanism among the Tungus." *Journal of the North China Branch of the Royal Asiatic Society*, 54 (1923): 246–249

———, *Ethnical Unit and Milieu: a Summary of Ethnos*, Shanghai: E. Evans and Sons, 1924

————, "Ethnological Investigations in Siberia, Mongolia and Northern China." *The China Journal of Sciences and Arts*, 1 (1923): 513–522, 611–621

————, "What is Shamanism?" *The China Journal of Science and Arts*, 2(3–4) (1924): 275–279, 368–371

————, *Social Organization of the Manchus: A Study of Manchu Clan Organization*, Royal Asiatic Society (North China Branch), extra volume 3, Shanghai: Kelly and Walsh, Limited, 1924; reprinted New York: AMS Press, 1973; translated into Japanese by Omachi Tokuzo and Toda Shigeyoushi, Tokyo: Toko Shoin, 1967; translated into Chinese, Hohhot, 1984

————, "Who are the Northern Chinese?" *Journal of the North China Branch of the Royal Asiatic Society*, 55 (1924): pp. 1–13

————, *Social Organization of the Northern Tungus with Introductory Chapters concerning the Geographical Distribution and History of these Groups*, Shanghai: The Commercial Press, 1929; reprinted Oosterhout: Anthropological Publications, 1966; reprinted New York: Garland Publishers, 1979; translated into Japanese by Kawakubo Teiro and Tanaka Katsumi, Tokyo: Iwanami Shoten, 1941; reprinted 1982

————, *Ethnological and Linguistical Aspects of the Ural-Altaic Hypothesis*, Beijing: The Commercial Press, 1931; reprinted Oosterhout: Anthropological Publications, 1970

————, *Psychomental Complex of the Tungus*, London: Kegan, Paul, Trench, Trubner and Co., 1935; reprinted New York: AMS Press, 1980

————, *A Tungus Dictionary: Tungus-Russian and Russian-Tungus*, Tokyo: The Minzokugaku Kyokai, 1944; 2nd edition, 1953

————, "Tungus Literary Language." *Asian Folklore Studies*, 50 (1991): 35–66

SHMIDT, OTTO YUL'EVICH

Otto Yul'evich Shmidt was a Soviet mathematician, astronomer, and geophysicist, and an Arctic explorer of the 20th century. As the first head of Glavsevmorput, the Chief Office of the Northern Sea Route, he was instrumental in organizing the Russian 1937 North Pole Expedition.

After graduating and earning a master's degree in 1916, Shmidt became an assistant professor at Kiev University. After the 1917 revolution, he worked in local and later in central government (Central Statistical Board, and State Publishing House). In 1928, he became a member of the Russian-German scientific expedition that took part in an ascent of the Fedchenko glacier (western Pamir).

From 1929 onward, Shmidt's career was connected with the Arctic. He headed the All-Union Arctic Institute expedition by the icebreaker *Georgy Sedov*, and organized the first scientific research and weather station on Franz Josef Land. In 1930, he headed another expedition aboard *Georgy Sedov*, which again visited Franz Josef Land, and then explored the western banks of Severnaya Zemlya. In 1932, Shmidt headed the expedition of the All-Union Arctic Institute aboard the ice-breaker *Alexander Sibiryakov* (captained by Vladimir I. Voronin). The *Sibiryakov* expedition was the first to pass from Arkhangel'sk to the Pacific Ocean during one season, thereby demonstrating the possibility of commercial use of the long-sought North East Passage. Soon after this expedition, the Soviet government made a decision to create a special organization, the Chief Office of the Northern Sea Route (Glavsevmorput), to coordinate work on sea-route development in the Arctic, and designated Shmidt as its head. Leading Glavsevmorput from 1932 to 1939, Shmidt demonstrated his talent as for Arctic development, scientific exploration, and economic development of the northern territories of the USSR. Glavsemorput's plan for development of the North, worked out under Shmidt's direction, assumed that industrial development of the polar regions would begin with a thorough study of the natural resources, economy, and traditional branches of the northern economy, and would require creation of its own food base and a considered resettlement policy. Together with large-scale economic activity, building of ports and shipyards, and transportation development by the Northern Sea Route and on rivers of the Arctic Sea basin (such as the Indigirka, Yana, Olenek, Khatanga), the Chief Office of the Northern Sea Route developed a network of scientific-research establishments and polar meteo-radiostations throughout the Arctic. To this end, Shmidt drew a number of famous scientists and talented young researchers to work in Glavsevmorput.

In 1933, an expedition aboard the icebreaker *Chelyuskin* (captained by Vladimir Ivanovich Voronin) was organized under Shmidt's leadership to attempt to repeat *Sibiryakov*'s success in navigating the Northern Sea Route. After the expedition arrived at the Bering Strait successfully, the ship was first stuck in ice, and then three months later on February 13, 1934 was struck by ice. The 104 expedition members with Shmidt at the lead were forced to disembark onto the ice. During an unprecedented voyage carried on drifting ice, the expedition did not interrupt their scientific explorations and were only picked up two months later by the Soviet pilots Anatoly V. Lyapidevsky, Mikhail V. Vodop'yanov, Sigizmund. Levanevsky, Nikolay P. Kamanin, Mavriky T. Slepnev, and Vasily S. Molokov, who took the expedition members to Alaska and then to Chukotka.

In 1936, Shmidt headed the routing of military ships from Leningrad to Vladivostok over the Arctic after Soviet-Japanese relations deteriorated. Torpedo boats, accompanied by the icebreaker *Litke*, the ships *Ermak*, *Lenin*, *Sadko*, *Sedov*, *Sibiryakov*, the *Anadyr* transport, and the tankers *Maikop* and *Lock-Batan* sailed the Barents Sea and in spite of difficult ice conditions for two months, the convoy arrived at Provideniya Bay on September 24. Thus, the first voyage of military ships in the Arctic was completed.

Subsequently, that same year, Otto Shmidt presented an idea to organize a drifting scientific station at the North Pole. The plan was to carry out the expedition with the help of aircraft landing on pack ice in the area of the North Pole. In 1937, this project was carried out under Shmidt's leadership. From May to June 1937, ANT-6 planes, piloted by Mikhail V. Vodop'yanov, Vasily S. Molokov, Aanatoly D. Alexeev, and Ilya D. Mazuruk made flights to the North Pole with the expedition members and equipment for the polar station. Shmidt arrived at the pole by the first plane. By June 6, station construction was completed and expedition members Pietr P. Shirshov, Ernst T. Krenkel, Evgeniy K. Fedorov, and Ivan D. Papanin were left to overwinter on the ice. Shmidt was conferred the title Hero of the Soviet Union for leadership of the expedition to the North Pole.

On leaving Glavsemorput in the late 1930s, Shmidt resumed his scientific activity as a professor at Moscow State University. In 1939, he was elected as vice-president of the USSR Academy of Sciences (a post he held till 1942), and from 1937 to 1949 he headed the Theoretical Geophysics Institute. From 1924 to 1948, he was a chief editor of the first edition of the *Bol'shaia sovetskaia entsiklopediia* [Great Soviet Encyclopaedia]. His book *Theory of Earth's Origin* was published in Russian in 1949, and later in English. Over the last years of life, Shmidt headed the geophysical department of the Moscow University, and edited the journal *Nature*.

Biography

Otto Yul'evich Shmidt was born on September 18, 1891 in the town of Mogilev, Belarus. His father, Yulius Fridrikhovich Shmidt, was German by origin and came from a peasant family of the Liflyandskaya province (now Latvia), and was engaged in small trade. His mother, Anna Fridrikhovna, also came from a peasant family. Otto was the eldest among five children. He was educated in Kiev, and taught on the physical-mathematical faculty of the St Vladimir University in Kiev. From 1920 to 1923, Shmidt served as professor of the Moscow Timber Technical Institute, from 1923 to 1926 as professor at the second Moscow University, and from 1926 to 1956 as professor at the Moscow State University. He was married twice, and had two sons: Sigurd and Vladimir from his first wife Vera Fedorovna Yanitskaya. Shmidt died on September 7, 1956 after a long illness in the village of Mozzhinka in Moscow region and was buried in Moscow. An icebreaker research ship constructed in the 1970s was named after him, and in 2000 the Otto Shmidt Laboratory for Polar and Marine Sciences opened in St Petersburg.

SARDANA BOYAKOVA

See also **Drifting Stations; Glavsevmorput (Chief Office for the Northern Sea Route); North Pole Air Expedition, 1937; Northern Sea Route; Voronin, Vladimir Ivanovich**

Further Reading

Duel', I.I., *Line of Life*, Moscow: Politizdat, 1977 (in Russian)
Matveeva, L.V., *Otto Yulievich Smidt*, Moscow: Nauka, 1993 (in Russian)
Nikitenko, N.F., *O.Yu. Smidt*, Moscow: Nauka, 1992 (in Russian)
Otto Yulievich Smidt: Life and Activity. 1891–1956, Moscow: Publishing House of the USSR AS, 1959 (in Russian)

SHRIMP

Shrimps (also known as prawns) are a suborder (Macrura) of decapod crustaceans (order Decapoda), with about 2000 species worldwide. Their body length may be from 1 to 30 cm. The body is elongate, usually compressed from the sides and bent at an angle at the join of the cephalothorax (front body part) with the long muscular abdomen—the main edible part of a shrimp. The first two or three pairs of walking legs usually bear chelae (pincers or "hands"). A tail fan (comprising a telson with paired uropod appendages) is located on the rear end of the abdomen. Using this tail, fan shrimps are capable of rapid salutatory (or jumping) movements in case of danger. Biramous abdominal appendages (pleopods) are used for swimming and for egg brooding in females (although some warm-water shrimps simply spawn eggs in the water). Shrimps are dioecious (i.e., separate sexes) or protandrous hermaphrodites (i.e., first appearing as males and then as females). They are both marine (pelagic or benthic) and freshwater inhabitants, and are predators and omnivores. Numerous bioluminescent species are known among marine pelagic shrimps. The development proceeds through several larval stages. Many shrimp species are commercially important. About 30 shrimp species are found in northern seas.

The most important commercial shrimp is the northern, or northern deepwater shrimp *Pandalus borealis*. It is distributed from west Spitsbergen and northern Barents Sea (in small quantities even in the Kara Sea) to Cape Cod and northern North Sea, and in the North Pacific and Far Eastern seas from the Bering Sea to the Japan Sea and Washington on the western US coast. Its body length can reach 13–14 cm, on average 6–7 cm, and the carapace length is up to 4 cm, usually 2–3 cm; the body mass is usually 6–7 g. Shrimps inhabit the muddy bottom at depths down to 1500 m, mainly at 200–400 m, at temperatures usually ranging from +0.5°C to 8°C.

Two types of aggregations of *Pandalus borealis* are known: one inhabiting deep fjords with a sill, where shrimps spend all their life (independent, or mother populations), and the other found on the open continental shelves, where independent populations develop only where a closed water circulation exists (e.g., on the Bering Sea shelf off Alaska). When such water circulations are absent, the populations are replenished by the advection of larvae from an outside mother population, and self-replenishment is absent (these are termed dependent, or pseudo-populations, and are common in the Barents Sea and off West Spitsbergen). Semi-independent populations also exist (e.g., in the central Barents Sea).

The shrimps undergo diurnal vertical migrations—ascending at night into midwater and descending during daytime to the bottom. In midwater, they feed on various planktonic animals (copepods, euphausiids), and on the bottom—on benthos (polychaete worms, small molluscs) and detritus; this species also feed on their own young. Young shrimps and males migrate more intensively than females. On the bottom, the shrimps position themselves with their head against the current. If threatened, the abdomen is bent rapidly 3–5 times. This drives the shrimp backward and an animal can cover 3–5 m in one series of tail strokes. It can slowly walk on or swim off the bottom, but not bury into the deposit.

This shrimp is a protandrous hermaphrodite, and its life cycle includes a change of sex: initially (in the 2–3rd year of life, at carapace length 1.5–2 cm) it matures as a male, reproduces for one or two years as a male, and then in the 3–5th year (at carapace length 2–2.5 cm) it goes through an intermediate stage, becomes a female, and reproduces as a female for one or two years more. In temperate waters near the southern limit of its range, some shrimps mature as females at once (primary females). Reproduction takes place from spring to fall. The female carries eggs under her abdomen on pleopods for 4–12, usually 8–10 months. Fecundity is 500–4000 eggs, half of which may be lost during the incubation time. Hatching is from winter to late summer. Egg diameter before hatching of the larvae is 1.7–2.0 mm. Larval development includes nine stages and lasts up to 5 months, during which time the larvae may be carried away by the currents for a distance of some hundred miles. The length of larva at hatching is 5, and 17 mm by the final larval stage when the adult descends to the ocean bottom. The duration of life is to 9–11 years, mostly 4–6 years.

Commercial concentrations of shrimps are formed, as a rule, in areas where warm and cold currents meet, on a muddy bottom. The reproductive potential of concentrations depends on water temperature during the larval settling to the bottom. The shrimps are fished by special shrimp trawl nets, usually at depths of 200–400 m; the catch is then frozen or canned. The yearly catch of *P. borealis* in 1998, according to the FAO statistics, was 304, 900 tons, in the northwestern Atlantic somewhat more than in the northeastern (169,500 and 135,400, respectively). It is fished by Canada (Atlantic, 78,900 tons), Greenland (69,600 tons), Iceland (62,700 tons but in 1968, 89,600 tons), Norway, including Svalbard (56,200), Faroes Islands (13,000), Denmark (8100), Estonia (7200), and Russia (5000 tons but in 1991, 25,300 tons).

Related species are distributed in the North Pacific, Far Eastern seas, and off the western coasts of America. Among these is humpy shrimp (dock shrimp, flexed shrimp) *Pandalus goniurus*, abundant, among other areas, in the Bering Sea, including the Gulf of Anadyr, and penetrating the Chukchi Sea; southward, it reaches the Japan Sea and Puget Sound. It inhabits depths down to 450 m, mostly 50–200 m. It feeds mainly on planktonic and benthic crustaceans. The shrimps mature as males in 2–2.5 years, becoming females in 3–6 years and live to 8 years. Fecundity is 2–3000 eggs. Their biology has much in common with that of *P. borealis*. The catch of the Pacific *Pandalus* in 1996 was 40,800 tons, including 25, 000 in Canada, 9900 in the United States of America, and 3000 in Russia (in 1998–4900 tons).

In the Barents and White seas, the sand shrimp *Crangon crangon* occurs, and is caught in large quantities in northern Europe. It lives on sandy and sandy-muddy bottom in shallow waters, burying in the sediment. Development occurs without sex changes. Also potentially commercially important are the large benthic predatory shrimps of the genus *Sclerocrangon*, reaching 13 cm in length. These shrimps are abundant in the Barents, Siberian, and Far Eastern seas. However, the quality of its meat is inferior to that of the northern shrimp.

K.N. NESIS

Further Reading

Berenboim, B.I., *Severnaya krevetka (Pandalus borealis) Barentseva morya (biologiia i promysel)* [Northern Shrimp (*Pandalus borealis*) of the Barents Sea (Biology and Fisheries)], Murmansk: PINRO, 1993 (in Russian)

Horsted, S.Aa. & E. Smidt, "The deep-sea prawn (*Pandalus borealis* Kr.) in Greenland Waters." *Meddelelser fra Danmarks Fiskeri- og Havundersøgelser*, N.S., Bd. 1, No.11, 1956

Proceedings of the International Pandalid Shrimps Symposium, Fairbanks, Alaska. University of Alaska Sea Grant College Program Report, No. 81–3, 1981

Squires, H.J., "*Decapod Crustaceans of Newfoundland, Labrador and the Canadian Eastern Arctic.*" Fisheries Research Board of Canada Manuscript Report Series (Biological), No. 810, 1965

SHRUB TUNDRA

Shrub tundra is the major vegetation type of mesic (moderately moist) environments in the southernmost latitudes of the tundra zone. It is especially abundant in the broad amphi-Atlantic portion of the Low Arctic from the Canadian and European Arctic to the Taymyr Peninsula, whereas in eastern Siberia and the amphi-Beringian sector tussock tundra is more abundant, in better drained and snow-covered slope bases and river valleys.

Shrub tundra communities are usually well stratified vertically into three layers. The shrub layer is dominated by birch (*Betula nana*) and several willow shrubs (*Salix phylicifolia, S. lanata, S. lapponum, S. glauca, S. pulchra*). In the southernmost part of tundra and in open woodland, the alder shrub *Alnus fruticosa* is common. The middle layer consists of abundant dwarf-shrubs such as crowberry (*Empetrum nigrum*), mountain cranberry (*Vaccinium vitis-idaea* subsp. *minus*), bog bilberry (*V. uliginosum* subsp. *microphyllum*), black bearberry (*Arctostaphylos alpine*), Labrador tea (*Ledum palustre*), and herbs such as cottongrass (*Eriophorum vaginatum*), cloudberry (*Rubus chamaemorus*), and several sedges forming a continuous herb-dwarf-shrub layer. The ground layer consists of mosses (*Hylocomium splendens, Pleurozium schreberi, Dicranum elongatum, Aulacomnium turgidum, A. palustre, Sphagnum girgensohnii,* and *Polytrichum alpestre*) and lichens (*Cladina mitis, C. rangiferina, Cetraria nivalis,* and *C. cucullata*).

The shrub layer height usually coincides with the winter snow depth, which is about 60–70 cm (maximum 1–1.5 m), usually permanent throughout winter. Further north and in exposed hills, the shrub layer becomes discontinuous, covering less than 50% with a reduced height of 30–50 cm, dominated by *Betula nana* and *Salix glauca*. Tundra gley soils are common for sandy to clay loam deposits; better-drained sand and loamy sand deposits are dominated by illuvial-humus soils and podzolized podburs. The soil texture and winter snow depth influence community composition, especially the ground layer. Better-drained and exposed habitats are rich in lichens, and the shrub layer is reduced. Shrubs grow in better snow-covered microdepressions.

Shrub tundra is a major reindeer pasture, especially in the European-West Siberian north, usually in spring and summer, but exposed, relatively poorly snow-covered habitats are also grazed in winter. Overgrazing leads to the loss of poorly trample-resistant fruticose lichens, especially *Ciadina rangiferina* and *C. stellaris*, replaced by less reindeer-edible lichens and mosses.

Shrub tundra is also widely distributed in the north of the boreal zone and within the transitional open woodland, where it occupies extreme environments unfavorable for tree growth, such as exposed hill tops and wet depressions. In lowlands, it is combined with various mire vegetation. Tall shrub tundra with a shrub layer more than 1 m high is usually recognized along with the low shrub tundra discussed above. Tall willow scrub (*Salix lanata, S. alaxensis,* etc.) is common for well snow-covered floodplains where willow thickets are combined with various meadows. Along rivers, shrub tundra penetrates far north even into the High Arctic. The southernmost tundra of northeastern Asia is characterized by the dominance of a unique tall-shrub pine *Pinus pumila* called *stlanik,* which is usually recognized as a special subzone. Vegetation of the middle and lower mountain slopes consists of tall shrub communities dominated by *stlanik* and, in slope depressions, by *Alnus fruticosa* with a low shrub layer of *Betula middendorffii* and some willows. The sparse ground layer between *Pinus pumila* shrubs consists of common dwarf-shrubs and fruticose lichens. Most of the species abundant in shrub tundra are latitudinally distributed throughout the Low Arctic, open woodland, and north of boreal zone with optima in the southernmost tundra.

VOLODYA RAZZHIVIN

See also **Dwarf-shrub Heaths; Lichen; Tundra; Tussock Tundra**

Further Reading

Aleksandrova, V.D., *The Arctic and Antarctic: Their Division into Geobotanical Areas,* Cambridge: Cambridge University Press, 1980
Bliss, L.C., "North American and Scandinavian Tundras and Polar Deserts." In *Tundra Ecosystems: A Comparative Analysis,* edited by L.C. Bliss, O.W. Heal & J.J. Moore, Cambridge: Cambridge University Press, 1981, pp. 5–24
———, "Arctic Ecosystems of North America." In *Polar and Alpine Tundra,* edited by F.E. Wielgolaski, Amsterdam: Elsevier, 1997, pp. 551–684
Bliss, L.C. & N.V. Matveyeva, "Circumpolar Arctic Vegetation." In *Arctic Ecosystems in a Changing Climate,* edited by F.S. Chapin III et al., San Diego: Academic Press, 1992, pp. 59–89
Chernov, Yu.I. & N.V. Matveyeva, "Arctic Ecosystems in Russia." In *Polar and Alpine Tundra,* edited by F.E. Wielgolaski, Amsterdam: Elsevier, 1997, pp. 361–507
Daniëls, F.J.A., "Vegetation of the Angmagssalik District, Southeast Greenland, IV. Shrub, dwarf shrub and terricolous lichens." *Meddelelser om Grønland, Bioscience,* 10 (1982): 1–78
Razzhivin, V. Yu., "Zonation of Vegetation in the Russian Arctic." In *The Species Concept in the High North—A Panarctic Flora Initiative,* edited by I. Nordal & V.Yu. Razzhivin, Oslo: Norwegian Academy of Science and Letters, 1999, pp. 113–130

SHTERNBERG, LEV YAKOVLEVICH

Ukranian-born Lev (Khaim) Yakovlevich Shternberg was a well-known scholar of ethnography of the peoples of the Russian Far East and a corresponding member of the Russian Academy of Sciences (1924). He was one of the founders of the discipline of Jewish ethnography in the USSR. He was also a journalist.

In 1881, he joined St Petersburg University, in the natural sciences division. Shternberg became an active member of the revolutionary illegal organization "People's Will," which fought against the Russian Monarchy. He was expelled from the University and was exiled from the capital. He joined the law division of Novorossisk University in Odessa, but four years later was arrested again and spent three years in prison (1886–1888). In 1889, he was exiled to Sakhalin Island (Russian Far East). Shternberg remained on Sakhalin for eight years (1889–1897). During his exile, he met the native people, Nivkhi, and became interested in their culture. He conducted field research all those years, particularly in 1891, 1893, 1895, and 1910.

His first scientific publication appeared in the ethnographic journal of Russia in 1893 and was devoted to the problems of family and clan structure, marriage, and ordinary law of the Giluak (Nivkh) people. V. Radloff, the director of the Museum of Anthropology and Ethnology in Petersburg, invited Shternberg to join the Museum's staff, where he worked as a senior ethnographer until his death in 1927. In 1919, he became the dean of the ethnographic department in the newly created Institute of Geography.

He published numerous articles and two monographs, including Shternberg, L.Ya., *Materialy po izucheniu Gilyazkogo yazuka i fol'klora*, Izdatel'stvo Academii Nauk, t. 1: St Petersburg, 1908 (*Gilyak Language and Folklore Study Data*, Volume1, Academy of Sciences Publishing House). Three monographs were published after his death by his disciples: Ia.P. Alkor (Koshkin) (editor), 1933 *Gilyaki, Orochi, Gol'du, Negidal'zy, Ainy*, Khabarovsk: Dal'giz; Ia.P. Alkor (Koshkin) (editor), *Semya i Rod u Narodov Severo-Vostochnoy Azii*, Leningrad, 1933 (*The Family and the Clan of the Peoples of North-Eastern Asia*). Shternberg's book, recently published in English (*The Social Organisation of the Gilyak*, edited by Bruce Grant, Anthropological Papers of the American Museum of Natural History, 1999, No. 82), is based on his last monographs. Shterneberg's students also published his lectures and notes on "primitive religion" (1936) (*Pervobytnaya religiya v svete etnograficheskogo issledovania (stat'i i lekzii)*, 1936, Leningrad (The primitive religion in the light of ethnographic study [articles and lectures])).

Shternberg became interested in the language, folklore, social organization, and religious life of the Nivkh people, in whose culture there remained many old traditions. Shternberg's interests were also influenced by a Polish exile, and later an ethnographer, B.O. Pilsudskii. In 1891, the administration of the Sakhalin Island suggested that Shternberg conduct the Census of Native population in the north of Sakhalin, among the Gilyaki and the Orochi. Later, he carried on the census among the Ainu of southern Sakhalin and the Gol'dy of Low Amur River basin. This was his first experience in demographic and ethnographic studies. He collected all possible materials, including those in ethnography, archaeology, and linguistics. Although his scientific method consisted of interviews rather than observations, he considered long-term fieldwork to be a basis for ethnographic exploration, as well as the necessity of knowing the indigenous language. He was the first to describe grammatical, phonetic, and lexical structures of the Nivkh (Gilyak) language, and collected examples of their language and folklore. Further investigations of Nivkh language showed some mistakes he made in the phonetic structure.

Shternberg did not receive an ethnographic education; his scientific worldview was eclectic. He followed the evolutionist theory, as Morgan and Engels did. He implemented a historical approach, but in general was an idealist. Culture was understood by him as a common life experience that creates remembrances, uniting peoples. He believed ethnography to be a science about mankind, which he regarded as something whole and unique.

Studying the social organization of the Gilyak, Shternberg uncovered an example of a group marriage. The publication was noted by F. Engels, who used Shternberg's data as a proof of his own conclusions on the evolution of family and state. Because of this review, Shternberg's works became broadly known in the USSR. In his investigations, Shternberg noted the survival of the Nivkh culture that was observed in the language structure and particularly in the terms they used in the family relationship. Shternberg's works considerably influenced the direction of future research, particularly in the study of "primitive societies," and the problems of their social organization. At the same time, they slowed the development of the new approaches. The old principle that was stated by Morgan and influenced Shternberg's approach about the clan as an economic unit could not be clearly traced in the Nivkh culture. The investigations made after Shternberg also did not confirm the existence of a three-clan model of the Gilyak marriage.

He wrote a number of articles on the history of ethnography, on ethnic history, social organization and religion of peoples of Far East, such as the Ainu, the Uilta (Orochi), and the Nanai (Gol'du). He was one of the first scholars who suggested the hypothesis about the southern origin of the Ainu people.

Shternberg was one of the founders of Leningrad ethnographic school, which had many well-known soviet ethnographers, such as Vasilevich, Kreinovich, and Zinzius. His influence on the further development of Russian/Soviet ethnography was considerable.

Biography

Lev (Khaim) Yakovlevich Shternberg was born in 1861 in Zhitomir, Ukraine. From an early age, he received a religious Jewish upbringing; from the age of 10, he went to a Russian school. Having come back to Zhitomir in 1897, he married Sarra Ratner, who was a teacher. They had a son, who later became a military surgeon. Since 1902, Shternberg worked in the Museum of Anthropology and Ethnography as a senior ethnographer. In 1919, he became the dean of the ethnographic department in the newly created Institute of Geography. Shternberg died in 1927 in Leningrad (USSR).

ANNA A. SIRINA

See also **Ainu; Nanai; Vasilevich, Glafira Makar'evna**

Further Reading

Alkor (Koshkin) (editor), Pamyati L.Ya. Shternberga (1861–1927). Ocherki po istorii znanii. 1930. VII [To the memoriam of L.Ya. Shternberg (1861–1927). Issues on the knowledge history, Volume VII, 1930], Leningrad(?)

Gagen-Torn, N.I., *Lev Yakovlevich Shternberg*, Moskva: Nauka, 1975

Grant, Bruce (editor), "L.Ia. Sternberg." *The Social Organization of the Gilyak.* With foreword and afterword by B. Grant, New York: Anthropological Papers of the American Museum of Natural History 82, 1999, pp. XXIII–LVI

Izvestia Instituta nasledia Bronislava Pilsudskogo. [Proceedings of the Institute of the heritage of Bronislav Pilsudskii], Yuzhno-Sakhalinsk, 2001. No. 5

Kan, Sergei, "The mystery of the missing monograph: or, why Shternberg's *The Social Organization of the Gilyak* never appeared among the Jesup Expedition Publications." *European Review of the Native American Studies*, 14(2) (2000): 19–38

Stanyukovich, T.V., Lev Yakovlevich Shternberg i muzei antropologii i etnografii//Sovetskaya etnografia. 1986. 5. S.81–91. (Lev Yakovlevich Shternberg and the Museum of the Anthropology and Ethnography//Soviet Ethnographia)

SIBERDIK CULTURE

The Siberdik Culture of Northeast Asia was distinguished by Nikolay Dikov in the early 1970s, after the discovery of the Siberdik and Kongo sites in the Upper Kolyma. He considered it a specific Early Holocene culture combining small flint and massive pebble tools. It is associated with the pebble complexes in the Northeast Asian paleolithic. There have been no other sites referred to the Siberdik Culture.

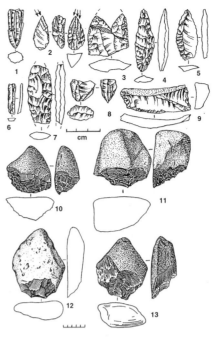

Siberdik Culture artifacts

Siberdik Culture artifacts: 1— conical microblade core; 2—burin; 3—biface; 4, 5, 7—points; 6—microblade; 8—wedge-shaped microblade core; 9—knives; 10–13—cobble tools (choppers). 1–13—stone.

The sites are located on the estuary capes of large tributaries of the Kolyma River, 35 km from one another. Cultural layers were deposited at the depth of 1–1.2 m, in sandy loam and sand sediments. The material study resulted in defining two stages in the culture. The early stage, radiocarbon-dated to 9740 BP, covered the materials from the Kongo Site lower level containing microblades, a conic core, a boat-shaped tool, burins on flakes, and large, chopperlike pebble tools. The late stage included the materials from the Kongo Site upper level and the Siberdik Site lower level, radiocarbon-dated to 8655–8020 BP. It contained microblades, leaf-shaped points, a wedge-shaped microcore, bifaces, knives and scrapers on flakes, and choppers.

The sites' cultural layers are reported to have contained the production spots with hearths, numerous flakes, reindeer, and horse bones. A spot on the Siberdik Site has been described, with frost cracks and horse teeth having ochre traces on the surface. Wooden artifacts have also been reported.

Special attention was given to choppers and choppings, that is, pebble tools weighing several kilograms, with sharp chopping edges formed by flaking the pebble edge with large spolls, without retouching the rest of the pebble surface. This led Dikov to the assumption that the Siberdik Culture had been the relic of the pebble Paleolithic culture that had existed in Northeast Asia in the Pleistocene era. He associated the pebble tools from Kongo and Siberdik with the pebble complexes on the Amur and in Primorye, studied by Alexei Okladnikov, and with the Pasika pebble complex of British Columbia, studied by C. Borden and originally dated to the late Pleistocene. Dikov considered the Siberdik choppers the missing part in the pebble culture chain between Siberia and America. These ideas were broadly discussed in archaeological publications, but the question is still far from being solved.

So far, it is difficult to say if the pebble paleolithic had really existed in Northeast Asia and, if so, how it was linked with America's pebble traditions because the Western Beringia's pebble complexes are still weakly studied and dated and the Pasika Complex has recently been redated to 6000–3000 BP. Besides, the sandy dune activity at Siberdik and Kongo might have mixed the materials from various levels, which is proven by numerous discrepancies marked in defining the material distribution in the layers of the Siberdik Culture sites. Pebble chopper and choppinglike tools have also been found in other Northeast Asia's cultures of the Late Pleistocene and Early Holocene.

Rough pebble tools are also characteristic of the later cultures in Kolyma and Chukotka; in the middle, Neolithic, level of the Siberdik Site, dated to 6300–4420 BP, pebble tools were also found with microblades, smaller flint tools, and pottery. Dikov assumed that the Siberdik Culture had been a barrier in the Upper Kolyma, preventing the Dyuktai and Sumnagin cultures from spreading eastward; however, the sites of both cultures have been discovered in Chukotka and Kolyma within the last decade.

Analyzing the paleohistory of Circumpolar Arctic colonization, J. Kozlowski and H.-G. Bandi defined the Siberdik Culture as representing the Pacific Coastal Tradition and traced the link between the Siberdik projectile points and those from the Japanese Islands. For such inferences, there are no grounds so far.

Further research in the Kolyma valley would lead to specifying the Early Holocene cultures in the North-East and to defining the material complexes of the Siberdik and Kongo sites, determining their cultural reference, which is not yet completely clear.

SERGEI SLOBODIN

Further Reading

Derev'anko, Anatoliy P. (editor), *The Paleolithic of Siberia: New Discoveries and Interpretation*, Urbana and Chicago: University of Illinois Press, 1998

Dikov, Nikolay N., "The Stages and Routes of Human Occupation of the Beringian Land Bridge Based on Archaeological Data." In *Quaternary Coastlines*, edited by P.M. Masters and N.C. Flemming, London: Academic Press London, 1983

Goebel, Ted & Sergei Slobodin, "The Colonization of Western Beringia Technology, Ecology, and Adaptation." In *Ice Age Peoples of North America: Environments, Origins, and Adaptations of the First Americans*, edited by Robson Bonnichsen & Karen L. Turnmire, Corvalis, Oregon: Oregon State University Press, 1999

Haley, Shawn, "The Pasika Complex Revisited." In *Early Human Occupation* in British Columbia, edited by Roy L. Carlson & Luke Della Bona, Vancouver: UBC Press, 1996

Kozlowski, Janusz & Hans-Georg Bandi, "The paleohistory of circumpolar Arctic colonization." *Arctic*, 37(4) (1984): 359–372

Mochanov, Yuri A., "Paleolithic Finds in Siberia: Resume of Studies." In *Beringia in the Cenozoic Era*, Rotterdam, New Delhi, edited by V.L. Kontrimavichius 1986

Powers, Roger W., "Palaeolithic man in Northeast Asia." *Arctic Anthropology*, 10(2) (1973): 1–106

Slobodin, Sergei B., "Northeast Asia in the late Pleistocene and early Holocene." *World Archaeology*, 30(3) (1999): 484–502

SIBERIAN (CHUKOTKAN) YUPIK

The ethnic label Siberian Yupik is not a self-designation, but the most commonly used English-language designation for the small groups of speakers of the Yupik branch of Eskimo languages residing in the Russian Far East. Alternative labels include Asiatic Eskimo and Siberian Eskimo, while the self-designations *Yuit* (singular) and *Yupigyt* (plural) are rarely used outside of the local context. According to the 1989 Soviet census, the total number of Siberian Yupik in the Soviet Union was 1700. Most of them live in the eastern part of the Chukotka Autonomous Okrug, on the Chukchi Peninsula close to the Bering Strait. Given that the Yupik residents of Chukotka do not see themselves as "Siberians" (Siberia is located further to the west in their view), Chukotkan Yupik would be the most accurate outside label.

Today, the Siberian Yupik constitute the largest ethnic group in only two settlements of the Chukchi Peninsula: Novo-Chaplino and Sireniki. In all other settlements of the either region, Russians or Chukchi are demographically dominant. Notwithstanding their small numbers, the Siberian Yupik are not a homogenous ethnic group. Until the late 19th century, there were three linguistically and culturally distinct groups. The *Nuvuqaghmiit* were centered around the village of Naukan (Nuvuqaq), which in 1958 was forcibly closed by Soviet bureaucratic intervention, and its population relocated to neighboring Chukchi settlements. The *Ungazikmiit* resided in and around the village of Chaplino (Ungazik), which was also closed by administrative order in 1958 and its population relocated to Novo-Chaplino. Today, the *Ungazikmiit*, who are closely related to the inhabitants of St Lawrence Island, Alaska, are the largest group of Siberian Yupik. Finally, the *Sighenegmeghey* were originally centered around the settlement of Sireniki. Although the village still exists today, the distinct language of the group,

Sirenikski, disappeared with the death of its last speaker in 1997. The contemporary Siberian Yupik of Sireniki are linguistically and culturally part of the *Ungazikmiit*.

Until the late 19th century, Russians and other early explorers did not distinguish the Siberian Yupik from their neighbors, the coastal Chukchi. Both groups were called Chukchi, despite the unrelated languages they spoke. The main reason for this confusion was that both ethnic groups engaged primarily in sea-mammal hunting activities, which distinguished them sharply from the Reindeer Chukchi of the inland tundras. Sea-mammal hunting activities of the Siberian Yupik and of the neighboring coastal Chukchi shared a number of general characteristics, with several kinds of seals and walrus being the most important animals economically. Bowhead whales, which were extremely important socially and ritually, were hunted by only a few large villages situated at capes facing the open sea. Forms of individual hunting, such as seal hunting at ice holes, prevailed during the winter. Boat crews staffed by 6–10 adult male hunters provided the framework for the organization of labor during summer and fall hunting. Sea-mammal hunting was traditionally defined as a male activity, although it happened that women fulfilled the social role of male hunters. The gathering of tundra plants, bird, duck, and goose eggs, as well as river fishing were necessary but auxiliary subsistence activities in all coastal villages. Plant gathering, the preparation and distribution of meat, the processing of hides, and the production and maintenance of clothing and skin-sewn gear were among the prime responsibilities of women.

The Siberian Yupik have interacted closely with the Chukchi reindeer herders of the inland tundra for centuries. The reindeer herders were in constant need of sea mammal fat and hides, while the coastal residents sought reindeer meat and hides. Social mobility between coastal and inland settlements occurred mainly among different Chukchi groups.

Permanent and semi-permanent villages were the most important social and political units for the Siberian Yupik. Larger villages tended to consist of two or more subgroups, which were generally named after their current or previous places of residence. Within coastal villages, the "whaling crew," a group made up of relatives and neighbors, was an important social unit, as was the extended family. Although the Siberian Yupik did have kin groups that resembled the so-called "clans" of the Yupik living on St Lawrence Island in the Bering Sea, it would be misleading to assume that these groups were based entirely on principles of unilinear descent. Siberian Yupik continue to employ a variety of ways of extending the range of "relatives," be it through naming practices or "spouse exchange." Marriages did not require any special wedding ceremony, nor the payment of bride-price or dowries, but

rather a period of bride-service, after which both spouses typically moved to the husband's family. There were no particular rules governing who an individual could or could not marry, but there was a general tendency to marry within one's own camp or village.

Bowhead whales were the most prominent animals in the ritual cycle of the Yupik hunters of the Chukchi Peninsula. The "ceremony of boats" in May, marking the beginning of the hunting season, and the ritual greeting of a hunted whale were the major ceremonies. Only the settlement of Nuvuqaq held a special "whaling festival," celebrated in winter after the closing of the whaling season and lasting for an entire month. The central theme of the whale rituals among the Yupik hunters of Chukotka was the "resurrection of animals," a way to guide them back to their "homeland." Animals, plants, and other features of the landscape were thought to be animated and to have spiritual "owners" or "masters" with whom humans had to interact properly. Male and female shamans had privileged access to the spiritual world, which they used to cure the sick, prevent misfortune, and predict the weather. The Chukchi Peninsula is exceptional within the circumpolar world in that until 1990 there had been few serious attempts at religious conversion through missionaries. Due to the lack of governmental control of the area, the Russian Orthodox Church had no significant presence on the Chukchi Peninsula prior to the Russian Revolution. After 1990, missionary influx from Alaska has been clearly outperforming the Russian Orthodox Church in financial and personnel investment.

In the 1930s, the impact of the Russian Revolution came to be felt on the Chukchi Peninsula. The traditional economic activities of the Siberian Yupik were first incorporated into consumer collectives and later into state farms. Starting in the late 1950s, the massive influx of Soviet citizens from the European parts of the Soviet Union gradually made local residents a minority in their own settlements. The following decades witnessed a sharp increase in the numbers of suicides and other violent deaths, and also a rise in alcoholism and other social problems.

The post-Soviet years have been characterized by extreme instability for the Siberian Yupik. Early on, optimism and high expectations about the changes to come prevailed. They were fueled by events such as a US-USSR agreement signed in 1989, which made visa-free travel for indigenous residents on both sides of the Bering Strait once more possible, after 40 years of Cold War separation. Local community leaders also started to engage in organizational activities geared toward renewed self-determination. In August 1990, the Regional Society of the Eskimos of Chukotka was founded, which is still active under its current name Yupik Eskimo Society of Chukotka. The Siberian

Yupik also joined the Inuit Circumpolar Conference (ICC), which has a regional office in Anadyr, the capital of Chukotka. At the same time, economic and social problems rose exponentially, as previous state subsidies were disappearing while ill-fated privatization attempts led to economic disaster and despair. It has only been since the late 1990s, when a new governor took office in Chukotka and economic recovery commenced in Russia, that the Siberian Yupik began to see a sustainable post-Soviet future for themselves.

PETER P. SCHWEITZER

See also **Chukchi Autonomous Okrug Chukotka; Eskimo-Aleut Languages; Yupiit; Yupik Eskimo Society of Chukotka**

Further Reading

Bogoras, Waldemar, *"The Eskimo of Siberia*, Leiden: Brill, 1913

Chichlo, Boris, "Les Nevuqaghmiit ou la fin d'une ethnie." *Études/Inuit/Studies*, 5(2) (1981): 29–47

Kerttula, Anna M., *Antler on the Sea: The Yupik and Chukchi of the Russian Far East*, Ithaca, New York: Cornell University Press, 2000

Krupnik, Igor, *Arctic Adaptations: Native Whalers and Reindeer Herders of Northern Eurasia*, Hanover, New Hampshire: University Press of New England, 1993

Krupnik, Igor, & Nikolay Vakhtin, "Indigenous knowledge in modern culture: Siberian Yupik ecological legacy in transition." *Arctic Anthropology*, 34(1) (1997): 236–52

Leont'ev, Vladilen V., *Khoziaistvo i kul'tura narodov Chukotki (1958–1970 gg.)* [Economy and culture of the peoples of Chukotka (1958–1970s)], Novosibirsk: Nauka, 1973

Menovshchikov, G.A., *Eskimosy: Nauchno-populiarnii istoriko-etnograficheskii ocherk ob aziatskikh eskimosov* [The Eskimos: a popular-science account of the historical ethnography of the Asiatic Eskimos], Magadan: Magadanskoe knizhnoe izdatel'stvo, 1959

Rubtsova, E.S., *Materialy po iazyku i fol'kloru eskimosov (chaplinskii dialekt)* [Materials about Eskimo language and folklore (Chaplino dialect)], Moscow: Izdatel'stvo Akademii nauk SSSR, 1954

Schweitzer, Peter P. & Evgeniy V. Golovko, "Local identities and traveling names: interethnic aspects of personal naming in the Bering Strait area." *arctic Anthropology*, 34(1) (1997): 167–80

Tein, Tassan S., "Shamans of the Siberian Eskimos." *Arctic Anthropology*, 31(1) (1994): 117–25

SIBIRYAKOV, ALEXANDER

Alexander Mikhailovich Sibiryakov was a Siberian businessman who financed many important Arctic expeditions in the late 19th century, and undertook many explorations of Siberia himself. Coming from a long line of Irkutsk merchants, he inherited several gold-mining companies after his father's death in 1874, and also became owner of the Lena-Vitim steamship line, the greatest steamship enterprise in the Lena River basin. In the early 1870s, he bought the Alexander-Nevsky glassworks and a papermaking factory. Moreover, in 1885, Sibiryakov founded a towing steamship line on Angara, and in 1894 the Amur Society of steamship line and trade. Thus, steamer proprietorship together with gold mining became the main spheres of Sibiryakov's commercial activity.

However, commercial activity was not Sibiryakov's only aim. In Sweden, he got to know Adolf-Erik Nordenskiöld, a famous geologist and polar explorer, and subsequently devoted himself to scientific practical work on the exploration of Siberia. Sibiryakov began by assisting Joseph Wiggins in 1875 to make a voyage from Europe to the mouth of Ob' Bay along the Northern Sea Route. However, Wiggins only reached Kolguev Island because he went to sea late. Wiggins's next voyage in 1876, financed by Sibiryakov and Gardiner, an English businessman, was a success, reaching the Yenisey mouth from England and sailing up along it to the Kureika River.

In 1876, with Sibiryakov's financial support, Nordenskiöld made a voyage from Norway to the Yenisey River on the schooner *Preven*. He discovered an island in the Yenisey mouth and called it "an island of Sibiryakov, by name of an ardent and generous organizer of various expeditions." But Nordenskiöld's main achievement was to show that in early August a trip from Europe to the Yenisey River mouth could be completed by ship. The same year, Sibiryakov allocated funds for the Society of German Expedition in Bremen for just one more expedition to the region of the river Ob'. The members of this expedition brought back to Germany more than 550 specimens of birds, 150 specimens of amphibians, 400 specimens of fish, about 1000 insects, a large number of rocks, and also ethnographic collections from Siberia. These were displayed at exhibitions in Germany, and Siberian collections enriched funds of Berlin Zoo Museum, museums in Munich, Stuttgart, and London.

Sibiryakov's participation in organizing Nordenskiöld's famous expedition along the North East Passage and around Eurasia in 1878–1880 was the most important venture he funded. Oscar Dickson, a Gothenburg businessman, and King Oscar II of Sweden and Norway, also subsidized the voyage, which began in July 1878. *Vega*'s voyage by the Northern Sea Route, wintering on Kolyuchinsky Bay, was a success. On July 20, 1879, the expedition passed through the Bering Strait, and on April 24, 1880 returned to Stockholm. This expedition convincingly demonstrated the possibility of voyage along the Northern Sea Route, and proved that all seas surrounding Siberia were available for navigation at a certain period of the year. The problem of trade and communication between Europe and Siberian rivers mouths was now resolved.

Sweden appreciated Sibiryakov's services. He was conferred an order of Polar Star, selected as an Honorary Member of the Swedish Anthropology and Geography Society, a corresponding member of the Society of army seamen, a member of scientific and literary societies in Gothenburg. In 1878, Nordenskiöld renamed Kuzkin Island as Sibiryakov Island in honor of the sponsor of the expedition.

During the 1870–1890s, Sibiryakov supported a series of expeditions, in the course of which the mouths of the Pechora, Yenisey, Ob', Amur rivers, the coasts of the Kara and Okhotsk seas, and land routes between rivers of Western and Eastern Siberia were explored. In 1879–1880, Sibiryakov financed A.V. Grigoriev's expedition on explorations in the Arctic Ocean. He also was one of the initiators and organizers of the Sibiryakov historical and ethnographic expedition (1894–1896), one of the most significant carried out by the East-Siberian Branch of the Russian Geographic Society. Valuable ethnographic material that became an object of interest to explorers for a long time was collected and published by the members of the expedition.

It should be noted that Sibiryakov not only financed various expeditions but also undertook several Arctic and taiga expeditions himself. For example, in 1880, he made an attempt to voyage from Scandinavia to the Yenisey mouth via the Kara Sea. In 1884, Sibiryakov set out on a new voyage from Arkhangel'sk up to the Ob' and Yenisey river mouths, but sea ice prevented him from completing the voyage. Then, he decided to stop on the Pechora River and achieve communication between Siberia and Europe via an overland route. Here, Sibiryakov was engaged in building of a land road between Ob' and Pechora, which was soon called the Sibiryakov highway.

Sibiryakov also invested in education and culture in Siberia. He contributed 100,000 rubles for the foundation of Tomsk University, the first in Siberia, 50,000 rubles for an establishment of a Higher Technical School, 950,000 rubles for openings of national schools, creation and maintenance of four primary specialized schools, and 12,000 rubles for the construction of a printing plant for the newspaper "Siberia." In 1882, he presented the Nordenskiöld expedition collections from Arctic Siberia and America to the Botany and Zoo Museums of the University.

In 1883, Sibiryakov donated 10,000 rubles to the Academy of Sciences, from which a prize for the best historical composition about Siberia is paid once a year. Moreover, he assigned large sums of money for building and improving churches and shelters for widows and orphans. For his charity, in 1893 A.M. Sibiryakov was confered the title of Honorary Citizen of the town of Irkutsk, and in 1904 D.I. Mendeleev and he were selected as Honorary Members of Tomsk University.

Sibiryakov's books and articles on problems of communication in Siberia and its relations with other countries were another product of his scientific and practical activity. He wrote about 30 articles, published between 1881 and 1914, mainly in German journals. Some of them were published by Sibiryakov in the book "About Siberian ways of communication and sea relations with other countries" (St Petersburg, 1907), including his thoughts "About autonomy of Siberia" instead of an introduction. Future routes of Siberian ways of communication were presented and described in detail in the book, which included interesting ethnographic observations, and geographic descriptions. In 1910 in Zurich, his last book "To the problem of foreign relations of Siberia with Europe" was published in German.

Biography

Alexander Mikhailovich Sibiryakov was born on September 26, 1849 in Irkutsk (Siberia), the oldest son of Mikhail Alexandrovich and Varvara Konstantinovna. He belonged to the seventh generation of one of the most ancient and influential families of Siberia. His father was a merchantman of the First guild, joint owner of a distillery, rich goldfields, the Bodaybinskaya railway, and a shipping company. After graduating from the Irkutsk grammar school, Alexander continued his education at the Zurich polytechnic school, then in Germany, France, Sweden, and other European countries.

In the early 20th century, Sibiryakov left his active commercial activity, delegated his business to his son, and left Irkutsk. He lived in Batumi, Nice, Paris, and Zurich. He died on November 2, 1933 in Nice and was buried in a Russian cemetery near Nice.

NINA VASILIEVA

See also **Nordenskiöld, Adolf Erik**

Further Reading

Boyakova, S.I., *Osvoenie Arktiki i narody Severo-Vostoka Azii* [Development of the Arctic and the peoples of the North-East Asia], Novosibirsk: Nauka, 2001

Gogolev, A.I., Izuchenie etnogeneza yakutov ssylnymi narodnikami (Uchastniki Sibiryakovskoi expeditsii)/ Osvoboditelnoe dvizhenie v Rossii i yakutskaya politicheskaya ssylka (XIX—nachalo XX v.) [Study of the Yakut ethnogenesis by the exiles (Members of the Sibiryakov expedition) / Liberation movement in Russia and Yakutia political exile (XIX—early XX century)], Yakutsk, 1990, p. 2

Oglezneva, T.N., *Ruskoe geographicheskoe obshestvo: izuchenie narodov severo-vostoka Asii. 1845–1917* [Russian Geographic Society: study of the North-East Asia peoples. 1845–1917], Novosibirsk, 1994

Solovieva, B.A., "Alexander Mikhailovich Sibiryakov." *Nature*, (9) (2000)

Vallenius, S., "Zagadka Sibiryakova" [Mystery of Sibiryakov]// Poisk, 1999, No. 1,2

SIEROSZEWSKI, WACŁAW LEOPOLODOVICH

Wacław Sieroszewski is a Polish writer and ethnographer, known for his work on Yakut (Sakha) culture. Arrested by the czarist police in 1880, Sieroszewski arrived as an exile in Yakutia (Sakha), where he spent the next 12 years. First, he resided in Verkhoyansk, from where he attempted an unsuccessful escape. Afterward, he was sent to remote parts of Yakutia, such as the settlements Andylakh and Engzhu. In 1885, he was allowed to settle down in Aldan and, later, in the region of Namsk. From 1892 until 1894, he lived in Irkutsk, and from 1894 until 1896–in St Petersburg. In 1898, he came back to Warsaw, but two years later he was arrested by the Czarist police again. Only the assistance of the Imperial Russian Geographical Society saved him from a second exile. Instead, he became a participant of the Society Far East expedition, where he collected, for example, material on Ainu culture together with Bronisław Piłsudski.

Sieroszewski's primary contribution to Arctic studies is related to his stay in Yakutia where he was married to a Yakut woman, Anna, and quickly learned the language. Apparently during the thorough preparation for the escape in 1882, he gathered his first material on the geography of the Verkhoyansk area, including human settlements. As a valued blacksmith, Sieroszewski could easily make contacts with Yakut people. He published several ethnographic articles in journals, and his main work, *Yakuty* [The Yakuts], was published in 1896 in St Petersburg.

In this work, Sieroszewski describes the climate, flora, and fauna of Yakutia, the history of the Yakut people, including a linguistic and cultural analysis, as well as myths and legends. He also presents an account of anthropological types of the inhabitants of Yakutia, their subsistence (hunting, agriculture, cattle breeding, and fishing), clothing, dwellings, handicraft, social organization, kinship terms, marriage rules, oral folklore, and religious beliefs.

Yakuty was highly praised at the time of publication, and it received the gold medal from the Imperial Russian Geographical Society. The criticism emerged later, especially with an article by V. Ionov (1914), which was concerned especially with the translation and interpretation of Yakut words as well as information on the Yakut religious beliefs. However, during its time, Sieroszewski's book was an extremely valuable and rich ethnographic account.

Nowadays, although criticized for its old-fashioned terminology patronizing the native population, Sieroszewski's work is still a valued reference book for researchers. With the collapse of the Soviet Union and the cultural independence of the Sakha Republic (Yakutia), this book also became a source of inspiration for intellectual leaders of the Sakha nation, looking for national symbols and ways of expressing Sakha national unity and specificity.

After the success of the first part of his work, Sieroszewski prepared the second volume. In 1901, he brought it to St Petersburg ready for publishing, but the manuscript was lost. It was discovered by Soviet researchers in 1927; however, by this time Sieroszewski was an active participant in the political life in Poland, supporting Józef Piłsudski, which was unacceptable to the Soviet authorities. His work could not be published in the Soviet Union.

The results of his second trip to Siberia and the Far East were presented in the work on Ainu people *Wśród kosmatych ludzi* [Among the Hairy People] published in 1927 in Poland, but did not have the same impact as his work on the Yakuts. Simultaneously, Sieroszewski was publishing novels and poems. Especially the novels *Na kraiu lesov* [At the edge of forests] and *Pobeg* [The Escape] give a vivid image of life in Siberia. He published under the pen-name Wacław Sirko.

Biography

Wacław Sieroszewski was born in 1858 in Wólka Kozłowska near Warsaw, at the time when Poland was a part of the Russian Empire. Sieroszewski's father was imprisoned after participation in the Polish uprising of 1863–1864 and later he had to flee from the country. His mother died soon afterward. During his years in the college in Warsaw and during his work as a locksmith at the railway workshops, Sieroszewski became involved with the socialist movement. He was arrested by the Czarist police in 1878 and sentenced to eight years of hard labor, which were exchanged for exile to Siberia. He spent 12 years there, married a Yakut woman, Anna, and had one daughter Maria, who became a teacher. In 1902–1904, he took part in the expedition of the Imperial Russian Geographical Society to the Far East, Mongolia, China, Korea, and Japan. From 1905, Sieroszewski remained in Poland and took active part in political life. During World War I, he fought in the Polish Legions under the command of Józef Piłsudski. Between World War I and II, he devoted himself to novel writing. He died in 1945, in Piaseczno near Warsaw.

AGNIESZKA HALEMBA

Further Reading

Ionov, V., "Obzor literatury po verovanyam yakutov." *Zhivaia starina*, III–IV (1914) 317–372

Kuczyński, Antoni, *Polskie opisanie świata* [Polish Description of the World], Wrocław: Wydawnictwo Univwersytetu Wrocławskiego, 1994

Sieroszewski, Wacław, "Kak i vo chto veruiut Yakuty" [How and in what the Yakuts believe]. *Sibirskii sbornik*, 2, (1891)

———, "Yakutskaia svad'ba" [The Yakut Wedding]. *Zhivaia starina*, III–IV (1894)

———, *Yakuty* [The Yakuts], St Petersburg: Imperatorskoe Russkoe Obshchestvo, 1896 (abridged version of this work was published in English in *The Journal of the Anthropological Institute*, 31, 1901)

———, *Wsród kosmatych ludzi* [Among the hairy people], Warsaw, 1927

———, In *Dzieła* [Collected Works], Volume I–XX, edited by Andrzej Lam & Jerzy Skórnicki, Kraków: Wydawnictwo Literackie, 1958–1963

Stepanov, S.A., "V.L. Seroshevskii i Yakutia" Foreword to Sieroszewski, Wacław Yakuty [The Yakuts], Moskva, 1993 (reprint)

Svenko, G., "Vaclav Seroshewskii I ego trudy o Yakutakh." *Izvestia sibirskogo otdelenia akademii nauk SSSR*, 1(151) (1969): 74–78

Tales by Polish Authors: Henryk Sienkiewicz, Stefan Żeromski, Adam Szymański, Wacław Sieroszewski, translated by E.C.M. Benecke, Oxford: B.H. Blackwell, 1915

SIKUSSAK

A type of very thick fast ice was first reported by Koch (1945) in north and northeast Greenland and was given the Greenlandic Eskimo name sikussak ("fjord ice like ocean ice"). Koch reported three areas of sikussak in May 1938 in Peary Land, whereas in earlier years (such as 1933, when he flew over the area) it had been more widely prevalent and had been responsible for holding calving icebergs in place against the edges of glaciers and preventing them from breaking out. There is no doubt that sikussak was more common in high-latitude fjords during the last glacial period, and may have been instrumental in bottling up Greenland icebergs. Conventionally, sikussak is now defined as very thick fast ice (i.e., ice anchored to the shore), more than 10 years old, with a thick snow cover.

In 1980, Wadhams observed ice of sikussak type in the fast ice at the mouth of Danmarks and Independence fjords in north Greenland in areas first reported by Koch. The ice had a highly developed surface drainage system, and a core drilled through 6.1 m of ice failed to reach bottom. A salinity record from the uppermost 4.6 m shows evidence of many years of alternating growth and surface melt. In these fjords, conditions prevail that differ from the Arctic Ocean as a whole: high snowfall (with high coastal mountains), low ocean heat flux (from the single-layer water structure in the fjord), and intensely cold air temperatures. Sikussak probably exists in other High Arctic coastal locations; for instance, there have been observations of fast ice "plugs" of 10 and 12 m in Nansen Sound and Sverdrup Channel in the Canadian High Arctic (Serson, 1972, 1974). Sea ice is, by comparison, usually about 3 m thick.

Very rarely, ice of sikussak type is observed in the Arctic Ocean pack. Cherepanov (1964) found that the 80 km^2 ice-floe on which the Russian drifting station NP-6 had been established was 10–12 m thick, with a crystal structure that was typical of slow congelation growth. A 1 km floe of mean thickness 9.2 m, apparently undeformed, was observed by submarine sonar near the North Pole (Walker and Wadhams, 1979). A 10–12 m thick floe was observed by A.R. Milne (personal communication) during an icebreaker voyage west of Prince Patrick Island. It is likely that these floes represent occasional breakouts from coastal source areas.

In the Antarctic, a source area for ice of sikussak type was discovered in 1986. During the Winter Weddell Sea Project experiment aboard FS *Polarstern*, a small number of floes of very high freeboard were observed in the pack (Wadhams et al., 1987). The origin of these floes was found to be bays along the edge of the nearby Fimbul Ice Shelf, from which icebergs had calved. The inlets "healed" themselves by growing multiyear fast ice. Protected from the drifting pack by the shelf edge geometry, the ice could keep growing from year to year with the special circumstances of high snowfall (mainly snow blown onto the ice surface by cold katabatic winds blowing over the ice shelf) and low oceanic heat flux (an outflow of very cold water from under the ice shelf). In this way, the ice could reach 11 m or more, and the occasional small breakouts of ice from these fast ice regions produced the isolated thick floes seen in the drifting pack.

The conventional thermodynamic models of ice growth in the Arctic (Maykut and Untersteiner, 1971; Semtner, 1976) predict that under normal Arctic Ocean ice conditions, undeformed sea ice will reach an ultimate equilibrium thickness of about 3 m after many years of winter growth and summer melt. Given the sensitivity of these thickness values to ocean heat flux, snowfall, and other factors, Walker and Wadhams (1979) set out to examine the conditions that could lead to sikussak formation. They ran the Maykut-Untersteiner model with an oceanic heat flux set to zero and an annual snowfall increased to 1.0 m, with air temperatures following the normal Arctic cycle. The ice thickness in the model reached 12 m in 65 years. Extrapolation of the annual curves of ablation and accretion showed that an equilibrium thickness of 20 m would be eventually achieved after about 300 years. Thus, there is little doubt that if fast ice is allowed to remain in place for many years whilst experiencing fjordlike conditions of high snowfall and no ocean heat flux, it will go on growing and will achieve exceptional thicknesses.

An intriguing possibility is that some ice that is conventionally viewed as shelf ice, that is, ice of terrestrial origin, may actually be very old fast sea ice, what may be termed super-sikussak. An Arctic example is the Ward Hunt Ice Shelf on the north coast of Ellesmere Island. Since the end of World War II, this ice shelf has been progressively breaking up, giving rise to the famous ice islands, several kilometers in diameter and 50 m or more thick, which have drifted in the Arctic Ocean and provided secure bases for drifting research stations. The most famous of all was Fletcher's Ice Island (T-3), which left the Beaufort Gyre in 1984 after 27 years and exited through Fram Strait, finally breaking up off southwest Greenland. It is also possible that "islands" reported by early explorers north of Ellesmere Island, Peary's "Crocker Land" and Cook's "Bradley Land," were actually ice islands. Unlike Antarctic ice shelves, Ward Hunt Ice Shelf is not actively fed by glaciers, and so is either a relic of the last glacial period or else, in whole or part, an accumulation of very thick, very slowly grown sea ice, with fabric properties resembling polycrystalline ice (including zero salinity) because of its very slow growth rate.

PETER WADHAMS

Further Reading

Cherepanov, N.V., "Structure of very thick sea ice." *Trudy Arkticheskogo i Antarkticheskogo Nanchno–Issledovatel' skogo Instituta,* 267 (1964): 13–18

Koch, L., "The east Greenland ice." *Meddelelser om Grønland,* 130 (part 3) (1945): 373

Maykut, G.A. & N. Untersteiner, "Some results from a time-dependent thermodynamic model of Arctic sea ice." *Journal of Geophysical Research,* 76(6) (1971): 1550–1575

Semtner, A.J., "A model for the thermodynamic growth of sea ice in numerical investigations of climate." *Journal of Physical Oceanography,* 6(3) (1976): 379–389

Serson, H.V., "Investigation of a plug of multi-year old sea ice in the mouth of Nansen Sound." Defence Research Establishment, Ottawa, Tech. Note 72–6, 1972, 4pp

———, "Sverdrup Channel." Defence Res. Establ, Ottawa, Tech. Note 74–10, 1974

Wadhams, P., "The seasonal Ice Zone." In *The Geophysics of Sea Ice,* edited by N. Untersteiner, New York: Plenum Press, 1986, pp. 825–991

Wadhams, P., M.A. Lange & S.F. Ackley, "The ice thickness distribution across the Atlantic sector of the Antarctic Ocean in midwinter." *Journal of Geophysical Research,* 92(C13) (1987): 14535–14552

Walker, E.R. & P. Wadhams, "Thick sea-ice floes." *Arctic,* 32(2) (1979): 140–147

SIMON, MARY

Mary May Simon was Canada's first Ambassador for Circumpolar Affairs, between 1994–2003. Her appointment in 1994 marked the first time an Inuk would hold an ambassadorial position in Canada. Following early work in broadcasting, Simon's career concentrated on the political arena. She worked extensively for the Inuit Tapirisat of Canada (ITC) and from 1986 to 1992, served as the first president of the Inuit Circumpolar Conference (ICC), where she was known particularly for developing close ties with Greenland. Simon's work has been recognized through appointments to the Order of Canada, the National Order of Québec, the Gold Order of Greenland, the Royal Canadian Geographical Society's 1998 Gold Medal, honorary doctorates from McGill and Queen's universities, and in 1995 she was named Chancellor of Trent University. In 1996, Simon received the National Aboriginal Achievement award for her environmental and circumpolar work; she was named to *Maclean's* magazine's 11th honor roll.

In 1988 Simon told participants at the Arctic Policy Conference Conference at McGill University, Montreal that "there must be a significantly expanded role for Inuit at the international level (Petrone 1988: 272)." She reiterated ICC's commitment to promoting international cooperation and world peace, and its declaration of the Canadian Arctic as a nuclear-free zone—a declaration Inuit continue to support, through various challenges by the United States and Canadian governments and corporate interests (Petrone, 1988: 265–271). Simon's opposition to President Ronald Reagan's Star Wars Strategic Defense Initiative has new currency in the light of pressures by the Bush administration to expand the United States' military presence in the Canadian, American, and Greenlandic Arctic in the new millennium.

Simon attributes her awareness of the internationality of Inuit to hearing Greenlandic music on her family's short-wave radio as they travelled among hunting and fishing camps in northern Québec, and to hearing her grandmother speak about her dream that Inuit from different countries would someday work together. Early formative experiences such as these contributed to her dedication to fostering international cooperation among Inuit and the Arctic nations.

Simon was drawn to a career in broadcasting in 1969 as an Inuktitut language producer and announcer on CBC Northern Service and a writer for *Inuit Today.* In 1973, she left journalism for politics, holding key positions with the Makivik Corporation representing the Inuit of Nunavik, and the ICC. Simon was first vice-president of Makivik from 1979 to 1982 and president from 1982 to 1985. In the 1970s, she cut her political teeth on the difficult process of signing and implementing the controversial James Bay and Northern Québec Agreement, Canada's first comprehensive land claim agreement. As Simon described it, "We were a rag-tag, poorly funded group of Inuit and Cree up against governments and very powerful industrial interests. When the Québec government announced that the largest hydroelectric development project in the world was to be built on our lands, we were more or less forced into the world of white politicians and businessmen (Simon, 2000: 18)."

The agreement left rifts and distrust among Inuit and Cree communities and constituencies in its wake. The most controversial element was the government's insistence that Nunavik's indigenous residents surrender and accept the final extinguishment of their Aboriginal rights to the territory covered by the Agreement. Some people have never accepted this compromise, and see Simon as one of the leaders who betrayed them. Similar feelings are expressed toward John Amagoalik and others who were instrumental in signing and implementing the later Nunavut Agreement. Simon's position is that despite its weaknesses, the Agreement "provided our people with a foundation on which to build new relationships within Canadian society (Simon, 2000: 19)."

Simon successfully opposed the Québec government's program to impose the French language on northern Québec through Bill 101 (1977). In the early 1990s, she was a member of the negotiating team that helped to create Nunavut Territory. In 1993, Simon was appointed co-director and secretary to the Royal Commission on Aboriginal Peoples, and in 1994, she was appointed Canada's ambassador for Circumpolar Affairs. Simon's responsibility in this capacity was to renew efforts to create an Arctic Council that would enhance Canada's links to other Arctic nations. In 1997, while continuing in this role, she assumed additional duties as ambassador to Denmark. In September 1998, the Arctic Council became a reality, formalized by the inaugural First Ministerial Meeting in Iqaluit. One of the results of this meeting was the creation of the "Iqaluit Declaration: An Agenda for 2000," which suggested priorities and projects for circumpolar cooperation and collaboration, including an initiative on the future of Arctic children and youth and an initiative to develop a northern foreign policy for Canada.

In June 2001, in Simon's dual role as Canada's ambassador to the Kingdom of Denmark and for Circumpolar Affairs, she addressed the tenth anniversary celebration of the Arctic Environmental Protection Strategy (AEPS). In a political climate that continues to challenge Inuit and other initiatives to protect the Arctic environment, Simon's presentation reiterated the objectives of what had become known as the "Rovaniemi Process." ICC had joined forces with the Nordic Saami Council and the Russian Association of Small Peoples of the North (now RAIPON) to lobby the governments of Arctic nations to include indigenous peoples in the AEPS. Simon's presentation emphasized optimism about the prospects for addressing issues such as transboundary pollution and heralded the release of the AEPS report on Arctic biodiversity. Among the efforts she praised was the collaboration between the Coalition of Canadian Aboriginal Peoples Against POPs and the Canadian negotiating team in enabling the signing of the POPs Global Convention in Stockholm in 2001.

Biography

Mary May Simon was born in Kangiqsualujjuaq on the western shore of Ungava Bay in Arctic Québec (now Nunavik) and spent much of her childhood and adolescent years camping, gathering, and hunting in and around the settlement of Kuujjuaq. She completed her formal education by correspondence and in Colorado. Her mother, Nancy, is an Inuk from Nunavik and her father, Bob May—originally southern Canadian—came north to manage the local Hudson's Bay Company post. She is married to the former CBC reporter Whit Fraser; they have three children and six grandchildren.

VALERIE ALIA

See also **Arctic Council; Arctic Environmental Protection Strategy; Inuit Circumpolar Conference (ICC); Makivik Corporation; Rovaniemi**

Further Reading

Petrone, Penny (editor), *Northern Voices: Inuit Writing in English*, Toronto: University of Toronto Press, 1988 (Please note that the entry on Mary Simon, on page 265 contains an error: the Arctic Policy Conference at McGill University is mislabelled the "Arctic Polar Conference")

Simon, Mary, *Inuit: One Arctic, One Future*, Peterborough, Ontario: Trent University, 1997

———, "From Kangiqsualujjuaq to Copenhagen: A personal Journey." *Northern Review*, No. 22, (Winter 2000): 17–22

———, *10 Years of Arctic Environmental Cooperation (Speaking Notes)*, Rovaniemi, Finland, June 11, 2001. Posted on the Arctic Council website: http://www.arctic-council.org/pmeetings/aeps10/simon.asp.

SIMPSON, THOMAS

Thomas Simpson is best remembered for his explorations, together with Peter Warren Dease, on behalf of Hudson's Bay Company during 1836–1839. His extensive surveys of the north coast of the North American continent filled in almost all the blanks left by the earlier explorations of Samuel Hearne, Alexander MacKenzie, William Beechey, John Franklin, John Richardson, George Lyon, George Back, and John Ross.

Simpson was an improbable explorer, sickly as a child, small in stature, and with a university education directed toward the ministry. It was his realization that he was unlikely to find a suitable living within the church that led him to accept employment in Hudson's Bay Company, arriving in Canada in 1829. Simpson's early years were uneventful but a winter journey from York Factory to the Red River settlement in 1831 gave the first signs that he had outgrown his fragile constitution. In correspondence, he mentions walking the full distance on snow shoes, avoiding the easier option of riding on the dog sled, describing winter travel as "a most healthy and strengthening exercise." (Alexander Simpson, 1845). Further experience accrued over the next five years on the annual four-to five-month return passage to York Factory. In 1833, he assisted with hiring men and making arrangements for Back's Great Fish River expedition.

The Hudson's Bay Company directors at this time, following unsuccessful attempts by Richard King to raise money in England in 1836 for a private expedition, realized the necessity of appearing to justify the company's charter, due for renewal in 1842, which granted them a monopoly on trade. The Company thus resolved to mount their own explorations with the instructions to "complete the discovery of the northern shores of this continent," to trace the coast "westwards ....whence Beechey's Barge returned" and "from Franklin's Point Turnagain eastward to the entrance of Back's Great Fish River" (Thomas Simpson, 1843). Thomas Simpson undertook the expedition planning but, presumably to avoid charges of nepotism, Governor George Simpson, his uncle, appointed a veteran of Franklin's second land expedition 1825–1827, Peter Warren Dease, as leader.

Dease set out on July 21, 1836 from Norway House for Fort Chipewayan on Lake Athapaska. Simpson summered at Red River before joining Dease in February 1837.

The expedition proper set out on June 1 traveling via Great Slave Lake and the Mackenzie River, reaching the Arctic coast of the Beaufort Sea on July 9, with a complement of 14 men in two purpose-built craft: *Castor* and *Pollux*. A second party was sent from the MacKenzie to establish, build, and supply winter quarters (Fort Confidence) on the northeastern arm (Dease Arm) of Great Bear Lake. The lesson of establishing secure winter quarters, well supplied with food, had been learned from the harsh deprivations suffered by the earlier Franklin land expeditions. The ocean party traveled west along the coast, passing Return Reef (Franklin's furthest west) on July 23 before encountering impassable ice conditions at "Boat Extreme" (the furthest point west reached in the boat) on August 1. A party of six men, including Simpson, then set out on foot, and borrowing an *umiak* (Inuit women's boat), reached Point Barrow (Beechey's furthest east) on August 4. Beechey, in fact, had observed this point only from offshore. The party then returned to Fort Confidence where they overwintered. Along their journey, they traded frequently with the Inuit whom they met and following their return to the fort they provided some winter relief for the starving local Indian population.

The following year the party ascended Dease River and crossed the barren ground, transporting their boats with them to the Coppermine River, which they descended, reaching the Arctic coast at Coronation Gulf on July 2, 1838. Progress eastward along the coast was slow with poor weather and unfavorable ice conditions, and several days were spent encamped at Boathaven near Franklin's furthest east, before open water allowed further advance along the unexplored coast. Progress, however, remained slow and realizing that they were unlikely to gain their objective and return safely that year, the expedition turned back to Fort Confidence on August 24, marking their furthest east, near Beaufort River, with a cairn (a large pile of stones).

The following year proved much more favorable for travel and Simpson rapidly recovered the ground traversed in 1838, pushing eastward beyond Beaufort River, reaching Back's Great Fish River on August 11, 1839 and Back's furthest east Point Ogle and Montreal Island on August 13, 1839, achieving his set mission. He then, however, decided to continue eastward along the coast in an attempt to link up with John Ross's earlier surveys of Boothia but he eventually turned back only partly successful on August 20, 1839, at a watercourse he named Castor and Pollox River, in honor of his trusty boats. Standing at the limit of his survey, Simpson remarked on the open water and the continuing coastline trending north east. This led some to conclude contentiously that Simpson was the first to complete the mapping of the North West Passage. Others have argued that the lack of clarity in the exact configuration of the coastline between Simpson's and Ross's surveys contributed to the difficulties experienced by survivors of John Franklin's *Erebus* and *Terror* expedition.

On his return to Red River, Simpson decided to visit England, setting out on June 6, 1840. He never arrived. Traveling initially with two voyagers of mixed blood, John Bird and Antoine Legros, they overtook a traveling party and were joined by Legros's son, Antoine Jr. and James Bruce. Simpson's chart detailed progress up until June 12, at which point events become obscure. It is clear that three men, Simpson, Legros Sr., and John Bird, died violent deaths from gunshot wounds. The survivors swore that Simpson shot his two companions before turning the gun on himself, following an argument over whether they should return to Red River. The authorities returned a verdict of suicide; but others painted a blacker scene. Several motives for Simpson's murder have been suggested, including Simpson's known antipathy toward people of mixed-blood generating hatred toward himself, and the theft of valuable documents relating to his discoveries.

Biography

Thomas Simpson, born on July 2, 1805 in Dingwall, Scotland was the son of a schoolmaster Alexander Simpson and his second wife Mary (neé Simpson). He was an unlikely explorer, described during childhood by Alexander, his brother, and biographer, as "weak and sickly in physical and timid in mental constitution." As a grown man, he was barely 5′5″ tall. Thomas was educated at the local school before entering Kings College, Aberdeen in 1824 to train for the ministry of the Church of Scotland. On leaving the University, he joined Hudson's Bay Company at the invitation of his uncle George Simpson, the Governor, arriving at Norway House, Canada in June 1829. He worked initially as a secretary but in 1836 was asked to plan an expedition on behalf of the Hudson's Bay Company to examine and map those parts of the northern coast of North America that had not been traversed by earlier expeditions. Simpson's explorations were successfully accomplished in association with the nominal expedition leader Peter Warren Dease, during the years 1836–1839. His meticulous journal was revised by Edward Sabine and published posthumously, largely unaltered. Simpson died under mysterious circumstances east of Winnipeg sometime between June 13 and 14, 1840. He was buried in the churchyard of the Red River Colony, and a memorial was put up in Dingwall by his brother Alexander. He did not live to receive his award of the gold medal of the Royal Geographical Society.

IAN HODKINSON

See also **Beechey, Frederick; Hearne, Samuel; Hudson's Bay Company; Mackenzie, Sir Alexander; North West Passage; Richardson, Sir John; Ross, Sir James**

Further Reading

Barr, William (editor), *From Barrow to Boothia: The Arctic Journal of Peter Warren Dease, 1836–1839,* Montreal: McGill-Queens University, 2001

Bryce, George, *Mackenzie, Selkirk, Simpson,* Toronto: Morang, 1903

The Dictionary of National Biography, *Simpson, Thomas (1808–1840),* London: Oxford University, 1885

Fernandez-Armesto, Felipe, *The Times Atlas of World Exploration: 3000 Years of Exploring, Explorers and Mapmaking,* London: Harper Collins, 1991

McArthur,Alexander, *A Prairie Tragedy: The Fate of Thomas Simpson, the Arctic Explorer,* Winnipeg: Mortimore, 1887

Neatby, Leslie, "Thomas Simpson (1808–1840)."*Arctic,* 40 (1987): 348–349

Simpson, Alexander, *The Life and Travels of Thomas Simpson, the Arctic Discoverer,* London: Richard Bentley, 1845

Simpson, Thomas, *Narrative of the Discoveries on the North Coast of America Effected by Officers of the Hudsons Bay Company During the Years 1836–39,* London: Richard Bentley, 1843

SIRIUS PATROL

The Sirius Patrol is a Danish military patrol covering Greenland's northeast and north coasts. The uninhabited part of East and North Greenland that lies north of 71°30′ N and the settlement Ittoqqortoormiit (Scoresbysund) composes the area that is under the supervision of the Danish Sirius Patrol. The Mesters Vig airport, Sirius headquarters Daneborg, Danmarkshavn weather station, and Station Nord are the only inhabited spots in this vast area.

From 1908, Norwegian and Danish trappers wintered and traveled in this area north to 77°30′, building small wooden cabins at a distance of a day's march with dogsled from each other. During World War II, Denmark and the United States came to an agreement on the need to patrol the northeast Greenland coast in order to be able to discover any German attempts to establish weather-reporting stations. Three experienced Norwegian trappers joined the 5–9 Danes and 2–4 Greenlandic dogsled drivers in the northeast Greenland Sledge Patrol, which operated for the last four winters of the war. This patrol was disbanded in 1945, but re-established on August 18, 1950 during the Cold War as a secret military sledge patrol under the name Operation Resolute. In 1951, the name was changed to Sledge Patrol Resolute, and in 1953 to Sirius Patrol to avoid misunderstandings with the weather station name Resolute Bay in northern Canada. Sirius is the name of the brightest star in the night sky. Also known as Alpha Canis Majoris/the Dog Star, it is to be found in the constellation Canis Major. The patrol is a Danish military unit under the Navy, Greenland Command, which has its headquarters in Ivigtut.

The Patrol's task today is still to inspect the uninhabited coast between Liverpool Land on the east coast and Nares Strait on the north coast, a stretch of about 2100 km on the map. During the winter—*c.*November 1 to June 15—dogsleds are used, and in summer small boats. Originally, the old trapping stations were used as lodging, in addition to tents, and the Patrol has helped to maintain a number of these. Today, some modern huts have been erected and tents are still used. In addition to the military aspect, the main tasks of the patrol are to maintain the Danish-Greenlandic sovereignty, to supervise the National Park, and to exercise police authority in the area. The unit consists of 12 men at a time, who are volunteers from any of the three Danish military services and who serve for 2 years in the Patrol, with half being relieved each year. The sledge patrols consist of two men and 11 dogs who can spend 4–5 months continually traveling. In addition to the headquarters at Daneborg, the Patrol also operates a summer station at Ella Ø (Ella Island).

In February–May 2000, six Danes marked Sirius' 50th anniversary by traveling with three dogsleds the

3500 km from Qaanaaq in the northwest to Mestersvig in the east. Four of the men had previously served in the Sirius patrol, one was the Danish crown prince Frederik, and a cameraman came in addition to document the expedition.

SUSAN BARR

Further Reading

Mikkelsen, Peter Schmidt, *Tusind dage med Sirius*, Copenhagen: Gyldendal, 1990
———, *Nordøstgrønland 1908–60*, Copenhagen: Dansk Polarcenter, 1994

SISIMIUT

Sisimiut means "the people at the fox caves." A town in West Greenland, 50 km north of the Arctic Circle, Sisimiut is the main town in Sisimiut Municipality. With its 5210 (August 2001) inhabitants, Sisimiut is the second largest town in Greenland. The landmark of Sisimiut is the 784-m-high mountain Nasaarsaaq (Kælingehætten) situated west of the town.

The first settlers who came to the area were the Saqqaq Culture people 4500 years ago. The Saqqaq people stayed in the area for more than 2000 years. The Dorset Culture people stayed in the area between 500 BCE and 1200 CE. In the 13th century, the first Thule Culture people arrived in the area.

In 1756, the Danish-Norwegian state established the colony of Holsteinsborg. The colony was named after Johan Ludvig Holstein (1694–1763), a highly influential official to the Danish king. The colony was first placed at Ukiivik (Sydbay) 40 km north of Sisimiut. Eight years later, the colony was moved to today's Sisimiut. A house from Ukiivik is still part of the old colonial town. Among the old houses is also the oldest Lutheran church in Greenland. The church was constructed and financed by the local Greenlanders in 1771 and began to be used in 1775.

At the beginning of the 19th century, a small industrial complex for the production of whale oil with a blubber cookery and a blacksmith was established in Holsteinsborg. It was the first land-based European production in Greenland.

In 1923, the Royal Greenland Trade Company (KGH) began to buy fish, and in 1924 the first fish-processing factory in Greenland was built in Sisimiut. In the beginning it produced halibut in tins. In the 1930s, shrimp was produced, and later until the collapse of the stock it was cod. Now, the factory produces shrimp and snow crabs. In 1931, Greenland's first shipyard was established next to the factory. From the beginning of this industrialization, Sisimiut flourished quickly. Today, Sisimiut is known as an enterprising town.

Since the 1990s, the tourist industry has been growing with a number of outfitters. Sisimiut offers cultural activities, dog sledging, snow mobiles, and in the summer whale safaris, trekking, fishing, and hunting.

Sisimiut has several educational institutions. In 1949, Greenland's first technical school was established. It later became the vocational school for carpenters. In 1962, *Knud Rasmussens Højskole* was established. It was extended in 1977 with *Kvindehøjskolen*. Sisimiut also hosts a school for the deaf, and a language school. Since 2000, Sisimiut has housed a technical high school (HTX). Danish Technological University has established a small branch in Sisimiut.

The harbor in Sisimiut is open all year round. Sisimiut is the most northern of the open-water towns. Since the 1960s, Sisimiut has had a heliport. In 1998, the airport was opened. In the late 1960s, the American army offered to build a road between Sisimiut and Kangerlussuaq. At that time, it was rejected by the administration in Greenland. In 2001, plans to build a road had been taken up again, this time by the local politicians.

The largest settlement in Sisimiut Municipality is Kangerlussuaq with 485 inhabitants (August 2001). It was established in 1941 as an American military base to support the traffic between USA and Europe during World War II. The American army left Kangerlussuaq in 1992. Since the beginning of the 1960s, Kangerlussuaq has played a key role as a center for civil air traffic. From 1970 to 2001, Kangerlussuaq was an area outside the Municipal division. Today, Kangerlussuaq has a comprehensive tourist industry with activities like dog sledging, muskox safaris, and trips to the ice cap. Two traditional settlements near Sisimiut are still inhabited: Sarfannguaq with 113 people (August 2001) and Itilleq with 138 people (August 2001).

KLAUS GEORG HANSEN

See also **Kangerlussuaq; Saqqaq Culture**

Further Reading

Bendixen, O., "Holsteinsborg Distrikt." In *Grønland i tohundredeaaret for Hans Egedes Landing,* Meddelelser om Grønland, Volume 61, edited by G.C. Amdrup et al., Copenhagen: Reitzel, 1921, pp 1–86
Blæsild, Benno, *Sisimiut = Holsteinsborg*, Publikationer fra Arktisk Institut nr 4, Charlottenlund: Arktisk Institut, 1989
Gad, Finn, *The History of Greenland,* 3 volumes. Volume 1: *Earliest Times to 1700*, London: C. Hurst, 1970. Volume 2: *1700–1782*, London: C. Hurst, 1973. Volume 3: *1782–1808*, Copenhagen: Nyt Nordisk Forlag, 1982
Hamilton, L.C., C. Brown & R.O. Rasmussen, *Local Dimensions of Climatic Change: West Greenland's Cod-to-Shrimp Transition.* University of New Hampshire, NAArc Working Paper 01–3. 2001
Haarløv, Niels et al. (editors), *Holsteinsborg; Sisimiut kommune, natur- og kulturforhold*, Copenhagen, 1980

Mathiesen, Jørgen & Frederik Lennert (editors), *Sisimiut Holsteinsborg 1756–1956*, Godthåb: Det Grønlandske Forlag, 1958

Møbjerg, Tinna, "New Aspect of the Saqqaq Culture." In *Fifty Years of Arctic Research. Anthropological Studies from Greenland to Siberia*, edited by K. Red, R. Gilberg Ferdinand & H.C. Gulløv, *Ethnographical Series*, 18 (1997): 1–320

———, "The Saqqaq Culture in the Sisimiut Municipality Elucidated by Two Sites Nipisat and Asummiut." In *Man, Culture and Enviroment in Ancient Greenland*, No. 4, edited by J. Arneborg H.C. Gulløv, Copenhagen: The Danish National Museum and Danish Polar Center, 1998

———, "New adaptation strategies in the Saqqaq culture of Greenland, c. 1600–1400 BC." In *Arctic Archaeology*, edited by Peter Rowley-Conwy, *World Archaeology*, 30(3) (1999)

SIUMUT

Siumut is a Greenlandic political party, of a moderate socialist orientation, in practice a Social Democratic party in style and ideological persuasion. Siumut, which means "forward," is the dominant Greenlandic political party, which has been in control of governmental power since the establishment of the Greenlandic Home Rule system in 1979. However, Siumut lost its absolute majority in 1983 and the party has since remained in power through shifting coalitions with either Inuit Ataqatigiit (IA, the Socialist Party) or Atassut (the Liberal Party). In later years, Siumut's voting base has been declining, but it remains the largest party in Greenland.

Currently, the party is led by Hans Enoksen, who is also the Greenlandic prime minister (Landsstyreformand). Enoksen took over from Jonathan Motzfeldt in 2002. Historically, there had been forerunners to a patriotic workers and fisherman party before Siumut; an Inuit Ataqatigiit (IA) appeared in 1963 and the Sukaq Party was formed in 1969. A Social Democratic party had also been established briefly around 1955, at the time when the first Greenlandic national labor union, Grønlands Arbejder Sammenslutning (GAS), was established. Motzfeldt had a political background in the Inuit party, where he was the editor of the party's newsletter *Inuit*.

Siumut was organized as a movement in 1975 and was officially established as a party in 1977 during the hectic political activities that dominated political life in Greenland in the 1970s. The foundations for Siumut were already established in 1971, when actors such as Motzfeldt, Lars Emil Johansen, and Moses Olsen decided to establish a political group. The arrangement began as a kind of practical consultation around the time when Moses Olsen became a Greenlandic member of the Danish parliament, while at the same time Motzfeldt and Johansen were elected to the Greenlandic Council (Grønlands landsråd). Olsen and Motzfeldt had already known each other from their student years in Copenhagen. Motzfeldt, the son of a hunter, had studied theology at the University of Copenhagen; Johansen, the son of a trade steward, had a teacher's certificate from Nuuk; and Olsen, the son of a fisherman, had studied in Denmark and at the University of Iceland.

Generally, an important stimulus to the establishment of the Siumut movement was the European Union (EU) issue, which came to a crescendo when Denmark joined the EU in 1972. There was great opposition in Greenland toward the EU, and the EU functioned as the major catalyst for a stepwise awakening of political demand for a Home Rule arrangement and for a nascent Inuit self-confidence. In this way, it also functioned as a catalyst for those forces, which became manifest in the Siumut party. The EU became a symbol for those motivational forces, which was triggered by the built-in tension in the modernization process that was articulated in Greenland's G-50 and G-60 reform programs (*see* **G-50, G-60**). In 1975, the party's newspaper *Sujumut* appeared for the first time under the slogan of a "New Politic" and with Moses Olsen as editor. In the first issue, the party declared that all natural resources in Greenland belonged to the indigenous people and it demanded that Greenland should control its own natural resources. The language and orientation in the party's first political proclamations were strongly influenced by socialist and nationalist ideas. As a general ideological outlook, it reflected many of the global political issues and the ideas of "anti-imperialism" as they been reflected among students in Copenhagen in the 1960s. The purpose was to challenge the prevailing paternalism of colonial power and to place Inuit in charge of their own affairs. At the bottom of the process lay a complex relationship of both identification and disassociation with the Danish system in which the actors had been inherently socialized. One both wanted to accept and reject it. The result of the first political turmoil was the creation of the new Home Rule government and it also resulted in Greenland's withdrawal from the EU. In later years, however, Siumut has highlighted the importance of a pragmatic and constructive relationship with Denmark and has refrained from the ethnocentric and nationalist appeals of other parties. In various situations, the party has stood firm on the principle articulated in the party manifesto of 1999, which states "that no one in Kalaallit Nunaat (Greenland) must ever be discriminated against because of birthplace, sex or religion." In the later years, the atmosphere in the party after 20 years in power is geared toward practical politics. On the issue of independence,

Siumut has stressed the Commonwealth with Denmark but at the same time has insisted on a greater Greenlandic role in foreign policy.

Generally, the modern Greenlandic State is very much the creation of the Siumut party, which has become a Greenlandic interpretation of a Scandinavian welfare state. Most of the party's political demands as they were articulated in the late 1970s have been realized. Thus, the current "pragmatism" in Siumut is the effect of an ideology that has realized many of its original goals. Despite a declining voting base, the party is still the central actor in Greenland's political life. It is also important to note that Agnethe Davidsen, a Siumut politician who received by far the highest personal vote in the last Municipal election, is mayor of Nuuk (Greenland's capital).

JENS KAALHAUGE NIELSEN

See also **Atassut; Greenland Home Rule Act; G-50; G-60; Inuit Ataqatigiit; Johansen, Lars Emil; Motzfeldt, Jonathan; Olsen, Moses**

Further Reading

Greenland's Home Rule Government website: http://www.gh.gl

Harhoff, Frederik, *Rigsfællesskabet (The Danish Commonwealth)*, Århus: Klim, 1993

Kaalhauge Nielsen, Jens, "Economic dependence, political autonomy and cultural identity in Greenland. Or Sweet dreams, harsh reality and ambiguous value patterns." In *Global and Local Socio-Economic Processes in the North, International Scientific Conference in Apatity,* Russia, March 18–21, 1999, edited by Gennady Lusin, Apatity: Institute for Economic Problems, Kola Science Centre RAS, 2001

Lyck, Lise, "Politics and Elections in Greenland with a Focus on Economy and Sustainable Development." In *Grønland and Arctic Economic and Political Issues*, edited by Lise Lyck, Nordic Press, 2001

Siumut website: www.siumut.gl

Skydsbjerg, Henrik, *Grønland 20 år med Hjemmestyret (Greenland, 20 years with the Home Rule Government),* Nuuk: Atuagkat, 2000

Thomsen, Hanne, *Between Tradition and Modernity*. Cultural and Social Research in Greenland 95/96, Nuuk: Ilisimatusarfik/Atuakkiorfik, 1996

SKRAELING ISLAND

Skraeling Island is located at 78° N and 74° W in the Canadian High Arctic, off the east coast of Ellesmere Island. The widest part of the island is about 1.5 km and the distance from northwest to southeast is about 2.0 km. A narrow, low isthmus connects the northern and the southern part of the island, except during extremely high tides. Shoals and rocky islets bordering the northeastern shore create secondary polynya conditions favorable to walrus and seals.

Over the centuries, the island has undoubtedly been given many different names by various Paleo- and Neo-Eskimo groups who settled there intermittently over the past 4500 years. In the fall of 1875, Sir George Nares anchored his ships, *Alert* and *Discovery,* in a bight a few hundred yards south of the island, which he named Three Sisters Island because of its three prominent points. Between 1898 and 1899, the Norwegian explorer, Otto Sverdrup, investigated the central east coast of Ellesmere Island. Possibly unaware of Nares's previous naming, Sverdrup renamed the little island, Skraeling Island, the term Skraeling being an old Norse term for Natives, be they Inuit or Indians.

Believing that Sverdrup's naming of the island reflected his discovery of ancient Native habitation sites, Peter Schledermann investigated the island in 1977 and discovered the remains of two large Thule culture winter sites and numerous traces of earlier Paleo-Eskimo encampments. The initial survey of the island was followed by 15 archaeological field seasons, involving excavation and testing of selected sites and eventually a complete survey of the central east coast of Ellesmere Island. The evidence from Skraeling Island and the entire Bache Peninsula region proved that this part of the High Arctic was the primary route for prehistoric migrations into Greenland. Furthermore, the Bache region had periodically supported relatively large prehistoric groups for extended periods of time.

The first people to set foot on Skraeling Island were part of what has been termed the Arctic Small Tool tradition (ASTt), an archaeological concept, that includes cultural remains left behind on Paleo-Eskimo sites stretching from western Alaska to Greenland, spanning an approximate time period from about 4500 BCE to 1200 CE. The earliest Paleo-Eskimo camps on Skraeling Island located between 15 and 24 m above present sea level, are part of the Independence I complex of the ASTt. When these sites were occupied, sea level was considerably higher than today, placing them close to the shore line at the time. Many of the central hearths from this early period are completely intact and contain ashes and boiling stones.

Human occupation of the High Arctic became more intermittent following the pioneering Paleo-Eskimo migrations into the area. Evidence from Skraeling Island indicates that population movements across Smith Sound occasionally originated from Greenland, particularly during the Saqqaq cultural period. However, more regularly northward movements came from the Canadian Arctic in the form of various stages of pre-Dorset, Early, and Late Dorset cultures. A significant intensity of human occupation in the Far North, between about 900 and 500 BCE, is reflected in a number of sites on Skraeling Island, which, like the rest of the Far North, also indicate a complete lack of human activities during the following 1200 years. The long period of abandonment was broken with the arrival of Late Dorset people migrating northward from the Canadian Arctic about 800 CE. The Late Dorset occupations are well represented on Skraeling Island. About 1250 CE, a new cultural tradition, originating in Alaska, pushed eastward into the High Arctic and Greenland. The pioneering families of these early Thule culture people wintered on many occasions on Skraeling Island, which has yielded the most important archaeological data pertaining to the lives of these early whale hunters. The same winter houses have also yielded one of the largest assemblage of Norse artifacts discovered in the New World, indicating close contact between Inuit and Norsemen in the High Arctic sometime around 1300 CE.

PETER SCHLEDERMANN

See also **Arctic Small Tool tradition; Devon Island; Ellesmere Island; Thule Culture; Vinland**

Further Reading

McCullough, K. M., *The Ruin Islanders: Early Thule Culture Pioneers in the Eastern High Arctic*, Ottawa: Canadian Museum of Civilization Mercury Series, Archaeological Survey of Canada Paper 141, 1989

Nares, G.S., In *Narrative of a Voyage to the Polar Sea During 1875–76 in H. M. ships Alert and Discovery; with Notes on the Natural History.* Edited by H. W. Fielden, *naturalist to the expedition*, London: Low, Marston, Searle and Rivington, 1878

Schledermann, P., *Voices in Stone: A Personal Journey into the Arctic Past*, Komatic Series, Calgary: Arctic Institute of North America, 1996

Sverdrup, O., *New Land: Four Years in the Arctic Regions*, translated by Ethel Harrier Hearn, London: Longmans, Green and Co., 1904

SKUAS AND JAEGERS

The Stercorariidae family of birds has seven species, of which four (great skua *Stercorarius skua*, Pomarine skua *S. pomarinus*, Arctic skua *S. parasiticus*, and long-tailed skua *S. longicaudus*) are typical breeders for the Northern Hemisphere, but three other species (*S. maccormicki*, *S. antarcticus*, and *S. chilensis*) are only found in the Southern Hemisphere. The great skuas are sometimes differentiated from the three other northern hemisphere species (the small skuas, collectively known as jaegers). The larger skuas (*Stercorarius skua*, and the three Southern Hemisphere species) are also sometimes classified as a separate genus, *Catharacta*.

Dimorphism in color is known for all skua species: there are pale, intermediate, and dark morphs. Some Arctic skua populations are composed almost entirely of the dark phase. There are some geographical correlations: the dark phase is more often seen in northern Europe and East Asia; the pale phase is more typical for high latitudes. Among Pomarine and long-tailed skuas, dark and intermediate phases are also known but they are less typical. The dark morphs of long-tailed skuas are rare, while Pomarine skuas have 1–20% of dark forms throughout its range.

The great skua breeds in the North Atlantic, while the Pomarine, Arctic, and long-tailed skuas have circumpolar distributions and breed in tundra of the Old and New World. All skuas of the Northern hemisphere inhabit tundra, coasts, and islands. They come to land only during the breeding season; the rest of the year they migrate and wander above the seas and oceans. The wintering areas of skuas are located mainly in the North Atlantic (all species) and North Pacific (all species except great skua). Long-tailed and Pomarine skuas also winter in the Arctic Ocean, and Pomarine skua can be found in the Indian Ocean and near the coasts of Australia.

Non-breeding birds of different age are distributed in different parts of their range: the older birds wander close to the breeding grounds but the younger birds are widely distributed throughout the whole wintering area.

Breeding Biology and Behavior

Skuas normally start breeding at the age of 4–5 years (for the long-tailed skua, cases of breeding at the age of 2 years are known, and great skuas do not start reproducing until the age of 9 years). The longest recorded lifespan is 16 years for a great skua. As a rule, they are monogamous, and keep partners for several years, although some cases of polygamy are known (e.g., a great skua breeding family was known consisting of one male and two females, having one nest with a clutch of three eggs).

During the reproductive season, skuas are territorial. They retain and defend their territories after arrival to the breeding grounds. The breeding pairs usually attack other skuas and predators within several hundred meters from the nest.

Nests are built inside the territory by both partners. Egg laying takes place in early June. Clutches normally consists of 1–2 eggs. Clutches of one egg are assumed to be replacements or occurring in years with limited food supplies. The incubation period is 24–29 days depending on species. Both partners may incubate the eggs; however, the female does the most. Chicks leave the nest 1–2 days after hatching, but stay around, usually within 500 m. Both parents feed the young. The fledging age varies in different species: the chicks of long-tailed skua start flying after 25 days, the great skua not till after 40 days.

All skuas have a large variety of vocalization and demonstrative behavior (Arctic skuas have more than 12 special calls). Display postures on the ground assume to be less varied than in gulls, but the aerial behavior is more elaborated, probably because of large territories and open habitats.

Long-tailed jaeger (small skua),
Bathhurst Island, Nunavut.
Copyright David R. Gray

Diet, Breeding Dynamics, Distribution, and Numbers

All species of skuas have a wide spectrum of food. During the breeding season, they eat lemmings, voles, insects, small birds, their eggs and young, and berries, while the main food of nonbreeding skuas is fish. Flocks of nonbreeding birds (up to several hundred individuals) are concentrated near the coast feeding on fish.

All species of skuas often obtain food by stealing it from other individuals of the same or different species. This manner in which food is obtained is named "piracy" or "food parasitism" or "kleptoparasitism."

During the breeding season, the main food for skuas are rodents. Since the abundance of lemmings in the tundra varies from year to year, the numbers and distribution of breeding skuas vary in different seasons. For example, in places where the density of lemmings is high, the Pomarine skuas breed throughout the range and have a high breeding density, becoming more abundant than all other species of skuas. If the number of lemmings is low, the Pomarines do not usually breed, they wander in tundra hunting small waders and their young, or move to the coast to feed on fish. Breeding of the long-tailed skua is also correlated with rodent abundance (northern Scandinavia); in Siberia, it can breed even in areas with a low density of lemmings, but with a commensurate reduced population.

In the North Atlantic, Arctic skuas mostly forage by kleptoparasitism—attacking other birds in the air and forcing them to drop food. They nest in colonies of up to several dozen pairs (such as at the Varanger Peninsula, Norway). If food is abundant (e.g., in peaks of lemming density) solitary skuas also breed in tundra (Siberia, Arctic tundras). There, the species is often widely distributed, but nests with low density. Its breeding numbers and distribution as well as breeding success depend mostly on lemming abundance but they can also feed on eggs and chicks, small birds, and even insects and berries.

The breeding density can vary and mostly depends on the food supplies of the area. Pomarine skuas in good years have a breeding density from 1.2 pairs per sq km (Wrangel Island) up to 7.0 pairs per sq km (Alaska). The breeding density of long-tailed skua (pairs per sq km) can vary from 0.002–0.63 (Sweden), 0.068–0.94 (Alaska), and 0.1 (northern Chukotka) to 0.8–1.2 (Yakutia) and 1.7 (Greenland). In the Varanger Peninsula, Arctic skuas breed in colonies of about 60 pairs in the vicinity of seabird colonies but in the tundra, they breed at a lower density. Breeding densities also vary by region: in the west, the number of breeding pairs of Arctic skua is higher, but in East Siberia the long-tailed skua is more abundant.

In breeding areas, skuas can be quite aggressive: if there are not enough lemmings to feed on, they start feeding on other birds and predate the clutches, young, and adults of small waders and passerines. That is why in different aboriginal dialects in Siberia, skuas are named "robbers."

E. LAPPO

Further Reading

Andersson, M. & F. Goetmark, "Social organization and foraging ecology in the Arctic skua *Stercorarius parasiticus*: a test of the food defendability hypothesis." *Oikos* 35 (1980): 63–71

Andersson, M., "Breeding behaviour of the long-tailed skua *Stercorarius longicaudus* (Vieillot)." *Ornis Scandinavica*, 2 (1971): 35–54

———, "Behaviour of the Pomarine skua *Stercorarius pomarinus* Temm. with comparative remarks on Stercorariinae." *Ornis Scandinavica*, 4 (1973): 1–16

———, "Reproductive tactics of the long-tailed skua *Stercorarius longicaudus*." *Oikos*, 37 (1981): 287–294

Andersson, M. & F. Goetmark, "Social organization and foraging ecology in the Arctic skua *Stercorarius parasiticus*: a test of the food defendability hypothesis." *Oikos* 35 (1980); 63–71

Arnason, E., "Apostatic selection and kleptoparasitism in the Parasitic Jaeger." *Auk*, 95 (1978): 377–381

———, "Clutch size in the long-tailed skua *Stercorarius longicaudus*: some field experiments." *Ibis*, 118 (1976): 586–588

Davis, J.W., "Breeding success and experience in the Arctic skua *Stercorarius parasiticus* (L.)." *Journal of Animal Ecology*, 45 (1976): 531–535

De Korte, J. & J. Wattel, "Food and breeding success of the Long-tailed skua at Scoresby Sund, Northeast Greenland." *Ardea*, 76 (1988): 27–41

Donald, P., *The Arctic Skua. A Study of Ecology and Evolution of a Seabird*, Cambridge and New York: Cambridge University Press, 1983

Flint, V.E., In *Semeistvo Pomornikovyie. Ptitsy SSSR. Family Stercorariidae* [Birds of the USSR], edited by V.D.Il'ichev & V.A. Zubakin, Moscow: Nauka, 1988

Maher, W.J., "Ecology of Pomarine, parasitic and long-tailed jaegers in Northern Alaska." *Pacific Coast Avifauna*, 37 (1974): 1–148

Manning, T.H., "Geographical and sexual variation in the long-tailed jaeger *Stercorarius longicaudus* Vieillot." Biol. Pap. Univ. Alaska No. 7, 1964, p. 16

Perdeck, A.C., "The early reproductive behavior of the Arctic skua, *Stercorarius parasiticus* (L.)." *Ardea*, 51(1) (1963): 1–15

Perry, R., "Natural history of the skuas." *Discovery,* 10 (1949): 389–392

Southern, H.N.M.A., "Dimorphism in *Stercorarius pomarinus* (Temminck.)" *Ibis*, 86 (1944) 1–16

SNOW

Snow consists of falling or deposited (lying) ice crystals that grew while floating, rising, or falling in the atmosphere. It is estimated that snowfall accounts for about 5% of the total precipitation reaching the Earth's surface, equivalent to approximately 3×10^{16} kg per year. About 10% of this snowfall contributes to ice sheets and glaciers, while the remainder forms temporary (forming most years, but unstable) or seasonal snow cover. Permanent snow and ice occurs mainly in Antarctica and Greenland, while temporary and seasonal snow cover is primarily a phenomenon of the Northern Hemisphere. In northern America, seasonal snow occurs roughly at latitudes north of 40° and temporary snow north of 30°. In western Europe, seasonal snow is confined to latitudes north of about 60° and mountainous areas, while temporary snow can occur almost everywhere except the southwestern Iberian Peninsula. In eastern Europe, seasonal snow is found at latitudes north of about 50°, and the zone of temporary snow extends southward into the Middle East at a latitude of about 35°. In Asia, seasonal snow occurs as far south as 30°. In the Southern Hemisphere, significant snow cover is largely confined to mountainous areas (the Andes in South America, the Drakensberg in South Africa, the Snowy Mountains in Australia, and the Southern Alps in New Zealand). The figure below illustrates the spatial distribution of snow cover in the Northern Hemisphere.

Northern Hemisphere snow cover varies between a minimum of around 4 million square kilometers in August and 46 million square kilometers (around 40% of the total land area) in January. The maximum amount of water stored as snow is about 3×10^{15} kg, which gives an average "residence time" (the time spent by a molecule of water as part of the snow pack) of about a month. This is in marked contrast to ice sheets where the residence time can be of the order of 10,000 years. The average snowfall over areas that receive it is around 2 m, with an average snow depth of about 15 cm. The maximum recorded snowfall in one year is 31 m (near Mount Rainier, Washington State, in 1971–1972), and the maximum recorded depth of snow is 11.46 m (at Tamarack, California, in 1911).

Apart from its effect on the Earth's albedo (*see* **Albedo**) and on atmosphere-to-surface energy transfer, snow cover plays an important part in the hydrological cycle, through evaporation and sublimation to the atmosphere and through the runoff of meltwater. While this runoff can be significant for hydroelectric power generation, irrigation, and freshwater supply, it is often significantly more variable and less predictable than from a drainage basin fed entirely by rain. Snow cover also has significance as a potential transport hazard, and for recreation. The global snow cover, and especially its southern boundary in the Northern Hemisphere, is a sensitive indicator of the global climate.

The Physics of Snow

The ice crystals of which snow is composed grow initially in a basically hexagonal form dictated by the molecular structure of water and the hydrogen bonds that form in the ice crystal, but many variations are possible depending on the temperature and degree of supersaturation at which they are formed. If the degree of supersaturation is low, the crystals generally form as simple hexagonal prisms, whereas high supersaturation and temperatures around −15°C produce dendritic plates in the form of symmetrical six-pointed stars (see Figure 2). Loose aggregates of these plates are generally referred to as flakes.

Freshly fallen snow (new snow) is a loose, porous aggregate of ice crystals, with a density typically between 0.05 and 0.3 Mg m^{-3}. The porosity of the snow is defined as the volume fraction of air, and is thus given by the formula

$$p = 1 - \frac{\rho}{\rho_i},$$

where ρ is the density of the snow and ρ_i is the density of pure ice (0.92 Mg m^{-3}). As the snow ages, it undergoes metamorphism through melting, sublimation, refreezing, and sintering, and through mechanical compaction by wind or by the weight of overlying layers of snow. Its density increases, its porosity decreases correspondingly, and the grains of ice become simpler in shape (exhibit fewer concavities). If this process continues far enough to produce a density of around 0.83 Mg m^{-3} (porosity around 10%), the pores no longer interconnect and it is more appropriate (and conventional) to describe the material as ice. Snow that has survived at least one summer is usually referred to as firn.

The quantity of snow in a snow pack can be specified by its thickness (measured perpendicular to the surface on which it lies) or its depth (measured vertically). The total amount of material contained within the snow pack is normally specified through the snow water equivalent (SWE), which is the depth of water that would be produced by melting the snow. This is given by

$$d_w = \frac{1}{\rho_w} \int_0^d \rho \, dz,$$

where d is the snow depth, ρ is its density at depth z, and ρ_w is the density of water. If the density ρ of the snow can be taken as constant, this formula is simplified to

$$d_w = \frac{\rho d}{\rho_w}.$$

The latent heat of fusion of pure ice is 330 kJ kg^{-1}, so that the heat input required to melt 1 cm of water from 1 m^2 of ice or dry snow at 0°C is 3.3 MJ. The thermal quality of snow is defined as the ratio of the heat input required to produce a given mass of water to the heat input required to produce the same mass of water by melting pure ice at 0°C. If the temperature of the snow is below 0°C, the thermal quality is greater than 1, since heat input is also needed to warm the snow to 0°C. The specific heat capacity of ice is 2.1 kJ kg^{-1} K^{-1}, so (e.g.) the thermal quality of snow at −20°C is around 1.13. On the other hand, if the snow is at 0°C and already contains some liquid water, the thermal quality will be less than 1. For example, snow with a density of 0.4 Mg m^{-3} and a liquid water content of 10% by volume has a thermal quality of 0.75. The melting of snow by warm air can be represented by a dependence on the number of *degree-days* of thaw. The number of degree-days is the integral of the positive Celsius temperature (negative temperatures are ignored) with respect to the time measured in days, and a commonly used assumption is that each degree-day of thaw will melt 0.5 cm of water. Thus, for example, 10 degree-days of thaw will produce 50,000 m^3 of meltwater from 1 km^2 of snow. Such an assumption forms the basis of snow hydrology models.

The thermal conductivity of snow increases with density, from about 0.01 W m^{-1} K^{-1} (comparable to that of thermal insulators such as glass wool and expanded polystyrene) at a density of 0.1 Mg m^{-3} to 2 W m^{-1} K^{-1} for pure ice. The presence of a snow pack on soil reduces the amplitude of thermal fluctuations in the soil, and can protect autumn-sown agricultural crops (e.g., winter wheat) during the winter.

Fresh snow has a particularly high albedo, typically between 80% and 90%, which is climatically significant. The albedo is uniformly high throughout the visible part of the electromagnetic spectrum, meaning that snow is white. As the snow ages, its albedo decreases as a result of weathering and the adsorption of dust or soot. An empirical relationship between age and albedo can be used, in the absence of other information, to estimate the age and hence density of a snow pack. Light is quite strongly attenuated on passing through snow, the intensity being reduced to 1% by about 20 cm of dry snow. Since the optical absorption by ice is negligible, this attenuation is almost entirely due to scattering at the interfaces between the ice grains and air.

In the microwave region, the dielectric constant of snow depends on the frequency, the density of the snow, and the amount of liquid water contained within it. Dry snow is practically transparent to microwave radiation, while a water content of only 0.5% by volume reduces the attenuation length to a few tens of centimeters, and when the water content is as high as 5% the attenuation length is only a few centimeters.

Mapping Snow Cover

Mapping of snow cover can be performed in situ for small drainage basins, by sampling the snow depth and characteristics at a number of locations and then interpolating and extrapolating from these measurements. This is not a practical approach for larger areas, and some form of remote sensing is needed. Aerial photography reveals the spatial extent of the snow cover very straightforwardly, because of the characteristically high albedo of snow. For quantitative measurement of the snow extent in areas of significant relief, it is necessary to correct the geometry photograph for distortions due to the viewing perspective. It is, furthermore, not possible to estimate the SWE from a single aerial photograph, although a series of photographs acquired throughout the accumulation season can allow the SWE to be estimated. Satellite remote-sensing observations in the visible and near-infrared (VIR) regions of the electromagnetic spectrum provide data similar to aerial photographs. There are advantages and disadvantages to

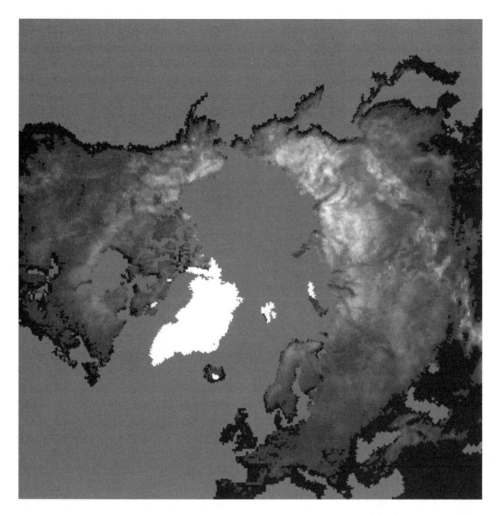

Estimate of the total snow amount (depth integrated over time) in the circumarctic region in 1986, shown as shades of gray. The primary data were derived from the NIMBUS-7 SMMR satellite microwave radiometer (Chang, A.T.C., J.L. Foster & D.K. Hall, "Nimbus-7 SMMR derived global snow cover parameters." *Annals of Glaciology*, 9(1987): 39–44), downloaded from the website at http://www.ngdc.noaa.gov/seg/eco/cdroms/gedii_b/datasets/b08/cs.htm, and further processed at the Scott Polar Research Institute, Cambridge.

both approaches. Compared with aerial photography, satellite imagery generally has a coarser spatial resolution but a correspondingly wider coverage. The data are normally digital, so easier to import into and process using a computer. The higher-resolution data sets are not generally available immediately after reception (there may be a delay of weeks or months), but, on the other hand regular, sampling of a given study area is normally automatic. Cloud cover introduces two difficulties in the analysis of VIR imagery of snow. The first of these is that, at wavelengths up to about 1.2 μm, the reflectances (albedos) of snow and optically thick cloud are very similar so that discrimination of snow from cloud is difficult. This problem can be resolved in various ways, including the analysis of spatial texture or the use of an observation at a wavelength of about 1.5 or 1.6 μm (unlike cloud, snow has a very low reflectance at this wavelength) or in the thermal infrared part of the electromagnetic spectrum. The second, more obvious, problem introduced by cloud is the fact that it obscures the Earth's surface from view, so that no data can be derived concerning the snow cover beneath it. Nevertheless, satellite VIR remote-sensing data are widely used for snow surveys. For example, Landsat

imagery, with a spatial resolution of 30 m, a swath width of 185 km, and a revisit period of 16 days (or less in favorable circumstances), can be used for large drainage basins, while Advanced Very High Resolution Radiometer (AVHRR) data, with a resolution of 1 km, a swath width of 2500 km, and several viewing opportunities per day, are used for regional and global snow monitoring.

Remote-sensing techniques in the VIR region offer some limited scope for discriminating wet snow from dry snow, since the albedo is reduced when the snow begins to melt; but this approach is difficult to apply in practice since it requires well-calibrated data with good atmospheric correction. It is also difficult to estimate snow depth or SWE from VIR data, as noted earlier. These factors have prompted interest in alternative remote-sensing methods for snow cover. Passive microwave measurements, detecting naturally occurring (black body) radiation at wavelengths between a few millimeters and a few centimeters, can be used to estimate the depth of dry snow and the onset of melting. However, the spatial resolution of passive microwave systems when operated from space is very poor, typically a few tens of kilometers, so this

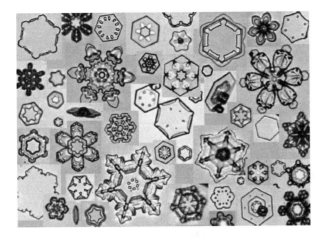

Mosaic of laboratory-grown snow crystals.
Courtesy of Kenneth G Libbrecht, California Institute of Technology (see http://www.snowcrystals.net)

technique is only actually useful for regional and global snow mapping. For basin-scale mapping, it can be used as an airborne technique, as can gamma-ray remote sensing. This technique uses the absorption of naturally occurring gamma radiation by an overlying snow layer to estimate the SWE up to about 30 cm. However, the greatest interest is currently being shown in the potential of Synthetic Aperture Radar (SAR) methods.

Spaceborne SAR images can give a spatial resolution of 10 m or better from a narrow swath (of the order of 100 km), and somewhat coarser from a wider swath. They are thus potentially suitable for monitoring at the drainage basin scale. At the operating wavelengths typical of spaceborne SAR systems (5–25 cm), dry snow is practically transparent and cannot be distinguished from snow-free terrain unless it is many meters deep. However, a wet snow cover (with a liquid water content of 1% or more) can generally be discriminated from snow-free terrain, provided it is more than a few centimeters deep, with an accuracy of at least 70%. Spaceborne SAR systems currently (2001) in operation probably cannot be used to extract more information than this, but it is likely that more sophisticated instruments scheduled for launch over the next few years will allow the estimation of various parameters of the snow pack, possibly including the SWE.

GARETH REES

See also **Precipitation and Moisture**

Further Reading

Bentley, W.A. & W.J. Humphreys, *Snow Crystals*, New York: Dover Books, 1962. (reissue of original 1931 edition)
Gray, D.M. & D.H. Male, *Handbook of Snow*, Toronto: Pergamon Press, 1981
Hall, D.K. & J. Martinec, *Remote Sensing of Ice and Snow*, London: Chapman & Hall, 1985
Kepler, J., *Strena, seu De Nive Sexangula*, Frankfort am Main: Godfrey Tampach (Reissued and translated by Clarendon Press, Oxford, in 1966 as '*The six-cornered snowflake*', edited by C Hardie), 1611
Kirk, R., *Snow* (2nd edition), Seattle: University of Washington Press, 1998
Mergen, B., *Snow in America*, Washington: Smithsonian Institution Press, 1997

SNOW HOUSE

Human shelters made of snow and ice have a long history, going back thousands of years to at least as far as the Ice Ages. However, snow houses present archaeologists with a dilemma because the structures leave no ruins, no traces, not even an outline where they stood when they melt away. What is certain is that long before vaulted constructions and arches had made it into European architecture, some of the Inuit groups inhabiting the northernmost regions of the North American Arctic had already perfected an ingenious way of cutting ice-blocks and arranging them into dome-shaped, hollow shelters, commonly known in English as an "igloo." The word igloo is actually an anglicization of an Inuit word (*igdlu* or *illu* in different dialects) that simply described house or dwelling (but no more). For snow houses, a separate terminology was in use: in Greenland, for instance, a snow house (which an English-speaker would call an igloo) is actually an *illuigaq*. An igloo has vast advantages over a tent: it is more spacious, more solid, more quiet, and drier. It offers almost 100% protection against a storm and it can be warmed to an extent that the temperature inside an igloo lies 50°C above that of the outside world. At an outside temperature of –46°C, for instance, the temperature of the sleeping platform inside the igloo would be –6°C, but at shoulder height a cosy +4°C would be measurable. Although the inside walls of an igloo would melt at temperatures above 0°C, a thin glassy layer of frozen water would soon cover the inside; moreover, accumulating snow from the outside would offset any melting that might occur on the inside. Building an igloo requires snow and a snow-cutting saw. The snow has to be of the right consistency; it must be neither too loose and fluffy nor too hard and compact. The ideal snow for an igloo is cuttable, wind-packed and light, and the ideal snow saw has a length of 50 cm and a serrated blade of 5 cm height. The site for the igloo need not necessarily be flat, but the construction always begins with a drawing in the snow of the circular outline of the igloo's base. A diameter of 180 cm (corresponding to the inside dimension of the igloo, because the freshly cut snow blocks will be placed at the outer edge of the circle) is regarded as ideal. The entrance of the igloo is planned in such a way that it is at right angle to the prevailing wind. Cutting the snow blocks is tricky and starts with the

A traditonal snow house built with blocks of snow, Igloolik, Northwest Territories, Canada.
Copyright Bryan and Cherry Alexander Photography

biggest block, which is destined to cover the entrance trench. The correct placing of the blocks, which should measure approximately 20 × 40 × 70 cm, is not easy, but initially not too difficult. As the work progresses, however, and the snow walls begin to bend inward, placement of the snow blocks must follow a spiral that at the end leaves open only the hole for the centerpiece of the snow roof. If a gas-cooker or even candles will be used in the igloo, an opening in the roof is essential so that the poisonous carbonmonoxide can escape. To put the last snow-brick in place is the easiest part of the whole operation. In the end, only the gaps between the snow blocks need to be filled with snow for wind-proofing. The finished igloo is a strong structure and can easily carry the weight of a polar bear (should one climb onto the igloo). The entrance trench is usually sufficient, but a tunnellike entrance can be fitted to the igloo during stormy weather. Inside the igloo, the deeper trench can continue, so that on either side of it the sleeping platforms are somewhat elevated. That way one can sit on the sleeping platforms as if they were benches, but one gives up valuable floor space. In another design, the entrance trench terminates just behind the entrance block, which makes entering and leaving the igloo more difficult, but increases the sleeping space. That simple igloolike shelters can also be constructed without snow blocks is something many Antarctic researchers, including this writer, had to learn during their survival training in Antarctica. At first, with spades and shovels (and in a real emergency even by hand) loose snow is heaped into a big pile. The weight of the small hill compresses the snow and after 2 h or so one can hollow out the hill and thus create space inside to shelter several people. This kind of shelter will not cave in and, like a true igloo, is

strong enough to carry the weight of a grown-up person, provided the excavations have not left the roof too thin. The most sophisticated snow houses are undoubtedly the so-called ice hotels, of which several now exist and cater to the adventure needs of Arctic tourists in a number of Arctic countries. One such hotel, built in 1991 in Jukkasjärvi (Swedish Lappland), is completely constructed with ice and accommodates 130 people a night on beds also made of ice.

V.B. MEYER-ROCHOW

See also **Housing**

Further Reading

Freuchen, P., *Book of the Eskimos*, Greenwich: Fawcett Crest Book, 1961
Shemie, B., *Houses of Snow, Skin, and Bone: Native Dwellings of the Far North*, Plattsburgh: Tundra Books, 1989
Weyer, E.M., *The Eskimos*, Hemden, Connecticut: Archon, 1962
Yue, C. & D. Yue, *The Igloo*, Boston: Houghton Mifflin, 1988

SNOW PATCHES

Snow patches (snow banks, snow beds) are formed in concave landforms where snow accumulates throughout the winter both in the Arctic and further south in the mountain alpine belt, for example in British Columbia. Snow patches are common over the circumpolar Arctic, but are especially important in oceanic mountainous areas with high winter precipitation, where long-lying snow may cover large areas. Sheltered from the sun, snow patches may remain nearly all year round, only melting at the height of summer. Long-lying snow turns into firn (coarse-grained snow and granular ice) and ice, representing an initial stage of glacier formation.

The major environmental effect of long-lying snow is a growing season much shorter than in neighboring habitats, due to reduction of solar radiation available for photosynthesis. This is especially important within the Arctic where the growing season is already short. Snow patches reduce temperature fluctuations and protect against severe winds. The soil texture is mostly intermediate to coarse due to leaching at the onset of melting. The down-slope portion of a snow patch habitat is usually rich in accumulated organic matter forming a rendzina-like soil.

Low Arctic snow-rich habitats can be subdivided into two types with different environmental effects, depending on the depth of snow. The depth of snow in extremely late-snow habitats is greater than 5 m, snow not melting until mid-July or later. Arctic and Arctic-alpine plants adapted to a very reduced growth season can survive here, forming open herbaceous and herb-prostrate willow (*Salix polaris, S. herbacea*) communities. *Salix polaris* is characteristic of very snow-rich habitats for both basic and acid soils in North America, whereas in the corresponding habitats in Scandinavia *S. polaris* is found only on basic soils, with *S. herbacea* as a counterpart on acid soils. Prostrate forbs such as *Koenigia islandica, Ranunculus pygmaeus, R. sulphureus, R. nivalis, Minuartia biflora,* and *Saxifraga hyperborean,* and grass *Phippsia algida* indicate very snow-rich environments over the circumpolar Low Arctic. Arctic willow and many snow-bed plants of the Low Arctic are also common in mesic tundra of the High Arctic. Most obligate snow patch species or chionophytes are probably of alpine or Arctic origin, which were already present at high latitudes before the disappearance of forests from the Arctic during the late Neogene. The humid cool climate of the early Pleistocene may have been favorable for the wide circumpolar distribution of most tolerant species, which now occupy a wide range of habitats in the High Arctic.

The diversity of plants and plant communities is much higher in late-snow habitats with a lower (2.5–5 m) snow depth and where snow melts by the end of June or the first half of July. Here, plant types range from herb-grass and low dwarf shrub-lichen heaths of well-drained gravely habitats dominated by *Cassiope tetragona, Phyllodoce caerulea,* and *Diphasiastrum alpinum* to prostrate willow (e.g., *Salix reticulata*) stands and meadows rich in tall herbs. Herb species composition varies widely over the circumpolar Low Arctic. Medium-depth snow patch habitats are more favorable to plant growth than either high snow depth patches or normally snow-covered habitats because of snow protection in winter, little permafrost, high organic matter accumulation in the hollows, and no major reduction in the growing season. Boreal and relict species are usually found in the snow patch meadows.

Snow patch habitat plant cover of the High Arctic is reduced to a sparse herb cover of *Phippsia algida, Ranunculus pygmaeus, Saxifraga hyperborea, S. tenuis* with fragmentary moss cover of genera such as *Calliergon, Drepanocladus, Bryum,* and *Campyllium.* Quite often, snow patches are altogether devoid of plants, especially if the snow does not thaw annually. Snow patch meadows are important summer pastures for ungulates like reindeer and snow sheep, and some rodents (e.g., ground squirrel) both in the Arctic and the alpine.

VOLODYA RAZZHIVIN

See also **Herb Slope**

Further Reading

Daniëls, F.J.A. "Vegetation of the Angmagssalik District, Southeast Greenland, IV. Shrub, dwarf shrub and terricolous lichens." *Meddelelser om Grønland Bioscience,* 10 (1982): 1–78

Gjærevoll, O., "The plant communities of the Scandinavian alpine snow-beds." *Kung. Norske. Vidensk. Selsk. Skr.,* 1 (1956): 1–405

———, "A comparison between the alpine plant communities of Alaska and Scandinavia." *Acta Phytogeographica Suecica,* 68 (1980): 83–88

Razzhivin, V. Yu, "Snowbed vegetation of far northeastern Asia." *Journal of Vegetation Science,* 5 (1994): 882–894

SNOWSHOE HARE

The snowshoe hare (*Lepus americanus*), also known as the snowshoe rabbit, received its common name from the large size of its hind feet, a feature allowing efficient travel over deep, soft, snow. It is also called the varying hare because of its regular seasonal change of color from white to brown. In Alaska, this hare is known by the Iñupiat name *ukallik* in the North Alaska dialect and *ukalliurak* in the Kobruk River dialect. In Yukon, the Vuntut Gwich'in name is *Geh.*

The snowshoe hare ranges across most of Canada, and throughout Alaska, down the Rocky Mountains, and into the northeastern United States. The northern distribution of the snowshoe hare follows the treeline. This hare is found wherever stands of spruce and aspen provide food and shelter. The northernmost part of the snowshoe hare range is the Mackenzie River Delta area of the Northwest Territories. Snowshoe hares are not usually found on the tundra beyond the treeline, preferring the forest cover. Distribution maps show some range overlaps with the larger arctic hare, but the two species rarely occur in the same area. Little is known of the habits of either hare in the main area of range overlap in Labrador.

A medium-sized hare with large ears and hind feet, the snowshoe hare is smaller than both the arctic hare and white-tailed jackrabbit. Females are larger than males, with an average weight of 1500 g compared to 1300 g for males. The total length is from 363 to 520 mm, with a tail length of 25 to 57 mm. In the northern part of its range, the fur is white in winter, although the base of the winter hair is brown. The ears are tipped with a ridge of black. In summer, these hares are dark or rusty brown with a grayish chin and belly, and a white undertail. The fall molt begins in September and the spring molt begins in March. Both may take about 70 days for the full change in color.

Active throughout the winter, snowshoes hares are nocturnal, sheltering under trees, logs, or bushes during the day and feeding around sundown and dawn. Although they may use simple forms or scrapes for resting, they do not dig tunnels in the snow. Posture and behavior are adjusted in response to specific weather conditions. Resting and grooming are an important part of daily activities. During rest, snowshoe hares reingest their soft feces, a system common to all hares, which ensures full use of food nutrients. Hares eat various kinds of plants, including grasses, dandelions, berries, fireweed, and clover in summer, and buds, twigs, and bark of woody shrubs and trees in winter. In the north, they select the bark of birch, willow, and spruce when other food sources are absent or snow-covered. Living most of their lives within a relatively small area, female snowshoe hares have a home range of about seven acres, and males about 18 acres.

Snowshoe hares have an unstructured mating system, in which males and females may mate with several individuals. Consequently, the young in a single litter may have different fathers. No individual males dominate socially. Litters of two to four young can be produced up to five times a year, between March and August. After a gestation period of 36 days, snowshoe hares are born in the open in a sheltered area. After birth, the mother leaves the young leverets alone, returning daily only to nurse them. Born with fur and open eyes the young grow rapidly, reaching adult weight within about four months. Weaning tales place after one month. Hares live for about four or five years in the wild.

Hare populations in the north are known for their repeated fluctuations in size, with a cycle of high population about every 9 to 10 years. During the cycle, population sizes range from as low as one hare per square mile (2.5 km^2) to over 3400 hares per square mile of favorable habitat. Changes in reproductive success may occur three years before changes in population numbers, a phenomenon not yet fully understood. It has been suggested that such changes in reproduction may be associated with body condition, which is affected by nutrition or predation pressure. However, recent studies have found no relation between body condition and cyclic changes in reproduction.

Recent long-term studies of snowshoe hare populations in the Yukon have increased our understanding of the complexity of hare cycles. High hare population densities on small islands at the peak of the cycle have been related to higher survival rates due to a reduction in the number and types of predators, rather than higher reproductive rates. At the low point in the cycle in the Yukon, snowshoe hare population dynamics are dominated by the interaction of food and predators.

Analysis of the hare fur records of the Hudson's Bay Company and dating of hare browse marks on white spruce trees during times of high hare density show that hare numbers, tree browse marks, and sunspot activity are all correlated. The snowshoe hare cycle may be regulated indirectly by solar activity through a cyclical impact on the climate that affects the whole boreal ecosystem.

The snowshoe hare is an important link in northern food chains between the plants and the carnivores, and is considered a key herbivore, or plant-eater, in the boreal forest. Changes in hare numbers in northern Canada have been correlated with changes in the numbers of Arctic ground squirrel, spruce grouse, ptarmigan, lynx, coyote, great horned owl, goshawk, raven, and hawk owl. In the northern Yukon and Northwest Territories, the chief predators of the hare are lynx, red fox, wolf, and the great horned owl.

Snowshoe hares are one of the most important of the small game mammals. In many parts of the North, hares are a regular and easy source of food. Due to their habit of using well-marked runways, hares are easily snared. The Vuntut Gwich'in of Old Crow, Yukon, hunt snowshoe hares for food by setting snares along trails or inside fences in suitable habitat. Hare skins are traditionally used for trimming garments and for women's hats and jackets. The skins are also cut into strips and braided for making blankets.

DAVID R. GRAY

See also **Arctic Hare**

Further Reading

Banfield, A.W.F., *The Mammals of Canada*, Toronto: University of Toronto Press, 1974

Boutin, S., C.J. Krebs, R. Boonstra, M.R.T. Dale, S.J. Hannon, K. Martin, A.R.E. Sinclair, J.N.M. Smith, R. Turkington, M. Blower, A. Byrom, F.I. Doyle, C. Doyle, D. Hik, L. Hofer, A. Hubbs, T. Karels, D.L. Murray, V. Nams, M. O'Donoghue, C. Rohner & S. Schweiger, "Population changes of the vertebrate community during a snowshoe hare cycle in Canada's Boreal Forest." *Oikos*, 74 (1995): 69–80

Burton, C., "Microsatellite analysis of multiple paternity and male reproductive success in the promiscuous snowshoe hare." *Canadian Journal of Zoology*, 80 (2002): 1948–1956

Krebs, C.J., T.N. Zimmerling, C. Jardine, K.A. Trostel, A.J. Kenney, S. Gilbert & E.J. Hofer, "Cyclic dynamics of snowshoe hares on a small island in the Yukon." *Canadian Journal of Zoology*, 80 (2002): 1442–1450

Murray, D.L., "A geographic analysis of snowshoe hare population demography." *Canadian Journal of Zoology*, 78 (2000): 1207–1217

Ranta, E., J. Lindstrom, V. Kaitala, H. Kokko, H. Linden & E. Helle, "Solar activity and hare dynamics: cross-continental comparison." *American Naturalist*, 149 (1997): 765–775

Sherry, E. & Vuntut Gwitchin First Nation, *The Land Still Speaks*, Whitehorse: Vuntut Gwitchin First Nation, 1999

Stefan, C.I. & C.J. Krebs, "Reproductive changes in a cyclic population of snowshoe hares." *Canadian Journal of Zoology*, 79 (2001): 2101–2108

Theau, J. & J. Ferron, "Influence des Conditions Climatiques sur le Comportement du Lievre d'Amerique (*Lepus americanus*) en semi-liberte." *Canadian Journal of Zoology*, 78 (2000): 1126–1136

Wilson, D.E. & S. Ruff, *The Smithsonian Book of North American Mammals*, Vancouver/Toronto: UBC Press, 1999

SOIL RESPIRATION

The total carbon emissions from soils at the global level have been estimated to amount to 60×10^{15} g carbon per year (*see* **Carbon Cycling**), an amount that approximates the annual global fixation of carbon in net primary production. Soil respiration is an indicator of the intensity of decomposition in the soil, and the significance of this process in the Arctic can hardly be overestimated since it is one of the key factors that determine the overall ecosystem carbon balance. A large part of the soil organic matter in Arctic regions consists of labile fractions, which could be easily transformed by microorganisms or available to plants, but that are currently withdrawn from exchange with the atmosphere because the soil is contained within the permafrost layer. Global warming, giving rise to changes in energy balance, will ultimately cause changes in the hydrology and thermal regimes of Arctic ecosystems. This may lead to enhanced soil respiration and decomposition of soil organic matter, which would greatly increase the emission rates of carbon dioxide from Arctic soils. However, if the main part of the stored organic matter is unresponsive to decomposition, the carbon cycle response to global warming may be relatively small. The sensitivity of the Arctic pool of soil organic carbon to climate change is currently not well understood.

All living organisms respire in order to generate energy for metabolic processes. The primary energy carrier in living organisms is the high-energy phosphate compound adenosine triphosphate (ATP). The energy needed for the synthesis of ATP is derived from oxidation-reduction processes in which electrons are transferred from an electron donor to a final electron acceptor. A wide variety of both organic and inorganic compounds may serve as electron donors and acceptors, but soil respiration is mainly concerned with the coupled redox reactions involving the breakdown of organic carbon compounds (heterotrophic respiration). Depending on the prevailing environmental conditions and the organism group in question, respiration may occur along various pathways that differ in their resultant yield of ATP. In the absence of any external terminal electron acceptor, other organic compounds may be reduced in a process called fermentation. This process results in an incomplete oxidation of the starting compound, with a relatively small release of energy and the synthesis of only a few molecules of ATP per molecule of reductant. However, when other external, inorganic electron acceptors are present, the substrate molecules can be completely oxidized to carbon dioxide (CO_2) and water with a higher yield of energy and synthesis of ATP. The maximum number of ATP molecules (38) per molecule of oxidized glucose is generated in the aerobic respiration pathway, in which the final electron acceptor is oxygen (O_2). The generalized process of aerobic respiration occurs according to the following simplified reaction, which is the reverse of photosynthetic carbon fixation in primary production (*see* **Carbon Cycling**):

$$C_6H_{12}O_6 + 6O_2 = 6CO_2 + 6H_2O + \text{energy}$$

Soils are often said to respire because of their ability to take up O_2 and give off CO_2 to the atmosphere. However, heterotrophic microbial respiration may also proceed anaerobically. In this case, the final electron acceptor is an inorganic molecule other than O_2, such as nitrate (NO_3^-), manganese (Mn^{4+}), ferric iron (Fe^{3+}), sulfate (SO_4^{2-}), or carbon dioxide (CO_2) (see Figure 1). The energy yield is low compared to aerobic respiration, but the utilization of alternate electron acceptors permits microorganisms to develop in environments where O_2 is absent. The anaerobic respiration pathway is therefore of great ecological importance since it renders microbial decomposition of organic matter in anoxic soils possible.

The term soil respiration is often used in the context of an ecosystem's carbon balance and covers a mixture of plant root and heterotrophic microbial respiration. Heterotrophic bacteria gain energy for cell growth and multiplication by oxidation of soil organic material to CO_2. Plant roots also use organic compounds for energy supply in root metabolism (growth and uptake of nutrients and water), but in this case the carbohydrates are synthesized in the leaves of the plants and translocated to the roots for oxidative breakdown. Oxygen is then supplied either from the soil or from the atmosphere through the plant tissues to the roots. In a constant climate, rates of soil respiration, carried out by obligate aerobic microorganisms, normally remain fairly constant until a certain low O_2 concentration is reached. A rapid decline in respiration rates can then be observed as facultative anaerobes and/or obligate anaerobes become active. This sequence may, for example, occur over depth in waterlogged soils, since diffusion of O_2 in water is very slow compared to diffusion in air (about 10–4 times). In wet tundra ecosystems where the water table is close to or at

Entry: Soil Respiration

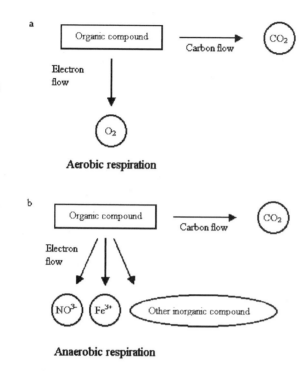

Electron and carbon flow in aerobic (a) and anaerobic (b) respiration.

contributions from plant root and heterotrophic microbial respiration may be difficult to separate out. Spot measurements of CO_2 emissions are commonly carried out by various chamber incubation techniques, in which the change in CO_2 concentration over time in an enclosed volume of air is measured. One obvious disadvantage of this technique is that the spatial heterogeneity of soil respiration may be difficult to cover accurately. Measurements of the integrated CO_2 emissions at larger scales may instead be carried out by micrometeorological techniques.

ANNA EKBERG

Further Reading

Christensen, T.R., S. Jonasson, A. Michelson T.V. Callaghan, & M. Havström, "Environmental controls on soil respiration in the Eurasian and Greenlandic Arctic." *Journal of Geophysical Research*, 103 (D22) (1998): 29015–29021

Illeris, L. & S. Jonasson, "Soil and plant CO_2 emission in response to variations in soil moisture and temperature and to amendment with nitrogen, phosphorus, and carbon in northern Scandinavia." *Arctic and Antarctic Alpine Research*, 31(1999): 264–271

Lloyd, J. & J.A. Taylor, "On the temperature dependence of soil respiration." *Functional Ecology*, 8(1994): 315–323

Oechel, W.C., G.L. Vourlitis, S.J. Hastings, R.C. Zuluet,a, L. Hinzman & D. Kane, "Acclimation of ecosystem CO_2 exchange in the Alaskan Arctic in response to decadal climate warming." *Nature*, 406(2000): 978–981

SOILS

Soils are natural bodies formed on the Earth's surface by the interaction between rock and living organisms (plants, bacteria, and burrowing animals), influenced by climate and topography. In the Arctic, defined as the area beyond the Arctic treeline, soils exist where vegetation exists. In the High Arctic, soils are discontinuous and intermittent with bare rock and ice.

Low temperatures and, in most places, the presence of permafrost are the dominant factors affecting the development of soils in the Arctic. Precipitation, which ranges in the Arctic from 100 to 1500 mm (annual average), is transformed into actual soil moisture in a complex way. Low temperatures lead to low evapotranspiration and a northward decrease in the ratio of liquid to solid precipitation. Permafrost is impermeable to the downward percolation of precipitation, meltwater, and river runoff. Permafrost is continuous in the Arctic, except for the European Low Arctic affected by the Gulf Stream, where it is discontinuous. As a result, soils range from being saturated almost all the time in most of the Low and Mid Arctic tundra, to being dry in the arid regions of the High Arctic and on steep mountain slopes.

Soil parent materials are diverse and contribute greatly to soil variability. Loose deposits (such as

the surface, O_2 penetration into the soil is therefore inhibited, and decomposition of soil organic matter occurs along various anaerobic pathways (*see* **Peatlands and Bogs**). One of the end products of anaerobic respiration occurring in environments with very low redox potentials is the radiatively active trace gas methane (CH_4). The populations of soil animals are often low in anaerobic environments, which further act to reduce soil respiration and decomposition of organic matter.

Apart from the O_2 concentration in the soil air, the amount of organic matter available for oxidation (the "food supply") is one of the main controlling factors of soil respiration. The chemical properties of the substrate are also of importance, since complex molecules are more refractory to breakdown than compounds that are simpler in their structures. Lignin (the major component of wood), for example, is a complex aromatic polymer of phenylpropane units, which is virtually stable to anaerobic degradation and it therefore does not decompose to any great extent in habitats where O_2 is absent. Soil temperature and moisture are other factors of substantial significance for soil respiration because of their direct relationship with the metabolic rates of both plants and microorganisms.

Soil respiration can be quantified by measuring the CO_2 emission at the surface. However, the individual frost-shattered rock and glacially deposited sediments) dominate the continental Arctic, whereas on many islands volcanic or calcareous solid rocks occur. Vegetation changes from continuous in the tundra to sparse in the polar desert. Soils are young (Holocene, or <10,000 years), because almost the entire area experienced either Pleistocene glaciations that stripped away older soils, or periglacial sedimentation on top of existing deposits.

Formation and Properties of Arctic Soils

No one soil-forming process is unique for the Arctic; however, the degree of their development, spatial extent, and combinations in particular soil profiles distinguish the Arctic from other regions. Cryogenesis is a process that is caused by the effects of frost on soils. Although also occurring in other regions, soil cryogenesis most completely manifests itself in the Arctic. Even though unfrozen water films and viable microorganisms occur within permafrost, identifiable soil-forming processes only develop above the permafrost, in a seasonally thawed layer called the active layer. The depth of thaw normally ranges from 20 to 200 cm depending on many factors. In general, mineral soils thaw deeper than organic soils, and those developed in coarse materials thaw deeper than those in fine materials. In the Arctic, solid permafrost associated with ice crystals, ice lenses, ice wedges, and massive ground ice dominates. Dry permafrost, which is loose with little ice, is less common, in contrast to the Antarctic. The impermeable permafrost prevents water percolation and supports lateral water flow on slopes. One of the striking features of Arctic environments that considerably affects soil movement and formation is the presence of patterned ground that exhibits regular symmetrical morphological patterns on the surface with a cell size from centimeters to several meters. Patterned ground is formed by frost cracking, ice wedge development, frost heave, stone movement, and ice segregation in soils. The main kinds of patterned ground are sorted polygons, nonsorted polygons, and ice-wedge polygons (see **Patterned and Polygonal Ground**). On gentle slopes, a viscous downslope movement of soil material called gelifluction is common, resulting in a pattern of lobate sloping terraces (see **Gelifluction Processes**). Soil mass movement associated with patterned ground results in disrupted soil horizons, broken horizon boundaries, burial of the fragments of the upper horizons, and similar features. A collective term for these processes is cryoturbation. Thixotropy, a soil's ability to flow under mechanical pressure, is characteristic of soils with a high silt content and affects their trafficability (or the ability to support the operation of farm machinery). Repeated freeze-thaw cycles favor disintegration of mineral grains in the soils in the Arctic. On the contrary, chemical weathering is impeded by low temperatures, and most clay minerals are inherited from parent materials.

Leaching and translocation of materials are weak in soils of the Arctic compared to soils in the boreal forest (taiga). Nevertheless, weak podzolization (formation of a poorly decomposed, acidic upper layer, a strongly leached gray layer, and a distinctive dark mineral-rich layer below) occurs on coarse materials in the Low Arctic, and isolated evidence of it can be found as far north as Svalbard. Strong mineralogical changes common in podzols under taiga are hardly possible in the Arctic; rather, iron coatings are removed from light-colored mineral grains producing the effect of bleaching.

The continental Arctic is dominated by plains and lowlands, which, in combination with permafrost, fine parent materials, and/or climate humidity explain the fact that most soils are wet or saturated and gley features develop in them. In these soils, iron, a principal coloring agent, is reduced to the ferrous state and is responsible for gray or bluish soil colors. The tundra is the only biome in which gleyed soils dominate upland areas. In East Siberia, however, gley does not develop in fine-textured upland soils. Low precipitation, oxygen-enriched melting water, and drainage provided by cryoturbations are responsible for its absence. The Russian name for these loamy nongleyed soils is cryozems.

A low content of ash elements in tundra plants and low microbiological activity lead to the accumulation of slightly decomposed organic matter. It forms surface organic soil horizons in addition to organic soils associated with peatlands. As the rate of accumulation depends on vegetation density, the process is best developed in the Low Arctic. Almost all peatlands in the Arctic are permafrost-affected, even in the relatively "warm" European tundra, where many mineral soils are permafrost-free. Oligotrophic bogs (i.e., with low levels of nutrients) represented by peat plateaus, polygonal peat plateaus, and palsas develop in the Low Arctic. In the High Arctic, fens are more common. They are richer in nutrients and have a thinner peat layer (see **Fens; Peatlands and Bogs**).

Salinization and secondary carbonate enrichment are better expressed in the High than in the Low Arctic. Soluble salts and carbonates appear in the soils developed in saline or calcareous materials, or near a sea coast where salt impulverization occurs. Otherwise, they are rare and not persistent, which is another important difference from the Antarctic.

Soil Classification

Until the 1970s, all classifications of soils of the Arctic were genetic, that is, by origin. Gorodkov, Tedrow,

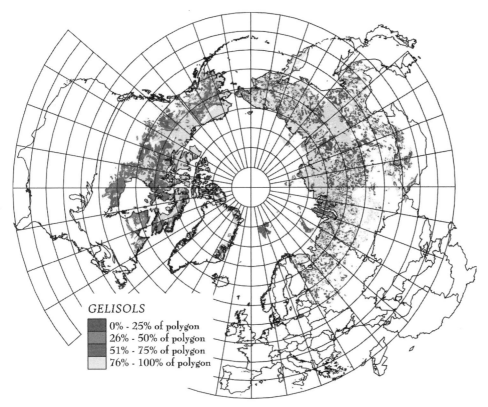

Distribution of Gelisols (permafrost-affected soils) in the Northern Hemisphere. From Tarnocai, C., J. Kimble, D. Swanson, S. Goryachkin, Ye.M. Naumov, V. Stolbovoi, B. Jakobsen, G. Broll, L. Montanarella & A. Arnoldussen, 2001 Northern Circumpolar Soil Map, Agriculture and Agri-Food Canada, ECORC, 960 Carling Avenue, Research Branch, Ottawa, Canada, 2001.

Everett, Liverovsky, Ivanova, and other explorers divided the soils based on soil-forming processes, such as podzolization, gleyzation, sod formation, peat accumulation, or salinization. Cryogenic processes were not considered to be soil-forming. Tundra gley, tundra bog, sod tundra, and Arctic soils were recognized in Russian classifications, and upland tundra, meadow tundra, bog tundra, Arctic brown, and polar desert soils were recognized in American classifications. Canadian pedologists (soil scientists) were the first to recognize cryogenic processes as soil-forming: in the 1970s, they included a Cryosolic order in their national classification. At the same time, US pedologists developed a new approach to classify world soils and called it Soil Taxomony. Genesis guided the selection of soil properties to separate classes within the highest categories, whereas soil properties that controlled processes were employed at lower levels, and quantitative diagnostic criteria were set. Artificial nomenclature indicated the position of every taxon in the classification. Most mineral soils of the Arctic fell into the Inceptisol order, which embraced soils whose common feature is a weak expression of soil-forming processes. In the 1990s, further development of Soil Taxonomy was undertaken, including permafrost-affected soils. Simultaneously, a World Reference Base for Soil Resources (WRB) supported by the UN Food and Agriculture Organization was developed based on a similar approach. Special high-level taxa were introduced to both systems to represent permafrost-affected soils.

In Soil Taxonomy, the Gelisol order contains soils, mineral and organic, with permafrost within 1-m depth, or between 1 and 2 m if cryoturbations and ice segregation are present. Gelisols are subdivided into three suborders: Histels (organic soils), Turbels (cryoturbated mineral soils), and Orthels (other soils). Further subdivision is similar to that of nonpermafrost soils and reflects the presence of gley, salts, sod, podzolic, and other features. Unique for the Gelisol order are Glacic and Ruptic-Histic subgroups, referring to the soils containing massive ground ice and those with a highly variable thickness of the organic layer.

In WRB, the Cryosol soil reference group encompasses mineral soils that have permafrost within 1-m depth. The group includes 19 lower level units, which reflect diversity of these soils. Histosols (organic soils) include ryic lower-level units for permafrost-affected organic soils. Ten other reference groups, such as Podzols, Gleysols, Cambisols, etc., include Gelic units, which encompass soils with the permafrost within 2-m depth.

Soil Taxonomy and WRB have been adopted in many countries. In Russia, the genetic approach to soil classifications is being further developed; however, more attention has been devoted recently to the correlation with the internationally adopted systems. The latest Russian classification (1997) recognizes one high-level taxon, cryozems, whose definition is based on cryogenic soil features. The taxon includes a few soils of semiarid and arid climates in which permafrost is supposed to affect soil formation to the greatest degree. Thus, it is incomparably narrower than Gelisols/Cryosols. Other soils of the Arctic belong to several high-level taxa, such as gleyzems, Al-Fe-humus, humus-accumulative, or metamorphic, whose definitions are based on soil genesis regardless of the presence or absence of permafrost.

Distribution of Soils in the Arctic

Traditional pedological subdivision of the Arctic more or less closely followed vegetation zones. Tedrow (1977) distinguished three soil zones in the North American Arctic: tundra, subpolar desert, and polar desert. He pointed out that podzolization does not exist in the polar desert, whereas gleyzation, peat formation, and salt and carbonate accumulation develop in all three zones, with gleyzation weakening and accumulations increasing northward. In the Soviet *Atlas of the Arctic* (1985), Tedrow's subpolar desert roughly corresponded to the northern subzones of the tundra. North of the tundra, on the Arctic islands, an Arctic zone was distinguished, characterized by a set of soil types, no one of which, however, was saline or calcareous. The polar desert dominated by saline and calcareous soils was only recognized in the North American Arctic. Later, based on new data, Goryachkin et al. (1998) questioned the existence of the polar desert soil zone in the Northern Hemisphere at all, with the possible exception for the Piri Land in Greenland. Sokolov and Konyushkov (1998) rejected a zonal approach arguing that moisture, and not a thermal zonality, is the primary control over pedological differentiation of the Arctic.

The concept of Gelisols/Cryosols changed soil maps of the Arctic dramatically. Cryogenic properties of the northern soils, most clearly distinguishing them from the soils of other regions became the priority of mapping. A soil map of the Northern circumpolar region was compiled based on Soil Taxonomy. Turbels varying in ice content absolutely dominate the Arctic. The proportion of Haplels increases northward, and in the Low Arctic some Histels occur. The High Arctic has a large amount of nonsoil components. Non-Gelisol soils occupy small isolated areas in the Low Arctic; examples are Cryods (podzols) in Scandinavia and Cryepts (young weakly developed soils) in the valleys of big rivers. Gelisols also develop beyond the southern limits of the Arctic, in the Subarctic, and in a part of the boreal zone, where they are intermittent with the soils of other orders (Figure).

Use of Soils in the Arctic

Traditionally, the main use of soils in the Arctic has been reindeer pastoralism. Where overgrazing takes place, the soils are easily damaged. Farming is normally not feasible in the tundra, although yields of grasses can be obtained in some areas, especially those that are permafrost-free or close to the treeline. Thus, in the USSR, 10,000 ha of artificial perennial grasslands were established in the Vorkuta area (Komi Republic) to support cattle. Artificial drainage of thermokarst lakes is practiced in places followed by the establishment of natural grassland. Industrial development of the Arctic is especially intense in Russia. Construction and traffic easily damage and contaminate permafrost soils. Unlike some other soils, removal of the organic layer of Gelisols/Cryosols causes drastic changes in the soil temperature regime. Erosion, thawing of permafrost and thermokarst are common responses, and, as a feedback, there is damage to the constructions themselves. Icy permafrost needs to be protected from thawing during and after construction. Dry permafrost is normally more stable and should be chosen for construction sites wherever possible.

Global Ecological Significance of Soils in the Arctic

Only recently have soils of the Arctic been recognized for their role in global climate equilibria and environmental issues. Climate Change that will be amplified in the Arctic may easily affect soil thermal regimes and, hence, the underlying permafrost. Precise estimates of the soil carbon stock in the Arctic are not known. Soils of the tundra biome (comprising Arctic, alpine, and Antarctic) probably constitute 14–16% of the global carbon pool. So far, they have been a sink for atmospheric carbon. With increased temperatures, they may turn into a source, except, probably, the High Arctic (*see* **Carbon Cycling**). A change in albedo due to a shorter snow period may be very important in increasing CO_2 flux. Melting permafrost should change freshwater runoff to the Arctic Ocean. Thus, feedbacks from the Arctic are expected to be strong, which accentuates the necessity to continue research in this fragile environment.

GALINA MAZHITOVA

See also **Gelifluction Processes; Peatlands and Bogs; Permafrost Hydrology; Soil Respiration**

Further Reading

Goryachkin, Sergei, Nina Karavaeva & Victor Targulian, "Geography of Arctic soils: current problems." *Eurasian Soil Science*, 5(1998): 520–530

Jackobsen, Bjarne, "Aspects of genesis, geography and evolution of soils in Greenland." in *Proceedings of the First International Conference on Cryopedology*, Pushchino, Russia, 1992, Pushchino: Russian Academy of Science, 1992

Kimble, John & Robert Ahrens (editors), *Proceedings of the Meeting on the Classification, Correlation, and Management of Permafrost-Affected Soils*—July, 1994, Linkoln, NE: USDA, Soil Conservation Service, National Soil Survey Center, 1994

Lal, Rattan, John Kimble & Bobby Stewart (editors), *Global Climate Change and Cold Regions Ecosystems*, Boca Raton, London, New York, Washington, District of Columbia: Lewis Publishers, 2000

Reiger, Samuel, *The Genesis and Classification of Cold Soils*, New York: Academic Press, 1983

Soil Survey Staff, *Soil Taxonomy* (second edition), United States Department of Agriculture, Natural Resources Conservation Service, 1999

Sokolov, Ilya & Dmitry Konyushkov, "Soils and the Soil mantle of the northern circumpolar region." *Eurasian Soil Science*, 11 (1998): 1303–1317

Tedrow, J.C.F., *Soils of the Polar Landscapes*, New Brunswick: Rutgers University Press, 1977

World Reference Base for Soil Resources, Rome: FAO United Nations, 1998

SOLOVETSKI ISLANDS

The Solovetski Islands are located in the northern area of the Onezhsky Bay of the White Sea, 165 km to the south of the Arctic Circle between 35 and 36 meridians. On the west, the Solovetsky Islands are separated from the main land by the Western Solovetskaya Salma Strait. The distance to Karelia is about 60 km. On the east, the archipelago is separated from the main land by the Eastern Solovetskaya Salma Strait. The distance to Onezhsky Peninsula is about 40 km.

The archipelago includes over 200 small and six large islands. The largest is Bolshoi Solovetsky Island (246 sq km). On its east there is Anzer Island (47 sq km), on the south–Bolshaya and Malaya Muksalma Islands (17 and 0.57 sq km), and on the west–Bolshoi and Maly Zayatsky Islands (1.25 and 1.02 sq. km). The total area is 347 sq. km. Bolshoi Solovetsky Island, Bolshaya, and Malaya Muksalma are connected by stone dams: in 1828, a 300-m stone bridge connected Bolshaya and Malaya Muksalma, and in the 1860s, a dam of about 1 km long was constructed to connect Bolshoi Solovetsky and Bolshaya Muksalma.

The topography of the area is hilly with domination of moraine landforms in the central parts of the islands and sea terraces in the periphery. The highest point of the archipelago is Golgofa (Calvary) Mount (107 m) on Anzer Island. The archipelago is located on the eastern edge of the Baltic crystalline shield. Thick glacial deposits—sand and boulders, which in the periphery have been derived by sea waves, overlay bedrock. At the glaciation time, the total area of the islands was about 30% of the current area. Due to compensatory elevation, the islands have risen by 20 m and are still rising by about 1 mm per year.

Domination of northeast winds in the spring and summer time and southwest winds in the autumn-winter season result in a cool summer, a lengthy autumn, and a relatively mild winter. The average July temperature is +12°C (max +31°C), and the average February (the coldest month) temperature is −11°C (min −36.5°C). The cooling effect of the White Sea makes spring and summer temperatures lower compared to those on the mainland. The annual precipitation varies between 400 and 600 mm. Snow depth varies, depending on the landforms and vegetation, being below 40 cm in the open areas and up to 1 m in the forest. Due to strong sea streams, the area several kilometers wide around the islands remains free of ice even in most severe winters.

There are 562 lakes on the islands but no rivers and very few brooks. The biggest lake Krasnoe (250 hectares) is located on Bolshoi Solovetsky Island. Lakes cover 13% of the total area of the archipelago. By origin, lakes are classified into three main types: glacial, glacial-tectonic, and relic. Lake depth varies from 2 to 15 m, reaching 33.5 m in the glacial-tectonic lakes. In the 16th century, a number of large lakes on Bolshoi Solovetsky Island were connected by canals. At the beginning of the 20th century, the canals were widened, deepened, and their banks were consolidated. The total canal length is about 1600 m.

Vegetation is varied and includes marshes, coastal grasslands, and various forests (fir woods, pine forests, mixed forests, birch crooked forest) covering 60% of the total area, and even the tundra (on Anzer Island). A significant area is occupied by man-made communities: irrigated marshes with heather bushes, meadows, and small-leaved woods on cleared space. At the end of the 19th century, a botanic garden was founded on Bolshoi Solovetsky Island, where one can find Siberian pine, Siberian larch, silver fir, ash tree, maple, hawthorn, and barberry, among others.

Fauna of the Solovetsky Islands is similar to the north taiga mainland fauna; however, its biodiversity is lower. Onshore mammals include fox, alpine hare, squirrel, and bank vole. In 1928–1929, muskrat was introduced. In the 16th century, reindeers from Lapland were brought there and inhabited the islands till 1944. In 1962, another attempt was undertaken to introduce reindeers on Solovki: 47 animals were brought from Kanin Peninsula, and in 1988 another 15 reindeers were brought from the Arkhangel'sk Oblast'. At present, there are several tens of reindeers inhabiting tundra ecosystems on Anzer Island.

Avifauna of the islands is much more rich. Over 200 bird species nest and rest on the islands during migrations from Western Europe to the Arctic. Among nesting Red Data Book species, there are fish hawk and erne. Small islands are nesting grounds for seagulls, arctic tern, common eider, and shell duck.

The first appearance of people on the islands dates back to the 5th millennium BP. Mesolithic sites on Bolshoi Solovetsky and Muksalma Islands belong to that period. Stone labyrinths, dolmens, and mounds are dated back to the Late Stone Age (2nd millennium BP). Major archaeological sites of the Late Stone Age culture have been found on Bolshoi Zayatsky Island. In the 12th and 13th centuries CE, people from the town of Novgorod visited the islands for hunting fur animals, sea mammals, and fishing.

In the 1430s, the Solovetsky Transfiguration male Monastery was founded on Bolshoi Solovetsky Island. After the Revolution of 1917, the monastery was closed down and in 1923–1939, its territory was used as one of the first GULAG sites, the Solovetsky Specialized Prison Camp. In 1967, the Solovetsky state historical, cultural, and natural reserve museum was established to preserve the unique historic, cultural, and natural sites. In 1990, the Solovetsky monastery recommenced its activities. In 1992, the Solovetsky historical and cultural complex was put into the Records of UNESCO World Heritage Sites.

The Solovetsky Archipelago is an administrative unit of the Arkhangel'sk Oblast'. The resident population is about 1000 people concentrated on Bolshoi Solovetsky Island. A number of monks from the monastery now live in separate houses on Bolshoi Solovetsky and Anzer Islands. Residents work in the tourist industry, in the museum, and in life-support services. In summer, algae harvesting occurs in shelf areas.

The islands are connected with the mainland by sea (during navigation) and by air (all year round) from Arkhangel'sk. Passenger and cargo ships come to Solovki from Kem, Belomorsk, Onega, Severodvinsk, Arkhangel'sk, and Murmansk.

GRIGORI TERTITSKI

See also **Arkhangel'skaya Oblast'; Labor Camps; White Sea**

Further Reading

http://www.solovky.ru

SOMERSET ISLAND

Somerset Island (Canada) lies across narrow Bellot Strait from the northernmost tip of the North American mainland, Boothia Peninsula. One of the mid-sized islands in the center of the Arctic Archipelago, it is about 9200 square miles in area, extending from Latitude 72–74° N and longitude 91–96° west. Barrow Strait separates Somerset from Cornwallis Island and the other islands of the High Arctic; Prince Regent Inlet separates it from Baffin Island to the east; and Peel Sound from Prince William Island to the west.

Its geographic names reflect Somerset's history of recent British exploration, but humans first occupied the island around 4000 years ago. Paleo-Eskimo hunters, bearing the distinctive tools of the Arctic Small Tool tradition, left the remains of tent rings scattered on many of the island's gravel beaches. At sea level then, these beaches are now many feet higher due to the isostatic rebound of the Arctic Islands since glaciation. Successive groups of Arctic peoples lived on Somerset, hunting marine mammals, caribou, and muskoxen. Most recently, Thule Culture whalers left the remains of large whalebone and stone houses. Thule Culture descendants were the Inuit whom European explorers encountered beginning in 1819. Much exploration took place along Somerset's east coast in search of the North West Passage, but the well-concealed entrance to Bellot Strait, often jammed with ice even during the openwater season, eluded discovery until 1851–1852.

Somerset Island consists of three physiographic regions. The northeast portion is mainly Paleozoic plateau, with numerous stream channels deeply eroded through soft earth. This plateau forms the steep cliffs (up to 2000 feet) of the north and west coasts. Sedimentary layers are visible in a subtle but distinctive palette, especially on clear midsummer nights. The plateau is arid. A cluster of diamondiferous kimberlite pipes are centered on Somerset.

A narrow strip on the island's west side, and about two-thirds of its southern portion are Precambrian upland of rocky, irregular terrain. Between the upland and the plateau lies lowland, drained by several lakes including large Stanwell-Fletcher Lake (in Inuktitut, *Tasealuk*). Muskoxen, Peary's caribou, raptors, and other common Arctic species frequent the lowland, where the foliage is thicker than elsewhere on Somerset. Prince Leopold Island, just off of Somerset to the northeast, is a rich bird rookery. Polar bears are abundant, especially on the north and east coasts. Cunningham Inlet on the north shore is an important beluga whale-calving site, drawing both polar bears and, recently, tourists.

Much of Somerset's human habitation occurred near Creswell Bay on the east coast. Fresh water from Stanwell-Fletcher Lake and the rest of the island enters Creswell through the Union River. Some historic buildings remain at Fort Ross near the east end of Bellot Strait, but the trading post was only open from 1937 to 1943. An Inuit outpost camp remained at

Creswell through the late 20th century. Idlout and his descendants were one of the last Canadian Inuit families to remain on the land after government settlements were created in the 1960s.

ELLEN BIELAWSKI

Further Reading

Dunbar, Moira & Keith Greenaway, *Arctic Canada from the Air,* Ottawa: Defence Research Board, 1956

Riewe, Rick, *Nunavut Atlas,* Edmonton: Canadian Circumpolar Institute and Tungavik Federation of Nunavut, 1992

SOMOV, MIKHAIL MIKHAILOVICH

Mikhail Mikhailovich Somov was a Soviet geographer, oceanographer, and a polar explorer. From early childhood, he became acquainted with the seas. After the Great October Revolution, Mikhail Somov Sr. headed a department in the Polar Institute for Oceanography and Fish Economy in Murmansk where he introduced his son to the North. Upon graduating from the institute as an engineer-hydrologist, Somov headed the Group of the Northern Seas in the Central Weather Institute in Moscow. For the navigation of 1938, the Group had developed one of the first long-range ice forecasts for the entire Northern Sea Route. Somov was also involved in the formation of scientific methodology for airborne ice reconnaissance, being among the first hydrologists to study sea ice states with the help of aircraft. His first scientific articles appeared at that time.

In the spring of 1939, Somov joined the staff of the Arctic Research Institute (ARI) and continued to study the patterns of hydrological and ice processes in the Arctic Ocean in order to create the reliable forecasts. In the summer, Somov participated as hydrologist-adviser in an expedition on board the icebreaker *I.Stalin.* *I.Stalin* was the first in history to complete a double-transit through the Northern Sea Route in a single season. The accurate ice forecasts made by Somov were of great importance for this success. In November of the same year, Somov became a postgraduate of the ARI. He worked on the Arctic expeditions as a hydrologist, providing forecasts and operational information for ship routing in the western segment of the Northern Sea Route. Under the supervision of N.N. Zubov, he also worked on his thesis, developing a method for ice forecast in the Kara Sea.

During World War II, Somov was engaged in the scientific-operational and prognostic support of the Navy and transport fleet operations in the Arctic, working at the Headquarters of the White Sea Navy flotilla in Arkhangel'sk and at the Headquarters of Marine Operations of the Main Administration of the Northern Sea Route in Dikson and in Moscow. From November 1941 to January 1943, he was in active military service. In spite of the war, Somov did not interrupt his scientific work and defended his thesis "Formation of the ice conditions of the Kara Sea" in April 1945. In his work, Somov suggested a generalized scheme of the annual cycle of ice cover development. He introduced into scientific circulation the idea that stable ice massifs formed in certain sea areas that affect navigation conditions.

In the postwar years, Somov continued to work at the ARI. In autumn 1945, he was dispatched as a hydrologist-observer to the airborne ice reconnaissance in the area of the Arctic Basin's "blanc spot." On October 2, 1945, during the polar night, the aircraft flew above the North Geographical Pole.

In 1946, Somov as a deputy expedition leader supervised researches on board the icebreaker *Severny Polyus* in the Central Arctic Basin. The expedition discovered an Atlantic layer spreading from the Greenland Sea in the intermediate ocean layer as far eastward as in the northern Chukchi Sea.

In 1948 and 1949, Somov headed one of the mobile scientific groups of the Airborne High-latitudinal Expeditions *North Pole-2* and *Sever-4* [North-4]. These expeditions made several important geographical discoveries in the Arctic, including the Lomonosov Ridge. On April 23, 1948, three airplanes landed at the North Pole for the first time in history. Here, M.M. Somov and P.A. Gordienko made an oceanographic station.

From April 1950 until April 1951, Somov was the head of the *North Pole-2* drifting expedition. A year-round complex of oceanographic, meteorological, and geophysical observations was undertaken at the station in one of the most inaccessible areas of the Arctic Ocean (76°01′–81°45′ N, 166°30′–167°48′ E). Somov personally conducted the oceanographic studies and collected valuable data on the distribution of Atlantic and Pacific waters to the eastern part of the Arctic Basin. He also tested a possibility of creating and preserving the runways on the drifting ice by regulating artificially the ice-floe surface melting. His research resulted in a thesis for a doctorate of geography "Drifting ice aerodromes," defended in 1954.

From 1951, Somov was the deputy director of the ARI on science. In spite of the responsible post, he continued participating as a hydrologist-observer in the airborne ice reconnaissance in the Arctic.

As one of the most experienced Arctic explorer and scientific expedition leaders, Somov was appointed head of the First Soviet Antarctic Expedition (1955–1957). The expedition set up a research Mirny Observatory in East Antarctica, carried out a wide range of studies under the program of the International Geophysical Year, and organized first Soviet inland Antarctic bases.

After his return from Antarctica in 1957, Somov was appointed the Deputy Director of the ARI (Arctic and Antarctic Research Institute—AARI, from 1958) on Antarctic studies and headed Soviet Antarctic scientific researches at the international level.

Up to 1964, in spite of health problems, Somov continued expedition work. Being the Head of the Soviet Antarctic Expeditions in 1962–1964, he personally was in charge of the summer seasonal activities. From 1964 until his retirement in 1967, Somov worked as a senior scientist in the AARI.

Somov's services were marked by numerous governmental awards. For successful fulfillment of the *North Pole-2* expedition, he was singled out with the USSR's highest distinction of honor, the title of Hero of the Soviet Union. The research expedition vessel *Mihkail Somov* (built at Kherson shipyard in 1975) was specifically designed for carrying out scientific observation and providing logistic operation in polar waters. Somov's fruitful activity in the area of polar research has also brought him international recognition. In 1959, the Swedish Society of Anthropology and Geography awarded him the golden "Vega" Medal. In 1961, the British Royal Geographical Society decorated Somov with the Golden Medal of the Patroness.

Biography

Mikhail Mikhailovich Somov was born on April 7, 1908 in Moscow into a family of modest noblemen, one on three children. Somov was married at the age of 24 to Serafima Grigorievna Somova (Generozova) with whom he had a son, Gleb. Several years after Serafima died, Somov married Elena Serebrovskaya. Somov died on December 30, 1973 in Leningrad. The main results of his work were published in the journal *Problemy Arktiki* [Problems of the Arctic] published by ARI. A list of his most important scientific papers includes: Construction calculation of the speeds of currents by the dynamic method between the hydrological stations of different depth, in *Meteorologiya I hydrologiya* [Meteorology and hydrology], 1938, No. 2 (in Russian); About construction of scheme of the ice drift in Polar Basin, in *Problemy Arktiki* [Problems of the Arctic], 1939, No. 5 (in Russian); On the direction of the ice forecasts development, in *Problemy Arktiki* [Problems of the Arctic], 1940, No. 1 (in Russian); The ice drift in the central part of the Arctic Basin, in *Problemy Arktiki* [Problems of the Arctic], 1940, No. 2 (together with N.N. Zubov) (in Russian); About influence of the Atlantic waters upon ice regime of the Kara Sea, in *Problemy Arktiki* [Problems of the Arctic], 1941, No. 3 (in Russian); Relation between the winter ice drift in the seas of the Soviet Arctic with the ice coverage of these seas in the consequent navi-

gation season, in *Transactions of the Arctic Research Institute*, 1943 (in Russian).

VERONIKA ZAKHAROVA

See also **Northern Sea Route**

Further Reading

Serebrovskaya, E.P. (Editor) *Mikhail Mikhailovich Somov. Vospominaniya druzei I znakomykh* [Mikhail Mikhailovich Somov. Memoirs of Comrades and Friends], Leningrad: Hydrometeoizdat, 1979

Somov, Mikhail, *Na kupolakh Zemli* [In the Cupolas of Earth], Leningrad: Lenizdat, 1978

Treshnikov, Alexey, "Mikhail Somov" in *Ikh imenami nazvany korabli nauki* [Namesake Research Vessels and the Researchers Whose Names They Bear], Leningrad: Hydrometeoizdat, 1984

SONG DUEL

The song duel occurred among the Inuit of Arctic North America and Greenland. (Apparently, Ivan Veniaminov, a Russian Orthodox missionary, also reported song duels among the Aleut, but as the original source is in Russian, they are not discussed here.) Generally, the purpose of the song duel was for two participants to fight through songs rather than physical combat. The participants were men (and sometimes women) who composed and performed songs about each other until one person was not able to reply and conceded the victory. Because the song duel was couched in humor, physical violence between the two parties was avoided. Since the song duel was an indirect means of social control, many 1950s and 1960s texts on anthropological law discussed this practice. However, song duels varied from region to region. For instance, song duels in Greenland occurred between men from different settlements, whereas song duels in Canada occurred between men living in the same settlement.

In West Greenland, the song duel was banned by missionaries in the 18th century, causing the practice to disappear by the early 1800s. In East Greenland, song duels continued until the mid-20th century. Early observers in Greenland were impressed that the Inuit maintained orderly social relations without physical sanctions even though they were "lawless." Later, many Europeans in Greenland attributed the increase in violence among the Inuit to the fact that song duels were no longer performed. A person initiated a song duel when he or she became jealous or resentful of someone from another settlement. The first party would challenge the second to a song duel and a time and place for the event were scheduled. Both parties then composed a series of songs about the other person, pointing out activities and behaviors that the other person committed that were considered inappropriate. Inappropriate behavior ranged from stealing from another's food cache to not providing for one's family. At the scheduled time, the two exchanged songs in front of both settlements until one person could not reply. Songs that produced the most laughter also determined the winner of a duel. When a winner was declared, several actions then took place. Sometimes, people from both settlements engaged in other contests of skill. This helped to channel aggressive tendencies into more peaceful activities. The ideal outcome was that a peaceful relationship between the participants and their settlements was established so that the exchange of material goods, marriage partners, and news of weather and hunting could occur. However, there are reports in which the loser and his settlement immediately departed. Although most duels were scheduled in advance, giving participants time to prepare songs, there were instances in which songs were improvised and performed on the spot. The end result of song duels was that physical violence was avoided. Not only was peace maintained between individuals and groups, but the youth learned what others felt was inappropriate behavior by listening to the songs and observing how transgressors were treated.

In Canada, outsiders recorded song duels among the Inuit through at least the mid-20th century. Based on the literature, it is unclear whether or not the practice has continued. These song duels occurred between participants, usually men, from the same settlement who were involved in a serious conflict. These men generally were not kin. As with the Greenland Inuit, the two participants exchanged songs of insult and accusation until one could no longer respond. The songs were composed to elicit laughter from the audience and the whole event was designed to be humorous, although an undercurrent of aggressiveness and animosity remained. Ideally, the audience's laughter diffused the negative feelings between the contestants and encouraged friendly behavior. Song duels did not necessarily resolve conflict, but rather encouraged what scholars Eckert and Newmark refer to as a "stable ambiguity." This is because song duels included elements of both joking and attacking, singing and arguing, and friendship and enmity. Although peaceful relations often occurred after a song duel, the conflict itself was not resolved and the issues behind the conflict were not openly discussed, which left the situation between the parties ambiguous. Song duels did allow everyone to witness the ridicule of another person's inappropriate behavior, which taught the rules of living to the young. Another genre of songs among the Canadian Inuit are "joking songs" in which song insults were exchanged, similar to the dueling songs. However, participants who exchanged "joking songs" shared a very friendly relationship and the event was only in fun. Since people in the community knew the participants of a song contest, they did not confuse which genre was employed in a particular situation.

In Alaska, song duels are still performed today in some areas, primarily in Yup'ik and Inupiaq communities where singing and dancing continued into the 20th century. In contrast to Greenland and Canada, Alaskan song duels occur between cross cousins (both men and women), otherwise known as "joking" or "teasing cousins," who could live in the same or different communities. Although an individual could have many such teasing cousins, since the cross-cousin relationship could also be determined through the grandparents' or even great-grandparents' generation, only a few are actually developed. Teasing cousins enjoy a close relationship, taking every opportunity to tease each other by calling names or insulting each other in public without getting angry. Since the relationship is based on a fun, close relationship, teasing cousins could point out inappropriate actions without violating the predominant rules of interpersonal behavior. Teasing includes the composition and exchange of songs. Since songs are performed within the community, everyone is witness to the ridicule of a transgressor, whose response ranges from being uncomfortable as the subject of the song to changing his behavior to conform to the rules of appropriate behavior. As in Canada, song contests diffuse interpersonal conflict and teach youth proper rules for living, but Alaskan song duels are closer to the Canadian "joking song" events in manner and intent than to the animosity exhibited in Canadian song duels.

Survival in the Arctic environment necessitated that individuals cooperate and live together in small communities. This created cultural norms that emphasized sharing and the avoidance of conflict. The song duel was an effective way to maintain peace, since they were employed to point out inappropriate behavior, but in a stylized and indirect manner that did not itself violate any rules.

DEANNA KINGSTON

See also **Music (Traditional Indigenous)**

Further Reading

Anderson, Wanni Wibulswasdi, "Song Duel of the Kobuk River Eskimo." *Folk,* 16–17 (1974): 73–81

Eckert, Penelope & Russell Newmark, "Central Eskimo Song Duels: A Contextual analysis of Ritual Ambiguity." *Ethnology,* 19(2) (1981): 191–211

Kleivan, Inge, "Song duels in West Greenland—joking relationship and avoidance." *Folk,* 13 (1971): 9–36

Rasmussen, Knud, *Intellectual Cultural of the Copper Eskimos. Report of the Fifth Thule Expedition, 1921–24,* Volume 9, Copenhagen, Nordisk Forlag, 1932

Rasmussen, Knud, *Intellectual Cultural of the Iglulik Eskimos. Report of the Fifth Thule Expedition, 1921–24,* Volume 7, Number 1, Copenhagen, Nordisk Forlag, 1929

————, *The Netsilik Eskimos: Social Life and Spiritual* Culture. *Report of the Fifth Thule Expedition, 1921–24,* Volume 8, Copenhagen, Nordisk Forlag, 1931

SOPER, J. DEWEY

J. Dewey Soper was one of Canada's first natural scientists of the 20th century to explore the Arctic and document its fauna and flora. Like others of his generation, it was a fascination with the Arctic, coupled with a quest for knowledge and pioneering spirit, that led Soper from his home on the Prairies to the Eastern Arctic. Over the course of his extended stays on Baffin Island between 1923 and 1931, he contributed thousands of specimens, many of them for the first time by a scientist, to the Natural History Museum (now the Canadian Museum of Civilization in Québec).

Soper's most notable discovery was the location of the nesting grounds of the lesser blue goose (*Anser caerulescens caerulescens*), later more accurately identified as a subspecies of the snow goose. While on expeditions, Soper spent an equal amount of time surveying the land and in this way played an important role in defining the geography of Canada.

Shortly after graduating from the University of Alberta with a degree in zoology, Soper was hired to collect specimens of flora, fauna, fossils, and geological samples for the National History Museum during the Canadian government's Eastern Arctic Patrol in 1923.

Leaving port from Québec City on July 9, his first voyage North involved living aboard the CGS *Arctic* while on its annual route to Greenland (where he received permission from the Danish government to collect specimens), the Devon and Ellesmere islands, and communities along the eastern coastline of Baffin Island. During stopovers, Soper made forays on land to collect the distinctive flora and small game found only during the Arctic growing season. Back on the ship, he spent hours pressing the plants and preserving the animal skins. His prize contribution from this trip, however, were the polar bear specimens he managed to capture as well as the frequent sightings that allowed him to make first-hand observations of them in abundance along the southern coast of Devon Island.

The following year, Soper was again hired by the National History Museum, this time for a two-year expedition based in Pangnirtung on Baffin Island. Again leaving Québec City aboard the CGS *Arctic* on July 5, he arrived in Pangnirtung 17 days later. Although there had been whaling stations and missions in the Cumberland Sound since the mid-1800s, when Soper arrived Pangnirtung consisted of little more than the newly opened Hudson's Bay Company post (1922) and the Royal Canadian Mounted Police (RCMP) detachment established the previous year (1923). Indeed, it was the recent formation of these two central agencies that allowed, for the first time, a scientist to work in this region for an extended period. Soper recalled that "Baffin Island was regarded as one of the largest virtually unexplored land masses in the northern hemisphere" (Soper, *Canadian Arctic Recollections Baffin Island 1923–1931*, p. 11). He set about collecting specimens during the warmer months and making topographical surveys during the winter season. Traveling by dog sledges and accompanied by Inuit guides, especially Akatunga, over the two years Soper explored and mapped an impressively extensive area, recording new landmarks as well as verifying or correcting previous ones, such as the altitudes of mountain peaks Odin, Asgard, Thor, and Tête des Cirques. The most difficult and memorable of his journeys during this period was from Pangnirtung to Kivitoo Point via the Pangnirtung Pass, a distance of 600 miles covered in 34 days. A second noteworthy exploration was from Pangnirtung to Foxe Basin on the west coast of Baffin Island, 650 miles covered in 37 days. From April to September 1925, Soper, accompanied by RCMP Constable Tredgold and Akatunga and his family, lived on the southeastern end of Nettilling Lake at Isoa, a traditional Inuit camping area but one previously uncharted by non-Inuit. Here, Soper caught a ringed seal (after which the lake is named) for scientific examination. The seal was later discovered to represent an unrecorded sub-species that was given the Latin name *Phoca hispida soperi*.

During the period of extended daylight, Soper recorded that he and his companions worked no less than 16 h to gather and preserve the abundant specimens for shipment back to Ottawa. They spent the remaining time conducting local explorations of the lake and river systems, in particular, the mouth of Amadjuak Lake. During this trip, Soper's attention turned to the blue goose migration and the question of their breeding grounds. Disappointed when the geese did not nest on Nettilling Lake, Soper deduced that their breeding grounds must lie between the Koukdjuak River and northern coast of Foxe Peninsula.

Toward the end of the two-year period, Soper made a one-way trip, from Pangnirtung to Cape Dorset, where he expected to meet the ship to return South. The route involved traveling and mapping new territory overland to Amadjuak Bay, with the final leg of the journey to be made by water following the coastline—a total of 525 miles over the course of 30 days. While finishing his summer at Cape Dorset, Soper met Inuit in the area who were reliable sources for

Iceberg near Cape Mercy, Cumberland Sound, Nunavut. Sketch by J. Dewey Soper (1975). *Photo published with permission from The Glenbow Archives, Alberta, Canada*

information about the blue goose (*kungovik*), and learned from an Inuit elder the approximate location of the birds' breeding grounds. This previously unknown information bolstered Soper's determination to return to the area.

It was not until 1928, however, that he was able to return to Cape Dorset and resume his quest. Even then Soper had to wait until the following spring in order to establish an observation site in advance of the annual migration. He spent the months conducting traverse surveys around the Foxe Peninsula. On this occasion, he established an astronomic station at Cape Dorset for surveying purposes such as reference points from the true meridian and to measure magnetic declination. A second major undertaking was to explore the unsurveyed area around the (later named) Hantzcsh River.

In mid-May Soper, along with five guides and dogteams, left Cape Dorset. They traveled to the site indicated by the Inuit elder, and further collaborated by one of his Inuit guides, Saila, at Bowman Bay over the course of seven days. Soper's team established their camp at the base of the stream now called Blue Goose River. By June 6, the migrations began arriving and on June 20, Soper recorded the first blue goose nest. Not long after, he wrote, "July 20 was a red letter day! On this date I was the first kabloona to see the wild young of the blue goose" (Soper, *Canadian Arctic Recollections Baffin Island 1923–1931*, p. 93).

Soper spent the following year at Lake Harbour, accompanied this time by his family. Because of an accident in early winter, the year's planned exploratory trip was canceled. Instead, Soper made ventures of a smaller scope that involved a few days travel but were nonetheless significant explorations of the river and stream systems inland from the community.

Above and beyond the numerous specimens collected for the National Museum and maps created for the Geological Survey of Canada, Soper left a written and visual legacy in his many scientific and popular publications, often illustrated with his own photographs and drawings. His published memoirs are a remarkable record of Arctic life and travel during this era when Inuit lived a seminomadic existence on the land. His trained sense of observation is coupled with a sensitive writing style, making his descriptions of the environment both accurate and poetic. In particular, the German naturalist Bernard Hantzsh seems to have held a particular meaning for him as the first ornithologist to reach the upper portion of Nettilling Lake in 1910 where he subsequently died of trichinosis. In Soper's relationship with Inuit, he was in keeping with the attitudes of his day, viewing them as a people perhaps less evolved yet untainted by modernism. He was, however, unstinting in his recognition and appreciation for the skill and knowledge of his guides upon whom his work and life depended. While scholars gain little insight into the thoughts of his Inuit guides during their journeys, it is apparent even from Soper's one-sided accounts that a mutual cross-cultural respect developed during their extended travels on the land. Soper's Inuktitut name was *Kiameate*, translating generally as "preserver of birds."

For his contributions to the broad field of natural history, Soper received numerous awards including an honorary doctorate from the University of Alberta (1960), the Commissioner's Award of the Northwest Territories (1978), and the Douglas Pimlott Conservation Award from the Canadian Nature Federation (1980). For his seminal work on Baffin Island, the Canadian Geographic Society named Soper Lake, Soper River, and Soper Highland in his honor. In 1957, the Canadian Government established the Dewey Soper Migratory Bird Sanctuary, a preserve of 3150 square miles whose international significance has been recognized by UNESCO.

Biography

Joseph Dewey Soper was born on May 5, 1893 in Guelph, Ontario. The family resettled in Edmonton, Alberta, in 1911 where Soper grew up, later studying at University of Alberta where he obtained a degree in zoology in 1922. Following his Arctic sojourns of 1923, 1924–1926, 1928–1929, and 1930–1931, he worked for the Canadian Wildlife Service as the first Chief Migratory Birds Officer for the Prairie Provinces from 1934 to 1948 and for Alberta, the Yukon, and Northwest Territories from 1948 until his retirement in 1952. He published over 100 scientific and popular articles, illustrated with his own drawings. Soper's photographs, paintings, sketches, field books, correspondence, and other papers are distributed among the Archives of the Canadian Museum of Civilization (Hull), National Archives of Canada (Ottawa), the Arctic Institute of North American at the University of Calgary, and the University of Alberta (Edmonton). He died on November 2, 1982 in Edmonton.

CHRISTINE LALONDE

See also **Baffin Island**

Further Reading

Martin, Constance, Search for the Blue Goose: J. Dewey Soper—The Arctic Adventures of a Canadian Naturalist, Calgary: Bayeux Arts Inc., 1995

Soper, Carolyn K., "A nurse goes to Baffin Island." The Beaver (Winter, 1964): 30–39

Soper, J. Dewey, "A faunal investigation of southern Baffin Island." National Museum of Canada Bulletin, Volume 53, Ottawa: National Museum of Canada, 1928

———, "Impressions of the Arctic." The Edmonton Journal, Edmonton: Alberta, December 29, 1923

———, "Intimate glimpses of Eskimo life in Baffin Island." The Beaver, 266 (4): 34–39, 64–65 and 267(1): 9–12, 66

———, "Ornithological results of the Baffin Island expeditions of 1928–29 and 1930–31, together with more recent records." Auk, 63 (1, 2, and 3) (1946) 1–24, 223–239, 419–427

———, Canadian Arctic Recollections Baffin Island 1923–1931, Saskatoon: University of Saskatchewan, 1981

———, Explorations by J.D. Soper 1924–26. In Southern Baffin Island, Ottawa: Department of the Interior, 1930

———, The Blue Goose, Ottawa: Department of the Interior, 1930

White, Peter, "J. Dewey Soper and the Representation of the Arctic." BlackFlash, 18(3) (2001): 4–11

White, Peter et al., Recollecting: J. Dewey Soper's Arctic Watercolours, Calgary: Nickle Arts Museum, 1995

SOUTHAMPTON ISLAND

Southampton is a Canadian island situated in the Keewatin region of Nunavut Territory. It is one of the ten largest Arctic islands with an area of 41,214 sq km (15,913 sq mi). Located between the Foxe Channel and Hudson Bay, the island is part of the Canadian Shield and the Hudson Bay lowlands. Some hills rise up to 600 m (1968 ft), but the surface reaches only 440 m (1444 ft). There has been no permanent ice cap on the island for about 5000 years. The coast is free from ice barriers between mid-July and November. The temperature varies in July between 4°C and 13°C (39–56°F), and between –34°C and –30°C (–29°F and –22°F) in February, and the annual precipitation average is of 282 mm (Environment Canada).

Typical Arctic vegetation is found everywhere except near the coast, where small willows, shrubs, and grassy meadows flourish. Walrus, beluga whales, seals, polar bears, Arctic hares, lemmings, Arctic fox, and short-tailed weasels are a few of the land and sea animals found on the island. Caribou and wolf populations disappeared from the island during the 1950s. Recently, caribou herds have been successfully reintroduced. Migratory birds like snow geese benefit from two protected areas: the Harry Gibbons Migratory Bird Sanctuary and the East Bay Migratory Bird Sanctuary.

The first people to inhabit the Island were the Paleo-Eskimo (Dorset Culture) at about 400 BP. Southampton is considered to be part of the core area of Dorset development. Thule immigrants replaced the Dorset less than 1000 years ago. The KkHh-2 site, dated between the 14th and 16th centuries CE, is considered to be "modified Thule." Neighboring Inuit described to the first explorers the Southampton inhabitants, the *Sallirmiut*, as the descendants of *Tuniit*, the inhabitants of Arctic before the Inuit came. It was later proposed that the *Sallirmiut* were possibly the last descendants of the prehistoric Dorset, but recent works disapprove this interpretation. Thomas Button came upon the island during an expedition for the North West Passage in 1613. He named the island in honor of the Earl of Southampton (England). The

Sallirmiut occupied the island when Button arrived. They died of European diseases following the establishment of the Cape Lowe Scottish whaling station in 1899. In spring 1903, only one woman and four children had survived. They were adopted by Inuit families and left the island. In 1924, the Hudson's Bay Company opened a trading post in Coral Harbor bringing Inuit from Baffin Island, Northern Québec, and Keewatin. The presence of fossilized coral in the region explains the harbor's name. During World War II, the Americans built a military transit base to Europe. It was thereafter used during the construction of the DEW Line stations.

Today, Coral Harbor is the only community on the island with 669 people, mainly Inuit (Statistic Canada, Census 1996). *Saaliq* is the Inuktitut name for the harbor, because of the flat island in front of the bay. Anglican and Catholic missions as well as a weather station, an RCMP detachment, a clinic, and, a school are present. A co-op, a northern store, public housings, and a hotel are other services and businesses available. Tourism, hunting, fishing, carving, and skin crafting are some of the major economic occupations in the community.

PIERRE DESROSIERS

See also **Button, Sir Thomas**

Further Reading

Clark, B.L., "The Lake site (KkHh-2), Southampton Island, N.W.T. and its position in Sadlermiut prehistory." *Canadian Journal of Archaeology,* 4 (1980): 53–81

Collins, Henry B., "Archaeological investigations on Southampton and Coats Islands, N.W.T." *National Museum of Canada Bulletin,* 142 (1956): 82–113

———, "The T 1 site at Native Point, Southampton Island, N.W.T." *Anthropological Papers of the University of Alaska,* 4(2) (1956): 63–89

Jefferson, C.W., J.E.M. Smith & S.M. Hamilton, *Preliminary Account of the Resource Assessment Study of Proposed National Park, Wager Bay—Southampton Island Areas, District of Keewatin,* Ottawa: Geological Survey of Canada, 1991

Mathiassen, Therkel, *Contributions to the Physiography of Southampton Island,* Coppenhagen: Gyldendal, 1931

Morrison, D.A., "Radiocarbon dating Thule culture." *Arctic Anthropology,* 26(2) (1989): 48–77

Rowley, Susan, "The Sadlermiut: Mysterious or Misunderstood?" In *Threads of Arctic Prehistory: Papers in Honour of William E. Taylor Jr.,* edited by David Morrison & Jean-Luc Pilon, Hull: Canadian Museum of Civilization, *Mercury Series,* 149 (1994): 361–384

Sabo, George, *Long Term Adaptations Among Arctic Hunter-Gatherers. A Case Study from Southern Baffin Island,* New York: Garland Publishing, 1991

Soubliere, Marion (editor), *Nunavut Handbook, 1999,* Iqaluit: Nortext, 1998

Sutton, George Miksch, *Eskimo Year: a Naturalist's Adventures in the Far North,* New York: Macmillan, 1934

SPACE WEATHER

Space weather arises from interactions between charged particles and the magnetic fields in the region between the Earth and the Sun. The aurora (or northern lights), magnetic substorms affecting radio communication, and radiation increases (X-ray and UV) during solar flares are manifestations of these solar-terrestrial interactions.

The Sun as a star generates energy from nuclear fusion of hydrogen to helium in its core. This energy travels outward from the Sun's interior and is emitted in two ways. The first is radiation in the form of heat and light from the Sun's surface, the visible disk also known as the photosphere. All living creatures on the Earth, plants and animals, benefit from this energy. The second mode of energy emission is the solar wind, which consists of particles of the Sun's outermost atmosphere, the corona. The solar wind blows away to distances beyond Pluto. Since the temperature of the corona is more than one million degrees kelvin, all the atoms in the corona are ionized, or dissociated into charged particles, mostly protons and electrons. The solar wind carries magnetic fields from the Sun.

As the solar wind particles approach the Earth, a few days after leaving the Sun, they tend to flow around the Earth at about a distance of ten Earth radii, because the Earth itself has a magnetic field like that of a bar magnet. As a result, the Earth is confined in a comet-shaped cavity in the solar wind. This cavity is called the magnetosphere. The magnetic field lines of the solar wind and those of the Earth connect on the boundary of the magnetosphere.

The solar wind and the magnetosphere together form a gigantic power generator, as the charged particles in the solar wind blow across the connected solar wind-Earth magnetic field lines. The generated power is more than one million megawatts. Like a neon sign, the aurora is a result of a high-voltage, high-vacuum electrical discharge powered by this generator (*see* **Aurora**).

The aurora appears along an oval-shaped, narrow belt in both polar regions. This belt is called the auroral oval, along which major auroral phenomena occur. Auroral activities in the polar regions are the only visible manifestations of solar-terrestrial relationships, namely, of space weather. In a sense, the auroral oval in both polar regions is the window from which space weather can best be observed.

Regions of strong magnetic field occur around complex sunspot groups. An intense eruption there causes parts of the corona to be blown away as clouds, causing a gusty wind. This phenomenon is called the coronal mass ejection (CME). When the clouds collide with the Earth's magnetosphere, the power of the solar wind-magnetosphere generator can increase more than ten times. As a result, the auroral discharge is increased. At the same time, the auroral oval shifts equatorward, often to the latitude of the continental US-Canada border.

The increased discharge currents in the magnetosphere and the ionosphere generate magnetic fields, which are recorded on the Earth as disturbances of the Earth's magnetic field, called geomagnetic storms. When CME clouds collide with the magnetosphere, the magnetic disturbance field shows a specific series of changes. The collision compresses the magnetosphere, causing a step-function-like change and signaling the arrival of a space storm. This phenomenon is called the storm sudden commencement (SSC). The magnetosphere then experiences a series of impulsive phenomena called substorms during which oxygen ions (O^+) flow out from the ionosphere to the magnetosphere, forming a belt of charged particles around the Earth called the ring current. This current flows westward around the Earth, depressing the Earth's magnetic field. This stage of a magnetic storm is called the main phase.

Auroral discharge currents also flow along the auroral oval with an intensity of about a few million amperes. The most intense part of this discharge current is called the westward auroral electrojet. The resulting magnetic disturbances and radio communication disruptions are most intense under the auroral oval.

This description is based on intense research efforts undertaken with ground-based instruments (e.g., all-sky cameras, photometers, magnetometers, and radio instruments) at many locations in the polar regions, rocketborne instruments, and spaceborne instruments.

Intense auroral activities and the accompanying discharge currents cause problems in electricity power grids, oil and gas pipelines, radio communication, satellite communication, radiation damage to satellites, and increased ionospheric drag causing difficulties in controlling spacecraft. The auroral discharge currents induce quasi-DC (direct) current on AC (alternating) current power lines. The added DC current on power lines causes problems in transformers and in other parts of the power grid, sometimes resulting in power blackouts in Canada and the northern United States. Effects of the aurora on GPS and other systems are at present being tested. The auroral discharge currents also induce electric current surges of up to 1000 amperes in oil and gas pipelines, requiring the Trans-Alaska Oil Pipeline to utilize various anticorrosion devices.

The ionosphere is greatly disturbed by auroral activities, making shortwave (HF, or high frequency) communication difficult or impossible. This effect is most serious in the polar regions. This is because high-energy electrons carrying the discharge currents cause ionizations in the lower part (the D region) of the ionosphere, which tend to absorb high-frequency waves. Satelliteborne systems can be damaged by being exposed to the discharge currents, which consist of flows of energetic electrons.

An intense eruption on the Sun's surface also produces low-energy cosmic rays, which can adversely affect human activity at both the space shuttle and orbiting space stations. Astronauts should avoid extravehicular activity after intense solar activity. These low-energy cosmic rays concentrate in the ionospheric region surrounded by the auroral oval, causing serious HF communication problems. This phenomenon is known as the polar cap absorption.

Monitoring of solar activities, auroral and geomagnetic storms, and forecasting their consequences on the Earth and the magnetosphere is necessary for "space weather forecasting." Although these consequences are global in nature, the storm effects are most intense along the auroral oval. The Sun is being observed by an international effort, including a few satellites between the Sun and the Earth, and solar activity data are assembled at the NOAA Space Environmental Research Lab at Boulder, Colorado.

S.-I. AKASOFU

See also **Aurora; Substorms; Upper Atmosphere Physics and Chemistry**

Further Reading

Akasofu, S.-I., *Physics of Magnetospheric Substorms*, Dordrecht: Reidel, 1977

——, *Aurora Borealis: The Amazing Northern Lights*, Anchorage: Alaska Geographic Society, 1979

Akasofu, S.-I. & S. Chapman, *Solar-Terrestrial Physics*, New York: Oxford University Press, 1972

Brekke, A. & A. Egeland, *The Northern Light: From Mythology to Space Research*, Berlin and New York: Springer, 1983

Carlowicz, M.J. & R.E. Lopez, *Storms from the Sun: The Emerging Science of Space Weather*, Washington, District of Columbia, Joseph Henry Press, 2002

Crooker, N., J.A. Joselyn & J. Feynman, *Coronal Mass Ejection*, Washington, District of Columbia: American Geophysical Union, 1997

Eather, R.H., *Majestic Lights*, Washington, District of Columbia: American Geophysical Union, 1980

Horwitz, J.L., D.L. Gallagher & W.K. Peterson, *Geospace Mass and Energy Flow: Results from the ISTP Program*, Washington, District of Columbia: American Geophysical Union, 1998

Suess, S.T. & B.T. Tsurutani, *From the Sun: Auroras, Magnetic Storm, Solar Flares and Cosmic Rays*, Washington, District of Columbia: American Geophysical Union, 1998

Tsurutani, B.T., W.D. Gonzalez, Y. Kamide & J.K. Arballo, *Magnetic Storms*, Washington, District of Columbia: American Geophysical Union, 1977

SPERANSKII, MIKHAIL

The prominent Russian statesman and legal reformer Mikhail Speranskii had a great impact on Russian constitutional reform in the early 19th century; also as

Siberia's governor general from 1819 to 1822, he reformed Siberia's administration. He was initially a teacher of mathematics, physics, and philosophy in a seminary, and held a secondary job as a private secretary of Duke Alexei Kurakin. With the ascension of Paul I, Duke Kurakin was appointed general prosecutor, and Speranskii held a post in his office. When Alexander I succeeded, Speranskii became state secretary, an exceptionally rapid rise through the civil service, and in 1802 he transferred to the Ministry of Internal Affairs.

Emperor Alexander I first became acquainted with Speranskii in 1806 and, impressed with his abilities, made him a close adviser. At the end of 1808, Speranskii was appointed a Deputy Ministry of Justice and worked on a project about Ulozhenie (code of law). At Alexander's request, Speranskii began to revise the civic code and work on constitutional reform of government, advocating a kind of constitutional monarchy, for which he was criticized by the conservative part of the nobility. Nevertheless, Speranskii succeeded in some reforms, the most important of which was the creation in 1810 of a State Council, the highest consultative body of the monarchy. As a result of intrigues by nobility who disliked his legal and financial reforms (including a tax on landed estates), in 1812 Speranskii lost his court position and was banished to exile in the town of Perm. Even in exile, he worked in the administration and was later transferred to be governor of the Penzensky Province.

On March 22, 1819, Speranskii, on appeal, was appointed as governor general of Siberia in Irkutsk with the aim of implementing administrative and socioeconomic reconstruction at the request of Alexander I. News about disorder and misuse of power in Siberia had come to St Petersburg, including the absence of food and subsequent hunger of local inhabitants and the disintegration of administrative machinery. The Czar had to take measures to strengthen local power in Siberia.

Speranskii revealed misuses of power by governor Pestel and of his secretary Treskin, who were sent to trial for graft and extortion, and with his huge plenary powers, formed a commission to study the administrative machinery of Siberia. The commission confirmed the necessity of administrative reforms and provided material for the reconstruction of state machinery in Siberia. At the same time as administrative reforms were occurring in relation to the Russian state, Speranskii paid attention to the system of governing the Siberian people, who were subjects of the Czar. According to his instructions, commissions were organized to study the beliefs and customs of each ethnic group.

As a result of Speranskii's work, several new laws were passed, the most important of which for the people of Siberia was "The Rules of management of the Siberian peoples," affirmed by the Czar on July 22, 1822. By this charter, the local (non-Russian) population of Siberia was divided into three categories of *inorodtsy* ("aliens" or literally, "of different stock"): settled, moving, and nomadic. The first category included indigenous peoples who lived in cities and who were busy with trade and service, the second included horsemen (Buryats, Yakut, and Chakas) who changed their place of living annually, and the third included the Even, Evenki, Yukagirs, Dolgans, Chukchi, Koryak, Nenets, Nanai, Ul'chi, and other aboriginal groups, who were hunters and fishers, moving from one place to another by rivers and lakes.

On public relations "foreigners" of the first category had rights and protections comparable to the Russian state krestyan (peasants) and were regulated under basic laws; "foreigners" of the second and third categories were a specific group, also compared to the Russian peasants, but distinguished from them by the system of control. Speranskii's administrative and economic reforms concerning the government of the Siberian people remained in place until the revolution of 1917.

In 1821, Speranskii returned to St Petersburg as a part of the State Council and Siberian Committee, as a manager of a commission on making laws. As a member of the Supreme Court, he participated in the trial of participants of the December 14, 1825 uprising in St Petersburg. From 1826, he headed two departments of the imperial chancellery, who published codifications of laws of the Russian Empire. Under Speranskii's guidance, the texts of the whole summary of laws of Imperial Russia were published in 45 volumes (1830). Speranskii was tutor to the future Czar Alexander II in 1835–1837, teaching him basic sciences. In 1838, he was appointed a chairman of the Department of Laws of the State Council.

Biography

Mikhail Mikhailovich Speranskii was born in January 1772 in the village of Cherkushino of Vladimirsky province. His father Mikhail Vasilevich was an administrative clergyman. In 1791, he graduated from the Alexander-Nevsky ecclesiastical seminary and remained there as a teacher before beginning his civil service career. On January 1, 1839, he received the title of a count. In February 1839, M.M. Speranskii died in St Petersburg and was buried there. He had a daughter Frolova E.M.—Bakhreeva. Most of Speranskii's legacy was published after his death.

PANTELEIMON PETROV

Further Reading

Chibiriaev, S.A., *Velikii russkii reformator: zhizn, deiatelnost, politicheskie vzgliady M.M. Speranskogo* [The Great

Russian Reformer: The Life, Work, and Political Views of M.M. Speranskii], Moscow: Voskresene, 1993

Fedorov, M.M., *Pravovoe polozhenie narodov Vostochnoi Sibiri* [The right position of the people of East Siberia], Yakutsk, 1978

Raeff, Mi., *Siberia and the Reforms of 1822,* Seattle: University of Washington Press, 1956

Raeff, M., *Speranskii: Statesman of Imperial Russia,* The Hague, 1957

Speranskii, M., O voennykh poseleniyakh [About military settlements], St Petersburg, 1825

———, *Proekty i zapisi* [Projects and notes], Moscow–Leningrad, 1961

———, *Obozrenie istoricheskich svedeniy o svode zakonov* [Review of historical informations about statute-book] St Petersburg, 1889

———, Plan gosudarstvennogo preobrazovaniya. Vvedenie k Ulozheniyu gosudarstvennykh zakonov [Plan of state reorganization. Introduction to state laws Ulozhenie], Moscow, 1905

———, *Polnoe Sobranie Zakonov Rossiiskoi Imperii* [Complete Collection of Laws of Imperial Russia], series 1, 45 volumes, St Petersburg, 1830

———, *Rukovodstvo k poyasneniyu zakonov* [Guide for explanation of laws], St Petersburg, 1845

Vagin, V., Istoricheskiia sviedieniia o dieiatelnosti grafa M.M. Speranskago v Sibiri s 1819 po 1822 god [*Historical information about the activities of count M.M. Speranskiy in Siberia from 1818–s1822*], St Petersburg, 1872

Whisenhunt, William Benton, *In Search of Legality: Mikhail M. Speranskii and the Codification of Russian Law,* Boulder: Eastern European Monographs, 2001

SPERM WHALE

Although this is probably the most familiar of all the great whales due to its distinctive large square head (Moby Dick was a sperm whale), it is still one of the least known of all large animals. *Physeter macrocephalus*, the largest member of the odontocetes (or toothed whales), is the only great whale with a single nostril at the front of its head; all the others have paired blowholes located much further back. Adult sperm whales have erupted teeth only in the lower jaw; these massive ivory pegs were occasionally carved into scrimshaw by Yankee whalers. Sperm whales are distributed from the tropics to Subarctic waters in both hemispheres, and migrate poleward in summer to feed. Females and juveniles are less likely to migrate far north, and only the large mature males are found in the polar seas, the Davis and Denmark straits, west of Jan Mayen, off western and northern Norway, and occasionally near Svalbard and in the Barents Sea. The largest male sperm whale is about a third again as big as the largest female. Weighing about a ton per foot, a big bull can be 60 ft long, while the females rarely attain 40 ft. They are dark in color; various authors have described them as "grayish brown," "lead-gray," or "dark brown." Both sexes have white lower jaws, and a mottling of white on the upper lip. There is usu-ally a white patch in the area of the belly, and the older males often have a whitish whorl on the end of the nose, the flattened area that is often referred to as the "forehead." When it exhales, the whale's spout is directed forward at about a 45° angle, which is a diagnostic feature at sea. The sperm whale has no dorsal fin, but it has a series of humps running down the midline of its back, the largest of which is located where the dorsal fin would be. On the underside, there is a curious notch, which defines the "post-anal hump." Aft of the flippers, the whale's body is deeply wrinkled, a characteristic that occurs in no other animal on earth. It is suspected that the hump and the corrugations on the whale's skin are somehow connected with its phenomenal diving ability.

In the spermaceti organ in the sperm whale's head, there is a huge reservoir of clear oil that may also have something to do with diving, but may be used to focus and resonate sounds. Sperm whales were hunted commercially in the 18th and 19th centuries for this oil. Like all odontocetes, the sperm whale relies on echolocation to find its food. It sends out sounds and processes the returning echoes to determine the nature of nearby objects, including its prey. But this only explains part of the problem: the whale still has to catch its food. Contrary to legend, sperm whales do not feed exclusively on giant squid. They probably do not feed on *Architeuthis* very frequently. Rather, the stomachs of captured sperm whales have revealed much smaller squid, but in much larger numbers. For years, cetologists have wondered how the sperm whale, operating in total darkness, was able to gather enough of the swift cephalopods to sustain itself. Finds of 5000–7000 beaks per whale are not uncommon, and one Soviet scientist found 28,000 upper and lower beaks in the stomach of a single whale, indicating a feeding frenzy in which 14,000 squid were consumed. It has been speculated but certainly not proven, since observations would require the prodigious diving capabilities of a sperm whale that the whales (and their smaller cousins, the dolphins) are able to stun their prey with focused bursts of sound, and then gobble them up at leisure.

We do not know what this animal does with a 20-pound brain, probably the largest brain of any animal that ever lived. (The blue whale, a much larger animal, has a much smaller brain.) It is likely that the large brain is involved in intraspecies communications; in addition to the echolocating functions, the sperm whale also communicates with its conspecifics by sound, using a complex arrangement of clicks, bangs, and wheezes. Sperm whales are among the deep-diving champions of the mammalian world, able to dive to 10,000 ft and hold their breath for an hour and a half. The substance known as ambergris (once used in the production of perfume) forms in the intestinal tract of some sperm whales, but we do not know why. Harpooned whales often vomit up lumps of this peat-like, waxy stuff, the largest of which weighed 983 pounds. The sperm whale lives in structured family groups, led by a dominant female, in an arrangement not unlike that of elephants. The babies, 14 ft long and weighing 2 tons when born, are nursed by their mothers for five years. The large bulls spend most of the year in high polar latitudes, visiting the family groups only during the winter breeding season.

Largely deepwater animals, sperm whales were not hunted by aboriginal whalers, probably due to their great size and because it is usually found far from shore. Indeed, they were probably first known from stranded specimens, and because they are so gregarious, they are notorious mass stranders, sometimes coming ashore to die in large numbers. Some of the more noteworthy records include 17 that died on shore at the mouth of the Elbe River in Germany in 1723; 31 sperm whales that died on a Brittany beach in 1784; on New Year's Day, 1956, 56 individuals died at Rancho San Bruno, Baja California; and in 1979, 41 sperm whales beached themselves at Florence, Oregon. So far, the only conclusions that can be drawn from these mass standings is that sperm whales stay together in death as in life; no assumptions can be made about parasite infestations, mass suicide, injured leaders, failure of the navigational system, or other possible explanations.

It may be an apocryphal tale, but the first sperm whales hunted by Yankee whalers are said to have been found by Captain Christopher Hussey in 1712 when he was hunting right whales and was blown far offshore in a storm. Within 20 years, an industry was born, and New England villages like Nantucket and New Bedford arose to the forefront of America's commercial centers. Thereafter, sperm whaling became one of America's flagship industries, and remained in the forefront for about 100 years, until various factors combined to reduce its importance and its popularity, such as the American Civil War (1861–1865), which swallowed up the young men who would otherwise have gone a-whaling, the California gold rush, and the 1859 discovery of petroleum in Pennsylvania.

With the demise of Yankee sperm whaling toward the end of the 19th century, the sperm whales were spared until Soviet and Japanese whalers discovered huge herds in the North Pacific, south of the Aleutian chain. (The Aleuts call the sperm whale *agidagikh*, and the Greenland Inuit refer to it as *kigutilik*.) During the 1960s, the height of North Pacific sperm whaling, the whalers were killing more whales every year than the Yankee square-riggers killed during their entire century-long fishery. Although they were heavily hunted during the 18th, 19th, and 20th centuries, sperm whales are now protected throughout the world under the International Convention for the Regulation of Whaling, and the population is believed to number more than 1,000,000 animals.

RICHARD ELLIS

See also **Whaling, Historical**

Further Reading

Berzin, A.A., *The Sperm Whale*. Izdatgel'stvo "Pischevaya Promyshlennost" Moskva, 1971 [Translated from the Russian by Israel Program for Scientific Translation, Jerusalem, 1972]
Caldwell, D.K., M.C. Caldwell & D.W. Rice, "Behavior of the Sperm Whale, *Physeter catodon* L." In *Whales, Dolphins and Porpoises*, edited by K.S. Norris, Berkeley: University of California Press, 1966
Ellis, R., *The Book of Whales*, New York: Knopf, 1980
———, *Men and Whales*, New York: Knopf, 1991
Mchedlidze, G.A., "Sperm Whales." In *Encyclopedia of Marine Mammals*, edited by W.F. Perrin, B. Wursig & J.G.M. Thewissen, London and San Diego: Academic Press
Norris, K.S. & G.W. Harvey, "A Theory for the Function of the Spermaceti Organ in the Sperm Whale (*Physeter catodon* L.)." In *Animal Orientation and Navigation*, edited by S.R. Galler, K.Schmidt-Koenig, G.J. Jacobs & R.E. Belleville, NASA, 1972, pp. 397–419
Norris, K.S. & B. Møhl, "Can odontocetes debilitate prey with sound?" *American Naturalist*, 122(1)(1983): 85–104
Rice, D.W., "Sperm Whale *Physeter macrocephalus* Linnaeus 1758." In *Handbook of Marine Mammals, Volume 4: River Dolphins and Larger Toothed Whales*, edited by S.H. Ridgway & R. Harrison, New York: Academic Press, 1989, pp. 177–233

SPORTING AND CULTURAL EVENTS IN CANADA

Arctic sporting and cultural festivals in Canada have a rich history. In the 1960s, the federal government provided funding for recreation programs in the Northwest Territories. The government's support of the development of recreation programs in the North coincided with the centralization and organization of northern life. As participation in traditional games and activities that were tied to seasonal festivities "out on the land" decreased, the government increased its efforts to provide consistent recreational programs (Paraschak, 1985).

Early attempts to bring ongoing recreation programs to the North were hampered by a severe shortage of facilities. Nevertheless, teachers, missionaries, and government officials from Southern Canada played crucial roles in facilitating the development of Eurocanadian sports in Canada's North, while local peoples also worked hard to keep their games alive. There are three main cultural/sporting festivals that have taken place in Canada's Arctic: the Northern

Games, the Arctic Winter Games, and the Dene Games.

Northern Games

According to Heine (2002), Inuit games were important for three reasons. First, games helped people to develop strength, endurance, and resistance to pain—all of which were important for survival. Second, the games had educational value that helped to prepare them for life on the land. Third, the games were used to celebrate culture. Glassford (1970) states that Inuit games were often associated with festivities such as whaling feasts and dark day celebrations. Glassford also found that at least one game, tug-of-war, was used to gain the favor of the spirit of the weather, with those born in the winter months pulling against those born in the summer months. If those born in the summer months won the game, it was believed that good weather would be on its way. In general, most games required very little equipment, equipment that could be quickly crafted from readily available materials, and very little space. These aspects of the sports helped to ensure that the Inuit, who were then primarily nomadic, could easily recreate the games when they moved camp (Glassford, 1970).

The Northern Games, an Inuit cultural/sporting festival, were established in July 1970 in response and resistance to the Arctic Winter Games (Paraschak, 1997). Some residents of Canada's North questioned the appropriateness of the Arctic Winter Games as they included only token Inuit games and were based on a southern-derived method of structuring sport. The first Northern Games took place in July 1970 and incorporated aspects of traditional games into a "euro-canadian-derived concept of a trans-Arctic festival in order to help create this emergent festival" (Paraschak, 1997: 12). The original Northern Games Committee consisted of Nellie Cournoyea, Billy Day, Reverand Doug Dittrich, Richard Hill, Tom Kalinek, and Kenneth Peeloolook (Wulf, 2002). Gerry Glassford, a researcher at the University of Alberta, also played a crucial role in helping to obtain funding for the Northern Games. The Northern Games philosophy encourages "participation over excellence and an atmosphere of camaraderie and self-testing rather than competitive equality" (Paraschak, 1997). Although competition is not the driving force, neither is time—the event schedule serves as only a rough guide.

Because the Northern Games had a non-Euro-Canadian sport focus, many federal government officials felt that they did not fit into a sports mandate. Instead, they viewed the Northern Games as cultural activities, thus making the acquisition of sport funding very difficult (Paraschak, 1983). As a result, although the Northern Games began as a trans-Arctic festival, funding difficul-

ties in the early 1980s caused the Games to change into regional festivals, which they continue to be today.

Some of the more popular Northern Games activities include Airplane, Arm Pull, Alaskan High Kick, Bench Reach, Blanket Toss, Caribou Leg Skinning, Drum Dancing, Fiddle and Guitar, Good Woman Events (include Bannock Making, Duck Plucking, Fish Cutting, Jigging and Square Dancing, Tea Boiling, Seal Skinning, and Sewing Competitions), Head Pull, Knee Jump, Knuckle Hop, Mouth Reach, Muskox Wrestling, Muskrat Skinning, One Foot High Kick, One Hand Reach, Two Foot High Kick, and Wrist Pull (Wulf, 2002). Although traditionally men and women did not compete in the same events, today it is common for women to participate in some male events, such as the kicking events.

Arctic Winter Games

The first Arctic Winter Games took place in Yellowknife, Northwest Territories in 1970, with Prime Minister Pierre Elliott Trudeau officially opening the Games. The Arctic Winter Games mirror the Canada Games, a southern Canadian multisport competition among provinces and the territories, and in the past included primarily Euro-Canadian sport that operated as a meritocracy based on skill (Paraschak, 1997). In fact, at the 1970 Arctic Winter Games, traditional arctic games were demonstrated but not contested. Arctic Sports were added as official events in 1974 (Paraschak, 1983) and Dene Games were added in 1990.

As time went by, the Games grew in size. Teams from Nunavut, Nunavik (Northern Québec), Northern Alberta, Greenland, and the Russian provinces of Magadan, Chukotka (and, for a short period of time, Tyumen) later joined the three original teams of Northwest Territories (which included Nunavut until the 2000 Games), Yukon, and Alaska. Nunavik dropped out of the Games in 1976 but rejoined as a guest participant in 2000.

The Arctic Winter Games, which are held every two years and welcome over 1000 participants, stress athletic competition, cultural exhibition, and social exchange. These philosophical tenets are supported through both sporting and cultural events at the Games.

Most athletes compete in regional trials to qualify for the Arctic Winter Games, which have offered a wide variety of events: Alpine Skiing, Arctic sports (Airplane, Alaskan High Kick, Arm Pull, Head Pull, Kneel Jump, Knuckle Hop, One Foot High Kick, One Hand Reach, Kneel Jump, Russian Sledge Jump, Russian Triple Jump, and Two Foot High Kick), Basketball, Badminton, Biathlon, Curling, Dene Games (Finger Pull, Hand Games, Pole Push, Snow Snake, and Stick Pull), Dog Mushing, Figure Skating,

Gymnastics, Hockey, Nordic Skiing, Snowboarding, Snowshoeing, Soccer, Speed Skating, Table Tennis, Volleyball, and Wrestling. Nevertheless, each Host Society must make decisions concerning which events they will and will not offer. For example, due to venue constraints, Figure Skating and Biathlon were not offered at the 2002 Games.

Dene Games

Dene Games take place in the Northwest Territories, where there is a concentrated population of Dene people. According to Heine (1999), Dene Games were heavily influenced by the connection between travel and life on the land. Strength and endurance were necessary for travel on the land, and endurance, speed, and accuracy were needed for hunting and were often practiced by playing traditional games (Heine, 1999).

The first Dene Games occurred in 1977 and were organized by the Dene-U Celebration Committee, a group that organized subsequent Games in 1978 and 1979 (Paraschak, 1983). In 1980, the Dene Games Association was created. Its first executive committee included Ted Blondin, Roy Erasmus, Tim Beaulieu, and Violet Camsell. The first Dene Games organized by the Dene Games Association took place in Rae in 1981. The Games continued in a multicommunity festival format until 1999. Since then, funding of the Dene Games has changed. Communities are now encouraged to use the current funding system to develop Dene Games within each community by holding workshops or small-scale festivals.

Popular Dene Games events include Axe Throwing, Bannock making, Bingo, Bow and Arrow Shoot, Canoe Races, Coin Toss, Dene Baseball, Drum Dancing, Dry Fish Making, Fish Filleting and Frying, Hand Games, Log Sawing, Spear Throw, Stick Pull, Tea Boiling, and Wood splitting.

Today, Inuit and Dene traditional games help contemporary individuals to stay in touch with the traditional skills that were necessary for survival in the old days. Although the Northern Games, Arctic Winter Games, and Dene Games are the most prevalent sporting/cultural festivals in Canada, other notable festivals, such as the annual World Indian-Eskimo Olympics, exist in other regions.

AUDREY R. GILES

Further Reading

Giles, A.R., "(An)Other in the (un)making: participation in sporting opportunities for Aboriginal peoples in Canada." *AVANTE*, 7(2) (2001): 84–91

Glassford, R.G. *"The life and games of the Traditional Canadian Eskimo." Proceedings of the First Canadian Symposium on the History of Sport and Physical Education,* Canada, 1970

Heine, M., *Dene Games: A Cultural and Resource Manual,* Yellowknife: The Sport North Federation & MACA (GNWT), 1999

———, *Arctic Sports: A Training and Resource Manual,* Yellowknife, Northwest Territories: The Sport North Federation and MACA (GNWT), 2002

Paraschak, V., Discrepancies between Government programs and community practices: The case of recreation in the Northwest Territories. Unpublished doctoral dissertation, University of Alberta, Canada., 1983

———, "A Look at Government's Role in Recreation in the Northwest Territories." In *Collected Papers on the Human History of the Northwest Territories,* edited by M.J. Patterson, C.D. Arnold & R.R. James, Yellowknife: Prince of Wales Northern Heritage Centre, 1985

———, "Variations in race relations: sporting events for native peoples in Canada." *Sociology of Sport Journal,* 14 (1997) 1–21

Wulf, A., *Northern Games,* Inuvik: Author, 2002

SPOTTED SEAL

Also known as the largha seal from the name given to it by the Tungus people who live along the shores of the Sea of Okhotsk, the spotted seal (*Phoca largha*) was long considered a subspecies of the harbor seal, but it has now been elevated to full species status. As with all phocids, males are larger than females; an adult male spotted seal will measure 5.5 ft (1.7 m) from nose to tail, and weigh up to 250 pounds (113 kg). Spotted seals reach sexual maturity at age seven or eight, and their life span is about 35 years. *Phoca largha* is found throughout the northern reaches of the Pacific, in the Chukchi, Okhotsk, and Bering seas, Kamchatka and the Commander islands, and the northern Sea of Japan, and there is a separate population in the Po Hai Sea and the Yellow Sea off China and Korea. Spotted seals are also found in North America, from Pt Barrow to the Pribilofs and the eastern Aleutians.

They are differentiated from harbor seals by their largely western Pacific distribution, somewhat smaller size, and that, unlike harbor seals, which breed on land, spotted seals breed on small, moving ice-floes. Although harbor seals may occupy much of the same western Pacific range as spotted seals, they do not interbreed because their breeding seasons are out of phase. During the breeding season, male and female spotted seals form pairs that remain together for about two months, separated from other couples. The gestation period is 11 months, including a delayed implantation period of up to four months. The pups, 18–25 pounds (8–11 kg) in weight and about 33 inches in length, are born in the shelter of ice hummocks or in crevices. They have a dense, wooly, whitish coat (lanugo) that is shed after two to four weeks. Mothers remain with their white-coated pups for the first few weeks, defending them against intruders, but when the pups shed their furry coats and become less buoyant and better able to dive, the mothers abandon them. Spotted seals can dive to 300 m (over 900 ft) and eat a variety of prey items, including capelin, pollock, herring, smelts, sand lance, and sculpins, as well as shrimps, octopuses, and small crabs. During the summer and fall, they congregate near rivers where anadromous fish, such as salmon, go to spawn in fresh water.

They are no more spotted than harbor seals, but their coloration is less variable, consisting usually of a pale silvery coat, darker on the back, and covered with dark spots and blotches. The doglike snout is believed to be responsible for Iñupiat legends concerning the seals' ability to come ashore and turn themselves into dogs, to see if the hunters are keeping the meat in a clean cache or if they are making the proper garments, and then returning to the sea as seals.

Because they inhabit areas far from human habitation and spend a portion of the year on ice-floes, spotted seals have not been as intensively studied as their relatives, the harbor seals. Little is known of their predators, but wandering polar bears sometimes catch them, and while swimming, they may be taken by killer whales or Greenland sharks. Except for a Japanese commercial hunt that continued into the mid-1970s, spotted seals have not been the object of a directed commercial fishery. The Japanese hunt, which was primarily off Sakhalin, was closed down when the Soviets enforced their 200-mile limit. To supply meat for their mink and fox fur farms in Siberia, the Soviets needed meat, and they harvested various whales and pinnipeds, including a few hundred spotted seals to feed the fur bearers. Alaska Native and Siberian subsistence hunters in Bering Strait and Yukon-Kuskokwim regions hunt the spotted seal for food, clothes, and fuel. Recent estimates suggest that there are probably 20,000 spotted seals in the Bering-Chukchi region, and another 130,000 in the Sea of Okhotsk.

There is concern that oil and gas exploration in the Chukchi and Beaufort seas may disturb the spotted seals, and will also threaten them with oil spills. The waters off Sakhalin Island and in the Sea of Okhotsk are about to be opened to massive oil and gas development, and Russian tanker traffic and extreme weather conditions makes an oil spill more than a little likely.

A new study, conducted on harbor seals by German researchers, has evidently answered the question of how pinnipeds are able to locate their fast-swimming prey if they cannot see very well underwater and they do not echolocate as dolphins do. To find food, they use their sensitive whiskers (vibrissae) to follow the minute hydrodynamic trails of fishes through the water. Blind but well-nourished seals have been observed in the wild, and in the study, blindfolded seals were able to track the wake of silent model submarines even when the path curved. (When the whiskers were covered, the seals failed to located the "prey object.") It is believed that the whiskers of a swimming seal vibrate with characteristic frequencies, and a change in this frequency, caused by the faint wake of a swimming fish, can be sensed by the seal.

RICHARD ELLIS

See also **Common (Harbor) Seal**

Further Reading

Burns, J.J., "Harbor Seal and Spotted Seal." In *Encyclopedia of Marine Mammals*, edited by W.F. Perrin, B. Wursig & J.G.M. Thewissen, London and San Diego: Academic Press, 2002

Dehnhardt, G., B. Mauck, W. Hanke & H. Bleckmann, "Hydrodynamic trail-following in harbor seals (*Phoca vitulina*)." *Science*, 293 (2001): 102–104

Haley, D., "Ice Seals." In *Marine Mammals of Eastern North Pacific and Arctic Waters*, edited by D. Haley, Seattle: Pacific Search Press, 1978, pp. 192–205

King, J.E., *Seals of the World*, Ithaca, New York: Cornell University Press, 1983

Naito, Y. & M. Nishiwaki, "Ecology and morphology of *Phoca vitulina largha* and *Phoca kurilensis* in the Southern Sea of Okhotsk and northeast of Hokkaido." *Rapports et Procès-Verbaux des Réunions,* 169 (1975): 303–312

Nelson, R.K., *Hunters of the Northern Ice*, Berkeley: University of Chicago Press, 1969

Reeves, R.R., B.S. Stewart & S. Leatherwood, *The Sierra Club Handbook of Seals and Sirenians*, San Francisco: Sierra Club Books, 1992

ST LAWRENCE ISLAND

St Lawrence Island or Sivuqaq (1983 sq mi/5135 sq km) lies in the Bering Sea between Alaska and Siberia. Most of the people live in two towns, Gambell (also called Sivuqaq) (population 653) and Savoonga (population 652), separated by 37 miles (60 km). Savoonga is 172 miles (277 km) from Nome and 102 miles (164 km) from Wales on the tip of the Seward Peninsula. Gambell is 61 miles (98 km) from Provideniya on the Chukotka Peninsula.

The island is 100 miles (161 km) long and 28 miles (45 km) wide at its widest point. This volcanic island is composed of three wider regions separated by two narrow sections, one 16 miles (26 km) and one 7 miles (11 km) wide. The topography varies from hilly to gently rolling. There are about 20 named hills ranging from 985 to 1970 ft (300–600 m) in height. Hundreds of ponds dot the tundra landscape. The climate is maritime and the weather is dominated by the moods of the Bering Sea. Cold, cloudy, foggy, rainy, and windy conditions prevail, with precipitation falling about 300 days out of the year. Gambell gets an annual average precipitation of about 375 mm, including 200 cm of snow. Comparable figures for Savoonga are annual precipitation, 250 mm, with 145 cm of snow. Recorded extreme temperatures for Gambell are −2°F/−19°C; for Savoonga, −34°F/−37°C. The average winter temperatures at Gambell range from −2°F/−19°C to 10°F/−12°C. The average summer temperatures range from 34°F/1°C to 48°F/9°C. Comparable figures for Savoonga are: summer, 40°F/4°C to 51°F/10.5°C; winter, −7°F/−22°C to 11°F/−12°C. The Bering Sea freezes over in mid-November; breakup occurs in late May. Marine mammals and birds take advantage of scattered areas of open sea that remain unfrozen during the winter.

The island has been occupied by Siberian and Alaska Yup'ik Eskimos for at least 2000 years. By the mid-1800s, there were 35 villages with a total population of about 4000. The population plummeted during the famine of 1878–1880. Reindeer were introduced in 1900 to provide a more steady food resource. President Roosevelt established a reindeer reservation on the island in 1903. Island residents elected not to participate in the Alaska Native Claims Settlement Act (ANCSA) of 1971, but opted instead to take title to the former federal reindeer reserve. St Lawrence Island is now owned entirely by its Native residents. The US Air Force operated a surveillance station on Northeast Cape for 20 years (1952–1972). Ten years later, the US Navy set up a communications base at the same site. Both services have long since abandoned the site, but left behind huge deposits of trash and toxic wastes including a fuel spill of some 220,000 gallons. Although both villages have scheduled air services and enjoy regular contact with the mainland via telecommunications and newspapers, traditional Yup'ik lifestyles have persisted. Walrus, whales, seals, and polar bears are harvested, as are other marine and land food resources. Islanders are renowned for their artistic creations, especially walrus ivory carvings. Housing is simple but essentially modern, with sanitary water and sewage systems either in place or projected.

J. RICHARD GORHAM

See also **Bering Sea; Siberian (Chukotkan Yupik); Yupiit**

Further Reading

Badten, Linda W., V. Kaneshiro, Marie Oovi & Steven A. Jacobson (editors), *Dictionary of the St Lawrence Island/Siberian Yupik Eskimo Language*, Fairbanks: Alaska Native Language Center, 1996

Braund, Stephen R., *The Skin Boats of Saint Lawrence Island, Alaska*, Seattle: University of Washington Press, 1988

Carius, Helen Slwooko, *Servukakmet: Ways of Life on St Lawrence Island*, Anchorage: Alaska Pacific University Press, 1979

Geist, William Otto & Froelich G. Rainey, *Archeological Excavations at Kukulik, St Lawrence Island, Alaska: Preliminary Report*, New York: AMS Press, 1976

Jolles, Carol Zane & Kaningok, "Qayuutat and angyapiget: gender relations and subsistence activities in Sivuqaq (Gambell, St Lawrence Island, Alaska)." *Etudes Inuit Studies*, 15 (2) (1991): 23–53

Rausch, Robert L. & V.R. Rausch, "The taxonomic status of the shrew of St Lawrence Island, Bering Sea (Mammalia: Soricidae)." *Proceedings of the Biological Society of Washington*, 108 (1995): 717–728

Rausch, Robert L., J.F. Wilson & P.M. Schantz, "A programme to reduce the risk of infection *by Echinococcus multilocularis*: the use of praziquantel to control the cestode in a village in the hyperendemic region of Alaska." *Annals of Tropical Medicine and Parasitology*, 84 (1990): 239–250

Staley, David P., "St Lawrence Island's subsistence diggers: a new perspective on human effects on archeological sites." *Journal of Field Archaeology*, 20 (1993): 347–355

Stringer, W.J. & J.E. Groves, "Location and areal extent of polynyas in the Bering and Chukchi seas." *Arctic*, 44 (1991): 164–171

Till, A.B. & J.A. Dumoulin, "Saint Lawrence Island." In *The Geology of Alaska*, edited by George Plafker & Henry C. Berg, Boulder: The Geological Society of America, 1994

Trust, K.A., K.T. Rummel, A.M. Scheuhammer, I.L. Brisbin & M.J. Hooper, "Contaminant exposure and biomarker responses in spectacled eiders (*Somateria fischeri*) from St Lawrence Island, Alaska." *Archives of Environmental Contamination and Toxicology*, 38 (2000): 107–113

STEFANSSON ISLAND

From the 19th century onward, western explorers traveled along the shores of Victoria Island in the Northwest Territories of Canada as the region was then called. Early on, only a few of them made short trips inland. Inuit people lived there and had done so for a long time (the Kitikmeot Inuit region). Today, the eastern part of Victoria Island and the other islands to the north and east of Victoria Island, as well as the northeastern part of the Canadian mainland, form the Nunavut territory of Canada.

The early explorers had an unclear view of the true shape and size of Victoria Island. During the first decades of the 20th century, scientists, hunters, and more seafarers clarified the picture, bringing home new geographic data while discovering more islands and the true features of islands in the Nunavut region, unknown outside the aboriginal population of present-day Nunavut.

During the extensive travels of the Canadian Arctic Expedition (1913–1918), led by Vilhjalmur Stefansson (1879–1964), expedition members stated (1917) that what had been thought of as a rather flat peninsula at the northeastern extremes of Victoria Island was in fact an independent, much smaller island. It is separated from the larger island by a narrow sound. Later, this island was named Stefansson Island to honor Arctic explorer Vilhjalmur Stefansson, a Canadian of Icelandic descent.

Stefansson Island has an area of 4463 sq km and is triangular in shape (the perimeter is 449 km). It is situated roughly at 73.20° N and 105.45° W. The McClintock Channel separates the island from the Prince of Wales Island and the Parry Channel and Melville Sound from Melville Island. The highest point only reaches some 256 m above sea level.

The bulk of the island is made of old, Precambrian bedrock. It forms a worn-down, rolling plain, denuded by the many Ice Age glaciers that have periodically covered the island. Many lakes and tarns, formed by glacial erosion, pockmark the plain. A lot of the bedrock is barren, with gravel and boulder deposits from the last glacial period. Wet lowlands constitute patches of continuous vegetation with a common tundra-type flora, many of them at lake shores or in depressions in the bedrock.

There are no permanent human settlements on Stefansson Island, although the island may have been a hunting ground for the Inuit living in the vicinity of Victoria Island. Besides small common mammals, bird life in summer, and trout in lakes or small rivers, the population of larger mammals consists of small herds or groups of muskox and Peary caribou.

There is hardly any tourist traffic on Stefansson Island but scientists have visited the island from time to time. The communities closest to Stefansson Island are Resolute Bay (Qausuittuq), 350 km to the northeast and Cambridge Bay (Ikaluktutiaq), some 450 km to the south.

ARI TRAUSTI GUÐMUNDSSON

See also **Canadian Arctic Expedition, 1913–1918
Victoria Island**

Further Reading

Thorsteinsson, Raymond & Tozer Edward, *Banks, Victoria and Stefansson Islands, Arctic Archipelago*, Ottawa: Geological Survey of Canada, 1962
Zoltai, S.C., "Stefansson Island." In *The Canadian Encyclopedia*, Edmonton: Hurtig, 1985, pp. 1,481 and 1,718

STEFANSSON, VILHJALMUR

Between 1906 and 1918, anthropologist and explorer Vilhjalmur Stefansson went on three expeditions into the Alaskan and Canadian Arctic, each of which lasted between 16 months and five years: the Anglo-American Polar Expedition (1906–1907), the Stefansson-Anderson Expedition (1908–1912), and the Canadian Arctic Expedition (1913–1918). On his return from the Arctic, Stefansson drew upon his Arctic experience, lecturing and writing about the Inuit, geopolitics, health, and a series of other issues. During his career, he published some 24 books and more than 400 articles on his travels and observations. He was a public figure in North America and Europe,

well known for his description of the "Blond Eskimo" (Copper Inuit), his discovery of new lands in the Arctic (including the islands of Brock, Borden, Mackenzie King, and Meighen), his approach to travel and exploration, and his theories of health and diet.

Stefansson was born in the Canadian Icelandic community at Arnes, Manitoba, but most of his childhood years were spent in North Dakota. After receiving his first academic degree in religious studies from the University of Iowa in 1903, Stefansson became affiliated with the Anthropology Department and the Peabody Museum at Harvard University. He was invited to participate in an expedition to the Arctic, to study indigenous groups along the Mackenzie River, and to collect artifacts for the Peabody and Royal Ontario Museums. During this expedition, other scientists and explorers employed Stefansson in a secondary role as an anthropologist and assistant. Stefansson's first expedition was relatively short and his ethnography was somewhat limited, although it provided interesting sketches of early fieldwork, Inuit society, and relations between "natives" and "whites."

Stefansson was determined to return to the Arctic for a second expedition, this time as the commander of an expedition of his own. His popularized articles based on the first expedition outlined a new, "friendly" approach to Arctic travel and exploration that appealed to potential sponsors. Stefansson argued that the costs of an expedition could be significantly reduced if one was prepared to live as the Inuit did. These articles caught the attention of the leading personnel of the American Museum of Natural History who offered Stefansson a contract. During the second expedition, Stefansson occupied a leading position, in charge of both logistics and research. Here, he appears in the role of an alert observer, keen to note minute details important for understanding social life in the Arctic. And in this case his field diaries are massive, with vocabularies, dictionaries, grammatical notes, descriptions of events, ethnographic observations, and drawings. The ethnographic observations offered in Stefansson's diaries and publications focus on a range of issues, including shamanism, religion, folklore, kinship, clothing, food, language, cleanliness, tattoo, concepts of time and labor, daily activities related to the organization of camps, and the collection and storing of food.

The third expedition was an extensive one, spanning five years. Here, Stefansson's role as geographic explorer and adventurer takes precedence for a variety of reasons, some of which have to do with the geopolitics of the time and the constraints of funding large-scale expeditions, involving teams of people and expensive equipment. Nevertheless, there was an important ethnographic element as two anthropologists were specifically hired for the expedition, Henri

Portrait of Vilhjalmur Stefansson.
Licensed with permission of the Scott Polar Research Institute, University of Cambridge, UK

Beuchat and Diamond Jenness. Accounts of the expedition are colored by an accident in which eleven of Stefansson's men lost their lives when their ship, the *Karluk*, became locked in ice, broke, and sank in November 1913. Over time, Stefansson's interests seem to have shifted from Inuit culture to the arctic natural environment, from ethnography to geography and exploration. The Inuit were removed from the center stage, and the Arctic, however "friendly," remained a natural space to be explored, conquered, and domesticated by Western "civilization."

Stefansson's Arctic practice and representation may be summed up by the notion of "Arcticality" implicit in his work, a notion that characterized the Arctic as a world of its own clearly separated from more temperate regions in terms of both culture and geography. Stefansson's notion of the "friendly Arctic" was the key to his career. He argued that arctic explorers and anthropologists often made the mistake of bringing their environment with them (food, clothes, methods of transport, and so on) while it would be far more productive and viable in the long run to adopt Inuit practices and flow with the Arctic environment. Pointing out that the Inuit saw no need to wage war with the environment in which they lived, he challenged the orthodox, literary notion of the Arctic as necessarily barren and desolate.

Stefansson was a serious fieldworker, learning the native language and participating in the social lives of the Inuit for years. A solid description of arctic societies, he argued, was more important than armchair speculations. One of the strengths of Stefansson's ethnography

from the second expedition may be credited to his intimate relationship with the Inuit Fannie Pannigabluk (?–1941), a widow originally from Alaska. Stefansson hired her as a seamstress and later she became both his key informant and his wife, in Inuit terms. Stefansson's fascination with the "Blond" Inuit and his controversial speculations about their Norse ancestry may also have been partly triggered by his own involvement with the Inuit. A few months before his first encounter with the Copper Inuit, the son of Stefansson and Pannigabluk, Alex Stefansson (1910–1966), was born.

Stefansson made quite an impression on the 20th century. One of his greatest scholarly contribution is his work on the voyages of Martin Frobisher (1576–1577), based on a variety of written sources. His major scholarly ambition, the editing of the *Encyclopaedia Arctica*, a massive 20-volume work that began in 1946, had to be aborted, largely, it seems, due to Cold War accusations of communist inclinations. More than anyone else, perhaps, Stefansson both mapped and defined the Arctic in Western discourse, paving the way for authentic accounts of Inuit society, more informed and less ethnocentric than those previously available. Although he was primarily known for his geographical explorations, he also contributed significantly to Inuit ethnography. Along with some others, Stefansson pioneered the standard anthropological methodology of extensive fieldwork and participant observation.

Biography

Vilhjalmur Stefansson was born on November 3, 1879 in the Canadian Icelandic community at Arnes, Manitoba. His parents, Ingibjorg and Johann Stefansson, along with 250 other colonists recruited by the Canadian government in 1877, left from north Iceland to settle near Winnipeg. In 1881, Stefansson's parents and their four children moved from Manitoba to Pembina County in North Dakota where Stefansson grew up in the Icelandic tradition. He attended university from the age of 18, first at the University of North Dakota and later at the University of Iowa and Harvard University. Late in his life, Stefansson married Evelyn Baird (now Stefansson Nef). He died in Hanover on August 26, 1962.

GÍLSI PÁLSSON

See also **Canadian Arctic Expedition, 1913–1918; Encyclopaedia Arctica; Eskimo; Exploration of the Arctic; Frobisher, Sir Martin; Jenness, Diamond; Inuit**

Further Reading

Diubaldo, Richard L., *Stefansson and the Canadian Arctic*, Montreal: McGill-Queen's University Press, 1978

Hunt, William R., *Stef: A Biography of Vilhjalmur Stefansson, Canadian Arctic Explorer,* Vancouver: University of British Columbia Press, 1986

LeBourdais, D.M., *Stefansson, Ambassador of the North,* Montreal: Harvest House, 1963

Pálsson, Gísli, *Writing on Ice: The Ethnographic Notebooks of Vilhjalmur Stefansson,* Hanover: University Press of New England, 2001

Stefansson, Vilhjalmur, *My Life with the Eskimo,* New York: Macmillan, 1913

———, *The Friendly Arctic,* New York: Macmillan, 1921

———, *The Three Voyages of Martin Frobisher,* Volumes 1 and 2, London: Argonaut Press, 1938

———, *Discovery: The Autobiography of Vilhjalmur Stefansson,* New York: McGraw-Hill, 1964

STELLER, GEORG W.

The German-born Georg Steller was the naturalist aboard the Second Kamchatka (or Great Northern) Expedition (1741–1743) under Vitus Bering, and during fieldwork in Alaska and Kamchatka, he described many new plant and animal species, including the marine mammals Steller's sea cow (now extinct) and Steller's sea lion.

Georg Steller came to Russia in 1734 after being educated at the universities of Wittenberg and Halle (Germany). After arriving in St Petersburg, he found work with the German botanist Johann Amann. When Steller heard of the Second Kamchatka Expedition under Captain Vitus Bering, he applied to join. Some of his German colleagues in St Petersburg—Johann Georg Gmelin and Gerhard Friedrich Müller—had already left for Siberia in 1733. Steller had no experience in Arctic exploration when he left in December 1737. He was to join Gmelin and Müller, and reached them in November 1738 in Yenisseisk after traveling via Moscow, Kasan, Ekaterinburg, and Tobolsk.

In February 1739, Steller was instructed by Gmelin and Müller to continue to Kamchatka. On the way, he undertook botanical research on the shores of Lake Baikal. The result of his research was Steller's main botanical work, *Flora Irkutiensis,* completed in December 1739. After several delays, Steller again left for Kamchatka in March 1740 and reached Okhotsk in May, where for the first time he met Bering and the other naval leaders of the expedition.

After arriving, Steller undertook several journeys on the Kamchatka Peninsula during his stay. His first trip was on the east coast, and in January-February 1741 he traveled to Cape Lopatka and the southern part of the peninsula studying the Itel'men and the Koryak. The Itel'men language was first recorded by Stepan Krasheninnikov, one of the students attached to Steller. Returning to Petropavlovsk, he was invited to take part in the American leg of Bering's expedition, sailing aboard one of the two ships, *St Peter,* in June 1741.

After sailing east toward the American coast, land was sighted in the middle of July and the ship anchored off Kayak Island. Steller was allowed to land for only six hours, during which he made detailed observations and described a single specimen of the jay that bears his name. Kayak Island is in the Gulf of Alaska some 50 miles southeast of Cordova. There is now a marine park encompassing the approximate landing site of Steller. He found a native camp, but no natives, and "exchanged some goods," leaving European items and taking native items. The ship continued in bad weather along the Alaskan southern coast. On August 28, Steller landed once more, this time on the Shumagin Islands, probably Nagai Island. Of the 15 larger islands comprising the Shumagin group, 13, including the Unga and Popof islands in outline, were described on a navigational chart.

After two months of further sailing, on November 6, *St Peter* landed at and was later wrecked on an uninhabited island off Kamchatka, which was named after Vitus Bering. The island is actually part of a group of islands, the Commander (Komandórskis) Islands, covering about 715 square miles and consisting of Bering and Medny (Copper) islands and two islets. After Bering's decision to overwinter, Steller was active not only in carrying out botanical and zoological research but also in acting as medical doctor and spiritual advisor. Although many of the crew, including Bering, died during the severe winter, Steller was able to gather and cook plants to combat scurvy. It was on Bering Island that Steller found the marine animal named Steller's sea cow, which he described along with other sea animals in his study "De bestiis marinis," which he actually completed on the island under harsh conditions, living in a dugout house. Other animals discovered by Steller were a cormorant (*Phalacrocorax perspicillatus*), Steller's sea eagle (*Haleaeetus pelagicus*), and Steller's sea lion (*Eumetopias jubatus*). Arctic foxes were also common on the island at the time of the overwintering of the expedition. From the wreck of *St Peter,* the crew built a smaller vessel and were able to return to Petropavlosk on August 26, 1742, carrying valuable fur pelts.

On his return to Petropavlovsk, Steller used the coming years to produce manuscripts on the American exploration and a "Description of the land Kamchatka" (published in German in 1774). In May-June 1743, he once more traveled to southern Kamchatka and the Kuril Islands. Later that year, he journeyed to the northeastern part of the peninsula (Karaga Island). In January 1744, Steller received information concerning the end of the expedition, and in August he left Kamchatka. Reaching Okhotsk, he took the route to St Petersburg via Yakutsk using the time for additional botanic observations. After the breakup of the ice, Steller continued westward in the spring of 1745. He traveled via Irkutsk and arrived in Tomsk in January and Tobolsk in March 1746. There he fell very ill and died in November.

Steller did not get the chance to publish his manuscripts in his own lifetime. However, Peter Simon Pallas (1741–1811), another German naturalist who with other scientists traveled extensively in Siberia from 1768 to 1774, published Steller's manuscripts in his journals "Stralsundisches Magazin" and "Neue Nordische Beyträge" (1769–1793) and also published a short biography of Steller.

Steller's work was undertaken during the reign of Empress Elisabeth I of Russia. Due to Steller's early death and fear from Russian authorities that the results of the Second Kamchatka Expedition and following expeditions would fall into the wrong hands, the results were suppressed for decades. But following the discoveries, no less than 42 expeditions between 1743 and 1764 set out to the newly discovered rich lands to hunt sea otters and sea cows. In 1825, the first Russian settlements were built on the Commander Islands, leading to Russian colonization of the Aleutian Islands and Alaska.

Biography

Georg Wilhelm Steller was born in Windsheim (now Bad Windsheim), Germany, on March 10, 1709. He was educated at school in Windsheim from 1713 to 1729. He studied theology at Wittenberg University in 1729–1731 and botany and medicine at Halle University in 1731–1734, and took part in the Great Northern Expedition from 1737 to 1743 as a scientist. He died in Tobolsk, Siberia, while returning to St Petersburg, on November 12, 1746. As Steller was a Lutheran, he was buried outside the city on the banks of the River Tura. The grave has now disappeared due to the rise of the river.

BERTIL HAGGMAN

See also **Bering, Vitus; Second Kamchatka Expedition**

Further Reading

Ford, Corey, *Where the Sea Breaks its Back: The Epic Story of Early Naturalist Georg Steller & the Russian Exploration of Alaska*, Boston: Little, Brown, 1966

Hintzsche, Wieland & Thomas Nickol (editors), *Die Grosse Nordische Expedition: Georg Wilhelm Steller (1809–1746): Ein Lutheraner erforscht Sibirien und Alaska*, Eine Ausstelklung der Frankeschen Stiftungen zu Halle, Gotha: Justus Perthes Verlag, 1996

Stejneger, Leonhard Hess, *Georg Wilhelm Steller, The Pioneer of Alaskan Natural History*, Cambridge, Massachusetts: Harvard University Press, 1936

Steller, Georg Wilhelm, *Beschreibung von dem Lande Kamtschatka*, Frankfurt and Leipzig: J.G. Fleischer, 1774

———, *Journal of a Voyage with Bering, 1741–1742*, edited by O.W. Frost, Stanford: Stanford University Press, 1988

———, *Steller's History of Kamchatka: Collected Information Concerning the History of Kamchatka, its Peoples, Their Manners, Names, Lifestyles and Various Customary Practices*, translated by Margritt Engel and Karen Willmore, Fairbanks: University of Alaska Press, 2003 (originally published in German, 1774)

STELLER'S SEA LION

Like the extinct flightless cormorant and sea cow, in addition to a species of jay and sea eagle, this species was first identified by and named after Georg Wilhelm Steller, the zoologist on Vitus Bering's 1741 voyage from Kamchatka to the Aleutians and Alaska. Also known as northern sea lions and *Eumetopias jubatus*, they are the largest of all sea lions. Males are much larger than females, and can weigh as much as a ton, while females do not exceed 700 pounds. The bulls are tan or cork-colored, noticeably darker on the head and neck; the females are lighter, and the newborn pups are black. This species breeds all around the perimeter of the North Pacific, in a wide arc that runs from southern California (particularly the Channel Islands), north past Oregon, Washington, Southeast Alaska, and through the Aleutians, where the largest colonies are found. The arc then sweeps westward, to incorporate the Commander Islands, the Kamchatka Peninsula, and the Sea of Okhotsk including Sakhalin Island. *Eumetopias jubatus* also establishes breeding colonies on the Kuril Islands and the northern Japanese island of Hokkaido.

Steller's sea lions are polygynous, with large bulls fighting to establish territories where they jealously guard their harems of females. The pups from the previous year's breeding are born 3 days after the females come ashore, and the mothers nurse their pups for 9 days before going out to sea to feed. The pups are quite precocious, and can walk and suckle within half an hour of birth, and can swim weakly within a few hours. After a month, the pups accompany their mothers on feeding trips. Both sexes reach sexual maturity at 3–8 years of age, but bulls do not establish territories until they are between 9 and 13 years old. Females can live up to 30 years, and males up to 20.

It is hard to imagine such abundant, massive animals as being "incidental," but because their range overlaps that of the northern fur seal and the northern elephant seal in so many areas, 19th-century sealers would often kill Steller's sea lions during their fur sealing and "elephanting" harvests. Compared to that of the fur seal, the pelt of *Eumetopias jubatus* known to the Aleuts as *seevitchie* is of almost no commercial value, but this distinction never bothered the sealers, and they killed the sea lions anyway. In California in the early 1900s, northern sea lions were killed because of complaints by fishermen that the sea lions were eating the fish that rightly belonged to the fishermen, and

Steller's sea lions, Lowrie Island, Forrester Island National Wildlife Refuge, Alexander Archipelago, Alaska.
Copyright Joel Satore / National Geographic Image Collection

later, in the Aleutians, pups were killed for their skins to make clothing. Most pinnipeds have a baculum or penis bone, and it is not surprising to learn that these bones were ground up and the powder sold as an aphrodisiac in certain Asian countries. North American sealers killed Steller's sea lions for "trimmings," which consisted of the genitals of bull seals, the gall bladder, and the whiskers. The penis and testicles were powdered and used to impart virility to humans; the gall bladder was used for medicine; and the heavy whiskers made wonderful toothpicks or opium pipe cleaners. The whole "set" of genitals, gall bladder, and whiskers fetched $2–5 in San Francisco, and because the pelts were not particularly useful, the animals were often killed just for the "trimmings" and the carcass left to rot on the beach. In the Aleutian Islands, Steller's sea lions are hunted by Alaska Natives as a traditional subsistence food.

In recent years, the Bering Sea and Gulf of Alaska populations of Steller's sea lions have declined drastically, and no one is quite sure why. In the 1960s, the total population was estimated at around 192,000 animals, but by 1994, it had dropped to an estimated 52,000, a reduction of about 75% in a 20-year period. Under the US Endangered Species Act (ESA), the species was listed as "threatened" in the eastern portion of their range, and "endangered" in the western. As of 1999, the population had fallen to around 20,000 animals, and the word "extinction" began to appear in discussions. Suggestions for the cause of this decline include "redistribution, disease, environmental perturbations (which may influence the quality and quantity of prey), and the synergistic effects of fisheries" (Loughlin et al., 2002), which seems the most likely.

Like northern fur seals, Pacific harbor seals, spotted and ringed seals, and some of the world's largest breeding colonies of kittiwakes, murres, and puffins, Steller's sea lions rely for sustenance on walleye or Alaska pollock (*Theragra chalcogramma*). The giant Alaska pollock trawl fisheries are hauling in fish on an unprecedented scale. The Alaska pollock catch in the Bering Sea rose from about 200,000 metric tons in the late 1970s to 800,000 metric tons in 1995. It has been estimated that nearly 90 billion pounds of pollock have been mined from the eastern Bering Sea since 1964. Unregulated pollock fishing in critical sea lion foraging habitat soared to record levels in the mid-1990s, with much of the winter catch concentrated in pollock spawning grounds near the sea lion population center.

As sea lion stocks continued to fall, the pollock fishery grew exponentially, increasing by 45% since 1990. The Alaskan pollock fishery accounts for about 40% of all commercially harvested seafood in the United States, and is the nation's largest fishery as well as the world's largest single-species commercial fish harvest. It appears in stores as "frozen whitefish," fish sticks, the patties used in fast-food fish sandwiches, and "imitation crab meat." In the spring of 1998, Greenpeace, the American Oceans Campaign, and Sierra Club Alaska sued the National Marine Fisheries Service (NMFS) under the Endangered Species Act for failing to protect the critical foraging habitat of Steller's sea lion. Since lack of food is the problem, they argued, it makes no sense to allow major fisheries to target pollock within the sea lions' critical habitat. The ESA requires that "reasonable and prudent alternative (RPA) measures" be taken to avoid inflicting any "adverse modification" on the critical habitat of a species. In December 1998, the NMFS sent shockwaves through the fishing industry by agreeing with the plaintiffs representing sea lions that fishery operations did create a situation of "food web competition." In July 1998, US District Court Judge Thomas Zilly upheld this finding and ordered NMFS to revise its RPA. Pollock fishing in critical sea lion areas has been curtailed, but it is not clear whether the reduction will allow the severely depleted Steller's sea lion populations to recover.

RICHARD ELLIS

Further Reading

Black, L.T. & R.G. Liapunova, "Aleut: Islanders of the North Pacific." In *Crossroads of Continents*, edited by W.W. Fitzhugh & A. Crowell, Washington, District of Columbia: Smithsonian Institution Press, 1988, pp. 52–57

Busch, B.C., *The War Against the Seals: A History of the North American Seal Fishery*, Montreal: McGill-Queens University Press, 1985

Calkins, D.G., D.C. McAllister, K.W. Pitcher & G.W. Pendleton, "Steller sea lion status and trend in Southeast Alaska." *Marine Mammal Science,* 15(2) (1999): 462–477

Gentry, R.L. & D.E. Withrow, "Steller Sea Lion." In *Marine Mammals of Eastern North Pacific and Arctic Waters*, edited by D. Haley, Seattle: Pacific Search Press, 1978, pp.166–171

Kenyon, K.W. & D.W. Rice, "Abundance and distribution of Steller sea lion." *Journal of Mammalogy,* 42(3) (1961): 223–234

Loughlin, T.R., "Steller's sea lion." In *Encyclopedia of Marine Mammals*, edited by W.F. Perrin, B. Wursig & J.G.M. Thewissen, London and San Diego: Academic Press, 2002

Merrick, R.L., T.R. Loughlin & D.C. Calkins, "Decline in abundance of the northern sea lion, *Eumetopias jubatus*, in Alaska, 1956–86." *Fisheries Bulletin,* 85 (1987): 351–365

Schusterman, R.J., "Steller Sea Lion—*Eumetopias jubatus* (Schreber, 1776)." In *Handbook of Marine Mammals, Volume 1, The Walrus, Sea Lions, Fur Seals and Sea Otter*, edited by S.H. Ridgway & R.J. Harrison, New York: Academic Press, 1981, pp. 119–141

STRATUS CLOUDS

Stratus clouds are relatively uniform grayish clouds that generally cover the entire sky. They form in the lowest part of the atmosphere, generally below 2000 m and often only a few hundred meters above the ground. Sometimes, the stratus clouds reach down to the ground, particularly on hilltops or in mountains. Stratus clouds at ground level are called fog. Usually, stratus clouds do not produce any precipitation and if they do it is generally in the form of drizzle, light rain, or light snow.

Atmospheric clouds at low levels generally form as a result of condensation of water vapor into liquid cloud droplets. The condensation can be a result of different atmospheric processes and interaction between the surface of the earth and the atmosphere. The formation of clouds is most often associated with ascending motion of the airmass where the clouds form. The upward motion reduces the pressure of the air and the airmass, including the water vapor, becomes colder and the vapor starts to condensate into droplets. Strong upward motion may result in thick precipitating clouds such as nimbostratus or cumulonimbus. On the other hand, stratus clouds form a layer or layers that are typically only a few hundred meters thick. If the airmass is sufficiently humid, only very little ascending motion may be sufficient to form a layer of stratus clouds. Stratus clouds and fog may also form without any large-scale ascending motion. Radiative cooling or cooling through contact with a cold surface such as ice or cold sea surface may lead to the formation of stratus clouds in a humid airmass. Stratus clouds in the Arctic may also form in a cold airmass that flows over a warmer sea surface and becomes convectively unstable.

Combined with other words that describe cloud types, the word stratus enters the combinations stratocumulus, altostratus, nimbostratus, and cirrostratus. Stratocumulus clouds bear strong resemblance to stratus clouds. They form in the lower part of the troposphere in a layer or layers and as the stratus clouds, the stratocumulus generally do not produce any precipitation. Unlike the uniform stratus clouds, the stratocumulus form a pattern of rounded cloudmasses, sometimes with clearings in between them. Altostratus is used for a grayish layer of uniform middle-level clouds, nimbostratus is a thick gray cloudmass that often produces rain or snow, and cirrostratus is a uniform layer of transparent high-level clouds. Cirrostratus clouds are located in the upper part of the troposphere at very low temperatures. They are made of ice crystals that produce a halo when the sun shines through them.

Stratus clouds are a particularly common feature in Arctic regions during the summer season. In the winter, the average cover of low clouds in the central Arctic is only about 20%, but from April to October, the average cover of low clouds is close to 70%. The persistence of the stratus clouds in the summer can be attributed to the absence of cloud dissipative mechanisms. There is no general subsidence that would dissolve the clouds, there are not many synoptic scale disturbances that may disrupt the stratus layers by vertical motion or precipitation, and there is little solar heating. Due to the low solar angle in the Arctic, longwave radiative cooling predominates over shortwave (solar) heating in the Arctic stratus. There is, in other words, a net radiative heat loss, which contributes to more condensation and sustainment of the Arctic stratus layers. The absence of strong solar heating and the cold surface of the ice and the Arctic Ocean hamper the formation of a convective boundary layer that could break up the stratus clouds.

Stratus clouds are frequently observed to form layers in the lowest part of the atmosphere. The layering of the clouds can be attributed to vertical variations of temperature and humidity in the large-scale flow. These vertical variations lead to differential radiation that can contribute to evaporation at levels inside the cloud layer and condensation at other levels.

The most important direct effect that stratus clouds have on the weather and the climate is through their insolation of the part of the atmosphere that is below the cloud layer and by reflection of solar radiation. The clouds strongly reduce solar radiation at the surface of the earth and can therefore lower daytime temperatures over land in the short term during the summer. On the other hand, the clouds hamper the net radiative heat loss in the atmosphere below them and thereby reduce its cooling. In the Arctic, the insolation effect of the stratus cloud is believed to cause an earlier start of spring than if no clouds were present.

In simulations of the global current and future climate, there are still considerable uncertainties and some of them are related to stratus clouds and cloud-related processes. This is of particular concern because simulations indicate that the Arctic is particularly vulnerable to global climate change.

Stratus clouds and fog can be a hazard for navigation at sea and it has a disturbing effect on air traffic. Before the times of modern equipment, navigation was based on the position of the sun and the stars in the sky and ships could easily become lost in fog or stratus. Arctic stratus was in this way a key element in the discovery of America by Europeans. The Icelandic sagas record that in the late 10th century, an Icelandic merchant, Bjarni Herjólfsson, sailed off for Greenland, but the ship was caught in fog and stratus, it was steered too far south where it missed Greenland, and ended up at the east coast of North America (Bergthórsson, 2000).

HARALDUR ÓLAFSSON

Further Reading

Bergthórsson, Páll, *The Wineland Millennium: Saga and Evidence*, Reykjavik: Mál og menning, 2000

Cotton, W.R. & R.A. Anthes, *Storm and Cloud Dynamics*, San Diego: Academic Press, 1989

Pinto, J.O. & J.A. Curry, "Role of radiative transfer in the modeled mesoscale development of summertime Arctic stratus." *Journal of Geophysical Research*, 102 (D12) (1997): 13861–13872

STURLUSON, SNORRI

Snorri Sturluson is probably the best known of Icelandic medieval saga authors, owing to his status as a politician and a man of the world. The main sources to his life are the works of his nephew, Sturla Þórðarson (1214–1284), who wrote an important section of the Sturlunga saga collection as well as the Hákonar saga, Hákonarsonar. Snorri also appears in some sagas of Icelandic bishops, most notably that of Guðmundur Arason (1161–1237).

Sturluson had a good start in life. He was the youngest son of an important chieftain, Sturla Þórðarson, who founded the clan of the Sturlungar. His two older brothers, Þórður (1165–1237) and Sighvatur (1170–1238), also became powerful chieftains and stretched the power of the clan well beyond that of their father. He spent his childhood and youth away from his family because he was sent away from home when he was three years old to be brought up at Oddi, in the southern part Iceland. Oddi was the home of the chieftain Jón Loftsson (1124–1197). This was part of a peace deal between his father and Jón Loftsson. At that time, Oddi must have been an important cultural center and it is said that candidates for priesthood did study there.

In 1199, Sturluson married into a fortune when he gained the hand of Herdís Bersadóttir (d. 1233), whose father was nicknamed "the wealthy." He inherited his wife's estate at Borg two years later. In 1206, he moved to Reykholt in the Borgarfjörður region. By then, he had become estranged from his wife, but not her wealth. Later on, he set up a home with Hallveig Ormsdóttir (d. 1241), reported to be the richest woman in Iceland. Following her death, he was resented by her sons because of his avarice, and they were involved in his slaying, later that very year.

In his youth, Sturluson was already seen as one of the greatest chieftains in Iceland. Although capable of being tough, he tended to be peaceful and he gained the respect of his peers. Between 1215 and 1235, he was probably the most powerful man in Iceland. He held the office of law-speaker for most of this period but his literary colleague and friend, the abbot Styrmir fróði Kárason (d. 1245), stood in for two longer intervals. He strengthened his ties with other chieftains through marital alliances, marrying his daughters to the chieftains Kolbeinn Arnórsson ungi (1209–1245), Gissur Þorvaldsson (1209–1268), and Þorvaldr Snorrason (d. 1228). Unfortunately, two of these marriages ended in failure and his sons-in-law turned on him, perhaps due to his excessive demands for financial compensation. The third alliance, however, produced a grandson, Einar Þorvaldsson (b. in 1227, still alive in 1286), who carried on Snorri's inheritance. One of his sons died young, while the other, Óraekja, was a turbulent man who often got into trouble.

Sturluson also courted the favor of Norwegian noblemen, sending youthful poems of praise to the kings Sverrir (d. 1202) and Ingi (d. 1217) as well as the earl Hákon galinn (d. 1214). The earl invited him to Norway, but died before Sturluson was able to take up his offer. He did, however, later visit the earl's widow in Gautland and during that time, it is assumed that he acquired knowledge of Swedish history and the pagan practices, which were only recently extinct there. This happened sometime during the years 1218–1220, during which Sturluson visited king Hákon (1204–1263) and earl Skúli Bárðarson (d. 1240) at the Norwegian court and became a royal retainer. He wrote panegyrics to Skúli, and received great favors from him. During this time, he undertook the task of subjugating Iceland to the Norwegian Crown.

Following increased pressure from his nephew, Sturla Sighvatsson (1199–1238), Sturluson again went to Norway in 1237. He was not known as a fighter, and in the works of his nephew, he often seemed to be contrasted negatively to the heroic Sturla Sighvatsson. In Norway, he became involved in the rebellion of earl Skúli against king Hákon, leaving Norway in 1239 in defiance of the king's ban. After quelling the rebellion, the king sent orders to his retainer in Iceland, Gissur Þorvaldsson, to arrest Sturluson and send him abroad, or kill him if he resisted capture. Gissur, although formerly his son-in-law, made no attempt to capture him but had killed him on September 23, 1241. His last words are reported to have been "eigi skal hfggva" (do not strike), a laconic if somewhat unheroic final speech. Órækja tried to avenge his father, but was largely unsuccessful and was forced out of the country by Gissur.

As can be seen from his poems to Norwegian noblemen, as well as his own manual on poetry, the *Prose Edda*, Sturluson was one of Iceland's greatest poets. In modern times, however, he is best known as one of the greatest medieval historians. He composed a separate Ólafs saga helga (the legend of St Olaf), which he then included in the collection of king's sagas known as *Heimskringla*. In this, he may have enjoyed the assistance of his friend Styrmir fróði, who is mainly known as one of the editors of the Icelandic Book of settlements (Landnámabók). Egil's saga (The saga of Egill Skallagrímsson) has often been attributed to Sturluson, and it is true that he once lived at Borg, where Egil also had resided, and was the chief magnate of that area in the period when Egil's saga must have been composed. In contemporary sources, little mention is made of Sturluson's literary active, apart from his skill as a poet.

The famous Norwegian sculptor, Gustav Vigeland (1869–1943), made two statues of Sturluson that are located in Reykholt and at Bryggens Museum in Bergen. Several artists have ventured to make a portrait of Sturluson, but in fact, it is not known what he looked like.

Biography

Snorri Sturluson (1179–1241) was born at Hvammur in the Dalir. His parents were Sturla Þórðarson (1115–1183) and Guðny Boedvarsdóttir (c.1147–1221). He grew up at Oddi, in South of Iceland. Later, he lived at Borg and Reykholt in the Western part of Iceland. He probably became a chieftain at an early age. He held the office of law-speaker of Iceland in 1215–1218 and 1222–1231. He became a courtier of the king of Norway. His first wife was Herdís Bessadóttir (d. 1233); they divorced. Their two children, Jón murti and Hallbera, died childless. His later wife was Hallveig Ormsdóttir (d. 1241), thought to be the wealthiest woman of Iceland. He had several illegitimate children, of whom the best known are Ingibjörg, Órækja (d. 1245), and Þórdís.

SVERRIR JAKOBSSON

See also **Grímsey**

Further Reading

Ciklamini, Marlene, *Snorri Sturluson.* Twayne's World Author Series, 493. Boston, 1978 *Snorri. Átta alda minning,* Reykjavík, 1979

Fix, Hans (editor), *Snorri. Beiträge zu Werk und Rezeption.* Ergänzungsbande zum Reallexikon zur germanischen Altertumskunde, 18, Berlin, 1998

Jóhannesson, Jón, *Sturlunga saga,* Magnús Finnbogason & Kristján Eldjárn (editors), 2 volumes, Reykjavík, 1946

Jónsson, Finnur (editor), *Heimskringla. Nóregs konunga sfgur af Snorri Sturluson.* Samfund til udgivelse af gammel nordisk litteratur, 23, 4 volumes, Copenhagen, 1893–1900

———, (editor), *Edda Snorra Sturlusonar,* Copenhagen, 1931

Nordal, Sigurður, *Snorri Sturluson,* Reykjavík, 1920

Paasche, Fredrik, *Snorre Sturlason og Sturlusgerne,* Oslo, 1922

Simon, John, "Snorri Sturluson. His life and times." *Parergon,* 15 (1976): 3–15

Vigfússon, Guðbrandur (editor), *Biskupa sögur,* 2 volumes, Copenhagen pp. 1858–1878

———, *Icelandic Sagas and Other Historical Documents Relating to the Settlements and Descents of the Nothmen on the British Isles. II. Hakonar saga and a fragment of Magnus saga* (Rerum Britannicarum medii ævi scriptores, 88), London, 1887

SUBARCTIC

Definitions of the boundaries of the Arctic reflect differing scientific, cultural, and political traditions (*see* **Arctic: Definitions and Boundaries**). Here, the Subarctic refers to a geographic zone of the Northern hemisphere, located between the Arctic zone to the north and the temperate zone to the south. By this definition, it includes the tundra, as well as the forest-tundra (taiga and birch forests) bordering in the boreal zone. The Subarctic is generally recognized to include southern Greenland, southern Alaska, the southern parts of Yukon Territory, Northwest Territories, and Nunavut, much of Québec, Newfoundland and Labrador, northern parts of the other Canadian provinces, and much of northern Norway, Sweden, Finland, and Russia in the boreal forest (taiga) zone.

Average temperatures in the Subarctic vary strongly between these regions, influenced by ocean currents, prevailing winds, and the distance from the continental interior. The coldest month's average temperature varies from −1.6°C in the Atlantic sector of the Subarctic to −37.9°C in the Siberian Subarctic. The warmest month's average temperature rises from 7.4°C on the coast to 11.4°C to the south and deep into the continent. In the Siberian Subarctic, the absolute range temperature is from −60°C to +33°C. Similar extremes of temperature are found in the North American Subarctic. On the cold shores of Hudson Bay and on the high Labrador plains, washed by the cold Labrador current from the east, the southern frontier of the Subarctic zone dips to a latitude of 50°; in western North America, the boundary is at a latitude of

60°. In Eurasia, the southern Subarctic boundary, which begins in the north of Scandinavia at a latitude of 70°, goes through the Arctic Circle, and only beyond the eastern side of the Lena River does it rise back down to a latitude of 70°.

The Subarctic is characterized by a low precipitation and extremely low evaporation. About 300–400 mm of precipitation falls in the tundra of Eurasia. More precipitation falls in the forest-tundra: 340–400 mm annual precipitation in the east of Eurasia, 500–600 mm in the west, and up to 700 mm in areas of frequent cyclonic storms, which are common here. In the continental sector of the North American Subarctic the annual precipitation is about 200–300 mm, in oceanic sectors up to 600–800 mm, and in Greenland up to 1000 mm. Zone and landscape differences depend mostly on thermal conditions, particularly in summer time.

Precipitation is mostly solid, and input to rivers mainly consists of snow. Widespread permafrost limits or even excludes subsoil input to rivers, although the depth of permafrost may be only a few inches in the southern Subarctic, and may be patchy or discontinuous. The presence of discontinuous permafrost is sometimes used to define the Subarctic, in contrast to the Arctic where permafrost is continuous. Ground ice frequently determines meso- and microrelief of the tundra and forest-tundra floor, with characteristic stone polygons, thermokarstic collapses (formed when permafrost thaws and weakens), pingos, solifluctional lobes and terraces, and thermo-erosive ravines (*see* **Ground Ice**).

Soils of the Subarctic are primitive, skeletal flat interfluves. On the lower reaches, they are gleyed (i.e., with reduced iron due to water saturation); in the southern areas, the soil shows signs of podzolization and thixotropy, with illuvial and humic horizons, in combination with peat moors (*see* **Soils**). Incomplete drainage due to permafrost and reduced decay rates due to low temperatures result in the accumulation of organic material as peat, while the concentration of available water at the surface in glacial depressions and frost cracks allows development of wetlands and bogs.

While the growing season is longer (3–4 months) than in the High Arctic (about 2 months), winters are still long and severe and plants must be adapted to cold, low precipitation, and the short growing season. During winter, crystals of snow and ice deposited by winds and snow-storms destroy tundra plants, which is why only low-growing shrubs can survive, sheltered by snow. These kinds of plants maximize the warmth of the Earth and surface air in their short growing period. In a forest-tundra subzone, Subarctic winds become less stable and powerful. The plant shelter of the Subarctic is commonly scattered birch trees (*Betula nana*, *B exilis*, and *B. mudendorfii*), willows

(*Salix lanata*, *S. glauca* and others), and shrubs (wild berry, red whortleberry, wild rosemary). As for herbage, only species adapted for severe conditions are found, for example, all kinds of herbs, moss, and tussock-forming sedges (such as tussocks of cotton-grass, *Eriophorum vaginatum*). The North America Subarctic is noticeable not only for circumpolar species but also for Arctic alpine dwarf shrubs, such as *Dryas integrifoli*, *Dupontia fischeri*, *Cassiope tetragona*, Labrador tea (*Ledum palustre*), and others. The flora of the southern forest-tundra Subarctic is richer and more diverse.

In the forest-tundra of Eurasia, sporadic stands of birch (*Betula tortiosa*), pine (*Pinus syevestris*), spruce (*Picea abies* and *P. obovata*), and larch (*Larix sibirica* and *L. gmelinii*) are found. The North American forest-tundra of the Subarctic has the same flora as Eurasia, but the dominant trees here are of different species—black spruce and white (*Picea mariana* and *P. glauca*), balsam fir (*Abies balsamea*), aspens (*Populus balsamifera*), juniper (*Luniperus communis*), and others.

The fauna of Subarctic tundra is richer than that of the polar deserts of the Arctic, but still has a low species diversity. The majority of animals, especially birds, migrate southward for winter, although across the Subarctic, overwintering animals include Arctic fox, lemming, hare, wolf, ermine, partridge, white owl, and gyrfalcon. In the mountains of the northeast of Siberia, black-headed marmot and some others are additionally found. In the North American tundra, moose, muskox, caribou (reindeer), and grizzly bear are typical. The fauna of forest tundra is more diverse, and enriched by some taiga animals occasionally seeking food or new habitat there.

INNOKENTY ZHIRKOV

See also **Arctic: Definitions and Boundaries; Birch Forests; Coniferous Forests; Dwarf-shrub Heaths; Peatlands and Bogs; Sedge Meadows; Taiga; Treeline; Tundra; Tussock Tundra**

Further Reading

Aleksandrova, V.D., *The Arctic and Antarctic: Their Division into Geobotanical Areas*, Cambridge: Cambridge University Press, 1980

Nuttall, Mark & Terry V. Callaghan (editors), *The Arctic: Environment, People, Policy,* London and New York: Taylor and Francis, 2000

Wielgolaski, F.E., *Polar and Alpine Tundra*, Amsterdam and New York: Elsevier, 1997

SUBLIMATION

The term sublimation describes the exchange of water vapor between ice and the overlying air during sub freezing conditions in which water molecules are transferred directly from the solid to the gas phase, or vice versa. Sublimation represents a significant term in Arctic hydrology and glacier mass balance given that temperatures are commonly sub-freezing. Sublimation is responsible both for the losses and gains of mass to the surface. Sublimation has a significant impact on human activity, in that it can represent a major force in removing snow, whence it could be used as a water resource or to insulate the surface from extreme cold. Snow fences and crop stubble represent means to reduce snow loss from sublimation and blowing snow (Pomeroy and Gray, 1995). Over ice where there is little or no melting and sublimation exceeds accumulation, blue ice regions develop. In Antarctica, these are sites where meteorites that have lain within the ice have been exposed and collected (Bintanja, 1999). Blue ice regions have also been observed in northeast Greenland. Sublimation occurs across the globe, and is not limited to the surface. Blowing snow is often associated with large atmospheric sublimation rates (Schmidt, 1972, 1982; Déry et al., 1998). Sublimation also occurs within clouds, for example, water vapor deposition onto ice crystals in the atmosphere, for example, forming rimed crystals called graupel. It may be important to consider the degree of moisture recycling within a volume, particularly for large areas. Water vapor fluxes at the surface may be contributed to by fluxes within the snow volume at depth (Albert, 1996; Colbeck, 1997). A number of books review the theory to derive sublimation rates given meteorological data (Monteith and Unsworth, 1990; Garratt, 1992), while Patterson (1994) states glaciological applications.

Physical definition: Sublimation arises from differences in the concentration of water vapor (humidity) over an ice surface and the overlying air. Without a turbulent mixing mechanism, however, such as the wind, sublimation only occurs slowly by molecular diffusion, for example, in temperature gradient or equitemperature snow metamorphism. Sublimation represents not only a mass flux, but is accompanied by the latent heat flux. For example, the addition of heat is required to propel water molecules into the gas phase from the relatively low kinetic energy solid phase. At 0° C, the latent heat required for sublimation is the sum of the heat of fusion (0.334×10^6 J kg^{-1}) and the heat of vaporization (2.501×10^6 J kg^{-1}). There is a 3% decrease in the latent heat of sublimation from $-30°C$ to $0°C$. The mass transfer of water vapor (Δm) and the amount of latent heat transfer to the surface or atmosphere by the phase changes of water is given by $\Delta m = Q_E \Delta t / L\rho$ where Q_E is the latent heat flux (W m^{-2}), Δt is the time interval (s), ρ is the density of liquid water (1000 kg m^{-3}), and L is the latent heat of fusion

and/or vaporization. Climatological Δm is commonly presented in units of mm water-equivalent depth. The latent heat flux influences the surface energy balance, and energy available for melt, by acting as a sink of energy, usually supplied by the atmosphere, in the common Arctic case of temperature inversions.

The term for bulk water vapor fluxes can sometimes be ambiguous when characterized by a combination of sublimation, deposition, evaporation, or condensation. The term deposition is used to refer to water vapor exchange from the atmosphere toward a snow/ice surface in a subfreezing state. Evaporation and condensation are also mass fluxes of water vapor but occur when the surface is at or above the melting point of ice, 0°C. The term evaporation is often used loosely to describe the water vapor exchanges for sites where there is occasional melting, for example, in Ohmura et al. (1999). Some use the term evaposublimation. The term sublimation has been considered to refer to the process of water vapor exchange to or from the surface (Kameda et al., 1997). It therefore helps to include a statement of the direction of the sublimation, either "away" or "toward" a surface. Given these considerations, some flexibility must be granted in the use of the term sublimation.

Across the Arctic, windy and relatively warm regions are where sublimation rates are greatest, particularly if air masses are dry. The windy lower reaches of the southern part of the Greenland ice sheet exhibit annual sublimation rates in excess of 130 mm (Box and Steffen, 2001). It should be noted that a significant portion of this total occurs for temperatures at the melting point and thus are predominantly caused by the process of evaporation. Given the constraint of sub-freezing temperatures for sublimation to occur, the sublimation rates for most places are significantly lower in their contribution to the annual total than evaporation.

A map of the surface water vapor flux distribution for the Arctic based on the HIRHAM regional climate model (Rinke et al., 1999) is presented in Figure. The values indicate the combined amount of sublimation and evaporation. Largest fluxes are found in the north Atlantic region where winds are strong, temperatures are relatively high, and there is an unlimited supply of water or ice. As sublimation is coming from ice only, the rates are smaller, with maxima found probably in the marginal ice zone (MIZ) or in the lower katabatic region of glaciers and ice caps. Large gradients in evaposublimation exist at the MIZ and along areas of high topographic relief, such as along the northern Scandinavian coast, Alaska, Iceland, and Greenland. A large gradient occurs across Svalbard, in association with the MIZ. Net deposition is found over the Greenland ice sheet plateau. Over the polar basin

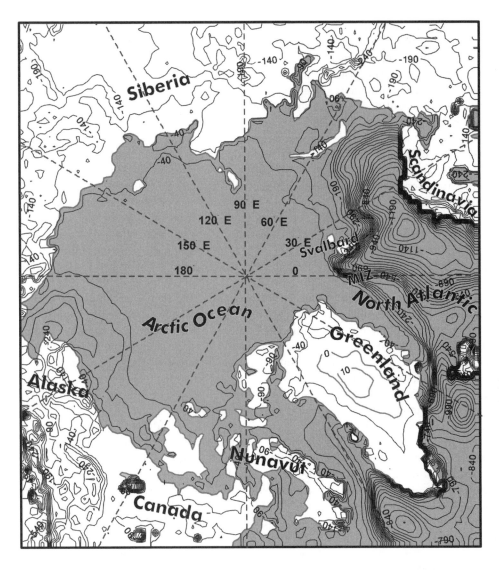

Evaporation map of the Arctic based on the HIRHAM regional climate model (Rinke et al., 1999). Values are mm water equivalence per year. Negative values indicate loss of water vapor from the surface. Map data courtesy of Annette Rinke, Alfred Wegener Institut für Polar und Meeresforschung, Potsdam, Germany.

ice pack, water vapor fluxes are between 20 mm a^{-1} and 50 mm a^{-1}. Values close to 80 mm a^{-1} occur over mountainous regions and ice caps near the polar basin. The large Canadian lakes are also sites of large evapo-sublimation values and gradients owing to high winds and dry air advection.

JASON E. BOX

See also **Glacier Ice; Sea Ice; Snow**

Further Reading

Albert, M.R., "Properties and Processes Affecting Sublimation Rates in Layered Firn." In *Glaciers, Ice Sheets and Volcanoes*, edited by S.C. Colbeck, Hanover, New Hampshire: US Army Cold Regions Research and Engineering Laboratory, 1996

Bintanja, R., "On the glaciological, meteorological, and climatological significance of Antarctic blue ice zones." *Reviews of Geophysics*, 37(3) (1999): 337–359

Box, J.E. & K. Steffen, "Sublimation estimates for the Greenland ice sheet using automated weather station observations." *Journal of Geophysical Research*, 106(D24) (2001): 33965–33982

Colbeck, S.C., "Model of wind pumping for layered snow." *Journal of Glaciology*, 43(143) (1997): 60–65

Déry, S.J., P.A. Taylor, & J. Xiao, "The thermodynamic effects of sublimating blowing snow in the atmospheric boundary layer." *Boundary Layer Meteorology*, 89 (1998): 251–283

Garratt, J.R., *The Atmospheric Boundary Layer*, Cambridge and New York: Cambridge University Press, 1992

Kameda, T., N. Azuma, T. Furukawa, Y. Ageta, & S. Takahashi, "Surface mass balance, sublimation and snow temperatures at Dome Fuji Station, Antarctica, in 1995." In *Proceedings of the NIPR Symposium on Polar Meteorology and Glaciology*, Volume 11, Japan: NIPR, Tokyo, 1997, pp. 24–34

Monteith, J.L. & M. Unsworth, *Principles of Environmental Physics* (2nd edition), London and New York: Arnold, 1990

Ohmura, A., P. Calanca, M. Wild, & M. Anklin, "Precipitation, accumulation, and mass balance of the Greenland ice sheet." *Zeitschrift für Gletscherkunde und Glazialgeologie*, 35(1) (1999): 1–20

Oke, T.R., *Boundary Layer Climates* (2nd edition), London and New York: Methuen, 1987

Patterson, W.S.B., *The Physics of Glaciers*, Oxford and New York: Pergamon Press, 1994

Pomeroy, J.W. & D.M. Gray, *Snowcover: Accumulation, Relocation and Management*, Saskatoon: Environment Canada (NHRI Science Report No. 7), 1995

Rinke, A., K. Dethloff, A. Spekat, W. Enke, J.H. Christensen, "High resolution climate simulations over the Arctic." *Polar Research*, 18(2) (1999): 1–9

Schmidt, R.A., Sublimation of Wind Transported Snow—A Model, Fort Collins, Colorado: USDA, 1972

———, "Vertical profiles of wind speed, snow concentration, and humidity in blowing snow." *Boundary Layer Meteorology*, 23 (1982): 223–246

SUBMARINES IN ARCTIC EXPLORATION

The idea of using a submarine for research under the ice of the Arctic Ocean dates back at least as far as 1901. In the summer of that year, an Austrian by the name of Hermann Anschutz-Kampfe planned to tow a submarine to the edge of the ice pack. From there, Anschutz-Kampfe planned to navigate to the Pole, submerging for 15 h at a time. Once submerged, he planned to use a 5000 candlepower underwater search light to look further north for open leads in the pack ice, leading ultimately to the North Pole.

Three decades after this novel idea, the Australian explorer Sir Hubert Wilkins became the first explorer to initiate the submarine exploration of the Arctic, and to learn firsthand of its difficulty. Wilkins's plan was to employ a submarine as a floating research platform, conduct meteorological and oceanographic research and observations while moored to ice-floes and while under way, and to reach the North Pole while submerged beneath the polar ice cap. The expedition brought together several famous names in exploration, including the American polar explorer Lincoln Ellsworth, who supported Wilkins financially and acted as Director of Scientific Research; the American inventor Simon Lake, whose company built the submarine used by Wilkins and who agreed to modify it for use in the Arctic; and the Norwegian Dr. Harald Sverdrup, one of the world's preeminent oceanographers, who joined the expedition as Chief Scientist.

On February 1, 1931, Wilkins signed a one-year lease with the US Navy for the use of an O-class submarine for one US dollar. The submarine, the O-12, was built in 1916 by the Lake Torpedo Boat Company of Bridgeport, Connecticut. It was 55 m long, had a normal complement of 29 submariners, and could reach speeds of 11 knots submerged, and 14 knots on the surface. It had been decommissioned and placed in reserve at the Philadelphia Navy Yard in 1924. The O-12 was towed across the Delaware River, to the Mathis Shipyard in Camden, New Jersey, where it was stripped of military armament, fitted with the latest scientific research equipment, and the superstructure modified to allow operation beneath the ice.

Wilkins's expedition was delayed several times during the spring of 1931, preventing him from reaching the polar ice cap in time to make a true attempt on the Pole. A snowstorm, of all things, briefly halted the expedition while still on Delaware River. Then, as the submarine entered New York Harbor, Assistant Radio Engineer Willard I. Grimmer fell overboard and drowned.

On March 23, 1931, at the Brooklyn Navy Yard, Wilkins's wife rechristened O-12 the *Nautilus*. The ceremony was attended by Jean Jules Verne, grandson of the author of *20,000 Leagues Under the Seas*, and the fictional source of both the O-12's new name and parts of its new mission. Following the ceremony, sea tests were run on the Nautilus at various locations off the New England coast, including a 30-m dive off Block Island in Long Island Sound. By this time, the expedition was already two months behind schedule.

On June 13, the starboard engine cracked a cylinder in mid-Atlantic. The port engine failed soon thereafter. An S.O.S. call brought the USS *Wyoming* to the rescue on June 15, which towed the *Nautilus* to Queenstown, Ireland, then Davenport, England for repairs. Not until August 5 was *Nautilus* able to leave from Bergen, Norway, after picking up scientific officers and equipment.

On August 19, 1931, *Nautilus* became the first submarine to encounter the ice of the Arctic Ocean. Three days later, Wilkins attempted to submerge the *Nautilus* under the ice but found that the diving planes had been carried away. He tried again on August 31, filling all four ballast tanks and diving beneath a meter of ice.

A week later, Nautilus docked at Longyearbyen, Svalbard, on its way out south from the ice. Storms en route to England forced Wilkins to return to Bergen, where the *Nautilus* was towed out and sunk in the fjord on November 20, 1931. A few artifacts—such as one of the control wheels—were salvaged before the submarine was sent to the bottom, and today these are displayed in the Fram Museum in Oslo.

Ten years after Wilkins's daring expedition, Dr. Waldo K. Lyon, a civilian physicist, and Lieutenant (j.g.) Roger Revelle, created an undersea acoustics research division for the US Navy, laying the foundations for what would become the Navy's Arctic Submarine Laboratory. In 1947, in the Chukchi Sea, the USS *Boarfish* (SS-327), commanded by J.H. Turner, became the first submarine to operate under the ice of the Arctic Ocean since Wilkins's attempt with the *Nautilus*. The Boarfish voyage was followed by submarine expeditions by USS *Carp* (SS-338), commanded by J.M. Palmer, to the Chukchi Sea in 1948; USS *Baya* (ESS-318), commanded by J.D. Mason, to the Chukchi and Bering seas in 1949; and USS *Redfish* (SS-395), commanded by J.P. Bienia, to the Beaufort Sea in 1952 and 1953.

In addition to the problems posed by ice and cold, these expeditions were also limited by the nature of the diesel-electric submarine, which required their commanders to resurface on a regular schedule to recharge the submarine's batteries. This problem was solved in 1954 with the introduction of the first nuclear-powered submarine, USS *Nautilus* (SSN-571). After a test voyage under the ice in 1957, Nautilus, under the command of W.R. Anderson, became the first submarine to cross the Arctic Ocean in the summer of 1958, driving under the North Pole on August 3. This triumph was amplified a year later when the USS *Skate* (SSN-578), under the command of J.F. Calvert, became the first submarine to surface at the North Pole. Honoring his last wish, the crew scattered the ashes of Hubert Wilkins at the pole.

Soviet and Western submarines hunted each other under the Arctic Ocean during the Cold War, and occasionally recorded exploration firsts. These included the first submerged transit of the Northwest Passage, by the USS *Seadragon* (SSN-584), G.P. Steele commanding, in 1960, and a winter rendezvous at the North Pole in 1984 by the USS *Gurnard* (SSN-662) and USS *Pintado* (SSN-672).

Following the collapse of the Soviet Union, the US Navy and the US National Science Foundation initiated a multiyear program beginning in 1993 to employ several of the now 30-year-old attack submarines as scientific research platforms under the Arctic Ocean. Beginning with a 63-day research cruise by the USS *Cavalla* (SSN-684), in 1995, these Science Ice Expeditions (SCICEX) mapped the Arctic Ocean floor, and recorded immense amounts of data on its character. These data helped to quantify the diminution of the Arctic Ocean's ice cover since the 1960s.

With the retirement in 2001 of the last of the Sturgeon-class submarines used for SCICEX missions, submarine exploration of the Arctic Ocean has entered a new phase, when data are increasingly collected remotely and continuously. Unmanned Autonomous Undersea Vehicles (AUVs) use heated buoys to melt up through the ice and transmit data to orbiting satellites, and undersea recording systems lowered down through the ice use sound sources and receivers to record the temperature of the seawater that the sound travels through.

P.J. CAPELOTTI

Further Reading

Arctic Submarine Lab History website: http://www.csp.navy. mil/asl

Hodges, Glenn, "The New Cold War: Stalking Arctic Climate Change by Submarine." *National Geographic Magazine,* 197 (3): (March 2000): 30–41

Leary, William M.& Waldo K. Lyon, *Under Ice: Waldo Lyon and the Development of the Arctic Submarine*, College Station Texas: A&M University Press, 1999

Shenton, Edward H. *Diving for Science: The Story of the Deep Submersible*, New York: Norton, 1972

Thomas, Lowell, *Sir Hubert Wilkins: His World of Adventure,* New York: McGraw–Hill, 1961

Wilkins, Sir George Hubert, U*nder the North Pole: The Wilkins-Ellsworth Submarine Expedition*, New York: Brewer, Warren & Putnam, 1931

SUBPOLAR GYRES

Strictly speaking, the term "subpolar gyres" is a misnomer since these gyres are located *poleward* of the respective polar fronts in both Northern and Southern Hemisphere oceans; hence, they belong to the respective *polar* zones, and therefore should be called the "polar gyres." Historically, however, the term "subpolar" has become universally accepted. The Northern Hemisphere's subpolar gyres are often called the "Subarctic gyres." The latter term does not have a Southern Hemisphere counterpart.

Subpolar gyres are known in the North Atlantic, North Pacific, and Southern Ocean. The subpolar gyres are cyclonic gyres, rotating counterclockwise in the Northern Hemisphere and clockwise in the Southern Hemisphere. The origin of subpolar gyres is linked to the curl of the wind field. The cyclonic circulation in subpolar gyres causes surface water divergence and upwelling of nutrient-rich deep waters that come to the surface to ensure the high productivity of subpolar gyres, especially during spring bloom when large amounts of chlorophyll change ocean color; this change is regularly observed from space.

The North Atlantic subpolar (Subarctic) gyre consists of the following currents: East and West Greenland, Baffin, Labrador, North Atlantic, and Irminger. Some authors extend this gyre into the Nordic Seas, in which case the subpolar gyres also comprises the North Atlantic Current Extension, Norwegian Atlantic Current, and West Spitsbergen Current, including the latter's retroflection that connects it to the West Greenland Current, thus closing the gyre. The West Greenland Current branches into the Davis Strait and Baffin Bay, where it retroflects cyclonically and joins the southward Baffin Current. The "Great Salinity Anomalies" (GSA) observed in the 1970s, 1980s, and 1990s (*Dickson et al.*, 1988; *Belkin et al.*, 1998) were transported by various branches of the Subarctic Gyre. The entire journey of the GSA 1970s around the northern North Atlantic took about 10 years, whereas similar journeys of the GSA 1980s and 1990s took only six to seven years to complete, thus providing evidence of the long-term acceleration of the North Atlantic subpolar gyre.

The North Pacific subpolar (Subarctic) gyre consists of the Oyashio Current and its northernmost eastward quasi-zonal extension associated with the Polar Front (Belkin et al., 2002), cyclonic Alaskan Gyre (Eastern Subarctic Gyre), Alaskan Stream, Aleutian Current, Kamchatka Current, and Kuril Current; the two latter currents form the western limb of the Western Subarctic Gyre. In the northern Gulf of Alaska, the deepwater Alaskan Stream is joined by the shallow-water Alaskan Coastal Current, then branches into the Bering Sea to form a cyclonic gyre over the deep western part of the sea, called the Bering Sea Gyre. The Kamchatka-Kuril Current branches into the Sea of Okhotsk to form the cyclonic Okhotsk Sea Gyre. The major North Pacific subpolar gyre thus includes four smaller cyclonic gyres.

In the Southern Ocean, there are two major subpolar gyres south of the Polar Front: Weddell Gyre in the Atlantic sector between 60° W and 30° E, and the Ross Gyre in the Pacific sector, between 180° W-120° W. Smaller cyclonic gyres exist in marginal seas around the Antarctic continent, especially well defined in the Indian sector. Such gyres are best defined in the Lazarev Sea, Riiser-Larsen Sea, Cosmonaut Sea, Commonwealth Sea, Pryudz Bay, and Davis Sea. A large cyclonic gyre circulation exists to the east of the Kerguelen Plateau, in the Southeast Indian Ocean. In the Pacific sector, in addition to the major Ross Gyre, there are cyclonic gyres in the Bellingshausen and Amundsen seas. Since the Southern Ocean's subpolar gyres are located in ice-laden waters, the cyclonic circulation patterns can be inferred from the sea ice-drift patterns and also from observations on icebergs caught in these gyres. The cyclonic circulation in the subpolar gyres results in upwelling and doming of isopycnals (equal density surfaces). Since the Southern Ocean vertical structure features a layer of warm deep water beneath a cold surface layer, the upwelling/doming brings the warm water closer to the upper layer. The upward heat flux from this warm subsurface water creates conditions favorable for development of polynyas, ice-free areas within sea ice cover that persist even in winter.

IGOR BELKIN

See also **Arctic Ocean; Oceanography; Salinity Anomalies**

Further Reading

Belkin, I.M., S. Levitus, J.I. Antonov & S.-A. Malmberg, "'Great Salinity Anomalies' in the North Atlantic." *Progress in Oceanography*, 41(1) (1998): 1–68
Belkin, I.M., R. Krishfield & S. Honjo, "Decadal variability of the North Pacific Polar Front: subsurface warming versus surface cooling" *Geophysical Research Letters*, **29**(9) (2002): DOI 10.1029/2001GL013806
Dickson, R.R., J. Meincke, S.-A. Malmberg & A.J. Lee, "The 'Great Salinity Anomaly' in the northern North Atlantic, 1968–1982." *Progress in Oceanography*, 20(2) (1988): 103–151

SUBSTORMS

Substorms or magnetospheric substorms are a transient process in which a significant amount of energy derived from interactions between the solar wind and the Earth's magnetosphere is suddenly released into the ionosphere (the ionized region of the Earth's upper atmosphere at 100–1000 km). The most noticeable manifestation of substorms is an explosive increase of auroral luminosity near the midnight sector (where "noon" is in the direction of the Sun, and time coordinates are reckoned from the magnetic poles). During substorms, strong magnetic disturbances also occur in the polar regions, and the magnitude of these disturbances can be as high as several thousands of nT on the Earth's surface (i.e., up to 5% of the Earth's geomagnetic field).

The concept and term of substorms were proposed by Syun-Ichi Akasofu in 1964. Initially, they were called auroral substorms. Later, Akasofu assembled the high-latitude ionospheric and magnetospheric processes associated with auroral substorms into a framework that was called magnetospheric substorms. With improving observational capability from ground-based and satellite instruments, understanding of substorms and the scope of research have been continuously evolving.

In general, a typical substorm can be divided into three phases. The first phase is called the growth phase, and lasts about one hour. During this period, ionospheric electric fields and currents in the polar regions gradually increase and magnetic field lines in the equatorial regions in the magnetosphere (> 6 Earth radii) gradually become stretched in the Sun-Earth direction. The second phase is called the expansion phase, and lasts only 20–30 minutes. The start of this period is represented by a sudden brightening of the auroral arc near the equatorward side of the auroral oval (an oval-shaped auroral luminosity that exists permanently in the polar ionosphere). This explosive increase of auroral luminosity normally occurs in the premidnight sector and is followed by a rapid poleward motion, resulting in an "auroral bulge" around the midnight sector. As the substorm progresses, the bulge expands in all directions and in the evening section forms a westward travel surge, which can move with a speed of more than 1 $km^{-1}s$ and quite often in a discrete jumping pattern. At the same time, localized structures of electric fields, currents, and plasma density develop in the ionosphere, and particle precipitation from the magnetosphere causes significant heating in the polar ionosphere. Meanwhile, the magnetic field lines in the equatorial regions of the magnetosphere become less stretched, which is called dipolarization. The third phase is called the recovery phase, which lasts several hours. During this period, auroral luminosity gradually decreases and the shape of the auroral oval gradually returns to that of the presubstorms period.

Some substorms are triggered by the southward turning of the interplanetary magnetic field (IMF), but others occur when the IMF turns northward after a long southward IMF period. Quite often, substorms are conjugate and explosive auroral development can be seen simultaneously in the ionospheres of the Arctic and Antarctic regions.

Cause of Substorms

Many theories have been proposed for the cause of substorms, which is still an on-going and controversial research topic. In general, without mentioning any specific substorm theory, a substorm may consist of two physical components. One is called the "directly driven" process and the other is called the "unloading" process. When the IMF turns southward, the magnetic merging of the Earth's magnetic field and the IMF at the dayside magnetopause increase, which leads to enhanced magnetospheric convection and more energy of the solar wind being deposited into and stored in the magnetosphere. Since the magnetosphere and the ionosphere are connected, the corresponding changes in the ionosphere induce increases in electric fields and currents in the polar regions. This is the so-called "directly driven" process and is probably a dominant process during the growth phase. The solar wind energy stored in the magnetosphere, mainly in the equatorial regions of the magnetosphere, can be suddenly released when some instability is triggered. This energy release occurs in an explosive manner, which causes the sudden brightening of the aurora in the polar ionosphere. This is the so-called "unloading process," which could be a dominant process during the expansion phase and could also be responsible for the occurrence of substorms during the northward IMF periods.

Relevance of Substorm Study to Human Society

The study of substorms tells us how energy from the Sun is deposited into and stored in the magnetosphere and ionosphere and how it is suddenly released and dissipated in the polar ionosphere. It also tells us how the solar wind interacts with the Earth's atmosphere and how these interactions change the electric fields, currents, plasma density, and neutral densities in the magnetosphere, ionosphere, and neutral atmosphere. But going beyond scientific research, the study of substorms also has significant impacts on the activities of human society.

Modern power grids are extremely complex and widespread. The dramatic changes in high-latitude ionospheric currents that occur during substorms can lead to induced currents and cause "surges" in power lines, which may lead to massive network failures, for example, a systemwide power failure occurred in Québec, Canada during March 13–14, 1989.

High–frequency (HF, or shortwave) radiowave communication depends on the reflection of radio waves from the ionosphere to carry signals over great distances. The highly structured plasma density in the polar ionosphere during substorms may cause absorption and fading of HF radio waves and make propagation of HF signals impossible.

Telecommunication companies use ultrahigh frequency (UHF) radio waves that penetrate the ionosphere and are relayed via satellites to other locations. The disturbed ionospheric conditions during substorms may cause degradation of the signals and or even completely block UHF communication with satellites.

The study of substorms will eventually give us the capability of forecasting when and where substorms will occur. This "space weather" information will provide some warning time during which preventive measures can be taken.

LIE ZHU

See also **Aurora; Space Weather; Upper Atmosphere Physics and Chemistry**

Further Reading

Akasofu, S.I. & J.R. Kan, *Physics of Auroral Arc Formation*, Washington: American Geophysical Union, 1981

Kan, Joseph R., Thomas A. Potemra, Susumu Kokubun & Takesi Iijima, *Magnetospheric Substorms*, Washington: American Geophysical Union, 1991

Kelley, Michael C., *The Earth's Ionosphere: Plasma Physics and Electrodynamics*, San Diego: Academic Press, 1989

Schunk, Robert W. & Andrew F. Nagy, *Ionosphere: Physics, Plasma Physics, and Chemistry*, Cambridge and New York: Cambridge University Press, 2000

Suess, Steven T. & Bruce T. Tsurutani, *From the Sun: Auroras, Magnetic Storms, Solar Flares, Cosmic Rays*, Washington: American Geophysical Union, 1998

Tascione, Thomas F., *Introduction to the Space Environment*, Malabar: Orbit Book Company, 1988

SUMNAGIN CULTURE

The Sumnagin Culture was proposed by Yuri Mochanov in 1966, on the basis of materials from sites (Bel'kachi I, Sumnagin, Ust'-Timpton, Ust'-Chirkow) excavated in the Lena River basin (Aldan and Vilyuy rivers), Yakutia. The materials were radiocarbon-dated back to 10,500–6000 BP, and indicate a transitional

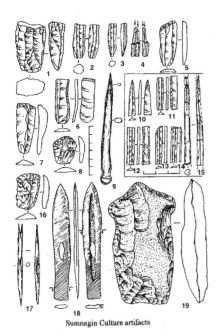

Sumnagin Culture artifacts

Sumnagin Culture artifacts: 1–3—prismatic cores; 4—polyhedral burin; 5, 7, 8, 16—scrapers; 6, 10–14—retouched microblades; 9—awl; 15—slotted point; 17—arrow point; 18—dagger; 19—adze. 1–8, 10–14, 16, 19—stone, 9, 15, 17, 18—bone.

culture between the late Paleolithic and Neolithic in Siberia, with the disappearance of wedge-shaped flint microblades.

In Northeast Asia at the Pleistocene-Holocene boundary, dramatic climate changes resulted in ecological changes. Global warming (the Holocene climatic optimum) resulted in the disappearance of glaciers, flooding of a great part of coastal areas as the sea level rose, and the spread of boreal forests far northward from the modern treeline. The Pleistocene mammoth fauna disappeared, and reindeer and the moose became the main objects of human hunting activities. This might have been one of the reasons for the disappearance of the preceeding Dyuktai Culture and the emergence of the Sumnagin, Final Paleolithic or Mesolithic, Culture in Yakutia. Mochanov associates its origin approximately with the influence of the Malta and Afontovo cultural traditions that existed to the west and the south from the Lena River basin in the Pleistocene. In all Yakutia, the Dyuktai complexes, with bifacial tools and wedge-shaped cores, had disappeared by the Early Holocene; instead, the Sumnagin Culture complexes became widespread, with unifacially retouched tools made on microblades, such as end scrapers, anglular burins, inserts retouched by the edge, knives. Blades and microblades were stroke-detached from conic and prismatic cores. Judging by a large number of retouched sideblades (60% of all finds), groove-insert bone and antler tools were wide-

ly used: points and knives, or daggers. So far, a few such tools with one side groove have been found. Simple bone arrow and dart points were also used. Other tools were bifacially percussioned adzes of long oval shape and oval axes with ears, both with the lanceolate cross section.

The Sumnagin people led a nomadic life and hunted moose in the taiga and reindeer in the tundra zone of the Arctic and Subarctic. Brown bears and, according to the Zhokhovo Site materials, polar bears were also hunted, and—very seldom (at the coastal sites)—walruses and seals.

The tendency of the cultural traditions with bifaces and wedge-shaped cores to be replaced with complexes based on obtaining blades from conic and prismatic cores and containing unifacial tools, no ceramics, and no ground tools can be generally traced around the entire Northeast Asia in the Early Holocene.

The Sumnagin Culture is supposed to have spread around the whole of Northeast Asia; however, there are no Sumnagin complexes found in Kamchatka, and there is no indubitable evidence of its existence on the Okhotsk Coast. Some Sumnagin sites have been found on the Taymyr Peninsula. Probably, various ethnic groups may be behind the vast spread of the Sumnagin archaeological culture; so it would be more correct and precise to talk about the Sumnagin Tradition represented by various local complexes or cultures in different parts of Northeast Asia.

On the Lower Kolyma, mostly the surface materials from the Panteleikha I-VIII and Piers sites have been referred to the Sumnagin Tradition, although the criteria by which the Early Holocene sites were distinguished there do not seem persuasive enough in the cases when it is done just by single microblades, prismatic or conic cores, or end scrapers of blades that are characteristic for the Neolithic, as well.

In Eastern Chukotka, the Sumnagin Tradition is represented by the Puturak Complex, which has not been radiocarbon-dated. The Puturak specificity in domination of large rough blades, bladelike flakes, and large subprismatic cores has been stressed, although microblades and microcores are also typical. The Puturak Site materials lay in the layers suffering from cryogenic and solifluction processes and may be mixed. They rather represent the remains of a workshop, which explains the absence of scrapers and burins in the tool kit.

More documented traces of the Sumnagin Tradition in Eastern Chukotka have been marked at the Achchen and Chelkun IV sites. From the cultural layer of the only radiocarbon-dated Early Holocene site in Chukotka, Chelkun IV (8150+/−450(MAG-719)), from the depth of 40 cm, prismatic core, microblades, and burins on blades were obtained. No end scrapers were found there; this can be explained by the functional character of the site (hunting camp).

In Western Chukotka, the Sumnagin Tradition is associated with the findings (basically surface, with no radiocarbon-dates) from Tytyl' I-III located on the shore of Lake Tytyl'. The declared originality of the Tytyl' Complex in some elements (diagonal burins and handle scrapers) would be a base for defining the criteria of local versions of the Sumnagin Tradition, but these elements are single, not typical for all Chuotka sites, and the complexes might have been mixed.

The example of the local and quite original Early Holocene complex in the Upper Arctic is the Zhokhovo Site located on Zhokhovo Island in the Novosibirsk Islands archipelago. Judging by radiocarbon-dates, the finds refer to the period between 8000 and 7800 BP. Like in the Sumnagin Culture, microblades and prismatic cores were presented there at the absence of bifacial tools. Bilateral and unilateral insert tools made from reindeer antlers, mammoth tusks, and walrus ivory, as well as household and hunting items of bone and wood retained at the site. The Zhokhovo tool kit differs from those of the Sumnagin Culture in the absence of end scrapers and the availability of ground adzes that appeared in Yakutia about 6000 BP, although one adze with a ground bit is 7000 years old.

The Sumnagin Tradition in the Kolyma is represented by the Buyunda Complex (Upper Kolyma) including the Buyunda III, Urtychuk IV, Jugajaka I (Point A), IV, and other sites. Their tool kits are characterized by conic and prismatic cores, blades and microblade artifacts (inserts unifacially retouched on the edges from the dorsal or the ventral side, angular burines, end scrapers, inserts with the retouch-sloped edge) absolutely dominating in the tool kit. At the Buyunda III site, a bifacially retouched adzelike tool was found. There, at the depth of 60–80 cm from the day surface, a stone-faced circular hearth was excavated. The teepeelike dwelling must have been ground or subsurface, with the natural microrelief hollow used. In the hearth, burned birch-tree bark remained. The charcoal obtained from the hearth was dated to 8135–7510 BP. The sites located on the mountain passes within the Okhotsk-Kolyma Watershed testify to hunting prevailing as the mode of life.

The Sumnagin Culture is thought to have spread to Alaska in the Early Holocene; there, it is presumably correlated with the Gallagher Flint Station and Anangula sites. About 6000 BP, over the whole area of its spread in Northeast Asia, the Sumnagin Culture was replaced with the Neolithic Syalakh Culture, having pottery and ground tools.

SERGEI SLOBODIN

See also **Dyuktai Culture**

Further Reading

Dikov, Nikolay N., *Drevniye kul'tury Severovostochnoy Azii* (Ancient cultures of Northeastern Asia), Moskow: Nauka, 1979

———, *Aziya na styke s Amerikoy v drevnosti* (Asia at the Joint with America: Stone Age on the Chukchi Peninsula), St.Petersburg: Nauka, 1993

Goebel, Ted & Sergei Slobodin, "The Colonization of Western Beringia Technology, Ecology, and Adaptation." In *Ice Age Peoples of North America: Environments, Origins, and Adaptations of the First Americans*, edited by Robson Bonnichsen & Karen L. Turnmire, Corvalis, Oregon: Oregon State University Press, 1999

Kiryak, Margarita A., *Arkheologiya Zapadnoy Chukotki* [Archaeology of Western Chukotka], Moscow: Nauka, 1993

Khlobystin, Leonid P., *Drevnyaya istoriya taymyrskogo Zapolyarya* (Ancient History of the Taymyr Circumpolar Area), St Petersburg: IMCH, 1998

Mochanov, Yuri A., *Drevneyshiye etapy zaseleniya chelovekom Severo-Vostochnoy Azii,* [The Earliest Stages of Settlement by Man of Northeastern Asia], Novosibirsk: Nauka, 1977

Mochanov, Yuri A. & Svetlana A. Fedoseyeva, "Main Periods in the Ancient History of North East Asia." In *Beringia in the Cenozoic Era*, Rotterdam, New Delhi, 1986

Pitul'ko, Vladimir B., "An early Holocene site in the Siberian High Arctic." *Arctic Anthropology*, 30-(1) (1993): 13–21

Powers, Roger W., "Palaeolithic man in Northeast Asia." *Arctic Anthropology*, 10-(2) (1973): 1–106

Slobodin, Sergei B., "Northeast Asia in the late Pleistocene and early Holocene." *World Archaeology*, 30-(3) (1999): 484–502

SUSTAINABLE DEVELOPMENT

Sustainability is a key concept in modern social and economic analysis. As a concept, it defines a system's capacity to rely on itself and become self-reproductive by its own means. This implies again that the system can control its interaction with its environment so that it does not jeopardize its capacity to be self-reliant, and yet take into account the implications of the fact that it is environment-dependent, not only with regard to social objects but also to Nature itself. The concept of sustainable development can be established within various levels and aspects of social analysis, such as cultural sustainability, ecological sustainability, and so on. Cultural sustainability implies that a social actor has cultural integrity, which can be defined as the irreversibility of certain features of its cultural value-system. One can also speak about political sustainability, which might correspond to the concept of self-determination. One also speaks about technological sustainability: in the case of the *Titanic* as a social system, the key issue was technological sustainability.

Central to the analysis of sustainable development in the Arctic are two forms of sustainability: economic sustainability and societal sustainability. These two kinds of sustainability are crucial to understanding industrial development. By economic sustainability, we refer to a social actor's capacity to establish a level of production that equals the sum of its consumption and investment, when these allocative streams are measured by the standards of the economic system. By societal sustainability, we indicate a society's capacity to control and fulfill the role pattern needed to maintain the general service level to which a society is normatively self-obligated. In other words, a society can obligate itself to maintain a certain hospital service to cure people for certain types of cancer, and so on.

Societal Sustainability

However, the term societal sustainability is not exhausted in the role-structure definition. On another level of analysis, it involves the overall question of social integration. Yet, the category of social integration is complex because the category of community can be analyzed in a hierarchy of theoretical level, and all levels correspond to a concept of sustainability. From an analytical point of view, society can be viewed as a complex containing ever-deeper configurations of societal sustainability. Therefore it is important that the axiomatic criteria of the systemic level of analysis are specified.

Generally, a social system is only really sustainable if its system is sustainable as a whole, that is, if it is culturally, societally, politically, economically, technologically, and ecologically sustainable. If one of these subsystems fail to become sustainable, the system will easily become dysfunctional and paralyzed. Again, the *Titanic* is a good example of how one dysfunctional subsystem can destroy the whole system. Generally, cultural sustainability is the most crucial issue of sustainability because it defines the social actor as an entity. However, for most cases of social analysis, the relevant level of analysis is that of societal sustainability, which is a more comprehensive concept than the more specialized fields of political and economic sustainability.

In addition to the systemic definition, the concept of sustainability will always imply an operational criterion. This criterion will specify those empirical properties by which a system's value pattern is historically defined. It will indicate what level of social reproduction corresponds to the concept "sustainable." Most often, this criterion will be defined from the social actor's point of view. That is, it will be natural to take the actor's value premises as a point of reference because the dynamics of a social system are not simply defined with regard to what it is, but to some degree to what its actors expect it to be. Therefore, what determines the relevant level of axiomatic crystallization is the normative pattern of orientation of the actors within the relevant system.

The processes of development and societal sustainability are not two unrelated concepts. By changing the level of complexity in each moment of history, the forces of development link the issue of sustainability to the reproductive logic of each evolutionary step. Hence, the Arctic could not choose to go back to a hunting society because a classic hunting society would not be able to sustain the current demographic base. From an empirical point of view, this means that sustainability as a boundary-maintaining system is a developmental concept, which implies that the question of sustainability with regard to the equilibrium of the institutional differentiation is a factor of time.

Because social systems, and all living systems, are characterized by openness to their environment, "sustainable" as an empirical concept will reflect this condition as long as a system-environment reference is defined. Sustainability must be analytically separated from autarky. Although the independent, self-sufficiency of autarky might remain an ideal, it is empirically a borderline case. Sustainability in a modern world is defined as a systemic point of stability within an interdependent process of developmental forces, where the strategic implications of sustainability are a moving equilibrium. With regard to the question of socioeconomic sustainability, the lack of sustainability in an open world-system environment most often correlates with the fact that the social system is out of touch with the center of developmental forces. It is not accidental that the systems that end up on the periphery of world development by and large are those systems that lack sustainability.

One major issue of sustainability is the vulnerability of the Arctic environment. As the Arctic societies become part of the modern world, they increasingly confront the problem involved when nature and modern technological society face each other. This meeting creates a series of problems with regard to the vulnerability of natural resources and a series of questions with regard to pollution. Modern harvest techniques are today so advanced that they can easily destroy the natural resource base unless strict regulation is applied. The threat with regard to overexploitation of marine mammals and other wildlife species is very real. The risk of industrial contaminants entering into food chains and disrupting ecosystems is also of great concern. It is particularly the persistent organic pollutants (POPs), heavy metal, and radionuclides that are the focus of research and political concern. To establish regulations on an international scale is a major task for the political players in the Arctic area, and has become one of the main tasks for the Arctic Council.

Obviously, the question of the sustainability of the ecological environment has certain objective criteria, which, for example, are explicated in the AMAP assessment report. However, environmental politics, including principles of animal rights, are a part of society's own self-definition and involve questions of societal sustainability. Increasingly, environmental politics involve various concepts and myths of the good society, which is quite natural because an Arctic society is a society in close connection with Nature, and the perception of Nature becomes a part of society's own self-perception. Hunting rules are not simply a sheer technical deduction from environmental data; they include perceptions of a "fair game for the animal" and various criteria of honor and pride. Hence, as an empirical system, the criteria for ecological sustainability and societal sustainability become part of an interrelated pattern.

Social and historical conditions within the Arctic vary greatly from place to place. The difference between Murmansk and Grise Fjord is staggering. Also, various societies in the Arctic exist in various historical stages of development.

Nonetheless, they have been subjected to globalization as an all-encompassing major force, which establishes a common point of analysis. However, when we analyze the circumpolar North today, we must not forget that, according to Gunnar Knapp, 85% of its population live in Russia. The average Arctic inhabitant is a Russian living in the northwestern part of Russia.

The regions and communities of the Arctic stand today at a juncture between tradition and modernity, where the current situation is still shaped by the Arctic's general historical condition of being a gigantic geographical hinterland at the absolute periphery of what in previous times would be regarded as civilization. Many of the structural problems in the Arctic today are problems of historical marginalization. This is true even if many of the original problems of marginalization, those of communication and transportation, have been overcome in part. Measured by various indicators, many communities of the Arctic suffer from problems that resemble those of the periphery, which characterize most developing countries. However, there is a paradox because if one looks at the World Bank's classification of countries measured by income per capita, then all the non-Russian Arctic communities are classified among the richest countries in the world.

Hence, if we analyze the non-Russian part of the Arctic, we obtain, on average, a picture of not only a comparatively high-tech, affluent Arctic measured by average income and technical infrastructure but also an Arctic whose industrial and societal structure is generally insufficiently developed and characterized by a weak pattern of sustainability. Many communities in the Arctic depend on transfer money from the South. This is also true in the case of the northern communities of Norway. In Greenland, the transfer money from Denmark accounts for 60% of the state budget; in Nunavut, the percent is significantly higher. In this way, many of the communities in the Arctic are characterized by a gap between their general standard of living and the capacity of their mode of production. The same pattern of substitution characterized the Soviet system. One important reason why the economy of Chukotka collapsed after the fall of the Soviet Union was because they were depending on a system of federal transfers, which were artificial from the point of view of sustainability. As a result, the population has declined to half because it is no longer profitable to live and work there. As a general rule, a great many societies in the Arctic are not sustainable industrially or societally on the current level of reproduction or in regard to their patterns of expectation. Iceland is one of the few clear-cut exceptions.

A general problem for many of the communities in the Arctic is that their income is based highly on a natural resource, often of a one-dimensional nature. Many coastal communities have traditionally built up an economy almost exclusively based on fishery. This is the case in Greenland, where fishery is the only sustainable industry and two-thirds of the income from this industry come from shrimp. A resource-based economy in a modern world faces many problems, of which the renewal of the natural resource is only one. One important problem is that the world market prices on many natural resource products involve an unstable and declining trend; this is one of the reasons why Royal Greenland is facing financial problems. Another reason is that in the case of fishery, the number of workers needed is steadily declining, so fishery is not an answer to the basic quest of securing employment in society. Also, fishery is potentially unstable, because of the great vulnerability of the marine environment and because of the risk of overfishing. The collapse of the Canadian fishery industry around 1992 is a case in point. The collapse of the cod fishery in Greenland is another.

Economic Sustainability

Communities of the Arctic are faced with the challenge of industrial differentiation in order to compete on the international market and attain the goal of economic sustainability. However, the challenge of differentiating the economy is a very difficult task because many societies in the Arctic are marked by insufficient societal differentiation, correlated with their historical marginalization, and a lack of the necessary well-rooted institutional structure. This is in part because the transformation to modernity occurred very fast or in a very abrupt manner, and has led to various degrees of social, cultural, and political disruption of the original matrix. This results in a transformation into a modern world that resembles the typical Third World pattern, where various elements of society proceed at different speeds and on different levels of penetration. This development pattern of asymmetrical penetration is also a phenomenon in the highly developed world but, there, the gap tends to close more quickly because of the highly developed communication structure and the depth and sophistication of the structure of societal capacities. In a social system that is insufficiently differentiated and incompletely institutionalized, the crystallizing effects of a new social component proceed slowly and might only reach the most cosmopolitan structures of the system. The result is a society that lacks societal sustainability with regard to the level of social reproduction that is necessary in order to become an adequate actor in the modern world. One criterion of this adequacy is economic sustainability, but this is only a visible symptom of the question.

In sum, the lack of societal sustainability normally means that a society is insufficiently differentiated and incompletely institutionalized. Societies where there is insufficient differentiation will normally have difficulties in establishing the necessary environment of social stimulation and communicative symbiosis that characterizes dynamic industrial clusters and a sensitive civil society environment. A society must, in general, have reached a certain threshold of institutional condensation in order to realize these goals. Cities are often the way in which social systems historically have established a powerful condensation and they are often the centers of economic growth. One cannot abstract the power of Iceland's economic structure from the fact that more than 60% of Iceland's population live in Reykjavik. The growth of the South Korean economy is also correlated with the fact that they command the fourth largest city in the world. The question is, however, whether the modern structure of telecommunication and the Internet highway will change the matrix by which social systems organize the condensation points of their social structure, which of course will have great consequences for the degree of sustainability for small communities in the Arctic.

Another important indicator of insufficient differentiation is education, where many communities in the Arctic, like Nunavut, tend to lag behind either in absolute or relative terms. Normally, these communities will lack a sufficient number of highly educated people to fill the role pattern of their society with regard to leadership positions in particular, but not exclusively. Growth in knowledge and technological savvy is the very backbone of any structurally solid and long-term sustainability. The real bottleneck to economic success starts with insufficiencies in the socializing forces institutionalized in the societal community.

Because Arctic societies and communities vary greatly in terms of the size and composition of their population, they also face various types of marked problems. Some communities in the Arctic like Greenland and the Canadian Northern territories are among the smallest of microsocieties and they are faced with certain intrinsic types of weaknesses, including the lack of economy of scale. Small states and societies are often too small to have a significant influence on the market in which they participate. They will be price-takers. Arctic communities will normally need a much larger economic space than their own territory in order for their economy to prosper.

In order to reach economic sustainability, Arctic societies need not only have to differentiate their industrial structure. They also need to focus on exports and become active players on the international market. Kenichi Ohmae has noted that only those actors who link up aggressively to the global economy and create a borderless economy, welcome foreign investment, and create natural economic zones, which he called "region states," can successfully win the competitive game of the world market. The key to modern development is to link with the global network of suitable locations. One of the ideas with the Barents Region is to create a zone of industrial cooperation and open up a new Arctic market that creates a borderless economy between Arctic Scandinavia and northwestern Russia. In this way, with regard to regionalism, the issues of sustainability and geopolitics converge at the same point.

Another important issue, that complicates the strategic choices involved in a differentiated strategy is that the Arctic society cannot simply pick and choose among the whole list of new industrial opportunities available on the international scene. If a high-income Arctic community wants to reproduce its standard of living, it will have to find a niche that corresponds to the typical industrial structure of the highly developed countries in the world, that is, generally high-tech industries and knowledge-based industries. Especially, it will become important to become a part of the expanding information technology (IT) industry, which is becoming one of the largest industries in the world. In the future, most jobs in the most advantaged parts of the world will be offered within this sector of knowledge-intensive industries or in sectors galvanized by its activities. In the United States of America, more people today work in the computer industry than in the auto, auto-parts, steel, mining, and petroleum-refining industries combined. Faced with this challenge, the various communities will have to find their own pathway into the modern information society and its knowledge-based industry in order to safeguard their current standard of living under the condition of sustainability. All this, however, places great pressure on society's capacity to upgrade its level of societal sustainability. Certainly, it will be impossible to make the full industrial jump into the modern information age unless the general societal capacities and the labor skills are sufficiently developed. Increasingly, the crucial edge in any industry or nation is the capacity to create and institutionalize intellectual capital; however, intellectual capital is just another name for a society's capacity to release the cognitive potential of its societal capacities. Generally, the solution to the problems of societal sustainability is a precondition for the adequate solution of economic sustainability.

In addition, the cultural element is a factor of its own. Cases from the North Atlantic Rim also show that the greatest barrier to successful industrial development often is the cultural mentality rooted in the symbolism of old industrial life worlds, which functions as a mental container of "object cathexis." In Cape Breton, it is the symbolism of the coal miner; in the Arctic, it might be symbols linked to the traditional way of life.

In this way, the battle of economic sustainability can first be won when the Arctic communities have been able to win the struggle of attaining the necessary level of societal sustainability. One key to this process is to provide optimal conditions for social communication. The aim is to create an impetus for the evolution of institutional intelligence, by establishing a total environment rich in stimulation. The new information technology establishes both a challenge and a promise in this regard.

One of the most fundamental characteristics of the North is that it is situated on some of the largest reserves of natural resources in the world. These have been utilized to various degrees, perhaps most systematically in Russia. However, the real potential of raw materials in the North is still unexploited, as in Greenland. Depending on the conjuncture of the world market, larger and larger parts of the Arctic world will be able to realize a sizable income from active exploitation of its raw materials. This development is in progress. One gigantic project is the Yamal-Europe pipeline in Russia, and gas and oil are already the foundation of the economy in the Hanty-Mansi and the Yamal-Nenets region of Russia. The agreement signed by Russia and China aimed at constructing a 2400-km pipeline is part of the overall picture. Also, both Canada and United States have signaled a need for a major expansion of the natural gas pipeline infrastructure in the North. However, the financial success, which is based on natural resource exploitation, raises important questions about a one-sided development of the economic structure of society. This state of affairs is often loaded with built-in problems, because it tends to sidetrack and restrict the forces of societal development. But even if a one-dimensional natural capital strategy in principle is a solution to economic sustainability, it does not follow that it necessarily is a solution to the question of societal sustainability. Generally, the development of a deeper matrix of societal differentiation is unlikely if the industrial development becomes reduced to opportunistic adaptation, rent seeking, survivalism, or various forms of one-dimensionalism. The real issue at stake is not only the social consequence of various forms of opportunistic adaptation but that the restriction of the dynamics of societal differentiation tends to backfire into the economic system. Another related issue is the danger of a Disneylandization of society, which is implicit in a one-dimensional development of tourism on a grand scale.

Direction for the Future

As the worldwide industrial development progresses, communities and policy-makers in the Arctic are faced with fundamental choices. Generally speaking, there are two major development forces at stake, each suggesting a possible direction for the future of the Arctic. As one of the main natural resource-base areas of the world, nothing would be more natural for the Arctic than to concentrate on the utilization of these resources and develop its industrial structure around that core. Generally, the question of economic sustainability will be solved. However, the cost side of this development involves the risk that the Arctic will become reduced to a raw material hinterland on the margin of the central activities of the world, and the level of sophistication of its societal differentiation will reflect this fact. All other things being equal, it will result in a development where the Arctic world will perhaps become rich but remain marginalized, with all the sociocultural consequences this implies. Also, some empirical research suggests, and some scholars argue, that resource-based economies are negatively correlated to economic growth and often correlated with low rates of savings, trade, investment, and education. However, a natural capital strategy has generally been the strategy that historically has been adopted in Arctic Russia and in the fishing communities of the North Atlantic. Often, society has been reduced to a natural resource machine, where everything has revolved around one single industrial activity. Certainly, very important forces within the Arctic geopolitical and historical situation will press the Arctic toward such a model.

All over the world today, the dynamics of industrial development is linked to the degree to which the general industrial structure can mobilize and codify learning processes embodied in the knowledge element of societal capacities. The crucial facilitator of this process is the IT industry with its various related industrial environments, including the multimedia industry. Advanced actors in the Arctic are increasingly linked up with this process because it is a part of the interactive process of globalization. Because modern social and industrial life is increasingly engulfed in an environment where knowledge and information transfer are built-in elements in the social situation, the most advanced communities in the Arctic will increasingly become involved in this process and facilitate their own agents of cognitive knowledge, despite various problems with regard to the level of education and the incomplete institutionalization of the social role-structure. If the policy-makers in the Arctic design a stimulating and rational environment for the actors, these actors might be able to upgrade the general industrial structure in the direction of industrial differentiation that works around the central forces of modern global development. In this way, Arctic communities might be able to link up to the industrial centers of the world and thereby become more than agents in a resource-rich hinterland of social marginalization. This industrial strategy will tend to enhance the level of societal differentiation and thereby increase the probabilistic chances for the institutionalization of more rich, multi-dimensional environments, where it is easier to limit the forces of out-immigration and provide a richer stimulation to cultural life. In this way, the Arctic will have the choice between two industrial strategies, which will determine its future. One is a strategy involving natural resources and the other is a strategy where Arctic society aims at more diversification. Both strategies can be economically sustainable, but will have a different impact on the configuration of societal differentiation. The real question is whether these two strategies are just two acceptable pathways to modernity or whether they manifest the difference between weak and strong sustainability.

Cultural Sustainability

The most difficult issue to deal with is the question of cultural sustainability, because there is no clear objective or inter subjectively recognized criteria for when the boundaries of a cultural system are violated and endangered. Indeed, culture is the most complex of all issues and is therefore a field of investigation where it is difficult to establish a unified scientific axiomatic framework. However, when we analyze the historical path of globalization phenomena, we will see that the rapid change in the linking of social systems poses a problem, if not a threat, for established cultural systems and traditional life worlds all over the Arctic. This is certainly not a new trend in world history. There has persistently been a battle between the basic values system of well-rooted cultural traditions and the forces of globalization in whatever form. Hence, Christianity as an early agent of the globalization forces succeeded in wiping out shamanism in Greenland. The Bolsheviks in Arctic Russia pursued the same task. The danger of rationalization, technologization, and homogenization of the modern world has been a current theme in Western intellectual thinking since the French Revolution and has been a repetitive theme for many scholars and thinkers of various ideological persuasions. Hence, thinkers like Arnold Gehlen, Theodor Adorno, Jürgen Habermas, Jose Ortega Y. Gasset, Julius Evola, and Martin Heidegger, among others, have articulated a warning against the development of the modern world. The main claim from these thinkers has been that the logic of the modern world is threatening the cultural sustainability of its life worlds.

Within the realm of life in the Arctic, the trend of globalization and modern development has posed a threat to the old structures and the cultural value system of indigenous society. Although the old ways of harvesting natural resources have continued to some extent and are still surrounded by a magic attraction, this whole pattern of life is in a state of siege and is potentially threatened. And indeed, in many places the old ways have been destroyed or are in the process of dissolving by steps. The globalization process—with its video games, rock music, mobile phones, computers, and modern consumption culture—tends to change and gradually eliminate traditional indigenous culture in almost all variables of daily life. Everything is in various stages of transition and often rapid, drastic change. Of course, some of the old pattern is still there, like pieces of wood floating down a stream. As in the case of Inuit culture, there is no simple way to judge the meaning of this process. It is not possible by axiomatic certainty to claim that fundamental Inuit values have been threatened and that the true Inuit culture is in a state of dissolution. It is possible to interpret what is happening as only an adaptive development of Inuit culture, which is not static but an evolving system. So the same phenomena can either be interpreted as a destruction of true Inuit-ness or a liberalization of its true potential as a cultural system. Larisa Abriutina has asked whether "real people" can survive in the 21st century. The answer depends on what we understand to be real. Indeed, the answer depends on how we define the structural logic of culture. However, it is clear that the ultimate meaning of the concept of sustainable development coincides with the cultural self-understanding of the task and the ultimate ends of a specific, historical society.

JENS KAALHAUGE NIELSEN

See also **Royal Greenland Globalization; Sustainable Development and Human Dimensions: Environmental Initiatives**

Further Reading

Auty, Richard M. (editor), *Resource Abundance and Economic Development*, Oxford and New York: Oxford University Press, 2001

Bartmann, Barry, "Patterns of Localism in a Changing Global System." In *Lessons from the Political Economy of Small Islands*, edited by Godfrey Baldacchino & David Milne, New York: Macmillian Press, St Martin Press & University of Prince Edward Island, 2000

Bond, James, "How Information Infrastructure is Changing the World." In *The Information Revolution and the Future of Telecommunication*, Washington, District of Columbia: World Bank, 1997

Castberg, Rune, "Economic Cooperation in the Barents Region: Potentials and Problems in Northwest Russia." In *The Barents Region: Cooperation in the Arctic Europe*, edited by Olav Schram Stokke & Ola Tunander, London: Sage, 1994

Caufield, Richard A., "Political Economy of Renewable Resources in the Arctic." In *The Arctic: Environment, People, Policy*, edited by Mark Nuttall & Terry V. Callaghan, New York: Harwood, 2000

Chance, N.A. & E.N. Andreeva, "Sustainability, equity and natural resource development in Northwest Siberia and Arctic Alaska." *Human Ecology*, 23(2) (1995): 217–240

Gray, Patty A., "Snezhnoe: where and west collide." *Transitions: Changes in Post-Communist Societies*, 4(6) (1997). 96–100

Gylfason, Thovaldur, "Natural Resources and Economic Growth: What Is the Connection?" *Paper for an International Conference on the Factors of Sustainable Economic Growth in Ukraine*, Kiev, Ukraine, June 25–26, 2001

Hannesson, Rögnvaldur, *Investing for Sustainability: The Management of Mineral Wealth*, Dordrecht, The Netherlands: Kluwer Academic Publishers, 2001

Kaalhauge Nielsen, Jens, "Teleonomy, the cognitive complex, societal capacities and social capital: elements for the theoretical analysis of institutional change." In *Greenland and Arctic Economic and Political Issues*, edited by Lise Lyck, *Proceedings of the Eigth Nordic Arctic Research Forum (NARF) Symposium*, Copenhagen Business School, January 22–23, 2000, Copenhaen: Nordic Press, 2001

Lyck, Lise, "Sustainable Development for Post-Sovereign Small Economies". *NARF-Conference*, Moscow: Nuuk, 1997

Martin, Thibault, "The Reflexive Community. Quest for Autonomy as a Coping Strategy in an Inuit Community." In *The Reflexive North*, edited by Nils Aarsæther & Jørgen Ole Bærenholdt, Copenhagen: Nord/Nordic Council of Ministers, 2001

Mayer, Jörg, Brian Chambers & Ayisha Farooq (editors), *Development Policies in Natural Resource Economies*, Cheltham, UK, and Northampton, Massachusetts: Edward Elgar, 1999

Nuttall, Mark, *Protecting the Arctic: Indigenous Peoples and Cultural Survival*, Amsterdam: Harwood Academic Publishers, 1998

OECD, *Politics to Enhance Sustainable Development*, Background report for the meeting of the OECD Council at Ministerial Level in May 2001, OECD, 2001

Pika, A. & D. Bogoyavlensky, "Yamal Peninsula: oil and gas development and problems of demography and health among indigenous population." *Arctic Anthropology*, 32(2) (1995): 61–74

Robin, Mansell & Uta When, *Knowledge Societies: Information Technology for Sustainable Development*, New York: Oxford University Press, 1998

Tykkyläinen, Markku, "Multicausal Theory of Local Economic Development and the Arctic." In *Development in the Arctic*, edited by Tom Greiffenberg, Copenhagen: Dansk Polar Center, 1998

Vitalis, Vangelis, *Measuring Sustainable Development*. OECD-Background paper, 2001

SUSTAINABLE DEVELOPMENT AND HUMAN DIMENSIONS: ENVIRONMENTAL INITIATIVES

Arctic work has historically centered around the environment, both in terms of a focus on the environment itself through exploration and research, and on indigenous peoples' traditional relations with the environment. These understandings of the Arctic can be seen, for example, in the International Polar Years (1882–1883 and 1932–1933), and the International Geophysical Year (1957–1958). The critical relationship between the environment and human dimensions can also be witnessed in the establishment of the journal *Arctic* as a part of research on what has been called North America's final frontier.

From such a background, Arctic research became established as an area of study in several disciplines, primarily in the natural sciences and anthropology. Thus, research on the Arctic has historically included only a limited human dimension; it has been a peripheral area for political action in general. Until recently, the limited extent to which the Arctic was included in political agreements mainly included areas such as anti-dumping agreements or polar bear protection. During the Cold War, the Arctic was viewed largely as a zone for potential conflict, and any extension of initiatives for the Arctic was hindered by United States-Soviet Union tensions. In the 1980s, under the influence of increasing Russian openness to cooperation and the increase in organization and growth of the environment as an issue area, stronger international cooperation on the Arctic developed. Scholars in the field have even occasionally referred to this period at the end of the 20th century as an Arctic boom or the "Age of the Arctic" (Young, 1986; Osherenko and Young, 1989).

One watershed event for Arctic organization was the speech of Soviet leader Mikhail Gorbachev in October 1987 in Murmansk, Russia. In his speech, Gorbachev stressed the importance of cooperation for protecting the natural environment of the North including "tundra, forest tundra, and the northern forest areas… and establishing a system to monitor the state of the natural environment and radiation safety in the region" (Gorbachev, 1987, para. 47). While he also suggested cooperation in other areas, Gorbachev placed the focus on the globally salient questions of environmental and civilian, non-military, cooperation, "effectively alter[ing] the calculation of what was and is possible in Arctic international relations (*Griffiths, 1992: ix*)." These expressions in the Gorbachev speech provided the impetus for Finland—which had historically been limited by the Soviet Union in its actions—to initiate and develop the Arctic Environmental Protection Strategy (AEPS), thus establishing an environmental focus for this Arctic cooperation. As a nonbinding environment-focused strategy, the Arctic Environmental Protection Strategy was established in 1991 through a declaration signed by the US, Canada, Russia, Norway, Sweden, Finland, Denmark-Greenland, and Iceland (which had come to be seen as Arctic "states" during the Cold War risk of conflict across the Arctic Ocean). The AEPS was managed through biannual ministerial meetings, coordinated by civil servants between these meetings, and organized in four working groups. The groups included the Arctic Monitoring and Assessment Program (AMAP), Conservation of Arctic Flora and Fauna (CAFF), the Protection of Arctic Marine Environment (PAME, mainly dealing with the effects of pollution on marine life), and Emergency Prevention, Preparedness and Response (EPPR, to respond to, for instance, oil spills).

Gorbachev's speech also reinforced the establishment of the International Arctic Science Committee (IASC) in 1990—an organization originally seen as a counterpart to the Scientific Committee on Antarctic Research (SCAR) that had already existed for the Antarctic since 1958. In turn, these developments sparked further organization, for instance, with states adapting their Arctic institutions to suit the needs of IASC, and the International Arctic Social Science Association (IASSA) established in 1990 in some conflict with IASC's focus on the natural sciences. While the International Arctic Science Committee initially adopted a largely environment-oriented direction, in later years the group included projects on the sustainable use of living resources. The International Arctic Social Science Association has included work on, among other things, identity and rapid cultural and social change.

The developments also sparked the creation of the Arctic Council, initiated by Canada, which eventually merged with the Arctic Environmental Protection Strategy. While the Finnish AEPS initiative largely placed the focus on the environment, the Arctic Council stressed sustainable development, and in that also human dimensions, a focus that represented a sizable difference between the initiatives. One of the factors that led to the Arctic Council's concerns was the extended global momentum for sustainable development that followed the 1992 UN Conference on Environment and Development. Another significant factor was the drive, especially by the indigenous nongovernmental organization the Inuit Circumpolar Conference (ICC) and Canada, to extend indigenous dimensions in the so far state- and environment-dominated cooperation. The Inuit Circumpolar Conference functions as a cooperation organ for Inuit/Eskimos in four states: Canada, USA (Alaska), Russia, and Denmark (Greenland). The Conference has prominently led in establishing priorities for its areas and suggested projects, for example, in developing the Arctic Council. In response to an ICC report on integration of indigenous knowledge and indigenous participation to the AEPS, the sustainable development direction in the emerging Arctic Council came to focus on indigenous peoples' economies. A task force with this aim was established in 1993 under the auspices of AEPS, and was extended into a working group on par with the AEPS environmental working groups in 1996, prior to the establishment of the Arctic Council later the same year. Coherent with this focus and with the historical foci of Arctic cooperation and established conflicts in Arctic waters, sustainable development at the outset largely came to discuss indigenous rights to marine mammal hunting (sealing and whaling).

Although the Canadian government institutionalized the Arctic Council with the aim to develop both an environmental and a sustainable development program, sustainable development often in this context come to be seen as impeding environmental protection. Conflicts often emerged over the sustainable development direction prior to and following the Council's establishment. The conservation-focused US, which came close to halting Arctic Council negotiations before its establishment, has to date insisted on reviewing projects on an ad hoc basis in order to shepherd marine mammal projects out of discussion. Other states have, for different reasons—either from a desire to work on the otherwise restricted marine mammal questions or from an agreement with the sustainable development principle—wished to establish a strategy on how to develop sustainable development as an Arctic Council aim and choose sustainable development projects.

Within Arctic research, there thus remains a conflict between environmental and sustainable development directions, largely targeting indigenous peoples' extent of hunting. This conflict still persists, for instance, in the difficulties of establishing a direction for work for Arctic Council sustainable development. While the environmental AEPS working groups were included in the Arctic Council following its founding, and formally through the last AEPS ministerial meeting in 1997, it took until 1998 to formally establish sustainable development as a working group in the Arctic Council, until the year 2000 to establish a framework document to direct its work, and until 2002 to develop further specifications of this framework document.

Despite these conflicts, sustainable development projects have flourished and have treated both environmental and human dimensions. Several cooperative examples include the study of ecological and cultural tourism, the role of forestry and reindeer herding in sociocultural and economic sustainability, and comanagement with respect to aboriginal people and traditional ecological knowledge. Most recently, the Survey of Living Conditions in the Arctic (SLICA)—initiated by the Greenland Home Rule government—has involved a comparative study of Inuit, Saami, and indigenous peoples of Chukotka in Russia. The concentration human relations with the environment and especially indigenous peoples is thus prominent, in keeping with historical Arctic foci.

One study that aims to extend a human dimension beyond these aspects is the Arctic Human Development Report (AHDR). This project aims to assess the state of sustainable development and community viability in the circumpolar north, including all Arctic residents. The project emerged from the Standing Committee of Parliamentarians of the Arctic Region (a body originally set up in 1994 to support the establishment of the Arctic Council) and was accepted in 2002 as an Arctic Council sustainable development project. The Arctic Human Development Report was inspired by, among other things, the environment-centered State of the Arctic Environment reports, which were developed under the Arctic Monitoring and Assessment Programme working group (AMAP, 1997; 1998). These reports included a limited human dimensions focus, primarily on impacts of indigenous people's traditional subsistence from pollution. The AHDR was thus intended to analyze the "social state" of the Arctic, and through its reporting, describe the Arctic from a human dimension viewpoint. This goal is based on the assumption that there are some common social denominators and shared concerns for the Arctic area. The Standing Committee of Parliamentarians of the Arctic region has also, developed under their own framework, an Inventory of Circumpolar Arctic Sustainable Development Initiatives, which includes a wide variety of educational, environmental, research, and other activities, evidencing both the variety of circumpolar initiatives and of sustainable development.

Environmental organizations such as the World Wide Fund for Nature/World Wildlife Fund (WWF) and the World Conservation Union (IUCN) have also initiated programs with limited human dimensions. Such organizations are otherwise involved with work primarily under the environment-directed working groups of the Arctic Council. For example, the World Wide Fund for Nature (WWF) has established an International Arctic Programme that also discusses the viability of indigenous cultures in the Arctic. The WWF's work on pollution furthermore impacts human dimensions. The World Conservation Union (IUCN) has also acknowledged an

Arctic approach including, among other things, a project on Arctic tourism in relation to protected areas.

The United Nations Educational, Scientific and Cultural Organization (UNESCO)-developed Man and the Biosphere-program (MAB) also established, as early as 1983, a MAB Northern Sciences Network (NSN) to facilitate MAB activities in northern regions, for example, on comanagement and climate change impacts. Among other bodies that prominently included human dimensions and environmental work is the Northern Forum, an organization for cooperation between subnational governments over an area wider than the Arctic, including, for instance, China, Japan, and Mongolia. The Northern Forum manages projects on a variety of issues, including reindeer management and health issues affecting indigenous peoples. Given its subregional focus, the Forum has also criticized the Arctic Council for including only state and not subregional governments, and thereby a limited human dimension.

The Barents Euro-Arctic Council (BEAR) exists within and for the European Arctic area and includes representation on both the state and regional levels. The Barents Council includes, as does the Arctic Council, participation by the Saami Council, a non-governmental organization representing Saami in four states: Norway, Sweden, Finland, and Russia. BEAR has adopted a rather broad focus on regional work, including, for instance, both economic and environmental cooperation, but the council suffered from not being able to attain funding for priority projects identified in its working groups. Human dimensions work in the Arctic thus differs largely both in terms of character and extent between areas. Human dimensions are often linked to a sustainable development component and are seen as extending an environmental focus that has motivated much work on the Arctic.

E. CARINA H. KESKITALO

See also **Arctic Council; Inuit Circumpolar Conference (ICC); Northern Forum; World Wide Fund for Nature (WWF) International Arctic Program**

Further Reading

AMAP, Arctic Monitoring and Assessment Programme, *Arctic Pollution Issues: A State of the Arctic Environment Report,* Oslo: Arctic Monitoring and Assessment Programme, 1997, website: http://www.grida.no/amap/assess/soaer-cn.htm (Accessed February 20, 2001)

———, *AMAP Assessment Report: Arctic Pollution Issues,* Oslo: Arctic Monitoring and Assessment Programme, 1998

Gorbachev, M., New Thinking in Arms Control: Speech in Murmansk at the Ceremonial Meeting on the Occasion of the Presentation of the Order of Lenin and the Gold Star to the City of Murmansk. Murmansk, 1 October 1987. Stockholm International Peace Research Institute Internet

Database, 1987, website: http://projects.sipri.se/ SAC/ 871001.html (Accessed February 20, 2001)

Keskitalo, E.C.H., *Negotiating the Arctic. The Construction of an International Region,* New York and London: Routledge,2003

Osherenko, G. & O.R. Young (editors), *The age of the Arctic,* Cambridge: Cambridge University Press, 1989

Scrivener, D., "Arctic environmental cooperation in transition." *Polar Record,* 35 (192) (1999): 51–58

Standing Committee of Parliamentarians of the Arctic Region, *Inventory of Circumpolar Arctic Sustainable Development Initiatives,* 2003 website: http://www.grida.no/parl/index.htm (Accessed May 12, 2003)

Tennberg, M., "*Arctic Environmental Cooperation. A Study in Governmentality,* Aldershot: Ashgate, 2000

Young, O.R., "The Age of the Arctic." *Foreign Policy,* 61 (1985–1986): 160–179

Young, O.R., *Creating Regimes. Arctic Accords and International Governance,* Ithaca and London: Cornell University Press, 1998

Young, O.R. & G. Osherenko (editors), *Polar Politics: Creating International Environmental Regimes,* Ithaca and London: Cornell University Press, 1993

SVALBARD

Svalbard is an archipelago in the Arctic Ocean, about midway between Norway and the North Pole. Svalbard comprises all islands between latitude 74° N and latitude 81° N and between longitude 10° E and longitude 35° E, including the sea within a territorial boundary 4 nautical miles from land. The archipelago is Norwegian territory, but is largely uninhabited except for the mining settlements at Longyearbyen and Barentsburg (a total population about 2400), and the international research stations at Ny-Ålesund. The principal islands are Spitsbergen, Nordaustlandet, Barentsøya, Edgeøya, Kong Karls Land, Prins Karls Forland, and Bjørnøya (Bear Island). The total area is 62,160 sq km (about 24,000 sq mi), which is only slightly smaller than West Virginia in the United States and almost 1.5 times the area of Denmark. With the exception of some coastal lowlands, the landscape is mountainous with many large and small glaciers. The highest peak (Newtontoppen) reaches 1717 m above sea level.

Geology

The geological history of Svalbard spans over 400 million years and comprises a fairly continuous succession of Precambrian metamorphic rocks, to Paleozoic and Mesozoic sedimentary rocks, as well as Tertiary to Quaternary strata. It is unusual in preserving a nearly complete geological record, compared to mainland Norway where only Precambrian rocks outcrop. Svalbard has been greatly affected by crustal movements along north-south trending lines with folding and thrusting of crustal blocks taking place over a long period of time. Rifting associated with the opening of the North Atlantic Ocean during the past 56 million years has separated Svalbard from its former position along northernmost Greenland, at that time located a few hundred kilometers further south compared to the present position.

Igneous and metamorphic bedrock comprises the deepest and oldest type of bedrock on Svalbard and is mainly found in western and northeastern Spitsbergen, in addition to the northern part of Nordaustlandet. Sedimentary rocks were laid down by rivers and in the ocean from Devonian to Tertiary times. Apart from gentle folding and thrusting, these consolidated deposits have remained undisturbed. Together, they have a thickness in excess of 15,000 m and form a huge trough-shaped structure extending from Isfjorden toward the south. The Tertiary deposits include coal layers, which have formed the basis for a mining industry on Svalbard. The youngest deposits are from the Quaternary period and are represented by unconsolidated glacial, periglacial, and fluvial deposits.

Climate

The climate of Svalbard is Arctic and the recent mean annual air temperature is about –6°C at sea level and as low as –15°C in the high mountains. Meteorological observations on Svalbard were initiated in 1912. From about 1915 to 1920, the mean annual air temperature increased rapidly from about –9°C to about –5°C. Following this temperature increase—which was concurrently experienced at several other North Atlantic measurement sites—the annual air temperature at sea level since 1930 has slowly declined to the present –6°C, although with 1–3°C interannual variations superimposed upon this trend. At Longyearbyen in central Spitsbergen, the coldest month is February with –15.2°C, the warmest month is July with 6.2°C and the mean annual air temperature is –5.8°C (average 1975–2000).

Precipitation measured at sea level is low, only about 200 mm per annum in central Spitsbergen and somewhat higher, about 400–600 mm along both the western and eastern coasts of the island. Precipitation increases with altitude, about 10–20% per 100 m, and glacier mass balance investigations as well as fluvial discharge measurements suggest that annual precipitation in the highlands may be in excess of 700–900 mm, even in the dry interior of Spitsbergen. Usually, April-May is dry, although large interannual differences are quite normal. The periods February-March and August-September tend to be comparatively humid, although very large interannual differences once again are to be expected. In addition, December-January may witness heavy snowfalls in some years. Snow is the dominant type of precipitation.

The effect of wind is significant, partly because of the strength, and partly because of the absence of high

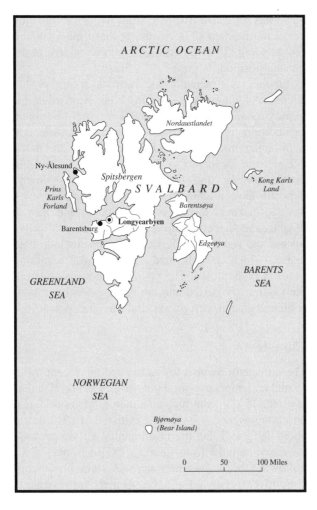

Svalbard, its main islands and towns.

usually ice-bound for most of the year. The polar sea ice in February-April usually extends to reach Bear Island about one-half of the way to northernmost Norway. Significant interannual variations in the extent of the sea ice cover are quite common, depending upon air temperature and wind conditions.

Longyearbyen has midnight sun from April 20 to August 23 and the sun is below the horizon from October 26 to February 16. Because of the influence of the atmosphere, the time of midnight sun is somewhat longer than the time of darkness. Reflectance of sunlight in the atmosphere likewise ensures that it is not completely dark before the sun is more than 6° under the horizon. The real "Polar Night" (i.e., 24 h of complete darkness) is therefore only experienced in Longyearbyen between November 14 and January 29. During the winter, the Northern Lights (Aurora Borealis) are a frequent phenomena.

Geomorphology

Svalbard falls within the zone of continuous permafrost and periglacial and permafrost-related terrain features are widespread in areas not covered by glaciers. At the coasts, the permafrost thickness is small, only 10–40 m, but increases to more than 450 m in the highlands. Terrain phenomena such as pingos, ice wedges, and rock glaciers are widespread, especially in the dry central regions of Spitsbergen. Snow avalanches are frequent, especially on downwind slopes. Periglacial features such as solifluction (gelifluction) lobes are found, although especially in the more humid western regions. In addition, various forms of patterned ground such as stone circles and stripes are widespread and well developed. Fluvial activity is important, especially during the spring melt (the nival flood), but remains so for most of the summer as well. Large braided river systems draining glaciers are found in most major valleys, transporting large amounts of sediments into the fjords. When these riverbeds dry up during the autumn, wind erosion of fresh fine-grained sediments lead to deposition of eolian sediments (loess) downwind the rivers. This process eventually ends when the winter snow cover is firmly established in October–November.

About 60% of the islands are presently covered by glaciers, many of which terminate with calving fronts into the ocean. Bjørnøya is the only major island within Svalbard without glaciers. In central Spitsbergen, most glaciers are comparatively small due to the dry climate, but along both the west and east coast of Spitsbergen large valley glaciers and ice caps dominate. On the eastern islands, Edgeøya, Barentsøya, and Nordaustlandet, several large ice caps are found. Due to low air temperatures and low precipitation, most glaciers in the dry interior of Spitsbergen move rather

vegetation such as trees. The dominant wind direction across the islands is from SSE toward NNW, although the local wind direction may vary greatly due to channeling effects by topography and according to the meteorological situation. Even during the summer, wind from northwest and north may bring cold polar air masses and snow showers to the islands within few hours. For this reason, snow may fall at any altitude in any month of the year. At sea level, the ground surface is usually snow covered from late September to early June, while altitudes above 600–800 m tend to be covered continuously by snow, except for peaked topography and wind-exposed slopes.

A branch of the North Atlantic Current reaches the west coast and northern tip of the main island Spitsbergen, keeping water open and navigable most years along the southern part of the west coast. Low temperatures and heavy icing conditions, however, make shipping operations during wintertime hazardous, especially for smaller vessels. The eastern cost of Spitsbergen and the coasts of the eastern islands are sluggishly, only 1–2 m per year and therefore are only little crevassed. In the more humid regions along the coasts, however, glacier velocities of more than 10–30 m per year and large crevasses are frequent. A significant number of glaciers in Svalbard from time to time advance with extraordinary high velocity, up to several kilometers during 3–6 years. This surge behavior is characteristic for at least 30% of all glaciers in Svalbard and possibly up to about 60% of all glaciers display this kind of behavior from time to time, with a recurrent interval of 50–100 years. A 30 km wide sector of the large ice cap on Nordaustlandet, Austfonna, between 1936 and 1938 experienced at surge advance of more than 20 km into the ocean. This is presumably the longest surge advance ever recorded at any glacier on this planet.

The mass balance of many glaciers in Svalbard is partly controlled by snowdrift during the winter and many glaciers for this reason face downwind, that is, toward NNW and northwest. Glaciers along the east coasts presumably receive huge amounts of snow from snow drifting across the sea ice cover during the winter, driven by southeasterly winds. Since the above-mentioned warming 1915–1920, many glaciers on Svalbard have experienced a negative mass balance, with corresponding retreat and thinning.

During the last glacial maximum during the Weichselian ice age, Svalbard glaciers extended beyond the present coast and terminated at the edge of the shelf to west. According to present opinion, the Svalbard glaciation at the last glacial maximum was coherent with an ice sheet covering the Barents Sea, representing a northern extension of the European ice sheet. Some of the highest mountains, especially along the western coast of Spitsbergen, may have escaped glaciation and protruded above the ice cover as nunataks.

At the end of the Weichselian, about 12,500 years ago, temperatures rapidly rose and glaciers in Svalbard melted back. Due to the eustatic sea-level rise brought about by the retreating North American and European Ice Sheets, coastal regions were submerged by the rising sea up to about 60–80 m above the modern coastline. Following this, isostatic effects of the decreasing ice load within the Svalbard region again brought about a relative sea-level fall to the present situation.

During the early part of the present interglacial, the Holocene, the mean annual air temperatures in Svalbard were presumably higher than now, up to 3–4°C, and glaciers and permafrost was reduced compared to modern conditions. Several of the present glaciers were presumably not in existence at that time. About 4000 years ago, a climatic change toward lower temperatures and presumably also wetter conditions began within the North Atlantic region and both glaciers and permafrost thickness have displayed a grow-

ing trend since then. Well-preserved plant remains found beneath a glacier near the town Longyearbyen, about 2 km upstream in relation to the present glacier terminus, were covered by the advancing glacier about 1600 years ago. Most glaciers on Svalbard attained their Holocene maximum extension only 80–100 years ago, at the end of the Little Ice Age.

Early History

Svalbard appears in 12th-century Icelandic and Norwegian written records, and early Norse knowledge about the archipelago is commonly assumed. The name Svalbard is thought to be of Norse origin, referring to "cold or barren coasts." Russian people (the Pomors) may have visited the archipelago early in the 16th century, but no solid proof of this or the Norse discovery of Svalbard has been presented. Undisputed, however, is the exploration of Svalbard by a Dutch expedition under the navigator Willem Barents in 1596.

Willem Barents made three voyages from the Netherlands in search of a North East Passage to Asia. The first vessel sailed on June 5, 1594, reached the northeastern extremity of Novaya Zemlya, and returned. A second expedition of seven vessels was sent out the following year, but too late in the season to be successful. On the third expedition, which started in May 1596, Barents discovered and named Spitsbergen (now Svalbard). There, his two vessels separated to conduct independent explorations. Barents and his crew spent a miserable winter frozen in at the northern tip of Novaya Zemlya. On June 13, 1597, they left in two open boats; Barents died shortly afterward. The survivors reached the shores of the Kola Peninsula where the second ship of the expedition rescued them. The Barents Sea, which he crossed in 1594, 1596, and 1597, and Barents Island in the Svalbard archipelago are named after him.

At the time of Barents' voyages, Svalbard was often considered as part of Greenland, assumed to extend from southernmost Greenland near the Norse settlements, north of Iceland, to Novaya Zemlya at the Russian coast. For this reason, shortly after the discovery by Barents, the Danish king Christian IV claimed Svalbard to be part of the Danish-Norwegian kingdom. Whalers of several nationalities, especially English, Dutch, Danish, Norwegian, and German, were active in the waters around Svalbard from early in the 17th century, reaching a culmination in the period 1630–1635 for hunting in the fjords and coastal waters of northwest Svalbard. Not only whales but also walruses and seals were the objects for hunting. Later in the 17th century, whaling moved toward the open sea west of Spitsbergen, near to the drift ice along northeast Greenland.

As the whaling activity changed character in the late 17th century, the European presence on the islands of Svalbard declined and was followed by Russian (the Pomors) dominance from the early 18th century. The Pomor people were living along the coasts of the White Sea in northwest Russia and during the 16th century they gradually extended their hunting activities into the Barents Sea area, presumably reaching Svalbard around the mid-17th century. Some investigations of remains from Russian buildings on Svalbard, however, indicate these to date from the previous century, and the question about the timing of the first Pomor discovery of Svalbard still remains to be solved. The Pomors traditionally used the name "Grumant" for Svalbard, presumably referring to Greenland.

Planned or by accident, wintering on Svalbard was attempted with varying degrees of success on several occasions before the Russian period, but the Pomors were the first to do this on a bigger and more organized scale. They mainly hunted walrus, but would also hunt various bird species, Arctic fox, Svalbard reindeer, and polar bears. Many remains of their wooden houses can still be found along the coasts of many islands in Svalbard. Following a series of bad years with low catches, loss of ships and crew the Russian period abruptly came to an end around 1750. Within a few years, however, this was followed by a surge of renewed Norwegian hunting activity (especially whales and walruses) around the archipelago, using new technology such as the steam engine and harpoon guns.

Research Expeditions

As Great Britain during the 18th century became the undisputed leading sea power, the Royal Navy became interested also in the Arctic waters. One naval expedition with two ships, the Constantine John Phipps expedition, in 1773 visited the Svalbard area with the purpose of investigating the geography of the area as well as looking into the possibilities of crossing the Arctic Ocean by ship. Unfortunately, however, shortly north of Nordaustlandet, both ships were stopped by solid sea ice and the expedition had to return to England.

The 19th century witnessed a significant number of scientific expeditions to Svalbard, mainly with the purpose of studying the geography of the archipelago and other adjoining Arctic regions, but also driven by a desire of displaying national strength. As one example among others, the famous German geographer August Peterman in 1868 argued for a German expedition to the North Pole using expressions such as "national strength" and "national importance." Several expeditions expressly wanted to use Svalbard as the basis for attempts to reach the North Pole, such as the ill-fated Andreé attempt in 1897 to reach the pole by balloon from northwest Spitsbergen.

The Norwegian geologist Baltazar Mathias Keilhau initiated systematic research on Svalbard in 1827. In the mid-19th century, when the emergent theory of past Ice Ages competed with Darwin's theory on the Origin of Species as the most contentious issue in contemporary natural sciences, outstanding scientists such as Otto Torell of Sweden came to Svalbard to experience the action of glaciers and ice caps. Additionally, other nations such as France were active, such as exemplified by the Recherché-expeditions in 1838 and 1839. In general, the main purpose was investigations of the physical geography of Svalbard, but biological, geological, and meteorological investigations were also carried out. These expeditions were followed by a series of expeditions in 1864–1873 by the famous Swedish-Finnish geologist Adolf Erik Nordenskiöld. The International Polar Year 1882–1883 also further stimulated research initiatives in the Svalbard area and other Arctic regions.

Mining Activities

On several occasions since the early 17th–century, ships had taken small amounts of coal from coastal exposures, but only for private use. The Norwegian skipper Søren Zachariassen presumably carried out the first commercial mining operation in 1899, in Isfjorden (about 40,000 kg), for later sale in Norway. This was only a small-scale undertaking, but following 1900, several coal companies were established in Norway with the purpose of initiating more comprehensive mining operations on Svalbard. A British-Norwegian company, Spitzbergen Coal and Trading Co., in 1905 established the first mining town—Advent City—on the northeast shore of Adventbay in central Spitsbergen. This mining attempt, however, was abandoned after few years, in 1908. A Norwegian-American company The Arctic Coal Company took over the area on the southwest side of Adventbay in 1905 and within a short time began mining operations. The American mining entrepreneur John M. Longyear founded the present main settlement Longyearbyen (Longyear City) on that occasion. Russian interests established themselves shortly after this with mining operations near the modern Russian settlement Barentsburg a few years before World War I. In 1916, the Arctic Coal Company was sold to the Norwegian company Store Norske Spitsbergen Kulkompani A/S (SNSK).

Norwegian national interest in supply of coal from Svalbard gradually grew, especially during the British war-induced blockade in 1917. Today, SNSK remains as one of the two coal mining companies excavating coal in Svalbard today. The other is Trust Arktikugol,

Mountains and glaciers on Prins Karls Forland by Forland Sound, Svalbard. *Copyright Bryan and Cherry Alexander Photography*

a Russian company mining the deposits in and around Barentsburg.

No permanent settlement took place on Svalbard until after coal mining began in the early 20th century. Since then, coal mining has been the major industry on Svalbard. Until recently, the Norwegian mining activity has mainly been concentrated around the town Longyearbyen in central Spitsbergen. Today, Longyearbyen is the chief port and administrative center of Svalbard. Other nations, such as Netherlands, Russia, and Sweden also established themselves with mining facilities in the early 20th century, although none of the mining activities carried out in the 20th century ever turned out to be profitable from an economical point of view. In the early 21st century, new large-scale Norwegian mining operations by Store Norske Spitsbergen Kulkompani A/S at the old Swedish mining town Svea (Spitsbergen) may for the first time turn out to be economically profitable.

The Svalbard Treaty

In the late 19th century, Norway was clearly the most heavily engaged nation on Svalbard, even though Svalbard internationally still was considered as *terra nullius*, a no man's land. For potential economical reasons, in 1871, it was considered by Norway and especially Sweden (at that time in union) to investigate the possibility of obtaining international recognition of a Norwegian claim to Svalbard. The Norwegian government was not entirely happy by this initiative, which soon was halted by Russia, who claimed traditional Russian interest in the region.

As tensions within the Swedish-Norwegian union grew until Norway's independence in 1905, the question about the sovereignty over Svalbard became a Norwegian national issue. From 1907, the Norwegian government initiated talks between nations with traditional interest on Svalbard, in order to resolve the question of the future status of the archipelago. This was followed up by an international conference in 1909, where a Norwegian administration of Svalbard was suggested in the invitation. The Swedish government, however, protested against this, instead suggesting a common Norwegian-Swedish-Russian council for Svalbard—a condominium model. United States and Germany, both having a potential economic interest in the area, objected to this model, as it would effectively remove Svalbard's terra nullius status. An international conference in Oslo on the future status of Svalbard was then prepared for June 1914. On the conference, growing international tension, especially between Germany and Russia, halted attempts toward agreement on the Svalbard issue and during the following war, further negotiations were suspended. The war, however, especially in Russia demonstrated the importance of free access to the Barents Sea, and the railway to Murmansk was constructed within a few years. Russian and subsequent Soviet interest in the Svalbard region for this strategic reason grew toward the end of the war. At the same time, various British interests argued for the importance of having a British naval base on Svalbard.

At the peace conference in Paris 1919–1920, Norway claimed sovereignty over Svalbard, partly as compensation for losses endured during the war, and partly based upon previous Norwegian activity in the area. France supported the Norwegian proposal; the United States and the UK were at least in principle positive. A somewhat modified treaty, giving sovereignty to Norway but also ensuring rights of foreign citizens, was finally signed on February 9, 1920. The sovereignty was formally put in to effect on August 14, 1925, the date from which Svalbard officially became a part of the Kingdom of Norway. The Svalbard treaty has later received acceptance from more than 40 nations. Neither Germany nor the Soviet Union was invited to participate in the negotiations in Paris. Germany, however, became a signatory power in 1925 and USSR in 1935, following recognition of the Soviet government by United States in 1934.

Limitations in Norwegian sovereignty were that all signatories should have equal rights to exploit mineral deposits in Svalbard, subject to Norwegian regulation. Norway was also supposed to work out a mining code and settle any conflicting property claims within the region. Also, according to the treaty, Svalbard should remain as a demilitarized area. The Norwegian government should recognize historical rights within the region, and regulations should be formulated in order to protect flora and fauna. This has later been specified in a comprehensive set of environmental regulations for Svalbard, addressing traffic, litter storage, pollution, and the management of wild life. Since the treaty came into force, the Norwegian Ministry of Industry has administered Svalbard, through a governor (Sysselmann) residing in Longyearbyen.

The Interwar Period

During the interwar period, most mining companies active in Svalbard experienced great problems and many of them terminated activities. Only the Norwegian company Store Norske Spitsbergen Kulkompani A/S and the Soviet state trust Arktikugeol continued coal mining during the 1930s. A little more than 300,000 tons coal were shipped from Svalbard each year during the period 1925–1929, mainly from the Norwegian mining activities. The interwar period was a golden period for wintering trappers and for sealing in the adjacent waters. Cod fisheries experienced a short upswing around 1930 when 20th-century temperatures reached their maximum following the marked increase from 1915 to 1920. At Ny-Ålesund in NW Spitsbergen, a landing station for cod was established at that time. In addition, tourism was becoming an industry during the prewar period, especially during the 1930s and a regular passenger route from Norway was established in 1934.

World War II

German troops occupied Norway in April 1940. This had, however, no immediate consequences for mining and other activities on Svalbard, as both Germany and the Norwegian government in exile in London wanted all Svalbard activities, including broadcast of daily meteorological observations, to continue as before.

Following the German attack on USSR in June 1941, the Barents Sea and Svalbard suddenly became strategically important in relation to supplying USSR from the west. Of special importance was access to meteorological observations from Svalbard for both protection and attack on convoys from UK to Murmansk. Not possessing the means to occupy and hold Svalbard at that time, the British and Norwegian administration decided to evacuate all people from Svalbard, an operation Norway effected in August–September 1941. The evacuation made most mining facilities inoperable, and stores of oil and coal were set on fire.

Shortly after the evacuation, the German Wehrmacht (armed forces) landed a small unit and established a meteorological station shortly southeast of Longyearbyen. This station was evacuated the following summer after being spotted by the British Royal Air Force; but throughout the war, the German army from time to time established both manned and sophisticated automatic meteorological stations at various sites in the Svalbard region, in order to acquire meteorological observations. The last unit of the German forces to surrender in World War II did so in September 1945 in Rijpfjorden, northernmost Nordaustlandet. Two years earlier, in September 1943, German warships—including the battleship Tirpitz—attacked Barentsburg, Grumant, and Longyearbyen, demolishing and burning most buildings and mining facilities. The Germans raided Svea and Ny-Ålesund in 1944.

The Postwar Period

In November 1944, when the Red Army was entering northernmost Norway via Finland, the Soviet Foreign Minister Molotov suggested revisions to the Svalbard treaty. According to the Soviet point of view, a joint Norwegian-USSR administration ought to govern Svalbard, and Bjørnøya (Bear Island) should become Russian territory. The Norwegian government refused this but agreed to open discussions regarding the future military status of Svalbard. The USSR reiterated its proposal in 1946, but the Norwegian government flatly rejected any discussions of changes in the treaty. The Soviet administration turned its attention to the nascent Cold War such that any revisions to the Svalbard treaty diminished in political importance.

Shortly after the war, Norway and the Soviet Union reestablished mining facilities on Svalbard. In 1949, Norway became a member of NATO, and in 1951, the Soviet Union protested against the establishment of a NATO joint command including Svalbard, although under the specific condition that no military structures be established on Svalbard. Later, in 1958–1959, USSR launched protests against Norwegian plans of establishing an airfield at Ny-Ålesund and in 1964 against the construction of a telemetry station at Ny-Ålesund, intended for communication with satellites operated by the European Space Research Organization (ESRO). In addition, the issue of establishment of a modern airport near Longyearbyen led to contacts between Norway and USSR. Eventually, the airport was opened in 1975 with Russian access to facilities as well. Today, this airport is vital for most activities on Svalbard, with scheduled daily flights to Europe and to local destinations (Svea and Ny-Ålesund) on Spitsbergen. It should be emphasized, however, that by tradition, local relations between the Norwegian and Russian population in Svalbard always have been friendly and remained so even during the Cold War.

During the final part of the 20th century, Norway invested heavily in development of Longyearbyen, especially in the years after 1990. At the same time, Russian mining operations were limited to Barentsburg, closing both Grumantbyen (1961) and Pyramiden (1998). Especially, the years following the collapse of USSR were difficult for the Russian population and mining industry. Before the reopening of Norwegian mining operations at Svea in 2000, diminishing coal reserves at Longyearbyen precipitated Norwegian plans for enhancing the tourist industry and establishment of a university (UNIS, see below) in Longyearbyen.

The size of the present population of Svalbard is not precisely known, but is estimated to be about 2400 (July 2000). Little more than 1420 persons live in Longyearbyen (78°N), the northernmost town on the planet and the largest settlement on Svalbard, followed by Barentsburg (about 850 inhabitants). Tourism now represents an important means of income for the population on Svalbard, as does the new university in Longyearbyen, although coal mining remains as the major economic activity on Svalbard. There is also some trapping of seal, polar bear, fox, and walrus, although of little economic importance.

Tourism

Tourism on Svalbard began as expeditionlike arrangements for English gentlemen and the leisure class in the latter half of the 19th century. Very soon, similar tourism from other nations such as, for example France, were initiated. After a few years, however, this was followed by cruise arrangements for larger groups of other people as well, often using whaling boats available in Norway. Even the American mining entrepreneur John M. Longyear, founder of Longyearbyen in 1905, first came to Svalbard as a tourist a few years before. The media attention created by the many dramatic attempts at reaching the North Pole from Svalbard no doubt contributed to the growing interest in visiting Svalbard as a tourist. In 1896, a small hotel was constructed at the coast of Adventbay in central Spitsbergen, near the present administrative center Longyearbyen, in order to make land-based tourism activities possible as well. This initiative represents the beginning of organized tourism on Svalbard.

Today, at the beginning of the 21st century, modern tourism on Svalbard is still centered on Longyearbyen, where an international airport, harbor, several modern hotels and other lodging facilities, restaurants, pubs, shops, indoor sport and swimming facilities, museum, and even a gallery are at hand. Cruises as well as land-based tours are arranged for tourists throughout the summer, while skiing and snow scooter tours are popular winter activities, especially from March to May. Each year, several thousands of tourists visit Svalbard.

UNIS

Since 1993, Svalbard has housed the northernmost university in the world, located in Longyearbyen and specializing in Arctic Geology, Arctic Biology, Arctic Geophysics, and Arctic Technology. The University Courses on Svalbard (UNIS) is a private foundation established by the Norwegian government and owned by Norway's four universities. The objective of the foundation is to offer university-level courses and to perform research relevant to Svalbard's geographical location in the High Arctic. In the longer term, UNIS will form the core of the Svalbard Science Center (SSC), an international Arctic center of expertise in research and education on Svalbard, which will also incorporate a large number of professional and scientific institutions represented on Svalbard.

Research Facilities in Ny-Ålesund

In Ny-Ålesund, the former Norwegian coal-mining company Kings Bay operates the world's northernmost permanent settlement, Ny-Ålesund (79°45′N), on a year-round basis. Infrastructure and other logistical services such as full board and lodging to scientists and research stations operating in Ny-Ålesund are provided by a permanent staff consisting of 20–30 people. Ny-Ålesund was founded as a mining settlement in 1917, but following a serious disaster in 1962, the Norwegian government in 1963 decided to stop further mining operations in this area.

The Norwegian Government later designated Ny-Ålesund to be the center for environmental research at Svalbard. All other activities in Ny-Ålesund must pay due consideration to the needs and demands of the research activities. The aim is to develop Ny-Ålesund into a leading international environmental research and monitoring station in the Arctic. Norway, Germany, Great Britain, Italy, Japan, and France all have established their own permanent research stations in Ny-Ålesund. Each year, scientists from at least fifteen nations come here to work on 120 different research projects.

OLE HUMLUM

See also **Barentsburg; Coal Mining; Longyearbyen; Norway; Svalbard Treaty**

Further Reading

Arlov, Thor B., *A Short History of Svalbard*, Tromsø, Norway: Norwegian Polar Institute, 1994

——, *Svalbards historie*, Oslo: Aschenhoug, 1996

Helle, Audun, *Geology of Svalbard*, Tromsø, Norway: Norwegian Polar Institute, 1993

Mehlum, Fridtjof, *Birds and Mammals of Svalbard*, Tromsø, Norway: Norwegian Polar Institute, 1990

Rønning, Olaf I., *The Flora of Svalbard*, Tromsø, Norway: Norwegian Polar Institute, 1996

SUERSAQ—*See* HENDRIK, HANS

SVALBARD TREATY

By the Svalbard Treaty of 1920, the Kingdom of Norway was given responsibility for and sovereignty over the Svalbard archipelago, Europe's northernmost territory. The Svalbard Treaty was signed at the Peace Conference in Paris on February 9, 1920 by Norway, the United States, Denmark, France, Italy, Japan, Netherlands, Sweden, the United Kingdom, and Ireland. As ratified by all signatory powers, The Svalbard Treaty came into force on August 14, 1925. This date has since been considered as an unofficial "national holiday" for Svalbard.

Viewed before as *terra nullis*, that is no man's land, the legal status of Svalbard was reconsidered in the second half of the 19th century due to increasing interest in scientific exploration and research. The import of the first coal from Svalbard to Norway in 1899 led to prospecting and mining by several companies from different states on Svalbard, resulting in an increase in conflicts on land occupation. After its independence from the union with Sweden in 1905, Norway made several attempts to improve the legal regime of the archipelago, resulting in a conference including all relevant powers in 1914, but the process was interrupted by World War I. In 1919, the Supreme Council of the Peace Conference in Paris agreed—based on a request by Norway—to establish a separate Spitsbergen Commission in order to examine the Svalbard question. The Svalbard Treaty focusing on nationalization rather than on the management of the archipelago area by an

international commission resulted from this commission. The decision to grant Norway sovereignty over the archipelago, and not to constitute an international territory or a mandate over Svalbard under the League of Nations, also helped to avoid the complexity of a permanent international administration. The commission emphasized the need for a final solution in the Svalbard question, and the installation of an effective administration on Svalbard. Although no explicit references were made, the neutral role of Norway and the desire for a stabile political situation in the European North most likely influenced the decision.

Background

The Svalbard Treaty is a so-called "open" treaty joined by 41 countries (2001). The treaty has two main aspects. First, Norway undertakes to accord to nationals of all signatories equal treatment in terms of economic activity within Svalbard, that is, the treaty ensures equal rights to the citizens of these countries on the archipelago, while Svalbard is still to be open to all countries, even those that did not sign the treaty. Second, Norway is obliged neither to create nor allow the establishment of any naval base or to construct any fortification in Svalbard, that is, the archipelago shall remain demilitarized.

Many conflicts over mining rights and ownership of Svalbard remained unresolved until the Svalbard Treaty was ratified. Based on article 8 of the Treaty, which establishes that Norway undertakes to provide mining regulations, the "Mining Code" was adopted by the Norwegian Royal decree of August 7, 1925, which regulated mining activities.

During World War II, Svalbard was first raided by German troops in August 1941, and in September 1943, the German battleships *Tirpitz* and *Scharnhorst*, with 10 destroyers, completed the devastation of the mines and mining installations by bombarding the islands. In 1944, the USSR—which had not signed the 1920 treaty but adhered to it on February 27, 1935—was refused a request to share with Norway in the administration and defense of Svalbard. After the war, the mining settlements were rebuilt. Coal-mining concessions operated by the USSR and later Russia account for about one-third of the coal shipped from Svalbard.

Coal mining is the major economic activity on Svalbard. The treaty of February 9, 1920 gives the 41 signatories equal rights to exploit mineral deposits, subject to Norwegian regulation. Although US, UK, Dutch, and Swedish coal companies have mined in the past, today only Norway and Russia have permanent economic activities. Within the archipelago, three mining settlements and four scientific stations operate. There is also some seal and fox hunting, and the tourist industry has considerably increased in importance during the last decade.

Today's Structure

Norwegian law is used on Svalbard, with the exception of any laws that conflict with the treaty. Thus, there are no restrictions, for example, on work permits as it would limit the commercial activities of other countries. Practically all Norwegians living on the archipelago are registered in their home municipality on the Norwegian mainland. In 1971, a local Svalbard council was established in Longyearbyen, with representatives from the different institutions and groups on Svalbard. The main function of the Council is to make recommendations, and not to adopt binding decisions. It is discussed (2001) if, and how to introduce a local democracy in the Norwegian settlements on Spitsbergen. Russia on its side has a consul in Barentsburg.

The treaty specified that Norway was not allowed to use Svalbard for its own profit—so all taxes there must be used only on the archipelago, resulting in a separate Svalbard-budget, although Norway can add money to this budget, which they do. The mining rights are handled by "Bergmesteren på Svalbard" (the Mining Inspector), while "Sysselmannen på Svalbard" (the Governor of Svalbard, also "notarius publicus"; helping judge in the under court) is the representative of the Norwegian Authorities on the archipelago. The Sysselmannen is responsible for example, for regular police duties, monitoring pollution and wildlife, and more. His office is located in Longyearbyen. Svalbard is juridically sorted under two Norwegian region's courts: Nord-Troms herredsrett and Hålogaland Lagmannsrett, both situated in Troms county on the Norwegian main land. While Sysselmannen is subordinated to the Norwegian Minister of Justice, other areas are subordinated to the respective national institutions like the Ministry of Trade and Industry, The Norwegian Directorate for Nature Management, or the Directorate for Cultural Heritage. The Norwegian Polar Institute located in Tromsø is the professional and strategic adviser of the Norwegian Government for issues on environmental protection.

Outlook

Norway was in practice reluctant to implement the formally granted sovereignty until the mid-1970s (Østreng, 1975). The establishment of the 200-mile Fishery Protection Zone (also called Spitsbergen Fishery Conservation Zone) through Norway in 1977 led to international dispute. Different interpretations of whether Norway is allowed under the Svalbard Treaty to give Norwegian fishermen exclusive fishing rights around Svalbard are the background for the disagreement. The Norwegian authorities intended to establish an economic zone in accordance with the introduction of exclusive economic zones (EEZ) in 1976, thereby granting Norwegian fisherman exclusive fishing rights. So far, Norwegian authorities have been able to establish and to maintain the Protection Zone around Svalbard and have additionally demonstrated a relatively successful management of fish stocks around Svalbard. This management of the fish stocks has to be seen in relation to the observation that in the Svalbard Zone most of the fishermen comply most of the time with the Norwegian regulations (Hønneland, 1998). In the discussion about Norwegian sovereign rights on the continental shelf and in the 200-mile zone, Norway claims—to the protest of other states—that the rights of other states under the Svalbard Treaty and the Mining Code do not apply in these maritime areas.

On the whole, however, the administration of the Svalbard archipelago, given to the Norwegian Authorities by the Svalbard Treaty, can be considered as successful, and has so far not led to serious conflicts. The Government of Norway stresses its objective for Svalbard to be one of the world's best-managed wilderness areas. "In event of a conflict between environmental targets and other interests, environmental considerations are to prevail within the limits dictated by treaty obligations and sovereignty considerations" (Royal Norwegian Ministry of Justice and the Police, 2000; see **National Parks and Protected Areas: Norway**). The Norwegian Government is strongly committed to remain and to exercise its sovereignty on Svalbard. Future challenges here are the focus on the Arctic areas in general, and the protection of the vulnerable environment in particular, especially in a time when tourism on the archipelago is increasing.

JOCHEN PETERS

See also **Svalbard**

Further Reading

Barr, Susan, *Norway's Polar Territories*, Oslo: Aschehoug, 1987

Hønneland, Geir, "Compliance in the Fishery Protection Zone around Svalbard." *Ocean Development and International Law*, 29(4)(1998): 339–360

Østreng, Willy, *Det politiske Svalbard*, Oslo: Gyldendal, 1975, pp. 109–117

Royal Norwegian Ministry of Justice and the Police. Report No. 9 to the Storting (1999–2000), Svalbard

Sing, E.C. & A.A. Saguirian, "The Svalbard Archipelago: The Role of Surrogate Negotiators." In *Polar Politics*, edited by Oran R. Young, & Gail Osherenko, Ithaca, New York: Cornell University Press, 1993, pp. 56–96

The Svalbard Treaty from 9 February 1920, Norwegian, English, and French version in Ulfstein, Geir: *The Svalbard Treaty: From Terra Nullius to Norwegian Sovereignty*, Oslo: Scandinavian University Press, 1995, pp. 513–532

SVERDRUP, OTTO

Of the great triumvirate of Norwegian explorers, Fridtjof Nansen, Roald Amundsen, and Otto Sverdrup, Sverdrup is probably the least well known, although his achievements as an explorer are certainly of a significance equal to those of the other two. Sverdup participated in six Arctic expeditions, of which he was leader of four. His Arctic career began in 1888 when he was 33 years of age, and already held his master's ticket in the Norwegian merchant marine. On hearing that a friend's brother, Fridtjof Nansen, was looking for volunteers to attempt the first crossing of the Greenland Ice Cap on skis, Sverdup volunteered and was accepted. They planned to be landed from the sealer *Jason* on the east coast of Greenland in July 1888, but ice prevented the ship from reaching the coast, and the six-man party was forced to try to reach shore in two boats. It took them ten days to do so, by which time they had been carried well south of their planned starting point by the ice drift; it took them a further two weeks to work their way back north to that starting point. After 40 days on the ice cap, they safely reached the first rocks and tundra on the west side. Since it was now late in the season, the party was forced to winter at Godthåb (present-day Nuuk) and did not return to Norway until May 1889.

Almost immediately, Nansen began planning for an even more challenging expedition. In 1884, various items, indisputably from the wreck of George Washington De Long's *Jeannette*, which had been crushed by the ice in June 1881 to the north of the Novosibirskiye archipelago, had been found on an ice-floe off the coast of southwest Greenland. Clearly, they must have been carried by ice drift across the Arctic Basin and south via the East Greenland Current. On this basis, Nansen conceived the idea of deliberately placing a specially built ship in the ice near where *Jeannette* had been crushed and allowing the ice drift to carry the ship along the same presumed trans-Arctic drift route. Scientific observations would be made throughout the drift. Sverdrup offered his services as captain of the expedition vessel and for three years (1890–1893) he was devoted almost entirely to supervising the construction of the ship. This remarkable vessel, named *Fram*, was designed and built by Colin Archer but every stage of its construction was supervised by Sverdrup.

Having taken *Fram* eastward via the Northern Sea Route, Nansen and Sverdrup deliberately allowed the ship to be beset northwest of the Novosibirskiye Ostrova (New Siberian Islands) in September 1893, and it began to drift slowly northwestward. By November 1894, it was clear that *Fram*'s drift course was not going to take it as far north as Nansen had calculated, and hence in late February 1895 Nansen and Hjalmar Johansen set off with two dog teams to get as far as possible, and then to make their own way south to Frantz

Josef Land, and home. This meant that from that date until mid-August 1896, when *Fram* emerged safely from the ice northwest of Svalbard, Sverdrup was in sole command of the ship. He was entirely responsible for the ship, its crew, and the scientific program for more than half the total duration of the famous ice drift.

Soon after *Fram*'s return to Norway, at Nansen's suggestion, Sverdrup began planning for another Arctic expedition aboard *Fram*, but this time he would be in sole command. The plan was to head north via Nares Strait, between Ellesmere Island and Greenland, then east along the north coast of Greenland to a suitable wintering site. From there, sled parties would explore the northernmost areas of Greenland and its unknown northeast coast; there was no intention of making an attempt at the Pole.

With a well-knit team of 16 men, *Fram* sailed from Norway on June 24, 1898. But in Smith Sound impassible ice blocked all attempts to push north; after a prolonged wait Sverdrup snugged his ship down in a secure bay, named Fram Haven at the north end of Rice Strait between Pim Island and Johan Peninsula on Ellesmere Island. The party spent the autumn hunting walrus and muskoxen for dog food and while thus engaged, Sverdrup and his men explored most of the Bache Peninsula area, discovering, in so doing, that it was a peninsula and not an island. Then, in the spring of 1899, two sledge expeditions made major thrusts westward across Ellesmere Island, one of them reaching the sea at the head of Bay Fjord.

That summer, Smith Sound and Kane Basin remained solidly packed with ice and Sverdrup was forced to abandon his original plan to explore northern Greenland. Well aware of the vast unknown lacuna that lay west of Ellesmere Island and north of Jones Sound, he decided to make it the alternative focus of his expedition. With this in view, he took *Fram* south and then west into Jones Sound and settled down for a second wintering in Harbour Fjord on the south coast of Ellesmere.

From there and from Goose Fjord, to which *Fram* moved in the summer of 1900, in a truly remarkable series of sledge trips over the next three summers Sverdrup and his finely tuned, well-coordinated team, explored the entire west coast of Ellesmere Island north to beyond the mouth of Nansen Sound, the entire coastline of Axel Heiberg Island, Amund and Ellef Ringnes islands, King Christian, Cornwall and Graham islands, as well as much of the north coast of Devon Island. In total, this represented one of the most impressive feats of polar exploration ever achieved, affected in an extremely workmanlike fashion with a minimum of fuss and fanfare.

It is not generally known that Sverdrup was involved in three further expeditions to the Arctic. In 1914, he was invited by the Imperial Russian government to take command of the whaling ship *Eclipse* to search the Kara Sea for any trace of the missing expeditions headed by Georgiy Sedov, Vladimir Rusanov, and Georgy Brusilov. He found no sign of them, but during the wintering off the Taymyr coast he played a major role in facilitating and guiding a precautionary evacuation of half the crews of the Russian icebreakers *Taimyr* and *Vaygach* of the Arctic Ocean Hydrographical Expedition, which had also been forced to winter in the ice of the Kara Sea. Then, in the spring of 1920, this time at the request of the Soviet government, Sverdrup took command of the icebreaker *Sviatogor*, and rescued the icebreaker *Solovei Budimirovich*, beset and drifting in the ice of the Kara Sea with a large number of passengers on board, and with its fuel and food supplies nearing exhaustion. Finally, in 1921, aboard the icebreaker *Lenin*, Sverdrup escorted a convoy of freighters to and from the mouth of the Yenisey River, thus contributing to the early stages of the buildup of the Soviet Union's important Kara Sea shipping operation.

Biography

Born on his father's farm, Haarstad in the Helgeland area of Norway on October 31, 1854, Otto Sverdrup spent his childhood among the fjords, forests, and mountains. He went to sea at the age of 17, sailing aboard both Norwegian and American vessels, and obtained his mate's ticket in 1878 and his master's ticket in the early 1880s.

From 1888 until 1902, Sverdrup's three most famous Arctic expeditions consumed his time and energies. For most of the year after his return home in 1902, he was busy writing his book, *New Land*, detailing the achievements of the expedition. Thereafter, for several years, he lived quietly in Oslo, In 1906, he was a member of a consortium that started a fruit plantation at Baracoa on the north coast of Cuba; next, he was a member of one of the ski-patrols that surveyed the route of the Oslo-Bergen railway across the Hardanger Vidda. In 1910, along with Ivar Fosheim, one of his companions on his last expedition aboard *Fram*, he was on a walrus-hunting expedition to Davis Strait. Then, in 1911, he took part in a whaling venture in the Aleutian Islands where he built a whaling station on Akutan Island and bought a floating factory ship. In 1913, he was back in the North Pacific, as captain of a ship chartered by friends who wanted to reconnoitre the forestry potential. In 1923, he helped to select a site for a coal port on Spitsbergen, and then he spent most of 1924 and 1925 trying to get a whaling operation off the ground in Granada in the West Indies.

Finally, in 1926 when Sverdup requested Prime Minister Gunnar Knudsen for some suitable employ-

ment for himself, the latter, on discovering that Sverdrup did not have any sort of pension, was able to persuade the Storting to award him a pension of 6000 Norwegian kroner.

Sverdrup appeared in public for the last time at Fridtjof Nansen's funeral on May 17, 1930; thereafter, he himself was bedridden for a few months and he died on November 26, 1930. Throughout the final decade of his life, Sverdrup had fought to save his old ship, *Fram*. Through his fund-raising efforts, by the spring of 1930, *Fram* had been completely restored and in the summer of 1936 the Fram Museum, which still houses the old ship in a special building in Oslo, was inaugurated by King Haakon.

During his expedition of 1898–1902, Sverdrup had taken possession of all the new lands he had discovered for the Norwegian crown, and he so informed King Oscar on his return to Norway in the autumn of 1902. For the next quarter century and beyond, his claim was to cloud Canadian-Norwegian relations, since Canada claimed all land north of its boundaries to the Pole. Sverdrup fought doggedly to make his claims a reality, suggesting repeatedly, for example, that a Norwegian police force should be sent to the islands he had discovered. Sverdrup did not win this fight; however, it was a dignified defeat. The dispute over sovereignty over the Sverdrup Islands, the name by which islands he discovered are still known, was settled between Norway and Canada in a gentlemanly manner that salved national pride. On November 11, 1930, the Norwegian government formally recognized Canada's title to the lands Sverdrup had discovered and explored. And in a related gesture, which was covered in the same article in many Canadian newspapers, the Canadian government paid Sverdrup $67,000 for his original maps, diaries, and documents relating to his expedition of 1898–1902. Before the month was over, Sverdrup was dead. In one of the great ironies of Arctic history, intense exploration for oil and gas in the early 1970s revealed that the Sverdrup Basin, underlying the islands in question, contained proven reserves of 10 trillion cubic feet of gas and 10 million barrels of oil.

WILLIAM BARR

See also **Nansen, Fridtjof; Sedov, Georgiy Yakovlevich**

Further Reading

Barr, William, "Otto Sverdrup to the rescue of the Russian Imperial Navy." *Arctic*, 27(1) (1974): 3–14

———, "The drift and rescue of *Solovei Budimirovich* in the Kara Sea, January-June 1920." *Canadian Slavonic Papers*, 20(4) (1978): 483–503

Belov, M.I., *Sovetskoe arkticheskoe moreplavanie 1917–1932 gg. Istoriia otkrytiia i osvoenia Severnogo morskogo puti, III* [Soviet Arctic navigation 1917–1932. The history of the discovery and exploitation of the Northern Sea Route, III], Leningrad: Izdatel'stvo "Morskoi Transport," 1959

Fairley, T.C., *Sverdrup's Arctic adventures*, London: Longmans, 1959

Kokk, D., *Otto Sverdrups liv*, Oslo: Jacob Dybwad, 1934

Nansen, Fridtjof, *The First Crossing of Greenland*, London: Constable and Co., 1890

————, *Farthest North. Being the Record of a Voyage of Exploration of the Ship "Fram" 1893–96 and of a Fifteen Months' Sleigh Journey by Dr. Nansen and Lieut. Johansen*, London: Constable & Co., 1897

Starokadomskii, Leonid Mikhailovich, *Charting the Russian Northern Sea Route. The Arctic Ocean Hydrographic Expedition 1910–1915*, translated and edited by William Barr, Montreal and Kingston: McGill-Queen's University Press, 1976

Sverdrup, Otto, *New land: four years in the Arctic regions*, London: Longmans Green and Co., 1904

————, *Under Russisk Flag*, Oslo: H. Aschehoug & Co., 1928

SWAINE, CHARLES

British explorer Charles Swaine is best known for failing in two attempts to locate the fabled North West Passage to the riches of the East, but he did have success in contributing to the general knowledge of the Arctic region. While mapping the Labrador coast, Swaine determined that there was no water connection between the Atlantic Ocean and the Hudson Bay through Labrador, as had been believed. His expeditions, probably the first organized attempts by American colonists to find a passage, also provided information about the Inuit as well as details about the Arctic climate and its minerals, flora, and fauna.

Swaine first gained fame as a clerk on the *California* when the vessel sailed from England in 1746 with the *Dobbs* to search for a North West Passage. The ships spent an ice-bound winter in Hudson's Bay before admitting defeat and returning to England in 1747. In 1748, Swaine published a two-volume history of the *California* expedition, *An Account of a Voyage for the Discovery of a North-West Passage by Hudson's Straights to the Western and Southern Ocean of America, Performed in the Years 1746 and 1747, in the Ship "California."* His interest in the Arctic continued, and he is presumed to be the anonymous author of *The Great Probability of a Northwest Passage in 1768, etc.* This work is often credited to Theodorus Swaine Drage, a cousin, but there is no evidence that this man served aboard the *California* or had the experience to make statements about navigation and Arctic conditions.

Probably a native of England, by 1750 Swaine had taken up residence in Chester Town, Maryland. He had a reputation for being an honest, straightforward man, and his experience with the *California* helped him to obtain a license from Governor Samuel Ogle of Maryland on November 3, 1750 to discover the North West Passage, explore the Labrador coast, open trade with Labrador, and improve the fishing and whaling in that region. Ogle and Swaine disclaimed any intention of interfering with the Hudson's Bay Company's monopoly on trade with Native Americans for Northern animal skins or of establishing clandestine trade with Greenland. Although he had the necessary knowledge to captain an Arctic ship, Swaine did not have the funds to finance the expedition and sought backers. About 1750, Swaine used Ogle's proclamation to persuade Benjamin Franklin, William Allen, and a number of other American merchants to support his Arctic expedition. The Philadelphia and New York traders who comprised the newly formed Northwest Company hoped to claim the prize of £20,000 offered by the British government for the Northwest route. The possibility of opening trade with Inuit in the Hudson Bay region served as an additional lure for these ambitious men to gamble their money.

The merchants purchased the schooner *Argo* in New England and fitted it out for its journey in Philadelphia. Swaine, in New England in 1752, searched for all available data about the Arctic, and arranged for a crew. Outfitted with provisions to last for 16 months, the *Argo* sailed down the Delaware River on March 4, 1753. She rounded Cape May and set sail to the North. As Swaine could not secure enough sailors in Philadelphia to man the ship, he deliberately set sail short-handed. By prearrangement, he put in at Portsmouth. There, he took on board ten whale men and purchased two cedar whaleboats. This delay detained the expedition until April 15, 1753.

Unfortunately for Swaine and his backers, the ice conditions were especially bad that year. In due time, the *Argo* was off Cape Farewell, the southern point of Greenland. Here, the ship ran into heavy ice flows and was essentially trapped for 14 days. Managing to break free, Swaine unsuccessfully attempted to sail to the northwest through Davis Strait. Forced by ice to turn back, the *Argo* then failed to enter Hudson Strait. It was now August and the waters along the shore of Hudson Bay were gradually becoming a solid mass of ice. In defeat, Swaine turned the ship to the south and explored the coast of Labrador from 65° to 56° N latitude.

He entered six inlets along the Labrador coast and sailed up these inlets as far as navigable water would permit. He then continued his explorations overland to the heads of the waters. Many of these inlets were unknown and had never been charted. Assisted by draftsman and mineralist John Patten, Swaine established that Labrador waters did not link the Atlantic Ocean and the Hudson Bay. The *Argo* left Labrador on September 20, 1753 and arrived in Philadelphia in the middle of November. Swaine returned with news about the Arctic and its peoples, as well as examples of flora and fauna. The samples of minerals and ore that Swaine had obtained on this voyage would spell doom for his next Arctic journey.

Gold-bearing quartz was among the collection that Swaine gathered in Labrador with the assistance of John Patten. On May 2, 1754, the *Argo* left Philadelphia on its second attempt to locate the North West Passage and Patten was again among the crew. Little knowledge remains of this trip, but it is known that Patten and a few other men left the ship in Labrador to locate gold deposits without Swaine's knowledge. While on land, all the men were killed by Inuit. The crewmen who remained on board the ship became discontented and refused to sail further. To avoid mutiny, Swaine abandoned the search and returned home in late October 1754. Swaine's backers lost faith and sold the schooner on December 4, 1754. Although much of Swaine's life is shrouded in mystery, it is believed that he never returned to the Arctic.

Biography

Charles Swaine is believed to have been born in England, date unknown. By 1750, Swaine had married and settled in Chester Town, Maryland. His wife's name and date of death are unknown, but in 1758 Swaine married Mrs. Hannah Boyte of Philadelphia. In 1755, he secured an appointment from Governor Robert Hunter Morris to be the commissary of the supplies raised by Pennsylvania for General Edward Braddock's troops during the Seven Years' War. He moved to Shippensburg and completed his work later that same year. He returned to Philadelphia by 1757 and was appointed Prothonotary of the city in that year. He also obtained additional positions as Clerk of the Orphans' Court of Philadelphia in 1757 and as Recorder of Deeds of Philadelphia in 1758. In 1758, he may have resigned these three positions because he accepted work as Clerk of the Peace, Prothonotary, Recorder of Deeds, Clerk of the Orphans' Court, and Clerk of Quarter Sessions of Northampton County. These offices were held until 1760 or 1761. In 1759, Swaine volunteered for militia duty because of continuing conflict with Native Americans. In 1763, he went into business with his son, known to history only as "Young" Swaine. In 1767 or 1768, he was in London completing work on *The Great Probability of a Northwest Passage: Observations on the Letter of Admiral DeFonte, who Sailed from the Callao of Lima on the Discovery of a Communication between the South Sea and Atlantic Ocean; And to Intercept some Navigators from Boston in New England whom he Met with, Then in Search of a Northwest Passage, Proving the Authenticity of the Admiral's Letter with These Explanatory Mapes the Account of Discovery of Part of the Coast and Inland Country of Labrador, Made in 1753.* Thomas Jefferys of Charing Cross published the work in 1768. Swaine was dead by the year 1780, when his wife was buried as a widow. The location of his death is unknown.

CARYN E. NEUMANN

Further Reading

Chidsey, Jr., A.D., *Charles Swaine,* read before the Northampton County Historical and Genealogical Society, Thursday, June 25, 1942

Eavenson, Howard N., *Map Maker and Indian Traders: An Account of John Patten, Trader, Arctic Explorer, and Map Maker; Charles Swaine, Author, Trader, Public Official, and Arctic Explorer; Theodorus Swaine Drage, Clerk, Trader, and Anglican Priest,* Pittsburgh: University of Pittsburgh Press, 1949

SWAN

Swans are the largest of all waterfowl and among the largest of flying birds, but there is but one species of truly Arctic swan, the tundra (collectively), whistling or Bewick's swan (*Cygnus columbianus,* known as *Qussuk* in Greenlandic, *Dvergsvanur* in Icelandic, and *Dvergesvane* in Norwegian). This species has a circumpolar distribution, represented in the New World by the nominate race *C. columbianus* (the tundra or whistling swan), which numbers some 170,000 individuals.

The majority of these breed in Alaska with lesser numbers in Canada, and the vast proportion of the population winters in coastal areas of both west and east coasts of the United States. Large numbers congregate about Chesapeake Bay, Virginia, and North Carolina, while in the west, the Bay area of California is important. In the Old World, two subspecies, *C. bewickii* and *C. jankowskii* (both known as the Bewick's swan), nest throughout the tundras of Europe and Asia; *C. jankowskii* breeds east from the Lena Delta and migrates southward to winter in Japan, Korea, and China (c.30,000 birds), while over 30,000 *C. bewickii* breed further west and winter in northwest Europe, mostly in the Netherlands and United Kingdom. All the subspecies are naturally pure white as adults, except when stained orange by the ochrous deposits to be found in their wetland feeding habitats, with black feet and bills. Those representatives of the races *bewickii* and especially *jankowskii* exhibit an extensive yellow patch on the bill. This yellow patch is sufficiently distinctive and unique as to enable individual recognition, a feature first recognized among wintering birds by Sir Peter Scott at Slimbridge, England, in the 1960s and on the basis of individual studies over many years since. The tundra swans of North America, by contrast, have almost entirely black bills. First-year birds are grayish with pink and black bills, associating with their parents for one or more winters.

Tundra swan.
*Photograph courtesy US
Fish and Wildlife Service*

Because of the short nature of the northern summer, their stay on the breeding areas of the tundra is limited to the *c*.130 days that such areas are snow and ice free. The species breeds in the lush low-lying flat open tundra areas that are early to thaw, characterized by abundant standing water or slow-flowing rivers with backwaters that provide abundant emergent vegetation that grows sufficiently to offer a rich food resource for the young. Throughout the breeding range, the species becomes rare within the treeline and avoids both areas of mountains and those associated with human disturbance. The nest is a huge mound of vegetation, often used in subsequent years, generally close to the water, up to a metre in diameter and anything up to 70 cm high, with a depression in the top to accommodate the 3–5 eggs. Only the female incubates for 29–32 days, but both parents care for the cygnets, which take 40–75 days to fledge (depending on breeding area, North American cygnets taking longer to fledge). Long-term studies show that the swans generally pair for life. Birds occasionally pair up in their second winter, more commonly in their third, but may breed first later than their third or fourth years. Individuals are known to have lived for well over 20 years in the wild. Counts of the proportion of young appearing each autumn on the wintering grounds show wide fluctuations, reflecting weather conditions in the arctic during the summer.

Although generally solitary in nature on the breeding grounds, tundra swans are highly gregarious and gather into flocks for migration and in winter. Satellite telemetry has demonstrated that throughout its range, the tundra swan undertakes long migrations between important staging areas, where abundant food resources enable the recouping of depleted energy stores en route to and from the breeding areas. Hence, swans from western Europe stop off in spring in Estonia and again in the White Sea before reaching their ultimate summering areas in the Russian Arctic, although they rarely move more than 600 km from one stopover to the next. Similarly, tracked spring migrating individuals in North America made movements of less than 500 km from wintering areas to prairie spring staging sites, but one bird is known to have traveled 1900 km between northern Saskatchewan and the Mackenzie River delta in one flight.

Tundra swans winter on estuaries, river floodlands and lakes, where the traditional foods were probably submerged, and emergent vegetation, especially the overwintering tubers of Fennel Pondweed, *Potamogeton pectinatus*, which are highly nutritious and available to the long-necked swans in shallow fresh and brackish waters. Increasingly as man has created pastureland in close proximity to traditional wetlands areas, throughout its range, the species has become a grazer of soft grasses and clover, as well as a gleaner of waste after agricultural harvest (e.g., grain, potatoes, and sugar beet in Britain and the Netherlands). Much of the change in habitat use appears voluntary, in the sense that the swans have shifted to exploit novel food sources without the loss of traditionally used habitats. Despite this movement to agricultural areas, the species invariably resorts to formerly used wetlands and open water (up to 10 km away) as safe nighttime roosts.

Many cultures celebrate the beauty and grace of swans in their mythology, and the pure white of northern swans, coupled with their large size, has undoubtedly contributed to many legends of humans being converted to swan forms. As long-distant migrants, folklore has cast the swan as the traditional harbingers of (especially bad) news; in old English, "it swans me" literally means, "I have a boding." This in turn has no doubt contributed to the cultural taboo of killing swans, despite their undoubted food value, for fear of killing a forebear or messenger. To the Inuit of the north, there are many myths involving swans, but their relationship is more functional, since the Iñupiat of northern Alaska slept on mattresses of swan skins and the Bering Strait Inuit made storage bags of the same material. Despite widespread protection, illegal hunting continues in Europe, since 44% of the dead birds analyzed contained lead shot; nevertheless, this population has apparently increased in number in recent years. In North America, hunting accounts for at least 4000 birds per year, although associated lead poisoning undoubtedly adds to this death toll, along with subsistence hunting and poaching, factors that may contribute to recent declines in the western flyway population in recent years.

TONY FOX

Further Reading

Lagerquist, J.E., M. Davidson & W.J. Foreyt, "Lead poisoning and other causes of mortality in Trumpeter (*Cygnus buccinator*) and Tundra (*C. columbianus*) swans in western Washington." *Journal of Wildlife Diseases,* 30 (1994): 60–64

Nolet, B.A., V.A. Andreev, P. Clausen, M.J.M. Poot & E.G.J. Wessel, "Significance of the White Sea as a stopover for Bewick's Swans *Cygnus columbianus bewickii* in spring." *Ibis,* 143 (2001): 63–71

Rees, E.C., "Distribution within the USSR of Bewick's Swans *Cygnus columbianus bewickii* marked in Britain." *Wildfowl Supplement,* 1 (1991): 209–213

Rees, E.C., J.M. Bowler & J.H. Beekman, "Bewick's Swan and Whistling Swan." *Birds of the Western Palearctic Update,* 1 (1997): 63–74

Scott, P., "The Bewick's Swans at Slimbridge." *Wildfowl Trust Annual Report,* 17 (1966): 20–26

Scott, P. & the Wildfowl Trust, *The Swans,* London: Michael Joseph, 1970

SWEDEN

The Kingdom of Sweden occupies about two-thirds of the Scandinavian peninsula with Finland and the Baltic Sea to the east. Norway occupies one-third of the peninsula to the west. The territory north of the Arctic Circle comprises 15% of Sweden's total area of 449,752 sq km (173,665 sq mi). In 1999, the population in Sweden was estimated at 8,861,426; of these, 258,094 live in Norrbotten County (as on December 31, 1999; Statistical Yearbook of Sweden, 2001).

Historically, Sweden has been divided into three major regions: Götaland, Svealand, and Norrland. Norrland (the Northland) is the large northern frontier region bordering on northern Norway, Finland, and the Gulf of Bothnia. Norrland comprises two-thirds of the territory of Sweden. Within Norrland, both Norrbotten County and Swedish Lapland occur.

Political Subdivisions

Today, Sweden has 24 counties (*län*). The Arctic area of Sweden comprises Norrbotten County (Norrbottens län). There are also two provinces (*landskap*), namely Lapland and Norrbotten. These provinces are remnants of an older system of political subdivision from, in many cases, the Middle Ages. Many Swedes today relate to the provinces for cultural and geographical identity, but they have no administrative meaning. In the case of Norrbotten province, this is secondary to the subdivision of county. Norrbotten County was decreed in 1810, but the geographical distinction of Lapland was, however, decided already in the 18th century through the so-called Lapland Border (*lappmarksgränsen*), which indicated the area in the north where no settlement originally was allowed. There is a province in Finland also called Lapland (*see* **Lappin Lääni**): the two areas were once one when Finland was a part of Sweden, and today the term Lapland could be said to refer to the Northern Cap or Nordkalotten area (*see* **Lapland**).

Major Cities and Towns

The administrative seat of Norrbotten County is Luleå with 70,694 inhabitants (1995), a marketplace since the Middle Ages mentioned in written documents for the first time in 1327 ("Lulu") and accorded city rights in 1621.

Piteå is an industrial town (18,171, 1995) in the southern part of Norrbotten County, on the coast of the Gulf of Bothnia. It grew from a Middle Age church center to receive town privileges in 1621. Like many northern towns (houses were built of wood), it was destroyed by a fire in 1666. Piteå was first mentioned in a document in 1314 as Pito.

Boden, northeast of Luleå, was formerly, until the end of the Cold War, a military town with six regiments. Most employment is still in the public sector (30,178, 1992). The town encompasses a large fortress, built around the turn of the last century, which is now a museum.

Karesuando, with 362 inhabitants (1994), is an important Saami center. Kiruna, with just over 20,000 inhabitants, is a young town. With an iron mine, a railway center on the Luleå-Narvik railway, it is also headquarters of Sweden's space exploration activities. Haparanda (6687, 1994) is dominated by the service industry and also has some smaller industries. It is a border town to Finland as well. The first settlements took place in the 16th century.

Population

The Arctic area of Sweden is inhabited by Swedes, Finns (mainly Tornedalians along the Torne River valley), and Saami, the Swedes being the dominant population. While the population grew between 1950 and 1960, it has diminished thereafter. Norrbotten County is the most thinly populated area of Sweden, with only three inhabitants per sq km. Of the total population, 66,729 (1995) lived in Lapland province while the rest lived in Norrbotten province, the coastal area of Norrbotten County. While this county is territorially the largest county in Sweden, the population is only between 2%–3% of Sweden's total population.

Traditionally, before the introduction of statistics in 1749, the population centers were along the coast of the Gulf of Bothnia, which had permanent residents and churches. An estimate of the population in the Middle Ages is therefore not possible and it was not until the 16th century that some information became available. The region Norrland then had less than 10% of the population, which in 1749 could be fixed at 8.2% growing to 11.5%, with Norrbotten County accounting for 59,000 inhabitants growing to 134,769 in 1900.

Most Swedes in the north are members of the Lutheran Church, but religion is playing an increasingly small role. Most Swedes do not go to church regularly. The pietistic Laestadian movement in northern Sweden is still alive. During the 19th century, shamans were regarded as prophets in the movement.

Due to snowy and cold winters, Swedes in the north are accustomed to skiing, which at various times made Sweden an important ski sport nation (World Championships and Olympic Games). Hunting is more common in northern Sweden than elsewhere in the country.

Historical Summary

Early recorded impressions can probably be found already in Tacitus Germania of the 1st century AD with the people of the Fenni, but the description is so tendentious and vague to say with certainty if they are to be regarded as ancestors of the Saami or any other particular people.

Later in the 6th century AD, the classical author Procopius described Thule (which can seemingly be identified with Scandinavia) and a tribe he called Skrithiphinoi. The land of this people was described as having exceedingly large forests. Procopius also mentions the midnight sun and the winter darkness: "For the sun at the time of the summer solstice never sets for forty days, but appears constantly during this whole time above the earth. But no less than six months later, at about the time of the winter solstice, the sun is never seen on this island for forty days, but never ending night envelops it" (History of the Wars, VI. XV. 6–7). Jordanes, also in the 6th century AD in Getica, makes a similar report about the Screrefennae on what is described as the Scandza Island, and the report of the historian of the Langobardi, Paul the Deacon, provides a detailed report on the Scritofini that makes their identification with the Saami reasonably certain.

When colonization started during the Middle Ages, Swedish administration was confined to the coast with permanent settlement and churches. The official presence in the inland was early established by the so-called birkarlar (traders), who by decree from 1277 taxed the Saami with whom they traded. As claims of Sweden-Finland, Denmark-Norway, and Russia overlapped, some areas were taxed by all three countries.

The first book on Lapland appeared in a Latin original in Frankfurt am Main in 1673, written by the academic Johannes Schefferus of Strassburg (1621–1679). He had been called to the University of Uppsala as professor of law and rhetoric. There were rumors on the continent that Sweden's astonishing victories on the battlefields during the Thirty Years' War (1618–1648) were due to the witchcraft of Lappish sorcerers in the armies of Gustavus Adolphus. It was important to put such rumors to rest by publishing an account describing Lapland as a true Swedish province with a spectacular, dignified population. Schefferus never went to the north, but had access to field material, reports sent in from clergymen, bailiffs, and other informants. On occasion, however, he met the fur-clad Lappish traders on the markets in Uppsala. The chapters in the book on sorcery and magic of the natives were printed separately in German and Dutch. The book was translated by an unknown young Oxford student, Acton Cremer, which makes for amusing reading of the erratic spelling of placenames. Published in 1674, it contains the 35 chapters of the Latin original.

The inhabitants of this far away, strange European land were described by Schefferus as being "of low stature" and "much given to superstition, which is no wonder while they live in the Woods among wild Beasts, and maintain little correspondance one with another … Furthermore they are beyond all imagination ferfull and mean spirited; above all things dreading War" (pp. 12–13). But Schefferus also wanted to present "their vertues" … "their veneration and due esteem of Marriage…. They also abhor theft…in Lapland there are no Towns and no man could be sure of any thing, if the People were inclined to thievery. They are likewise charitable to the poor…supplying them with stock whereon to live Farther they are civil and

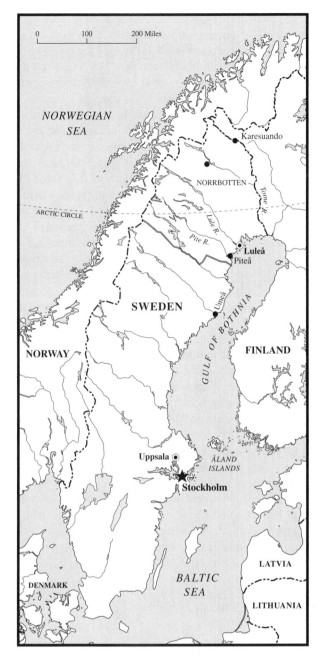

Sweden and main and northern cities and rivers.

also carried detailed accounts of plants and animals. There is actually not much of a description of the towns and landscape. On traveling to "Pithoea" (Piteå), Linnaeus remarked on June 13:

> The fields in this part of the country are excellent, being extensive and level, the soil consisting of sandy and argillaceous earth. The crops are abundant, provided the corn be not injured by frost as it had the proceding year. Owing to this misfortune, I found bread made of spruce fir bark at present in general use. (pp. 199–200)

On the way to Piteå, Linnaeus passed Skellefteå, "consisting of two principal streets and several cross ones, with a church. The houses are about three hundred and fifty or four hundred, and their white chimneys give them a cheerful aspect" (p. 203).

Arriving in Luleå on June 22, he wrote that "the new town of Lulea is very small, situated on a peninsula, encompassed by a kind of bay. The soil is extremely barren. Indeed the town stands on a little eminence, which is a mere heap of stones, with seasand in their interstices. It seems as if the sea had carried away all the earth, and, like a beast of prey, had left nothing but the bones, throwing sand over them to conceal its ravages" (p. 235).

Saami Population

The attitude of the Swedish administration in the north has passed through several periods, each dominated by a certain course of action. A central territorial and fiscal policy from 1550 to 1635 was deeply disturbing to the Saami. The basic result was that it triggered a transformation from a hunter-gatherer society to a reindeer pastoralist society. At the same time, schooling was introduced (1617) and in 1619 the first books in Saami were published. The Saami were thus subjugated to state power. During a period of the 17th century (1653–1673), mining policy came to play an important role. In 1635, a Saami, Peder Olsson, had found silver ore at Nasafjäll close to the Norwegian border. Mining started the next year and Lapland was introduced in the imagination of the Swedes as a possible treasury. It became important with territorial policy and to keep the Saami on Swedish territory. Nasafjäll was a disappointment but new finds retained interest in the far north. As the Saami were burdened with demands of transportation at the mines, it led to conflicts. When mining authorities resorted to force, this led to migration from the mining areas. Soon, policy changed to remunerated transport and things quietened down.

The next period (1673–1749) has been described as colonization policy without Saami participation. The first settlement proclamation was introduced in 1673, which underlined the need for farming and clearing of land for agricultural use. A new proclamation had little

hospitable to Strangers, whom they with much kindness invite to their Huts…Lastly they are sufficiently ingenious, making for themselves all sorts of tools and implements for their fishing and hunting" (pp. 14–15).

The famous Carolus Linnaeus in 1732 started an exploration of Lapland for the Academy of Sciences. Being alone for most of the journey, he traveled 3000 miles in five months. He collected and catalogued flowers, plants, trees, and animals and described the physical beauty of the region. Much of his travel record (*A Tour in Lapland*, first published in English in 1811) was devoted to the Laplanders (the Saami), but effect as the first one. There was basically no surplus farming population willing to take up farming under harsh conditions in the northern forests. At the same time, the Saami religion was forced underground by the formation of parishes. After 1749 (to 1846), Saami participation in the colonizing efforts was supported. The next settlement ordinance (1749) accorded settlement privileges also to the Saami. Trade flourished and at the middle of the 18th century the Saami dominated the economy in the north but the population remained static, and by the 19th century the great immigration of Swedes and Finns to the coastland had taken over. The following period (1846–1913) witnessed the introduction of more negative views toward the Saami. They were described as unsteady, suspicious, drunkards, and childlike. The Saami were relegated to a lower stage of development and their disappearance was often seen as inevitable. Forestry industry introduced a large number of Swedes and Finns in the 1870s, and from that time domination of the non-Saami started. General law was introduced, and special legislation was abandoned. Swedish became the dominant language and assimilation views came to be introduced. Saami livelihood was distinguished from Swedish-Danish agricultural livelihood. After 1913, for around 60 years a segregation policy dominated. The nomads could only be protected by separation from the general population, was the general argument, and separate legislation for the nomadic Saami was introduced. Grazing rights for the reindeer herds were connected to the Saami villages. To enforce the grazing rights, a special bailiff organization was set up with increasing power over the life of the Saami. This administration was abandoned at the beginning of the 1970s, paving the way for Saami self-government.

The attitudes of Swedes and Finns toward the Saami have developed much according to the official view of the Saami, but although differences exist one can say that racism does not play an important role. The large majority of the Saami also live in the same way as their Swedish or Finnish neighbors. They wear the same clothes, live in the same kind of houses, and do the same jobs. They fish, farm, and work in factories.

The attitudes of the Saami toward their neighbors can be said to be that of acceptance, while they are keenly aware of their Saami origin.

Economy

The economy in the far north is to a large extent based on natural resources like mining, hydroelectric power, and forestry, and traditional heavy industry. During recent years, undergone extensive rationalization and restructuring processes.

Many northerners feel that high economic benefits from the abundant natural resources have not been reinvested back into the area. There have also been problems of depopulation, which at present seem to have diminished somewhat (although the population today is lower than in, for instance, 1980). Especially, the rural areas are in danger as over 80% of the population of Norrbotten County live in towns.

The aims in the economy have largely been fulfilled, but the complicated transfer from industrial society to information society is especially problematic in a harsh climate and in thinly populated areas. One special problem is broadband connection for the Internet in the thinly populated north. The transformation has started, but much investment is still needed in IT companies to keep northern economy alive and future directed.

A reduction in public sector employment has taken place in Sweden during the 1990s, but these reductions have not been so drastic in the Arctic. Large areas are suitable for adventure tourism and recreation. To protect the unique Arctic landscape, a number of national parks have been created. With increasing urbanization in areas like Holland and the Ruhr in Germany, the possibility of adventure and ecological tourism in the far north is high in one of the last wildernesses. Thus, tourism is looked upon as a future industry.

The economic benefits of the Arctic for Sweden have been substantial. Much of the wealth of the country has been produced in the far north and, among northern Swedes, there is the suspicion that part of the country has not received the reinvestment deserved for the great benefit the country has harvested in terms of, for instance, hydroelectric power, forestry, and mining. But there has been substantial investment in the north, mainly in infrastructure. Perhaps more could have been done to improve the conditions of living in the north. Thus, it is questionable if the aims have been fulfilled in terms of investment. In terms of reaping the benefits of the natural resources in the north, the aims have certainly been fulfilled by Stockholm.

Development and Integration

Development in the north came later than in the south. Harsh climate and long travel distances prevented colonization. It was not until industrialization, which came relatively late in Sweden, and forestry beginning in the late 19th century that the Swedish Arctic developed in earnest. Iron ore mining in the Kiruna-Gällivare area and the Luleå-Narvik railway were important developmental factors.

Northern Identity

The Arctic area, especially the vast interior of Lapland, is very distinct from other parts of Sweden in terms of nature. There are few areas in the

European Union that offer such grandeur and natural beauty. As population increases on the continent, Swedish Lapland could offer much for visitors from the great urban sprawl on the continent. In terms of city life, the population centers are not much different from those further south in Sweden, except Saami habitation.

In the self-image of Sweden, the Arctic area cannot be said to have played a significant role. As a centralized state, the self-image of the country was concentrated in Stockholm. Until the 20th century, the north has been really integrated, but both north and south in Sweden have been peripheral. The Lake Mälaren area with Stockholm and Uppsala has been the only "real" Sweden for those in power and in media. Thus, Sweden along with France have been the countries most opposed to the regional development within the European Union. The further away from Stockholm, the less important the basic rule. Norrbotten and Lapland no doubt have suffered from that self-image.

To the world, the north in Sweden has always been presented as exotic and nontypical. Part of this image has of course been used to attract visitors to the Arctic. In historical times, the image of Lapland as mystical and dangerous could have been useful, for instance, during the Thirty Years' War, when Sweden participated as a leading power (1630–1648). But steps were also taken to present Lapland as a natural part of Christian Sweden (Schefferus above). In modern times, this has been replaced by presenting the north as exotic and unusual to prospective visitors.

BERTIL HAGGMAN

See also **Kiruna; Lapland; Norrbotten; Saami**

Further Reading

Baudou, E., Norrlands forntid—*ett historiskt perspektiv*, Förlags AB Wiken, Höganäs, 1992
Heininen, Lassi & Tuija Katermaa (editors), *Regionalism in the North*, Rovaniemi, Arctic Centre 1993 (Arctic Centre Reports 8)
Hofsten, E. & H. Lundström, *Swedish Population History: Main Trends from 1750 to 1970*, Stockholm: Statistiska centralbyrån, 1976
Linnaeus, Carl, *A Tour in Lapland*, New York: Arno Press & The New York Times, 1971
Schefferus, Johannes, *The History of Lapland* (a facsimile reprint of the original English edition of 1674), Stockholm: Rediviva, 1971

SYALAKH CULTURE

The Syalakh Culture existed in Northeast Asia 6200–5200 BP. It was identified by Y.A. Mochanov in 1966, after the excavations at the multi-layer

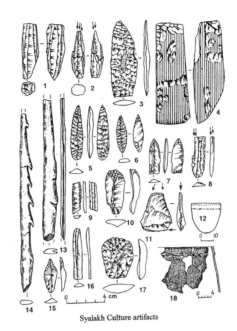

Syalakh Culture artifacts: 1—core; 2—polyhedral burin; 3—bifacial knife; 4—polished adze; 5, 6—points; 7—point on blades; 8—angle burin on microblade; 9—bilateral retouched microblade; 10—scrapers; 11—angle burin; 12—pottery vessel form; 13—slotted point; 14—barbed harpoon head; 15—perforator; 16—microblade; 18—potsherd. 1–11—stone, 12, 18—ceramic; 13, 14—bone.

Bel'kachi I Site. The most typical sites of this culture were found in Yakutia, in the valleys of the Lena, Vilyuy, and Aldan rivers. The Syalakh sites have also been marked on the Taymyr Peninsula and in Western Chukotka. The Syalakh Culture is supposed to have been formed in the process of Transbaikal people assimilating the Sumnagin Culture at the end of 5 million BC. At the multi-layer sites in Yakutia, the Syalakh materials always overlay the Sumnagin levels.

The emergence and spread of the Syalakh Culture in Northeast Asia are associated with the start of the Neolithic, marked by the first appearance of ceramic and ground tools. Ceramic is the most characteristic feature that distinguishes the Syalakh Culture from other Neolithic cultures in Yakutia. The comparatively high-quality pottery was egg-shaped, with parabolic cross-sections, round bottoms, and technical imprints of knitted net, which served as the base for forming the vessels, on the outer surface. Vessels reached 35 cm in diameter. They were ornamented with one row of holes under the rim. The purpose of the holes has not been determined so far: they are either a decoration, or a technological element vital for producing and firing pottery. Similar holes were present on Yakutia pottery of the following Neolithic cultures until the second millennium BP. In the early stage, vessels were decorated with one or two narrow horizontal plastic bands. In the final stage, pottery was decorated with indents around the rim.

In the stone tool production technique, the Early Holocene microblade technology remained. For producing microblades, prismatic and conic cores were still used. Microblades were used to make about 50% of tools: perforators, end scrapers, angle and dihedral burins, some arrow points, and sideblades for bone insert tools (points and knives).

A very important technological element was the bifacial retouch that had almost never been used in the Sumnagin Culture. In the tool kit, bifacial leaf-shaped arrow points and knives, reaching 10 cm by length, end scrapers on flakes with retouched backs, angle burins, and perforators on flakes prevailed. The first polyhedral burins with core-shaped bodies appeared, later widely spread in the northeastern Neolithic. Grinding was used for finishing rectangular adzes.

From that period on, the use of arrows and bows has been explicitly fixed in Yakutia. Before, partly retouched microblades might have been used as arrow points, or bone insert points with microblades as sideblades.

The barbed harpoons found at the Bel'kachi I Site, containing the Syalakh materials of 5270 BP, suggest that at that time active fishing as well as the production of special fishing tools started. Net sinkers were also found.

The economy of the Syalakh people was based on moose and reindeer hunting, augmented by seasonal river and lake fishing and bird hunting. Hunting the migrating animals determined their nomadic mode of life as well as their dwelling type, surface and portable, teepeelike.

Some pictures on Yakutia petroglyphs have been referred to the Syalakh Culture. They were painted with ochre on the rocks. Images of moose, reindeer, and less often of bears, wolves, or dogs prevail. Pictures presented the scenes of animal breeding or death. Most figures are in motion. Images of people occur seldom. The Syalakh Culture was replaced by the Bel'kachi Culture at the end of the third millennium BP.

SERGEI SLOBODIN

Further Reading

Alekseyev, Anatoly N., *Drevnyaya Yakutia: neolit i epokha bronzy* [Ancient Yakutia: Neolithic and Bronze Time], Novosibirsk: Nauka, 1996

Argunov, Vasily G., "Syalakhskaya neoliticheskaya kul'tura na territorii Severo-Zapadnoy Yakutii" [The Syalakh Neolithic Culture on the Territory of Northwestern Yakutia]. in *Arkheologicheskiye issledovaniya v Yakutii* [Archaeological Research in Yakutia], edited by Yu.Mochanov, Novosibirsk: Nauka, 1992

———, *Kamenniy vek Severo-Zapadnoy Yakutii* [Stone Age of Northwestern Yakutia], Novosibirsk: Nauka, 1990

Kochmar, Nikolay N., *Pisanitsy Yakutii* [Painted Petroglyphs of Yakutia], Novosibirsk: Nauka, 1994

Mochanov, Yuri A. (editor), *Arkheologicheskiye pamyatniki Yakutii (basseyny rek Aldana i Olyokmy)* [Archaeological Sites in Yakutia: Aldan and Olyokma River Basins], Novosibirsk: Nauka, 1983

———, "The early Neolithic of the Aldan." Arctic Anthropology, 6(1) (1969): 95–103

Mochanov, Yuri A., Svetlana A. Fedoseyeva, "Main periods in the ancient history of North East Asia." In *Beringia in the Cenozoic Era*, Rotterdam, New Delhi, 1986

Mochanov, Yuri A., & Vitaly E. Larichev (editors), *Arkheologicheskiye pamyatniki Yakutii (basseyny rek Vilyuy, Anabar i Olenyok)* [Archaeological Sites in Yakutia: Vilyuy, Anabar, and Olenyok River Basins], Novosibirsk: Nauka, 1991

Mochanov, Yuri A., *Mnogosloynaya stoyanka Bel'kachi I i periodizatsiya kamennogo veka Yakutii* [Bel'kachi I Multi-layer Site and Yakutia Stone Age Periodization], Moscow: Nauka, 1969

SYKTYVKAR

Syktyvkar is the capital of the Republic of Komi in the Russian Federation. Situated in the northeast of the European part of Russia, Syktyvkar occupies the banks of two rivers, the Sysola and the Vychegda in the Pechora Basin, and is surrounded by taiga. The distance to Moscow is 1410 km. Of the population of 230,900 (*Goskomstat Rossii*, 1999), 54.3% are Russians and 33.6% are Komi.

Evidence of the first hunters and fishermen in this location dates back to the Neolithic. The first written mention of a permanent village at the mouth of the Sysola was in 1586. Trade was the main occupation of its residents due to the favorable location. In 1780, the village became the town of Ust-Sysolsk by a nominal decree of the Empress Catherine II. The town was given its coat of arms: a sleeping bear in its den due to the large number of bears in the area. Trading items were fish, cedar (Siberian pine) nuts, cloth, footwear, tableware, tea, and sugar. Trading between Siberia and European Russia was important, particularly cast iron produced in the Urals. In 1918, Soviet power was established in the town. In 1921, Ust-Sysolsk became the capital of the newly formed Komi Autonomous Oblast'. In 1930, it was renamed as Syktyvkar ("a town on the Sysola" in Komi). In 1936, the Oblast' was renamed the Komi Autonomous Soviet Socialistic Republic and in 1994 the Republic of Komi.

Industrial development of the city started in the 1930s with the construction of a sawmill. However, it did not expand until the 1960s, when a timber industrial complex began operation. At present, Syktyvkar has a highly developed economic infrastructure with 230 enterprises (1998). Dominant industries are timber, wood-working, pulp, and paper making. The Stock Company "Syktyvkar Timber Industrial Complex" is the most powerful enterprise of this kind in the north of European Russia. "Komitex," a factory of non-woven materials, is the biggest producer of oil-cloth in Russia. Other industries include electric power generation, civil engineering, machine-manufacture, food production and processing, and clothes manufacturing. Recently, the "Belkomur" company headquartered in Syktyvkar has started constructing the Arkhangel'sk-Syktyvkar-Perm' railway, and the "Bauxite Timan" company is starting the development of raw materials for the aluminum industry. Railways connect Syktyvkar with Moscow and the towns of the Republic. Motor car roads extend in three directions. The Syktyvkar airport has regular flights to 16 Russian cities and charters flights abroad.

The six institutes of the Komi Scientific Center, Ural Division of Russian Academy of Sciences, are located in Syktyvkar. There is a University and several Higher Education Establishments, three theaters, and a number of museums and libraries. Since perestroika, when acceptance was reestablished between the republican authorities and religious organizations, the city has been the center of the Syktyvkar-Vorkuta diocese of the Russian Orthodox church.

GALINA MAZHITOVA

See also **Komi Republic**

Further Reading

Berkhin, Ilya, *Istoriya Syktyvkara* [History of Syktyvkar], Syktyvkar: Komi Publishing, 1980

Knyazeva, Galina, *Lesnoi kompleks Respubliki Komi: problemy perestroiki i formirovanie novoi modeli* [Timber complex of the Republic of Komi: problems of perestroika and development of a new model], Moscow: Moscow State University, 1996

Melnikova, Natalia (editor), *Syktyvkar*, Syktyvkar: Komi Republican Printing House, 2000 (text in Russian and English)

Obedkov, Anatoly, *Stolny gorod Syktyvkar* [Capital city of Syktyvkar], Syktyvkar: Prolog, 1996

Rogachev, Mikhail & Aleksandr Tzoi, *Ust-Sysolks: stranitzy istorii* [Ust-Sysolsk: pages of history], Syktyvkar: Komi Publishing, 1989

Roshchevsky, Mikhail, Albert Vaneev & Nikolai Timonin (editors), *Respublika Komi. Entziklopedia* [The Republic of Komi. Encyclopedia], Volume 3, Syktyvkar: Komi Publishing, 2000

Saveleva, Eleonora (editor), *Istoriko-kulturny atlas Respubliki Komi* [Historical–Cultural Atlas of the Republic of Komi], Moscow: Drofa, 1997

T

TAIGA

Taiga is dense, thick, difficult to traverse, coniferous forest with wind-fallen trees and marshy soil. In terms of geography and geobotany, taiga is a continuous area of coniferous boreal forests located in the northern temperate zones of North American and Eurasia. The term itself originates from southern Siberian Turkic-Mongol (*taiga, taig, taika, daika*), where the meaning of it was narrower: dense coniferous mountain forest rich in wildlife. A large number of tree species are found in taiga. The dominant composition of species consists of dark-needle taiga (spruce, fir tree, cedar pine) and light-needle taiga (spruce, larch, birch). Taiga may also be defined as a climate zone: the northern limit of taiga corresponds approximately to the July isotherm of +10°C and its southern border corresponds to +18°C. Within these limits, taiga occupies vast spaces, spreading southward for 2000 km in Eurasia and for 1500 km in Northern America.

A certain amount of warmth and moisture is necessary for self-sufficient development of taiga landscapes: 70–100 kcal cm^{-2} of solar radiation per year, 25–35 kcal cm^{-2} of radiation balance per year, a maximum temperature of 12–19°C, and a growing season in Eurasian taiga of 70–150 days, and in northern North America of 60–100 days, although sometimes longer. Winter temperatures vary drastically within various sectors. Near the Atlantic coast of Eurasia, the average temperature in January is −3°C to 4°C, in east Siberian taiga (in Yakutia) down to −50°C, in north American taiga of the Pacific coast from 0°C to −10°C, on the Atlantic coast −4° to 5°C, and in the continental sector −20°C and below. Annual amplitudes of absolute temperatures reach 104°C in east Siberian taiga and 96°C in North America.

The amount of precipitation in taiga varies considerably. Annual precipitation is usually 500–700 mm, but within inner-continental sectors of Eurasian taiga (e.g., Yakutia) it decreases to 180–250 mm and in North American taiga (in Alaska and Canada Northwest Territories) to 280–340 mm. In near-oceanic sectors of Eurasian taiga, annual precipitation reaches 800–1000 mm, in North American taiga up to 1500 mm, and in its Pacific sector (on the expository mountain slopes) up to 4200 mm. Approximately 50–70% of precipitation evaporates in taiga. The following annual water balance figures are characteristic of typical east Siberian taiga: precipitation 750 mm, evaporation 450 mm, surface flow 200 mm, groundwater flow 100 mm, and net soil moisture 550 mm.

Runoff is smoother in taiga, as evaporation is lower in taiga landscapes due to shading by trees, and rainfall and snowmelt are held by the forest grass and hygrophilous undergrowth (moss, reindeer moss, etc.). Runoff is lowest in the continental sectors of taiga: less than 50 mm in eastern Siberia, less than 100 mm to the east from the Rocky Mountains of North American taiga, and much higher near the oceanic sector of taiga of both continents: 500–800 mm, often 800–1000 mm and higher, especially on the oceanic mountainous slopes (up to 3000 mm and higher).

Perennial permafrost is widespread in taiga landscapes of eastern Siberia and northern sparsely forested subzones of west Siberian and North American taiga. The so-called "drunken forest" (tilted trees) develops when the active layer thaws. Large areas of swamp, wooded swamp, and peat bog can be found within poorly drained lowlands in the taiga, particularly in thermokarst depressions (formed when permafrost thaws and weakens).

Taiga is divided into latitudinal subzones: northern, middle, and southern. The dominant forest verdure consists of dark-needle and light-needle taiga. The floristic composition of taiga is not large. European

Aerial view of taiga (boreal forest) with a newly frozen river in the autumn, Yamal, Western Siberia.
Copyright Bryan and Cherry Alexander Photography

dark-needle taiga trees are mostly European spruce (*Picea albies*), Siberian spruce (*P. obovata*) in the eastern zones, and the Siberian fir tree (*Abies sibirica*). The Siberian cedar pine (*Pinus sibirica*) is rarer. In west Siberian dark-needle taiga, one can also find Siberian larch (*Larix sibirica*). In Far Eastern dark-needle taiga, Ayan spruce (*P. ajanensis*) dominates over white-bark fir tree (*Abies nephrolepis*) and Sakhalin fir tree (*A. sachalinensis*). In North American dark-needle taiga, white spruce (*P. glauca*), black spruce (*P. mariana*), tamarack larch (*L. laricina*), and balsamic fir tree (*A. balsamea*) are typical. In west Siberian light-needle taiga, Siberian larch (*L. sibirica*) dominates; in east Siberian taiga, it is Kayander larch (*L. cajanderi*) and Gmelin larch (*L. gmelini*), and rarely chosenia (*Chosenia*). On sandy and rocky soils of Eurasian taiga, regular pine dominates; on sands and in the southern subzone of North American taiga, banks pine (*P. banksiana*), white pine (*P. stobus*), and red pine (*P. resinosa*) dominate.

The undergrowth in taiga is rather poor: birch (*Betula*), aspen (*Populus tremula*), and alder (*Alnus*) are common. In the southern subzone of Eurasian taiga where soil is rich, the undergrowth and admixture are made up of rowan (*Corbus aucuparia*), honeysuckle (*Lonicera xylosteum*), and linden (*Tilia cordata*); in European taiga, it is holly maple (*Acer platanoides*), elm tree (*Ulnus laevis*), hazel (*Corylus avellana*), and rarely cutting oak (*Quercus robus*); in North American taiga it is balsamic poplar (*Populus balsamifera*), sugar maple (*Acer saccharum*), white elm (*Ulnus*

Americana), linden (*Tilia americana*), black ash (*Fraxinus nigra*), and others. For herbal-shrub taiga layer cowberry, bilberry, great bilberry, ledum, marsh myrtle (Cassandra, Chamaedaphne) and other boreal species dominate; for the ground layer it is green and sphagnum mosses, and for dry taiga it is reindeer mosses.

The podzol type of soil formation dominates in taiga, with the abundant groundwater leading to leaching of nutrients and iron, calcium, and aluminum from the surface humus layer. A characteristic gray or white upper soil layer forms, underlain by red soil where these are redeposited.

In taiga, there are more permanent animals than in tundra, but not as many as in deciduous forest. Widespread tundra animals such as wolf, fox, deer, hare, badger, otter, weasel, ermine, roe, hedgehog, and others are common in taiga habitats as well. The typical Eurasian taiga animals are beaver, squirrel, brown bear, chipmunk, sable, wood lemming, glutton, lynx, elk, musk deer, and hedgehog, and the birds are capercaillie, heath cock, hazel grouse, eagle owl, little owl, crossbill, and woodpeckers. In the North American taiga, black bear, coyote, skunk, marten, American mink, musk rat, porcupine, American elk, and caribou reindeer are more typical. In the Pacific taiga, grizzly bears are also found; in the mountainous taiga of the Cordillera, ram, gray marmot, snow goat, mountain deer are typical, and in the mountainous taiga of Eurasia, bighorn sheep, sable, and black-capped marmot are also found.

Taiga is the main supplier of wood and pulp fibers to the world. In Scandinavia and Finland, large-scale exploitation of the taiga has resulted in most old forests being replaced by intensively managed secondary forests. In Russia, which has about 60% of the world's total boreal forest, Karelia, the Arkhangel'sk Region, and the Komi Republic have mostly intact primary forest, but forestry is continuously moving into previously untouched areas. Parts of Alaska and Canada also have pristine taiga.

Human activities such as extensive logging and mining have resulted in decreased species diversity and total numbers of animals. Although commercial forestry may replace trees, this tends to be monoculture, and the old-growth forests with decaying wood and undergrowth provided a wider range of habitats and species diversity. However, there are some positive results: some of the vanishing species have been restored (sable, bighorn, and black-headed marmot) or are invading the new habitat (muskrat, American mink, and European polecat). Taiga is also the habitat for representatives of other biomes, such as wild boar, aurochs, wood bison, coyote, porcupine, raccoon, and others; 70% of taiga nesting birds are migratory birds. The reptiles of the southern taiga of Eurasia are usually adder, grass snake, and viviparous lizard. Mosquitoes are especially numerous in taiga. Typical species of insects are the following: bark beetles, ants, silkworms, saprophytes, and others.

INNOKENTY ZHIRKOV

See also **Boreal Forest Ecology; Coniferous Forests**

Further Reading

Kaplan, E., *Taiga: Biomes of the World*, New York: Marshall Cavendish, 1996
Taiga Rescue Network website: http://www.taigarescue.org/
Van Cleve, K., F.S. Chapin III, P.W. Flanagan, L.A. Viereck & C. T. Dyrness (editors), *Forest Ecosystems in the Alaskan Taiga: A Synthesis of Structure and Function*, New York: Springer, 1986

TANNER CRAB

Tanner crabs (snow crabs) belong to the genus *Chionoecetes* of the crab family Majidae (spider crabs). There are five species in the northern parts of the Atlantic and Pacific and in the Arctic. One species (*C. opilio*) inhabits the North Pacific, Far Eastern seas, Chukchi Sea, and Northwest Atlantic; others inhabit the Pacific. They are edible and commercially important. Most important are the *C. opilio* (snow crab or queen crab in the northwest Atlantic), *C. bairdi*, and *C. tanneri* (both or all called tanner crab collectively).

The carapace or exoskeleton of tanner crabs is a wide, flattened oval up to 10–15 cm wide. Antennae and antennules are short, and the eyes sit on stalks. They have five pairs of legs, of which the first pair of legs are large, strong chelae or pinching claws. The chelae are so sharp that crabs may cut set nets; thus these crabs are called "cutter crabs" in Russian. The walking legs (second to fifth pairs) are long and widened. The abdomen, as in other crabs, is short, bent under the body, and much wider in females than in males. The rostrum (a forward-pointing projection between the eyes) is short, with a triangular incision. The shell color is yellowish-brown, pinkish, or orange-red.

The snow crab *C. opilio* is a Pacific and Northwest Atlantic species, distributed from the Bering Strait to Korea Strait, southern Japan, and British Columbia, also in the Chukchi and Beaufort seas, reaching Wrangel Island and the area off the Mackenzie River estuary, also off southwestern Greenland, Labrador, Newfoundland, in the Gulf of St Lawrence, and off Nova Scotia (southward to the Gulf of Maine). In 1996, it was found, although in very small numbers, in the southeastern part of the Barents Sea westward of Novaya Zemlya, at depths of 100–300 m and ocean bottom temperatures of 2–3°C. In general, it lives on the shelf and continental slope up to a depth of 650 m, mainly from 70–100 to 200–300 m, on sandy and muddy bottoms, at bottom temperatures from 0°C to 7°C. Males are larger than the females. Mating takes place in spring and summer. During that time, the males fight fiercely with one another (male chelae are much larger than the female's) and many males lose (autotomize or self-amputate) damaged limbs. The females stop feeding before spawning, and may spawn about 40,000 eggs in one clutch. Eggs are incubated in the female's abdominal flap for one or even two years. Larvae usually hatch the following spring. The pelagic larval stage lasts 3–5 months, with the larvae molting many times. Late in summer or in fall, the megalopa (or settling) larvae stop swimming and descend to the ocean bottom and molt to the benthic stage. They become sexually mature at the age of 4–5 years. In some places, the crabs, particularly males, undergo rather long seasonal migrations, descending during the summer into colder waters. The duration of their life is 7–10 years. They feed upon bottom invertebrates such as polychaete worms, crustaceans, molluscs, and echinoderms. This crab is fished in the Gulf of St Lawrence, near Newfoundland and in adjacent areas, in the Bering, Okhotsk, and Japan seas.

The shallow-water tanner crab *C. bairdi* is predominantly a shelf-living species, distributed from the Bering Sea to Hokkaido and Oregon, not quite penetrating into the northern Bering Sea. In 1995–1997 it was found in considerable numbers in the eastern

Sea of Okhotsk off western Kamchatka. It lives at depths up to 500 m, mostly at 250–300 m. It is fished predominantly off Alaska. The deepwater Tanner crab *C. tanneri* occurs in American waters from Bering Sea to Baja California; at 400–1100 m, it is fished off British Columbia. The deepwater (300–2100 m) North Pacific *C. angulatus* and *C. japonicus* (at 500–2700 m) living in the Japan Sea are also fished.

Tanner crabs are caught with traps, and to a lesser extent by trawl nets and seines. The meat from claws and walking legs is utilized. The early catch of all species of the genus *Chionoecetes* in 1998, according to the Food and Agriculture Organization (FAO) statistics, is 194,500 tons, including 75,200 tons in Canada (Atlantic side), in USA (Pacific side) 114,200 tons, and 4700 tons in Japan. In former years, the stock and catch of tanner crabs in the North Pacific and Bering seas were much higher than now (the USA catch in 1991 was 162,000 tons, and the Japanese one in 1993 was 32,400 tons), but from the early 1980s off Alaska and from the late 1980s off Japan, overfishing was noted and catches dropped significantly.

K.N. NESIS

See also **King Crab**

Further Reading

"High Latitude Crabs: Biology, Management, and Economics." *Proceedings of the International Symposium on Biology, Management, and Economics of Crabs from High Latitude Habitats*, Anchorage, Alaska, USA, October 11–13, 1995; University of Alaska Sea Grant College Program Report, No. AK-SG-96-02, 1996

Jamieson, G.S. & W.D. McKone (editors), *Proceedings of the International Workshop on Snow Crab Biology*, December 8–10, 1987, Montreal, Québec, Canadian Fisheries and Aquatic Science, Manuscript Report, No. 2005, 1988

Paul, A.J. (editor), *Bibliography of Research on Snow Crab (Chionoecetes opilio)*, Alaska Sea Grant Publications, No. AK-SG-00-01, 2000

Proceedings of the International Symposium on King and Tanner Crabs, November 28–30, 1989, Anchorage, Alaska USA, Alaska Sea Grant College Program Report, No. AK-SG-90-04, 1990

TAQRAMIUT NIPINGAT

Taqramiut Nipingat Incorporated ("The Northerners' Voice")—or TNI—is a nonprofit Inuit-controlled Canadian corporation that produces radio and television programs aimed at Inuit audiences. It was founded in 1975, with support from government grants, by a group of young Nunavik aborigines anxious to express themselves through the new medium of television (which had just been introduced to the Canadian Arctic), and to bring local contents to northern broadcasting. Its main office was originally in Salluit, Arctic Québec, but it later moved to Montreal. TNI's stated mandate is to provide communication services to the Inuit of Nunavik, to strengthen Inuktitut, the language of the eastern Canadian Inuit, and to promote traditional and contemporary culture.

It was not until 1972 that the newly launched telecommunication satellite *Anik* enabled Canada's northern regions to receive television signals. Several communities, including all of Nunavik's villages, however refused at first to be connected to television networks, because programming did not reflect Inuit interests. This explains why TNI—which was operating out of Nunavik—put its original efforts into audio production (although video cassettes were also produced). In 1976, it linked six villages by satellite, thus inaugurating community radio in the North. It was only in 1983 that television became available to the households of Nunavik.

TNI now produces various types of television programs: interviews with Inuit elders or well-known personalities; documentaries on traditional hunting and fishing activities; and reporting on northern festivals, or on local political, religious, or sports events. Most of this programming is in Inuktitut. Programs are sold to the three Arctic and/or native Canadian television networks: Canadian Broadcasting Corporation's (CBC's) northern service, Television Northern Canada (TVNC), and Aboriginal Peoples' Television Network (APTN). TNI is Canada's oldest producer of Inuit television, since its establishment antedated that of Nunavut's Inuit Broadcasting Corporation (IBC), founded in 1981. Other Inuit producing houses include the Inuvialuit Communication Society (Inuvik, Northwest Territories), Labradormiut (Nain, Labrador), and Isuma Productions (Igloolik, Nunavut).

TNI's programming—and that of its subsidiary, Taqramiut Productions Inc.—is generally appreciated by audiences, although competition by Canadian and American mainstream television channels—several Arctic communities have access to more than 50 channels—is hard to beat. An audience research conducted in 1984 in Nunavik showed that interest for programs in Inuktitut increased with age. These programms were listened to by 67% of all respondents over 54 years of age, by 59% of the 45–54 age group, 56% of those between 35 and 44, 37% of the 25–34 group, 22% of those between 19 and 24, and only 13% of adolescents between 13 and 18 years of age. The situation may have improved since, because TNI and other Inuit producers started diversifying their production, introducing, among other novelties, programs for children, feature films, and music shows. Competition from southern television is still strong, but the TV screen, which now partly reflects local language and culture, cannot be considered anymore a perfect instrument for cultural ethnocide, as it often was during the 1980s and early 1990s.

LOUIS-JACQUES DORAIS

See also **Inuit Broadcasting Corporation**

Further Reading

Anonymous, *TNI-NNBAP Audience Research Preliminary Report (Television)*, Montreal: Quithe Communications Inc., 1984
———, "TVNC: TV about us!." *Makivik News* (1991): 14–17
Boulay, R., J.P. Lamonde & Gilles Larochelle, *Communications Media Development Plan for the Native Communities*, Québec: Department of Communications, 1983
Graburn, Nelson H.H., "Television and the Canadian Inuit." *Études/Inuit/Studies*, 6(1) (1982): 7–17
Valaskakis, Gail G. & Charles Hill, *An Assessment of Project Naalakvik I*, Salluit: Taqramiut Nipingat Inc., 1979

TARYA CULTURE

The Tarya Culture unites a group of archaeological sites in central and southern Kamchatka (Russian Far East) dated at between 5200 and 2200 years before present (years BP). The first sites were studied by Vladimir Il'ich Iokhel'son (Waldemar Jochelson) in Avacha Bay in 1910–1911; later on, in the 1960–1990s, Nikolay Dikov, Tamara Dikova, and Aleksey Ponomarenko continued research on the Tarya Culture.

People of the Tarya Culture were the first to use stone tools and pottery in the Kamchatka Neolithic, an era formed on the basis of local Early Holocene (13,000 to 5000 years ago) cultures, with new elements appearing from outside Kamchatka. The Tarya sites are located in both continental and coastal parts of Kamchatka. Two groups of Tarya sites have been distinguished: South Kamchatkan (Avacha Level II and III; Kopyto II; Zhupanova Level III; Bol'shoy Kamen') and Central Kamchatkan (Domashneye Ozero, Zastoychik, Kultuk). The former are located mostly along the shores of Tarya Bay, Avacha Bay, and Zhupanov Firth, and the latter are located in the Kamchatka River valley. Judging by the dates, the South Kamchatkan group appeared first (3rd to 2nd millennia BC). Later, in the 1st millennium BC, its influence spread over the continental areas as far as Central Kamchatka.

Materials of the lower Level III of the Avacha Site located on the shore of Avacha Bay provide the earliest evidence of the Tarya Culture (radiocarbon-dated to 5200 years BP). At that time, a comparatively small climatic warming was marked.

The Tarya assemblage is represented by its exceptional stone tools. Most of them were made of chert, chalcedony (a form of quartz), and obsidian (a glassy volcanic rock), abundant in Kamchatka. They include

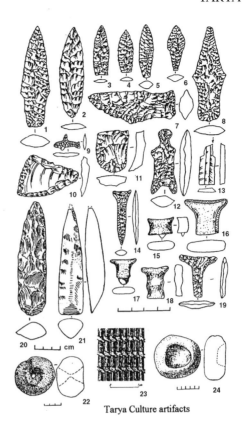

Tarya Culture artifacts: 1–6, 8—point; 7, 10—knives; 9—zoopomorphic figurine; 11—scraper; 12—anthropomorphic figurine; 13—angle burin on microblade; 14–19—labrets; 20, 21—adzes; 22—sinker; 23—twinning mat fragment; 24—oil lamp. 1–22, 24—stone, 23—grass.

projectile points, knives, scrapers, axes, ground adzes, perforators, burins, and engravers. Projectile points include leaf-shaped, triangular with notched bases, and stemmed ones. Knives are represented by leaf-shaped or oval bifaces and a highly specific type of humpbacked, bifacially retouched knives with handles. Side and end scrapers were produced on blade flakes. Some retouched and burinated flakes served as perforators and burins. Shale-ground adzes had a sharpened back and a unilaterally convex or triangular cross section, and were preformed by flaking. Microblades, produced from prismatic cores, and scrapers and burins made on them are typical of the Central Kamchatkan group of sites.

Tarya people hunted for land and sea mammals and birds and were engaged in fishing; bone fragments of fish, birds, and sea mammals have been found at the sites. Tarya hunting tools are represented only by stone tools. No bone tools for the specialized sea mammal hunting with harpoons and leisters (a forklike antler or bone fishing harpoon) were found; however, they might simply have never been retained. The sites located on the seashore, in estuaries, and valleys of fish-rich rivers testify to the beginning of exploration of the sea resources of Kamchatka at that time, originally in the form of gathering. Evidence of fishing with nets is provided by the two types of pebble sinkers found: oval, with a biconical hole drilled in the center, and flat, with symmetrical notches on the sides for attaching lines. Indirect evidence of hunting sea mammals for their fat is found in the form of stone oil lamps dated at 3000 years BP. These were made of flattened pebbles with subtriangular hollows for fat notched on the flat side. The killer whale figurine from Level II of the Avacha Site (1st to 2nd millenia BC) is of similar significance as evidence for seal hunting. At the sight of a killer whale, seals would hurry out onto the shore, where they were caught by a man with a spear and a bow.

Two types of Tarya dwellings can be distinguished: summer and winter ones. Summer homes were located on the shore at river estuaries and along the banks of spawning rivers. They were light framework structures, possibly cache-type on piles, or below-ground ones for summer and fall fishing and sea mammal hunting at rookeries. Winter dwellings were located at convenient high capes and at lakesides. These were semi-subterranean dwellings, subrectangular or oval to 0.8 m deep, and reached 6–13 m across. Settlements consisted of three or more dwellings. Some dwellings had one or more side exits toward the sea, the lake, or the river. They had a log ceiling supported by the rectangular frame covered with sod, with two exits: through the side and through the top. The latter served both as a chimney and as a sunroof. In the center, there was a large hearth with several smaller ones around it. Hearths were not faced with stones. The dwelling floor was covered with birch bark or grass. At 3000 years BP, Tarya people knew how to make textile from nettle fibers; a small burnt fragment of such a textile was found in the burned dwelling at the Avacha Site.

A few ceramic findings have been reported, with the obscure shape of vessels. Tarya people must have cooked mostly in pots made from birch bark; abundant remains have been found at the sites. Water was heated with pebbles warmed in the fire and put in the bark or wooden vessels; such pebbles have also been found in abundance.

The characteristic feature of the Tarya Culture is labrets, face ornaments inserted into special cuts in the lips, cheeks, or nasal septum. They were made of stone and bone. Labrets from hard rock (including obsidian) were first retouched for shape and size, and sometimes, although not always, ground. Labrets from soft, sedimentary rock were produced by grinding. Some labrets were made from bone and walrus ivory. There are sharpened pins with oval cross sections, blunt flat pins, and stud-shaped labrets. Some of them reach 10 cm in length; the average length is about 3 cm, and the width is 1 to 3–4 cm. Labrets must have been associated with

the initiation ritual for boys and girls. The variety of labret shapes and types supposedly reflects the variety of tribal or clan unions within the Tarya Culture. The Old Itel'men Culture that originated from it contains no labrets.

Another peculiarity of the Tarya Culture is chipped-stone zoo-and anthropomorhpic figurines. One can distinguish those of a human and of a killer whale; some are supposed to represent a dog and a bear.

Judging by the great succession in stone tools, the Tarya Culture can be considered as the base for the Old Itel'men Culture that replaced it at the end of the 1st millenium BC and developed the harpoon complex for sea mammal hunting.

SERGEI SLOBODIN

Further Reading

Dikov, Nikolay N., *Arkheologicheskiye pamyatniki Kamcgatki, Chukotki i Verkhney Kolymy* [Archeological Remains in Kamchatka, Chukotka, and the Upper Reaches of the Kolyma], Moscow: Nauka, 1977

———, *Drevniye kul'tury Severo-Vostochnoy Azii* [Ancient Cultures of Northeastern Asia], Moscow: Nauka, 1979

Dikova, Tamara M., *Arkheologiya Yuzhnoy Kamchatki v svyazi s problemoy rasseleniya aynov* [South Kamchatka Archaeology in Connection with the Ainu Occupation Problem], Moscow: Nauka, 1983

Dumond, Don E. & Richard L. Bland, "Holocene prehistory of the northernmost North Pacific." *Journal of World Prehistory,* 9(4) (1995)

Johelson, Waldemar I., *Archaeological Investigations in Kamchatka,* Publication 383, Washington, District of Columbia: Carnegie Institution, 1928

Michael, Henry N., "The Neolithic Cultures of Siberia and the Soviet Far East." In *Chronologies in Old World Archaeology,* edited by Robert Ehrich, 2 volumes, Chicago: University of Chicago Press, 1992

Ponomarenko, Aleksey K., *Drevnyaya kul'tura itel'menov Vostochnoy Kamchatki* [Ancient Culture of the East Kamchatka Itelmen], Moscow: Nauka, 1985

TASIILAQ

Tasiilaq, formerly known as Ammassalik, is the largest town in East Greenland and the central town of the municipality of Ammassalik with a total population of 2911 inhabitants (as recorded in 2000). In addition to the town of Tasiilaq (with a population of 1705), the area includes the villages of Isortoq (129 inhabitants), Tiniteqilaaq (146 inhabitants), Ikkatteq (two inhabitants), Kulusuk (332 inhabitants), Qernertivartivit (one inhabitant), Kuummiit (389 inhabitants), and Sermiligaaq (207 inhabitants). The total population has been stable since the beginning of the 1990s.

The total area of the municipality of Ammassalik is 243,000 square kilometers, making it the largest in Greenland, although only 33,500 square kilometers are not permanently covered with ice. In the north, the municipality borders Ittoqqortoormiit, and on the south, Nanortalik.

The town of Tasiilaq is picturesquely situated within a fjord surrounded by high mountains and divided into two by a small river that flows down through the Flower Valley. Tasiilaq is located near the Arctic Circle and has a warm and dry summer and relatively mild winters. Summer flora in the Ammassalik area is lush with Arctic plants, berries, and flowers. There is a rich fauna, with polar bears, narwhal, whales, and seals.

When the town was founded in 1894, it was named Ammassalik (meaning "the place with the Ammassat (capelin)"), although in 1997 the name was changed to Tasiilaq. The present name is the East Greenlandic equivalent to the West Greenlandic name *Tasiusaq*, meaning "the place at the lakes." Tasiilaq is surrounded by one of the most astonishing landscapes in Greenland, which, together with its rich cultural life, has contributed to its popularity among tourists in Greenland. During the year, several thousand tourists arrive from Iceland by helicopter from the main airport in Kulusuk in Greenland.

Permanent connection to Europe and colonization by Denmark was established with the *konebådseks-pedition* (the Umiaq expedition) by the Danish naval captain Gustav Holm in 1884–1885. At that point in time, approximately 400 persons comprised the settlement's population, who suffered severely due to vanishing resources, malnutrition, and disease. In 1894, the natural harbor at Tasiilaq established a trade station, becoming the essential hub for connections between the Danish colonial authorities and East Greenland.

Up until World War II, hunting characterized the Tasiilaq region; however, after the war and particularly during the 1960s, cod fisheries emerged as a promising trade, and investments were made in order to stimulate the economic base. The fish resource fluctuates however; hence presently, the town's economic base comprises transfers of external monetary sources with limited contributions from fisheries and hunting. The transfers sustain the life of the town and its vocational training school, administrative, and social services, providing the population with economic and social conditions equal to other parts of Greenland.

The natural habitat in East Greenland is both beautiful and harsh and characterized by the fierce *piteraq*, a katabatic wind (an air current or wind moving down a slope with high speed because of extreme cooling conditions) that regularly strikes the town with tremendous force and causes severe destruction. Architecture must be designed to withstand the piteraq's wind speed of up to several hundred kilometers per hour.

Tasiilaq's economy depends upon transfers of money from the Home Rule government. Public services generate 55% of Tasiilaq's jobs, while 22% of the population is employed in hunting and fishing. Trade and business services employ 15% and the building industry comprises 8% of the workforce. There are several weekly flights to the municipality via the capital, Nuuk, and the airports in Kangerlussuaq, Keflavik, and Reykjavik in Iceland. These routes are particularly utilized during the sailing season from the beginning of July to the end of October. Outside the sailing season, weekly helicopter flights to all settlements other than Ikkatteq and Qernertivartivit serve the community and its visitors.

Tasiilaq's first church, constructed in the traditional Greenland colonial style of wood, painted red, with a shingle roof and spire, dates from 1908 and has since been beautifully restored. Today, the church houses the local museum with a collection of art and artifacts from both recent and ancient history of the municipality. The town built a new pentagonal church in 1986 with interior designs by the Greenlandic artist Aka Høegh.

RASMUS OLE RASMUSSEN

See also **Holm, Gustav**

Further Reading

Berthelsen, Christian, Inger H. Mortensen & Ebbe Mortensen, *Kalaallit Nunaat Atlas, Greenland,* Nuuk: Atuakkiorfik, 1992

Nielsen, Niels, Peter Skautrup & Christian Vibe (editors), *J.P. Trap Danmark, bind XIV, Grønland,* Copenhagen: Gads Forlag, 1970

Rasmussen, Rasmus Ole, "Formal economy, renewable resources and structural changes in West Greenland." *Études/Inuit/Studies,* 24(1): (2000), 48–78

Statistics Greenland, *Greenland 2000–2001. Statistical Yearbook,* Nuuk: Statistics Greenland, 2001

www.ammassalik.gl/Turisme

TATSHENSHINI/ALSEK

The Tatshenshini/Alsek River flows through northwest British Columbia through the Saint Elias Mountains, joining the Alsek River just before the Alaska border in southwestern Yukon to flow toward the Pacific in southeast Alaska. It is one of the few rivers to breach the coastal range, and has been used as a trade route by both native peoples and early European explorers. Both rivers are large-volume, fast-flowing glacial rivers in their upper reaches, terminating in a large delta-estuary at Dry Bay in the Gulf of Alaska.

Nearly one million hectares in size, the Tatshenshini-Alsek River valleys are protected under British Columbia law as a Class "A" Provincial Park. Taken together with the Wrangell-St Elias National

Park and Glacier Bay National Park in Alaska, and Yukon's Kluane National Park Reserve, this created the largest international protected area in the world. The Tatshenshini-Alsek watershed was also designated a United Nations World Heritage Site in 1993, for its wildlife and biodiversity, and wilderness values. A mining proposal in the late 1980s to open an open-cast copper mine at Windy Craggy Mountain above the confluence of the rivers in northwestern British Columbia was a major factor in the environmental campaign to create the Provincial Park.

The Tatshenshini-Alsek is one of the three major salmon-bearing rivers on the northern Pacific coast, serving the commercial fishery in the Deep Bay area. In the mid-19th century, rich salmon resources supported numerous fishing villages and a relatively large aboriginal (Tutchone) population, but today only Klukshu, Yukon is occupied. A breach of an ice-dammed lake on the Alsek in the late 1800s generated massive floodwaters that swept an entire village into the valley below. Today, the river supports a thriving tourist white-water-rafting business.

The Tatshenshini has ecosystems ranging from sea level to over 15,000 ft and consequently has a high biodiversity with abundant grizzly bears, wolves, mountain goats, moose, bald and golden eagles, peregrine and gyr falcons, and trumpeter swans. The area is also home to many rare species such as the "blue" or "glacier" bear, and is home to about half of British Columbia's Dall's sheep population. Rare birds include the king eider and Stellars' eider.

GILLIAN LINDSEY

Further Reading

Ministry of Tourism, Sustainable Development Branch, *Tatshenshini Alsek River Use Study,* Victoria, 1992
Searle, R., "North America's wildest river." *Wildlife Conservation,* 96(1) (1993): 8

TATTOOING

Most indigenous peoples of the Arctic practiced tattooing to some extent. Although tattoos served a variety of personal and social functions in the past, outside forces such as missionization, disease, and modernity have paved the way for relinquishing tattoo customs in the present. Only a handful of Yupiget individuals from Chukotka and St Lawrence Island retain traditional tattoos: all date from the early 20th century. One St Lawrence Island Yupiget woman is the last living tattoo artist and designer.

Archaeological evidence in the form of a carved human figurine from the Dorset Culture demonstrates that tattooing was practiced as early as 3500 years ago.

Moreover, the remains of several mummies discovered in Bering Strait and Greenland indicate that tattooing was an element basic to ancient traditions. This is corroborated in mythology because the origin of tattooing is sometimes associated with the creation of the sun and moon.

Ethnographically, the first reference to tattooing practices in the Arctic was probably recorded by Sir Martin Frobisher in 1576. He briefly described women with facial tattoos living in Frobisher Bay. As a general rule, expert tattoo artists were almost always respected elderly women. Their extensive training as skin seamstresses facilitated the need for precision when stitching or puncturing the human skin with tattoos. Tattoo designs were usually made freehand, but in some instances a rough outline was first sketched upon the area of application. The typical tattoo kit consisted of a bone or steel needle, sinew thread, and a compound liquid pigment composed of lampblack, urine, and lubricating seal oil; in some regions, gunpowder, graphite, and plant juices were used. Oftentimes, tattoo pigments were believed to possess apotropaic properties and, as the needle and sinew were drawn through the skin, the tattoo artist chanted special words to facilitate the process. Several sittings were required to complete the desired pattern.

The concepts of tattooing were as varied as the pigments used by the tattoo artist. Among the Yupiget, funerary tattoos (*nafluq*) consisted of small dots at the convergence of various joints: shoulders, elbows, hip, wrist, knee, ankle, neck, and waist. These tattoos protected a pallbearer from spiritual attack. Joints became the locus of tattoo because it was believed that malevolent spirits entered the body at these points, as they were the seats of the soul(s). Urine and tattoo pigments, as the nexus of dynamic and apotropaic power, prevented the evil spirit from penetrating the pallbearer's body.

Nearly every attribute of the human dead was also believed to be equally characteristic of the animal dead, as the spirit of every animal was believed to possess semihuman form. Yupiget men, and more rarely women, were tattooed when they killed seal, polar bear, or harpooned a bowhead whale (*aghveq*) for the first time. Like the tattoo of the pallbearer, "first-kill" tattoos (*kakileq*) consisted of small dots at the convergence of various joints. Again, the application of these tattoos impeded the future instances of spirit possession at these vulnerable points. *Kakileq* were also important to other aspects of the hunt; they helped harpooners hit their targets. Similar tattoos on the North Slope of Alaska doubled as whaling charms, serving to bring the whale closer to the umiaq. This type of sympathetic magic was also manifest in the stylized "whale-fluke" tattoos adorning the corners of men's mouths. Fittingly, these symbols were applied as part of first-kill observances among the Yupiget as well as by other groups in the Arctic.

Tattoos also recalled an ancestral presence and could be understood to function as the conduit for a visiting spiritual entity, coming from the different temporal dimensions into the contemporary world. Vladimir G. Bogoraz and Sergei Rudenko noted that the Yupiget and Chukchi tattooed anthropomorphic spirit-helpers onto their foreheads and limbs. These sticklike figures, more appropriately named "guardians" or "assistants," protected individuals from evil spirits, disasters at sea, unknown areas where one traveled, strangers, and even in the case of new mothers, the loss of their children.

Chin stripes were more commonly found than any other tattoo motif. Most notably, they were tattooed on the chin as part of the ritual of social maturity, a signal to men that a woman had reached puberty. To increase their fertility, childless Chukchi women tattooed slightly sloping parallel lines on the cheeks, usually consisting of three tightly grouped bands. Two diverging lines also ran from high up on the forehead down over the full length of the nose. These tattoos distinguished Chukchi and Yupiget women in the afterlife from men. In Igloolik, Canada, the tattooing of women's thighs ensured that newborns would see something of beauty as they entered this world. Intricate scrollwork on the cheeks, tattoos on the arms, wrists, and hands of Yupiget and King Island women combined family or clan designs to form a genealogical marker. Similar tattoos on the forearms of Aleut women represented a family's respective whaling boat.

Tattoos were also utilized as a curative agent. Inuit (or Eskimos generally) and Yupiget, in particular, like many other circumpolar peoples, regarded living bodies as inhabited by multiple souls, each residing in a particular joint or bodily area. As noted, these regions were often tattooed. Interestingly, many joint-tattoos correspond to classical acupuncture points and it is not surprising that the Aleuts, as well as the Yupiget, utilized "tattoo-puncture" to relieve those aching joints that were affected by spiritual possession.

Apparently, this potent medical technology reached Greenland in the distant past. Radiocarbon dated to the 15th century AD, the Qilakitsoq mummies have revealed that a conscious, exacting attempt was made to place dot-motif tattoos at important facial loci, each corresponding to acupuncture points utilized today to cure facial disorders. Several ivory dolls from the Old Bering Sea Culture and Punuk Culture excavated from St Lawrence Island illustrate ancient continuity in curative tattooing practices spanning thousands of miles and hundreds of years.

Regardless of the medical implications of the tattoo and its origins, it is apparent that the practice of tattooing among Arctic peoples was quite homogenous. Tattooing was a graphic image of social beliefs and values expressing the many ways in which Arctic peoples attempted to control their bodies, lives, and experiences. Tattoos provided a nexus between individual and communally defined forces that shaped perceptions of existence.

LARS KRUTAK

See also **Qilakitsoq Mummies**

Further Reading

Bogoras, Waldemar (also Bogoraz, Vladimir, G.), *The Chukchee*, 3 volumes, Leiden: Brill, and New York: Strechert, 1904–1909, reprinted New York: AMS, 1975

Krutak, Lars, "St Lawrence Island joint-tattooing: spiritual/medicinal functions and intercontinental possibilities." *Études/Inuit/Studies*, 23(1–2) (1999): 229–252

———, "The Arctic." In *Tattoo History: A Source Book*, edited by Steve Gilbert, New York: Juno Books, 2000

Rudenko, Sergei I., "Tatuirovka aziatskikh eskimosov" [Tattooing of the Asiatic Eskimo]. *Sovetskaia etnografiia*, 14 (1949): 149–154

TAYMYR (DOLGAN-NENETS) AUTONOMOUS OKRUG

Taymyr (Dolgan-Nenets) Autonomous Okrug is located in the Far North of eastern Siberia to the north of the Arctic Circle, between the estuaries of the Yenisey and Khatanga rivers and also including the offshore Severnaya Zemlya Archipelago. Established on December 30, 1930, it is an autonomous district within Krasnoyarsk Kray, and includes four administrative regions: Dikson (center: village Dikson), Ust'-Eniseysky (center: village Karaul), Khatangsky (center: village Khatanga), and Dudinsky (center: city Dudinka). Within its territory, there is also the city of Noril'sk that is administratively subordinated directly to Krasnoyarsk Kray. The cities of Talnakh, Kaierkan, and Oganer and village Snezhnogorsk are subordinated to Noril'sk.

The total area of Taymyr Autonomous Okrug is 879,900 km². The administrative center is the city of Dudinka located in the lower course of the Yenisey River. The total population on 01.01.2000 was 44,100 people (not taking into account the Noril'sk administrative area, which has a population of 259,900). About 20% of the population of the okrug is indigenous, of whom 4900 are Dolgans, 2800 Nenets, 900 Nganasans, 300 Evenks, and 200 Enets. Other major ethnic groups in Taymyr are Russians, Belarussians, and Germans,

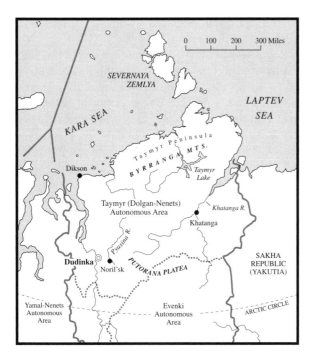

Location of Taymyr (Dolgan-Nenets) Autonomous Okrug and main cities and rivers.

and there are a total of over 60 nationalities. The severe climate and permafrost have meant that people have not settled here in large numbers: development and life support costs are 3.5–12 times higher than in the central areas of Russia, and the population is mainly concentrated in the south, between the towns Dudinka and Noril'sk. The change to the market economy and high inflation rates severely worsened the working and life conditions in the North, stimulating emigration from the area. Migration balance in the okrug is negative. The unemployment rate is about 4%.

Dolgans make up the majority of the indigenous people in Taymyr Autonomous Okrug, inhabiting mainly the Khatanga and Dudinka areas. They have the most recent ethnic history of the indigenous peoples (*see* **Dolgans**). They speak the Dolgan dialect of the Yakut language. Dolgans are Orthodox believers, and some still have Russian family names given to their ancestors by Russian Orthodox priests. The Dolgans' traditional occupations include domestic reindeer breeding, hunting for wild reindeers and fur-bearing animals, and fishing. Domestic reindeer breeding is most developed in the Khatanga area, where the number of reindeer in a collective farm may reach several thousands. Reindeer nomadic routes are traditional: tundra in the summer time and forest-tundra in winter.

The Nenets are the second most populous indigenous group of the okrug, having a wider population base across a vast territory from the Nenets Autonomous Okrug of the Arkhangel'sk region and the Yamal-Nenets Autonomous Okrug of the Tyumen Oblast'. The Nenets are also traditionally reindeer herders, but unlike the Dolgans, they have retained animistic beliefs (*see* **Nenets**).

Nganasans live only in the Taymyr area. In former times they were the most northern people who had well adapted to the severe climate. In the 1989 all-Russia census, there were only 849 Nganasans registered (*see* **Nganasans**).

Russian pioneers from Moscow, Arkhangel'sk, Tula, and Tver' started to populate the banks of the Yenisey and Pyasina rivers in the 16th century. It was first mentioned in 1667 in the tribute chronicles of Mangazeya. Records of Dudinka date back to 1610–1611.

Land and Resources

Taymyr Okrug is the only subject of the Russian Federation entirely located north of the Arctic Circle. Cape Chelyuskin at the tip of the Taymyr Peninsula is the most northern point of the continental Eurasian and Russian mainland. The cape is named after a member of the Great North Expedition, Semyon I. Chelyuskin, who first reached this point in May 1742. There is a small settlement named Chelyuskin connected with Khatanga by irregular air communication.

Landforms of Taymyr Peninsula may be zoned into three areas: North Siberian Lowland located between the Khatanga River and southern piedmont of the Byrranga Mountains, Byrranga Mountains (elevations up to 1119 m) stretching in several parallel chains in the east-west direction, and a coastal plain with gentle hilly landforms. The Taymyr lowlands are the largest unbroken tundra landscape in Eurasia.

The climate of the area is Arctic and Subarctic with severe long winters (up to 10 months) and cool summers. A typical feature is the frequent and abrupt change of the weather. The average air temperature −32°C in January is and 2–13°C in July. The annual precipitation is abot 250 mm. Snow cover is formed in late September, and lost in mid-June. Permafrost occurs all over the area. In summer, the sun shines 24 h a day, and plants and animals accelerate their growth and development.

The Arctic and nival deserts and semideserts occupy the northern part of Taymyr. Vegetation in its central part is represented by lichen, moss-cotton-grass, moss-sedge and shrub tundra. Forest-tundra with thin larch forests and shrubs covers its southern part. The extreme northern point of wood species worldwide (Siberian larch at 72°50′) is located in the okrug. Dominant soils in the area are typical tundra and peat-gley soils; in the south podzolic soils occur, and in the Yenisey flood plain meadow soils occur.

Lake Taymyr located near the southern terrace of the Byrranga Mountains is the largest water body of the area (*see* **Taymyr Lake**). Its shore is deeply cut. From September to June, the lake is frozen. Due to its shallowness (the major part of the lake is about 5 m deep and less), it cools and freezes rapidly. Water level decreases along as ice depth grows, and by the end of the wintertime ice reaches the bottom. About 80% of the lake's area gets frozen down to the bottom. Common fish species include loach, whitefish, burbot, grayling, and omul. Lake Taymyr and the adjacent tundra are the habitat of numerous birds, such as swans, geese, ducks, rough-legged buzzards, and peregrines. In 1983, the lake was included in the Taimyrsky nature reserve (zapovednik).

Flora and Fauna

Taymyr fauna includes reindeer, argali, Arctic fox, wolf, lemming, ermine, and hare. The population of wild reindeer in the Taymyr Peninsula is the largest in Eurasia (up to 1,000,000). Bird species include snowy owl and partridge. On the coast of the Arctic Ocean, polar bear, walrus, seal, and white whale are found. In summer, the coastal tundra is an important nesting ground for numerous migratory birds (ducks, geese, swans, waders, loons, or divers), including the dark-bellied brent goose, and the endangered lesser white-fronted goose and red-breasted goose. Commercial fish species include sturgeon and salmon. In 1975, muskoxen were brought from Canada and Alaska and reintroduced into Taymyr Peninsula, which they inhabited in former times. Having completely adapted to the new environment in the Putorana reserve, their population increased so much that a number of animals were transported to Sakha (Yakutia) Republic.

There are three zapovedniks or state nature reserves in the Taymyr Autonomous Okrug: the Bolshoi Arktichesky reserve (on the islands and coast of the Taymyr Peninsula, total 4.2 million ha), Taimyrsky biosphere reserve (a UNESCO Man and Biosphere Reserve), and Putorana reserve. These are sometimes collectively known as the Great Arctic Reserve, Russia's largest protected area. The total protected area is over 11% of the territory of the okrug.

The Putorana reserve was established in 1988. Its area is 1.9 million ha. It comprises the Putorana Plateau with deeply cut relief and flat tops, headstreams of the Pyasina and Kheta rivers, and tributaries of the Nizhnaya Tunguska River. Dominant ecosystems of the area include larch sparse forests, mountainous tundra, and polar deserts. The main protected species is the putorana argali, or wild sheep. The Putorana Plateau is under preparation for inclusion into the UNESCO World Heritage List.

The Taymyr reserve was established in 1979. Its area is 1.3 million ha. It includes the southwestern part of Taymyr Lake, tundra and bog ecosystems, and larch wood plots. Resident species are Arctic fox and reindeer; nesting birds are red-breasted goose, bean goose, swan, and peregrine falcon.

Environmental Status of the Area

Environmental pollution caused by the activities of the joint stock company RAO Noril'sk Nickel is an urgent problem that seriously impacts the natural environment of the Taymyr Okrug. Long-term emissions of sulfur dioxide from the ore smelters and deposition of aerosols and heavy-metal particles in the area have had a severe impact on approximately 13 million ha of virgin tundra and reindeer grazing land. From Noril'sk, dead lichen and trees due to acidic emissions stretch 90 km southward and 120 km southeast, copper concentrations in mosses around the smelter complex are twice those of background levels, and heavy metals pollute the aquatic environment. The area in the vicinity of Noril'sk is generally recognized as a zone of severe environmental degradation, and long-range atmospheric transport may cause circumpolar contamination.

Natural Resources

Although the rate of geological survey in the Taymyr Autonomous Okrug is the lowest in Russia, there are prospected resources of oil and natural gas, and prospective areas for molybdenum, copper, titanium, gold, polymetallic ores, mercury, stibium, fluorite, phosphorites, iron, slates, and salt have been revealed. The area has coal resources estimated at 92 billion tons, although the only currently operating coal mine, Kotui, will be exhausted in a few years. There are placer gold and platinoids producing plots in the area. Recent geological prospecting has revealed over 30 oil and gas fields in the area. Potential hydrocarbon resources of the Taymyr Okrug comprise about 20% of all potential resources of the Siberian Platform. Three operating gas fields form a gas-producing area in the north of the eastern Siberia. Natural gas is supplied from the Messoyakha gas field to Noril'sk via a gas pipeline 260 km long.

Economy

Taymyr Autonomous Okrug is the most economically underdeveloped subject of the Russian Federation by all macroeconomic indices. The okrug's share in the gross regional product is about 0.02% of the Russian gross output. The largest industrial enterprise is the coalmine "Kotui." Other industries include fish-processing plants in Khatanga and Dudinka. The Noril'sk industrial area and Ust' Khatanga Power Plant are located within the territory of the okrug, but are subordinated directly to the Krasnoyarsk Kray administration.

The rural economy of the area is not diverse. It specializes in reindeer breeding, hunting and fur trapping, and fishing. Cattle breeding and poultry keeping are not highly developed. A major share of its production belongs to collective farms and husbandries; however, the shares of family and tribal husbandries are growing from year to year, reaching over 35% of the total rural production in 1998. Currently, there are 27 farms and husbandries in the okrug with various forms of property, of which 13 are collective farms.

Communications

Close to the northern border of the Taymyr Autonomous Okrug is the Northern Sea Route: the Dikson-Khatanga section 1730 km long leads into the Kara and Laptev seas, and the Yenisey low stream as far as Igarka town (928 km). Railroad Dudinka-Noril'sk-Talnakh connects the town of Dudinka with the Noril'sk industrial area. Its length is 89 km; the maximal permitted speed is 50 km h^{-1}. The road is not connected with the main railroad network of Russia; it plays the role of an access road to the Dudinka seaport. There are 85 km of motor roads with hard surface, 175 km of earth roads, and 6000 km of seasonal (winter) roads crossing the territory of the okrug.

Navigable waterways are the rivers of Yenisey and Khatanga, and the Northern Sea Route. The main ports are Dudinka, Dikson, and Khatanga. Noril'sk has an airport connecting the city with Moscow and other major cities of Russia.

GRIGORI TERTITSKI

See also **Dikson; Dolgan; Dudinka; Khatanga; Krasnoyarsk Kray; Nganasan; Nenets; Noril'sk; Taymyr Peninsula; Yenisey River**

Further Reading

Anderson, D., *Identity and Ecology in Arctic Siberia*: The Number One Reindeer Brigade, Oxford: Oxford University Press, 2000

Müller, H.H., P. Prokosch & E. Syroechlovsky, *Nature Reserves on Taymyr*, Oslo: WWF Arctic Program

TAYMYR LAKE

Taymyr Lake, the largest freshwater lake north of the Arctic Circle, lies in a tectonic down-faulted valley at 73–75° N and 99–108° E, in the Dolgano-Nenet Autonomous Okrug, northeastern central Siberia, in a polar desert environment. The lake is very irregular in shape due to many bays, but is generally elongated with a length of 250 km and a width (excluding bays) of 15–20 km. The northern shore of Taymyr Lake is rocky with the steep cliffs of the Byrranga Mountains rising to 50–100 m; its southern banks are formed by smooth pebble hills and are seldom higher than 10 m.

In 1973, the surface area (along with small additional connected lakes) was estimated as 6129 km^2. The area of the lake is gradually decreasing, and hydrologists predict that the lake will disappear completely in the next 400–500 years. The reason is that Taymyr Lake is a relict of Pleistocene sea transgressions. Taymyr Lake is extremely shallow, with an average depth of 2.9 m and a maximum depth of 20 m. Sand bars make up more than 70% of its bottom, while silts cover around 25%. The total water volume is 13.7 km^3.

From radiocarbon isotope dating (Bol'shiyanov et al., 2001), it is known that from 40 to 20,000 years ago alternating stages of intense sedimentation and erosion took place, followed by a catastrophic loss of water 16,800 years ago, corresponding to the last sea regression. In the last 10,000 years, water level rises and falls (of 5–10 m compared with today's level) have been recorded. The annual changes of water level are 5–6 m following spring floods in July, and by the end of winter the lake loses 75% of its peak water volume.

The drainage basin of Taymyr Lake is about 126,000 km^2, and its largest tributary, accessible by river steamboats, is Verkhnyaya Taymyra. Other notable tributaries are the Bikada, Severnaya, Zapadnaya, and Tarada rivers. The only river flowing out of the lake is Nizhnyaya Taymyra. Its drainage basin covers over 34% of the total basin of the lake system. Melted snow water in the lake feeds outward river flow.

The climate around Taymyr Lake is relatively mild as the Byrranga Mountains protect the area from severe north winds. The average January temperature is −25°C, and the average temperature in July is +9.7°C; annual precipitation is low, and only in May does snow cover reach 45–50 cm. Ice depth in the lake is 200–212 cm. Ice is present from September to May or June, and more than 85% of the lake bottom becomes frozen. Open water remains for 40–80 days, its temperature being less than 0.1°C.

In the lake, there are no higher aquatic plants, and no molluscs. There is a low volume of benthic fauna (Tendipedidae, Polychaeta, Nematodes, Bryozoa), with a biomass of 0.2–2 g m^{-2}. However, the plankton fauna is fairly rich (Diatomea, Rotatoria, Copepoda, and Oligochaeta), and its biomass in early September is 0.12 g m^{-3}. Besides freshwater fauna, there are relict marine crustacean species (*Limnocnus macrorus*, *Pallasea quadrispinosa*, *Gammaracanthus loricatus*, *Mysis oculata*) and Baikal species (*Manajunkia baicalensis*, *Hislopia placoides*, *Echinogamma rus*). Fish are represented by 20 species, most of them being sigs (*Coregonus sardinella, C. peled, C. muksun*), loaches (*Salvenius taimyricus, S. alpinus, S. boganidae, S. tolmachoffi, S. drjagini*), burbot, stickle-backs, and others. Many birds live in the lake during the summer migratory period, including sandpipers (*Pluvialis apricaria, P. squatarola, Limosa lapponica, Charadrius hiaticula, C. morinellus*), geese (*Anser albifrons, Branta ruficollis*), ducks (*Clangula hyemalis, Somateria spectabilis, S. stelleri*), gulls (*Larus hyperboreus, L. argentatus, Sterna paradisaea*), peregrine falcons, skuas, and loons.

The famous Russian explorer Alexander Theodor von Middendorf was the first to visit and describe Taymyr Lake in the 1840s. Later, the lake was passed by Nikolai N. Urvantsev during his geological expeditions in the 1930s. The first expedition to study Taymyr Lake was sent by the Institute of the Arctic and Antarctic from Leningrad in 1943. Six members of the team started from Noril'sk and crossed 1000 km of lifeless tundra with loaded reindeer. They then wintered in tents on the northern bank of the lake monitoring hydrology and biology. Up to now, the shores and surroundings of the lake have been unpopulated. Geological parties, scientific groups, and rarely indigenous hunters visit it. In 1983, the southwestern part of the lake was included in the Taimyrsky nature reserve (zapovednik).

LEONID M. BASKIN

See also **Byrranga Mountains; Taymyr Peninsula**

Further Reading

Adamenko, V. & A. Egorov, (editors), *Geographiya ozer Taymyra* [Geography of Taymyr Lakes], Leningrad: Nauka, 1985

Bol'shiyanov, D., G. Fedorov & L. Savel'eva, "Izmeneniya prirodnoy sredy poluostrova Taymyr v pozdnem neopleistotsene I golotsene" [Natural Environment of Taymyr Peninsula Changes during Late Neopleistocene and Holocene]. In *Taymyr. Malochislennye narody. Prirodnye usloviya. Fauna* [Taymyr. Indigenous People. Nature Conditions. Fauna], edited by Nikolay Lovelius, St Petersburg: Khatanga, 2001

Greze, V., "Taymyrskoe ozero" [Taymyr Lake]. *Izvestiya Vsesoyuznogo Geographicheskogo obshchestva*, 79(3) (1947): 289–302

Pavlov, Dmitriy & Kseniya Savvaitova, *Raznoobrazie ryb Taymyrskogo poluostrova* [The Diversity of Fishes of Taymyr Peninsula], Moscow: Nauka, 1999

TAYMYR PENINSULA

The Taymyr Peninsula is located between the Yenisey estuary of the Kara Sea and Khatanga Bay of the Laptev Sea. Its extreme northern point is Chelyuskin Cape. The area of the peninsula is about 400,000 km². It stretches in the west-east direction for about 1000 km, and in the north-south direction for over 500 km.

The landforms of Taymyr are various and picturesque. Its northern coast is flat and low, forming the Northern Taymyr Lowland. The center of the peninsula is occupied by the Byrranga Mountains comprising a number of ridges stretching in the southwest-northeast direction. The mountains' height varies from 500–700 m in the west to 1000–1100 m in the east (the greatest height is 1146 m). A small area (50 km²) of modern glaciation is located in the eastern part of the mountains. The North Siberian Lowland occupies the southern part of the Taymyr Peninsula.

The large area and complicated relief of the peninsula result in a varied climate. In western Taymyr, the climate is milder with higher precipitation compared to its eastern part. Temperature and precipitation differences between north and south are small in spite of long distances.

In western Taymyr, the mean annual air temperature is about –12°C; the mean temperature is –28°C in January and 3–4°C in July. There are 260–270 days per year with temperatures below 0°C. The annual precipitation is 250–270 mm, snow being possible in any season. Snow cover lasts for about 250 days.

In eastern Taymyr, the mean annual temperature drops down to –14°C to –15°C; the mean January temperature is –33°C to –35°C. The mean air temperature in July is 3–4°C. Annual precipitation is lower: 220–240 mm; however, in the Byrranga Mountains it increases up to 295 mm. There are 270–300 days with daily temperatures below 0°C.

The largest rivers in the region are the Pyasina (818 km) flowing from Pyasina Lake to the Kara Sea; Verkhnyaya Taymyra (567 km) flowing to Taymyr Lake; Nizhnyaya Taimyra (187 km) flowing from Taymyr Lake to the Kara Sea; and the Khatanga (227 km) flowing to the Laptev Sea.

The freezing period on the rivers starts in early October and lasts over 250 days. In spite of the fact that precipitation in the summer is considerably higher than the total amount of snow, water from melted snow is the main source for the rivers of Taymyr (60% of the total runoff), while rainwater and groundwater constitute only 40% of the runoff. A considerable amount of the summer precipitation infiltrates into the thawing-out soil strata and replenishes the stock of groundwater. Some summer precipitation is lost in evaporation. The period of most intensive snow melting determines the rivers' hydrological regime: floods occur during the second half of June after snowmelt, and the lowest runoff occurs in the winter, when small rivers may freeze through.

The Taymyr lakes are of various origins: there are glacial-tectonic, glacial, thermokarst, sea lagoon, and river flood lakes. Most lakes, mainly small (several hectares) thermokarst lakes, are located within the lowlands. Lakes in the Byrranga Mountains are rather scarce. However, the largest lake in Eastern Siberia, Lake Taymyr, is located there (*see* **Taymyr Lake**). Its area is 4370 km², and 80% of its area has a depth below 1 m in the low water period. Only the northern part of the lake is deep (down to 26 m). In mid–October, the lake becomes frozen and is ice-covered for about 10 months. By the end of winter, the ice depth reaches 2 m and more; therefore, most of the lake area gets frozen through. In the Quaternary Age, this region was in the area of sea transgressions; therefore, the water is slightly mineralized and there are representatives of relict marine fauna.

Permafrost occurs all over the Taymyr territory, even on the bottoms of some of the bays. Its depth reaches 600 m (in the Byrranga Mountains), and the depth of seasonal thawing is 0.5–1.5 m.

The process of soil formation in the northern and mountainous areas of the peninsula is extremely slow. Dominant soil types in the area are primitive polygonal, gley, turf and mountainous Arctic soils. Tundra peat-gley soils with a peat layer of 20–25 cm occur in the north of the North Siberian Lowland.

Almost all of Taymyr is woodless. In the Byrranga Mountains and in the extreme north of the peninsula, vegetation cover is fragmentary. Bare soil sites alternate with spots of moss-lichen vegetation and bogs (in flat areas). Lichen, moss-lichen, and shrub tundra in combination with bogs cover the Byrranga Piedmont and lowland in the south of Taymyr. Forest-tundra areas occur in the extreme south of the peninsula.

Severe climatic conditions, particularly the low temperatures, result in poor invertebrate fauna and lack of amphibians and reptiles in Taymyr. The bird fauna is very rich in summer (over 100 species). Similar to other Arctic regions, migrant birds such as geese, ducks, gulls, and waders form the basis of the ornithofauna in the peninsula. In addition, settled birds such as rock ptarmigan (*Lagopus mutus*) and willow ptarmigan (*Lagopus lagopus*) are abundant in places. Among the species nesting in Taymyr, the following birds are registered in the Russian Red Data Book of endangered species: red-breasted goose (*Rufibrenta ruficollis*)—over half of the total population, lesser white-fronted goose (*Anser erythropus*), Baikal teal (*Anas formosa*), and white-tailed eagle (*Haliaeetus albicilla*).

In the Taymyr coast, walrus (*Odobenus rosmarus*), seals, and polar bear (*Ursus maritimus*) can be found. The tundra is the habitat for the world's largest population of reindeer (*Rangifer torandus*). After the sharp decline of commercial hunting of reindeer in the 1990s, its population reached 800,000. Among other mammals, the collared lemming (*Dicrostonyx torquatus*), Siberian lemming (*Lemmus sibiricus*), Arctic fox,

wolf, common weasel (*Mustela erminea*), and mountain hare (*Lepus timidus*) are common. Muskox (*Ovibos moschatus*) was reintroduced from Canada and Alaska in 1975. Among the mammals inhabiting Taymyr, walrus and polar bear are registered in the Red Data Book.

The rivers and lakes are rich in fish, most fish species belonging to the salmon family (Salmonidae): muksun (*Coregonus muksun*), nelma (*Stenodus leucichthus nelma*), sardine cisco (*Coregonus sardinella*), Arctic cisco or omul (*Coregonus autumnalis*), taimen (*Hucho taimen*), and Arctic char (*Salvelinus alpinus*). In the Yenisey estuary area, Siberian sturgeon (*Acipenser baeri baeri*) is found. Other common fish species include Arctic grayling (*Thymallus arcticus*), white spotted pickerel (*Esox lucius*), burbot (*Lota lota*), and perch (*Perca fluviatilis*).

About 15% of Taymyr's area is occupied by the Bol'shoy Arktichesky (Great Arctic) and Taimyrsky nature reserves. There is no industry developed in the peninsula. Coal deposits have been prospected in the Byrranga Mountains, but they are not being developed. Most of the population is concentrated in a few settlements located on the coast and on the largest rivers: Ust'-Port, Ust'-Tareya, and Dikson. Dikson was founded to supply the Northern Sea Route; it has an airport and a seaport. There are no roads in Taymyr that can be used all year round. In the summer, communication between the settlements occurs via riverways, and in the winter via seasonal roads. Aviation is the only all-year-round transport. The Dolgans, Nenets, and Nganasans are the indigenous peoples of the area. Most of them live in settlements; a few are nomadic. Commercial fishing and hunting are the main occupations of the local population. Reindeer breeding is not common.

OLGA BYKOVA

See also **Byrranga Mountains; Dikson; Khatanga River; Taymyr (Dolgan-Nenets) Autonomous Okrug; Taymyr Lake; Yenisey River**

Further Reading

Taimyro-Severozemel'skaya oblast'. Fiziko-geograficheskaya kharakteristika (Taimyr-Severnaya Zemlya area. Physiographic description), Leningrad: "Gidrometeoizdat," 1970 (in Russian)

TAZ RIVER

The head of the Taz River is located in the Sibirskije Uvaly Uplands. From here, the Taz River flows north, crossing the Tazovsky and Krasnoselkupsky administrative regions of the Yamal-Nenets Autonomous Okrug of the Russian Federation and draining into

Tazovskaya Bay (Taz River estuary) of the Kara Sea in the Arctic Ocean. The river has a total length of 1401 km, and the area of its catchment basin is about 150,000 km². The largest tributaries are the Khudosei (409 km), Tol'ka (391 km), Bolshaya Shirta (301 km), and Chaselka (295 km) rivers.

Flowing across a wide valley, the river is meandering and forms numerous arms and branches. The floodplain width varies from 3 km in the upper course to 20 km in the lower course. The mean current velocity decreases from 0.7 ms⁻¹ in the upper reaches to 0.3 ms⁻¹ near the mouth. River input is mainly from snowmelt and the summer-autumn rains. A typical characteristic of the water regime is a high spring flood that starts 2–3 weeks before ice breakup and drifting. In the upper course, the flood occurs at the end of April, and in the lower course it occurs at the end of May. Water level rise during the spring floods can reach over 9 m. The mean duration of high water during floods is 24–26 days, and the mean duration of water abatement is 40–60 days. In late August, high rainfall causes a second water rise; however, this is significantly lower than in the spring. In winter, the water level is at its lowest. At the river mouth summer river levels are influenced by northern and southern winds, which cause fluctuations in the river level of up to 2 m. The freezing-over period lasts from October to the end of May. By the end of April, the ice depth reaches 1.5 m.

The Taz River is home to 18 fish species belonging to six classes: sturgeon (Acipenseridae), salmon (Salmonidae), carp (Ciprinidae), pickerel (Esocidae), darter (Percidae), and cod (Gadidae), including Siberian sturgeon (*Acipenser baeri baeri*), which is listed in the Russian Red Data Book of endangered species. Some species such as Siberian sturgeon (*Acipenser baeri baeri*), nelma (*Stenodus leucichthus nelma*), muksun (*Coregonus muksun*), sardine cisco (*Coregonus sardinella*), peled (*Coregonus peled*), Siberian whitefish (*Coregonus lavaretus pidschian*), and broad whitefish (*Coregonus nasus*) are semimigratory and spend the winter in Tazovskaya Bay. In summer, they return to the river for spawning and feeding. Commercial fishing is developed only in the lower reaches of the Taz River.

The river crosses zones and subzones of the northern taiga, forest-tundra, and southern tundra. The upper reaches are forested (including the floodplain). Dark-needle coniferous forests and birch woods cover marshy areas. Larch and pine forests occur on well-drained sites. Forest vegetation is found to the north along the floodplain and river terraces as far as the tundra zone.

The river is navigable from the mouth for 450 km upstream as far as the settlement of Krasnoselkup. Settlements located upstream are accessible by river only during floods. The navigation period lasts about 3–3.5 months. Other settlements on the riverbanks are Tazovsky, Gaz-Sale, Sidorovsk, Krasnoselkup, Tolka, and Ratta. Their total population is about 20,000. Sel'kups, one of the indigenous peoples of the Arctic, inhabit the middle and head areas of the river and its tributaries. Nenets inhabit the lower reaches of the river.

Russian settlers first came to the Taz River area in the 16th century. Mangazeya, the first Russian town in the Arctic and an advance fur trading post in the north of Siberia, was founded in 1601 somewhat to the north of the Arctic Circle. In the summer, its population reached 5000. In 1672 by order of the Czar, the center of Russian trade in Siberia was removed to Turukhansk, a settlement on the Yenisey River. By the present time the river has washed away most of the former Mangazeya settlement.

Within the latest 30 years, the population in the central settlements (Tazovsky, Gaz-Sale, Krasnoselkup) has increased due to migrants from other parts of the country, connected with the development of oil and gas fields in the river basin. In the upper river reaches, commercial logging has been carried out, although in recent years logging volumes have decreased. In 1986, the Verkhnetazovsky Reserve was established with an area of over 6300 km².

GRIGORI TERTITSKI

See also **Kara Sea; Tyumen Oblast'; Yamal Peninsula**

Further Reading

Malik, L.K., "Reki." In *Prirodnye usloviya osvoeniya Tazovskogo neftegazonosnogo raiona* [Rivers. In Natural Environment of the Taz Oil-and-Gas Bearing Region], Moscow: Nauka, 1972

TEIN, TASYAN

Tasyan Sergeyevich Tein, the first and only Siberian Yupik Eskimo archaeologist, who devoted his life to studying the ancient past of his people, was born in an old Eskimo settlement of Naukan, Chukotka, in 1938. The settlement was located on the Bering Strait, at Cape Dezhnyov, the easternmost point of Asia. Naukan, with its semi-subterranean dwellings built from drift, stones, and sod, was one of the oldest and most crowded settlements on the coast of Chukotka. Tasyan's father, Tein, was an Eskimo hunter; his mother, Nakayuk, also an Eskimo, ran the house. They had five children. As Eskimos did not have last names, Tasyan took his father's name as a surname. He spent his childhood in Eskimo settlements, helping his father with hunting, fishing, and gathering bird eggs on the nearby rocks. Taysan garnered his knowledge of Eskimo life not from books on ethnography, but, rather, through life experiences.

In 1958, the Naukan settlement was closed, and its people were moved to the settlement of Nunyamo near the large administrative center, the settlement of Lavrentiya. Despite threats from the local shaman Tapkalyn, who opposed education and believed it would bring disasters upon families, Tasyan's parents supported his education. In 1959, he entered the Teachers' College in Anadyr and graduated in 1964. In 1965, Tein worked as a teacher and mentor at the Nunyamo Boarding School in Chukotka. The next year, he entered the State Pedagogical Institute in Magadan. In 1969, after graduating as a teacher of history and social studies, he was sent to work at the boarding school on Wrangel Island. In late 1971, Tein was invited to conduct research at the Magadan Regional Museum, where he worked in the Pre-revolutionary Period department. Accompanied by a mobile exhibition, he visited many Chukotka settlements in order to lecture on the history of the peoples of the North. At these various settlements, Tein collected ethnographic materials necessary for further research analysis.

In late 1974, Tein was invited to the graduate school at the Laboratory of History, Archaeology, and Ethnography of the Northeastern Interdisciplinary Research Institute, Far North Scientific Center of the USSR Academy of Sciences. His research supervisor was Nikolay Dikov; his topic of study was titled "Archaeology of Ancient Eskimos." In 1975, together with Dikov, he conducted the first archaeological investigations on Wrangel Island. The expedition that he led found undisputable traces of the island's ancient people dating to the Stone Age. The most important find was the only (so far) Paleo-Eskimo site in the Russian Northeast, Chyortov Ovrag. He led prospecting excavations there, which resulted in stone-stemmed spear points and the toggling harpoon point. In addition to Chyortov Ovrag, some Eskimo archaeological sites of the later period (1st millennium AD) were found on the island in 1975. Tein conducted further excavations and materials analysis, and in 1976, 1977, and 1981, he found numerous stone tools.

The total excavated area was 246 m². The site had been initially radiscarbon- dated at 3360 BP. Howevr, later Tein obtained additional data on Chyortov Ovrag, resulting in an estimation of 3260–2930 BP, which confirmed the original dates obtained by Dikov. These studies led Tein to the conclusion that "the similarities in hunting and working tools with the Paleoeskimo stone industry of Alaska and, to some extent, Greenland, testify to the connection between the Wrangel Paleoeskimo Culture with the cultures of North American Eskimos" (Tein, 1979: 58). Specifying the origin of the first inhabitants of Wrangel Island, he noted that they had come from North America and Greenland, not from the coast of Asia. At the same time, Tein surmised that the ancient roots of the Paleo-Eskimo Culture had been in continental Asia, from where they migrated to North America and Greenland, and that they "created the material and spiritual culture of sea mammal hunters, having preserved the relic element of their ancestors' culture" (Tein, 1979: 58).

Simultaneously, Tein studied the Eskimo sites at Cape Ryrkaypiy on the Chukchi Sea shore, at Cape Billings, Cape Yakan, and on Ratmanov Island, in the middle of the Bering Strait. At Cape Billings, he investigated a Birnirk time dwelling. In 1979, on Ratmanov Island, he studied a site of the Okvik and Old Bering Sea periods. In 1985, at Cape Yakan (the Schmidt District), he researched an ancient Eskimo site of the Punuk stage (AD 300–1200). These studies allowed Tein to distinguish some new Old Eskimo Culture sites of Okvik-Old Bering Sea, Birnirk, and Tule-Punuk stages. He obtained hundreds of archaeological artifacts representing various periods in the culture of Asian Eskimos.

Tein assigned comprehensive characteristics relating to economic and social usage to many material culture items that have been previously undefined; he traced the evolution of hunting tools, for example, within the Old Eskimos' social life. He also specially studied the Eskimo use of whale baleen. He offered a new interpretation of "rich" and "poor" burials at Eskimo burial grounds. Contrary to the idea of property differentiation on the Old Bering Sea Stage, he believed that rich and poor graves represented more or less successful sea mammal hunters.

In his research, Tein emphasized the issues of Eskimo religion. While writing his dissertation "Old Eskimo Culture of Northern Chukotka, Including Wrangel and Ratmanov Islands," he prepared a series of papers and books on this topic as well as on Eskimo ethnography. He also dealt with the history of the Eskimo open skin boat, *baidar* (or umiak), and concluded that there had originally been one center of sea mammal hunting, not two, as it was assumed.

Moreover, Tein was specifically interested in the problem of emerging and developing Eskimo traditional festivals. He demonstrated a connection between the sea mammal hunters' festivals and their religious ideas, rituals, and hunting. Studying Eskimo dancing and musical instruments, Tein revised the Punuk date of the drum on the basis of the fragments found at the Ryrkaypiy Site and concluded that Eskimo dancing had appeared in the Ancient Bering time, in the 1st millennium BC.

Biography

Tasyan Sergyeyevich Tein, the Russian Eskimo archaeologist, was born in Naukan, Chukotka, in 1938, of Eskimo parents. He graduated from the Teachers' College in Anadyr, Chukotka (1964), and from the department of history at the State Pedagogical Institute, Magadan (1969). He worked as a teacher at various boarding schools in Chukotka, until in 1971 he started his research at the Magadan Regional Museum. In 1974, Tein entered the graduate school under the supervision of Nikolay Dikov, with whom he conducted his first archaeological excavations on Wrangel Island in 1975. Later on, he worked independently and made a significant contribution in studying the Old Eskimo Culture as well as Eskimo ethnography. In 1988, he took part in the organization and scientific supervision of the Soviet-American Eskimo national festival. In 1991, he successfully presented his Candidate thesis in Leningrad. He is married, with one child. Tein retired in 1997.

SERGEI SLOBODIN

See also **Dikov, Nikolay; Wrangel Island**

Further Reading

Denisov, Ye., "Oshibki starogo shamana" [Errors of the Old Shaman]. *Magadanskaya Pravda,* June 10, 1977

Ogryzko, Vyacheslav, "Tasyan Mikhailovich Tein." In *Pisatyeli I literatury malochislennykh narodov Severa I Dalnyego Vostoka* [Writers and Literatures of Native Peoples of the North and Far East], Part 2, Moscow: Literaturnaya Rossiya, 1999

Tein, Tasyan, "Arkheologicheskiye issledovaniya na o.Vrangelya" [Archaeological Investigations on Wrangel Island]. In *Noviye arkheologicheskiye pamyatniki Severa Dal'nego Vostoka* [New Archaeological Monuments of the North of the Far East], Magadan: NEISRI, 1979

———, "Kul'toviye amulety s o.Ratmanova" [Cult Amulet from Ratmanov Island]. In *Novoye v arkheologii Severa Dal'nego Vostoka* [New in Archaeology of the North of the Far East], Magadan: NEISRI, 1985, pp. 109–115

———, *Drevneeskimosskaya kul'tura Severnoy Chukotki, vklyuchaya ostrova Vrangelya i Ratmanova* [Old Eskimo Culture of Northern Chukotka, Including Wrangell and Ratmanov Island], Dissertation Synopsis, Leningrad: Institute of Archaeology, 1991

———, "Shamans of the Siberian Eskimo." *Arctic Anthropology*, 30(1) (1993): 35–47

———, "Traditions, rituals and beliefs." *Anthropology and Archaeology of Eurasia*, 31(3) (1993): 82–86

Yeryomenko, Zh., "Uchonost' samoy vysokoy proby" [Erudition of the Highest Alloy]. *Magadanskaya Pravda,* May 14, 1992

TELECOMMUNICATIONS

Telecommunications is a commonly used expression that is not always precisely defined. Here, telecommunications will be defined as electronic two-way communication (e.g., by telegraph, telephone, or computer). Together with mass communication and direct (oral) communication, telecommunications covers all aspects of communication.

Mass communication is defined as both electronically transmitted one-way communication (e.g., radio, television, or film) and physically transmitted (i.e., printed) visual communication (newspapers and books). Direct (oral) communication is defined as the spoken word. This article will concentrate mainly on telecommunications in the Arctic, with some history of radio and television usage.

Telecommunications is often divided into telecommunications equipment (telegraph, telephone, fax machine, etc.) and information technology (computer, satellite, Internet, etc.). Information technology is thus only a subset of the broader category of telecommunication.

Telecommunications in the Arctic is generally characterized by sparsely populated areas with small populations. National infrastructures are limited. In the larger cities (i.e., cities with more then 5000 inhabitants), Asians and Europeans are often in the majority, while in the smaller cities and villages, the Inuit, Indians, or other native groups are in the majority. Several different languages and scripts are in use. Thus, small, scattered, isolated, and heterogeneous communities are the common picture in the Arctic. In addition, the harsh Arctic climate and geography contribute to the difficulties of building up a telecommunication infrastructure as it is known in other parts of the world. These two conditions, the small, scattered, isolated, and heterogeneous communities and the harsh Arctic climate and geography, influence the use of telecommunications in two diametrically opposite ways.

To the small, scattered, isolated, and heterogeneous communities, on the one hand, the use of telecommunications brings obvious advantages, such as aid in emergencies, rapid transfer of news, commercially important information, and weather data. Thus, since the 1900s, different generations of telecommunications have been introduced rapidly in the Arctic. On the other hand, the harsh Arctic climate and geography has spelt trouble for generations of engineers. Therefore, the different generations of telecommunication systems over the last 100 years have been established with often very limited capacity. Thus, the introduction of telecommunications in the Arctic can be characterized as early, but with limited capacity.

Telecommunications in the Arctic shows a more or less uniform history all around the Pole. The focus here will be on telecommunications in the areas from

Chukotka in the west to Greenland in the east. Typically, the first telecommunication stations to be established in these remote areas were military radio telegraphy stations at the beginning of the 20th century. Early Arctic expeditions were also able to use radio telegraphy to communicate their position (such as that of Robert Peary to the North Pole in 1909), raise distress calls (such as the Russian Arctic Ocean Hydrographic Expedition in 1915), or report scientific data (such as on the Russian manned drifting station, North Pole-1, in 1939). In the 1930s shortwave radios were introduced, and in the 1950s and 1960s, people in some areas had access to telephones and television. Common public access to information technology in telecommunications was introduced to most of the areas as late as the 1990s.

At first, the establishment of telecommunication stations in the Arctic had no influence in most places on the local indigenous people. The telecommunication stations served military interests and only in emergency situations was the equipment used for civilian communication. Here, the history in Greenland differs from other areas in that the radio telegraphy stations served primarily an administrative purpose and local people had access to the radio telegraphy stations from their start in 1925.

Chukotka

The first Russian Arctic radio telegraphy station was constructed in Anadyr (at that time Novo-Mariinsk) in 1912. It was a Russian Navy station with a 40-m mast. The station was constructed as one of several stations that covered the Russian Arctic Ocean coast and islands, from Franz Josef Land in the Barents Sea to Wrangel Island in the Chukchi Sea.

From 1934, a network of shortwave radio stations was built and operated by Glavsemorput, the Chief Office for the Northern Sea Route. These polar stations served the ships traveling the Northern Sea Route between Murmansk and Vladivostok with weather forecasts and information on ice situations. A polar station was built in Provideniya, at the southeast coast of the Chukotka Peninsula, in 1937.

In 1970, the satellite TV station ORBITA began construction of a network in the Russian North. This gave television access to the larger cities and villages in Chukotka. In the remote villages, television became available in the first half of the 1980s.

In the late 1980s, A&T AlasCom provided Provideniya with an automatic telephone system. Telephone lines have since been extended to many small villages. All rural villages in Chukotka should soon have access to telephony through satellite connections with the help of a program by the Chukotka government to establish good telecommunication connections in rural Chukotka however, a large demand for mainline services remains unsatisfied. Wireless Internet access became available in Anadyr and dial-up access in the eight regional centers in Chukotka from 1998. Russia as a whole had 18 million Internet users in 2002 (up by 4.3 million from 2001), but broadband data are not available in northern Russia.

Alaska

The history of telecommunications began in Alaska in 1900. That year, the US Army Signal Corps began to build the Washington-Alaska Military Cable and Telegraph System (WAMCATS). In 1903, it linked Alaska by wire to the rest of the United States with the following words: "Alaska is now open to civilization." Thus, Alaska was the first area in the North to get cabled telegraph stations, used and maintained by the army. Commercial and nonmilitary traffic was permitted.

In 1936, the system was reorganized as the Alaska Communication Systems (ACS, later Alascom), but military communications still had first priority. In 1946, the first telephone system was established, and civilian access increased. At statehood in 1959, most remote villages were connected to a telecommunication system, with wireless (VHF) stations replacing land lines. From 1971, when Alascom was formed, Alaska's telecommunications became commercially rather than military based.

Alascom launched its first communications satellite (Aurora I) in 1982 and a second (Aurora II) in 1991. Not until 1997 were proper Internet connections introduced in Alaska by AT&T Alascom. At the end of 2001, approximately 69% of Alaska's population had Internet access, ranking first of the states.

Canada

As in Chukotka and Alaska, the first telecommunications in Canada's North was established by the military, with army radio telegraphy stations first installed at Dawson City and Mayo Landing in the Yukon in 1923.

The Canadian North was the first area in the Arctic to be served by communications satellite, with the launch of the satellite Anik in 1973. The Inuit name of the satellite indicated its purpose, which enabled 17 communities in the Arctic to receive certain television and radio stations. However, in the federal government's plan of 1993 to get Canada wired, the North was left out of the plan. Although all villages in the Canadian North today have access to the Internet through Canada's telecommunications satellites, satellite service is a monopoly and the cost of bandwidth is high.

As a central part of preparations for the new territory Nunavut in 1999, plans were made for the extensive use of Internet-based telecommunications. Many of these plans still await execution.

Greenland

As early as 1854, and only nine years after the establishment of the world's first wired telegraph line in the United States, Schaffner was given concession on a telegraph line between Europe and America. It was part of the plan that the undersea cable should be taken via Greenland. After some years, the plans were however abandoned.

In 1901, the first local wire telegraph was established. A major milestone in the history of telecommunication in Greenland occurred in 1925, when four radio telegraph stations were established. Only one year later, in 1926, the first radio broadcasting took place. During World War II, it became more common for people to have a radio. Among the about 20,000 Inuit in Greenland in 1944, more than 400 households are assumed to have had a radio.

In the 1970s, a UHF network connected Greenland internally. This network was modernized and digitalized in 1996 and Greenland became the second nation in the world with a 100% digital telecommunication network. Greenland's neighbor to the east, Iceland, had, as the first nation, reached that goal only a few months before. 1996 was also the year in which access to the Internet was established, and by 2001, 100% of the population had access to the Internet. It is estimated that at least 50% of the 55,000 people in Greenland are using the Internet. Broadband data are not available.

Today

Taking an overview of the Arctic today allows four areas to be identified: the Nordic countries (except Greenland); Greenland; Canada and Alaska; and finally Russia and Siberia. In the Nordic countries (minus Greenland), conditions are relatively good. Most places have access to broadband. Provision is regulated to some extent, but in most places there is competition in providing voice, data, and wireless in the area. Public access to the Internet is widespread.

Greenland is part of the Nordic countries, but with regard to telecommunications it is anomalous. Here, there is still no access to broadband. Provision is highly regulated, with no competition in providing voice and data. On the other hand, public access to the Internet is relatively good.

For northern Canada and Alaska, the situation is that broadband exists, but it is not widespread. Provision is deregulated, and public access to the Internet is poor.

For the 2–3 million people in the northern parts of Russia and Siberia, the situation is not good. No broadband access reaches so far north in the area. The provision of telecommunications is almost without regulations, and public access to the Internet is poor.

The Future

One of the major concerns in modern telecommunications in the Arctic is still the question of organizing access to telecommunications. In most places, the spread of telecommunications still heavily relies on satellites. In most areas, some kind of monopoly or concession is given to one company in providing access to telecommunications. The liberalization of the telecommunications market that has taken place in most of the world has not yet fully reached the Arctic. Here, Alaska is an exception.

One of the major elements in the discussion for and against strong monopolies is the question of securing full access for the most remote settlements under a more or less liberal market. It is now clear that the telecommunications monopolies who served the Arctic areas well during the industrialization period now cannot provide the needs for more proactive citizens because of the demands of information society, and the remaining elements of monopoly have now become a drag on the development of the public use of telecommunications.

Internet

Even though a major part of the Arctic now has access to the Internet, it does not look as if the Arctic can keep up with developments in the rest of the western world through the Internet. In addition to the lack of high-speed Internet access in the Arctic, communities also lack a general high level of education. These two factors alone make it very difficult, for example, for new media businesses to be established in the Arctic.

On the one hand, access to the Internet has opened up new possibilities for obtaining access to updated and relevant information, which seems to bring the Arctic closer to the rest of the world. Schools and libraries are currently the largest users of Internet access, for example, in northern Canada. On the other hand, easy communication could be part of the argument for pulling the few human resources out of the Arctic, which seems to take the Arctic even further away from the rest of the world.

The Internet is being used more and more for buying products that are not provided to Arctic communities locally and also for long-distance education from educational institutions that are not situated in the Arctic.

Access to the Internet has opened up the potential for strengthening Arctic communities, but this is still not taking place. It could, for example, help provide local, public, and other relevant information on the Internet in the local languages. But these potentials are still not fully explored by Arctic communities.

KLAUS GEORG HANSEN

See also **Information Technology**

Further Reading

Alia, Valerie, *Uncovering the North*: *News, Media, and Aboriginal People*, Vancouver: UBC Press, 1999

Christensen, Neil Blair, *Inuit in Cyberspace: Embedding Offline Identity Online*, Copenhagen: Museum Tusculanum Press, 1999

Hansen, Klaus Georg, "IT-sektoren i et magt perspektiv" [The ICT sector in a power perspective]. In *Demokrati og magt i Grønland* [Democracy and power in Greenland], edited by Gorm Winther, Aarhus: Aarhus University Press, 2003, pp. 162–194

Information and Communication Technology in the Arctic; *An International Conference of the Arctic Council*, Akureyri, Iceland, October 20–21, 2003; http://vefir.unak.is/ICTConference. Visited: November 6, 2003

Nunavut telecommunication needs: community teleservice centres: a supplementary report of the Nunavut Implementation Commission/Nunavut Implementation Commission [S.l.]: Nunavut Implementation Commission, 1995

TERN

Most adult terns (there is no sexual dimorphism) are white and gray birds with a black head and a more or less forked tail. Among the 33 species of true terns (genus *Sterna*) and the three species from the genus *Chlidonias*, five can be found in the Arctic. The small black tern (*Chlidonias niger*) and the large Caspian tern (*Sterna caspia*) only just penetrate the taiga zone. In Canada, they breed as far north as the Great Slave Lake; in Europe, they reach Scandinavia. The common tern (*Sterna hirundo*) is more widespread and its ranges also include eastern Siberia and northern Scandinavian. Both the Caspian tern and common tern breed further south in the tropics. The Aleutian tern (or Kamchatka tern: *Sterna aleutica*), on the other hand, is restricted to the Bering Sea. This and the Arctic tern (*Sterna paradisaea*) are the only true terns of the Arctic region. The latest has a circumpolar range extending as far north as Ellesmere Island in Canada, Kap Morris Jesup in Greenland, Svalbard, Franz Josef Land, and many other Siberian islands. Due to their light flight, terns are sometimes called "sea swallows." Natives rather use morphologic traits in their names: forktailed gull (Cree Indians), drooping feathers (Nunamiut Eskimo for the Arctic tern), etc.

The rare Aleutian tern (33 cm; 75–80 cm wingspan) is a gray bird, which has a typical head: white forehead and black cap, lores, and bill. Its tail and rump are white, and its legs are black. It is restricted to Siberia and Alaska during the breeding season, but is not globally threatened. The population size of this endemic tern could be lower than 15,000 pairs (5–10,000 pairs in Alaska, 2100 pairs on Sakhalin Island, 1000 pairs along the Sea of Okhotsk, and 500 in Kamchatka). Its winter range, still largely unknown, seems to include the Philippines.

The Arctic tern is the most common and the more widespread of the five Arctic species. With the exception of the tropical sooty tern (*Sterna fuscata*), which has an estimated population exceeding 25 million pairs (and some colonies of more than one million birds), the Arctic tern is also one of the most numerous terns on earth. The adult has approximately the same size (33–36 cm; 76–85 cm wingspan) as the Aleutian tern, a clearer back (light gray), a very long tail that juts out from the folded wings when the bird is sitting, red legs and bill, and a black forehead and crown without distinct lores. Most Arctic terns breed in the Arctic region, mainly above the treeline, but some small populations are also found further south to the northern coasts of the United States, Ireland, Great Britain, and sporadically in western France.

Ireland and Great Britain host 10% of the world population estimated at 0.5–1 million pairs, but the largest numbers are found in Greenland (several 10,000 pairs), the Barents Sea (more than 100,000 pairs), Iceland (100–400,000 pairs), and Siberia (several 100,000 pairs?). Alaska and Canada also have large populations but their sizes remain unknown.

The largest colonies are found on offshore islands and skerries, which foxes cannot access, but smaller colonies and isolated pairs also breed on the mainland coasts and inland (on lakes, marshy tundra, or large river shores). In the northern part of their breeding range, Arctic terns lay one or two eggs (more rarely three) on bare ground (sand, gravel, or rock) in an unlined shallow scrape. Sabine gulls, eiders, long-tailed ducks, waders, and even divers sometimes breed with Arctic terns in mixed colonies, where they benefit from tern aggressiveness against predators (and humans!). In the North, most eggs are laid in July, when the ice has gone. Hatching occurs after 3 weeks of incubation, and another 3–4-week period is needed before the fledglings start to fly. In cold summers or when a second clutch has to be laid (to replace drowned or predated nests), some young stay at the colony until late August or early September, a time when snow falls and wind storms seriously affect their survival rate. If they survive (20% die in their first year), Arctic tern can live for more than 30 years, but

Arctic tern (*Sterna paradisaea*).
Copyright Paul Nicklen/National Geographic Image Collection

before returning to the Arctic to breed (usually at the age of 4), young terns will spend more of their time offshore.

Arctic tern feed on small fish (sand eels, capelin, herring, stickleback), crustaceans, amphipods, polychaetes, molluscs, insects, and other invertebrates that they locate from a perch or by flying a few meters above the water. In summer, most prey comes from shallow water along the seashores, but feeding in fresh water is not rare and is of course the rule for inland breeders. Like other seabirds, Arctic terns are often chased by skuas when they come back to the colony to feed their young. They are harassed until they drop their prey or arrive at a large colony where other terns chase the skuas to defend their nests.

Apart from its high adaptation to a harsh polar environment, migration is unquestionably the most interesting trait of an Arctic tern's life history. From the Arctic where most breed, they fly offshore all the way round the world to the Southern Hemisphere and, with the exception of some juveniles that may winter in equatorial waters, most "overwinter" (it is summer there) around the Antarctic continent, where they find an environment similar to that of their breeding grounds. With a round flight of 20–50,000 km and despite its relatively small size (close to 100 g), the Arctic tern is therefore regarded as the animal with the longest annual migration route on Earth. Incidentally, it also enjoys more daylight than any other animal, spending most of the year under Arctic or Antarctic summer.

The Arctic tern is protected over most of its range, sometimes for long as in Iceland: 1882 (but only in 1981 in Norway). Some Arctic tern populations have increased in regions where egging stopped or was reduced, but most seem to have decreased in the 20th century. In Scotland and north Norway, for example, where overfishing has reduced the stock of its main prey (sand eels), Arctic tern populations have declined drastically in the 1980s. In other regions, oil spills can result in massive losses for such a pelagic bird. Locally (e.g., West Greenland), illegal shooting and egging (allowed until July 1) also reduce the size of the colonies close to settlements.

OLIVIER GILG

See also **Seabirds; Gulls**

Further Reading

Anker-Nilssen, Tycho, Vidar Bakken, Hallvard Strom, Alexander N. Golovkin, Vitali V. Bianki & Ivetta P. Tatarinkova, "The status of marine birds breeding in the Barents Sea region." *Norsk Polarinstitutt Rapportserie*, 113 (2000): 1–213

Boertman, David, Anders Mosbech, Knud Falk & Kaj Kampp, *Seabird Colonies in Western Greenland*, Copenhagen: National Environmental Research Institute, 1996

Cramp, Stanley & K.E.L. Simmons, *Handbook of the Birds of Europe the Middle East and North Africa,* Volume 3, Oxford: Oxford University Press, 1983

Del Hoyo, Joseph, Andrew Elliot & Jordi Sargatal, *Handbook of the Birds of the World*, Volume 3, Barcelona: Lynx Edicions, 1996

Godfrey, W. Earl, *Les Oiseaux du Canada*, Ottawa : Musées nationaux du Canada, 1986

Harrison, Peter, *Seabirds*, London: Christopher Holm, 1983

Hohn, E. Otto, "Mammal and bird names in the Indian languages of the Lake Athabasca Area." *Arctic*, 26(2) (1973): 163–171

Irving, Laurence," The naming of Birds by Nunaliut Eskimo." *Arctic*, 6(1) (1953): 35–43

THALBITZER, WILLIAM

William Thalbitzer, founder of Danish Eskimology, acquired a degree from the University of Copehagen in 1899 with Danish studies as principal and English and Latin as subsidiary subjects. He wanted to study a non-European language and was advised to study Greenlandic Inuit language. Thus, a lifelong study of Inuit languages and culture started. In 1900 and 1901, he traveled in Disko Bay, and reached Upernavik. He carried out phonetic and grammatical studies. His teacher, Professor Otto Jespersen, was known for his contribution to the elaboration of a phonetic alphabet. This material was an important part of Thalbitzer's publication in 1904: *A Phonetical Study of the Eskimo Language*. He included Western Inuit/Yuit languages, but was in part too uncritical of his sources. Many of them were not written by philologists.

In 1905–1906, he was in Ammassalik in East Greenland, where he carried out phonetic studies again and recorded songs, legends, and other kinds of texts. The Lutheran mission had started in Ammassalik in 1894, and here Thalbitzer met several angakkut (shamans) not yet converted to Christianity. Back in Copenhagen, he was asked to prepare for publication material from Amdrup's expedition in East Greenland in 1898–1900. This material was published in 1909, but he continued to examine East Greenlandic ethnographical and archaeological material, which was published in 1912. For some reason, he was not able to study a large part of Holm's ethnographical collection from Ammassalik, and because of this, his analysis was insufficient. His work was subjected to a hard critique, and his conclusion—partly based on dialectological material—that the Ammassalik district was populated both from the north (1914: 146 f.) and south was not accepted until many years later.

Thalbitzer presented *Eskimo* in Franz Boas's *Handbook of American Indian Languages* in 1911. With northwest Greenlandic phonetic and grammatical patterns, he described Inuit languages. It is partly outdated. He regarded the Mackenzie Delta area as a border for eastern and western Eskimo dialects.

In Danish notes by Rasmus Rask in 1916, he published material on the relation between Aleutic and Greenlandic languages, and thereby gave a scientific documentation for comparative Inuit linguistic studies. Rask met some Aleuts in St Petersburg in 1818. His hypothesis on the origin of Eskimo culture in central Siberia is also based on language studies. In the same period, Danish ethnographers pointed to Barren Grounds west of Hudson Bay as the original home of the Eskimo culture. Also in connection with this hypothesis, Thalbitzer's theories were weakened by his limited knowledge in Paleo-Siberian languages.

Thalbitzer's third publication on Eskimo Languages, in 1923, dealt with *East Greenlandic: Language and Folklore*. It was an important source material. He prepared a comparative dictionary of Eskimo languages and an East Greenlandic dictionary, but these were not published.

The review of the first volume of his work on Ammassalik Eskimo, published in 1914, was also a hard critique. The first volume presented Holm's ethnographical work on the Ammassalik group in English, and for many years it was the main work on the ethnography of East Greenlanders. The next volumes from 1923 and 1941 were based on his own studies, and contained songs, legends, shamanistic traditions, social organization, and the like. He demonstrated a clear admiration of the Inuit culture in his detailed description.

Thalbitzer had continued contacts with the Greenlandic community. He was in southwest Greenland in 1914; later on, he visited Greenland in 1924, and three times in the 1930s. Finally, he visited Ammassalik in 1950. In the 1930s, he had some publications in Greenlandic: a book on East Greenlandic songs (1931) followed by a pamphlet on Greenlandic spiritual culture (1932). In 1939, *Inuit Songs and Dances from Greenland* was published with Greenlandic, Danish, and English text. Here, he presented both traditional songs from East and West Greenland, early dance music of European origin, and contemporary Greenlandic songs with both Greenlandic poets and composers. In the same period, he participated in discussions of the need for a modernized Greenlandic orthography, but this was not accepted. In addition to the popularity of Kleinschmidt's orthography, another important factor influencing its lack of acceptance was that—seen in retrospect—Thalbitzer presented the idea before he elaborated his system. It began as a proposal of phonetic replacement of symbols for voiceless fricatives (inclusive voiceless lateral), but he developed it to stronger acceptance of phonemic full assimilation of former diphthongs and consonant clusters. For this mixture of phonetic and phonemic principles, he gave no explanation, and this lack was a difference between his early formulations and his later examples. This weakened his argument.

Thalbitzer was a musical person. In his dialectological studies, the melody of the speech was a part of his description, and his interest in Inuit music was always strong. He had already about 1905 recordings of speech and songs both in West and East Greenland with the Edison phonograph. In his description, artistic intuition played an important role. He had a vivid admiration of the Inuit culture, especially in East Greenland for which he had great respect. Thalbitzer published a series of works, diaries, and so on from East Greenland: Hansêraqs Dagbog (1933), Chr. Rosing: Østgrønlændere (1946), and Johan Petersen's diaries (1957). He is reputed to have said to an American Congress in 1924: *"The world needs to be Eskimo-ized."*

Biography

William Thalbitzer was born in 1873, and began to teach Greenlandic (Eskimo) culture at the University of Copenhagen in 1920. His teaching included linguistic, cultural, religious, and social issues as comparative Inuit studies, with the main focus on Greenland. But he also included themes from neighboring people. In connection with this study, he became *professor extraordinarius* in 1926, with Eskimo culture and language as his subject. He retired from this chair in 1945. Thalbitzer died in 1958.

ROBERT PETERSEN

Further Reading

Thalbitzer, William, "A phonetical study of Eskimo language." *Meddelser om Grønland (MoG)*, 31(I—XII) (1904): 1–405
———, "Ethnological description of the Amdrup collection from East Greenland." *MoG*, 28 (1909): 329–542; The Heathen Priest of East Greenland (Angakut), XVI, 1910
———, Amerikanisten Kongress in Vienna 1908, pp. 447–467; Wien 1911. "Eskimo (A Grammatical Sketch)." In. F. Boas: *Handbook of American Indian Languages. Bulletin of the Bureau of American Indian Languages*, 40(1), Washington, pp. 971–1070
———, "*Grønlandske Sagn om Eskimoernes Fortid. Populcåra etnologiska skrifter*, Volume 11, Stockholm, 1913
———, "The Ammassalik Eskimo. Contribution to the ethnology of the East Greenland natives." *MoG*, 39–40 1914–1941
———, "Et Manusskript af Rasmus Rask om Aleuternes Sprog sammenlignet med Grønlændernes." *Kgl. Danske Videnskabernes Selskabs Oversigt*, 3 (1916): 211–249
———, *Tunumiut taigdliait*, Nûk, 1931
———, *Kalâleq*. Kalåtdlit itsarnitsat ilerquisa ilait, Nûk, 1932
———, *Fra Grønlandsforskningens første Dage*. Festskrift fra Københavns Universitet, København, 1932
———, *Inuit Sange og Danse fra Grønland/Eskimo Music: Songs and Dances from Greenland/Inuit kalåliussut erinarssûtaisa qîtataisalo ilait*, Copenhagen, 1939
———, *Uhlenbeck's Eskimo-Indoeuropean Hypothesis. A Critical Revision*, Traveax du Cercle linguistique de Copenhague, I, 1945, pp. 66–96
———, "Grønlands Litteraturhistorie." In: *Grønlandsbogen* II, edited by K. Birket-Smith, København, 1950, pp. 225–250.

THERMOHALINE CIRCULATION

More than two-thirds of the Earth's surface is covered by ocean water. This water is constantly in motion and is driven basically by three processes: tidal forces (i.e., forces originating by the gravitational attraction between the Earth, moon, and sun), wind stresses (i.e., differential (shear) forces that are imposed by near-surface winds at the air-water interface), and vertical or horizontal density gradients between different parts of the ocean. The latter process, which is the main subject of this entry, is controlled by the temperature (thermo) and the salinity (or the relative content of various salts; haline) of ocean waters. The circulation caused by density gradients is thus called thermohaline circulation, a term first introduced by Stommel (1961).

While this explanation seems straightforward, a closer look leads to a more cautious approach. In fact, an examination of the relevant literature reveals that there are at least seven different and mutually inconsistent definitions of the term thermohaline circulation in use (Wunsch, 2002). Furthermore, thorough investigations of large-scale, three-dimensional ocean currents reveal that density-driven circulations might not be as paramount as some authors conclude, who essentially link the entire global ocean circulation to thermohaline circulation. Instead, it has been argued that wind-induced mass fluxes in combination with tidal forcing are more significant processes in driving global circulation (Wunsch, 2002). However, this does not diminish the importance of thermohaline circulation as a process, particularly when it comes to circulations at high latitudes. Before addressing this subject more closely, a few general principles will be explained.

Basic Principles and Quantification of Thermohaline Circulation

Changes in the density of sea water (dρ) are determined by the following equation of state:

$$d\rho = \alpha\, dT + \beta dS + k\, dp$$

where $\alpha = \partial\rho/\partial T$ is the thermal expansion coefficient representing the change of density with temperature T, $\beta = \partial\rho/\partial S$ is the haline contraction coefficient, which represents the change of density with salinity S (where salinity has traditionally been defined as the total amount in grams of dissolved substances contained in 1 kg of sea water; more recent definitions link salinity to the electrical conductivity of sea water, through the so-called practical salinity unit, psu), and $k = \partial\rho/\partial p$ is the compressibility of sea water and represents the change in density with varying (hydrostatic) pressure p.

Because variations in ocean water densities are relatively small, oceanographers have introduced a new quantity, called σ_t, which is defined as

$$\sigma_t = \rho - 1000 \text{ kg m}^{-3}$$

The density of ocean water is usually close to 1025 kg m^{-3} (typically, it varies between 1020 and 1028 kg m^{-3}), that is, $\sigma_t = 25$ kg m^{-3} (often, the unit kg m^{-3} is omitted, even though incorrectly; thus, for usual sea water, one often finds $\sigma_t = 25$). For fresh water with a density close to 1000 kg m^{-3}, $\sigma_t \approx 0$ k m^{-3}. Figure 1 graphically represents the variation of density (given as σ_t values) as a function of temperature and salinity; also shown are the temperatures of the freezing point (lower line) and of the density maximum (upper line) for water at varying salinities.

Since in general $\alpha < 0$, $\beta > 0$, and $k > 0$, seawater density decreases with increasing temperature, except at temperatures below the density maximum (i.e., at approximately 4°C), and increases with increasing salinity and pressure. While usually taken as constant, α, β, and k all vary with temperature, salinity, and pressure. This implies that a complete quantification of seawater density requires computations of several polynomial expressions involving about 50 terms.

However, in most cases, ocean water density increases with depth, mainly because of decreasing temperatures and increasing salinities and pressures. This implies that the ocean is usually stably stratified, that is, lighter water masses are underlain by denser

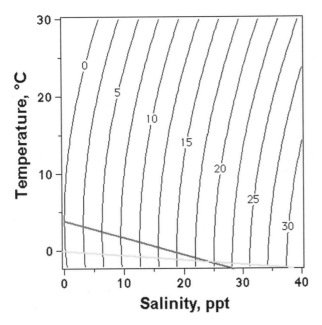

Figure 1: Isolines of σ_t values as a function of temperature and salinity; also shown are the temperatures of the freezing point (lower line) and of the density maximum (upper line) for water at varying salinities (Weeks and Ackley, 1982).

water and no vertical circulation (other than that induced by wind-driven turbulence) can be observed. Only at places where surface waters attain densities higher than the water masses below is down-welling of water initiated.

It easily follows from the above that density-driven circulation in the "real" ocean and its complex interdependency on various time-and space-dependent oceanic but also atmospheric parameters requires numerical models to describe it properly. To this end, coupled global ocean-atmosphere circulation models have been developed (e.g., Manabe and Stouffer, 1988) and utilized in order to understand the role of thermohaline circulation in the global climate system. While descriptions of such models are beyond the scope of this entry, the following section briefly describes some basic mechanisms and implications of altered thermohaline circulation in the North Atlantic.

Deepwater formation in the North Atlantic

There are three places in the world ocean where thermohaline circulation plays a decisive role in ocean water modification and in the generation of so-called deep water: the northern North Atlantic (Norwegian, Greenland, and Iceland seas), and the Ross Sea and Weddell Sea in Antarctica (Rahmstorf, 2002). At these places, surface waters are cooled and release heat and/or become more saline (as salt is expelled from the ice lattice as sea water freezes) up to the point where their density exceeds the density of the underlying water and they sink to form North Atlantic Deep Water (NADW) and Antarctic Bottom Water (AABW). These deepwater masses are high in dissolved oxygen and nutrient contents and are found throughout the deep global ocean, thus playing an essential role in renewing and ventilating the abyssal parts of the seas.

It has been demonstrated that the formation of NADW and AABW, which comprise a flow of 15 ± 2 Sv (where 1 Sv or Sverdrup $= 10^6$ m^3 s^{-1}) and 21 ± 6 Sv, respectively (Rahmstorf, 2002), is part of a larger system of ocean currents often called the global ocean conveyor belt (Broecker, 1991), as shown in Figure 2.

While the formation of AABW seems to be relatively stable, processes in the North Atlantic are extremely sensitive to external boundary conditions. This relates particularly to the introduction of fresh water to the ocean, which may lead to a reduced if not a complete collapse of NADW formation. It has been shown that three distinct circulation modes can be distinguished based on paleoclimatic evidence: the stadial, interstadial, and the Heinrich mode, during which NADW is formed in the subpolar North Atlantic, the Nordic Seas (as today), and hardly at all, respectively

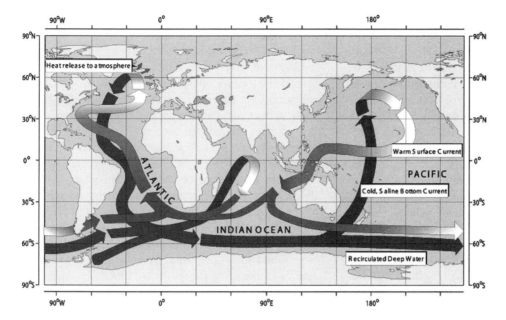

Figure 2: Schematic depiction of global ocean circulation pathways, the Global Ocean Conveyor.
Courtesy W. Broecker (LDEO, USA), modified by E. Maier-Reimer (MPIfM, Germany)

(Rahmstorf, 2002). Because of their occurrence during stadial (i.e., a glacial period), and interstadial (i.e., a period of comparatively warm climate between two glaciations, particularly of the Pleistocene epoch), and so-called Heinrich events (i.e., during periods of intense calving of sediment-laden icebergs from the Laurentide Ice Sheet to the North Atlantic), these modes have been linked to climate development of the Northern Hemisphere. This is because the shift in NADW formation from northerly to more southerly positions (interstadial and stadial, respectively) leads to the retreat of warm (Gulf Stream) water to more southerly regions, thus depriving central and northern Europe of its major "heat engine".

The thermohaline circulation exerts a negative feedback mechanism to global climate warming in the Northern Hemisphere. With rising temperatures, more fresh water will be released at high latitudes, either through increased precipitation or enhanced ice melting. This will result in lowered surface densities at the sites of NADW formation and will slow down or even shut off thermohaline circulation. Without thermohaline circulation, the northward transport of heat will be reduced, creating a negative feedback (i.e., a cooling). In contrast, in the Southern Hemisphere less heat will be exported northward, leading to a positive feedback to global warming (i.e., a further warming). This process has been numerically modeled (Velinga and Wood, 2002).

MANFRED A. LANGE

See also **Denmark Strait; Fram Strait; Greenland Sea; Oceanography**

Further Reading

Broecker, W.S., "The great ocean conveyor." *Oceanography*, 4(1991): 79–89

Manabe, S., & R.J. Stouffer, "Two stable equilibria of a coupled ocean-atmosphere model." *Journal of Climate*, 1(9) (1988): 841–866

Rahmstorf, S., "Ocean circulation and climate during the past 120,000 years." *Science*, 419 (2002): 207–214

Stommel, H., "Thermohaline convection with two stable regimes of flow." *Tellus*, 13 (1961): 224–230

Velinga, M., & R.A. Wood, "Global climate impacts of a collapse of the Atlantic-thermohaline circulation." *Climate Change*, 54 (2002): 251–267

Weeks, W.F., & S.F. Ackley, The growth, structure, and properties of sea ice, US Army Cold Regions Research and Engineering Laboratory, Hanover, New Hawpshire, USA CRREL Monograph 82–1, 1982

Wunsch, C., "What is the thermohaline circulation?." *Science*, 298 (2002): 1179–1181

THERMOKARST

Thermokarst is an important erosional geomorphic process unique to areas underlain by ice-rich permafrost. The International Permafrost Association glossary defines thermokarst as "the process by which characteristic landforms result from the thawing of ice-rich permafrost and or melting of massive ice" (van Everdingen, 1998). The importance of thermokarst is often discussed in terms of its potential occurrence as an impact on human activity (e.g., as a response to the construction of pipelines and highways) or global warming; however, it should not be forgotten that thermokarst is a naturally occurring erosional process. The term thermokarst was introduced by Russian geologist M.M. Ermolaev in 1932 to describe dissected topography in northern Siberia caused by the melting of ground ice (Shumskii, 1964). It first appears in the English literature in 1945 in S.W. Muller's report "Permafrost or permanently frozen ground and related engineering problems."

Even though thermokarst topography is somewhat similar in appearance to karst and sinkhole terrain produced by solution weathering in limestone regions, the nature of the thermokarst process is entirely different. The current usage of the term thermokarst applies to processes and landforms associated with the thaw of all forms of ground ice irrespective of origin (French, 1996). It therefore includes both the thaw degradation of epigenetic ground ice (developed in previously deposited rock or sediment) as well as the formation of dead ice topography caused by melting buried glacier ice in disintegration moraines. This has not always been the case, as thaw subsidence in glacial sediments has often been called "glacier karst" in the glacial geology literature (Sugden and John, 1976). The importance of this pertains to the interaction between glaciers and permafrost as well as the paleoenvironmental reconstruction of glacial landscapes. Thermokarst occurs throughout the Earth's polar regions, but is best known from locations in Siberia, the Canadian Arctic, and Alaska, where vast areas have been affected.

The nature and magnitude of thermokarst are directly related to two important variables: the thermal stability of the upper part of permafrost, including the depth of the active layer, and ground ice contents. The stability of permafrost reflects a thermal equilibrium controlled by the mean ground surface temperature and the ground's geothermal gradient. Ground surface temperatures are controlled by the surface energy balance along with vegetation and snow cover. Seasonal fluctuations in the ground surface temperature, which are driven by the annual cycle of solar radiation and surface energy balance relationships, produce annual fluctuations in the upper 10–20 m of the ground thermal regime, including the active layer. The active layer is a thin layer above the permafrost that freezes and thaws annually. Generally, the active layer depth varies very little from one year to the next. However, any change in the ground surface conditions (natural or anthropogenic) or in summer climate patterns will change the surface energy balance and the depth of the active layer. Any number of things may lead to an increase in the active layer depth, most notably (a) warmer summer temperatures, (b) change in surface moisture conditions, (c) change in or removal of surface vegetation, and (d) removal of a layer of sediment. If the subsequent increase in thaw depth results in melting of ground ice, then thermokarst may result. Ground ice differs from most other common minerals on the Earth's surface in that over most of its distribution and duration, it is very close to its melting point. The potentially unstable nature of ground ice makes it highly sensitive to slight increases in ground temperature. When the ground ice content exceeds the saturated moisture content of its enclosing sediments, the surplus is called excess ice. The thawing of permafrost containing excess ice will result in a net lowering of the ground surface proportional to percent volume of excess ice. For example, the thaw of a 1 m layer of permafrost containing 20% excess ice will result in a net subsidence of 20 cm. The water released by melt of excess ice is called supernatant water.

Two types of thermokarst are described in the literature: thermokarst subsidence and thermal erosion. Thermokarst subsidence is primarily vertical in direction, while thermal erosion involves lateral planation and is a backwearing process, that is, a sideways recession of a slope that does not alter its general shape (French, 1996). Thermokarst subsidence tends to occur in flat to low relief areas and often produces surface ponding and shallow depressions. A well-known example of this type of thermokarst from the Russian literature is the development of "alas" landscapes in central Yakutia. Alas landscapes involve several stages beginning with the thaw and collapse of an area containing well-developed ice-wedge polygons. This leaves a regular pattern of residual mounds that eventually degrade to form a steep-sided depression containing a tundra pond.

By comparison, thermal erosion occurs on slopes where melting of exposed ground ice causes the slope face to retreat laterally. In this case, large pools of supernatant water and liquefied sediment collect at the base of the exposure and then gradually flow away, keeping fresh ice exposed and sustaining the process. Very distinctive "C-shaped" depressions called retrogressive thaw slumps are a common expression of thermal erosion.

In its simplest form, thermokarst may occur as a local, minor land surface subsidence when an increase in active layer depth thaws permafrost with low excess ice contents. However, thermokarst is rarely simple and tends to include complex feedbacks that can result in widespread (hundreds to thousands of square meters) and uneven surface subsidence on the order of several meters. It may take several years for the various feedbacks to run their course and a new thermal equilibrium to be established. This type of thermokarst produces closed depressions or a hummocky terrain.

There is widespread consensus that permafrost will be one of the Earth's systems most affected by global climate change. Not only will the effects of climate change be observed sooner in the Arctic than anywhere else, but the magnitude of change is predicted to be greater. Given the delicate nature of permafrost thermal regimes, thermokarst is potentially one of the most significant outcomes of global climate change.

WAYNE POLLARD

See also **Environmental Problems; Geomorphology; Ground Ice; Permafrost; Permafrost Hydrology; Permafrost Retreat**

Further Reading

French, H.M., *The Periglacial Environment*, (2nd edition), London: Addison-Wesley, Longman, 1996

Muller, S.W., *Permafrost or Permanently Frozen Ground and Related Engineering Problems*, United States Engineers Office, Strategic Engineering Study, Special Report 62, 1945

Shumskii, P.A., *Principles of Structural Glaciology*, New York: Dover, 1964

Sugden, D.E. & B.S. John, *Glaciers and Landscape*, London: Edward Arnold, 1976

van Everdingen, R.O., *The International Permafrost Association Multi-Language Glossary of Permafrost and Related Ground-Ice Terms*, Calgary, Alberta: The Arctic Institute of North America, University of Calgary, 1998

THULE AIR BASE

The Danish-Greenlandic polar explorer Knud Rasmussen used the name "Thule" when he, together with another Danish polar explorer, Peter Freuchen, established the trade post *Kap York Stationen Thule* close to the Inughuit settlement of Uummannaq in 1910. Today, Avanersuaq (northern Greenland) is also called Thule. The United States established Thule Air Base in 1951 in a valley created by a former glacier near the Danish colony, Thule, and the Inughuit settlement of Uummannaq. In the local Inuktun language, this valley is called *Pituffik*, which means "the place where the dogs are tied up."

In a Defense Agreement of April 9, 1941 between Denmark and the United States, the latter was allowed to establish military bases in Greenland for defense purposes. Ten years later, the agreement was renewed on April 27, 1951. During World War II, the Americans maintained 17 military installations principally in the South and Central of Greenland. The Danish intended to end the 1941 Defense Agreement after the war, but the United States was reluctant to do so because of the growing antagonisms between the USSR and the United States during the Cold War. From 1947 onward, Greenland's strategic role was therefore redefined from being an important link between North America and Europe to being a primary, strategic aerial base against USSR's industrial centers. Greenland, regardless of its political relation with Denmark, had to be occupied in case of war. Denmark joined NATO in 1949 and the renewed Defense Agreement remains valid as long as the NATO treaty is valid.

Thule Air Base was built in 1951, its location made possible by the forced resettlement of the Inughuit to Qaanaaq (about 140 km or 90 miles north). The immense base, which housed more than 10,000 soldiers, cost one billion US dollars to construct. It was established within the rich hunting territory near the Inughuit settlement of Uummannaq. Although the Thule Hunting Council exercised political and juridical authority in the local area, it was only informally informed about the construction several months after the work had well advanced and before the defense treaty between Denmark and the United States was signed.

The creation of the Thule Air Base created immediate myriad conflicts for the local Inughuit. The expansions at the base negatively affected the ecosystem on which the local hunters depended and led to economic deficiencies. One-third of the entire population in the Thule district (altogether 27 families of 116 people) was relocated to Qaanaaq in haste in 1953 when the United States decided to enlarge the base to include antiaircraft guns exactly where the indigenous settlement lay. This information appeared in a classified letter from the Prime Minister's office to the Danish Parliament's Finance Committee of May 1954, one year after the relocation. Officially, the relocation was presented as a wish from the local population and the Thule Hunting Council. Jens Brøsted and Mads Fægteborg (1985) argued that the construction of the base was an infringement upon the Thule population's local laws, was inconsistent with the principles of the defense agreement, broke international law, and resulted in the unconstitutional confiscation of property. Brøsted later demonstrated in 1995 that the defense agreement contained secret appendices—a disclosure that had hitherto been denied by successive Danish government leaders. The secret appendices, which at no time were presented to the Danish Parliament, demonstrated the agreement's unconstitutionality. These charges have yet to be addressed by either Danish or Greenlandic officials. An admission has, however, been given to the Greenlandic government that all security matters are to be discussed between the two governments, the two parliaments, and among top-level officials from both countries.

The surviving relocates of Uummannaq and their descendants have subsequently sought compensation for their lost hunting and fishing grounds and have demanded the right to return. The Inughuit began making claims for compensation as early as the 1950s. With the 1985 publication of Brøsted and Fægteborg's research, the municipality of Thule reiterated its claim for compensation against the Danish government. In a letter to the Danish Minister of Greenlandic Affairs,

Aerial view of the US Air Force base at Thule, an American strategic site near the Dundas Mountain, Northwest Greenland.
Copyright Bryan and Cherry Alexander Photography

the then premier of the Greenlandic government wrote that neither legal nor moral foundation for the claims existed. Both the Danish and the Greenlandic governments admitted, however, that problems existed in Thule, and consequently the Danish government began negotiations with the US government, which resulted in diminishing the base area by 50%. About 1500 sq km of land were returned to the Inughuit.

In 1998, the Greenlandic government in Nuuk supported the Thule claim for compensation. Their line of action, however, had little to do with punitive damages rewarded for the loss of territories. The government was concerned with civilian air traffic to and from Thule and the question of financing a civilian airport at Thule if negotiations concerning civilian traffic via the base failed. The Danish government refused to discuss compensation, but was willing to consider a transit agreement for civilian traffic with the Americans.

The Inughuit of Thule had not been satisfied with the work of the government-appointed committee, nor the political efforts made in Nuuk in 1999. In 1996, they had formed the organization *Hingitaq 53* ("The Discarded 1953"). This group filed a lawsuit on behalf of the Inughuit against the Danish government in 1996 at the Eastern Danish High Court. In 1999, the High Court stated: "There is no reason to assume that a decision to relocate was made by the Hunters' Council ... more that any wish was brought forward about a joint relocation of the settlement ... [and so] it must

apply that the decision to relocate the settlement was taken solely by the Danish authorities." The High Court's judgment commented on the lack of notice of the relocation and criticized Denmark for not notifying the Inughuit so that they would have had the opportunity to prepare their move. The High Court also referred to the International Labour Organization's Convention No. 169 of 1989, which constituted the Inughuit as a distinct people with indigenous rights to be guaranteed by the government. In other words, Denmark had acted illegally and was ordered to pay compensation. The High Court, on the other hand, decided that the Inughuit had no legal right to return to their ancestral lands. The Inughuit, desiring the right to return and in protest of the small compensation, appealed to the Danish Supreme Court in 1999. The Supreme Court rejected the claims in late 2003 and upheld the 1999 Court of Appeals verdict.

In February 2003, the Dundas Peninsula (about 7 km^2), located near the base, was returned to Greenland. However, the indigenous population protested at the manner in which the Americans returned their land because they were not involved in the negotiations. At the time of the return, reports on potential pollution had not been released, but it was suspected that the dumps of the Dundas Peninsula remained heavily contaminated (according to the Defense Agreement of 1951, the United States was not required to clean the area, and this decision was upheld in a February 2003 memorandum signed by the governments of the United States, Denmark, and Greenland). The municipality of Qaanaaq claims that there are more than 20 heavily contaminated dumps within the existing and former defense area of Thule.

Today, all the former military installations, including Narsarsuaq Air Base (1941–1958), Søndre Strømfjord Air Base (1942–1992), and the Distant Early Warning (DEW) Line Stations Dye 1, 2, 3, and 4 (1960–1992), no longer exist. Thule gradually changed from being a vantage point of operations for the strategic air force of the United States, to serving as a logistics base for high-technology installations in and around the base vicinity. Thus, by the end of the 1950s, the United States built one of the world's largest radar installations at the Thule Air Base devised as a "missile shield" against attacks. Several events, however, spurred discussion concerning military security in the 1980s as well as the continuing American presence in Greenland. These debates, however, primarily took place in the Danish media, in the Danish Parliament, and among Danes. The Government of Greenland asked for a report on the American installations from the Danish Minister of Defense. During the following debate in the Greenlandic Parliament, Aqqaluk Lynge (chairperson of the Inuit Ataqatigiit Party from 1980 till 1992) stated that each time a public debate about the Thule Air Base was initiated, the answer was that this was purely a Danish/American matter. Lynge referred to, among other things, the Inuit Circumpolar Conference's interest in making the Arctic a nuclear-free zone and, in the end, demilitarizing the Arctic. The Greenlandic Parliament passed a resolution requesting to be kept informed about defense matters. In 1984, the Parliament passed a resolution, by request of Inuit Ataqatigiit, to reject any deposit of nuclear weapons, and to prohibit their transportation in and through Greenland territory, both in peace and wartime.

In 1987, the Danish newspaper *Information* raised the question as to whether a new radar system (LPAR) at Thule Air Base was inconsistent with the Anti-Ballistic Missile Treaty between the US and the USSR (signed, ratified, and put into effect in 1972). The US officially withdrew from the ABM Treaty, effective June 2002. On December 17, 2002, the US formally requested from the UK and Denmark use of facilities in Fylingdales, England, and Thule, Greenland, respectively, as part of the National Missile Defense (NMD) program. Controversy continues in Greenland regarding the American NMD program and its presence in Greenland (with much resistance coming from the left-leaning political party, Inuit Ataqatigiit, which opposes NMD activity in Thule). Currently, the United States, Denmark, and Greenland remain in negotiations with regard to the American "Missile Shield" program,

aimed at reducing the threat from various "rogue states," including Iraq and North Korea.

Internal disputes on security matters persist in Greenland, but, in general, the politicians are more united and pragmatic today. The Inughuit population of Thule remains unsatisfied with the negotiations between the Greenlandic and Danish government on matters regarding Thule Air Base. In February 2003, when the United States relinquished a small part of the Thule defense area, local politicians, Inuit Ataqatigiit politicians, the Inuit Circumpolar Conference, and many citizens of Greenland held the biggest demonstration in the history of Greenland against the governments (United States, Denmark, and Greenland), leading to the signing of the agreement governing the return of the Dundas Peninsula.

In recent years, the Parliament and the Government of Greenland have adopted a new attitude toward Denmark. Although Greenland won partial Home Rule in 1979, Denmark still manages the state's foreign, defense, and security policy. The missile defense initiative has provided an avenue for current Greenland Premier Hans Enoksen to argue for changes to the 1951 Defense Agreement. As a result, the Danish government is working with Greenland to identify and possibly propose updates to the agreement in the light of developments in the past 50 years. According to the US Secretary of State, Colin Powell, and his Danish counterpart, Minister of Foreign Affairs, Per Stig Møller, a new defense agreement is out of the question, but both parties are willing to make amendments to the existing agreement. As of October 2003, it is not clear if Greenland will accept this.

MADS FÆGTEBORG

See also **Greenland; ILO Convention No. 169; Inuit Ataqatigiit; Lynge, Aqqaluk; Militarization of the Arctic in Russia; Militarization of the Arctic in the West; Political Issues in Resource Management; Qaanaaq; Relocation; Thule Culture**

Further Reading

Brøsted, Jens & Mads Fægteborg, "Expulsion of the Great People. When U.S. Air Force Came to Thule." *Native Power*, edited by Jens Brøsted et al., Bergen–Oslo–Stavanger–Tromsø: Universitetsforlaget AS, 1985

———, *Thule fangerfolk og militæranlæg*, Copenhagen: DJØF, 1985

———, *Thule fangerfolk og militæranlæg*, Copenhagen: Akademisk Forlag, 1987

Claesson, Paul (editor), *Grønland—Middelhavets Perle*, Copenhagen: Eirene, 1983

Fægteborg, Mads, *Grønland i dag—en introduktion år 2000*, Copenhagen: Arctic Information, 2000

———, "Snegle ændrer køn ved Pituffik." *Sermitsiaq* (Nuuk), August 29, 2003

Lynge, Aqqaluk, *The Right to Return*, Nuuk: Atuagkat, 2002

THULE CULTURE

Thule is the archaeological term for the material culture representative of the ancestors of modern Inuit people. Danish archaeologist Therkel Mathiassen, following his work with Knud Rasmussen's Fifth Thule Expedition in 1921–1924, first defined the Thule Culture. Excavations such as those at the site of Naujan, in Repulse Bay, Canada, revealed that material from a distinct culture with many uniform characteristics lay underneath many modern Inuit sites. In 1927, Mathiassen published "Archaeology of the Central Eskimos II: The Thule Culture and its Position Within the Eskimo Culture" as part of the *Report of the Fifth Thule Expedition 1921–24*, in which he systematically described Thule material culture.

Thule is generally considered to be derived from the Old Bering Sea and Okvik cultures in the Bering Strait region of northwest Alaska, and from Birnirk and Punuk cultures on the northern coast of Alaska, all of which are considered part of the "Neo-Eskimo" stage of Arctic prehistory (as opposed to the earlier "Paleo-Eskimo"), also known as the "Arctic Whale Hunting Culture" or the "Northern Maritime Tradition." These associations are based mainly on the reliance of each culture on marine resources, and most particularly the common use of equipment such as float gear, which is seen as a great technological improvement, allowing open water whale hunting from kayaks and umiaks.

While some Neo-Eskimos remained in what is now Alaska to develop Western Thule Culture, others moved rapidly east. The speed of this migration is demonstrated by the impressive uniformity shown in site remains and artifacts from this period, as well as a remarkably similar language across the Arctic. Thule dates are somewhat problematic, but researchers generally consider the culture as entering the Canadian Arctic around AD 1000. One of the reasons commonly postulated for its rapid expansion was the climatic warming of the 10th and 11th centuries AD, which extended eastward the summer range of whales and other marine mammals, perhaps encouraging hunters to follow. Other theories consider the richness of the Lancaster Sound region in general or the availability of metal in the east. Evidence from harpoon head typologies suggests that there were two waves of Thule migration. In the eastern Arctic, Thule is often divided into three periods: Early (first Thule in a specific area), Classic (Ruin Island types), and Late/Historic (modified Thule).

Thule sites are found from western Siberia to Greenland. Principal sites include Cape Krusenstern (western Alaska), Walakpa, and Kurigitavik (Pt Barrow region), Nelson River (Banks Island), and Clachan (Coronation Gulf) in the western Arctic, Naujan, Silumuit (west Hudson Bay), Brooman Point, Qariaraqyuk, Nunguvik, and Mittimatalik in the Canadian High Arctic, and Thule, Comer's Midden, and Qeqertaaraq in Greenland, among many others.

Debate continues over the fate of the Dorset people (*c*.900 BC–*c*.AD 1500) who occupied the eastern Arctic prior to Thule arrival. No evidence of violence

Large Thule Culture site featuring a village with whalebone house foundations, Brooman Point, Bathurst Island, Nunavut, August 1974.
Copyright David R. Gray

yet exists between the two populations, and whether they even met is held in contention. Thule sites do tend to be found on Dorset middens. However, researchers suggest that either the Dorset were unable to adapt to changes in the environment, and died out before Thule pioneers arrived, or that the increased burden placed on resources by the more competitive newcomers forced them further into the margins, with the same results. A third suggestion claims that the Dorset culture was integrated with Thule, but again little evidence currently exists to support this theory.

Contact and trade between Thule groups are evidenced by the distribution of iron, amber, soapstone, and walrus ivory. Norse contact is suggested by historical sources, and in fact the Norse settled in southwest Greenland. There are archaeological finds of Norse materials on Thule sites, and the resulting mix of Norse and Thule cultures is termed Inugsuk Thule. Archaeological finds in North Greenland and northeast Ellesmere Island seem to show earlier contact, but its nature and extent with these more distant Thule groups remain unclear.

A typical Thule inventory was impressively diverse, reflecting a varied diet and subsistence economy, and a highly specialized technology, particularly in organic materials, that allowed them to adapt to almost any Arctic environment. Hunting tools included toggling harpoons with open socket-shafts and ice picks, lances, salmon spears, bird darts, bolas, throwing boards, and bows and arrows. Knives and other cutting tools were generally made of polished slate. Bow and hand drills, adzes, mattocks, wedges, clubs, flint flakers, ulus, scrapers, and needles were common utensils. Copper and iron were known from the early period and grew in importance. Soapstone, pottery, and baleen were used to make equipment such as lamps and bowls. Driftwood served as an important resource used in house construction and various tools and utensils. For transport, kayaks and *umiaks* were both used, as were toboggans and dog sledges, allowing greater hunting ranges. Snow goggles equipped people against the glare of the sun.

Artistic expression included the decoration of implements with incised motifs, both naturalistic and geometric. Thule people carved human figures of driftwood, most commonly female but also male, often missing facial features, arms, and feet. Carvings made of animals and birds are rendered simply and reflect the cultural importance of the sea. Although Thule art is often considered clumsier than that of preceding cultures such as Dorset and Old Bering Sea, finds of drums suggest the vitality of dance and music.

Thule tended to construct groups of houses near the shore for easy access to marine resources. These houses could consist of dozens of structures, possibly representing winter aggregation. The winter houses were semi-subterranean, generally built of stone, sod, and whalebone, with narrow underground passageways that acted as cold-traps, and opened onto paved floors. Raised platforms existed for sleeping, and cloverleaf and other shaped houses often show evidence of several sleeping platforms, suggesting domiciles for extended families. Temporary dwellings are harder to define in the archaeological record, but snow houses are suggested by finds of snow knives, and skin tents for summer dwellings are represented by rings of stones. Thule dead were buried in heavy stone cists or burial chambers.

The cooling climate, ultimately resulting in the "Little Ice Age" of the 14th to the 16th centuries, perhaps led Thule people to adopt the way of life that characterized their Inuit descendants.

JENNIFER I.M. NEWTON

See also **Birnirk Culture; Collins, Henry B.; Fifth Thule Expedition; Mathiassen, Therkel; Old Bering Sea Culture**

Further Reading

Appelt, Martin, Joel Berglund & Hans Christian Gulløv (editors), *Identities and Cultural Contacts in the Arctic*, Copenhagen: Danish National Museum and Danish Polar Centre, 2000

Dumond, Don E., *The Eskimos and Aleuts*, (revised edition), London: Thames and Hudson, 1987

Mathiassen, T., "Archaeology of the Central Eskimos I: Descriptive Part." *Report of the Fifth Thule Expedition 1921–24*, Volume IV, Copenhagen. Gyldendalske Boghandel, Nordisk Forlag, 1927

———, "Archaeology of the Central Eskimos II: The Thule Culture and its Position Within the Eskimo Culture." *Report of the Fifth Thule Expedition 1921–24*, Volume IV, Copenhagen: Gyldendalske Boghandel, Nordisk Forlag, 1927

Maxwell, M., *Prehistory of the Eastern Arctic*, Orlando: Academic Press, 1985

McCartney, Allen P., *Thule Eskimo Culture: An Anthropological Retrospective*, Ottawa: National Museums of Canada, 1979

McCullough, K.M., *The Ruin Islanders: Thule Culture Pioneers in the Eastern High Arctic*, Archaeological Survey of Canada Mercury Paper 141, Ottawa: Canadian Museum of Civilisation, 1989

McGhee, Robert, "The past ten years in Canadian Arctic prehistory." *Canadian Journal of Archaeology* (6) (1982): 65–77

TIDES

Tidal motion in the Arctic Ocean influences sea ice distribution and generates periodic leads or openings in the pack ice associated with divergence and convergence over the tidal cycle. These periodic openings of the pack ice cover influence both heat exchange between the ocean and the atmosphere and the rate of ice production. Tides are also responsible for maintaining the basic level of turbulence beneath the ice cover and in close proximity to the bottom. Mixing and stirring due to tides is especially strong along the Eurasian continental shelf, and also plays an important role in the deep Arctic Ocean where the general circulation appears to be extremely weak.

Tides in the Arctic Ocean generally propagate in the same fashion as in ice-free water bodies. The long tide wave of several hundred kilometers in length has a very small surface inclination. On such surfaces, the pack ice cover behaves like a flexible membrane, which weakly damps the vertical mode of motion but strongly resists the horizontal motion. Due to friction damping at the ice-water boundary, the water particles near this boundary move slower than in the deeper layers. This leads to the occurrence of the boundary layer in the tidal flow and variability of the tidal motion along the vertical direction.

Tides along the coastline of the Arctic Ocean are known from observations; however, in the Central Basin, tides are inferred from hydrodynamical models. Tidal heights are composed of a sum of simple waves, which are called constituents. Their periods are clustered around 12- and 24-h bands. The first are known as semidiurnal tides (or constituents); the latter are called diurnal tides (or constituents). The major contribution to tides in the Arctic Ocean is related to the semidiurnal constituents M_2 and S_2, and diurnal constituents K_1 and O_1. The numbers 1 and 2- denote the diurnal and semidiurnal constituents, respectively. The strongest component of all tidal waves is usually M_2; it is caused by the moon's attraction. The S_2 constituent is of solar origin. The strongest constituent in the diurnal band of oscillations is K_1; it is of the mixed luni-solar origin. The O_1 constituent is forced by the moon's attraction.

Tides in every location are associated with the vertical movement of the free surface. The time interval between two successive peaks (or troughs) is called the period, and sea level due to the tide repeats itself after one tidal cycle (period). The sea-level changes in time cause horizontal tidal currents. A water particle transported by tidal current follows a closed elliptical path during one tidal cycle, that is, in one cycle it runs along an elliptical path, returning to its initial position. The magnitude of the tidal current is given along the major axis of such a tidal ellipse.

The largest component of the tide in the Arctic Ocean is the semidiurnal M_2 (period 12.42 h). Since the tide-producing force for this constituent in the Arctic Ocean is very small, the origin of this wave is generated in the Atlantic Ocean. The M_2 tide entering the Arctic Ocean between Greenland and Scandinavia is divided at Spitsbergen into two branches. The main tide enters through the Greenland Sea and the second tide propagates around Scandinavia toward the White Sea. The latter has an amplitude in northern Norway of about

1 m. In the White Sea, at the entrance it grows to about 2–3 m and in the shallow Mezen Bay in the southeastern White Sea the amplitude is greater than 4 m.

The M_2 wave in the main basin of the Arctic Ocean propagates counterclockwise during one period around an amphidromic point (a point of zero tidal amplitude) located off the Canadian Archipelago. The tidal amplitude is zero at an amphidromic point, and it increases toward the shoreline. While traveling in the Arctic Ocean, the M_2 wave undergoes transformation. When it impinges on the North Siberian Shelf, its amplitude diminishes through bottom friction. Along the North Siberian Shelf the amplitude is about 20–30 cm, and further the amplitude decreases to 5–10 cm at the Alaskan shore. The M_2 tidal currents in the deep basin are quite small—of the order of 2 cm s^{-1}. The strong currents were observed along the coasts in the shallow water of the Barents Sea, especially over Spitsbergenbanken and close to Bear Island. The strongest currents, often up to 2 m s^{-1}, occur at the entrance to the White Sea. Along the North Siberian Shelf, especially in the region of the New Siberian Islands, the M_2 tide currents are often of the order of 50 cm s^{-1}. The variability of the tidal currents is much stronger compared to the tidal levels, because currents depend on the local conditions: for example, the currents along Alaska Beaufort Sea coast are of the order of 5–10 cm s^{-1}, but in the narrow entrances to the coastal lagoons they can be enhanced several times. Amplitudes of the second semidiurnal constituent S_2 (period 12 h) are much smaller, but the general picture of the wave propagating counterclockwise in the main basin is very similar to the M_2 wave. Generally, diurnal tides K_1 (period 23.93 h) and O_1 (period 25.82 h) have amplitudes smaller than the M_2 tide and their currents over shallow regions are also small compared to M_2.

However, in some regions around Alaska and the Canadian Archipelago, the amplitudes of diurnal tides are close to semidiurnal tides. In these regions, the semidiurnal tides were damped by friction. The diurnal tides propagate differently from the semidiurnal tides. This difference occurs in the currents. The diurnal tides generate regions of enhanced tidal currents along the shelf break at a depth of several hundred meters. These are so-called topographic trapped shelf waves. The discovery of the enhanced diurnal tidal currents in the entire water column above the Yermak Plateau (depth about 700 m), by measuring currents below the drifting pack ice, showed the importance of this mechanism for deep processes in the Arctic Ocean. Along the shelf break in the Arctic Ocean and in the Nordic Seas, the tidal models predicted about 26 locations where diurnal trapped shelf waves occur. These are locations where the bathymetry (contours of the seafloor) at the shelf break (where the continental shelf falls away sharply to the deep ocean floor) shows irregular features such as seamounts and canyons. The tidal energy due to diurnal tides, dissipated over these 26 locations, is larger than the energy dissipated over the entire Arctic Ocean. Because large tidal currents occur either along the shelf (for the semidiurnal constituents) or at some locations along the shelf break (for the diurnal constituents), the nonlinear effects are important factors in the tidal dynamics of the Arctic Ocean. These effects are determined by averaging tidal current over a tidal period. If the average current is not equal to zero, a residual (or steady) current is generated over the tidal cycle. This residual current constitutes a measure of the nonlinear effects. Therefore, the water particle in such tidal currents during one tidal cycle will depict an open ellipse with the initial and the final positions after one tidal period at the different locations. A well-known example of the steady motion due to oscillating tide is the circular ice motion around Bear Island in the Barents Sea. The individual ice-floes circle around the island in a few days. The role of the strong tidal currents over shallow coastal regions is connected to the generation of the tidal fronts. Strong currents induce vigorous mixing (homogenizing) of the water salinity and temperature along the vertical direction in the shallow water. These tidally mixed coastal regions are separated from the open ocean by tidal fronts. The well-known tidal front is located around Bear Island and Spitsbergenbanken. Tidal fronts occur along the entire Eurasian shelf; the fronts in the White Sea and around the New Siberian Islands are especially well described. Their position is often defined by a tidal velocity of about 50 cm s^{-1}.

The periodic tide motion through divergence/convergence processes generates a periodic change in the ice compactness distribution, causing periodic openings and closings in the pack ice in calm weather (see Leads). Grounded icebergs on the Spitsbergenbanken, and in other shallow domains, give the best visualizations of the elliptically shaped traces caused by the tidal motion. In a field of drifting ice-floes, grounded icebergs induce trailing wakes (similar to an icebreaker), which, on satellite imagery, reveal the size of the tidal ellipses.

A major feature of the Arctic tides is the seasonal change of the tidal constituents. In most regions of the Arctic Ocean, the seasonal changes from summer to winter in the pack ice compactness result in the diminishing of the tide amplitude by about 3% and in a time lag of 5% of a tide period. Locally, especially in proximity to the shore-fast ice (ice attached to the shore), these differences occur in a wider range. Canadian observations from Tuktoyaktuk revealed a strong dependence of the tide on the ice cover. The M$_2$ amplitude changes from 16 cm during summer to 11 cm during winter. The seasonal time difference is one-sixth of a tide period.

Tidally induced motion of the pack ice interacts with other motions of the ice cover caused by the wind and permanent currents. The most interesting phenomena generated through these interactions are polynyas, that is, permanently or semipermanently open water surrounded by ice. The largest polynya occurs along the continental slope of the East Siberian and Laptev seas. Tidally induced motion is also one of the main factors in generating and sustaining polynyas in the region of the Lincoln Sea, Chukchi Cap, Yermak Plateau, and Northeast Water Polynya.

Tidal research and the history of the Arctic tide research till 1960 are well described by Defant (1960). New developments have been summarized by Gjevik and Straume (1989) and Kowalik and Proshutinsky (1994). A basic understanding of the principles of tidal theories can be gleaned from Macmillan (1966). Tidal phenomena in the oceans and research methods to study tides are described by Pugh (1987).

ZYGMUNT KOWALIK

See also **Leads; Polynyas**

Further Reading

Defant, Albert, *Dynamical Oceanography*, Volume II, Oxford: Pergamon Press, 1960

Gjevik, Bjorn & Trygve Straume, "Model simulations of the M2 and K1 tide in the Nordic Seas and the Arctic Ocean." *Tellus*, (1989) 73–96

Kowalik, Zygmunt & Andrey Proshutinsky, "The Arctic Ocean Tide." In *The Polar Oceans, and Their Role in Shaping the Global Environment*, edited by O.M. Johannesen, R.D. Muench & J.E. Overland, Washington District of Columbia: American Geophysical Union, 1994

Macmillan, Donald, H., *Tides*, New York: Elsevier and London: CR Books, 1966

Pugh, David, *Tides, Surges and Mean Sea-Level*, Chichester: Wiley, 1987

TIKSI

Tiksi is a port on the Lena River at the Laptev Sea coast in the Sakha Republic (Yakutia), Russian Federation. Tiksi was established as a polar station and reindeer herding community in 1934 to develop the Northern Sea Route. It received the status of workers' settlement in 1939. Its name originates from the Yakut word *tiksii* meaning "a place of destination" or "moorage." The relief of the ulus and Tiksi is mountainous and plain. The average January temperature is from −32°C in the north and down to −40°C in the southeast. The average July temperature is +4°C in the north and +14°C in the south. The annual precipitation is 150–200 mm in the north and 250–300 mm in the south. Aboriginal traditional economies are reindeer herding, fishing, and hunting.

Tiksi is the gateway to the sea of the Sakha Republic. In a short period of time, Tiksi became a key seaport on the Northern Sea Route. Cargo is delivered through Tiksi to almost all Arctic regions, of the Sakha Republic as well as to neighboring regions, including the ports of the Taimyr and Chukotka Autonomous okrugs. Cargo is delivered from Murmansk and Vladivostok by the Northern Sea Route and from Yakutsk by the Lena River.

The distance from Tiksi to Yakutsk is 1270 km by air and 1703 km by river. In the period of full flowering of the Northern Sea Route, the population of Tiksi numbered approximately 11,900 people in 1989, although from 1990 –to 2000 the population declined sharply due to the decline in sea cargo delivery. Recently, the settlement's life has been reinvigorated as a result of international expeditions that travel annually to Tiksi to conduct research in the Lena Delta and on the Novosibirsky Islands (New Siberian Islands).

The Siberian Division of the Institute of Cosmophysical Research and Aeronomy (of the Russian Academy of Sciences) conducts monitoring of aurora borealis, thermal regime, and large-scale circulation of the upper atmosphere at the Polar Geocosmophysical Observatory in Tiksi. The Institute of Permafrost's Siberian Division (also under the auspices of the Russian Academy of Sciences) monitors geothermal conditions and performs research on aerosol geochemistry in the terrestrial atmosphere of Tiksi.

Tiksi is home to a shipping company, a large seaport, a hydrographic station, a reinforced concrete plant, and various other building enterprises. The aircraft company located in Tiksi currently operates for the entire Arctic shore zone of Yakutia. The town is home to a recreational center, clubs, secondary sports and music schools, and a folklore and arts museum. The polar station is located nearby.

Tiksi administers the Ust-Lenski Nature Reserve and Lena-Delta Resource Reserve, embracing the Lena Delta and the Novosibirsk Archipelago. Tiksi is the administrative center of the Bulunski ulus, Sakha Republic, which covers 223.6 sq km.

VLADIMIR VASILIEV

See also **Lena River; Northern Sea Route; Sakha Republic (Yakutia)**

TLICHO—*See* DOGRIB (TLICHO)

TLINGIT

The northernmost Northwest Coast group of Native Americans, the Tlingit live on the Alaskan coast from Yakutat south to the British Columbia border. The Tlingit language comprises different but related dialects, including the northern Tlingit, southern Tlingit, and the now nearly extinct Tongass Tlingit.

Although prior to the 18th century the Tlingit inhabited the entirety of the southernmost portion of Alaska, during the late 18th and early 19th centuries, the Haida drove the Tongass Tlingit out of southern Prince of Wales, Dall, Long, and Sukkwan islands. At the same time, the northern Tlingit were driving the Eyak and Athapaskan from Dry and Yakutat bays. At the time of contact with Russian settlers (*c.* late 1700s), the estimated Tlingit population numbered approximately 14,800. The Tlingit speak a language related to Athapaskan and are the northernmost Northwest Coast group. Like their neighbors on the British Columbia coast, the Tlingit economy is based primarily on salmon. They traditionally lived with their extended families in large cedar-plank houses lined along beaches. During the summer, Tlingit moved to smaller fishing camps.

Anthropologists suggest that the Tlingit individual's role within society is determined by a rigidly structured social organization composed of two exogamous, matrilineal moieties (one of two basic complementary tribal subdivisions): the Ravens and the Wolves (who are referred to as the Eagles in some Tlingit communities). A number of extended family groups called lineages constitute each moiety; each lineage, in turn, is composed of one or more house groups, whose members claim a common origin. Tlingit hierarchically rank individuals within the house, houses within the lineage, and lineages within the moieties.

The moieties are considered equal opposites. The two house chiefs of the highest ranking lineage houses in each moiety possess the highest status within a village. Until quite recently, numerous reciprocal obligations connected these two halves—one married a member of the other moiety, opposites performed funerary functions, built the large plank houses that held extended families, and attended potlatches.

An individual's status is exceedingly important among the Tlingit. One of the most important indications of rank is the crest, which takes the form of artistic icons as well as the stories about those images. Both refer to interactions in mythic times with certain beings who provided the families with considerable wealth and status. The creation of an artwork illustrating a crest (the visual depiction of lineage history and status) was the responsibility of one's opposite. If that individual was unskilled as an artist (a not uncommon occurrence), he hired and paid the most talented artist available for the task.

Any ritual service performed by a moiety opposite was paid for with gifts. The most formal of such ritual gift giving was the funerary potlatch, during which a family paid its opposites for attending to the funeral of a high-ranking individual, rebuilding his house, and, in some communities, erecting a memorial totem pole.

Two groups of guests are invited to the Tlingit potlatch: the opposite moiety lineage who had done the work, and another opposite moiety lineage from a more distant village. Dressed up in their best finery, the guests enter the house of the host, assuming carefully selected seating positions appropriate to their ranking. For several days, the guests provide entertainment of dancing, singing, imitating animals, or performing amusing skits, some of which mock foreigners such as the Athapaskans. Both rivalry and competitive spirit exist between the two groups of visitors, who try to catch each other's mistakes and at times hurl insults at each other.

After the entertainment period, the hosts become involved in the event, presenting their nieces and nephews, displaying cherished heirlooms of clan regalia, making speeches about their lineage and its high position, and thanking their guests for contributing labor. For several days, the hosts distribute thousands of dollars worth of blankets to pay their guests for not only the actual work they did, but also, and perhaps even more importantly, to validate their claims for status. By accepting these "payments," the guests acknowledge that their hosts are indeed as aristocratic as they claim, their regalia as estimable, and their young nobles worthy inheritors of high positions.

Among most Northwest Coast groups, shamans played an important role in society. Shamans were responsible for curing the sick, controlling the weather, guaranteeing adequate fish runs, combating witches, and providing assistance during battle by interacting on a personal level with both benevolent and malevolent supernaturals. The shaman typically experienced a supernatural calling in his or her adolescence, went on a spirit quest during which spirit assistants made themselves known, and usually apprenticed to an older shaman.

The Tlingit cultures featured an elaborate form of shamanism, and a large variety of shamanic artworks. According to Tlingit beliefs, the shaman received his calling at about the age of puberty, after which he went on an eight-day vision quest, during which time he lived in an isolated place and deprived himself of food and fresh water. Animals destined to become his helping spirits approached him and protruded their tongues, evincing their spirit power. The initiate excised all the animal tongues and assembled them in a special charm. After this quest, the novice shaman returned to his community, where he either inherited his predecessor's regalia or had new regalia made. Charms, rattles, costumes, and masks depicted the helping spirits that the novice encountered on his vision quest. After this initiatory experience, the novice shaman typically apprenticed with an older shaman, who instructed him in the practices of shamanism.

The Russians who first settled in Alaska at the end of the 18th century interfered relatively little with Tlingit culture. The colony was sold to the United States in 1867; the influx of whites during the late 19th-century gold rushes signified the end of Tlingit autonomy. Shortly thereafter, settlers, government officials, missionaries, and tourists began to intercede with Tlingit life and culture. By 1920, the population had plummeted to 3895.

By the mid-20th century, the Tlingit, whose population was gradually increasing, became a political force to be reckoned with. In 1912, they founded the Alaska Native Brotherhood, an organization intended to promote Native advancement and combat discrimination. The most significant event in 20th-century Alaskan Native economic and political life occurred with the passage of the Alaska Native Claims Settlement Act (ANCSA) in 1971, which gave Natives title to 44 million acres—10% of the land—and $962.5 million in compensation. Regional and village corporations were formed to administer the land and the investment of the funds. Under the ANCSA, Tlingit (along with the smaller number of Haida who lived in southeast Alaska) formed the Sealaska Regional Corporation and ten village corporations. Sealaska received 200,000 acres of land, and the village corporations received surface rights to 23,000 acres. Sealaska and the village corporations are presently involved with logging, fishing, and tourism.

ALDONA JONAITIS

See also **Alaska Native Claims Settlement Act (ANCSA); Haida; Shamanism**

Further Reading

Dauenhauer, Nora Marks & Richard Dauenhauer, *Haa Shuka, Our Ancestors: Tlingit Oral Narratives*, Seattle: University of Washington Press, 1987; *Haa Tuwunaagu Yis, for Healing Spirit: Tlingit Oratory*, Seattle: University of Washington Press, 1990; *Haa Kusteeyi: Our Culture. Tlingit Life Stories*, Seattle: University of Washington Press, 1994

de Laguna, Frederica, "Under Mount St Elias: the history and culture of the Yakutat Tlingit." *Smithsonian Contributions to Anthropology*, 7 (1972)

Emmons, G.T., *The Tlingit Indians*, edited by F. de Laguna, Seattle: University of Washington Press, 1991

Jonaitis, Aldona, *Art of the Northern Tlingit*, Seattle: University of Washington Press, 1986

Kan, Sergei, *Symbolic Immortality: The Tlingit Potlatch of the Nineteenth Century*, Washington District of Columbia: Smithsonian Institution Press, 1989

Krause, Aurel, *The Tlingit Indians: Results of a Trip to the Northwest Coast of America and the Bering Straits*, Seattle: University of Washington Press, 1956

Swanton, John, *Social Conditions, Beliefs, and Linguistic Relationship of the Tlingit Indians*, New York: Johnson Reprint Corporation, 1970 (originally published 1908)

TOFALARS

The Tofalars (Tofa) are a small Siberian minority with a specific subsistence and culture, and are thus considered one of the recognized ethnic groups of northern Russia. Formerly named "Karagas" after one of the major Tofalar clans, the Tofalars live on the northeastern taiga slopes of the East Sayan range in the south of Eastern Siberia, over an area of about 27,000 sq km. The region is usually called Tofalaria after the name of the indigenous people, but although the Tofalar national district with a center in the Alygdzher village existed from 1939 to 1951, it is no longer an administrative unit. In 1951, Tofalar and Verkhne-Gutar village soviets were created within the administrative borders of Nizhneudinsk district of the Irkutsk province of Russia. The Tofalars live in the three villages of Alygdzher, Nerkha, and Verkhnya Gutara, which were built during the period of forced settlement from 1927 to 1932.

The Tofalar population numbered 731 in the 1989 Soviet Census, and this number has remained relatively stable for centuries. Before the 1917 Russian Revolution, their numbers decreased during periods of poor harvests and epidemics. In Soviet and post-Soviet periods, the special policy of northern privileges in the sphere of education and health care contributed to an increase in the number of Tofalar.

The Tofalar language is a Turkic language of the Altaic group closely related to Tuvan. The language is in serious decline with very few native speakers. Almost everyone can speak Russian; some Tofalar also speak the Buryat language. Education in the schools is conducted in Russian. The Tofalar written language was created only in 1986 by V.I. Rassadin, who used the Cyrillic script as a base.

According to archaeological data, the ancestors of the Tofalars were nomadic hunters and gatherers. Living in the neighborhood of the Buryat, Soyot, Kamasinzy, Uryanhai, and Tuva-Todzha peoples led to the adoption of the Turkic language over the original Samodian. The first contact with Russians began in the 17th century, when Nizhneudinsk fort (*ostrog*) was built at the foot of East Sayan range, on the banks of the Uda River.

The *aal*—a community joining two to five monogamous families all sharing a common male ancestor—formed the basis of Tofalar society. Because of the nomadic subsistence lifestyle, the community structure was not stable, decreasing in number in winter and increasing in summer. These communities were joined into clans (*nen*), of which there were eight. Every clan was nomadic within the boundaries of a clan hunting ground. The Russian administration established five administrative clans. The clans united and formed a tribe (*khaptygay*), which elected its chief, called *starosta* (*shulenga*). Once a year, the chief organized the annual gathering of the clans where important questions, such as judicial problems, tax payment, and trade, were discussed and solved. The tax payment (or *yasak*) to the Russians consisted of pelts and furs (mainly sable).

Today, more than 50% of Tofalar families are mixed. Although the practice of endogamy (restricting marriage to within the community) no longer exists, the Tofalar self-consciousness is preserved.

Traditionally, the Tofalars led a nomadic lifestyle throughout the year, wandering in the mountains and foothills of the East Sayan range. Their subsistence economy was based on fur trapping and hunting of land animals. They bred reindeer and (at least since before the 17th century) horses for transport. The Tofalars, having the largest and strongest domesticated reindeer in northern Eurasia, used the animals not only for carrying loads but also for riding. The Tofalar style of riding is essentially different from many taiga nomads of Eurasia through its use of stirrups and saddle-girth in the reindeer harness. Also, the rider is seated on the left side of the reindeer's back. Preparation of yogurt and sour cheese from fermented reindeer milk testifies that their culture of forest hunters and reindeer breeders of Samodian origin adopted Turk and Mongol delicacies.

During the year, the Tofalar wandered along more or less constant routes, making temporary camps, consisting of conical hide tents, on their way. In summer, traveling by horse, they bred reindeer in the high mountains, where there was plenty of reindeer moss, and where wind kept mosquitoes away. In autumn and winter, while the horses pastured in the intermountain hollows, the Tofalar hunted in the taiga foothills for fur animals such as sable and squirrel, using reindeer for transport.

Tofalar hunted for musk deer, wild deer, Manchurian deer, elk, and sometimes brown bear. They dried and cured meat for storage. In the past, the Tofalar hunted using bows and arrows, and since the 17th and 18th centuries, rifles have predominated. Dogs have been a mainstay for Tofalar hunting, and hunting remains the primary subsistence of the present-day Tofalars, who rely on tracking animals near lakes or natural salt reserves, or chases. The tradition of sharing the hunting game among relatives and neighbors has been preserved. The gathering of tubers of sarana, wild onion and wild garlic, berries, and cedar (Siberian pine) nuts constituted the essential part of the Tofalar subsistence diet. Since the middle of the

20th century, harvesting of cedar nuts has played an important role in their business.

From 1926 to the mid-1930s, the Tofalars were forcibly settled, their traditional hunting lands became state property, and reindeer breeding was collectivized. Special hunting and reindeer-breeding brigades were created. New economic incentives, such as stockbreeding for milk and vegetable production, were introduced. Children were sent to schools, and a health care system was organized. In the late 1960s, the collective farms (*kolkhozes*) were replaced by hunting and reindeer-breeding farms, in which 60% of the entire Tofalar population worked. Recent attempts to develop private economy conflict with the community traditions. Although reindeer numbers have decreased by a factor of two during the last 10 years, reaching fewer than 1000, some of the Tofalars still work as breeders. Most of the men hunt for fur animals during the autumn season and for land animals throughout the year.

The Tofalars believe in "lord spirits" of nature and animals. They believe that the world consists of three spheres: of these, the "middle world" is populated with numerous lord spirits of land, mountain passes, and animals. The "low world" is the realm and the possession of the dead, and the "upper world" is populated by supreme forces and spirits. Tofalars perform rituals dedicated to these spirits.

In the past, the Tofalars had a shaman (*kham*), who provided assistance and cures for disease and misfortune, and possessed the ability to predict the future. Both men and women could act as shamans. Because of Buryat and Tuva-Todzha influences, Tofalar shamanism retained some features of Lamaism. In the 17th century, the Tofalar became acquainted with Christianity through the Russian Orthodox Church. Shamanism and Christianity lost their influence in the 20th century under the attack of Soviet atheism.

ANNA A. SIRINA

See also **Reindeer Pastoralism**

Further Reading

Dioszegi, V., "Zum Problem der ethnischen Homogenitat des tofischen (karagassischen) Shamanismus." In *Glaubenswelt und Folklore der Sibirischen Volker*, Budapest: Akadémiai Kiadó, 1963
Donahoe, B. "Hey, You! Get offa my Taiga!." *The Troubled Taiga: Cultural Survival Quarterly* (spring 2003)
Harrison, K.D., "Tofa." In *Encyclopedia of the World's Minorities*, edited by C. Skutsch, New York and London: Routledge, 2004
Krivonogov, V.P., "K sovremennoy etnicheskoy situazii v Tofalarii" [On the present-day ethnographic situation in Tofalaria]. *Sovetskaya Etnografia*, 5 (1987): 81–90
Mel'nikova, L.V., *Tofy* [The Tofa], Irkutsk: Vostochno-Sibirskoe knizhnoe idatel'stvo, 1994
Melnikova, A.I., *Tofas. Historical and Ethnological Essay*, Irkutsk, 1994
Petri, B.E., "Okhotnich'i ugod'ya i rasselenie karagas" [Hunting Grounds and Distribution of the Karagas]. *Collection of the Proceedings of the Professors and Teachers of the Irkutsk State University*, Vyp. 13, Irkutsk: Irkutsk University, 1927
Sergeev, M.A., "Tofalary." In *Narody Sibiri*, edited by M.G. Levin & L.P. Potapov, Moscow: Russian Academy of Sciences, 1956; as *The Peoples of Siberia*, Chicago: Chicago University Press, 1964
Vainshtein, S.I., "Rodovaia structura i patronimicheskaia organizazia u tofalarov" [Clan structure and patronymic organization among the Tofalar]. *Sovetskaya Etnografia*, 3 (1968): 60–67
———, *Mir kochevnikov Tsentra Azii* [The World of the Nomads of the Central Asia], Moscow: Nauka, 1991

TOKAREV CULTURE

The Tokarev culture existed on the northern Okhotsk coast in northeast Asia in the first millennium BC to the beginning of the first millennium AD. Typologically, the culture is Neolithic; however, its later stage appears related to the Paleo-metal Age. The Tokarev culture was developed when bands from the Kolyma region settled on the eastern coastal areas. Another considerable formative influence was the Amur area cultures, which is reflected in Tokarev ceramics, designs, and the appearance of metal.

Similar stone assemblages can be found in Priamur'e, Primor'e, on Kamchatka, the Kuril Islands, Sakhalin Island, and in Pribaikal'e during the second to first millennium BC. Typological likeness of stone implements from sites in west Chukotka and the artefact complex of the Tokarev culture are, however, not evidence of the transition of west Chukotka inhabitants to the Okhotsk coast. Also, there is no basis for establishing a definite influence of the Ymyiakhtakh culture on the Sea of Okhotsk maritime cultures. Very interesting finds are ornaments—pendants and amulets—made of small oval pebbles and ground slabs. Grinding, carving, and drilling were widely used in the preparation of these ornaments. The pendants were decorated with notching along the edge, as well as with incised lines. Among them are representations of birds, marine mammals, and humans.

The wealth of stone artifacts attests to the significant role of stone in the economy of the Tokarev culture. A variety of bone tools were also used: punches, awls, compound fishhooks, arrowpoints, darts, leisters (a forklike antler or bone fishing harpoon), needles, and needle cases.

The specialized tools of maritime hunting (barbed and toggling harpoon heads) appeared on the Okhotsk coast during the second half of the first millennium BC. The toggling harpoon heads are similar to those of the Dorset culture and the Okhotsk culture of the Kuril islands in the presence of a barb, an open socket, and the placement of the line hole. Barbed harpoon heads have analogs in the cultures of Kachemak I (Alaska), in the Aleutian Islands (Chaluka), and in the Okhotsk culture. The appearance of a harpoon complex on the Okhotsk coast can be tied to influence from the Paleo-Eskimo cultures of Alaska. Close similarities may be observed among the cultures of the Aleutian Islands, the Canadian Arctic, and the Okhotsk coast, which can be explained by strong connections between the early North Pacific cultures and those of the Arctic North American coastal regions.

The ceramics of the Tokarev culture are represented by vessels of pot-shaped form with turned-back rims and flattened bottoms. The vessels were decorated with hatching, punctate stamps, and incised lines. The lower parts of small, undecorated, pointed-bottomed, thin-walled vessels were found. The Tokarev ceramic ornamentation is very similar to that of the Lower Amur region. One vessel was decorated with rows of deeply punched, short slanted lines forming a zigzag with three links.

Iron began to spread onto the Okhotsk coast at the end of the first millennium BC. Burin or graving instrument hafts or handles, fitted in antiquity with iron blades, were found on some sites. Iron artifacts probably spread onto the Okhotsk coast from the Priamur'e and Primor'e tribes. However, iron was used very rarely in this period.

Copper tools (a piece of an awl and a knife) were found on Spafar'eva Island. The knife has a pointed copper blade of triangular cross section, wrapped by a thin layer of birch bark and inserted into a bone handle of oval cross section. It is similar to a bronze knife from the Ust'-Mil' I site in Yakutia.

Large settlements were found on Spafar'eva Island, where 34 house depressions were discovered, and at Cape Vostochnii, where 26 house depressions were counted. The dwellings have shallow roughly circular basins, 5–9 m in diameter. The depressions are 0.4–0.7 m deep. The rectangular hearths are lined with vertically set stones.

Sites on the islands of Spafar'eva, Nedorazumeniia, and Zav'ialova are located at some distance from the mainland coast, which attests to the existence of boats among the early population.

The Tokareva people engaged in maritime procurement, hunting, fishing, and collecting. Bones of marine mammals (including whales), deer, and bears were found in the sites. The primary objects of the hunt were small seals. Hunting of large sea mammals (whales and walruses) was evidently random. The early hunters also could have utilized whales stranded on the shore.

A.I. LEBEDINTSIV

See also **Old Bering Sea Culture; Old Koryak Culture**

Further Reading

Lebedintsev, A.I., "Maritime cultures of the north coast of the Sea of Okhotsk." *Arctic Anthropology*, 35(1) (1998): 296–320
———, *Early Maritime Culture of North Western Priokhot'e*, Anchorage: National Park Service, 2000

TOLL, BARON EDWARD VON

In 1885–1886, the Russian Academy of Science organized the first scientific expedition to the Novosibirskiye Islands (New Siberian Islands). Its main goal was the thorough exploration of the archipelago complemented by topographic surveys of the shoreline. The naval doctor Alexander von Bunge was appointed as chief of the expedition, and the young scientist Baron Edward von Toll was appointed as his assistant. At the end of 1884, von Toll left St Petersburg, and went through Irkutsk, Yakutsk, and Verkhoyansk, and came to the Kazach'je settlement. Here, he spent the winter of 1885–1886 preparing for the voyage to the Novosybirskye Islands. By March 1886, 20 sledges and 240 sled dogs were accumulated near Cape Svyatoy Nos. In the middle of May 1886, the travelers reached Kotel'ny Island.

The year 1886 was characterized by heavy ice conditions in the region of the Novosibirskiye Islands; Sannikov's Strait and Big Lyakhov Island were covered by ice throughout the summer. Regardless of the difficult weather conditions during the summer of 1886, von Bunge researched the Lyakhov Islands, while von Toll traveled all around Kotel'ny, Fadeevsky, and Novaya Sybir' Islands. He named the low sandy plain as "Bunge's Land." Various geological observations followed and paleontology specimens were collected. At the beginning of August 1886, von Toll saw, completely distinct from the northwest shore of Kotel'ny Island in the sea, the contours of four mountains joined to the low plain. From that time, he believed in the existence of a mysterious "Sannikov's Land." His Evenk guide V. Gergeli also saw this land many times.

The Bunge-Toll expedition in 1885–1886 brought back enormous amounts of scientific data that clarified the geological structure, flora, and fauna of the Novosibirskiye Archipelago. Returning from this expedition, von Toll went to Germany in 1887–1888. On April 19, 1889 he was elected as a member of the Imperial Russian Geographical Society. In 1890, during the International Geographical Congress, von Toll made the acquaintance of Fridtjof Nansen, who was preparing for his famous expedition on *Fram*. Nansen asked von Toll about the details on the ice and weather conditions in the eastern part of the Laptev Sea and ow has over 300,000 visitors every year. In the , Greenland received over 3000 tourists annual- 35,000 tourists per year are expected in the first e of the 21st century. In Alaska, the number of s has increased by 50% since the mid-1980s to l million a year (more than 1.4 million in 2001). The increase in cruise ship travel is the ry driver of growth in Alaskan tourism, with an l growth rate of 11.69% since 1991.

lay, most Arctic countries promote themselves rist destinations through government-run depart- of tourism. However, the emergence of locally l and controlled tour companies has given many nous communities opportunities to diversify economies as traditional subsistence activities e increasingly marginalized, and at the same ain control of an industry that outsiders have vise dominated. In this way, local communities ginning to use tourism to develop strategies for etermination and cultural survival. Tourism is onsidered to play an important role in strategies th sustainable development and environmental vation, and sustainable tourism projects are sup- l by the Arctic Council.

lopment of Tourism

ts have been traveling in the Arctic for pleasure, ture, or geographical and personal discovery since t the mid-19th century, when small expeditions l steamers and whaling boats visited Alaska and rd. As more steamer services became available Yukon River, as well as more extensive coastal , tourists were able to visit remote parts of Alaska, s Nome, the Aleutian Islands, and the interior, had previously been accessible only to explorers, sts, the military, and government officials. The entury growth in Arctic tourism was fueled not by improved access and ease of travel, but by a for a "last frontier," and popular writings by early ers, adventurers, and literary figures such as Jack n, John Muir, and Robert Service.

e image of a vast forbidding wilderness, a land of ual cold and darkness, has contributed much to peal of Arctic and Subarctic regions as tourist ations. Such images are reinforced by tour com- , who market the Arctic as a land of superlatives tremes, where nature can still be experienced as d pristine. The media attention created by the dramatic attempts at reaching the North Pole no also contributed to the growing interest in visit- aces such as Svalbard, Greenland, and northern a as a tourist. Synonymous with the idea of the rn regions as the last frontier is the history of pioneers. Tourism development in Alaska and

the Yukon Territory has capitalized on nostalgia asso- ciated with the gold rush and the idea of the Arctic as a frontier, with mines, pipelines, oil production com- plexes, and military installations all packaged as industrial heritage for touristic consumption, while former gulags (labor camps) such as those at Perm and on the Solovetsky Islands aim to prevent people from forgetting the horrors of the communist system.

At the start of the 21st century, the variety of tourist activities is wide and diverse, ranging from sightsee- ing in urban areas, specialized adventure tourism, guided walking, wildlife, ornithological tours, sport fishing and sport hunting, cruise ships, dog mushing, cross-country skiing, and visits to Santa Claus (claimed variously for Rovaniemi Santa Claus Park, in northern Finland, Santa Claus House in North Pole, a small town in Alaska and Uummannaq and Nuuk in Greenland). Increasingly, tour companies offer "cul- tural tourism," so-called ecotourism (ecological or environmentally responsible tourism), and "sustain- able tourism." Travelers may arrive by air, by cruise ship, by highway, or by ski tour to the North Pole. The Alaska Highway, constructed during World War II to provide, through Canada, a land link for the military between Alaska and the rest of the United States, has become an adventure in itself. Some 10% of summer visitors to Alaska enter by road from Canada, in camper vans and recreation vehicles. Cruise ships attempt to sail through the North West Passage, Russia's Northern Sea Route, and also break their way through the ice to the North Pole.

Impacts of Tourism

Tourism requires infrastructural changes, for example, transport and accommodation. However, it is a com- monplace remark that tourism contributes to social change and the destruction of the very things that the industry both promotes and depends upon, such as local cultures and the natural environment. Ironically, since many Arctic travelers seek the chance to visit places not yet accessible to the "tourist," regions that were once "remote" and "untouched" are also threat- ened by the inevitable encroachment of mass tourism as tour companies capitalize on this desire.

The appearance of tourists is mainly seasonal, and during summer months may involve a high proportion of local people in servicing directly, and indirectly, the needs and demands of tourists, rather than indigenous- ly generated needs. In this way, tourism produces dependency relationships, and local people may also become dependent on outsiders for seasonal or long- term employment when primary industries such as fishing decline. Tourism often develops in areas at the same time as they are experiencing rapid social

shared with him a plan to reach the North Pole on a ship specially equipped for prolonged drift, frozen into sea ice. Von Toll was also asked by Nansen to help him with the delivery of sled dogs from Siberia.

In 1892, the Russian Academy of Science sent von Toll to northern Yakutia for the description and trans- portation of a mammoth's body, which was discovered near the Cape of Svyatoy Nos in 1889, to St Petersburg. Along the way, the scientist made an agreement with two Norwegian hunters Alexander I. Trontheym and I. Tor'ersen, who lived in Siberia, about the delivery of sled dogs for Nansen to Khabarovo and to the Olenek River mouth.

In the spring of 1893, von Toll and hydrographer Evgeny A. Shileyko made a trip to Kotel'ny Island for the continuation of geological investigations and for the preparation of the provision depots for Nansen. Siberian gold industrialist Nikolay F. Kelkh paid the expenses for the depots. Von Toll made two depots on Kotel'ny Island and one more on Maly Lyakhov Island. During this voyage, he significantly augment- ed his geological survey of the region.

During the return journey, von Toll and Shileyko crossed virtually unknown regions of northern Yakutia along the route from Bulun to the mouth settlement (Olenek River), the mouth of Anabar River, Khatanga, and on to Dudinka, and made various investigations. The total length of this voyage was more than 25,000 km. E.A. Shileyko also determined 38 astronomical positions. This expedition strengthened von Toll's con- fidence about the existence of "Sannikov's Land."

Two books published in 1897–1899 ("The fossil ice of Novosibirskiye Islands, their relationship to mam- moth's dead bodies and glacial period" and "Essay of Novosibirsky Archipelago's geology and fundamental tasks of polar regions exploration") were the result of von Toll's two polar expeditions. These explorations remained the fundamental and practically the only work concerning geology, geomorphology, and paleo- geography of Novosibirskiye Islands till the 1950s.

The Russian Geographical Society awarded von Toll and Shileyko the N.M. Przheval'sky Grand Silver Medal and a monetary prize for the successful expedi- tion of 1893.

In the summer of 1896, von Toll was sent by the Russian Geographical Society on an official journey to Norway. There, in August, he took part in the ceremo- nial greeting of Nansen and *Fram*. The Norwegian gov- ernment gave von Toll an award for his help to Nansen.

In May 1899, admiral S.O. Makarov invited von Toll to take part in the first navigation of icebreaker *Ermak* from Tromsø to the region of west Spitsbergen. During this voyage, *Ermak* reached 81°28′ N.

The idea of reaching "Sannikov's Land" was still alive in von Toll's mind. In 1898, he proposed to the

Russian Geographical Society the organization of a large polar expedition, during which explorations would reach this land, overwinter and inspect it in detail, and then to return to Vladivostok. In 1900, such an expedition was organized and was named the Russian Polar Expedition. Its main goals were various scientific explorations of northern Taymyr and the Novosibirskiye Islands and to search for the hypothet- ical "Sannikov's Land."

On June 21, 1900, the schooner *Zarya* left St Petersburg, which marked the beginning of von Toll's last expedition (see Russian Polar Expedition, 1900–1902). Despite the enormous scientific material collected by the participants, the accomplishments of this expedition were darkened by the death of six men—von Toll, astronomer F.G. Zeeberg, guides Nikolai Protod'yakonov and Vasily Gorokhov (in the autumn of 1902, they apparently drowned in the sea on the way from Bennett Island to the New Sibir' Island), doctor German E. Valter (died from a heart attack dur- ing the wintering in the beginning of January of 1902), and stoker Trofim Nosov (who, by accident, was wounded by sailor Nikolay Bezborodov and died from gangrene in September 1902). On its return, the schooner *Zarya* could not enter the mouth of the Lena River due to its large draught and decrepit hull; there- fore, the crew left it in Tiksi Bay and this legendary ship was later destroyed by sea waves. Its remnants could be seen for many years until the beginning of the 1940s.

Nowadays, more and more researchers have con- cluded that as head of the Russian Polar Expedition, von Toll made some erroneous decisions, which led this well-equipped expedition to such disastrous results. Toll could not get along with *Zarya*'s captain Nikolay N. Kolomeytsev and sent him off to Dixon Island to organize a provision depot, although it had already been passed by the ship. Had he made such a depot on Kotel'ny Island, *Zarya* would have been more mobile. Captain Fyodor A. Matisen said that Toll had simply wanted to leave the ship because it became a burden to him. Analyses of the remains of the expedi- tion on Bennett Island led to the conclusion that there had been a conflict between Toll, Zeeberg, and the guides, which accelerated the death of the group.

The reasons for the disappearance of von Toll's group are still not entirely clear. However, his scientif- ic works through exploration of the Novosibirskiye Islands' nature remain a valuable source.

Biography

Edward (Eduard Vasiljevich) von Toll was born on March 2 (14), 1858 in Revel (now Tallinn, Estonia). He graduated from the natural history department of Derpt University and, at first, worked in marine zoology. In

1882, he investigated Mediterranean fauna and the geological structure of Menorka Island. For this research, he was granted a Ph.D. degree. In 1885–1886 he was a member of the first Russian Expedition to the Novosibirskiye Islands. In 1887–1888, he studied the geological structure of the Harz and Thuringian forests. In 1892–1893, he explored the nature of northern Yakutiya and Kotel'ny Island. During 1895–1896, he investigated the geological structure in Latvia on the shore of Riga's Bay of Baltic Sea and around the town of Mitava (Elgava). He is presumed to have drowned in 1902 in the East Siberian Sea.

FEDOR ROMANENKO

See also **Bunge, Alexander von; Russian Polar Expedition, 1900–1901**

Further Reading

Chaykovsky, Yu.V., "Pochemu pogib Eduard Toll?" [Why was Edward Toll lost?]. *Voprosy istorii estestvoznaniya i tekhniki* [Problems of natural science and technical history], 1 (1991): 3–14

"Russkaya polyarnaya expeditsiya na yakhte Zarya pod nachal'stvom E.V. Tollya (1900–1903)" [Russian Polar Expedition on the Yacht "Zarya" headed by E.V. Toll (1900–1903)]. In *Istoriya otkrytiya i osvoeniya Severnogo Morskogo Puti* [History of Discovery and Development of the Northern Sea Route], Chapter 14 edited by Ya.Ya. Gakkel' & M.B. Chernenko, Volume II, Leningrad, 1962

Shparo, D.I. & A.V. Shumilov, *Tri zagadki Arktiki* [Three mysteries of Arctic], Moscow, 1982

Toll, E.V., *Die Russische Polarfahrt der "Sarja" 1900–1902. Aus den hinterlassenen Tagebuchern*, Berlin, 1909

———, *Plavanie na yakhte "Zarya"* [Yacht "Zarya" Navigation], Moscow, 1959

Vittenburg, P.V., *Zhizn' i nauchnaya deyatel'nost' E.V.Tollya* [The life and scientific activities of E.V.Toll], Moscow, 1960 (in Russian)

TORELL, OTTO

Before the middle of the 19th century, despite the efforts of figures such as the German geologist Karl Ludwig Giesecke and the Swedish zoologist Sven Lovén, the study of science did not hold pride of place in the investigations of the polar regions. It tended to be carried out in addition to the prescribed duties of naval officers or others on voyages in the north, and, as stated in a memorandum from the Admiralty, did not "require the use of nice apparatus and instruments…so that men merely of good intelligence and fair acquirement may be able to act upon them" (Herschel, 1871: iii–iv). Swedish glacial geologist Otto Torell was one scientist who contributed to the reversal of this tendency; he proposed the scientific study of the Arctic as a goal and not just as a supplement to commercial or geographical investigations.

Born on June 5, 1828, Torell grew up in the coastal town of Varberg in southwestern Sweden. The young

Torell was precocious: at the age of only 16, he entered Lund University, where he studied with Sven Lovén, who introduced him to the study of marine invertebrates. Torell's study of marine fauna indicated to him that the climate in southern Scandinavia had once been similar to that of the Arctic, and led him to the then unorthodox speculation that an Ice Age had occurred in that area. Little fieldwork had been carried out in this area of research, and Torell determined to study glaciers and inland ice, including their deposits and striae, in a variety of geographical regions. His field observations were to lay the foundation for the modern understanding of the Pleistocene glaciations.

In 1856, Torell began his fieldwork with a trip to Switzerland. The next year, he spent nearly six months traveling in Iceland, investigating glaciers, glacial geology, and local marine zoology. The year 1858 witnessed his most important expedition yet. For three months, he and his party studied the west coast of Spitsbergen from the Norwegian fishing boat *Frithjof*. Perhaps the most important aspect of this trip was that it introduced two of Torell's young colleagues to the Arctic: the zoologist August Quennerstedt and the mineralogist Adolf Erik Nordenskiöld. The party collected a vast number of plant and animal fossils on both land and sea. These were used not only for helping to date the geological strata of the island but also for determining the climatic conditions that had previously existed.

After a research trip to Greenland in 1859, Torell organized and led the most ambitious scientific expedition that had ever been sent to the Arctic. Unlike his earlier expeditions, which Torell had funded himself, the Swedish Arctic Expedition of 1861 received contributions from the Swedish Parliament and Crown Prince Oscar, and gained the approval of the Royal Swedish Academy of Sciences, the Royal Geographical Society in London, and a variety of other major scientific bodies. The expedition included nine scientists (an unprecedented number), including Nordenskiöld, who was second-in-command.

The Swedish Arctic Expedition embraced three objectives: a comprehensive scientific investigation of Spitsbergen and the seas around it; a reconnaissance for establishing a triangulation network for future measurements of an arc of meridian; and a geographical excursion to the north. The plan was unique both in its emphasis on science and in the careful distinction between its scientific and geographical aims. Further, it was designed so that the scientific studies—most importantly those of land ice, zoology, and botany, but also including geomagnetics, meteorology, and oceanography—could be accomplished even if the geographical survey proved impossible.

The expedition left Norway on May 10, on two ships: the brigantine *Aeolus* and the yacht *Magdalena*.

They sailed up the west coast of Spitsbergen before finding shelter in Sorgfjorden on the northeast corner of the island. When after a wait of some weeks the excursion northward had to be forsaken due to difficult ice conditions, the two ships parted company to work in different sections of the archipelago. The five scientists aboard *Magdalena* carried out studies first in Wijdefjorden and then, successively as they headed south, in Magdalenefjorden, Smeerenburgfjorden, Krossfjorden, Kongsfjorden, and the vicinity of Isfjorden. They then headed north to meet *Aeolus* near Dansköya.

In the meantime, *Aeolus*, with Torell and Nordenskiöld, sailed to the previously little-known Murchisonfjorden, where the participants divided into three groups to investigate the northern and western parts of Nordaustlandet and the area of Hinlopenstretet. A geographical-geological group consisted of Torell, Nordenskiöld, the Danish Arctic expert Carl Petersen (famed for his participation in several Franklin searches), and four crew. Two excursions in a small boat (July 10–23, and July 27–August 24) gathered an exceptional amount of data, giving rise to the future use of small craft in such scientific operations. From July 11, to August 23, Karl Chydenius, using another small boat and also taking four men, led the reconnaissance for a future arc measurement. Meanwhile, *Aeolus* moved carefully around Hinlopenstretet and off northwestern Nordaustlandet, primarily conducting biological excursions under Anders Malmgren. The party united in late August, met up with *Magdalena* at Dansköya, and then they all returned to Norway.

The scientific program of the Swedish Arctic Expedition had exceeded all expectations and resulted in a wealth of data in a wide variety of scientific disciplines. Moreover, Torell's pattern of comprehensive investigation was assumed by Nordenskiöld and eventually became the model for other European and American scientific expeditions. In fact, the significance of the expedition was such that paleobotanist A.G. Nathorst claimed: "With Torell's expedition of 1861 scientific polar research had been founded. The radical influence which this research had on the various areas of research in the natural sciences can only be hinted at' (Nathorst, 1900: 458).

Despite its success, the expedition of 1861 was Torell's last scientific investigation in the Arctic. When the Swedish government sent another expedition in 1864, it ignored Torell—despite the ideas having been his as well as the funding of much of the earlier research—and selected Nordenskiöld as its leader. Torell returned to his position at Lund University, where he was made professor in zoology and geology in 1866. In 1871, he was appointed head of the Geological Survey of Sweden, where he remained until

1897. During this time, he att[...] for his research into the Weich[...]

Biography

Otto Martin Torell was born [...] June 5, 1828. At the age of on[...] University, where he became [...] rounding the most recent Pleis[...] organizing and funding sci[...] Switzerland (1856), Iceland [...] (1858), and Greenland (1859), [...] Arctic Expedition of 1861 to S[...] dition established the pattern o[...] tigation that later became [...] European and American scient[...] rise to Torell being credited as [...] scientific polar exploration. A[...] did not return to the Arctic, bu[...] of zoology and geology at Lund [...] head of the Geological Survey [...] earned an international reputatic[...] to the most recent Ice Age. He [...] 1900 at Charlottendal, near Sto[...]

See also **Nordenskiöld, Adolf [...]**

Further Reading

Chydenius, Karl, *Svenska expeditione[...] under ledning af Otto Torell [...] Spitsbergen in the Year 1861 Und[...] Torell], Stockholm: P.A. Norstedt, [...]

Herschel, John, *A Manual of Scientif[...] the Use of Officers in Her Majesty[...] General* (4th edition), London: Joh[...]

Holmström, Leonard, "Otto Torell." [...] *Förhandlingar*, 23 (1901): 391–46[...]

Liljequist, Gosta H., High Latitudes[...] Polar Travels and Research, Sto[...] Research Secretariat, 1993

Nathorst, Alfred, "Otto Torell, den [...] forskningens grundläggre." *Ymer*, 2[...]

Quennerstedt, August, "Minnen från er[...] 1858." *Lunds Studentkalender*, 1 (1[...]

TOURISM

Tourism is the world's fastest gro[...] expanding into the circumpol[...] extremely high costs of travel al[...] hotel infrastructure have in the pas[...] of visitors to the High Arctic, the c[...] tourism in the second half of the 2[...] search for remote or "untouched[...] tremendous growth. For example, [...] just a few thousand visitors each [...]

change, and while it contributes to social and economic transition, the success of tourism can become necessary for the economic survival of some areas.

Arctic Tourism and Economic Development

Tourism is important for the economic development of Arctic regions. For example, tourism is currently Alaska's major growth industry, generating $1.6 billion in revenues each year. While most Arctic visitors arrive in summer, tourism industry officials increasingly promote local winter sporting events for international tourists, such as annual dog sledding races (e.g., the Iditarod and the Yukon Quest), the annual Arctic Team Challenge in Ammassalik in East Greenland, and the Drambuie Ice Golf Championship, played on the sea ice in Uummannaq in northwest Greenland, while tourists are attracted to various parts of the Arctic in the coldest, darkest months to view the aurora borealis.

In northern Scandinavia, tourism has long been well-established and both local Scandinavians and indigenous Saami people rely heavily on the industry during the summer months.

In Greenland, while future exploitation of nonrenewable resources is as yet uncertain, tourism is seen to provide a lucrative and immediate source of revenue. In 1992, Greenland Tourism, a Home Rule-owned company was established to develop and coordinate tourism in the country. A development of this scale requires major infrastructural changes, for example, in transportation and accommodation. At present, most visits are short term, with the majority of tourists arriving on cruise ships or on guided excursions. Although an increase in tourism would bring much-needed revenue to the country, it could also result in specific problems if allowed to go unchecked. This is true for other parts of the Arctic.

Svalbard has been popular as a cruise-ship destination since the 1890s. From the 1990s, increasingly larger vessels brought 15,000–20,000 passengers annually, and helicopters and light aircraft can be chartered for sightseeing and trips to other settlements. New hotels have sprung up in Longyearbyen.

Parts of Siberia and Russia's Far East long closed to foreign visitors only became open in 1991 following perestroika (the policy of economic and governmental reform instituted by Mikhail Gorbachev in the Soviet Union in the mid-1980s). Travel on the Trans-Siberian Express from Moscow to Vladivostok or vice versa has always been a popular way of traveling through Russia, with the opportunity now to stop at cities and towns previously barred. Tourism in Chukotka and Yakutia (Sakha Republic) is currently undeveloped due to the harsh winter climate, long distances, the lack of infrastructure, inaccessibility, and dependence on air transport, but has large potential for cultural tourism in

relation to indigenous crafts (whale ivory carving), subsistence lifestyle, and wildlife tours. The last decade of the 20th century witnessed a tremendous growth in ecotourism in northern Russia. The Kamchatka volcanoes and, in particular, the geysers in Kronotsky National Park are popular destinations, and in 2002, Kamchatka companies invested $2.3 million in local tourism infrastructure development (construction of small hotels and bases, and purchase of necessary tourism equipment). Expedition cruises travel around Chukotka, Kamchatka, and the Kuril islands, and occasional icebreaker tours travel to the nature reserve on Wrangel Island.

Hunting tourism is popular in Chukotka and Kamchatka, with trophy hunting by foreign hunters and wildlife viewing by eco tourists. World Wildlife Fund/Russian Far East under a grant from USAID assisted many of the nature preserves in the Khabarovsk and Primorsk krays to build the necessary infrastructure and trails to host small groups of ecotravelers and student groups.

Community-Based Tourism

Indigenous culture is increasingly popular as the main attraction after scenery and wildlife, with tourists striving to experience reality and to have less superficial contact with people and places. Such ethnographic tourism has been well documented by anthropologists and sociologists. There is a growing market eager to consume images of indigenous peoples and to understand something of their relationship with the environment.

The remoteness of Arctic villages (many of which are only accessible by air) and traditional Native culture is attractive to tourists in search of authenticity. However in general, it is very difficult for travelers to visit Native villages independently; for example, there are virtually no roads in Kamchakta, and all transport must be by helicopter. In the United States, the Alaska Native Claims Settlement Act of 1971 made many villages and their lands in effect private reserves, often making it necessary for visitors to have permits before entering a community.

A currently fashionable argument in social science tourist literature is that tourism done well and with community participation can empower local communities. Arctic tourism represents an interesting test case as to the effectiveness of this, as in many parts, such as Alaska, Canada, and Greenland, indigenous communities are participating in environmental and cultural tourism projects at both the planning and implementation stages, as well as benefiting from the outcome. Nickels et al. (1991) have described how tourism development in Baffin Island in Canada's eastern Arctic is viewed by residents of Inuit communities as a potentially viable industry. While people remain ambivalent about the cultural and environmental impacts, their main fears "revolve around the potential lack of community involvement in the industry and the possibility that tourists may break local rules" (Nickels et. al, 1991: 166).

Capitalizing on tradition, local heritage, and wildlife as a tourism resource and determined that communities should benefit directly from tourism, several Native-owned tour companies have also emerged in Alaska over the last few years, and offer examples of community tourism development for other parts of the Arctic. Many of these companies are owned by village corporations, which were established as profit-making enterprises by the Alaska Native Claims Settlement Act of 1971. Alaska Native communities see tourism as an opportunity for developing cash-earning enterprises based on the desire of other people to experience wilderness and visit non-Western societies, and at the same time it allows local people to gain control of an industry that outsiders have otherwise dominated and profited from. Linked to indigenous political movements that emphasize the importance of indigenous knowledge for sustainable development, locally controlled tourism also represents an opportunity for Arctic communities to educate visitors about indigenous ways of life and about human-environment relationships. Alaskan Native leaders see the local control of tourism as an industry that can form part of diversified local economies and at the same time regulate the numbers of visitors to Native lands (Nuttall, 1998). Local communities are increasingly supported in their efforts by the State of Alaska Division of Community and Economic Development, which produces the *Alaska Community Tourism Handbook*, with advice on how to develop tourism in small, rural communities.

Conclusion

Research into the possible environmental, economic, and cultural impacts is necessary and appropriate management structures and policies need to be adopted if tourism is to proceed in the best interests of communities and the environment.

As tourism grows in areas seldom used to visitors other than scientists, government officials, and the occasional adventurer, serious questions need addressing. Will resource management decisions meet the needs of the tourism industry first, and the needs of local people second? Will tourism in remote Arctic regions create dependency relationships? How sustainable can tourism really be? How possible is it to balance social and environmental needs with economic profit and the survival of the tourism industry? How far will tourism transform, revitalize, or redefine indigenous culture? How far will community members be consulted and be made aware of tourism development plans? As local communities, tourism boards, and tour operators work to adopt policies and guidelines to ensure sustainable tourism development, answers to some of these questions may result from promising work currently being carried out under the auspices of the Arctic Council's Sustainable Development Working Group (SDWG) project "Ecological and Cultural Tourism." This project aims to develop a framework for sustainable Arctic tourism called SMART (Sustainable Model for Arctic Regional Tourism), defined by a set of common principles and supported by a set of best practice and resulting benefits. One objective is to define sustainable tourism practices and to award businesses in the tourism sector for achieving them, possibly through an Arctic-market recognition scheme for sustainable tourism businesses. SMART will assist mainly local small-to-medium-sized businesses in the Arctic tourism sector to adopt economically, environmentally, and culturally sensitive tourism practices, as well as create tools and resources to be used by local businesses in tourism development and in vocational training programs.

MARK NUTTALL

See also **Alaska Native Claims Settlement Act (ANCSA); Arctic Council; Aurora; Economic development; Handicrafts/Tourist Art; Images of Indigenous Peoples; Images of the Arctic; Labor Camps; London, Jack; North Pole; Service, Robert; Sustainable Development**

Further Reading

Grenier, A., *Ship-Based Polar Tourism in the Northeast Passage—A Case Study*, Rovaniemi: University of Lapland, 1998

Hall, C.M. & M.E. Johnston (editors), *Polar Tourism: Tourism in the Arctic and Antarctic Regions*, Chichester: Wiley, 1995

Nickels, S., S. Milne & G. Wenzel, "Inuit perceptions of tourism development: the case of Clyde River, Baffin Island, N.W.T." *Etudes Inuit Studies*, 15(1) (1991): 157–169

Nuttall, M. *Protecting the Arctic: Indigenous Peoples and Cultural Survival*, London and New York: Harwood, 1998

TRADE

For hundreds of years, international trade in the Arctic was an appendix to indigenous peoples' subsistence economies and a barter economy with neighboring tribes and early explorers. Foreign trade from the 16th century was driven by southern traders or explorers in search of trade routes, and based on the exchange of luxury or scarce items from the Arctic (sea otter, polar bear, beaver, marten, and fox furs; whale and walrus ivory; falcons for hunting; reindeer meat and skins;

train oil rendered from whale blubber) for ordinary southern consumer goods (such as alcohol, sugar, tobacco, and from the beginning of the 1830s, coffee) and for weapons for hunting. Taxation by Russia and Sweden on their northern colonies was also paid in the natural resources of the region.

By the time of the Industrial Revolution, Europe needed increased energy for lighting, and foreign trade shifted character. Whaling became essential, to supply oil for Europe's lamps. This marked the start of the regime, still ongoing, with the Arctic as a hinterland resource for economic development at more southern latitudes. This regime is now concentrated on minerals—metals and precious stones—and on energy, but also includes other primary products from forestry and fisheries.

The international Arctic trade regime includes exports from Arctic territorial lands that have few primary resources of high quality, and imports of all types of consumer and investment goods from southern centers. It is an export-import pattern similar to that found in many underdeveloped countries. Each of the various economies of the crcumpolar North has a specialization: in Alaska it is salmon, metals, and oil and gas; in Canada forestry, metals, and energy; in Greenland shrimp; in Iceland cod; in Norway cod, salmon, and energy; in Sweden iron and forestry; in Finland forestry; and in Russia minerals and energy. Only Iceland, Norway, and Alaska have managed to diversify their production base, mainly by the development of tourism and of knowledge-intensive third-sector private goods productions.

The trade is characterized by investments from the southern centers in the Arctic states and by transportation systems, with logistics being designed and decided outside the Arctic and without Arctic ownership (although this is not the case in Iceland). As a consequence, the main capital accumulation from trade takes place outside the circumpolar North.

Volume of Trade and Balance of Payments

International trade is primarily a decisive factor in the developed countries of the Western World, but world trade and trade in relation to GDP are world wide—including in the Arctic—increasing. All economies develop to become more open, that is, exports and imports in relation to GDP are increasing. Furthermore, the volume of tradables compared to nontradables is increasing. Although the volume of trade is increasing all over the Arctic, the Arctic economies as well as many underdeveloped countries have difficulties in achieving the same dynamics in the trade development as the developed economies in general. There are three main reasons for this delay in

dynamics: the Arctic economies are less diversified; export of raw material is a derived demand from business cycles, making prices more volatile; and nontradables compared to tradables in the Arctic mixed economies, in Greenland, and in Russia are a larger fraction of the production than the averages found in most Western economies.

Only Iceland and Alaska have complete balance of payments accounts. Greenland has with respect to merchandise, but only rudimentary information concerning services. Norway, Sweden, and Finland have national account information at the county level. Canada has information on interprovincial trade. For Russia, no valid information exists. Iceland and Alaska have managed their balance of payments problems. Yukon has a surplus. Greenland has a deficit, which is covered by the block grant from the Danish state.

Management of Trade

Foreign trade followed early expeditions to explore the Arctic. As these expeditions were normally financed by the state, the state has been heavily involved in Arctic foreign trade from the start. The general development has been firstly state financed, then monopoly trade based on state licenses or establishment of trade companies, and finally a more free trade-based system with different degrees of regulation. Exceptions are Russia and Greenland, Russia because of the command economy and Greenland because of the Danish administration of the colony, Greenland being until 1953 the only part of the circumpolar North having a formal colonial status.

The heavy state impact and responsibilities on trade are still found in many Arctic trade structures: (1) Trade in Alaska—and Canada but to a less degree—mirrors a *market* economic system, trade in Russia mirrors a *command* economy system, and trade in Iceland, Norway, Sweden, and Finland mirrors a *mixed* economy system. The Greenland system is unique in character. (2) Trade has a military dimension, implying a weight on domestic trade compared to international trade, and with the international trade relations decided in the centers of the states and often at the political level and not in the Arctic. (3) Trade has a social element, a survival dimension with focus on procurement and delivery. (4) In the present-day international foreign trade relations and institutional setup—NAFTA (The North American Free Trade Agreement) for Alaska and Canada, the EU (European Union) for Iceland, Norway, Sweden, and Finland (only Sweden and Finland are members of the EU, but Norway and Iceland are included in the EEA (European Economic Agreement) or European Economic Space including free trade of goods inside the EU), Russia by the WTO relation—all the eight

Arctic states are members of the WTO (World Trade Organization).

Today, international trade in the Russian Arctic is, to a large degree, a result of bilateral agreements and a rather uncontrolled capitalism due to laws and institutions not being in place after the end of the command economy epoch. Greenland has a rather unique setup. Denmark is a member of the EU and so was Greenland originally. The Faroe Islands, part of the Danish Realm and since 1948 with Home Rule, was able to decide for itself if they wanted EU membership when Denmark joined the EU in 1973, and they said no. At that time, the negotiations on Home Rule for Greenland had started, and Greenland was promised a referendum on membership when Home Rule was established. The Greenlanders also voted no to EU membership and consequently, after prolonged negotiations, Greenland left the EU in 1983. Greenland is the only jurisdiction that has ever left the EU. Greenland is a member of the WTO and has an OLT-OCT agreement.

Greenland Foreign Trade

Greenland foreign trade is dealt with here specifically, because it is unique and also throws the other foreign trade systems in relief. Private merchants from the Danish Realm followed in the footsteps of expeditions to explore Greenland from the mid-1600s. When Hans Egede came to Greenland in 1721, the main purpose was to baptise the Inuit. This implied establishment of a new social structure that also set rules for trade. The main focus was to protect the Inuit from violence exerted by foreigners. As his brother Niels Egede was one of the largest merchants at that time, the rules were set from an inside knowledge on foreign trade. Also, the Herrnhuter missionaries from Germany who later came to South Greenland established trading rules, which is why trade rested on Danish law plus societal regulation in Greenland for hundreds of years. However, in the 1770s, it was felt in Denmark that a closer agreement between the regulation in Denmark and in Greenland was needed, and the Royal Greenland Trade Company was established as a state company in 1774 (see **Royal Greenland Trade Company**). The basic idea was a state trade monopoly, and as such it functioned till 1948. It implied that trade was based on exchange ratios: not on world market prices, but on administered prices. In 1782, it was formalized in "Instrux til Handelen og Hvalfangerne på Grønland" (Act on the Relations between the Royal Greenland Trade Company and the Whalers). It ordered fixed prices throughout Greenland. The monopoly and fixed price construction were not undisputed. Especially in the 1830s, when most of the trade monopolies ended their days, it was also heavily debated in Denmark whether the monopoly should continue. Some private merchants wanted to break the monopoly, referring to the new liberal trade regimes in Europe. In 1851, a law was passed by the Danish Parliament that free trade should be allowed in Greenland; however, the Danish state inspector in Greenland, Hinrich Johannes Rink, was against it, and succeeded in having a flexible adjustment period connected to the law. It was an effective delay and as the oil prices, which was the reason for the Danish merchants' interest, started to fall, the discussion ended and the implementation of the law was never effectuated. It implied that private international trade did not come to Greenland. In 1906, a new arrangement was discussed, a split between administration and trade, and it became law in 1908. The idea was that trade should be in balance. However, already in 1912 it was given up, as it was found impossible to make this split. In 1925, it was decided that if trade was run with surplus, the surplus should be used to the benefit of the Greenlanders. In order to avoid price volatility influencing the life of Greenlandres, still more administered prices were added . A system developed without any true market prices. Even today, this system is the basis for prices in Greenland. It is the *ensprissystemet*, whereby all over Greenland the prices of the same products in the Home Rule-owned shops (the rest of the old Royal Greenland Trade Company) are uniform. However, today privately owned shops in most towns in Greenland buy their goods wholesale in the Home Rule-owned trade corporation. Only the cooperative society has their own delivery from the Danish cooperative system. The old monopoly for ship transportation is today practiced by another Home Rule-owned company named Royal Arctic Line Ltd. The implication of these systems is that price competition almost does not exist in Greenland and that prices do not relate to market prices. The system is very problematic for Royal Greenland Ltd., the Home Rule-owned corporation that exports Greenlandic prawns and has to sell at market prices.

The prices in Greenland were set to protect people from the consequences of competition; the idea was that prices should not mirror market interests but the Greenland people's needs. In the former Soviet Union, prices were also administered, not however for the benefit of people living in the Russian North but for the benefit of all Russians. The reason for administered prices in Greenland is still the reason for people in Greenland wanting to continue the present price system.

The Arctic and Globalization

Globalization is the regime of today. It implies that international economic relations include international foreign trade as well as foreign direct investments.

Alaska has foreign direct investments from corporations as well as from transnational corporations. So has Russia, but at a much lower level. The Canadian foreign investments are mainly from the United States and from transnational corporations. Foreign direct investments in Greenland are almost nonexistent. The level of foreign direct investments in the Arctic territories of the Nordic states is relatively low, Iceland included. Globalization is most dominant in Alaska (at a mature level) and in Russia (at the very first level). Iceland has a high level of outward-oriented globalization with a modest level of inward globalization. Greenland still has a pronounced bilateral relation to Denmark concerning trade as well as investments. The Arctic territories of the other Arctic states are more characterized by internationalization than by globalization.

LISE LYCK

See also **Globalization and the Arctic**

Further Reading

ISER (Institute of Social and Economic Research publications) reports, books and periodicals from 1961 to 2001

Lyck, Lise (editor), *Constitutional and Economic Space for the Small Nordic Jurisdictions*, Stockholm: Nordrefo, 1997

———, *Arctic International Trade*, New Social Science Monographs, Copenhagen: Copenhagen Business School, 1999

Statistics Canada, *Interprovincial Trade in Canada 1984–1996*, Ottawa: Ministry of Industry, Government of Canada, 1998

Statistiske årbøger, Grønlands Statistik (Statistical Yearbooks, The Greenland Statistical Bureau, Nuuk)

TRANS-ALASKA PIPELINE

The Trans-Alaska Pipeline runs 800 miles (1300 km) south across the state of Alaska from Prudhoe Bay on the Arctic Ocean to the ice-free deep sea port at Valdez, on the Gulf of Alaska. The pipeline, which is both above and below ground, has a 48-inch diameter and a design life of 30 years. The volume of oil flowing through the pipe was about 1 million barrels per day as of 2001. The pipeline is owned by the Alyeska Pipeline Service Company, which was responsible for design and construction, and is responsible for the operation and maintenance of the pipeline. The company employs more than 2000 people (2000) in Alaska, and is a joint venture between six pipeline companies.

Oil revenues are the major source of income to Alaska. In 1999, the state received nearly $1 billion in revenue from oil production. Since oil production began on the North Slope in 1977, the state has received more than $46 billion in taxes and royalties. The flow from this pipeline accounts for 17% (2001) of annual US oil production.

The need for a pipeline to exploit the Alaskan oil reserves was accelerated in 1973 by the OPEC embargo of oil to the United States. Between the time that oil was first discovered at Prudhoe Bay in 1968, and 1973, the project was delayed due to the absence of any agreement on a pipeline route and the need for an environmental impact statement. From April 29, 1974 when construction began, the time required to complete the construction of the pipeline, pump stations, access roads, and marine terminal was 3 years and 2 months (to June 20, 1977). The Trans-Alaska Pipeline was the largest privately financed construction project at the time with a total cost of $8 billion (1977 US dollars). The northern part of the pipeline parallels the Dalton Highway, which was planned to service pipeline construction.

The construction workforce peaked at 28,072 in October 1975. A total of 29 construction camps were used during construction, which varied in size from 3480 beds to 112 beds. The total weight of materials shipped to Alaska was approximately 3 million tons; the largest single piece shipped was a floating tanker berth weighing 3250 tons. The gravel used for the entire project was approximately 73 million cubic yards in total.

Transporting oil at temperatures warm enough to maintain an even flow rate meant that in permafrost soils, the pipe could not be buried along its entire length. Field programs of boring and oil sampling in the years before construction began determined the soil characteristics, including permafrost conditions, and hence the aboveground or belowground configuration along the route. In areas where the ground is a well-drained gravel or solid rock, and thawing does not cause any instabilities, the pipeline was buried. In areas of thaw-sensitive soils, where heat from the oil in the pipeline might cause ground thawing and instability, the pipeline was elevated on supports above ground. The aboveground portion of the pipeline is 420 miles long, and the belowground portion of the pipeline is 380 miles long.

The aboveground section consists of 78,000 vertical supports that were placed in drilled holes or driven into the ground at 60 feet intervals. To allow for thermal expansion or contraction, the insulated and covered aboveground sections were built in trapezoidal or zigzag sections, which convert changes in pipe length to sideways movement. In this pattern, thermal expansion deforms the pipe between the fixed anchors, changing the formal trapezoid into a gentle "S" curve. The pipeline design permits 96 inches of sideways movement per section due to heat expansion, and 50 inches sideways movement in the opposite direction due to cold contraction. Another 24 inches of sideways movement is permitted in the

Trans-Alaska Pipeline.
Copyright Karen Kasmauski/National Geographic Image Collection

event of an earthquake. In the earthquake zones, the pipeline rests on teflon sliders with bumpers on each side of the pipe.

In areas of thaw-sensitive soils, special devices known as thermal syphons were installed to maintain the soil in a frozen stable condition around the vertical pipeline supports. Insulation on the aboveground sections is designed to keep the oil at the pipe wall between −20°F and +145°F. The operating flows for these temperatures are as low as 600,000 barrels a day, and as high as 2 million barrels a day. The operating range for the pipe itself is of 215°F. The temperatures can range from a −70°F, when the pipe is empty in midwinter, to a maximum of 145°F. Over this temperature range, the pipe expands more than 18 inches in a typical 1200-foot aboveground section. Aboveground sections, secured between fixed anchor installations, range from 700 to 1800 feet in length.

The belowground sections were installed in ditches that were typically 8 feet wide, and 8–16 feet deep; the maximum buried depth of the pipeline is 49 feet. Zinc strips are buried alongside the pipeline to provide corrosion protection.

In some small sections of the pipeline, where burying the pipe in thaw-sensitive soil was necessary because of highway and animal crossings, or natural hazards, other special provisions were used. In these sections, the pipeline was insulated and buried in a refrigerated ditch. Refrigeration plants circulate chilled brine through loops of pipe to maintain the soil

around the pipes in a stable frozen condition. There are 23 buried pipeline sections for animal crossings, and over 500 animal crossings to allow migrating caribou and other species to cross the pipeline.

To operate the pipeline, 12 pump stations were originally constructed: in 2001, two pump stations are not operating, and two are on idle status. The entire system is operated from the Operations Control Center located in Valdez, but can also be operated independently at each pump station. There are four leak detection systems that use pressure deviation, flow rate deviation, flow rate balance, and line volume balance to detect and locate leaks.

The volume of oil in the pipeline from Pump Station 1 to the marine terminal is approximately 9 million barrels. Pig launching and receiving facilities are located at three locations along the length of the pipeline (a pig is a robotic device that cleans the inside of the pipe). The marine terminal has a holding capacity of 9.18 million barrels in crude oil tanks.

Production from existing Cook Inlet and North Slope fields is declining, and will continue to decline. Development of the North Slope's 35 trillion cubic feet of natural gas recoverable reserves will be in the forefront of oil and gas activity in the region over the next two to seven years.

KENNETH R. JOHNSON

See also **Dalton Highway; North Slope; Oil Exploration; Prudhoe Bay**

Further Reading

Coates, Peter A., *The Trans-Alaska Pipeline Controversy: Technology, Conservation, and the Frontier*, Bethlehem, Pennsylvania: Lehigh University Press, 1991

Dixon, M., *What Happened to Fairbanks? The Effects of the Trans-Alaska Oil Pipeline on the Community of Fairbanks*, Boulder, Colorado: Westview Press, 1978

http://fairbanks-alaska.com/trans-alaska-pipeline.htm

http://www.alyeska-pipe.com

http://www.alaskachamber.com/OilandGas.htm

TRANS-ARCTIC AIR ROUTE

By 1929, the 1919 flight of the British R-34 dirigible was still the only successful round-trip flight between Europe and the United States (the first nonstop one-way flight having been made by Alcock and Brown earlier that year). Aircraft, still in their relative infancy, were limited by their short range to making short hops, from New York to Boston, Boston to Nova Scotia, Nova Scotia to Greenland, and so on, across to Europe. New York was the favored terminus for these sea hops, as it had been for Charles Lindbergh when he flew the Atlantic solo from Newfoundland to Paris in 1927. But Lindbergh carried no payload, and the challenge for other pilots was to use similar technology on a more northern route to establish regular, passenger-carrying air routes from the United States to Europe.

The Great Circle route is the most direct ocean crossing, but is still nearly 2000 miles from Ireland to Newfoundland. No aircraft existed in the late 1920s that could carry a payload that far, and the weather over that direct stretch was often horrendous, with disastrous fogs around Newfoundland and vicious westerly prevailing winds, making a return trip from Europe a continuous battle. Beginning in 1928, northern air route pioneers such as Parker "Shorty" Cramer, a pilot, like Lindbergh, from the midwestern United States, sought to use existing aeronautical technology to fly north of the bad weather. As Cramer himself wrote, to create a northern air route that was "several hundred miles shorter between important cities of America and Europe than the proposed Southern Route Via Bermuda and the Azores... The Northern Route, with no jump exceeding 500 miles, will permit existing planes to carry normal payloads of profitable size" (cited in Capelotti, 1995: 44).

But as Cramer discovered, at the eventual cost of his life, the difficulties encountered in establishing a North Atlantic air route were considerable. No infrastructure existed to handle landplanes or support them once on the ground; where open water existed for flying boat operations, there were no marked channels, no channel sweeping equipment, no loading gear, and no accommodations for pilots or passengers.

In April 1928, an aircraft crossed the Atlantic from east to west, when the Junkers W33 *Bremen* made the flight from Ireland to Greely Island off the coast of Labrador. In August 1928, Cramer flew with Bert J.R. "Fish" Hassell in a Stinson monoplane called the *City of Rockford*, from Rockford, Illinois, to a forced landing in Greenland, where the flight came to an end. The resulting two-week trek off the ice cap and re-emergence after being given up for dead made both pilots famous. In April 1929, Cramer made a flawless survey flight in a Cessna monoplane from Nome, Alaska, over the Siberian wastes, and a return via Nome to New York. Cramer's 1929 expedition in a twin-engine Sikorsky S-38 flying boat was planned to take him, fellow pilot Robert Gast, and a *Chicago Tribune* aviation reporter north over northern Québec, over Remi Lake, Rupert House, and Port Burwell, Labrador, to Greenland, Iceland, Norway, to a landing in Berlin. But the lack of any aviation infrastructure north of 55° N led to the sinking of the S-38 at Port Burwell in July 1929.

The development of such essential infrastructure, both physical and informational, was the object of several expeditions that followed the 1929 sinking of the S-38. Gino Watkins's British Arctic air route expedition landed at Ammassalik on Greenland's eastern shore in 1930, complete with a ski-equipped plane, to attempt the still-unachieved first hop over the Greenland ice cap. Harvard University's Alexander Forbes set sail aboard the schooner *Ramah* in 1931, with two seaplanes on board, to chart the coast of northern Labrador, the very kind of geographic legwork essential to any northern route's success. Lindbergh and his wife Anne Morrow Lindbergh completed long pioneering flights across northern Canada to Asia in a single-engine Lockheed Sirius in 1931, and then to Greenland in 1933.

In June 1931, Cramer piloted "Survey Plane No. 1," a small Bellanca seaplane, across the northern route. He lifted off in early August 1931, with a Canadian radio operator, Oliver Pacquette, and accomplished the first west-to-east crossing of the Greenland ice cap. He continued on from Ammassalik to Reykavik, then to the Faroes, and then the Shetland Islands. The Bellanca seaplane left Lerwick in the Shetlands for one final 200-mile hop to the coast of Norway on August 9, but was never heard from again. A month later, the wreckage of the Bellanca was located about 300 miles southeast of Lerwick. Neither Cramer nor Pacquette were ever found.

The Soviet Union took up the challenge of pioneering a Trans-Arctic air route even further north in the mid-1930s, sponsoring a series of long-distance flights that included attempts to fly from Moscow over the pole to the United States. In July 1936, Soviet pilot Valery Pavlovich Chkalov flew a Tupolev ANT-25

5600 miles from Moscow to an island off the Kamchatka Peninsula. Chkalov followed up this record-breaking success in June 1937, with a 5300-mile Ant-25 flight from Moscow, over the pole, to Washington State, the first flight between Russia and the United States over the Pole.

Spectacular as these flights were, they were eclipsed by one led by Professor Otto Shmidt, head of Russia's Arctic Institute. Shmidt planned and executed a large aerial expedition to both fly to and land at the North Pole in the summer of 1937. The expedition left Moscow in March of that year and, after waiting out unfavorable weather on Rudolf Island in the Franz Josef Land Archipelago, made its first landing at the pole on May 21. In the days that followed, three more converted Tupolev TB-3 bombers arrived at the Pole, until enough supplies were landed to enable four men to remain at the Pole for nine months. The ice station at the Pole drifted steadily south, arriving near Greenland in early 1938, where the four men were picked up by two Russian icebreakers (*see* **Drifting Stations**).

By the start of World War II, US President Franklin Roosevelt in early 1941 ordered that a series of northern air route bases be established in Greenland. Important airports were constructed at Narsarsuaq and Kangerlussuaq. Short-range fighters could then fly directly to the aid of the British, and avoid shipment aboard freighters with its risk of sinking by German U-boats. By the time these bases were operational however, larger and longer-range aircraft were flying directly over the northern air route from Labrador to England.

P.J. CAPELOTTI

See also **Air Routes**

Further Reading

Armstrong, Edward R., *America-Europe via North Atlantic Airways over the Armstrong Seadrome System of Commercial Ocean Transit by Airplane*, Wilmington, Delaware: The Armstrong Seadrome Development Co., 1927

Barry, Jim, *Flying the North Atlantic*, London: B.T. Batsford, 1987

Bleriot, Louis, *Wings over the Sea: Are Landing Places Necessary for the Commercial Aerial Crossing of the North Atlantic?*, Washington, 1936

Capelotti, P.J., *Explorer's Air Yacht: The Sikorsky S-38 Flying Boat*, Missoula, Montana: Pictorial Histories Publishing, 1995

Forbes, Alexander, *Northernmost Labrador Mapped from the Air*, New York: American Geographical Society, Special Publication No. 22, 1938

———, *Quest for a Northern Air Route*, Cambridge: Harvard University Press, 1953

Glines, C.V. (editor), *Polar Aviation*, New York: Franklin Watts, Inc., 1964

Hassell, Col. Bert R.J., *A Viking with Wings*, Bend, Oregon: Maverick Publications, 1987

McCannon, John, *Red Arctic: Polar Exploration and the Myth of the North in the Soviet Union, 1932–1939*, New York: Oxford University Press, 1998

Ridgway, John, *Gino Watkins*, London: Oxford University Press, 1974

TRANSPOLAR DRIFT

Sea ice in the Arctic Ocean is in continuous motion and the study of ice drift has significant scientific and applied values. But until the end of the 19th century, the judgments of scientists about ice drift in the Arctic Ocean were based on unfounded assumptions.

Observations on ice motion collected during Fridtjof Nansen's expedition on the vessel *Fram* in 1893–1896 were the first data used for quantitative estimates of ice drift and its dependence on wind and current. Along with the analysis of ice drift as a physical phenomenon, studies of ice dynamics through the middle of the 20th century aimed to establish the scheme of general ice circulation in the Arctic Ocean. The studies were based on analyses of atmospheric pressure, drift of ships and polar stations, and air reconnaissance data. Only in the mid-20th century were numerous observations made during Soviet expeditions to the central Arctic used by Soviet scientist Zalman Gudkovich to create an improved model of ice motion in the Arctic Ocean. This scheme could be considered as the first scientifically based theory, which, in general, corresponds to our current knowledge on ice drift.

According to the model, there are two important features of large-scale ice drift in the Arctic Ocean: transpolar drift in the Eastern Hemisphere and anticyclonic circulation (Beaufort gyre) in the Western Hemisphere. On average, the areas of these features are approximately equal. The transpolar drift begins in the northern part of the Chukchi Sea, travels to the vicinity of the North Pole and further to the Fram Strait between Greenland and Svalbard. The Beaufort gyre is located between the North Pole and Alaska, with the center of rotation approximately at 80° N and 150° W.

Along its way, the transpolar drift widens, absorbing heavy ice of the Beaufort gyre from the right side and predominantly first-year ice of the Russian marginal seas (Chukchi, East Siberian, Laptev, and Kara) from the left side. The average velocity of ice drift changes insignificantly along the first two-thirds of transpolar drift. At the last third of transpolar drift, approaching Fram Strait, the velocity of ice drift begins to increase. The most significant acceleration of ice drift near Fram Strait occurs in winter. The described spatial changes in ice drift velocity lead to a divergence of drifting ice at the approaches to Fram Strait. This explains the frequent appearance of openings in ice cover over the Atlantic side of the Arctic Ocean.

After Fram Strait, ice of transpolar drift continues to accelerate along the eastern coast of Greenland. It takes slightly more than half a year for ice to pass along the eastern Greenland coast from Fram Strait to the southernmost point of Greenland. Ice reaching that point usually turns around Greenland and continues its motion along the southwestern coast of Greenland.

The location of the boundary between transpolar drift and the Beaufort gyre is very variable. The intensification of transpolar drift is accompanied by the widening and large absorption of Beaufort gyre ice. When transpolar drift weakens, even ice from Russian marginal seas could be taken into the Beaufort gyre circulation.

Ice drift is subject to seasonal changes, but the picture of general ice motion is on average the same, with the main features of general ice circulation in the Arctic Ocean, transpolar drift and the Beaufort gyre, persistent year-round. The average velocities of drift in transpolar drift do not change significantly in the seasonal cycle, but the width of transpolar drift increases in summer because of a smaller area occupied by the Beaufort gyre.

On average, the drift of ice from the Chukchi Sea and the East Siberian Sea to Fram Strait takes 3–4 years. Ice absorbed by transpolar drift from the Laptev Sea reaches Fram Strait in 2–3 years and from the Kara Sea in 1–2 years.

Development of our knowledge on ice drift since the 1950s became possible due to new observation methods and technical equipment, including the Soviet and American drifting manned stations and other expeditions, automated drifting weather stations, and observations from airplanes and satellites. Accelerated collection of data on ice drift corresponds to the beginning of the International Arctic Buoy Program in 1979 and the deployment of automatic buoys on Arctic ice cover. Ice drift velocities can also be calculated on the basis of comparison between two successive satellite images. Passive microwave and synthetic aperture radar (SAR) images, giving information on ice cover state under any weather conditions, have found wide application in the study of features of ice drift fields over the entire Arctic Ocean.

Short-term ice drift trajectories are complex, and mostly depend upon wind. Due to extreme variability in wind direction and speed, instantaneous ice drift changes its direction over a wide range. Instantaneous ice drift is also characterized by great spatial variability of its velocity. The velocity of ice drift usually adjusts to changes in wind speed within 3–6 h.

The relative contribution of wind and current into ice drift depends on the temporal scale of averaging. Thus, over a daily period, the contribution of current is less than one-third. But over a three-month period, only one-third of the total drift is explained by the influence of wind and two-thirds of the drift are related to surface current. As the time averaging scale increases, the structure of ice drift becomes simpler. There is a certain stability in ice drift, mostly related to the influence of quasipermanent surface currents independent of local winds. Despite interannual variability of ice drift, the main features of general ice drift and trajectories of ice motion remain approximately the same year after year. Therefore, large-scale predominant ice motion in the Arctic Ocean on the whole, and in transpolar drift in particular, mostly corresponds to the system of surface currents.

Wind could be considered as a main factor causing both drift and surface currents. It explains a significant resemblance between the fields of wind, ice drift, and surface currents. Large-scale general motion of ice cover in the Arctic Ocean corresponds to the system of surface currents, formed and supported by the atmospheric circulation in the north polar area, in particular, the persistence of high-pressure air masses over the western Arctic region, stimulating clockwise rotation of surface winds and waters.

IGOR APPEL

See also **Arctic Ocean; Beaufort Gyre; Drifting Stations; Sea Ice**

Further Reading

Aagard, K. & E.C. Carmack, "The role of sea ice and other fresh water in the Arctic circulation." *Journal of Geophysical Research C*, 94 (1989): 14485–14498

Emery, W.J., C.W. Fowler & J.A. Maslanik, "Satellite-derived maps of Arctic and Antarctic sea ice motion: 1988 to 1994." *Journal of Geophysical Research*, 24(8) (1997): 897–900

Gudkovich, Z.M., "Dreif L'dov v Tsentral'noy Chasti Arcticheskogo Basseyna" [Ice drift in the central part of the Arctic Ocean]. *Trudy Arkt. I Antarkt. Inst.*, 87 (1957): 106

Hibler, W.D., Arctic Ice-Ocean Dynamics. In *The Arctic Seas: Climatology, Oceanography, Geology, and Biology*, edited by Yvonne Herman, New York: Van Nostrand Reinhold, 1989

Pfirman, S., R. Colony, D. Nurnberg, H. Eicken & I. Rigor, Reconstructing the origin and trajectory of drifting Arctic sea ice. *Journal of Geophysical Research*, 102 (1997): 12575–12586

TRANSPORT

Transport is often considered the key issue to Arctic development and living. Economic growth is severely limited without effective transport systems. The vast areas of the Arctic require transport hubs, of which there are few.

One of the most important hubs is Anchorage in Alaska. Called the "Air crossroads of the world," it is located almost equidistant (via the polar great circle routes) from New York and Tokyo and only slightly farther from London. It is a port of call for cargo carriers from three continents and a midway stopover on numerous intercontinental flights. It is served not only by Alaska Airlines and other Alaskan airlines, but by most of the internationally well-known carriers. From Anchorage, it is possible to fly to New York, Seattle, and other major US cities.

An important transport hub is also characterized by having many different kinds of transport possibilities. This is also the case for Anchorage. A transport hub concentrates the population, and half of the population in Alaska (250,000) lives in Anchorage. Anchorage is connected by road to Fairbanks via the Glenn Highway, and from there the legendary two-lane Alaska Highway to Dawson Creek in British Columbia was built in 1942. It was built for military purposes and extends to the old gold-mining areas. Anchorage is also a rail headquarter. A rail shuttle connects it to the Prince William Sound ferry arrivals. The Alaska Marine Highway system operates to Valdez, Whittier, and Seward, which all have direct rail or road access to Anchorage. There is only limited direct ship connection due to the tides of the Cook Inlet.

Another important hub in the Arctic, although minor, is Reykjavík, the capital of Iceland. Besides being served by Iceland air and other Icelandic air carriers, Reykjavík is served by international airlines, especially Scandinavian Airlines System (SAS). It includes connection to the main cities in Europe, New York and Canada, and Greenland and the Faroe Islands. Furthermore, there is a well-developed road system around Iceland. Reykjavík is also the base for Eimskip Ltd., the huge Icelandic shipping company with transport to destinations in Europe and America, etc.

Tromsø in Norway also has some hub characteristics. It not only has flight connections to Europe but also road connections to Oslo, Sweden, and further north to Russia and the Norwegian Sea Route; in addition, it is the stopover of many cruisers. Combined with Norwegian regional policy, the transport links have made Tromsø a center.

Canada, with most of the population along the US border, has another hub structure related to the capitals of the provinces and with no real Arctic hubs, although Whitehorse, the capital of Yukon, with its logistic position, has some central hub features and can be a hub in the summertime. Whitehorse has flight connections to Vancouver, Edmonton, and Alaskan cities. It is also possible to drive or to sail via the Alaskan ferry to Port Chilkoot, and during the summer season tourists more than double the size of the population. Gander in Newfoundland formerly had a central link position in the North Atlantic air route system, but its importance has decreased due to the technical development of aeroplanes and the use of polar flight routes.

Murmansk cannot be counted as a hub position in spite of its size, due to the relatively low transport frequency and transport being mainly to Russia alone. At present, the Northern Sea Route is not a real transport corridor due to lack of capital and economic potential. However, Lawson W. Brigham estimated that at the end of the 1980s, the annual level of operation of the Northern Sea Route was 600 freight voyages carrying six million tons of cargo. The road network to other places is not so well developed.

Arctic Sweden and Finland as well as Greenland have no transport hubs. The fact that nuclear energy has not developed into a world energy regime has prevented the hub development of Murmansk.

In total, the Arctic has few hub positions and only Anchorage can be considered a real global hub. It implies that labor division and competition is limited and is a hindrance for the development of Arctic competitiveness in the production of differentiated (heterogeneous) goods.

Transport Prices

Transport prices can be extremely high in the Arctic and almost a barrier to transport. This is mainly an impact of the monopoly elements, bad management, and some degree of low transport quantity. Prices in Greenland are the highest and prohibitively high for economic development. To give an example, to go to Upernavik in Greenland from Copenhagen costs about 2500 US dollars; for the same price, it is possible to go three times around the globe.

Arctic Transport Practice

Alaska has the best functioning and most effective transport system in the Arctic. In Alaska, it is not unusual to have your own car, boat, and plane. There is a plane per 65 inhabitants, more than 40,000 pilots, and about 1000 airports. The road network is more limited, with about 12,500 miles of road. The Alaska railroad was constructed in 1923. It runs 470 miles from Seward to Whittier, the deepwater ports of South Alaska, through Anchorage to the Denali National Park and Fairbanks. The Alaska Marine Highway has two ferry systems. The Southeast System serves 15 towns in Alaska's Panhandle. The Southwest System links 12 towns in Prince William Sound, the Kenai Peninsula, and Kodiak Island.

In Canada, there are about 60 communities spread across Canada's northern territories. Most have mainly local transport, but about ten have more contact with the outside world through tourists, visitors, and public employees. This is the case for Fort Smith, once the territorial capital of the Northwest Territories and founded as a Hudson's Bay Company fur-trading post in 1874. Other large communities with good transport connections are Hay River, Fort Simpson at the Mackenzie Highway, Iqaluit (the capital of Nunavut) and Inuvik, both among the larger settlements. In Yukon, transportation is concentrated on the capital Whitehorse and other destinations are mainly served from Whitehorse. Many small airlines plus the main national airline provide regular connections to the communities; furthermore, highways in Yukon are used by a bus system, in addition to private cars. Traditional Arctic transportation such as dog sledges and snow scooters still play a large role in local transport.

Finland has a well-developed collective transport system, including buses, railways, and air transport. Also, the number of cars is high. Transport prices are moderate.

In Greenland, the high prices for air transport imply that travel is often a part of the wage system (free travel) and only a minority of air passengers are private customers. The ferries are much cheaper to use, and are used mainly by people who themselves pay for their transport. There are no railways in Greenland and no roads link the cities together. Many people own boats and cars. In the summer, boats are used to travel to settlements and nearby towns. During the winter, people drive cars on the ice; it is normally easier to travel around in wintertime. Also, dog sledges (mid- and North Greenland) and snow scooters are popular transport means. In spite of the limited road network, Greenland (and especially Nuuk) has an extremely high number of taxis in relation to the number of inhabitants.

In Iceland, collective and private transport includes a domestic airline and buses plus a well-developed road system and many private cars. Iceland has no railways.

In Norway, the main sea route for goods and passengers is the Hurtigruten from Bergen to Kirkenes in the north of Norway. A highway runs from Oslo (the capital of Norway) to the north of Norway, and a railway runs along the coast and from Narvik to Kiruna in Sweden. A domestic airline flies along the coast and has regular connections to Svalbard (Norwegian territory). With buses and many private cars, Arctic Norway has both a well-functioning collective and private transport system.

Russia has few private cars, and bad and few roads. The collective transport system that formerly functioned well has drastically deteriorated in quality since the economic transition to a market economy. Traditional good transportation in the Arctic and Subarctic has been by the great rivers (Lena, Yenisey) to the Arctic Ocean, and onward to Asia and Europe by sea. However, the prestigious Northern Sea Route Project along the coast of Arctic Russia has almost fallen apart due to lack of capital and investment. The Trans-Siberian railway links container ports in Russia's Far East to northern Europe, connecting the ports of Japan and South Asia via an overland route to European consumers.

Sweden has a well-developed collective transport system including the railway, roads, and planes. It is expensive to fly, but the railway is a cheaper alternative based on subsidies. Also, the number of cars is high, and the road quality is good.

Arctic Transport History and Development

The history of transport is mainly transport of goods by ship. Valuable resources had to be brought out of the Arctic and deliveries to the Arctic were small, implying a double transport cost, as the ships were without cargo one way. In this way, the Arctic hinterland position was further deepened by the transport cost structure. Even after World War II, when passenger transportation and imports of consumer goods and investment goods for modernization increased, it has been difficult to manage the cargoes in a cost-efficient way and the shipping monopolies have not made it easier.

The history of shipping is also the history of shipbuilding from the old wooden barques and brigs to modern steel ships. Each part of the Arctic has its own story about ships that, for hundreds of years, have been the only means of contact with the rest of the world: it is a story of long and true service, with many ships capsizing and disappearing with whole crews. Arctic shipping even has its own Titanic story: the Danish ship *Hans Hedtoft*, named after the Danish Prime Minister and said to be unsinkable, sank on its maiden voyage to Greenland on January 30, 1959. All 95 on board perished when it hit an iceberg. Only one of the lifebuoys was later found, and it is now placed in the church in Qaqortoq (Greenland).

During World War II, many ships were lost due to German submarine activities. This put pressure on the establishment of an air transport route and for developing the pilot air transport trials over the North Atlantic into a reliable transport connection. It was an immense task to develop the air connection as quickly as needed, but proved possible to realize, with military air bases being established, for example, in Greenland to stage a Europe-America air route. After the war, it was evident that development of the concept to have civilian air transport established as the cost of constructing the airports was already paid. However, political questions spoilt some of the efficiency potential. The first was the question of Greenland. Henrik Kauffmann, the Danish ambassador to the United States, had been in the United States during the war, and had an unusually powerful position as he had negotiated the US deliveries to Greenland as the war had disrupted the transport delivery line from Greenland to Copenhagen. The United States wanted to buy Greenland or at least to continue to have some military bases in Greenland, while Denmark wanted reintroduction of Danish sovereignty. In this political climate, a civilian air route linking Greenland to the United States was impossible. Secondly, when the Cold War became a reality, Arctic cost-efficient flying became impossible as circumpolar flying became impossible politically.

As a consequence, polar flying had to develop according to political realities, but it was possible to achieve some extra efficiency when airplanes were further developed. A milestone of this development was achieved in 1952, when SAS (Scandinavian Airlines System) operated the first passenger flight via Thule in Greenland to California in 1952. It took 24 hours. This development diminished the economic rationale in the remaining part of the North Atlantic Sea Route, especially for Gander in Canada. Iceland managed to achieve economy in the air route by changing its business idea to linking to the European capitals in continental Europe.

In Alaska, severe political barriers hindered the expansion to develop business-oriented air routes, and this has been the core element behind the strong position that Alaska holds in air transportation today.

In Russia, the command economy and military logic governed transport development. Road construction in remote regions in the Soviet era concentrated on strategic sites, and providing access, for example, to the gold fields of Kolyma (Magadan). Transport in the Arctic has been badly affected in the last ten years due to the economic transition.

LISE LYCK

See also **Air Routes; Alaska Highway; Anchorage; Dalton Highway; Icebreaker; Kolyma Highway; Murmansk; Northern Sea Route; Reykjavík; Trans-Siberian Railway; Tromsø**

Further Reading

Brigham, Lawson W., "Soviet Arctic marine transportation." *Northern Perspectives*, 16 (1988)

Savours, A., *The Search for the North West Passage*, New York: St Martin's Press, 1999

Young, Oran R., *Arctic Politics* Hanover: New England University Press, 1992

TRANS-SIBERIAN RAILWAY

The Trans-Siberian Railway is one of the most significant transport routes not only in Eurasia but also in the world. Politically, the railway connects Moscow in central Russia with Vladivostok on the Pacific.

Economically, it links the eastern ports of the Russian Federation (Vladivostok, Nakhodka, Vostochny, Vanino, and Zabaikalsk) with western European countries via Moscow. The railway is a basic means of connecting the Urals with the Far East, but also has significance on a local level.

Usually abbreviated to "Trans-Sib" in Russia, the name Trans-Siberian Railway was an English nickname, which quickly took root and became widely used: the literal translation from Russian would be "Great Siberian Way." Trans-Sib passes through the territories of 14 regions, three territories, two republics and one autonomous region of the Russian Federation and 87 towns. The railway crosses 16 large rivers: the Volga, Vyatka, Kama, Tobol, Irtysh, Ob', Tom, Chulym, Yenisey, Oka, Selenga, Zeya, Bureya, Amur, Khor, and the Ussuri.

Construction of the railway started at the newly founded port of Vladivostok in 1891 and at the western end in 1892, and the main route to Mocow was completed in 1903. The first track was officially laid in an area close to Vladivostok on May 19 (31), 1891 (all dates are given in the old and new, in parenthesis, styles), when heir to the throne Nikolai Alexandrovich, future emperor Nikolai II, attended an opening ceremony. Actual construction began a little sooner, at the beginning of March 1891, when construction of the section Miass to Chelyabinsk commenced.

China gave Russia permission to build the original eastern segment of the Trans-Sib through Manchuria, instead of following a much longer route along Russia's border. The railway was completed on October 21 (November 3), 1901 when engineers of the Chinese Eastern line who had laid track from the western and eastern ends of the line met together. Regular rail traffic along the full length of the railway was impossible at that time for both economic and technical reasons, however.

Regular communication by railway between the capital of the Russian empire, St Petersburg, and the Pacific Ocean ports of Vladivostok and Dalni was established by the railway in July 1903 when the Chinese Eastern line passing through Manchuria went into regular operation. On July 1 (14), 1903, the Great Siberian Way went into full-length service, except for one break in the journey to ferry trains over Lake Baikal on a special ice-breaking train ferry. A continuous track ran between St Petersburg and Vladivostok after the Circum-Baikal railway was completed on September 18 (October 1), 1904, the most costly and technically demanding section (with 39 tunnels over 53 miles). One year later, on October 16 (29), 1905, the Circum-Baikal railway operated regularly as a section of the Great Siberian Way. For the first time in history, it was possible for passenger trains to travel from the Atlantic shore (from Western Europe) to the Pacific shore (to Vladivostok).

The political situation after the Russian-Japanese War of 1904–1905 necessitated the replacement of the Chinese Eastern line with an alternative route through Russia's territory, north from Vladivostock via Khabarovsk to rejoin the main line at Chita. This section, known as the Amur Railway, was completed on October 5 (18), 1916 with the construction of a bridge over the river Amur near Khabarovsk and the commencement of rail traffic over it.

The cost of construction for the period 1891–1913 was 1,455,413 roubles.

The current length of the main passenger route of the Trans-Siberian railway (from Moscow to Vladivostok) is 9288.2 km (5771.7 miles), making it the longest railway on Earth, running as it does across almost all of Eurasia. The tariff length (used to calculate the cost of tickets) is a little longer at 9298 km (5778 mi), not the same as the concrete one, because of cargo lines at various sections. The Trans-Sib track width is 1520 mm (5 ft).

Today, the starting point of the Trans-Sib is the Yaroslavsky Railway Station in Moscow, and the end point is Vladivostok Main Railway Station. But early on, till the mid-1920s, the gateway to Siberia and the Far East was Kazansky (then Ryazansky) Railway Station, and at the start of Trans-Sib's existence (the beginning of the 20th century) it was Kursko-Nizhegorodsky (now Kursky) Railway Station in Moscow. Before the Russian revolution in 1917, the starting point of the Great Siberian Way was Nikolaevsky (now Moscovsky) Railway Station in St Petersburg, then the capital of the Russian Empire. Furthermore, Vladivostok was not always the end point; for a brief time, from the end of the 1890s up to the Russian-Japanese war in 1904–1905, the end of the Great Siberian Way was the end of the branch of the Chinese-Eastern Line at Port Arthur, a strategic port on the East Chinese Sea on the leased Chinese Liaotung Peninsula.

Up to the end of the 1920s, there were two main routes of Trans-Sib. From 1903, the route was from Moscow (via Ryazan, Ryazhsk, Penza, Syzran, Samara, Ufa, Chelyabinsk, Kurgan, Petropavlovsk, Omsk, Krasnoyarsk, Irkutsk, Baikal, Mysovaya, Verkhneudinsk, Chita, Manchuria, Kharbin, Grodekovo) to Vladivostok. For a short period only (1897–1900), Moscow Siberian trains passed via Tula, Uzlovaya, Ryazhsk, and thereafter by the route given above. From 1906, the route was from St Petersburg: via Cherepovets, Vologda, Bui, Shar'ya, Vyatka, Perm, Nizhniy Tagil, Ekaterinburg, Kyshtym, Chelyabinsk, Omsk, then on to Vladivostok by the route above. In 1909, the route from Perm to Ekaterinburg was closed down and a shorter

railway via Kungur was built. Similarly, in October 1913, the route from St Petersburg was made shorter, passing from Ekaterinburg via Tyumen to Omsk.

Up to April 1905, the South Manchurian line from Harbin via Changchun to the port of Dalni and Port Arthur belonged to Russia.

The major Trans-Sib route as it is recognized today was formed from the beginning of the 1930s, when normal operation of the shorter Chinese Eastern line became impossible, firstly because of political conflicts and secondly because the South Uralian way was becoming too overcrowded due to the start of Soviet industrialization.

The main route is now: Moscow, Yaroslavskaya, Yaroslavl, Main, Danilov, Bui, Shar'ya, Kirov, Balezino, Perm-2, Sverdlovsk-Passenger (Ekaterinburg), Tyumen, Nazyvaevskaya, Omsk-Passenger, Barabinsk, Novosibirsk-Main, Mariinsk, Achinsk1, Krasnoyarsk, Ilanskaya, Taishet, Nizhneudinsk, Zima, Irkutsk-Passenger, Slyudyanka-1, Ulan-Ude, Petrovsky Zavod, Chita-2, Karymskaya, Chernyshevsk, Zabaikalsky, Mogocha, Skovordino, Belogorsk, Arkhara, Khabarovsk-1, Vyazemskaya, Ruzhino, Ussuriisk to Vladivostok. Up to 1949, Trans-Sib's main route passed along the Circum-Baikal railway via Irkutsk, along the Angara River to Baikal station, then along the shore of Lake Baikal to Slyudyanka station. In 1949–1956, two routes were in use: the old one along the Lake Baikal shoreline and a new mountain pass one.

The route of main Trans-Siberian trains was changed in June 2001, after which they passed through Vladimir, Nizhny Novgorod, and Kotel'nich instead of the northern path through Yaroslavl and Shar'ya. The new route reduces the journey time by approximately 3 hours.

In December 2002, electrification was complete, made up of 6142 km (Danilov to Balezino 836 km, Mariinsk to Guberovo 512 km, Sibirtsevo to Vladivostok 180 km) at alternating current (~25 kV), and 2877 km (Moscow, Yaroslavskaya, Danilov 356 km, Balezino to Mariinsk 2521 km) at direct current (3 kV).

The basic advantages of Trans-Sib are reduced delivery time of freight and cost of transportation. Russian railway operators continue running container deliveries from South Asian countries to Northern Europe. The transport time by Trans-Sib is less than 9 days. The whole transit time from Vostochny Harbor near Nachodka to Buslovskaya Railway Station on the Russian-Finnish border is 11–12 days, to Brest 12.5 days, and Berlin 14.5 days. The average transit time of container deliveries by rail from the ports of Japan to Western European ports is 17 days, and from Korean ports it is 16 days. The rail route from South Asian countries to European consumers can be three times faster than the shipping route passing through the Pacific, Indian, and Atlantic oceans.

The cost of container transportation through Trans-Sib from the port of Yokogama to the Finnish port of Kotka is $1350 for the 20-ft container and $2173 for the 40-ft container. The average transportation costs of a 20-ft container from Japanese ports to Scandinavian ports, including loading costs in the departures and arrival ports, are $1750–2150 for the 20-ft container and $3000–3500 for the 40-ft container, depending on quantity, container capacity, and regularity of the traffic.

There is also accelerated customs freight handling by the joint instructions of the Russian Custom Committee and the Ministry of Railway, adopted in 1997.

About this time, foreign businessmen formed the unfavorable image of Trans-Sib (as well as all Russian transportation networks) as an unsafe route for freight delivery. Now, Russian railway operators monitor that transit container deliveries are on time and give cargo owners information on the quickest way to get freight through Russian territory.

The Russian Ministry of Railways and the Ministry of Internal Affairs have accepted measures that ensure the safety of freight transported on Trans-Sib. Container trains are now accompanied by specialized security divisions and, because of these measures, no transit goods have been lost since 1998. It is difficult, however, to alter stereotypical image in a short time.

It is clear that the logistics of Trans-Sib is not only the delivery of materials, but also covers functions necessary to make deliveries possible and/or meaningful. For example, if goods originate in Japan and must be delivered in Germany, Russia cannot facilitate this goal itself because the railway runs only as far west as Moscow. It is easy for people to say "just transport it over the Trans-Sib," but the main problem is how to get the goods to Trans-Sib. Therefore, the problem of Trans-Sib expansion is the first one. At present, three main players take part in the dividing of Trans-Sib transit container traffic: Finland, the Baltic states, and Russia itself. There is a fourth railway route under construction from Moscow via Warsaw to Berlin and Paris. In addition, in the southeast part of Finland, there are rail terminals for container handling; about 24 freight trains cross the Russian-Finland border daily.

Other problems are connected with the development of Trans-Sib East divisions. The first project was thought of a hundred years ago, when in 1896 the French engineer L. De Lobel proved the possibility of tunnel traffic under the Bering Strait. But the terms for investment were unacceptable to Russia, and the State Duma blocked its realization. Fifty years later, Stalin tried to construct a 10 km tunnel under the Tatarsky straits to connect Sakhalin Island and the mainland. A tunnel under the straits was begun in the 1940s, and apparently workers made it almost to the halfway point. But the project was abandoned after Stalin's death, and it is now not clear if the digging done half a century ago could still be used.

This idea was revived in 2000 by the Russian government. Apart from a tunnel, a new project also proposes a 40 km bridge over the Pacific connecting Sakhalin Island and the Japanese island of Hokkaido. Russian Railway Ministry officials say the massive infrastructural investments would pay for themselves in 15–20 years. Railway Ministry officials believe that due to the assured increase in cargo transit between Europe and Japan alone, the Russian budget could earn an additional 20 billion roubles (about $750 million) annually.

The project would probably attract $10 billion in new foreign investment from countries looking to invest in Asia, including Japan and the United States, in the near future.

There could be not only geographical but also technological expansion, by creating a new system for changing wheels on Russia's west border or by the creation of additional broad track railways in some West European countries. There is also an interesting idea to organize so-called redistribution centers.

The diversity of port activity has now been realized. Specialized terminals for container transshipment operate, in addition to St Petersburg, in three Finnish ports (Helsinki, Kotka, and Hamina) and in three ports in the Baltic States (Tallinn, Riga, and Klaipeda). In December 2000, a new container terminal, the largest in Finland, capable of handling up to 500,000 TEU (twenty-foot equivalent units, or an 8×8×20 ft container) annually, was inaugurated in Mussalo. Kotka Port is expected to become the number one port in the Baltic Sea in the near future. Many ports are specialized in handling Trans-Sib transit cargo. There is strict competition between the Baltic ports.

ELENA G. EFIMOVA

Further Reading

Braunburg, Rudolf, *Die Transsibirische Eisenbahn: terra magica*, Lucern: Reich Verlag, 1997

des Cars, Jean & Jean-Paul Caracalla, *Die Transsibirische Bahn. Geschichte der langsten Bahn der Welt*, Zurich: Verlag Orell Fussli, 1987

Marks, Steven G., *Road to Power: The Trans-Siberian Railroad and the Colonization of Asian Russia*, Ithaca, New York: Cornell University Press, 1991

Pifferi, Enzo, *Trans Sibirien. Auf der langsten Bahn der Welt*, Augsburg: Weltbild Verlag, 1996

Richmond, S. & M. Vorhees, *Trans-Siberian Railway: A Classic Overland Route*, Victoria, Australia: Lonely Planet, 2002

Sutyrin, S.F., E.G. Efimova & E. Riccio, "Russia as a logistical intermediary on Euroasian space." Vestnik Sankt-Petersburgskogo universiteta. *Seria Ekonomika* (2) (2001)

Thomas, Bryn, *Trans-Siberian Handbook*, New York and London: Trailblazer, 2000

Tupper, Harmon, *To the Great Ocean: Siberia and the Trans-Siberian-Railway*, Boston: Little, Brown & Company, 1965
http://www.transsib.ru/Eng/

TRAPPING

Furs have been critical to the survival of peoples in the cold Arctic environment. Long before contact with Europeans, northern indigenous peoples traded among themselves for furs as well as other products. Three hundred and fifty years ago, the search for furs led to extensive exploration and colonization of the circumpolar region, Russia moving into Siberia and onward to the Pacific, and Europe moving into and across North America. In Canada, the fur trade is seen as the major factor driving the exploration and development of the country in its early stages. The fur industry continues to be most widespread, as well as socially and economically important in Canada, parts of the United States, and the Russian Federation.

Experiences with the fur trade varied, including exploitation by greedy traders, starvation caused by too much focus on fur harvesting, enhanced trade and intertribal relations, and increased economic diversity and autonomy. That traders and trappers had a mutually dependent relationship is clear. For many aboriginal peoples today, fur harvesting continues to be an important part of their income, contributing furs for domestic use or for cash sales or trade. This often provides the only cash income some aboriginal households make, and it is critical to supporting their other subsistence harvesting activities. Trapping and other subsistence activities also represent an important cultural, social, and spiritual link to the land and its resources.

Different peoples harvested in different ways: the ancient Inuit used deadfall traps of balanced rocks to catch foxes; Evenki herdsmen rode reindeer and used hunting dogs to chase sables into trees where they could be shot, or used heavy log traps to catch Arctic fox or wolverine; Inuit and Athapaskan Indians used net traps to entangle caribou; noose traps or snares were commonly used in Siberia and North America for small game; and Siberian trappers also used pitfalls for Arctic foxes. European traders brought metal traps, which became widely used. These have evolved over time, but include leg-hold traps, body-traps, and box traps, used in different ways according to the habitat and species being trapped.

Two alternative forms of the fur harvest occur in the North. Fur farming was introduced in Russia in the 19th century, and carried on through Soviet collective and state farms. In the Yukon and Northwest Territories of Canada, fur farming was attempted but never particularly successful. In Alaska, the majority of the fur harvest (60–70%) used to come from the large herds of fur seals on the Pribilof Islands, managed and harvested under the North Pacific Sealing Convention (this was halted in 1983).

Now, fur farms (mostly outside the Arctic) contribute 85% of the global fur trade, raising mainly mink and fox. Two-thirds of this takes place in northern Europe, 11% in North America, and the rest in Argentina, the Baltic States, Ukraine, and Russia. Manufacturing takes place close to traditional markets, such as the United States, Canada, France, Germany, Italy, Austria, the Nordic countries, and Greece. Hong Kong and China are increasingly involved as well.

In response to concerns about the cruelty of leg-hold and other traps, research had begun in Canada in 1973, by a Federal/Provincial Committee on Humane Trapping, to improve the efficiency, humaneness, conservation, and safety of traps. This was continued by the Fur Institute of Canada (representing provincial and territorial governments, the fur industry, some aboriginal groups, and trappers' associations), which has spent over $14 million to develop standards and technology for humane traps and testing. In addition, Woodstream Corporation in Pennsylvania, the world's largest manufacturer of traps, has carried out research, and developed new traps. As time went by, it became apparent that the real aim of the animal rights participants was not to improve humaneness, but to end trapping and killing of animals altogether.

After the successful antisealing campaign (*see* **Seal Skin Directive**; **Animal Rights Movement and Renewable Resources**), the trapping industry was targetted by animal rights activists in the 1970s and 1980s. In 1983 and again in 1985, the CITES meetings considered resolutions to ban trade in furs caught in leg-hold traps (most wild furs); these failed because, among other reasons, none of the species are endangered. In 1984, the European Parliament considered a resolution to ban the sales of fur products in EEC nations, to end trapping in EEC nations, and to press non-EEC nations to eliminate the fur trade. This was withdrawn because of pressure from fur ranchers within the EEC, who felt that their own markets would be destroyed.

In 1988, a proposal was made, first in Britain, and then in the European Parliament (EP) and the EEC Commission, for "cruelty tagging" furs that came from countries where animals were "mainly" or "often" caught in leg-hold traps. In 1991, the European Community again proposed a ban on the import of furs caught in leg-hold traps; the legislation would take effect in 1995, when leg-hold traps would be banned in Europe as well (they are still manufactured and used there for "pest" animals). Ironically, the ban was not justified on the basis of animal welfare, but on (unfounded) management concerns for "threatened or endangered species of wild fauna" (the species remain unendangered).

Canada, Russia, and the United States fought this regulation together, as a regional group that exports much of the fur to Europe. In 1997, Canada, Russia, and the European Union signed an Agreement on International Humane Trapping Standards, which sets out trap performance requirements for 19 wild species. The United States joined in 1998 with a separate "set of principles" similar to the Canada/Russia/European Union agreement. Canada and Russia agreed to ban certain types of traps for certain species, in a specified time (much of this had already occurred, such as banning leg-hold traps on land for beaver and muskrat). Only those species that go to European markets are covered by the new rules, and others are not included because they are ranched in Europe.

After the experience with the antisealing campaign, northern native peoples took more aggressive action in response to the antitrapping campaigns: through Indigenous Survival International, they worked alone and with their governments to lobby and educate American and European publics about the cultural and economic realities of their communities and the impacts of such a ban. Aboriginal representatives toured Europe to meet with parliamentarians, government officials, and welfare organizations. European parliamentarians and journalists were taken to visit trappers in the North, to observe the reality of their lifestyle and harvesting practices.

It has been predicted that banning the fur trade will have disastrous effects on northern aboriginal peoples, including health, social, cultural, and economic disruption. Also, if trappers and indigenous peoples are removed from their land-based economy and lifestyle, the wilderness will be opened up for industrial activities and resource extraction, which will have even more negative effects on the furbearer populations and northern ecosystems.

Fundamentally, the antifur move breaks commitments undertaken by nations in the UN Covenant on Economic, Social and Cultural Rights (1966), the Rio Declaration on Environment and Development (1992), the Draft Universal Declaration on the Rights of Indigenous Peoples (1994), the ILO Convention concerning Indigenous and Tribal Peoples in Independent Countries (1989), Article XI of the General Agreement on Trade and Tariffs, and Article 3 of the Convention on Biodiversity. All of these recognize the rights of indigenous peoples to the use of resources for social, cultural, and economic purposes.

The trapping issue highlights the philosophical differences between northern and southern peoples, and between urban and rural residents. The fur industry continues to be valuable and important to a significant portion of the circumpolar countries. In Canada, there are at least 75,000 trappers (half of them aboriginal) and another 25,000 employed in fur ranches, manufacturing, and retailing; the fur industry as a whole generates $600 million per year. In the United States, 50,000 people are employed, plus 1400 retailers and 100 manufacturers, leading to $1.2 billion retail sales in 1995. In the European Union itself, 175,000 are employed directly in the fur trade, plus 50,000 in supply trades, generating more than $6 billion in retail trade. The value of the fur industry in Europe makes the proposed European Union bans on fur imports seem even more hypocritical.

HEATHER MYERS

See also **Fur Trade; Hunting, Subsistence; North Pacific Fur Seal Convention; Seal Skin Directive**

Further Reading

Elias, Peter Douglas, *Northern Aboriginal Communities: Economies and Development*, North York, Ontario: Captus University Publications, 1995

Freeman, M.M.R. (editor), *Endangered Peoples of the Arctic: Struggles to Survive and Thrive*, Westport, Connecticut: The Greenwood Press, 2000

Fur Institute of Canada website: http://www.for.ca/

Herscovici, Alan, *Second Nature: The Animal Rights Controversy*, Toronto: CBC Enterprises, 1985

International Fur Trade Federation, n.d., International Fur Trade Today website: http://www.iftf.com/today.html

Lynge, F., *Arctic Wars: Animal Rights, Endangered Peoples,* Hanover: University Press of New England, 1992

Maracle, R., "Impacts of the European Union (EU) regulation 3254/91 on the aboriginal peoples of Canada;" n.d., http://www.inac.gc.ca/pubs/report.html

Myers, Heather, "From fur to fir: lessons for the BC forest industry from the anti-fur campaign." *Forestry Chronicle,* 77(1) (2001): 77–84

Nelson, Richard K., *Make Prayers to the Raven: A Koyukon View of the Northern Forest,* Chicago: The University of Chicago Press, 1983

TREELINE

The treeline is the transition between boreal forest and tundra ecosystems. It is a major global biogeographic boundary, separating the circumpolar boreal forest (Subarctic) from the Arctic tundra. The term "treeline" has been used to refer to a number of different boundaries, including, among others, the limit of continuous forest, the limit of tree-sized individuals, or the limit of any individuals of the tree species. These can be quite different, as discussed below.

In North America, black spruce (*Picea mariana*) and white spruce (*Picea glauca*) form the treeline, although other trees (e.g., tamarack, *Larix laricina*) can regionally be found north of spruce. In Alaska, trees are found only to the south of the Brooks Range. The treeline is

The treeline ends in sparse stunted growth at the edge of tundra, Churchill, Canada.
Copyright Bryan and Cherry Alexander

located almost at the Beaufort Sea in the Mackenzie Delta region of northwest Canada, and curves to the south of Hudson Bay in central Canada. It again curves northward in eastern Canada and is a broad zone covering several degrees of latitude in Québec and Labrador. In Eurasia, the treeline roughly follows the coast of the Arctic Ocean with a strip of tundra less than a couple of hundred kilometers wide. Spruce, larch (*Larix*), and birch (*Betula*) all form treeline in different regions. In mountainous regions, such as Labrador and Scandinavia, the treeline is more difficult to define, as there are both latitudinal and elevational treelines, and the interaction of these makes a complex of landscapes. Spruce, pine (*Pinus*), and birch may be important treeline species in these regions.

The treeline can be abrupt or diffuse and is better considered a transition region (ecotone) than an actual line on the landscape. This transition region, the forest-tundra, can be compressed into a small area (a few kilometers), or spread over several degrees of latitude. Where the treeline is relatively broad, it can be further subdivided into zones. Where the transition is abrupt, these zones would be compressed or less noticeable. A description of these zones illustrates important processes influencing the treeline. The example given below is from the well-studied treeline region of northern Québec, but this description can probably be applied, with some modification, elsewhere.

The southern limit of the ecotone is the boreal forest. The boreal forest is a conifer-dominated ecosystem that is circumpolar in extent. Except in eastern Siberia, the dominant evergreen conifers are spruce, with codominants that vary by region, and can include, for example, pine, larch, fir (*Abies*), birch, or poplar (*Populus*). Usually, one or several species of spruce comprise the treeline species, but there are regional exceptions. Several characteristics serve to distinguish the boreal forest from the forest-tundra. The key aspects are that the entire landscape, from the low-lying areas to the hilltops are covered by trees, and that after a fire, the trees regenerate, usually from seed. Fire is an important process in the dynamics of the boreal forest, and the trees are adapted to the presence of periodic fires that burn large patches of the forest. The boreal forest at its northern limit is an open community, with widely spaced trees and intervening areas covered by shrubs or lichen. Yellow lichens can give this open forest a characteristic appearance, called the lichen woodland.

At the northern limit of the forest-tundra is the tundra. The tundra, under the influence of Arctic air all year round, is a herb and shrub-dominated ecosystem with no trees. Of course, it is possible to find outliers of the tree species well to the north of the treeline. Individuals or small populations of spruce or other tree species can be found well north of the typical location. These are of some interest for study, as they may indicate times when the treeline was further north than at present. Trees can persist for years or centuries under unfavorable conditions, once established, as the most critical time for survival seems to be the first few years of the seedling's life. Alternatively, these outlier individuals or populations may have become established in some way during several particularly favorable years and persisted north of the usual tree limit since then. When trees persist for years under less than favorable conditions, they tend not to grow to full stature, and remain relatively small, with branches clustered close to the ground. This shrub form of spruce is called krummholz, from the German word meaning "twisted wood," and that describes it well.

The treeline ecotone—the forest-tundra—has characteristics of both of these ecosystems. Here, it is important to think of the vegetation structure on a regional basis—the landscape on the scale of several tens of square kilometers. In the forest-tundra, there is a gradation from south to north. Toward the south, the forest-tundra region resembles the boreal forest, whereas toward the north, it resembles the tundra.

Starting in the southernmost section of the forest-tundra, one starts to observe subtle changes indicating an environment less favorable for tree growth. Spruce (or other species) grow to normal height, but only in the valleys. The summits of the hills begin to sustain tundra. After a fire, there generally will be tree reproduction, but only in the valleys. To the north, the area of tundra begins to be greater and greater as larger portions of the hilltops remain covered by tundra. The local altitude of the tundra portion of the landscape decreases.

Continuing to the north, the relative area of the tundra increases. Furthermore, the spruce become smaller in stature and most have a krummholz form. Trees tend to be found only on more protected areas of the landscape, where the snow accumulates to a greater depth in winter and moisture accumulates from spring snowmelt or seepage. Regeneration typically occurs by vegetative means (layering) rather than by seeds. After a fire, there is no tree regeneration.

The causes of treeline have been studied for years, and treeline has been correlated with a number of climate parameters, for example, the location of the 10°C July isotherm (line of constant temperature; see maps in **Arctic: Definitions and Boundaries**). The most generally accepted explanation of the large-scale location is that the treeline is associated with the mean position, in summer, of the Arctic front. This is itself a major transition in the atmosphere, separating Arctic from tropical air masses. Arctic air masses tend to be colder and drier and with less cloudiness than the modified tropical air that is characteristic of the boreal region in summer. The growing season is shorter and, combined with the low temperatures, leads to an environment where trees cannot survive and grow if a region is dominated by Arctic air masses all year. At a local scale, the distribution of snow seems to be important in permitting the survival of spruce. The snow

protects the branches from abrasion and desiccation in winter.

K. GAJEWSKI

See also **Arctic: Definitions and Boundaries; Boreal Forest Ecology; Treeline Dynamics**

Further Reading

Bryson, R., "Air masses, streamlines and the boreal forest." *Geographical Bulletin*, 8 (1966): 228–269

Crawford, R.M.M., *Studies in Plant Survival*, London: Blackwell, 1989

Larsen, J., *The Northern Forest Border in Canada and Alaska*, New York: Springer, 1989

Payette, S., "The forest tundra and present tree-lines of the northern Québec-Labrador Peninsula." In *Tree-Line Ecology*, edited by Pierre Morisset & Serge Payette, Québec: Université Laval Press, 1983

Scott, G., *Canada's Vegetation*, Montréal: McGill-Queens University Press, 1995

Stevens, G. & J. Fox, "The causes of treeline." *Annual Review of Ecology and Systematics*, 22 (1991): 177–191

TREELINE DYNAMICS

The geographic location of the treeline varies through time: it can move northward when climate conditions are favorable, and retreat southward under less favorable conditions. The processes involved in northward and southward movement are, however, quite different, so that the natures of advancing (northward movement) and retreating (southward movement) treelines are quite different. The rapidity of the movement is different as well.

Several methods are available to study treeline dynamics. For short-term dynamics, that is, changes on the order of years to decades, tree-ring and age-structure analysis can be used. For longer-term dynamics, centuries to millennia, pollen analysis of sediment cores is appropriate. Dating preserved tree trunks found north of the present-day treeline can be used to indicate a period when the treeline had advanced northward.

The position of the treeline moves northward when the climatic conditions in the tundra become favorable for tree growth. The conditions permitting establishment of a tree vary among species, but in general trees need a certain length of growing season, sufficient precipitation, and warm enough conditions during the growing season. Winter temperatures are apparently less important, provided the tree was able to harden in the autumn or late summer. Snow depth is important, and sufficient snow is needed to protect the needles from desiccation or abrasion. Frequently, at the northern limit of a tree species, trees only grow in more protected areas where there is an accumulation of snow.

Propagules of tree species can be transported long distances, either across the snow surface in winter, or along watercourses in spring or summer. When they become established, the tree will grow, but only if there are several years of favorable conditions. The first few years of a tree's growth are the most critical. Once the tree has established, it can probably persist through several unfavorable years. Those trees that do establish can become seed sources for the region and, in this way, large areas of tundra can become forested in a relatively short time.

There is evidence that trees can persist for years or centuries with no seed reproduction. That is, once established, a tree can continue to live even though local conditions are unfavorable for sexual reproduction. During this time, the tree can continue to reproduce asexually, for example, by layering. Layering is the process whereby the branches of the tree produce roots if they should become buried away from the source tree. These can eventually become new plants independent from the source tree, and in this way a dense group of individuals can become established in a small region. These probably persist for many years.

Southward movements of the treeline occur by a very different dynamics. If the environment should be unfavorable for tree reproduction in the forest-tundra, the trees can probably persist for a long time period, although growth may be reduced and there may be no reproduction by seeds. The trees may adopt a shrub form and reproduce by layering. Trees will not disappear from the landscape until a fire kills the individuals. Since the environment is unfavorable for reproduction, there will be none after the fire. In this way, the treeline "moves" southward, as patch after patch of forest are killed with no subsequent reproduction.

Tree-ring studies are used to study the relation between interannual climate variability and tree growth. These studies, now available from around the circumpolar region, show that ring width and wood density are typically correlated with summer temperatures. Not surprisingly, these studies record an irregular alternation of decades of above- and below-normal growth, but different treeline regions have different chronologies. That is, in a particular decade, trees may record below-normal growth in one region, but above-normal growth in another. This means that results from one region cannot be extrapolated to others. In some cases, the cool climate in the years following a major volcanic eruption suppressed tree growth across large regions. Several studies have noted an increase in tree reproduction in the recent past in North America, suggesting ameliorating climate in the past few decades.

The postglacial variations in treeline have been studied in many regions. The study of pollen diagrams from North America shows significant differences in treeline movements during the Holocene from east to west. Except for small local regions, spruce trees (*Picea glauca* and *Picea mariana*) make up the treeline across North America. In Alaska, spruce arrived from the east and migrated westward after 9000 years BP (radiocarbon years before present), arriving in western Alaska by 6000 years BP. Smaller movements both eastward and northward have occurred in the past 8000 years. In the Mackenzie Delta region of Canada, spruce arrived early, and the treeline was located north of the present-day limit between 10,000 and 7000 years BP. It then retreated southward, remaining around 50 km north of the present-day limit until 3500 years BP, subsequently retreating further southward. In central Canada, spruce was found north of the present-day limit between 5000 and 3500 years BP, retreating southward subsequently. In eastern Canada, trees moved to the present-day limit shortly after the region was deglaciated around 6000 years BP. Although there are no north-south movements of treeline recorded, there is a suggestion of a gradual deforestation of the forest-tundra in the past 2000 years.

In Fennoscandia, a zone of mountain birch (*Betula pubescens* spp. *tortuosa*) is located between the tundra and the open pine forest, whereas the spruce limit is further south. Birch arrived first, in the early Holocene, probably spreading north of the present-day limit. Pine arrived 1000–2000 years after birch. Between 5000 and 3000 years BP, both the pine and birch northern limits retreated south; at the same time, spruce arrived at its northern limit. During the past 3000 years, there has been increased human activity in the region, and this has affected the plant populations.

Across much of Russia, including Siberia, several species of larch (*Larix*), tree birch (*Betula*), and one species of spruce (*Picea obovata*) are important in the treeline region. Trees moved northward after the last glaciation, reaching the modern limit around 10,000 years BP. The treeline then advanced to nearly the present-day Arctic Ocean coastline between 9000 and 7000 years BP, retreating southward to the present-day position between 4000 and 3000 years BP.

K. Gajewski

See also **Treeline**

Further Reading

D'Arrigo, R., G. Jacoby, M. Free & A. Robock, "Northern hemisphere temperature variability for the past three centuries: tree ring and model estimates." *Climatic Change*, 42 (1999): 663–675

Gajewski, K., S. Payette & J.C. Ritchie, "Holocene vegetation history at the boreal forest-shrub tundra transition in northern Québec." *Journal of Ecology,* 81 (1993): 433–443

Hyvarinen, H., "Absolute and relative pollen diagrams from northernmost Fennoscandia." *Fennia*, 142 (1975): 3–23

Kremenetski, C.V., L.D. Sulerzhitsky & R. Hantemirov, "Holocene history of the northern range limits of some trees and shrubs in Russia." *Arctic and Alpine Research*, 30 (1998): 317–333

TRESHNIKOV, ALEKSEI FEDOROVICH

MacDonald, G. & K. Gajewski, "The Northern Treeline of
Canada." In *Geographical Snapshots of North America*,
edited by D. Janelle, New York: Guilford Press, 1992
Ritchie, J.C., *Past and Present Vegetation of the Far Northwest
of Canada*, Toronto: University of Toronto Press, 1984

TRESHNIKOV, ALEKSEI FEDOROVICH

Aleksei Fedorovich Treshnikov was a Russian
oceanographer, polar explorer, geographer, and distinguished scientist. He organized and headed the Arctic
expedition on the floating station (1954–1955) and
two expeditions to the Antarctic (1956–1958,
1967–1968). While he was studying oceanography,
one of Treshnikov's tutors in the university was the
President of the Russian Geographical Society, Y.
Shokalsky (1856–1940). Treshnikov was influenced
by this outstanding scientist. In 1938, Treshnikov participated in the hydrographical expedition that measured the water currents in the shallow eastern part of
the Kara Sea. He analyzed these data in his master's
thesis, and this work was acknowledged by Shokalsky.

In 1939–1946, Treshnikov worked in the Arctic
expeditions that studied the hydrology and ice regime
of the Nordic seas. He was intensively involved in the
hydrometeorological support of the Northern Sea
Route navigation, particularly in sea-ice forecasting. At
that time, he prepared several atlases and navigation
manuals and published two monographs and sketches
on hydrometeorology. He received his Ph.D. in 1946.

Since 1948, Treoshnikov was intensively involved
in the Russian program of exploration of the Central
Arctic. He was a participant of several expeditions to
the North Pole and head of the multidisciplinary
research team, which performed systematic oceanographic and geophysical measurements on drifting ice
sheets. They discovered the large anomaly of the geomagnetic field, which traverses the whole Arctic
Ocean. They also discovered the large ridge at the bottom of the Arctic Ocean in the vicinity of the North
Pole and, through bathymetric survey and measurements of the deep ocean water temperatures, estimated the height and aspect of the ridge. Russian polar
expeditions "North 2" and "North 4" in 1948 confirmed that there is a 1800 km (1100 miles) long and
2500–3000 m high ridge on the bottom of the Arctic
Ocean from the New Siberian Islands through the
North Pole to Ellesmere Land. It is called Lomonosov
Ridge. This ridge divides the Arctic Ocean into two
parts with quite different properties and organic content of the deep waters. In 1949, Treshnikov received
the highest state award of the Soviet Union.

In 1954–1955, Treshnikov organized and headed
the research expedition North Pole 3. The research
group set up a camp on the ice sheet 400 km to the east
from the North Pole, and then drifted along the transect coming through the Pole. The drifting camp came
across the Lomonosov Ridge and studied the ocean
bathymetry near the North Pole. Additional data were
obtained by another station North Pole 4, headed by E.
Tolstikov, which started from Wrangel Island and
drifted to the north. These stations collected valuable
data on the bathymetry and hydrobiology of the Arctic
Ocean, the structure and drifting routes of the sea ice,
and Arctic meteorology, and made measurements of
the magnetic fields. Data from the Arctic expeditions
North 2, 3, and North Pole 3, 4 were summarized and
analyzed in Treshnikov's monograph "Arctic
Oceanography." These scientific expeditions found
that the waters of the Pacific Ocean penetrate up to the
North Pole, and play an important role in the circulation of the surface waters in the Arctic.

Treshnikov was the head of four Russian expeditions to the Antarctic. In 1955–1958, his expedition
reached the central Antarctic, and on December 16,
1957 founded the "Vostok" station on the South
Geomagnetic Pole. His second trip was on board the
plane Ilushin-18, which made an experimental flight
from Moscow to the Antarctic in 1963. In 1967–1968,
Treshnikov was the head of the Thirteenth Russian
Antarctic Expedition, and came around Antarctic on
board the ship *Ob*. In the summer of 1973, he made his
fourth trip to the Antarctic rescuing the *Ob*, which was
jammed in the massive floating ices. He wrote a book
"Ice Regime in the Southern Ocean," where he summarized the findings of his expeditions to the Antarctic,
and participated in "The Atlas of Antarctic," for which
he was awarded the State Prize of the USSR in 1971
and the Gold Medal of the Geographic Society.

While the director of the Arctic research institute in
Leningrad, he organized the continuous meteorological observations on tens of stations in the Arctic, on
drifting ice-floes, which were supported by the observations from the ships. He was one of the organizers of
the international research programs on global atmospheric processes (PIGAP) and ocean-atmosphere
interactions in the polar regions (POLEXP). He wrote
more than 200 scientific papers, books, and reports on
the geography of the Nordic countries and oceanography of the Arctic and Southern Oceans.

Treshnikov was the dean of the oceanography
department of the Leningrad State University, lecturing on the world oceans' geography. In 1981, he
became the director of the Limnology Institute of the
Russian Academy of Science. Since 1976, he was
Corresponding Member, and since 1982 a Member of
the Russian Academy of Science. For more than 10
years, he was the vice-president, and since 1980 the
president of the Russian Geographical Society. He was
a member of the editorial board of several scientific

journals and periodicals. Treshikov was an educator and progressive intellectual of the 20th century. He was seriously concerned about environmental problems and natural resources. He wrote several popular books, among them "On the Novosibirsk Island," "A Year on Ice," "Near the Earth's Poles," and "Around the Antarctic."

Biography

Aleksey Fedorovich Treshnikov was born into a peasant family in the village of Pavlovka, Simbirskaya Oblast' (province) on April 14, 1914. He went to rural primary school. From the age of 15, he provided for himself. In 1934, he entered the Leningrad State University, faculty of Geography, Geology, and Soil Sciences. After graduating from the university, Treshnikov began working in the Arctic research institute (since 1958, the Arctic and Antarctic research institute) in Leningrad. At that time, this was one of the world-leading polar research centers. Treshnikov worked there for more than 40 years; during 1960–1981, he was a director of the institute. His works included *Atlas Antarctidy* [Atlas of Antarctic], 1966–1969 and *Istoria Otkrytiai i Issledovania Antarctidy*, [History of Discovery and Exploration of Antarctic], 1963. Treshnikov met Tatiana Nikolaevna Makarevich (1917–1993) at the university in 1938; they married in 1939. They had two daughters: Ksenia and Natalia. Treshnikov dedicated his book *Moi Poliarnje Puteshestvia* [My Polar Expeditions] (1985) to Natalia. Treshnikov died in Leningrad, on November 17, 1991.

M. BELOLUTSKAIA

Further Reading

Gramberg, I.S., D.A. Dodin & N.P. Laverov, *Arctica na poroge tret'ego tysiatcheletiia* [The Arctic on the threshold of the third millennium], St Petersburg: Nauka, 2000

Treoshnikov, A.F., *Moi poljarnye pyteshestvija* [My polar travellings], Moskva: Mysl, 1985

TROMS

Troms county in Norway lies north of the Arctic Circle between Finnmark county and Nordland county. The administrative center and largest town is Tromsø (*see* **Tromsø**). Troms county faces the Norwegian Sea in the west, Finnmark county, Finland and Sweden to the east, and Nordland county to the south.

The county, which has an area of 25,954 km², has a very rugged coastline, with long and deep fjords, and there are many large offshore islands. All the larger islands are connected to the mainland by bridges. Harstad, the second largest town, is located on Norway's largest permanently inhabited island, Hinnøya (2198 km²). Between Harstad and Tromsø, we find Finnsnes, the youngest city (1.01.2000) in Troms county, and located at the bridge to the second largest island of Norway, Senja (1590 km²), with the Andersdalen National Park (69 km²). South we find the highest island of Norway, Andørja (1277 m).

Of the coastline's many fjords, the largest is Lyngenfjorden east of the Lyngen Alps, one of the most marked mountainous areas in Norway with their pointed peaks, deep ravines, glaciers, and rapids. Jiekkevarri (1833 m), the highest peak of the county, is part of the Lyngen Alps. In 2001, work began to establish a landscape protection area of 978 km². Inland there is Dividalen National Park (743 km²). The landscape of Dividalen varies from lowland forests of pine and birch to low hills and mountain plateaus with lakes and bogs interspersed throughout. A sparse pine forest is home to lynx and wolverine. Large numbers of tame reindeer from Sweden come to graze in the park during summer. At Treriksrøysa (Three Countries Cairn) in the National Park, the borders of Finland, Sweden, and Norway meet. A more than 800 km long marked hiking trail (Nordkalottruta) from Karasjok (Finnmark county) to Sulitjelma (Nordland county) passes through all three countries. The Reisa National Park (803 km²) is found in the northern part of the county. Here, the landscape changes from the deep fjords to the large highlands (*vidda*), mostly used as reindeer pasture.

The climate is influenced by the topographic conditions, with a distinct variation of the weather inland and along the coast. The warm Gulf Stream keeps the coast ice-free, with an average temperature in February around −2°C, while the long valleys inland have temperatures, from −6°C to −9°C. The lowest temperature ever measured along the coast is −15°C, while inland it is −35°C. The average summer temperature is 11–12°C at the coast, and 14°C inland, with maximum summer temperatures around 30°C. The annual precipitation is 750 mm along the coast, 300–600 mm inland, with the Skibotn valley as an extremely dry area (less than 300 mm). Along the coast there is the possibility for large amounts of snow, in Tromsø up to 2.40 m snow depth. Midnight Sun occurs from May 21 to July 23, and winter darkness from November 25 to January 21 (Tromsø).

Population and Government

Troms county has a population of 151,777 (Statistics Norway, 2000), of which about 40% live in the capital Tromsø. In Troms, besides more modern immigrants from all over the world, live the ethnic groups of the Saami people, Kven (immigrants from Finland), and Norwegians. Tromsø (population 61,182) is the

Location of Troms and main towns, islands, and rivers.

administrative center: there are 25 municipalities, of which Harstad (23,038), Finnsnes (11,139), and Målselv (7011) are the largest. Harstad, the second largest town by population, flourished during a rich herring fishery at the beginning of the 20th century, and is now a shipbuilding center and port serving the North Sea oil fields.

The municipalities in the northern part of the Troms county benefit from the distinct Norwegian model for regional development. The county parliament has 45 members, with six representatives at the Stortinget (national parliament).

Economy

The county is mainly mountainous; much of its interior supports only livestock raising (sheep and goats). Along the coast and on the islands, fishing is dominant. Traditionally, agricultural activity took place by "combination"-farmers, combining farming with fishing, while nowadays fishing has become more specialized, and the combination of farming and regular work like in the construction business and services has become more common. There is a small industrial sector, mostly fish processing, shipyards, wood industry (particleboard production), and ferrosilicon production at Finnsnes. A number of minerals are found in Troms, but only the graphite ore at Skaland on the island of Senja is exploited on a commercial basis. A number of military installations and the "Brigade Nord" of the Norwegian Army are located in the municipalities of Bardu and Målselv.

The travel patterns have changed from along the coast in the beginning of the 1900s, to be based on roads today. There are no railroads in the county, but the E6 runs through the inner part of the county and a good network of secondary roads. Communications are also by the Hurtigruten (Costal Steamer), speedboat connections, and domestic air services (Bardufoss, Evenes, and Tromsø airfields), and locally by bus and ferries.

The importance of fish farming is increasing. Aquaculture is about to become Norway's second-most important export industry after oil, and salmon fish farms are spread along the coast of Troms. The University of Tromsø runs an aquaculture research station at the island Ringvassøya. In the municipality of Kvæfjord in the southern part of the county, there is large strawberry production.

History

More than 9000-year-old rock carvings evidence the earliest known settlements. In the 8th century, the northern border for Norwegian settlement was in Troms, according to the report from the Norwegian chief Ottar to English King Alfred the Great. The first church of the county was built in Tromsø in 1250. In 1787, the first migration of farmers from southern Norway started to Troms, at this time unpopulated in the inner parts of the county—their particular dialect still exists.

Due to its proximity to the poles, Arctic sailors were recruited from Troms for national and international Arctic expeditions. A number of sealing and whaling vessels had their home port in the fjord Balsfjord. During World War II, the battleship *Tirpitz* sank outside Tromsø. Only the northernmost parts of the Troms county were burned to the ground under the withdrawal of the German troops in 1944/1945.

JOCHEN PETERS

See also **Finnmark; Nordland; Norway; Saami; Tromsø**

Further Reading

Barrett, Rob, Jakob Møller & Ivar Bjørklund (editors), *Bird Life,* Tromsø: University of Tromsø, Tromsø Museum, 1994
Eliassen, Jens-Eric, *Coastal and Fjord Resources of Nordland and Southern Troms Counties,* Tromsø: Fiskeriforskning, 1994
Johnson, Pål Espolin, *Norway's Coastal Voyage to the Top of the World,* Oslo: Cappelen, 2000
Kristoffersen, Ivan (editor), *Troms—Bygd og by i Norge,* Oslo: Gyldendal norsk forlag, 1979
Mørkved, Brynhild & Arne C. Nilssen (editors), *Plant Life,* Tromsø: University of Tromsø, Tromsø Museum, 1993
Norway North of 65, Oslo: Oslo University Press, 1960
Riste, Olav, *Norway's Foreign Relations: A History,* Oslo: Universitesforlaget AS, 2001
Statistics Norway website: http://www.ssb.no/english/
Troms County website: http://www.troms-f.kommune.no/

TROMSØ

Tromsø, from the Old Norse *trums*, interpreted as "current" or "current water," is the largest city in the northern Norway region, and also a fishing port. The city center is located on Tromsø Island (21.7 km²) in the Norwegian Sea, connected by a bridge and an undersea tunnel with the mainland. Tromsø municipality extends to additional islands and the mainland. The international airport of Tromsø, opened in 1964, has mostly domestic flights, but is also the main starting point for flights to Longyearbyen, Svalbard. As the seat of Troms county, Tromsø is the administrative and cultural center of northern Norway.

Tromsø received the rights for trade (city foundation) in 1794, but the settlement is much older (according to 9000-year-old archaeological findings), and the first church here was built in 1252. The warming by the Gulf Stream, its sheltered harbour, which is ice-free all year round, and the rich fishing grounds are considered as the main reason for the settlement. For its high northern latitude (69°40′ N and 360 km north of the Arctic Circle), the climate is mild, with an average temperature of −4.4°C in January to a maximum of 12.5°C in July. Midnight Sun occurs from May 21 to July 23, and the Dark Period occurs from November 25 to January 21.

During the last 100 years, Tromsø has undergone very rapid development, from 6700 (1900) to 61,182 (2003) inhabitants. Due to its role in education and polar research, and as a service center in the northern Norway region, Tromsø is expected to continue to grow. The main industries are fishing and fish processing, shipbuilding, brewing, oil industry, and tourism.

With its location this close to the North Pole, polar explorers like Fridtjof Nansen, Roald Amundsen, and Adolf Erik Nordenskiöld exploited the local knowledge and experience when setting off on expeditions. Today, it is the starting point for many cruise ships. The Norwegian government was based in Tromsø for a short period during World War II, before the king and government fled to exile in Britain in 1940. In 1944, the British air force sank the German battleship *Tirpitz* at Håkøya.

Tromsø has several pseudonyms, for example, "Paris of the North" (due to the relatively well-dressed women at the beginning of the 19th century, and today used to describe the lively nightlife), "Gateway to the Arctic" (illustrating its importance as a center for supplies and trade of the Arctic hunters, a recruiting place for Arctic sailors, and a starting point for the whaling and sealing vessels).

The Mack Brewery (the northernmost brewery in the world) is one of the few remaining industry enterprises in Tromsø; the public administration and service sector, together with shops, hotels, and restaurants stands for almost two-thirds of all employees. The islands around Tromsø are characterized by enterprising fishing villages; the Norwegian Seafood Export Council from its head office in Tromsø coordinates most of the export.

Arctic Cathedral (*Ishavskatedralen*), Tromsø.
Copyright Bryan and Cherry Alexander Photography

In addition to its key position in Arctic research in Norway and in general, Tromsø is a center for education and culture in the North. The University of Tromsø, established in 1968, is the northernmost university in the world, with almost 7000 students. The Northern Lights Observatory (Finnmark), founded in 1927, is today a part of the University of Tromsø. A ground station receiving data from meteorological and Earth observation satellites and the EISCAT station (Svalbard) are located close to the city. Since 1998, the Norwegian Polar Institute (NP) is located in Tromsø.

The city hosts museums of art, history, natural science, polar expeditions, and trade. Other tourist highlights include the Arctic Cathedral (*Ishavskatedralen*), Polaria (the Norwegian Centre for Polar Knowledge), and the funicular to the Storsteinen, a nearby cliff and viewing point 420 m high.

JOCHEN PETERS

See also **Finnmark; Norway; Svalbard; Troms**

Further Reading

Dahl, Håvard (editor), *Northern-Norway: A Way of Life,* Tromsø: University of Tromsø, Tromsø Museum, 1997

Libæk, Ivar, *A History of Norway: From the Ice Age to the Age of Petroleum*, Oslo: Grøndahl Dreyer, 1999

Møller, Jakob J., Per K. Reymert & Øystein Steinlien (editors), *Earth Science*. Tromsø: University of Tromsø, Tromsø Museum, 1992

Norwegian Polar Institute website: http://www.npolar.no/

Rian, Erlend (editor), *Tromsø (English)*. Trondheim: Aune, 2000

Statistics Norway website: http://www.ssb.no/english/

Tromsø gjennom 10000 år, Tromsø: Tromsø Municipality, 1994–1996

Tromsø Municipality website: http://www.tromso.kommune.no/1090.asp

TROPHIC LEVELS

Ecologists consider trophic (feeding) levels in reference to an organism's position in the food chain, or how many steps away from feeding on plant material the organism in question is. Organisms of the first trophic level, also called primary producers, comprise green plants and photosynthetic protists (simple organisms such as algae, foraminifera, ciliates, and flagellates), blue-green bacteria, and other microbes. Herbivores form the second trophic level, as do plant detritivores because both consume the primary productivity of the green plants in the living or dead state, respectively. The third trophic level comprises predators, parasites, and parasitoids (basically predators that feed from the inside of their prey and kill it) that consume living animals in the second trophic level. The fourth trophic level comprises predators and parasitoids that consume living elements from the third level. Animals that consume animal detritus can be considered to be on the third level according to this scheme. Because of the complexity of food webs, not all organisms can be neatly defined as belonging to a single trophic level. Arctic fox are well appreciated as predators (third level) on lemmings (second level) that consume mostly plant material (first level). Foxes may fall prey to raptors or larger carnivores, such as wolves or polar bears (now fourth level) that are mostly third-level consumers, and the corpses of all animals are consumed by flies and other invertebrates (consuming at third, fourth, and fifth trophic levels) and they themselves may be eaten by birds, fish, etc. In practical terms, there are rarely more than four or five trophic levels in any ecosystem.

The eminent ecologist Charles Elton laid the foundation for the trophic-dynamic approach to ecology. This was further formalized by Lindeman (1942), who presented ecological communities through the ideas of energy exchange through the trophic levels rather than through diversity (numbers of species), abundance (numbers of individuals), or biomass (weight of organisms, wet or dried). In general, animals in higher trophic levels tend to be larger than those in lower levels. The exceptions are parasites, animals that hunt cooperatively (such as wolves), and parasitoids (such as various wasps (Hymenoptera) and bristle flies (Diptera: Tachinidae) of the Arctic) that inject their larger prey with eggs. For large predators to live on small prey, their prey must be abundant and the predators must have special feeding structures as do filter feeders, such as many aquatic insect larvae (mosquitoes, caddis flies), aquatic Crustacea (fairy shrimp, *Daphnia* spp., etc.), a host of marine invertebrates, and among the vertebrates the baleen whales epitomize the idea.

The trophic ratio is the ratio of the number of species of predators:prey. When the kinds (trophospecies) of predators and prey are ecologically related trophically, the ratio is usually just over 1 (in the Arctic, the species richness of terrestrial vertebrate predators is greater than the species richness of terrestrial herbivores). In general, the proportions of a fauna that comprise top predators (they have no predators of their own) and that do not prey on anything but plants (basal trophospecies) are 28% and 19%, respectively. About 50% of all animals are predators that can become prey. Thus, species in an ecological community may be better considered as existing in a trophic continuum within a food web. The relatively high proportion of the fauna that is predatory, coupled with the relatively depauperate fauna, has been argued to be, at least in part, the reason for extreme oscillations in populations (e.g., lemming plagues, and the classical population cycles of boreal lynx and hares). In the Arctic, there are not enough species of prey and of predators to damp out the oscillations.

Food webs describe the interactions of organisms in a community as they relate to each other trophically. Food webs can be highly complex. Some of the best understood food webs are from lakes, including some from the Arctic, where biological diversity and the numbers of possible interspecific interactions are low. Partial food webs in the Arctic have been elucidated for marine and terrestrial ecosystems. Various techniques have been used, especially the ratios of stable isotopes of nitrogen and carbon that are differentially taken up from the environment by different organisms and passed on through the food chain. The trophic cascade hypothesis has been invoked, but not without modern debate, to explain the diversity, abundance, activities, and forms of organisms in food webs. Top predators, such as Arctic char in some Arctic lakes, influence the diversity, abundance, and forms of their crustacean prey. In lakes without char, large Crustacea (fairy shrimp, tadpole shrimp) are often present, but where char are present such prey are absent. In lakes with predatory tadpole shrimp, the smaller Crustacea that comprise their prey are translucent and inconspicuous.

A classical area of ecology has been the study of trophic pyramids. On land, the biomass (mass of living organisms) of primary producers is the highest, and that of top predators is the lowest. In marine and aquatic systems, the reverse often operates. The differences can be explained by the relative rates of reproduction of the main primary producers. In marine and aquatic environments, unicellular algae reproduce quickly, yet are removed by herbivores almost as quickly as they are produced. Thus, the carbon, nutrients, and energy they capture are transferred to the next tropic level quickly, and so on up the chain to predators such as fish (e.g., Arctic char, trout, grayling, whitefish, cod, haddock, dab, sea bass, and so on), which represent the highest biomass. These effects are especially important in the Arctic polynya. On land, primary productivity occurs much more slowly and the carbon, nutrients, and energy in more complex plants are less accessible to herbivores. As ecologists have come to understand the dynamics of more and more ecosystems, the pyramid model has been found to be rather simplistic.

The importance of understanding the trophic standing of organisms and of food webs is close to human concerns for at least three reasons. First, it is through food webs that environmental contaminants disperse through life on Earth, as is especially true in the Arctic. A wide array of pollutants find their way into the Arctic environment by global atmospheric circulation. There, the pollutants enter the food web, bioaccumulating (increasing in concentration) as they ascend the tropic levels (*see* **Bioaccumulation**). Thus, high concentrations of radionucleotides, heavy metals, and persistent organic chemicals are present in marine and terrestrial mammals and birds. These levels have become so high in indigenous human populations that there is global, and of course local, concern. Second, overutilization of renewable resources by people has caused major environmental disruptions throughout the world. For the Arctic, commercial depletion of whale stocks has impacted traditional ways of life. Overfishing threatens to erode the balance of the relative abundances of various organisms in marine and aquatic ecosystems, as it has on Grand Banks and elsewhere. The consequences have been suggested to be simplification and shortening of the food chain and food web, and inversion of at least parts of the normal marine trophic pyramid. Third, there are issues of wildlife management within and beyond the Arctic. For example, the overabundance of migratory snow geese in parts of the Hudson Bay lowlands seems to have changed the biota, and the way in which the ecosystem functions, of the saltmarshes.

PETER KEVAN

See also **Food Webs; Primary Production; Secondary Production**

Further Reading

AMAP, *AMAP Assessment Report: Arctic Pollution Issues*, Oslo, Norway: Arctic Monitoring and Assessment Programme (AMAP), 1998

Bliss, L.C., *Truelove Lowland, Devon Island, Canada: A High Arctic Ecosystem*, Edmonton, Canada: University of Alberta Press, 1977

Calow, P. (editor-in-chief), *The Encyclopedia of Ecology & Environmental Management*, Oxford: Blackwell Science, 1998

Golden, H.E. & L.A. Deegan, "The trophic interactions of young Arctic grayling (*Thymallus arcticus*) in an Arctic tundra stream." *Freshwater Ecology*, 39 (1998): 637–648

Jefferies, R.L. & R.F. Rockwell, "An overabundance of lesser snow geese and an apparent trophic cascade." *Integrative and Comparative Biology*, 42 (2002): 1250

Levinson, H., J.T. Turner, T.G. Neilsen & B.W. Hansen, "On the trophic coupling between protists and copepods in arctic marine ecosystems." *Marine Ecology—Progress Series*, 204 (2000): 65–77

Lindeman, R.L., "The trophic-dynamic aspect of ecology." *Ecology*, 23 (1942): 399–418

Lovejoy, C., L. Legendre & N.M. Price, "Prolonged diatom blooms and microbial food web dynamics: experimental results from and Arctic polynya." *Aquatic Microbial Ecology*, 29 (2002): 267–278

May, R.M., *Stability and Complexity in Model Ecosystems. Monographs in Population Biology No. 6*. Princeton, New Jersey: Princeton University Press, 1974

Remmert, H., *Arctic Animal Ecology*, Berlin: Springer-Verlag, 1980

Sato, M., H. Sasaki & M. Fukuchi, "Stable isotope compositions of overwintering copepods in the arctic and subarctic waters and implications to the fishing industry." *Journal of Marine Systems*, 38 (2002): 165–174

Srivastava, D.S. & R.L. Jefferies, "A positive feedback: herbivory, plant growth, salinity, and the desertification of an Arctic salt-marsh." *Journal of Ecology*, 84 (1996): 31–42

TSIMSHIAN

The Tsimshian are an indigenous people of North America. Tsimshian territory lies mainly in the northwest of the Canadian province of British Columbia, straddling two parallel physiographic areas within the western section of the Canadian Cordillera. This area encompasses the watershed of the lower Skeena River from east of Kitselas Canyon down to the Pacific Ocean coast, and includes the archipelago of islands from the mouths of the Skeena and Nass rivers south to the Estevan group. In addition, they have territory around Metlakatla, Alaska, on Annette Island.

The Tsimshian are surrounded by aboriginal people sharing a similar lifestyle and heritage. The neighboring Nisga'a and Gitxsan are the most similar, culturally and linguistically. Nisga'a territories lie in the same Coast Mountain zone as the Tsimshian, but also extend into the Central Plateau and Mountain Area of the Interior System (Holland, 1976). The Gitxsan are entirely in this interior area, and the territorial boundary between them and the Tsimshian approximates the geoenvironmental boundary. Culturally and linguistically more distant are the Haida on the Queen Charlotte Islands, the Haisla further south in the Kitimat Range, the Kwakiutl also to the south, and the Tlingit to the north.

The referent of the term Tsimshian is problematic. For the Tsimshian themselves, the term applies only to the people of the lower Skeena River and adjacent coast. Many outsiders, including many academic writers, call this particular group the Coast Tsimshian or the Tsimshian Proper, and use the term Tsimshian generically as a label for the Tsimshian, Nisga'a, and Gitxsan First Nations. The term Tsimshianic is better for the larger grouping.

The Tsimshian call their language Sm'algyax, or Algyagm Ts'msyeen, the language of the Tsimshian. Nisga'a and Gitxsan are considered separate, but closely related languages in the Tsimshianic language family (Halpin and Seguin, Thompson and Kinkade, both in Suttles, 1990). There is well-accepted evidence of a southern language or dialect in the southern portion of the coastal territory (Kitkatla, Hartley Bay, and Klemtu), but it is not much used today.

Other neighboring nations speak languages from the Wakashan family (the Haisla people in Kitamaat) and from the Haida language isolate. Tsimshians understand these languages only with foreign language training, which, in the past, many Tsimshians received. Today, all Tsimshians speak English, and some Tsimshian can understand other languages, such as French.

Like many aboriginal languages in Canada, Sm'algyax is endangered. Two significant causes of this situation are the historic ethnocentric practices of Christian Churches and the assimilative policies of the Canadian government to undermine indigenous ways of life (Ts'msyeen Sm'algyax Authority, 2001). These pressures continue but many communities are organizing effective resistance with language research, language programs, and other forms of language training that are encouraging a return to Sm'algyax. Today, language training is available in several public schools, the regional university, and many community-operated language classes. Communities are developing this training themselves, usually under the sponsorship of elders and hereditary chiefs, and often with the support of schools and universities. These educational developments attract non-Tsimshian students as well.

Population figures for the Tsimshian are difficult to ascertain. A number of Tsimshian people are not active in their community, or live away from the territory and are not in touch with their community political structures for census purposes, or do not self-identify as Tsimshian on the census. The Tsimshian Tribal Council (TTC) estimates that 10,000 people belong to its member communities, but fully inclusive population estimates for all Tsimshian could be twice as high. The Canadian government recognizes 7207 status Indians as Tsimshians.

The Tsimshian live in communities called Galts'ap or Ts'ap, terms translated by a variety of English words including tribe, town, and village. Of their galts'ap, three communities are primarily coastal and represented by the Indian Reserve towns of Hartley Bay, Kitkatla, and Kitasoo. Another 11 galts'ap traditionally lived along the lower portion of the Skeena River, owning the various mountainous valleys of the major tributary streams that flowed into the Skeena. The lower nine formed a loose residential confederation in the coastal town of Metlakatla. When the fur trade post of Port Simpson was built in the 1830s, during the early mercantile period of Tsimshian history, these nine groups, along with some families from other galts'ap, created a new town site at Port Simpson now called Lax Kw'alaams. A portion of this composite community, along with other individuals and families, moved to Alaska in 1885 as a result of religious controversy within the Anglican Church and established New Metlakatla.

Furthest up the Skeena are the sister communities of Kitsumkalum and Kitselas, the 10th and 11th of the Skeena River Tsimshian communities. They are sometimes called the Canyon Tsimshian because their main towns were located at the canyons on the Kitsumkalum

his managed landscape was redefined as a wilder-
s by colonial forces coveting the resources.
adian governments alienated resources from the
uup, transforming them into resources for the new
nomy, and severely restricting indigenous use to
itional activities (McDonald, 1994). Nonetheless,
munity reliance on laxyuup resources continues,
hin the context of contemporary legislation, and is
ended. Tsimshian struggles for aboriginal rights
economic reforms resist the dominant classifica-
of Tsimshian resources and subsistence in terms
raditional and commercial use. This distinction is
de within a politicized environment of land claims,
riginal rights, and treaty negotiations; however, in
light of the long history of Tsimshian involvement
global trade, it seems artificial.

Tsimshian Houses belong to larger social units.
ditionally, the fission of a lineage could result from
pulation growth or the immigration of members.
w Houses could form under the leadership of a sen-
titleholder from the original House. Barbeau (1917,
29) and McDonald (1994, 2003) have noted the
portance of these related groups for mutual eco-
mic assistance, political alliances, ceremonial sup-
rt, and military aid. Barbeau (1929) saw the groups
clans, but Boas (1916) and McDonald (2003) iden-
ed the term *wil'naat'aL*, a concept Adams (1973)
opted theoretically, but controversially, to describe a
urcating system in Gitxsan society.

All Houses, and all individual Tsimshian, belong to
e of four matrilineal and exogamous groups called
ex in Sm'algyax and confusingly designated as
ns or tribes or crests in English. They are the
nhada (raven or raven/frog for the Nisga'a and
txsan), Gisbutwada (killerwhale/blackfish or fire-
ed for the Nisga'a and Gitxsan), Laxgibuu (wolf),
d Laxsgiik (eagle). The pteex have important social
d ceremonial functions.

In a matrilineal system, the father belongs to a dif-
ent lineage from the children in a marriage. Among
e Tsimshian, the paternal lineage has great impor-
ce throughout the life of the individual (McDonald,
03) for social, cultural, and ceremonial purposes
eguin, 1986). These obligations are grounded in the
ternal lineage, but can involve the larger wil'naat'aL
d pteex relations of the father.

The religious views and worldviews of the
imshian came under heavy attack from the Christian
urches and colonial government, with destructive
nsequences on the integrity of the belief system and
e actions of practitioners. In his description of the
ditional religious beliefs of the Tsimshian, Boas
916) noted the importance of Heaven as the ruler of
stinies, giver of values and morals, and a helper of
ople. For Guedon (in Seguin, 1986), the basis of the

Tsimshian world view was a personalized and multidi-
mensional universe where beasts, objects, and all living things communicate. Some entities, the halaayt,
were capable of transmuting from one dimension to
another. Guedon also described functional variation
among practitioners (curing, harming, politics, entertainment, initiation) and variation by social status. A
model has been presented of the wholeness and
integrity of Tsimshian culture based on an axiomatic
tension between the five symbolic categories of the
potlatch, winter ceremonials, crests, spirits, and light,
with light being the all-pervading source and summary of the culture. Throughout the colonial period, various Christian churches opportunistically employed
syncretic practices. Most Tsimshians identify themselves as Christian or do not practice a religion. There
has not yet occurred the same cultural recovery in religious belief witnessed in other aspects of culture, but
the syncretic practices now help perpetuate indigenous
Tsimshian spiritual values within the Christian context.

Politically, the Tsimshian have a long and effective
history of actively building relationships with neighboring peoples, national and regional governments,
and international organizations. Their central organization is the TTC, formed to facilitate and coordinate
the Tsimshian comprehensive claim process. Integral
to their current political work is their participation in a
long and ever evolving list of organizations that fight
for aboriginal rights and other issues. Two examples
are participation in the First Nations Summit, which
represents the interests of First Nations working to
negotiate treaties with the provincial and federal governments, and the Northwest Tribal Treaty Nations,
which works to advance and protect the common interests of the member First Nations.

JAMES ANDREW McDONALD

Further Reading

Adams, John W., *The Gitskan Potlatch, Population Flux,
Resource Ownership, and Reciprocity*, Toronto: Holt,
Rinehart and Winston, 1973

Barbeau, Marius, "Growth and Federation in the Tsimshian
Phratries." In *Proceedings of the 19th International
Congress of Americanists* 1915, 1917, pp. 402–408

———, *Totem Poles of the Gitksan, Upper Skeena River,
Ottawa*: Department of Mines, 1929 (National Museum of
Canada, Bulletin 61)

Boas, Franz, *Tsimshian Mythology, Based on Texts Recorded by
Henry W. Tate*. 31st Annual Report, 1909–1910, Bureau of
American Ethnology, 1916, pp. 27–1037

Garfield, Viola, *Tsimshian Clan and Society*, Seattle: University
of Washington Press, 1939

Holland, Stuart S., *Landforms of British Columbia, A
Physiographic Outline*. in British Columbia Department of
Mines and Petroleum Resources, Bulletin No. 48, Victoria:
The Government of British Columbia, 1976

and Skeena rivers. They occasionally call themselves the freshwater Tsimshian because they are the most inland and, traditionally, tended to maintain winter residences inland.

Settlement patterns changed with the industrial era, which could be dated to the first cannery on the Skeena in the 1870s, although it should be noted that commercial production and sale of fish, lumber, and other commodities actually started a hundred years earlier. The colonial town of Port Essington was a major industrial/cannery center at the mouth of the Skeena River and depended, originally, on indigenous labor. At the request of the main industrialist, an alliance was created, based on the participation of Kitsumkalum and Kitselas, to ensure a constant supply of fishermen and cannery workers for the canneries there. The town lasted a little more than 80 years. With the resource depleted and technology changing, the canneries centralized in the nearby rail terminal of Prince Rupert, causing Tsimshian demographics to shift again. One consequence was the reestablishment of the town site of Kitsumkalum in the early 1960s, with an economic emphasis on employment in the forest industry.

Port Essington was one among a number of industrial and agricultural centers that appeared on the coast during the 20th century, attracting Tsimshian people while jobs were available. Most of those settlements disappeared in favor of larger centers like Prince Rupert, Port Edward, Terrace, and Thornhill, which continue to have significant Tsimshian populations. Tsimshians in these urban centers live "off-reserve," a term associated with restrictive government policies limiting residency on the Indian Reserve.

Recent changes in these policies enabled many families to return to their home communities. The resulting, often large population growths on some reserves simultaneously revitalized the communities, placed great pressures on the social infrastructure, and created numerous new challenges to the cultural, social, and political life of the reserves. An indication of the magnitude of the impact is the 400% growth of the village of Kitsumkalum within five years.

Today, Tsimshian people live throughout the world. Their reasons for moving away include employment opportunities, educational opportunities, personal preferences, and government assimilation policies such as the adoption policies that removed children from their homes into highly assimilationist, often foreign environments. Most Tsimshians migrate within the province of British Columbia, but sizable populations live in Washington State and Alaska, and there are individuals scattered elsewhere in Canada and the United States. A few live in Europe and Asia. The size of the diaspora is not known, but every year different Tsimshian organizations, especially Band Councils

and the TTC, receive information ... ing to establish communications w... munity. These migrants may not I... that is also part of the Tsimshian h...

Tsimshians focus on the relatio... matrilineal corporate group and i... central feature of their society. The... House (waap or wilp) consists of a... hold includes affines, plus a variet... viduals and, in precolonial times, sl... Individuals can become attached t... ceremonial adoption or the absor... related lineage.

The House group is identified wi... ed territories (laxyuup), additional... cific resource sites such as fishing st... nonmaterial resources such as songs... crests, and other privileges. Hou... owned by the lineage and managed... structure with the senior titleholder... steward. Today, there is a strong s... territories are not normally perm... from a House, and cannot be approp... by a colonial power, a point driven... tions with the Canadian and provin... The structure and resources of the ... were dramatically impacted by colo... early 20th century (Garfield, 1939), ... relationship with the Canadian feder... evolve.

Traditionally, the laxyuup is th... many resources needed to sustain the... industries, and to make them wealthy... resources of the laxyuup are car... Socially, the laxyuup is the home c... place where children learn how to be... are taught the culture, and learn the... ancestors. Spiritually, the laxyuup be... the House and the galts'ap. The lax... people, connecting them to their pa... generations. Kitsumkalum elders s... embodies the culture. These values... context of the Canadian state.

The Tsimshian used an extensive ra... from their laxyuup in accordance... management principles that created a... scape (McDonald, 2003). Boas's (191... 19th-century seasonal cycles was giv... by Garfield (1939) and updated by M... in the context of a cultural ecology c... under colonial rule. Some writers have... theme of starvation stalking the tow... the spring, but elders refer to the abu... laxyuup, which they describe as storag... (McDonald, 2003).

McDonald, James Andrew, "The Marginalization of a Cultural Ecology: The Seasonal Cycle of Kitsumkalum." In *Native Peoples, Native Lands*, edited by Bruce Cox, Ottawa: Macmillan, 1987, pp. 109–218

———, "Building a moral community for the 21st century: Tsimshian potlatching, implicit knowledge, and everyday experiences." *Cultural Studies*, 9(1) (1994): 125–144

———, "Social change and the creation of underdevelopment: a northwest coast case." *American Ethnologist*, 21(1) (1994): 152–175

———, *People of the Robin: The Tsimshian of Kitsumkalum*, Edmonton: CCI Press, 2003 (Solstice series; no. 1)

Seguin, Margaret, "Understanding Tsimshian Potlatch." In *Native Peoples, The Canadian Experience*, edited by R.B. Morrison & C.R. Wilson, Toronto: McClelland and Stewart, 1986, pp. 556–585

Suttles, Wayne (editor), *Handbook of North American Indians Northwest Coast*, Volume 7, Washington, District of Columbia: Smithsonian Institution, 1990

TUKTOYAKTUK

The hamlet of Tuktoyaktuk, Northwest Territories, is an Inuvialuit community located on the shores of the Beaufort Sea, east of the Mackenzie Delta, at 69°27′ N 133°05′ W. The community is 137 km north of Inuvik, and it is the most northerly community on mainland Canada. The permafrost terrain of the community is characterized by tundra polygons and small shallow lakes.

The population was estimated at 979 in 2000, with approximately 88% of the population being Inuvialuit. The mean annual precipitation is 138 mm, and the mean annual temperature is –10°C, with a mean summer temperature of 4°C and a mean winter temperature of –29°C. The ocean ice breaks up in late June, and freezes again in late October.

Tuktoyaktuk derives its name from the Inuvialuit place name for "resembling a caribou," which is the shape of the point of land that the community originally occupied. The community has open ocean on one side, and a sheltered harbor on the other side. Tuktoyaktuk was established as the port of choice for the Mackenzie River traffic, serving community resupply and commercial requirements during the 1930s. A Hudson's Bay Company store and Anglican and Roman Catholic missions were also established in the 1930s.

The introduction of fur trading into the region encouraged the Inuvialuit of the Tuktoyaktuk area to focus on trapping furs instead of their subsistence economy of hunting and fishing. Trapping continued to be the principal means of economic livelihood until the early 1950s, when the DEW Line and government services introduced a wage-based economy to the community.

Interest in the Mackenzie Delta as a potential source of oil and gas began in the early 1960s. Tuktoyaktuk was selected as a base of operations for the offshore operations because the community possessed the only adequate natural harbor in the delta area, and had an adequate runway. In the 1970s and early 1980s, 53 significant oil and gas discoveries were made in the Mackenzie Delta-Beaufort region. The estimate of the total resources discovered up to 1989 was 1.01 billion barrels of recoverable oil, and nine trillion cubic feet of marketable gas.

Oil-and gas-related activity in the Tuktoyaktuk region declined after the early 1980s and into the late 1990s. In 2000, the Mackenzie Delta was once again very active with natural gas exploration activity. The region produced exploration bids totaling $466.6 million in 2000, which are spending commitments for the next 5 years. These dollars will translate into direct employment and logistical support opportunities for the entire region, including Tuktoyaktuk. A future natural gas pipeline from the region is emerging as a viable project in the foreseeable future.

Tuktoyaktuk has had an ongoing problem with shoreline erosion that has been documented for the past 60 years, and has necessitated the abandonment of several buildings. The shoreline continues to erode at the north end of the community in spite of efforts to protect it. Global climate change is seen to enhance this problem in the future, and may require the community to relocate buildings in the future.

KENNETH R. JOHNSON

Further Reading

http://www.maca.gov.nt.ca/resources/communityresult.asp?ComCode=405

http://www.stats.gov.nt.ca/CPWeb/Commasters/TUK_basepage.html

Welcome to Canada—North West Territories, November 1998, Community Economic Development Services, RWED, GNWT

TUNDRA

The term "tundra" is derived from the Finnish word *tunturi* for sparse woodlands and barrens (where vegetation is absent or poorly developed) near the treeline. Tundra therefore usually refers to treeless areas beyond the climatic limit for the growth of trees and has therefore been applied to Arctic, Antarctic, and alpine regions. Tundra can also be a general geographic designation for areas with permafrost, as well as part of a proper name for a specific treeless area, especially in Russia, where maps may reveal place names such as the Bol'shezemelskaya (Big Land) Tundra or the Yamal (Land's End) Tundra.

In botanic terms, terrestrial biologists define the Arctic as those lands poleward of the climatic limit of trees and agree that the flora is that of a single region.

Despite its occurrence over several disjunct landmasses, the Arctic is comprised of a single biome, the tundra, which also encompasses so-called polar desert systems in the far north. The vascular flora (i.e., plants that have pipelines carrying water and nutrients around the plant) of Arctic tundra is severely diminished, comprising mainly low shrubs and herbs, and similarity between Arctic continents is high (c.60%), extremely so in High Arctic zones with more severe climates and soils (up to 90%). Although similarity of the nonvascular flora is also high on a circumpolar basis, species richness of bryophytes (mosses and hepatics, or liverworts) and lichens tends to be higher than that of vascular plants within a given landscape.

Compared to more temperate ecosystems, Arctic tundra vegetation has low species diversity, simple structure, and low annual primary production, approximately one-half that of temperate grasslands. Nonetheless, tundra ecosystems support large populations of wild and semidomestic animals highly valued by both nonnative and indigenous peoples, and they supply critical nesting habitats for immense numbers of shorebirds, waterfowl, and other birds.

Evolution of the Tundra Flora

Among flowering plants, the tundra comprises a distinctive flora, the majority of species being confined to or at least most abundant in areas north of the forest boundary, although some species range widely from temperate to boreal forest regions. It is generally agreed that most Arctic phanerogams (plants with visible seeds, which are dominated by perennial herbs) evolved before the development of Arctic tundra environments. The assumed evolutionary origins traditionally include mainly alpine habitats, although other likely candidates include coniferous forests, steppe, and sparsely wooded areas, such as the Central Asian highlands, where taxa would have become adapted to cool, dry, open situations. The Early Tertiary fossil plant record from the present Arctic lands appears to be that of a deciduous forest flora of plains and open country of a presumably temperate climate. Interestingly, more than half of the modern species are of polyploid origin, although the reasons for this have yet to be satisfactorily explained.

According to bryologist Howard Crum, mosses and hepatics are extremely ancient, dating at least to the Upper Carboniferous (300+ million years BP). Most Mesozoic and Cenozoic bryophytes known from North America belong to genera and, perhaps, even to species still growing on the continent. There are few mosses of widely disjunct bipolar distribution. A group of strictly Arctic bryophytes extends more or less continuously around the Arctic Ocean basin. In fact, this region has proven to be so unexpectedly rich in endemic (i.e., naturally occurring only in the Arctic) species that it may very well have been a primary center for the dissemination of bryophytes during interglacial and post-Pleistocene times, much as the late Swedish taxonomist and phytogeographer Eric Hultén had suggested for higher plants. Truly Arctic bryophyte species are not even closely related systematically or phylogenetically to those of temperate regions immediately to the south, and most certainly have not evolved directly from them. The closest relatives of these species, where they exist, occur in very distant parts of the world, usually in the Southern Hemisphere, which are characterized by ancient and primitive floras, a further indication of antiquity.

The traditional view is that the circumpolar Arctic endemic cryptogams (flowerless and seedless plants that reproduce by spores, e.g., ferns, mosses, algae, and fungi) are Tertiary relics. The lichenologist John Thomson has suggested that isolated montane habitats extant in the Miocene (15 million years BP) could well have provided conditions suitable for the origin of Arctic-alpine species. Contrary to the bryophytes, the Southern Hemisphere is the center of distribution of several lichen genera, which are thought to have evolved there and which are represented in the Northern Hemisphere by only one or two species. Already in the Early Cretaceous (140+ million years BP), the flora of Antarctica comprised a wide variety of lichens and bryophytes.

Generally speaking, the ranges of most cryptogams are geographically broader than those of phanerogams, and many more species are widely disjunct over the world. Similar to phanerogams, the moss, hepatic, and lichen floras of mountains in both North America and Eurasia share a very significant circumpolar/Arctic-alpine or Arctic-montane element. It thus seems even more likely in the case of cryptogams than of higher plants that the majority of species originated before the retreat of forests and other temperate vegetation, with their occurrence in the tundra reflecting tolerance of polar environments rather than evolution in response to the selection pressures exerted by such conditions.

Development of Modern Tundra

In both polar regions, there is evidence of four major periods of glacier growth and decay during the Pleistocene. The most recent Wisconsin or Würm glaciation began its major retreat about 14,000 years BP, although substantial areas of the Arctic are believed to have become deglaciated only 5000–10,000 years BP. Warmer Mesozoic climates began cooling in the late Cretaceous and continued cooling through the Tertiary, with coniferous and deciduous forests persisting at high latitudes until the late Pliocene, when the onslaught of glaciations spread Arctic conditions far to the south of the present northern treeline. Recolonization by plants and animals followed each glacial retreat, and it was during this period that the modern tundra assemblages began to take shape.

Contemporary tundra vegetation types range from tall shrub tundra (2–5 m high), to dwarf-shrub heath and dry tundra (5–20 cm high), and graminoid-moss tundra (*see* **Dry Tundra; Dwarf-Shrub Heaths; Shrub Tundra**). Such landscapes have a total plant cover of 80–100%, including an abundance of cryptogams in most sites, sometimes with cover values well over 50%. Soils are permanently frozen, with only the upper portion, the so-called active layer, thawing in summer. The active layer is typically 20–60 cm, except in riparian areas along rivers where it may be up to 100–200 cm deep. These river habitats are where the tallest shrubs develop through a combination of wind protection, from deep snow banks in winter, and deeply thawed soils in summer, for adequate root development. The timing of snowmelt has a significant influence on species distribution, particularly in the High Arctic. There is also a very strong correlation between shrub height and average snow depth, especially in the Low Arctic.

How Many Species?

The late Arctic-alpine taxonomists Áskell and Doris Löve believed that the original Arctic flora probably had about 1500 vascular species and had reached a largely circumpolar distribution prior to the onset of Plio-Pleistocene glaciations. However, each successive glaciation certainly caused the extinction of some species and the modern Arctic flora ended up with only about 1000–1100 species of higher plants, depending on the taxonomic treatment and the limits of the territories considered as Arctic. If subspecies are included, the vascular total is closer to 2000. The nonvascular circumpolar flora also shows at least a general relationship with latitude in that High Arctic diversity appears impoverished compared to low Arctic, Subarctic, and boreal regions. The moss flora thus ranges from 105 species on northern Ellesmere Island, to 415 species for the North Slope of Alaska, and 530 species for the Russian Arctic. Broadly similar patterns are evident for hepatics, with 43 species reported from northern Ellesmere Island, 135 species from South Greenland, and 205 species from the Russian Arctic. Among lichens, 186 species are listed for the whole of Ellesmere Island, 331 species for Baffin Island, 965 species for the North American Arctic, 1078 species for the Russian Arctic, and over 1300 species for the circumpolar Arctic (not including synonyms).

Summer warmth is considered the dominant macroenvironmental control delimiting vascular plant vegetation distribution in the Arctic, although a mosaic rather than a zonal pattern is most helpful in understanding local biological diversity. Within a given bioclimatic zone, factors such as moisture, nutrient status, soil chemistry and wind become important controls, as evidenced by change along local catenas (i.e., along a local sequence of soils of about the same age) in a number of landscapes. Gross distributional patterns among Arctic cryptogams are not so easily explained, although there can be pronounced differences between both cryptogamic and noncryptogamic floras of adjacent areas where substrates vary even slightly in age since deglaciation or in chemical status. This is often the case among bryophytes, which may be sensitive to subtle spatial and temporal changes in factors such as soil texture, moisture, and pH.

Functional Differences between Low and High Arctic Tundra

The circumpolar north is roughly divided into two regions—High and Low Arctic—based on differences in biogeography, climate, and edaphic (soil) features. The division into Low and High Arctic has been mapped, with phytogeographic subdivisions within each major zone. The High Arctic, in general, differs from the Low Arctic in having very low-growing plant communities—polar desert and polar semidesert—with only 10–30% cover of vascular plants. Tundra heath/dwarf shrub communities, sedge meadows, and wet tundra with continuous vascular plant cover and a variety of growth forms, which are abundant in the Low Arctic, are very minor components and usually restricted to coastal lowlands (*see* **Dwarf-Shrub Heaths; Sedge Meadows; Wet Tundra**). Taken together, relatively productive terrestrial ecosystems such as these, sometimes referred to as "polar oases," comprise only a tiny fraction (*c*.1%) of the surface area of the High Arctic, yet are critical to the region's terrestrial food chain providing essential summer habitat for many herbivores, for example, muskox, caribou (reindeer), and microtines. Cottongrass tussocks (*Eriophorum vaginatum*) are important in terms of structure, function, and surface hydrology in many Low Arctic and Subarctic ecosystems, and can also burn readily in dry summers. However, so-called tussock tundra is absent in the High Arctic (*see* **Tussock Tundra**).

Other differences between the High Arctic compared to the Low Arctic include (1) a shorter growing season (2–2.5 months versus 3–4 months), (2) cooler summers (July mean 2–8°C versus 4–11°C), (3) less precipitation, (4) less biomass and slower decomposition, (5) eight species of land mammals versus 10–15 species, (6) 10–20 nesting birds versus 30–60 species, (7) vascular flora of 360+ versus about 600 species, (8) richer bryophyte flora but with fewer species of *Sphagnum* and therefore extremely limited peatlands and bogs, (9) poorer invertebrate faunas, and (10) significantly slower soil-forming processes.

Dynamics of Tundra Vegetation and Soils

To early observers, Arctic ecosystems appeared to be so thoroughly affected by the natural disturbance regimes associated with frozen ground—on a variety of sloped and level soil surfaces—that "stability," as represented by so-called "climax communities," was simply absent. Several others have also acknowledged the strong relations between vegetation and periglacial geomorphology. Recent thinking incorporates the various disturbance regimes into a theoretical framework in which the factors limiting directional succession and individualistic responses of species and communities are necessarily accounted for and alternative stable states are possible. Periglacial erosional processes, such as thermokarst, shallow-layer detachment slides, and gelifluction processes, are still considered important, especially in regions with ice-rich permafrost. However, herbivory is increasingly seen as a force to contend with—both as a form of natural "disturbance" in itself and as a potential limiting factor during succession. This is particularly the case in the relatively lush lowland and coastal tundra ecosystems with high herbivore densities and complex plant-animal interactions (*see* **Plant-Animal Interactions**).

In order to better understand the role of vegetation dynamics in the conservation of tundra ecosystems, it is necessary to draw attention to general system structure and production characteristics as a context for physical disturbance. The most productive Arctic ecosystems often have 2–4 species, contributing 60–80% of the vascular plant production. This relationship is seldom true for the cryptogams, where species richness is much greater and productivity is broadly shared. Most vascular plants are perennial, long-lived species ranging in age from 5 to 7 years for individual graminoid stems to 50 to 100+ years for tussock graminoids and deciduous shrubs. With regard to community structure, tundra is considered to be "root biased" since root:shoot ratios can be as large as 10–20:1. The traditional view is that an impact of insufficient intensity to open the root mat in these root-biased systems will have little impact on species coexistence. However, recent studies have demonstrated that even minimal mechanical disturbance (such as off-road vehicle traffic) can have lasting impacts on tundra vegetation and soils, particularly in the High Arctic.

Surface hydrology is extremely important for the development and maintenance of tundra. In coastal areas, raised beach ridges resulting from isostatic rebound may extend intermittently across vast lowlands, with the result that regionally significant mire complexes can develop. Prominent examples include the meadow systems of the Hudson Bay lowlands and northern Devon Island in Canada. In such permafrost areas, surface moisture and drainage appear to be related more to the pattern of snow accumulation and runoff than moisture derived from the thawing active layer. Where slope is more significant, such as on the coasts of northern Baffin Island and southern Novaya Zemlya, closed tundra vegetation can still develop when adequate moisture is available via snow patches, which can persist until the middle of August. Studies on Cornwallis Island and Axel Heiberg Island in the Queen Elizabeth Islands have found that as much as 80% of the annual precipitation can be lost directly into the atmosphere through evaporation, leaving only 20% for runoff, which occurs mostly during and immediately after the melt period. However, this does not necessarily mean that there is inadequate moisture for plant growth. For example, glacial meltwater available throughout the growing season allows for the development of small but ecologically significant wetlands even in relatively warm and dry High Arctic landscapes such as the area around Lake Hazen on Ellesmere Island.

Tundra Classification and Plant Categorization Schemes

The methods and nomenclature for characterizing tundra vegetation, vegetation-soil units, and plant groups vary considerably throughout the Arctic, and often even within individual countries. The substantial difficulties in comparing the respective classifications resulting from these different approaches have become most evident in recent years through, for example, the international effort to create a circumpolar Arctic vegetation map (CAVM; see separate entry). CAVM scientists are currently collaborating to develop a legend framework that seeks to overcome these difficulties. The following provides a brief overview of the major historical and contemporary classification schemes for tundra vegetation/soils and plant groups.

Physiognomy

Physiognomic approaches have generally been preferred in the North American Arctic. This is at least partly because workers there have tended to use only vascular floristics, which are inadequate for tundra vegetation classification due to the wide ecological

Cottongrass on summer tundra in July, Senyarinskiya, Chuktotka.
Copyright Bryan and Cherry Alexander Photography

amplitude of the most prominent plant species. The principal unit is the "formation" and vegetation units have typically been described by characterizing the dominant structure and plant life forms. Examples include dwarf-shrub heath, sedge-moss meadows, tussock tundra, and cryptogam-herb tundra. Another approach is to emphasize the structure of the combined soil-vegetation unit. Examples include hummock-hollow terrain, frost-boil tundra, high-center, low-center, and ice-wedge polygons (patterned ground formed when contraction and expansion of permafrost creates ice-filled cracks that meet in a geometric pattern to enclose a low or high central area), and soil polygons. The major advantage of the physiognomic approach is that it allows nonspecialists to visualize the terrain and general tundra structure/appearance. The disadvantage is that for specialists it reveals nothing about vegetation composition and therefore little about the ecology of a particular system, for example, prevailing soil conditions such as moisture, texture, and pH.

Geobotany/Phytosociology

Until recently, classification of tundra vegetation using traditional geobotanical or phytosociological methods was limited to the Eurasian Arctic. Floristic-sociological methods are mostly rooted in the so-called Braun-Blanquet approach to classification and interpretation of communities. Plant communities are conceived as types of vegetation recognized by their floristic composition.

The underlying assumption is that the full species compositions of communities better express their relationships to one another and environment than any other characteristic. The basic units are called "associations." These are differentiated based on "character species," which possess different degrees of "fidelity."

The advantage of the phytosociological approach is that the Latin name given the association (e.g., *Caricetum stantis*) is derived directly from the character taxon or taxa and therefore immediately conveys some sense of community ecology to a specialist. Traditional disadvantages include the long apprenticeships required of would-be practitioners, the need to accurately identify the full range of vascular and nonvascular species within all "relevés" or sample plots, and the ostensibly subjective nature of both the field sampling and interpretation of the results. Computer-based approaches employing multivariate statistics have lately helped to add a more objective element to the analysis and interpretation of field data. Unfortunately, the challenge of nonvascular taxonomy, in both the field and the laboratory, remains a significant deterrent to many students outside of Europe and Russia.

Growth Forms, Life Forms, Strategies, and Functional Types

Other approaches to categorizing tundra plants have emphasized plant growth form, life history and, more recently, physiological "strategies." Growth form systems are quite old and are based on the gross morphology (architecture) of plants as they affect vegetation structure. The concept is therefore free of any hypotheses about adaptation. Life forms are considered types of plants having the same kind of morphological and/or physiological adaptation to a certain ecological factor. Life forms usually focus on specific plant characteristics, whereas plant strategies refer to coadapted traits fitting generalized environmental constellations. In practice, this distinction is somewhat arbitrary since most schemes adopt a position between these two extremes. Plant functional types are based on the growth forms traditionally recognized by Arctic ecologists. Recent research by F. Stuart Chapin III, Gaius Shaver, and colleagues has endeavored to objectively define functional types based on multivariate analyses of plant traits in order to develop a framework for predicting vegetation responses to, and effects on, ecosystem processes.

The above categorization systems have generally been applied to both vascular and nonvascular plants. The ecological "indicator value" of poikilohydric (i.e., active at high humidity, becomes dormant when water is scarce) bryophytes and lichens has long been well known. The life form systems of Heinjo During and Jeffrey Bates therefore focus on water relations, since water is one of the most important environmental factors for both groups of plants. With regard to growth forms, mosses are divided into at least two groups based primarily on the positioning of reproductive organs via their respective branching patterns: acrocarpous (erect, tufted) and pleurocarpous (lateral, spreading). Recent research argues for the additional distinction of cladocarpous forms based on differing perichaetial positions. Hepatics are divided into leafy and thallose forms, but little work has been done to investigate their respective adaptations to ecological factors. Lichen growth forms are typically divided into crustose (crustlike), foliose (leafy), and fruticose (branched). More so than in bryophytes, lichens can be further grouped according to substrate preference, for example, species growing, respectively, on soil (terricolous), rocks (saxicolous), bark/wood (corticolous), and leaves (folicolous). Among lichens, statistically significant relationships have been demonstrated among survival strategy/growth form, mode of asexual reproduction (see below), and substratum preference.

Plant Reproduction

Within even a relatively small area of tundra, one may encounter a wide variety of sexual and asexual means of plant reproduction. The predominantly belowground allocation of biomass in tundra ecosystems has led many to believe that tundra species have largely substituted asexual methods of reproduction for sexual means. However, among vascular plants, taxa never producing seed are very rare and taxa producing copious amounts of seeds are common, even among those taxa with highly developed means for rapid vegetative growth. Particularly in communities characterized by rhizomatous graminoids, plants can easily resprout from intact tillers and then continue to spread vegetatively. Recruitment from the "seedbank" (including viviparous propagules) may also occur, most notably in disturbed patches resulting from either natural or anthropogenic causes. In general, seeds of most species germinate only on warm microsites (15–20°C). In the High Arctic, seed production can be more reduced and infrequent, and viability very low, especially among meadow-forming graminoids.

In bryophytes and lichens, asexual propagation predominates. This is the case in bryophytes, despite the fact that some 50% of the taxa are dioecious. Among lichens, asexual propagation is commonly achieved either by specialized propagules or simply by broken-off fragments, although these processes are less common among crustose forms. The advantages of such vegetative strategies are a greater survival for propagules and a rapid invasion of new habitats.

Anthropogenic Effects

Human impact is more extensive within the tundra biome now than at any time in the past. While dramatically different from Low and Subarctic regions, where most applied ecological studies of tundra to date have been based, the more remote High Arctic is also threatened by development and environmental change. Existing and potential environmental problems include direct habitat loss from gas and oil exploration and production, and other nonrenewable resource developments, for example gold and coal mining. Additional to these are the indirect effects of climate change and global warming (see **Global Change Effects**).

BRUCE FORBES

See also **Dry Tundra; Flora of the Tundra; High Arctic; Lichen; Mesic Tundra; Polar Desert; Shrub Tundra; Subarctic; Treeline; Tussock Tundra; Vegetation Distribution; Wet Tundra**

Further Reading

Bates, Jeffrey W., "Is 'life-form' a useful concept in bryophyte ecology?." *Oikos*, 82 (1998): 223–237

Bliss, Lawrence C. & Nadya V. Matveyeva, "Circumpolar Arctic Vegetation." In *Arctic Ecosystems in a Changing Climate: An Ecophysiological Perspective*, edited by F. Stuart Chapin III, Robert L. Jefferies, James F. Reynolds, Gaius R. Shaver & Josef Svoboda, New York: Academic Press, 1992, pp. 59–89

Chapin III, F. Stuart & Christian Körner (editors), *Arctic and Alpine Biodiversity: Patterns, Causes and Ecosystem Consequences*, Berlin: Springer, 1995

Chapin III, F. Stuart, M. Syndonia Bret-Harte, Sarah E. Hobbie & Hailin Zhong, "Plant functional types as predictors of transient responses of Arctic vegetation to global change." *Journal of Vegetation Science*, 7 (1996): 347–358

Chernov, Yuri I., *The Living Tundra*, Cambridge: Cambridge University Press, 1985

Crum, Howard, "Evolutionary and Phytogeographic Patterns in the Canadian Moss Flora." In *The Evolution of Canada's Flora*, edited by R.L. Taylor & R.A. Ludwig, Toronto: University of Toronto Press, 1966, 29–42

During, Heinjo J., "Ecological Classifications of Bryophytes and Lichens." In *Bryophytes and Lichens in a Changing Environment*, edited by Jeffrey W. Bates & Andrew M. Farmer, Oxford: Clarendon Press, 1992, pp. 1–31

Hultén, Eric, *Outline of the History of Arctic and Boreal Biota During the Quaternary Period*, New York: Wheldon & Wesley, 1937 (1972 reprint)

Jonasson, Sven, Terry V. Callaghan, Gaius R. Shaver & Lena A. Nielsen, "Arctic Terrestrial Ecosystems and Ecosystem Function." In *The Arctic: Environment, People, Policy*, edited by Mark Nuttall & Terry V. Callaghan, Amsterdam: Harwood Academic Publishers, 2000, pp. 275–313

Komárková, Vera & Jay D. McKendrick, "Patterns in Vascular Growth Forms in Arctic Communities and Environment at Atkasook, Alaska." In *Plant Form and Vegetation Structure: Adaptation, Plasticity and Relation to Herbivory*, edited by Marinus J.A. Werger et al., The Hague: SPB Academic, 1988, pp. 45–70

Longton, Royce E., *Biology of Polar Bryophytes and Lichens*, Cambridge: Cambridge University Press, 1988

Löve, Áskell & Doris Löve, "Origin and Evolution of the Arctic and Alpine Floras." In *Arctic and Alpine Environments*, edited by Jack D. Ives & Roger G. Barry, London: Methuen, 1974, pp. 571–603

Murray, David F., "Breeding Systems in the Vascular Flora of Arctic North America." In *Differentiation Patterns in Higher Plants*, edited by Krystyna N. Urbanska, New York: Academic Press, 1987, pp. 239–262

Rogers, R. W., "Ecological strategies of Lichens." *Lichenologist*, 22 (1990): 149–162

Shaver, Gaius R., Ann E. Giblin, Knute J. Nadelhoffer & Edward B. Rastetter, "Plant Functional Types and Ecosystem Change in Arctic Tundras." In *Plant Functional Types: Their Relevance to Ecosystem Properties and Global Change*, edited by: T.M. Smith, Herman H. Shugart & F.I. Woodward, Cambridge: Cambridge University Press, 1997, pp. 153–173

Sonesson, Mats & Terry V. Callaghan, "Strategies of survival in plants of the Fennoscandian tundra." *Arctic*, 44 (1991): 95–105

Thomson, John Walter, "Distribution patterns of American Arctic Lichens." *Canadian Journal of Botany*, 50 (1972): 1135–1156

Wielgolaski, Frans-Emil (editor), *Ecosystems of the World 3. Polar and Alpine Tundra*, Amsterdam: Elsevier Science, 1997

Young, Steven B., *To the Arctic: An Introduction to the Far Northern World*, New York: Wiley Science, 1989

TUNGUS

The term Tungus has been used as the pre-1930 name for the Evenki; the name for both the Even and Evenki peoples; and a general term for a number of peoples living in Northeast Asia, including the Even, Evenki, Dolgan, Negidal, and Solon (the so-called Northern Tungus) as well as the Nanais, Orok, Orochi, Udege, and Ulchi. In the latter case, the denomination is based on the similarity of the languages (except in the case of the Dolgan), and partly other cultural features, of these peoples. In the widest sense, the term Tungus and particularly its derivative Tungusic (in Soviet and Russian literature: Tungus-Manchu) refer to the whole language family, including Evenki and all the languages genetically related to it. The Tungusic (Tungus-Manchu), Turkic, and Mongolic language families form the Altaic group, which is best viewed as an areal rather than a genetic unit.

The origin and initial settlement area of the Tungus have been debated for more than a hundred years, but there are few definite results. A synopsis of this discussion was recently published by Turov (1998), who revised the theories of Shirokogorov (1933), Okladnikov (1950), Vasilevich (1969), Tugolukov (1985), and others. Turov compares the various disciplinary approaches in the debate and suggests including the criterion of self-identification. The studies of Anderson (2000) and Vitebsky (1992: 225) among the Even and Evenki imply that ethnonyms and ethnic self-identification are often directly connected with the livelihood of a certain group.

Most scholars would agree with Glafira M. Vasilevich's hypothesis, according to which the Tungus appeared as an entity in the mountainous areas around Lake Baikal, although others locate the initial settlement area somewhere along the River Amur. Before AD 500, some Tungus had migrated into the vast expanses of the Siberian taiga, while other Tungus groups stayed in the transition zone between taiga and steppe. The variety of natural habitats and the various peoples with which the Tungus came into contact led to the development of a number of different subgroups and forms of livelihood. The division between Even and Evenki was fostered by the immigration of the Yakut into the basin of the Lena River (after AD 1200): to the northeast of the settlement area of the Yakuts, the Tungus groups gradually developed into an ethnically distinct entity, the Even.

By 1900, the Tungus (Evenki and Even) settlement area reached from the tundra of the Taymyr Peninsula in the north to the steppes of Mongolia and Manchuria in the south, and from the Ob'-Yenisey watershed in the west to the Sea of Okhotsk and areas beyond the Kolyma River in the east. Groups of Even live on Kamchatka, and Evenki live on Sakhalin Island. Based on the census of 1897, Patkanov (1912, Volume 1: 83) estimated the number of all "Tungus" (Tungusic) inhabitants of Russia at between 76,000 and 79,000, and the number of what he calls the "Tungus proper" (Evenki and Even) between 62,000 and 64,500.

The connotation of the Tungus (Evenki and Even) as "reindeer people" derives from the use of domesticated reindeer among many (but not all) Tungus groups. However, they kept domesticated reindeer not for slaughter, but as a means of transport in order to hunt for elk and wild reindeer. Reindeer herding can be considered as the focal point of Tungus culture and identity. The hunting of fur animals (e.g., sable) became important only after the Russian conquest of Siberia in the 17th century and the introduction of fur tribute payments (yasak). In the steppe region, Tungus were engaged in cattle and horse breeding and gradually mixed with the Buryat and other Mongol groups. Some Tungus groups in Manchuria became sedentary agriculturalists. Tungus peoples along the Amur River engaged mainly in fishing, whereas those in the neighborhood of the Koryak also pursued the hunting of sea mammals.

The northern Tungus were socially organized in patrilineal clans, and leadership within the clan was mainly determined by personal authority. During the 18th and 19th centuries, the clan system gradually disintegrated owing to the worsening economic situation of the Tungus (which was mainly caused by tribute payments and encroachments on hunting and fishing grounds by other ethnic groups). Mikhail Speranskii's reforms in 1822 as governor general of Siberia accelerated the transition from the traditional clan system to a merely administrative one.

Animistic worldviews and shamanism were characteristic for all Tungus peoples. The word "shaman" is derived from the Evenki and Even word *saman* (*haman*, *shaman*). Christian missionary activity was at its strongest in the late 19th and early 20th century, but usually led only to nominal membership in the Christian church. Most Tungus in the Baikal region and Mongolia shared shamanic and lamaistic religious beliefs.

A first comprehensive ethnographic description of the Tungus was written by Ides on the basis of his journey in 1695. The actual scientific and ethnographic exploration of Siberia started with Daniil Messerschmidt's expedition (1720–1727) to the Lower Tunguska River and Transbaikalia. Further scientific journeys include those of Gerhard Friedrich Müller and Yakov Lindenau (participants in the Bering expedition of 1733–1743), Johann Gottlieb Georgi (who took part in Pallas's expedition of 1768–1774), Alexander Middendorf (1843–1845), and Matthias Alexander Castrén (1840s). The latter wrote the first grammar of the Tungus (Evenki) language. In the Soviet period, comprehensive research on the Even and Evenki languages was carried out by V.I. Tsintsius and Glafira Makar'evna Vasilevich, who both worked at the Herzen Institute and promoted literacy in the indigenous languages among northern Tungus peoples.

In 1924, the Soviet government established the Committee of the North as the main institution to deal with the affairs of the Tungus and other indigenous peoples. This committee played a major role in defining national (later: autonomous) areas (okrugs) for the numerically small peoples of Siberia in 1930–1931. At this time, the name Tungus was officially replaced by the ethnonyms of the various groups.

JOACHIM OTTO HABECK

See also **Dolgan; Evenki; Evens; Nanai; Nedigal; Northern Altaic Languages; Orochi; Orok; Udege; Ul'chi**

Further Reading

Anderson, David G., *Identity and Ecology in Arctic Siberia: The Number One Reindeer Brigade*, Oxford: Oxford University Press, 2000

Okladnikov, A.P., "K izucheniiu nachal'nykh etapov formirovaniia narodov Sibiri" [On the study of the initial stages of the formation of the peoples of Siberia]. *Sovetskaia Etnografiia*, 2 (1950): 36–52

Patkanov, S., *Statisticheskiia dannyia, pokazyvaiushchiia plemennoi sostav naseleniia Sibiri, iazyk i rody inorodtsev* [Statistical data showing the tribal composition of the population of Siberia, language and clans of the natives], Volumes 1–3, St Petersburg: Russkoe Geograficheskoe Obshchestvo, 1912

Shirokogorov, S.M., *Social Organization of the Northern Tungus: With Introductory Chapters Concerning Geographical Distribution and History of These Groups*, Shanghai: Commercial Press Ltd., 1933

Sirina, Anna, "The Evenkis." In *The Small Indigenous Nations of Northern Russia: A Guide for Researchers*, edited by Dmitriy A. Funk & Lennard Sillanpää, Vaasa: Åbo Akademi University, 1999, pp. 62–69

———, "The Evens." In *The Small Indigenous Nations of Northern Russia: A Guide for Researchers*, edited by Dmitriy A. Funk & Lennard Sillanpää, Vaasa: Åbo Akademi University, 1999, pp. 70–76

Tsintsius, V.I., *Sravnitel'nyi slovar' tunguso-man'chzhurskikh iazykov: Materialy k etimologicheskomu slovariu* [Comparative dictionary of the Tungus-Manchurian languages: materials for an etymological dictionary], Volumes 1–2, Leningrad: Nauka, 1975–1977

Tugolukov, V.A., *Tungusy (evenki i eveny) Srednei i Zapadnoi Sibiri* [The Tungus (Evenki and Even) of Central and West Siberia], Moskva: Nauka, 1985

Turov, M.G., "K probleme etnogeneza i etnicheskoi istorii evenkov" [On the question of ethnogenesis and ethnic history of the Evenki]. *Etnograficheskoe Obozrenie*, 3 (1998): 12–25

Vasilevich, G.M., *Evenki: Istoriko-etnograficheskie ocherki (XVIII–nachalo XX v.)* [The Evenki: historico-ethnographic outline (18th–early 20th century)], Leningrad: Nauka, 1969

Vitebsky, Piers, "Landscape and Self-Determination among the Eveny: The Political Environment of Siberian Reindeer Herders Today." In *Bush Base: Forest Farm: Culture, Environment and Development*, edited by Elisabeth Croll & David Parkin, London and New York: Routledge, 1992, pp. 223–246

TUPILAK

In Greenland, the term *tupilak* (plural *tupilait*) was originally used to denote the physical representation through which supernatural misfortune was passed. Today, tupilait objects, figurines, or statues remain among Greenland's most important carved souvenirs.

A tupilak was a magical creation that was believed to embody supernatural powers. Anyone knowledgeable in sorcery could create tupilait in order to bring or detract misfortune, but absolute secrecy was needed. Various objects were used to form the tupilak's physical body. The skeleton was made from animal and human bones; earth, moss, and seaweed were used to sculpt flesh and muscles; and found materials such as fur might be used to embellish the object further. The materials were tied together or wrapped in a piece of hide and could only be touched by the sorcerer's thumb and little finger. Invoking magical songs and chants while blowing over the bundle, the tupilak was brought to life. The tupilak was believed to acquire its strength by sucking the sexual organs of its creator, who was ceremonially dressed with his *anoraq* reversed and the hood hiding his face. The tupilak generally appeared to be an animal, with the odd ability to transform its body into all the different animals it was made from, or like a strange being, constructed of different animal parts.

The tupilak's only task was to kill its creator's enemy. It was designed as a magic tool or intercessor, without its own will. The sorcerer incorporated into the body of the tupilak parts of his or the victim's own fingernails, hair, or a little piece of clothing. According to legend, these things enabled the tupilak to track down its victim. If seal bones were used, for example, it was believed that the tupilak could swim and that it possessed the ability to drown its victims; if bird bones were used, it could fly. Once a tupilak had fulfilled its task, it disappeared. Only if its victim had superior magical powers, or if he or she consulted an *angakoq* (a shaman) for help could the tupilak be turned against its creator. The maker's only chance for survival was to publicly confess to the secret creation of a tupilak. Normally, the creator of a tupilak would rather be killed by his or her own tupilak than to reveal its existence, the admission of which would bring shame to the family because it was considered taboo to engage in such "black magic."

While tupilait may once have been prevalent throughout Greenland, during colonial times the concept survived only in remote areas such as East Greenland. When the Danish researcher William Thalbitzer inquired into peoples' religious beliefs in the Ammassalik area in East Greenland in 1905, he found that tupilait were still feared by the people. Tupilait were believed to be invisible to ordinary people; only

Tupilak carved from walrus ivory, depicting a mythical, fearsome figure living on the Northwest Greenland Inland Ice, date unknown.
Copyright Bryan and Cherry Alexander Photography

shamans could see them. The *angakoq* Mitsivarniannga of Ammassalik dared to carve several wooden tupilait in response to Thalbitzer's queries, thereby breaking the taboo that "outsiders" could never see the spirit figures. When nothing destructive happened to Mitsivarniannga as a result of his public carvings, greater numbers of Inuit began to carve tupilak images, first in driftwood and later in Arctic ivory (sperm whale teeth, narwhal and walrus tusks), bone, and antler.

While early tupilait figurines were carved with knives, later tupilait figures were made with electric drills. Originally, eyeholes were filled with baleen or blackened with lamp sod; later, black plastic combs were used as inlays for the eyes. With time, the tupilait carvings became increasingly grotesque, limited only by the materials and the makers' imaginations. The cultural beliefs in the magical power of the tupilak eventually subsided; today, tupilait comprise Greenland's most popular souvenir carving. Furthermore, the term "tupilak" is used to denote nearly all Greenlandic carvings, ranging from pure fantasy figures to other mythical beings or types, such as the *naligateq* (intestine eater) or *qivittoq* (mountain wanderer). The *naligateq* is represented as an old woman with a polar bear's or dog's head emerging from her belly. An *angakoq* was believed to pass the old woman on his way to visiting the spirits responsible for the fertility of land mammals. The *naligateq* tried to make the *angakoq* laugh as she distorted her strange body. If the shaman laughed, the *naligateq* could eat his intestines, but if he withstood, she must let him pass. The *qivittoq*, on the other hand, was a hermit or mountain wanderer who had left his home or was expelled from his community for murder. By living alone in the Arctic, the *qivittoq* developed supernatural powers and became a ghost who could spread fear and terror. Often, *qivittoq* figures were depicted with oversized ears to suggest their acute sense of hearing needed for survival.

VERENA TRAEGER

See also **Art and Artists (Indigenous); Shamanism**

Further Reading

Gilberg, Rolf, "Tupilakken—den usynlige dræber og turistfiguren." *Grønland, Charlottenlund: Det Grønlandske Selskab*, (2001): 67–79

Hansen Hart, Jens Peder, Jørgen Meldgaard & Jørgen Nordqvist (editors), *The Greenland Mummies*, Nuuk-Copenhagen: Christian Eilers, 1991

Kaalund, Bodil, *The Art of Greenland. Sculpture. Crafts. Painting*, Berkeley, Los Angeles and London: University of California Press, 1983

Petersen, Robert, "Den Grønlandske Jens Erik Sørensen, Tupilak." In *Grønlandsk Kunst. Natur og Magi*, edited by Aarhus: Aarhus Kunstmuseum, 1987, pp. 49–51

TURNER, LUCIEN M.

Lucien McShan Turner was an American natural scientist and ethnologist, known for his descriptions of the birds and mammals of Alaska, Labrador, and the Ungava Bay area of Arctic Québec, but whose main contribution to science lies in his ethnological sketch of the Ungava District Inuit and, to a lesser extent, Naskapi Indians. This monograph was the first to describe in a systematic way the material culture, social organization, and religious beliefs of these peoples.

During his boyhood years, he developed a lifelong friendship with Robert Ridgway (1850–1929), who would become a noted ornithologist and curator of birds at the US National Museum in Washington. Ridgway encouraged Turner's interest in natural sciences and taught him taxidermy. Both of them started collecting birds and snakes.

Turner joined the US army's Signal Corps in 1874. The Corps hired him to keep meteorological records, first in Alaska and then in Ungava. It was understood that his meteorological work would leave him with enough free time to collect birds, mammals, and ethnological material because, through his friend Ridgway, he signed an agreement with the US National Museum for providing them with specimens in natural history and ethnology, and for writing descriptive reports on his findings.

For his first tour of duty with the Signal Corps (1874–1877), he was headquartered in St Michael's, a Yup'ik community of southwestern Alaska, which, until 1867, had been a Russian commercial and military outpost. There, he collected faunal specimens as well as Yup'ik artifacts. In 1878, Turner was transferred to the Aleutian Islands for a second tour of duty (1878–1881). He complained that he had much more meteorological work to do, but he still had time to collect specimens, write on Alaskan birds, and learn Russian. His Alaskan data, both zoological and ethnological, would be published some years later, in 1886.

Meanwhile, Turner had returned to Illinois, but after a few months, he signed up again with the Signal Corps. This time, he was sent to the other end of the North American Arctic, in the Ungava District of Canada's Northwest Territories (now part of the province of Québec). On September 1, 1882, Turner arrived at the Hudson Bay Company post of Fort Chimo (now Kuujjuaq) after a 63-day boat trip from Québec City. This journey had included stops along the Labrador coast, where Turner had made some zoological observations.

Turner spent two years in Fort Chimo (1882–1884). He had now become an experienced naturalist and ethnologist, and was ready to make the utmost of his scientific abilities, in a region that had never been thoroughly studied yet. He carried out meteorological work for the Signal Corps, but he also collected thousands of zoological specimens as well as Inuit and Naskapi implements. Turner also wrote a lot. In 1883, he suffered so severely from writer's cramp that he was unable to use his right hand for over three months.

Turner was assisted by Maggie Brown, the part-Indian (and, possibly, part-Inuit) wife of the post's cooper. She taught Turner Inuktitut and helped him collect Inuit myths and stories. She died in 1883, when she was just starting to teach him Naskapi. This might explain why his Naskapi material is more incomplete than his Inuit data.

On September 4, 1884, Turner left Fort Chimo to sail back to the United States. He seems to have lived for some years in Washington, District of Columbia, with his family, working on his collections and publications at the US National Museum (Smithsonian Institution). Between 1888 and 1895, he lived for a time in Indiana as an employee of the US Bureau of Pensions, and then in the state of Washington, working at unspecified businesses and collecting local fauna.

Turner was not a theoretician. His scientific contribution resides in the thousands of zoological and ethnological specimens from Alaska and the Ungava District that are still part of the Smithsonian collections. He also published a lot, principally in the Smithsonian series, and has left hundreds of pages of unpublished manuscripts and photos, which remain with the Smithsonian archives.

Turner was the very first scientist to describe the Ungava Inuit and Naskapi, and to divide the former into subgroups ("southerners," "northerners," and "people from the other side (of the Ungava Peninsula)"), a classification still in use. As a matter of fact, his monograph from 1894, *Ethnology of the Ungava District*, stands, with those by Petitot (Mackenzie), Boas (Baffin), Holm (East Greenland), and Murdoch (northern Alaska), among the first book-length accounts of an Inuit group. Like most anthropological monographs from this period, a good part of Turner's *Ethnology* is concerned with material culture, but it also includes very precious pages on mythology and religion. Turner was the first and last scholar to have observed the Ungava natives before their conversion to Christianity. A few weeks before he left Fort Chimo in 1884, Reverend Edmund J. Peck had arrived there from Little Whale River on Hudson Bay. Through his—and others'—ministry, Anglicanism would soon replace shamanism in the Ungava District.

Biography

Lucien McShan Turner was born on June 20, 1848 in Mt Carmel, Illinois, and raised there (according to one source, he was born in Maineville, Ohio). Turner was married to Mary E. Lutz, and they had two sons, Jesse J. (born 1872) and Eugene S. (born 1878). Turner worked as a teacher. He found, though, that this job was not satisfying enough. What he was really interested in was natural sciences, but in the absence of any formal scientific training, he could not be hired by a research institution. Largely self-taught in natural sciences, he worked for a total of ten years (1874–1884) as a meteorologist for the US army's Signal Corps, in Alaska and in the Ungava District of Canada's Northwest Territories. His stays in the Arctic enabled him to collect extensive zoological and ethnological specimens, and observation data for the US National Museum (Smithsonian Institution).

His publications include *Contributions to the Natural History of Alaska* (US Government Printing Office, 1886), "On the Indians and Eskimos of the Ungava District, Labrador" (*Proceedings and Transactions of the Royal Society of Canada*, 1888), and *Ethnology of the Ungava District, Hudson Bay Territory* (Bureau of Ethnology, Smithsonian Institution, 1894). Unpublished manuscripts by Turner (such as a 600-page dictionary and grammar of the Ungava dialect of Inuktitut) are to be found at the Smithsonian archives in Washington, District of Columbia Nothing is known of Turner's life after 1895, except that he died in San Francisco on April 8, 1909. At his death, no obituary was published in any scholarly journal.

Louis-Jacques Dorais

Further Reading

Balikci, Asen, "The Eskimos of the Québec-Labrador Peninsula: Ethnographic Contributions." In *Le Nouveau-Québec. Contribution à l'étude de l'occupation humaine*, edited by Jean Malaurie & Jacques Rousseau, Paris-La Haye: Mouton & Co., 1964

Harper, Francis, *The Friendly Montagnais and Their Neighbors in the Ungava Peninsula*, Lawrence: University of Kansas Museum of Natural History, 1964

Turner, Lucien M., *Indians and Eskimos in the Québec-Labrador Peninsula*, foreword by Asen Balikci, Québec: Presses Coméditex, 1979 (*fac-simile* edition of *Ethnology of the Ungava District*, 1894)

———, *Indiens et Esquimaux du Québec. Inuit et Nenenot de l'Ungava*, préface de Bernard Saladin d'Anglure, Montréal: Desclez Éditeurs, 1979 (translation of *Ethnology of the Ungava District*, 1894)

TUSSOCK TUNDRA

Tussock tundra is named for the dominance of the cottongrass tussock *Eriophorum vaginatum* in mesic tundra of the Low Arctic, although the vegetation type also includes other tussock-forming sedge and dwarf shrubs, lichen, and mosses. The landscape comprises ankle-high clumps of springy plants, often in a marsh or bog.

Although cottongrass tussock is distributed circumpolarly in the Low Arctic and in the taiga (northern needle-leaf forest of the boreal zone), it is especially abundant in the amphi-Beringian portion of the Low Arctic and northern taiga. Dwarf shrub-cottongrass tussock-peatmoss tundras cover vast areas from the Kolyma to Mackenzie rivers, but more limited areas westward in Yakutia and Taymyr (Russia) and eastward in the Northwest Territories (Canada). The tussock-forming sedge *Eriophorum vaginatum* is a conspicuous dominant in most stands, although other sedges and deciduous shrubs may be dominant. Along with *E. vaginatum*, there are several tussock-forming sedge and cottongrass species, but only *Carex lugens* is also abundant in Chukotkan and Alaskan Low Arctic. Dwarf shrubs *Betula nana* spp. *exilis, Salix pulchra, S. hastata, Vaccinium uliginosum* spp. *microphyllum, V. vitis-idaea* var. *minus, Ledum decumbens,* and *Empetrum subholarcticum* are permanent and abundant components of tussock tundra.

The most common mosses include *Hylocomium splenilens, Dicranum elongatiim, Aulacomnum turgidum,* and *Tomenthypnum nitens,* and the lichens *Cetraria cucullata, C. nivalis, Cladina rangiferina, C. amaurocraea, Dactylina arctica,* and *Thamnolia vermicularis. Sphagnum* mosses are also abundant especially where drainage is poor. Buds of cottongrass tussock are hidden deep inside the tussock providing effective protection against fire, and the plant is quite often the only plant surviving after tundra fire. Tussock tundra is an important summer range for reindeer.

Tussock tundra communities usually occur on plains, lowlands, or gentle slopes on gleysolic soils of intermediate drainage with seasonal thaw depth (active layer) about 40–60 cm. The thickness of the active layer is the major environmental constraint of cottongrass tussock tundra. In the taiga, the distribution of cottongrass tussock communities is mostly restricted to bogs but in eastern Siberia and in western North America, where continuous permafrost is distributed far south, cottongrass tussock open forests are abundant. Their floristic and structural composition is very similar to that of the tussock tundra plus trees. Due to poor drainage, resulting from the thin active layer, which acts like the water table of a bog, the dwarf shrub-tussock vegetation is physiognomically, structurally, and environmentally close to bog vegetation. In the amphi-Atlantic portion of the Low Arctic, dwarf shrub-tussock tundra is less abundant because the distribution of these communities negatively correlates with the depth of the active layer, which in the amphi-Atlantic sector and the West Siberian north is much deeper than in the East Siberian and amphi-Beringian areas.

The occurrence of Low Arctic and northern taiga tussock vegetation can be explained by peculiarities of the Pleistocene environmental history of East Siberian, Beringian, and Alaskan biota. A tundra-steppe biome of Pliocene origin existed here throughout the Pleistocene. It was accompanied by a cold dry, ultracontinental climate, specific cryogenic weathering, widespread permafrost throughout the Pleistocene and Holocene, and fine-textured (loess) sediments. The environment of this nonglaciated area was stable throughout the Pleistocene. Along with the predominant cold and dry herb steppe, the dwarf shrub-tussock tundra was a permanent component of the tundra-steppe landscape. During the second stage of Pleistocene/Holocene transition (11,000–8000 years ago), the tundra-steppe biome disappeared, which led to the predominance today of dwarf shrub-cottongrass tussock tundra on the northeastern Siberian and amphi-Beringian landscapes.

VOLODYA RAZZHIVIN

See also Mesic Tundra; Polar Steppe; Tundra

Further Reading

Aleksandrova, V.D., *The Arctic and Antarctic: Their Division into Geobotanical Areas*, Cambridge and New York: Cambridge University Press, 1980

Bliss, L.C., "North American and Scandinavian Tundras and Polar Deserts." In *Tundra Ecosystems: A Comparative Analysis*, edited by L.C. Bliss, O.W. Heal & J.J. Moore, Cambridge: Cambridge University Press, 1981, pp. 5–24

Chapin III F.S., G.R. Shaver & R.A. Kedrowski, "Environmental controls over carbon, nitrogen, and phosphorus chemical fractions in *Eriophorum vaginatum* L. in Alaskan tussock tundra." *Journal of Ecology*, 74 (1986): 167–196

Razzhivin, V.Yu., "Zonation of vegetation in the Russian Arctic." In *The Species Concept in the High North—A Panarctic Flora Initiative*, edited by I. Nordal & V.Yu. Razzhivin, Oslo: Norwegian Academy of Science and Letters, 1999, pp. 113–130

Walker, D.A., J.G. Bockheim, F.S. Chapin III, W. Eugster, F.E. Nelson & C.L. Ping, "Calcium-rich tundra, wildlife, and the "Mammoth Steppe." *Quaternary Science Reviews*, 20 (2001): 149–163

Walker, M.D., D.A. Walker & N.A. Auerbach, "Plant communities of a tussock tundra landscape in the Brooks Range Foothills, Alaska." *Journal of Vegetation Science*, 5 (1994): 843–866

TUTCHONE

The Tutchone inhabit southwestern and central Yukon Territory as well as a small part of northern British Columbia. They occupy the plateau lying between the Rocky Mountains to the east and the Pacific Cordillera to the southwest. This plateau is the realm of the tundra. Down in the valleys and around numerous lakes grows a thick taiga. The environment is Subarctic. The principal settlements in which they presently live are Burwash Landing (Kluane First Nation), Haines Junction (Champagne/Aishihik First Nation), Lake Laberge (Ta'an Kwach'an First Nation), Carmacks (Little salmon/Carmacks First Nation), Pelly Crossing (Fort Selkirk First Nation), and Mayo (First Nation of Nacho Nyak Dun). In 1998, the overall Tutchone population was 2881 (statistics of the Council of Yukon First Nations).

History of Migration and Settlement

On the basis of linguistic evidence, Athapaskans migrated from Siberia to Alaska about 8000 years ago. By 6000 years ago, they most probably had reached the Yukon Territory (Krauss and Golla, 1981; Krauss, 1998). Some archaeological sites in the Tutchone territory are as old as 4000 years and some may go back to 8000 years (Gotthard, 1987). Permanent direct contacts with Eurocanandians was late: in 1898, associated with the discovery of gold in the southwestern Yukon. In the past 50 years, some Tutchone from various areas have migrated to Whitehorse, the administrative capital of the Yukon Territory, where they mingled with members from other Yukon Indian groups. In 1998, Whitehorse was the home of 961 status Indians (the Kwanlin Dun First Nation). A few Tutchone individuals have also moved to southern Canadian urban areas, but no reliable data are available. Others have intermarried with the Nabesna to the west (at Beaver Creek) and with the Tlingit to the south.

Language

The Tutchone people spoke two related languages (northern Tutchone (Mayo, Pelly Crossing, Carmacks) and southern Tutchone (Laberge, Haines Junction, Burwash)), which were themselves part of a group of 43 different languages belonging to the Athapaskan family. There were also dialectical variations within each of these two languages. Today, most people speak English. Only 400 individuals are really fluent in their native language and most of these are people over 40 (Krauss, 1998). However, an attempt is being made to revive the two languages through the local public schools.

Social Organization and Kinship Systems

In the mid-19th century, northern and southern Tutchone counted around 1400 individuals (epidemics transmitted through intertribal trade had decimated the original population). These were divided into some 14 regional bands, whose members met only twice a year. The rest of the year, each band split into nomadic camps, the largest having no more than 50 members. There existed a form of social stratification with chiefly rich families, poor families, and some domestic slaves. Kinship was matrilineal (descent from the mother) and matrilocal (residence of couple with bride's family). Among the northern Tutchone and the most southern Tutchone, the population was divided into two exogamic matrimoieties (the Crows and the Wolves). Intramoiety sexual relationships were punished by death. The ideal marriage was with a first-degree bilateral cross-cousin (if possible, a young man was married to his father's sister's daughter or his mother's brother's daughter). Kinship terminology was of the Iroquoian type. Polygyny (one man having more than one wife, often sororal, i.e., the wife's sisters) and polyandry (one woman having more than one husband, often fraternal, i.e., the husband's brothers) were legitimate forms of marriage. The levirate and sororate were normal marriage obligations, where following the death of a spouse or some cases during the lifetime of the spouse, the widowed husband or wife was permitted to marry the younger sibling, who was also required to provide security for the children. Among the southernmost Tutchone (Champagne First Nation), the influence of Tlingit Indians was strong. Cousin kinship terminology was of the Crow type, and moieties were subdivided into matriclans. Today, matriliny and matrilocality are still very important elements of the culture.

Traditional Means of Subsistence

Large mammals such as moose and woodland caribou were the most important game animals. They were caught principally with snares and also with bows. Large herds of tundra caribou also wintered on the Tutchone Plateau. They were trapped with the use of corrals. However, due to poor food resources, they regularly abandoned the Tutchone area, often for periods as long as 60 years. Dall's sheep and mountain goats were hunted where available. The most important small mammals (hares, muskrats, and gophers) were snared by women. Mammals contributed roughly 45% of the diet. Fish provided another 45%. King and dog salmon (chum) were caught in fish traps in the summer and fall, respectively. Most freshwater fish were caught with nets or traps when and where they were running. However, rare fishing lakes with a narrow inlet where a fishnet could be set under ice, were regarded as "gold mines" for they allowed people to avoid winter starvation. The long process of drying meat and fish for winter use was women's responsibility. Root and berry collecting represented no more than 10% of the diet. Native foods, especially fish, still provide 60% of the diet. Trapping and trading in skins and furs is a centuries-old practice (earlier trade was between groups, particularly with the Tlingit).

Traditional Religions and Worldviews

Religion is a form of shamanism. According to Tutchone myth, the raven rebuilt the world we see today after a flood covered all the land. Today's ravens are simple embodiments of the first raven. Beaver Man came after to solve the problems left behind by the raven. Neither the raven, Beaver Man or any other entity are worshiped or regarded as gods or deities. Rather, the natural world is considered to be full of various powers. Animals and a few natural elements (thunder, etc.) are deemed to have special powers (zäak) that all humans strive to acquire through dreams. This allows them to heal fellow humans. After death, people are reincarnated or choose to go and live on the sun forever. At the death of a person, a funerary potlatch is held involving important exchanges between members of opposed moieties. Witchcraft is clearly distinguished from religion. Today, some Christian lore is incorporated into the native worldview.

Regional Government and Organizations

Northern Tuchone First Nations are regrouped into the Northern Tutchone Tribal Council and Southern Tutchone into the Southern Tutchone Tribal Council. These First Nations and their Tribal Councils are members of the Council of Yukon First Nations. Land

Claim Settlements and Agreements for Self-Government have recently been signed between each First Nation and the Yukon Territorial Government as well as the Canadian Federal Government: Champagne/Aishihik and the Nacho Nyak Dun in Mayo (1993); Carmarck/Little Salmon (1997); Selkirk (1997); Ta'an Kwach'an at Lake Laberge (2001); and Kluane (2003). Some Tutchone First Nations are presently reviving their more traditional political structure based on a balance between the two moieties.

DOMINIQUE LEGROS

See also **Northern Athapaskan Languages**

Further Reading

Clark, D. & R. Morlan, "Western subarctic prehistory: twenty years later." *Canadian Journal of Archaeology,* 6 (1982): 70–94

Cruikshank, Julie, *Life Lived Like a Story: Life Stories of Three Yukon Native Elders (In Collaboration with Angela Sidney, Kitty Smith, and Annie Ned),* University of Nebraska Press and Vancouver: University of British Columbia Press, 1990

Gotthardt, Ruth, *Selkirk Indian Band: Culture and Land Use Study,* Whitehorse (Yukon): Yukon Renewable Resources, 1987

Krauss, Michael E., "The condition of Native North American languages: the need for realistic assessment and action." *International Journal of the Sociology of Language,* 132 (1998): 9–21

Krauss, Michael E. & Victor K. Golla, "Northern Athapaskan Languages," edited by J. Helm, *Subarctic. In Handbook of North American Indians,* Volume 6, edited by W.C. Sturtevant, Washington: The Smithsonian Institution, 1981, pp. 67–85.

Legros, Dominique, *Structure socio-culturelle et rapports de domination chez les Indiens tutchone septentrionaux du Yukon au dix-neuvième siècle,* Ph.D. Thesis, University of British Columbia, 1981, 1098 pp. (sur microfilm à l'U.M.I. Ann Arbor, Michigan, et à la Bibliothèque Nationale du Canada, Ottawa, Ontario (No. C.T. 56751 ISBN 0-315-08834-6)) (an English translation of this work is being completed by Yukon Heritage as of 2003)

———, "Réflexions sur l'origine des inégalités sociales à partir du cas des Athapascans tutchones." *Culture,* II(3) (1982): 65–84

———, "Commerce entre Tlingits et Athapascans tutchones au XIXe siècle." *Recherches Amérindiennes au Québec,* 14(2) (1984): 11–24

———, "Wealth, poverty, and slavery among XIXth century Tutchone Athapaskan." *Research in Economic Anthropology,* VII (1985): 37–64

———, "Communautés amérindiennes contemporaines: structure et dynamique autochtones ou coloniales." *Recherches Amérindiennes au Québec,* XVI(4) (1987): 47–68

———, "A propos des bandes patrilocales: illusions théoriques et réalités ethnographiques." *Journal de la Société des Américanistes (Paris),* 74 (1988): 125–161

———, "Vendetta et cérémonie de la paix chez les tutchones (Yukon): pour une critique de lien nature et violence fait par saint Augustin, Hobbes et Lévi-Strauss." *Recherches amérindiennes au Québec,* XXX(2) (2000): 33–50

McClellan, Catharine, "My Old People Say: An Ethnographic Survey of Southern Yukon Territory," 2 volumes. *Publications in Ethnology 6 (1 & 2),* Ottawa: National Museums of Canada, 1975

McClellan Catharine, Lucie Birkel, Robert Bringhurst, James A. Fall, Carol McCarthy & Janice R. Sheppard, *Part of the Land, Part of the Water: A History of the Yukon Indians,* Vancouver: Douglas & McIntyre, 1987

TYRRELL, JOSEPH BURR

During the closing years of the 19th century, officers of the Geological Survey of Canada carried out an impressive amount of primary geographical exploration of an enormous area of northern Canada while fulfilling their primary task of geological reconnaissance. Albert Peter Low, Robert Bell, and Richard McConnell immediately come to mind. However, perhaps the most impressive of these exploring geologists, in terms of the distances covered and the audacity of the journeys, was Joseph Burr Tyrrell.

His reputation is mainly based on his two expeditions across the Barren Lands of the Keewatin in 1893 and 1894, but these expeditions followed from an expedition to the Subarctic the previous year. In 1892, accompanied by D.B. Dowling, Tyrrell started from Prince Albert and traveling almost entirely by canoe, reached as far as Fond du Lac on Lake Athabasca, Black Lake, and Wollaston Lake through areas that were largely terra incognita (unknown territory). On Black Lake Tyrrell was told by the local Chipewyan of a major river flowing north across the tundra, and was shown the start of the portage route that led to this river.

Tyrrell decided that on his next expedition he would find this river and follow it to its mouth. On his return to Ottawa, he persuaded his boss, Dr. Alfred Selwyn, that he should undertake such an expedition the next summer. His party was quite small: his brother James, who had previous geological experience and had wintered in the Arctic, three Iroquois canoemen from Caughnawaga, and three Métis from northern Saskatchewan.

The party traveled to Edmonton in May, then overland by wagon to Athabasca Landing and by canoe to Fond du Lac, which they reached on July 1. Having located the Chipewyans' route, they headed almost due north via a series of portages and lakes to Selwyn Lake and then over the height of land to Wholdaia Lake (named Daly Lake by Tyrrell) at the headwaters of the mysterious river (the Dubawnt), which Tyrrell wanted to explore.

Four days later, they found the outlet from this complicated lake and headed downstream. On August 7, they reached Dubawnt Lake, seen previously by only one white man, Samuel Hearne. The vast lake was still largely ice-covered, but they were able to proceed along shore-leads; however, they were windbound at times. They found the outlet on August 17 and continued downriver. On August 25, they reached Beverly Lake; from there, the route now took them east via Aberdeen Lake, Schultz Lake, and Baker Lake to the head of Chesterfield Inlet. By September 12, they had reached the open waters of Hudson Bay.

Tyrrell's party was now faced with an 800-km coastwise trip along the Hudson Bay coast, late in the season. They shot the occasional caribou, but shortage of food was a constant problem. As October began, the fast ice began to form along the shore and finally on October 14 it forced them to spend the night in the canoes, baling continually to keep afloat. The next morning they managed to get ashore, and soon the entire party was being cared for at Churchill.

They still had 1600 km to cover to reach Winnipeg. Setting off on snowshoes with dogsleds on November 5, their first destination was York Factory, but the Nelson River was still open and they had to wait ten days before they could cross. They thus arrived at York Factory on November 24; from there, their route took them south via Oxford House to Norway House, then south along the full length of Lake Winnipeg, to reach Selkirk on New Year's Day, 1894. The total distance covered on this trip, by canoe, sled, and snowshoes, was some 5100 km.

From the Inuit he had encountered, Tyrrell had heard of another major river, the Kazan, to the east of and approximately parallel to the Dubawnt, and decided to explore it. Although sponsored by the Geological Survey, the expedition was largely financed by Robert Munro-Ferguson, aide-de-camp to the governor-general, Lord Aberdeen, whom Tyrrell had met socially and who wanted to experience a tundra "safari," and by the governor-general.

Tyrrell, Munro-Ferguson, and party left Selkirk by steamer on June 16, 1894. Disembarking at Grand Rapid on June 22, they began their canoe trip from there, bound for Brochet at the head of Reindeer Lake. From here, their route led north up the Cochrane River, over the height of land into the headwaters of the Thlewiaza, down that river, and over another height of land to Kasba Lake, in the headwaters of the Kazan. They reached Kasba Lake on August 5. From here, they continued generally northward down the Kazan via Ennadai and Angekuni lakes.

They reached Yathkyed Lake on August 31. The next day, they started on a series of portages eastward to Ferguson Lake, at the head of Ferguson River; on September 18, they reached Hudson Bay. As they started south along the coast, they were a week ahead of the previous year's schedule and the weather was much more pleasant. They reached Churchill on October 1 and Norway House on November 24. Continuing south down the shores of Lake Winnipeg, they reached Selkirk on June 7 in a horse-drawn sleigh. Tyrrell estimated

the total distance he had covered from Grand Rapid to Selkirk at about 1700 miles (2700 km).

These two expeditions represent Tyrrell's major contribution to the exploration of the Canadian Arctic. But he also mounted two further exploring expeditions, less well known but still of real significance. In 1898, the Geological Survey of Canada dispatched him to the Yukon to survey the area from the Yukon River west to the Alaskan boundary. He reached Skagway on May 27, 1898 and, ignoring the frenzy of the gold rush, headed north via the Dalton Trail and down the Nordenskiöld River to its confluence with the Yukon, surveying the geology and assessing the mineral potential as he went. Thereafter, he paid a brief visit to Dawson City and the goldfields; in a week, he assembled a comprehensive knowledge of the potential of the goldfields. By mid-October, he was back in Ottawa.

Tyrrell's last exploration trip to the North took place in 1912. The northern boundary of Ontario, which till then had angled southwest from the Albany River to just north of the Lake of the Woods, was pushed north to Hudson Bay. At the same time, its boundary with Manitoba was set at its present location, some 300 km southeast of the Nelson River. But by a special dispensation, Ontario was granted a strip, 8 km wide, for building a railway to the mouth of the Nelson River and an area for a town site and port on the Nelson estuary. Tyrrell was hired to survey this strip and also the town site and port site and to conduct a general geological survey of the newly acquired area of Ontario. Traveling north to Norway House by steamer with two companions, Tyrrell reached there on June 7, 1912 and York Factory on July 12. Tyrrell then surveyed a town site on the east side of the Nelson estuary and located a site for a railway bridge over the Hayes River. In late August, he and an assistant sailed from York Factory in the Hudson's Bay Company's schooner eastward along the coast to Fort Severn. On September 4, they headed up the Severn River by canoe. Traveling via a series of lakes and many portages, via Trout Lake, Cat Lake, and Lac Seul, they reached Sioux Lookout and the railway on October 23. Tyrell had surveyed the entire route and had investigated the geology of the country through which they passed.

Biography

Joseph Burr Tyrell was born at Weston, Ontario, on November 1, 1858, the son of William and Elizabeth Tyrrell. Joseph was educated at Weston Grammar School and Upper Canada College and was enrolled at the University of Toronto in 1876, graduating in 1880 with a focus on geology, mineralogy, biology, and chemistry. Despite his obvious bent for the natural sciences, at his father's urging he next enrolled in Law at

Osgoode Hall; one year later, Tyrell was able to persuade his father that he should take a job with the Geological Survey of Canada.

For his first year, he was employed unpacking and identifying the Survey's collection of specimens following its move from Montreal to Ottawa. His fieldwork began in 1883 when he assisted George Dawson on surveys of the Rocky Mountains and the Rocky Mountain Trench. In 1884, he led a field party for the first time, surveying a vast area from the Bow River to the North Saskatchewan and from the Saskatchewan border west to the Rockies. In a single week in 1884, he discovered the rich dinosaur beds near Drumheller along the Red Deer River (now the site of the Royal Tyrrell Museum of Paleontology) and the coal seams, which became the mainstay of Drumheller's economy for most of the 20th century. Over the next four years, Tyrrell surveyed much of western Manitoba, from Lake Winnpeg west to the Saskatchewan border, especially Duck and Riding mountains. Then in 1892–1894, he was engaged in the three expeditions in the Subarctic and Arctic that were to make his name as an explorer. Between the 1893 and 1894 field seasons, he married Mary Edith Carey.

In the subsequent few years with the Geological Survey, Tyrrell's surveys covered much of west-central Manitoba, north of the Saskatchewan River, and west of the Nelson River. Then in 1898, he was dispatched to the Yukon to survey the land along the Dalton Trail. On his return, denied a promotion he felt he deserved, he resigned from the Geological Survey.

He then returned to the Klondike, but as a mining consultant, and made a considerable amount of money. In December 1905, he returned to Ottawa, where he continued to operate as a mining consultant but with his focus on northern Ontario. It was this that led to his last northern expedition, to the mouth of the Nelson River, in 1912. In 1924, Tyrrell became president and managing director of Kirkland Lake Mine—an extremely profitable enterprise. But in 1928 a heart attack forced him to give up all his mining interests. Instead, he devoted his energies to his apple orchards on the Rouge River, near Toronto. He died on August 26, 1957. Apart from his own contributions to the exploration of the Canadian Arctic, he also made important contributions by publishing edited versions of the journals of David Thompson, Samuel Hearne, and Philip Turno.

WILLIAM BARR

See also **Hearne, Samuel**

Further Reading

Inglis, Alex, *Northern Vagabond. The Life and Career of J.B. Tyrrell*, Toronto: McClelland and Stewart, 1978

Loudon, W.J., *A Canadian Geologist*, Toronto: Macmillan Co. of Canada, 1930

Tyrrell, James W., *Across the Sub-Arctics of Canada*, London: Fisher Unwin, 1898

Tyrrell, Joseph B., "An expedition through the barren lands of northern Canada." *Geographical Journal*, 4 (1894): 437–450

———, "A second expedition through the Barren Lands of northern Canada." *Geographical Journal*, 6 (1895): 438–448

———, "Report on the Doobaunt, Kazan and Ferguson Rivers and the North-west Coast of Hudson Bay." *Geological Survey of Canada Annual Report*, New Series 9, 1896 (publ. 1898), Report F

———, "Hudson Bay Expedition, 1912." *Report of the Ontario Bureau of Mines*, 1913, pp. 161–209

———, *David Thompson's Narrative of His Explorations in Western North America 1784–1812*, Toronto: Champlain Society, 1916

———, *Journals of Samuel Hearne and Philip Turnor*, Toronto: Champlain Society, 1934

Zaslow, Morris, *Reading the Rocks. The History of the Geological Survey of Canada 1842–1972*, Ottawa: Macmillan Co. of Canada, 1975

TYUMEN'

Tyumen' is a river port on the lower Tura River, and the administrative center of Tyumen' Oblast' in central Russia. The city is located in the southwestern part of the West Siberian Plain, about 150 miles from the Kazakhstan border. The population is about 560,000, swelled in recent years by the discovery of rich oil and gas reserves in the region. The River Tura, a tributary of the Ob' River, flows eastward from the Urals, and is navigable in summer.

Tyumen', one of the oldest Russian towns in Siberia, was founded in 1586 by Russian military leaders. Supported by 300 Cossacks, they took and destroyed a Tatar 14th-century settlement and stronghold named Chingi-Tura, replacing it with a fortress and settlement. Tyumen' became the center of Russian imperial expansion into Siberia, with much of the population migration from Russia to Siberia going through the city. Today, as many centuries ago, major roads from the Urals to Siberia cross Tyumen'. In 1761, when the settlement officially obtained the status of a city, the male population of Tyumen' was 2314, consisting of tradesmen, coachmen, craftsmen, and peasants. The population was mostly Russians (there were also 74 Tatars). The city served as a fortress against raids by steppe nomads from the south as well as a trade center in connection with Bukhara khanship in Central Asia. At the beginning of the 19th century, Tyumen' hosted more than 2000 craftsmen, and became the largest craft center in western Siberia. The city's regular layout is related to its military past. Rows of houses first lined the main road from Moscow to Siberia, and then parallel streets were built. The general city plan was created when Russia was ruled by Catherine the Great, at the end of the 18th century. All Tyumen' churches were rebuilt in stone at that time. In 1855, there were 25 streets, nine bridges, ten churches, a monastery, a city hall, a hotel, a college, and 1800 houses (19 of stone). The main square with its market and city hall, and all churches still stand today. In 1885, the railroad from Tyumen' to Ekaterinburg was constructed, and some years later the Trans-Siberian Railway also reached Tyumen'.

Tyumen' is today an industrial center with many manufacturing plants for machinery, electric equipment, lathe construction, medical instruments, woodwork, fishery, and woolen cloth. The new era began in the 1960s with the discovery of huge oil and gas deposits in the surrounding area. Tyumen' became the capital of the richest Russian province, and the headquarters for oil services in the region. Large chemical plants, as well as factories for oil-producing machinery and pharmaceuticals, were built. In 1970, the population had grown to 269,000 in Tyumen'. Five universities and institutes, two theaters, and two museums lead the long list of cultural, scientific, and research institutions of the city.

Tyumen' is a beautiful and well-organized city. The main part of the city with governmental and public institutions is located on the right, high bank of the Tura River. The lower left bank hosts the industrial part of the city, and from time to time suffers spring floods. The climate of Tyumen' is continental, with severe winters (average winter temperatures of −17°C) and warm summers (the average July temperature is +16°C). The average annual precipitation is 457 mm, with 142 rainy days per year. Snow cover usually begins in mid-November and lasts till mid-April. Tyumen' is surrounded by forests, first by birch forests on old clearings, then pine forests further than 30 km. The city of Tyumen' flourishes as the capital of the rich West Siberian oil and gas province, as a major transportation junction for river and rail freight, and as a promising industrial center.

LEONID M. BASKIN

See also **Tyumen' Oblast'**

Further Reading

Bespalova, A., *Zhivoie proshloe. Pisateli 19 veka o Tyumeni* [Living Past. Writers of 19th Century on Tyumen'], Sverdlovsk: Sredne-Ural'skoe knizhnoe izdatel'stvo, 1987

Bud'kov, S., N. Vokulev & S. Vlasova. *400 let Tyumeni. Sbornik dokumentov I materialov* [400 Years of Tyumen. Materials and Documents], Sverdlovsk: Sredne-Ural'skoe knizhnoe izdatel'stvo, 1985

Dunin-Gorkavi, A., *Tobol'skii Sever* [The North of Tobol'sk], 2 volumes, Moscow: Libereya, 1996

Dunin-Gorkavi, A. & S. Zavarikhin, *V drevnem centre Sibiri* [In the Ancient Center of Siberia], Moscow: Iskusstvo, 1987

Klepikov, V., *Tyumen—vorota Sibiri. Khronika, dokumenty,1586–1986* [Tyumen—Gateway to Siberia. Chronicles and Documents], Sverdlovsk: Sredne-Ural'skoe knizhnoe izdatel'stvo, 1986

Kopylov, D., V. Knyazev & V. Retunskii, *Tyumen'* [Tyumen'], Sverdlovsk: Sredne-Ural'skoe knizhnoe izdatel'stvo, 1986

Kruzhinov, V., *Tyumen: vekhi istorii* [Tyumen: Marks of History], Ekaterinburg: Sredne-Ural'skoe knizhnoe izdatel'stvo, 1997

Sokova, Z. (editor), *Tyumenskii istoricheskii sbornik* [Tyumen' Historic Works], Volume 3, Tyumen: Tyumenskii Gosudarstvennii Universitet, 1999

Zabolotnyi, E. (editor) *Zemlya Tyumenskaia: entsiclopediya v litsakh* [The Tyumen' Land: Encyclopedia of Persons], Tomsk: Izdatel'stvo Tomskogo Gosudarstvennogo Universiteta, 2000

Zhuchenko, Boris & Sviatozar Zavarikhin, *Tyumen' architekturnaiya* [Tyumen' in Architecture], Sverdlovsk: Sredne-Ural'skoe knizhnoe izdatel'stvo, 1984

TYUMEN' OBLAST'

Tyumen' Oblast' belongs to the West Siberian economic region of the Russian Federation, and the Urals federal okrug. The oblast includes the Tyumen' administrative center and the Yamal-Nenets and Khanty-Mansi autonomous okrugs, which are independent subjects of the Russian Federation. Tyumen', the capital of the oblast, is the oldest city in Siberia, founded in 1586. The population of Tyumen' city is 560,000. The population of the area is 3,243,500, of which over 70% (2,477,900) reside in urban areas. Russians make up the majority (83%) of the population, with Tatars (9.4%), Ukrainians (1.8%), Germans (1.4%), and indigenous Khanty, Mansi, and Nenets making up the remainder. There has been significant inward migration of settlers working in the oil and gas sector.

The area of Tyumen' Oblast' is 1,435,200 km² (comprising 8.4% of the territory of Russia, the third largest region in Russia). The oblast stretches in the north-south direction for 2100 km from the Kara Sea of the Arctic Ocean to the steppes of Kazakhstan. The extreme northernmost point is situated on Yamal Peninsula (73°30′ N). The extreme south point is on the border with Kazakhstan (55°10′ N).

Tyumen' Oblast' covers most of the West Siberian Plain. The folded Hercynian basement is overlain by thick Mesozoic-Cenozoic sedimentary cover, in which one of the world's largest oil and gas deposits was formed. The first gas strike in the Tyumen' area was in 1953 near the village of Berezovo. The first oil strike occurred in the basin of the Shalym River in 1960. Now the region produces about 87% of Russia's gas and 66% of its oil and gas condensate, and has attracted significant foreign investment for the production and sale of petroleum. The richest oil deposits are situated in the mid-reaches of the Ob' River (Khanty-Mansi Autonomous Okrug). Further to the north, oil fields are gradually being replaced by gas, gas condensate, and oil-gas deposits.

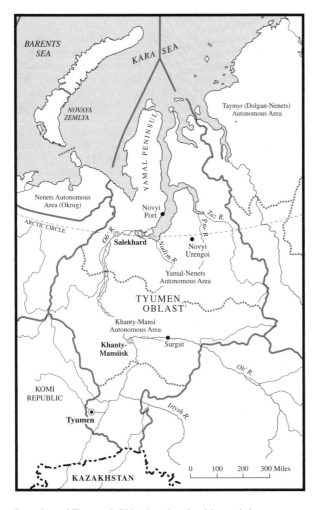

Location of Tyumen' Oblast' and main cities and rivers.

Lying to the east of the Urals, the region generally has low, plain relief, and is shaped like a giant amphitheater facing the Kara Sea. The western and eastern parts of the area are piedmont elevated plains with absolute elevations up to 250 m. Relief of the central areas is formed by alternating elevated plains (150–200 m), medium-height plains (100–150 m), and lowland (below 100 m). Lowlands stretch along the Irtysh and Ob' rivers. They are surrounded by well-drained uplands (local name "materik"—mainland). The northernmost region is a coastal lowland with absolute elevations below 85 m.

The relief of Tyumen' Oblast' is of various genesis and age. The northern lowland is the youngest part of the West Siberian Plain, consisting of marine sediments deposited during the Quaternary transgression of the Arctic Ocean, and has widespread permafrost forms (thermokarst sinkholes, frost mounds, polygonal tundra). Hilly relief of glacial and fluvial-glacial genesis is typical in the central part of the area. Glaciers did not cover the southern part. Its relief, with swampy sandy plains and numerous lakes (local name

"polesjie"), was formed under the influence of Quaternary sedimentation.

Permafrost is a characteristic feature of the area. The northern part of the area (approximately from the latitude of Novyi Urengoi to the north) is located in the area of continuous permafrost with both modern and paleo-permafrost, with permafrost thickness reaching 450 m. Thawed ground occurs only under riverbeds and big lakes. Permafrost occurrence to the south of Novyi Urengoi (as far as the border of Yamal-Nenets Autonomous Okrug) has a layered structure: the frozen upper layer (10–100 m) is underlain by thawed ground, and below this (at depth 150–400 m) paleo-permafrost occurs. South of the Yamal-Nenets Okrug border as far as the Konda and Demjanka rivers, there is relic permafrost at depths of 150–400 m. The southern part of the oblast has no permafrost.

The climate of the oblast is continental. Winter lasts for 8 months in the polar regions and 6 months in the southern areas. The average January temperature varies from −24°C to 27°C on Yamal, Gydan, and Taz peninsulas to −16°C in the city of Tyumen'. The absolute temperature minimum is −57°C (Novy Port on the Taz Peninsula). In Tyumen, the lowest registered temperature is −50°C. The depth of snow cover is 60–70 cm on the eastern slopes of the Urals, and 80–85 cm in the basin of the Taz River (middle course). In the southern open plains, it is about 30 cm. The depth of snow cover on the Kara Sea coast is below 20–25 cm. In the southern areas, summer begins around May 10–20, and in July in the Arctic areas. The average July temperature varies from 4–5°C in the north to 18–19°C in the south. Precipitation is highest in the forest zone (500–600 mm), decreasing both in the north and south directions down to 400 mm and less. The highest rainfall occurs in summer.

The rivers all drain to the Kara Sea. The Ob' River and its tributaries, the Irtysh, Taz, Pur, Nadim, are the major rivers in the area. The area of the Ob' River basin (2,990,000 km^2) is the fifth largest in the world (after Amazon, Congo, Mississippi, and La-Plata) and the largest in Russia. The length of Ob' with its tributary Irtysh is over 5400 km. Rivers in the area characteristically have spring floods and long periods of low water in summer-autumn and winter. The main sources of river feeding are snowmelt and summer rains. About 70–80% of the flow occurs in spring and summer. Stream velocity is only 0.4–0.6 ms^{-1}. The slow flow and significant north to south extent cause ice jams at the time of ice drifting. This phenomenon is connected with different times of opening in the upper and lower courses of the rivers, which leads to blocking of the stream, quick water rising, and floods.

There are more than 500,000 lakes in the area, of which 15 are over 100 km^2. The number of lakes is especially large in Yamal-Nenets (over 300,000) and Khanty-Mansi (200,000) okrugs. Almost all lakes are fresh. However, in the forest-steppe zone, there are lakes with mineralized water.

Bogs occupy over 50% of the Tyumen' area, which is generally a lowland between the Ob' and Irtysh rivers. Bogs of Western Siberia hold about 490 km^3 of water, which exceeds the total annual flow of the Ob' River by 20%. Tyumen' Oblast' crosses several vegetation zones, from the tundra in the north to taiga and forest-steppe in the south.

Soils of the area change from thin tundra-gley soils in the tundra zone to leached chernozem in the forest-steppe zone. In the taiga zone, there occur various types of podzolic soils. Soil salinization processes are typical for forest-steppe soils.

There are three state nature reserves in Tyumen' Oblast'—Malaya Sos'va (92,200 ha), Yugansky (622,800 ha), and Verhkne-Tazovsky (631,300 ha)—and 35 game reserves (zakazniks). The Red Data Book of Tyumen' Oblast' includes the following endangered species: dalmatian pelican, great cormorant, black stork, red-breasted goose, stiff-tailed ducks, osprey, golden eagle, merlin, peregrine falcon, and white and hooded cranes. Reindeer, elk, roe, Arctic fox, sable, squirrel, fox, and muskrat are hunted for game, as are wood grouse, black grouse, partridge, and waterfowl. Commercial fish include sturgeon, salmon, and whitefish.

Oil and gas production is the main industry (81.8% of industrial output) of the oblast. Other industries include energy production (10.9%), machinery and metalwork (2.2%), woodwork and the paper and pulp industry (0.7%), the food industry (1.8%), and the textile industry (0.2%). There is little arable land in the north, but some agriculture in the south. Farming includes cattle breeding, reindeer breeding, and poultry keeping. The fur trade is also well developed. Transportation and infrastructure are well developed, the Ob' and Irtysh rivers are navigable in summer, and there are road and rail links between Tyumen' (which is on the Trans-Siberian Railway), Moscow, St Petersburg, or Yekaterinburg.

GRIGORI TERTITSKI

See also **Khanty-Mansi Autonomous Okrug; Ob' River; Tyumen'; Yamal-Nenets Autonomous Okrug; Yamal Peninsula**

Further Reading

Glatter, Pete, *Tyumen: The West Siberian Oil and Gas Province*, London: RIIA, 1997

Regiony Rossii: Statisticheskii Sbornik [Regions of Russia: Statistical Handbook], 2 volumes, Moscow: Goscomstat of Russia, 2000

Official site of Tyumen' Oblast' website: http://www.adm.tyumen.ru/

U

UDEGE

The Udege people (in the 19th century, Russians grouped them with the Orochi to the north, and Chinese people called them the *Tazy*) are an indigenous people of the Primorsk and Khabarovsk territories in the far southeast of Siberia, which became part of the Russian Empire in 1860. The Udege originated through extensive interactions with different peoples, such as the Orochi, the Nanais, and the Ul'chi. Later on, Udege came into contact with the Chinese, the Man'chzu, and the Koreans, and since the 19th century with the Russians. Today, they live on the tributaries of the Ussuri River, on the rivers Anuyi and, Khungari, and on the eastern slope of the Sikhote-Alin range. The well-known Russian ethnographer Vladimir K. Arsen'ev described them as "the people of the forests." After periods of Soviet collectivization and amalgamation, some Udege were settled in the villages of Ostrovnoe, Krasnyi Yar, Verkhnii Pereval, Olon, and Agzu in Primorsk territory, and in the villages of Gvasyugi, Kuka, Snezhyi, Rassvet, and Arsen'evo in Khabarovsk territory.

Udege or Udegei is their self-designation, later adopted by the Russians. There are about 1600 Udege people (according to the 1989 Soviet Census). They speak the Udege language, which belongs to the Tungusic-Manchurian group of the Altaic language family. The Udege mostly speak Russian; some also speak Orochi and Nanais. Up to the present time there has been no written Udege language; however, students may study the spoken language in school.

In the past, the Udege people were divided into five clans—Kamandziga, Kyalundzyuga, K'ya, Kimonko, and Geonka—which in turn were broken into many smaller units. By the 20th century, eight territorial groups were in existence, namely the Khungari, Anyui, Khor, Bikin, Big Ussuri, Samargi, Maritime, and Kur-Urmi. Each group consisted of two to three units called *zamula* in the Udege language, between which there existed some marriage relations. The specific social institution *zamula* (*dokha*) was characteristic only for some indigenous peoples of the Amur River basin.

The basis of Udege society was the large family. Marriages among clans were widespread, and one family might be offered a special payment for the bride from another family. The youngest brother, according to the levirate custom, had to marry the widow of the eldest brother upon the latter's death.

The Udege shared and borrowed several cultural elements from the Tungus (also a fishing and hunting subsistence culture). Udege traditions such as dog breeding, semi-subterranean dwellings, and clothing made of fish skin and seal pelts were combined with Tungus cultural elements, such as conical dwellings (*chum*), boats made of birch bark, the baby cradle, and the apron.

Hunting and fishing were the basic occupations of the Udege. The majority of the Udege were primarily hunters, using bows and arrows, spears, hinges, and nets. Only since the 18th and 19th centuries have they employed rifles to hunt elk, deer, musk deer, fur animals, and sea mammals. Small-scale fishing comprised the primary subsistence among the groups who lived along the rivers draining into the Sea of Japan, and along the Khungari and Anyui rivers. Here, they harpooned salmon during the spawning season in September and October. The Udege borrowed nets and seine from the Russians. Since the end of the 19th century, the Russian industrial fishery has been developed within Udege settlement areas.

Some southern Udege groups in contact with Chinese and Russians developed small-scale crop growing to include wheat, barley, and vegetables (potatoes, onion, and garlic). They gathered berries, fern, wild garlic, and onion. The gathering of roots of ginseng (*olondo*) was particularly important because the Udege used these as currency in trade with the Chinese. During the reign of the Soviet Union (1922–1991), the Udege began to develop collectivized cattle breeding and agriculture.

In winter, Udege lived in semi-subterranean dwellings with ridged roofs. Several kin families lived in each dwelling. Some Udege dwellings resembled the Chinese fanza (or huts).

According to the Udege worldview, the universe was divided into three spheres: the sky world (*ba nani, ugu buga*), the middle world, and the underground world. The Udege believed in the existence of the soul, reincarnation of the soul, and transformation. The souls of dead relatives lived in the underground world (*khegi ukhe ba*). The Udege buried their dead in wooden boats on the surface of the land.

Although Christianity was widespread by the end of the 19th century, the Udege preserved many of their traditional beliefs, including shamanism. They especially revered and did not hunt the Siberian tiger (*kuti mafa*), considering it as a supernatural ancestor. As with the majority of indigenous peoples of the Russian Far East, they participated in bear ceremonialism. The Udege shamans performed many rituals: they treated the sick, ensured hunting success, and accompanied the souls of the dead to the underworld. The shamans performed their rituals in special clothes, and wore a wooden (birch-bark) mask, which seemed to embody the patron-spirit of the ancestor. The shamans used drums, in common with many Far Eastern shamans.

Under the Soviet Union, an emphasis on cultural and education standards led to the training of Udedge scientists, writers, artists, doctors, and teachers; nonetheless, some elements of their traditional culture were lost.

The Association of Indigenous People of Primorsk region was created in 1990 and united 2500 native people belonging to the Udege, the Nanais, and the Orochi. The association defends the interests of these people and preserves the environment. The traditional lifestyle of these peoples depends on the resources of the forest: wild animals trapped for fur, fish, and game animals. In 1990–1991, prompted by a proposal of the international timber industry to increase logging in the area of Bikin River, the association began campaigning for the creation of traditional land-use territories for a few village councils within the territory and the right to determine use of their lands.

ANNA A. SIRINA

See also **Bear Ceremonialism; Nanai; Northern Altaic Languages; Orochi; Shamanism; Tungus**

Further Reading

Arsen'ev, V.K., *Lesnye lyudi -Udegeizy*, [The Udege—the peoples of the forests], Vladivostok, 1948

Kimonko, D.B., *Tam, gde bezhit Sukpai: Povest'* [Where the Sukpai flows: story], Khabarovsk: Book Publishing House, 1950 (was translated into French and German)

Krushanov, A.I., (editor), *Istoria i kul'tura udegeizev* [The history and the culture of the Udege], Leningrad: Nauka, 1989

Lar'kin, V.G., *Udegeizy: istorico-etnograficheskii ocherk s serediny XIX a. do nashich dney* [Udegeizy: history and ethnography essay since the middle of the 19th century till today], Vladivostok, 1958

Podmaskin, V.V., *Dukhovnay Cultura Udegeizev XIX–XX vv. Istorico-etnograficheskie ocherki* [The spiritual culture of the Udegezu people. The essays of history and ethnography], Vladivostok, 1991

Przheval'skii, N.M., *Puteshestvie v Ussuriskom krae. 1867–1869 gg* [The trip in the Ussuri region], Vladivostok, 1949

Shnirel'man, V.A., *Bikinskie Udegeizy: Politica i Ecologia// Isslrdovania po Pricladnoi i Neotlozhnoy etnologii: IEA, No 43* [The Udege of the Bikin River: the policy and the ecology//Urgent and applied studies], 1993.

Smolyak, A.V., *Etnicheskie prozessy u narodov Nizhnego Amura i Sakhalina* [Ethnic processes among the Low Amur and Sakhalin Island's peoples], Moscow: Nauka, 1975

Starzev, A.F., *Material'naya Kultura Udegeizev (vtoraya polovina XIX–XX vv)* [The material culture of the Udegeizy (the second half of the 19th–20th century)], Vladivostok, 1996

UL'CHI

The Ul'chi are an indigenous people living on the lower Amur River in Russia's Far East. In 1897, they lived in 39 villages, from the villages Addi and Kulgu in the north to Ukhta in the south. Soviet relocations concentrated most Ul'chi people in the village of Bulava, which is their communal center today. A minor part of the population lives in towns along the Amur River, including Khabarovsk and Komsomol'sk-na-Amure. Their self-designation is *Nani* (*na*=land, earth; *ni*=people), a name also used by the Nanais and Orochi. Other names used are *Mangun* from *Mangu*, the name of the Amur River in the Tungusic languages, and introduced by the 19th-century Amur expedition headed by Gennadyi Nevel'skoi, and *Ul'cha, Ol'cha* (reindeer people, from *ula*=reindeer). Ul'chi is the official Russian name.

Ethnogeography

According to archaeological evidence, the Ul'chi are related to the ancient Mesolithic population of the lower Amur, which was influenced by unknown newcomers in the third millennium BC. Their culture has many common elements with the neighboring peoples of the Amur basin (the Nanais, Nivkhi, Manchurians, Negidals, Evenki, and Ainu).

The first Russian records relating to the Ul'chi date back to the 17th century, when first attempts were undertaken to make them pay *yasak* (a tribute in the form of furs). Russian colonization of the Amur River basin by Russian Cossacks and Russian peasant migrants first began in the middle of the 19th century, and has since diluted Ul'chi settlement and exerted a great impact on their culture, economy, and social development.

Population Level

The total number of Ul'chi in the Russian Federation in the Soviet census of 1989 was 3173, with 72% living in rural areas. Of the total number, 2028 lived in the Ul'chi District at the lower Amur River, and others in the cities of Khabarovsk (207), Komsomol'sk-na-Amure (133), and in the Nikolaevsk District to the north (114).

The 1897 census counted 1455 Ul'chi. After a severe decline at the beginning of the 20th century (1926 census: 758), the population level has increased continuously to the present number.

Language

The Ul'chi people speak the Ul'chi language, which was considered until the 1930s to be a dialect of the Nanai language. Along with the languages of other peoples of the Amur region, the Ul'chi language belongs to the Tungusic-Manchurian branch of the Altaic family. It lacks ancient Altaic relics and is much closer to Tungus than to Manchurian. Ul'chi writing was created in the 1970s to 1980s on the basis of the Russian alphabet.

While the population has been increasing constantly until 1989 (date of the most recent census), the decrease in the number of native speakers (from 85% in 1959 to 35% in 1989) is alarming. Since nearly all Ul'chi speakers are over 40 years old, the language must be deemed nearly extinct. Russian has taken over as the main language in all areas of modern life.

Lifestyle and Subsistence

The Ul'chi led a sedentary mode of life based on fishing and, secondarily, hunting and trapping. Fishing was a year-round activity with climaxes during the salmon migrations. The migratory routes of the salmon also determined the distribution of the Ul'chi villages along the eastern bank of the main channel of the Amur River. Fish was not only the main food source for people but also for their dogs, which they kept in large numbers for pulling sleds.

Hunting was of secondary importance. They mostly hunted fur animals—mainly sable, but also weasel, squirrel, otter, and fox. Prior to the introduction of guns, hunting was carried out with bows and arrows and spears. Pelts were in great demand among Russian and Chinese merchants. When sables became rare in the Amur area at the end of the 19th century, the Ul'chi hunters would leave for long expeditions to other river basins and Sakhalin Island to find them. Moose and wild reindeer were hunted throughout the year. Marine mammals, especially otter and sea lion, were hunted on the coast of the Tatar Strait. The Ul'chi traveled there in small groups across Lake Kizi.

The Ul'chi lived traditionally in small villages, consisting of two to five houses, with both summer and winter dwellings. The ancient winter dwelling, *khagdu*, is a frame structure of poles and logs with a double-pitch roof and a dirt or clay floor, heated by two fireplaces.

The main means of summer transport were boats: plank punt boats, *ugda*, canoes, *omorochki*, and small birch-bark boats; in winter, the Ul'chi used skis and dogsleds of the Amur type, which were narrow and light and had bent runners.

Russian large-scale commercial fishing in the Amur River later forced the Ul'chi to compete and to develop their subsistence into a commercial undertaking. Because of the greatly increased scale of fishing, hunting became less important—by this time, there were also far fewer fur animals on the Lower Amur. To earn a living, the Ul'chi gradually had to take on occupations formerly unknown to them, such as agriculture, forestry, and service jobs. Horse breeding and haymaking were also introduced.

In recent years, commercial overfishing reduced stocks and led to quota regulations severely affecting the indigenous population's subsistence. Recent environmental damage has almost abolished the fishing trade and deprived people of their customary diet. The pollution of the Amur River with phenols and heavy metals from cellulose and mineral processing factories and a timber mill kills fish stocks, degrades the quality of the natural environment, and causes health problems among the population. Fish stocks have been depleted by a factor of 20 from 1960 to 1990. In addition, timber felling in water-protection zones of the Amur River has a detrimental effect on water regulation, affecting both fishing and transportation.

Society and Social Structure

Traditionally, most Ul'chi families were small and based on single marriages, while a few families were large and polygynous. They were approximately of 30 clans. The families belonging to one clan lived dispersed and met only for a few annual celebrations, for instance, bear festivals. The main function of the clan was the regulation of the marital custom of exogamy, marrying outside the clan.

Everyday life was regulated by the local community independently of the clan structure. Each family used land and water resources independently, without defined areas belonging to a clan or a community. Disputes were solved by the community, and neighboring families helped each other in cases of need.

Religion

The Ul'chi had an animistic worldview; all parts of nature like the sun, the stars, mountains, rivers, forests, and hunting grounds had guardian spirits. The guardian spirits were worshipped according to certain rites, including sacrifices. Important rituals were regularly devoted to the water guardian spirit *Tem* and the taiga guardian spirit *Duente Edeni*. Every family had their own tree in the taiga, where they worshipped the local guardian spirit.

The shamanism of the Ul'chi has much in common with that of the Nanais. The shamans, women among them, were subdivided into several categories in terms of their power. Those of the highest category would convey the souls of the dead into the next world.

Like most Arctic indigenous people, the Ul'chi also worshipped the bear; several taboos were connected with the bear hunt and the breeding of bears, as well as the associated feasts (*see* **Bear Ceremonialism**). Another highly developed cult was that of twins: twins and the mothers of twins were considered sacred, and were given special burial rites.

By the end of the 19th century, the Ul'chi had officially converted to the Russian Orthodox church through a number of mission schools, but their innate religious beliefs were not really changed.

Folklore

The folklore of the Ul'chi features shaman tales of spirits, animals, and their origin. Numerous famous shamans were good narrators, who performed their rites with special theatricality. The Ul'chi spiritual culture is known for its musical folklore. Music accompanied the bear festival and various other rites, and musical chanting was an element of shaman rites. Characteristic musical instruments are one-string violins, pipes, Jew's harps, and the unique instrument called the musical log. The musical and choreographic arts are represented by bear dances, performed at the bear festival, and are also associated with the twin cult and shaman dances.

The decorative arts of the Ul'chi are represented by ornamentation of wood, bone, and metal (by men), and of fish skin and birch bark (by women). Ritual spoons, ladles, and other housewares were embellished with intricate carving.

WINFRIED K. DALLMANN

See also **Nanai; Northern Altaic Languages; Tungus**

Further Reading

Aizenshtadt, A.I., "Muzykal'nyi fol'klor narodnostei Nizhnego Priamur'ia" [Musical folklore of the lower Amur peoples]. In *Muzykal'ny ifol'klor narodov Sibiri i Severa* [Musical Folklore of the Peoples of Siberia and the North], Moscow: 1966

Boiko, V.I. & V.A. Timokhin, "Traditsionnoe v obikhode nanaitsev i ul'chei segodnia" [Traditions in the daily life of the Nanais and Ul'chi]." In *Materialy konferentsii "Etnogenez narodov Severnoi Azii"* [Proceedings of the conference "Ethnogenesis of the peoples of Northern Asia"], Volume 1, Novosibirsk, 1969, pp. 183–206

Ivanov, S.V., A.V. Smoliak & M.G. Levin, "Ul'chi" [The Ulchi]. In *Narody Sibiri*, edited by M.G. Levin & L.P. Potapov, Moscow: Russian Academy of Sciences, 1956; as *The Peoples of Siberia*, Chicago: Chicago University Press, 1964

Messhtyb, N.A., "Traditsionnye sredstva sokhraneniia zdorov'ia nanaitsev i ul'chei" [Traditional means of preserving the health of the Nanais and Ulchi]. In *Rossiiskii etnograf* [Rusian ethnographer], Volume 12, Moscow: 1993

Shrenk, L.I., *Ob inorodtsakh Amurskogo kraia* [On the native inhabitants of the Amur territory], 3 volumes, St Petersburg: Tip. Imp. Akadem,i nauk, 1883, 1898, 1903

Smoliak, A.V., *Ul'chi (khoziaistvo, kul'tura i byt v proshlom i nastoiashchem)* [The Ulchi: ecology, culture and way of life in the past and present], edited by S.I. Vainshtain, & B.O. Dolgikh, Moscow: Nauka, 1966

———, "O nekotorykh starykh traditsiakh v sovremennom bytu ul'chei" [Old Ulchi traditions in contemporary life]." In *Drevniaia Sibir': Materialy po istorii Sibiri* [Ancient Siberia: Materials on the history of Siberia], Volume 4, *Bronzovyi i zheleznyi vek Sibiri* [Bronze and iron age in Siberia], Novosibirsk: 1974, pp. 319–338

———, "Osnovnye cherty shamanizma nanaitsev i ul'chei" [Basic features of the shamanism of the Nanai and Ul'chi]." In *Antropologiia istoricheskaia etnografiia Sibiri* [Anthropology and historical ethnography], Omsk: 1990, pp. 141–149

Sunik, O.P., "Ul'chi, ikh iazyk i fol'klor" [Ul'chi language and folklore]." In *Narodnosti Severa: problemy i perspektivy ekonomicheskogo i sotsial'nogo razvitia: tezisy dokladov i soobshcheny Vsesoiuznoi nauchnoi konferentsii* [Ethnic groups of the North: problems and prospects for economic and social development. Abstracts of reports and communications at the All-Union scientific conference], Novosibirsk: 1983, pp. 218–221

———, *Ul'chski Iazyk: issledovaniia i materialy* [The Ul'chi language: research and data], Leningrad: 1985

Zolotarev, A.M., *Rodovoi stroi i religiia ul'chei* [The Ul'chi clan system and religion], Khabarovsk: Dalgiz, 1939

http://www.raipon.net/Web_Database/ulchy.html

ULTRAVIOLET-B RADIATION

Ultraviolet (UV) light, an extension of the visible solar spectrum beyond the blue and violet into shorter wavelengths and higher energy, is not detected as visible radiation by the eyes of humans and most mammals.

For some birds and the vast majority of insects, however, UV radiation represents a color that can be seen on feathers, the wings of butterflies, flower petals, and even fruits. The high energy of UV radiation can damage animal tissue or affect functions, for example, inhibiting photosynthesis in phytoplankton, where adaptations have not evolved to screen out UV.

Solar UV radiation is usually subdivided based on wavelengths (UV-A, 320–400 nm; UV-B, 290–320 nm; and UV-C, 200–290 nm). UV-B and UV-C are the most readily absorbed by plants and animals. UV-B makes up no more than 1.5% of the solar spectrum. However, unlike UV-A (which passes virtually unhindered through the ozone of the stratosphere 15–50 km above the Earth's surface) and UV-C radiation (which is successfully absorbed in the upper atmosphere), UV-B is only partially attenuated by ozone levels. A thinning of the ozone layer, therefore, affects UV-B the most. Ozone levels in the upper atmosphere were first observed to be decreasing in 1985, initially observed over the southern polar region and by the mid-1990s over the Arctic as well. A loss of 10% stratospheric ozone from the late 1970s to 2000, affecting latitudes higher than 30° N and 30° S, is generally accepted, while individual ozone hole episodes over the Arctic may reach 20–40%. While no consensus to date has been reached on the amount of ozone depletion that is directly attributable to man-made chemicals such as chlorofluorocarbons (CFCs) or freons (liquid fluorocarbons), which have made it to the upper atmosphere, there is little doubt that CFCs can interact with ozone in such a way that the amount of harmful UV radiation that reaches the Earth's surface increases.

A 1% loss of ozone, it is thought, results in an increase in UV-B radiation of around 1.5%. Ozone destruction is aggravated by very low temperatures, and this explains why ozone thinning was first recognized over Antarctica and why the so-called "ozone hole" is particularly massive during the winter months. In absolute terms, UV radiation levels in high latitudes are still much below those received in the Archaean era (c.3500–3000 Ma, when the only life forms were cyanobacteria), and also those in tropical countries and on the summits of mountains. What scientists are concerned about is the speed with which UV-B levels in particular have been rising in the polar regions since the late 1970s. Plants and animals of these regions, adapted to relatively low levels of UV radiation over many millions of years, may find it hard to cope with rapid increases in these levels. The long daylight hours and the increased reflectance from snow and ice also magnify the effects of UV levels for Arctic peoples and ecosystems.

UV radiation does not penetrate far into the body, being mostly absorbed in the surface 0.1 mm of, for instance, the skin and eyes. In fact, UV is required to synthesize vitamin D in the skin. Prolonged exposure to UV radiation in humans appears to reduce the body's resistance to tumors and to be involved in causing melanomas, DNA damage, photoconjunctivitis, photokeratitis, basal and squamous cell carcinomas, as well as senile cortical cataract and macular degeneration of the eye. Snowblindness, a common Arctic eye problem due to reflected UV radiation from snow and ice, has long been mitigated by indigenous peoples by the use of goggles. The irradiation dose is strongly influenced by the abundance of ozone, solar zenith (highest point) angle (and therefore time of day and season), volcanic discharges and tropospheric aerosols, cloud cover, degree of shade, geographic latitude, altitude, and surface albedo. Snow, sea surf, and white house paint (in that order) have been suggested to be more important in relation to human cataractogenesis than generally realized, due to their reflectance characteristics. Humans tend to direct their vision downward and, at least during spring when snow still covers the ground, eyes can receive more reflected UV from below than from the Sun above. Spring is also the time of greatest ozone depletion, and the time when biological systems are most susceptible.

One problem in assessing the specific actions or roles of UV radiation and exposure is that individuals and species of humans, animals, and plants exhibit different degrees of tolerance toward the potentially harmful UV effects. As UV wavelengths increase from UV-C to UV-A, the role of the eye lens as an attenuator becomes increasingly more important, while that of the cornea (100% effective for wavelengths of around 280 nm) decreases. In human eyes the cornea and the lens together absorb approximately 98% of the UV-B, and thus protect the retina against any damage. However, effective UV-B radiation can penetrate clear water down to at least 8 m, potentially affecting fish and zooplankton. The possibility that rising UV-B levels in conjunction with an exposure to pollutants can interfere with an eye's normal protective mechanisms and cause blindness has been shown in farmed salmon treated with specific chemicals against fish lice. Fish that have eggs and larvae in shallow waters in early spring would be most vulnerable: this includes many commercially important species such as herring, pollock, cod, and salmon. At the bottom of the food chain, UV radiation is known to inhibit algal photosynthesis, but the responses of plant communities as a whole are not fully known.

To make meaningful predictions of the consequences of the global and especially circumpolar rises in UV levels, molecular, genetic, cellular, and biochemical investigations must support research on cell and tissue interactions, and laboratory-based findings need to be reconciled with observations in the field. Field monitoring of UV radiation in the Arctic began only in 1989, and research on the effects of increased ultraviolet radiation on terrestrial and aquatic ecosystems and societies and settlements in the Arctic is still at an early stage.

V.B. MEYER-ROCHOW

See also **Ozone Depletion**

Further Reading

AMAP, *AMAP Assessment Report: Arctic Pollution Issues*, Oslo: Arctic Monitoring and Assessment Program (AMAP), 1998

Ayala, M.N., R. Michael, & P.G. Söderberg, "Influence of exposure time for UV radiation-induced cataract." *Investigative Ophthalmology and Visual Science,* 41 (2000): 3539–3543

Cockell, C.S., "Biological effects of high ultraviolet radiation on early Earth—a theoreticalevaluation." *Journal of Theoretical Biology*, 193 (1998): 717–729

Crutzen, P.J., "SSTs—A threat to the Earth's ozone shield." *Ambio*, 1 (1972): 41–51

De Fabo, E.C. & F.P. Noonan, "Ultraviolet-B radiation and stratospheric ozone loss: potential impacts on human health in the arctic." *International Journal of Circumpolar Health*, 59 (2000): 4–8

Farman, J.C., B.G. Gardiner & J.D. Shanklin, "Large losses of total ozone in antarctica reveal seasonal ClO_x/NO_x interaction." *Nature*, 315 (1985): 207–210

Hessen, D.O. (editor), *UV Radiation and Arctic Ecosystems*, Berlin: Springer, 2002

Meyer-Rochow, V.B., "Risks, especially for the eye, emanating from the rise of solar UV-radiation in the Arctic and Antarctic regions." *International Journal of Circumpolar Health*, 59 (2000): 38–51

Munakata, N. et al., "Comparisons of spore dosimetry and spectral photometry of solar UV radiation at four sites in Japan and Europe." *Photochemistry and Photobiology*, 72 (2000): 739–745

Oikarinen, A. & A. Raitio, "Melanoma and other skin cancers in circumpolar areas." *International Journal of Circumpolar Health*, 59 (2000): 52–56

UMIAK

Also written as *umiaq* or *oomiak*, the umiak is a large, open skin boat distributed from Siberia to Greenland. The Aleut might have called it *baidaras* (or baidarka), but in modern times this term designates the two-hatch kayak. The inhabitants of St Lawrence Island called it *anyaq* (i.e., "boat") or *anyapik* (i.e., "authentic boat"). The Koryak had skin boats closely similar to the umiak but with an elongated oval shape. Distinctive forms are also found for the Koniag (Alutiit) and Chugach Eskimo. The existence of a small umiak *umiahalurak*, a little open retrieval boat, is mentioned in northwest Alaska and also in the Central Arctic. In the eastern Arctic, the name "woman's boat" was often used in recent times because of its exclusive use as a traveling craft in historic times. However, this interpretation is contested and the term umiak seems preferable.

It is usually 6–9 m (20–30 ft) long, about 1–2 m (4–6 ft) wide, and 0.5–1 m (2–3 ft) deep. This double-ended and flat-bottomed boat is lightweight (two to four men can lift it), offers a large capacity (loads of more than 2 tons or more than 20 people), and has a similar design with light regional differences.

The framework is built right side up by men using driftwood or sometimes bone (whale ribs) and ivory. The keel is made of timber and runs from stem to stern. The ends are attached by a post and the upper part fits to the headboard. The flat bottom is constituted of floor timbers crossing the keel transversally and is delimited by longitudinal bilge stringers. The gunwales are connected to the bilge stringers by side ribs that are bridged by outer stringers. The transversal seats or thwarts rest on a pair of inner stringers. The pieces are lashed together with skin thongs and/or attached with either bone pins, pegs, and/or scarphs (simple slash, or locking, notches). The extended gunwales in Greenland were separate pieces of wood called horns.

The cover was prepared by women, and usually made of bearded sealskin; depending on the region, seal, walrus, beluga, caribou, and even polar bear skins have been reported. The hides, previously tanned and with hair removed, were patched together using needle and thread (braided sinews). The necessary number of skins varied according to the specie's size and the dimensions of the boat. For example, it would take about five walrus skins to cover a 9 m umiak. The cover was tightened to the framework by thongs passing over the gunwales and fastened to the uppermost pair of stringers. For waterproofing and upkeep, oil was applied regularly on the skin's surface. Traditionally, alligatorlike mythical animals and also humanlike figures were occasionally painted on the sides of the umiaks of the Bering Sea. Today, white paint is often used to prevent skin from getting damaged and to make it waterproof.

To preserve the skin cover as long as possible, the boat could be either stored for the winter or left on a rack by the shore to protect it from animals. A cover could last about 4–5 years. If an accident damaged the skin, the hole was quickly concealed with blubber; once ashore, it was patched with skin or, in modern times, with brass or aluminum.

Ancestrally, to propel the umiak, paddles, oars, sail, and dog traction were used. The western boats were originally paddled, while in the eastern Arctic, women used oars and men used paddles. The first appearance of the sail is unknown, but it seems to have been used since the first European explorers reported its use. The

Oleg Ukutagin drags an umiak (*baidarka*) while hunting at the floe edge, Chukotka.
Copyright Bryan and Cherry Alexander Photography

square sail limited the boat to following the wind; however, at the beginning of the century, the adoption of the triangular sail allowed it to go windward. The sails were made of light skins, intestines, and, later on, cloth. Dogs harnessed to the boat trotted on the beach and tugged the boat when traveling near the seashore or riverbank (inland). On icy surfaces, the umiak was also occasionally transported on dogsleds. The outboard motor was adopted for the first time in certain regions as early as the 1920s. In this case, the frame of the umiak was modified to fit the motor (at the stern or at the off-center). Nonetheless, the paddles were still used during hunting expeditions when necessary to approach prey silently. The skin float, or *avataq*, lashed along the gunwales, was another piece of equipment for the umiak that gave greater stability in rough seas or for whaling.

The umiak is a multipurpose craft for hunting seal, walrus, whale, and other animals like ducks (with a firearm). Fishing is also another activity possible with the umiak. Historically, the umiak was mainly used as a whaling and traveling boat. Men, traveling by umiak, occasionally raided neighboring tribes in the Bering Strait. For seasonal migrations, the umiak could contain several families with all their equipment and their dogs. When landing, it was lifted ashore and overturned so that it could serve as a temporary shelter or windbreaker. In almost every region, the umiak was put on a rack during winter and used for storing food and household articles.

The *umialik* or *angyaellk* (for the St Lawrence Island) was the umiak owner, a skilled hunter and leader of the whaling crew. He had social prestige and influence on his crew (20–30 people), who cooperated in its regular maintenance.

The origin of the umiak is unclear, but in the east Arctic zone it is generally recognized that the umiak was introduced by the Thule culture 1000 years ago. Historically, the umiak was said to be absent in Central Arctic regions, but archaeological researches gave evidence of its past existence. The umiak gradually disappeared during this century almost everywhere, except for the Bering Sea area. This situation is often explained by the difficulty of finding skin for recovering the frame, the scarcity of the whale population, or simply the adoption of wooden boats.

PIERRE DESROSIERS

See also **Kayak; Thule Culture; Transport**

Further Reading

Adney, Edwin Tappan & I. Chapelle Howard, *Bark and Skin Boats of North America*, Washington: Smithsonian Institute, 1983

Arima, E.Y., *Report on an Eskimo Umiak Build at Ivuyivik, P.Q., in the Summer of 1960*, Ottawa: Dept of Northern Affairs and National Resources, 1963

Braund, Stephen R., *Skin Boats of St Lawrence Island*, Washington: University of Washington Press, 1988

Hughes, Charles C., "Saint Lawrence Island Eskimo." In *Arctic*, edited by David Damas, Washington: Smithsonian Institution, 1984

Nelson, Esward William, *The Eskimo About Bering Strait*, New York: Johnson Reprint Corporation, 1971

Nelson, Richard K., *Hunters of the Northern Ice*, Chicago: The University of Chicago Press, 1969

Petersen, H.C., *Skin Boats of Greenland*, Roskilde: Greenland Provincial Museum and Viking Ship Museum, 1986

Snaith, Skip, *Umiak, an Illustrated Guide*, Eastsound: Walrose and Hyde, 1997

Turner, Lucien M., "Ethnology of the Ungava district, Hudson Bay Territory." *Bureau of Ethnology* (Smithsonian Institution), 7 (1889–1890): 165–350

Victor, Paul-Emile & Joelle Robert-Lamblin, *La Civilisation du Phoque, jeux, gestes et techniques des eskimo d'Ammassalik, ville*, Paris: Armand Collin, Raymond Chabaud, 1989

UN CONVENTION ON THE LAW OF THE SEA

The United Nations Convention on the Law of the Sea was opened for signature on December 10, 1982 at Montego Bay, Jamaica, and entered into force 12 years later on November 16, 1994. Its official languages are Arabic, Chinese, English, French, Russian, and Spanish. German is the unofficial language. The Convention is held in the Secretary-General of the United Nations depository. The Secretariat is the Division for Ocean Affairs and the Law of the Sea (DOALOS) of the Office of Legal Affairs of the United Nations.

The United Nations Convention on the Law of the Sea (UNCLOS) creates a comprehensive legal framework governing the world's oceans and seas and their uses and resources. The scope of UNCLOS is wide ranging and contains 320 articles and nine annexes, relating to navigational rights, territorial sea limits, the contiguous zone, exclusive economic jurisdiction, the continental shelf, legal status of resources on the seabed beyond the limits of national jurisdiction, passage of ships through narrow straits, conservation and management of living marine resources, protection of the marine environment, scientific marine research regime, and development and transfer of marine technology. In addition, it provides a comprehensive and binding procedure for the settlement of disputes between States.

Background

Attempts have been made through the years to regulate the use of oceans in a single convention acceptable to all nations. The oceans were being exploited as never before, and as a result were generating a multitude of claims, counterclaims, and sovereignty disputes. The oceans had become the newest arena for conflict and instability in the world.

Among the factors rendering the freedom-of-the-seas doctrine obsolete were declining fish stocks, and increasing tension between distant-water fishermen and coastal nations' rights over fishing resources; the prospects of rich harvesting of resources on the seafloor; the increased presence of maritime powers with, for example, nuclear submarines charting deep waters and designs for antiballistic missile systems to be placed on the seabed; super tankers ferrying oil from the Middle East to European and other ports, passing though congested straits; and the global spread of pollution.

Recognizing the need, Ambassador Arvid Pardo of Malta, on November 1, 1967, addressed the General Assembly of the United Nations and called for "an effective international regime over the seabed and the ocean floor beyond a clearly defined national jurisdiction." This led to the convening of the Third United Nations Conference on the Law of the Sea in 1973.

Treaty Process

The preamble of the UNCLOS states that the Convention is based on the premise "that the problems of ocean space are closely interrelated and need to be considered as a whole." The desire for a comprehensive Convention arose from the recognition that traditional sea law was disintegrating and that the international community could not be expected to behave in a consistent manner without dialogue, negotiation, and agreement.

Participant States represented every region of the world, all legal and political systems, and all degrees of socioeconomic development. They composed coastal States, States described as geographically disadvantaged with respect to ocean space, archipelagic States, island States, and land-locked States. Not surprisingly, each of the more than 150 countries came to the negotiations with unique and disparate positions on key issues.

The threshold issue that needed to be resolved before any other issues could be addressed was reaching consensus on setting jurisdictional limits for States. All subsequent issues would depend on clearly defining the line separating national and international waters. While every State agreed that a coastal State, in accordance with international law, has complete jurisdiction and control over its territorial sea (a belt of water along its shoreline), States did not initially agree on the width of this belt.

The UNCLOS was adopted as a package, to be accepted as a whole in all its parts without any reservation on any aspect. On December 10, 1982, signatures from 119 delegations representing 117 States, the Cook Islands (at that time a self-governing associated state), and the United Nations Council for Namibia were appended to the Convention. In addition, one ratification, that of Fiji, was deposited that day. The Convention came into force on November 16, 1994, one year after Guyana became the 60th State to adhere to it. In total, the UNCLOS has been signed by 159

States and has been ratified or acceded to by more than 140 States and the European Community.

Impact of UNCLOS

A number of important political and economic changes have taken place in the ten years that have elapsed since the adoption of the UNCLOS, some directly affecting the deep seabed mining provisions of the Convention and others affecting international relations in general. Mining of minerals lying on the deep ocean floor outside of nationally regulated ocean areas had raised many concerns, especially from industrialized States. A subsequent Agreement relating to the implementation of Part XI (mining minerals in the international seabed) of the Convention was adopted on July 28, 1994 and came into force on July 28, 1996. It established the International Seabed Authority, headquarters in Jamaica, to organize and control activities in the deep seabed beyond the national jurisdiction and to administer the resources.

The definition of the territorial sea has brought relief from conflicting claims. Navigation through the territorial sea and narrow straits is now based on legal principles. The right of landlocked countries of access to and from the sea is now stipulated unequivocally. The right to conduct marine scientific research is now based on accepted principles and cannot be unreasonably denied.

The International Tribunal for the Law of the Sea, which has competence to settle ocean-related disputes arising from the application or interpretation of the UNCLOS, is established and operating. The aim of the UNCLOS is universal participation in the Convention in its entirety. As such, no one State can claim that it achieved all it desired without making concessions. Every State benefits from the provisions of the Convention and from the certainty that results from the establishment of a body of international law relating to the law of the sea.

SHANNON BENTLEY

Further Reading

Brown, E., "Dispute Resolution and the Law of the Sea: the UN Convention regime." *Marine Policy*, 21(1) (1997): 17–43

Dolzer, R. & T. BuB, "International marine environmental protection: the legal framework." In *Protecting our Environment: German Perspectives on a Global Challenge*, St Augustin: Konrad Adenauer Stiftung e.V., 2000

Dzidzornu, D.M., "Coastal State obligations and powers respecting EEZ environmental protection under Part XII of the UNCLOS: descriptive analysis." *Colorado Journal of International Environmental Law and Policy*, Volume 8(1) (1997): 283–321

Guruswamy, L., "The promise of the United Nations convention on the Law of the Sea (UNCLOS): justice in trade and environment disputes." In *Ecology Law Quarterly*, Volume 25, No. 2, Berkeley: School of Law (Boalt Hall), University of California, 1998

Kolossovsky, I.K., "The future of the UN Law of the Sea Convention and maintenance of legal order and peace in the oceans in the 21st century." In *The Role of the Oceans in the 21st Century*, Honolulu: The Law of the Sea Institute

Mann Borgese, E., *Ocean Governance and the United Nations,* Halifax: Centre for Foreign Policy Studies, Dalhousie University, 1996

———, "The Law of the Sea: unfinished business." *Natural Resources Forum*, Volume 23(2) (1999): 105–114

Mensah, T.A., "Law of the Sea: The International Tribunal and the protection and preservation of the marine environment." In *Environmental Policy and Law*, Volume 28, No. 5, Amsterdam: IOS Press, 1998

———, "The competence of the International Tribunal for the Law of the Sea outside the Framework of the Convention on the Law of the Sea." *Collected Papers of Zagreb Law School*, 51(5) (2001): 877–883

Ogley, R., "Between the devil and the Law of the Sea." In *The Environment and International Relations*, London: Routledge, 1996

Sohn, L.B., "Managing the Law of the Sea: Ambassador Pardo's forgotten second idea." *Columbia Journal of Transitional Law*, 36(1/2) (1997): 285–305

UNITED STATES OF AMERICA

United States of America (USA), or the United States (US), is a country of 3.7 million sq mi (9.5 million sq km) in North America. The US consists of 50 states and a federal district, Washington, District of Columbia, the capital. The 48 contiguous states of the continental US lie north of Mexico and south of Canada, and stretch from the Atlantic Ocean in the east to the Pacific Ocean in the west. The island state of Hawaii lies in the Pacific Ocean at 21° N 157° W. The state of Alaska, the largest of the 50 states at 656,000 sq mi (1.7 million sq km), occupies the northwest portion of North America. Alaska is bounded on the north by the Arctic Ocean, and more than a quarter of the state lies north of the Arctic Circle. Thus, the US is one of the eight Arctic nations of the world (together with Russia, Finland, Sweden, Norway, Iceland, Denmark/Greenland, and Canada), and held the chairmanship of the Arctic Council from 1998 to 2000.

The US is the fourth largest country in the world, with 6.4% of the total land surface area. In 2000, the population was 286 million, or 4.6% of world population. The US economy is the largest in the world, with a gross national product of $9.6 trillion in 2000, or 30% of the gross world product. The US also leads the world in energy production (19%) and consumption (25%). The US contains abundant natural resources, including oil and natural gas, minerals, forests, and much arable land. The Appalachian Mountains separate the eastern seaboard from the vast central plains of the Midwest and Great Plains states. The western US contains the rugged Rocky Mountains, the arid Great Basin, the deserts of the Southwest, and coastal mountain ranges. More than 70% of the US population live in urban areas; the largest city is New York city. The US government is a federal republic with executive, legislative, and judicial branches. National elections are held every four years for President and other offices.

Prehistoric human settlement of what is now the US goes back at least 12,000 years to the Clovis Culture, descendants of the people who crossed the Bering land bridge during the last Ice Age. Another wave of migration about 5000 years ago brought the ancestors of the Eskimos to Alaska and Canada (Alaska Natives and indigenous peoples of the Arctic). Norse explorers visited the northeastern US around AD 1000 (Norse settlement of the North Atlantic). Following the voyage of Columbus to the Caribbean in 1492, European exploration accelerated over the next several hundred years, dominated by the Spanish, English, and French. The Spanish established the first European settlement (1565) in Florida. In the 1600s and 1700s, the English settled the eastern seaboard, while the French controlled Québec (Canada) and the Mississippi Valley down to Louisiana. The American colonists became increasingly frustrated with British rule, and declared independence in 1776. General George Washington led the colonial rebels to victory in the American Revolution (1775–1783) and was elected the first president in 1789. In 1803, the Louisiana Purchase (from France) doubled the size of the country, extending it beyond the Mississippi River. Throughout the 1800s, westward expansion led to the conquest or seizure of new US territory, notably from Mexico and Native American tribes. The California gold rush (1848–1849) and the completion of the first transcontinental railroad (1869) spurred westward migration. The US fought a bloody Civil War (1861–1865) over slavery and secession. The Union prevailed and slavery was abolished. In 1867, the US purchased Alaska (from Russia) through the efforts of Secretary of State William Seward. Alaska became known as Seward's Folly because of its supposed uselessness. By the 1890s, the continental US was settled from coast to coast and the Native Americans were effectively displaced. Between 1881 and 1920, 23 million immigrants entered the US, the largest population flux ever recorded. At the start of World War I (1914), the US declared neutrality, but entered the war against Germany in 1917. The 1920s witnessed an industrial and financial boom that collapsed in 1929, inaugurating the Great Depression. New social and economic measures were enacted under President Roosevelt's New Deal in the 1930s. The US again declared neutrality at the start of World War II (1939), but the Japanese attack on Pearl Harbor (Hawaii, 1941) precipitated US entry into a war in the Pacific as well as the war in Europe. The postwar period saw the rise of two rival superpowers, the US and the USSR, engaged in a "cold war" of world domination and arms buildup. The socially turbulent 1960s brought the civil rights movement, the environmental movement, and protests against the Vietnam War (1964–1973). Since the collapse of the USSR in 1991, the US has been the world's sole superpower.

The US exploration of the Arctic goes back to 1850 when Lieutenant De Haven of the US Navy commanded two of the 11 ships on a search for the Franklin expedition. Kane led a small expedition (1853–1855) that wintered in Kane Basin and traced part of the coast of Greenland. Hall spent much of the 1860s exploring the Arctic and learning the ways of the Eskimos. In 1871, he pushed north of Kane Basin all the way to the Arctic Ocean. Lieutenant DeLong hoped to reach the North Pole from the other side of the Arctic, sailing north through Bering Strait in 1879. His ship became locked in the pack ice for two years and was finally crushed near the New Siberian Islands. Three years later, remnants were found on the southwest coast of Greenland, inspiring Nansen's famous drift in the *Fram*. The US had two research stations as part of the First International Circumpolar Year (1882–1883), one at Pt Barrow, Alaska, and one on Ellesmere Island under Lieutenant Greely, whose party met a tragic fate. Robert Peary, another US Naval officer, became obsessed with attaining the Pole. After two expeditions to northern Greenland in the 1890s and two thwarted polar attempts in the early 1900s, Peary finally reached the North Pole by dogsled in 1909 with Henson and four Eskimos. Macmillan, a member of Peary's expedition, went on to make 28 voyages of Arctic exploration over the next 40 years. Aviator Richard Byrd claimed the first overflight of the North Pole in 1926. The US military maintained weather stations along the east coast of Greenland during World War II, and developed a strong interest in the Arctic after the war due to the proximity of the USSR across the top of the world (Geopolitics of the Arctic). US Navy submarines have patrolled under the ice since 1958, and a radar network (the Distant Early Warning line) was constructed in the 1950s from Alaska to Greenland. Oil was discovered on the North Slope of Alaska in 1968, and the Trans-Alaska pipeline was completed in 1977, despite environmental concerns. Controversy now surrounds the proposed oil drilling in the Arctic National Wildlife Refuge.

US scientists have conducted research at more than 30 manned drifting stations in the Arctic Ocean since 1952, including two during the International

Geophysical Year (1957–1958). In 1997, a joint US/Russian agreement led to the release of previously classified US Navy submarine data and Russian data from 40 years of their drifting stations. The Greenland Ice Sheet Project 2 (GISP2) completed five years of drilling in 1993 to recover an ice core more than 3000 m long. The ice core record preserves properties of the climate dating back more than 100,000 years. Current US research is sponsored by the National Science Foundation, the National Aeronautics and Space Administration, the National Oceanic and Atmospheric Administration, the Office of Naval Research, and other government agencies, and focuses on sea ice, ice sheets, climate, and global change effects.

HARRY L. STERN

See also **Alaska**

Further Reading

Mirsky, Jeanette, *To the Arctic!*, New York: Knopf, 1948
The Columbia Encyclopedia, Ithaca, New York: Columbia University Press, 1993
The Statesman's Yearbook 2002, New York: Palgrave, 2001
The World Almanac and Book of Facts 2002, New York: World Almanac Books, 2002

UNIVERSITIES AND HIGHER EDUCATION ESTABLISHMENTS, NORTH AMERICA AND GREENLAND

Education has been a lifelong process since people first inhabited the North. Indigenous peoples learned to extract their food, clothing, and shelter from the natural resources available on land and water. A holistic worldview incorporated continuing education into the daily lives of indigenous peoples. Education was an inherent process that occurred during daily activities, ensuring cultural stability and community. The direction of lessons for individual learners was often determined by the learner's aptitude and by the needs of the community. Long before the founding of western models of universities and higher education establishments, indigenous peoples of the Arctic had established their own distinct institutions and societies aimed at research in the pursuit of knowledge. Teaching and learning are known to have taken place in formal and informal settings. Formal institutions such as Medicine Lodges and Sweat Lodges were created for traditional teachings and ceremonies. Societies were created for the exchange of ideas and sharing knowledge such as the Medewin Society for healing and medicine. Informal teaching took place in the experiential learning of daily life, enabling people to gain new knowledge and to develop proficiency in various skills. Teaching and learning roles remained interchangeable over the course of a lifetime.

Changes in the daily life of northern indigenous peoples have occurred as a result of forced assimilation to western values, including attitudes toward education. The transformation from subsistence-based societies to wage-based societies has altered the content and delivery of higher education among Arctic indigenous communities and has presented an ongoing challenge to universities and higher education establishments in the Arctic. Universities and higher education establishments, which are modeled on the European prototype, have begun to dot the circumpolar map. These relatively new institutions address numerous issues in the delivery of education, including climate, landscape, community, culture, family patterns and relationships, socioeconomic status, gender barriers, and language.

In Canada, there are over 50 universities and colleges with northern programs or northern interests. A number of these institutions are affiliated with the Association of Canadian Universities for Northern Studies (ACUNS). ACUNS was established to bring together scholars, northern communities, governments, and national and international organizations interested in northern scholarship. Canadian programs vary widely in scope and size, from formal northern institutes and centers to informal groups of scholars with northern research interests. Several such institutes and centers are recognized internationally for their circumpolar interests, including GÉTIC (Groupe d'études inuit et circumpolaires) of Laval University in Québec, CINE (Centre for Indigenous Nutrition and the Environment) of McGill University in Québec, NHRU (Northern Health Research Unit) of the University of Manitoba in Manitoba, AINA (Arctic Institute of North America) of the University of Calgary in Alberta, and CCI (Canadian Circumpolar Institute) of the University of Alberta in Edmonton, Alberta. Athabasca University in northern Alberta has taken the lead in developing the University of the Arctic's online learning environment. Three colleges and one university stand out as full-fledged northern institutions serving the needs of northern peoples: Nunavut Arctic College in Nunavut, Aurora College in the Northwest Territories, Yukon College in Yukon, and the University of Northern British Columbia in British Columbia.

In Greenland, the Home Rule government is determined to ensure that Greenlanders do not have to leave their homeland to pursue higher education. The University of Greenland in Nuuk is dedicated to serving the educational needs of and studies relevant to Greenlanders. Higher education establishments also include a college of education, a socioeducational college, and a number of business colleges. Vocational programs have been introduced and 14 local vocational colleges have been set up to provide training in the trades, business, and service industries. The Danish Polar Center in Greenland provides services and logistics support to research projects in Greenland, publishes information for scientists and the general public, and operates a library. Numerous Danish and foreign institutions are involved in academic research in Greenland.

In the United States, the Arctic Research Consortium of the United States (ARCUS), with a similar mandate and scope as ACUNS, lists over 30 universities and colleges with northern programs or northern interests. American programs differ in scope and size, from Arctic research institutes on university campuses to academic discussion groups on Arctic themes. Many of the institutes are recognized internationally for their circumpolar interests, including the Institute for Arctic Studies of Dartmouth College in New Hampshire, Byrd Polar Research Center of the Ohio State University in Ohio, the Institute of Arctic and Alpine Research and the Arctic System Science Data Coordination Center of the University of Colorado in Colorado, the Polar Science Center of the University of Washington in Washington, the Center for Northern Studies in Vermont, the Glaciology and Arctic Science Institute of the University of Idaho in Idaho, as well as the numerous research units and institutes of the University of Alaska in Alaska. In Alaska, the Consortium for Alaska Native Higher Education (CANHE) with university, college, and community representation was formed to support the formation of a state college system controlled by Alaska Natives. Among these is Ilisagvik College, which was founded to provide an education based on the Iñupiat cultural tradition and is committed to reinforcing Iñupiat culture, language, values, and knowledge.

The multiplicity of needs of the indigenous peoples that represent the majority of the Arctic population in North America and Greenland means that programs need to be developed and implemented by and with indigenous peoples for indigenous peoples. This approach can be illustrated in the roles that indigenous peoples are reclaiming in terms of sharing indigenous knowledge and expertise within academia. Such an approach offers culturally relevant academic curricula in institutions of higher education. The recently launched University of the Arctic endeavors to meet this approach.

HEATHER CASTLEDEN

See also **Arctic Research Consortium of the United States (ARCUS); Association of Canadian Universities for Northern Studies (ACUNS); Education; Indigenous Knowledge; University of the Arctic**

Further Reading

Allerston, Rosemary, "Learning for life." *Up-Here,* 16(6) (2000): 38–43

Battiste, Marie, "Enabling the autumn seed: toward a decolonized approach to Aboriginal knowledge, language, and education." *Canadian Journal of Native Education*, 22(1) (1998), 16–27

Grant, Agnes, "The Challenge for Universities." In *First Nations Education in Canada: The Circle Unfolds,* edited by M. Battiste & J. Barman, Vancouver: UBC Press, 1995

Haig-Brown, Celia, *Taking Control: Power and Contradiction in First Nations Adult Education*, Vancouver: UBC Press, 1995

Johnson, Peter, "University of the Arctic." *Arctic,* 52(3) (1999): iii–iv

Langlais, Richard & Outi Snellman (editors), *Learning to be Circumpolar: Experiences in Arctic Academic Cooperation,* Publications in the University of the Arctic Process No. 5, Rovaniemi, Finland: University of Lapland, 1999

Senkpiel, Aron, "North to North: the new discourse." *Northern Review* (21) (summer 2000): 11–18

Senkpiel, Aron, Kenneth Coates & Judith Kleinfield (editors), "Education in the North." *Northern Review* (12–13) (summer/winter 1994)

Smith, Linda, *Decolonizing Methodologies: Research and Indigenous Peoples*, London: Zed Books, 1999

University of the Arctic, *Shared Voices: University of the Arctic Newsletter*, No. 1–7; http://www.uarctic.org/publications. html, 2000–2001

UNIVERSITIES AND HIGHER EDUCATION ESTABLISHMENTS, RUSSIA

The beginning of higher education in Russia dates from the founding of the Academic University as part of the St Petersburg Academy of Sciences in 1725. It was, however, closed because of a shortage of students. The true starting point for Russian universities is accepted as 1755, when the Imperial Moscow University (now Moscow State University) was founded by the famous Russian scientist Mikhail V. Lomonosov. In 1802–1805, Derpt (now Tartu University in Estonia), Kharkov, and Kasan universities were established in the territory of the Russian Empire, and the main school of the Grand Duchy of Lithuania, established since the 16th century, was renamed Vilno University. In 1816, Warsaw University was founded, and in 1819, St Petersburg University (on the site of the Pedagogical Institute, founded in 1806).

Privileged groups of the population received education outside universities, at boarding schools or lyceums, so university students came from a range of social groups. University towns supplied the country with educated public officers, doctors, and teachers, and the towns themselves became educational, scientific, and administrative centers.

The common Charter of the Russian universities was approved in 1804 and provided autonomy for universities, headed by the Council of Professors. All internal issues, including disciplinary ones, were considered by the university's court. According to the Charter of 1835, rectors were appointed by the Czar, and professors were appointed by curators from the Ministry for Education. In 1863, the universities made an attempt to restore self-government, but the Charter of 1884 canceled their autonomy once and for all.

In 1863–1865, for the first time in the history of Russian higher education, women were allowed to attend universities as external students. In the 1870s, women's higher medicine courses were opened in Moscow and St Petersburg, and physical-mathematical and historical-philological courses in Kazan and Kiev.

After the Great October Revolution, the universities were reorganized along socialist lines. Higher education became free and available to all, regardless of social origin, race, nationality, language, sex, and faith. In 1919–1920, all university programs were restructured along political and ideological lines, and natural sciences were extended with new departments opened, for example, in biology, physics, chemistry, and mechanical and electric engineering.

Industrialization demanded qualified technical specialists; therefore, at the end of the 1920s and the beginning of the 1930s on the basis of separate departments of some universities, industry institutes were established such as the Siberian Mining Institute in Irkutsk in 1930 (now the Irkutsk State Technical University). The higher education network was greatly expanded in Soviet Russia. New institutes and universities were opened in every union and autonomous republic; for instance, Irkutsk State University was founded in 1918, Samarkand University (Uzbekistan) in 1927, Tyumen's Institute of Higher Education (now Tyumen State University) in 1930, and the University of Kazakhstan in 1934. Higher education was established even in those provinces where the indigenous population had no written language prior to the October Revolution. So, in 1934, the Yakutsk Pedagogical Institute was founded; this was reorganized into the Yakutsk (Sakha) State University in 1956.

In the 1920s, the Soviet government gave high priority to the education of the northern indigenous peoples. Teacher-training colleges and special departments within universities were set up to train schoolteachers from the northern regions to teach both in the native language and in Russian; for example, the Department of Russian Language of the State Pedagogical University in Leningrad (now St Petersburg's Herzen State Pedagogical University) operated teacher-training courses in northern languages from 1930.

Today, higher education in Russia is regulated under the Federal Education Act and the Federal Higher and Postgraduate Education, both of 1996. In 1990, there were 514 various higher education establishments in Russia, with a total of 2,800,000 students. In 2000, Russia had more than 1000 government and non-government universities, academies, institutes, higher military schools, and other higher education establishments with a total of almost 4,000,000 students.

Every Russian citizen, foreign national, or stateless person is eligible to enter a Russian higher education institute, provided he or she supplies a certificate of general secondary education and passes entrance tests set by individual universities. Foreign nationals are accepted within quotas established by international agreements. Every year, the Russian Federation Ministry for Education approves the Entrance Regulations. Normally a student has to take several exams: one for the selected speciality, a written test of the Russian language, and very often a foreign language test is required (one mentioned in the school certificate).

From 2004, following tests in five regions from 2001, students in their final school year take the Unified State Exam as an entry exam to higher education establishments. Where candidates have equal scores, orphans, applicants from families with many children, and victims of the Semipalatinsk nuclear testing ground and of the Chernobyl nuclear power station disaster are given preference. The Russian Federation Ministry for Education also recommends preferential terms for indigenous northern minorities, refugees from disaster areas, handicapped individuals, and discharged military service persons (and veterans of military operations). All university and higher institution students are granted deferral of military service, which is mandatory for citizens of the Russian Federation.

Traditionally, the Moscow State University is rated number one in Russia for the quality of training, modern teaching methods, and careers of its graduates. Among the best are the Russian Academy of Economics named after G.V. Plekhanov', Moscow Physical Technical Institute, Russian State University for Humanities, Russian University of Friendship of Nations, Moscow State Academy of Law, Moscow Academy of Medicine named after I.M. Sechenov', and St Petersburg State University. The Novosibirsk State Academy of Medicine, Saratov State University, Kazan State University, and Bashkir State Medical University are also highly ranked.

Several universities have departments with northern programs researching the languages and literature of the peoples of the Far North, Siberia, and Far East, including the Faculty of Far North Peoples of the Herzen State Pedagogical University (St Petersburg), Department of the Siberian Peoples Languages and Folklore, Humanities Faculty of the Novosibirsk State University,

Research Center on Ethnic and Language Relations, Institute of Linguistics, Russian Academy of Sciences, and Siberian Languages Sector, Philology Institute of the Russian Academy of Sciences Siberian Division.

LILIA VINOKUROVA

See also **Circumpolar Universities Association; Herzen Institute; Institute of Peoples of the North; University of the Arctic**

Further Reading

Letopis Moskovskogo universiteta, 1755–1979 [Annals of the Moscow University, 1755–1979], Moscow: izdatelstvo MGU (Moscow State University Press), 1979

Obrazovanie 2000: spravochnik. Moscow: Nauchno-tekhnichesky centr Universitetsky, 2000 [Education 2000: the directory, Moscow: Scientific and technical centre "University"]

Rossiysky statistichesky agegodnik, Ofisialnoe izdanie [The Russian statistical year-book: The official issue], Moscow: State Statistic Committee Press, 1999

Vysshie i srednie spesialnyie uchebnye zavedeneya Rossii, 1998–1999, Spravochnik [Higher Education Establishments and Professional Schools in Russia, 1998–1999], Moscow: Arbat-Inform Press, 1998

Vysshee obrazovanie v Rossii:statisticheskyi sbornik. Centr issledovaniya I statystiki nauki [Higher Education System in Russia: the statistical collection], Moscow: Centre of Research and Statistics of a Science Press, 1998

Vysshie uchebnyie zavedeneya Rossii po respublikam, krayam I oblastyam;ofisialnaya informastiya dlya postupaustikh v vuzy. Spravochnik [Higher Education Establishments in the republics, regions, districts of Russia: official information for school post-graduates. Guidebook], Moscow: Logos Press, 1997

UNIVERSITY OF THE ARCTIC

The University of the Arctic is a network of over 50 universities, colleges, research institutes, and other organizations concerned with higher education and research in and about the circumpolar region. It has no students and no campus, and is not a degree-awarding institution; however, students registered at any of the member institutions (from Canada, Faroe Islands, Finland, Greenland, Iceland, Norway, Russia, Svalbard, Sweden, and the United States) are eligible to participate in the University of the Arctic programs such as the Bachelor of Circumpolar Studies (BCS), which may be a full degree program or incorporated as credits into local degree programs.

The concept of the University of the Arctic as an international nongovernmental organization was first proposed to the Arctic Council in 1997. A feasibility study undertaken by a working group of the Circumpolar Universities Association reported to the Ministers of the Arctic Council in 1998, and the first University of the Arctic Interim Council meeting was held in Fairbanks, Alaska, in December 1998. A secretariat, formerly called the Circumpolar Coordination Office, was founded in Rovaniemi, Finland, by the University of Lapland in January 1999, and the Interim Council was replaced by the Council in November 2000. The University was officially launched in June 2001, and the first students completed the introductory course of the BCS in May 2002.

The University's Council, working with a board of governors, directs program development and delivery. The Council is composed of institutions of higher education and other organizations concerned with higher education and research in the circumpolar North, such as the Arctic Athabascan Council, RAIPON, Association of Canadian Universities for Northern Studies, Canadian Polar Commission, and GRID-Arendal (a Resource Information Database project of the United Nations Environment Program).

The University's curriculum includes both social and natural sciences—the lands, peoples, and issues of the circumpolar North—and incorporates specialized field schools in northern locations for young researchers. Higher education programs are planned to be accessible even to those in small and remote communities, and access initiatives include the online Arctic Learning Environment (ALE) portal, and the Circumpolar Mobility Program (CMP) incorporating the north2north student exchange program. ALE supports distant learners, and pilot delivery of online BCS courses began in January 2003. Open learning aims to give northern local and indigenous peoples outside the traditional university system an opportunity to further their education and acquire new skills. A further program of the University aims to strengthen the role of northerners in research and knowledge generation through dialogue on contemporary northern issues among northerners and with the rest of the world, through close links with the Circumpolar Universities Association and Northern Research Forum.

GILLIAN LINDSEY

See also **Circumpolar Universities Association; Northern Research Forum**

Further Reading

University of the Arctic website: http://www.uarctic.org/
Bachelor of Circumpolar Studies website: http://www.uarctic.org/bcs/

UPERNAVIK

Upernavik is a municipality and town located between Svartenhuk Peninsula (Nunavik in Greenlandic) and Melville Bay in northwest Greenland. The largest municipality in this part of the country, Upernavik comprises a total area of 199,000 sq km. Only 10,000 sq km are free of ice cover. In the northern parts of Upernavik, the inland ice reaches the sea at several places, dividing the ice-free areas into two portions. North of the 71st parallel, darkness reigns from November until February, but midnight sun occurs from May until August. Relatively warm and nutrition-rich deep-sea water rises to the surface, generating excellent conditions for a fertile plankton production in the northern part of Baffin Bay, and at the same time it creates a situation with permanent open water, that is, ice-free conditions, and consequently an abundant fauna.

The town of Upernavik is situated on a small island in Baffin Bay and was founded as a whaling and sealing base in 1771. During the 20th century, however, fisheries expanded, and today halibut fishing and processing dominates Upernavik's economy. The town serves as a municipal administrative center with a hospital and a school. Graphite deposits are located, although not produced, nearby. The name "Upernavik" means "spring place" in Greenlandic, and its total population is 2902 (as recorded in 2000), with 1143 inhabitants residing in the town. The remainder of the population is distributed among the 11 settlements in the municipality: Upernavik Kujalleq (population 186), Kangersuatsiaq (255), Aappilattoq (213), Tussaaq (one), Naajaat (52), Innarsuit (161), Tasiusaq (231), Nutaarmiut (64), Ikerakuuk (17), Nuussuaq (192), and Kullorsuaq (387).

To the northwest on Kingittoq (Kingigtoq) Island, the Greenlander Pelimut (in Danish, *Filemon*) found, in 1824, an early 14th-century runic stone that told of three men who wintered there. Three lines of runes are carved into the clay-mica-slate stone (measuring 10×3×2 cm) along with the year 1333. This indicates that the Norse settlers had reached as far North as Kingittoq in the 14th century and had made contact with the Inuit population. The Norse hunted walrus for its skin, a desirable and valuable commodity. During the latter part of the 17th century, the Dutch hunted whales in the area, and hunters consequently named several of the localities including Zwarten Hoek and Vrouwen Eylande. Danish colonization began in 1771, and during the next 150 years sea mammal hunting dominated cultural activity in the municipality, primarily seals and walruses, in addition to a variety of birds. Within the territory of Kingittoq, a large number of steep bird cliffs exist such as those found on the islands Qaarsorsuaq and Aapassuit, north of Tasiusaq, the latter being the largest in Greenland.

In the early part of the 20th century, the warming period and the expansion of the cod stock had a limited effect on fisheries in Upernavik. The cooling of the water since the 1970s has led to an increase in the numbers of fisheries for Greenland halibut, and a tendency to overfish in southerly waters, which has caused a decline

in the average size of the fish. The fisheries further north, therefore, realize greater profits. Approximately 27% of the employment in Kingittoq relies upon fishing and hunting, surpassed only by the public service and administration sector, which comprises 41% of the total number of employees. In addition, 15% of the population works in retail and wholesale trade.

Upernavik includes all of the amenities and features one would expect from a larger town in Greenland. The town provides general services such as a museum, a hospital, a home for the elderly, and a kindergarten. Moreever, at the end of the 20th century, Upernavik began preparing for an expected boom in tourism. With beautiful and dramatic landscapes, exquisite nature, kayaking and dogsled rides, and a friendly and open population, experts expect that tourism will emerge as a significant income source. Helicopters serviced the town until the opening of an airport close to Upernavik, which increased accessibility tremendously.

RASMUS OLE RASMUSSEN

See also **Baffin Bay**

Further Reading

Berthelsen, Christian, Inger H. Mortensen & Ebbe Mortensen (editors), *Kalaallit Nunaat Atlas, Greenland*, Nuuk: Atuakkiorfik, 1992
Nielsen, Niels, Peter Skautrup & Christian Vibe (editors), *J.P. Trap Danmark, bind XIV, Grønland*, Copenhagen: Gads Forlag, 1970
Rasmussen, Rasmus Ole, "Formal economy, renewable resources and structural changes in West Greenland." *Études/Inuit/Studies*, 24(1) (2000): 48–78
Statistics Greenland, *Greenland 2000–2001. Statistical Yearbook,* Nuuk: Statistics Greenland, 2001
http://www.upernavik.gl/

UPPER ATMOSPHERE PHYSICS AND CHEMISTRY

The upper atmosphere is here taken to be all parts of the Earth's atmosphere that lie above the troposphere (the weather layer). In the Arctic, the upper atmosphere begins somewhere between 5 and 10 km above the Earth's surface (lower over a depression, higher over a high-pressure ridge). It extends out to several hundred kilometers from the Earth. The air in the upper atmosphere is very thin, becoming progressively thinner with increasing distance from the Earth's surface. Altogether, about 20% of the total amount of air in the atmosphere is in the upper atmosphere.

Composition

At the base of the upper atmosphere, the main gases are the same as at the Earth's surface—nitrogen (78%), oxygen (21%), argon (1%), and carbon dioxide (0.04%). All other gases found in trace amounts in the troposphere are also found at the base of the upper atmosphere. One distinct difference between the troposphere and the upper atmosphere is that the latter is much dryer—air in the troposphere can hold up to 4% water vapor, whereas in the upper atmosphere water comprises less than 0.001%. This means that clouds are very rare in the upper atmosphere. Higher up in the upper atmosphere, gas molecules are steadily broken apart by solar radiation. This leads to the formation of new compounds and to the presence of gases in atomic rather than molecular form. Up to about 100 km altitude, the gases are well mixed and the proportions of the nonreactive constituents remain the same. Above 100 km, the density of each gas decreases with increasing height at a rate depending on the atomic or molecular weight. The gas that dominates furthest out in the atmosphere is the lightest, namely hydrogen.

Effects of Solar Radiation

The Sun emits both electromagnetic and particle radiation, which heat and ionize the air in the upper atmosphere and dissociate molecules. Electromagnetic radiation (light) travels in straight lines from the Sun to the Earth. This leads to strong differences in the effects of solar electromagnetic radiation between summer and winter in the Arctic (and the Antarctic). Solar particle radiation is generally steered toward the polar areas by the Earth's magnetic field, and equally to the two hemispheres, irrespective of season. Both electromagnetic and particle radiation from the Sun vary over the Sun's 10–11 years "solar activity cycle." This leads to strong 10–11-year variations in ionization, temperature, and composition of the upper atmosphere.

Stratosphere

The lowest part of the upper atmosphere, directly above the troposphere, is called the stratosphere. Solar ultraviolet radiation is much stronger in the upper atmosphere than at the Earth's surface, where the stratosphere almost completely absorbs the highest-energy ultraviolet rays. Absorption of ultraviolet radiation by the air leads to a strong increase of temperature with increasing height up to about 50 km. This temperature maximum is called the stratopause and the region below it is called the stratosphere. Temperatures increase from about –50°C at the lower border of the stratosphere to between –10°C and +10°C at the stratopause. Solar ultraviolet radiation in the upper atmosphere also breaks apart molecular bonds and leads to the separation of atoms and, at lower heights,

to the formation of new molecules. The most important of these molecules is ozone, formed when oxygen molecules are dissociated by ultraviolet radiation. The stratosphere contains most of the ozone in the atmosphere. Although ozone is formed mainly at low latitudes, where the sun is high in the sky and the intensity of ultraviolet radiation is strong, it is transported toward the poles by winds. This means that the largest accumulations of ozone are over the Arctic and the Antarctic. Ozone absorbs part of the Sun's ultraviolet light which is not otherwise absorbed by the atmosphere, and so protects life-forms on the Earth's surface from this aggressive radiation (see **Ultraviolet-B Radiation**). The changes in solar ultraviolet radiation during the solar cycle lead to a few percent variation in the ozone amounts.

Ozone Depletion

In recent decades, the natural accumulation of ozone has been disturbed by new chemical reactions involving mainly chlorine, released into the atmosphere by humans. Chlorine is one of the constituents of freons (a chlorofluorocarbon or CFC), which were developed by industry to be very stable under normal atmospheric conditions. They are not broken down in the troposphere and are insoluble in water (rain). This means that freons can be transported intact into the stratosphere. Once in the stratosphere, they are slowly broken apart by solar ultraviolet radiation, releasing their chlorine to form less stable compounds. Chlorine reacts with oxygen and with ozone in such a way as to transform ozone back to oxygen. After achieving this, the chlorine remains free to react with a new ozone molecule, so that just a few chlorine atoms can destroy many ozone molecules. Less ozone allows more ultraviolet light to reach the Earth's surface. Ozone depletion is worst over the Antarctic, during the Antarctic spring. The situation over the Arctic has not become so severe, for reasons of geography (see **Ozone Depletion**). Research has shown that the rate of ozone destruction is accelerated up to two orders of magnitude if clouds form in the ozone layer.

Polar Stratospheric Clouds

Clouds in the winter stratosphere are known as polar stratospheric clouds (see **Polar Stratospheric Clouds**). Sometimes (but not always) they can be seen from the ground as brilliantly colored "nacreous" or "mother-of-pearl" clouds. Such clouds have been observed over northern and southern Scandinavia, and occasionally even over the British Isles, for as long as scientific records have been kept (at least 100 years). Clouds in the upper atmosphere form only at extremely low temperatures because of the very low water content. During polar winter, a cold air mass forms in the stratosphere circulating around the pole and is called the polar vortex. Over the Antarctic, the circulating winds are relatively undisturbed and the air in the polar vortex remains isolated from the air outside. It cools steadily during the sunless winter months and temperatures drop well below the limit needed for clouds to form, and remain low for most of the winter. In the Arctic, the winds circling the polar vortex are disturbed by the winds below, which have to climb up and down over several mountain chains. As a result, the air in the vortex is less isolated and warmer. Clouds in the Arctic stratosphere are a relatively rare occurrence. Although polar stratospheric clouds have, in recent years, become a major factor in depleting stratospheric ozone, it is important to remember that they are not the cause. Without the chlorine released from man-made industrial chemicals (such as freons), the ozone layer would have remained in its natural state.

Stability

An important characteristic of the upper atmosphere in general, and the stratosphere in particular, is that it is "stable"—meaning that there is very little mixing of the air in the vertical direction. This is due to the strong increase in temperature with increasing height. It means that chemical species such as freons will be transported very slowly upward or downward once they have reached the stratosphere. The only way for freons to leave the atmosphere is for them first to be broken apart by solar ultraviolet radiation in the stratosphere, to form new chemicals that are water soluble, and then to be mixed back into the troposphere where they can be removed by rain. The downward mixing of stratospheric air takes place primarily at the boundary between the Arctic (or Antarctic) and midlatitude airmasses. Unfortunately, the process is slow and it is expected to take many tens of years before anthropogenic chlorine can be removed from the upper atmosphere.

Atmospheric Waves

A further important process in the stratosphere is the propagation of waves. Both large- and small-scale waves are generated in the lower atmosphere and travel up into the stratosphere. These may be reflected back, absorbed, or allowed to propagate further, depending on the state of the winds and temperatures in the stratosphere. The propagation of waves through the atmosphere is the primary process in the atmosphere by which heat is transported from low- to high latitudes, for example, keeping Arctic temperatures at

reasonable levels even during the long polar night. Strong correlations have been found between temperatures in the stratosphere and the Sun's 10–11-year cycle of "solar activity." This has led to the suggestion that changes in heating of the stratosphere due to changes in ultraviolet radiation during the solar cycle can change the way in which waves are affected by the stratosphere. This in turn could affect the way in which heat is transported to the Arctic. This is a very active research field and results, as yet, are only preliminary. It is hoped that this line of investigation might provide an explanation for 10–11-year climate cycles sometimes reported from different locations in the Arctic (and from other parts of the globe).

Mesosphere

The part of the atmosphere between about 45 and 90 km altitude is known as the mesosphere. The temperature at the lower edge is about +10°C in summer, and −10°C in winter. Temperature decreases with increasing height in the mesosphere until, at the upper edge (mesopause), it is around −70°C and −150°C in summer. The mesosphere contains less than 0.1% of the air in the atmosphere, but is nonetheless an important part of the Earth's protection against radiation from space.

Solar Proton Events

In addition to the electromagnetic radiation that we receive as heat and light, the Sun also emits considerable quantities of high-energy particles—protons with mega-electron-volt energies—and high-energy X-rays. These are largely absorbed by the atmosphere in the mesosphere. Emission of high-energy protons from the Sun takes place during "solar proton events." Such events typically last for a few days and occur 10–20 times during a typical 10–11-year cycle of solar activity, mostly close to the time when the Sun is most active. Solar protons are steered by the Earth's magnetic field and reach the upper atmosphere only at high latitudes. They ionize the upper atmosphere (primarily the mesosphere), and the strong ionization prevents radiocommunications from traveling through the atmosphere. This leads to the phenomenon of "polar cap absorption," where shortwave radio communications become impossible over the whole polar cap. Sometimes, the solar protons have such high energies that they penetrate far into the stratosphere and even closer to the Earth's surface. In such cases, they can become a danger for passengers and crew in aircraft crossing the polar areas. Normally, flight routes will be changed to avoid this danger (*see* **Space Weather**).

Noctilucent Clouds

At the very top of the mesosphere, at heights between 80 and 87 km, noctilucent clouds are found (*see* **Noctilucent Cloud Formation**). These are very thin clouds that appear only during the summer months. They occur in the Arctic (and the Antarctic) and extend equatorward to about 60° latitude. In fact, they are observed most easily from locations outside the Arctic (or Antarctic), when they can be seen lit up by sunlight long after sunset, contrasted against a dark sky. Since they occur only during summer (late May to early August in the Northern Hemisphere), they are hard to see in the Arctic (or Antarctic) since the Sun there does not get far enough below the horizon to give sufficient contrast against the background sky. Measurements have shown that in the Arctic, at about 86 km altitude in summer, the temperature can fall below −150°C. The low temperatures are caused by the same process as the cooling in a refrigerator—air is forced to move upward in the mesosphere over the summer polar caps. It expands and cools as it moves upward to a region with lower pressure. The very low temperatures attained allow water ice to form even though the water content of the air is extremely low, thus forming the noctilucent clouds.

In recent years, there have been a number of reports that noctilucent clouds are becoming increasingly common. However, the evidence is inconclusive. Reanalysis of earlier data sets, and analysis of data sets from new locations do not support the idea that there has been an increase in the occurrence of noctilucent clouds, at least not during the last 40 years. However, all analyses and all data sets so far presented do show a strong 10–11-year cycle in noctilucent clouds. A complete explanation for this cycle has not yet been found; however, it may be related to the solar-cycle effects on ozone and heating of the stratosphere and, through this, to effects on the propagation of upper-atmosphere waves.

Polar Mesosphere Summer Echoes

Noctilucent clouds are closely related to the phenomenon of polar mesosphere summer echoes (PMSE). These are strongly enhanced echoes seen by satellite radars at frequencies close to 50 MHz from heights between 80 and 90 km, in the Arctic, during summer. PMSE are thought to be due to very small ice particles, the precursors of noctilucent clouds. It is easier to make quantitative observations of PMSE than of noctilucent clouds. Appropriate scientific radars operate continuously in a number of locations. Their observations are not dependent on good weather and the exact magnitude of the effect can be easily monitored. So far, PMSE have been monitored regularly only since

about 1990, so it will be many years before their study can help resolve the questions posed by noctilucent cloud observations. However, it is to be expected that they will eventually provide an explanation of the 10–11-year cycle in noctilucent clouds and resolve the question of whether or not there is a long-term trend.

Thermosphere

The atmospheric layer above about 100 km height is called the thermosphere, and marks the beginning of the ionosphere (the partially ionized plasma region that coexists with the uppermost layers of a planet's atmosphere). It is characterized by very high temperatures. These vary from about 300°C at times of low solar activity to about 1000°C when the Sun is more active. The thermosphere contains only ten- millionths of a percent of the Earth's atmosphere. Perhaps surprisingly, it was for a long time the best-understood part of the upper atmosphere. This is a result of the strong ionization of the thermosphere, which results from the solar extreme ultraviolet and X-ray radiation and, in the Arctic, from high-energy electrons that rain down from space and cause the spectacular northern lights (the aurora borealis). The ionization makes the thermosphere susceptible to study by radio waves, whereas the aurora makes it visible to the naked eye.

Aurora

The aurora (see separate entry) comprises light emissions from atoms and molecules excited by collisions mainly with electrons that have energies of a few kilo-electron-volts. Sometimes protons with similar energies are the cause of the excitation. The electrons and protons come from the outer reaches of the Earth's atmosphere. They are accelerated by electric fields that arise as the plasma wind from the Sun (the solar wind) buffets the Earth's magnetosphere—the zone around the Earth where the ionized atmosphere is contained by the magnetic field. The accelerated electrons and ions are steered toward the Arctic (or Antarctic) by the Earth's magnetic field—they travel along the magnetic field lines and it is here that magnetic field lines from the outer boundaries of the magnetosphere descend into the atmosphere.

In the outer reaches of the atmosphere, there are very few atoms and molecules so that the chance of a collision with an accelerated electron or proton is small. As the air density increases toward lower altitude, collisions become more and more frequent. By about 100 km altitude, the accelerated electrons and protons have generally lost their energy through collisions with the air. The different colors in the aurora are due to excitation of different gases. The most common color, green, comes from atomic oxygen. Red at high altitudes can be produced by hydrogen. Purple-red at lower heights, often forming a lower border to a green auroral curtain, comes from molecular nitrogen.

One topic of lively debate in the Arctic is whether it is possible to hear the aurora. Many residents in the Arctic report that they have heard crackling or "whooshing" sounds from the aurora. Most usually, they report that this happened in very cold weather (which means below −20°C), with the ground covered in snow and the sky crystal clear. Very few people report having heard the aurora more than once, even though they may have lived in the Arctic all their lives. The extreme thinness of the air at the height of the aurora (about 100 km) makes it extremely difficult to generate a sound wave that could travel down and be heard in the very dense atmosphere at the ground. Also, those who have heard the aurora usually report an immediate connection between movement in the aurora and hearing a sound. This would not allow any time for a sound wave to travel the long distance, usually several hundred kilometers, from the aurora to the observer. (This can be compared with the easily detectable delay of several seconds between seeing a lightning flash a few kilometers away and hearing the peal of thunder.) So far, no scientific measurements of sound from an aurora have been made and the reason for this phenomenon remains a mystery.

Substorms

Intense aurora are often observed as part of a well-organized sequence of events—an auroral substorm. A substorm (*see* **Substorms**) usually begins with a weak auroral arc extending east-west across the sky. Over a period of an hour or two, the arc drifts equatorward and may brighten slightly and fade again one or more times. Finally, a surge of bright aurora will appear, moving in from the west, and the whole sky will be filled with intense aurora for many minutes. Such substorms are thought to be a result of a steady buildup of energy in the magnetosphere, fed in by favorable conditions in the solar wind. The reasons as to why the energy is suddenly released are not well understood, although sometimes the release appears to be triggered by changes in the solar wind.

During an auroral substorm, the air in the upper atmosphere is highly ionized and highly electrically conductive. Often, there are also strong electric fields associated with the substorm. This leads to powerful electric currents flowing over hundreds of kilometers at heights about 120 km above the Earth's surface. The electric currents generate a magnetic field that can easily be detected at the Earth's surface. The magnetic field generated by auroral currents can be as large as a few percent of the Earth's normal magnetic field. Rapid changes in the magnetic field due to rapid changes in the aurora induce secondary currents in any electrical conductor on the Earth's surface. This can be a serious problem for electricity supply networks, causing current surges and overloading. Power supply companies in the Arctic must take steps to avoid such problems, particularly on those occasions when extreme conditions in the solar wind lead to a major magnetic storm, a situation with exceptionally large substorms.

Methods of Study

The earliest possibilities to study the upper atmosphere were provided by the visual, electrical, and magnetic effects associated with the aurora. Cameras and spectrometers recorded the aurora and determined which atoms and molecules were responsible for emitting the auroral light. Magnetometers recorded the effects of the strong electric currents flowing in auroral arcs. Riometers (relative ionosphere opacity meters) recorded the absorption of cosmic radio-noise due to strong increases in ionization in the upper atmosphere associated with auroral displays. Ionosondes (ionospheric sounders using transmitted radio wave pulses) also measured the ionization changes. All of these techniques have been in use for more than 50 years, some for more than 100 years. Geophysical observatories were established at many places in the Arctic to study the aurora, the main ones being in Fairbanks (Alaska), Tromsø (Norway), Kiruna (Sweden), Sodankylä (Finland), and Apatity (Russia). These observatories are still in use today and form the basis of well-established international monitoring and research networks.

Possibilities to study the atmosphere between about 10 and 100 km heights were developed somewhat later. For about 40 years, sounding rockets, scientific balloons, and research aircraft have been available to make measurements directly in the upper atmosphere. At the present time, more than 1000 standard instruments measuring temperature, pressure, humidity, and wind are released each day into the upper atmosphere from sites around the globe using weather balloons. The more sophisticated aircraft, research balloons, and sounding-rocket platforms can carry specialized instruments to measure, for example, the composition of the air, the size and shape of cloud droplets and crystals, electrical properties, and the incoming radiation reaching the atmosphere. Such measurements can be made only infrequently. The major bases in the Arctic for civilian sounding-rocket and balloon launches are at Poker Flat (Alaska), Andøya (Norway), and Esrange (Sweden).

In the last 20–30 years, remote-sensing instruments placed on the ground or on satellites have also been developed to study the upper atmosphere (*see* **Satellite Remote Sensing**). Lidar (laser-radar) systems measuring mainly upper-atmosphere clouds, temperature profiles, and ozone profiles are permanently installed at many places (in Sweden, Norway, Svalbard, Greenland, Canada, and Alaska). In many cases, these have been complemented by "MST" (mesosphere-stratosphere-troposphere), "MF" (medium frequency), and "meteor" radar systems, which provide further information on layering in the atmosphere and on winds. Much more powerful "incoherent-scatter" radars have been installed in Norway, Svalbard, and Greenland (earlier also in Alaska) to study the extremely thin ionized gas in the uppermost parts of the atmosphere, above about 80 km altitude. To measure atmospheric composition and temperature, spectrometers are used both from the ground and from satellites. These examine in detail the spectrum of electromagnetic radiation emitted or absorbed by the atmosphere. The most important recent satellite mission in this respect has been UARS (Upper Atmosphere Research Satellite).

In the last 20 years, satellites have also been launched to make direct measurements at the outer boundaries of the magnetosphere in order to improve understanding of the auroral acceleration processes. The most recent such satellite mission is CLUSTER, which comprises four identical satellites each measuring electric fields, magnetic fields, plasma waves, and the energy spectra of charged particles.

SHEILA KIRKWOOD

See also **Aurora; Space Weather; Substorms**

Further Reading

Andrews, David G., *An Introduction to Atmospheric Physics*, Cambridge: Cambridge University Press, 2000

Bone, Neil, *The Aurora, Sun-Earth Interactions*, Chichester, England: John Wiley and Sons, 1994

Brekke, Asgeir & Alv Egeland, *The Northern Light: From Mythology to Space Research*, Berlin, Heidelberg, New York, Tokyo: Springer-Verlag, 1983

Gadsden, Michael & Wilfried Schröder, *Noctilucent Clouds*, Berlin, Heidelberg, New York, Tokyo: Springer-Verlag, 1989

Hargreaves, John K., *The Solar Terrestrial Environment*, Cambridge and New York: Cambridge University Press, 1995

Hobbs, Peter V., *Introduction to Atmospheric Chemistry*, Cambridge and New York: Cambridge University Press, 2000

IPCC (Intergovernmental Panel on Climate Change, WMO-UNEP), Section 6.11, "Solar Forcing of Climate." *In Climate Change 2001: The Scientific Basis, Contribution of Working Group I to the Third Assessment Report of the Intergovernmental Panel on Climate Change*, edited by J.T. Houghton, Y. Ding, D.J. Griggs, M. Noguer, P.J. van der Linden & D. Xiaosu, Cambridge and New York: Cambridge University Press, 2001, pp. 380–385

URAL MOUNTAINS

The Urals (in Russian *Ural'skii khrebet*, and in the Tatar language meaning "belt") are a mountain range in west-central Russia, dividing the plains of Eastern Europe from the West Siberian lowlands of marshy basins, and mark the major part of the traditional boundary between Europe and Asia. The mountains extend north-south for more than 2000 km (1240 miles) from the Arctic Ocean to its southern end near where the Ural River bends from north-south to east-west in the steppes of Kazakhstan. In the Russian Arctic and Subarctic, the Urals straddle the border between the Yamal-Nenets Autonomous Okrug and the Komi Republic, and between Khanty-Mansi Autonomous Okrug and the Komi Republic. The mountain range is relatively narrow, on average 40–70 km (24–43 mi) and up to 150 km (93 mi) in some places. The mountain system comprises several parallel ridges and valleys, with an average height of 400–500 m (1300–1600 ft).

The mountains constitute the western portion of the Ural orogenic belt, a wider zone of deformation now partially buried beneath the later deposits of western Siberia, which stretches north from the Aral Sea in Kazakhstan and has had a long geological history. Today, the mountains are generally worn down and low in relief, with several low passes providing major transportation routes eastward from Europe into Siberia. Thick Paleozoic strata laid down in the ocean in the Carboniferous-Permian (about 250 million years ago) were uplifted, folded, and faulted, particularly in the eastern part, during the collision of the east European craton with Siberia and Kazakhstan in the middle to late Paleozoic. Tectonic movements were accompanied by periods of magmatic activity and interchanged with subsidence, erosion, and local sea transgressions. A new period of uplift, folding, and thrusting began in the Late Paleocene. The northern Urals were glaciated during the Quaternary, with ice sheets reaching 58° N in the western slopes and 61° N at the eastern slopes, and glaciated forms are obvious in the relief of the northern Urals.

According to differences in trends, height, and geological structures, the mountain system of the Urals is divided approximately into five major sections from north to south. The northernmost Polar Urals, extending in a 390 km arc from the Arctic Ocean in the northeast to the Yamal-Nenets Autonomous Okrug toward the southeast, are typically alpine. The mountains form a ridge 20 km wide, its highest point being Mt

Paiy-Er (1500 m). The next section southward is the highest segment of the range, the Nether-Polar Urals (mainly in the Komi Republic), comprising three mountain chains 80–100 km wide, of which the eastern chain marks the watershed between the East European and West Siberian rivers and is adorned by the highest Urals mountains—Mt Narodnaya (1894 m), Mt Karpinskii (1815 m), and Mans'i-N'er (1764 m). Both the Polar and Nether-Polar Urals have present-day glaciers. The Northern Urals, 50–60 km wide, are a longitudinal bunch of chains with their highest peaks such as Telpos-Iz (1617 m) and Denezhkin Kamen' (1498 m) at the northern and southern ends, respectively. Elsewhere, the Northern Urals are mostly between 900 and 1500 m, with flattened summits, the remnants of ancient peneplains uplifted by recent tectonic movements. The lower Central Urals rarely exceed 490 m. The Southern Urals continue southwestward, forming several parallel ridges. The eastern ridge is low (670–850 m) and the western ridge higher (generally less than 1220 m, the highest point being Yaman-Tau, 1639 m).

Dense taiga in the southern slopes, chiefly fir, pine, and larch, give way in a diffuse transition zone to isolated larch and eventually tundra further north. The western slopes receive more precipitation. Spruce on the western slopes in the south has been clearcut, which led to the creation of a UNESCO World Heritage Site to conserve the untouched Komi Forests in the northern Urals.

The Urals are one of the richest mineral-bearing areas in the world. More than 1000 types of minerals are known to occur, many of which were first discovered there, such as uralite, ilmenite, and the element ruthenium. The deposits include almost every commercially useful mineral, with many occurring in very large deposits, including iron, copper, chromium, and bauxite. Iron-ore deposits in the Urals include magnetite, hematite, limonite, and natural ferroalloys with titanium, chromium, and vanadium. Besides copper and bauxite, other nonferrous ores, including lead, zinc, beryllium, and precious metals (gold, silver and, above all, platinum), are widespread in the Urals. Many minerals used in the chemical industry, such as potassium, magnesium, and arsenic, are mined here. On the southwestern flank of the Urals lies the Volga-Ural oil field. Bituminous coal and lignite deposits are extensive but of poor quality. The Urals are famous for precious and semiprecious stones like amethyst, morion (a rare black quartz), topaz, jasper, malachite, and marble.

The largest rivers in the Urals flow west: the Kama (length in the Urals 1073 km) and Belaya (1410 km) rivers are tributaries of the Volga, and at the southernmost part of the Urals the Ural River (1340 km) rises within the mountains and drains into the Caspian Sea. Lakes are commonly small and rather shallow (19 m maximum). There are artificial reservoirs such as Kamskoye (1810 sq km) and Votkinskoye (1120 sq km).

The Urals were known from ancient times and were first mentioned in works by Herodot and Ptolemeus, in the 5th and 2nd centuries BC, respectively. The first maps of districts in the Urals were made under the leadership of Vasily Tatishchev, a historian and geographer who was a government official and was ordered to develop Urals factories and mines in the 1720s. Pyotr Rychkov gave the first geographic descriptions of the Southern Urals in 1755 and was the first to name the whole mountain system as "the Urals." From 1768 to 1774, the naturalist and scientist Peter Pallas (since 1767, he moved from Germany to Russia to be a member of the Academy of Science) traveled throughout southern Russia, including the Urals. In 1847, the Russian Geographic Society began its activity in the Urals and the expedition leader E. Hoffman was the first to describe the whole system in general. The first geological map of the Urals was made in 1881 by Aleksandr Karpinskii.

The most ancient records of human population in the Urals are Paleolithic cave paintings (300,000 years old) in Permskaya Oblast'. From 2000 BC the Urals became a center of metallurgy in north Asia. Bronze artifacts from the Urals have been found across Eurasia from Lake Baikal to the Mediterranean. At that time, tribes of Indo-Europeans inhabited the Urals. From the 1st century AC, nomads invaded from the East. In the 9th and 10th centuries, Turkish peoples came from the Aral steppes and assimilated the Finno-Ugric tribes as well as the Sarmats, who spoke Iranian, thus forming the ancestors of the Bashkir people. Peoples of the Ugric group (Khanty and Mansi) represent remnants of the aboriginal population from the first millennium BC and still inhabit the eastern slopes of the Northern and Middle Urals. The Nenets in the Polar Urals are representatives of an ancient Samodian group, as are the Finno-Permic group—Komi, Udmurt, Komi-Permyaki, now inhabiting the western slopes of the mountains (*see* **Northern Uralic Languages**). Russians appeared in the Urals from the 11th century. The first were tribute collectors from Great Novgorod. They founded some Ural settlements, which later became cities (Solikamsk, Vyatka, Cherdyn', and Kotel'nich). Merchants of the Stroganoff family colonized the vast territories along Kama, Perm', and Chusovaya rivers in the 15th and 16th centuries. Later, under Peter the Great and Catherine the Great, the same other areas were colonized by businessmen from the Demidov clan, who established several metallurgy plants at the Middle and Southern Urals.

Today, the population of the Urals comprises about 73% Russians, 8.5% Tatar, 5.3% Bashkir, 3%

Ukranians, and 3% Udmurt. In addition, there are small numbers of Mordva, Chuvash, Komi-Permyak, Belorussians, Mari, Kazakhs, and Jews. The largest cities are Ekaterinburg (in Soviet time, Sverdlovsk), which is a metallurgy center (population 1,266,300); Chelyabinsk, also metallurgy, machinery, and tubes (1,083,000); Perm' (1,009,700); Ufa (1,091,200), chemistry, machinery; Orenburg (523,600); Nizhniy Tagil (390,900); Magnitogorsk (357,000); and Izhevsk (376,000) (figures for January 2000, http://www.mojgorod.ru/cities/pop2000_3.html).

The Urals provide one-quarter of the total Russian industrial production, and in particular a high proportion of the weapon industry, employ one-fifth of the total labor force, and provide 10% of the Russian wheat harvest. The Ural industry declined drastically in the 1990s because of the collapse of military industries. Unemployment was as high as 8%, more than 55% of the population had an income below the poverty line, and the birth rate declined from 18.5 in 1987 to 7.9 in 1993. Now, industry in the Urals is rapidly recovering. Rich natural resources, an educated population, skilled professionals, and developed infrastructure promise a prosperous future for the Urals.

LEONID M. BASKIN

Further Reading

Aleksashenko, N., N. Minenko, V. Zapariy, A. Irbe & A. Safronov, *Istoriya Urala s drevneishikh vremen do kontsa 19 veka* [The Urals History from Ancient Time to the End of the 19th Century], Ekaterinburg: Izdatel'stvo "CB-96." 1998

Dobrokhotov, F., *Ural severnyi, srednii, yuzhnyi. Spravochnaya kniga* [The Northern, Middle and Southern Urals. Handbook], Petrograd: Izdatel'stvo Suvorina, 1917

Golikova, S., N. Minenko & I. Poberezhnikov, *Gornozavodskie tsentry I agrarnaya sreda v Rossii* [Mining Centers of Russia and Agriculture Environment in Russia], Moscow: Nauka, 2000

Harris, James R., *The Great Urals: Regionalism and the Evolution of the Soviet System,* Ithaca: Cornell University Press, 1999

Kirillov, A., A. Mamleev & B. Kirillov, *Ural ekonomikcheskii. Reformy. Resul'tatu. Perspectivy* [Economic of the Urals. Reforms. Results. Perspectives], Ekaterinburg: Izdatel'stvo Ural'skii Rabochiy, 1999

Komar, I. (editor), *Rossiyskaya Federatsiya. Ural* [Russian Federation. The Urals], Moscow: Mysl', 1969

Kuftyreva, N., *Ural. Fisiko-geograficheskaya characteristika* [The Urals. Physics-Geographical Characteristics], Trudy kafedry geografii Moskovskogo oblastnogo pedagogicheskogo instituta imeni N.K. Krupskoy, Volume 44, no. 8, 1961, pp. 5–41

URBAN CLIMATES

A city's climate is quite different from that of the surrounding countryside, and these differences are caused by a number of factors. First, energy consumption and fuel combustion in factories, houses, and cars produce waste heat, moisture, gases, and particles, including carbon monoxide, soot, and other products, which modify the temperature, precipitation, fog frequency, and other climatic parameters in and around a city. Second, the concrete, brick, and asphalt masses of the city have different reflectivities (albedos) to sunlight than surrounding fields and forests, and different heat storage capacities. Third, the buildings themselves present a different large-scale surface "roughness" to the wind, so that the energy balance of the city is likely to be different from that of the surroundings areas. Since the energy balance (the partitioning of the available solar energy into heat available to warm the ground, warm the air, cause evaporation, and so on) determines the climate of any particular region, climatic differences between the city and its surroundings can be expected.

Table 1 (after Landsberg) shows the differences in climatic parameters between urban and rural environments.

Arctic Versus Non-Arctic Cities

Although much of the Arctic is sparsely populated, nearly two million people, including a relatively large indigenous population, live north of the Arctic Circle. In Russia, large urban centers include Vorkuta and Noril'sk with populations exceeding 100,000 and

TABLE 1. Average changes in climatic parameters caused by urbanization

Element	Comparison with rural environment	
Contaminants	Condensation nuclei and particulates	10 times more
	Gaseous admixtures	5–25 times more
Cloudiness	Cover	5–10% more
	Fog, winter	100% more
	Fog, summer	30% more
Precipitation	Totals	5–10% more
	Days with less than 5 mm	10% more
	Snowfall	5% less
Radiation	Global	15–20% less
	Ultraviolet, winter	30% less
	Ultraviolet, summer	5% less
	Sunshine duration	5–15% less
Temperature	Mean annual	0.5–1.0°C higher
	Winter minima	1–2°C higher
Wind speed	Annual mean	20–30% less
	Extreme gusts	10–20% less
	Calms	5–20% more
Relative humidity	Winter	2% less
	Summer	8% less

After handsberg (1981).

Murmansk with about 500,000 people. While Arctic towns in Scandinavia and North America are smaller, there are about 30 towns in the Arctic with more than 10,000 inhabitants. More people live in cities than ever before and these urban centers create their own unique climates.

The climate and pollution chemistry of Arctic cities is controlled by entirely different factors than those of mid- or low-latitude cities, as shown in Table 2. This table compares Fairbanks (Alaska), a small city in the Subarctic at latitude 65° N, with Los Angeles at latitude 34° N. The two cities probably represent the extreme ends of the climate and pollution settings of urban regions.

The climate and associated pollution problems of Arctic cities are thus quite different from those of mid-latitude cities; the peculiarities of Arctic city climates are further discussed in the subsequent sections.

Heat Islands

Urban climates in the Arctic differ most from the climates of their surroundings in winter. This is due to the unusually steep temperature inversions near the ground and the generally low wind speeds that characterize many populated Arctic regions in winter. Both factors tend to prevent pollutants, moisture, and heat from escaping the urban environs. High pollution levels and the so-called "urban heat islands" result, the latter produced by trapping of the escaped heat from

TABLE 2. Spectrum of climate and pollution settings

	Fairbanks in winter	Los Angeles in summer
	Low-temperature ice fog/ pollution	Smog
Temperature	−30°C to −60°C	30–40°C
Temperature inversion	30°C/100 m (surface)	10°C/100 m (above ground)
Radiation	None during winter, ~980 W m^{-2} in summer	High (>1000 W m^{-2})
Saturation vapor pressure	Low (0.5 mb at −50°C)	High (42.43 mb at 30°C)
Chemistry	Reducing atmosphere	Oxidizing atmosphere
	No photochemical reaction	Maximum photochemical reaction
	"Wet" air chemistry	"Dry" air chemistry
	(Low absolute water content but condensed form present)	(High absolute water content but condensed form absent)

buildings, thus raising air temperatures up to several degrees above those of the surrounding terrain. The primary cause of the heat island is anthropogenic waste heat. The per capita energy use of Fairbanks, expressed as energy density flux (W m^{-2}) for the urban area, is very high and is comparable to that of Los Angeles and exceeds that of Hong Kong by a factor of six.

Typical heat island temperatures in Fairbanks (Alaska) were measured to be up to 10°C higher than the surroundings, and occasionally as high as 14°C in winter. During summer, the heat island disappears in the daytime, except for a short period in late spring when the snow has melted in the city but not in the surroundings. During nighttime in summer, the heat island reaches intensities almost as great as in winter. These heat island effects are a problem in analyzing long-term climate trends, since they may reflect growth in population and energy use rather than true climate trends, and must be taken into account.

Ice Fog

Ice fog is another distinctive feature of urban climate in the Arctic; it is a form of low-temperature pollution. It is produced when water vapor condenses into droplets, which then supercool and eventually freeze at temperatures well below the normal freezing point of water. The source of the water vapor is primarily combustion of fuels in cars, heating plants and industrial facilities of northern urban centers, and ice fog forms when temperatures are −30°C or lower. Steep temperature inversions initiate ice fog events; they are produced under clear sky conditions with strong radiational cooling of the surface and can reach values of 10–30°C/100 m. Ice fog develops and can eventually envelop entire northern cities; its vertical thickness and its density increase as temperatures continue to fall.

Ice fog "crystals" generally have spherical or slightly irregular forms with sizes peaking at 8 μm when the source is car exhaust, 16 μm from open water, and 26 μm from heating plants. The spherical or irregular shape gives a dull, graph appearance to the ice fog, quite unlike regular ice crystals. Ice fog is important in Arctic cities since it reduces visibility and often hampers both aircraft and automobile operations. Below −40°C, street-level visibility can drop to less than 30 m.

Air Pollution

Reduction in visibility is not the only consequence of ice fog to urban climate. When ice fog forms, the temperature inversion initially starting at the surface is lifted to the top of the fog layer. This changes the highly stable boundary layer over cities affected by ice fog to a neutrally buoyant one and allows free mixing of pollutants throughout the fog layer. Pollutants such as carbon monoxide (CO) emitted by cars at the ground diffuse throughout the fog layer, instead of being trapped near the ground. CO levels thus decrease near the ground during ice fog, but sulfur dioxide (SO_2), which is produced by burning coal and is mostly emitted from tall smokestacks, is mixed down to the surface, increasing the concentration near the ground.

Air pollution, as another feature of urban climate, is a well-known phenomenon in cities at lower latitudes and is not a new problem. Even in antiquity, people noted that urban air was different from rural air, and they were concerned about it. A reference to "the pestilential vapor and soot" of Rome already appears in the odes of Quintus Horatius Flaccus about 24 BC. In the Middle Ages, London became the prototype of urban pollution. The situation prompted several monarchs to prohibit burning coal in the 13th, 14th, and 16th centuries. The problem persisted until a particularly severe episode in 1952 caused 4000 excess deaths and led to legislation that converted London and other English cities into "smokeless" zones.

Among the principal urban atmospheric pollution constituents are CO, SO_2, oxides of nitrogen (NO, NO_x), and a number of organic compounds, as well as aerosols including a variety of elements such as lead (from gasoline—although this is probably no longer a big problem), carbon (soot), vanadium, aluminum, and other metals produced from the combustion of fuels in cars, power plants, and houses. The per capita fuel consumption in Arctic urban centers is much higher than at lower latitudes; car engines started at low temperatures are inefficient and produce excess quantities of carbon monoxide. In Fairbanks (Alaska) and other northern cities, CO levels may exceed permissible standards several times each winter.

GUNTER WELLER

See also **Climate; Microclimates**

Further Reading

Benson, C., Ice Fog: Low Temperature Air Pollution Defined with Fairbanks, Alaska as Type Locality." *Geophysical Institute Report UAG R-173*, University of Alaska, 1965

Landsberg, H.E., *The Urban Climate*, New York: Academic Press, 1981

Stonehouse, B. (editor), *Arctic Air Pollution*, Cambridge and New York: Cambridge University Press, 1986

Weller, G., *"Ice Fog Studies in Alaska."* *Geophysical Institute Report UAG R-207*, University of Alaska, 1969

URBANIZATION

For the first time in history, half the world's population now lives in cities. All over the world, globalization and urbanization are two forces that are closely linked. Urbanization is an old force in the shaping of history. A rapid increase in the population in Paris was an important factor that set the stage for the French Revolution. In the modern world, the size of cities continues to grow. In 1800, the world's 100 largest cities had an average of 200,000 inhabitants; in 1950, the average had reached 2.1 million and today it is more than 5 million.

There are many reasons why urbanization is such a penetrating and irresistible force in the world. One very important reason is that it is an engine for economic growth. In most places in the world, the growth sector is usually concentrated in cities. If certain minimum institutional conditions are favorable, cities create strong agglomerate effects and reduce "transaction costs." This is because dynamic cities create favorable networks of handy markets, labor, support, and cultural stimulation, and reinforce certain advantages of proximity. Although communication and information technologies, in principle, have broken the quasi-monopoly of cities on fast, direct communication, it has also revealed the importance of geographical proximity, face-to-face encounters, direct access, and just-at-hand environments. Especially, large and middle-sized cities can offer their citizens a variety of cultural and social diversification, with which the small cities and the villages cannot compete.

Urban development varies greater from place to place in the Arctic, from large urban complexes in Russia and southern Alaska, through middle-sized concentration in Norway and Iceland, to tiny scattered small concentrations in northern Canada and Greenland. Some of the largest cities in the North are Murmansk, Archangel'sk, Petrozavodsk, Vorkuta, Uhta, Syktyvkar, Nizhnevartovsk, Surgut, Neftejugansk, Nojabrsk, Novyi Urengoi, Noril'sk, Yakutsk, Nerjungri, Magadan, and Petropavlovsk-Kamchatsky in Russia, Anchorage in Alaska, Tromsø in Norway, Oulu in Finland, and Reykjavík in Iceland.

The numbers and sizes of cities in the Arctic are strongly correlated with the demographic pattern. Gunnar Knapp estimated a total population of 10.5 million inhabitants of the Arctic in 1990, of which no less than 8.9 million (85%) are inhabitants of the Russian Arctic. Knapp also showed that less than 10% of the population of the North are indigenous people and the Inuit do not amount to more than about 1% of the total population of the Arctic. However, one must also take into account that since the collapse of the Soviet Union, there has been a major out-migration from the Russian North. Calculations on the basis of the World Gazetteer indicate that the population of the Russian North in the turbulent years of the 1990s had probably declined to around 8 million.

The main population concentration in the Arctic lies in the Barents region (i.e., the Scandinavian North and Northwestern Russia). Hence, within an area of less than 10% of the total landmasses of the Arctic, almost 55% of its population resides. Not surprisingly, it is here that the two largest Arctic cities, Murmansk and Arkhangel'sk, are located. Murmansk has 369,000 inhabitants and Arkhangel'sk has 359,000. The Barents region also includes Petrozavodsk, the capital of the Karelian region, which has 280,000 inhabitants. Among the largest cities of the Arctic are Anchorage in Alaska with 260,000 inhabitants and Surgut with 275,000, Nizhnevartorsk with 232,000, and Syktyvkar with 229,000. Yakutsk, the capital of the Saha Republic, has 194,000 inhabitants. But Noril'sk, Vorkuta, Magadan, Petropavlovsk-Kamchatsky, and Reykjavík are also among the major cities of the North. Although many of the Russian cities in the North are large, they are still too small to be placed within the group of the 20 largest cities in Russia. The Asian part of Russia covers 45.9% of the Arctic landmasses, and some parts of its region also have a fairly high population density compared with other regions of the Arctic.

Outside these areas of concentration, the population of the Arctic is extremely small and scattered. This is particularly true with regard to the Canadian North and Greenland. The two areas cover 35.6% of the total landmasses of the Arctic, but contain only 1.3% of its inhabitants. Even remote areas in the Russian Asian North have a much higher population density than the Canadian North. The only region in all of the Russian Asian North that reaches Canadian population density standards is the Evenki Autonomous Okrug, whose capital Tura has only 5000 inhabitants. Obviously, the cities in the Canadian North and in Greenland are very small. Yellowknife has 18,000 inhabitants, Iqaluit around 5000, and Nuuk around 14,000. However, Chukotka in Russia also has a very small population due to a drastic decline in the number of nonnatives in the region after the collapse of the Soviet Union. Hence, the capital of Chukotka, Anadyr, is small, with only 11,000 inhabitants, and the total population is only 68,000.

From an urbanization and demographic point of view, the demographic structure of the Arctic region varies greatly. The highest population concentration is found in the Barents region. The lowest urbanization degree is found in the Canadian Arctic and Greenland. Indeed, twice as many people live in Iceland than in the Canadian North and Greenland combined. Alaska and the Asian part of Russia lie in between these two areas with regard to level of urbanization and population density.

The population of the Arctic is steadily growing. According to Gunnar Knapp, the total population in the Arctic has almost doubled since 1960 and has increased five times since 1930. The main impact is the growth in the number of inhabitants in both the European and Asian part of Russia. The highest growth rate is found in Asian Russia: especially the Yamalo-Nenets and the Khanty-Mansi regions have high growth rates, and the Yakutsk region's rate is on the level of Canada. Alaska had high growth rates, its population having increased ten times since 1920, but it is lower than the growth rate in Asian Russia. However, Alaska's growth rate is higher than the combined Russian rate.

In summary, with respect to volume and growth, the two most expanding areas are the Asian part of Russia and Alaska. Sometimes in the future, we might expect that the largest cities in the Arctic will be found in the Asian part of the Russian North. It is possible that Murmansk and Arkhangel'sk might drastically expand if the regions prosper from a major gas and oil bonanza. The city of Anchorage in Alaska characterized the expansion and speed of urbanization, typical of many cities in the Arctic. In 1929, the city of Anchorage had a population of 2736 and today it is a city with 260,000 inhabitants. In 1929, the population of the city represented 4.6% of the population of Alaska but in 1999 the ratio had grown to 41.7%.

Despite various historical differences, the same trend toward a steadily increasing urbanization occurs all over the Arctic. Even in the least demographically concentrated part of the Arctic, the forces of urbanization are very clear. Iqaluit in Nunavut is growing rapidly, particularly after it became the seat of the new provincial government, and Nuuk in Greenland is growing steadily despite a huge shortage of houses. Its municipal council has initiated a major expansion of the city, which will create a new suburb located on the Marlene mountain; this step will facilitate a substantial increase in the city's population. Right now, one out of four Greenlanders live in Nuuk; within a decade or two, we might expect one out of three.

The case of Nuuk in Greenland illustrates how cities tend to absorb and aggregate social capacities and why they are considered engines of industrial development. In 1999, the population of Nuuk was 24.19% of Greenland's total population; however, the importance of Nuuk within the Greenlandic national power structure is not reflected by the sheer demographic numbers. Nuuk's share of the total income and tax income in Greenland is a better indicator. These shares were 33% and 36%, respectively. Also, Nuuk had the highest average income of all cities in Greenland. Nuuk was also the city with the highest population growth in the years from 1970 to 1999. The city had the highest ratio of people in the productive age group between 15 and 65. Nuuk also had the highest proportion of Danes, which is correlated with the fact that the central administrations and the large enterprises are located in the city. Half of Greenland's students are living in Nuuk, where the university, Ilisimatusarfik, is located. Some other revealing figures from 1996 provide an indication about the distribution of the land-based industry in Greenland. The numbers indicate that almost six out of ten of the land-based industries were located in Nuuk and about seven out of ten consultant firms. The same pattern was clear when one looks at the distribution of PCs per household. In the mid-region, where Nuuk is located, 45% of the households had access to a PC, although only 14% had access in the North and Eastern areas. The number of people in Nuuk with a higher education was three times higher than in the Disko area and almost 12 times higher than in the Northern and Eastern part of Greenland. All these indicators show very clearly that Nuuk acts as an engine for industrial development in Greenland, and that the city attracts social and industrial forces into its orbit out of proportion to its demographic base.

Russian urbanization varies from the general pattern of other places, where the incentive for urban growth most often was various market opportunities, which brought many immigrants to the North. In Russia, most of the urbanization of the North occurred during the 74 years of Soviet rule. The drive in promoting urbanization in Soviet Russia was based on bureaucratic power and political coercion. Large-scale immigration from European Russia into the Central Asia and the Siberian Far East was a mixture between compulsory displacement and socio-economic encouragement. As a result, more than half the population in the Yakutsk republic is today of European descent. Forced labor was also important for the urbanization process in Arctic Russia. Hence, Noril'sk and Vorkuta, two major cities in the Russian North, were originally established as Stalinist forced labor camps in the 1930s. Today, they are both mining cities and suffering from social problems related, in part, to the great turmoil that followed the collapse of the Soviet Union. The municipality of Vorkuta is broke, and hospitals, public transportation, and schools are barely functioning. Also, the city's heating plant is in permanent crisis. Rising unemployment and rapidly worsening living conditions forced thousands of people to leave this outpost in the North.

Generally, the years following the collapse of the Soviet Union have been a period of social and economic transformation of Russian cities in the North, because the cities depended on a system of industrial paternalism based on subsidies. Many cities experienced a dramatic decline and an out-immigration to central European Russia. Murmansk's population fell from 440,000 inhabitants in 1989 to 369,000 in 2001.

In the same period, Magadan's population, in the Russian Far East, fell from 152,000 to 118,000. At the same time, a new urban era in the Russian North is slowly taking shape as cities from Murmansk to Anadyr are linking up with the global economy and making various trade deals with other regions.

JENS KAALHAUGE NIELSEN

See also **Demography and Population; Industrial Development**

Further Reading

Demco, Grigory J., Grigory Points & Zhanna Zayonchkovskaya (editors), *Population Under Press. The Geodemography of Post-Soviet Russia,* Boulder, Colorado: Westview Press, 1999

Kaalhauge Nielsen, Jens, "The role of Nuuk's industry within the frame of Greenland's societal development—an analysis with special emphasis on the concepts of social capital and societal capacities." Paper presented at the MOST CCPP Workshop, Joensuu, Finland, November 15–19, 2000. Scheduled to be published in 2002. The paper is featured at MOST CCPP website: www.uit.no/MOSTCCPP/Huhmari/JOE_pap/

Knapp, Gunnar, "The Population of the Circumpolar North." In *The Arctic: Environment, People, Policy,* edited by Nuttall, Mark & Terry V Callaghan, Amsterdam: Harwood, 2000

Putnam, Robert D., *Making Democracy Work: Civic Traditions in Modern Italy,* Princeton, New Jersey: Princeton University Press, 1993

USHAKOV, GEORGIY

By the time of the Russian Revolution of 1917, very little of the Russian Arctic remained to be explored and mapped. It is noteworthy that the two major remaining lacunae, namely Ostrov Vrangelia (Wrangel Island) and Severnaya Zemlya, were filled by the efforts of one man, Georgiy Alekseevich Ushakov. In 1926, the Soviet government decided to establish a settlement on the previously uninhabited Ostrov Vrangelia, in the Arctic Ocean north of Chukotka. In 1921, the Canadian Arctic explorer Vilhjalmur Stefansson, in an attempt to force the Canadian government to claim sovereignty over Ostrov Vrangelia, had dispatched a trapping party of four men and one Alaskan Eskimo woman to the island. All four men died, but in 1923 their place was taken by a party of 12 Alaskan Eskimos led by a trapper and prospector, Charles Wells. In 1924, this party was forcibly removed by a Soviet party from the gunboat *Krasnyi Oktiabr'* led by B.V. Davydov.

Clearly, however, the best defense against a repetition of this kind of foreign encroachment would be to establish a permanent Soviet presence on the island. It was decided to relocate several Eskimo families from the eastern tip of Chukotka, where the hunting and trapping economy was badly depressed, to Ostrov

changes have resulted in more open water, that is, longer periods of ice-free conditions, greater precipitation in winter, and consequently diminished conditions for wintering of animals such as reindeer, fox, hare, and ptarmigan.

In the 17th and 18th centuries, Dutch whalers regularly explored Uummannaq and the surrounding region, but never created any permanent settlement. The Danish colonial authorities arrived in 1761 and brought with them new types of equipment such as nets for catching seals, which resulted in a marked increase in hunting activity. Fisheries were of limited importance prior to the 20th century, but the present expansion in fisheries for Greenland halibut has resulted in a marked increase in the economic performance. Most notably in the villages, increased incomes have generated marked changes in the social structure.

A tradition of small-scale coal mining for home consumption has been sustained in a number of localities in the municipality, and for a short period of time—until 1924—commercial coal mining existed. The largest mining activity in the municipality, however, has been the mining of marble at Maarmorilik and, more recently, the nearby mining of zinc, lead, and silver in the Black Angel mine, both situated in one of the fjords close to the town. Although the majority of miners came from outside Greenland, mining activity had a tremendous economic impact on the municipality, as the local miners used a portion of their income to invest in equipment for fisheries, thereby founding the present-day fishing industry.

Uummannaq boasts a marked potential for tourism with activities such as dog sledging, fisheries, hunting, whale watching, and other types of recreation available in abundance.

RASMUS OLE RASMUSSEN

See also **Coal Mining; Maarmorilik; Mining; Qilakitsoq Mummies**

Further Reading

Berthelsen, Christian, Inger H. Mortensen & Ebbe Mortensen (editors), *Kalaallit Nunaat Atlas, Greenland*, Nuuk: Atuakkiorfik, 1992

Nielsen, Niels, Peter Skautrup & Christian Vibe (editors), *J.P. Trap Danmark, bind XIV, Grønland*, Copenhagen: Gads Forlag, 1970

Rasmussen, Rasmus Ole, "Formal economy, renewable resources and structural changes in West Greenland." *Études/Inuit/Studies*, 24(1) (2000): 48–78

Statistics Greenland, *Greenland 2000–2001. Statistical Yearbook,* Nuuk: Statistics Greenland, 2001

http://www.ummannaq.gl

V

VAIGACH

Vaigach (Ostrov Vaygach) is a large island 105 km long by 44 km wide (area 3398 sq km) off northeast European Russia, between Kara Sea and Barents Sea. The island is less than 8 km (5 miles) from the Russian mainland, lying between the Yugorsky Peninsula and Novaya Zemlya. Explored by travelers in search of the North East Passage, it is named after the Russian captain who discovered it in the 16th century. Administratively it is part of the Nenets Autonomous Okrug.

The island is north of the Arctic Circle, has no trees, and is covered with tundra, mosses, and lichen. There are numerous shallow lakes, which become frozen to the bottom in winter. The climate is Arctic marine, with relatively mild winters (average temperature −17°C), cool summers (average temperature 5.9°C), and frequent rain and fogs. Two small villages, Vaygach and Varnet, are on the island. However, until the beginning of the 20th century, there were no permanent residents on the island, only visiting seafaring marine mammal hunters. The island was historically a sacred place for the Nenets, probably due to it being inaccessible and far from the mainland. It retains very high cultural and spiritual significance for the Nenets people due to the many sacred natural monuments and shrines that still exist. Excavations in Vaigach shrines in the 1980s showed that these sacred places are centuries old and already existed in the 10–11th centuries. The shrines and sanctuaries remained untouched until the mission to convert the Nenets to Christianity in the 18th and 19th centuries, when a number of cult places were destroyed and idols burnt. The Nenets people hid some of these from the missionaries and saved them.

During Soviet collectivization, several Nenets families with a herd of reindeer were brought to Vaigach for permanent residence, and a Polar Station and radio station were set up. From 1930 to 1935, lead-zinc ore was extracted, and the population in Varnet increased due to gulag prisoners being brought in to work in the mines. Mining terminated due to the flooding of mines by underground waters. Currently, industrial activity is restricted on Vaigach, although zinc, copper, and lead deposits are known. The resident Nenets population is today probably less than 100, carrying out reindeer breeding, fishing, and hunting.

Vaigach Island has a high floral diversity, and is an important waterfowl breeding site (e.g., for Bewick swan, white-fronted goose, lesser white-fronted goose, king eider, and others). The land mammal fauna includes Arctic fox, wolf, lemming, and wild reindeer. Marine mammals have been extensively hunted, but polar bear, Atlantic walrus, beluga, bearded and ringed seal, and narwhal are found.

For its cultural history and relatively high biodiversity, part of Vaigach Island was declared a state wildlife reserve in 1983, with protection for polar bears and eider ducks. There are plans by Nenets Autonomous Okrug to further expand the protection as a *zakaznik*, to conserve the protected species in the Russian Red Book (tundra swan, falcon, white-tailed sea eagle, and white-billed diver) and other bird and marine mammal species.

GILLIAN LINDSEY

See also **Nenets Autonomous Okrug**

Further Reading

Byarsky, P.V. & V.P. Stolyarov (editors), *Ostrov Vaigach: Kul'turnoe i prirodnoe nasledie Kniga 1: Pamiatniki istorii osvoeniia Arktiki*, Moscow: Rossiiskii NII kul'turnogo i prirodnogo naslediia, 2000

VAN DE VELDE, FRANZ

Among the numerous Catholic and Protestant missionaries who came to the Canadian Arctic from the end of the 19th century, some are particularly noteworthy, not for their conversion of the natives to Christianity, a mission on which there is no intention to make any assessment here, but rather for their contribution to a greater knowledge of the past and present cultures of the North. Oblate priests Guy-Marie Rousselière (well known for, among other things, his archaeology work), Lucien Schneider (recognized for his fundamental contribution to the study of the language of Nunavik), and Franz Van de Velde belong to this category of "ethnographer-missionaries," whose works strongly enriched knowledge of the Inuit.

Van de Velde settled in the Arctic in 1937 and left permanently only in 1986, exerting his ministry in three communities for very unequal durations: from 1938 to 1965 in Arviligjuarq (Pelly Bay), then two years in Iglulik (Igloolik), and Sanirajaq (Hall Beach). Of these periods, it is undeniably the first one, spent among the Arviligjuarmiut, which profoundly marked the man who the Inuit called "Ataata Vinivi." Van de Velde served as a witness as well as an actor of the fundamental changes experienced by the Inuit during these decades.

The Belgian missionary arrived on April 23, 1938 at Arviligjuarq, one of the most difficult communities to access. He was welcomed by Pierre Henry, a French Oblate who had arrived three years earlier to establish the mission. Both priests cohabitated until Henry's departure in 1945. Van de Velde harnessed himself to his task with enthusiasm and patience, demonstrating his sincere interest in the Inuit life and culture. Before his arrival at Arviligjuarq, Van de Velde spent a few months in Naujat (Repulse Bay) in order to learn the Inuit language, which he mastered quickly. His curiosity led him to ask numerous questions of the Inuit in order to interpret and understand their myths, songs, hunting practices, etc., which he then recorded. Van de Velde wrote prodigiously, producing an abundant ethnographic work on the Arviligjuarmiut that scholars continue to reference today.

Although a Catholic by conviction with precise objectives for being in the Arctic, Van de Velde generally refrained from making definitive assessments on the Inuit culture and its specific characters; he expressed nuanced views on what he saw and heard. For example, in his article of 1954 on infanticide, he described this practice as being "cruel," but refused to moralize on the subject (Van de Velde, 1954). He also seems to have circumvented what Inuit representations and shamanism were, highlighting what brought them closer to the Catholic faith. In a paper from 1956, he established a parallel between the *tornrark (tuurngaq)*, "the spirit which helps the hunter and protects him," and the guardian angel of the Catholic doctrine. He also compared the realms of the Inuit and Christian afterlife and defined a series of convergences between the shaman and the priest, the latter of whom attempted to mediate the former. Van de Velde concluded that a missionary ought not to abuse his authority and must try to live in a manner similar to the Inuk, hence acquiring a rich and extensive knowledge of the Inuit material life and social norms. He described, for example, in detail the rules governing the sharing of seals hunted at the *aglu,* analyzing the partnership habit among hunters whereby they called themselves by the name of the piece of meat that they would get after the portioning of the carcass. He also made a toponomy survey of the region of Arviligjuarq, collecting Inuit place-names and their English translations. Van de Velde published numerous papers detailing aspects of Inuit religion, mythology, ethnography, and cultural customs. One such example is his description of the *kauttalik,* the copper hammer seal: "the *kauttalik* is a kind of seal, extremely rare, it is said, in which Pelly Bay's Eskimo believe firmly. Does this involve a purely legendary animal, or on the contrary, is there any basis to this belief in reality, I know nothing of it, since I have never seen nor met with an Eskimo who saw a seal fulfilling all the conditions to be a true *kauttalik*" (Van de Velde, 1960).

In 1945, Van de Velde introduced the practice of carving on ivory and stone in order to create objects to sell. This activity became successful, particularly after the establishment of the Distant Early Warning (DEW) line station near the community. In 1970, the missionary published a biographical dictionary of the Inuit artists of Arviligjuarq, in which he paid significant and sensitive tribute.

Van de Velde worked for many years on the transcription of an Inuktitut document known as "the Awongaitsiark diary" written by the Inuk Awongaitsiark between 1958 and 1964 at the missionary's request. This unique document, written in Inuit syllabic orthography, describes not only the daily activities of the community in all their social and personal aspects but also significant conflicts and crises. Van de Velde transcribed the text into Roman writing and then translated it into French. A translation into Dutch was later proposed by the anthropologist C.H.W. Remie, under the missionary's supervision, in 1978.

Another critical piece of scholarship carried out by Van de Velde included an 800–page production of the genealogy of the population of Arviligjuarq, written between 1980 and 1984 while he was living in Sanirajaq. In the text, he detailed over one hundred families, analyzing the genealogy of each individual. In addition to data that could be described as marital status, it provides a large number of life accounts including factual events, many of which he subjectively interprets through character and behavior analyses.

Biography

Franz Adélaide Marie Joseph Van de Velde was born on November 28, 1909 in Landskouter, Belgium, to Arthur Van de Velde (1867–1956) and Gabrielle Lanens (1879–1969), who ran an agricultural enterprise (distillery, miller's trade, farming). He was the second of eight children, three of whom served religion. Van de Velde attended the Jesuit High School in Aalst and then studied at a seminary. He was ordained in 1935 and joined the Oblates of Mary Immaculate. He left Europe to go to Arctic Canada in 1937, where he stayed for almost 50 years in Arviligjuarq (Pelly Bay), Igloolik, Sanirajaq (Hall Beach), and Kugaaruk.

As a missionary, Van de Velde wrote extensively and brought back from his long stay in the Arctic numerous notebooks, recordings, and photographs. These objects are now housed in various archives, including the Katholiek Universiteit Leuven (Louvain, Belgium), Museum of Central Africa (Tervueren, Belgium), and Archives Deschâtelets (Ottawa, Canada). Among several honorary distinctions, he was decorated with the Order of Canada and the Royal Order of Belgium. In 1986, Van de Velde returned to Belgium for health reasons, and died there on February 22, 2002. He was 93 years old.

GUY BORDIN

See also **Mary-Rousseliere, Father Guy; Missionary Activity; Shamanism**

Further Reading

Brandson, L.E., *Carved from the Land: The Eskimo Museum Collection*, Diocese of Churchill, Hudson Bay, 1994

Remie, C.H.W., "Culture change and religious continuity among the *Arviligdjuarmiut* of Pelly Bay, N.W.T., 1935–1963." *Études/Inuit/Studies*, 7(2) (1983): 53–77

Van de Velde, Franz, "Infanticide among the Eskimo." *Eskimo*, 34 (1954): 6–8

———, "Religion et morale chez les Esquimaux de Pelly Bay." *Eskimo*, 39 (1956): 6–16

———, "Rules governing the sharing of seal after the 'aglus' hunt amongst the Arviligjuarmut." *Eskimo*, 41 (1956): 3–7

———, "Les règles de partage des phoques pris à la chasse aux aglus." *Anthropologica*, 3 (1956): 5–15

———, "Fat, symbol of Eskimo well being and prosperity." *Eskimo*, 48 (1958): 16–17

———, "Quaint customs and unusual stories of the Arviligjuarmiut: seal chase." *Eskimo*, 54 (1960): 7–8

———, *Canadian Eskimo Artists, a Bibliographical Dictionary: Pelly Bay*, Yellowknife, NWT: Government Press, 1970

———, *Canadian Eskimo Artifacts*, with Eric Mitchell, Ottawa: Canadian Arctic Producers, 1970

———, "Coutumes des Natjilingmiut: le premier phoque." *Eskimo*, N.S. 21 (1984): 18–19

———, *Statistiques objectives sur la population netjilique*, Volumes I–IV, Hall Beach, 1979, 1980, 1981, 1984

———, "Counting on one's fingers in Inuktitut." *Eskimo*, N.S. 29 (1985): 10–12

VANSTONE, JAMES

James VanStone, a 20th-century American scholar, conducted research in Alaskan archaeology, ethnohistory, and ethnography, in Chipewyan Athapaskan ethnography, and in Inuit and Athapaskan change with European contact. He pioneered work in ethnoarchaeology, ethnohistory, and the translation of Russian ethnohistorical sources on Alaska. His 51-year academic legacy includes over 140 articles, books, and monographs.

VanStone's outstanding contribution to Arctic scholarship was never limited to a single discipline or subdiscipline. His writing wove the story of postcontact Native life in Alaska based on his research expertise in archaeology, ethnography, ethnohistory, in museum and material culture studies, and through translating Russian historical sources. VanStone's careful, thorough attention to the minutiae of history, and his outstanding academic standards, lent his work a value that was only enhanced by his humility and humanity.

VanStone lived in Pt Hope, Alaska, for a year's study, which resulted in the 1962 publication of *Point Hope: An Eskimo Village in Transition*. This and *The Changing Culture of the Snowdrift Chipewyan* (1965) remain reference points in studies of northern communities and culture change. In *Athapaskan Adaptations*, VanStone set out a clear summary of the people he called "the most interesting hunters and gatherers on the North American continent" (1974: ix). Incorporating a critical evaluation of the state Athapaskan research at that time, he described the division of Athapaskans into two major groupings: those living in the Arctic drainage and those in the Pacific drainage. Few anthropologists had, according to VanStone, attempted to understand the region as a whole, and this division was exacerbated as Athapaskan land claims remained in conflict on opposite sides of the United States and Canada boundary, usually to the detriment of Athapaskan culture. VanStone noted that researchers tended to seek discrete external influences on Athapaskan culture (to the east for Arctic drainage peoples, to the west for those on the Pacific side) rather than recognize and examine the cultural unity suggested by the Athapaskan language and geographical distribution.

Between 1963 and 1979, VanStone integrated ethnohistory, archaeology, and ethnography in his analyses of Alaska Native culture change from the 1700s to the mid19th century. His fieldwork for this effort took him repeatedly to the Kuskokwim and Nushagak river drainages in Alaska, and his *Ingalik Contact-Ecology: An Ethnohistory of the Lower-Middle Yukon, 1790–1935* (1979) is one of the two major monographs resulting from his archaeological fieldwork and ethnohistorical studies on the Yukon River drainage.

VanStone's 1959 essay "Russian Exploration in Interior Alaska, an Extract from the Journal of Andrei Glazunov" was one of the first scholarly treatments of Russian language sources on Alaskan history. He continued to translate and interpret historical Russian works and methodologically apply that insight to Alaska ethnohistory throughout his career. He also contributed greatly to the development of productive research relationships among scholars on the Soviet and US sides of the Bering Strait. Well before the end of the Cold War, VanStone led American participation in a joint American-Soviet working group on behalf of the American Council of Learned Societies and the former USSR Academy of Sciences.

In the meantime, VanStone's editorship at the journal *Fieldiana* (published by the Field Museum of Natural History of Chicago, Illinois) meant that he documented several important Museum collections, including Chilcotin material from British Colombia, Blackfoot and Cree material from Alberta, and southern Chippewa material.

VanStone also served as associate editor of *Arctic Anthropology* from 1961 to 1989. Along with Wendell Oswalt, he founded *Anthropological Papers of the University of Alaska* in 1952, and edited these volumes up until 1957. VanStone's scholarship led him to develop an exceptional Arctic library that is today part of the Smithsonian Institution Arctic Studies Center in Anchorage, Alaska. VanStone was a major force in the organization of the Arctic and Subarctic volumes of the Smithsonian's *Handbook of North American Indians* (edited by William C. Sturtevant and published in 1978); he authored four chapters on peoples of southwest and central Alaska, as well as one on museum and archival sources on Subarctic Alaska. VanStone's Russian contacts and his work contributed largely to the Smithsonian's "Crossroads of Continents" exhibition and to the Field Museum's major exhibition on Northwest Coast and Arctic peoples.

Biography

James VanStone and his twin sister Suzanne were born in Chicago, Illinois, on October 3, 1925. He grew up in Cleveland, Ohio. As a teenager, VanStone contracted polio; his recovery required both a long convalescence at home, where his mother nursed him, and later back surgery. His adult life in the Alaskan bush and villages contradicted the advice of his doctors. VanStone drove dog teams and paddled in Inupiaq skin boats.

VanStone received a B.A. in art history from Oberlin College in Oberlin, Ohio (1948), and a master's degree in plains archaeology and a Ph.D. in Alaskan archaeology from the University of Pennsylvania in

Philadelphia (1950 and 1954, respectively). J. Louis Giddings, a colleague at the University of Pennsylvania, introduced VanStone to the North in 1950. In 1951, as part of his doctoral research, VanStone excavated at Kotzebue (Alaska) and published his findings in the *Anthropological Papers of the University of Alaska* (Vol. 3, No. 2., 1955).

After teaching anthropology at the University of Alaska, Fairbanks (1951–1958) and the University of Toronto (1959–1966), VanStone spent the remainder of his career as curator of North American archaeology and ethnology at the Field Museum of Natural History in Chicago (1966–1993; Emeritus 1993–2001)

ELLEN BIELAWSKI

See also **Athapaskan; Northern Athapaskan Languages**

Further Reading

Fitzhugh, William & Aron Crowell, (editors), *Crossroads of Continents: Cultures of Siberia and Alaska,* Washington, District of Columbia: Smithsonian Institution Press, 1988

Pratt, K.L., W.L. Sheppard & W.E. Simeone (editors), "*No boundaries: papers in honor of James W. VanStone.*" *Arctic Anthropology,* 35(2) (1998)

———, "Russian Exploration in Interior Alaska, an Extract from the Journal of Andrei Glazunov." *Pacific Northwest Quarterly,* 50(2) (1959): 37–47

———, *An Archaeological Collection from Somerset Island and Boothia Peninsula, N.W.T.,* Toronto: Royal Ontario Museum Occasional Paper 4, 1962

———, *Point Hope: An Eskimo Village in Transition,* Seattle: University of Washington Press, 1962

———, *The Changing Culture of the Snowdrift Chipewyan,* National Museum of Canada Bulletin 209, 1965

———, *Eskimos of the Nushagak River,* Seattle: University of Washington Press, 1967

———, "Ethnohistorical Research in Southwestern Alaska: A Methodological Perspective." In *Ethnohistory in Southwestern Alaska and the Southern Yukon: Method and Content,* edited by Margaret Lantis, University of Kentucky Press, 1970

———, *Athapaskan Adaptations: Hunters and Fishermen of the Subarctic Forests,* Aldine, Chicago, 1974

———, *Ingalik Contact-Ecology: An Ethnohistory of the Lower-Middle Yukon, 1790–1935,* Chicago, Illinois: Field Museum of Natural History, 1979

VanStone, James, "An annotated ethnohistorical bibliography of the Nushagak River Region, Alaska." *Fieldiana* (special issue) 54(2)

VASILEVICH, GLAFIRA MAKAR'EVNA

The Russian pedagogue, linguist, and anthropologist Glafira Makar'evna Vasilevich was a significant scholar of the Evenki (Tungus) language and culture. A student at the department of ethnography in the Institute of Geography in Petrograd in 1920–1924, Vasilevich was among the first group of students to graduate from this department, which was committed to the ethnography of the various peoples of Siberia. Vasilevich graduated in December 1924 and the following summer set off for her first expedition to the Tungus, organized by the State Committee of the North. In its attempt to integrate the indigenous peoples of Siberia into a socialist society, the Soviet government aimed at promoting literacy and creating an indigenous intelligentsia. Vasilevich and her colleagues contributed to the development of alphabets and textbooks for the various native languages.

After the first expeditions and several years of working with Evenki students who were sent for higher education to Leningrad, she developed the Evenki alphabet in 1927. This officially approved alphabet was first written in Latin, and since 1937 has been written in Cyrillic characters. Vasilevich's students helped to disseminate the alphabet and textbooks to the areas they had come from. Through her scholarship, Vasilevich assisted Evenki students in creating a first body of Evenki literature. She translated Evenki stories into Russian and some well-known works of Russian poets into Evenki. Vasilevich and her students also undertook the task of translating the canon of texts that the Communist Party had approved for public education and Soviet enlightenment.

The Evenki language textbooks of the first generation were all written by Vasilevich, who also compiled a number of dictionaries. Furthermore, she authored the pedagogical literature for teaching the Evenki language. One of the purposes of her expedition in 1935–1936 was to supervise and instruct teachers in village schools of the Evenki National Area (today the Evenki Autonomous Okrug). During her various expeditions, Vasilevich collected material not only on the Evenki language but also folkloric and ethnographic data. The ethnographic results of her expeditions in the late 1920s and 1930s have been published in the journal *Sovetskii Sever*.

In the early 1940s, Vasilevich's research shifted from pedagogy to anthropology, in large part a result of her appointment as researcher in the Institute of Ethnography of the Academy of Sciences of the USSR in 1941. That same year, World War II, the blockade of Leningrad (September 1941–January 1943), and temporary evacuation to Tashkent temporarily impeded and interrupted her academic work.

After 1945, Vasilevich published mainly on Evenki ethnogenesis and history, folklore, linguistics, toponymy (the study of place-names), and material culture. Drawing on her vast fieldwork material and sound knowledge of other Siberian peoples, she contributed not only to the ethnography of the Evenki but also to general anthropological issues, such as the origins and development of reindeer herding in Eurasia. Shamanism and religious beliefs of the Evenki played an important role in her writings after 1960. At the same time, she started to publish in German and in English.

Two key monographs were published in the last years of her life: *Istoricheskii fol'klor evenkov* [Historical Folklore of the Evenki] in 1966, and *Evenki* [The Evenki] in 1969. The latter, in particular, has become a standard text for Evenki studies. A number of works ready for publication were issued after her death. The other academic effects have presumably gone to the archive of the Russian Academy of Sciences. Vasilevich bequeathed her personal library and travel photographs to the Republican Library of Yakutia in Yakutsk.

Vasilevich's systematic and comprehensive study of Evenki language, folklore, and ethnography provides the basis for contemporary and future research. The quality of her scholarship was grounded in her continuous contacts and friendship with the Evenki community in Leningrad and her own participation in Evenki life during her extensive fieldwork.

Vasilevich conducted and participated in 11 expeditions to Siberia between 1925 and 1969. She visited numerous areas inhabited by Evenki. Her Evenki nickname was *Engesi* ("the strong one"). Her usual way of conducting fieldwork was to join a group of Evenki hunters in a village or trading post and to set off with them for the forest, where she would stay for several months.

Biography

Glafira Makar'evna Vasilevich was born on March 15, 1895 in St Petersburg, Russia. She attended an all-girls high school (*Petrovskaia zhenskaia gimnaziia*), graduating in 1912. She subsequently worked for the postal service, and after 1919 in school education. From 1920 to 1924, Vasilevich studied at the Institute of Geography, Petrograd, in the department of ethnography. After graduating in 1924, she prepared for her first expedition to the Tungus (Evenki) in 1925 and subsequently worked as research assistant at the subfaculty for Northern Peoples of the Department of Ethnography. Until 1931, she taught courses in ethnography of the Tungus peoples and Tungus (Evenki) language at various educational institutions in Leningrad. In 1931, Vasilevich was appointed as a reader in Evenki language at the Herzen Institute (Pedagogical Institute). In 1941, she took a position at the Institute of Ethnography of the Academy of Sciences of the USSR (Leningrad branch) and worked as senior researcher until her death in Leningrad on

April 21, 1971. Glafira Makar'evna Vasilevich did not marry or have children.

JOACHIM OTTO HABECK

See also **Evenki; Northern Altaic Languages; Tungus**

Further Reading

Menges, Karl H., "Glafira Makar'jevna Vasilevič." *Ural-Altaische Jahrbücher*, 46 (1974): 141–145

Romanova, A.V. et al., *G.M. Vasilevich—krupneishii sovetskii tungusoved (K 70-letiiu so dnia rozhdeniia)* [G.M. Vasilevich—the Most Prominent Soviet Tungusologist], Iakutsk: Iakutskoe knizhnoe izdatel'stvo, 1965

Taksami, Chuner, "Glafira Makar'evna Vasilevich." *Sovetskaia Etnografiia*, 5 (1971): 184–186

Tsintsius, V.I., "Pamiati Glafiry Makar'evny Vasilevich." In *Voprosy iazyka i fol'klora narodnostei Severa*, edited by B.N. Putilov, Iakutsk: Iakutskii filial SO AN SSSR, 1972

Uray-Köhalmi, Käthe, "In memoriam Glafira Makar'evna Vasilevich." *Acta Orientalia Academiae Scientiarum Hungaricae*, 27(1) (1973): 131–133

Vasilevich, G.M., *Istoricheskii fol'klor evenkov: skazaniia i predaniia* [Historical Folklore of the Evenki: Tales and Legends], Moskva and Leningrad: Nauka, 1966

———, "The Acquisition of Shamanistic ability among the Ewenki (Tungus)." In *Popular Beliefs and Folklore Tradition in Sibera*, edited by V. Diószegi, Bloomington: Indiana University; The Hague: Mouton, 1968

———, "Shamanistic Songs of the Ewenki (Tungus)." In *Popular Beliefs and Folklore Tradition in Sibera*, edited by V. Diószegi, Bloomington: Indiana University; The Hague: Mouton, 1968

Vasilevich, G.M. & A.V. Smoliak [Smolyak], "The Evenks." In *The Peoples of Siberia*, edited by M.G. Levin & L.P. Potapov, Chicago: University of Chicago Press, 1964

VDOVIN, INNOKENTIY STEPANOVICH

Innokentiy Stepanovich Vdovin was a 20th-century Russian ethnologist and linguist who specialized in the culture and in the languages of Chukchi and Koryak and other peoples of the Far North-East of Asia. Vdovin belonged to the first generation of Russian ethnologists who had begun their scientific career at the time of the early years of Soviet Union. A disciple of Vladimir Germanovich Bogoraz, Vdovin was knowledgeable in both the material and spiritual culture of Chukchi and Koryak.

Having graduated from secondary school, Vdovin worked as a teacher in the Far East (Khabarovsk Autonomous Territory), and later, in 1927–1930, in the small settlement Karaga in Kamchatka. In 1930, after moving to Leningrad, Vdovin studied at the Northern Department of the Leningrad State Pedagogical Institute named after A.I. Herzen. In his final year in 1932, due to a lack of skilled teachers in northern schools, Vdovin, together with his other schoolmates, went to western Chukotka and worked as a teacher for two years (1932–1934). While working among the Koryak in Kamchatka, and later among the Chukchi in Chukotka, Vdovin learned the Koryak and the Chukchi languages. Later, Vdovin was able to record and translate the folkloric texts in Koryak dictated by the performers of stories and legends. In 1934, Vdovin returned to Leningrad and began work at The Institute of the Peoples of the North, where in 1935 he became a postgraduate researcher. By 1932, Vdovin had participated in the creation of the Chukchi written language (a project led by Bogoraz and his colleagues), first on the basis of alphabet in Latin letters (the so-called Standard Northern Alphabet), and after 1936 on the basis of the Cyrillic alphabet. Vdovin authored more than 24 primary school textbooks devoted to the Chukchi language between 1935 and 1994.

Vdovin defended his thesis "The History of Relations of Russians and Chukchi Before the Beginning of 20th Century" in the year that Leningrad was besieged by German World War II troops, on December 4, 1941. From 1942 to 1946, Vdovin lived near Irkutsk in Russia, where he served as the director of the local pedagogical college. After returning to Leningrad at the end of the war, Vdovin joined the department of northern languages at the Institute of Language and Thought, named after N.Ya. Marr of the Academy of Sciences of the USSR (since 1950, Leningrad Branch of the Institute of Linguistics; since 1992, The Institute of the Linguistic Researches of Russian Academy of Sciences). He was concurrently teaching at Leningrad University, an institution in existence from 1948 to 1952, and that merged with the Northern Department of Leningrad State Pedagogical University in 1953. In 1954, Vdovin published his first monograph—*The History of Studies in the Paleosiberian Languages*—a scholarly work that is still considered widely relevant. In 1956, due to conflicts with his fellow linguists who also specialized in the Chukchi and the Koryak languages, Vdovin left the Institute of Linguistics and became a scientific worker of the department of the peoples of Siberia at the Institute of Ethnography, named after N.N. Mikluho-Maklay, and today called the Museum of Anthropology and Ethnography (Kunstkamera), where he worked till his death.

At the Institute of Ethnography, Vdovin continued his own research and that of his mentor, Vladimir Bogoraz, which dealt with the traditional Chukchi culture. Vdovin's doctoral thesis, *Essays in History and the Ethnography of Chukchi*, was published as a monograph in 1965. His *Essays on the Ethnic History of the Koryaks* (1973) analyzed the ethnogenesis of the Koryak, the history of various territorial groups of Koryak of the coast of the Sea of Okhotsk and Kamchatka, as well as the Aliutors, whom Vdovin regarded as one of the groups of Koryak.

Vdovin later studied the traditional religious beliefs and the shamanistic practices of the peoples of Siberia. He organized several significant collective research projects and was one of the forerunners in the nascent study of Siberian shamanism in the 1970s and 1980s, studying, in particular, the history of collective consciousness of the aboriginals of Siberia as a response to the dominant Marxist-Leninist ideology in the human sciences at that time. Vdovin was one of the first scholars in Russia to analyze shamanism not as a specific religious system but as a social institution that was based on animistic religious beliefs. In addition to religion and shamanism, the significant subject of Vdovin's scientific career comprised the problem of ancient ethnic contacts of Koryak and Chukchi with other peoples of the Far North-East of Russia, including the Inuit, the Evens, and the Yukagirs. In an essay on the "Problems of the Ethnogenesis of the Itelmens," Vdovin presented the original idea that the Itel'men genetically do not belong to the Chukchi-Kamchadal or the Chukchi-Koryak group, and the similarities in the culture and language between the Itel'men and Chukchi and Koryak relate to the later territorial connections and contacts.

Biography

Innokentiy Stepanovich Vdovin was born on December 9, 1907 in the Irkutsk Province of Russia. He worked as a teacher in the Far East (Khabarovsk Autonomous Territory), and in the small settlement Karaga in Kamchatka between 1927 and 1930. He moved to Leningrad in 1930, where he studied at the Northern Department of the Leningrad State Pedagogical Institute. In 1932, Vdovin traveled to western Chukotka where he taught for two years (1932–1934). He returned to Leningrad in 1934, attending the Institute of the Peoples of the North, where in 1935 he became a postgraduate researcher. After World War II, Vdovin held a number of faculty positions at the Leningrad Institute of Language and Thought, Leningrad University, and the Institute of Ethnography, where he taught until his death. Vdovin had two sons; one of them, Boris Vdovin, specializes in the ecology of the Polar regions. Vdovin died on December 25, 1996 in St Petersburg.

A. BURYKIN

See also **Bogoraz, Vladimir Germanovich**

Further Reading

Vdovin, I.S., *Istoriya izucheniya paleoaziatskix yazykov* [The History of Studies in the Paleo-siberian Languages], Moscow and Leningrad, 1954

———, *Iz istorii otnosheniy chukchey i eskimosov Alyaski* [From the History of Relations of Chukchi and the Eskimos of Alaska], Moscow, 1964

———, *Ocherki etnicheskoj istorii koryakov* [Essays on the Ethnic History of the Koryak], Leningrad, 1973

———, *The Traces of Aleut-Eskimo Culture on the Kamchatka Pacific Shore,* Moscow, 1966

———, *Issledovaniya shamanizma narodov Sibiri i Severa* [Researches of Shamanism of the Peoples of Siberia and North], Moscow, 1973

———, (editor), *Priroda i chelovek v religioznyx predstavleniyax narodov Sibiri I Severa* [Nature and Man in the Religious Ideas of the Peoples of Siberia and North], Leningrad, 1976

———, (editor), *Material'naya kul'tura narodov Sibiri i Severa* [Material Culture of the Peoples of Siberia and North], Leningrad: Nauka, 1976

———, (editor), *Problemy istorii obshchestvennogo soznaniya aborigenov Sibiri* [The Problems of History of the Collective Consciousness of the Aboriginals of Siberia], Leningrad, 1981

VEGETATION DISTRIBUTION

Compared to more temperate ecosystems, Arctic vegetation has low species diversity and a simple structure. Vegetation distribution has two main elements: the gross distribution, or phytogeography, of the individual plant taxa; and the distributions of the respective plant communities formed locally within a given region from components of the available flora. Climatic parameters, in particular, summer temperature, change drastically from the treeline in the south to the polar desert of the far north with a concomitant latitudinal shift in vegetation composition and cover. The primary trend in Arctic vegetation distribution is therefore the reduction in plant cover from 100% in the tundra ecosystems of the south to less than 1% in the more northerly polar deserts.

Many different schemes employing diverse terminologies have been used to classify units or zones along the latitudinal gradient of the Arctic. The concept of landscape "zones" is prevalent in Eurasia, whereas "biome" is more widely used in western literature. Among Russian scientists, there is now a complicated system for the division of Arctic vegetation zones. According to the simplest Russian scheme, the Arctic is divided from north to south as follows: polar desert zone, tundra zone, Arctic tundra subzone, typical tundra subzone, southern tundra subzone, and forest tundra subzone. Within a given zone, factors such as moisture, nutrient status, and wind become important controls, as evidenced by change along a local sequence of soils of about the same age (catena) in a number of landscapes.

There is also disagreement on the problem of Arctic classification among western vegetation scientists. In North America, including Greenland, the most commonly used classification is a division into High Arctic and Low Arctic, although various subdivisions have been delineated within these two regions based on floristic richness and/or vegetation physiognomy. The most widespread tundra vegetation complexes in the Low Arctic consist of tussock tundra, sedge meadows, and shrub tundra. The High Arctic contains some isolated sedge meadow systems in so-called polar oases, but is primarily divided between polar desert and polar semidesert communities. In polar semideserts, vascular plants contribute 5–20% cover and mosses and lichens contribute 50–80%. Polar deserts have a maximum of 5% vegetation cover.

North American soil scientists recognize three major soils zones: polar desert, subpolar desert (both High Arctic), and tundra (mostly Low Arctic). Proportionally, most of the lands designated as High Arctic exist in North America, encompassing the northern Canadian Shield and the Arctic Archipelago. In Eurasia, by way of comparison, true High Arctic landscapes with polar desert vegetation are mostly limited to the islands of the Arctic Ocean. Due to the different substrates in these two regions, contrasting definitions of what constitutes polar desert vegetation have developed in North America and Eurasia. Eurasian soils tend to be finer grained, thus holding more moisture, and support a greater diversity of vascular and nonvascular plant species. Another important factor is the parent material.

While it seems certain that most Arctic plants evolved before the development of tundra environments, substantial areas of the Arctic are believed to have become deglaciated only 5000–10,000 years BP. The modern distribution and composition of tundra vegetation is therefore a relatively recent development based on paleoecological analyses. Beringia was first postulated by the late Swedish botanist Eric Hultén as the land bridge connecting Alaska with Siberia to account for the distribution of certain groups of Arctic plants in eastern Asia and western North America. Beringia is central to the understanding of present-day Arctic and alpine ecosystems because of the role this land bridge served for the migration of cold-adapted plants (and animals) throughout the Pliocene and Pleistocene (*see* **Beringia**). During the latter period, so-called steppe tundra ecosystems were much more widespread (*see* **Polar Steppe**). Some scientists believe that contemporary analogs for steppe tundra occur in isolated well-drained habitats, such as south- and west-facing river bluffs and on pingos in modern-day Beringia.

Trees were absent from the steppe tundra, which characterized much of Pleistocene Beringia because of the cold, dry climate. The present-day treeline, or forest-tundra ecotone, is variously a function of temperature, precipitation, permafrost, wind, fire, herbivory, or any combination of these and other factors. It is now known that there are many other "treelines" as one moves northward from the forest edge to the High Arctic. The mosaic of vegetation types that characterize the various zones described above becomes simpler from south to north as the flora becomes progressively more impoverished. For example, disappearance of the cottongrass *Eriophorum vaginatum* denotes the circumpolar "tussock line," beyond which tussock tundra does not occur. Similar lines exist for dwarf shrubs, and other vascular plants as well, and have been correlated with mean July temperature.

To some extent, gross distribution patterns of Arctic bryophytes and lichens parallel those of flowering plants, but fewer species are restricted to high latitudes. The majority are also widespread in boreal, or in boreal and temperate regions, commonly with extensions to alpine areas. Most, perhaps 80% of the bryophytes and 70% of the lichens, have circumpolar distributions. There is a small cosmopolitan, and a significant bipolar element. Small amphi-Atlantic, amphi-Beringian, and other disjunct elements are also represented, but there are few local endemics. Of particular phytogeographical significance are the small temperate disjunct, and the larger circumpolar Arctic elements, both believed to be remnants of an early Tertiary flora formerly existing in Arctic regions under temperate or subtropical conditions.

The present species are thought to have persisted throughout the Pleistocene in refugia from which they have subsequently radiated to varying extents. Arctic recolonization by the more widely distributed taxa is seen as having occurred by migration from both northern refugia and regions south of the Pleistocene ice boundary. Contemporary bryophyte and lichen distributions have much to do with substrate pH. For example, the sedge meadows of widely disparate lowlands in the Canadian Arctic Archipelago with contrasting parent materials (granitic/acidic versus dolomitic/alkaline) can have up to 85% or more of their vascular taxa in common. However, the same meadows may share only 30% or less of their bryophyte taxa. In general, Arctic bryophytes and lichens are more sensitive than vascular plants to subtle spatial and temporal changes in moisture, chemical, and other environmental conditions.

BRUCE FORBES

See also **Circumpolar Arctic Vegetation Map; Coniferous Forests; High Arctic; Lichen; Polar Desert; Sedge meadows; Shrub Tundra; Treeline; Tundra; Tussock Tundra**

Further Reading

Aleksandrova, Vera Danilovna, *Vegetation of the Soviet Polar Deserts*, translated by Doris Löve, Cambridge: Cambridge University Press, 1988

Bliss, Lawrence C., "Arctic Tundra and Polar Desert Biome." In *North American Terrestrial Vegetation* (2nd edition), edited by Michael G. Barbour & William Dwight Billings, Cambridge and New York: Cambridge University Press, 2000, pp. 1–40

Chernov, Yuri I. & Nadya V. Matveyeva, "Arctic Ecosystems in Russia." In *Ecosystems of the World 3. Polar and Alpine Tundra*, edited by Frans-Emil Wielgolaski, Amsterdam: Elsevier Science, 1997, pp. 361–507

Daniels, Fred J.A. & J.G. de Molenaar, "Dry Coastal Ecosystems of Greenland." In *Ecosystems of the World 2A: Dry Coastal Ecosystems, Polar Regions and Europe*, edited by Eddy van der Maarel, Amsterdam: Elsevier Science, 1993, pp. 39–50

Edlund, Sylvia A., "Bioclimatic Zones in the Canadian Arctic Archipelago." In *Canada's Missing Dimension: Science and History in the Canadian Arctic Islands,* Volume 1, edited by C.R. Harington, Ottawa: Canadian Museum of Nature, 1990, pp. 421–441

Elvebakk, Arve, "A New Method for Defining Biogeographical Zones in the Arctic." In *Arctic Research: Advances & Prospects*, edited by V.M. Kotlyakov & V.E. Sokolov, Moscow: Nauka, 1990, pp. 175–186

Hultén, Eric & Magnus Fries, *Atlas of North European Vascular Plants North of the Tropic of Cancer*, Königstein: Koeltz Scientific Books, 1986

Markon, Carl J. & Donald A. Walker, *Proceedings of the Third International Circumpolar Arctic Vegetation Mapping Workshop*, Open-File Report 99-5511999, US Geological Survey, 1999

Matveyeva, Nadya & Yuri Chernov, "Biodiversity of Terrestrial Ecosystems." In *The Arctic: Environment, People, Policy*, edited by Mark Nuttall & Terry V. Callaghan, Amsterdam: Harwood, 2000, pp. 233–273

Oksanen, Lauri & Risto Virtanen (editors), "Geographical Ecology of Northernmost Fennoscandia." *Acta Botanica Fennica*, 153 (1995): 1–110

Virtanen, Risto, "Arctic and Oroarctic vegetation patterns in Northern Europe as a consequence of topography, climate, bedrock conditions and grazing." *Acta Universitatis Ouluensis*, A282 (1996)

Walker, Marilyn D., Fred J.A. Daniëls, & Eddy van der Maarel (editors), "Circumpolar Arctic vegetation." *Journal of Vegetation Science*, 5 (1994): 758–920

Young, Steven B., *To the Arctic: An Introduction to the Far Northern World*, New York: Wiley Science, 1989

VENIAMINOV, IVAN—*See* ARCHBISHOP INNOCENT

VERKHOYANSK RANGE

The Verkhoyansk Range in the eastern Sakha Republic (Yakutia) is one of the largest mountain ranges in Siberia. It is a watershed for the Lena, Omoloi, Yana, Indigirka, and Aldan rivers. The Verkhoyansk mountains reach from the Lena Delta on the Laptev Sea south to the middle reaches of the Aldan in an arc 1000 km (600 miles) long, running approximately northwest to southeast. The range is a fold and thrust belt, formed as a result of the collision between two large blocks of continental crust in the late Jurassic–early Cretaceous period, and further uplifted in the mid-Quaternary of several hundred meters. The range separates the eastern edge of the Central Siberian Plateau from the North Asia Craton.

The northern part of the Verkhoyansk Range begins at the Lena Delta and reaches the Dyanyshka tributary, parallel to and east of the Lena River. The width of the range here is 180–250 km. The central backbone of the range, beginning at the Lena Delta, is the Kharaulakhsky Range (430 m high in the north and 990 m in the south). The Kunga Ridge to the east and the Tuora-Sis Ridge to the west lie parallel to the Kharaulakh Range. The ranges consist mainly of shales, sandstones, limestones, with some intrusive igneous rocks (diabases). The Orulgan mountains to the south (average 1700–1900 m, highest peak, 2281 m) continue the main Verkhoyansk Range. From north to south, the OgonnerTaga and Sietindinsky ranges extend to the east, the Jarjansky and Byrandya ranges lie to the west, and several other small mountain chains (Kuiellyakh, Unduiluing, Serille, Namykyt, and Selenchan-Sise) lie parallel to the Orulgan mountains. These ranges consist of Triassic clay and sand shales, covered with young Mesozoic sediments on the western sides.

The central portion of the Verkhoyansk Range lies between the Dyanyshka and Tompo rivers, where it is called the West Verkhoyansk Range. Unlike the northern part of the mountain system, there are no parallel mountain chains to the east and the north; instead, the range gradually descends east to the Yana Plateau. This central part of the range aligns with the Tumara River from north to south, then to the southeast. The Keltersky, Tygyndzhinsky, Muniysky, Muosuchansky, Sorkinsky, Bygynsky, Buoruolakhsky, Kuturginsky, Chochumsky, and Ust-Viluisky mountain chains lie parallel to the Lena to the west of the main range, from Dyanyshka up to Tumara.

The southern part of the Verkhoyansk Range consists of three mountain ranges: the Tompo River up to Kukhtui Range to the southeast; the Beredjinsky Range to the northeast; and the Yudomo Maysky Range to the south. The width of the mountain system is 160–240 km. The southern part of the Verkhoyansk Range consists of three independent mountain ranges from the west to the northeast—Sette-Daban, Skalistyi, and SuntarKhayata.

The Sette-Daban Range is located to the east of the Aldan River section, stretching to the north from the Tompo River up to the southern curve of the Allakh-Yun River. The range length is approximately 250 km; the maximum height is 1988 m. The rocky range to the east of Sette-Daban joins the Suntar-Khayata Range in the east. Its length is 320 km, reaching a peak at Khalyinsky Golets (2403 m). The range is divided into parts by the Aldan River tributaries (Menkuile, Vostochnaya Khandyga, Tyry, and Khanda). The Suntar Khayata Range is the largest in the southern part of the Verkhoyansk mountain system, measuring 450 km in length. At a height of approximately 2000–2300 m, the Mus-Khaya mountain (2797 m) is the highest peak in the entire Verkhoyansk Range.

The Verkhoyansk mountain chain is asymmetrical; its western slope reaches higher than its eastern one. Thus, the western and southern sides of the range have a lower base level for erosion and are scarred with valleys in the form of narrow canyons; the eastern and northern ones, in contrast, are more gently sloping, and merge gradually with the Central Siberian Plateau.

The Verkhoyansk Range was glaciated in the Late Quaternary. Today, glaciers are found above 1800 m: 47 glaciers (total area 20 km^2) are found on the Orulgan Range, and 250 (246 km^2) glaciers on the Suntar-Khayata Range. The climate is severely continental: the world's lowest temperatures have been recorded in the town of Verkhoyansk, which is also characterized by the world's greatest temperature ranges (extremes of −70°C to 36°C). The harsh winter temperatures preserve permafrost throughout the range.

The northern Verkhoyansk Range is in the polar desert biome, with tundra vegetation found on the mountainsides below 1200 m, and further south the range is forested. The treeline is found at an altitude of 1150 m in the central part of the mountain system, and at up to 1370 m to the east. Trees are of the light-needle taiga type: Dahurian larch (deciduous), birch, poplar, and aspen.

Rich in minerals, the first recorded information about silver ore in the Verkhoyansk mountain system (on the Endybal River) occurred in 1748; from 1765 to 1775, mining was conducted here. This region was subjected to detailed geological exploration in the 1930s–1950s, and recent offshore petroleum interest has led to further study of onshore structures. The mountain system and adjoining table-lands and uplands are rich in quartzvein systems bearing nonferrous metals: gold, silver, lead, tin, tungsten, zinc, and copper. Moreover, gold has been mined in placers in the southern mountains. Nezhdaninsky is a rich deposit in the south Verkhoyansk Range, which has been mined since 1975, but the difficult conditions (due to permafrost and severe climate) require further development to accelerate production.

PAVEL KAZARYAN

See also **Lena River**

Further Reading

Atlasov, I.P., "Orulgansky khrebet" [The Orulgan range]. *Transactions of the Arctic Institute*, 99(1), (1938)

Geologicheskie pamyatniki Respubliki Sakha (Yakutia) [Geological Monuments of the Sakha Republic (Yakutia)], Novosibirsk: AS SR (Y), 1997, p. 80

Layer, P.W., L.M. Parfenov, V.A. Trunilina, & A.G. Bakharev, "Age and tectonic significance of granitic belts within the Verkhoyansk fold and thrust belt, Yakutia, Russia." *Geological Society of Ameircan Abstracts with Programs Cordillerian Section*, 27(A60) (1995)

Parfenov, L.M., "Tectonics of the Verkhoyansk-Kolyma Mesozoides in the context of plate tectonics." *Tectonophysics*, 199(1991): 319–342

VESTMANNAEYJAR (WESTMAN ISLANDS)

The Vestmannaeyjar (Westman Islands) are a group of small islands, about 10 miles (16 km) south of Iceland. The Vestmannaeyjar are generally counted as 15 or 18 islands, with about 30 smaller rocks. From the island of Surtsey in the southwest to Elliðaey in the northeast, the Westman Islands cover a distance of 31 km in a straight line. The entire Westman Island area is 38 km long and 29 km wide. Heimaey (13.4 km^2) and Surtsey (1.9 km^2) are the largest islands. Seventeen sites of volcanic activity have been recognized and studied. The oldest islands were probably formed in volcanic eruptions about 10,000 years ago, and the youngest island, Surtsey, was created in a series of volcanic eruptions from 1963 to 1967.

The Vestmannaeyjar are among the windiest places in Iceland, although this can partly be explained by the fact that the weather station is located at Stórhöfði, 122 m above sea level. The wind force at Stórhöfði has reached up to 200 km per hour (as recorded in October 1963). The average temperature is one of the highest in the country, and is especially high during the winter months.

Approximately 150 plants and 80 species of insects are found on the Vestmannaeyjar Islands. The puffin is the characteristic bird of the islands. Some birds, such as the manx shearwater, are not found anywhere else in Iceland.

The people's principal means of existence include fishing, fowling, and farming. Great colonies of gannets and other waterfowl breed in these islands. As the islands are characterized by steep cliffs, ropeclimbing is a common practice to seek both fowls and eggs. The puffin has been hunted for food since the 19th century, when the catch totaled approximately 330,000 puffins per year. In more recent years, this number has decreased to approximately 60–80,000. Formerly, catching fulmar was an important part of people's livelihood, but this declined in importance during the 20th century. Despite difficult surroundings, the islanders kept up to 1200 sheep until the advent of fisheries made other occupations more profitable.

The only island with any population to speak of is Heimaey. By the mid-19th century, 48 farms had been established on the island, with roughly 500 inhabitants. The mechanization of the fishing industry however, at the beginning of the 20th century, led to an increase in population. The population of the islands quadrupled between 1900 and 1920, largely due to increased productivity gained from the use of motorboats in fishing. More and more people settled in the town on Heimaey, generally known as Vestmannaeyjar. The population of the islands rose to around 4700 in 1960, and has maintained a steady level since then, despite setbacks during the volcanic eruption in 1973.

According to Icelandic tradition, the islands are named after the Celtic slaves of the first settler, Ingólfr Arnarson. They slew his foster-brother Hjörleifr, and then fled to the islands, where Ingólfr sought and killed them all. The term "west man" is, however, rarely used by Celts in medieval Icelandic medieval sources, but it is more commonly used for Norsemen who lived in the British Isles.

According to the Book of Settlements (Landnámabók), during the first decades there were few permanent residents of Vestmannaeyjar, although it was the site of a fishing station there. Fishing was mainly carried on in late winter, from January or February until May, in open rowboats. It nevertheless proved to be profitable, and the islands became the subject of foreign interest. Around 1400, the islands had come into the private ownership of the Danish king, who ruled until 1874. English fishermen, who began to frequent Icelandic waters between the 13th and 16th centuries, also coveted the islands and built fortified camps there. The English captured the Danish governor and established a permanent camp in Vestmannaeyjar until 1558, confiscating all Danish property and controlling all trade and fishing.

In 1627, Algerian pirates ravaged the islands, taking nearly 300 people into slavery and killing more than 30. Although attempts to collect ransoms were unsuccessful, one of the priests in the islands was killed in the raid, but the other, Ólafur Egilsson (1564–1639), was taken into captivity and then sent to Copenhagen to negotiate the release of the captives. Twenty-seven Icelanders were eventually returned.

Most of the islanders were tenants of the English Crown and lived in endemic poverty. When the first consultative assembly was founded in Iceland in 1843, voting rights were dependent upon the ownership of property, a qualification that disenfranchised the entire constituency. Thus, the Vestmannaeyjar Islanders did not send a representative to the first Icelandic parliament. Nevertheless, they managed to operate a school around 1750, long before the advent of such institutions in other parts of Iceland. The Vestmannaeyjar Islands became a municipal township in 1918.

Vestmannayjar is best known for the eruption of a volcano, formerly believed to be extinct, on Heimaey in 1973. On a night in January of that year, the earth erupted only 200 m from the edge of the town. Within a few hours, the cleft had extended almost completely through the island. Fortunately, almost the entire fishing fleet was in the harbor and the weather conditions were good. The entire island was evacuated during the night and into the early hours of the following morning. A portion of Heimaey disappeared under lava, and is today buried under black volcanic ash. When the eruption ended in June, the town was cleaned and later partly rebuilt. Although the eruption cost no lives, it wreaked tremendous economic damage to the islanders.

SVERRIR JAKOBSSON

See also **Iceland**

Further Reading

Einarsson, Þorleifur, *The Surtsey Eruption. In Words and Pictures*, (2nd edition), Reykjavík, 1966

Eyjólfsson, Guðjón Ármann, *Vestmannaeyjar. Byggð og eldgos*, Reykjavík, 1973

Gíslason, Guðlaugur, *Útgerð og aflamenn. Ágrip af sögu útgerðar í Vestmannaeyjum*, Reykjavík, 1984

Guðnason, Haraldur, *Við Ægisdyr. Saga Vestmannaeyjabæjar*, 2 volumes, Reykjavík, 1982, 1991

Johnsen, Sigfús M., *Saga Vestmannaeyja*, 2 volumes, Reykjavík, 1946

Jónsson, Sigurgeir, *Vestmannaeyjar*, Reykjavík, 2000

Jósepsson, Þorsteinn and Steindór Steindórsson, *Landið Þitt Ísland*, 5 volumes, (2nd edition), Reykjavík, 1980–1984

Kålund, P.E. Kristian, *Bidrag til en historisk-topografisk Beskrivelse af Island*, 2 volumes, Copenhagen, 1877, 1882

Karlsson, Gunnar, *Iceland's 1100 Years. The History of a Marginal Society*, London, 2000

Rúriksson, Björn, *The Westman Islands*, Seltjarnarnesi, 1995

VIBE, CHRISTIAN

The Danish zoologist Christian Vibe made his first trip to Greenland in 1936 as an undergraduate student participating in a Danish expedition to northwest Greenland, where he studied the birds and the deep-sea fauna of the Melville Bay area.

In 1939, Vibe joined the Danish Thule-Ellesmere Land Expedition (1939–1940). From its permanent winter quarters at the northern coast of Murchison Sound, the expedition made several trips by dogsled or boat in the Thule area. In the spring of 1940, Vibe and a small group of Inuit traveled by dogsled across Smith Sound to explore the eastern areas of Ellesmere Island. Based on his studies, Vibe wrote "The Marine Mammals and the Marine Fauna in the Thule District with Observations on Ice Conditions in 1939–1941" in *Meddelelser of Grønland* (the oldest journal on Arctic subjects) on marine mammals and ice conditions in the eastern edges of the North Water in northern Baffin Bay (Smith Sound). Vibe's experiences in Thule triggered a lifelong interest in the physical and biological conditions in polynyas and in long-term fluctuations in the Arctic environment.

While returning from Ellesmere Island in the spring of 1940, Vibe and his team learned of the German occupation of Denmark. During the occupation, there was no regular contact between Greenland and Denmark, and Vibe remained in Greenland until the liberation in May 1945. In 1941, he moved to Nuuk (formerly Godthåb)—the largest town in Greenland—where he served through the war years as a meteorologist, editor of the local newspaper (*Grønlandsposten*), and a radio broadcaster. In 1948, Vibe joined the newly established Greenland Zoogeographical Studies Unit at the Zoological Museum of Copenhagen and spent many years studying the fauna in Greenland. He collected numerous specimens of both terrestrial and marine vertebrates as well as invertebrates for the Zoological Museum. Moreover, Vibe coordinated the local reporting of hunting statistics. In recognition of his work, new animal species and subspecies were named after him, for example, a crane fly (*Dicranomyia vibei*), an anthonomid fly (*Fucellia vibei*), and an aphid (*Thrips aphis vibei*). Until he retired in 1983, Vibe served as a special advisor to The Danish Ministry of Greenland.

Vibe's doctoral thesis, *Arctic Animals in Relation to Climatic Fluctuation* (1967), analyzed long-term data based on Greenland hunting statistics. He studied the Greenlanders' catch of mammals in relation to long-term variation in ice conditions over almost 200 years. A landmark study on the effects of climatic fluctuations on animal abundance, Vibe's work is even today, frequently cited within the scientific community.

During his scientific career, Vibe was concerned about Greenlanders' ability to make a living from harvesting the markedly fluctuating living resources of their country. In Greenland, muskox lived only on the east coast, while the vast majority of the Greenlanders lived on the western coast. Hence, in order to provide Greenlanders with access to a stable resource, Vibe made two expeditions (1961 and 1966) to northeast Greenland. Where he caught 27 muskox calves, which he then transplanted to the Kangerlussuaq (Søndre Strømfjord) area in Central West Greenland. By 2000, this group had grown to a population of 7000–10,000 species that are now harvested for local consumption under an annual quota of 2200. In 1986, Vibe transplanted another 21 muskox from central to north west

Greenland, where the population has now grown to several hundred animals.

Moreover, Vibe contributed significantly to the conservation and protection of Arctic wildlife. While recognizing the traditional rights of the Arctic peoples to exploit their living resources, Vibe also realized early that hunting could only be sustained with careful guidelines for conservation and protection. In 1966, he was one of the founding members of the Polar Bear Specialist Group, formed under the auspices of the International Union for the Conservation of Nature (IUCN). The work of this group led to the Agreement on the Conservation of Polar Bears in 1972, which was the first agreement of any kind on conservation in the Artic. A visionary agreement, it was the first to recognize the need to protect habitat as well as animals. During 1973–1975, 1977, and 1979, Vibe led field expeditions to study polar bears in northeast and Northwest Greenland. He spearheaded the introduction of Greenland's first Law on Protection of Nature (1972), the establishment of the large national park in North and northeast Greenland (1974), and the Melville Bay Game Reserve (1978).

Vibe's contributions spanned a wide range of species and topics, including marine and land mammals, birds, invertebrates, wildlife protection, and the study of the effects of climatic fluctuations. He wrote over 100 scientific and popular articles, and three books with personal accounts on his experiences in Greenland in 1936–1945. In addition, Vibe produced six films on expedition life and wildlife in Greenland and gave public lectures in order to raise public and private funds for his expeditions.

Biography

Christian Vibe was born on March 16, 1913 in the village of Raved in southern Jutland in Denmark. His parents Jacob Petersen Vibe (born on September 22, 1877) and Sofie Dorothea Vibe (née Petersen, born on June 24, 1877) had five children. Both parents came from farming families and were farmers themselves.

Vibe graduated with a master of science degree in 1939 in natural history (zoology, botany, and geology) at the University of Copenhagen; he earned his doctorate of philosophy at the same university in 1967. In 1936, Vibe participated as an undergraduate student in a Danish expedition to northwest Greenland. In 1939, he joined the Danish Thule-Ellesmere Land Expedition (1939–1940) and subsequently lived in Nuuk (Greenland) from 1941 to 1945. Until his retirement in 1983, Vibe traveled in Greenland nearly every year. In his marriage with Grete Vibe (neé Glentoft), Vibe had one son. Vibe died in Farum on June 23, 1998.

ERIK W. BORN

Further Reading

Meldgaard, M., & E.W. Meldgaard, "Videnskab med vision og hjerte. Nekrolog over Dr. phil. Christian Vibe." [Science with vision and heart. Dr. Phil. Christian Vibe, obituary]. *Dansk Naturhistorisk Forenings Årsskrift Nr.* 9 (1997/1998): 61–65

Vibe, Christian, "The marine mammals and the marine fauna in the Thule District (Northwest Greenland) with observations on ice conditions in 1939–41." *Meddelelser om Grønland,* 150(6) (1950): 1–115

———, "Arctic animals in relation to climatic fluctuations." *Meddelelser om Grønland,* 170(5) (1967): 1–227

VICTOR, PAUL-ÉMILE

The French explorer, writer, ethnologist, and logistician Paul-Émile Victor (also known by the diminutive PEV) was one of the most well-known French polar explorers of the 20th century.

After engineering courses in Lyon (France), he studied the sciences, ethnology, and literature at the Institute of Ethnology in Paris. Victor then enrolled in the French Navy so that he could learn to sail.

In 1934, he convinced commandant Jean-Baptiste Charcot, a veteran Arctic and Antarctic explorer, to take him and his three companions to Ammassalik, a remote and poorly known Inuit settlement that was considered to be nearly prehistoric on the southeast coast of Greenland. That was the first winter Victor spent in the Arctic, with Michel Perez, Fred Matter and Robert Gessain, a famous French anthropologist. In 1936, returning to Greenland, he crossed the ice cap from the west coast to the same eastern settlement, this time accompanied by Perez, Gessain, and a young Dane who soon became a well-known artist and archaeologist, Eigil Knuth. At the end of this second expedition, while the others went back to Europe, Victor began his second wintering, which lasted for 14 months. Adopted by a local family, he shared and carefully observed their culture. He brought back several thousand ethnographic drawings, artifacts (which he donated to the Musée de l'Homme in Paris), and a newfound knowledge of the East Greenlandic culture.

When World War II erupted in 1939, Victor had already sharpened his dog sledging skills through travels in the Alps and Lapland (with doctors Raymond and Michel Latarget). Hence, he was sent to Scandinavia and Finland as a naval attaché. When the armistice was signed in 1940, Victor emigrated to the United States, where in 1941 he enrolled in the Air Force and later became an instructor at the Polar Training School, founding the Search and Rescue squadron for Alaska, Canada, and Greenland.

In 1947, he returned to France and established the Expéditions Polaires Françaises (French Polar Expeditions, EPF). For 30 years, Victor directed this institution and organized several dozen expeditions both in the Arctic and in the Antarctic region. In 1990, before the logistics of the French expeditions were transferred to the French Polar Institute, the EPF had organized 65 expeditions, employed more than 3000 participants, traveled 450,000 km with tracked vehicles, and published 500 monographs and 1000 scientific articles in different fields.

In addition to his career as an explorer, Victor was an acknowledged writer. He published 40 scientific, technical, and science texts, most of them dealing with polar topics. *Boréal: la joie dans la nuit* (My Eskimo Life), first published in 1938–1939, related his experience with the East Greenland Inuit. Victor considered his greatest accomplishment to be the printing, in the early 1990s, of his ethnographic material collected in 1934–1937 that had been lost for nearly 50 years. He had personally published several ethnographic studies, such as comprehensive studies on the cup-and-ball game in 1938 and "Cat's Cradle" or "String Figures" in 1940 (other monographs published with Robert Gessain include studies on the kayak in 1969, the Greenlandic drum in 1973, and jack games in 1974). But when Joëlle Robert-Lamblin and Catherine Enel, two scientists who pursued the French ethnological tradition in East Greenland, analyzed and published Victor's notes, drawings, and the translation of the traditional songs he had recorded, the scientific community suddenly discovered that he had not only been a pioneering explorer but also a surprisingly advanced man of science.

Victor received the highest award (Great Gold Medal) from the Royal Geographical Society of London, the Royal Scottish Geographical Society, the Royal Geographical and Ethnographic Society of Sweden, as well as the Great Cross of the French Legion of Honor. Today, a permanent exhibition recalls his life at the Paul-Emile Victor Centre of Prémanon, a quiet village of his home region, the Jura Mountains.

Biography

Paul-Émile Victor was born in Geneva, Switzerland, on June 28, 1907. He was given the first name Paul-Eugène at birth. His father owned a pipe factory. Victor spent his childhood in St Claude, a small village of the Jura Mountains (eastern France) and then at Lons-le-Saunier. He studied at the École centrale de Lyon. At the age of 27, he organized his first Arctic journey to Ammassalik (East Greenland). The ethnological material that he later published was collected during this trip and a second wintering in 1936–1937. After World War II, Victor returned from Alaska, where he was in charge of a search and rescue squadron, to

Paris, where he established the French Polar Expeditions in 1947. There until 1976, Victor led French polar research both in the Arctic and the Antarctic region. Among his international activities, Victor actively contributed to the signing of the Antarctic Treaty in Washington, District of Columbia, on December 1, 1959. He was also chairperson of the Scientific Committee on Antarctic Research (SCAR). In the 1960s and 1970s, he immersed himself into the conservation of humankind and their environment, supported among others by his long-time friend Jacques-Yves Cousteau.

In 1977, he retired to Bora-Bora, a tropical island of French Polynesia. In 1987, for his 80th birthday, he went for the last time to Adélie Land, the French sector of Antarctica, and then to the geographical North Pole. In 1988, an exhibition presenting the documents he had collected in Greenland attracted more than 100,000 visitors at the Musée de l'Homme in Paris. Following his last wishes, his body was submerged in the warm waters of the lagoon from the French polar supply ship, the *Durmont d'Urville*. Paul-Émile Victor had three children (Jean-Christophe, Daphné, and Stéphane) from his first marriage with Eliane Decrais and one son (Téva) from his second wife Colette Faure de la Vaulx. He died in Bora-Bora on March 7, 1995.

OLIVIER GILG

See also **Gessain, Robert**

Further Reading

Monestier, Marianne, *Paul-Émile Victor; ou, L'aventure intelligente,* Paris: Desclée, De Brouwer, 1974

Orphelin, Catherine, *Paul-Emile Victor: mémoires et rêves d'un humaniste*, Marseille, France: AGEP, 1992

Victor, Paul-Emile, *Boréal: la joie dans la nuit* (My Eskimo life), translated from French by Jocelyn Godefroi, New York: Simon & Schuster, 1939

———, "Contribution à l'ethnographie des Eskimo d'Angmagssalik." *Meddelelser om Grønland*, 125(7) (1940): 1–213

———, *The French Polar Research Expeditions, 1948–1951; A Report,* New York: French Embassy Press and Information Division, 1950

Victor, Paul-Emile, & Joëlle Robert-Lamblin, *La civilisation du phoque: jeux, gestes et techniques des Eskimo d'Ammassalik*, Bayonne: Armand Colin-Raymond Chabaud, 1989

———, *La civilisation du phoque: légendes, rites et croyances des Eskimo d'Ammassalik*, Bayonne: Raymond Chabaud, 1993

VICTORIA ISLAND

Victoria Island, at 212,200 km^2 and just slightly smaller than Great Britain, is the second westernmost island of the Canadian Arctic Archipelago. Roughly square-shaped and indented by several deep inlets, the island's southern coast faces the northern shores of the American continent. Geological outcrops are mostly from the pre-Cambrian and Paleozoic ages, with a preponderance of sedimentary rocks (mostly limestone and dolomites) and some intrusive rocks: diabase and gabbro. Devoid of glaciers, the topography of Victoria Island is mainly one of moraine-covered lowlands and drumlin fields, except for the Shaler Mountains that run from Prince Albert Sound (west coast) to Hadley Bay (north coast) with spectacular gabbro scarps. Postglacial emergence rises between 50 and 75 m and, where the shoreline consists of till or limestone rubble, raised beaches are ubiquitous, providing excellent camping grounds.

Victoria Island's climate is definitely polar with a mean high of −30.0°C in January and 11.9°C in July (low of 3.9°C). The average annual precipitation is 13.6 cm, 6.8 cm rainfall, and 76.8 cm snowfall (Cambridge Bay). Permafrost is permanent, the snow cover remains from late September until June, and the sea-ice sheet remains from late October until mid-July. In recent years the weather has become more unpredictable, probably due to global climate change.

Sparse tundra vegetation—Arctic willows in protected valleys, grassy and boggy lower grounds, lichens on rocky plateaux—manages to feed rather large numbers of muskoxen and caribou grazing in tiny herds. Other resident species include white foxes, wolves, ptarmigans, and Arctic owls. Waterfowl is abundant in summer. Lakes and rivers are rich with freshwater and anadromous fish. Ringed and bearded seals and polar bears populate the sea waters and coastal areas in good numbers.

Victoria Island has been a gateway to the eastward migrations through the North American Arctic for over 10,000 years. The Copper Eskimo (Inuinnait), so named by Vilhjalmur Stefansson because of their use of local copper, lived both on the mainland and on the island. Inuinnait relied primarily on winter seal hunting at breathing holes and summer caribou hunting complemented by lake fishing.

As most exploration was launched from the East and whalers from the West harvested only the Beaufort Sea, island reconnaissance was belated. Victoria Island's key explorers included John Rae (1849–1850), Robert McClure (1850–1851); Richard Collinson (1851–1853); and Vilhjalmur Stefansson (1911, 1914–1918). Of the many trading posts established from the 1920s, two became Inuit settlements in the 1950s. In Cambridge Bay (69° N 105° W), the construction of a Distant Early Warning (DEW) Line station attracted many Inuit. It became the largest community in the area, the headquarters of Kitikmeot Administrative Region in 1981, and the capital of western Nunavut in 1999. Cambridge Bay's population increased from 815 in 1981 to 1351 in 1996 (Canada Censuses), 1500 estimated in 2001. The population of Holman (71° N 118° W) grew from 295 in 1981 to 423 in 1996 and has since stabilized, as several families moved elsewhere for jobs. Wage employment has become the major source of income in both communities, but hunting, the only source of fresh meat, remains important. As Holman is part of the 1984 Inuvialuit Final Agreement, the island was partitioned between the Northwest Territories and Nunavut in 1999.

BÉATRICE COLLIGNON

See also **Beaufort Sea; Inuvialuit Settlement Region; Nunavut; Stefansson Island**

Further Reading

Collignon, Béatrice, *Les Inuit, ce qu'ils savent du territoire*, Paris: L'Harmattan, 1996

Condon, Richard, *The Northern Copper Inuit, A History*, Toronto: University of Toronto Press, 1996

Freeman, Milton (editor), *Inuit Land-Use and Occupancy Project*, Ottawa: DINA, 1976

Jenness, Diamond, *The Life of the Copper Eskimo—Report of the Canadian Arctic Expedition 1913–1918—Southern Party 1913–1916*, Volume XII, *A*, Ottawa: F.A. Acland, 1922

Maxwell, John B., *The Climate of Canadian Arctic Islands and Adjacent Waters*, Ottawa: Environment Service, 1980

Thorsteinsson, Raymond & Tozer Edward, *Banks, Victoria and Stefansson Islands, Arctic Archipelago*, Ottawa: Geological Survey of Canada, 1962

VIKINGS

Víking is the Old Norse term for "raider" or "pirate." In modern usage, the Viking Period defines the period from *c*.AD 750 to 1050 in the history of what is now Denmark, Iceland, Norway, Sweden, and southern Greenland. Finland was a separate cultural entity, but shared some of the material trappings of the Viking Age. The Viking Period is marked by the transition from pagan to Christian religion; colonization; high mobility; increased trade; raiding; population increase; new ship technology, relatively widespread literacy, and a general shift from chiefdoms and minor kingdoms to the beginnings of centralized states.

The origin of the word *viking* is unclear. Suggestions include *vika*, a rowing shift, *Viken*, the Viking Period name for Oslo, *vík*, the Old Norse word for "bay," and Anglo-Saxon/Latin *wic/vicus*, meaning trade center. Although today we speak of "Vikings" to denote all Scandinavians of that period, "Norse" is a more accurate term. The people of the Viking period referred to themselves in terms of their geographic home area and reserved the word "viking" for a man participating in a

raid. Raiding was usually seasonal, but a high proportion of males took part in at least one raid, as it was an excellent way to obtain honor and goods.

A wide-reaching expansion of Nordic peoples is what most characterizes the Viking Age. The expansion occurred in all directions and embraced four elements: raids, trade, mercenary service for foreign rulers, and colonization. The raids and trade resulted in seasonal bases, many of which became permanent towns.

The Viking Raids

The earliest recorded raid was on England, in 789, followed by a raid on the monastery of Lindisfarne (Northumbria) in 793. Raids on Ireland and Scotland, the Frisian coast, and what is now Germany began about the same time, and eventually reached as far as Spain, Italy, and northern Africa. The first recorded attack on Frankia took place in 799. After Charlemagne's death in 814, when Frankia was divided by civil war, Vikings established themselves in bases in the Loire, Somme, and Seine rivers. They participated as mercenaries on all sides in the war and terrorized the surrounding areas even after the war ended in 843. To avoid further raids, a great portion of the royal revenue was paid in ransom to the Vikings. This *Danegeld* was first paid in Paris in 845, and over the next 50 years the Vikings received as much as 30,000 lb in silver in France alone, and several times those amounts in England. In France the situation improved after 911, when Charles the Simple granted land around Rouen to the Norwegian Hrolfur (Rollo), which, under Rollo's son, became Normandy.

Trade

The raids were interspersed with trade to continental Europe via the German rivers and along the coast to western Europe. The most extensive trade network was between Swedes and the Orient via the Russian rivers. The Swedish Norse ventured as far south and east as Constantinople and Baghdad. At the latter market, they obtained goods from India and China that had arrived via the "silk road." Archaeologists have found Chinese silks in the Swedish town of Birka and a lizard purse from India in a burial in northern Sweden.

Imported goods were primarily luxury items: jewellery, silk and velvet, copper alloys, tin, foods such as spices, nuts, and wine, and lavish household objects. In exchange the Norse offered furs, leather, sea mammal oil, walrus ivory, and slaves. In northern Norway, Sweden, and Finland, some of these latter products were obtained by taxation and through trade with the Saami. Iron stock was exported from Finland to the Frankish area, where fine damascened sword blades were manufactured and then exported back to the northern countries. There was also considerable trade between the various Norse groups, in items such as pork, flour, malt and hops, household vessels of soapstone, whetstones, bone and antler products, and iron stock.

Trade was generally confined to ports of trade and towns, controlled by a chieftain or king. Important ports of trade included Kaupan in Norway, Ribe in Denmark, Löddeköpinge in Sweden, and Eyrar in Iceland. Birka (Sweden), Haithabu (now Schleswig, Germany), and Oslo, Trondheim, and Bergen (Norway) were major towns. In other areas, Vikings were active in Staraja Ladoga (Russia), Wolin (Poland), Dorestad (Frisia), York (England) and Dublin (Ireland), as well as numerous other places.

Mercenary Services

Vikings worked in the service of foreign rulers, often fighting each other in the process. The famous Varangian guard at the royal court in Constantinople lasted long after the Viking Period.

Political Systems and Social Organization

Political and religious power lay in the hands of nobles. Control was gained by personal leadership, military prowess, and number of followers. Loyalty was bought with land grants, the distribution of gifts, ostentatious feasting, and the display of wealth. In return, the nobles offered military protection and material support.

The basic social unit was the farm, inhabited by a nuclear family. Not all farms were equal. The owners of large estates controlled and collected rent from a number of satellite farms. The large estates invariably occupied the most productive lands, and the halls of prominent chieftains were not only larger but more elaborate than the dwellings on satellite farms. The largest known chieftain's hall, at Borg in northern Norway, is 83 m long, five times as long as a standard farm dwelling. There was also a considerable labor force of both free and enslaved individuals. A chieftain had his own paramilitary force of personal retainers, usually young men from prominent families who gained honor and prowess through the opportunity to participate in wars, trade, and raids. Competition between leaders was an incentive to warfare. Dominance over rivals, their lands, and supporters eventually led to the formation of large kingdoms in what became Denmark, Norway, and Sweden. In Denmark this process was more or less completed in the late 10th century by Harald Bluetooth; and in Norway in the early 11th century by Olaf Tryggvason and Olaf Haraldsson (Olaf the Holy). The process was not completed in Sweden until after the Viking Age.

Colonization

From the late 9th century and onward, the Norse settled permanently in Danelaw in northern and eastern England. By the end of the 9th century, much of Scotland, including the Hebrides, Orkneys, and the Shetland Islands, had become Norse chiefdoms. While some of the local inhabitants were taken as slaves, many of the Norse also married into local families. The Faroes were settled around 825. Situated in the Atlantic, halfway between Scotland and Iceland, they were inhabited by only a few Irish hermits. In Iceland, too, the only previous inhabitants were Irish hermits. Large-scale settlement began shortly after 871±2, according to radiocarbon dates on volcanic ash. The settlement was a highly organized undertaking, probably led by chieftains. Most of the settlers came from Norway, Norse Scotland, and Ireland, with some individuals from Sweden. In 930, Icelandic chieftains established the *Althing*, an open-air yearly assembly that served as a common point for negotiations and settlement of disputes.

In about 985/986, emigration took place from Iceland to southwestern Greenland, which was uninhabited at that time. This Norse colony lasted for almost 500 years. From Greenland, there was further exploration along the North American coast to Vinland, probably as far as the Gulf of St Lawrence (*see* **Vinland**).

Slavery

Slavery existed throughout the Viking Period. Slaves were generally taken in raids and then sold on European slave markets. Other slaves, for domestic service, were either born into slavery, or offered themselves as slaves in return for subsistence. Slaves were not necessarily ill treated. A slave could operate a small farm and, by hard work, obtain his freedom. However, at his death his farm was inherited by his former master. Even as a freed man he could not vote on the *thing* and was obliged to pay rent to his former master for the rest of his life.

Position of Women

Free women enjoyed greater rights before Christianization. A woman could initiate divorce and was entitled to retain her dowry. During the absence of her husband on Viking or trading voyages, she ran the estate or farm, and may have controlled some of the trade. However, her inheritance was less than a brother's if any, and female infanticide was not uncommon. Female slaves had few, if any, rights. Female slaves were also kept as concubines.

Economy

The mainstay of the economy was livestock farming. Because of the high latitudes of the Nordic countries (55° N to 72° N), the short growing season, and the relative scarcity of arable soil, cereals could be grown successfully only in Denmark, southern Sweden, and southern Norway. Barley, rye, and oats were the chief crops. Denmark produced wheat in some quantities. Cattle, as well as sheep and goats, were raised for milk, meat, and wool. Pasture land was augmented by a *shieling* system, in which livestock were moved to summer pastures at some distance from the farm. Even in Greenland, dairy farming dominated in the Viking Period. Farming was supplemented with hunting and fishing. Furs and walrus teeth were an important source of revenue through trade.

Language, Writing, and Literature

At the beginning of the Viking Age, all Norse people spoke Old Norse, which by that time had become distinct from the common Germanic language of northern Europe. By the end of the Viking Period, differences in dialect between East and West Norse were noticeable, but it was not until the 13th century that the differences became sufficiently distinct to form ancestral Norwegian, Danish, and Swedish. In Iceland, change has been much slower so that modern Icelandic differs little from Old Norse.

Writing also became common in the Viking Age. The alphabet used was the 16-rune *futhark*, derived from the 24-rune Old Germanic futhark. Runic inscriptions have survived primarily on memorial stones (so-called runestones), but texts on preserved birch bark, wood, and wax indicate that literacy was relatively widespread. Latin script was introduced with Christianity but did not completely replace runic script, which continued in secular use into modern times.

Most of the literature pertaining to the Viking Age postdates it. Oral traditions of story-telling, "sagas," were an important aspect of the culture. Writing of the sagas began in the 11th century, and reached florescence in the 13th century when most of the so-called Icelandic sagas were written.

The ability to compose poetry was particularly admired. Court poets enjoyed special privileges. While prose was simple and close to spoken expressions, poetry was intricate, abounding in mythological references and elaborate metaphors. An important function of poetry was to produce a flattering picture of a king or chieftain. Among the best-known pieces of literature are the *Edda* and *Heimskringla* (compiled in the 13th century).

Religion

The Viking Age marks a transition from paganism to Christianity (Roman Catholicism). The pagan religion was polytheistic, the gods termed *aesir* and the goddesses *vanir*. The chief gods were Thor, Odin, and Frey. Thor was probably regarded as the most powerful god, but Odin was the god of the upper classes and warriors. Frey was the fertility god and brother of Freyja, goddess of fertility, war and an ancient deity in Norse society. Christianization was gradual and directly related to the expanding power of kings who used the introduction of the new religion as a tool to form even wider alliances. In Denmark, Norway, Iceland, and Greenland, Christianization was completed by the early 11th century, and later in Sweden. Following pagan tradition, chieftains and kings remained religious leaders, and the churches were owned by them. This entitled them to the tithes due the church, a powerful incentive for the introduction of the new religion.

The pagan elite were generally cremated and placed in burial mounds, stone rings, cairns, or stones aligned in the shape of a ship. Impressive mounds can be found at Borre in Norway and Jelling in Denmark. Norwegian ship burials include the large ships at Oseberg, built around 820, and the slightly later Gokstad and Tune ships.

Technology

The greatest technological achievement of the period was in ship construction. Although sailing ships had been developed already in the 8th century, it was not until the 9th century that large oceangoing sailing ships became relatively common. The ships were plank-built, mostly open, with a shallow keel. Excavated ship remains have shown that there were many specialized forms, including the oceangoing merchant *knarr*, coastal and river ships, warships, fishing boats and, for landing places, shallow prams and boats. The large ships, built by professional master boat builders, were costly, and only the elite could afford them. Navigation was by dead reckoning and the position of the sun and stars. Latitude could be determined, but not longitude.

Iron was produced both for domestic purposes and for trade. The raw material was bog or lake ore, which was smelted in small furnaces. Large production centers were located in forested areas in Norway, Sweden, and Finland.

Art

Professional artists produced spectacular wood carvings to decorate ships, furniture, wagons, sleds, saddles, and door frames. Art was valued by the elite as a means to impress others. A common motif is a highly stylized ribbonlike animal. Runestones were sometimes heavily decorated in this style, and occasionally the carver signed his name. Another art form, the so-called "picture" stones on the island of Gotland, consists of painted upright stones, often keyhole-shaped and depicting mythological scenes. Integral to the art motifs were symbolic meanings that could be understood by most people, and some may have been regarded as having magical powers.

BIRGITTA WALLACE

See also **Archaeology of the Arctic: Scandinavian Settlement of the North Atlantic; Eirík the Red; Norse and Icelandic Sagas**

Further Reading

Almgren, Bertil (editor), *The Viking*, New York: International Book Society, a division of Time-Life Books; translation of Swedish edition published by Tre Tryckare, 1964

Bigelow, Gerald F. (editor), "The Norse in the North Atlantic Conference." *Acta Archaeologica*, 61 (1990), Copenhagen: Munksgaard, 1991

Crumlin-Pedersen, Ole (editor), *Proceedings of the Nordic Seminar on Maritime Aspects of Archaeology,* Roskilde, March 13–15 1989, Roskilde: Viking Ship Museum, 1991

Fitzhugh, William W. & Elisabeth I. Ward, (editors), *Vikings: The North Atlantic Saga*, Washington, District of Columbia: The Smithsonian Institution, 2000

Foote, Peter G. & David M. Wilson, *The Viking Achievement: A Survey of the Society and Culture of Early Medieval Scandinavia,* New York: Praeger, 1970

Graham-Campbell, James, Colleen Batey, Helen Clarke, R.I. Page & Neil S. Price (editors), *Cultural Atlas of the Viking World*, Abingdon, Oxfordshire, England: Andromeda Oxford, and New York: Facts on File, 1994

Iversen, Tore, *Trelldommen. Norsk slaveri i middelalderen,* Historisk Institutt, University of Bergen, Skrifter 1, Bergen: University of Bergen, 1997

Jesch, Judith, *Women in the Viking Age*, Woodbridge: Boydell Press, 1991

Norwegian Archaeological Review, Oslo: University of Oslo, 1968

Pulsion, Phillip & Kirsten Wolf (editors), *Medieval Scandinavia. An Encyclopedia,* New York and London: Garland Publishing, 1993

Roesdahl Else & David M. Wilson (editors), *From Viking to Crusader. Scandinavia and Europe 800–1200*, translation from Danish, Norwegian, Swedish, and German by Helen Clarke, with additional translations by Joan F. Davidson, Gillian Fellows-Jensen, Ingemar Jansson, David Liversage, Clifford Long & Kirsten Williams, Copenhagen: Nordic Council of Ministers in collaboration with The Council of Europe, The 22nd Council of Europe Exhibition, 1992

Skre, Dagfinn, "Aristocratic dominion and landownership in Norway AD 200–1100." In *Settlement and Landscape*, edited by C. Fabech & J. Ringvedt, Proceedings of a Conference in Århus, Denmark, May 4–7, 1998, pp. 415–422

Steinsland, Gro, *Den hellige kongen*, Oslo: Pax forlag, 2000

VILKITSKII STRAIT

Vilkitskii Strait, one of the major navigation straits in the Arctic Ocean, is the main and southernmost connection between the Kara and Laptev seas on the Northern Sea Route in the Russian Arctic. Located along the northern coast of the Taymyr Peninsula, the 110 km (68 mi) strait separates Bolshevik Island of the Severnaya Zemlya islands from the Russian Arctic mainland. The northernmost point of the continent of Asia, Cape Chelyuskin, lies along the southern shore of Vilkitskii Strait at 77°43′ N and 104°15′ E. A lighthouse (wooden framework tower) stands 2.4 km (1.5 mi) southeast of Cape Chelyuskin. The narrowest width of the strait, between Cape Chelyuskin and the southern coast of Bolshevik Island, is 55 km (34 mi); the western entrance is 81 km (50 mi) wide and the eastern entrance in the Laptev Sea has a width of 90 km (56 mi). The prevailing depths in Vilkitskii Strait are 100–200 m (228–656 ft), and ships of any size and draft can make passage.

The strait is named after Captain Boris A. Vil'kitskii of the Imperial Russian Navy, expedition leader in 1913–1915 of the Arctic Ocean Hydrographic Expedition (1910–1915) and captain of the icebreaking survey ship *Taimyr* during the same period. On September 3, 1913, the expedition discovered a new group of islands north-northwest of Cape Chelyuskin, which was named Emperor Nicholas II Land (now Severnaya Zemlya). Earlier, Nordenskiöld's *Vega* became the first ship to anchor off Cape Chelyuskin on August 19, 1878 and to subsequently transit (west to east) Vilkitskii Strait during the first through voyage of the Northern Sea Route (1878–1879). The polar ship *Fram* sailed along the southern coast of Vilkitskii Strait on September 10, 1893 en route the Laptev Sea to commence Fridtjof Nansen's Arctic Ocean drift. The first east to west through passage of the Northern Sea Route also included transit of Vilkitskii Strait: the *Taimyr* and *Vaigach* under Captain Vil'kitskii made passage in September 1914 only to winter over along the western shore of the Taymyr Peninsula. During World War II, the German armed merchant cruiser *Komet* completed a voyage from the Barents Sea to Bering Strait and transited Vilkitskii Strait on August 26, 1941. Since the USSR buildup of the Northern Sea Route during the 1960s, Vilkitskii Strait has been the principal link between eastern and western regions of the Russian maritime Arctic. Compulsory icebreaker escort and pilotage within the strait are mandated by navigation regulations.

The high-latitude position and approximate east-west orientation of Vilkitskii Strait are conducive to the presence of extensive sea ice. Landfast ice along the Taymyr coastline and around Severnaya Zemlya can be present until August. Regional clusters of multiyear ice in the northeast Kara Sea and western Laptev Sea (designated the North Kara and Taymyr summer ice massifs) can project south from the central Arctic Ocean and clog both approaches to the strait. Westerly winds can create very difficult ice conditions for ship transit in the western approaches. Consequently, there are a few days each year when Vilkitskii Strait is completely ice-free. A two-way flow of surface currents has been observed in the strait: a main eastward current in the southern half of the strait and a westward flow along the north shore. Regional winds can influence both surface flows and local ice conditions.

Past Soviet decrees on historic waters, the establishment of straight baselines (embracing the approaches), and Law of the Sea rights accorded to coastal Arctic states have led Russia to declare the legal status of Vilkitskii Strait as internal waters. Thus, complete Russian sovereignty is asserted. This position remains a contentious issue with the United States, which maintains that the ice-covered straits in the region are international and subject to the right of transit passage by ship.

LAWSON W. BRIGHAM

See also **Northern Sea Route**

Further Reading

Brigham, Lawson W. (editor), *The Soviet Maritime Arctic*, London: Belhaven Press, 1991

Ostreng, Willy (editor), *The Natural and Societal Challenges of the Northern Sea Route: A Reference Work*, Dordrecht, The Netherlands: Kluwer Academic Publishers, 1999

Starokadomskiy, L.M., *Charting the Russian Northern Sea Route: The Arctic Ocean Hydrographic Expedition 1910–1915,* translated and edited by W. Barr, Montreal: Arctic Institute of North America and McGill-Queen's University Press, 1976

Vaughan, Richard, *The Arctic: A History*, Phoenix Mill, UK: Alan Sutton, 1994

VIL'KITSKII, BORIS ANDREEVICH

In the closing years of the czarist regime in Russia, the Russian Navy, through its Chief Hydrographic Directorate, mounted a serious attempt at surveying the Northern Sea Route along the Arctic coast of Russia. For this purpose, two identical, small steel-hulled icebreakers were launched in the autumn of 1909 in St Petersburg. Named *Taimyr* and *Vaigach,* they sailed from St Petersburg on November 10, 1909 and reached Vladivostok on July 16, 1910. From 1910 to 1913, voyages of the Arctic Ocean Hydrographical Expedition carried out surveys further and further west (*see* **Arctic Ocean Hydrographical Expedition, 1909–1915**).

The head of the Chief Hydrographic Directorate, Andrei Ippolitovich Vil'kitskii, was instrumental in the planning of the surveys. His son, Boris Andreevich Vil'kitskii, was a naval graduate of the Hydrographic Department. From its inception, he had wanted to participate in the expedition, but his father, anxious to avoid any hint of nepotism, had opposed any such appointment. But in 1913, he was appointed to the expedition after his father's death with impressive results.

At the start of the 1913 season, Captain Ivan S. Sergeyev was in overall command, but two newcomers commanded the two ships: Captain P.A. Novopashennyi was in charge of *Vaigach* and Captain Boris Andreevich Vil'kitskii was in charge of *Taimyr.* The two ships sailed from Vladivostok on July 9, 1913 and by July 20, were at Bukhta Provideniya, coaling from a collier. During this operation, Sergeyev suffered a stroke; he was evacuated south and Vil'kitskii assumed command of the expedition. On this occasion, *Taimyr* assumed a more northerly course than previously and on August 20 northeast of Novaya Sibir', the vessel encountered a small, rocky island, which was named Ostrov Vil'kitskogo (Vilkitsky Island). A landing was made and the Russian flag was hoisted. The next morning, *Taimyr* lay off Bennett Island, but rough seas precluded a landing. After the two ships had made a rendezvous off Ostrov Preobrazheniya, they headed north along the east coast of the Taymyr Peninsula. To their disappointment, right at Cape Chelyuskin they found an unbroken field of heavy ice, its edge running away to the northeast. Following it north in the hopes of finding a route west farther north, on September 2, they sighted a low island, initially named Ostrov Tsesarevicha Alekseia (now Ostrov Malyi Taimyr).

The next morning, they sighted a high mountainous coast; they followed it northward, although a belt of fast ice kept them some distance offshore and hence they were unable to determine whether it was a single landmass with some deep inlets, or an archipelago with several straits running through it. The latter is in fact the case. On September 4, a landing was made at a headland named Mys Berga; the Russian flag was raised, a gun salute was fired, and Vil'kitskii read a proclamation claiming the new land for the Czar. Initially named Zemlia Imperatora Nikolaia II, it was subsequently renamed Severnaya Zemlya (North Land). Pushing on north, the two ships were finally blocked at the cape later named Mys Arkticheskii, and in fact the northern tip of the archipelago. Returning south, they still found ice blocking access to the south coast of the archipelago. Landings were made on Ostrov Tsesarevicha Alekseia and at Cape Chelyuskin, the northernmost point of Eurasia, where a cairn was built, and another small island (Ostrov Starokadomskogo) was discovered. On the way back east, a landing was made on Bennett Island. By November 25, the two ships were back at Vladivostok.

For the 1914 season, the two icebreakers were ordered to complete the through passage to Arkhangel'sk. They sailed from Vladivostok on June 7, but there were several delays before they got down to their main task. Among other things, they spent some time trying unsuccessfully to get through the ice to rescue the survivors of Vilhjalmur Stefansson's expedition aboard *Karluk*, marooned on Wrangel Island. *Vaigach* even lost a propeller blade and suffered some hull damage in these attempts.

By September 2, both ships were back at Cape Chelyuskin; that year, the strait between the mainland and Zemlya Imperatora Nikolaia (later named Proliv Vil'kitskogo) was largely free of ice, and they easily cruised along the north shore of the strait. But once in the Kara Sea, they encountered heavy ice; both ships were nipped and suffered some damage. Finally, by September 24, 1914, they were firmly beset and started a wintering in the ice off Bukhta Dika on the west coast of the Taymyr Peninsula. It was some consolation that they made radio contact with *Eclipse*, which, under the command of the veteran Arctic captain Otto Sverdrup, had been sent north in search of three missing Russian expeditions and was wintering in the Kara Sea some 275 km southwest of the Russian ships. *Eclipse* played a vital role in acting as a radio relay station passing messages to *Taimyr* and *Vaigach* from St Petersburg and vice versa.

In case the ice did not break up in the summer of 1915, it was decided to evacuate half of the crews of *Taimyr* and *Vaigach* first to *Eclipse*, escorted by Sverdrup and his men, and then by a reindeer caravan, organized from St Petersburg, overland to Gol'chikha on the Yenisey. This operation was executed successfully in July-August 1915. In the event it was not needed. The two icebreakers got under way without much difficulty in early August. They reached Arkhangel'sk on September 16, 1915, only the second expedition to complete the transit of the North East Passage.

The results of the expedition's work were substantial. In terms of geographical exploration, they had discovered Severnaya Zemlya, the last major landmass to be discovered on the Earth's surface, as well as smaller islands such as Malyi Taimyr, Strarokadomskogo, and Vil'kitskogo. On the basis of their surveys, charts and pilots were produced for the entire Siberian coast and the outlying islands from Bering Strait to Cape Chelyuskin. In addition, very valuable data had been collected in the areas of oceanography, sea ice distribution, botany, and zoology.

Immediately after the Revolution, the Soviet government planned a rather ambitious Arctic Ocean Hydrographic Expedition into the Kara Sea; Vil'kitskii was to be in overall command. But with the British-French-Canadian-American Intervention at Arkhangel'sk, these plans came to naught. However, Vil'kitskii did take command of a much more limited expedition, which the White Russian government and the Interventionists dispatched aboard *Taimyr* and *Vaigach* to the Kara Sea in 1918. Its aims included the establishment of a radio station at Dikson, whereby the White government at Arkhangel'sk might maintain contact with Kolchak's government at Omsk. Then in 1919, Vil'kitskii commanded a more ambitious Kara Sea expedition, aimed at transporting military supplies and personnel to Omsk, and bringing a return cargo of grain from the Ob' estuary. Vil'kitskii commanded *Taimyr*, which escorted four freighters to Nakhodka on the Ob' estuary and back.

Biography

Boris Andreevich Vil'kitskii was born on March 22 (April 3), 1886 at Pulkovo, the son of Andrei Ippolitovich Vil'kitskii, head of the Chief Hydrographic Directorate of the Imperial Russian Navy. Graduating from the Naval College in 1903, he served initially with the First Pacific Ocean Squadron, based at Port Arthur. He was severely wounded during the siege of Port Arthur in the Russo-Japanese War in 1905 and received several decorations for valor. He graduated from the Hydrographic Department of the Naval Academy, and thereafter served with the Baltic Fleet.

After his Arctic Ocean Hydrographic Expedition voyages, early in 1920, Vil'kitskii, along with many other White officers, emigrated to London. This did not end his Arctic activities, however. In both 1923 and 1924, at the request of Sovkomneshtorg, and working for Arkos, he led two convoys of ships from London to the Kara Sea and back, sailing aboard *Rusanov* in the first case, and aboard *Malygin* in the second.

Vil'kitskii made his home in Brussels and worked for many years as a hydrographer in the Belgian Congo. He died in Brussels on March 6, 1961 at the age of 75. Ostrov Vil'kitskogo and Proliv Vil'kitskogo, separating Severnaya Zemlya from the mainland, are named after him.

WILLIAM BARR

See also **Arctic Ocean Hydrographical Expedition, 1909–1915; Severnaya Zemlya**

Further Reading

Arngol'd, E.E., *Po zavetnomu puti* [Along the long-sought route], Moscow, 1929

Barr, William, "A Tsarist attempt at opening up the Northern Sea Route: the Arctic Ocean Hydrographic Expedition 1910–1915." *Polarforschung*, 45(1), (1975): 51–64

———, "The Arctic Ocean Hydrographic Expedition 1910–1915: an overview." *Polar Geography and Geology*, 9(4), (1985): 257–271

Evgenov, N.I. & V.N. Kupetskii, "Russkii poliarnyi issledovatel' B.A. Vil'kitskii." *Letopis' Severa*, 4 (1964): 223–228

———, *Nauchnie rez'ultaty poliarnoi ekspeditsii na ledokolakh "Taimyr" i "Vaigach" v 1910–1915 godakh* [Scientific results of the polar expedition on board the icebreakers "Taimyr" and "Vaigach" in 1910–1915], Leningrad: Izdatel'stvo "Nauka", 1985

Kuskin, I.E., "The Arctic Ocean Hydrographic Expedition, 1910–1915." *Polar Geography and Geology*, 15(4) (1991): 299–309

Pinkhenson, D.M., *Problema Severnogo morskogo puti v epokhu kapitalizma. Istoriya otkrytiia i osvyeniia Severnogo mosrskogo puti*, II [The problem of the Northern Sea Route during the capitalist era. The history of the discovery and exploitation of the Northern Sea Route, II], Leningrad: Izdatel'stvo "Morskoi Transport, 1962

Starokadomskii, Leonid Mikhailovich, *Charting the Russian Northern Sea Route: The Arctic Ocean Hydrographic Expedition 1910–1915*, translated and edited by W. Barr, Montreal: McGill-Queen's University Press, 1976

VINLAND

Vinland was an area of North America explored by the Greenland Norse, sometimes in partnership with Icelandic traders. Oral traditions of their exploits were written down in Iceland in the late 13th century. Two major accounts exist: *Saga of Eirík the Red* and the *Saga of the Greenlanders*. There are also a few fragments in other sagas. The documents are commonly referred to as the *Vinland Sagas* and known throughout history in the Scandinavian area. The texts became accessible to the rest of the western world in 1837 when they were published in Latin, and subsequently in English, French, and German. Their publication stirred a lively interest, especially in North America, and speculations began as to the location of Vinland.

According to *Saga of the Greenlanders*, the coasts of North America were first sighted by an Icelandic trader, Bjarni, son of Herjolf, when blown off course between Iceland and southwestern Greenland. Bjarni observed three distinct regions, all with their specific attributes, the northernmost of them located on the latitude of southern Greenland. Leif Eriksson, son of Eirík the Red, in Greenland later explored these areas. Although the historical record remains unclear, scholars believe that Eriksson, in conjunction with other Greenlanders, named the three regions, thus claiming control over them. From north to south, they were Helluland (Land of Flat Rocks), Markland (Land of

Forests), and Vinland (Land of Wine). Eriksson explored Vinland, where he found wild grapes, and established a base, *Leifsbudir* (or Leif's Camp). The *Saga of the Greenlanders* describes four subsequent expeditions, all headed by members of Eriksson's family: Thorvald, who was killed in an encounter with Aboriginal people; Thorsten and his wife Gudrid, who never reached Vinland; the Icelander Thorfinn Karlsefni in partnership with two other Icelanders; and finally Eriksson's sister Freydis in partnership with an Icelandic trader.

In the *Saga of Eirík the Red*, the five expeditions were reduced to two. Bjarni was not mentioned, and Eriksson replaced him as the accidental discoverer. The four successful expeditions were combined into one mega-expedition led by Thorfinn Karlsefni. Vinland has two rather than one base. *Straumfjord* (Fjord of Currents) is described as a year-round base in the northern part of Vinland, and *Hóp* (Tidal Lagoon) is a temporary summer camp in the southern part. The text described grapes that grew at Hóp and vines attached to large trees, but not at *Straumfjord*. At Hóp, large numbers of Aboriginal people were recorded with deadly battles ensuing. In contrast, no native inhabitants were recorded at Straumfjord.

Icelandic research on sagas has shown that the *Saga of Eirík the Red* was compiled in order to honor a direct descendant of Thorfinn Karlsefni and Gudrid, and was written down by another, later descendant. The role of Thorfinn Karlsefni and Gudrid has therefore been magnified to suit the occasion, but at the same time the saga provides richer details of the bases. Leif's Camp in the *Saga of the Greenlanders* appears as a conflation of Straumfjord and Hóp.

Suggestions as to the location of Vinland have ranged in locales from Virginia in the southern United States to Newfoundland in the north. Many accounts have focused on New England because it was believed that this area formed the northern limit of land suitable for grape growing. The archaeological findings at L'Anse aux Meadows at the northern tip of Newfoundland's Northern Peninsula indicate that Vinland comprised the coasts surrounding the Gulf of St Lawrence. L'Anse aux Meadows corresponds in all aspects to Straumfjord of the *Saga of Eirík the Red*. Like Straumfjord, it was a large, year-round base, from where the occupants sought areas farther south where grapes grew wild. The evidence points to eastern New Brunswick, which is the northern geographical limit for wild grapes in North America, an area that also has the tidal lagoons of Hóp and, at the time of the Norse, had perhaps the largest Aboriginal population in Atlantic Canada, the ancestors of the Mi'kmaq.

From the documentary evidence, it is clear that the incentive for the Vinland voyages was exploration for resources not present in Greenland. Colonization was not a motive, as pastures were plentiful in Greenland, and its small population could not support further splintering. The voyages were soon abandoned as the costs outweighed the profits. It was farther to New Brunswick than to Norway and Europe, and whatever could be obtained in Vinland could equally well be purchased in Europe, along with many other necessities not present in Vinland, such as various metals, spices, exotic textiles, glass, and jewelry. Vinland also lacked the social and family connections present in Europe.

The Norse and the Aboriginal People

The *Vinland Sagas* describe encounters between the Norse and Aboriginal people, whom the Norse termed *Skrælings*, not only at Hóp but also in Markland, the area north of Vinland. The people who inhabited Markland at the time would have been the ancestors of the Innu, and possibly Dorset Eskimos. Encounters in Vinland, although peaceful at times, disintegrated into violence.

Other Norse Finds in North America

In addition to L'Anse aux Meadows, a number of sites, artifacts, and inscriptions in locations ranging from New England in the east to Minnesota in the west and Oklahoma in the south have been alleged to be Norse. All these finds have other explanations. Genuine Norse finds have been found on Thule Inuit sites in the Arctic. A wide assemblage consisting of over a hundred 13th-century objects such as chain-mail, boat nails, an oak box, woolen cloth, a small sculpture, and a carpenter's plane were excavated from 1977 to 1995 at a Thule site from the same period on Skraeling Island off the east coast of Ellesmere Island. A fragment of a bronze balance found on another Thule Inuit site on the western coast of Ellesmere may ultimately have come from the same site. A small, extant Thule Inuit carving from Baffin Island portrays a Norseman in a 13th-century cloak. In addition, a few iron and copper alloy fragments remain, scattered widely on Aboriginal sites all over the eastern Arctic. The extent of contact they represent remains unclear. A late 11th-century Norwegian coin Blue Hill in Maine on Penobscot Bay probably reached its destinations via Aboriginal trade routes from northern Labrador.

BIRGITTA WALLACE

See also **Eirík the Red; Eriksson, Leif; Norse and Icelandic Sagas; Vikings**

Further Reading

Ashe, Geoffrey (editor), *The Quest for America*, London: Pall Mall Press; New York: Praeger, 1971

Bergersen, Robert, *Vinland Bibliography. Writings Relating to the Norse in Greenland and America*, compiled and annotated by Robert Bergersen, University Library "Ravnetryk" 10, Tromsø: University of Tromsø, 1997

Bigelow, Gerald F. (editor), "The Norse in the North Atlantic Conference." *Acta Archaeologica*, 61 (1990): 166–197, Copenhagen: Munksgaard, 1991

Fitzhugh, William W. & Elisabeth I. Ward (editors), *Vikings: The North Atlantic Saga*, Washington, Distrtict of Columbia: The Smithsonian Institution, 2000

Halldórsson, Ólafur, *Grænland í miðaldaritum*, Reykjavik: Sögufélag, 1978

Ingstad, Anne Stine & Helge Ingstad, *The Norse Discovery of America*, Volumes I and II; Volume I: *Excavations at L'Anse aux Meadows, Newfoundland 1961–1968*; Volume II: *The Historical Background and the Evidence of the Norse Settlement Discovered in Newfoundland*, Oslo: Oslo University Press, 1986

Jones, Gwyn, *The Norse Atlantic Saga, Being the Norse Voyages of Discovery and Settlement to Iceland, Greenland, and North America*, a new and enlarged edition, Oxford and New York: Oxford University Press, 1996

McGhee, Robert, "Contact between native North Americans and the Medieval Norse: a review of the evidence." *American Antiquity*, 49(1) (January 1984): 4–26; *Journal of the Society for American Archaeology*, 1984

McGovern, Thomas H., "The Vinland Adventure: A North American Perspective." *North American Archaeologist*, Volume 2, No. 4, Farmingdale, New York: Baywood Publishing, 1980–1981, pp. 285–308

Schledermann, Peter, *Voices in Stone. A Personal Journey into the Arctic Past*, Calgary: The Arctic Institute of North America of the University of Calgary, 1996

Sigurðsson Ingi & Jón Skaptason (editors), "The Norse in the North Atlantic: The L'Anse aux Meadows Settlement in Newfoundland." In *Proceedings, The International Congress on the History of the Arctic and Sub-Arctic Region*, June 18–21, 1998, Reykjavík: University of Iceland Press in co-operation with the Institute of History, University of Iceland, the Ministry for Foreign Affairs and External Trade of Iceland and the Stefansson Arctic Institute, 2001, pp. 486–500

VIZE, VLADIMIR

Vladimir Iul'evich Vize is unique as a scientist who participated in Arctic expeditions under both the czarist and Soviet regimes. His first northern experience came in 1911 when he was involved in an expedition to the Kola Peninsula (Kol'skyi Poluostrov), where he collected ethnographic materials and especially Saami folklore. In 1912–1914, he participated as a geographer in Georgiy Sedov's ill-fated North Pole expedition aboard the *Sv Foka*. Along with geologist M.A. Pavlov, Vize made a trip across the north island of Novaya Zemlya by dogsled in the spring of 1913. He also coordinated weather observation programs at the expedition's wintering sites at Pankrat'eva Peninsula on Novaya Zemlya and at Tikhaya Bukhta (Quiet Bay) on Franz Josef Land.

In 1921, Vize made the first of many cruises as a Soviet scientist. Aboard the icebreaker *Taimyr*, he surveyed the coast and inshore waters of Baydaratskaia Guba (west of Pol. Iamal) and the east coast of Novaya Zemlya from Cape Zhelaniia south to Zaliv Blagopoluchiia. His next expedition was aboard the icebreaker *Malygin*, which in the summer of 1924 was assigned to support the Kara Sea Expedition, that is, freighters bound to and from the mouths of the Ob' and Yenisey rivers. Vize conducted oceanographic investigations while *Malygin* patrolled the ice edge as the freighters made the round-trip across the Kara Sea further south.

In 1928, Vize went north as the expedition leader for the first time, again on board *Malygin*. Along with the icebreaker *Krasin*, *Malygin* attempted to rescue the Italian expedition of Umberto Nobile from its camp on the ice to the east of Svalbard where they had taken refuge after the crash of the dirigible *Italia*. Despite difficult ice conditions, *Malygin* pushed north to the east of Svalbard, reaching the latitude of Kong Karls Land. If *Krasin* had not rescued the survivors from Nobile's camp, either *Malygin,* or the aircraft that it carried, would have reached the camp shortly afterward. As always, Vize was conducting oceanographic investigations throughout the cruise.

In 1929, Vize found himself in the familiar surroundings of Franz Josef Land, as the deputy leader of a Soviet expedition that established the first Soviet High Arctic weather station at Quiet Bay, in part to counter Norwegian claims to the archipelago. The expedition vessel *Georgy Sedov* also established a record high latitude of 82°14′ N to the north of the archipelago. At the start of the 1930 season, as chief scientist, Vize was back on Franz Josef Land again, this time on board *Georgy Sedov*. The expedition resupplied the weather station at Quiet Bay, and then headed east across the Kara Sea to land a small party led by Georgiy Alekseevichy Ushakov intended to explore and map Severnaya Zemlya. En route, the expedition discovered what would be named Vize Island, whose existence Vize had predicted on the basis of ice-drift studies. After landing Ushakov and his party on Domashnyi Island off the west coast of the Northern Land, *Sedov* pushed north and discovered the ice-capped island of Shmidta.

The 1931 season found Vize back on Franz Josef Land, this time on board *Malygin*, and leader of a rather unusual enterprise that was both a tourist cruise and a scientific expedition. *Malygin* had been chartered by Inturist and visited a number of historic sites in the archipelago. At Quiet Bay, the ship made rendezvous with the dirigible *Graf Zeppelin*, in part for an exchange of mail for the benefit of philatelists. After a swing east into the Kara Sea, *Malygin* returned to the Barents Sea by the spectacular Strait of Matochkin Shar that divides the islands of Novaya Zemlya.

In the summer of 1932, Vize was the chief scientist on board the icebreaker *Sibiryakov* during its attempt at the first one-season transit of the Northern Sea Route. Within sight of Cape Serdtse-Kamen', near the Bering Strait, the ship lost its propeller in heavy ice. The captain, using improvised sails made from tarpaulins and lifeboat sails, managed to sail his steel steamer out of the ice to where a waiting trawler took it in tow. Vize returned north again in 1933, this time in charge of the scientific programs on board *Sibiryakov*, but with the less ambitious objective of resupplying the weather station on Cape Chelyuskina. The trip was nevertheless challenged by heavy ice and the expedition explored several island groups, including the Arkticheskogo Instituta Islands in the Kara Sea.

In the light of the outcome of *Sibiryakov*'s voyage in 1932 and the even less successful results of *Chelyuskin*'s voyage in 1933–1934, in the summer of 1934 a further attempt was made to complete a one-season transit of the Northern Sea Route. Vize served as the head scientist on the icebreaker *Fedor Litke,* the chosen vessel. *Litke* completed the passage in one season, from Vladivostok to Murmansk, but sustained damage to its bows from colliding with solid ice to free the ships of the First Lena Expedition that had wintered off the east coast of the Taymyr Peninsula. The expedition reached Murmansk and Leningrad safely on September 20, and October 7, respectively. Vize performed his usual oceanographic and meteorological work along the way.

For the first time in six seasons, in 1935 Vize did not go north, but in 1936 he served as deputy head of the scientific group on board the *Sadko* on what was called the Second High Latitude Expedition. The plan was to establish a weather station on one of the De Longa Islands, and then to push north from there to occupy an oceanographic station in the central Arctic Basin. The expedition was eventually aborted after being diverted by rescuing several ships, including the *Yermak*, the *Litke*, and the *Rusanov,* from dangerous ice.

In 1937, *Sadko* was again dispatched to the Laptev Sea to carry out the aborted plan of 1936, with Vize leading the scientific party. *Sadko* reached Genrietty Island, where the crew established a weather station. Thereafter, *Sadko* visited the Zhannetty, Zhokhova, and Bennetta islands; it was the first Soviet vessel to visit any of the De Long Islands group. By September 13, *Sadko* was bunkering at Tiksi. Thereafter, it was called upon to assist various vessels in navigating dangerously heavy ice in the Vilkitski Strait. Since there would be little opportunity for scientific work, Vize and seven other scientists transferred to the freighter *Belomorkanal*, which was eastbound for Bering Strait, encountering no ice and reaching Vladivostok safely on October 21, 1937. This was Vize's final Arctic voyage.

Biography

Vladimir Iul'evich Vize was born on February 21, (March 5), 1886 at Tsarskoye Selo (now Pushkin), Russia. After leaving school, he moved to Germany and studied at the Göttingen University and Halle University, returning to St Petersburg in 1910 to continue his studies of meteorology and oceanography. In 1918, he joined the staff of the Chief Geophysical Observatory, initially as an adjunct and then as a full-time staff member working on geophysics and oceanography. In 1921, Vize moved to the Chief Hydrographic Administration and in 1922 to the Central Administration of Marine Transport and the Hydrological Institute, as a meteorologist and hydrologist.

In 1928, Vize became senior hydrologist at the Institute for the Study of the North, and in 1930, when that institute became the Arctic Research Institute, he was appointed deputy director, a post that he held for much of his subsequent career. He became a corresponding member of the Academy of Sciences in 1933, and a professor at Leningrad State University in 1945. He died in Leningrad on February 19, 1954. Apart from his vast research on Arctic meteorology, oceanography, and ice forecasting, he was also one of the leading Soviet Arctic historians. Vize was awarded the State Prize of the USSR in 1946, two Orders of Lenin, and the Order of the Red Banner of Labor. Vize Island in the Kara Sea, Cape Vize in northwestern Novaya Zemlya, and Cape Vize near the Soviet station of Mirnyy in Antarctica are named after him.

WILLIAM BARR

See also **Sedov, Georgiy Yakovlevich**

Further Reading

Barr, William, "Sedov's expedition to the North Pole 1912–1914." *Canadian Slavonic Papers*, 15(4) (1973):499–524
———, "The Soviet contribution to the *Italia* search and rescue, 1928." *Polar Record,* 18(117) (1977): 561–574
———, "The first tourist cruise to the Soviet Arctic." *Arctic*, 33(4), (1980):671–685
———, "The voyage of *Sibiryakov*, 1932." *Polar Record*, 19(120) (1978):253–266
Belov, M.I., *Sovetskoe arkticheskoe moreplavanie 1917–1932 gg. Istoriia otkrytia I osvoeniia Severnogo Morskogo Puti*, III [Soviet Arctic navigation 1917–1932. The history of the discovery and exploitation of the Northern Sea Route, III], Leningrad: Izdatel'stvo "Morskoi Transport", 1959
———, *Nauchnoe i khoziaystvennoe osvoenie Sovetskogo Severa 1933–1945. Istoriia otkrytiia i osvoeniia Severnogo Morskogo Puti, IV* [Scientific and economic development of the Soviet North 1933–1945. The history of the discovery and exploitation of the Northern Sea Route IV], Leningrad: Gidrometeorologicheskoe Izdatel'stvo, 1969
Vize, Vladimir Iu., *Na "Sibiriakove" i "Litke" cherez ledovitie moria* [Aboard *Sibiriakov* and *Litke* in icy seas], Moscow/Leningrad: Izdatel'stvo Glavsevmorputi, 1946
———, *Morya Sovetskoi Arktiki* [Seas of the Soviet Arctic], Moscow/Leningrad: Izdatel'stvo Glavsevmorputi, 1948

VLAMINGH, WILLEM DE

A Dutch naval officer, Willem de Vlamingh was born in 1640 on a small Frisian island in the Netherlands called Vlieland. Similar to many inhabitants of Vlieland, de Vlamingh began a career at sea at an early age. In the beginning, he sailed on a whaling ship to the north but soon after undertook voyages of discovery, searching for the North East Passage. In 1664, at the age of 24 years, de Vlamingh sailed along the west coast of Novaya Zemlya, off the coast of Russia in the Arctic Ocean, to the north. He rounded the north cape of the island and continued his voyage in the Kara Sea on the east side of Novaya Zemlya in an east-south-east direction till 74° N, when he saw the coast of Tartarije. According to Nicolaes Witsen (1705), de Vlamingh called the land of this coast Jelmerland. The area was drawn for the first time as the coast of the continent on the chart of Asia, which was published by Witsen in 1687, stating that "Jelmerland [was] discovered by master Willem De Vlamingh on August 4, 1664." De Vlamingh convinced his principal, Jacob Jelmersz Cock from Amsterdam, that he had discovered the North East Passage. Cock decided to ask the Netherlands States-General for a charter to sail to China and Japan along this route. When he did not receive an answer quickly enough, Cock turned to the King of Denmark, who considered himself to be the ruler of the polar area, and asked and received a charter to sail into the North East Passage.

Until 1688, de Vlamingh sailed to the north to catch whales, walrus, and seals almost every year. Amsterdam merchants fitted a fleet of three galliots (long, narrow Dutch merchant sailing ships) to catch whales and walrus as well as to discover unknown northern countries in 1668. De Vlamingh was chosen to command this small fleet, and because there was a supercargo on board one of the ships, the goal of this expedition must have been also to establish new trade contacts. The results of de Vlamingh's voyage were most likely disappointing.

In 1677, his ship—*De hoop op de Walvisch*—was captured by a French man-of-war and a ransom was paid to free it. In 1688, on de Vlamingh's last voyage to the Polar seas, he hired some Norwegian farmers in Massø on Magerøya Island off the coast of Norway to sail with him to Novaya Zemlya to catch whales. After the campaign, the farmers returned home safely and, according to documentary sources, they were well paid.

From 1688 onward, de Vlamingh sailed several times to Batavia in Dutch East India, and in 1696–1697 he commanded the last Dutch Southland expedition with three ships. This expedition made him the first person to land on Amsterdam Island and St Paul in the Indian Ocean. Later, on this same trip, he explored the west coast of Australia. On February 3, 1698, de Vlamingh departed from Batavia and on April 17, of the same year he arrived in Cape Town, South Africa. The most recent information that historians have compiled about de Vlamingh is that he left Cape Town on May 8, 1698 to sail home to the Netherlands. It is assumed that he died some time shortly after that date, perhaps on his journey homeward.

Biography

Willem de Vlamingh was born on November 28, 1640 on Vlieland, in the West Frisian Islands of the Netherlands, the son of Hessel Dircksz and Trijn Cornelis. He was educated as a seaman and sailed as a whaling commander to the Spitsbergen and Novaya Zemlya islands. In 1668, he married Willempje Cornelis from Amsterdam. In 1664, he searched for the North East Passage and observed the coast of Tartarije. He commanded the Dutch Southland expedition in 1696–1697. Willem de Vlamingh died sometime in or soon after 1698.

LOUWRENS HACQUEBORD

See also **North East Passage, Exploration of**

Further Reading

Jong, C. de, *Geschiedenis van de oude Nederlandse Walvisvaart*, Deel 2, Bloei en achteruitgang 1642–1872, Johannesburg, South Africa, 1978

Schilder, G.G., *De ontdekkingsreis van Willem de Vlamingh in de jaren 1696–1697*, Deel 1, Werken uitgegeven door de Linschoten-vereeniging, Deel LXXVIII, Martinus Nijhoff, 's Gravenhage, 1976

Vlamingh, Willem de, *Gedachtenisse der voornemelykste bevindingen int vergat de Geelvink door mij Willem de Vlamingh, gedestineert naer Zuijtlant en vooreerst de eijlanden Tristant de Conha, St. Pouwel en Amsterdam aen te doen, God verleent ons geluck en behoude rijs*, National Archive, The Hague (logbook written by Willem de Vlamingh on board the *Geelvinck*, May 3, 1696 to March 20, 1697), 1697

VOLCANOES AND VOLCANIC ACTIVITY

Where molten rock (magma) ascends from the Earth's interior to the surface, magmatic gases become separated from the magma and the molten rock solidifies as different types of eruptives, including lava. The eruptive channel, or volcano, is always a crack or a fissure. Repeated eruptions in a confined area lead to the formation of a large mountain. Such volcanic centers may develop into high, cone-shaped stratovolcanoes or they may become broad and gently sloping composite shield volcanoes. In some cases, a circular depression forms at the summit of the volcano following exhaustion of the subterranean magma source. In other instances, a deep depression forms during highly explosive eruptions in a volcano. Generally, such subsidence forms are termed calderas.

Evidence of Arctic volcanic activity in the period after the last glacial period of the Ice Age (Pleistocene), during the past 10,000 years (Holocene), is linked to plate margins or in hot spots above mantle plumes. Plate margins and hot spots may converge. At subduction zones, two tectonic plates collide and one of them sinks. Continental volcanism occurs at these convergent margins, characterized by stratovolcanoes, highly developed, often acid (silicic) magmas, and explosive eruptions. In the Arctic, this type of volcanic activity is currently found in the Alaska Peninsula and Aleutian Islands, onward to the Kamchatka region. At divergent plate margins (rift zones), two tectonic plates part. Within oceanic crust they form mid-oceanic ridges, but are also found inland (e.g., in eastern Africa). Oceanic volcanism is characterized by volcanic fissures and calderas, primitive, basaltic magmas, and primarily effusive activity. In the Arctic, this type of volcanic activity occurs on the submarine part of the Mid-Atlantic Ridge and in Iceland. Hot spot activity in the Arctic is found, for example, in Iceland (where a rift system and a hot spot are superimposed) and on Jan Mayen Island to the north of Iceland, where it causes off-rift activity, partly similar to continental volcanism. Off-rift activity is also found in Iceland, in three lateral zones, in addition to the main oceanic, rift-type activity.

Volcanic eruptions occur when excess magma pressure at depth is high enough to force magma through an existing tectonic fissure or fault, or to form a fissure on its own. Magma contains gases, which expand as the hot magma ascends, promoting the eruption process. In the volcanic vent, degasing causes the magma to boil rather quietly, spurt, or erupt violently, depending on the gas content, pressure, and the local conditions. Volcanic gases escape from the vent and the eruptive material is ejected as lava—flowing on the ground or piling up—and tephra—flying as loose material through the air or forming a pyroclastic flow within a hot cloud of ash. The magma temperature, magma type (chemical/mineral content), and the conditions at the vent, for example, presence of water, influence whether effusive eruptions (predominantly

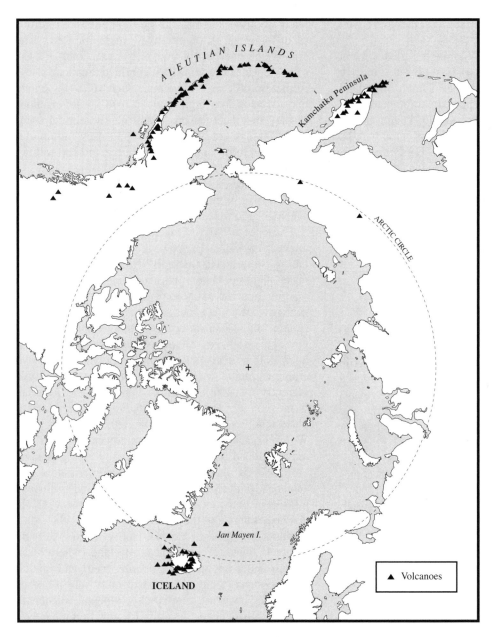

Distribution of volcanoes within the Arctic and Subarctic.

lava but very little tephra) or explosive eruptions (tephra is produced but little or no lava) are dominant.

Volcanic activity in glaciated areas has characteristic features. Eruptives cannot flow freely from an eruptive vent 100–2000 m beneath glacier ice. Instead, eruptives pile up in a confined space within the ice. Meltwater floods (*see* **Jökulhlaups**) accompany such eruptions. High external pressure (from meltwater and ice) and rapid cooling of the magma beneath ice cause lava to form rounded pillow lava at first, usually with a glassy crust at the water-chilled margin. Finally, decreasing pressure and flash boiling of water may induce a different eruption phase. The eruption gradually changes into a tephra-producing, phreatic (or steam-driven) eruption

as the eruption penetrates the ice. Glassy tephra covers the underlying pillow and breccia formation. The eruptive vent may become isolated from meltwater and emit lava, which caps the volcano. Water and heat alter the tephra glass, and cement the grains together by forming new mineral deposits in the loose mass. It becomes compact and the tephra changes color. Tephra and breccia from eruptions in water are termed hyaloclastites.

Russian Far East

Kamchatka Peninsula in the Russian Far East is one of the most active volcanic regions along the Pacific Rim,

Shishaldin Volcano, one of many active volcanoes in the Aleutian Chain, Unimak Island, Aleutian Islands, Alaska. It is claimed to be one of the three perfect cones in the world.
Copyright Joseph Baylor Roberts/National Geographic Image Collection

where the Pacific plate subducts beneath the continental margin, forming the Kamchatsko-Kuril volcanic island chain. The older Okhotsk-Chukotka volcanic belt extends from the Chukotka Peninsula to the Sea of Okhotsk. Kamchatka has about 300 volcanoes, of which at least 29 are active, including Klyuchevskaya Sopka, the highest volcano on the Eurasian continent at 4750 m. Klyuchevskaya is a stratovolcano that is very active, with eruptions about once every two years. The 1956 eruption of Bezymianny, a 2282 m stratovolcano in the Klyuchevskaya group that had been apparently dormant in historic time, destroyed the summit, lowering the height by some 600 ft, forming a caldera roughly a mile across. The eruption style and resulting landform are very similar to the 1980 Mt St Helens eruption. Since 1955, Bezymianny has been one of the most active of Kamchatka's volcanoes.

Alaska

Along the southern edge of the Bering Sea and onto the Alaska Peninsula, a volcanic arc delineates the subduction of the Pacific plate beneath the North American plate. The offshore chain of volcanic islands (the Aleutians) continues inland as a line of volcanoes along the edge of the continent (the coastal Aleutian Range on the Alaska Peninsula). The concentration of volcanoes in the Cook Inlet region coincides with the highest density of population in Alaska.

Other Alaskan volcanoes that have been active in the Holocene occur in southeastern Alaska and in the Wrangell Mountains, with a few in interior Alaska and in western Alaska as far north as the Seward Peninsula.

Most of Alaska's 40 active volcanoes are of continental type, large individual volcanoes, some with smaller associated volcanoes or cinder cones. Most of them are glaciated stratovolcanoes, many have developed a caldera, and there are some lava shields as well. Among the well-known volcanoes are Mt Katmai (2047 m) and Pavlof (2519 m), on the Alaskan Peninsula. The former is a complex stratovolcano with a 5 km wide caldera and a lake. The eruption in 1912 is among the world's largest in historical times and it included a glowing pyroclastic flow. The eruptive tephra volume reached 30 km^3, filling an adjacent valley, the Valley of Ten Thousand Smokes, with hot ash deposit up to 200 ft thick in places. This thick hot ash heated groundwater below the deposit, causing fumarole or steam vents that lasted 15 years. The Novarupta lava dome rose in the main eruptive vent and a new flanking volcano, Trident, erupts from time to time. Pavlof, which is a classic stratovolcano, has had more than 40 eruptions since 1790, the last one in 1997. The nearby Pavlof's Sister is more timid, with one historical eruption in the 18th century. A series of eruptions in the peninsula volcano Veniaminof (2507m) started in 1993. There are at least 13 other active volcanoes on the peninsula. The Wrangell mountains in the east of Alaska count in as a region of volcanic activity, with eight volcanoes: stratovolcanoes, shield volcanoes, and smaller composite cones. The Wrangell shield volcano (4317 m) and Churchill (4766 m) are two of the better known "fire mountains." The former erupted in 1902, but the other has apparently been quiet during the Holocene period. Augustine is a cone of a stratovolcano, rising out of the sea, in Cook Inlet. It has erupted explosively at least eight times since 1812. There are four other stratovolcanoes at the inlet; among them are Redoubt (3108 m), which erupted in 1989–1990 causing substantial damage, and Spurr, erupting in 1992.

Iceland

Iceland was built entirely by eruptive and intrusive activity during the past 15–20 million years. Iceland is situated on top of the North Atlantic Mid-Ocean Ridge, where plates part at an average rate of 2 cm per year. The periodic volcanic activity is caused by magma upflow under the divergent plate margins, and by magma upflow in a mantle plume (hot spot), which is presently active beneath the central part of Iceland. Holocene volcanic activity is confined to a central rift zone (in two parts) and three lateral volcanic zones. The rift-zone volcanism is characterized by basaltic fissure eruptions, formation of dozens of lava shields, and a number of large central volcanoes, set with calderas. Individual lava flows may cover up to 900 km^2 and have a volume of 15–20 km^3. The volcanic activity in the lateral volcanic zones displays somewhat different features, such as more explosive activity, the formation of stratovolcanoes, and more evolved eruptive rock types. There is volcanic activity at the seafloor off the south coast and on the mid-ocean Reykjanes Ridge in the southwest. Occasionally, an island rises out of the sea during a volcanic event (e.g., Surtsey in 1963–1967). Submarine volcanic activity also occurs at the mid-ocean ridge north of Iceland (Kolbeinsey Ridge), stretching toward the North Pole. There are about 30 volcanic systems in Iceland, most of which support a large, central volcano, and hundreds of individual craters, lava shields, and crater rows as well. An eruption occurs every fourth year on average. A number of volcanic systems are in heavily glaciated highlands. Subglacial eruptions become predominantly phreatic (explosive) and produce tephra and large meltwater floods or jökulhlaups. Among the active subglacial volcanoes are Grímsvötn and Katla. Grímsvötn erupts once a decade on an average, but the eruptions tend to be rather small. The last eruption occurred in 1998. Katla is noted for about 20 eruptions in historical records; the last one was in 1918. It

produced a jökulhlaup with a peak discharge of 100,000–200,000 m^3 s^{-1}. Other well-known volcanoes are Askja (last eruption in 1961) and Krafla in northeastern Iceland. In Krafla, a volcano-tectonic episode in 1975–1984 caused nine effusive fissure eruptions and a 7–8 m widening of the fissure swarm. Hekla (1495 m) is a ridge-shaped stratovolcano in southern Iceland. It has erupted frequently and sometimes violently in prehistoric times and 18 times since the 12th century; the last eruptions occurred in 1991 and 2000. The eruptions of Öræfajökull (2119 m), Iceland's highest and largest volcano, in 1362, the Laki eruption in 1783, and the Heimaey eruption in 1973 are examples of volcanic events, causing damage to pastures, farms, and towns. In 1783–1785, a famine, partly caused by climatic deterioration due to the Laki eruption, killed 20% of the population and 50% of the livestock. In 1973, an eruption destroyed some 40% of the buildings in the town on the main island of Vestmannaeyjar.

Geothermal activity is associated with volcanism. In Iceland, geothermal energy is used for domestic heating (90% of buildings), greenhouse farming, aquaculture, health spas, industrial use, and to generate electricity.

Jan Mayen

Jan Mayen is a volcanic island 550 km northeast of Iceland, claimed and governed by Norway. The island is approximately 50 km long and 5–10 km wide (377 km^2). The only settlement is a military and scientific installation with a staff of a few dozen. Jan Mayen lies within a transverse fracture zone in the North Atlantic rift system. The volcanic activity is associated with a small mantle plume (hot spot) and the leaky, transverse fault system. The system links the Kolbeinsey Ridge rift zone with the Mohns Ridge rift zone to the north. The island is set with Pleistocene and Holocene volcanic fissures, but is dominated by a large, symmetrical stratovolcano, Beerenberg (2277 m). Beerenberg, the northernmost active subaerial volcano on Earth, is mostly covered by glaciers. The record of Holocene volcanic activities is not known in detail, but Beerenberg has apparently erupted at least six times from 1732 to 1985. The last two eruptions occurred in 1970 and 1985. Both were flank eruptions, the former quite large, and both producing tephra and lava flows.

Gakkel Ridge

Volcanic features on Gakkel Ridge, a slow-spreading mid-ocean ridge extending across the Arctic Ocean beneath the polar sea ice cap, have recently been identified. At such slow-spreading ridges, it was previously thought that melt production would be diminished, but topographic highs of *c*.500–1000 m in areas of recent seismic activity are thought to be areas of submarine eruptions.

ARI TRAUSTI GUÐMUNDSSON

See also **Arctic Mid-Ocean Ridge; Jökulhlaups**

Further Reading

Decker, R. & B. Decker, *Volcanoes*, New York: Freeman, 1989

Edwards, M.H., G.J. Kurras, M. Tolstoy, D.R., Bohnenstiehl, B.J., Coakley & J.R. Cochran, "Evidence of recent volcanic activity on the ultraslow-spreading Gakkel Ridge." *Nature*, 409 (2001): 808–812

Gudmundsson, A.T., *Volcanoes of Iceland*, Reykjavík: Vaka-Helgafell, 1995

Rennick, P. (editor), *Alaska's Volcanoes*, Fairbanks: Alaska Geographic, 1991

Sigurdsson, H. (chief editor) et al., *Encyclopedia of Volcanoes*, New York: Academic Press, 1999

Simkin, T. & L. Siebert, *Volcanoes of the World*, (2nd edition), Tucson, Arizona: Geoscience Press, 1994

Wood, C.A. & J. Kienle, *Volcanoes of North America*, Cambridge and New York: Cambridge University Press, 1990

VOLES—*See* MICROTINES (LEMMINGS, MOLES)

VORKUTA

Vorkuta, a town in the Komi Republic of Russia, is located 160 km north of the Arctic Circle near the western foothills of the Ural Mountains and is surrounded by tundra containing massive islands of permafrost. Seventy percent of the total population of 92,600 is Russian (*Goskomstat Rossii*, 1999). A settlement in this location first appeared in 1931, as a result of the discovery and exploration of the Vorkuta coalfield, part of the Pechora coal basin. The basin is one of the largest in the former Soviet Union territory, and one-third of its coal is valuable for coking (creating fuel). In 1934, Vorkuta's first mine became operational. In 1937–1941, the Northern-Pechora Railway was constructed, connecting Vorkuta with Moscow and northwestern Russia. Vorkuta grew rapidly and in 1943 became a town. During World War II, when the German army occupied Donbass, another large coal basin in European Russia, Vorkuta was the only supplier of fuel and coking coal for Leningrad and northwestern Russia. Along with Magadan, Noril'sk, and several other places, Vorkuta was one of the sites of the Gulag, the Main Directorate for Corrective Labor Camps built for criminals and political prisoners under Joseph Stalin's reign in the early 1930s. From 1934 to 1960, several hundred thousand prisoners passed through the Vorkuta Gulag camps, and many thousands of them died. The number of prisoners reached a maximum of 60,000 in 1945–1947. They labored in construction, geological prospecting, mining, and agriculture.

At present, coal mining and preparation is the leading industry in Vorkuta; a total of 13 mines extract over 13,000,000 tons of coal per year (1999). Other vital industries include civil engineering, heavy motor transport enterprises, clothing manufacturing, and food processing. Numerous geological, geophysical, coal, oil, and gas prospecting companies are located in Vorkuta. During the Soviet period, dairy cattle operations were developed near Vorkuta and 10,000 ha of perennial meadows were artificially established in the tundra to provide forage. Communications, in addition to the railway, include an airport with regular flights to several Russian cities. Roads for motor vehicle transportation connect the mines and settlements surrounding the town. The planned construction of the Ukhta-Inta-Vorkuta highway is aimed at improving communication infrastructure in the region.

In spite of permafrost distribution, the town is dominated by five- and nine-story buildings. There are several prospecting institutes, branches of two higher education establishments, and a number of middle education establishments.

Perestroika (Mikhail Gorbachev's program of economic, political, and social restructuring started in 1986) and rapid privatization of state property in Russia were followed by social and economic crises, which were especially difficult in northern regions. In 1995, 60% of the coal mines of the Republic of Komi were unprofitable, but began to slowly improve by the early years of the 21st century. The northern territories continue to serve as the main suppliers of energy and raw materials. In Vorkuta, coal extraction is currently stabilized at a level of 20,000,000 tons per year. Large towns with developed infrastructures, such as Vorkuta, built in the extreme north during the Soviet period, will further serve as centers supporting the development of new areas.

GALINA MAZHITOVA

See also **Coal Mining**

Further Reading

Dedeev, Vladimir & Stepanov Yury (editors), *Resursy i narodnohoziaistvennoe ispolzovanie uglei Pechorskogo ugolnogo basseina* [Resources and economic use of the coal of the Pechora coal basin], Syktyvkar: Komi Publishing, 1988

Negretov, Pavel,. *All Roads Lead to Vorkuta*, Benson, Vermont: Chalidze Publication, 1985

Roshchevsky, Mikhail, Albert Vaneev & Nikolai Timonin (editors), *Respublika Komi. Entziklopedia* [The Republic of

Komi. Encyclopedia], Volume 1, Syktyvkar: Komi Publishing, 1997

Saveleva, Eleonora (editor), *Istoriko-kulturny atlas Respubliki Komi* [Historical-Cultural Atlas of the Republic of Komi], Moscow: Drofa, 1997

Uyshkin, Nikolai, Valentina Vityazeva & Vitaly Lazhentzev (editors), *Respublika Komi: economicheskaya strategiya vhozhdeniya v XXI vek* [The Republic of Komi: economic strategy for entering the 20th century], Proceedings Science Conference, March 13–14 1995, Syktyvkar: Commission on the Assessment of Productive Forces, 1996

Zherebtzov, Igor, *Gde ty zhivesh: naselennye punkty Respubliki Komi. Istoriko-demograficheskii spravochnik* [Where do you live: towns and settlements of the Republic of Komi. Historical-demographic reference book], Syktyvkar: Komi Publishing, 1994

VORONIN, VLADIMIR IVANOVICH

The Russian polar seafarer Vladimir Ivanovich Voronin was born in a large Pomor village on the White Sea coast. Sea life for Pomors typically begins early in life. At the age of eight years, Volodya went to Murman with his father for fishery as a Pomor ship's boy *zuiok* (ringed plover). In winter, he studied in a parish college, and each summer went to sea. Sailing experience allowed Voronin to enter Sumskiy Sea School of coastwise navigators at the age of 16 years. Upon graduation, he joined a steamship engaged in supply operations along the White and Barents seashores.

In 1913, Voronin passed the state examination in Archangel'sk for the rank of short-voyage captain, which allowed him to sail as a captain's senior mate on board large cargo-passenger steamships between Archangel'sk, Murmansk, and Norway for the next six years. In 1916, he passed the examination in the Archangel'sk Sea College and became a long-voyage navigator. For the first time in 1918, Voronin sailed as a captain, taking command of the steamship *Kandalaksha*.

In 1920–1921, as leader of the steamship *Kanin*, Voronin participated in the Kara Sea expeditions organized by the Soviet government to deliver Siberian bread and grain to Archangel'sk. Here, the young captain gained his first large experience of navigation under heavy ice conditions. In 1922–1923, Voronin conducted supply voyages to Novaya Zemlya; the following year, he sailed between Murmansk and London.

In 1926, Voronin was appointed as captain of the *Georgy Sedov*, an icebreaking vessel. Annual seal hunting expeditions to the White Sea for six years enriched his experience of ice navigation, and Voronin became one of the best-known ice captains of the North.

In 1928, Voronin received orders to voyage to the northern Barents Sea to investigate harp seal hunting along the ice edge. However, following news of the crash of Umberto Nobile's dirigible and the subsequent disappearance of Roald Amundsen's airplane, Voronin was requested to search for the missing people near Franz Josef Land. During a voyage that lasted more than two months, the *Georgy Sedov* sailed over 3000 miles, predominantly in heavy ice. Although no traces of the missing people were found, the oceanographic and cartographic studies conducted during the expedition resulted in invaluable data in the field of Arctic marine studies.

In 1929–1930, Voronin captained the *Georgy Sedov* for an expedition under the auspices of the All-Union Arctic Institute. During the first voyage, led by Otto Shmidt, the northernmost weather station in the world was established in Tikhaya Bay (Franz Josef Land). The following year, the expedition conducted a complex of oceanographic and meteorological studies in the northern Barents and Kara Seas, discovered several islands (one of them was named after Voronin), and delivered the research team led by Georgiy Alekseevich Ushakov to Severnaya Zemlya.

In 1932, under Voronin's command, the icebreaking vessel *Alexander Sibiryakov* made the first single-season transit through the North East Passage. The expedition, led by Shmidt, successfully sailed from Archangel'sk to the Bering Sea, rounding for the first time from the north the Severnaya Zemlya archipelago. The voyage was dramatic and challenging: at the approach to the Bering Strait, heavy ice broke the propeller shaft, the ship came to a halt, and the captain ordered the crew to raise the tarpaulin sail. With fair wind, the ship entered the North Pacific and was towed to Petropavlovsk-Kamchatsky. The historic voyage of *Sibiryakov* is considered to be the event that initiated the Northern Sea Route as a transport thoroughfare.

The success of *Sibiryakov* led to a repeat of the transit voyage along the Northern Sea Route on board the cargo ship *Chelyuskin*. Otto Shmidt was again the expedition leader and Voronin was appointed captain. On July 16, 1933, the vessel left Leningrad. In spite of the harsh ice—and the fact that the ship was not adapted for independent sailing in ice—Voronin was still able to lead the *Chelyuskin* to the Chukchi Sea. Here, the ship became trapped in heavy ice and started to drift. On February 13, 1934, a powerful ice pressure broke the ship hull and 104 crew members found themselves on drifting ice. The rescue operation by aircraft was completed by April 13. On this day, Captain Voronin was the last of the crew to abandon the ice camp.

The loss of the *Chelyuskin* did not diminish Voronin's conviction in the possibility of regular sailing along the Northern Sea Route. He actively supported the construction of new and potent icebreakers for the Northern Sea Route and organization of the scientific-operational support of Arctic navigation.

In 1935, Voronin was appointed the captain of the icebreaker *Ermak* to escort transport vessels in the Kara Sea. The year 1938 has become an important landmark in Voronin's polar career. That year, the *Ermak* began Arctic navigation unusually early, in the month of February, as it was necessary to first rescue the North Pole drifting expedition. On March 15, the icebreaker successfully delivered Ivan Dmitrievich Papanin's team to Leningrad.

Voronin subsequently took command of the flagship *Iosif Stalin*, the most imposing icebreaker in the country, whose construction Voronin had vigorously fought for. He spent only two navigation seasons, however, on board the icebreaker. A serious illness and a complicated operation forced Captain Voronin to leave the Arctic for almost two years.

In late 1941, barely recovered from illness, he was appointed an officer of the White Sea Navy Flotilla and participated in the routing of battleships along the Northern Sea Route. In April 1943, Voronin returned as a flag-captain to the *I. Stalin*. Under its escort, the allied convoys from Europe and convoys of transport vessels from the east sailed to Archangel'sk.

By now the most experienced ice navigator in the country, in 1946 Voronin departed to Antarctica as a captain and director of the first Soviet whaling flotilla, the *Slava*. Then Voronin returned to the Northern Sea Route and escorted cargo vessels as the commander of the *I. Stalin* for the next five years.

The Arctic navigation season of 1952 was the last for Captain Voronin. On October 18, he suddenly died from a cerebral hemorrhage on the pilot bridge while traveling in the Laptev Sea. For his services in labor and battle, Voronin was bestowed with numerous orders and medals. His name is immortalized on the Arctic and Antarctic charts, in namesakes of an icebreaker and fishery vessels.

Biography

Vladimir Ivanovich Voronin was born on October 17, 1890 in Sumsky Posad settlement (a large Pomor village in Archangel'sk province). His father was a fisherman, and his mother was a housekeeper. He graduated from Sumskiy Sea School of coastwise navigators in 1908, and soon after that he married a young Pomor woman, Pelagea Mikhaleva. They had three sons, all of whom became naval officers. Voronin devoted 54 years of his life to the sea. Principal Arctic expeditions that were captained by Voronin included those to Franz Josef Land (1928), Franz Josef Land, northern Kara Sea and Severnaya Zemlya (1930), both on board *Georgy Sedov;* the Northern Sea Route transit in a single season aboard *Sibiryakov* (1932); Northern Sea Route transit on board cargo vessel *Chelyuskin* (*1933–1934*); the rescue of Ivan Dmitrievich Papanin's expedition on board *Ermak* (1938); and the escort of northern convoys onboard *I. Stalin* (1942–1945). Voronin died in 1952 and was buried in St Petersburg.

VADIM VORONIN

See also **Northern Sea Route; Papanin, Ivan Dmitrievich**

Further Reading

Belov, Mikhail, *Istoriya otkrytiya i osvoeniya Severnogo moskogo puti, 3. Sovetskoe arkticheskoe moreplavanie 1917–1932* [History of the Discovery and Development of the Northern Sea Route, Volume 3, Soviet Arctic Seafaring 1917–1932], Leningrad: Morskoy Transport, 1959

———, *Istoriya otkrytiya I osvoeniya Severnogo moskogo puti, 4. Nauchnoe I khozyaystvennoe osvoenie Sovetskogo Severa 1933–1945* [History of the Discovery and Development of the Northern Sea Route, 4. Scientific and Economic Exploitation of the Soviet North 1933–1945], Leningrad: Gidrometeorologicheskoe izdatelstvo, 1969

Lupach, V. (editor), *Russkie moreplavateli* [Russian Seafarers], Moscow: Voennoe izdatelstvo Ministerstva oborony SSSR, 1953

Vize, Vladimir, *Na Sibiryakove i Litke cherez ledovitye morya. Dva istoricheskikh plavaniya v 1932 I 1934 gg* [Onboard *Sibiryakov* and *Litke* through the Ice Covered Seas. Two Historical Voyages in 1932 and 1934], Moscow-Leningrad: Izdatelstvo Glavsevmorputi, 1946Seleznev, S.A., *Ledovy kapitan* [The Ice Captain], Archangel'sk: Archangelskskoe knizhnoe izdatelstvo, 1969

——— *Morya Sovetskoy Arktiki* [The Seas of the Soviet Arctic], Moscow-Leningrad: Izdatelstvo Glavsevmorputi, 1948

WADERS

The plovers, sandpipers, snipes, and their close relatives represent the taxonomic suborder *Charadrii*, collectively known in English as waders (also known as *Timmiat sinaarmiutat* in Inuktitut, and shorebirds in North America). In the breeding season, these are birds of open landscapes such as the northern tundras, temperate grasslands, and arid regions further south. Outside of the nesting period, waders tend to gather in large numbers to do as their name implies, to wade in soft mud and shallow waters along the shore to find their food. As a result, many species are relatively long-legged, but the group is typified by its enormous adaptive radiation. The plovers, for instance, have short bills and large eyes and typically pick their invertebrate prey, located by eye, from the surface. By contrast, sandpipers have slightly longer bills and find their buried prey deep in the substrate by probing with the sensitive tip of their bills. Snipe and woodcock often have extremely long bills and, with their cryptic nature, exploit a range of terrestrial as well as wetland habitats probing soft substrates. Wader species straddle the globe, and many different species exploit the brief but productive Arctic summer as a reproduction habitat, before moving south, often making dramatic migrations to the Southern Hemisphere to winter.

Gray Plover (*Pluvialis squatarola* Anngilik (Greenlandic), Tundralo (Norwegian), Grálóa (Icelandic), black-bellied plover (North America))

In its striking breeding plumage, a white area extends across the forehead crown and nape of the gray plover, separating the black belly, chin, and face from the black and white mottled back. In winter, the plumage is subdued grayish and heavily speckled black on the back. In all plumages, its dumpy, rounded stature, longish legs, and short stout bill are distinctive. The species breeds on the tundra in Siberia and Greenland and winters on estuarine habitats along the eastern Atlantic, East Africa throughout Asia to Australia, numbering over 275,000 specimens; in western Europe, numbers have shown signs of increase in recent years. The gray plover also breeds throughout Arctic North America and this population of 50,000 winters in the southern United States and the neotropics. In addition to relying on sight to locate its prey on the mud surface, this species is unusual for feeding at night and for its habit of maintaining feeding territories in the nonbreeding season, gathering only in large numbers at high-tide roosts.

Dunlin (*Calidris alpina* Saarfaarsuk (Greenlandic), Myrsnipe (Norwegian), Lóuþræll (Icelandic), red-backed sandpiper (North America))

The dunlin's distinctive breeding plumage, black belly, reddish back, and finely streaked white undersides make this small sandpiper quite unlike any other. Its sturdy, long, and very slightly downward curved bill is also distinctive. In flight, its white wing bar and rump contrast with the dark center to the rump and upper parts. Dunlin breed in wetlands throughout Arctic Russia (subspecies *alpina* east to the Lena Delta numbering perhaps 1.6 million birds, *sakhalina* further east with perhaps up to 1 million individuals), Alaska (*pacifica* and *sakhalina*), Canadian Arctic west of Hudson Bay (*hudsonia*), and northeast Greenland (*arctica* numbering 15,000 birds). Greenland and western Russian birds winter mostly on coastal wetlands, exploiting intertidal mudflats throughout Europe, Africa, and southeast and southern Asia, while *sakhalina* winter in eastern and southeastern Asia. North American birds winter along east and west coasts and are showing signs of recent declines. Adult molting precedes autumn migration, so the young leave the breeding grounds before the adults, arriving in discrete flocks that persist into the winter.

Knot (*Calidris canutus* Qajorlak (Greenlandic), Polarsnipe (Norwegian), Rauðbrystingur (Icelandic))

This chunky, short-legged but large sandpiper is a true transcontinental traveler. All its races undertake flights of 2000–6000 km, often completely over open water. In the Old World, the knot breeds in the High Arctic on the Russian tundra (the nominate race *canutus*, which winters off West Africa mostly on Banc d'Arguin, Mauritania), on New Siberia Islands (probably *canutus*, which migrates along the east coast of Asia, possibly down to Australia), and in the far eastern tundra of Russia (*rogersi*, which winters in Australia and New Zealand). In the New World, it nests in northern Greenland and High Arctic northeast Canada (the subspecies *islandica*, which winters in Britain and North Sea coasts), in the central Canadian Arctic (*rufa*, which winters in Patagonia and Tierra del Fuego), and on Wrangel Island and in Alaska (*roselaari*, which migrates down the Pacific coast to winter in the Gulf of Mexico). In this way, some populations of the same species make huge trans-equatorial migrations, while Greenland birds must cross the Greenland Ice Cap to make the shorter journey to Europe. The large variation in nonbreeding latitudes means that the various populations are exposed to different and often erratic photoperiod (recurring cycles of light and dark periods of constant length) regimes, yet still manage to maintain highly complex migratory patterns.

Red-Necked Phalarope (*Phalaropus lobatus* Svømmesnipe (Norwegian), Óðinshani (Icelandic), northern phalarope (North America), Naluumasortoq (Greenlandic), saarraq/saurraq (strictly the skin of a red-necked phalarope in Inuktitut))

Red-necked phalaropes are extremely abundant, numbering populations of perhaps over 2 million individuals in both the Russian and North American Arctic regions. However, recent studies have shown dramatic declines in their numbers, and they have completely disappeared from areas where they were once extremely numerous in the Bay of Fundy in North America. Phalaropes are highly unusual among waders in that they are primarily aquatic (swimming and feeding on the water) and the males are less brightly colored than,

and are courted by, the females. The males also incubate the eggs for 18–20 days and tend the young to fledging (after *c.*20 days) alone, the females leaving after the last egg has been laid to court other males elsewhere. This species is confined to freshwater pools with abundant emergent vegetation in summer, breeding on lake margins and pools; however, outside of the breeding areas, red-necked phalaropes are pelagic (found only at sea), often in the Southern Hemisphere and frequently far from the coast. Ringing recoveries from northern Scandinavian birds suggest that these winter in the Arabian Sea, Gulf of Aden, and Persian Gulf, but little is known about where these birds winter, or their population size or trends.

TONY FOX

See also **Seabirds**

Further Reading

Cramp, S., The Birds of the Western Palearctic, Volume 3, Waders to Gulls, Oxford: Oxford University Press, 1984

Duncan, C.D., "Phalaropes in the Bay of Fundy." In *Bay of Fundy Issues: A Scientific Overview. Workshop Proceedings, Wolfville, Nova Scotia, January 29 to February 1, 1996*, edited by J.A. Percy, P.G. Well & A.J. Evans, Environment Canada Atlantic Region Occasional Report No. 8, Sackville, New Brunswick: Environment Canada, 1997

Hale, W.G., *Waders*, London: Collins, 1980

Hayman, P., J. Marchant & A.J. Prater, *Shorebirds: An Identification Guide To The Waders of The World*, London: Helm, 1991

Johnsgaard, P.A., *The Plovers, Sandpipers and Snipes of The World*, Lincoln: University of Nebraska Press, 1981

Morrison, R.I.G., Y. Aubrey, R.W. Butler, G.W. Beyersbergen, G.M. Donaldson, C.L. Gratto-Trevor, P.W. Hicklin, V.H. Johnston & R.K. Ross, "Declines in North American shorebird populations." *Wader Study Group Bulletin*, 94 (2001): 34–38

Piersma, T.N. Davidson, "The migration of knots." *Wader Study Group Bulletin*, 64 (1992)

Rose, P.M. & D.A. Scott, "Waterfowl Population Estimates." *Wetlands International Publication* (2nd edition), Volume 44, Wageningen: Wetlands International, 1997

WALRUS

Walruses are the largest pinnipeds (the order of mammals that includes seals, sea lions, and walruses) of the Arctic. Both male and female walruses have large ivory tusks. The Latin name, *Odobenus rosmarus*, means "tooth-walking sea horse." There is only one existing species of walrus. However, based on morphology and genetic divergence, two subspecies are recognized: Pacific walrus (*O. divergens*) and Atlantic walrus (*O. rosmarus*). The systematic status of a third subspecies, the Laptev walrus (*Odobenus rosmarus laptevi*), is debatable.

Walruses feed almost exclusively on bottom-dwelling bivalve molluscs. They prefer coastal shallow

A mother and juvenile Atlantic walrus approach the edge of an ice-floe, Igloolik, Canada.
Copyright Norbert Rosing/National Geographic Image Collection

water areas with drifting ice. Therefore, they occur year-round in the major polynyas. Pacific walruses, which basically constitute one population, are distributed in the Bering and Chukchi sea areas. The entire population of this subspecies is estimated at around 200,000 animals. The Atlantic walrus is found in eight more or less separate subpopulations from the eastern Canadian Arctic to the Kara Sea of the western Russian Arctic. Genetic analyses indicate that Atlantic walruses west and east of Greenland became separated by postglacial events. The number of Atlantic walruses is only vaguely known. Walruses in the five Canadian and West Greenland subpopulations perhaps number 15,000 in total, whereas the total number in the three putative subpopulations to the east of Greenland approximately number 3000–4000. The population of Laptev walruses that is confined to the Laptev Sea of central Siberia has been estimated at 4000–5000.

Male walruses grow larger than females. Adult males reach an average body length of *c.*320 cm and a body mass of 1200–1300 kg, whereas females are *c.*275 cm and weigh approximately 800–900 kg. Males may reach a body weight of *c.*2000 kg. Walruses can live up to *c.*40 years of age.

Walruses are easily distinguished by their tusks that are enlarged upper canines. Males have thicker tusks than females. The tusks are used for fighting with other walruses, as a defense against polar bears and killer whales, and to aid in hauling out on ice-floes. Tusk and body size is important for establishing hierarchy within a group of walruses. The heavy structure of the skull and lower jaw is an adaptation to frequent direct contact with ice and to a special foraging behavior. In its mouth cavity, a walrus can create a negative pressure (up to −119 kPa), which is used to extract the soft parts of the bivalve molluscs from their shells. The other teeth are peglike and are usually worn down to the gum line. Their shape and the presence of an unusually thick layer of cementum (an external bony layer covering the dentin of the part of a tooth normally within the gum) suggest that these teeth are mainly used for creating clacklike sounds underwater. The mystacial vibrissae on the muzzle are sensory organs that are used to find and select benthic (bottom-dwelling) prey. The bivalve molluscs are taken between the lips, and the soft parts are sucked from the shells and swallowed. The empty shells are left on the seafloor. The walrus propulses strong water jets from its mouth or waves with its front flippers in order to excavate the invertebrate prey. An average foraging dive lasts approximately 5 min, during which time a walrus may eat 40–60 molluscs.

Walruses sometimes also prey on seals or swimming birds and rely to a large extent on their sense of smell. The anatomy of the retina of the eye indicates that they have color vision. The hind flippers can rotate forward and are used when walking on land or ice; however, unlike sea lions, walruses have no pinnae (a projecting body part such as wings or fins). The color of the skin is brownish but can vary from gray to reddish. Walruses molt their sparse pelage (coat) during the summer when they spend about 30% of the time hauling out on ice-floes or terrestrial haul-outs. The skin is thick and tough as an adaptation to frequent contact with ice and rocks. Its thickness also protects it against jabs from the tusks of other walruses. The skin on the neck of adult males is covered with fibrous tubercles. Walruses have a negative buoyancy; therefore, they have pharyngeal pouches or "air sacs," which can be inflated when they need to rest in the water. These pouches are probably also used by the adult males for producing various underwater sounds during the mating season.

Walruses are highly gregarious and congregate on the ice or at their traditional terrestrial haul-out sites in herds of a few to hundreds of animals. The two sexes are usually separate for most of the year, but in some areas both sexes and all age classes are found together on land. Walruses emit a variety of sounds such as barking, grunting, snorting, roaring, and whistling, which have a social role. The Inuit word for walrus *aveq* stems from the most common of walrus sounds—"aauk."

Female walruses attain sexual maturity at an average age of six years, although some may ovulate already at four years of age. Males become sexually mature at between seven and ten years of age. The males do not usually participate in the mating until they have reached full body size, which occurs between 12 and 15 years of age. The penis bone can measure up to *c*.60 cm long, and the females have a well-developed clitoris. Walruses are polygynous, having more than one female mate at a time. During the mating season (January to April), the adult males use a variety of underwater sounds (taps, knocks, strums, and bell-like sounds) to attract estrus females. Copulation usually occurs in the water. Gestation lasts about 15 months (including a period of delayed implantation of four to five months). The female gives birth to a single 60 kg calf in May or June. The calf is usually weaned during its second year, by which time it has learned the complicated foraging pattern. Most reproductive females produce a calf every third year. A high degree of maternal care probably allows the walrus to produce fewer offspring than other pinnipeds. Theoretically, a walrus population has an annual net increase of about 2–5%.

Intense exploitation in the 18th and 19th centuries by commercial whalers and sealers (for ivory, oil, and hides) greatly reduced most walrus populations. To this end, Canada banned commercial hunting in 1867, the United States in 1941, and Russia in 1992. The Pacific walrus population has recovered, whereas several Atlantic walrus subpopulations still appear to be severely depleted. Nowadays, the Pacific walrus is legally hunted for subsistence purposes by native peoples of Alaska and Russia, and the Inuit living in Canada and Greenland hunt the Atlantic walrus. The subpopulations at Svalbard (1972) and the western Russian Arctic (1956) are fully protected. The East Greenland and Svalbard-Franz Josef Land subpopulations have shown recent signs of increase.

ERIK W. BORN

See also **Marine Mammal Hunting; Marine Mammals**

Further Reading

Born, E.W., "*Odobenus rosmarus* Linnaeus 1758—Walross." In *Handbuch der Säugetiere Europas, Band 6*, Meeressäuger, Teil II: Robben- Pinnipedia, edited by R. Duguy & D. Robineau, Wiesbaden: AULA-Verlag, 1992, pp. 269–299

Born, E.W., I. Gjertz, & R.R. Reeves, "Population assessment of Atlantic walrus (*Odobenus rosmarus rosmarus* L.)." *Norsk Polarinstitutt Meddelelser* (138) (1995)

Fay, F.H., "Ecology and biology of the Pacific Walrus, *Odobenus rosmarus divergens*, Illiger." *North American Fauna No. 74*, Washington: United States Dept. of the Anterior, Fish and Wildlife Service, 1982

———, "Mammalian species. *Odobenus rosmarus.*" *American Society of Mammalogists*, 238(1985): 1–7

Fay, F.H., L.L. Eberhardt, B.P. Kelly, J.J. Burns & L.T. Quakenbush, "Status of the Pacific walrus population, 1950–1989." *Marine Mammal Science*, 13(4)(1997): 537–565

Reijnders, P.J.H., G. Verriopoulos & S.M.J.M. Brasseur, "Status of pinnipeds relevant to the European Union." *IBN Scientific Contributions 8*, The Netherlands, 1997, pp. 160–182

WARFARE, HISTORICAL

Indigenous warfare in the Arctic and Subarctic regions is one of the least studied topics in modern anthropology, but it was a common feature of early ethnographic writings in the region to mention and often describe in detail conflict and violence among northern peoples. Much of the lack of emphasis on violence among northern peoples is likely a product of anthropologists' often-unacknowledged cultural biases and beliefs concerning the peaceful nature of many northern peoples. But this assumption is not supported in any reading of the literature. Jean Briggs states that: "Readers of Canadian Inuit ethnography, my own *Never in Anger* in particular, have sometimes concluded that Inuit are always and everywhere peaceful and pacific. Nothing could be further from the truth" (Briggs, 1994: 156). Katherine Reedy-Maschner and Herbert Maschner found in their analyses of warfare in three different regions of the north—the Subarctic, the Aleutian Islands, and the northern Northwest Coast—that warfare had been a regular aspect of intergroup relations for thousands of years (Maschner and Reedy-Maschner, 1998; Maschner, 1997). In the Bering Strait and northwest Alaska, Owen Mason also found that warfare had played an important role for at least two thousand years, and Ernest Burch has clearly demonstrated the widespread character of Iñupiat wars over the last few hundred years (Mason, 1998; Burch, 1974). In nearly all ethnographic and ethnohistoric accounts, from the Netsilik to the Aleut, Yupik, and Iñupiat, and from the Chipewyan to the Gwich'in, wars between families, bands, and villages were commonplace among many northern peoples.

The causes of indigenous northern conflicts fall under the broad category of striving for status and prestige rather than material motivations for aggression such as territory or food. Almost all conflicts tended to be rooted in either real or imagined revenge motives, and while most conflicts remain in the past, some occasionally resurface. Revenge was enacted to maintain the pride and often increase the status of a particular group that had been wronged or injured in some way, or simply to inflate the status of males who participated in the conflict. Often, underlying conflicts involved arguments related to women, such as sexual access, infidelities, broken marriages, incest, and other private familial issues. A multitude of examples could be used to describe northern conflicts, but the Gwich'in-Inuit case is perhaps the best studied. The Gwich'in-Inuit border was such a risky zone that eastern Gwich'in bands expected an almost annual clash with their Mackenzie Inuit neighbors; between 1825 and 1855, there were approximately thirty Gwich'in casualties (see Krech, 1979). The numbers of deaths for the western Gwich'in appear to have been greater than those of the eastern Gwich'in fighting against the Inuit. A dispute over women (the sources of which remain unclear) in the mid-19th century ended in a battle in which 20 Gwich'in were dead, but only two Nunamiut were wounded. The Gwich'in had guns by the 1820s, and stockpiled ammunition for defense against the Mackenzie Inuit, while the Inuit did not have guns until after the 1850s. Only when the Gwich'in ran out of ammunition did the Inuit instigate hostilities using bows and arrows as their primary weapons. Cornelius Osgood wrote that the primary cause of Gwich'in war against the Inuit was to capture their possessions; however, he explains that "many of these things have more of a trophy value, serving to enhance the prestige of the owner, than any important place as useful objects" (Osgood, 1936 [1970]: 86). Osgood cites the desire to acquire prestige as the second most common cause of Gwich'in warfare, noting that "A powerful chief often becomes such because he is a great war leader" and the gwich'in commonly lamented the cessation of fighting as a means of attaining esteem and power.

A rare and spectacular case of prehistoric conflict in this same region was found at the site of Saunaktuk in the Mackenzie Delta along the modern Inuit-Gwich'in border. Forensic evidence gathered from the examination of the scattered remains of 35 Inuit women, children, and elderly revealed facial mutilation, defleshing of the heads, decapitation, severed joints and muscles, split and gouged bones with signs of marrow extraction, and severed hands and feet. Human bones were randomly strewn amidst animal bones and detritus. Melbye and Fairgrieve's research, in which they studied oral narrative traditions of the Inuit and the Gwich'in, surmises that while the Inuit men hunted beluga, the Gwich'in most likely tortured and massacred the family (Melbye and Fairgrieve, 1994: 57–77). Dating to approximately AD 1250, the remains are a physical and prehistoric reminder of the massacre witnessed by Samuel Hearne at Bloody Falls 500 years later (and documented in his text *A Journey from Prince of Wales's Fort in Hudson's Bay to the Northern Ocean, 1769–1772*).

The Yupik peoples have powerful oral histories for the origin of war. One such narrative begins with two young boys playing with bone-tipped darts or arrows in a *kashigi* (the men's house). One boy accidentally shoots the other boy in the eye and blinds him. The father of the offending boy told the injured boy's father to poke out one of the eyes of his own son in retribution. The father of the injured boy was so angry that he blinded the boy in both eyes. Then the blind boy's father avenged that offense by killing the other boy. The dead boy's father attacked, and thus began an irreversible escalation in which the men in the village allied themselves with one or the other father until the entire village, and eventually the entire region, was at war. Indeed, as Ann Fienup-Riordan indicates, the historic regional groups appear to have emerged from these warring factions that most anthropologists believe began around AD 1100 and continued until the early contact period in the 18th and 19th centuries. These historical conflicts are often referred to as the "Bow and Arrow Wars" or the "Warrior Days" by storytellers. Researchers' familiarity with the Yupik war narratives derive from oral histories and ethnohistoric records. While details have been added and deleted over time, these stories nonetheless provide a complicated picture of tribal relations over the course of several centuries. Over a dozen independent political groups tended to compete for status within a vast area, often moving village locations hundreds of miles to avoid a conflict, or kayaking hundreds of miles to participate in one. Alliances shifted continuously, as did the fortunes of war (Fienup-Riordan, 1994).

In the Gulf of Alaska and then westward into the Aleutian Archipelago, anthropologists have documented extensive warfare among the Alutiiq (Pacific Eskimo) and Unangan (Aleut) peoples. Fleets of kayaks carried warriors hundreds of kilometers across the north Pacific in search of status, revenge, and honor, motivations that were regarded as immensely practical (Maschner and Reedy-Maschner, 1998). The Alutiiq-Unangan frontier was an area of intense discord before the arrival of the Russians in the 1760s, creating large border regions that remained unoccupied. After entire Alutiiq settlements had been destroyed by the Unangan, revenge wars became so frequent that the inhabitants of the Shumagin Islands, located on the Unangan-Alutiiq border, were either living in fortresses or on military expeditions.

In summary, there is a nearly 2000-year archaeological record of violent conflict in the Arctic region, and it appears that nearly every ethnographically described group participated in warfare with its neighbors.

HERBERT D. G. MASCHNER

See also **Aleut; Alutiit; Eskimo; Fur Trade; Gwich'in; Hearne, Samuel; Inuit; Iñupiat; Mackenzie Delta; Yupiit**

Further Reading

Balikci, Asen, *The Netsilik Eskimo*, New York: Natural History Press, 1970

Briggs, Jean, *Never in Anger,* Cambridge, Massachusetts: Harvard University Press, 1970

———, "'Why Don't You Kill Your Baby Brother': The Dynamics of Peace in Canadian Inuit Camps." In *The Anthropology of Peace and Non-Violence*, edited by Leslie Sponsel & Thomas Gregor, Boulder, Colorado: Lynne Rienner, 1994

Burch, Ernest S., "Eskimo warfare in Northwest Alaska." *Anthropological Papers of the University of Alaska*, 16(2) (1974): 1–14

Fienup-Riordan, Ann, "Eskimo War and Peace." In *Anthropology of the North Pacific Rim*, edited by W.W. Fitzhugh & V. Chaussonnet, Washington, District of Columbia: Smithsonian Institution Press, 1994

Hearne, Samuel, *A Journey from Prince of Wales's Fort in Hudson's Bay to the Northern Ocean, 1769–1772*, edited by R. Glover, Toronto, Canada: Macmillan, 1958

Krech III, S., "Interethnic relations in the lower Mackenzie River region." *Arctic Anthropology*, 16(2) (1979): 102–122

Maschner, H.D.G., "The evolution of northwest coast warfare." In *Troubled Times: Violence and Warfare in the Past*, edited by D. Martin & D. Frayer, Langhorne, Pennsylvania: Gordon and Breach, 1997

Maschner, H.D.G. & K.L. Reedy-Maschner, "Raid, retreat, defend (repeat): the archaeology and ethnohistory of warfare on the North Pacific Rim." *Journal of Anthropological Archaeology*, 17 (1998): 19–51

Mason, O.K., "The contest between the Ipiutak, Old Bering Sea and Birnirk Polities and the origin of whaling during the first millenium A.D. along Bering Strait." *Journal of Anthropological Archaeology*, 17 (1998): 240–325

Melbye, J. & S.I. Fairgrieve, "A massacre and possible cannibalism in the Canadian Arctic: new evidence from the Saunaktuk Site (NgTn-1)." *Arctic Anthropology*, 31(2) (1994): 57–77

Osgood, C., *Contributions to the Ethnography of the Gwich'in*, Yale University Publications in Anthropology, No. 14, New Haven: Reprinted by Human Relations Area Files Press from the 1936 edition, 1970

WASTE MANAGEMENT

Waste management may be described as the method of collecting, treating, and ultimately disposing of the by-products of human activity. Human activity may be a community where people live, or the manufacturing and industry that produce the things for the community to function. In warm climates, waste management has changed significantly in the past 50 years because of technology, environmental and public health impacts, and public awareness. In the Arctic, waste management has also been changing, but in ways quite different because of the influences of the climate, size, culture, and politics of this vast region.

From an environmental science perspective, the Arctic is considered to have tremendous assimilative capacity for wastes such as municipal wastewater because of the nutrient deficient nature of Arctic waters. However, the dispersion of municipal wastewater on a scale to take advantage of the assimilative capacity is very often cost prohibitive, and subject to the inherent challenges of cold and isolation.

Wastewater disposal in Arctic communities is a problem of increasing proportion for communities and government agencies. The increasing population of most Arctic communities, and the increasing demands of water use have dictated that past disposal practices such as discharge into the local landfill site are no longer appropriate. Increasing awareness of public health and environmental concerns has also focused the need to implement wastewater treatment and disposal systems that resolve both these concerns.

Prohibitive costs and inappropriate technology often dictate that domestic wastewater may not receive treatment, and may be discharged close to a community. This puts the local residents at risk for contact with pathogenic organisms in the wastewater. Microorganisms are known to survive for long periods below $0°C$; hence, frozen sludge may still be contaminated.

The tremendous change over the past 30 years in waste management practices has been most profound in the smaller communities, where the use of the "honey bucket" (in the absence of flush toilets) remains a recent memory. In fact, the complete transition from honey bucket to pump-out sewage disposal systems has not yet occurred in all northern communities, and consequently many communities maintain a central disposal lagoon or pit in the landfill.

The majority of communities employ some sort of detention system for waste treatment, such as a pond or wetland area for municipal wastewater treatment. Many of the systems are not engineered; therefore, the effluent quality has been highly variable. Mechanical-type systems have been applied in some cases where land for a lagoon may not be available, or where treatment requirements demand a consistent high-quality discharge. However, the past application of mechanical systems in communities has ultimately been unsuccessful; therefore, communities generally favor the use of simpler technologies of wastewater detention or retention.

The application of mechanical systems in industry has had greater success. The permanent camp facilities of the north have been able to successfully apply more sophisticated technology in their wastewater treatment and solid waste management responsibilities because of their financial and technical resources.

Solid waste management in Arctic communities is unique in the application of common waste management practices. Factors such as location, road construction, drainage, cover material, and reclamation may each become critical factors for developing a viable waste management scheme for an Arctic community.

A factor unique to the Arctic has been, until recently, the favored use of landfill burning as a means of volume reduction. The continued use of landfill burning in the Arctic had significant merit because it melted the snow that would accumulate in the landfill along with the waste, and ultimately use precious landfill space. Cover material is a critical factor for both landfill operation and landfill reclamation. The scarcity of granular material in most Arctic communities creates a competition for whatever material is available. The obvious priority of road construction material over landfill cover material creates the need to utilize whatever material is available in an efficient manner.

Solid waste management in the Arctic communities has been overlooked in the past for a variety of reasons, but this trend has changed with the recognition of a need for waste management, and the demands by the regulatory authorities. A key objective is to develop waste management practices appropriate to the Arctic environment.

The regulatory framework for waste management in communities and industry may involve issuing a "water license" with stipulated requirements for the quantity of water used and the quality of any waste discharge. The requirements of a water license often include aboriginal interests related to subsistence hunting, and other traditional activities.

In recent years, the regulatory requirements have placed greater demands on communities and industry, and a much higher degree of scrutiny than has been experienced in the past. This is a function of a number of factors, including increased public accountability and the right-to-know, and a demand for increased compliance with national and international laws and regulations. Also, the burden of proof that any proposed activities will not harm communities or the environment now rests with a community or an industry. This burden of proof may include full-cost accounting, where industries must provide an adequate security deposit to avoid public liability for any cleanup, reclamation, perpetual care, and monitoring.

A strong interest in cumulative effects management has emerged in the Arctic. This management system demands monitoring of overall environmental quality trends and measures to ensure that human activities stay within defined thresholds to protect ecological integrity and sustainable communities.

Past resource development, and military observation activity in the north have generally had limited responsibilities for short-term remediation or long-term monitoring. This has left a significant legacy and concern for residents of the north and their senior governments. There are a wide variety of remaining waste disposal issues that include petroleum spills, hazardous waste dumps, and mine tailings (*see* **Environmental Problems**). Concerted efforts for remediation of sites are under way and have been under way since the mid-1980s.

The Arctic is changing and its communities are preparing for a future that will include more development, and also provide for an unparalleled opportunity to protect the integrity of ecosystems, communities, and the sustainable way of life they support. Northerners are receiving a central role in any decision-making around this potential development.

KENNETH R. JOHNSON

See also **Ocean Dumping**

Further Reading

Canadian Arctic Resources Committee. website: www.carc.org/2002/april/ResponsibleMining.htm
Government of the Northwest Territories website: www.gov.nt.ca/RWED/library/eps/industrialwastedischarges.pdf
Mackenzie Valley Land and Water Board website: http://www.mvlwb.com/html/index.html

WATKINS, GINO

Gino Watkins, a significant British Arctic explorer of the 20th century, studied engineering and geography at Cambridge University, and attended Raymond Priestley's lectures on polar exploration. He was introduced to J.M. Wordie, who offered him a place on a 1927 Greenland expedition. This expedition was postponed, and so in 1927 Watkins organized and led his first Arctic expedition. When reporting his expeditions, Watkins minimized heroics and privation, describing the Arctic as a cheerful land where hardship was incidental to a satisfying life. He believed that polar air routes were inevitable, and that aircraft would maximize survey time on polar expeditions.

Watkins was concerned to repay sponsors' support through geographical and scientific discoveries; thus, he chose personnel for their technical competence, as well as their open-mindedness and hence adaptability. By the end of his third expedition, he was acknowledged to be one of the truly great Arctic explorers by such eminent authorities as Lauge Koch, Knud Rasmussen, Vilhjalmur Stefansson, Frank Debenham, and J.M. Wordie.

Watkins was an innovator, who, on his first expedition, replaced the traditional reindeer skin sleeping bags with eiderdown and successively doubled the fat in sledging rations on his first, second, and third expeditions. Other items, including tents, were also redesigned. Whenever possible, local animals were included in the diet, and he insisted that members of his Greenland expeditions learn from East Greenlanders to be proficient kayakers, hunters, and dog drivers.

Although unconventional, Watkins's expeditions were considered highly successful. He never called for volunteers, knowing that unpleasant or risky tasks would overwork the willing members. Rather, he invited participation and, in doing so, inspired a "relentless devotion to duty," as one expedition member wrote. Sometimes considered daring or lucky, Watkins believed that some risks had to be taken if anything important was to be accomplished. Modest about his own accomplishments, he nevertheless always praised his companions' contributions.

Edge Island 1927

This Svalbard island was chosen as it was scientifically unknown. Leaving Tromsø on July 27, 1927, the expedition landed on the north coast of Deevie Bay, and traversed the island to Cape Heuglin. Watkins's party consisted of C.T. Dalgety, N.C. Falcon, V. Forbes, A. Lowndes, A. Michelmore, H.T. Morshead, and R. Woolley. The Royal Geographical Society of Cambridge University as well as the members financed the expedition.

Encountering many foggy days, Watkins became convinced that aircraft were invaluable for Arctic surveying. Returning to Tromsø on August 31, he considered plans for an expedition to Franz Josef Land, believing that those islands would be a link in a future polar air route.

Watkins was elected a Fellow of the Royal Geographical Society (RGS) and also received the RGS Cuthbert Peek Award for his work on Edge Island.

Labrador 1928–1929

The RGS asked Watkins to summarize the Canada-Newfoundland boundary dispute; finding Labrador's interior scarcely charted, he decided to explore the region with funding from the RGS. Unsuccessful in obtaining a survey aircraft, travel was by canoe and dogsled. Starting from Northwest River on July 25, 1928, his five-man party surveyed the headwaters of the Hamilton River, returning to the coast on September 30, 1928. In early November, they left by dogsled for Hopedale, arriving on Christmas Eve of the same year. They went inland from Northwest River on February 2, 1929, exploring the Unknown Falls region in mid-March. On April 16, they left Northwest River for Battle Harbor. They then continued by motorboat to Forteau, from where they walked to Blanc Sablon to connect with a ship for Newfoundland in early May.

Expedition members D. Best, L. Leslie, J.M. Scott, and R. Michelin (the summer party), and Michelin and Scot (the winter party) accompanied Watkins; Best and Michelin were Labrador trappers.

Even when short of food, Watkins would not travel or hunt on Sundays out of respect for trappers' religious beliefs. Never motivated by the commercial benefits of his findings, Watkins recognized Labrador's forestry, mineral, and hydroelectric potential, and spoke of these matters in the hope that businesses would support exploration of the region.

East Greenland 1930–1931

The British Arctic Air Route Expedition left Tromsø, calling in to the Faroe Islands to embark the West Greenland sled dogs earlier delivered there by J.M. Scott. Arriving in late July, a base camp was established about 50 km west of Ammassalik. Expedition members included E.W. Bingham, F.S. Chapman, A. Courtauld, N.H. D'Aeth, H.I. Cozens, W.E. Hampton, P. Lemon, M. Lindsay, Q. Riley, J. Rymill, J.M. Scott, A. Stephenson, and L.R. Wager.

The East Greenland expedition objectives included surveying the coastal mountains from Kangerlussuaq southward, obtaining meteorological records from the coast and the ice cap, and determining the ice cap's topography. Expedition aircraft were used for surveying, and biological, geological, and magnetic studies were undertaken by dogsled and boat travel. When conditions prevented travel and surveying, Watkins and others lived with Greenland families in order to learn their hunting methods.

The crew made numerous coastal and ice cap journeys, and established a meterological station at 2500 m altitude on the ice cap; this station was manned by Courtauld alone from December 6, 1930 until May 5, 1931. Mapping was carried out north to Mt Forel and Kangerlussuaq, and south along the coast by sled and small boat. Lindsay, Scott, and Stephenson surveyed by dogsled south to Imivik, and then traversed the ice cap to Ivittut. Members Hampton and Riley completed another ice cap crossing, leaving the base on August 15, 1931 and reaching the west coast on October 14, near Holsteinsborg (Sisimiut).

On August 15, 1931, Watkins, Courtauld, and Lemon undertook a 960-km open-boat voyage, taking seven weeks to reach Nanortalik, which demonstrated to Watkins that he could live off the sea throughout the year. This realization fueled plans for future expeditions.

On returning to England, Watkins received the Royal Geographical Society's highest award (The Founder's (Gold) Medal), the Bruce Medal of the Royal Society of Edinburgh, and Denmark's highest award for Arctic work, the Hans Egede Medal. All members of the expedition received the British Polar Medal, the first time it had been awarded since 1876.

East Greenland 1932–1933

The Depression made funding impossible for a proposed trans-Antarctic expedition, but Watkins obtained limited funding from Pan American Airways, the RGS, and other sponsors that allowed Chapman, Riley, and Rymill to accompany him to East Greenland to extend the earlier meteorological, surveying, and biological work for a further year. Costs were minimal, as Watkins's hunting would feed the expedition. On August 20, 1932, Watkins left to hunt seals in a fjord where calving glaciers (the process by which ice breaks off a glacier's terminus) were a known risk; later that day, his water-filled kayak was found, but his body was never recovered. The expedition continued its work for the full year as planned under Rymill's leadership.

Subsequently, Rymill took over planning and leadership of the 1934–1937 British Graham Land Expedition that Watkins, out of necessity, had to postpone in 1932 for lack of funding. In addition to Rymill, other members of Watkins's Greenland expeditions participating in the Graham Land expedition included Bingham, Hampton, Riley, and Stephenson.

Biography

Henry George Watkins was born on January 27, 1907 in London, where he grew up with his younger brother Tony and sister Pam. He was always very close to his family, spending as much time as he could with them when not in the Arctic. Therefore, it was a shock when his mother died suddenly, just months before he was leaving on his Labrador expedition in 1928. He became engaged to Margaret Graham just before leaving on his last expedition in 1932. Watkins learned hunting from his father, an army colonel, and was introduced to climbing while attending private school. Watkins became an expert alpine skier and mountaineer, and learned to fly. At Cambridge University, he was an indifferent student, but excelled in subjects he wished to master.

Watkins died in Lake Fjord, near Ammassalik, on August 20, 1932. A memorial cairn was erected in 1932 overlooking the fjord where he died. A public appeal to establish the Gino Watkins Memorial Fund (to support Arctic expeditions) was generously supported, and for many years after his death, the public imagination was fired by his Arctic exploits and Courtauld's lonely vigil on the Greenland ice cap.

MILTON FREEMAN

See also **Rasmussen, Knud; Stefansson, Vilhjalmur**

Further Reading

Chapman, F. Spencer et al., *Northern Lights: The Official Account of the British Arctic Air Route Expedition 1930–1931*, London: Chatto and Windus, 1934

Lindsay, Martin, *Those Greenland Days: The British Arctic Air Route Expedition 1931–1932*, Edinburgh, London: Blackwood, 1932

Scott, J.M., *The Land that God Gave Cain: An Account of H.G. Watkins' Expedition to Labrador, 1928–1929*, London: Chatto and Windus, 1933

———, *Gino Watkins*, (8th edition), London: Hodder and Stoughton, 1951

Scott, J.M., F. Debenham & W. Goodenough, "Henry George Watkins." *Geographical Journal* 80(4) (1932): 273–280

WATT, CHARLIE

Born in 1944, Charlie Watt is a native Inuit leader from Kuujjuaq in northern Québec. Today, he is a senator who is best known for his instrumental role in the negotiation of the James Bay and Northern Québec Agreement of 1975.

That controversial agreement was signed after heated negotiations between native leaders and the Canadian government over the proposed James Bay hydroelectric dam project that flooded Aboriginal lands. Watt lobbied to halt the project altogether, but in the end he was able to mediate a compromise with the government, which gave the largely native communities who lived near James Bay a monetary settlement for the damage caused by the massive project. The sizeable compensation package has since facilitated the construction and upgrading of public services in Québec's native villages.

Watt's 30-year political career has been marked by many accolades. In 1984, he was appointed to the Senate, and in 1994 he was made an officer of the Order of Québec. Watt also received a prestigious National Aboriginal Achievement Award in 1994 for improving the lives of Inuit in Northern Québec.

Watt played a key role in drafting section 35 of Canada's constitution, which recognizes the rights of Aboriginal people. Bringing economic development to the north has always been a high priority for Watt. His senatorial work has fostered a number of native-owned businesses including Air Inuit, the first native-owned airline in Canada.

Watt was also an instrumental member of the standing senate committee on Aboriginal peoples, which was charged with studying the relations between native peoples and the Government of Canada. In conducting his research, Watt traveled across Canada listening to the concerns of native communities. The recommendations of the standing committee—that the government respect native peoples' right to self-government—were delivered to the Canadian Parliament in 2000.

Watt is also a member of the Senate committee on fisheries and has participated in trade missions to Asia. In both capacities, he has worked to bring increased business investment to his home region and to the Arctic in general. In the 21st century, his work focuses on developing funds for the Arctic char industry in Inuit communities, promoting ecotourism in the Far

North, and bringing native-produced products to the global market.

Although Watt is now often engaged in political battles in Canada's capital, Ottawa, he returns home to his people and the small community where he grew up almost every weekend.

Biography

Senator Charlie Watt was born in 1944 in Kuujjuaq (Strong Chimo), in Québec, on June 29, 1944. Watt's mother, Daisy Watt (1921–2001), was one of Kuujjuaq's best-known elders, and mother to another of Nunavik's most accomplished leaders, the Inuit Circumpolar Conference (ICC) Chair, Sheila Watt-Cloutier. He is married to Ida Epoo and they have five children: Donald, Robert, Lisa, Billy, and Charlene.

KOREY CAPOZZA

See also **James Bay and Northern Québec Agreement; Watt-Cloutier, Sheila**

WATT-CLOUTIER, SHEILA

Chair of the Inuit Circumpolar Conference since 2002, Sheila Watt-Cloutier is recognized for her untiring efforts on behalf of Arctic indigenous peoples worldwide and, in particular, the Aboriginal peoples of northern Canada. She champions many critical contemporary issues, including persistent organic pollutants (POPs), sustainable development, traditional ecological knowledge, northern education, and the impact of climate change on northern regions among others. Her distinctive and authoritative voice as an Inuit leader is heard internationally at the highest political levels as well as at the local level in northern communities.

In her former capacity as president of the Inuit Circumpolar Conference (Canada) and vice-president of the Inuit Circumpolar Conference, Watt-Cloutier played a prominent role during negotiations leading up to and during the Global Convention on Persistent Organic Pollutants in the late 1990s. The Inuit Circumpolar Conference (Canada) used its observer status to lobby, inform, and educate participants during the international conferences sponsored by the United Nations Environment Programme (UNEP). During the second meeting of the Intergovernmental Negotiating Committee in Nairobi (Kenya) in 1999, Watt-Cloutier presented an Inuit carving of a mother and child to Klaus Topfer, executive director of UNEP, and this powerful carving came to represent the conscience and heart of the negotiations.

During the various international meetings of the Global Convention, Watt-Cloutier and other northern leaders successfully focused world attention on the impact of POPs on the Arctic region. These toxic, long-lasting contaminants are carbon-based products and by-products of industrial activities that originate in Europe, Asia, the United States, and other areas south of the Arctic. Through the process of condensation and evaporation known as the "grasshopper effect," POPs travel by air, wind, and water currents, and are deposited in Arctic regions after encountering low temperatures. POPs include the following pollutants: polychlorinated biphenyls, DDT, furan, dioxin, lindane, mirex, heptachlor, endrin, toxaphene, and chlordane.

While the impact of these pollutants has largely been construed as an environmental issue, Watt-Cloutier has identified significant negative ramifications beyond environmental concerns for Inuit culture, health, and traditional way of life. During the mid-1980s, POPs were detected in alarmingly high rates in the breast milk and blood of Inuit mothers in northern Québec and southern Baffin Island. Subsequent studies revealed that POPs have a high lipid solubility, and bioaccummulate and biomagnify in the fatty tissues of marine mammals such as beluga whale and seal—the mainstay of the traditional diet of many northern peoples. Recent evidence suggests that consuming these contaminated foods has devastating consequences for human health, including neurological, endocrinological, and behavioral disorders. Consequences are particularly dire for women as POPs have been linked to high rates of breast cancer and reproductive disorders, afflictions and mutations that are additionally transferred intergenerationally through the placenta and breast milk. Watt-Cloutier asserts that traditional country foods are an integral part of Inuit culture and that they play an important role not only in nutrition and health but also in the maintenance of spiritual, social, and economic values and practices.

Watt-Cloutier is notable for her adroitness and skill in raising the profile of northern Aboriginal peoples on the international stage and in creating effective partnerships between Aboriginal organizations and governments. She has been particularly active in the area of sustainable development. The Inuit Circumpolar Conference has promoted sustainable development since 1986 with the adoption of a series of strategies and reforms outlined in *Towards an Inuit Regional Conservation Strategy*.

Through her involvement with the Sustainable Development Working Group of the Arctic Council and the Inuit Circumpolar Conference, Watt-Cloutier helped to establish links with the Russian Association of Indigenous Peoples of the North (RAIPON). One result of this partnership was a project strengthening regional governments in northern Russia and stressing practical aspects of comanagement of land and natural resources. As president of the Inuit Circumpolar Conference

(Canada), she coordinated annual humanitarian missions to Russian Aboriginal groups in Chukotka supported by North American government agencies and northern organizations such as the North Slope Borough in Barrow, Alaska. Additionally, the Inuit Circumpolar Conference (Canada) has implemented sustainable development projects with Mayan and Garifuna Indians in Belize. Watt-Cloutier emphasizes that sustainable development is more effectively achieved when projects and policies bring Aboriginal peoples and organizations together to learn from one another.

Watt-Cloutier has stressed the importance of establishing partnerships between Aboriginal organizations, government agencies, and the research community when addressing the potential impacts of climate change in the north. She has urged a bridging of the gap between Western scientific rationalism and the Aboriginal worldview in order that both perspectives may be brought to bear on the issue of climate change. Much is unknown about the consequences of climate change, but it is assumed by most scientists that the Arctic is one of the regions that will be most significantly affected. Watt-Cloutier has highlighted the role played by traditional ecological knowledge (TEK) and Inuit wisdom in identifying and investigating environmental problems, including climate change.

According to Fikret Berkes, Milton Freeman, and other scholars, TEK is acquired by Aboriginal peoples through the establishment of a long and intimate connection with the land. In the north, TEK can be used to identify changes in sea ice conditions, animal health and behavior, species density, and climatic patterns. Watt-Cloutier has recommended that TEK and other Aboriginal knowledge systems assume a more prominent role in dealing with current issues, including climate change.

Watt-Cloutier has earned the respect and admiration of her peers and colleagues, who commend her for her passionate commitment to northern Aboriginal peoples. She has fearlessly entered the realms of Arctic health, education, environment, politics, and culture, and demonstrates how all are interrelated and equally important. She insists that the world sees the human face—the Inuit face—when contemplating significant issues affecting the Arctic region.

Biography

Sheila Watt-Cloutier was born in Kuujjuaq, Northern Québec, Canada, on December 2, 1953. Her mother, Daisy Watt (1921–2002), was one of Kuujjuaq's best-known elders and was recognized throughout Nunavik for her skills as a healer, interpreter, and musician. Her brother, politician Charlie Watt, was appointed to the Canadian Senate in 1983 and was made an Officer of the Order of Québec in 1984. At the age of 10, Watt-Cloutier was sent to Nova Scotia and Churchill, Manitoba for schooling. At McGill University in Montreal, she took counseling courses as well as occupational and training sessions dealing with education and human development. In the mid-1970s, she worked as an Inuktitut interpreter for the Ungava Hospital and worked to improve health conditions and education in Nunavik over the next 15 years. From 1991 to 1995, she worked extensively as an advisor in a review of the education system in northern Québec, resulting in the groundbreaking report "Siatunirmut—The Pathway to Wisdom," compiled and published by the Nunavik Educational Task Force in 1992. Watt-Cloutier oversaw the administration of the Inuit land-claims body established under the James Bay and Northern Québec Agreement as corporate secretary of Makivik from 1995 to 1998. She entered politics in 1995. She has two grown-up children and a grandson. Her daughter is a well-known traditional Inuit throat-singer, drum-dancer, and singer. Her son is a pilot and the youngest captain ever employed by Air Inuit. Watt-Cloutier currently resides in Iqaluit, Nunavut, Canada.

JOANNA KAFAROWSKI

See also **Inuit Circumpolar Conference (ICC); Persistent Organic Pollutants (POPs); Russian Association of Indigenous Peoples of the North (RAIPON)**

Further Reading

Berkes, Fikret, Sacred Ecology: *Traditional Ecological Knowledge and Resource Management*, Philadelphia: Taylor and Francis, 1999

Canadian Arctic Resources Committee, "Arctic contaminants: an unfinished agenda." Northern Perspectives, 25(2)(1998): 1–22

———, "Persistent organic pollutants—are we close to a solution?." Northern Perspectives, 26(1)(2000): 1–20

Downie, David Leonard & Terry Fenge (editors), *Northern Lights Against POPs: Combatting Toxic Threats in the Arctic*, Montreal and Kingston: McGill-Queen's University Press, 2003

Freeman, Milton, "The nature and utility of traditional ecological knowledge." *Northern Perspectives*, 20(1)(1992): 7–12

Inuit Circumpolar Conference (Canada) website: www.inuit circumpolar.com

Nunavik Educational Task Force, *Final Report of the Nunavik Educational Task Force*, Lachine: Québec, 1992

Watt-Cloutier, Sheila, "Becoming aware of another form of violence." *Makivik News* (42) (1997) (spring issue): 48–50

———, "Capturing spirit." *Makivik News* (43) (1997/1998) (winter issue): 11–13

———, "Honouring Our Past, Creating Our Future: Education in Northern and Remote Communities." In *Aboriginal Education: Fulfilling the Promise*, edited by Lynne Davis, Louise Lahache & Marlene Castellano, Vancouver: University of British Columbia Press, 2000

Wilson, Simon, Janine Murray & Henry Huntington (editors), *AMAP Assessment Report: Arctic Pollution Issues*, Oslo: Arctic Monitoring and Assessment Program, 1998

WEASEL

Only two members of the weasel family (*Mustelidae*) can be considered truly Arctic species: the wolverine and the ermine. Others that inhabit the north in Alaska and reach the treeline in northern Canada are the least weasel, American marten, American mink, and river otter. The range of the Siberian weasel (*Mustela sibirica*) may also extend into tundra areas in eastern Siberia.

The ermine (*Mustela erminea*), known as the short-tailed weasel in North America and stoat in Great Britain, has a wide distribution in the Northern Hemisphere. In North America, it is found throughout Alaska and all of Canada except parts of the prairies. The range extends throughout the Arctic islands, to northern Ellesmere Island and Greenland, but ermine are never locally abundant. This weasel is also known by several variations of the Inuit name—*tegiak* or *tiriaq*. In Eurasia, the ermine is found from Kazakhstan north to the Arctic coast and possibly on some Siberian Arctic islands.

The ermine's summer coat is brown above with a yellow-white underside. The entire coat is white in winter, except for the tail, which is tipped with black in all seasons. The fur of northern weasels is more dense than that of southern weasels. Although several weasels are called ermine by the fur trade, the short-tailed weasel makes up the bulk of the furs traded. Male ermine are generally larger than females, with an average length between 235 and 270 mm. Weasels breed in April and the young, usually about seven, are born the next May, depending on latitude.

Short-tailed weasels are found in a wide range of habitats from sea level to alpine tundra, including forests, tundra, meadows, and lakeshores. In the north, their main prey species are brown and varying lemmings, and nestling birds, especially snow buntings. They may be important in controlling lemming population cycles. It is likely that they also prey on young Arctic ground squirrels and young Arctic hares.

Ermine travel on the snow surface and burrow under the snow to use runways made by lemmings. With good color and night vision, ermine are primarily nocturnal, and the low light of Arctic winter likely causes no hardships. Remaining active during the winter, ermine catch lemmings by pursuing them in their burrows under the snow. Ermine often take over the burrow of their prey and winter nests are found lined with masses of lemming fur. Excess food may be cached for later use, particularly in fall and winter.

Ermines are in turn hunted by wolverine, Arctic and red foxes, and snowy owls. Weasel skulls are often found in snowy owl pellets. Ermine show little fear of humans and may become established in and around field camps. Their rapid and erratic movements make them a difficult subject for photography.

Although weasels were not prominent in traditional native use in North America, their skins were used to decorate clothing. The Copper Inuit of the western Canadian Arctic prized ermine skins highly for use on their ceremonial dancing caps and suspended them from the back of their coats as charms for luck in hunting or against sickness.

Weasel, Nunavut, Canada.
Copyright Paul Nicklen/National Geographic Image Collection

The range of the least weasel (*Mustela nivalis*) just reaches the southern boundaries of the Arctic. Although this tiny weasel is usually found from the treeline south, it has been recorded from Herschel Island on the Yukon's north coast. The least weasel is found in Alaska, in most of the Yukon, and on the mainland in much of the Northwest Territories, but not in northern tundra areas or in Nunavut. In Eurasia, its range includes the Arctic coast except the northernmost tundra areas of Siberia. The smallest of the carnivores, this weasel seldom exceeds 200 mm in length. Like the ermine, the least weasel is brown and white in summer, and turns white in winter; however, its short tail does not have a black tip. Least weasels prey on voles and mice and take over their nests, often lining them with the fur of their prey. This species is hunted by great horned and other owls. Due to its size and rarity, the least weasel is of little significance to the fur trade.

DAVID R. GRAY

See also **Wolverine**

Further Reading

Banfield, A.W.F., *The Mammals of Canada*, Toronto: University of Toronto Press, 1974

Corbet, G.B., *The Mammals of the Palaearctic Region: A Taxonomic Review*, Ithaca, New York: British Museum/ Cornell University Press, 1978

King, Carolyn M., "Mustela erminea." *Mammalian Species*, 195 (1983): 1–8

Maher, William J., "Predation by weasels on a winter population of lemming, Banks Island, Northwest Territories." *Canadian Field-Naturalist*, 81 (1967): 248–250

Packard, Jane M. & L. David Mech, "An observation of a wild weasel, *Mustela erminea*, moving its pups." *Canadian Field-Naturalist,* 105(1) (1991): 110–111

Simms, David A. "Spring and summer food habits of an ermine (*Mustela erminea*) in the Central Arctic." *Canadian Field-Naturalist,* 92(2) (1978): 192–193

Simpson, Mark R., "Observation of an arctic groundsquirrel, *Spermophilus p. parryi*–short-tailed weasel, *Mustela erminea*, interaction." *Canadian Field-Naturalist,* 104(3) (1990): 473–474

Youngman, Phillip M., *Mammals of the Yukon Territory*, Ottawa: National Museum of Natural Sciences, Publications in Zoology, No. 10, 1975

WEATHER

Weather may be humankind's most widely discussed topic. The influence of the weather ranges from inconsequential to catastrophic, and dictates many of the decisions made by humans. Weather and climate have been a major factor in the settlement, development, and evolution of the Arctic. Indigenous peoples survived in the Arctic because they understood the natural environment and adapted to its demands. Weather influenced every aspect of their lives, including where they lived.

Weather is the general term for the conditions prevailing in the atmosphere, especially in the layer near the ground, over a short period of time or at a specific time at any one place. Climate describes the average weather conditions throughout the seasons over a fairly wide or very extensive area of the Earth's surface and considered over many years (usually 30–35 years), and usually describes extreme and infrequent events.

Temperature, humidity, sunshine, pressure, wind, cloudiness, precipitation, and the presence of fog or mist are all taken into account when describing weather.

Seasons and Solar Radiation

Solar radiation is the fundamental driver of global climate. The angle of the sun at a location on Earth determines the season, and in the Arctic the season of the year influences weather conditions more than any other location on the Earth.

Although four seasons make up the Arctic year, the Arctic winter is long and the summer is short. In the Arctic, the sun does not rise high in the sky at any time of the year, and the sun always strikes the ground at an oblique angle. Sun angle, or the height of the sun in the sky, controls the Arctic climate, not the fraction of the year the sun is above the horizon (which is the same everywhere on Earth). The lower the angle of the sun, the larger the area of ground a given amount of solar energy strikes, and the greater the amount of energy absorbed by a thicker atmosphere. Snow and ice have a high albedo (reflectivity) that also reduces the amount of solar radiation absorbed at the Earth's surface.

During the long polar night of Arctic winter when the sun never rises, which varies in length from a single day on the Arctic Circle to six months at the pole, no solar radiation reaches the ground. If it were not for the arrival of air masses from the south, temperatures would drop to very low levels. Winter ends when breakup begins, which is usually not before June in the High Arctic.

Air and Ocean Circulation

The height of the sun is not the only control on Arctic weather. The cold is moderated by warmth reaching the Arctic from the south in the form of warm air masses and warm ocean currents. Circulation of air and ocean reduces temperature extremes, and without global circulation the poles would be colder and the tropics warmer.

In the winter, a cold low-pressure vortex in the middle and upper troposphere caps the pole. Westerly winds, winds that blow from the subtropical high-pressure area to the temperate low-pressure area between 35° N and 65° N and are predominantly from the southwest in response to the equator-pole temperature gradient, flow around this vortex. These westerly jet streams at the periphery of the vortex play a vital role in the development and steering of the surface cyclones (low atmospheric pressure) and anticyclones (high atmospheric pressure). Areas beneath the periphery of the vortex generally experience a succession of eastward-moving frontal cyclones, whereas regions under the cold core of the vortex experience persistent cold non-frontal low systems.

At the surface in high nothern latitudes, the vortex is obscured by a complex pattern of high- and low-pressure areas. The surface atmospheric pressure in the Arctic is characterized by semipermanent (i.e., long-term average) highs and lows, within which traveling cyclones lasting only a day or so form. Stable deep troughs (a narrow elongated region of low barometric pressure between two areas of higher pressure) are located over eastern North America and Eastern Siberia in winter (the Icelandic Low and the Aleutian Low), and these have a great influence on midlatitude cyclones. Atlantic cyclones move northward into Baffin Bay, where they contribute significantly to the maritime regime of the eastern Canadian Arctic. The central Canadian Arctic and the central and eastern Siberian Arctic are dominated by high-pressure conditions in winter and spring (the North American High and the Siberian High). Spring is the only season when there is a semipermanent Arctic high-pressure system. In summer, the polar vortex contracts and weakens. Although the major trough is at that time centered over Baffin Island, weak cyclonic activity is widespread in the Arctic. Lows on the Arctic front affect both northern North America and northern Siberia.

Surface weather is strongly influenced by the high degree of stability of the lowest layer of the atmosphere, which is stable because of radiational cooling over snow and ice. Surface weather over much of the Arctic and Subarctic depends on the local effectiveness of anticyclones and cyclones in either intensifying or breaking down this very cold stable layer. The center of anticyclones is characterized by calm clear conditions and is often associated with temperature inversions. Most of the surface weather factors, including cloud cover, precipitation, winds, and temperature change, are associated with the presence and passage of cyclones.

Temperature

Some of the more common misconceptions of the Arctic are that it is intensely cold year-round, snow and ice perpetually cover land, and winter is continuous. In contrast, a great variety of temperature and climate conditions can be found in the Arctic, including maritime, coastal, and continental climates.

Summer temperatures across the Arctic are relatively uniform. Diurnal temperature ranges are less in summer than in any other season in the Arctic. The mean temperature of the warmest month is 10°C in the southern Arctic, and is only 10° warmer in the High Arctic. In continental tundra areas, maximum daily temperatures may reach 25°C, and temperatures of 20°C are occasionally recorded at 80° N latitude. In much of the Arctic, the little snow that accumulates over winter melts with the onset of warm summer temperatures.

In the summer, the temperature varies on a 24-hour basis. Even in the midnight sun, the sun is higher when it is to the south at midday, creating warmer temperatures than when it is to the north at midnight. Temperatures in mid-summer tend to remain above freezing, although frost is possible at any time. Summer ends when freeze-up begins, usually in August or September.

Winter temperatures across the Arctic are more variable than summer temperatures. The mean temperatures in the coldest month vary from −5°C to −10°C in the southern Arctic, to −30°C to −35°C in the High Arctic. Extreme minimum temperatures below −70°C have been recorded.

Temperature inversions, a phenomenon in which there is a temperature increase with increasing height instead of the normal decrease, are observed in all Arctic regions. Inversions are most prominent over pack ice.

Precipitation and Moisture

As one moves toward the pole, Arctic climates become drier and more desertlike, since low temperatures limit atmospheric water content. Although precipitation decreases with increasing latitude, the ability of air to hold moisture decreases and humidity increases, making abundant moisture available in areas that are classified as polar desert. The relative humidity of the air above the Arctic Ocean in the winter is always close to 100%, reaching a maximum in mid-winter and a minimum in June over ice and August over water. Precipitation in the Arctic ranges from 70 to 200 mm, most of it falling as snowfall.

In Arctic regions, snow or ice covers the ground for a significant part of the year. Snow and ice significantly modify air masses crossing the region. Precipitation is largely related to the passage of cyclones (a system of winds circulating anticlockwise round a center of low barometric pressure) over open water, and as large areas of open water are uncommon, the occasional open water areas in winter become important heat and moisture sources. Air masses cool when traveling over ice and snow, reducing the water-holding capacity of the air to the extent that much of the Arctic is considered a cold desert.

Wind is an important factor in the distribution of snow, and particularly windy sites may have little or no snow cover even in the winter. The coldness of Arctic air causes precipitation to take the characteristic form of small, dry, hard snow particles that are easily redistributed by wind to produce blowing-snow storms. The heaviest snowfalls usually arrive in October, after which the air becomes so cold that it can carry only negligible amounts of moisture. Thereafter, snow is swept off ridges and accumulates in hollows as its distribution is influenced by wind conditions.

Weather Phenomenon

Numerous weather phenomena are common to the Arctic, including ice blink, water sky, whiteout, and Arctic mirages.

On cloudy days, sunlight that penetrates the clouds is reflected back and forth between the ground surface and the underside of clouds. Ice blink is a streak of dazzling brightness on the underside of distant clouds, where they are lit from below by sunlight reflected up from a surface of snow or ice. Water sky is the converse of ice blink. A dark patch appearing on the otherwise bright ceiling of cloud over a snow-covered world shows that something dark occurs below, nearly always a patch of open water in the pack ice.

Whiteout, an optical phenomenon, is produced by a combination of overcast sky (diffuse, shadowless illumination) and an unbroken snow or ice surface. Whiteout also refers to blowing snow conditions when visibility is restricted.

Mirages occur when the temperature of the air near the ground changes greatly over a short vertical distance. Over Arctic sea ice, air temperatures commonly rise as one goes upward (an inversion), and these changing temperatures can produce mirages. Light travels slightly faster through warmer air, creating an object that is viewed from a distance to appear displaced and distorted.

Clouds and Fog

Clouds over the Arctic Ocean are least in winter and spring and greatest in summer. The cloud maximum in summer is unique to the Arctic and is contrary to cloud patterns in midlatitudes. In the winter, the combination of frozen ground and ocean and the absence of sufficient incoming radiation for evaporation create a limited supply of moisture to the atmosphere.

The vertical motion of air favors cloud conditions under cyclonic conditions and clear sky under anticyclonic conditions. Clouds are also created over moist surfaces with high evaporation rates, and when moisture-laden air is cooled as it rises over a high relief barrier.

Low cloud and fog are especially characteristic of coastal areas and broken pack ice in summer. The melting of pack ice in summer leads to the formation of persistent fog and low cloud. Summer fog is generally caused by advection (horizontal movement) of relatively warm and moist air, such as the air over melting ice or cold water, moving over a cooler surface, such as sea ice, causing the lower layers of air to chill below the dew point. Advection fog is most prevalent from June to September, is patchy and tends to be short in duration, and rarely forms in winds over 20 knots. During the winter, small patches of fog form over open water leads in the pack ice. This phenomenon, sometimes referred to as Arctic sea smoke, develops when cold air flows over open water and moisture and heat are rapidly released into the air.

Ice fog often forms during the Arctic spring. Ice fog is a mist of tiny ice crystals floating in the air. Often, these conditions produce the appearance of halos around the sun (caused by light refracting through the ice crystals) and other optical displays such as sun dogs (two bright spots on either side of the sun, lying on the halo if one is present) and sun pillars. Although only parts of the circle may be visible, the halo is always of the same radius, since hexagonal ice refracts rays from the sun by an angle of 22° (or about the span between the thumb and little finger if one holds the arm outstretched to the sun). Ice fog typically reduces visibility at ground level without obscuring the sun.

Wind and Wind Chill

Over the Arctic Ocean, surface wind velocities are characteristically light, between 8 and 10 knots. Annual mean wind speeds are greatest at exposed coastal locations near cyclone tracks, where storms are most frequent.

Windy conditions are associated with the passage of fronts and low-pressure systems. Winds of around 5 knots will cause unconsolidated snow to drift along the ground surface, at speeds of 10–15 knots; this snow will lift into the air. Once drifting snow reaches a height of 6 feet, it is referred to as blowing snow. This phenomenon commonly occurs on half of the days in the winter season in many parts of the Arctic.

The combination of wind and low temperatures can produce much greater heat loss from exposed flesh than the air temperature alone would suggest. Wind chill provides an estimate of apparent temperature and is useful to determine the risk of frostbite. Wind chill is a significant factor in determining the safety of outdoor travel in the winter months in the Arctic.

Arctic Weather and Climate Change

Northern environments and communities are entering a period of unprecedented change. Emissions of greenhouse gases due to human activities are altering the atmosphere and are expected to change global climate in ways that may be detrimental to our environmental, social, and economic systems. An increasing body of observations provides convincing evidence of a warming world. Changes in the climate system over the past 50 years are expected to continue throughout the 21st century and persist for many centuries to come. The Intergovernmental Panel on Climate Change (IPCC) concluded in its Third Assessment Report that "the confidence in the ability of models to project future climate has increased" and "there is new and stronger evidence that most of the warming observed over the last 50 years is attributable to human activities" (Watson, 2001).

The northern environment is demonstrating clear scientific and observational evidence of climate change, evidence that strongly supports the current IPCC models and predictions on global climate change. It is commonplace for northern residents to discuss unusual weather conditions in casual conversation. Local observations appear to concur with the science and, in some cases, provide insights into local and regional conditions that smaller global climate models do not detect.

Northern regions are extremely vulnerable to projected climate change and its impacts. Because of a variety of positive feedback mechanisms, the North is likely to show the effects of climate change more rapidly and more severely than any other area on the earth. Changes in the polar climate are likely to affect the rest of the world through increased sea levels from melting of the cryosphere (permafrost, glaciers, sea ice), increased warming of lower latitudes from slowing of oceanic transport of heat, and increased greenhouse gas levels through carbon dioxide and methane emissions from peatlands. Human activity in the North will be affected by these physical and ecological changes, and there will be economic benefits and costs. Benefits may include new opportunities for shipping, lower operational costs for the oil and gas industry, lower heating costs, and easier access for tourism. Costs may include reduced transportation capabilities across frozen ground and water, sustainability of traditional lifestyles, and implications of reductions in sea ice on trade and defense.

AYNSLIE OGDEN

See also **Climate; Climate Change; Intergovernmental Panel on Climate Change (IPCC); Polar Lows; Polar Vortex; Precipitation and Moisture; Windchill**

Further Reading

Ahrens, Donald, *Meterology Today: An Introduction to Weather, Climate, and the Environment*, Pacific Grove, California: Brooks/Cole, 2000

Burroughs, William J., *Watching the World's Weather*, Cambridge and New York: Cambridge University Press, 1991

Burroughs, W.J. et al., *Weather: Nature Company Guides,* Time Life, London 1996

Houghton, J.T., Y. Ding, D.J. Griggs, M. Noguer, P.J. van der Linden & D. Xiaosu (editors), *Climate Change 2001: The Scientific Basis, Contribution of Working Group I to the Third Assessment Report of the Intergovernmental Panel on Climate Change (IPCC)*, Cambridge and New York: Cambridge University Press, 2001

Lamb, H.H., *Climate, History and the Modern World*, London and New York: Routledge, 1995

Ludlum, David M., *The Audubon Society Field Guides: Weather*, New York: Knopf, 1993

Pielou, E.C., *A Naturalist's Guide to the Arctic*, Chicago: University of Chicago Press, 1994

Sater, John et al., *Arctic Environment and Resources,* Washington, District of Columbia: The Arctic Institute of North America, 1971

Watson, R. (editor), *Climate Change 2001: Synthesis Report. Contribution of Working Groups I, II, and III to the Third Assessment Report of the Intergovernmental Panel on Climate Change*, Cambridge, UK: Cambridge University Press, 2001

WEGENER, ALFRED VON

Alfred Von Wegener was a German-born explorer and scientist who studied in Heidelberg (Germany), Innsbruck (Austria), and Berlin, where he obtained his doctorate in astronomy in November 1904. In 1905, Wegener followed his brother Kurt to the aerological observatory in Lindenberg to work as a technical meteorological assistant under Richard Assmann (1845–1918). In 1906, Alfred and Kurt Wegener established the world record at that time of over 52 h in a hot air balloon. Due to his meteorological expertise, Wegener was the only German to be invited to participate in the Danish Greenland expedition (1906–1908) under the leadership of Ludwig Mylius-Erichsen (1872–1907). Wegener was the first researcher to apply kites and air balloons to study the polar atmosphere up to 3000 m height. He used data collected during the Greenland expedition to finish his habilitation thesis in 1909 on "Die Drachen- und Fesselballonaufstiege bei der Grönlandexpedition."

He was subsequently offered a position as docent (lecturer) in meteorology and astronomy at the University in Marburg (Germany). During this time, Wegener published the summary of his lectures on meteorology in *Thermodynamics of the Atmosphere* (1911), which was the standard textbook in Germany for many years. Therein, he proposed a new mechanism for raindrop formation—the Wegener-Bergeron-Findeisen procedure—that is still used today for studying rain.

In 1912, Wegener returned to Greenland for his second expedition (1912–1913), during which he and his three companions nearly died when climbing a calving glacier. This was the first expedition to overwinter on the Greenland ice cap and to make the longest crossing ever of the Greenland ice cap on foot. The expedition traversed 750 miles of barren snow and ice to heights over 3000 m. The crew survived the trip only due to the assistance of Inuit. As a result, Wegener collected and published a wealth of meteorological and glaciological data, which made him the leading expert in Arctic meteorology among his peers. After returning from Greenland, he married Else, the daughter of Wladimir Köppen, who was the leading meteorologist in Germany at that time.

Wegener was an extremely efficient scientist who worked in many disciplines. He published 170 articles and books, most of them dealing with meteorology but also on astronomy, meteorites, geology, and geophysics. He is perhaps best known for his contributions concerning the continental drift, the concept of drifting continents and widening oceans. In autumn 1911, Wegener read a publication on the fossil records of the west and east coasts of the Atlantic Ocean in which the authors concluded that these continents had once been connected by a now sunken land bridge. A brilliant interdisciplinary scientist, Wegener incorporated these results with those from paleontology, climatology, and geology into a complex of theories about the continental drift. He presented his ideas on January 6, 1912 at the meeting of the Geological Association in Frankfurt and four days later in Marburg. His interdisciplinary theory caused much controversy and was especially disregarded by geologists.

Nonetheless, Wegener continued to work on his groundbreaking ideas during World War I, when he served at the German Army weather broadcasting service after being wounded in 1914. In 1915, he published the influential *Die Entstehung der Kontinente und Ozeane* [The Origin of the Continents and Oceans]. In the third edition (published 1922) of this book, he concluded that about 200 million years ago, the supercontinent Pangaea (from the Greek word for "all lands") broke apart and the continents started to move. The international scientific community largely ignored his concept until the book's third edition was translated into English. Again, his theory provoked hostile reactions and was finally rejected. Forty more years would pass before discoveries in paleomagnetism and seafloor mapping would convince the scientific community that Wegener's proposals regarding modern plate tectonics were correct.

The dispute over the continental drift had a disastrous impact on Wegener's scientific career. In 1919, he became head of the theoretical meteorological department of the Seewetterwarte Hamburg and taught at the University of Hamburg, but he never received a full professorship at a German university. He was finally appointed professor of meteorology and geophysics at the University of Graz in Austria in 1924. In 1929, he traveled to West Greenland with Johannes Georgi, Fritz Loewe, and Ernst Sorge to prepare for a large meteorological campaign the following year. In spring 1930, Wegener arrived in Greenland with 21 other scientists and technicians for his fourth and final expedition to Greenland. The plan was to establish three meteorological observatories along 71° N: one at the west edge of the ice cap, one at the east edge, and one in the middle of transect. Wegener's group arrived at the west coast of Greenland on April 15, but due to the ice conditions it took until June 17 to land all their equipment in the base camp. Within a month, they had established the west station and by July 30 had reached the midcap station called "Eismitte." For the third station, a separate expedition had landed on the east coast of Greenland. Station Eismitte was located about 400 km from the west coast at an elevation of 3000 m. Weather conditions in 1930 were unusually harsh so that only a limited amount of supplies were brought to Eismitte, where Georgi and the glaciologist Ernst Sorge were planning to overwinter. Therefore, Wegener decided to start a rescue expedition from the base camp on September 30 with the meteorologist Fritz Lowe, 13 Greenlanders, and 15 dogsleds. Progress was slow, and all but one Greenlander gave up and returned to the base station. After 30 days, they finally arrived at Eismitte, where Georgi and Sorge had dug a housing shelter into the firm ice. On November 3, Wegener and the Greenlander Rasmus Villumsen started their way back to the base camp. Lowe had to stay with Georgi and Sorge as his feet and fingers were severely frost bitten. Wegener never returned to the base camp, so a search started in April 1931. Wegener's body was found on May 12, 1931, buried in the ice by Villumsen with great care. The latter was never found. Wegener's body was left on the Greenland ice cap, the site marked with an iron cross.

To honor Wegener's remarkable contributions to science, the main German polar research institute (founded in 1980) was named Alfred Wegener Institute for Polar Research. Furthermore, the German meteorological society honors outstanding scientists with the Alfred Wegener Medal every 3 years.

Biography

Alfred von Wegener was born in Berlin, Germany, on November 1, 1880. He received his doctorate in astronomy in 1904 and finished his habilitation thesis in meteorology in 1909. From 1909 to 1919, he worked at the University of Marburg, Germany, as a docent. Wegener was meteorologist at the Seewetterwarte in Hamburg until 1924, when he became a professor of meteorology and geophysics at the University of Graz in Austria. He participated in four expeditions to Greenland (1906–1908, 1912–1913, 1929, and 1930), where he died in 1930 (exact date unknown) during his last expedition.

ROLF GRADINGER

See also **Mylius-Erichsen, Ludwig**

Further Reading

Hughes, P., "The meteorologist who started a revolution." *Weatherwise*, 47(1994): 29–35

Körber, H.-G., *Alfred Wegener*, Leipzig: Teubner, 1980

Reinke-Kunze, C., *Alfred Wegener—Polarforscher und Entdecker der Kontinentaldrift*, Basel: Birkhäuser, 1994

Schwarzbach, M., *Alfred Wegener—The Father of Continental Drift*, Madison, Wisconsin: Science Tech, 1986

———, *Alfred Wegener und die Drift der Kontinente*, Stuttgart: Wiss. Verlgs, 1989

Wegener, Alfred von, *Drachen- und Fesselballonaufstiege*, København: Bianco Lunos Bogtrykkeri, 1909

———, *Die entstehung der kontinente und ozeane*, Germany: Braunschweig, F. Vieweg & sohn akt.-ges., 1922 [*The Origin of Continents and Oceans*], translated from the third German edition by J.G.A. Skerl, New York: Dutton, 1924

Wegener, Else von (editor), *Greenland Journey: The Story of Wegener's German Expedition in 1930–31, as Told by Members of the Exposition and the Leader's Diary*, Glasgow and London: Blackie & Son, 1939

———, *Alfred Wegener—Tagebücher, Briefe, Erinnerungen*, Wiesbaden: Brockhaus, 1960

Wegener, Kurt von, *Wissenschaftliche Ergebnisse der Deutschen Grönland-Expedition Alfred Wegeners in den Jahren 1929 und 1939/31*, 7 Bände, Leipzig, 1933–1940

Wutzke, U., *Der Forscher von der Friedrichsgracht—Leben und Leistung Alfred Wegeners*, Leipzig: Brockhaus, 1988

———, *Durch die weiße Wüste. Leben und Leistungen des Grönlandforschers und Entdeckers der Kontinentaldrift Alfred Wegener*, Gotha: Perthes, 1997

WELLMAN, WALTER

Walter Wellman was a lifelong journalist and Washington (District of Columbia) correspondent for a major Chicago newspaper, but his abiding passion was exploration. He carried out five expeditions toward the North Pole (three of them by airship); an expedition to Watling Island (San Salvador) in the Bahamas to locate the first landfall of Columbus; and, in 1910, an aborted airship flight across the Atlantic Ocean.

In 1893, at the age of 35, Wellman journeyed to Norway to study ice conditions around Spitsbergen (Svalbard) and, in the process, found a short cut to the North Pole. In the spring of 1894, Wellman sailed for Spitsbergen on a Norwegian ice steamer called *Ragnvald Jarl*, eventually pitching camp in early May

at British sportsman Arnold Pike's House on the shores of Virgo Harbor, a locale soon to figure prominently in the history of polar aviation. On May 10, Wellman sailed north and east on the *Jarl* and arrived at the Seven Islands 48 hours later, an extremely speedy passage. At the Seven Islands, Wellman's good fortune turned. After leaving the *Ragnvald Jarl* and taking to sledges and aluminum boats, Wellman's party scarcely progressed north when a courier overtook them and reported that ice had holed the *Jarl* along the western shore of tiny Walden Island. Apparently undismayed by the disaster, after sending *Ragnvald Jarl*'s crew south in search of rescue, Wellman turned and again started north. By this time, the summer sun had warmed the pack ice into a mass of shifting slush. With sledges now being useless, Wellman ordered his dogs shot. Exhausted and freezing, with their clothes and equipment soaked by slush and falls into open leads of subfreezing water, Wellman's men hauled the boats back to Walden.

This experience led Wellman to his first consideration of the use of some method of aerial exploration in the Arctic. "…[P]ushing and pulling the heavy sledges and boats over the rough ice on this expedition," Wellman later wrote, "the idea first came to me of using an aerial craft in Arctic exploration. Often I looked up into the air and wished we had some means of travelling that royal road where there were no ice hummocks, no leads of open water, no obstacles to rapid progress" (Wellman, 1911: 35).

In the spring of 1898, Wellman chartered another ice steamer, *Frithjof*, and headed north to Franz Josef Land, with three other Americans (Evelyn Briggs Baldwin, Quirof Harlan, and Edward Hofma) and five Norwegians (Paul Bjørvig, Bernt Bentzen, Daniel Johansen, Emil Ellefsen, and Olaf Ellefsen). "To our imaginations," Wellman wrote, "[Franz Josef Land] presented itself as a paradise of opportunity" (Wellman, 1911: 42). Since Wellman used no aeronautical apparatus on this expedition, his aerial ambitions were confined to a brief and ultimately futile search for the missing Swedish balloonist Salomon August Andrée and his crew. Wellman's dash for the pole in the spring of 1899 failed off the east coast of Rudolf Island. Wellman then sent Baldwin to the north and east, where Baldwin discovered and mapped several islands and straights around Wilczek Island.

In 1906, Wellman's newspaper provided the necessary funds to build an airship in Paris, and a large airship hangar and expedition base camp at Virgo Harbor. But the hangar was not completed until August and, when tested, the airship's engines promptly self-destructed. Wellman returned to Virgo Harbor in the summer of 1907 with an airship configured by Melvin Vaniman, who had scrapped the original Louis Godard car and designed one of his own. He built the new car with steel tubing and steel-reinforced wood, 115 ft long and 12 ft wide at its open top. The car tapered inward from the top, down to a narrow catwalk, underneath which a long, steel 1200-gallon fuel tank formed the keel. Vaniman wrapped the car in oiled silk to protect the crew from wind, and mounted a more powerful propulsion. He selected a Lorraine-Dietrich 75 hp engine, driving two propellers mounted, not fore and aft, but side by side, on booms riding out from the sides of the car. August 1907 came and went, and still the airship remained tethered in her shed. The winds did not abate until early September, at which time Wellman ordered a short trial flight of 15 miles. This was the first time a motorized airship had flown in the Arctic.

Wellman tried for the pole one last time, in the summer of 1909. About 60 miles north of the hangar at Virgo Harbor, the trailing ballast line that Wellman called an "equilibrator" fell off. The disaster caused Wellman to turn the airship around and receive a rescue tow from a nearby Norwegian survey ship, the *Farm*.

In the fall of 1910, Wellman built a new dirigible. With this new dirigible, Wellman flew in a huge arc past Cape Cod and then southeast for over 1000 miles—a far greater distance than that from Virgo Harbor to the Pole—before engine trouble forced the journalist and his crew to abandon ship not far from Bermuda. Wellman brought the ship down within a mile of a passing steamer, which delivered him and his crew to shore. This Atlantic adventure set a record for the longest airship flight to that moment in aviation history. After the failure of the Atlantic flight in 1910, Wellman lived on until 1934, but he never got into another airship.

Biography

Walter Wellman was born in Mentor, Ohio, in 1858, and died in New York City of liver cancer in 1934. He founded a newspaper, the *Cincinnati Evening Post*, at the age of 21. In 1884, he became the Washington (District of Columbia) correspondent and political reporter for the *Chicago Herald* and its successor, the *Record-Herald*. He remained as a Washington correspondent until 1911. His book about his polar expeditions was published in 1911 as *The Aerial Age*. Other significant articles on polar subjects authored by Wellman include "Where is Andrée?" (1898); "Sledging Toward the Pole" (1900a); "An Arctic Day and Night" (1900b); "The Polar Airship" (1906); "By Airship to the North Pole" (1907a); and "Will the America Fly to the Pole?" (1907b).

P.J. CAPELOTTI

See also **Andrée, Salomon August; Franz Josef Land; Race to the North Pole**

Further Reading

Capelotti, P.J., "A preliminary archaeological survey of Camp Wellman at Virgohamn, Danskøya, Svalbard." *Polar Record*, 30(175) (1994): 265–276
———, *The Wellman Polar Airship Expeditions at Virgohamna, Danskøya, Svalbard; A Study in Aerospace Archaeology*, Oslo: Norwegian Polar Institute, Meddelelser Nr. 145, 1997
———, *By Airship to the North Pole: An Archaeology of Human Exploration*, New Brunswick: Rutgers University Press, 1999
——— (editor), *The Svalbard Archipelago: American Military and Political Geographies of Spitsbergen and Other Norwegian Polar Territories, 1941–1950*, Jefferson, North Carolina: McFarland Publishers, 2000
Mabley, Edward H., *The Motor Balloon "America,"* Brattleboro, Vermont: Stephen Greene Press, 1969
National Geographic Magazine, "Walter Wellman's Expedition to the North Pole." April 1906
Scientific American, "The Fate of Vaniman." July 20, 1912
Stevens, George E., "Walter Wellman: journalist, explorer, 'astronaut'." *The* [Lake County, Ohio] *Historical Society Quarterly*, 11(3) (1969)
Toland, John, *The Great Dirigibles*, New York: Dover, 1972
Van Dyck, Herman, "The evolution of the Wellman/Vaniman airships, Parts One—Three." *Jack Knight Air Log—The Zeppelin Collector*, January, April, July 1996
Vaniman, Melvin, "Revolutionizing air travel." *Aircraft*, May 1912
Wellman, Walter, *The Aerial Age; A Thousand Miles By Airship Over the Atlantic Ocean; Airship Voyages Over the Polar Sea; The Past, the Present and the Future of Aerial Navigation*, New York: A.R. Keller, 1911

WEST NORDIC COUNCIL

The West Nordic Council was established in 1985 as the West Nordic Parliamentarian Council of Cooperation. Its charter was revised in 1997, with the aim of promoting collaboration and cooperation between the Western Nordic countries: the Faroe Islands, Iceland, and Greenland. The West Nordic Council is also an associate member of the Arctic Council, which consists of six parliamentarians from each of the three countries. The council's representatives are politically selected and represent the balance of party politics in each member state. It has a presidium with three members from the member countries. The chairperson of the West Nordic Council from 2000 to 2001 was Ole Lynge from Greenland, and from 2001 to 2002 Hjalmar Arnason, a member of the Icelandic parliament, served. The current president is Jógvan á Lakjuni of the Faroe Islands.

The charter of the council stipulates that Iceland will finance half of the council's financial expenditures, while the Faroe Islands and Greenland each pay one-quarter. The council secretariat has so far been located in the Icelandic parliament, *Althingi*.

The primary goal of the West Nordic Council is to promote West Nordic interests, to be guardians of the natural resources, fishery and culture of the North

Atlantic area, and to promote issues with regard to communication, trade, and the environment. In addition, it functions as a link between Nordic and Arctic interests. Cooperation between the West Nordic Council and the Nordic Council is based on various formalized agreements, and the West Nordic Council has been represented at all sessions and thematic conferences at the Nordic Council since 1996.

One of the first tasks of the West Nordic Council was to reconstruct the Thjodhildar church and Eirík the Red's farm in Greenland. The council also initiated a conference in Tórshavn on the Faroe Islands about women in politics in June 1999. The council proclaimed its theme for the year 2001 as West Nordic Hunting Culture. As a part of the agenda, the West Nordic Council hosted a conference on traditional hunting in Akureyri in Iceland in June 2001, and created a traveling exhibition, Hunters of the North, in 2002. The West Nordic Council has also proclaimed 2002 as "the year of traffic" and 2003 as "the year of health."

In recent years, the West Nordic Council has met with the challenge that the attention and the donation of money from the Nordic Council have been influenced by the tendency in the Nordic Council to look eastward after the breakup of the Soviet Union. Hence, the Nordic Council has increasingly been involved in politics related to the Baltic regions, to the Barents region (North West Russia), and to cooperation with the European Union.

JENS KAALHAUGE NIELSEN

See also **Barents Region; Nordic Council of Ministers**

Further Reading

West Nordic Council website: www.vestnordisk.is/

WESTERN TELEGRAPH EXPEDITION

In the mid-19th century, the United States developed an infrastructure that made the breadth of their territory smaller. In 1861, the Western Union Telegraph Company created the first transcontinental telegraph line, shortly followed by the government's transcontinental railroad. However, attempts to lay a telegraph cable across the Atlantic would fail five times; an alternate route began as early as 1857, and was pursued intensively in the mid-1860s. Both cables expressed the ideological climate of Manifest Destiny; the alternative would run 5000 miles through British Columbia and Yukon Territory, through Russian America, across the Bering Strait and through Siberia to Nikolaevsk on the Sea of Okhotsk, whereupon the line would be extended to Europe. The entrepreneur Perry McDonough Collins inspired the venture, having obtained a charter from the Russians and garnered the

support of then-Senator William Seward, shortly to become the secretary of state who orchestrated the purchase of Russian America.

Collins merged with Western Union to commence the project. Organizers believed that the difficult Arctic environment as well as diplomatic relations with Russia required military efficiency to accomplish the task. Throughout the American Civil War, Colonel Charles Bulkley proved himself and the US Military Telegraph Corps adept at constructing and maintaining lines in Confederate territory since December 1861; thus, the North Pacific project would be commanded by Bulkley. Second in command was Captain Charles Scammon, on leave from the Revenue Cutter Service, in charge of operations in the Bering Sea. Heading the Land Service was Frank Wicker, and under him the Russian engineer Serge Abasa, in charge of the Siberian Division. The American Division, which comprised both the efforts in Canada and Russian America, was led by Edward Conway in British Columbia and Robert Kennicott in Alaska.

Colonel Bulkley determined that two submarine cables would span Bering Strait: the first from Cape Nome to Plover Bay, then another across Anadyr Bay to the mouth of the Anadyr River, whereupon the cable would travel southward toward Petropavlosk. Many of the men had left Civil War battlefields to join the teams leaving San Francisco in 1864–1865 for Canada, Russian America, and Siberia. For the next few summers, Scammon's fleet of six ships transported both men and supplies to the primary landing points: St Michael, Grantley Harbor, Kelsey Station on the Anadyr River, and Gizhiga, on the northern shores of the Sea of Okhotsk.

During winter months, the parties would reconnoiter possible routes, while the summers would be used to clear the paths, cut poles, and construct the stations and routes. The divisions hired local laborers to do the major work: cutting poles, clearing land, and planting the poles. They would also, in the tradition of Euro-American exploration, take advantage of native hospitality—utilize their trade networks, their food supplies, and their knowledge of the region. The assistance and generosity of native peoples were crucial to not only the successes of the expeditions, but to saving the lives of its men. In British Columbia, Conway's fatigued party would at times rely on the scattered groups of First Nations; the Siberian Division interrupted the trading networks and cultural customs of Chukchis in the far north and the Kamchadals and the "less friendly" Koryak of Kamchatka; the Russian-America Division utilized Athapaskan and Inuit hunters to assist in collecting museum specimens.

The British Columbia party began in the late summer of 1864. Work at first went faster than the team was supplied, and in the winter of early 1865 division leader Conway sent separate parties to explore possible telegraph routes. By the end of 1865, the telegraph line had nearly reached the Yukon Territory, and would continue northward in the spring of 1866.

In the summer of 1865, Scammon's ships sailed again; at Sitka, in southeast Alaska, the party had initially caused friction with Alaska natives, requiring the diplomacy of both Bulkley and Kennicott. But eventually, they traded with and enlisted the labor of many natives for the American Division, and Scammon's ships parted ways. One dropped off Kennicott, his men, and supplies at St Michael, near the Yukon River delta, by mid-September. Another ship deposited the Siberian Division at Petropavlovsk; by September, Scammon's ship had explored up the Anadyr River, engaging in an uneasy trading relationship with the Chukchi people. Twelve men were then dispatched to the mouth to construct the coastal route from Anadyr Bay to the Bering Strait. Although they immediately constructed a winter camp, the Chukchi mercifully took them into their village for the winter. Amidst uneasiness wrought from Chukchi mistrust of the explorers as spies for the Russians, one Chukchi served as a guide to lead two men south downriver.

Meanwhile, Abasa divided those left at Petropavlovsk into two parties to explore the possible route, and all met in Gizhiga by the end of the following winter, 1866. By the summer the entire division, including those from the Anadyr River, rendezvoused at Anadyrsk, whereupon they organized residents to cut poles for the telegraph.

The Russian-America Division made less progress than the other divisions, most likely due to the organization of the party. Unlike all the other commanders, Robert Kennicott was not a military man, but instead a naturalist who had spent time with the Hudson's Bay Company collecting for the Smithsonian Institution, and who most recently had been curator of the Chicago Academy of Sciences. His goal in Alaska therefore had a distinctly scientific dimension, where before the goals of government exploration would supersede those of natural history. Kennicott organized the party by separating the military men from Scientific Corps, whose main duty was to collect specimens and data. In fact, many naturalists, later to be recognized as Alaskan experts, enlisted in the Scientific Corps, including William Healey Dall, the artist and naturalist Henry Elliott, and the painter Frederick Whymper. The structure of the party not only reflected the uneasy relationship between quasi-military ventures and subsidiary scientific rigor, but also the romantic tradition in exploration, with the naturalists' later volumes dramatizing the journey.

Most of the Scientific Corps had dispersed throughout the territory. Kennicott, however, died in the spring of 1866, leaving William Healey Dall in charge. But this work did not go on much longer; in March 1867, not only were the negotiations for the sale of Russian America underway, but Western Union decided that the Atlantic cable's final success rendered obsolete work on the Collins Overland Line, even though they had spent over three million dollars. The Telegraph Expedition was recalled.

By June 1867, word reached the Russian-America Division about the sale of Alaska to the United States, accompanied by the cease work order. By July, the scattered party had gathered all portable items to Nulato and boarded ship for San Francisco. Dall, however, after loading specimens bound for the Smithsonian, decided to stay another year as the first naturalist in the new US territory—in 1870 publishing the work *Alaska and its Resources*, the first definitive account of the territory.

By September 1867, work had ceased for all divisions, but many supplies remained on-site in anticipation of the eventual failure of the Atlantic cable, a failure that never came.

ANNETTE WATSON

Further Reading

Bush, Richard, *Reindeer, Dogs, and Snowshoes: A Journal of Siberian Travel and Explorations*, New York: Harper and Brothers, 1871

Dall, William Healey, *Alaska and its Resources*, Boston: Lee and Shepard, 1870

Dwyer, John B., *To Wire the World: Perry M. Collins and the North Pacific Telegraph Expedition*, Westport, Connecticut: Praeger Publishers, 2001

Pettus, Terry, "Expedition to Russian America." *Beaver* [Canada], 293 (1962): 8–19

Postnikov, Alexei, "Prodazha Aliaskii I Mezhdun Arodnaia Telegrafnaia Ekspeditsiia" [The Sale of Alaska and the International Telegraph Expedition] *Voprosy Istorii Estestvoznaniia i Tekhniki* [Russia], 1(1997): 3–38

Sherwood, Morgan, *Exploration of Alaska, 1865–1900*, Fairbanks: University of Alaska Press, 1992

Whymper, Frederick, *Travel and Adventure in the Territory of Alaska*, New York: Harper and Brothers, 1871

WESTMAN ISLANDS—*See* VESTMANNAEYJAR (WESTMAN ISLANDS)

WET TUNDRA

Wet sedge tundras cover 880×10^6 ha in the circumpolar Low Arctic and 132×10^6 ha in the High Arctic. Wet tundra is less uniform than tussock tundra (922×10^6 ha) since it is less dependent on a single species. Nonetheless, cottongrass is typically abundant

Purple Saxifrage is the first plant to flower among the summer tundra meltpools, Northwest Greenland.
Copyright Bryan and Cherry Alexander Photography

or even dominant. The most common cottongrass of wet tundra on a circumpolar basis is *Eriophorum angustifolium*, a multiheaded, mat-forming species that is often best developed in flat areas with standing water present during most of the summer. The most common sedge is *Carex aquatilis* (including *C. stans*). Diversity in microtopography is a prerequisite for local diversity in the composition of wet tundra. For example, the wet coastal tundra at Barrow, Alaska, is dominated by a single species—*C. aquatilis*—with a few secondary species—*E. angustifolium*, *E. scheuchzeri*, and *Dupontia fisheri*. Although the vegetation changes character every few meters in response to changes in microrelief and drainage, it is due more to minor species such as mosses and grasses since *C. aquatilis* and *Eriophorum* are ubiquitous. This pattern is characteristic of wet sedge meadows throughout the Arctic.

Arctic wetlands are vital to water storage in an environment that is generally water-poor after the first few weeks of spring melt. Wetlands can assimilate nitrogen for long periods of time because they are the most important sites of denitrification by microbial populations, indicating that Arctic wetlands can remove excess nutrients. Tundra wetlands purify inflowing water by trapping sediment and by transforming or retaining, for example, phosphorus and toxicants. In this respect, Arctic wetlands are functionally similar to many temperate wetlands.

Vascular plants such as *C. aquatilis* can photosynthesize at temperatures as low as $-4°C$. This and other clonal graminoids of wet tundra have been shown to respond to added nitrogen and phosphorus with increased biomass. Root:shoot ratios of tundra graminoids as high as 10–20:1 facilitate growth in an environment of low nutrient availability, enhancing the productivity of tundra wetlands. Near Barrow, Alaska, estimates of aboveground primary production for *Carex* range from 89 to 370 g m^{-2}. Belowground biomass for *Carex* vegetation has been reported to be 3119 g m^{-2}. Vertebrate herbivores feed on the aboveground biomass so that much of the tundra's production is unavailable to these species. The graminoids *C. aquatilis*, *C. stans*, *Eriophorum*, and *Dupontia* are preferred forage for caribou (reindeer), muskox, microtine rodents, and lesser snow geese because of their nutritional quality and digestibility.

Research with Low Arctic populations of *C. aquatilis* has shown that shoots may not live for more than 2 years, but that the "tiller clump" of roots, rhizomes, and stem bases where they emerge successively may live up to 4 years after aboveground growth ceases. Since individual rhizomatous tillers may live 4–7 years, there is a total life of tiller clumps of 5–8 years (to 10 years). *Carex*, with 90% of its biomass below ground, invests proportionally more tissue in roots than other wetland graminoids (e.g., *E. angustifolium* and *D. fisheri*), and is most successful in nutrient-poor situations. In contrast to *Dupontia* and *Carex*, the longer-lived (from 5 to 8 years) *Eriophorum* tillers lose rhizome connections and become physiologically independent within 2–3 years, although the root system of this species is replaced annually. In High Arctic wet tundra, shoot longevity in populations of *C. stans* and *E. angustifolium* is 5–8 and 7–10 years, respectively.

The clonal growth form is an extremely important factor in determining the resistance and resilience of mechanically disturbed tundra graminoids. A primary reason for this is that mortality can affect modules individually, without necessarily causing the death of whole genets (or clonal populations). In the rhizomatous graminoids described above, genets spread widely and intermingle. A single lethal incident may thus remove modules of different genets but rarely all modules of a single genet. Disturbance is known to increase shoot turnover in rhizomatous tundra graminoids. The percentage of flowering shoots is thought to be a good measure of the vitality of many northern wetland plants, although allocation to sexual reproduction may vary widely among years. In general, moist tundra resists mechanical disturbance better than wet tundra, but it is less resilient once disturbed.

BRUCE FORBES

See also **Peatlands and Bogs; Sedge Meadows; Tussock Tundra**

Further Reading

Botch, Marina S. & V.V. Masing, "Mire Ecosystems of the U.S.S.R." In *Ecosystems of the World 4B, Mires: Swamp, Bog, Fen and Moor*, edited by A.J.P. Gore, Amsterdam: Elsevier, 1983, pp. 95–152

Brown, Jerry, Kaye R. Everett, Patrick J. Webber, Stephen F. MacLean Jr. & David F. Murray, "The Coastal Tundra at Barrow." In *An Arctic Ecosystem: The Coastal Tundra at Barrow, Alaska,* edited by Jerry Brown, P.C. Miller, L.L. Tieszen & F.L. Bunnell, Dowden, Stroudsberg, Pennsylvania: Hutchinson & Ross, 1980, pp. 1–29

Daly, Tom, Martin Raillard & Josef Svoboda, "Niche differentiation of *Carex aquatilis* var. *stans* and *Eriophorum triste* sharing the wet meadow habitat in Sverdrup Pass, Ellesmere Island, N.W.T." *Musk-Ox*, 37 (1989): 68–75

Ford, Jesse & Barbara L. Bedford, "The hydrology of Alaska wetlands: a review." *Arctic and Alpine Research*, 19 (1987): 209–229

Murray, Janine L. & Josef Svoboda, "Available nitrogen and phosphorus content in streams feeding wet sedge meadows at Sverdrup Pass, Ellesmere Island, N.W.T." *Musk-Ox*, 37 (1989): 54–59

Shaver, Gaius R., L.C. Johnson, D.H. Cades, G. Murray, J.A. Laundre, E.B. Rastetter, K.J. Nadelhoffer & A.E. Giblin, "Biomass and CO_2 flux in wet sedge tundras: responses to nutrients, temperature, and light." *Ecological Monographs*, 68 (1998): 75–97

Tarnocai, Charles & Stephen C. Zoltai, "Wetlands of Arctic Canada." In *Wetlands of Canada*, edited by C.D.A. Rubec, Montreal: Polyscience, 1988, pp. 27–53

Webber, Patrick J., "Spatial and Temporal Variation of the Vegetation and its Productivity." In *Vegetation and Production Ecology of an Alaskan Arctic Tundra*, edited by Larry L. Tieszen, Berlin: Springer, 1978, pp. 37–112

WEYMOUTH, GEORGE

Captain George Weymouth (sometimes spelled Waymouth and occasionally confused with John Waymouth, the captain who aided the Hudson mutineers on their arrival off the coast of Ireland in 1611) led two voyages across the Atlantic. His work influenced later explorers, particularly Henry Hudson, although he is poorly known today. In part, this is because Weymouth's discoveries were so rapidly overshadowed by Hudson's own in the same areas.

Little is known with certainty about Weymouth's early life. In order to have been selected to command a voyage of exploration in 1602, he must have been old enough to obtain significant sailing and navigation experience. This was probably acquired on trading voyages around the English coast, across the English Channel to Europe, and in the Mediterranean. Weymouth may have also gained experience on one of the many late Elizabethan voyages to the east in search of spices, fighting the Spanish Armada of 1588, or even on one of John Davis's explorations to the Arctic between 1585 and 1587. Certainly, it was the publication of Davis's journals in 1601 that led to Weymouth's first voyage.

On December 31, 1600, Queen Elizabeth I granted 218 knights and merchants of the City of London a Royal Charter as the East India Company. One of the knights, Sir Thomas Smythe, was a firm believer in the existence of a short, polar route to the spices of Asia, and became the leading proponent of northern voyages of exploration over the succeeding generation. His first venture was to send Weymouth to complete Davis's work and sail through a North West Passage.

Weymouth was so certain of success that he stated that, in the case of failure, he would waive all payment. He also included among his crew a preacher to convert the "heathen" spice islanders. Weymouth took the bark *Discovery* (55 tons) on the first of its five voyages to the north in the spring of 1602. Weymouth's intention was to sail through the open water that Davis suggested existed to the north and west of the strait he discovered. He was prepared to overwinter in the north should this be necessary, but at 68°53′ N, his crew refused to go further and forced Weymouth to return south. As an alternative, Weymouth attempted to force a passage through Hudson Strait, which had been recognized by Davis and which he had named the "Furious Overfall."

Weymouth entered Hudson Strait close by the north shore and sailed west by south for 100 leagues. This would place him close to Cap de Nouvelle-France, farther than anyone else had ventured, but still around 200 km short of Digges Island and the entrance to Hudson Bay proper. Unfortunately, ice forced Weymouth to retreat and he returned to England without having accomplished his goal.

After his failure of 1602, and his presumed lack of payment, Weymouth appears to have lost interest in the north. His 1605 voyage had the dual purpose of exploring new fishing grounds off the New England coast and prospecting a suitable settlement for English Catholics. Since the cod spawning grounds had been discovered off the coast of Maine, the focus of the North American fishery had moved south from Newfoundland and Nova Scotia. If this could be combined with discovering a suitable place to relocate troublesome Catholic dissidents, so much the better. The voyage was planned and equipped by Sir Thomas Arundell and other Plymouth merchants. Weymouth sailed on March 5, 1605 in the *Archangell*, heading south to 41°30′ and reaching the North American coast at Cape Cod. From there, he sailed north across the Gulf of Maine to Monhegan Island, where he went ashore and noted good timber, abundant fresh water, and rich fish stocks. He also noted the Burnt and Allen islands and suggested they would make good sites for settlement.

Using the *Archangell*'s shallop, Weymouth explored St George's River and the surrounding coast. He even attempted to head inland toward some distant mountains, but was forced to give up due to heat and exhaustion. Having collected the information required by Arundell, Weymouth returned to England in the fall of 1605.

Weymouth's second voyage is also notable for including the first recorded case of kidnapping on the New England coast. Five natives, possibly including Squanto who was later known to the Plymouth settlers, were forcibly taken on board the *Archangell* and brought to England. There, three of the captives were handed over to Sir Ferdinando Gorges of the Plymouth Company. Gorges returned the men to New England with a later mapping expedition led by Captain John Smith.

James Rosier's journal of Weymouth's 1605 voyage was published that same year and was in Hudson's possession when he sailed to the same area four years later. In fact, Hudson's journal of his third voyage suggests that he was following Weymouth's track in the Gulf of Maine. In addition, before Hudson sailed in search of the North West Passage in 1610, he obtained the then unpublished log of Weymouth's 1602 voyage from his friend Peter Plancius.

Like many of the explorers of that time, Weymouth sank into obscurity after his return in 1605.

Biography

Nothing is known of George Weymouth, including his birth date and place, prior to 1602. His first voyage was a follow-up of John Davis's discoveries. In the summer of 1602, Weymouth was prevented from sailing farther north than Davis by his mutinous crew, but did succeed in sailing farther into Hudson Strait than any previous explorer. He was prevented from discovering Hudson Bay by heavy ice. Weymouth's second voyage in 1605 was to discover new fishing grounds and a suitable place for the settlement of Catholics. During the summer, Weymouth and his crew explored Cape Cod, St George's River, and the islands in the Gulf of Maine. They also captured five natives, who were brought back to England. Despite the success of his second voyage, George Weymouth does not appear to have been given command of any of the later ventures to the north or the east and nothing is known of his life after 1605. The date and place of his death are also unknown.

JOHN WILSON

See also **Davis, John; Hudson, Henry**

Further Reading

Johnson, Donald S., *Charting the Sea of Darkness: The Four Voyages of Henry Hudson*, Camden: International Marine, 1993, and New York: Kodansha, 1995

Purchas, Samuel, *Purchas His Pilgrims—in Five Books, The Third Part, Voyages and Discoveries of the North Parts of the World, by Land and Sea, in Asia, Europe, the Polare Regions, and in the North-West of America*, London, 1625

Rosier, James, *A True Relation of the Most Prosperous Voyage Made this Present Year 1605 by Captain George Weymouth*, London, 1605

Sanders, Ronald, *Lost Tribes and Promised Lands*, New York and London: HarperCollins, 1992

WEYPRECHT, KARL

German explorer Karl Weyprecht attended the first Great German Geographers Day in Frankfurt on July 23, 1865, where he heard August Petermann's (1822–1878) lecture entitled "The Exploration of the Arctic Central Region by a German Northern Journey." Petermann outlined his theory of an ice-free and navigable polar sea and then suggested that Weyprecht be the leader of his proposed project.

Petermann's attempts to get a ship either from the Austrian or from the Prussian government, however, were in vain. In June 1866, the Austro-Prussian War erupted. On July 20, 1866, Weyprecht served in the naval battle of Lissa (led by Admiral Wilhelm von Tegetthoff) on board the ship *Drache*; he was subsequently decorated with the Order of the Iron Crown III. With his plans for polar exploration temporarily aborted, Weyprecht followed his duties as a naval officer and sailed to Mexico on board the wheel-steamer *Kaiserin Elisabeth* in support of the Austrian Emperor Maximilian, remaining there for an entire year in 1867.

Early in January 1868, Weyprecht traveled to Pula (the naval city in Croatia on the Adriatic Sea) and there met Petermann to start preparations for an Arctic journey. But he was soon required to resign from the leadership of what would be the First German Northpolar Expedition for reasons of health: he had caught a marsh fever while in Mexico. Fellow German explorer Karl Koldewey (1837–1908) was given command of the *Grönland* yacht.

Weyprecht, still in poor health, joined the Austrian Adriatic Coast Mapping Commission, where he served between 1869 and 1870. In December 1870, he was sent to Tunis for the observation of the solar eclipse. Moreover, during fall of that year, Weyprecht made the acquaintance of Julius von Payer (1841–1915), who had just successfully returned from the Second German Northpolar Expedition. That meeting finally brought Weyprecht back to Arctic exploration.

On May 10, 1871, Weyprecht presented his plan for a greater Austro-Hungarian Polar Expedition to the Geographical Society in Vienna. The plan was financially supported by the Austrian Count Wilczek (Graf Johann Nepomuk), enabling Weyprecht and his crew to set out on a preliminary expedition on the chartered barge *Isbjörn*. Leaving Tromsø (Norway) on June 20, 1871, their intent was the examination of the ice conditions between the Spitsbergen archipelago and the Novaya Zemlya islands; this would enable them to advance further to the north in the future. They returned successfully and optimistic on October 4 the same year.

Finally, preparations for the Austro-Hungarian North Pole Expedition could be finished. Again financed in large part by Count Wilczek, the three-mast schooner *Tegetthoff* set sail in Bremerhaven on June 13, 1872 with Weyprecht as commander of the ship and Payer as the leader of the land journeys. The official order was to ascertain whether the North East Passage was navigable. The North Pole was only a secondary target.

After a wintering beset in drifting ice, the *Tegetthoff* incidentally sighted and explored what Payer would name (Kaiser) Franz Josef Land on August 30, 1873. The archipelago was explored by Payer on several sled journeys, while Weyprecht continued his observations on board the ship. Having endured another winter, the ship had to be abandoned on May 20, 1874, and the long, difficult journey south began in three boats on sledges. Finally, the entire party was rescued by a Russian ship and arrived safely in Vienna on September 25, 1874.

They were showered with honors upon their lucky return; Weyprecht was decorated with the Knight's Cross in Vienna in September 1874, and in May 1875 he received the Gold Medal of the Royal Geographical Society, London. Nonetheless, Weyprecht had come to the conclusion that their scientific observations had not been productive because the data collected could not be directly compared and used in a broader context. He presented a paper—"Fundamental Principles of Scientific Arctic Investigation"—to the Academy of Sciences, Vienna, for the first time on January 18, 1875, and for a second time at the 48th Meeting of German Scientists and Physicians in Graz, Austria, on September 18, 1875.

Weyprecht's proposals, along with those of Georg von Neumayer (director of the German Hydrographic Office, who pleaded for the Antarctic research), were presented at the Second International Congress of Meteorologists in Rome in April 1879. Topics of discussion included the possible establishment of fixed stations in the Arctic and Antarctic regions for simultaneous hourly meteorological and magnetic observations around the poles.

As early as October 1879, the First International Polar Conference in Hamburg had led to the creation of the "International Polar Commission," with Neumayer as its first president. Detailed planning for the First International Polar Year (1882–1883) with eight (and subsequently 14) stations had begun. Weyprecht would likely have been appointed leader of the Austrian station at Jan Mayen had he not died on March 29, 1881.

Biography

Karl Weyprecht was born on September 8, 1838 in Michelstadt, Germany. In 1856, after he had finished his education in Darmstadt, he was accepted as a provisional sea cadet at the Austrian Naval Academy in Trieste. Between 1860 and 1862, he served on the frigate *Radetzky* under the command of Wilhelm von Tegetthoff, and from 1863 to 1865 he was instruction officer on the training ship *Hussar*.

His interest in science and subsequent meetings with August Petermann and later with Julius Payer led Weyprecht to turn his attention to polar exploration. Right before the inception of the Austro-Hungarian North Pole Expedition on February 18, 1872, Weyprecht received his Austro-Hungarian citizenship. Tragically, Weyprecht died on March 29, 1881 in his hometown, Michelstadt, Germany, without having seen his plans come true.

HERMANN F. KOERBEL

See also **Franz Josef Land; Koldeway, Karl; North East Passage, Exploration of; Payer, Julius; Petermann, August**

Further Reading

Gravier, Gabriel, *Notice nécrologique sur Karl Weyprecht, découvreur de la Terre François-Joseph*, Rouen: Impr. de Espérance Cagniard, 1882
Ihne, E., *Der Nordpolarforscher Carl Weyprecht* [The Northpolar Explorer Carl Weyprecht], Friedberg, 1913
Weyprecht, Karl, "Die Nordpolar-Frage und die verschiedenen Pläne zu ihrer Lösung" [The northpolar-question and the

different plans for its solution]. *Mittheilungen der Geographischen Gesellschaft in Wien*, 12 (1869) 413–427

————, *Die Nordpol-Expeditionen der Zukunft und deren sicheres Ergebniss, verglichen mit den bisherigen Forschungen auf dem arktischen Gebiete* [The North Pole expedition of the future and its certain results, compared with past researches in the Arctic region], Wien, 1876

————, *Die magnetischen Beobachtungen der Österr.-Ung. Arktischen Expedition* 1872–74 [Magnetic observations of the Austro-Hungarian Arctic expedition 1872–74], Wien, 1878

————, *Die Metamorphosen des Polareises—Österr.-Ung. Arktische Expedition 1872–1874* [Metamorphoses of polar ice—The Austro-Hungarian Arctic expedition of 1872–1874], Wien: Moritz Perles, 1879

WHALING, HISTORICAL

Scholars do not know when whaling started in northern seas; however, it is likely that Stone Age hunters used stranded whales, because whalebones have been found in the refuse piles of Neolithic sites in the countries around the North Sea. The fact that whales are depicted in Stone Age rock carvings in Norway together with hunted animals also suggests that humans hunted whales in that period too. Whales were probably driven ashore with boats and then killed.

In the 9th century, the Norseman Ottar told King Alfred of England that Norsemen drove whales into small fjords and trapped and killed them. The practice as Ottar described it has continued in modern times in the Orkneys, Shetlands, and Newfoundland, and is still done in the Faroes. In the same period, the religious text *Miracula Sancti Vedasti* (Miracles of St Vedast, written c.875) mentions whales that are hunted by ships from various monasteries in the English Channel Sea. This text demonstrates that the hunt, in which the participants shared the catch, was communal. Here whale hunting probably for the first time was an organized activity with the intention to kill as many whales as possible.

Archaeological evidence shows that around the Bering Strait, people from the Okvik, Old Bering Sea, Punuk, Birnik, Thule, and Inugsuk cultures were developing bowhead or Greenland right whale (*Balaena mysticetus*) hunting roughly in the period between 0 and AD 1000. The economy of the Thule culture was even based on bowhead whaling. Its people learned whaling techniques from the Punuk culture before they migrated to East Canada and Greenland.

The Norse settlers in Greenland hunted the narwhal (*Monodon monoceros*) and exported its ivory in the 11th century. The Inuit hunted narwhal and beluga (*Delphinapterus leucas*) as far back as scholars know and probably even supplied the Norse settlers with ivory.

From the 11th and 12th centuries, the people around the Bay of Biscay coast hunted the Nordkaper or Northern right whale (*Eubalaena glacialis*). From

historical sources, scholars know that the whales were chased with rowing boats, captured with hand-thrown harpoons, towed back to base, and processed on the beach in front of the village. This simple but effective technology performed the basis of commercial whaling. In fact, the Basques were the first commercial whalers, producing for a growing international whale oil market. The Basque sold whale oil in France, Spain, the Netherlands, and England. This commercial aspect most likely caused the decline in the number of whales in the Bay of Biscay. The fact that females and calves were often killed accelerated the decline. However, during this period of decline, Basque cod fishermen discovered a whaling ground in the Grand Bay in Newfoundland, which they decided to exploit.

The Grand Bay Whaling

At the end of the 15th century, Newfoundland and its rich cod banks were discovered. The English started the exploitation of these grounds, soon followed by fishermen from Brittany, Portugal, and the Basque country. The Basques discovered a whaling ground in Newfoundland with many Nordkapers and bowheads, two species that were easy to kill because they moved slowly.

Historians do not know precisely when the Basques began their whaling activities off Newfoundland, but between 1550 and 1600, whaling flourished in the Grand Bay. According to historical sources, the Basques outfitted an average of 15 ships a year, but at least 30–40 ships participated in the exploitation during peak years. According to written sources, the Basques caught approximately 300 whales annually and another 150 were killed but lost. Archaeological research in Red Bay (Labrador, Canada), the center of the Basque whaling industry, showed try-works with three to six small ovens made of rocks in a row, cooperages with canvas walls, and roofs covered with red tiles, small living quarters, some lookouts, and a cemetery. The structures were small and were found scattered over a great area. The whales were most likely processed alongside the ship, and the blubber was towed ashore where it was boiled to produce oil.

Basque whaling in the New World declined at the beginning of the 17th century when West European countries such as England and the Netherlands started whaling in Spitsbergen. The expanding whaling industries in these countries hired many Basque whalers as experts. At the same time, the control of the whale oil market was shifting from the Basque country to the West European countries. In addition to these economic factors, climatic change may have precipitated a general shift to the north of the ice edge and the ice edge-associated bowheads. Already by the 1580s, the catch was beginning to decline and the ships were returning half-empty. Although the Basques continued whaling until the middle of the 17th century, it was a declining industry.

The Spitsbergen Whale Fishery

After the discovery of Spitsbergen in 1596 and Henry Hudson's voyage to this archipelago in 1607, several years elapsed before whaling commenced in this area. High prices for grain resulted in the stagnation of the production of vegetable oils and fats. The increasing demand for these products caused a switch from vegetable to animal oils and fats. Only when the supply of whale oil from the original areas of production dried up did the English and Dutch merchants, with the help of Basque experts, decide to launch into whaling in 1611 and 1612.

In the first years in Spitsbergen, keen competition among whalers of different nationalities thrived, especially between the English and the Dutch. In the Netherlands, this competition led to the foundation of the Dutch whaling company called the *Noordsche Compagnie*. Unlike the English Muscovy Company, which was a trading company solely controlled by a small band of London merchants, the Dutch company was an association of independent enterprises or chambers from several Dutch ports, with a collective charter from the Dutch government. *Noordsche Compagnie* was a cartel of whaling enterprises in which agreements were made fixing catches and prices. In this way, the Dutch whaling trade became a reasonably well-organized enterprise, with 10–20 ships and an annual catch of approximately 300 whales.

On Amsterdam Island in Northeast Spitsbergen, the Dutch established a whaling settlement that they called *Smeerenburg*. Excavations of Dutch and Norwegian archaeologists from 1979 to 1981 have determined that this settlement originally consisted of eight try-works. The settlement comprised 15 houses: dwellings, cooperages, storehouses, a smithy, a bottling room, and a fortress to protect it against opponents. According to historical sources, *Smeerenburg* must have also had a church. From 1620 until 1650, about 200 men worked and lived in *Smeerenburg* in the summer. In the 1630s, two attempts were made to winter in the settlement. The first attempt was successful, but when the second failed and all winterers died, no new attempts were made. Now that the Dutch had their settlement at Spitsbergen, winches could be used to haul the whale on the beach, flense the animal, and turn the whale over. The Dutch whaling company existed from 1614 to 1642.

After the Dutch discovery of Jan Mayen in 1614, Dutch whaling concentrated and continued there for several years. Only a few ships sailed on for the west coast of Spitsbergen in the years after then until 1625. Dutch whalers also built whaling stations at Jan Mayen. In the Walrus Bay (Kvalross bukta), they maintained six to seven try-works, from which almost no remains were found during two archaeological surveys (1983 and 1988). On the Jan Mayen whaling grounds, the Dutch used a new whaling technique: they hunted the whale on the high seas with single-masted ships and brought the dead whales ashore to be processed using both oars and sails.

In the 1620s, it became clear that the Spitsbergen whaling trade was not as lucrative as some merchants had expected. A number of important investors turned their backs on the trade. In the years 1625–1630, the Dutch company experienced a crisis, but at the beginning of the 1630s, former interest revived because of high whale oil prices. During this period, the Dutch fleet was divided into two parts: one for Jan Mayen and the other for Spitsbergen. At Spitsbergen, the Dutch company tolerated interlopers because the whaling grounds shifted to the high seas more and more. Under the pressure of these interlopers, no further extension of the charter was requested in 1642, and whaling became accessible to every Dutch shipowner.

Many commanders and harpooners formerly serving the *Noordsche Compagnie* now voyaged to the Arctic seas on their own account. Part-ownership took over the Dutch trade, and whaling entered a new phase of development in which investors could spread the risk by buying shares in different ships. Many families became involved in whaling, and a tradition developed in small ports in the country and on the islands along the northern coast of the Netherlands and Germany. The annual average number of ships fitted out from Dutch ports increased from 50 in 1642–1665 to 126 in 1665–1700.

While Dutch whaling prospered, English whaling declined. The English settled in the southern bays of Spitsbergen and inadvertently drove the foreigners to the better northern hunting grounds. Moreover, the organization of the English company was overly restrictive; discussions over monopoly rights of the Muscovy Company seemed interminable, and the company spent a great deal of time, money, and energy fighting English interlopers from London, Hull, and Great Yarmouth. Not until 1670 was English whaling free for everyone, but by then the industry had floundered.

When the price of oil started to rise in the 1640s, merchants from German ports such as Hamburg and Bremen became interested in whaling too, capitalizing on the opportunity to enter the trade. The Germans' early activities were so successful that they soon maintained a fleet of 40 ships whaling in the Spitsbergen bays.

With so many ships and people in a limited number of bays suitable for whaling, maintaining shore stations became increasingly difficult. The working season was

Vintage 19th-century print of a Greenland whale being approached by a catcher boat. Source unknown. *Copyright Bryan and Cherry Alexander Photography*

made much shorter by not only a lack of organization, but also due to climate change that caused Spitsbergen bays to freeze for longer periods.

The Dutch, soon followed by the Germans, moved to the whaling grounds along the edge of the west ice between Spitsbergen and Iceland. They even followed the whales into the ice pack and processed the killed whales alongside the ships again. The blubber was put into barrels and boiled in the homeports. Until the end of the 18th century, Dutch whalers dominated European whaling. French, Basque, and even English whaling declined under Dutch pressure. Finally, the French and English were buying the bulk of their whale products in the Netherlands. In 1672, the English government placed a duty on imported oil in the hope of preventing the import of Dutch whale oil. Whale oil imported by English ships was free of tax, and the New England colonists, who in the meantime had begun offshore whaling in the western Atlantic, only had to pay a reduced tax on oil sold on the English market. The English whaling trade experienced a crisis and even ceased for a while.

In the second half of the 18th century, due to changing climate circumstances and continuing whaling, the number of whales decreased to such an extent that whaling profitability dropped severely. In the 19th century, the Spitsbergen population became exterminated, and halfway through the century whaling finally ceased completely in this area.

American Offshore Whaling

Evidence suggests that North American offshore whaling started as early as the first half of the 17th century.

The first New England settlers discovered whales washed up and stranded on the beaches. They were familiar with the economic value of blubber and baleen, but it is not clear how they learned whale-hunting techniques. The New England settlers may have brought a knowledge of whaling with them from England, but they more likely learned it from their Dutch neighbors in the south.

The native people of New England were, however, already whaling before the first British settlers arrived. The colonists may have followed the basic approach of the natives, which was similar to the whaling technique used by the Basques and the Dutch. A combination of native knowledge of whaling and European technology and capital may explain the success of North American whaling. At any rate, by about 1650, offshore whaling began in New England. European settlers hired Indians as oarsmen and lookouts while colonists provided the capital. In the 1680s, offshore whaling had spread to all the main communities along the New England coast, reaching its pinnacle in the 1720s.

At the turn of the century, Nantucket Island, off Cape Cod, Massachusetts, became the leading whaling center in America. Whaling had become a well-established tradition here, so commonly practiced that the local school in East Hampton closed during the whaling season. Lookouts were placed at several points along the east coast, and whaling crews with extremely fast boats were ready to go at the very first sign. Once killed, boats towed the whales ashore using oars and sails. Following the Dutch precedent, whalers installed a winch on the beach to haul the animal ashore, turn it over, and strip the blubber. The chopped blubber was placed in carts and brought to the furnaces near the settlement, while the meat was left behind on the beach. Whaling in Nantucket was cooperative, as it was in the Netherlands in the same period. Every whaler received a share of the revenues proportional to his investment.

In 1712, the Nantucket captain Christopher Hussey killed the first sperm whale (*Physeter macrocephalus*). The inhabitants of New England had already seen stranded specimens of this type, although they had never hunted it because there were plenty of right whales, which were easier to catch. The sperm whale produced less oil than the right whale, but it yielded additional products such as ivory, ambergris, and spermaceti (used for perfume and candle making). Although the hunt for right whales continued, the sperm whale replaced the former, causing a rapid growth in whaling after 1712. New hunting methods and technologies were required to hunt sperm whales. Because the sperm whale had to be chased on the high seas, voyages lasted longer and bigger ships were necessary. Whalers stripped the blubber from the whale alongside the ship as well as once the vessel had come ashore. The cold climate of the Arctic could preserve blubber for quite some time, but sperm whaling also took place in the temperate zone, where the preservation was hindered. Therefore, the ship had to return to the port for stripping several times during the season. In the 1760s, boiling oil on board ships was introduced again. In early times, the Basques and probably the Dutch boiled on board, but for practical reasons and safety this new technique was used less frequently.

The Davis Strait Fishery

Although notarial acts and other documents of the time suggested that the Dutch were already trading and hunting in Davis Strait in the last decade of the 17th century, the Dutch Davis Strait whale fishery began in earnest in 1719. In the 1720s, an average number of 67 Dutch whalers were sailing annually to this hunting ground. The Dutch Davis Strait fishery lasted throughout the 18th century, reaching its peak in 1732 with 137 ships. However, their activity declined rapidly in the 1780s, and after 1794 regular Dutch sailings ceased. The last Dutch whaling voyage to the Davis Strait occurred in 1826 when Klaas Hoekstra's galliot *Harlingen* was beset in the ice and sank. During the period of the Davis Strait fishery, the Dutch whaling activities were divided over the two hunting areas east and west of Greenland. The popularity of the Davis Strait fishery was most likely assisted by the potential of trading with the Greenlanders as well.

In addition to the Dutch, Germans hunted in Davis Strait until 1826. German whalers from Hamburg and Bremen had close contacts with their Dutch peers, often sharing catches and losses.

High whale oil prices and encouragement by the authorities also brought Danish whalers to Davis Strait. From 1749 to 1758, the Danish sent four ships to Spitsbergen and Davis Strait annually; from 1775 to 1788, they made 200 voyages from Denmark to both whaling grounds. The British not only followed the Dutch and Germans into the west ice near Spitsbergen but also to Davis Strait. Although British whalers were heavily subsidized, their revived whaling trade was not tremendously successful. Only in 1749 when higher bounties coincided with increasing prices for whale products did the British whaling fleet grow. Not until the 1770s did whalers from Hull and Witby sail to Davis Strait on a regular basis. In 1786, Britain outfitted 168 ships in English ports for the whale fisheries east and west of Greenland. The following year, this figure increased to 217, and in 1788, 222 whale ships sailed from Great Britain. Scotland was also active, and the number of ships outfitted by Scottish merchants rose to 31 by 1787. By then, the British whaling industry was so well established that the government could reduce the bounties on whaling.

The apex of British whaling east and west of Greenland continued until the end of the 1820s. However, in the west ice east of Greenland whalers complained about the reduced size of the killed whales. The Davis Strait fishery was more successful, especially when in the second decade of the 19th century, British whalers discovered a new whaling ground in Pond Inlet and Lancaster Sound. W. Gillies Ross (1979) counted 2406 voyages to Davis Strait, most undertaken by British whalers from 1820 to 1910. However, half of the voyages took place during the first 20 years of this 90-year period, and already in the mid-1830s the first signs of depletion in the northern whale stock were noticed, and the number of British whale ships gradually declined.

In 1840, whalers from New England and Scotland established a land-based whale fishery in Cumberland Sound that lasted until 1860, when the number of whales declined in this fishery too. The American and some Scottish whalers moved to Hudson Bay, where they started a fishery based on wintering and cooperation with the natives. This predominantly American fishery lasted only a few years.

In 1857, shipowners in Hull, England, sent a steam tender to accompany their whaler, ushering in the era of steam into whaling history. The introduction of the steam whaler, however, failed to revive British whaling activities. Whales grew scarce in the old whaling grounds, and the market for whale products declined. However, the waning of the Davis Strait fishery was slow; whalers from Peterhead, Scotland, Dundee, Scotland, and New England remained active up until 1893, 1913, and 1917, respectively.

The Northwest Whaling Trade

In 1835, while searching for new whaling grounds, the *Ganges* from Nantucket captured the first right whale off the northwest coast of America exploiting a nascent whaling ground. The American fleet doubled in six years, and due to the long voyages from the east coast to the Pacific, the ships grew considerably larger. The distance between the whaling ports and the hunting grounds demanded special carrier vessels. By the mid-1800s, the American fleet contained 75% of the world's whaling fleet.

The northwest whaling trade started off the coast of Kamchatka and moved to the Okhotsk Sea, where right and bowhead whales thrived. Within two decades, both whale populations were exterminated in this sea. During the period from 1847 to 1867, mostly Americans made 1391 voyages to the Okhotsk Sea. During the first decade of this period, 8240 bowheads and 3600 right whales were killed. From 1848 to 1910, 2712 voyages were made to the Bering Strait and the Chukchi and Beaufort seas by mostly American whale ships. Over half of these voyages took place within the first two decades of the period. In 1855, a drastic decline in bowhead catches led to the abandonment of the whaling efforts north of Bering Strait. The whalers believed the western Arctic's catch to be depleted. However, declining catches in the Okhotsk Sea persuaded the American whalers to return in force through Bering Strait in 1858. Of the original population of approximately 30,000 bowheads, whalers killed 18,600, two-thirds of that number in the first 20 years. This dramatic depletion shows that newly discovered whaling grounds attracted intensive hunting activities, resulting in a rapid reduction of the population to a small proportion of its original size. Depletion of the whale stock made whaling less profitable and no longer attractive for American capital investment. The whaling trade was considered too risky to invest capital; meanwhile, competition with other investment possibilities like the cotton industry was increasing in North America. Further difficulties arose for American whalers who frequently lost their crew to the gold mining rush on the west coast. Because the US transcontinental railway shortened the distance between the whaling grounds, carrier vessels were no longer needed, and San Francisco subsequently rose in importance as a whaling port.

In the late 1840s, a whaling industry emerged in Baja California near San Diego, which was based on the hunt of the gray whale (*Eschrichtius robustus*). As on the east coast of the United States, natives had known of and used this whaling ground for centuries. Whaling companies, often family enterprises, and independent of the oceangoing whaling ships, took over this whaling ground. Companies set up shore stations with try-works, storehouses, and lookouts. The industry used small schooners and sloops to take the whale-boats out to the sea. Whalers towed and flensed (stripped of skin and blubber) their catch to the beach in the same way as had been done in New England 150 years earlier. The slaughter of female and young whales grew to such a level within a few years that the gray whale herd severely declined, and after the 1878 gale, the San Diego whaling industry ended.

In the 19th century, the American Civil War greatly affected the whaling trade. The whaling fleet was reduced from 514 to 263 ships in 1866. At the same time, oil was discovered in Pennsylvania, and soon the market for whale products collapsed.

The North Atlantic Fin Whale Hunt

The combination of a harpoon gun and a steam whaler in 1863 by the Norwegian Svend Foyn made it possible to kill fast-moving fin whales. This technical development allowed for new whale stocks at a time when known whale stocks were almost depleted. On the coast of northern Norway on Foyn's initiative, whalers built several shore stations to process the dead whales. In 1885, 30 whale ships from 20 Norwegian companies killed 287 whales; by 1891, 70 ships had killed 3000 whales in the Norwegian Sea, making Norway the world's leading whaling nation. By thus increasing the catch, the Norwegians ignored the dramatic effect of whaling on the stock of whales. Soon, no whales remained within a certain distance of the Norwegian shore stations. Five companies consequently moved to Iceland and established a whaling station at Onundarfjordur in 1889. From that station, hunters killed 1296 blue whales between 1889 and 1900. Other Norwegian stations were established on Spitsbergen, the Faroes and Hebrides islands, and Newfoundland. Within eight years, Norway had established 18 shore stations.

This intensive whaling worried the fishermen in northern Norway, who believed that it would adversely affect the fisheries. Therefore in 1904, whaling was prohibited in the waters of northern Norway for ten years. However, the Norwegian companies continued their trade outside the waters of Norway, moving to other areas to continue coastal whaling. The consequences were dramatic near Iceland, where in 1902, 30 ships killed 1305 whales; however, ten years later, the catch dropped to 152 whales. The government imposed drastic measures to save the whales around Iceland; in 1913, the government initiated a ban on all whaling in 1915 that would remain in effect for ten years.

Modern whaling came to Japan from Russia. In 1898, the Russian Pacific Whaling Company began to operate using Norwegian equipment and methods. The result surprised the traditional Japanese net whalers, and that same year the Japanese Ocean Whaling Company also began using Norwegian equipment and methods. Later, the Japanese company even hired Norwegian gunners. The Japanese-Russian war of 1904–1905 ended the Russian Whaling Company, but the Japanese expanded their industry because of an increasing demand for whale meat for human consumption.

The hunting pressure on the whale stocks expanded worldwide, and whale stocks decreased rapidly. To save the natural resources, the International Whaling Commission (IWC)—composed of delegates of the whaling countries—was established in 1946. The Commission tried to protect the different species one by one to ensure their survival by fixing quotas by stock. Whaling continued until 1982 when the IWC adopted a moratorium on all commercial whaling from 1986 onward.

The moratorium on commercial whaling remained in effect until 1996, when the Norwegian government decided that the minke whale population in the North Atlantic Ocean had grown large enough to stand a restrictive commercial hunt. At the Commission's 2001 meeting in London, participants discussed the possibility of resuming commercial whaling of certain species.

LOUWRENS HACQUEBORD

See also **Bowhead (Greenland Right) Whale; Fin Whale; Gray Whale; International Whaling Commission (IWC); Jan Mayen; Sperm Whale; Whaling, Subsistence**

Further Reading

Ellis, Richard, *Men and Whales*, New York: Knopf, 1991

Gillies Ross, William, "The annual catch of Greenland (Bowhead) whale in waters north of Canada, 1719–1915." *Arctic*, 32 (1979): 91–121

Hacquebord, Louwrens, "A historical-archaeological investigation of a seventeenth century whaling settlement on the west coast Spitsbergen in 79 North Latitude." Smeerenburg Seminar, *Rapport serie* No. 38, Oslo: Norsk Polar Institute, 1987, pp. 19–34

———, "Three centuries of whaling and walrus hunting in Svalbard and its impact on the Arctic ecosystem." *Environment and History*, 7 (2001): 169–185

Hacquebord, Louwrens & Wim Vroom, *Walvisvaart in de Gouden Eeuw; opgravingen op Spitsbergen*, Amsterdam: Bataafse Leeuw, 1988

Jackson, Gordon, *The British Whaling Trade*, London: Adam & Charles Black, 1978

Jacob, Hugo K., Kim Snoeijing & Richard Vaughan (editors), *Arctic Whaling*, Groningen: Arctisch Centrum, 1984

Oesau, Wanda, *Schleswig-Holsteins Grönlandfahrt auf Walfischfang und Robbenschlag vom 17.-19. Jahrhundert*, Hamburg: Glückstad, and New York: J.J. Augustin, 1939

Proulx, Jean Pierre, *Whaling in the North Atlantic: From the Earliest Times to the Mid-19th Century*, Ottawa: Parks Canada, 1986

Starbuck, Alexander, *History of the American Whale Fishery: From its Earliest Inception to the Year 1876*, Volumes 1 and 2, New York: Argosy-Antiquarian, 1964

Tonnessen, Johan N. & Arne O. Johnsen, *The History of Modern Whaling*, London: C. Hurst & Co, 1982

Webb, Robert Lloyd, *On the Northwest; Commercial Whaling in the Pacific Northwest 1790–1967*, Vancouver, British Columbia: UBC Press, 1988

WHALING, SUBSISTENCE

Aboriginal subsistence whaling was first formally recognized in a global international treaty as being distinctive from commercial whaling operations when the International Convention for the Regulation of Whaling (ICRW) opened for signature in Geneva on January 16, 1931. The ICRW came into effect on January 16, 1935 and included, as Article 3, the statement that the Convention did not apply to coastal dwelling aboriginal people, provided that they used what were considered exclusively native craft propelled by oars or sail, such as canoes and pirogues; that they did not carry firearms; and that the products from whale hunting were for their own use. The 1946 Convention, which created the International Whaling Commission (IWC), carried this forward and recognized that aboriginal peoples are permitted to hunt whales for subsistence purposes. It allowed a specific exception to the general ban on the commercial catching of gray and right whales when the meat and products were to be used exclusively for local consumption by aboriginal people.

In 1975, the IWC adopted a new management procedure for commercial whaling, which led to recognition of the need for a separate and specific management regime for aboriginal subsistence whaling. This occurred during a period of controversial debates over the status of the bowhead whale stock hunted off Alaska by Iñupiat Eskimos. In 1977 and the years following, the annual bowhead whale kill was considered by some scientists to exceed what the then-estimated population could sustain.

The 1946 Convention or its associated schedule of regulations does not formally define aboriginal subsistence whaling, although provisions speak of establishing "catch limits for aboriginal whaling to satisfy aboriginal subsistence need" (paragraph 13 (a) of the ICRW). An ad hoc Technical Committee Working Group on Development of Management Principles and Guidelines for Subsistence Catches of Whales by Indigenous (Aboriginal) Peoples met immediately before the 1981 IWC Annual Meeting and agreed to the following definitions:

- *Aboriginal subsistence whaling* means whaling for purposes of local aboriginal consumption carried out by or on behalf of aboriginal, indigenous, or native peoples who share strong community, familial, social, and cultural ties related to a continuing traditional dependence on whaling and on the use of whales.

- *Local aboriginal consumption* means the traditional uses of whale products by local aboriginal, indigenous, or native communities in meeting their nutritional, subsistence, and cultural requirements. The term includes trade in items that are by-products of subsistence catches.
- *Subsistence catches* are catches of whales by aboriginal subsistence whaling operations.

The 1982 Annual Meeting of the IWC adopted a Resolution agreeing to develop a distinct management regime for aboriginal subsistence whaling, which includes recognition of the nutritional, subsistence, and cultural needs of the aboriginal peoples affected. Bowhead whaling off Alaska, whaling in Greenland, Siberian gray whaling, and humpback whaling in the Caribbean are regulated by the IWC under its aboriginal subsistence whaling scheme. The catch limits to satisfy aboriginal subsistence need are established in accordance with certain principles. For stocks above the maximum sustainable yield (MSY) level, aboriginal subsistence catches are permitted up to 90% of MSY; for stocks below the MSY level, catch levels are set so as to permit the stocks to rebuild to the MSY level. A standing Aboriginal Subsistence Whaling Subcommittee of the IWC considers documentation on nutritional, subsistence, and cultural needs relating to aboriginal subsistence whaling and the uses of whales taken for such purposes, and provides advice to the IWC Technical Committee.

The current regulations governing commercial whaling activities still include specific exemptions for aboriginal subsistence whaling from the general controls and limitations spelled out by the IWC, even if whale stocks hunted by aboriginal peoples are considered to be seriously depleted. This contrasts with the refusal of the IWC majority to recognize that some nonaboriginal whalers have a similar subsistence need to kill whales. Nonaboriginal subsistence whaling is considered unacceptable even in cases where the whale stocks in question are not considered endangered by the IWC's Scientific Committee (and even when the Committee has concluded that the catch is sustainable). This inconsistency derives primarily from a misunderstanding over the appropriate use of the terms "aboriginal" and "subsistence," and also from a confusion of how to accept arguments put forward by nonaboriginal whaling communities for the recognition of cultural continuity and cultural, economic, and nutritional needs.

The IWC definition of subsistence fails to take account of the complex interplay between informal and formal economic activities, and also ignores the fact that many nonaboriginal whalers engage in subsistence while aboriginal hunters engage in monetized economic exchange. The majority of member countries have trouble with accepting that aboriginal subsistence hunts do not operate outside a monetized economy and that commercial hunts have important cultural and subsistence aspects, even though these aspects have been well documented at the IWC. For example, Japanese and Norwegian delegates have presented rich evidence in support of the cultural aspects of small-type coastal whaling and the very similar dependence of their coastal communities on whales and whaling as found in Arctic aboriginal communities, while the kind of whaling carried out in Chukotka during the 1950s to the end of the Soviet era characterized by the IWC as aboriginal subsistence whaling was, in fact, a state-run enterprise carried out by nonaboriginal (and nonlocal) whalers who were paid a wage to hunt. The meat and by-products of the hunt supported the cash economy of coastal communities in northeastern Russia, where many of the inhabitants depended on employment from fur farming. In Greenland, where whaling is also classified as an aboriginal subsistence activity, the whale hunt has involved wage employment of both local and nonlocal people and the sale of whale meat and other products since the mid-1700s.

An encompassing definition of subsistence would include "all the uses to which a species may be put," while a mode of subsistence would be "the aggregate of extractive processes characterizing a particular population." In this sense, subsistence for Arctic peoples is a way of life bound up with the harvesting of renewable resources, rather than meaning, as the commonplace misunderstanding of the term does, that subsistence is found among people who are disadvantaged and on the margins of survival. For whaling cultures, subsistence encapsulates an intricate web of human-environmental relations, irrespective of what kinds of technology are used, or whether the hunters and their households consume the food produced directly, or whether it is shared, traded, or sold beyond the local community.

Whaling has nutritional, cultural, social, and spiritual importance for many aboriginal and nonaboriginal peoples. However, aboriginal peoples are looking to the hunting of marine mammals as a way to enhance opportunities for economic development. The general view within the IWC is that aboriginal subsistence whaling must be regulated within the broad concept of sustainable use. Revisions to the IWC aboriginal subsistence whaling management regime and work on an Aboriginal Subsistence Whaling Procedure aim to ensure that subsistence hunting does not seriously increase the risk of extinction to an individual stock. Aboriginal subsistence whaling is at the very center of

An Inuit hunter harpoons a narwhal from his kayak, Northwest Greenland.
Copyright Bryan and Cherry Alexander Photography

debate over appropriate approaches to marine mammal conservation and harvesting in the Arctic. On the one hand, aboriginal peoples claim the right both to continue whaling and to develop domestic and international markets for whale products. On the other hand, scientists, environmentalists, and antiwhaling groups express concern over depleting whale stocks and abhorrence at the commercial nature of whaling. As commercial whaling has declined as an economic activity in recent decades, so subsistence whaling by aboriginal peoples has attracted more attention over the last few years from the IWC and environmental organizations concerned with whale conservation. As a consequence, the future for aboriginal subsistence whaling is increasingly uncertain as the regime undergoes revision and while the very meanings of aboriginality and subsistence are undergoing critical reevaluation and rethinking.

The definition of whaling by indigenous peoples of the Arctic as aboriginal subsistence whaling has proved in many ways to be an imposition, by restricting indigenous peoples from developing their resources in ways that seem appropriate and defined in terms of their own cultural and economic needs. The category of aboriginal subsistence whaling also excludes nonaboriginal coastal whaling communities. Small-type coastal whalers in Japan and Norway are subject to the ban on commercial whaling, but argue that they have cultural traditions and nutritional needs similar to the aboriginal peoples who are permitted to whale because the IWC recognizes the socioeconomic and cultural importance of whaling for northern aboriginal communities.

Whaling for Arctic peoples is embedded within, and cannot be separated from, the social, cultural, and economic bases of survival. For this reason, comanagement and small-scale community-based development is aiming to integrate the values, perspectives, opinions, and environmental knowledge of indigenous peoples with scientific approaches to resource management. Aboriginal subsistence continues to be at the forefront of environmental debate concerning the importance of hunting and its role in providing a sustainable economic base for Arctic coastal communities. Many commentators see the IWC as moving toward an explicit antiwhaling stance, rather than maintaining its original role as a regulatory body. The future of subsistence hunting, especially whaling, is dependent on working out appropriate definitions that will allow hunting activities to exist within the framework of the market economies that characterize the modern Arctic. The IWC category of aboriginal subsistence whaling is not based on any real substantive definitions of what the IWC understands by "aboriginal" and "subsistence." Indigenous peoples are represented as "traditional" if they only hunt for their own consumption, yet "modern" if they wish to sell the products of the catch.

Aboriginal marine mammal hunters have acted to counter the extent of management by the IWC and currently exercise a degree of control over the regulation and management of subsistence whaling. Inuit and other coastal peoples have formed their own organizations concerned specifically with the importance of subsistence activities for the survival of Inuit culture, or cooperate with other whaling communities to produce community-based strategies for whale management. These organizations, among them the Alaska Eskimo Whaling Commission (AEWC), the Greenland Hunters and Fishers Association (KANPK), the Inuit Circumpolar Conference (ICC), and the North Atlantic Marine Mammal Commission (NAMMCO), work to ensure that subsistence whaling in the Arctic is monitored and controlled by and for the communities that depend on it, thereby safeguarding its future. This work has set a precedent for the management of marine resources by and for indigenous peoples elsewhere and demonstrates how indigenous knowledge may be used to feed into scientific research. Whales and whaling have assumed political and symbolic potency as indigenous peoples claim the right to hunt marine mammals in a sustainable way.

MARK NUTTALL

See also **Alaska Eskimo Whaling Commission; Greenland Hunters and Fishers Association (KANPK); Hunting, Subsistence; International Convention for the Regulation of Whaling; Marine Mammal Hunting; North Atlantic Marine Mammal Commission (NAMMCO)**

Further Reading

Caulfield, R.A., *Greenlanders, Whales and Whaling: Sustainability and Self-determination in the Arctic*, Hanover and London: University Press of New England, 1997

Donovan, G.P., *The International Whaling Commission and Aboriginal/Subsistence Whaling: April 1979 to July 1981*, Reports of the International Whaling Commission (Special Issue 4), Cambridge: IWC, 1982

Freeman, M.M.R., E. Wein & D. Keith, *Recovering Rights: Bowhead Whales and Inuvialuit Subsistence in the Western Canadian Arctic*, Edmonton: Canadian Circumpolar Institute, 1992

Friedheim, R.L. (editor), *Toward a Sustainable Whaling Regime*, Seattle: University of Washington Press and Edmonton: Canadian Circumpolar Institute (CCI) Press, 2001

Gambell, R., "International management of whales and whaling: an historical review of the regulation of commercial and Aboriginal subsistence whaling." *Arctic*, 46(2)(1993): 97–107

Lynge, F., *Arctic Wars, Animal Rights, Endangered Peoples*, Hanover: University of New England Press, 1992

Stevenson, M., A. Madsen & E. Maloney, (editors), *The Anthropology of Community-Based Whaling in Greenland*, Edmonton: Canadian Circumpolar (CCI) Press, 1997

WHITE WHALE—*See* BELUGA (WHITE) WHALE

WHITE SEA

The White Sea is located in the northwest of the Russian Federation, between 68°40′ and 63°48′ N latitude and 32°00′ and 44°30′ E longitude. The White Sea is mostly landlocked and has only one marine border, with the Barents Sea. It is thus isolated from the rest of the Arctic Ocean. The area of the White Sea is nearly 90,000 km², and its average depth is 67 m. The topography of its seabed is rough and complex. The north part of the White Sea is shallow, with the depth not more than 50 m, and the northwest part (Kandalaksha Bay and the adjacent central region) is up to 350 m deep. The maximum tide is up to 7 m.

The climate of the White Sea is transitional from oceanic to continental. Winter is long and severe, with average temperatures from −14°C to −15°C in February. Summer is cold and moderately wet with average temperatures from 8°C to 10°C in July. Water temperature is low and variable from site to site, with appreciable seasonal changes. Temperature varies at the water surface in winter from −0.5°C to −0.7°C in the bays and decreasing to −1.9°C in the north part of the White Sea, according to salinity values. The sea is ice-covered for half the year, but the ice cover is not solid and the sea is kept open for transport by ice-breakers. Water temperature increases in summer up to 14–15°C at the water surface, but decreases quickly with depth to −1.4°C at 130–140 m.

Freshwater input to the White Sea is approximately 228 km³ per year, mainly as river flow. Three rivers flow into the White Sea: Severnaya Dvina, Mezen', and Onega, which are responsible for most (75%) of the freshwater input. The salinity of the White Sea is not stable and can change from 10 to 30 ppm ($g^{-1}l$), depending on the site, season, and depth. Maximum salinity is observed in winter, and the minimum in spring and summer. The highest salinity values usually occur in the north part of the White Sea, in the vicinity of the Barents Sea.

There are six main ports along the White Sea seashore: Arkhangel'sk, Onega, Belomorsk, Kandalaksha, Kem', and Mezen'. Kandalaksha is one of the oldest settlements, and was mentioned for the first time in chronicles of the 12th century. Arkhangel'sk is the main sea and river port on the White Sea shore and also an important rail junction. Timber, building materials, chemical products, technical equipment, fish, and fish products are the main part of cargo. There is an industrial center too, with sawmills, pulp and paper, hydrolytic, and shipbuilding industries. Many people, including tourists, travel by sea, too. The White Sea is connected with the Baltic Sea by a canal 140 miles long from Belomorsk to St Petersburg.

There are many marine resources that flourish in the White Sea. Fish, marine animals, and seaweed are among them. Navaga, White Sea herring, smelt, codfish, and salmon are the main commercial fish.

Greenland seal and ringed seal are the main marine animals hunted for their fur.

VLADIMIR IL'INSKII

See also **Arkhangel'sk; Barents Sea; Severnaya Dvina**

Further Reading

Berger, Victor & Salve Dahle, *White Sea: Ecology and Environment*, Tromsø, 2001

Dobrovol'skii, Aleksei & Zalogin Boris, *Morya SSSR* [Seas of the Soviet Union], Moscow: Moscow University Publishing House, 1982

Pantiulin, A.N., *"O formirovanii i izmenchivosti structuri vod Belogo morya"* [Formation and changeability of water structure in White Sea]. In *Biologicheskie resursi Belogomorya* [Biological resource of the White Sea], edited by P.M. Matekin, Moscow: Moscow State University Publishing House, 1990

Prochorov, Alexandr (editor), *Sovetskii Enciklopedicheskii Slovar'* [Soviet Encyclopedic Dictionary], Moscow: "Soviet Encyclopedia," 1985

Zenkevich, Lev, *Biologiya morei SSSR*, Moscow: Academy of Science of USSR Publishing House, 1963; as *Biology of the Seas of the USSR*, New York: Wiley, 1963

WHITE-FRONTED GOOSE

The white-fronted goose (*Anser albifrons*, or *Nerleq* in Greenlandic) breeds in the entire Arctic region except for northern Scandinavia, Iceland, and Svalbard. Four subspecies have been recognized, all grayish-brown with a white forehead and black barring on the underparts of the adults. The geese are medium-sized, length 65–90 cm from bill to tail, and 2–3 kg in weight.

The Greenland subspecies *flavirostris* (Greenland greater white-fronted goose) is easily distinguished by the orange bill, dark brown plumage, and heavy black barring. The other subspecies have a pink bill and, in general, a paler brown plumage. Young birds lack the white front and barrings. The lesser white-fronted goose is a separate species (*Anser erythropus*) that is somewhat smaller than *Anser albifrons*, has dark plumage, dark underbars, and a yellow eye ring. The subspecies *albifrons* (greater white-fronted goose) breeds in western and northern Siberia, *frontalis* (Pacific white-fronted goose) breeds from eastern Siberia to Arctic Canada, and *gambelli* (Gambel's white-fronted goose) breeds in Alaska. The lesser white-fronted goose breeds from Scandinavia to the Anadyr Peninsula of northeast Siberia. The breeding habitat for all subspecies is taiga and open tundra close to marshes, lakes, ponds, and rivers. The goose can also be found near the coast. The white-fronted goose is a migratory bird that winters in the United States, Europe, and central and East Asia. The winter habitats are boglands, marshes, farmland, and natural and seminatural grasslands.

The white-fronted goose population can be separated into up to ten different "flyway" populations, of which the majority are increasing their size. The total wintering population numbered approximately 2.7 million birds in 1997, with flyway populations varying between 8000 and 790,000 birds.

The different flyway populations leave the wintering grounds between mid-March and mid-April. Somewhere between the wintering grounds and the breeding range, the geese stage at stopover sites for two to three weeks before continuing their migration. The geese arrive at the breeding grounds in early to mid-May, and start breeding in late May to early June. To be able to migrate the 3000–5000 km to the breeding areas, the geese must build up stores of fat and nutrients during the last month on the wintering grounds. The stopover sites are used by the geese to rebuild energy stores so that upon arrival in the breeding range they are able to cope with the often harsh weather conditions, which offer poor feeding possibilities. It was previously thought that most geese build up condition only on the wintering grounds, but recent studies have revealed that the geese must feed on or near the breeding grounds to be able to breed successfully. The female goose needs fat and especially protein to produce a full clutch of four to seven eggs. Fat is obtained from feeding on the underground stems of common cottongrass *Eriophorum angustifolium*, viviparous knotweed *Polygonum viviparum*, and marsh arrowgrass *Triglochin plaustre*. Proteins are obtained from the latter plant species, but especially from fresh foliage of grasses, sedges, and herbs. Calcium for the eggshells is acquired from underground plant parts and from associated soil minerals.

The white-fronted goose is normally solitary nesting, with mean nest densities of 0.4 – 4.6. Aggregations of up to 300 nests per km² have been found in the albifrons subspecies, where it breeds in association with gull colonies on islands or nests of the peregrine falcon (*Falco peregrinus*). The nest is often placed on a tussock or hillock on a gently sloping hill overlooking nearby lakes and marshes. The female goose incubates the eggs for a period of 25–27 days. During this period, the female leaves the nest only for up to 3% of the time spent incubating. These short feeding trips are not sufficient to maintain her body mass and the female goose might lose about 40% of her body mass by the end of incubation. The male goose stays vigilant through most of the incubation period, but has time to feed in the nearby marshes. At the time when the goslings are hatched, the male would have lost about 20% of his weight, but he continues to lose weight because it is most important that he remain watchful in order to defend the goslings from predators. Predators are mainly Arctic foxes (*Alopex lagopus*) and ravens

Greater white-fronted goose (*Anser albifrons*).
Photo by Dave Menke, courtesy US Fish and Wildlife Service

(*Corvus corax*), which especially exploit eggs and goslings. Arctic foxes can occasionally kill an adult breeding or molting bird, and white-tailed eagles Haliaeetus albicilla have been observed attacking spring staging geese. Two weeks after hatching, the goslings feed on horsetail (*Equisetum* spp.) and herbs such as *Stellaria* and *Polygonum*, a diet completely different from the adult diet. In the following weeks, the differences in the gosling and adult diets become less apparent, and constitute fresh leaves of grasses, sedges, and herbs. The goslings are able to fly at approximately six weeks of age.

The white-fronted geese have, like other goose species, only one body molt every year, and the most conspicuous of these is the wing molt. The duration of the wing molt is three to four weeks, and the development of the flying feathers is more rapid than in many duck species, indicating an adaptation in Arctic breeding goose species to the short Arctic summer. Immature geese and failed breeding birds molt in July, while breeding birds molt about two weeks later. Immatures and failed breeders migrate in most subspecies northward to safe moulting sites, which contain refuge lakes or rivers and abundant food. The Greenland subspecies has no such conspicuous molt migration, and molt takes place in the breeding range. During molt, up to one-third of the total body protein content is shed. Despite this loss over a relatively short period, geese are able to meet their energy and protein demands by moderate feeding, and do not have to deplete their energy and nutrient reserves. During this period, proteins are degraded from the breast muscles and built into leg muscles. These changes are ascribed to disuse-use of the muscle groups.

The autumn migration starts in September and the white-fronted geese reach their wintering grounds around October and November.

The white-fronted goose is nowadays heavily hunted with annual goose bags of about 15% in the *albifrons* and *flavirostris* populations. The lesser white-fronted goose *Anser erythropus* is globally threatened, with the population having decreased by nearly 90% since the early part of the 20th century, and in Fennoscandia the population may only represent 30–50 breeding pairs. In all white-fronted goose breeding and molting areas, local people gather eggs and catch molting geese for meat and down. In Greenlandic myths, geese give back sight to blinded people by squirting their feces into people's eyes.

CHRISTIAN M. GLAHDER

Further Reading

Batt, B.D.J., A.D. Afton, M.G. Anderson, C.D. Ankney, D.H. Johnson, J.A. Kadlec & G.L. Krapu (editors), *Ecology and Management of Breeding Waterfowl*, Minneapolis: University of Minnesota Press, 1992

Cramp, Stanley & K.E.L. Simmons (editors), *Handbook of Birds of Europe, the Middle East, and North Africa: The birds of the Western Palearctic*, Volume 1, Oxford: Oxford University Press, 1977

del Hoyo, Josep, Andrew Elliott & Jordi Sargatal (editors), *Handbook of the Birds of the World,* Volume 1, Barcelona: Lynx Edicions, 1992

Glahder, Christian Martin, *Sensitive Areas and Periods of the Greenland White-Fronted Goose in West Greenland. Spring Staging and Molt as Important Bottleneck Periods in the Annual Cycle of the Goose Subspecies*, Ph.D. thesis, Denmark: National Environmental Research Institute, 1999

Madsen, Jesper, Gill Craknell & Tony Fox (editors), *Goose Populations of the Western Palearctic. A Review of Status and Distribution*, Wetlands International Publ. No. 48, The Netherlands, Wageningen: Wetlands International; Denmark, Rönde: National Environmental Research Institute, 1999

Owen, Myrfyn, *Wild Geese of the World. Their Life History and Ecology*, London: Batsford, 1980

Rose, P.M. & D.A. Scott (compilers), *Waterfowl Population Estimates* (2nd edition), The Netherlands, Wageningen: Wetlands International, 1997

Salomonsen, Finn, *Grønlands Fugle. The Birds of Greenland*, Copenhagen: Munksgaard, 1950

———, "The moult migration." *Wildfowl,* 19 (1968): 5–24

WHITEHORSE

Whitehorse, capital of the Yukon Territory, Canada, straddles the Yukon River near the Alaska Highway at kilometer 1476. The city has served as a major transportation center for the Yukon Territory since its origins in the 1890s, when it was a temporary stopping point for gold seekers on their way to the Klondike Gold Rush at Dawson City. The White Pass and Yukon Route Railway from Skagway, Alaska, to Whitehorse was completed in 1900, and resulted in the establishment of a permanent community. The city, which was incorporated in 1950 and has a population of 19,157 (1996), takes its name from the Whitehorse Rapids, which were a significant hazard to navigation on the Yukon River.

The White Pass and Yukon Route Corporation, and its subsidiary, the British Yukon Navigation Company, which operated steamboats on the Yukon River, dominated the economy of the community for most of its existence, providing jobs and economic opportunities. The railway facilitated the shipment of soldiers and supplies to Whitehorse for the building of the Alaska Highway in 1942–1943. The US military also expanded the Whitehorse airport as part of the Northwest Staging Route, and built an oil refinery. It lodged thousands of soldiers in the community until World War II ended. The Canadian military took over the operation and maintenance of the highway from 1946 until 1964, when it was turned over to civil administration. The large military presence in Whitehorse declined rapidly after the change, but the town's population soon recovered. The federal government moved the territorial capital from Dawson City to Whitehorse in 1953.

Whitehorse benefited from federal construction projects in the 1950s, when a large federal office building, a bridge across the Yukon River, a new hospital, a large high school, and new housing for public servants were constructed. A hydroelectric dam was constructed on the Yukon River south of the town site in 1959, creating Schwatka Lake. This lake was named after Lt. Frederick Schwatka of the US Army, who led two expeditions into the Yukon in the 1880s. Steamship traffic on the Yukon River ceased in 1955 and three majestic riverboats were marooned on the riverbanks in the city. Two of these, the *Whitehorse* and the *Casca*, burned in 1974, leaving only the SS *Klondike*, which has since been restored by Parks Canada. Other attractions in Whitehorse include the Whitehorse Rapids Fishway, the Old Log Church, the Beringia Interpretive Center the Takhini Hotsprings, the Transportation Museum, and the McBride Museum.

STEVEN SMYTH

See also **Alaska Highway; Yukon River**

Further Reading

Coates, K. & W.R. Morrison, *Land of the Midnight Sun: A History of the Yukon*, Edmonton: Hurtig, 1988

———, *The Federal Government and Urban Development in Northern Canada After World War II: Whitehorse and Dawson City, Yukon Territory*, B.C. Studies, No. 104, Vancouver: University of British Columbia, winter, 1994–1995

WILDERNESS

"The universe of the wilderness is disappearing like a snow bank on a south-facing slope on a warm June day" (Robert Marshall, "The Universe of the Wilderness is Vanishing," quoted in Foreman, 1991: 69).

According to Cassell's *Concise English Dictionary* (1994), *wilderness* is an uninhabited or uncultivated land, a desert; a waste, a scene of disorder or confusion. In Webster's *Third New International Dictionary* (1966), wilderness is defined as a tract of land or a region (as a forest or a wide barren plain) uncultivated or uninhabited by human beings; an empty or pathless area or region. The concept of wilderness in western culture has its roots in Judeo-Christian fundamentalism. Europeans brought this concept with them to North America as they set out to tame the wilderness of the continent's western frontier. A related term is *terra nullius*, a land that is devoid of people. The latter is a legal concept used by Europeans when they first arrived in North America. They sought to justify their claim to own all the land by pretending that no one else had been there first. Due to this confluence of geography and history, much of the abundant literature and legislation treating wilderness is North American in origin.

George Perkins Marsh's *Man and Nature* (1864) was the first book to attack the American myth of the superabundance and the inexhaustibility of the earth. Marsh, whose text is considered to be the fountainhead of the conservation movement, wrote that "man has too long forgotten that the earth was given to him for usufruct alone, not for consumption, still less for profligate waste" (Marsh, 1864: 36).

Other writers have also profoundly influenced thinking about nature. Henry David Thoreau's most famous quote from the essay "Walking," published in the *Atlantic Monthly* (June 1862), is surely "in wildness is the preservation of the world" (quoted in Nash, 1982: 84). It was publicity-minded mountaineer John Muir, more than any other individual—not coincidentally based largely on his late 19th-century experiences in Alaska—who launched the nature preservation movement. Muir's travels coincided with the disappearance of the western frontier in the contiguous United States. In the 1930s, forester Robert Marshall championed the concept that some wilderness should be preserved, even in heavily populated regions. Marshall was the first person to recognize that wilderness preservation in Alaska could involve whole watersheds, entire mountain ranges, and intact ecosystems. Instead of wilderness being islands in a sea of civilization, the proportions were reversed in the Arctic. Still later, Rachel Carson's *Silent Spring* (1962) gave a voice to the modern environmental movement in the 1960s and Edward Abbey's *Monkey Wrench Gang* (1975) inspired radical strains of environmentalism in the 1970s. In the 1980s, Harvard biologist Edward Wilson stirred the discipline with his thesis that many defend nature because of *biophilia*, an inherent love for nature.

In his controversial 1995 essay on "The Trouble with Wilderness," historian William Cronon wrote that

> preserving wilderness has for decades been a fundamental tenet, indeed a passion, of the environmental movement, especially in United States. Ever since the 19th century, celebrating wilderness has been an activity mainly for well-to-do city folks. Rural people generally know far too much about working the land to regard underworked land as their ideal. There are other ironies as well. The movement to set aside national parks and wilderness areas followed hard on the heels of the final Indian wars, in which the prior human inhabitants of these regions were rounded up and moved onto reservations so that tourists could safely enjoy the illusion that they were seeing their nation in its pristine, original state. Meanwhile, its original inhabitants were kept out by force, their earlier uses of the land redefined as inappropriate or even illegal. To this day, for instance, the Blackfeet continue to be accused of "poaching" in Montana's Glacier National Park, on lands that originally belonged to them and that were ceded by treaty only with the proviso that they be permitted to hunt there. (Cronon, 1996: 42–34)

The idea of designated "wilderness areas" has long been linked not only with conservation but also with recreation. Forest ranger Aldo Leopold held the opinion that "wilderness areas are a series of sanctuaries for the primitive arts of wilderness travel, especially canoeing and packing" (Leopold, quoted in Foreman, 1991: 63). Leopold was responsible for the world's first wilderness area, New Mexico's Gila in 1924, which was administratively established by the United States Forest Service. However, Marshall, the founder of the Wilderness Society in 1935, instituted a system for protecting "wildlands" on the US National Forests. So-called "wilderness areas" were to be more than 100,000 acres, and "wild areas" less than 100,000 acres. The Wilderness Act of 1964 established a National Wilderness Preservation System, initially composed of the preexisting wilderness and wild areas on the national forests. The protection of the existing and establishment of new roadless wildlands has been a key goal of wilderness advocacy groups like Earth First in the 1980s and Wild Earth from the 1990s onward.

A turning point in the human relationship with the natural world was the advent of herding and agriculture some 15,000 years ago. As geographer Clarence Glacken wrote, "forest clearance was required for the extension of civilization, for public health, and for the promotion of agriculture necessary for this extension" (Glacken, 1967: 691). In *Wilderness and the American Mind* (1982), Roderick Nash observed that the domestication of animals and plants had an impact not only on the earth but also on thought. For the first time, humans conceived of themselves as distinct from nature. Until there were domesticated animals, it was impossible to distinguish them from wild ones. Until there were fenced fields and walled cities, "wilderness" had no meaning. Everything was simply habitat that humans shared with other creatures. Chief Standing Bear of the Ogalala Sioux recognized that only to the white man was nature a wilderness and the land infested with "wild" animals and "savage" people. For nomadic hunters and gatherers such as the Sioux, it made no sense to distinguish wilderness from civilization or wild from tame animals.

Scientists as well as anthropologists have noted that the concept of wilderness is equally alien to indigenous Arctic cultures. According to anthropologist Richard K. Nelson, referring to the Koyukon Athapaskans' homeland in northwestern Alaska, "the fact that westerners identify this remote country as wilderness reflects their inability to conceive of occupying and utilizing an environment without fundamentally altering its natural state. But the Koyukon people and their ancestors have done precisely this over a protracted span of time" (Nelson, 1983: 246). Biologist Dave

Klein has similarly written that "indigenous peoples are at the top of trophic relationships within Arctic ecosystems and view themselves as a part of nature. Their lifestyles and very existence have been dependent upon a sustained harvest of resources from the land without altering nature" (Klein, 1994: 1). In short, indigenous peoples are traditionally at home in these so-called wild and barren Arctic lands. At the same time, contemporary indigenous communities are diverse when it comes to practicing environmental conservation within their respective homelands. During the debate over petroleum exploration in Alaska's Arctic National Wildlife Refuge (ANWR), the Athapaskan Arctic Village has consistently fought against development, whereas the Iñupiat village of Kaktovik has lobbied in favor of development.

BRUCE FORBES

See also **Conservation; Environmentalism**

Further Reading

Butler, Tom (editor), "The Wildlands Project." *Wild Earth*, 10(1)(2000): 1–112

Cronon, William, *Changes in the Land: Indians, Colonists, and the Ecology of New England*, Hill and Wang: New York, 1983

———, "Trouble with Wilderness; or Getting Back to the Wrong Nature." In *Uncommon Ground: Rethinking the Human Place in Nature*, edited by W. Cronon, New York: Norton, 1996, pp. 69–90. Originally published in the *New York Times Magazine*, August 13, 1995

Davis, John (editor), "Opposing wilderness deconstruction." *Wild Earth*, 6(4) (1997): 1–105

Foreman, Dave, *Confessions of an Eco-Warrior*, New York: Harmony Books, 1991

Glacken, Clarence, *Traces on The Rhodian Shore; Nature and Culture in Western Thought from Ancient Times To the End of the Eighteenth Century,* Berkeley: University of California Press, 1967

Klein, David R., "Wilderness: A Western Concept Alien to Arctic Cultures." *Information North*, 20(3)(1994): 1–6

Leopold, Aldo, *A Sand County Almanac*, Oxford: Oxford University Press, 1949

Marsh, George Perkins, *Man and Nature*, Cambridge: Harvard University Press, 1864

Marshall, Robert, *Alaska Wilderness* (2nd edition), Berkeley: University of California Press, 1970

Nash, Roderick, *Wilderness and the American Mind* (3rd edition). New Haven: Yale University Press, 1982

Nelson, Richard K., Make Prayers To the Raven: A Koyukon View of the Northern Forest, Chicago: University of Chicago Press, 1983

Oelschlaeger, Max, *The Idea of Wilderness: From Prehistory to the Age of Ecology*, New Haven: Yale University Press, 1993

Peepre, Juri & Bob Jickling (editors), *Northern Protected Areas and Wilderness*, Whitehorse: Canadian Parks and Wilderness Society and Yukon College, 1994

Shepard, Paul (editor), *The Only World We've Got*, San Francisco: Sierra Club Books, 1996

Thomas Jr., William L. (editor), *Man's Role in Changing the Face of the Earth*, Chicago: University of Chicago Press, 1956

Turner, Frederick, *Beyond Geography: The Western Spirit Against the Wilderness*, New Brunswick: Rutgers University Press, 1983

Wilson, Edward O., *Biophilia*, Cambridge, Massachusetts: Harvard University Press, 1984

WILDLIFE MANAGEMENT: ENVIRONMENTAL INITIATIVES

Arctic wildlife management is subject to international conventions and the national laws that implement these conventions. Wildlife species may also migrate across one or more national boundaries, necessitating and giving rise to regional management. Wildlife comanagement regimes are developing, based on joint decision-making by local users and indigenous peoples, and governments. For example, comanagement regimes in northern Canada have arisen under aboriginal and treaty rights and land claim agreements, and involve Inuit and First Nations, as well as federal and territorial governments. Similarly, comanagement regimes are also found in Alaska, Scandinavia, and the former Soviet Union.

One example of Arctic wildlife management is found in the case of migratory species that travel across national boundaries and are subject to international conventions, national legislation, and comanagement. Such species include beluga whales, polar bears, caribou, and reindeer. Polar bears are a noteworthy example as they are a marine and terrestrial species. Other than breeding periods, polar bears spend much of their lives on land fast ice and can migrate over vast distances. Canada, the United States, Denmark, Greenland, Norway, and Russia are members of the Agreement on the Conservation of Polar Bears and Their Habitat, 1973. The agreement provides for joint management and the sharing of research. It also provides that polar bears may be harvested by local people using the traditional methods in the exercise of their traditional rights and in accordance with the laws of that country. Indigenous peoples in Alaska and Canada are involved in a subsistence and commercial harvest of polar bears. For example, Canada has a management regime for polar bears that is established under international conventions, land claim agreements, and federal, territorial, and provincial regulation. The Inuvialuit and the Inuit peoples harvest polar bears for commercial and subsistence purposes in the Northwest Territories and the Nunavut Territory. Local communities receive quotas for harvests of polar bears, which the community can then use for a traditional hunt, or transfer to sport hunters for a fee.

Beluga whales are another migratory species subject to international agreements, national legislation, and comanagement regimes. The whales are a medium-sized cetacean belonging to the group known as odontocetes or toothed whales, and their name is derived from the Russian word for "white." Beluga whales occur throughout Arctic and Subarctic waters, and are found in ice-covered regions in winter and spring and in coastal waters in summer and autumn. For example, the Bering Sea population is estimated to be 25,000, and winters in the drifting ice of the Bering Sea, moving in the summer to concentrate from the coast of Bristol Bay, Alaska to the Mackenzie River delta, Canada. The Inuvialuit of Canada, the Iñupiat peoples from Alaska, and other peoples in Russia harvest the Bering Sea population for subsistence purposes.

The Bering Sea population is subject to international and national management. The Inuvialuit and the Iñupiat are signatories to the Inuvialuit Iñupiat Beaufort Sea Beluga Whale Agreement, which requires them to cooperatively manage beluga whales in accordance with the Beaufort Sea Beluga Management Plan (Canada) and the Alaska Beluga Whale Committee Management Plan. In Canada, the approach to managing this population is derived from regulations under the national Fisheries Act, and the Inuvialuit Final Agreement, a land claim agreement that recognizes Inuvialuit harvesting and management rights for freshwater and marine species. The Beaufort Sea Beluga Management Plan is based on extensive community consultation, and includes stakeholders such as the Inuvialuit, government, and industry. Inuvialuit participation includes incorporation of traditional ecological knowledge, and the involvement of the Inuvialuit in research and monitoring. The Canada-Greenland Joint Commission on the Conservation and Management of Beluga and Narwhal recognizes that the two countries share management of beluga and narwhal populations that migrate between their waters.

Caribou migrate in large herds through northern and coastal regions of North America. The Porcupine caribou herd comprises 160,000 animals that seasonally migrate over about 260,000 square kilometers in Alaska, and the Yukon and Northwest Territories. Multijurisdictional arrangements for this herd involve the US and Canadian governments, Inuit, and First Nations; it includes national governments, three state or territorial governments, eight native land claim agreements, five national parks or preserves, two native special management areas, and two specific ordinances. National and international agreements have been negotiated, and create management boards that apply to Canada, and Canada and the United States, respectively.

In 1985, the Porcupine Caribou Management Board was formed to supervise the caribou herd and its Canadian habitat pursuant to an agreement between the governments of Canada, the Yukon and Northwest Territories, the Inuvialuit, and First Nations. The Board has the mandate to conserve the caribou herd for sub-sistence use by Inuvialuit and First Nations, while recognizing that other users may share the harvest. The Porcupine Caribou Management Board has eight representatives, with two representatives from the Council of Yukon First Nations and the government of the Yukon Territory, and one representative from the governments of Canada and the Northwest Territories, the Inuvialuit, and the Gwich'in. In 1987, Canada and the United States signed an international conservation agreement creating the International Porcupine Caribou Board. A plan was accepted as a framework for coordinating international aspects of herd management in 1993. Five management agencies work with the herd: Canadian Wildlife Service, US Fish and Wildlife Service, Government of Yukon, Government of the Northwest Territories, and the Alaska Department of Fish and Game. Research and logistics are coordinated by the Porcupine Caribou Technical Committee, which consists of biologists from five agencies.

Other regions of the Arctic demonstrate integrated approaches to wildlife, and consider the rights of indigenous peoples. One example is reindeer herding by indigenous peoples, and the protection of herding rights and grazing ranges. Domesticated reindeer are genetically similar to caribou, and are herded by the Saami peoples in Scandinavia, and Saami peoples and other indigenous peoples in Russia. All these countries protect reindeer herds and the herding rights of these peoples, and have shared management involving herders for seasonal grazing ranges of these herds.

Common environmental issues exist throughout the Arctic for wildlife. These issues include transboundary air and marine pollution; negative impacts from resource-oriented economic development such as hydrocarbons, hydroelectric generation, and mining; and the impacts of climate changes on marine and coastal species and ecosystems. For example, the Porcupine caribou herd and the Bering Sea beluga population will be affected by hydrocarbon developments in coastal and offshore regions of the Beaufort Sea. In the Komi Republic and the Nenets Autonomous District, and western Siberia regions of the former Soviet Republic, oil and gas production is connected with major environmental hazards. Oil exploration and extraction in the Komi Republic have damaged and reduced the winter pastures of the reindeer, and oil spills in 1994 and 1995 at the Kolva River have affected villages of Komi reindeer herders. Contamination and pollution originating in one area of the Arctic or outside the Arctic can negatively impact other regions of the Arctic. Moreover, climate change also impacts Arctic wildlife populations. For example, polar bears are negatively affected by climate change, given their dependence on ice cover and thickness, while at the same time there may be increasing open waters for beluga whales.

Climate change could lead to a complete decline in reindeer husbandry in the former Soviet Union. If the mean annual temperature increases by 5°C, the biological preconditions for reindeer herding may no longer exist as—if the treeline proceeds to the coast of the North Polar Sea—there will be no tundra left.

Considering these different species, Arctic wildlife management can be said to conserve species and habitat, while recognizing the uses and rights of indigenous peoples and local communities.

MAGDALENA A.K. MUIR

See also **Agreement on the Conservation of Polar Bears; Alaska Beluga Whale Committee; Conservation; Hunting, Subsistence; Inuvialuit Comanagement Bodies; National Parks and Protected Areas; Nunavut Wildlife Management Board; Political Issues in Resource Management; Sustainable Development**

Further Reading

Caulfield, R.A., *Greenlanders, Whales and Whaling: Sustainability and Self-Determination in the Arctic*, Hanover, New Hampshire: University Press of New England, 1997

Freeman, M.M.R., "Polar Bears and Whales: Contrasts in International Wildlife Regimes." In *Issues in the North*, edited by J. Oakes & R. Riewe, Edmonton: Canadian Circumpolar Institute, 1996, pp. 175–181

Huntington, H., *Wildlife Management and Subsistence Hunting in Alaska*, Seattle: University of Washington Press, 1992

Muir, M.A.K., "Wildlife management in Alaska and northern Canada, and the development of circumpolar approaches." *Wilderness in the Circumpolar North Conference*, Anchorage, Alaska, May 15–16, 2001

Muir, M.A.K., & L.N. Binder, "Traditional knowledge and northern wildlife management." *International Federation of Library Associations and Institutions Conference*, Khon Kaen, Thailand, August 16–19, 1999 (see http://www.ieels.com/publications/1999-wildmantradknow.pdf)

Osherenko, G., *Sharing Power with Native Users: Co-management Regimes for Arctic Wildlife*, Canada: Canadian Arctic Resources Committee, 1988

WINDCHILL

The concept of "windchill" is one that quantifies the subjective sensation of cold, and the objective danger of frostbite to exposed flesh, experienced by human beings when cold air is in motion as a result of wind. Many factors contribute to the degree of discomfort experienced by human beings in cold windy conditions, including insolation, humidity, the quality and amount of clothing worn, and the physical fitness, body temperature, metabolic rate, and psychological condition of the subject. However, the single most important factor is the rate at which heat is lost from exposed flesh. This factor is almost solely responsible for determining the conditions beyond which frostbite

occurs, and is principally governed by the air temperature and the wind speed. The rate at which heat is lost from the body is increased when air that has been warmed by the body is transported away by air movement.

Early investigations of the phenomenon date to the 1920s, but the most famous study was probably that performed by Siple and Passel in Antarctica in 1941. From their observations of the rate at which water froze in containers, Siple and Passel derived an empirical formula for the rate of heat loss as a function of air temperature and wind speed. This formula, or the slightly modified version of it produced by A. Court in 1948, still forms the basis of many official estimates of windchill. The Siple-Passel-Court formula is, however, rather unrealistic. One major problem is that it predicts that, for a given air temperature, the windchill increases with wind speed only up to about 25–30 m s^{-1}, and actually decreases somewhat as the wind speed increases beyond this value. This behavior is a consequence of the simple model used by Siple and Passel to fit data derived over a comparatively limited range of wind speeds, and it has led to the misleading and potentially dangerous belief that wind speeds above about 20 m s^{-1} have little additional cooling effect. Since about 1970, beginning with the work of R.G. Steadman, models of windchill have been developed that are based on human physiology rather than on the freezing of containers of water. Unlike the Siple-Passel-Court formula, these predict that the rate of heat loss from exposed skin increases monotonically with increasing wind speed. Unfortunately, these models do not yet seem to have been incorporated into most graphs and tables of windchill.

Windchill can be expressed in essentially three ways: as the rate of heat loss from exposed skin, as an "equivalent temperature," and as subjective sensation of cold. None of these is entirely satisfactory. Subjective categories of cold, typically ranging from "cool" through "very cold" to "freezing cold," will differ between individuals and their circumstances. The rate of heat loss calculated on the basis of some of the more recent work may differ by a factor of two or more from that calculated from the "standard" Siple-Passel formula, so that a quoted figure is useless unless one knows the formula that was used to generate it. Similar remarks apply to the use of equivalent temperatures. These are calculated as the air temperature required to produce the same rate of heat loss under some standard conditions (for e.g., for the Siple-Passel formula this is a wind speed of 5 mi h^{-1}, whereas some of Steadman's work assumes still air and a clothed individual), and are an attempt to provide a number that a nonexpert can assimilate. But one may object that few people are likely to be able to interpret the difference between an equivalent temperature of say –30°C and one of –40°C, and that the calculations are in any case again model-dependent. Furthermore, experience shows that people have a tendency to believe that the equivalent temperatures are somehow "real," and should determine, for example, the concentration of antifreeze needed in a car's radiator.

A serious danger arises from the existence of more than one formula for calculating the rate of heat loss, and hence the equivalent temperature, from the environmental conditions. This is that safety criteria appropriate to one model may be mistakenly applied to another. For example, an air temperature of –30°C and a wind speed of 5 m s^{-1} gives a rate of heat loss from exposed skin of about 1370 W m^{-2} according to one of Steadman's formulas, but over 2000 W m^{-2} from the Siple-Passel formula. A typical subjective scale derived from the Siple-Passel formula would categorize the former rate of heat loss as "very cold," whereas a rate of 2000 W m^{-2} would be classified as "freezing cold," with a strong risk of frostbite. Paradoxically, this danger is an argument in favor of using verbal descriptions instead of quantitative measures of windchill, especially in the case of frostbite, which is far from being a subjective condition.

GARETH REES

See also **Precipitation and Moisture; Weather**

Further Reading

Barry, R.G. & R.J. Chorley, *Atmosphere, Weather and Climate* (6th edition), London: Routledge, 1992

Bluestein, M., "An evaluation of the wind chill factor: its development and applicability." *Journal of Biomechanical Engineering*, 120 (1998): 255–258

Court, A., "Windchill." *Bulletin of the American Meteorological Society*, 29 (1948): 487–493

Osczevski, R.J., "The basis of wind chill." *Arctic*, 48 (1995): 372–382

Quayle, R. & Steadman, R. "The Steadman wind chill: an improvement over present scales." *Weather and Forecasting*, 13 (1998): 1187–1193

Rees, W.G., "A new wind-chill nomogram." *Polar Record*, 29 (1993): 229–234

Siple, P.A. & C.F. Passel, "Measurements of dry atmospheric cooling in subfreezing temperatures." *Proceedings of the American Philosophical Society*, 89 (1945): 177–199

Steadman, R.G., "Indices of windchill of clothed persons." *Journal of Applied Meteorology*, 10 (1971): 674–683

Thompson, R.D. & A. Perry (editors), *Applied Climatology*, London: Routledge, 1997

WOLF

The gray wolf was first scientifically described by the Swedish biologist Carl Linnaeus in 1758. Belonging to the *Canidae* family, the species name, *Canis lupus*, combines the Latin words for dog and wolf. Taxonomists have recognized over 32 subspecies of the gray wolf. Several circumpolar subspecies of the gray wolf are known as Arctic wolves and those on the treeless plains of the north are called tundra wolves. The wolf of the Canadian Arctic islands, *Canis lupus arctos*, is most commonly referred to as the Arctic wolf. The local people have their own names for these white wolves: *Amarok* (Inuit), *Amagok* (Inuvialuit), and *Amaguk* (Iñupiat).

In the northern parts of their mainland range, wolves vary greatly in color. In the northern Arctic islands and Greenland, wolves may be pure white or white with blackish or reddish markings, especially on the shoulders and tail. Pups are usually darker in color for their first year of life.

In winter, the wolf coat consists of a dense underfur, which provides suitable insulation, plus the coarser outer coat for protection and warmth. With warmer summer temperatures, the extra wool is shed, leading to a period of distinctly shaggy appearance.

Adult females weigh 18–55 kg and adult males weigh 20–80 kg, depending on the subspecies. The total length (nose to tip of tail) ranges from 1.37 to 1.52 m for females, and from 1.27 to 1.64 m for males.

The gray wolf is a social animal and functions in a group or pack that is basically a family group of five to eight wolves. Packs are held together by strong ties between the members, reinforced as pups grow up together or by courtship behavior between two mature adults. Order within a pack is maintained by a dominance hierarchy system in which the adult male dominates the adult female and pups.

Wolves communicate through posture, howling and other vocalizations, and through scent marking. Howling functions in assembling the pack, advertising the occupation and extent of the pack's territory, and expressing distress or contentment. Scent marking involves depositing urine or feces on conspicuous objects within a pack's range, usually by dominant males, and probably plays a role in territory advertising.

Male and female wolves breed only once a year, commonly in the spring, but timing varies with the latitude. Litters of five or six pups are born after a gestation period of nine weeks. Wolf pups are usually born in the early spring in a den dug by the female in soft soil. On the treeless tundra, dens are commonly located in eskers deposited by glaciers. Dens used in the High Arctic are usually traditional sites used for hundreds of years, featuring many old bones and the luxurious vegetation that develops from the increased fertilization.

Pups remain within the den for about two weeks, and then begin venturing outside as they develop mobility in mid-summer. Adults carry meat back to the pups at the den site in their stomachs, and disgorge it for the pups. During late summer, the pups are moved from the birth den to rendezvous sites where the pack

Gray wolf (*Canis lupus*).
Photo by Gary Kramer, courtesy US Fish and Wildlife Service

spends much time. In the fall, the pups begin to accompany the adults on some hunting trips. The curiosity and playfulness associated with life around the den decreases when they begin traveling.

Wolf pups on the Arctic islands face the hardships of nomadic life much earlier than temperate region wolves, since they leave the summer den sites or home-sites by mid-July. In Alaska, wolf packs with pups extend the use of summer rendezvous sites until early or late September. After that time, the adults set a grueling pace for the pups as they begin traveling with the pack.

The major prey species of the wolf are the large ungulates: moose, caribou, and muskoxen. When attacking large prey, wolves use various strategies however, the success ratio of approaches to successful attacks is low. Wolves are also opportunists and feed regularly on smaller mammals and birds. In summer, the diet expands to include the eggs, young, and adults of the many species of birds that come to the Arctic to breed.

Arctic wolves normally cover great distances in their travels in search of food. Northern wolves travel alone, in pairs, or in packs of up to 15 or more individuals. Territory size varies with different habitats and depends on the numbers and kinds of prey available. In Alaska, territories may be up to 13,000 sq km in size. Wolves will fight when neighboring packs trespass on their territory, often resulting in mortality.

Mortality among northern wolf pups during their first winter is high. Wolves may live to 16 years, but 10 years is an old age for wolves in the wild. Injuries suffered during attacks on large prey are likely numerous and can be fatal. Wolves suffer from many parasites and diseases: flukes, roundworms, tapeworms, lice, ticks,

mites, rabies, distemper, arthritis, and cancer. Other mortality factors include starvation, attacks on lone intruders, and all the various methods that humans have invented for killing wolves.

The gray wolf has had a great diversity of relationships with humans over the last thousands of years. Early humans tamed wolves and domesticated them, resulting in the development of the domestic dog. In the Canadian Arctic, Inuit hunters encouraged their sled dogs to breed with wolves to retain their desirable characteristics.

Although wolves still live throughout the large wilderness areas of both North America and Eurasia, their present range is greatly reduced in area due to human activities. About 200 years ago, gray wolves were more widely distributed than any other mammal of historic times. In North America, wolves can be found from Alaska and Yukon west to Labrador on the eastern coast, and to the tip of Ellesmere Island in the north.

Wolves have always been trapped and hunted throughout the north for their pelts, which are used for making or trimming clothing. In most areas, governments set up a bounty system to reward hunters and trappers for killing wolves. Over the last 20 years, conservation organizations lobbied for an end to the bounty system and for more ecologically sound policies on wolf and big-game management. In most jurisdictions, the bounty system was eliminated in the 1970s. In the Canadian Arctic, wolves are still sought by native hunters. In the west, in both Canada and Alaska, controversial wolf hunts promoted by wildlife departments have created major divisions between conservationists and governments.

Wolves were exterminated in most European countries over the past 400 years. Small remnant populations of wolves survive in France, Italy, Spain, Finland, and parts of the Middle East. In Asia, wolf populations have also been decimated. In the former Soviet Union, wolves were actively exterminated, with more than 220,000 wolves killed during the 1980s. Substantial numbers probably remain in remote areas on the Russian and Mongolian steppes. Wolves were thought to have been extirpated in East Greenland in the late 1930s. However, wolves have reentered Greenland from Ellesmere Island, and by 1983 wolves were again seen in their southernmost former range in east Greenland and were breeding there by 1988.

The gray wolf is listed as threatened (rather than endangered) under the United States Endangered Species Act, and none of the Canadian subspecies are officially listed as endangered, threatened, or vulnerable. However, a recent report on the status of wolves in the Canadian Arctic islands concludes that the numbers of wolves on the High Arctic islands are low and not likely to exceed several hundred individuals.

In many remote stations, wolves still face problems in their relationships with humans because of open garbage dumps and hand-feeding. A wolf infected with rabies presents the only situation where a wolf attack is likely to occur. In 1995, three wolves attacked personnel at CFS Alert, a military station on northern Ellesmere Island. One individual was knocked down by a wolf, and two others were bitten. The wolf tested positive for rabies, the first known case of rabies for this part of the Arctic.

On the positive side, the wolf has become a popular symbol of wilderness and an attraction for thousands of visitors to national and provincial parks, many of whom attend wolf-howling excursions.

DAVID R. GRAY

Further Reading

Carbyn, Lu.N. (editor), *Wolves in Canada and Alaska: Their Status, Biology, and Management,* Ottawa: Canadian Wildlife Service (Report Series No. 45), 1983

Carbyn, Lu.N., S.H. Fritts & D. Seips (editors), *Ecology and Conservation of Wolves in a Changing World,* Edmonton: Canadian Circumpolar Institute (Occasional Publication No. 35), 1995

Gray, David R., "Interactions between wolves and muskoxen on Bathurst Island, N.W.T., Canada." *Acta Zoologica Fennica,* 174(1983): 255–257

———, *The Muskoxen of Polar Bear Pass,* Markham: National Museum of Natural Sciences/Fitzhenry and Whiteside, 1987

———, "The use of muskox kill sites as temporary rendezvous sites by Arctic wolves with pups in early winter." *Arctic,* 46(4)(1993): 324–330

Kuyt, Ernie, *Food Habits of Wolves on Barren-Ground Caribou Range,* Ottawa: Canadian Wildlife Service (Report Series No. 21), 1972

Mech, L. David, *The Arctic Wolf: Living with the Pack,* Stillwater, Minnesota: Voyageur Press, 1988

———, *The Wolf: The Ecology and Behaviour of an Endangered Species,* New York: Natural History Press, 1970

WOLVERINE

The wolverine (*Gulo gulo*) is a member of the family Mustelidae, which also includes weasels, otters, skunks, martens, and fisher. Other names by which the wolverine has been known include devil bear, woods devil, and *carcajou* (French).

The wolverine has a circumpolar distribution that coincides with the boreal forests and tundra of the Northern Hemisphere. It occurs in Eurasia, North America, and the Canadian Arctic archipelago as far north as Ellesmere Island. The Eurasian distribution extends from Scandinavia across Siberia to the Bering and Chukchi seas, although this distribution may not be continuous due to regional population declines. In North America, its range is north of latitude 37° N, while in Eurasia it is above latitude 50° N. Populations of wolverines in the western United States appear to constitute peninsular extensions of populations existing in Canada, except for a population in the mountains of northern and western California. The animal no longer appears to occur in the north central United States.

The wolverine is the largest terrestrial member of the Mustelidae. Males can weigh 20 kg or more, while females typically weigh up to 12 kg. The combined head and body length can be as much as 1050 mm, and the tail can be as long as 260 mm. Although the wolverine may appear somewhat bearlike, its behavior and movement are distinctly characteristic of the weasels. The wolverine is a powerfully built animal with apparent adaptations for winter survival, as it does not hibernate. The skull is robust, and the dentition and jaw muscles are powerful, all of which enable the wolverine to forage on frozen carcasses during the winter. They have tremendous physical endurance, and can travel up to 40 miles a day. Wolverines will fiercely defend a food source or their territory.

The pelage is dark brown with a characteristic pale buff stripe running laterally along the side from the shoulders to the rump. As with other mammals, the pelage consists of a dense underfur for insulation, and coarse, outer guard hairs. In some individuals, there is a prominent white hair patch on the neck and chest. A light-colored facial mask may also be distinct in some individuals. Wolverines communicate by means of vocalizations and scent markings. They also possess well-developed anal musk glands in common with other members of the Mustelidae.

The wolverine occupies a variety of habitats, from forest regions to tundra. Their selection of habitat is probably influenced more by prey availability and freedom from human interference than by any other factors. Wolverine travel extensively and require large home ranges. Male home ranges may be as large as 622 sq km and encompass the ranges of up to six females. Female home ranges are smaller, up to 260 sq km. However, the size of the range used may vary considerably, and may fluctuate seasonally. Natal dens are usually located under snow, often at higher elevations where snow lasts longer and human interference may be absent.

Little is known about the population dynamics of the wolverine due to its reclusive nature and naturally low population density. In Scandinavia, density estimates ranged from one wolverine per 200–500 sq km, while a United States study reported considerably smaller ranges and higher densities. The young leave the mother after the first year and disperse to available territories. Replacement of individuals lost due to mortality may be hampered due to an inherently low reproductive rate. The estimated life span in the wild is seven years, although captive animals have lived for 17 years.

Some populations throughout its range are considered threatened, primarily due to habitat changes resulting from human activity. The wolverine population in eastern Canada has declined significantly, and the animal is listed as endangered.

Wolverines appear to have a polygamous mating system, whereby males seek out females in estrus, and thus may mate with more than one female during a season. The home range of a male usually includes that of several females, thereby increasing the opportunities for a male to mate. Females are believed to be monestrus, with breeding occurring between May and August, although females may not produce litters every year. Wolverines exhibit delayed implantation, whereby the blastocyst does not implant in the uterus until sometime between November and March following fertilization. Parturition occurs 30–50 days after implantation of the blastocyst, and the average litter size is 2–3. The young wolverines are born fully furred and weigh approximately 84 g. They attain adult size by their first winter, but may remain in the mother's home range until they reach sexual maturity at 1–2 years of age. The success of a pregnancy depends upon the food supply and the physical condition of the mother. In years when food is scarce, and the female is in poor condition, litter production may be inhibited. Recent studies have indicated that, in fact, not all females produce young every year.

The wolverine is an opportunistic feeder that occupies an upper trophic level in food chains. Wolverine are capable of taking ungulates (reindeer, elk, cattle, and sheep) in a weakened condition or when the snow is soft, enabling the wolverine to stay on top while the prey sinks into the deep snow. During the winter, the wolverine relies heavily on scavenging ungulate carcasses, either those taken by other carnivores or perishing due to natural causes. At other times of the year, wolverine prey on smaller animals, such as hares, ptarmigan, and ground squirrels. The wolverine caches food for future use, and its ability to locate these food caches under deep snow is legendary.

Wolverines are known to kill domestic sheep and reindeer in northern Europe. Wolverines are taken by trappers for their pelts. Because of their low population density, their impact on a local economy can only be minimal. Nonetheless, they have been extensively hunted in Scandinavia because of their attacks on domestic livestock. Among some First Nations of Canada, the wolverine, respected for its strength and cunning, is the subject of many mythologies. The wolverine was also considered to be a powerful spirit, and was acquired as a spirit helper by some shamans.

ROBERT W. EDWARDS

See also **Weasel**

Further Reading

Blair, W. Frank et al., *Vertebrates of the United States*, New York: McGraw-Hill, 1957

Ingles, Lloyd G., *Mammals of the Pacific States, California, Oregon, and Washington*, Stanford: Stanford University Press, 1965

Jones Jr., J. Knox et al., *Mammals of the Northern Great Plains*, Lincoln: University of Nebraska Press, 1983

McNab, Brian K., *Carnivore Behavior, Ecology, and Evolution*, Volume 1, [Chapter 12,] edited by John L. Gittleman, Ithaca: Cornell University Press, 1989

Nowak, Ronald M., *Walker's Mammals of the World* (5th edition), Baltimore: Johns Hopkins University Press, 1991

Sandell, Mikael, *Carnivore Behavior, Ecology, and Evolution*, Volume 1, Chapter 6, edited by John L. Gittleman, Ithaca: Cornell University Press, 1989

WOODLANDS

Woodlands are open forests characterized by widely spaced trees. These landscapes do not have a continuous canopy cover; the proportion of overhead foliage in these ecosystems ranges between 25% and 60%.

In the Arctic, woodlands occupy the transitional zone between the northern boreal forest and Arctic tundra. Arctic woodlands are delineated by the timberline to the south (the northern limit of the continuous forest) and the treeline to the north (the northern limit of tree growth). As one travels north from the timberline, trees become smaller and sparser, gradually giving way to large open areas and then treeless tundra. Circumpolar countries use different terms to describe this area, but it is often referred to as the forest-tundra ecotone.

Climate is the major factor determining the northern limit of Arctic woodlands. The primary limitation to tree growth is the lack of summer warmth. The treeline is difficult to map precisely because the change from forest to woodland to tundra is a gradual one. Treeline species are different across the Arctic, and include spruce, pine, birch, aspen, and larch.

The position of the treeline has changed over time. Since the last glaciation, both the timberline and the treeline, and the forest-tundra woodlands in between, have advanced northward and retreated southward a number of times. Both the treeline and timberline will react to short- and long-term climate fluctuations. The processes of soil formation and plant colonization are enhanced during periods of favorable climate conditions, advancing the treeline northward. Cooler climates, human activities such as livestock grazing and logging, and forest fires are factors linked to southern retreat of the treeline.

Woodlands provide important habitat for many species of Arctic flora and fauna. However, few, if any, plant species are unique to the forest-tundra ecotone, and the forest-tundra has fewer plant species than the tundra or the boreal forest. With the obvious exception of trees, plant species found in this transitional zone tend to be the same as those found on both sides. True tundra species and true forest species tend to do poorly in this intermediate zone, while more ecologically flexible species thrive. The lower species richness of the forest-tundra woodlands may also be linked to climate, as this zone roughly coincides with the mean summer position of the Arctic front.

Tree species that occupy this landscape have unique adaptations that allow them to survive in this environment, including growth forms, stature, and methods of regeneration. The growing season is short and cool, and plants must survive both the deep cold of winter when plants are dormant and spells of cold in the summer during the growing season. However, cold temperatures are only one factor in this environment that plants have adapted to; other factors are the short growing seasons, drought, frost heaving, strong winds, and poor soils. Krummholz (from the German word meaning "twisted wood") is a common growth form at the northern end of the forest-tundra woodlands—the shape of these slow-growing, short-stature, gnarled trees is the result of severe environmental stress.

Frozen ground underlies much of this region. Generally, permafrost is discontinuous beneath woodlands in the forest-tundra ecotone. Some species, such as spruce and larch, are shallow-rooted and can thrive in areas where there is a shallow active layer, while others, such as birch and poplar, have a deep taproot that requires a deeper layer of unfrozen ground. Tree height is limited by the depth of the soil it is rooted in, which is defined in part by the active layer in these northerly regions. Therefore, in addition to warmth, permafrost affects the size of trees as one travels northward from forest to tundra.

Most birds and mammals spend much of their time in any given year in either the forest or the tundra, and either depending on the forest-tundra woodlands for part of their life cycles, or as a migration corridor. Forest-tundra woodland mammals face challenges of cold and hunger in winter months. Some species, such as caribou, have a thick coat of insulating air-filled hairs, while many small mammals, such as voles and shrews, spend much of the winter in sheltered tunnels beneath the snow. Many mammals, such as bears, increase their fat reserves during the summer, while others, such as caribou and muskoxen, lose weight in the winter to reduce their need for food. Carnivorous species have an easier time finding nutrition during the winter than herbivorous species. Migratory birds link this region to nearly every other region in the world.

Arctic woodland ecosystems are particularly sensitive to disturbance and change. Human industrial activity in this region has a history that extends back several centuries, and today there are few areas at or near the treeline that have not been disturbed. Dams, roads, mines, pipelines, and transmission lines are but a few examples of activities that have fragmented the Arctic woodland landscape. Commercial logging tends to be at a lower intensity in the woodlands than the boreal forest to the south. Forest-tundra woodlands are also vulnerable to the effects of acid rain, long-range transport of pollutants, increased ultraviolet radiation, and climate change. Due to the harsh climate conditions, these regions are relatively slow to recover from disturbance.

Climate change is expected to influence habitats more severely at high latitudes than any other region on the earth. Forest-tundra woodlands are carbon sinks; however, with increased global warming and subsequent warming and drying of peat, this region may become a carbon source, enhancing the greenhouse effect through what is called a positive feedback mechanism. The treeline, timberline, and woodlands in the transition zone are expected to move northward encroaching into the tundra. Melting permafrost, increased frequency and severity of forest fires, and insect and disease outbreaks are also projected for much of this region (*see* **Impacts of Climate Change**). The rapid pace of change that is projected for these ecosystems will be especially risky for species with a narrow habitat range, limited dispersal capability, and low climatic tolerance. Those species that have a relatively large distribution and greater climatic tolerance will be less at risk.

Much of the woodlands of the Subarctic region between Arctic tundra and boreal forest remain in a relatively natural state; however, this region is no longer remote and invulnerable to human activity. Since the fate of this region is largely dependent on what happens in the rest of the world, it is important for all nations, including the eight Arctic countries, to make conservation of these unique and globally important ecosystems a priority.

AYNSLIE OGDEN

See also **Coniferous Forests; Treeline; Tundra**

Further Reading

Brown, R.J.E., "Permafrost as an Ecological Factor in the Subarctic." In *Ecology of the Subarctic Regions*, UNESCO, *Proceedings of the Helsinki Symposium. Ecological Conservation*, 1(1970): 129–140

CAFF (Conservation of Arctic Flora and Fauna), *Arctic Flora and Fauna: Status and Conservation*, Helsinki: Edita, 2001

Chapin, F.S. & C. Koroner (editors), *Arctic and Alpine Biodiversity: Patterns, Causes and Ecosystem Consequences*, Berlin: Springer, 1995

Jonasson, S., T.V. Callaghan, G.R. Shaver & L.A. Nielsen, "Arctic Terrestrial Ecosystems and Ecosystem Function." In

The Arctic: Environment, People, Policy, edited by M. Nuttall & T.V. Callaghan, Amsterdam: Harwood, 2000

Krebs, J.S. & R.G. Barry, "The Arctic Front and the Tundra-Taiga boundary in Eurasia." *Geographical Review*, 60(1970):548–554

Kullman, L., "Tree-limit rise and recent warming: a geoecological case study from the Swedish Scandes." *Norsk Geografisk Tidsskrift*, 54(2000):49–59

Malcolm, J.R., C. Liu, L.B. Miller, T. Allnutt L. Hansen. *Habitats at Risk: Global Warming and Species Loss in Globally Significant Terrestrial Ecosystems*, Gland, Switzerland: World Wild Fund for Nature, 2002

Pielou, E.C., *A Naturalist's Guide to the Arctic*, Chicago: University of Chicago Press, 1994

Tuhkanen, S., "The Northern Timberline in Relation to Climate." In *Sustainable Development in Northern Timberline Forests, Proceedings of the Timberline Workshop*, May 10–11, 1988, Whitehorse, Canada, edited by S. Kankaanpaa, T. Tasanen & L.L. Sutinen, Finnish Forest Research Institute, Research Papers 734, 1999, pp. 29–61

Van Cleve, L., F.S. Chapin, P.W. Flanagan, L.A. Viereck & C.T. Dyrness (editors), *Forest Ecosystems in the Alaskan Taiga*, New York: Springer, 1986

Veijola, P., *The Northern Timberline and Timberline Forests in Fennoscandia*, The Finnish Forest Research Institute, Research Papers 672, 1998

WORLD COUNCIL OF WHALERS

The World Council of Whalers (WCW) is a non-governmental organization established in 1997 to facilitate communication among, and provide assistance to, the world's whaling societies. Discussions among whalers and government officials on ways to increase cooperation among whalers began in 1992 in Glasgow, Scotland, and continued in 1993 (Kyoto, Japan), 1994 (Halifax, Canada), and 1996 (Berkeley, California). The Berkeley meeting was attended by whalers and representatives of whaling societies from the Arctic, the North Atlantic, the Caribbean, the North Pacific, Southeast Asia, Oceania, and Australasia. Under leadership provided by the Nuu-Chah-Nulth Tribal Council (representing several North Pacific whaling First Nations), a founding meeting to approve a Constitution and appoint the first Executive Board was held in Vancouver, Canada, in January 1997.

The objectives of WCW include facilitating cooperation among those engaged in, or planning to engage in, sustainable whaling activities; providing a voice for whalers' interactions with individuals and organizations whose activities may affect whalers' rights, actions, and well-being; supporting sustainable and equitable whaling operations; promoting respect and understanding for the cultural and social needs and concerns of producers and consumers of whale products; assisting whaling communities to remain aware of issues that may affect their livelihoods, health, and cultural integrity; and identifying and engaging the knowledge of whalers and other experts in solving technical and scientific problems associated with whaling-related activities.

These objectives are pursued through meetings and workshops, maintaining a website, and responding to individual requests for information. The Council convenes general assemblies and conferences to bring together whalers, whaling community representatives, government officials, parliamentarians, researchers, students, and journalists from over 20 countries. Such meetings have been held in 1998 (Victoria, Canada), 1999 (Reykjavik, Iceland), and 2000 (Nelson, New Zealand). The theme of the Council's meeting in 2000 was *Sustaining Food, Health, and Traditional Values Through the Sustainable Use of Martine Resources,* and attracted over 250 delegates from 22 countries: Aotearoa/New Zealand, Australia, Bermuda, Canada, Cook Islands, Denmark, Dominica, Federated States of Micronesia, Faroe Islands, Fiji, Greenland, Iceland, Japan, Norway, Philippines, Russia, Saint Lucia, Scotland, Switzerland, Tonga, United States, and Zimbabwe. The 2002 assembly was held in Tórshavn (Faroe Islands).

Arctic peoples participating in these meetings include Canadian Inuit from Nunavut, Inuvialuit Settlement Region (Western Arctic), Nunavik, Inuit Tapirisat of Canada, ICC-Canada, and the Canadian parliament. Greenland delegates include members of the greenland Parliament (Landsting) and Home Rule government, Inuit Circumpolar Conference (ICC), and Greenland Association of Hunters and Fishers (KNAPK). Yupik and Chukchi delegates have also attended from Chukotka at each of the meetings.

WCW is incorporated under the laws of Canada, with a secretariat in Brentwood Bay, British Columbia, Canada. Its executive Board consists of a chairperson, vice-chairperson, secretary/treasurer, and regional members representing the Arctic, the North Atlantic, the Caribbean, and the South Pacific. The Council is funded by organizational, sustaining, and individual membership dues. Grants and contributions from governments and foundations, meeting registrations, and in-kind support from host organizations cover the cost of conferences and assemblies.

MILTON M.R. FREEMAN

See also **Alaska Eskimo Whaling Commission (AEWC); Greenland Hunters and Fishers Association (KNAPK); International Whaling Commission (IWC); Inuit Circumpolar Conference (ICC); Whaling, Historical; Whaling, Subsistence**

Further Reading

World Council of Whalers website: www.worldcouncilofwhalers.com

WORLD WIDE FUND FOR NATURE (WWF) INTERNATIONAL ARCTIC PROGRAM

The World Wide Fund for Nature (WWF) International Arctic Program, based in Oslo, Norway, works to protect the biological diversity of the Arctic in a sustainable manner. Formed in 1992, WWF's International Arctic Program maintains six key targets:

1. In cooperation with northern residents and other important stakeholders, WWF desires a circumarctic network of representative, permanently protected areas by 2010, targeting in particular unfragmented wilderness in marine, freshwater, and terrestrial habitats.
2. In cooperation with northern wildlife users, WWF aims to conserve and, if necessary, restore wide-ranging Arctic wildlife species, such as caribou and reindeer, muskox, bears, wolverine, wolves, walrus, whales, and migratory waterbirds, to secure viable populations by 2010.
3. By 2005, WWF wants all Arctic nations to establish requirements for land- and resource-use plans for all Arctic natural regions.
4. By 2005, WWF aims to develop and implement ecoregion action plans for the Bering and Barents seas, including measures to ensure sustainable fisheries.
5. By 2010, WWF wants carbon dioxide (CO_2) emissions in industrialized countries to have fallen 10% below 1990 levels as a first step in reducing threats to Arctic ecosystems that are particularly sensitive to climate change. To meet this target, Arctic nations should move quickly to ratify the Kyoto Protocol and make drastic reductions in CO_2 emissions.
6. By 2007, WWF wants the levels of at least 30 of the most hazardous industrial chemicals and pesticides eliminated or drastically reduced, with special emphasis on persistent organic pollutants (POPs) and endocrine disrupting chemicals, through implementation of the 2001 International POPs Treaty and other pollution-prevention initiatives.

WWF's International Arctic Program helps to both coordinate and promote WWF's Arctic conservation work in WWF offices in Canada, the United States, Russia, Norway, Denmark, Finland, and Sweden, and runs its own conservation program.

The International Arctic Program conducts advocacy work with international, national, regional, and local governments, the Arctic Council, and other international and national political and environmental organizations to help achieve its goals. It also carries out public awareness work internationally to develop a greater understanding of Arctic issues and provides limited funding for scientific research to further an understanding of the threats confronting Arctic biodiversity.

SAMANTHA SMITH

See also **Conservation**

Further Reading

WWF Arctic Program website: http://www.ngo.grida.no/wwfap/

WRANGEL ISLAND

Wrangel Island (Vrangelya Ostrov) is located on the border of the East Siberian and Chukchi seas, between 70° and 72° N, and 177° E and 176° W. De Long Strait separates the island from the Siberian mainland, with a minimum width of 140 km. The island has an area of *c.*6000 km². Despite being generally barren, rocky, and frozen, it has a highly diverse fauna and is *zapovednik* (nature reserve) and an International Biosphere Reserve. Ownership of the island has been the subject of international dispute between Russia and the United States since the 19th century.

The eastern, western, and central portions of the island have three parallel mountain ranges—the Tsenralnyje, Mineeva and Evstifeeva mountains, and Zapadnoye Plateau in the west, which are dissected by the wide valleys of Mamontovaya, Gusinaya, Klark, Neizvestnaya, Krasny Flag rivers between their ridges. The largest peak Mt Sovetskaya in the Tsentralnyje mountains rises up to a height of 1096 m. The large northern ("Tundra Akademii") and narrow southern portions are plains. The climate of Wrangel Island is Arctic maritime, with an average July temperature of 2.4–3.6°C and an average February temperature of–24.7 to 24.9°C. Annual precipitation is 229–247 mm, more than half of which falls in the form of snow. Snow cover remains for 240 days of the year. Ten small atmospheric glaciers formed by blowing ice and snow occur in Tsenralnyje and Mineeva mountains.

Plant and animal diversity is extremely high compared to other islands of the Arctic Ocean at the same latitude; for example, the number of vascular plant species is more than 390 whereas other comparable islands have less than 200 species. There are several evident reasons for this high biodiversity. The island was largely nonglaciated during the late Pliocene and Pleistocene glaciations when the island was a mountainous part of the huge Beringia landmass joining Asia and America. During marine transgressions, the island was and remains today the largest refugium of Arctic shelf flora and fauna, where many species are signs of trans-Beringian migrations and unique Pleistocene biomes. For example, woolly mammoths inhabited the island 7390–3730 years ago, that is, for as long as 6000 years after the estimated extinction of mammoths on the Siberian continent. Landscape, bedrock, and local climate diversity provide suitable environments for the survival of relicts; the island's isolation has prevented colonization by mainland Subarctic species in recent times. Lack of competition with acidophilous Subarctic species enables intense speciation in typically Arctic taxa of genera *Papaver, Potentilla, Taraxacum, Oxytropis*, etc. At least nine species and subspecies are endemic to the island or coendemic, occurring in one or more localities of the northern Chukotkan mainland (e.g., *Papaver gorodkovii, P. uschakovii, Oxytropis wrangelii, Poa vrangelica*). Nearly 100 species of the island flora are represented by morphologically different populations compared to the mainland populations. Dwarf and prostrate shrubs with cushion forbs dominate throughout the mountain portion of the island, but dwarf willows (*Salix* spp.) can reach nearly 1 m in height in intermontane valleys. Spared during the last Ice Age, relics of Pleistocene tundra-steppe landscapes also remain in internal and southern Wrangel Island. Acidic cottongrass tussock tundra with Subarctic dwarf shrubs is relict and survives in a few spots. The northern plain is covered by typically Arctic polygonal tundra dominated by *Deschampsia borealis, Artemisia tilesii, Alopecurus alpinus, Salix polaris*, etc., and cottongrass-sedge (*Carex stans, Eriophorum polystachyon, E. medium*) bogs rich in non-Sphagnum mosses are common.

The island fauna is one of the most diverse throughout the Arctic and includes many rare species. Wrangel and Herald islands have about 80% (350–500 pregnant bears) of the polar bear breeding population of the Chukotkan region. Rocky slopes covered with snow are excellent sites for polar bear dens. Some areas support 6–12 bears per square kilometer. The majority of the bear population remains at sea throughout the year. In the 1950s, domestic reindeer were introduced to the island. The reindeer quickly began to damage the tundra ecosystems, cropping vegetation in areas and trampling nesting sites for snow geese, in addition to eating their eggs. Muskoxen were reintroduced to the island in 1975, with an initial population of 20 animals that has increased several times since. The Arctic fox also inhabits the islands, feeding mostly on Siberian and collared lemmings and remains from polar bear kills. Each summer, about 10,000 walruses occupy the beaches of the island. The ringed seal and bearded seal are also plentiful. Fifty species of migratory birds and waterfowl come to the islands each year to nest. Eight kinds of seabirds nest in large rookeries on the cliffs and rocky shores of the islands. The black-legged kittiwake, pelagic cormorant, and glaucous gull are common birds in rookeries. The snowy owl builds its nest in a depression on the ground, feeding primarily on lemmings. Brent geese, eider ducks, and snow geese frequent the more than 900 lakes of Tundra Akademii to raise their young. Rare birds include Ross's gull, buff-breasted sandpiper, and spoon-billed sandpiper. The colony of lesser snow geese on Wrangel Island is all that remains of the large colonies in Siberia a century ago. The population decline is likely being driven by long-term poor weather conditions on the breeding grounds (which causes fewer young to be produced) and high harvest rates (the population decline from 120,000 nesting birds in 1970 to fewer than half that number in the 1990s).

In the early 1820s, during his Arctic expedition, Ferdinand von Wrangell tried to find the island, which had been seen by Chukchi natives. In 1867, the American whaler Thomas Long saw the island and named it in honor of Wrangell. Until the 20th century, the island was uninhabited and several countries competed from the beginning of the century for it. A Russian expedition was sent to the island in 1911, and in 1916 the Russian government claimed it. The Canadian explorer Vilhjalmur Stefansson sent four young university students and an Inuit woman to the island in 1921, intending to claim it for Britain; however, all except one member of the group perished. In 1924, a Soviet vessel forcibly removed a small colony of Inuit established there by the United States in 1923, and in 1926 the Soviet Union established a permanent colony on the island. During Soviet times, there was a small town on Wrangel Island, but today only a few people of the meteorological station and nature reserve reside there permanently. Since 1976, the area has been designated an International Biosphere Reserve to preserve the integrity of the unique community of Arctic wildlife.

VOLODYA RAZZHIVIN

See also **Stefansson, Vilhjalmur; Wrangell, Baron Ferdinand Petrovich von**

Further Reading

Ovskynikov, Nikita, *Polar Bears: Living with the White Bear*, Voyager Press, 1999
Stewart, J.M.,*The Nature of Russia*, New York: Cross River Press, 1991
Vartanyan, S.L., V.E. Garutt & etc A.V. Sher, "Holocene dwarf mammoths from Wrangell Island in the Siberian Arctic." *Nature,* 362(1993): 337–340

WRANGEL PALEO-ESKIMO CULTURE

In the second to first millenia BC, in the Arctic zones of America and Canada from Greenland to Alaska, the Paleo-Eskimo Independence I, II, Saqqaq, Pre-Dorset, Dorset, Old Whaling, Norton, Choris, and Ipiutak cultures were formed. Starting with the Independence II

Culture, there is clear evidence of people using toggle harpoons for hunting sea mammals. All of the aforementioned cultures are regarded by most researchers as Paleo-Eskimo. In the Asian Arctic adjacent to the Bering Strait, the Paleo-Eskimo Tradition was represented by the Wrangel Asian Paleo-Eskimo Culture. It was distinguished by Nikolay Dikov in 1976, after the 1975 research of the Chyortov Ovrag site on Wrangel Island in the Chukchi Sea, 150 km from the northern coast of Chukotka. The site excavations and the culture studies were continued by Tasyan S. Tein in 1976–1977 and in 1981. To date, this is the only known Paleo-Eskimo site in Chukotka.

The site is located on the southern coast of the island, on an 8-m-high cape, in Krasin Bay. A creek flowing to the sea is found adjacent to the site. Not far from the site there had been walrus rookeries, which are presently deserted. The cape surface is rocky, covered with sod, with some exposed spots. Findings were made on the surface, in the sod, and under it, in the humus layer at a depth of 15–60 cm. The total area of excavations on the Wrangel Paleo-Eskimo site exceeded 284 m². The cultural layer contained several hearths and a trash pit filled with walrus, seal, bird, and polar bear bone fragments. Six radiocarbon dates ranging from 3360 to 2851 BP were obtained from the hearths found on the site. On the whole site area, archaeologists have found bone and stone artifacts.

Lithic (stone) tools obtained from the surface and from the excavations have been represented only by retouched items. Only the blades of subtriangular or oval-shaped adzes (a cutting tool with a thin, arched blade) with the sublanceolate/oval cross section had been ground. The tool kit consisted of biface stemmed projectile points and knives, leaf-shaped and oval bifaces (spear points and knives), unifacial knives on blades and flakes, retouched flakes, stemmed end and side scrapers on flakes, oval scrapers, burins on flakes, and carvers. The artifacts were made from black siliceous shale and chert. Neither ground slate knives nor pottery characteristic for Neo-Eskimo cultures were found at the site.

Walrus ivory was used to carve three ice picks and a toggle harpoon head. The toggling harpoon head was of archaic type, with an asymmetrical spur, a single-line hole, open socket, lashing groove for a binding to secure the foreshaft in the socket, and an open bed for an endblade with a lashing groove on the opposite face. Dikov believed that stemmed bifacial points had been used as endblades.

No analogs to the Wrangel Culture and no cultures that might have been the basis for its formation have been found in Chukotka so far. Dikov and Tein suggested that Alaska's Paleo-Eskimo cultures might have been the origin of the Wrangel Paleo-Eskimo Culture.

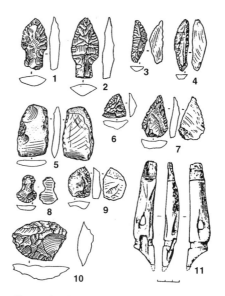

Wrangel Asian Paleo-Eskimo Culture artifacts

Wrangel Paleo-Eskimo Culture artifacts: 1, 2—points; 3–4, 7—unifacial knives; 5—adze blade with the polish bit; 6, 8, 9—scrapers; 10—knife biface; 11—toggling harpoon head. 1–10—stone, 11—ivory.

Dikov traced the similarity of the Wrangel lithic tools with those from the Greenland Paleo-Eskimo Independence II Culture and from the Cape Krusenstern Palisades II site in Alaska. However, the Old Whaling Culture (Cape Krusenstern) is closer to Wrangel by virtue of its age and stone tools. Here J.L. Giddings found the single toggle harpoon head with a single-line hole and open socket that was similar to the Wrangel version. Some similarities can be traced in other tools, for example, stemmed end scrapers, side-notched points, and knives on flakes. The Old Whaling Culture dates to 3170 BP.

Likewise, comparing juxtapositions of lithic tools, especially of humpback knives unknown in Alaska, Dikov credibly suggested cultural links between the Wrangel Culture and the Neolithic cultures of Kamchatka, primarily Tarya and North Okhotsk.

Wrangel Island is still the earliest maritime-adapted, sea mammal hunters' culture known in Northeast Asia. Its people used boats and hunted sea mammals in the open sea.

SERGEI SLOBODIN

See also **Arctic Small Tool Tradition; Dikov, Nikolay; Tein, Tasyan; Wrangel Island**

Further Reading

Ackerman, Robert E., "Prehistory of the Asian Eskimo Zone." In *Handbook of North American Indians, Volume 5: Arctic*, edited by D. Damas, Washington, District of Columbia: Smithsonian Institution, 1984

Dikov, Nikolay N., *Arkheologicheskiye pamyatniki Kamcgatki, Chukotki i Verkhney Kolymy* [Archeological Remains in Kamchatka, Chukotka, and the Upper Reaches of the Kolyma], Moscow: Nauka, 1977

———, *Drevniye kul'tury Severovostochnoy Azii* [Ancient Cultures of Northeastern Asia], Moskow: Nauka, 1979

———, "The oldest sea mammal hunters of Wrangell Island." *Arctic Anthropology*, 25(1) (1988): 80–93

Dumond, Don E. & Richard L. Bland, "Holocene prehistory of the northernmost North Pacific." *Journal of World Prehistory*, 9(4) (1995): 401–451

Giddings, J. Louis & Douglas D. Anderson, *Beach Ridge Archaeology of Cape Krusenstern: Eskimo and Pre-Eskimo Settlements Around Kotzebue Sound, Alaska,* Washington, District of Columbia: National Park Service, 1986

Tein, Tasyan S., "Arkheologicheskiye issledovaniya na o.Vrangelya" [Archaeological Research on Wrangell Island]. In *Noviye arkheologicheskiye pamyatniki Severa Dal'nego Vostoka* [New Archaeological Sites of the North of the Far East], Magadan: NEISRI, 1979

———, *Tayna Chyortova Ovraga* [The Secret of the Devil's Gorge], Magadan: Magadan Printing Hause, 1983

WRANGELL, BARON FERDINAND PETROVICH VON

Admiral Baron Ferdinand Petrovich Vrangel (von Wrangell) was a Russian naval officer who became an outstanding polar explorer and administrator in Russian Alaska in the 19th century.

In 1817, Wrangell was appointed to the *Kamchatka* ship, which set off for a two-year voyage around the world under Vasilij M. Golovnin's command . The *Kamchatka* commander appreciated young von Wrangell, and upon Wrangell's return from the voyage Golovnin recommended him for appointment as the head of an expedition for exploration of the northern coasts of eastern Siberia.

The northern Siberian coasts and some islands—as early as the 17th century—were examined more than once by Cossacks, and were partly described by naval officers and geodesists. However, the tools and methods of exploration in the 17th and even 18th centuries were imperfect, because by the early 19th century, these maps were obsolete. Moreover, the Russian government was interested in legends concerning the existence of settled lands in the north from New Land (Novaya Zemlya) and opposite the mouth of the Kolyma River. In 1819, the Naval Ministry decided to organize two expeditions in order to document the northeastern coast of Siberia and the attendant searches of new lands in the Arctic Ocean. These included the Yansky and Kolymsky expeditions led by dog teams, headed by lieutenants Petr F. Anzhu and Wrangell, respectively. Fedor F. Matyushkin (a warrant officer), Petr T. Kozmin (a navigator), August F. Kiber (a doctor), Savelij Ivannikov (a fitter), and Michail Nekhoroshkov (a sailor) were members of the Kolymsky expedition under Wrangell's command. The expedition embarked from St Petersburg in late March of 1820.

In early November of that same year, the expedition arrived in Nizhnekolymsk, Russia. They spent that winter buying food and equipment for the expedition. From February to March of 1821, Wrangell and Kozmin, the expedition's navigator, surveyed the coast beginning at the mouth of the Kolyma River up to Shelagski Cape, a point on the north coast of Chukchi Autonomous Okrug. After a ten-day rest in Nizhnekolymsk, Wrangell and his team set off on March 26, 1821 on sledges for the second trip on ice. During this trip, the expedition discovered a small island—Chetyrekhstolbovyi—and documented Bear Islands, a group of small islands opposite the mouth of the Kolyma River in the East Siberian Sea. In the summer of 1821, Wrangell engaged in astronomical and geographical observations in the mouth of the Kolyma River, while his fellow travelers explored the Great Anyi Basin and conducted a survey of the seacoast from the mouth of the Malaya Chukochiya up to the mouth of the Indigirka River. Wrangell made his third trip exploring the seacoast between the Kolyma River and Chaun Bayin during the spring and summer of 1822. During this third trip in Chukotka, he collected data and described various Chukotka settlements. In the spring of 1823, Wrangell undertook searches of an unknown land for the fourth time, simultaneously describing the coast to the east of the Shelagsky Cape. As a result of his ethnographic research, Wrangell mapped a hypothetical location of a mountainous island to the east of the Yakan Cape. Forty-four years later, in 1867, an American whaleboat (the *Thomas Long*), not far from the site Wrangell had indicated, discovered land that was subsequently named Wrangell Land after the explorer. On May 10, 1823, Wrangell's expedition returned to Nizhnekolymsk, and in August of 1824 to St Petersburg.

Wrangell's Kolyma expedition made vital contributions to the field of Arctic exploration. For the first time, the expedition was able to precisely mark the Arctic Ocean coast from the Indigirka River mouth up to the Kolyuchinsky Bay on a map. Moreover, the expedition documented valuable scientific observations of nature and the Northeast Asia nations. Wrangell and his fellow-campaigner Petr Anzhu confirmed the existence of a so-called "great polynya" (an oceanic area that remains either partially or totally ice-free at times and under climatological conditions where the surface waters would be expected to be ice-covered), a discovery that served as a basis for subsequent voyages in the Arctic Ocean, namely, the discovery of the Northern Sea Route by Niels A.E. Nordenskiold. The German geographer Karl Ritter wrote the preface for Wrangell's expedition description, which was first published in

German in 1839 as Narrative of an Expedition to the Polar Sea, in the Years 1820, 1821, 1822 & 1823. The text was subsequently translated into English and French. In 1841, Wrangell's text was published in Russia followed by a second edition in English in 1842.

At the conclusion of the Kolyma expedition, Wrangell was appointed commander of a military ship Krotkij, intended to deliver provisions and goods for Kamchatka. In August 1825, the Krotkij embarked and returned in September 1827, at which time Wrangell was appointed commander of the Elizaveta frigate.

In the winter of 1828, the Council of Directors of the Russian-American company recommended Wrangell for an administrative post in the American Russian colonies. Wrangell accepted, and in March 1829 he was made a captain of the first rank with appointment as a governor of the NorthAmerican colonies of Russia. In November 1830, Wrangell and his family arrived at Sitka (what was once New Archangel in Alaska), where he spent five years as governor. In this position, Wrangell enjoyed positive and friendly relations with the inhabitants of Sitka, primarily due to his efficient exploitation of trades and humane treatment of aboriginals. In 1835, Wrangell left the colonies returned home via Mexico.

On his return to Russia in 1838, he was appointed director of the department of ship timber of the Naval Ministry and subsequently elected head of the Russian-American Company. Two years later, he became the company's chief director, a position Wrangell held until 1849. In 1854, he was appointed director of the Hydrographic Department, then as chairperson of the Academic Committee on revision of Naval Criminal Laws, and in 1855 as chairperson of the Academic Committee and an inspector of navigators. In May 1856, Wrangell served as manager of the Naval Ministry, and was made admiral the following year. Wrangell's initiative led to, among other significant gains, the technical rearmament of the Russian Fleet. Serious illness, however, forced Wrangell to end his civil service. In June 1857, he was discharged from his post at the Naval Ministry and was appointed to the Russian State Council. While in retirement, Wrangell initiated numerous important reforms of the Russian Naval Fleet. In 1845, he cofounded the Russian Geographic Society. He was highly critical of the sale of Alaska to the United States in 1867.

Biography

Ferdinand Petrovich Vrangel (Baron Ferdinand Petrovich von Wrangell) was born on December 29, 1796 in the town of Pscov, Estonia, to a nobleman's family. His ancestors came from Denmark in the 13th century and had settled in Estonia, which joined the Russian Empire in the 18th century. An orphan, Wrangell was raised by relatives who, seeing the boy's aptitude, sent him to the Naval Military cadet school in St Petersburg in 1807. In 1815, Wrangell graduated with honors and achieved the rank of warrant officer. In 1829, Wrangell married Baroness Elizaveta Vasilievna Rossilion. They had three children: two daughters, who died early, and a son, Ferdinand, who became a famous naval officer. Wrangell retired to his family estate Ruil' in Estonia during the last years of his life. He died of heart failure at the age of 74 in Derpt (Tartu), Russia, on May 25, 1870.

SARDANA BOYAKOVA

See also **Chukchi Autonomous Okrug (Chukotka); Kolyma River; Second Kamchatka Expedition; Wrangel Island**

Further Reading

Davydov, Yu.V., *Ferdinand Vrangel*, Moscow: Geigraphgyz, 1959
Pasetsky, V.M., *Ferdinand Petrovich Vrangel*, Moscow: Nauka, 1975
Wrangell, Ferdinand Petrovich, Narrative of an Expedition to the Polar Sea, in the years 1820, 1821, 1822 & 1823, London: Madden, 1840; reprinted Fairfield, Washington: Ye Galleon Press, 1981

Y

YAKUTIA—*See* **SAKHA REPUBLIC (YAKUTIA)**

YAKUTS

The Yakuts (from the Evenki word *Yakoltsy*), or *Sakha* as they call themselves, are an indigenous people of northeastern Siberia in the Russian Federation. The Yakut people number over 400,000, and form the vast majority of the indigenous population of the Sakha Republic (Yakutia). Yakuts occupy a considerable area of the Arctic. The main Yakut groups are the Amginsky-Lensky (between the Lena, Lower Aldan, and Amga, on the Lena left bank), Vilui (in the Vilui Basin), Olekminsky (in the Olekma Basin), and the northern group (in the tundra zone of the Anabar, Olenek, Kolyma, Yana, and Indigirka rivers). They speak Yakut, which is of Turkic origin and has local Central, Vilui, northwestern, and Taymyr dialects. Since Yakuts are the major group in Yakutia, Yakut is also spoken by many of the other indigenous groups such as Evenki living in Yakutia, by Russian old settlers resident in Yakutia, and is the language of newspapers, radio, and television.

Traditional Yakut culture has some features (such as pastoralism and cattle breeding) typical of the population of the southern Siberia steppe, whereas all the other eastern Siberian peoples are hunter-gatherers. Language, anthropological data, and Yakut legends point to a compound and heterogeneous origin of the Yakuts, with some influence from the Tungus population of the northern taiga as well as Turkic-Mongol elements from the Baikal region. The Turkic precursors to the Yakut are thought to have penetrated northward from the Baikal area about 1000 years ago, reaching the middle Prilen'e region by the 13th to 15th centuries, having assimilated the local population en route.

Society

By the time of early contact with the Russian colonizers in the 1620s, Yakuts lived in Central Yakutia. Some groups lived in Vilui, at the mouth of the Olekma and Upper Yana rivers. They were divided into 35–40 "tribes," each having 2000–5000 people. Intertribal quarrels and Russian imposition of the yasak tribute (paid in furs) forced Yakuts to settle in outlying districts, mainly to the northwest and northeast. Tribes were subdivided into smaller groups: "father's kins" or patriarchal families (aga-uusa) and smaller "mother's kins" or matriarchal families (ije-uusa). There were customs of vendetta, hospitality to travelers, and gift exchange. A military aristocracy (toions) emerged; each toion had one to three or rarely up to 20 slaves, and were wealthy, having the most livestock and the best pasture land. The slaves lived with their families, often in separate yurtas, and men served in a toion's military squad. There were other kinds of dependence, for example, the custom to give cattle to poor men to pasture, or feed in winter; destitutes and orphans being dependent on a rich man; later, hired workers became common. A professional merchant class appeared in the 19th century, trading furs with the Russians. Hunting and fishing, reindeer pasture, and haymaking areas were in private ownership, for communal use by the clan. The Russian administration, however, tried to slow down the growth of land ownership.

During Russian administration, Yakuts were divided into clan communities, headed by clan leaders (knyaztsy) and united into districts or naslegs, which were headed by elected leaders consisting of kin elders. Members of the community had kin and nasleg meetings. Naslegs united into uluses under an elected ulus head.

Polygamy was practiced up to the 19th century; moreover, wives lived separately and had their own household duties. Exogamy (marrying outside the tribe, trying to find a fiancée in another village or ulus) was practiced. Payment of a bride price or kalym preceded a marriage. A fiancé's relatives took part in kalym collection, and a fiancée's relatives in its distribution. A fiancé got a fiancée's dowry, half the value of the kalym, partly in cattle, but mainly in clothes and utensils. A wedding was accompanied by games and dances.

Lifestyle and Subsistence

Cattle and horse breeding were the main traditional occupations. Men looked after horses, and women looked after cattle. Despite severe winter temperatures, Yakut horses were pastured all the year round. In summer, cattle were grazed, and in winter they were kept in cattle sheds with hay for fodder. The Yakuts took up haymaking before the arrival of the Russians. Yakut cattle were remarkable for their endurance, but were unproductive, and milked only in summer.

Fishing was usually with seine nets, made of horsehair; landing nets were also used. Usually the Yakuts fished in summer, but they also fished in ice holes in winter; in autumn, they arranged a collective fishing, the catch being divided among all participants. For poor people who had no cattle, fishing was their main subsistence.

Hunting was more common in the North, where it was a main source of food (Arctic fox, hare, reindeer, elk, and birds). Hunting for meat and furs (bear, elk, squirrel, fox, hare, and birds) was known in the taiga by the time of the Russians' arrival in the 1620s. Traps, bow and arrows, and spears were the main hunting tools, and from the 18th century firearms were also used.

Milk was the main food, especially in summer, although it was rarely used fresh. Kumys, an alcoholic drink, was fermented from mare's milk; yogurt, cream, and butter were made from cow's milk. Yakuts drank clarified butter or used it with kumys. Yogurt was frozen in preparation for winter storage, adding berries and roots to it in large birch bark vessels. Fish was the main food for poor people in the northern uluses, where there were no cattle; they ate raw, boiled, and fried fish. Meat was eaten mainly by rich people; it was boiled, fried, and frozen. Horseflesh was particularly appreciated as a delicacy. In the 19th century, barley flour was introduced, from which the Yakuts made unleavened scones and thick pancakes.

The Yakuts gathered pine and deciduous sapwood, roots, greenery, and berries. Sedentary agriculture was adopted from the Russians in the middle of the 17th century; up to the middle of the 19th century, it was weakly developed. Its spread was promoted by Russian exiles banished to Yakutia, who began to grow wheat, oats, and potatoes.

Wood, birch tree, fur, and leather processing were developed; the Yakuts made various dishes, footwear, and clothes from leather, and cords and embroidery from horsehair.

Iron working, which had a trade value, was also developed by the Yakuts prior to the arrival of the Russians. They were one of the few northern Russian ethnic groups to work metal. They melted iron in forges, and from the 20th century forged purchased iron. Iron was used to decorate clothing, particularly shamans' costumes, and to make bells and cooking pots. Silver and copper casting and engraving were also widespread. In the 19th century, mammoth bone-carving was common.

The Yakuts traveled mainly by riding on horseback, and loads were carried by pack horses. They also wore skis sheathed with horse leg skin, and used sledges drawn by ox or in the north by reindeer. Boats were constructed from birch bark or board.

Yakuts who owned livestock alternated between summer and winter camps. Winter settlements were near the hayfield, and consisted of one or three yurtas (tents); summer camps near pastures consisted of about ten yurtas. Yurtas had inclined walls made of thin logs or poles on a rectangular log frame and a lower gabled roof. Walls were covered with clay mixed with manure; the roof was covered with bark. The tents had an earthen floor; rich men often had a plank floor. A house was arranged according to cardinal points: the entrance was in the eastern side, windows (made of ice) were in the southern and western sides, and the roof was from the north to south. There was a hearth (osokh), a cylindrical pipe made of poles and covered with clay on the right side from the entrance, in the northeast corner. In winter, the tent was constantly heated; it was also aired well.

A cattle shed (khoton) was added to the northern side of the yurta; its construction was like the yurta, and separated from the house by a thin partition. There was a tethering pole, decorated with carvings, near the yurta. The tent and grounds were enclosed with fence poles.

Summer tents did not differ from winter tents. Instead of the khoton, there was a cattle shed (titik) for calves. A conical construction from poles, and covered with birch bark (urasa), was used up to the late 19th century. From the 18th century, six- or eight-cornered log yurtas with a pyramidal roof were known. Since the second half of the 18th century, Russian log cabins and also various mixed types of houses became common.

Clothing

Traditional clothing for men and women consisted of short leather trousers, fur underclothes, leather footwear, and a single-breasted caftan (in winter made of fur, and in summer made of horse or cow skin with wool inside). Among the rich, the caftan was made of fabric traded from merchants. The caftan was pleated at the shoulders with wide sleeves tapering at the cuff; a shirt with a turn-down collar appeared later, apparently due to the influence of the Russians. Men tied a leather belt with a knife around their waists. A festive women's long fur caftan, which was very expensive and mainly used in rich families, was widespread and often hereditary; a festive women's fur cap with a high flat woolen top, a round silver badge (tuosakhta), other decorations, and a long back part made of deer fur was also typical. Footwear consisted of winter high boots made of reindeer or horse skin with the fur outside; and summer boots were made of soft leather with a boot-top covered with smooth woolen cloth. Women's long fur stockings were decorated with appliqué. A rich woman's dress was decorated with embroidery, appliqué work, and silver ornaments: chains, ear-rings, bracelets, and rings were also worn.

Religion and Folklore

The Russian Orthodox Church became widespread in the 18th to 19th centuries. Christian practices such as visiting church, wearing crosses, and icons in the front corner of the yurta were combined with beliefs in various spirits, such as the kind spirits of ajyy, the harmful abaasy spirits, and spirits of deceased shamans and spirit-owners. Elements of totemism were retained: each clan or family had an animal protector, which they were forbidden to kill or name. The universe consisted of several worlds: Urung Ajy Toion was considered to be god or head of the Upper World and Ala Buurai Toion was head of the Lower World. The cult of Ajyysyt, a female divinity of fertility, was important. The Yakuts sacrificed horses to the spirits living in the Upper World, and cows to the spirits in the Lower World. There was a major spring-summer festival (ysyakh), accompanied by kumys sprinkling from big wooden vessels (choroon), games, and sport contests; "white shamans" (ajyy ojuuna) led the ysyakh. Shamans—both men (ojuun) and women (udagan)—often came from the same family. Each shaman had his spirit protector whose representation as a copper badge was sewn on the shaman's chest, and an animal double. Shaman tambourines were oval and broad-rimmed.

Yakut folklore consisted of bogatyr epics (such as the olonkho); chanting by special narrators (olonkhosuts); historical legends bylyrgy sesenner (ancient stories), including stories about the Yakut ancestors Omogoi and Ellei who came from the south along the Lena River; fairy tales, especially fairy tales about animals; and proverbs and riddles. Yakut songs were of two types: solemn songs were sung in a falsetto voice (kylysakh), creating an effect of two-voice singing (musical fragments of olonkho, addresses to spirit protectors, algys or blessings, and song improvisations or toyuks were sung in this way); and love, dance, comic and other songs, and songs for the osuokhai circular dance were sung in the usual voice. Special kinds of singing were connected with shamanism. The Jew's harp (khomus), violin, and percussion instruments represented traditional musical instruments. Circular osuokhai and game dances were also common.

Wood and mammoth ivory carving, copper, silver, and gold engravings, silver blackening, weaving from horsehair, dyeing with alder pigments, processing of leather, fur, embroidery, and appliqué work were developed. Ornamentation is mainly geometrical, with symmetrical scrolls, meanders, and palmettos used in engraving and birch bark work; the two-horned motif is typical. Prevailing colors are black, red, yellow, and blue.

Today

Following the formation of the Yakut Autonomous Soviet Socialist Republic (ASSR) in 1922, towns, modern industry and mining, transport, and communication all developed. Collectivization from 1930 led to the formation of Yakut settlements in new villages. People were forced to work for state farms and cattle-breeding collectives, and the nomadic way of life and clan structure more or less ended. Today the Yakuts base their life on democracy and civil freedom, and farms are being returned to the private sector.

VASILY IVANOV

See also **Northern Altaic Languages; Sakha Republic (Yakutia)**

Further Reading

Balzer, M.M., "Yakut." In *Encyclopedia of World Cultures*, Volume 6, Boston: G.K. Hall & Co., 1991

Crate, S., "Sakha" (Yakut). In *Encyclopedia of the World's Minorities*, edited by C. Skutsch, New York and London: Routledge, 2004

Ionova, O.V., "Zhile i khoziaistvennye postroiki Iakutov" [Dwellings and economic buildings of Yakuts]. *Transactions of the Ethnography Institute of the AS SSSR*, Volume 18, 1952

Istoria Iakutskoi ASSR [History of the Yakut ASSR], Volume 1, Moscow-Leningrad, 1955; Volume 2, 1957; Volume 3, 1963

Ivanov, V.N., *Sotsialno-ekonomicheskie otnosheniia u Iakutov (XVII vek)* [Social and economical relations among Yakuts (17th century)], Yakutsk, 1966

Jochelson, Vladimir Il'ich, *The Yakut*, New York: American Museum of Natural History, 1933

Konstantinov, I.V., "Proiskhozhdenie yakutskogo naroda i ego cultura" [Origin of the Yakut people and their culture]. *Yakutia and its Neighbours in Ancient Times*, Yakutsk, 1975

Ksenofontov, G.V., *Uraankhai sakhalar. Ocherki drevnei istorii yakutov* [The Uraankhai Sakha. Essays of ancient history of Yakuts], Volume 1, Irkutsk, 1937

Maak, R.K., *Viliuisky okrug* [Viliui district], Moscow, 1994

Seroshewsky, V.L., *Iakuty. Opyt etnograficheskogo issledovaniia* [Yakuts. Knowledge from ethnographic research], St Petersburg, 1897

Tokarev, S.A., *Obshestvennyi stroi iakutov XVII–XVIII v* [Social structure of Yakuts of the 17th–18th century], Yakutsk, 1945

———, "The Yakuts." In *Narody Sibiri*, edited by M.G. Levin & L.P. Potapov, Moscow: Russian Academy of Sciences, 1956; as *The Peoples of Siberia*, Chicago: University of Chicago Press, 1964

Vitebsky, P., "Yakuts." In *The Nationalities Question in the Soviet Union*, edited by G. Smith, London and New York: Longman, 1990

YAKUTSK

Yakutsk is the capital of the Sakha Republic (Yakutia), Russian Federation, and is also a major port on the Lena River, 1703 km upriver from the Arctic Ocean port of Tiksi. Yakutsk is one of the oldest Siberian cities. A Strelets (Russian army) detachment led by the Cossack Peter Beketov founded the city in 1632 as the Lensk fortress on the eastern bank of the Lena River in its middle stream. In 1634, the fort was moved upstream due to frequent floods. However, the new location was short-lived, with further flooding threatening dwellings. In 1643, Peter Golovin, the first military governor of the Yakut District, left the fortress and built a new fortress further upstream on the west bank. This new fortress was named Yakutsk, and is on the site of present-day Yakutsk.

Until the mid-20th century, the population of Yakutsk grew slowly due to its remoteness and poor inward migration. In the late 17th century, the population of Yakutsk numbered 1000 people, 2500 in the late 18th century, 7315 in 1917, and 219,523 in 1984. From the 1960s, mining activity (particularly of diamonds) brought large numbers of new workers to Yakutsk, mainly Russians. The current population numbers approximately 200,000 (about 25% of the entire population of the Sakha Republic), of which about 60–70% are Russians and 30–40% are Yakut.

Yakutsk was of great significance to Russia as the base for further conquest of the North and East to the Pacific, and from where numerous exploration and scientific expeditions orginated. Russian Cossacks and merchants annexed the entire Asian Northeast to the Sea of Okhotsk for Russia from the 1630s to the 1650s. Expeditions by Ivan Moskvitin, Semen Shelkovnikov, Vasily Poyarkov, Yerofei Khabarov, Semyon Dezhnev, Vladimir Atlasov, and many others started from Yakutsk, surveying inland areas and making important discoveries along the Arctic and Pacific coasts. These expeditions discovered the strait between Asia and America (Dezhnev), Kamchatka (Atlasov), and the Amur River (Poyarkov and Khabarov). Until the mid-19th century, political, economic, and cultural contacts between Russia, Pacific coastal areas, and Russian America took place only through Yakutsk by roads from Irkutsk to Yakutsk, Okhotsk, and Ayansk. Only with the development of the Amur River did Yakutsk lose its role as an important transport hub.

The name and territory covered by the region of which Yakutsk is the capital has been changed several times. From 1641, Yakutsk was the center of the large Yakut District. The district stretched from the upstream Lena River to the Okhotsk coastal areas and Kamchatka. It was the political, military, administrative, trade, and cultural center of a region encompassing almost the entire Siberian Northeast, and a center for collection of the fur tribute. From 1852, Yakutsk was the center of the Yakut Oblast' with province rights headed by a governor. Until Russia's 1917 October Revolution, Yakutsk was a focal point of political and criminal exile. Many political dissidents—representatives of all revolutionary stages—were sent to Yakutsk.

Soviet rule was established in Yakutsk on July 1, 1918. Since April 27, 1922, Yakutsk has been the capital of the Autonomous Soviet Socialist Republic of Yakutia. Since 1990, Yakutsk has been the capital of the Sakha Republic (Yakutia).

During the Soviet years, the city experienced noticeable changes, developing into a focus for economic, research, and cultural activities. The Yakutsk State University was founded here in 1956, and the Science Center of the Russian Academy of Sciences uniting nine research institutes, the Sakha Academy of Sciences comprising six institutes, several national higher education institutions, an agriculture academy, and several secondary vocational training institutions are also located in the city. In addition, the National Museum of Northern History and Culture and its subbranches, the Museum of Fine Arts, the state literature museum, geology museum, permafrost museum, the Yakut Drama Theatre, Russian Drama Theatre, Opera and Ballet Theatre, National Philharmonic Society, and National Library are all based in Yakutsk.

Yakutsk has a continental climate with a mean monthly temperature ranging from –45°C to approximately 20°C. Annual rainfall is low, but spring floods on the Lena are caused by rapid snowmelt in conjunction with jams during ice breakup. In May 2001, many buildings were damaged in the worst floods for more than a century. The city has no rail links, and main transportation is by river traffic or air.

VLADIMIR VASILIEV

See also **Lena River; Sakha Republic (Yakutia)**

YAMAL PENINSULA

The Yamal Peninsula is located in the extreme north of the West Siberian Plain, and juts northward into the Kara Sea. In the Nenets language, yamal means "the end of the earth." To the west, the peninsula is washed by Baidaratskaya Bay and Kara Sea, and to the east by Obskaya Bay. In the north, the Malygin Strait separates it from Belyi Island. The Yamal Peninsula stretches in the north-south direction for 750 km between 73° N and the Arctic Circle. Its width varies from 140 to 240 km; its area measures 122,000 km².

Yamal Peninsula is a low, largely flat plain, mostly at about 60–70 m above sea level; the highest elevation is 90 m. Coasts are commonly low and flat; however, here and there they rise above the sea in the form of terraces up to 20–30 m high. Flat portions of the coast often have narrow sandy spits and low islands (called koshki). To the west of Yamal Peninsula, the Sharapovy and Maresalskiye Koshki stretch for 80–90 km. Yamal's northern lower part is composed of marine Quaternary sandy-clay sediments. The southern part bears the mark of glaciation in the form of moraine ridges, hills, and sandy low plains. Marine sediments wash and overlay much of the moraine sediments (near Neito Lake). Outcrops of older rocks that are the extension of the Urals Piedmont occur in the southern part of the peninsula in the Sobkey Ridge.

Yamal's location in the permafrost zone results in poor soils. By the end of summer, the Yamal peat bogs thaw out to less than 40 cm depth. Sandy-clay sediments sometimes contain ice wedges; peat bogs contain ice lenses. Lowland areas often contain laccoliths. Low evaporation and permafrost cause excessive humidity of the tundra soil in spite of the small amount of annual precipitation.

The climate of Yamal is severe. Mean annual air temperatures are below zero and vary from –6.6°C in the south to –10.2°C in the north of the peninsula. Summer is short and cool; frosts may occur through the whole season. The mean air temperature in July ranges from +12°C to +14°C in the southern part of the peninsula to +4°C to +5°C in the north, although individual daily highs may reach +28°C. In the summer, the entire peninsula has almost constant sunlight for three months. Winter is long, windy, and frosty. The mean annual temperature in January is –21°C to –25°C, and lows may reach –56°C. The sun does not rise above the horizon during two winter months.

The presence of the Arctic Ocean strongly impacts the weather regime: western areas are characterized by high relative air humidity, extremely high cloudiness, and frequent fogs (over 80 days per year). Annual precipitation is 250–300 mm, occurring mainly in the summer time in the form of drizzle. Due to permafrost and little thaw, the infiltration of precipitation is very

Aerial view of tundra in the autumn on the Yamal Peninsula, Western Siberia.
Copyright Bryan and Cherry Alexander Photography

low. Evaporation is also low; thus, precipitation is nearly all converted to surface runoff. Snow cover is formed in late September. Its depth varies greatly: on open sites the snow is blown out, and in the windless areas it accumulates to 1–2 m depth. In winter, the northwest cyclones often bring snowstorms and sharp rises of air temperature. The number of days with snowstorms amounts to 150 per year.

The main rivers of the Yamal Peninsula include the Schuchya (585 km), Yuribey (400 km), Kharasavey (210 km), Mordy-Yakha (200 km), and Seyakha (165 km). The freezing-over period begins in late October; opening usually occurs in May. The rivers are characterized by slow stream and shallow depth. They meander in shallow, wide valleys. High sandy riverbank steeps (up to 20–30 m) occur in the head and middle courses of the rivers. The lower courses of the river valleys are low and boggy.

Yamal Peninsula is rich in lakes, mostly small, up to several hundred meters in diameter. They are often circular, filling up small depressions formed due to thawing of ground ice. Most lakes are closed; however, some are connected with rivers and other lakes. Larger lakes with diameters up to 10–20 km include the Nei-To, Yambu-To, Yarro-To, and Yasavey-To lakes. These lakes fill up moraine depressions, have complicated shapes, and are rather deep. The lakes commonly freeze in late October. Ice on large lakes melts only by mid-summer.

Severe climate and poor, boggy soils of the peninsula have resulted in poor tundra vegetation. The Arctic tundra in the north is gradually replaced by the typical moss-lichen tundra further south, which in turn is replaced by shrubs and forest-tundra in the southeast of the peninsula. Variations of the Arctic tundra in combination with the tundra and grass bogs and coastal meadows comprise the dominant vegetation type in the north of Yamal. Further south, in the middle part of the peninsula, a subzone of moss-lichen tundra occurs that is characterized by various kinds of small shrub tundra in combination with raised and lowland bogs, and thickets of osier dogwood. Vegetation cover of the shrub tundra subzone is typically composed of the mosaic of dwarf birch tundra, tundra osier-beds, alder bushes, and bogs. Forest-tundra covers the southern part of Yamal. Complexes of moss-lichen and shrub tundra, and lowland bogs alternate with sparse woods of Siberian larch (*Larix sibirica*). Lowland sedge bogs and boggy meadows occur along the coasts and wide river floodplains.

Lemmings are the most typical mammals on the peninsula and are the primary food for another common animal, the Arctic fox. Another pair of common animals in Yamal that are connected with each other by predator-prey relations, comprise wolves and reindeer. Wild reindeer are not numerous; instead, most reindeer in Yamal have been domesticated. Reindeer grazing is practiced throughout the peninsula, and the entire district of Yamal-Nenets Autonomous Okrug is the grazing area for the largest domestic reindeer herd in Russia, about 500,000 head. Fewer than 200,000 reindeer live on the peninsula.

Yamal is the habitat for many birds. Rock ptarmigan (*Lagopus mutus*), willow ptarmigan (*Lagopus lagopus*), snowy owl (*Nyctea scandiaca*), rough-legged buzzard (*Buteo lagopus*), and waders are quite common. The coast is a nesting and molting site for numerous geese and ducks. Many rare and endangered bird species such as the peregrine (*Falco peregrinus*), gyrfalcon (*Falco gyrfalco*), white-tailed eagle (*Haliaeetus albicilla*), Bewick's swan (*Cygnus bewickii*), red-breasted goose (*Rufibrenta ruficollis*), and lesser white-fronted goose (*Anser erythropus*) nest in Yamal.

Yamal's rivers and lakes are rich in fish. White spotted pickerel (*Esox lucius*), peled (*Coregonus peled*), sardine cisco (*C. sardinella*), muksun (*C. muksun*), and broad whitefish (*C. nasus*) are most frequent.

Yamal Peninsula is one of the major gas-producing areas in Russia. Twenty gas, oil, and gas-condensate fields have been prospected within its territory, with reserves estimated at 10 trillion m³. Planned development, and construction of a pipeline, is currently on hold.

Russians have maintained a presence in Yamal since the 11th century. The Yugor and Samodian tribes were first mentioned in the Old Russian chronicles in 1096. In 1265, Yugra was annexed to the Novgorod Princedom and started paying tribute to Russian princes. Coastal dwellers (Russians living on the White Sea coast) sailed to Obskaya Bay to trade with the Nenets. Their route went past Novaya Zemlya via the Kara Sea as far as Belyi Island and then to the south around Yamal. Since the foundation of the city of Mangazeya on the River Taz in 1601, Russians mastered the way across Yamal from the Mordy-Yakha River via the system of rivers and lakes to Obskaya Bay, then to Tazovskaya Bay and up the Taz River to Mangazeya. Interest in Yamal recommenced at the beginning of the 20th century in connection with the development of the Northern Sea Route. In the 1970s and 1980s, with the discovery of the large gas fields, the population steadily rose with a large influx of Russian-speaking immigrants, stimulating industrial development.

Yamal's territory belongs in part to Yamalsky and Priuralsky Administrative Districts of the Yamal-Nenets Autonomous Okrug. The population is concentrated in settlements on the coast. The population of the Yamalsky Administrative District numbers approximately 15,000; indigenous peoples, the Nenets, comprise over 50% of the population. About 5000 of these are nomadic. The main occupation of the local population is reindeer breeding, hunting, and fishing. Yar-Sale in the southern part of the peninsula is the center of the Yamalsky District.

GRIGORI TERTITSKI

See also **Gas Exploration; Yamal-Nenets Autonomous Okrug**

Further Reading

Dobrinskii, L.N. (editor), *Priroda Yamala* [Nature of Yamal], Ekaterinburg: Nauka, 1995 (in Russian)

Golovnev, A.V., G. Osherenko, Yu.P. Pribylskii & D.L. Schindler, *Indigenous Peoples and the Development of the Yamal Peninsula*, Lysaker, Norway: Fridtjof Nansen Institute, 1998 (INSROP Working Paper 112)

Pika, A. & D. Bogoyavlensky, "Yamal Peninsula: oil and gas development and problems of demography and health among indigenous populations." *Arctic Anthropology*, 32 (1995): 61–74

Sisko, R.K. (editor), *Yamalo-Gydanskaya oblast'. Fiziko-geograficheskaya kharakteristika* (Yamal-Gydan area. Physiographic description), Leningrad: Gidrometeoizdat, 1977 (in Russian)

YAMAL-NENETS AUTONOMOUS OKRUG

Yamal-Nenets Autonomous Okrug (YNAO) belongs to the West Siberian economic region and Ural Federal district. YNAO is an independent unit of the Tyumen Oblast' and lies in the extreme north of the West Siberian lowland, which encompasses the largest wetland (technically a peatland) in the world. It occupies a territory of some 750,600 km², or nearly 1.5 times the size of France. The region includes three major peninsulas, Tazovsky, Gydansky, and Yamal (*see* **Yamal Peninsula**), as well as several groups of islands in the Kara Sea. In the west, the region covers a large portion of the Polar Urals, with foothills consisting of bedrock outcrops extending onto the base of Yamal Peninsula. The length of YNAO from north to south is 1200 km and from east to west 1130 km. The northernmost tip of Yamal Peninsula lies at 73°30′ N latitude, 800 km north of the Arctic Circle. In the Nenets' own language, "Yamal" means roughly "the end of the earth" or "land's end."

YNAO is often referred to as "the land of rivers and lakes." Large navigable rivers include the Ob', Pur, Taz, Schuchya, Sob, Longot-Yugan, and Messoyakha. There are about 48,000 rivers and estimates of the number of lakes range from 3000 to 5000. The largest are the lake complexes Neito and Yarato on north-central and southeastern Yamal Peninsula, respectively.

The climate is not quite as continental as neighboring Taymyr Peninsula, but is still characterized by extremely cold winters and short, reasonably warm summers with frequent fogs in the north and west coming in from the Kara Sea. In January, average temperatures are –23°C to –27°C, with an absolute maximum of –3°C and an absolute minimum of –59°C. In July, average temperatures are 5–16°C, with an absolute maximum of 37°C and an absolute minimum of –5°C. In summer, the sun does not descend below the horizon for 45 days at Mys Khammeny, 70 days at Seyakha, and for almost 100 days on Bely Island. The ground is completely covered with snow for 210 days annually in Salekhard and Urengoy, 230 in Mys Khammeny, and 250 in Sabett.

YNAO is characterized by frozen ground and encompasses three zones of permafrost distribution from south to north: sporadic, discontinuous, and continuous. The Yamal Peninsula lies entirely within the continuous permafrost zone. Ice-rich permafrost is widespread in all three zones and is susceptible to thermokarst erosion from both natural and anthropogenic surface disturbance. As a result, much of the terrain is considered moderately to extremely unstable for purposes of engineering and infrastructure developments (roads, bridges, pipelines, etc.).

According to Russian botanist Boris Yurtsev, the Yamal-Gydan West Siberian subprovince is characterized phytogeographically by a low floristic richness due to gaps in the ranges of species with predominantly montane, east Siberian or western (amphi-

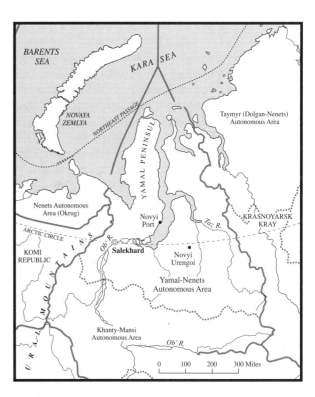

Location of Yamal-Nenets Autonomous Okrug and main towns and rivers.

Atlantic) distributions. Much of the Yamal region's tundra consists of polygonal lowland mires or bogs, open dwarf-shrub tundra vegetation, and graminoid-moss meadows. Well-drained portions of ice-wedge polygons are dominated by deciduous (*Betula nana*) and evergreen (*Ledum decumbens*) dwarf shrubs, while saturated troughs are typically filled with aquatic sedges (*Eriophorum* and *Carex* spp.) and grasses. The forest-tundra transition zone covers a broad band coincident with the southern portions of Yamal and Taz peninsulas, and most maps depict the latitudinal treeline as running approximately through the city of Salekhard on the Arctic Circle (*c*.66°33′ N). Upright bushes of alder (*Alnus fruticosa*) and willow (*Salix* spp.) are common on slopes in the Polar Urals and in riparian zones well north onto the Yamal Peninsula. Shrub willow is generally ≤30 cm in height on the open tundra, although individuals of ≥1 m can occur in riparian zones. These zones comprise prime habitat for moose (*Alces alces*), causing their ranges to overlap with those of reindeer (*Rangifer tarandus*). South of the Ob' River delta, sparse lichen woodlands of Siberian larch (*Larix sibirica*) give way to more or less closed forest in the southernmost parts of YNAO.

The relative biodiversity of Yamal on a global scale is insignificant, but does include some rare, ecologically vulnerable species. About ten kinds of birds and small mammals and seven vascular plants are included in the Russian Federation Red Book, and it seems that none appear there for a lack of being studied. Substantial populations of terrestrial wildlife still exist, although some fur-bearing species are subject to hunting and trapping, both licit and illicit, and available records indicate that some preferred game species have been significantly reduced in recent years, primarily by non-Natives. The Arctic fox (*Alopex lagopus*) is considered to be particularly at risk due to poaching and destruction of dens in association with petroleum development. The Gydansky zapovednik (nature reserve), which includes Arctic tundra and forest-tundra of the northern tip of the Gydansky Peninsula, seashore, and the neighboring islands of the Kara Sea, was established in 1996 and covers an area of 8780 km^2. This coastal area is important for migratory waterfowl, some of which, such as the red-breasted goose, are threatened. The Upper Taz zapovednik, established in 1986 at the junction of Podkamannaya Tungusska River with the Yenisey, has bogs and northern taiga.

Precious mineral deposits suitable for industrial mining occur in the Polar Urals, as well as some rare metals and various nonferrous metals such as lead, zinc, and copper. Prospecting here for deposits of semiprecious stones, diamonds, and emeralds has also yielded promising results. In addition, the mining of barite deposits is under way. After industrial processing, this mineral is used by the petroleum industry for refining oil, as well as in medicine.

Russia has approximately 47 trillion cubic meters of gas reserves, about 80% of which are located in western Siberia. The region thus contains the largest known deposits of natural gas in the world. As such, the petroleum industry occupies the leading place in the industrial structure of YNAO. YNAO supplies more than 90% of the total natural gas and 12% of the total oil extracted in Russia. Twenty-seven percent of the region's working population are employed in the petroleum industry: exploration, extraction, and transportation. The main branches are oil, gas, and gas condensate production. The volumes of petroleum and gas condensate production are 30,496 thousand tons per year and for natural gas 523,324 million cubic meters per year (1998). In 2002, Gazprom and the administration of the YNAO sent the federal government a draft law intended to make Yamal a "region of strategic interests." The aim is to ensure the company's goal of increasing its annual output to 530 billion cubic meters by 2010 as production from its massive Urengoi and Yamburg fields begins to decline. In so doing, Gazprom demonstrated its intention to concentrate on developing its Yamal reserves over the natural gas potential of eastern Siberia. One

reason is the relative ease of transporting gas from Yamal Peninsula. While eastern Siberia is almost devoid of infrastructure, the established Yamal-Europe pipeline is currently capable of pumping 18 billion cubic meters of gas annually, a figure that could rise to 60 billion once a second line is completed, most likely via Poland.

The types of environmental degradation commonly associated with the petroleum industry are many. The three most widespread types of surface disturbance are off-road vehicle traffic, exploratory drilling, and sand excavation. Other impacts include road and railway construction; blowing sand and dust from quarries and, especially, roads; housing; processing facilities; pipelines and power transmission lines; waste fluids from drill holes; oil spills; marine and air traffic; and seismic survey trails. Some of these impacts (e.g., vehicle tracks) continue to be common and widespread all across the Russian Arctic, despite the existence of relevant regulations since the 1980s, primarily due to a lack of enforcement. The negative consequences associated with the development of gas deposits on Yamal have consequences for all spheres of life in the region, including socioeconomic, demographic, health, and political situations.

YNAO (formerly a national region) was founded by the USSR on December 10, 1930. In 1944, the Tyumen Oblast' was established to the south and YNAO was included within the oblast. As an independent subject of the Russian Federation, YNAO was included in the Tyumen Oblast' in August 1994. It has 22 administrative and territorial entities, of which six are towns of regional subordination, nine are industrial settlements, and seven are districts. The territory of YNAO itself consists of these seven districts: Shurishkarsky, Priuralsky, Yamalsky, Tazovsky, Purovsky, Krasnoselkupsky, and Nadymsky.

The largest cities (number of inhabitants on January 1, 1999) are Salekhard (32,900), Noyabrsk (98,500), Novy Urengoy (91,800), and Nadym (47,100). The combined population of the region in 2003 was *c.* 504,200, with 83% of people living in towns and the rest in smaller settlements or mainly on the tundra (news from Information Agency "Sever Press": http://www.salekhard.ru/sevpress3/1803.html). A net increase of *c.* 2000 people was recorded during 2003, primarily due to in-migration from southern former republics of the USSR, which is significant because most northern regions of Russia have been losing people since the collapse of the Soviet Union. About 27% of the population is aged 16–29. Indigenous people who are officially members of the so-called "small peoples of the North" comprise 6.7% of the total population, or *c.* 33,100 people. Of these, about 12,000 are nomads moving with the reindeer herds. Besides

Russian, linguistic groups represented include the northern Samoyedic languages (Nenets, Enets, Nganasan, Sel'kup) and Ob'-Ugrian languages (Khanty and Mansi). Educational facilities comprise some 465 institutions including 209 preschool, 156 secondary, 6 vocational schools covering 28 different professions, and 40 local branches of higher education from state institutions in Tyumen, St Petersburg, and Moscow.

Regional agriculture specializes in reindeer breeding, fur farming, and hunting. The Yamal Nenets have exploited reindeer via hunting and/or husbandry in northwest Siberia for several hundred years. Yamal Peninsula serves as the northern endpoint of an annual reindeer migration route that, for most animals and modern herders, covers several hundred kilometers from the forest-tundra in the south to the typical tundra. For the reindeer, and the herders or their hunting predecessors, this migration has been taking place for at least a millennium, probably longer. The population of semidomestic reindeer has increased steadily since World War II and now numbers nearly 600,000 animals managed by approximately 12,000 people. This comprises 37% of the total reindeer population in Russia, including wild reindeer. Since the early 1900s, there are very few wild animals remaining in the region, mainly in remote areas such as Bely (White) Island, north of Yamal Peninsula. Fifty-six percent of agricultural income in YNAO comes from reindeer breeding.

The city of Salekhard (formerly Obdorsk) was founded by Cossacks in 1595 during the reign of Ivan the Terrible, and celebrated its 400th anniversary in 1995. Salekhard is the historical and political center of the autonomous region. It is also a node for culture and education, its museum housing an extensive collection on the history of exploration in the Ob' River's northern territories.

The region of the northern Ob' is believed to have been originally populated during the last Ice Age. Materials dating to the Neolithic and even earlier have been unearthed in YNAO with artifacts and utensils of bronze and metal from the period 5000 BC found in the oil fields of Surgut. During the 1990s, extensive investigations of archaeological monuments, sites of worship, and other sacred places of the indigenous population were undertaken with the purpose of maintaining their protection in the face of ongoing development and operation of the region's gas deposits. The best-researched ancient settlement is that of Ust Polui within the boundaries of modern-day Salekhard. In the first and second millennium BC, these households contained items of bronze and iron. A complete woman's body dating from about 2000 BC was found in 1995. The peoples referred to as Samoyed (self-eaters) were first referred to in an 11th-century Russian manuscript.

Evidence for the long history of reindeer management in the region mentioned above comes from several places, including Yarte 6, a major archaeological site near the south shore of the Yuribei River on west-central Yamal Peninsula. The latest archaeological material at Yarte 6 dates from the 11th to 12th centuries, but there is evidence for domesticated reindeer as early as AD 600. However, at that time only a few reindeer were partly domesticated, perhaps only for riding or as hunting decoys. Even in the 12th century, there were probably still relatively few semidomesticated animals compared to wild ones.

BRUCE FORBES

See also **Gas Exploration; Nenets; Novyi Urengoi; Ob' River; Oil Exploration; Salekhard; Taz River; Tyumen Oblast'; Yamal Peninsula**

Further Reading

Alexeev, S. et al. (editors), *Znakom'tes Yamal!* [Meet Yamal!], St Petersburg: Russian Collection, 1998 (in Russian)

Chernov, Yuri.I. (editor), *Red Book of the Yamal-Nenets Autonomous Okrug*, Ekaterinburg: Urals University Press, 1997 (in Russian)

Dobrinskii, L.N. (editor). *Priroda Yamala* [Nature of Yamal], Ekaterinburg: Nauka, 1995 (in Russian)

Fedorova, Natalia (editor), *Ushedshie v kholmy* [Gone to the hills: culture of the coastal residents of the Yamal Peninsula during the Iron Age], Ekaterinburg: History and Archaeology Institute, 1998 (in Russian)

Forbes, Bruce C., "Reindeer herding and petroleum development on Poluostrov Yamal: sustainable or mutually incompatible uses?." *Polar Record*, 35 (1999): 317–322

Golovnev, Andrei V. & Gail Osherenko, *Siberian Survival: The Nenets and Their Story*, Ithaca: Cornell University Press, 1999

Golovnev, Andrei V. & G.S. Zaitsev, *Istoria Yamala* [History of the Yamal], Ekaterinburg: History and Archaeology Institute, 1992 (in Russian)

Haruchi, Sergei, S. Sohlberg & P. Sulyandziga, *The Conservation Value of Sacred Sites of Indigenous Peoples of the Arctic: A Case Study in Northern Russia*, Moscow: RAIPON, 2002

Khitun, Olga & Olga Rebristaya, "Anthropogenic Impacts on Habitat Structure and Species Richness in the West Siberian Arctic." In *Wilderness in the Circumpolar North*, compiled by A.E. Watson, L. Alessa & J. Sproull, Ogden, Utah: USDA-FS, Rocky Mountain Research Station, 2002, pp. 85–95

Pika, Alexander & D. Bogoyavlensky, "Yamal Peninsula: oil and gas development and problems of demography and health among indigenous populations." *Arctic Anthropology*, 32 (1995): 61–74

Podkoritov, F.M., *Olyenedstvo Yamala* [Reindeer Herding on Yamal], Sosnovyi Bor: Leningrad Atomic Electrical Station, 1995 (in Russian)

WRH (Association of World Reindeer Herders), *Reindeer Husbandry in Yamal Nenets Autonomous Okrug*, Working Paper No. 4/99, Tromsø: WRH, 1999

YANA RIVER

Yana, a river in the Sakha Republic (Yakutia), rises in the Verkhoyansk mountains and drains northward into the Yansky Bay of the Laptev Sea east of the Lena River. The source of the Yana River is two rivers in the mountains at over 1000 m, the Doulgalakh and Sartang rivers, and after their confluence the river is named the Yana River. The length of the river is 872 km, the area of the river basin is 238,000 km², and the area of the river's delta is 10,200 km².

In the upper mountainous reaches, the riverbed is narrow with many rapids. The river enters a plain after it flows out of the Verkhoyansk mountains, and meanders strongly. The river basin is in the zone of continuous permafrost and sometimes coastal precipices on the plain uncover large ground ice deposits. When the tributary Adycha River flows into the Yana River, the latter becomes forked into channels, creating islands. The Yana River has about 52 quite large (>1000 km² basin area) tributaries; the main tributaries are the Doulgalakh (507 km), Sartang (620 km), Adycha (715 km), and Bytantai (586 km) rivers.

There are about 40,000 lakes in the Yana River basin. From May to August, when the river attains 90% of its annual flow due to rapid spring snowmelt and rain in July and August, floods are common. The spring flood height fluctuates from year to year but may reach 9 m. The highest water levels recorded were in the river port of Verkhoyansk (11.4 m in 1918) and Kazachie village (13.6 m in 1967). The maximum flow rate during the flood at Verkhoyansk District is 2840 m³ s⁻¹ and 12,400 m³ s⁻¹ at Jangky District. The river freezes at the beginning of October and becomes clear of ice from the end of May to the beginning of June. The average freezing-over period is 225–240 days. At Verkhoyansk District and at Ust-Yansk at the mouth of the river, the river is ice-free for only 105 days per year. At Jangky District, it freezes for 43 days. The river is thus navigable only for a short period in the summer.

In the delta, 60% of flow is taken by the main channel, 20% takes the right channel, and the remaining flow is distributed on a number of other deltaic channels (Samandon, Kochevaya, Dourganova, Ilin-Shar, Taryngnaakh, and others).

The area of wet tundra lowland between the Yana and Indigirka rivers is an important, although not well studied, flyway for migrating birds from the Sea of Okhotsk coast on their way toward the Lena Delta at the Arctic Ocean. It is also a mass geese molting site (it is estimated that each year, over 30,000 geese migrate to the wetlands between the Yana and Kolyma rivers), and a breeding ground for Steller's and spectacled eiders and Baikal Teal.

Hunting is a common and widespread threat to all ducks and geese in northern Siberia, where, for example, eiders are an important local food source. The spectacled eider Somateria fisheri is hunted in the Yana River delta, but the species is thought to be endangered due to its decline in the Alaskan breeding sites.

INNOKENTY ZHIRKOV

See also **Verkhoyansk Range**

Further Reading

Chistyakov, G.E., D.D. Nogovitsyn & M.V. Yakoushev, *Gidroenergeticheskie resoursy basseina reki Yany* [Hydroenergetic resources of the Yana river basin], Moscow, 1970

Resursy poverkhnostnykh vod SSSR [Resources of the shallow water of the USSR], Volume 17, Leningrad, 1972

Syroechkovski Jr., E.E. & C. Zockler, "Threatened waterfowl in the lower Yana river, Yakutia, Russia." *TWSG News No.10*, 1997, pp. 26–29

YASAK

Yasak (the word is of Turkic origin, sometimes spelt iasak) was a form of tax or tribute that non-Russian hunters in Povolzhye (Volga region) and Siberia were required to pay to czarist Russia. The system began in Povolzhye in the 15th–16th centuries, and in Siberia in the 17th century. Yasak was paid in the form of sables, foxes, beavers, martens and other furs, and sometimes by cattle; the Chukchi paid in the form of walrus tusk. From the 18th century, yasak was paid in monetary form (in Povolzhye from the 1720s, in Siberia from 1822). This slightly changed the enslaving nature of yasak in the regions where hunting remained the main occupation of the indigenous population.

Unlike the waggon (kibitochnaya) tax collected from the "nomadic indigenous peoples" of Central Asia, yasak from the "unsettled indigenous peoples" of Siberia was the personal income of the Czar. At first, the Siberian Command, and then from 1763 the Cabinet of his Imperial Majesty, was in charge of yasak collecting. Yasak collection existed up to the February Revolution in 1917, but it was an infinitesimal part of the income of the last Czar (130 thousand roubles in 1913).

Yasak payment served as an outward expression of citizenship, or recognition of Russian sovereignty. Yasak was named individually for each tribe or kin, "according to men and trades." There was a land yasak among the Kungur Tatars and Bashkirs of the Perm region, and a stock or cattle yasak among some Siberian peoples; among the Yakuts, yasak was estimated according to the total number of cattle.

Men between 18 and 50 years old, except those ill or injured, paid yasak (later, from 16 to 60 years old). They were called yasak people and were recorded in the yasak books. The number of yasak payers was periodically checked by taking a census. The first census of such kind was taken in 1642 in Yakutia, which caused an uprising of the indigenous population. The Yakut governor responded by changing the procedures to force even more of the population to pay yasak. A full list of yasak payers in the Yakutsk District is given in the yasak book of 1648, when there were 7304 sables and 43 foxes in the yasak treasury. In 1700, there were 9203 yasak payers from whom 7629 sables and 5980 red foxes were collected, from 35 central districts of the region.

Abuses by local Siberian military leaders and governors (who often collected yasak in their personal names) and also ordinary yasak collectors caused repeated attempts (beginning in 1763) to regulate yasak payment. In 1763–1789, the First Yasak Committee, headed by D.I. Chicherin, a Siberian governor, changed yasak levy with the purpose of increasing the amount paid to the treasury. Yasak was then levied taking into consideration the payers' land quality and quantity, their hunting trade, and their cattle-breeding state. The Committee strove for timely and stable collection of yasak. It conducted the government's policy on preventing abuses by the governors, military leaders, and their subordinates (the yasak collectors), improvement of the yasak regime, preservation of the population's paying capacity, and maintenance of the Siberian nations in peace and order. Official functionaries of the local residents were charged to collect yasak. Everything was in the political and fiscal interests of the government. The Committee legalized the replacement of fur yasak with money.

Subsequently, it was decided to change the order of yasak imposition in connection with the introduction of "The Rules of management of the Siberian peoples" in 1822 (Mikhail Speranskii's reforms), which in turn caused the publication of "The Yasak Committee regulations" and an organization of the Second Yasak Committee in 1826. In conformity with the regulations, the division of the indigenous peoples into "settled, nomadic and unsettled ones" was adopted as a basis for taxation; "settled indigenous people" were imposed a monetary tax; and "nomadic and unsettled ones" paid yasak in the form introduced in 1763. In 1828–1834, the Committee in Yakutsk introduced a new yasak-tax policy of the government in accordance with which yasak was included in the class system of taxes and duties distribution; from four classes of the population, the first two paid yasak together with taxes and duties, and the rest did not pay. The Second Yasak Committee tried to introduce so-called "equalizing land use," but this decision was not implemented. After the Committee's work, Yakut toionat (leaders)

had the best lands, and the main burden of yasak fell on the ordinary members of the tribes.

Amanats (native hostages) and shert (an oath) were used to compel natives to pay yasak. Amanats served as a guarantee of yasak payment. One or two representatives (usually rich or powerful) of the local population from each ulus (region) who were captured through opposition to the Russian authorities or simply evaded yasak payment were held in the Russian fort for some time. The authorities were normally well disposed to them and fed them at the government's expense. They could be replaced some time later, if their relatives agreed to pay. It was advisable to take amanats among the nomadic inhabitants of the Arctic tundra in any case, because it was very difficult to find their nomad camps. Another means of compulsion to pay yasak was shert. Russian called shert any non-Christian oath, whereby the local inhabitants swore an oath to pay not only their own yasak, but from all the ulus people.

The burden of yasak and abuses during its levy caused an increase in nonpayment, poverty of yasak people, and unrests and uprisings. For example, in the middle of the 17th century, I.F. Golenitshev-Kutuzov, a Yakut military leader, took about 23,000 sable skins appropriated by him to Russia. In addition to paying tribute, yasak people had to perform various duties, such as working on roads or military service, for the imperial government's benefit. Gradual replacement of fur yasak with money brought it closer to a tax. By the late 19th to early 20th centuries, yasak by fur was levied only from the Chukchi, Maya Tungus (Evenki), and Yukagirs, and the rest paid in monetary form.

VASILY IVANOV

Further Reading

Bakhrushin, S.V., *Yasak v Sibiri v XVII v* [Yasak in Siberia in the 17th century], "Sibirskie ogni", 1927, No. 3

Basharin, G.P., *Istoria agrarnykh otnosheniy v Yakutii (XVIII–ser. XIX v.)* [History of agrarian relations in Yakutia (18th to middle of the 19th century), Moscow: Nauka, 1956

Gurvich, I.S., *K voprosu ob evolutsii yasachnogo sbora v Yakutii* [On the problem of evolution of yasak collection in Yakutia], Reports on the fifth and sixth scientific sessions of the Yakut branch of the AS SSSR, History and philology, Yakutsk, 1954

———, *Ethnicheskaya istoria severo-vostoka Sibiri* [Ethnic history of North-East Siberia], Moscow: Nauka, 1966

Ivanov, V.N., *Socialno-economicheskie otnoshenia u Yakutov. XVII vek* [Social-economic relations in Yakutia. 17th century], Yakutsk, 1966

———, *Vkhozhdenie Severo-Vostoka Asii v sostav Russkogo gosudarstva* [The North-East Asia joint to the Russian state], Novosibirsk, 2000

Istoria Sibiri s drevneishikh vremen do nashikh dnei [History of Siberia beginning with the ancient times up to nowadays], Volume 2, Leningrad: Izdatelstvo Nauka, 1968

Istoria Yakutskoi ASSR [History of the Yakut ASSR], Volume 2, Moscow, 1957

Sofroneev, P.S., *Yakuty v tret'ei polovine XVIII veka* [Yakuts in the first half of the 18th century], Yakutsk, 1972

Vdovin, I.S., *Ocherki istorii i etnographii Chukchei* [Essays of history and ethnography of the Chukchi], Moscow-Leningrad, 1965

YELLOWKNIFE

The capital of the Northwest Territories, Yellowknife is located at 62°276′ N latitude and 114°226′ W longitude, on the shore of Great Slave Lake. Yellow metal comprises part of the city's history—first, copper, used by the Chipewyans two centuries ago, and then gold, which was developed in the 1930s.

The Yellowknife Chipewyan Indians moved into the area in the early 1800s, but the Dogrib Dene repopulated the area, part of their traditional hunting area, about two decades later. The aboriginal peoples' annual subsistence livelihood depended on the area's moose, caribou, fishing, berries, and furs. People could travel north to the Barren Lands, where huge caribou herds migrated and congregated in spring and fall, or they could harvest their food and resources farther south in the boreal forest.

Yellowknife's remote location kept the area's gold from being developed until the 1930s, although it had been discovered 40 years before by passing Klondike gold-rush miners. As part of the federal "Roads to Resources" policy in the late 1950s, the Mackenzie Highway was built from Edmonton to Hay River and then to Yellowknife. Presently, there is year-round road access (except during freeze-up and breakup of the Mackenzie River) and daily air service.

Gold drove the development of the city, but presently local gold deposits are diminishing and gold prices are falling. Exploration and development of Beaufort Sea and Mackenzie Valley hydrocarbons and the Norman Wells Pipeline in the 1970s and 1980s ushered in a period of activity in planning, assessment, and development. Today, diamond mines northeast of Yellowknife, and other mining exploration and development may become the city's next economic focus. Federal, territorial, and municipal governments are still the largest employers in the local economy, with transportation and other service industries also being significant. Yellowknife provides health care, education, and commercial services for many outlying communities. Tourism is a growing sector, including Aurora Borealis tours in the winter.

Yellowknife became a Municipal District in 1953, with its own mayor. In 1967, it became the capital of the Northwest Territories, when administration of the Territories was moved north. It is the only city in the Northwest Territories, and had a population of 18,028 in 2000 (Northwest Territories Bureau of Statistics). The population is 80% nonnative, 9% Dene, 7% Métis, and 3% Inuit.

Lying in the northern part of the Subarctic, Yellowknife enjoys warm, relatively short summers and cold winters; the city residents enjoy extensive and varied outdoor pursuits, as well as an active cultural life of fine art, crafts, theater, film, and live music. The city presents a combination of historical buildings, including some early structures now renovated into restaurants, shops and stylish homes, and modern skyscrapers, malls, and designer homes built onto rocky outcrops. The Pre-Cambrian shield provides a rolling rocky landscape studded with lakes and rivers. Many rock outcrops still show "polish" from the last glaciation over 25,000 years ago.

Generally perceived to enjoy a clean northern environment, Yellowknife suffered elevated levels of arsenic for a period in the 1960s and 1970s. Ore roasting released an arsenic-rich dust that settled over Yellowknife; residents were tested for arsenic levels. Tailings ponds attempt to control contaminants now, but with the closure of the Giant Mine (one of the two gold mines remaining in Yellowknife) governments and local residents face a huge problem, that is, how to deal with the decades-old stockpile of arsenic built up by the mine.

HEATHER MYERS

See also **Great Slave Lake; Mackenzie River; Norman Wells**

Further Reading

Bone, R.M., *The Geography of the Canadian North*, Don Mills Ontario, Canada: Oxford University Press, 1992

Northern Frontier Visitors Association, *Northern Frontier Travel Directory*, Yellowknife, Northwest Territories: Northern Frontier Visitors Association, 2000

Payne, A.V., *Quin Kola: Tom Payne's Search for Gold*, Okotoks, Alberta, Canada: Crossfield Publishing, 2000

Wade, F., "Old Yellowknife." *Above and Beyond*, 13(1) (January/February 2001), 45–49

Yellowknife Seniors' Society, *Yellowknife Tales: Sixty Years of Stories from Yellowknife*, Yellowknife, Northwest Territories, Canada: Outcrop, The Northern Publishers, 2000

YENISEY RIVER

The Yenisey River is one of the longest rivers of the world. More than 4092 km (2540 miles) long from the Bolshoy (Great) Yenisey source to its outfall into the Kara Sea of the Arctic Ocean, the river has more than 500 tributaries in a drainage basin of area 2,580,000 km^2 (996,000 square miles) and has an annual discharge of 591 km^3, making it the largest Russian river in terms of runoff. The Yenisey flows north along the natural tectonic boundary between West and Central Siberia, and crosses all bioclimatic zones of northern Asia, from the deserts of Central Asia through the taiga to the polar desert of the Taymyr Peninsula. All of its major tributaries flow from the Central Siberian Plateau to the east.

The river is known as the Yenisey from the confluence of the Bolshoy (Great) Yenisey and Maly (Little) Yenisey at the city of Kyzl in the republic of Tuva. The Upper Yenisey has four main tributaries: the Khemchik (320 km), Abakan (514 km), Us (236 km), and Oya (254 km) rivers. In its upper reaches, the Yenisey flows in the Tuva Basin. Below the Khemchik River mouth, it crosses the West Sayan Mountains. Formerly, the river crossed the ridge through a rocky canyon about 100 m wide with many rapids. Today, the Sayan Reservoir occupies this canyon for 313 km, supplying the Sayanskaya hydroelectric station. Having crossed the West Sayan Ridge, the Yenisey flows through the Minussinsk Basin. It has three large tributaries here: the Tuba (119 km), Mana (475 km), and Kan (629 km). Before the creation of Krasnoyarsk Reservoir in the 1970s, the Yenisey was 600–1000 m wide here, had many islands, and a fertile floodplain with ancient agriculture. Today, almost the entire Minussinsk part of the Yenisey is flooded by the 388-km-long Krasnoyarsk Reservoir (the dam of Krasnoyarskaya hydroelectric station is 40 km above Krasnoyarsk).

The Yenisey gradually becomes wider to the north, being 300–700 m wide in the upper reaches, up to 10 km in the lower reaches, and over 70 km at the delta. North of Ust'-Port, the delta begins where the river becomes divided into channels separated by numerous islands. In the lower reaches, the Yenisey's discharge increases by a factor of 1.5–3 owing to substantial contributions from three large tributaries: the Angara, Podkamennaya Tunguska, and Nizhnyaya Tunguska.

The Angara River flows out of Lake Baikal, and is 1779 km long with a drainage basin of area 1,040,000 km^2; its average annual discharge before the construction of hydropower stations was 15 km^3 (a volume 1.5–1.6 times greater than the Yenisey above its confluence with the Angara). In the 1950s to 1980s, three large hydroelectric stations were built on the Angara—Irkutskaya, Bratskaya, and Ust'-Ilimskaya stations—with a total annual capacity of up to 50,000 million kWh. The Angara is navigable along its length (except in the area of the hydroelectric dams).

The Podkamennaya (Stony) Tunguska is 1865 km long with a drainage basin of 240,000 km^2, and an average annual discharge of 5.6 km^3. It has many rapids, but is navigable in the lower reaches in spring. The Nizhnyaya (Lower) Tunguska is 2989 km long, with a drainage basin of 473,000 km^2. The average annual discharge is 11 km^3. In spring, it is navigable in the lower reaches.

Below the confluence with the Nizhnyaya Tunguska, the Lower Yenisey has many other large tributaries, including the Kureyka (888 km, including the 170-km-long Kureyka Reservoir), Sym (694 km), Big Kheta (646 km), Turukhan (639 km), Yeloguy (464 km), and Khantayka (174 km long, including the 85-km-long Khantayka Reservoir).

The Yenisey is fed mainly by snowmelt runoff (50% and more) and rainfall runoff (30%); groundwater supplies no more than 20%. Before, the Yenisey runoff was regulated by reservoirs, discharge occurred mainly in spring and summer (75–85%), with high spring floods following ice melt. The water temperature in July in different parts of the Yenisey was 16–25°C. Freeze-up began on the Upper and Middle Yenisey in the second half of November and on the Lower Yenisey at the end of October; ice breakup occurred at the end of April and end of May to the beginning of June accordingly. The duration of freezing over was 150–230 days, with an ice-free period of 120–160 days. The maximum ice thickness was 80–140 cm on the Upper and Middle Yenisey and 90–150 cm on the Lower Yenisey. In spring, large ice jams were typical. During spring floods, water level could increase by more than 20 m.

After the creation of a series of reservoirs in the Yenisey Basin, the water regime changed significantly, especially in the southern part. Below the dams, maximum spring water levels decreased and winter levels increased; summer water temperature decreased (in July by 2–9°C) and autumn temperature rose. The start of the autumn freeze-up was delayed by up to 10–40 days, and the ice-free period increased by 2–20 days. Breakup in spring is 2–20 days earlier. Each year, a large area of unfrozen water 50–500 km long exists on Yenisey near Krasnoyarsk below the Krasnoyarsk hydroelectric station dam.

The Yenisey is navigable along almost (3487 km) its entire length; only the dams of Sayno-Shushenskaya and Maynskaya hydroelectric stations prevent through navigation (the Krasnoyarsk station has a lift for ships). On the Middle Yenisey, the Kazachinskiy and Ossinovskiy rapids also complicate navigation. The main cargo is lumber, and the main ports are Igarka, Dudinka, and Krasnoyarsk.

From the 1960s to 1980s, five hydroelectric stations (Krasnoyarskaya, Sayano-Shushenskaya, Maynskaya, Kureyskaya, and Khantayskaya) were built in the Yenisey Basin (excluding the Angara Basin), with a combined annual generation capacity of up to 45,000 million kWh. The total potential of power resources of the Yenisey (without tributaries) is about 190,800 million kWh.

More than 30 species of fish live in the Yenisey River. The main commercial species are whitefishes (*Stenodus leucychthis* or nelma, *Coregonus sardinella* or cisco, *C. tugun*, *C. autumnalis* or omul, *C. peled* or peled, *C. nasus* or tschirr, *C. lavaretus*, *C. muksun* or muksun), as well as *O. osmerus*, *Esox lucius* (pike), *Rutilus rutilus* (roach), and *L. lota* (burbot). In the 1950s, the annual catch of each of these species was 150–600 tons, and 100 tons of sturgeon (*Acipenser baeri*) and starlet (*A. ruthenus*). Now centralized fishing on Yenisey is disorganized, and poaching (especially for sturgeon) is widely developed. As a result, the Yenisey population of sturgeon has decreased dramatically. The lower reaches of small coastal islands and lagoons of the Yenisey are a summer haven for migrant waterfowl (ducks, geese, and swans) from the south.

Seven state nature reserves are situated in the Tenisey Basin: Azas State Nature Reserve, in the Tuva mountain taiga and steppes (300,390 ha); Sayano-Shushensky Biosphere State Nature Reserve, in West Sayan Ridge (390,400 ha); Stolby State Nature Reserve, in East Sayan Ridge (47,156 ha); Central Siberian Biosphere State Nature Reserve (972,017 ha); Tungusskiy State Nature Reserve (place of fall of the Tungusskiy meteorite in 1908; 296,562 ha); Putoransky State Nature Reserve (1,887,000 ha); and Bol'shoy Arktichesky (Great Arctic) State Nature Reserve on the coastal Arctic tundra and Kara Sea islands (4,200,000 ha).

H.V. ROGACHEVA

See also **Dudinka; Igarka; Kara Sea; Krasnoyarsk Kray; Taymyr Peninsula**

Further Reading

Arefyeva, V.A., "Gidrologiya" [Hydrology]. In *Srednyaya Sibir* [Central Siberia] (Series: Prirodnye usloviya i estestvennye resursy SSSR [Natural Conditions and Resources of the USSR]), edited by I.P. Gerasimov, Moscow: Nauka, 1964, pp. 132–188

Bakhtin, N.P., *Reka Yenisey* [The Yenisey River], Leningrad: Gidrometeoizdat Pubs, 1961

Petenkov, A.V., "Yenisey" [The Yenisey]. In The Yenissey Encyclopaedia, Krasnoyarsk: KOO Assiciation Russkaya Encyclopedia Pubs, 1998, pp. 183–184 (in Russian)

Shooty, M.E. & E.E. Teodoronskaya, "Reki i gidroenergeticheskiye resursy" [Rivers and hydropower resources]. *In Lesnye resursy Krasnoyarskogo kraya i perspektivy ikh promyshlennogo ispol'zovaniya* [Natural conditions of Krasnoyarsk Territory], Moscow: USSR Acad. Sci. Pubs, 1961, pp. 231–249 (in Russian)

YMYAKHTAKH CULTURE

The Ymyakhtakh Culture represents the latest stage in the Neolithic and the transition to the metal working period in northeast Asia, dated by 4200–3200 years BP.

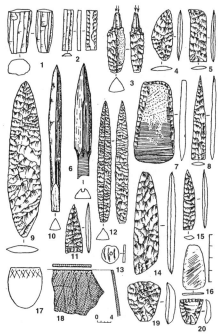

Ymyakhtakh Culture artifacts

Ymyakhtakh Culture artifacts: 1—core; 2—retouched microblade; 3—polyhedral burin; 4, 5, 15—sideblade inset; 6—slotted point; 7—polished adze; 8, 10, 11, 12—arrow points; 9—spear point or knife; 13—pendant; 14, 16—knives; 17—pottery vessel form; 18—potsherd with a check-stamped design; 19, 20—scrapers. 1–5, 7–9, 11–12, 14, 15, 19, 20—stone, 6, 10—bone, 13—shell, 16—bronze, 17, 18—ceramic.

Over 300 Ymyakhtakh sites were found in the Arctic and Subarctic taiga and tundra. They were located along riverbanks and lakeshores. The first Ymyakhakh sites in Yakutia were found by Aleksyey Okladnikov in the 1940s. Some sites, primarily Bel'kachi 1, excavated in the 1960s, allowed Yuri Mochanov to distinguish the specific Ymyakhtakh Culture. Later on, it was studied by Svetlana Fedoseyeva, who presented a comprehensive description of Ymyakhtakh sites and complexes. The most typical sites were found in Yakutia, on the Lena (Siktyakh Level VI, Lake Ymyakhtakh), the Aldan (Sumnagin Level VI–VII, Bel'kachi I Level III), the Vilyuy (Tuoy-Khaya, Ust'-Chirkow), the Olyokma (Kurung II, Novy Leten II), and the Indigirka (Burulgino) rivers; on the Taymyr Peninsula (Kholodnaya II, II); and in the Lower Kolyma (Pomazkino). The strong influence of the Ymyakhtakh Culture was marked in western Chukotka, and partially on eastern Chukotka and Upper Kolyma.

The emergence of the Ymyakhtakh Culture is associated with the influence of southern cultural traditions, from the cultures located between Lake Baikal and the Zeya River. These cultures affected the Bel'kachi Culture in Yakutia that existed from 5000–4000 years BP, accepted some of its elements, and, finally, replaced it. At that time, in addition to the continued wide use of lithic tools, copper and bronze artifacts appeared. Metal items came to Yakutia with the new population from Siberia that had already possessed them as well as by exchange.

The most characteristic indicator of the Ymyakhtakh Culture at the North East sites is the rectangular or rhomboid check-stamp pottery or the linear pattern produced by the ornamented forming paddle. Some ceramics had a plain, not ornamented, surface. The pottery was round, round- or sharp-bottomed, with a series of holes under the rim (circling it) or a roll. Vessels were 10–30 cm in diameter, with bodies up to 40 cm high. The decorating ornament consisted of straight or zigzag lines on the vessel body. The specific feature of the Ymyakhtakh ceramic is the use of reindeer wool or, less often, plant fibers (grass, fir needles) and its multilayer structure. The pots were made by layers, placing as many as two to three layers successively on the walls and five on the bottom. Judging by the ceramic quality, the pots were burned in the bonfire by the open method. There is great similarity of the check-stamped Ymyakhtakh ceramic with that of Alaska's Nortoy and Choris cultures, although their direct origin from the Ymyakhtakh Culture is still doubtful. In the western direction, the check-stamped ceramic spread up to the Kola Peninsula.

In the Ymyakhtakh lithic industry, the microblade technique continued. The microblades were detached from prismatic and conic cores. Microblades were used to make sideblades for composite tools, perforators, and angle burins. But they were no more important than in previous times: the microblades made just a few percent of all findings and almost disappeared in the later stages.

Among lithic tools, typical for Ymyakhtak are trihedral and quadrihedral file and small triangular arrow points; rectangular, bifacially retouched sideblades; polyhedral burins with trihedral retouched handles; subtriangular bifacial knives; large (up to 20 cm long) bifacially retouched spear points or knives; small ground adzes, rectangular in the plane, with lanceolate cross-section; and subtriangular, completely retouched scrapers. End scrapers on flakes and stemmed points were also used.

The finds of bone, antler, and mammoth ivory are represented by spindlelike arrow and spear points, needles, needle cases, armor plates, chisel handles, insert tools, spoons, and bow facings.

Some of Yakutia petroglyphs refer to the Ymyakhtakh Culture. All of them were painted; there were no carvings. They present pictures of men, with fewer images of animals. Anthropomorphic figurines are pictured standing, sitting, dancing, with their hands up. The pictures were painted in mineral ochre of various shades. Profile images appeared. The animalistic pictures are mostly stylized.

The Ymyakhtakh people were moose and reindeer hunters; this hunting mode of life was supplemented by fishing and gathering. The nomadic life determined the teepeelike type of dwelling made of poles covered by skin, which is still used by reindeer herders in the North.

The Ymyakhtakh influence on western Chukotka was visible in such elements as check-stamp ceramic, trihedral points, polyhedral burins, rectangular adzes, and the like found in the North Chukotkan Culture. Art items were represented by ornamented bone artifacts and small flat disk-shaped beads cut from freshwater shells.

Several separate Ymyakhtakh interments and burials, both individual and group, are known. Interments include Kullaty (Middle Lena), Ichchilyakh, and Buguchan (Lower Lena). Burials include Pomazkino (Lower Kolyma), Chuchur-Muran, and Diring-Yuryakh (Middle Lena). The least typical of all burials referred to Ymyakhtakh is Diring-Yuryakh. All interments were accompanied by rich burial kits. Numerous sets of well-made arrow and spear points, burins, sideblades, scrapers, beads, pottery, and bone tools were placed in graves. The burial rituals and kits differed. There were soil graves as well as stone cases. In some interments, pottery was found and the ritual of covering the deceased with ochre was observed. This element is not observed in other graves. In some cases, corpses were burned. Most burials were oriented along the river; some were located perpendicular to it. At the Diring-Yuryakh, the antique case of grave robbery for copper or bronze artifacts was observed. In some burials, the ritual of placing animals (sable, hare), birds, and fish into the grave was followed. Hunting tools (arrow and spear points) were found both in male and in female graves.

The bone armor plates found at the Ymyakhtakh sites testify to intertribal military conflicts, although no property differentiation or distinguishing rich graves from poor ones has been observed in the burial ritual.

Anthropological examination of skulls from the burials shows that the Ymyakhtakh people referred to the Mongoloid race. They are believed to have participated in forming several ethnic groups of the modern Natives of Northeast Asia, particularly of the Yukagir and Chukchi ethnos formation, although scholars have not come to the final agreement on this issue so far.

SERGEI SLOBODIN

See also **Bel'kachi Culture**

Further Reading

Alekseyev, Anatoliy N., *Drevnyaya Yakutia: neolit i epokha bronzy* [Ancient Yakutia: The New Stone and Bronze Ages], Novosibirsk: Nauka, 1996

Dikov, Nikolay N., *Drevniye kul'tury Severovostochnoy Azii* [Ancient cultures of Northeastern Asia], Moskow: Nauka, 1979

Fedoseyeva, Svetlana A., *Ymyakhtakhskaya kul'tura Sever-Vostochnoy Azii* [The Ymyakhtakh Culture of Northeast Asia], Novosibirsk: Nauka, 1980

Kashin, Vitalii A. & Valentina V. Kalinina, *Pomazkinskiy arkheologicheskiy kompleks kak chast' tsirkumpolyarnoy kul'tury* [Pomazkino Archaeological Complex as a Part of the Circumpolar Culture], Yakutsk: Institute of the Native Peoples of the North, 1997

Khlobystin, Leonid P., *Drevnyaya istoriya taymyrskogo Zapolyarya i voprosy formirovaniya kul'tur severa Azii* [Ancient History of Taymyr and the Formation of the North Eurasian Cultures], St Petersburg: IMCI, 1998

Kiryak, Margarita A., *Arkheologiya Zapadnoy Chukotki* [Archaeology of Western Chukotka], Moscow: Nauka, 1993

Kochmar, Nikolay N., *Pisanitsy Yakutii* [Painted Petroglyphs of Yakutia], Novosibirsk: Nauka, 1994

Mochanov, Yuri A., *Mnogosloynaya stoyanka Bel'kachi I i periodizatsiya kamennogo veka Yakutii* [Multi-layer Belkachi I Site and Yakutia Stone Age Periodization], Moscow: Nauka, 1969

————, "The Ymyiakhtakh Late Neolithic culture." *Arctic Anthropology*, 6(1) (1969): 104–114

Mochanov, Yuri A. & Svetlana A. Fedoseyeva, "Main periods in the ancient history of North East Asia." In *Beringia in the Cenozoic Era*, Rotterdam, New Delhi, 1986

Okladnikov, Aleksey P., *Yakutia Before its Incorporation into the Russian State*, Montreal and London: McGill-Queen's University, 1970

Slobodin, Sergei B., *Verkhnyaya Kolyma i kontinental'noye Priokhotye v epokhu neolita i rannego metalla* [Upper Kolyma and Continental Priokhotye in the Time of Neolithic and Early Metal], Magadan: NEISRI, 2001

YUKAGIR

The Yukagir (alternative spellings are Yukaghir, jukagir, Russian jukagirskij), or Odul and Wadul (meaning "mighty" or "strong") as they used to call themselves, today consist mainly of two groups living in the basin of the Kolyma River in the Republic of Sakha (Yakutia). These include the Upper Kolyma Yukagirs, whose main settlement is the village of Nelemnoye beside the Yasachnaya River in Verkhnekolymsk Ulus, and the Tundra Yukagirs, in the settlements of Andruskino and Kolymskoye in Niznekolymsk Ulus. Small groups of Yukagirs also live in other settlements in these districts, such as Zyrianka, Cherskiy, and Srednekolymsk and in the republic's capital Yakutsk. There are several dozens of people who do not speak the Yukagir language but call themselves Yukeghirs around the lower reaches of the Yana and Indigirka rivers.

When the Russians first made contact with the Yukagirs in the 1630s, they occupied a huge territory, from the lower reaches of the Lena River in the west to the Anadyr Basin in the east, and from the shores of the Arctic Ocean in the north to the upper reaches of the Yana, Indigirka, and Kolyma rivers in the south.

They consisted of a large number of separate groups, such as the Chuvan, Khodyntsy, Anauls, and Omoks, who spoke kindred languages but had no political unity. It is estimated that the Yukagirs in total numbered between 5000 and 10,000 people in the 1650s. But during the next three centuries, they underwent the greatest recorded decline among north Siberian peoples. Thus, the 1859 census revealed no more than 2500 Yukagirs; the 1897 census, 1500; and the 1927 census, 443. Wars with other invading indigenous peoples, the Evens, Yakuts, and Chukchi, greatly reduced the Yukagir population. In the 1700s, the Chuvan, the eastern branch of the people, were almost exterminated after losing a series of wars, supported by the Russians, against the Chukchi. Even more disastrous was the introduction of European diseases: a series of smallpox epidemics caused numerous deaths between 1691 and 1885 and epidemics of measles killed many. Widespread syphilis was responsible for making people sterile, thus reducing the birth rate. During the 19th century, the migration of wild reindeer, the main game animal of the Yukagirs at the time, ceased in widespread areas. At the same time, fish-spawning runs were low. This resulted in a hunger catastrophe. In 1897, most of the members of the Omolon Yukagirs, a branch of the Upper Kolyma group, starved to death. The few who survived settled among the Russians in Srednekolymsk. Changing ethnic membership may also have contributed to the steady decline of the Yukagirs. Censuses for the purpose of fur taxation were taken infrequently and the amount of tribute was calculated on the basis of the numbers shown; thus, the rapidly declining Yukagirs often found themselves paying taxes for dead men. By joining demographically expanding groups, they could ease their tax burden.

Despite centuries of decline, the Yukagir population has undergone a remarkable growth within the last decades. According to the 1989 census, there are 1112 Yukagirs. Strikingly, the 1979 census gave a figure of 500. This outstanding increase can easily be explained; according to legislation, the Yukagirs enjoy certain economic privileges, such as special hunting and fishing rights. Thus, most children born of mixed parentage are being registered as Yukagirs.

The Yukagir language belongs to the so-called Paleo-Asiatic group, in which, however, it occupies a special place. It is conventionally considered a genetically isolated group; yet, most probably, it can be affiliated with the Uralic family. The Upper Kolyma and Tundra Yukagirs speak two almost completely mutually incomprehensible dialects. Today, only the oldest generation is competent in the native language. For all under 60, the first language is Russian or Yakut. The youngest generation is practically monolingual; they only speak Russian, although the Yukagir language has been mandatory for all school children in Nelemnoye and Andruskino since 1986/1987.

The Yukagirs are believed to be the oldest of the present-day indigenous peoples of northeastern Siberia, but precisely when the culture was formed is not known. It seems certain, however, that the Yukagirs are closely connected to the development of the Evens as an ethnic group. In general, the Yukagirs have adopted a large number of cultural traits from the Evens and Evenki. Reindeer breeding among the Tundra Yukagirs is evidently one of these. Traditionally, this group kept only a few domesticated reindeer, mainly for transportation, while they lived from hunting wild reindeer. However, since collectivization in 1929, they have moved toward large-scale reindeer breeding. The Upper Kolyma group, conversely, have remained hunters and fishermen, and the dog is, even today, their only domesticated animal. At present, they live mainly from hunting elk, which reemigrated into the area in large numbers in the 1970s and have taken over the position of wild reindeer as the most important food staple. They also trap sable in winter.

Little is known about the traditional social organization of the Yukagirs. It seems certain, however, that ranking did exist. High status was thus attached to the clan elder, distinguished warriors, hunters, and shamans. Even today, many traits of the egalitarian hunting society are apparent, such as a lack of exclusive property in hunting land and the obligation to share meat among relatives and friends. According to Vladimir Il'ich Jochelson (Vladimir Il'ich Iokhel'son), the first scholar who studied the Yukagirs, strangers could freely join the clan, and thus a Yukagir clan used to comprise two groups: kinsmen by blood and members by adoption. This system has prevailed among Yukagir hunters, who call all those who hunt together kin-members, independent of blood ties and ethnic affiliation. Jochelson suggested that the Yukagirs were traditionally patrilineal, while the Soviet ethnographers Stepanova, Gurvich, and Khramova argue for an aboriginal matrilineal descent group. In any case, since the turn of the century, the Yukagirs have functionally been a bilateral grouping, that is, individuals select their kin on both the mother's and father's side.

Traditionally, each Yukagir clan had its shaman. In addition, it also had dead shamans as spirit protectors of the clan. When a clan shaman died, his flesh was removed from his bones, dried, and divided among the clan members as amulets. However, during the 1700s, this cult disappeared entirely. Shamans continued to exist until the 1950s, but they became a kind of household shaman and had neither a special dress nor a drum. They assisted hunters in times of starvation by using magic to force the spirits to provide game animals and helped cure sickness. Today, no shamans are

left among the Yukagirs, but many of their former functions have been taken over by laypersons and have become a sort of do-it-yourself activity. An example of this involves the interpretation of dreams as omens, which used to be the task of the shaman; however, today it is something people figure out for themselves. Another traditional belief, which still exists, is the idea that dead relatives are reincarnated in newborn children. Ideas that humans and animals can exchange appearances and perspectives are present in many Yukagir myths and play an essential part in the practical activity of hunting. The hunter thus attempts to bring the elk into the open by imitating its bodily movements and sound. In general, Yukagirs conceive of hunting as an act of sexual seduction.

The collapse of the USSR and the state farms in 1991 brought about changes in political and economic organization. In 1992, the first obshchina, Yukaghir, was established in Nelemnoye. Originally intended as an organ of aboriginal self-government, it evolved as an economic enterprise, engaged in hunting, fishing, and small-scale horse breeding. Due to economic problems and internal conflict, the obshchina split and two more obshchinas were formed: Teki Odulok and Odul. However, these were also plagued by economic problems, and in 1993 they all reunited into the obshchina Teki Odulok. Approximately one-third of Nelemnoye's population belong to this obshchina. Still, obshchina members barely eke out a living, depending on a combination of subsistence hunting and fishing and the pensions of older family members. In 1993, the wages of the obshchina were recorded at one-third of the Sakha republic's minimum. The failure of the obshchina organization led to calls for more control over traditional land and its natural resources. Since 1995, Yukagir leaders have been fighting for legislation enshrining special self-governing status, Suktul, for the two Yukagir communities Nelemnoye and Andruskino. It would give them their own administration, police and flag, as well as absolute control over the natural resources of their territories. In 1998, the law on the Suktul was passed in the Yakut parliament, Iltylmen, but to date it has not been implemented.

RANE WILLERSLEV

See also **Chukchi-Kamchadal Languages; Chuvan; Iokhel'son, Vladimir Il'ich**

Further Reading

Jochelson, Waldemar, In *The Yukaghir and the Yukaghized Tungus*, edited by Franz Boas, New York: The American Museum of Natural History, 1926

Morin, Françoise & Bernard Saladin d'Anglure, "Ethnicity as a Political Tool for Indigenous Peoples." In T*he Politics of Ethnic Consciousness*, edited by Cora Govers & Hans Vermeulen, New York: Macmillan Press, 1997, pp. 157–194

Pedersen, Morten Axel, "Totemism, animism and North Asian indigenous ontologies." *Journal of the Royal Anthropological Institute*, 7 (2001): 3

Stepanova, M.V., I.S. Gurvich & Khramova, "The Yukagirs." In *The Peoples of Siberia*, edited by M.G. Levin & L.P. Potapov, Chicago: University of Chicago Press, 1964, pp. 788–798

Vakhtin, Nikolai, *The Yukaghir Language in Sociolinguistic Perspective*, Leningrad, USSR: Institute for Linguistics Academy of Science, 1991

Willerslev, Rane, *The Hunter as a Human "Kind": Hunting and Shamanism among the Upper Kolyma Yukaghirs in Siberia*, North Atlantic Studies, Volume 4, 2001

YUKON NATIVE LANGUAGE CENTER

The Yukon Native Language Center (YNLC) is a training and research facility that provides a range of linguistic and educational services to Yukon First Nations and to the general public. YNLC is administered by the Council of Yukon First Nations, with funds provided by the Government of Yukon.

YNLC works in partnership with First Nations communities and individuals to provide literacy training, research, and program support for the Native languages of the Yukon Territory: Gwich'in, Hän, Upper Tanana, Northern Tutchone, Southern Tutchone, Interior Tlingit, Tagish, and Kaska. It often helps First Nations Elders to document Yukon native traditions, oral history, personal names, and place names. The Center also assists First Nations and other organizations with translations, transcriptions, and signage.

In 1977, the Yukon Native Languages Project (YNLP) was created through the joint sponsorship of the Council of Yukon Indians, now the Council of Yukon First Nations, and the Government of Yukon. Requests for native language teaching in the schools were increasing, and the YNLP, under the direction of linguist John Ritter, started to develop curriculum, instructor training, and material for the native language courses that were appearing in the Territory. In 1980, the YNLP produced the curriculum guide Teaching Yukon Native Languages, which has since been used in many jurisdictions beyond the Yukon. In 1985, the YNLP was renamed the Yukon Native Language Center (YNLC). In 1988, YNLC moved to its present location on the Whitehorse campus of Yukon College.

In 2003, YNLC employed eight staff members. During the school year 2001–2002, YNLC provided 54 days of instruction to more than 333 students in 19 separate training sessions. These sessions included various teacher training sessions, literacy sessions, and special sessions requested by First Nations groups.

YNLC offers training and certification for Yukon Aboriginal Teachers. YNLC staff teach the Certificate (3-year) and follow-up Diploma (2-year) courses for Native Language Instructors at Yukon College. The most important aspect of these programs is the practicum component, and graduates and students currently enrolled in these programs serve as teachers in many communities of the Yukon, British Columbia, Northwest Territories, and Alaska. YNLC also works with the University of Alaska Fairbanks in implementing an Associate of Applied Science Degree Program in Native Language Education. In 2002, there were 70 Certificate graduates, 20 Diploma graduates, and 5 AAS degree graduates from the Yukon.

YNLC develops teaching and learning materials for all the Yukon aboriginal languages. These include a curriculum guide, language lesson booklets and tapes, dictionaries and reference materials, and, most recently, a range of interactive multimedia materials. A complete list of the Center publications can be found on its website at www.yukoncollege.yk.ca/ynlc

YNLC plays an important role as a regional and international Center. It maintains relationships with such organizations as the Gwich'in Cultural and Social Institute (Tsiigehtchic, NWT), the Tanana Chiefs Conference (Fairbanks, Alaska), the Mount Sanford Tribal Consortium (Chistochina, Alaska), the Tok Branch of Interior Campus, UAF (Tok, Alaska), and with individual school districts in British Columbia, the Northwest Territories, and Alaska.

ANDRÉ BOURCIER

See also **Alaska Native Language Center; Northern Athapaskan Languages**

Further Reading

McClellan, C., L. Birckel, R. Bringhurst, J.A. Fall, C. McCarthy & J.R. Sheppard, *Part of the Land, Part of the Water*, Vancouver: Douglas & McIntyre, 1987

Pettigrew, C.J., "Yukon native language instructors: the struggle for recognition." *Women's Education des femmes*, 8(1) (June 1990): 15–18

Wright, R., "Beyond words." *Saturday Night Magazine*, 103(4) (April 1988)

YUKON RIVER

The Yukon River, 3185 km long, is the fourth longest and the fifth largest river (in terms of volume) in North America, and the second longest in Canada. It is unique in that it starts in a originates of small lakes close to the Pacific Ocean in the northwestern part of the province of British Columbia, flows northwest across Yukon Territory past the International Boundary of the 141st meridian into the state of Alaska, reaches its northernmost point at Fort Yukon where it nudges the Arctic Circle, and then runs west and south to empty into the Bering Sea. The river is a huge arc from sea to sea that is half in Canada, half in the United

States, and covers a drainage area of 855,000 sq km. The name Yukon is John Bell's—Hudson's Bay Company English fur trader—interpretation of the Gwich'in (Indian/First Nations) word for "Great River." The Aleut-Eskimo word given by the Russian fur trader, Andrey Glazunov, for this river also means "Great River." Glazunov (in 1835) and Bell (in 1844) were the first nonaboriginals to see the Yukon River.

In the Upper Yukon River Valley, the principal tributaries are the Teslin, Pelly, White, Stewart, and Klondike, and the main settlements today are Atlin, Teslin, Carcross, Whitehorse, Carmacks, and Dawson City. In the Middle Yukon River Valley, the main tributaries are the Porcupine, Tanana, and Koyukuk; the main communities (of 23) are Eagle, Circle, Fort Yukon, Beaver, Stevens, Rampart, Tanana, Ruby, Galena, Koyukuk, Nulato, Grayling, and Anvik where Glazunov first encountered the river, and the cultural crossroad of Holy Cross where the Athapaskans of the interior meet the Yup'ik Eskimos of the delta. In the Lower Yukon River Valley, the main river divides into the various sandbar and island-studded channels of the immense Yukon Delta, which, with the neighboring Kuskokwim Delta, makes up the largest single mass of intertidal habitat in the Western Hemisphere. Finally, by three main mouths and several minor ones, the Yukon River empties into the Bering Sea. About a dozen small Yup'ik Eskimo communities strung along the riverbanks include Russian Mission, the first Russian American Company fur trading post established on the Yukon River in 1837.

The Yukon River is generally slow-moving, shallow, and braided, navigable for only three months in summer but travelable by ice road in winter. It has been a major travel artery through the interior of Yukon and Alaska, since the earliest inhabitants are believed to have crossed to the American continent by a natural land bridge over the Bering Sea some 40,000 years ago. Aboriginals, fur traders, missionaries, miners, soldiers, and road construction workers depended on it for transportation and sustenance. Steamboats (sternwheelers) carried people and cargo between communities on the Yukon River and its major tributaries from 1869 to the 1950s when roads largely replaced rivers, especially on the Canadian side. Communities on the American side still depend on the river for hunting, fishing, trapping, and transportation, despite modern airplanes.

Despite the river's continental Subarctic climate (very cold winters, warm summers, little precipitation), it sustains a rich plant and animal life. Pacific salmon, historically the most abundant of the Yukon River's 18 species of fish, has a 3000-km annual migration run, which is one of the longest of any fish in the world. Since 1998, the numbers of chum and chinook salmon have decreased drastically, and since 2000 fishing has been tightly controlled by the Canadian-American Yukon River Salmon Agreement in order to preserve stocks. Moose, bear, caribou, sheep, goats, and furbearers (such as wolves, wolverine, lynx, and beaver) are common. Environmentalists fear that the large Porcupine barren-ground caribou herd, which ranges throughout the Porcupine River area, is threatened by plans to drill for oil in the Arctic National Wildlife Refuge and by pipeline proposals to bring oil and gas to southern markets.

Birdlife is especially abundant. The Yukon-Charlie Rivers National Preserve in the Middle Yukon River hosts the largest population of breeding peregrine falcons in North America. The Yukon Flats National Wildlife Refuge in the Middle Yukon River and the Yukon Delta National Wildlife Refuge in the Lower Yukon River provide outstanding breeding and feeding habitats for waterfowl—particularly geese, ducks, and swans—arriving from all four American flyways. Marine mammals—seals, sea lions, walrus, and beluga whales—are very important to the subsistence lifestyle of natives in the Lower Yukon River and along the adjacent coast.

LYN HANCOCK

See also **Dawson; Whitehorse**

Further Reading

Karpes, Gus, *Exploring the Upper Yukon River, Whitehorse to Carmacks*, Hancock House, 1998
———, *Exploring the Upper Yukon River, Carmacks to Dawson City*, Hancock House, 1998
Rennick, Penny (editor), "The Upper Yukon Basin." *Alaska Geographic Quarterly*, Volume 14, No. 4, Alaska Geographic Society, 1987
———(editor), "The Middle Yukon River." *Alaska Geographic Quarterly*, Volume 17, No. 3, Alaska Geographical Society, 1990
———(editor), "The Lower Yukon River." *Alaska Geographic Quarterly*, Volume. 17, No. 4, Alaska Geographical Society, 1991
The Yukon River Basin Committee (Yukon, British Columbia, Canada), Report on the Yukon River Basin Study, September 1984

YUKON TERRITORY

The Yukon Territory is located in the far northwest of mainland Canada, between Alaska, the United States, and the Northwest Territories, south of the Beaufort Sea, and north of British Columbia. It has an area of 483,450 sq km.

Situated in the Canadian Cordillera, the Yukon Territory is a mountainous region possessing Canada's highest mountains. Mt Logan, at 5971 m, is Canada's highest mountain, located in the St Elias range of mountains along the southwestern border of the

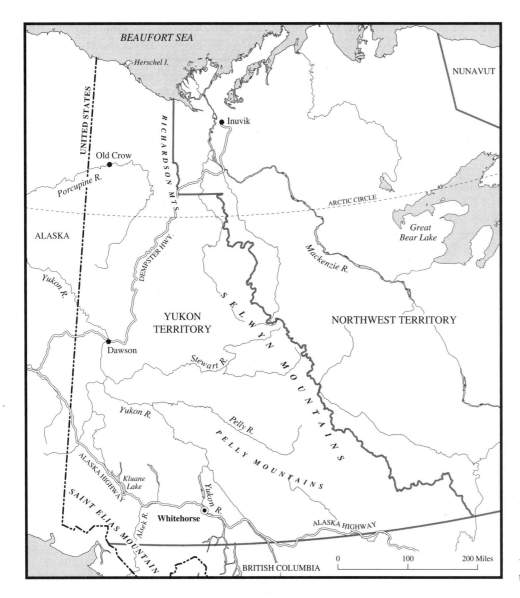

Yukon Territory and main towns and rivers.

Territory. Between the coastal ranges on the west and the Selwyn and Ogilvie mountains in the east lies the large Yukon Interior Plateau, which has an average elevation of 1200 m. A tundra plain lies along the 200 km Arctic coastline. Yukon's largest island, Herschel Island Territorial Park, is located just off the Arctic coast in the Beaufort Sea.

The Yukon has had a varied geologic history. Thick sediments were deposited over existing rocks from the late Precambrian to the late Mesozoic and early Tertiary times. In the Rocky Mountain area, the sedimentary rocks were folded, faulted, and eroded over a long period of time, creating saw-toothed ridges. In the region west of Watson Lake, the sedimentary strata were deformed and intruded by granitic rocks in Mesozoic times, producing mountains that were heavily eroded to almost flat surfaces, over which lava flows spread during the Tertiary era. The land was sub-

sequently uplifted, and then deeply dissected, forming mountain ranges and plateaus. Pleistocene era ice sheets covered most of the Yukon, giving the Territory its present landscape.

The Yukon's lakes and rivers are as spectacular as its mountains. The Yukon River is the second longest in Canada, and drains almost two-thirds of the Territory. The headwaters of this magnificent river are the large, crystal-clear lakes in northern British Columbia and southern Yukon: lakes Bennett, Marsh, Tagish, and Laberge. The Yukon River flows northwesterly some 3185 km from these lakes, through central Yukon and Alaska, before emptying into the Bering Sea. Other major rivers include the Alsek, which flows westward into the Gulf of Alaska to join the Tatshenshini; the Liard, which flows easterly into the Mackenzie River; and the Pelly River, which drains the Wernecke and Ogilvie mountains into the

Mackenzie. The Firth, Babbage, and Blow rivers flow northward across the Yukon's North Slope into the Beaufort Sea.

Climate

The Yukon has a Subarctic climate that is heavily influenced by two major features: the warm, moist air and storms in the Gulf of Alaska, and the cold Arctic air masses over the Beaufort Sea. The southern Yukon benefits from frequent intrusions of warm, moist air from the Pacific during the winter months, but may also experience weeks of below average temperatures when high-pressure ridges from the North settle in during the winter season. Most of the Yukon experiences very dry conditions. The total annual precipitation ranges from approximately 50 mm in dry valleys to as much as 600 mm in the coastal mountains. More precipitation falls in the winter months than during the summer, but the average depth of winter snow is only 50–70 cm.

Average January temperatures range from −20°C to −32°C, but the dry air makes the cold more tolerable for most people. The extreme low temperature of − 62.8°C (−81°F) was recorded at Snag in the western Yukon in February 1947. The average July temperature is about 14°C, although summer days can reach 32°C. The frost-free period varies considerably around the Territory, averaging 90 days in Dawson City, but only 70 days at higher elevations in southern Yukon.

Flora and Fauna

Most of the Yukon lies south of the treeline, and thus most of the vegetation can be described as Subarctic and alpine. Boreal forests cover about 57% of the territory, with white spruce, black spruce, lodgepole pine, tamarack (larch), aspen, and balsam fir being the predominant species. There are more than two hundred flower species found in the Yukon. Some of the more well-known species include anemones, yellow potentilla, monkshood, Arctic poppy, harebell, wild rose, lupines, lousewort, and wintergreen (Pyrola). The official flower of the Yukon is the fireweed, while the official tree is the subalpine fir.

The Yukon is the home of a variety of species of large mammals, including the black bear, grizzly bear, caribou, mountain sheep, mountain goat, moose, and wolf. It has North America's largest population of grizzly bear and Dall's sheep. Small numbers of polar bear and muskox range along the Arctic coastal plain. In the southern Yukon, mule deer can occasionally be seen along the highways. Elk and bison were reintroduced into the Yukon from the 1950s onward, and there have been a small number of confirmed sightings

of cougar. Deer, elk, and muskox are protected from hunting.

There are 14 species of smaller furbearers that live in the Yukon, many of which are actively trapped for their pelts. The more valuable species include lynx, marten, muskrat, beaver, wolverine, Arctic fox, colored fox, coyote, mink, and fisher.

There are approximately 214 species of birds found in the Yukon, including at least 21 species of hawks and owls. Bald and golden eagles are commonly seen through most of the Yukon in the summer months. Gyrfalcons and peregrine falcons are less common, but can be seen in more remote areas of the Territory.

Many species migrate to or through the Yukon, including trumpeter and tundra swans, snow and brant geese, northern pintail, common eiders, greater and lesser scaup, and sandhill cranes, to name just a few. The official Yukon bird is the raven, which lives year-round in the Yukon, and is renowned for its intelligence.

Population and Government

With a population of just over 30,000 people occupying a large land area, the Yukon has one of the lowest population densities in Canada. There are approximately 7300 people of aboriginal descent living in the Yukon, representing about 21% of the population. There are four levels of government in the Yukon: federal, territorial, First Nation, and municipal. The federal government owns and controls the public land, water, and resources of the Yukon, but the Yukon and First Nations governments have been negotiating the transfer of federal programs to local control through First Nation land claim negotiations and devolution negotiations, which have been ongoing since 1973. As of May 2001, seven of 14 First Nation land claim negotiations had been completed, and devolution negotiations were nearing completion. The seven First Nations with land claim agreements also have self-government agreements, which authorize them to enact laws governing their settlement lands and their citizens.

Communities

Yukon's population is disbursed among communities of varying sizes. Whitehorse, the capital, has the largest population with approximately 24,000 people. The remaining communities are Watson Lake, Dawson City, Mayo, Faro, Ross River, Haines Junction, Burwash Landing, Destruction Bay, Beaver Creek, Old Crow, Teslin, Pelly Crossing, Carmacks, and Carcross. Some rural districts have hamlet status with a limited form of local government, but no taxing authority.

Culture

The Yukon has a rich and diverse mix of aboriginal and nonaboriginal cultures. There are 14 First Nations representing eight different language groups. A number of programs have been developed in the past decade to revive the teaching and use of aboriginal languages, and these have been achieving some success. Major public celebrations of aboriginal culture include National Aboriginal Day (June 21) and the Commissioner's Potlatch.

There is a small but vibrant francophone community that operates its own school board and sponsors many social activities. A variety of services are provided in the French language by the federal and Yukon governments.

History

Aboriginal peoples had inhabited the Yukon for at least 18,000 years before White explorers, prospectors, and fur traders arrived in the area in the 1800s. Early contacts were generally friendly, although the trading post at Fort Selkirk was burned down by coastal Tlingits in 1852 when it threatened their trading monopoly with inland tribes.

The Klondike Gold Rush of 1896–1898 resulted in the creation of the Yukon Territory on June 13, 1898. The Yukon soon had self-government, and elected its first Member of Parliament in 1902. However, by 1918 the population of the Territory had declined drastically, and the federal government cut funding and programs in the Yukon, and reduced the size of the Territorial Council to three members. The Yukon remained an undeveloped backwater of Canada until World War II, when the Japanese invasion of the Aleutian Islands galvanized American resolve to build the Alaska Highway and the Canol pipeline through the Yukon. These projects had a major and lasting impact on the Yukon. Isolated aboriginal communities were suddenly located on a major transportation thoroughfare. The shipment of goods into the Territory became cheaper, and new services catering to the trucking and "rubber-tire" tourist industries sprang up.

The postwar era witnessed political and economic development. The elected Yukon Council sought additional responsibilities from the federal government, and the Yukon Act was amended several times between 1953 and 1974 to expand the size of the Council and to create the Advisory Committee on Finance, among other things. In 1970, the Executive Committee was created by a Directive from the Minister of Indian and Northern Affairs to Commissioner Smith. This Committee served as a partially elected, partially appointed Cabinet until 1979, when the last appointed member was removed by a ministerial directive, and the Yukon became governed by a wholly elected Executive Council.

From 1970 to 1978, territorial political parties emerged and some ran slates of candidates in territorial elections. However, it was not until 1978 that political parties were officially recognized in the Elections Act, and three local parties ran slates of candidates in the election that year: the Liberal Party, the Yukon New Democratic Party, and the Yukon Territorial Progressive Conservative Party. The Yukon has had a party-based system of government since that year, which distinguishes it from the Northwest Territories and Nunavut, its sister territories, which have consensus forms of government. The Yukon elected its first Liberal Government in April 2000. There are 17 members in the Yukon Legislative Assembly: 11 Liberals; 5 New Democratic Party; and 1 Yukon Party. Nationally, the Yukon is represented by a Liberal Senator in the Senate of Canada, and a Liberal Member of Parliament in the House of Commons.

STEVEN SMYTH

See also **Alaska Highway; Council for Yukon First Nations (CYFN); Council for Yukon Indians Umbrella Final Agreement; Herschel Island; Whitehorse; Yukon River**

Further Reading

Cameron, K. & G. Gomme, *The Yukon's Constitutional Foundations, Volume II, A Compendium of Documents Relating to the Constitutional Development of the Yukon Territory*, Whitehorse: Northern Directories Ltd., 1991

Cameron, K. & G. White, *Northern Governments in Transition: Political and Constitutional Development in the Yukon, Nunavut and the Northwest Territories*, Montreal: The Institute for Research on Public Policy, 1995

Coates, Ken S., *Best Left as Indians: Native-White Relations in the Yukon Territory, 1840–1973*, Montreal: McGill-Queen's University press, 1991

Coates, Ken S. & William R. Morrison, *Land of the Midnight Sun: A History of the Yukon*, Edmonton: Hurtig Publishers Ltd., 1988

Smyth, S., *The Yukon's Constitutional Foundations, Volume I, The Yukon Chronology, 1897–1999*, Whitehorse: Clairedege Press, 1999

Wright, Allen A., *Prelude to Bonanza: The Discovery and Exploration of the Yukon*, Whitehorse: Arctic Star Printing Inc., 1980

YUPIIT

The Yupiit (singular Yup'ik or Yupik) are an Inuit people of western Alaska. Yup'ik settlements are traditionally located in the broad lowland delta of the Yukon and Kuskokwim rivers and along the Bering Sea coast from the mouth of the Yukon River to Bristol Bay.

Sloughs, streams, and lakes are everywhere in the Yupiit region; from the air, it appears to be as much water as land. Due to the abundance of riverine, lacustrine, and marine resources, the Yupiit concentrated along the Bering Sea coast and up the rivers, as well as in certain locations between the two river systems, where inland lakes and waterways provide abundant fish. Yupiit have also depended upon migratory waterfowl and fur-bearing animals, as well as berries and greens. The majority of the region is treeless tundra. Low hills and coastal cliffs characterize some areas; there are spruce trees and more topographical relief higher up the rivers, as well as stands of spruce around Dillingham. Spring flooding carries driftwood down the rivers, and Yupiit historically used this material extensively. People lived in driftwood-framed, sod-covered, semi-subterranean houses. Winter settlements were semipermanent and larger than those found in the eastern Arctic; during other seasons, smaller family groups dispersed into camps to harvest available resources. In the summer, people used open skin boats (umiak) and kayaks to travel and hunt; in the winter, transportation was by foot and dogsled.

The region has a long history of occupation, probably at least since 4500 BP. Dumond (1984) suggested that with a developing emphasis on coastal resources, population and sedentarism increased, and local cultural divergences emerged through the first millennium AD. The subsequent Thule tradition is associated with early Bering Strait cultures. Thule spread widely throughout the Arctic around 1000 BP, although its relationship with the historic Yup'ik population remains unclear. One scenario suggests that Thule spread east from this region of Alaska, while another hypothesizes a Thule movement into the area from the north.

The Central Alaskan Yup'ik language is most closely related to Alutiiq (also called Pacific Yup'ik or Sugpiaq), spoken in Prince William Sound, the tip of Kenai Peninsula, Kodiak Island, and Alaska Peninsula, and to the languages of St Lawrence Island and Chukotka (Central Siberian Yupik and Naukan Siberian Yupik) (Fortescue et al., 1994). Inland neighboring groups include the Deg Hit'an (Ingalik) and Dena'ina (Tanaina) Athapaskans, whose languages are unrelated to Yup'ik.

Linguistic evidence suggests that at one time there was a Yup'ik continuum from St Lawrence Island and the opposing shore of Chukotka northward and across the Bering Strait, through the Seward Peninsula and south to the Pacific coast of Alaska. Within the last 500 years, this continuum was apparently broken by Inuit movement into the Seward Peninsula. The Yup'ik languages are more sharply differentiated than the different dialects of Inuit, which form a rough dialect continuum. Today, people speak a number of localized dialects of Central Alaskan Yup'ik. To some extent, these dialects reflect historic regional groupings, although epidemics, missionization, schooling, and economic development led to population dispersals and reaggregations that complicate this picture.

Regional groups (or societies) in the 1900s, as described by contemporary elders, were composed of one or more settlements linked by kinship ties. Group identity was primarily based on shared dialect, personal names (which link namesakes to living and dead kin), generally endogamous marriage ties, a common resource base, and political alliance (Shinkwin and Pete, 1984). Yupiit tend to identify more strongly with a village than a larger regional grouping.

Kinship continues to be the primary basis of community. Yup'ik kinship is reckoned bilaterally. Parallel cousins, designated by sibling terms, are differentiated from cross cousins, with whom one maintains a close and often joking relationship. Grandparents and grandchildren tend to be close, and the relationship with a surviving grandparent may be reinforced when a grandchild is named after that grandparent's deceased spouse. Naming (through which a name-soul comes to reside in the recipient), partnerships (historically quite extensive), adoption, and other often multiply overlapping extensions of interpersonal ties foster a wide network of local and more distant relations. Marriage was historically easily dissolved, and men and women spent much of their time in gender-segregated activities. Prior to missionary influence, women maintained separate multiple-generation households, while men shared a common residence in the qasgiq (or qasgit (plural) if the settlement was a large one). Young boys resided with their female relatives until they were old enough to move in with the men. In the qasgiq, men made tools, wooden containers, ceremonial objects, and weapons. Fire-bathing was also an important men's activity in the qasgiq. In their homes, women manufactured clothing, baskets, and mats, as well as other items needed for daily life. While labor was typically divided by gender, however, roles were not rigid, and men and women cooperated in tasks that required multiple skills, such as the manufacture of boats.

Yupiit subsistence activities remain important, with per capita harvests among the highest in Alaska. Subsistence also forms a basis for Yupiit identity in that these activities (fishing and hunting) and the consumption of traditional foods are important to a shared sense of ethnicity. Women and men continue to be active partners in subsistence pursuits. Fish (the word for which is synonymous with "food") is still a mainstay of the diet, and catching and preserving large quantities of salmon, in particular, require the labor of many family members. Commercial fishing, the primary source of cash in recent decades, contributes to keeping salmon central to Yup'ik life. Land and sea mammal hunting, pursued primarily by men, is a more solitary activity, with women typically completing the processing of the catch back in the village.

The general worldview of Yupiit is similar to that described for other Inuit peoples. In a sentient world, balance and reciprocity need to be maintained among humans, living and dead, and between humans and the nonhuman "persons" (yuit) of animals, weather, plants, and other entities. Yupiit developed an elaborate winter ceremonial cycle to renew and maintain these relationships. In the qasgiq, a series of multiday rituals involved hosting neighbors, reciprocal gifting, masked dances, and shamanic activity (see **Bladder Ceremony; Messenger Feast**). Numerous prescriptions (alerquutet) and proscriptions (inerquutet) were the foundation for personal and spiritual safety and right relationship. Ritual life today focuses on Christianity (mainly Russian Orthodox, Catholic, or Moravian), but older principles of right relationship remain important, as do hosting and feasting.

Today, the communities of Bethel (population 5471) and Dillingham (population 2466) serve, respectively, as regional centers for the Yukon-Kuskokwim Delta and Bristol Bay villages. Village populations range from less than 100 to over 1000, with the majority in the 250–500 range. The total Yup'ik population of the area is less than 30,000 (population estimates are based on US Census Bureau, Census 2000 Summary File 1). Contemporary political, territorial, and economic organization is evolving, in the intersection of the provisions of the Alaska Native Claims Settlement Act (ANCSA) with local-level organizations (such as Village Councils and Indian Reorganization Act Councils) and state and federal governments. The ANCSA corporations in the Yup'ik homeland are the Bristol Bay Native Corporation and Calista.

PHYLLIS MORROW

See also **Alaska Native Claims Settlement Act (ANCSA); Bladder Ceremony; Eskimo-Aleut Languages; Indigenous Worldviews; Inuit; Messenger Feast; Siberian (Chukotkan) Yupik**

Further Reading

Dumond, Don E., "Prehistory of the Bering Sea Region." *Handbook of North American Indians, Volume 5, Arctic*, Washington, District of Columbia: Smithsonian Institution, 1984

Fienup-Riordan, Ann, *The Nelson Island Eskimo: Social Structure and Ritual Distribution*, Anchorage: Alaska Pacific University Press, 1983

———, *Eskimo Essays: Yup'ik Lives and How We See Them*, Rutgers, New Jersey: Rutgers University Press, 1990

———, *Hunting Tradition in a Changing World: Yup'ik Lives in Alaska Today*, Rutgers, New Jersey: Rutgers University Press, 2000

Fortescue, Michael, Steven Jacobson & Lawrence Kaplan, *Comparative Eskimo Dictionary. Alaska Native Language Center Research Paper Number 9*, Fairbanks, Alaska: University of Alaska Fairbanks, 1994

Shinkwin, Anne & Mary C. Pete, "Yup'ik Eskimo societies: a case study." *Etudes/Inuit/Studies*, 8 (supplementary issue) 1984

YUPIK—*See* **SIBERIAN (CHUKOTKAN) YUPIK**

YUPIK ESKIMO SOCIETY OF CHUKOTKA

The Yupik Eskimo Society of Chukotka, designed for all Asian Eskimo communities, was established in August 1990. Until the year 2000, the Society was called "Eskimo Society of Chukotka Yupik" and was administered by co-chairpersons elected by each community. Since 2000, a single chairperson—Lyudmila Ainana (Aynganga)—has headed the Society.

The society is a member of the Russian Association of Indigenous Peoples of the North (RAIPON) whose chairperson is a member of the coordination council of RAIPON. The Yupik Eskimo Society is also a member of the Inuit Circumpolar Conference (ICC).

The main objectives of the Yupik Eskimo Society comprise conservation of the culture, language, and traditional lifestyle of the Asian Eskimos. For more than eight years, the Society has been actively working for the revival of traditional bowhead whaling, which has been the apex of marine mammal hunting among all Inuit. Since its establishment, the Society has contributed to research programs associated with the organization of the international Beringia Park; since 1994, the Society has spearheaded Russian-American programs devoted to monitoring marine mammals as well as investigation and conservation of traditional subsistence of the indigenous peoples of Chukotka. The Yupik Eskimo Society's biological research on the bowhead whale and other marine mammals substantially expanded and refined existing concepts and data in the field.

The Society additionally and significantly maintains relations with families of Asian Eskimos who left Chukotka for Alaska in the late 19th and early 20th centuries, in particular, for St Lawrence Island.

LYUDMILA BOGOSLOVSKAYA
TRANSLATED BY PETR ALEINIKOV

See also **Ainana, Lyudmila; Siberian (Chukotkan) Yupik**

Z

ZAGOSKIN, LAVRENTII ALEKSEEVICH

Lavrentii Alekseevich Zagoskin was well known as a Russian explorer of Alaska in the 19th century, who became interested in far travel when he studied in the Kronshtadt Naval School. Zagoskin studied under Pavel Mikhailovich Novosilsky, a participant in the Faddey Faddeyevich Bellinsgausen and Mikhail Petrovich Lazarev expedition that resulted in the exploration of Antarctica (1819–1821). In May 1823, Zagoskin began his military service as a reefer (a junior naval officer or *gardemarine*), and subsequently served in the Russian Navy for 26 years. In the spring of 1826, he made his first six-month voyage to the North Sea, England, and Lübeck, Germany. Zagoskin graduated from the Kronshtadt Naval School in 1826 and was sent to Astrakhan on the Caspian Sea, where he spent eight years. In January 1832, he was promoted to lieutenant, and three years later he was sent to the Baltic Sea, where he served on frigates *Kastor* and *Alexandra*. While in the Baltic Zagoskin, he wrote his *Memoirs of Caspiy*.

In 1838, Zagoskin was given a position in the Russian-American Company; he left St Petersburg in late December and arrived in Okhotsk, Russia, in mid-summer. As a captain, he led his brig *Okhotsk*, crossed the Pacific in two months, and in October 1839 he reached New Archangel (today Sitka, Alaska). In this same company, Zagoskin served several years on the brig *Elena* cruising through the Pacific between New Archangel and Okhotsk. During one of his voyages returning from Fort Ross, California, Zagoskin made the acquaintance of Russian scientist Ilya Gavrilovich Voznesensky, who worked for the Russian Academy of Science in St Petersburg and inspired Zagoskin's interest in the natural sciences, particularly mineralogy, entomology, and zoology.

Activities in the Russian-America Company were largely associated with the fur trade, and the manager Adolf Karlovich Etolin was concerned about how to retain control of the fur industry. Merchants from Kolyma (or Kolima) were buying furs from Chichi, who exchanged them directly from Inuit living on the coasts of the Bering Strait. Etolin sought to discover how furs from the continental regions of Alaska were transported to the coast. In the spring of 1842, Etolin organized an expedition to the continental parts of Alaska to explore the valleys of the Kuskokwim and Yukon rivers, which he believed to be along the fur-trading routes. These rivers were first mentioned by Baron Ferdinand von Wrangell, and up until 1839 had been unexplored. The second task of the expedition was to explore the upper reaches of Yukon and Kuskokwim rivers in order to find new places for beaver trade. Etolin asked Zagoskin to head the expedition.

The brig *Okhotsk* left New Archangel with six passengers on May 4, 1842, and two months later, after traversing the Pribulov, Unalaska, and Shumaginsli islands, arrived in St Michael's redoubt (a protective retreat or settlement). St Michael's redoubt was founded in 1833 on Seward (formerly St Michael) Island in the Norton Sound close to the mouth of the Yukon River. Here Zagoskin established a camp and remained for four months. During this time, he conducted meteorological observations, measured ebb and flow, collected plant samples and minerals, documented the dates of birds and fish migration, and studied the vertical transect of permafrost in the well. Moreover, he investigated the history of St Michael's redoubt, its Russian colonizers, and indigenous peoples. In his diary, Zagoskin described, for example, the summer and winter Inuit clothing; using information from the native peoples, he made a survey of 38 settlements to the north of Unalekleek River, including Pt Barrow, Alaska, and adjacent territory to the east.

In December 1842, Zagoskin's expedition left St Michael's redoubt and went along the coast of Norton Sound to the entry of the Unalakleet River. Zagoskin traveled through the Unalakleet River valley deep into continental regions of Alaska up to the Yukon (formerly Kwihpak) River, and in January 1843 he reached the Nulato redoubt on the right bank of the Yukon that had been established as a Russian blockhouse in 1938. He remained here for more than six months exploring the Yukon and Koyukuk rivers and searching the paths to the Kotzebue Sound, an inlet in the Chukchi Sea. In the summer months, Zagoskin explored the upper stream of Yukon and reached the mouth of Tanana River (a Yukon tributary), from where he returned by kayak to Ikogmut, the Inuit settlement. Zagoskin explored and mapped approximately 700 km of the Yukon River beginning 80 km upstream from Nulato. In November and December 1843, he traveled the path between the Yukon and Kuskokwim rivers and through the village Paimayt. In the summer of 1844, he started from the Eskimo settlement Ikogmute to the upstream Kuskokwin River, returning to Norton Sound through the Yukon. Zagoskin returned to New Archangel in September 1844.

In May 1845, Zagoskin traveled to Okhotsk, and at the end of the year returned to St Petersburg, where he had begun his journey six years earlier. He returned with several large zoological, botanical, and mineralogical collections and published his materials with a map that indicated 40 geographically referenced settlements in the *Annals of the Russian Geographical Society*. In 1848, Zagoskin authored a two-volume book about his expedition, in which he described the cultural traditions of the indigenous peoples and provided geographical descriptions of the continental regions of Alaska with precisely referenced maps of the lower Yukon and Kuskokwim rivers and coasts of the Bering Sea.

In 1848, Zagoskin retired from the Navy and moved to the village of Ostrov, located 20 km outside of Moscow. In 1849, he was elected a member of the Russian Geographical Society and received an award from the Russian Academy of Science. In 1850, Zagoskin sold his family estate and released most of his peasants to become involved in civil activities. He was elected the chief of the military volunteers during the Crimea War, and from 1861 to 1864 served as a judge, mediating among Russian landlords and peasants. Not content to retire from scientific endeavors, he planted a garden of apple trees and made daily meteorological observations studying the impact of climate on crop yield. In 1935, Alaskan resident Antuanetta Gotovickaia translated Zagoskin's book *Lieutenant Zagoskin's Travel in Russian America, 1842–1844*

into English. The copy of this typewritten translation is housed in the United States Library of Congress under the title *L. Zagoskin, Account of Pedestrian Journeys in America in the Years 1842, 1843 and 1844* (Sanct Petersburg, 1847, 2 parts).

Biography

Lavrentii Alekseevich Zagoskin was born to a family of military officers in the village of Nikolaevka, in the Penza Oblast' (province) of Russia on May 21, 1808. His father was Aleksei Nikolaevich Zagoskin, a retired naval officer. There were four children in the family, including Lavrentii's siblings Elizaveta, Aleksei, Dmitrii, and Varvara. Zagoskin's great-grandfather Lavrentii Alekseevich Zagoskin battled under the flag of Russian Czar Peter the Great. Zagoskin spent his childhood in the military pension, and in 1822 he entered the Naval School in Kronshtadt. He served as a naval officer on the Caspiy and Baltic seas. In 1842–1844, Zagoskin organized the largest Russian expedition to the continental regions of Alaska, western and southern parts of Norton Sound, lower Unalakleet and Yukon River and its tributaries, Kuskokwim River and the lower Koyukuk River. He discovered the mountain ridge between the Yukon territory and the eastern coast of the Norton Bay, explored the Kotzebue Sound, studied the climate of Alaska, and published his meteorological data collected over this two-year period. Alexsei Zagoskin experienced the tragedy of his eldest son Nikolai, also an officer, committing suicide by gunshot. Zagoskin's granddaughter Nadezhda Petrovna Glasko assisted with the editing of her grandfather's book when it was reissued in Russia in 1956. Zagoskin died on January 22, 1890 in the village of Abacumovo in the Ryazan province of Russia.

M. BELOLUTSKAIA

Further Reading

Pasetskii, V.M., *Russkii otkritija v Arctice,* Volume 1 [Russian discoveries in the Arctic], St Petersburg: Admiralteijstvo, 2000

Postnikov, A.V., *The Mapping of Russian America. History of Russian -American Contacts in Cartography*, Milwaukee: University of Wisconsin Press, 1995

Zagoskin, L.A., *Vospominanija o Caspii, jurnal "Sjin Otechestva," tchast 177* [Memoirs of Caspy, Journal "Son of Motherland," part 177], St Petersburg, 1836

———, *Peshehodnaja opis tchasti Ruskich vladenii v Americe, proizvedennaja leitenantom Zagoskinjim v 1842, 1843, 1844 godach* [Account of pedestrian journeys in the Russian possessions in America in the years 1842, 1843, 1844], Tchast I, St Petersburg, 1847, tchast II, St Petersburg, 1848

———, *Lieutenant Zagoskin's Travel in Russian America, 1842–1844*, translated by H.N. Michael & P. Rainey, Toronto: University of Toronto Press, 1967

List of Contributors

Aiken, Susan. Canadian Museum of Nature, Ottawa, Canada. Articles contributed to *Encyclopedia of the Arctic*: FLORA OF THE TUNDRA.

Akasofu, Syun-Ichi. International Arctic Research Center, Fairbanks, Alaska. Articles contributed to *Encyclopedia of the Arctic*: SPACE WEATHER.

Aleinikov, Peter A. Center for Traditional Subsistence, Institute of Heritage, Moscow, Russia. Articles contributed to *Encyclopedia of the Arctic*: AINANA, LYUDMILA; DOG SLEDGE IN NORTHERN EURASIA; YUPIK ESKIMO SOCIETY OF CHUKOTKA.

Alia, Valerie. Centre for Research in Media and Cultural Studies, University of Sunderland, England. Articles contributed to *Encyclopedia of the Arctic*: ABORIGINAL IDENTITIES; ERASMUS, GEORGES; IMAGES OF INDIGENOUS PEOPLES; KENOJUAK; KUPTANA, ROSEMARIE; MEDIA; NAMING; OFFICE OF POLAR PROGRAMS, NATIONAL SCIENCE FOUNDATION; PITSEOLAK, PETER; RADIO GREENLAND (KNR); SIMON, MARY.

Anderson, David G. Department of Anthropology, University of Aberdeen, Scotland. Articles contributed to *Encyclopedia of the Arctic*: REINDEER PASTORALISM.

Anderson, Douglas. Department of Anthropology, Brown University, Rhode Island. Articles contributed to *Encyclopedia of the Arctic*: ARCTIC WOODLAND CULTURE; BIRNIRK CULTURE; CHORIS CULTURE; GIDDINGS, LOUIS; IYATAYET.

Anisimov, Oleg. Department of Climatology, State Hydrological Institute, St Petersburg, Russia. Articles contributed to *Encyclopedia of the Arctic*: ICE JAMS; PERMAFROST.

Aporta, Claudio. Department of Anthropology, University of Alberta, Edmonton, Canada. Articles contributed to *Encyclopedia of the Arctic*: NAVIGATION, INDIGENOUS.

Appel, Igor. Independent scholar, Washington, D.C. Articles contributed to *Encyclopedia of the Arctic*: POLYNYAS; TRANSPOLAR DRIFT.

Barber, Valerie. Forest Sciences Department, University of Alaska, Fairbanks. Articles contributed to *Encyclopedia of the Arctic*: LAND BRIDGES AND THE ARCTIC CONTINENTAL SHELF; MOUNT MCKINLEY (DENALI).

Barr, Susan. Directorate for Cultural Heritage, Oslo, Norway. Articles contributed to *Encyclopedia of the Arctic*: FIALA, ANTHONY; INGSTAD, HELGE; JAN MAYEN; LONGYEAR, JOHN; NANSEN, FRIDTJOF; SIRIUS PATROL.

Barr, William. Arctic Institute of North America, University of Calgary, Canada. Articles contributed to *Encyclopedia of the Arctic*: ANZHU, PETR FEDOROVICH; BADIGIN, KONSTANTIN SERGEYEVICH; KOLDEWAY, KARL; MIDDENDORFF, ALEXANDER; MIDDLETON, CHRISTOPHER; MUSKOX; SEDOV, GEORGIY YAKOVLEVICH; SVERDRUP, OTTO; TYRRELL, JOSEPH BURR; USHAKOV, GEORGIY; VIL'KITSKII, BORIS ANDREEVICH; VIZE, VLADIMIR.

Barry, Roger. National Snow and Ice Data Center (NSIDC), University of Colorado, Boulder. Articles contributed to *Encyclopedia of the Arctic*: CLIMATE: RESEARCH PROGRAMS.

Basinger, James. Department of Geological Sciences, University of Saskatchewan, Saskatoon, Canada. Articles contributed to *Encyclopedia of the Arctic*: FOSSILS: PLANT SPECIES.

Baskin, Leonid. Severtsov Institute of Ecology and Evolution, Russian Academy of Sciences, Moscow, Russia. Articles contributed to *Encyclopedia of the Arctic*: BILIBINO; BYRRANGA MOUNTAINS; KHANTY-MANSIISK; KHLOBYSTIN, LEONID; KOLYMA RANGE; PALANA; PENZHINA RIVER; PETROPAVLOVSK-KAMCHATSKY; SHEEP; TAYMYR LAKE; TYUMEN'; URAL MOUNTAINS.

Belkin, Igor. Graduate School of Oceanography, University of Rhode Island, Narragansett. Articles contributed to *Encyclopedia of the Arctic*: ATLANTIC LAYER; BEAUFORT GYRE; BERING SEA; GULF OF ALASKA; GULF STREAM; ICE ISLANDS; ICEBERGS; NORTH ATLANTIC DRIFT; OCEAN FRONTS; SALINITY ANOMALIES; SUBPOLAR GYRES.

Belolutskaia, Marina. Department of Biophysics, St. Petersburg Medical University, Russia. Articles contributed to *Encyclopedia of the Arctic*: ALASKA TREATY (CONVENTION FOR THE CESSION OF THE RUSSIAN POSSESSIONS IN NORTH AMERICA TO THE UNITED STATES); CHERSKII, IVAN; KROPOTKIN, PETR; PAPANIN, IVAN DMITRIEVICH; RUSSIAN AMERICAN COMPANY; TRESHNIKOV, ALEKSEY FEODOROVICH; ZAGOSKIN, LAVRENTII ZAGOSKIN.

Belolyubskaya, Varvara Grigorievna. Office of International Programs, Sakha State University, Yakutsk, Russia. Articles contributed to *Encyclopedia of the Arctic*: LITERATURE, RUSSIAN.

Bennett, John. Canadian Polar Commission, Ottawa, Canada. Articles contributed to *Encyclopedia of the Arctic*: CANADIAN POLAR COMMISSION; ROWLEY, GRAHAM.

Bentley, Shannon. Attorney and Policy Analyst, Port Gamble S'Klallam Tribe. Articles contributed to *Encyclopedia of the Arctic*: CONVENTION FOR THE PROTECTION OF THE MARINE ENVIRONMENT OF THE NORTH-EAST ATLANTIC (OSPAR); DECLARATION ON THE PROTECTION OF THE ARCTIC ENVIRONMENT (1991); UN CONVENTION ON THE LAW OF THE SEA.

Berge, Anna. Alaska Native Language Center, University of Alaska Fairbanks. Articles contributed to *Encyclopedia of the Arctic*: KLEINSCHMIDT, SAMUEL.

Beringer, Jason. School of Geography and Environmental Science, Monash University, Australia. Articles contributed to *Encyclopedia of the Arctic*: SEWARD PENINSULA.

Berteaux, Dominique. Canada Research Chair in Conservation of Northern Ecosystems, Université du Québec à Rimouski, Canada. Articles contributed to *Encyclopedia of the Arctic*: LAND MAMMALS: RESEARCH PROGRAMMES.

Bielawski, Ellen. Arctic Institute of North America, University of Calgary, Canada. Articles contributed to *Encyclopedia of the Arctic*: ALASKA FEDERATION OF NATIVES (AFN); ANCHORAGE; DENBIGH FLINT CULTURE; DOGRIB; INDIGENOUS KNOWLEDGE; INDIGENOUS WORLD-VIEWS; SOMERSET ISLAND; VANSTONE, JAMES.

Bjerregaard, Peter., Statens Institut for Folkesundhed, Copenhagen, Denmark. Articles contributed to *Encyclopedia of the Arctic*: HEALTH AND DISEASE IN THE ARCTIC; HUMAN POPULATION TRENDS; INTERNATIONAL UNION FOR CIRCUMPOLAR HEALTH; MEDICAL SCIENCE IN THE ARCTIC.

Bocking, Stephen. Environmental and Resource Studies Program, Trent University, Ontario, Canada. Articles contributed to *Encyclopedia of the Arctic*: ENVIRONMENTALISM.

Bockstoce, John. Independent scholar, South Dartmouth, Massachusetts. Articles contributed to *Encyclopedia of the Arctic*: RAINEY, FROELICH.

Bogoslovskaya, Lyudmila. Department of Subsistence and Traditional Economies, Institute of Natural and Cultural Heritage of Russia, Moscow. Articles contributed to *Encyclopedia of the Arctic*: DIAMOND MINING.

Bordin, Guy. Institut national des langues et civilisations orientales, Paris, et Laboratoire d'ethnologie et sociologie comparative, Université de Paris X-Nanterre, France. Articles contributed to *Encyclopedia of the Arctic*: VAN DE VELDE, FRANZ.

Born, Erik W. Greenland Institute of Natural Resources. Articles contributed to *Encyclopedia of the Arctic*: VIBE, CHRISTIAN; WALRUS.

Bourcier, Andre. Yukon Native Language Centre, Yukon College, Whitehorse, Canada. Articles contributed to *Encyclopedia of the Arctic*: YUKON NATIVE LANGUAGE CENTRE.

Box, Jason. Byrd Polar Research Center, Ohio State University, Columbus, Ohio. Articles contributed to *Encyclopedia of the Arctic*: SUBLIMATION.

Boyakova, Sardana Iljinichna. Arctic Centre, Institute of Humanitarian Research, Yakutsk, Russia. Articles contributed to *Encyclopedia of the Arctic*: DAURKIN, NIKOLAY; GLAVSEVMORPUT (CHIEF OFFICE FOR THE NORTHERN SEA ROUTE); KOBELEV, IVAN; KOLCHAK, ALEXANDER; SHMIDT, OTTO YUL'EVICH; WRANGELL, BARON FERDINAND PETROVICH VON.

Brandson, Lorraine E. Eskimo Museum, Churchill, Canada. Articles contributed to *Encyclopedia of the Arctic*: CHURCHILL.

Breen, Katie. Département de chimie-biologie, Université du Québec à Trois-Rivières, Canada. Articles contributed to *Encyclopedia of the Arctic*: CURLEY, TAGAK; INUIT TAPIRIIT KANATAMI; MICROBIAL MATS.

Brigham, Lawson W. U.S. Arctic Research Commission, Anchorage, Alaska. Articles contributed to *Encyclopedia of the Arctic*: ARMSTRONG, TERENCE; EAST SIBERIAN SEA; ICEBREAKER; KARA SEA; LANCASTER SOUND; NORTH WEST PASSAGE; VILKITSKII STRAIT.

Bronshtein, Mikhail. State Museum of Oriental Art, Moscow, Russia. Articles contributed to *Encyclopedia of the Arctic*: ARUTYUNOV, SERGEI.

Bryce, Robert M. Head Librarian, Montgomery College, Maryland. Articles contributed to *Encyclopedia of the Arctic*: GILDER, WILLIAM HENRY.

Burykin, Alexis. Institute of Linguistics, St Petersburg, Russia. Articles contributed to *Encyclopedia of the Arctic*: BILIBINO NUCLEAR POWER PLANT; CHARCOT, JEAN-BAPTISTE; CHUKCHI-KAMCHADAL LANGUAGES; IVANOV, SERGEI VASIL'EVICH; LEVIN, MAXIM; MENOVSHCHIKOV, GIORGYI; OKLADNIKOV, ALEXEI; VDOVIN, INNOKENTIY STEPANOVICH.

Bykova, Olga. Institute of Geography, Russian Academy of Sciences, Moscow, Russia. Articles contributed to *Encyclopedia of the Arctic*: GREAT STALIN RAILWAY; IGARKA; NOVYI URENGOI; OROCHI; SALEKHARD; SEL'KUP; TAYMYR PENINSULA.

Callaghan, Terry. Abisko Research Station, Royal Swedish Academy of Sciences, Abisko, Sweden. Articles contributed to *Encyclopedia of the Arctic*: BIODIVERSITY: RESEARCH PROGRAMMES; COPSE.

Callaway, Donald G. National Park Service, Alaska Regional Office. Articles contributed to *Encyclopedia of the Arctic*: NATIONAL PARKS AND PROTECTED AREAS: ALASKA.

Capelotti, Peter. Division of Social and Behavioral Sciences, Penn State University Abington College, Pennsylvania. Articles contributed to *Encyclopedia of the Arctic*: ANDRÉE, SALOMON AUGUST; COAL MINING; ELLSWORTH, LINCOLN; LEIGH SMITH, BENJAMIN; PETERMANN, AUGUST; PHIPPS, CONSTANTINE; RUSSIAN CIVIL WAR; SUBMARINES IN ARCTIC EXPLORATION; TRANS-ARCTIC AIR ROUTE; WELLMAN, WALTER.

Capozza, Korey. Investigative reporter, San Francisco, California. Articles contributed to *Encyclopedia of the Arctic*: KANGERLUSSUAQ; RED DOG MINE; WATT, CHARLIE.

Castleden, Heather. Department of Earth and Atmospheric Sciences, University of Alberta, Edmonton, Canada. Articles contributed to *Encyclopedia of the Arctic*: HEALTH: ENVIRONMENTAL INITIATIVES; UNIVERSITIES AND HIGHER EDUCATION ESTABLISHMENTS, NORTH AMERICA AND GREENLAND.

Chan, Laurie H. M. Centre for Indigenous Peoples' Nutrition and Environment, McGill University, Quebec, Canada. Articles contributed to *Encyclopedia of the Arctic*: FOOD USE OF WILD SPECIES; HEALTH: RESEARCH PROGRAMMES.

Chaturvedi, Sanjay. Department of Political Science, Panjab University, Chandrigarh, India. Articles contributed to *Encyclopedia of the Arctic*: GEOPOLITICS OF THE ARCTIC; IMAGES OF THE ARCTIC.

Chernova, Natalia V. Zoological Institute, Russian Academy of Sciences, St. Petersburg, Russia. Articles contributed to *Encyclopedia of the Arctic*: CAPELIN; COD; HERRING; REDFISH.

Chiarenzelli, Jeffrey R. Department of Geology, State University of New York at Potsdam. Articles contributed to *Encyclopedia of the Arctic*: LICHEN.

Christensen, Torben R. Department of Physical Geography and Ecosystems Analysis, University of Lund, Sweden. Articles contributed to *Encyclopedia of the Arctic*: BIOGEOCHEMISTRY; CARBON CYCLING; GLOBAL CHANGE EFFECTS.

Collignon, Beatrice. Institute of Geography, Université de Paris, Sorbonne, France. Articles contributed to *Encyclopedia of the Arctic*: HOUSING; INUVIALUIT; PLACE-NAMES; VICTORIA ISLAND.

Colt, Stephen G. Institute of Social and Economic Research, University of Alaska-Anchorage. Articles contributed to *Encyclopedia of the Arctic*: ALASKA NATIVE CLAIMS SETTLEMENT ACT (ANCSA).

Conroy, James W. H. Celtic Environment Ltd., Environmental Consultants, Banchory, Scotland. Articles contributed to *Encyclopedia of the Arctic*: BRUCE, W.S.; NORTH EAST PASSAGE, EXPLORATION OF.

Corbett, Helen. Arctic Institute of North America, University of Calgary, Canada. Articles contributed to *Encyclopedia of the Arctic*: NORTH PACIFIC FUR SEAL CONVENTION; PRIBILOF ISLANDS.

Cowing, Charles O. Elisha Kent Kane Historical Society, New York. Articles contributed to *Encyclopedia of the Arctic*: KANE, ELISHA KENT.

Cronenwett, Philip N. Office of Leadership Giving, Dartmouth College, Hanover, New Hampshire. Articles contributed to *Encyclopedia of the Arctic*: BARTLETT, ROBERT; BRITISH ARCTIC EXPEDITION, 1875-1876; ENCYCLOPAEDIA ARCTICA (1946); MARKHAM, SIR ALBERT H.

Crump, John. Arctic Council Indigenous Peoples Secretariat, Copenhagen, Denmark. Articles contributed to *Encyclopedia of the Arctic*: CANADIAN ARCTIC RESOURCES COMMITTEE (CARC); RELOCATION.

Cruwys, Liz. Scott Polar Research Institute, University of Cambridge, England. Articles contributed to *Encyclopedia of the Arctic*: HAVEN, EDWIN J. DE; RASMUSSEN, KNUD.

Csonka, Yvon. Department of Social and Cultural History, Ilisimatusarfik - The University of Greenland, Nuuk, Greeland. Articles contributed to *Encyclopedia of the Arctic*: ETHNOHISTORY.

Dallmann, Winfried. Norwegian Polar Institute, Tromsø, Norway. Articles contributed to *Encyclopedia of the Arctic*: CHUVAN; NANAI; NEGIDAL; NIVKHI; OROK; ULCHI.

Danks, Hugh. Canadian Museum of Nature, Ottawa, Canada. Articles contributed to *Encyclopedia of the Arctic*: INSECT LARVAE; INSECTS; MOSQUITOES.

Derocher, Andrew. Department of Biological Sciences, University of Alberta, Edmonton, Alberta, Canada. Articles contributed to *Encyclopedia of the Arctic*: AGREEMENT ON THE CONSERVATION OF POLAR BEARS; BEARS; MARINE MAMMALS; NARWHAL; POLAR BEAR.

Desrosiers, Pierre M. Avataq Cultural Institute, Montreal, Canada, and Université Sorbonne, Paris, France. Articles contributed to *Encyclopedia of the Arctic*: BAFFIN ISLAND; PRE-DORSET CULTURE; PRINCE PATRICK ISLAND; SOUTHAMPTON ISLAND; UMIAK.

Diamond, Beverley. Articles contributed to *Encyclopedia of the Arctic*: MUSIC (CONTEMPORARY INDIGENOUS).

Dick, Lyle. Western Canada Service Centre, Parks Canada, Vancouver, Canada. Articles contributed to *Encyclopedia of the Arctic*: ELLESMERE ISLAND; PEARY, ROBERT E.; RACE TO THE NORTH POLE.

Dickson, Graham. Independent scholar, Toronto, Canada. Articles contributed to *Encyclopedia of the Arctic*: FLOE EDGE; GREENLAND SHARK; LEADS.

Distad, N. Merrill. University of Alberta Library, Edmonton, Alberta, Canada. Articles contributed to *Encyclopedia of the Arctic*: BAFFIN, WILLIAM; BEECHEY, FREDERICK; BUTTON, SIR THOMAS; DAVIS, JOHN; FOXE, LUKE; FREUCHEN, PETER; FROBISHER, SIR MARTIN; MACKENZIE, SIR ALEXANDER; MACMILLAN, DONALD BAXTER; MARKHAM, SIR CLEMENTS R.

Dixon, John C. Department of Geosciences, University of Arkansas, Fayetteville. Articles contributed to *Encyclopedia of the Arctic*: FROST AND FROST PHENOMENA; GELIFLUCTION PROCESSES.

Dorais, Louis-Jacques. Département d'Anthropologie, Université Laval, Québec, Canada. Articles contributed to *Encyclopedia of the Arctic*: ASSOCIATION INUKSIUTIT KATIMAJIIT; ESKIMO-ALEUT LANGUAGES; GROUPE D'ÉTUDES INUIT ET CIRCUMPOLAIRES.; KUUJJUAQ; PETERSEN, ROBERT; QUMAQ, TAAMUSI; TAQRAMIUT NIPINGAT; TURNER, LUCIEN M.

Dore, Jonathan. Writer and editor, British Columbia, Canada. Articles contributed to *Encyclopedia of the Arctic*: BARROW, SIR JOHN; JACKSON, FREDERICK; LYON, GEORGE FRANCIS; SCHWATKA, FREDERICK.

Dumond, Don E. Department of Anthropology, University of Oregon, Eugene. Articles contributed to *Encyclopedia of the Arctic*: ARCHAEOLOGY OF THE ARCTIC: ALASKA AND BERINGIA; NORTON CULTURE.

Ebbin, Syma Alexi. Research Fellow, Institutional Dimensions of Global Environmental Change (IDGEC), and Eastern Connecticut State University. Articles contributed to *Encyclopedia of the Arctic*: FISH; FOOD WEBS, MARINE; SALMON.

Eberle, Jaelyn J. Curator of Vertebrate Paleontology, University of Colorado Museum, Boulder. Articles contributed to *Encyclopedia of the Arctic*: FOSSILS: ANIMAL SPECIES.

Edwards, Robert. Manager/Environmental Scientist, Mitretek Systems, San Antonio, Texas. Articles contributed to *Encyclopedia of the Arctic*: KING WILLIAM ISLAND; NORTH WEST COMPANY; WOLVERINE.

Efimova, Elena G. School of Economics, St Petersburg State University, St Petersburg, Russia. Articles contributed to *Encyclopedia of the Arctic*: TRANS-SIBERIAN RAILWAY.

Ehrlich, Alan. Mackenzie Valley Environmental Impact Review Board, Yellowknife, Canada. Articles contributed to *Encyclopedia of the Arctic*: BIOCONCENTRATION; GREAT SLAVE LAKE.

Einarsson, Arni. Institute of Biology, University of Iceland, Reykjavík. Articles contributed to *Encyclopedia of the Arctic*: Mývatn Lake.

Ekberg, Anna. Department of Physical Geography and Ecosystems Analysis, Lund University, Sweden. Articles contributed to *Encyclopedia of the Arctic*: Peatlands and bogs; Soil respiration.

Elias, Scott. Institute of Arctic and Alpine Research, University of Colorado at Boulder. Articles contributed to *Encyclopedia of the Arctic*: Beringia; Environmental history of the Arctic.

Elling, Henrik M. Arctic Environmental Secretariat, Danish Polar Center, Copenhagen, Denmark. Articles contributed to *Encyclopedia of the Arctic*: DANCEA (Danish Cooperation for Environment in the Arctic).

Ellis, Richard. Research Associate, American Museum of Natural History, New York. Articles contributed to *Encyclopedia of the Arctic*: Blue whale; Common (harbor) seal; Dolphins and porpoises; Fin whale; Gray whale; Grey seal; Hooded seal; Killer whale; Minke whale; Northern bottlenose whale; Northern fur seal; Pilot whale; Ribbon seal; Sea otter; Sei whale; Sperm whale; Spotted seal; Steller's sea lion.

Espiritu, Aileen A. Faculty of History, University of Northern British Columbia, Prince George, Canada. Articles contributed to *Encyclopedia of the Arctic*: Ainu; Collectivization.

Etzel, J. Brent. Thomas Tredway Library, Augustana College, Rock Island, Illinois. Articles contributed to *Encyclopedia of the Arctic*: Amagoalik, John; Council for Yukon First Nations (CYFN); Moses, James Kivetoruk.

Evans, David J.A. Department of Geography and Geomatics, University of Glasgow, Scotland. Articles contributed to *Encyclopedia of the Arctic*: Eskers; Fjords; Glacial deposition; Glacial erosion; Glacial geomorphology; Glaciers; Ice sheets; Kames; Moraines; Nunataks.

Evans, Michael Robert. School of Journalism, Indiana University, Bloomington. Articles contributed to *Encyclopedia of the Arctic*: Handicrafts/tourist art; Inuit Broadcasting Corporation.

Eveno, Stéphanie. Independent scholar, Montreal, Canada. Articles contributed to *Encyclopedia of the Arctic*: Athapaskan; Bureau of Indian Affairs.

Fægteborg, Mads. Nature and Peoples of the North, Copenhagen, Denmark. Articles contributed to *Encyclopedia of the Arctic*: Arctic Leaders' Summit; Brun, Eske; Greenland Home Rule Act; Inuit Circumpolar Conference (ICC); Inuit Party; Johansen, Lars Emil; Lynge, Aqqaluk; Lynge, Augo; Lynge, Finn; Motzfeldt, Jonathan; Rosing, Hans Pavia; Thule Air Base.

Falk, Marvin W. Alaska & Polar Regions Collections, Elmer E. Rasmuson Library, University of Alaska Fairbanks. Articles contributed to *Encyclopedia of the Arctic*: Dalton Highway; Krauss, Michael E.

Farynowski, Lise. Department of Economic Development, Yukon Territorial Government, Whitehorse, Canada. Articles contributed to *Encyclopedia of the Arctic*: Josie, Edith; McLaughlin, Audrey.

Fast, Phyllis. Department of Alaska Native Studies, University of Alaska Fairbanks. Articles contributed to *Encyclopedia of the Arctic*: Gwich'in; Hensley, Willie; Mallot, Byron.

Filler, Dennis. NORTECH Environmental & Engineering Consultants, Fairbanks, Alaska. Articles contributed to *Encyclopedia of the Arctic*: Prudhoe Bay.

Fletcher, Chris. Department of Anthropology, University of Alberta, Edmonton, Canada. Articles contributed to *Encyclopedia of the Arctic*: Adoption; Innu.

Fondahl, Gail. Department of Geography, University of Northern British Columbia, Prince George, Canada. Articles contributed to *Encyclopedia of the Arctic*: Russian Federal Law Guaranteeing the Rights of Native Sparse Peoples of the Russian Federation; Russian Federal Law on Clan Communes (Obshchinas); Russian Federal Law on Territories of Traditional Nature Use.

Forbes, Bruce. Arctic Centre, University of Lapland, Rovaniemi, Finland. Articles contributed to *Encyclopedia of the Arctic*: Conservation; Environmental problems; Habitat loss; Polar steppe; Reindeer; Sedge meadows; Tundra; Vegetation distribution; Wet tundra; Wilderness; Yamal-Nenets Autonomous Okrug.

Forbes, Donald. Geological Survey of Canada, Bedford Institute of Oceanography, Dartmouth, Canada. Articles contributed to *Encyclopedia of the Arctic*: Coastal erosion.

Forchhammer, Søren. The Danish Institute for Advanced Studies in the Humanities, Copenhagen, Denmark. Articles contributed to *Encyclopedia of the Arctic*: Olsen, Jørgen; Olsen, Moses.

Fox, Anthony. Department of Wildlife Ecology and Biodiversity, National Environmental Research Institute, Denmark. Articles contributed to *Encyclopedia of the Arctic*: ALASKA NATIVE SCIENCE COMMISSION; BRENT GEESE; CIRCUMPOLAR ARCTIC VEGETATION MAP; DIVERS OR LOONS; EIDER; FELL-FIELDS; GULLS; HERB SLOPES; QEQERTARSUAQ; SWAN; WADERS.

Fox, Stephanie Irlbacher. Scott Polar Research Institute, University of Cambridge, Cambridge, England. Articles contributed to *Encyclopedia of the Arctic*: DEPARTMENT OF NORTHERN AFFAIRS ACT (1953); GOVERNMENT OF THE NORTHWEST TERRITORIES LEGISLATION (1966-); GWICH'IN COMPREHENSIVE LAND CLAIMS AGREEMENT; INUVIK; LAND CLAIMS; NORTHWEST TERRITORIES; SELF-GOVERNMENT.

Freeman, Milton. Canadian Circumpolar Institute, University of Alberta, Edmonton, Canada. Articles contributed to *Encyclopedia of the Arctic*: EGEDE, INGMAR; HIGH NORTH ALLIANCE; INTERNATIONAL CONVENTION FOR THE REGULATION OF WHALING; INTERNATIONAL WHALING COMMISSION (IWC); MARINE MAMMAL HUNTING; WATKINS, GINO; WORLD COUNCIL OF WHALERS.

Fryer, Paul. Department of Geography, University of Joensuu, Finland. Articles contributed to *Encyclopedia of the Arctic*: HERZEN INSTITUTE; KOLA PENINSULA.

Fuglei, Eva. Norwegian Polar Institute, Tromsø, Norway. Articles contributed to *Encyclopedia of the Arctic*: ARCTIC FOX.

Funk, Dmitrij. Department of the North and Siberian Peoples, Institute of Ethnology and Anthropology, Russian Academy of Sciences, Moscow, Russia. Articles contributed to *Encyclopedia of the Arctic*: POPOV, ANDREI; SANGI, VLADIMIR.

Funston, Bernard. Northern Canada Consulting. Articles contributed to *Encyclopedia of the Arctic*: CAPACITY BUILDING.

Gajewski, Konrad. Department of Geography, University of Ottawa, Canada. Articles contributed to *Encyclopedia of the Arctic*: HOLOCENE; PRINCE OF WALES ISLAND; QUATERNARY PALEOCLIMATOLOGY; TREELINE; TREELINE DYNAMICS.

Gavrilo, Maria. Arctic and Antarctic Research Institute, St Petersburg, Russia. Articles contributed to *Encyclopedia of the Arctic*: AUK; FULMAR; GUILLEMOT; KING EIDER; PECHORA DELTA.

Gibbons, Russell. The Frederick A. Cook Society, Pennsylvania. Articles contributed to *Encyclopedia of the Arctic*: HENSON, MATTHEW.

Gilberg, Rolf. Department of Ethnography, National Museum of Denmark. Articles contributed to *Encyclopedia of the Arctic*: HENDRIK, HANS (SUERSAQ); HOLTVED, ERIK; MYLIUS-ERICHSEN, LUDWIG; QAANAAQ; SACHEUSE, JOHN.

Giles, Audrey. Faculty of Physical Education and Recreation, University of Alberta, Canada. Articles contributed to *Encyclopedia of the Arctic*: SPORTING AND CULTURAL EVENTS IN CANADA.

Gilg, Olivier. University of Helsinki, Finland. Articles contributed to *Encyclopedia of the Arctic*: BYLOT ISLAND; GESSAIN, ROBERT; GREBE; KITTIWAKE; RAPTORS; SEABIRDS; TERN; VICTOR, PAUL-EMILE.

Gjertz, Ian. Zoological Museum, Oslo, Norway. Articles contributed to *Encyclopedia of the Arctic*: BARENTSBURG; BEAR ISLAND; HOEL, ADOLF; LONGYEARBYEN.

Glahder, Christian Martin. National Environmental Research Institute, Denmark. Articles contributed to *Encyclopedia of the Arctic*: BARNACLE GOOSE; ITTOQQORTOORMIIT (SCORESBYSUND); PINKFOOTED GOOSE; WHITE-FRONTED GOOSE.

Glazov, Mikhail. Institute of Geography, Russian Academy of Sciences, Moscow, Russia. Articles contributed to *Encyclopedia of the Arctic*: KOLGUYEV ISLAND; NENETS AUTONOMOUS OKRUG.

Gorham, Richard. United States Public Health Service (Retired). Articles contributed to *Encyclopedia of the Arctic*: ALASKA PENINSULA; ALASKA RANGE; BOREAL FOREST ECOLOGY; BROOKS RANGE; CONIFEROUS FORESTS; FAIRBANKS; FRESHWATER ECOSYSTEMS; KENAI PENINSULA; MOOSE; NORTH SLOPE; ST LAWRENCE ISLAND.

Gosliner, Mike. Marine Mammal Commission, Bethesda, Maryland. Articles contributed to *Encyclopedia of the Arctic*: MARINE MAMMAL PROTECTION ACT.

Gradinger, Rolf. School of Fisheries and Ocean Sciences, University of Alaska Fairbanks. Articles contributed to *Encyclopedia of the Arctic*: FRAM STRAIT; GREENLAND SEA; LARGE MARINE ECOSYSTEMS; PLANKTON; WEGENER, ALFRED.

Gray, David Robert. Canadian Museum of Nature, Ottawa, Canada. Articles contributed to *Encyclopedia of the Arctic*: ALERT; ARCTIC HARE; BANKS ISLAND; BATHURST ISLAND; CANADIAN ARCTIC EXPEDITION, 1913[-]1918; COPPERMINE RIVER; CORNWALLIS ISLAND; DALL'S SHEEEP; GRAY, DAVID, JR; GRAY, DAVID, SR; HAZEN, LAKE; MACKENZIE KING ISLAND; MELVILLE ISLAND; NATIONAL PARKS AND PROTECTED AREAS: CANADA; OLD CROW FLATS; SACHS HARBOUR; SNOWSHOE HARE; WEASEL; WOLF.

Greene, Tammy R. Department of Anthropology, University of Alaska Fairbanks. Articles contributed to *Encyclopedia of the Arctic*: HRDLI?KA, ALEŠ; KAYAK; MURDOCH, JOHN; NELSON, EDWARD.

Grinev, Andrei. Department of History, St Petersburg Humanitarian University of Trade Unions, Russia. Articles contributed to *Encyclopedia of the Arctic*: SECOND KAMCHATKA EXPEDITION.

Grønn, Jenny Fossum. Norwegian Archive, Library and Museum Authority, Oslo, Norway. Articles contributed to *Encyclopedia of the Arctic*: ARON FROM KANGEQ.

Guðmundsson, Ari Trausti. Línuhönnun, consulting engineers, Reykjavík, Iceland. Articles contributed to *Encyclopedia of the Arctic*: ICE CAPS; JÖKULHLAUPS; NATIONAL PARKS AND PROTECTED AREAS: ICELAND; REYKJAVÍK; STEFANSSON ISLAND; VOLCANOES AND VOLCANIC ACTIVITY.

Gultepe, Ismail. Cloud Physics Research Division, Meteorological Service of Canada, Ontario. Articles contributed to *Encyclopedia of the Arctic*: POLAR FRONTS.

Gunn, Anne. Recourse Wildlife and Economic Development, Government of the Northwest Territories, Canada. Articles contributed to *Encyclopedia of the Arctic*: CARIBOU HUNTING.

Habeck, Joachim Otto. Siberian Studies Centre, Max Planck Institute for Social Anthropology, Germany. Articles contributed to *Encyclopedia of the Arctic*: PECHORA BASIN; TUNGUS; VASILEVICH, GLAFIRA MAKAR'EVNA.

Hacquebord, Louwrens. Centre for Canadian Studies, University of Groningen, the Netherlands. Articles contributed to *Encyclopedia of the Arctic*: BARENTS, WILLEM; BOWHEAD (GREENLAND RIGHT) WHALE; CARTOGRAPHY; VLAMINGH, WILLEM DE; WHALING, HISTORICAL.

Häggman, Bertil. Director, Center for Research on Geopolitics, Sweden. Articles contributed to *Encyclopedia of the Arctic*: BERING, VITUS; ELLEF RINGNES ISLAND; LAPLAND; LAPPIN LÄÄNI; MUNK, JENS; NORDENSKIÖLD, ADOLF ERIK; NORRBOTTEN; STELLER, GEORG; SWEDEN.

Håkon Hoel, Alf. Associate Professor, Department of Political Science, University of Tromsø. Articles contributed to *Encyclopedia of the Arctic*: FISHERIES, COMMERCIAL.

Halemba, Agnieszka Ewa. Siberian Studies Centre, Max Planck Institute for Social Anthropology, Germany.

Articles contributed to *Encyclopedia of the Arctic*: PILSUDSKI, BRONISLAW PIOTR; SIEROSZEWSKI, WACLAW LEOPOLDOVICH.

Hancock, Lyn. Lyn Hancock Enterprises, British Columbia, Canada. Articles contributed to *Encyclopedia of the Arctic*: MACKENZIE DELTA; MACKENZIE RIVER; YUKON RIVER.

Hansen, Klaus Georg. Sisimiut Museum, Greenland. Articles contributed to *Encyclopedia of the Arctic*: GRAAH, WILHELM A.; KOCH, LAUGE; SISIMIUT; TELECOMMUNICATIONS.

Hansen, Steffen Stummann. Danish Polar Center, Copenhagen, Denmark. Articles contributed to *Encyclopedia of the Arctic*: ARCHAEOLOGY OF THE ARCTIC: SCANDINAVIAN SETTLEMENT OF THE NORTH ATLANTIC; HATT, GUDMUND; NØRLUND, POUL; ROUSSELL, AAGE.

Harington, C. Richard. Canadian Museum of Nature, Ottawa, Canada. Articles contributed to *Encyclopedia of the Arctic*: PLEISTOCENE MEGAFAUNA.

Harper, Kenn. Researcher and writer, Iqaluit, Canada. Articles contributed to *Encyclopedia of the Arctic*: ALPHABETS AND WRITING, NORTH AMERICA AND GREENLAND; BERNIER, JOSEPH-ELZEAR; EBIERBING, HANNAH [TOOKOOLITO] AND JOE; EENOOLOOAPIK; MINIK; PECK, EDMUND JAMES; PRYDE, DUNCAN; QILLARSUAQ.

Harrington, Fred H. Psychology Department, Mount Saint Vincent University, Nova Scotia, Canada. Articles contributed to *Encyclopedia of the Arctic*: CARIBOU; PUFFINS; RAZORBILL.

Harrison, Christopher. Geological Survey of Canada, Calgary. Articles contributed to *Encyclopedia of the Arctic*: GEOLOGICAL HISTORY OF THE ARCTIC.

Haukkala, Hiski. Finnish Institute of International Affairs, Helsinki, Finland. Articles contributed to *Encyclopedia of the Arctic*: INTERNATIONAL COUNCIL FOR EXPLORATION OF THE SEA (ICES); NORTHERN DIMENSION (OF THE EUROPEAN UNION).

Hausner, Vera. Department of Biology, University of Tromsø, Norway. Articles contributed to *Encyclopedia of the Arctic*: BIRCH FORESTS; NATIONAL PARKS AND PROTECTED AREAS: NORWAY.

Haysom, Veryan. Lawyer and researcher, Mahone Bay, Canada. Articles contributed to *Encyclopedia of the Arctic*: LABRADOR INUIT ASSOCIATION; LABRADOR INUIT LAND CLAIMS AGREEMENT IN PRINCIPLE.

Headland, Robert. Scott Polar Research Institute, University of Cambridge, England. Articles contributed to *Encyclopedia of the Arctic*: HERBERT, WALLY.

Heckathorn, Ted. Author, Idaho Falls, Idaho. Articles contributed to *Encyclopedia of the Arctic*: AMADEO, LUIGI, DUKE OF ABRUZZI; AMUND RINGNES ISLAND.

Heginbottom, John Alan. Emeritus Scientist, Geological Survey of Canada, Natural Resources Canada. Articles contributed to *Encyclopedia of the Arctic*: ARCTIC PILOT PROJECT; GROUND ICE; PERMAFROST RETREAT; PINGOS.

Heijnen, Adriënne. Center for North Atlantic Studies, Aarhus Universitet, Denmark. Articles contributed to *Encyclopedia of the Arctic*: ICELANDERS.

Heinrichs, John. Department of Geosciences, Fort Hays State University, Kansas. Articles contributed to *Encyclopedia of the Arctic*: BAFFIN BAY.

Henderson, Ailsa. Department of Political Science, University of Toronto, Canada. Articles contributed to *Encyclopedia of the Arctic*: HAPPY VALLEY; INUIT QAUJIMAJATUQANGIT; LOW LEVEL FLIGHT TRAINING; NORWEGIAN SAAMI PARLIAMENT.

Heyne, Eric. English Department, University of Alaska Fairbanks. Articles contributed to *Encyclopedia of the Arctic*: LITERATURE, NORTH AMERICAN.

Hodkinson, Ian D. School of Biological and Earth Sciences, Liverpool John Moores University, England. Articles contributed to *Encyclopedia of the Arctic*: BELCHER, SIR EDWARD; BELLOT, JOSEPH-RÉNÉ; CLAVERING, DOUGLAS C.; DEVON ISLAND; DISKO ISLAND; HEARNE, SAMUEL; JAMES, THOMAS; SIMPSON, THOMAS.

Hovelsrud-Broda, Grete K. North Atlantic Marine Mammal Commission, Tromsø, Norway. Articles contributed to *Encyclopedia of the Arctic*: NORTH ATLANTIC MARINE MAMMAL COMMISSION (NAMMCO).

Huebert, Rob. Department of Political Science, University of Calgary, Canada. Articles contributed to *Encyclopedia of the Arctic*: ARCTIC WATERS POLLUTION PREVENTION ACT (1971); MILITARIZATION OF THE ARCTIC IN THE WEST.

Hugason, Hjalti. Faculty of Theology, University of Iceland, Reykjavík. Articles contributed to *Encyclopedia of the Arctic*: CHURCHES IN ICELAND AND THE SCANDINAVIAN ARCTIC, ESTABLISHMENT OF.

Humlum, Ole. Department of Geology, The University Courses on Svalbard, Norway. Articles contributed to

Encyclopedia of the Arctic: FAROE ISLANDS; ROCK GLACIERS; SVALBARD.

Hund, Andrew J. Case Western Reserve University, Ohio. Articles contributed to *Encyclopedia of the Arctic*: DAAVI SUVVA FESTIVAL; EYAK; RADIOACTIVITY.

Huntington, Henry. Huntington Consulting, Eagle River, Alaska. Articles contributed to *Encyclopedia of the Arctic*: ALASKA BELUGA WHALE COMMITTEE; ARCTIC COUNCIL; ARCTIC RESEARCH CONSORTIUM OF THE UNITED STATES (ARCUS); BARROW.

Husebye, Sylvi Jane. Barents House, Kirkenes, Norway. Articles contributed to *Encyclopedia of the Arctic*: BARENTS COUNCIL; BARENTS REGION; BARENTS REGIONAL COUNCIL.

Ignat'eva, Vanda Borisovna. Institute of Humanitarian Research, Yakutsk, Russia. Articles contributed to *Encyclopedia of the Arctic*: NIKOLAEV, MIKHAIL E.

Il'inskii, Vladimir V. Biological Department, Moscow State University, Russia. Articles contributed to *Encyclopedia of the Arctic*: MICROBES; WHITE SEA.

Ingólfsson, Ólafur. Department of Geology, The University Centre in Svalbard, Longyearbyen, Norway. Articles contributed to *Encyclopedia of the Arctic*: FOSSIL PERIGLACIAL PHENOMENA; QUATERNARY PALEOGEOGRAPHY; QUATERNARY PERIOD.

Isherwood, William. Lawrence Livermore National Laboratory, California (Retired). Articles contributed to *Encyclopedia of the Arctic*: NORTH MAGNETIC POLE.

Ivanov, Vasily Nikolaevich. Institute of Humanitarian Research, Yakutsk, Russia. Articles contributed to *Encyclopedia of the Arctic*: YAKUTS; YASAK.

Jacobs, Peter. Ecole d'Architecture de paysage, Université de Montréal, Canada. Articles contributed to *Encyclopedia of the Arctic*: JAMES BAY AND NORTHERN QUÉBEC AGREEMENT; JAMES BAY HYDROELECTRIC PROJECT; KATIVIK ENVIRONMENTAL QUALITY COMMISSION; KATIVIK REGIONAL GOVERNMENT; MAKIVIK CORPORATION; NUNAVIK; NUNAVIK POLITICAL ACCORD; RAGLAND MINING PROJECT.

Jakobsson, Sverrir. University of Iceland, Reykjavík. Articles contributed to *Encyclopedia of the Arctic*: AKUREYRI; ARNASSON, INGOLFUR; COD WARS; ERIKSSON, LEIF; FINNBOGADOTTIR, VIGDIS; GRÍMSEY; HUSAVIK; NORSE AND ICELANDIC SAGAS; ODDSSON, DAVID; STURLUSON, SNORRI; VESTMANNAEYJAR (WESTMAN ISLANDS).

Jastrebski, Chris. Ecological Logistics & Research, Matheson, Canada. Articles contributed to *Encyclopedia of*

the Arctic: GREAT BEAR LAKE; INUVIALUIT CO-MANAGEMENT BODIES; NUNAVUT WILDLIFE MANAGEMENT BOARD; SCULPIN.

Jensen, Jens Fog. Institute of Archaeology, University of Copenhagen, Denmark. Articles contributed to *Encyclopedia of the Arctic*: DORSET CULTURE; INDEPENDENCE CULTURE; KNUTH, EIGIL.

Jessen, Mette-Astrid. Greenland Home Rule, Department of Environment and Nature, Nuuk, Greenland. Articles contributed to *Encyclopedia of the Arctic*: NATIONAL PARKS AND PROTECTED AREAS: GREENLAND.

Jóhannesson, Guðni Th. Centre for Research in the Humanities, University of Iceland. Articles contributed to *Encyclopedia of the Arctic*: ICELAND.

Johnson, Kenneth R. Cryofront Journal of Cold Region Technology, Alberta, Canada. Articles contributed to *Encyclopedia of the Arctic*: ALASKA HIGHWAY; DISTANT EARLY WARNING (DEW) LINE; IQALUIT; NANISIVIK; NORMAN WELLS; TRANS-ALASKA PIPELINE; TUKTOYAKTUK; WASTE MANAGEMENT.

Johnston, Vicky. Canadian Wildlife Service, Yellowknife, Canada. Articles contributed to *Encyclopedia of the Arctic*: PRINCE CHARLES ISLAND.

Jolles, Carol Zane. Anthropology Department, University of Washington, Seattle. Articles contributed to *Encyclopedia of the Arctic*: DIOMEDE ISLANDS.

Jonaitis, Aldona. University of Alaska Museum, Fairbanks. Articles contributed to *Encyclopedia of the Arctic*: HAIDA; TLINGIT.

Jones, E. Peter. Bedford Institute of Oceanography, Dartmouth, Canada. Articles contributed to *Encyclopedia of the Arctic*: OCEANOGRAPHY.

Kadas, Robert. Department of Foreign Affairs and International Trade, Ottawa, Canada. Articles contributed to *Encyclopedia of the Arctic*: NORTHERN DIMENSION OF CANADA'S FOREIGN POLICY.

Kafarowski, Joanna. Natural Resources and Environmental Studies program, University of Northern British Columbia, Canada. Articles contributed to *Encyclopedia of the Arctic*: MACLEAN, EDNA AGHEAK; NATIONAL PARKS AND PROTECTED AREAS: FINLAND; WATT-CLOUTIER, SHEILA.

Kallenborn, Roland. Norwegian Institute for Air Research, Norway. Articles contributed to *Encyclopedia*

of the Arctic: PERSISTENT ORGANIC POLLUTANTS (POPS); POLLUTION: ENVIRONMENTAL INITIATIVES; POLLUTION: RESEARCH PROGRAMMES; POLYCHLORINATED BIPHENYLS (PCBS).

Kaplan, Lawrence D. Alaska Native Language Center, University of Alaska Fairbanks. Articles contributed to *Encyclopedia of the Arctic*: LANGUAGES OF THE ARCTIC.

Karpoff, Jonathan. School of Business Administration, University of Washington, Seattle. Articles contributed to *Encyclopedia of the Arctic*: AMUNDSEN, ROALD; EXXON VALDEZ; HALL, CHARLES F.; MCCLURE, SIR ROBERT.

Kassam, Karim-Aly. Arctic Institute of North America, University of Calgary, Canada. Articles contributed to *Encyclopedia of the Arctic*: HUMAN ECOLOGY; HUNTING, SUBSISTENCE.

Kattsov, Vladimir. Voeikov Main Geophysical Observatory, St Petersburg, Russia. Articles contributed to *Encyclopedia of the Arctic*: GENERAL CIRCULATION MODELLING.

Kazaev, Andrey Vasilievitch. Arctic Centre, Institute of Humanitarian Research, Yakutsk, Russia. Articles contributed to *Encyclopedia of the Arctic*: ODULOK, TEKKI.

Kazaryan, Pavel Levonovich. Institute of Humanitarian Research, Yakutsk, Russia. Articles contributed to *Encyclopedia of the Arctic*: KOLYMA HIGHWAY; LENA RIVER; VERKHOYANSK RANGE.

Kennedy, Michael P.J. Department of English, University of Saskatchewan, Canada. Articles contributed to *Encyclopedia of the Arctic*: ALOOTOOK IPELLIE; SEDNA: THE SEA GODDESS.

Kent, Neil. Scott Polar Research Institute, University of Cambridge, England. Articles contributed to *Encyclopedia of the Arctic*: EGEDE, HANS; EGEDE, POUL; KIRUNA; LAXNESS, HALDOR; ROVANIEMI.

Keskitalo, Carina. Department of Social Studies, University of Lapland, Finland. Articles contributed to *Encyclopedia of the Arctic*: SUSTAINABLE DEVELOPMENT AND HUMAN DIMENSIONS: ENVIRONMENTAL INITIATIVES.

Kevan, Peter G. Department of Environmental Biology, University of Guelph, Canada. Articles contributed to *Encyclopedia of the Arctic*: ECOLOGY AND ENVIRONMENT; INVERTEBRATES, TERRESTRIAL; PLANT REPRODUCTION AND POLLINATION; QUEEN ELIZABETH ISLANDS; TROPHIC LEVELS.

Kingston, Deanna M. Department of Anthropology, Oregon State University. Articles contributed to *Encyclopedia of the Arctic*: INUPIAT; KING ISLAND; MASKS; MUSIC (TRADITIONAL INDIGENOUS); SONG DUEL.

Kirkwood, Sheila. Atmospheric Research Programme, Swedish Institute of Space Physics, Sweden. Articles contributed to *Encyclopedia of the Arctic*: UPPER ATMOSPHERE PHYSICS AND CHEMISTRY.

Klokov, Konstantin. Department of Social Geography, St Petersburg State University, Russia. Articles contributed to *Encyclopedia of the Arctic*: ECONOMIC INVENTORY OF THE (SOVIET) POLAR NORTH, 1926/27; INDIGIRKA RIVER.

Koerbel, Hermann F. Arctic Research Consortium Austria. Articles contributed to *Encyclopedia of the Arctic*: PAYER, JULIUS; WEYPRECHT, KARL.

Kovacs, Kit. Norwegian Polar Institute, Tromsø, Norway. Articles contributed to *Encyclopedia of the Arctic*: BEARDED SEAL; BELUGA (WHITE) WHALE; HARP SEAL; RINGED SEAL.

Kowalik, Zygmunt. Institute of Marine Science, University of Alaska Fairbanks. Articles contributed to *Encyclopedia of the Arctic*: TIDES.

Krutak, Lars. National Museum of Natural History, Smithsonian Institution, Washington, D.C. Articles contributed to *Encyclopedia of the Arctic*: REPATRIATION; TATTOOING.

Kulchyski, Peter. Department of Native Studies, University of Manitoba, Canada. Articles contributed to *Encyclopedia of the Arctic*: BOAS, FRANZ; COLONIZATION OF THE ARCTIC; DENE; INDIGENOUS RIGHTS; NUNAVUT FINAL AGREEMENT; SAHTU LAND CLAIMS AGREEMENT.

Kuzmin, Sergius L. Institute of Ecology and Evolution, Russian Academy of Sciences, Moscow, Russia. Articles contributed to *Encyclopedia of the Arctic*: ADAPTATION; AMPHIBIANS; FOOD CHAINS; MARINE BIOLOGY; REPTILES.

Lalonde, Christine. Associate Curator of Inuit Art, National Gallery of Canada. Articles contributed to *Encyclopedia of the Arctic*: IVORY CARVING; SOPER, J. DEWEY.

Lamoureux, Scott. Department of Geography, Queen's University, Kingston, Canada. Articles contributed to *Encyclopedia of the Arctic*: CORNWALL ISLAND.

Lange, Manfred A. Institute for Geophysics, University of Münster, Germany. Articles contributed to *Encyclopedia of the Arctic*: CLIMATE CHANGE; ICE AGES; ICE SHELVES; PANCAKE ICE; THERMOHALINE CIRCULATION.

Langgård, Karen. Department of Greenlandic Language and Literature, Ilisimatusarfik/University of Greenland. Articles contributed to *Encyclopedia of the Arctic*: LITERATURE, GREENLANDIC.

Lantto, Patrik. Department of historical studies, Umeå university, Sweden. Articles contributed to *Encyclopedia of the Arctic*: SAAMI.

Lappo, Elena G. Institute of Geography, Russian Academy of Sciences, Moscow, Russia. Articles contributed to *Encyclopedia of the Arctic*: SKUAS AND JAEGERS.

Lappo, Georgy M. Institute of Geography, Russian Academy of Sciences, Moscow, Russia. Articles contributed to *Encyclopedia of the Arctic*: ARKHANGEL'SK.

Lapteva, Elena. Institute of Biology, Komi Science Centre, Ural Division of Russian Academy of Sciences, Russia. Articles contributed to *Encyclopedia of the Arctic*: OB' RIVER.

Laugrand, Frédéric. Faculté de Théologie et de Sciences Religieuses, Université Laval, Québec, Canada. Articles contributed to *Encyclopedia of the Arctic*: CHURCHES IN GREENLAND AND THE NORTH AMERICAN ARCTIC, ESTABLISHMENT OF; ELDERS; MARY-ROUSSELIERE, FATHER GUY; MISSIONARY ACTIVITY; MYTHOLOGY OF THE INUIT; NOMADISM; SCHNEIDER, LUCIEN.

Lebedintsev, Alexander I. Northeastern Interdisciplinary Scientific Research Institute, Russian Academy of Sciences, Far-Eastern Branch, Vladivostok, Russia. Articles contributed to *Encyclopedia of the Arctic*: OLD KEREK CULTURE; TOKAREV CULTURE.

Lee, Molly. University of Alaska Museum, Fairbanks. Articles contributed to *Encyclopedia of the Arctic*: ART AND ARTISTS (INDIGENOUS); NALUKATAK.

Légaré, André. Government of the Northwest Territories, Yellowknife, Canada. Articles contributed to *Encyclopedia of the Arctic*: BATHURST MANDATE; GWICH'IN RENEWABLE RESOURCES BOARD; GWICH'IN SETTLEMENT AREA; GWICH'IN TRIBAL COUNCIL; NUNAVUT; SAHTU RENEWABLE RESOUCES BOARD; SAHTU SETTLEMENT AREA.

Legge, Scott S. Department of Anthropology, University of Kent, Canterbury, England. Articles contributed to *Encyclopedia of the Arctic*: NUTRITION AND FOOD; PHYSICAL ANTHROPOLOGY OF THE ARCTIC.

Legros, Dominique. Department of Sociology and Anthropology, Concordia University, Montreal, Canada. Articles contributed to *Encyclopedia of the Arctic*: PETITOT, FATHER; TUTCHONE.

Lehtola, Veli-Pekka. Thule Institute, University of Oulu, Finland. Articles contributed to *Encyclopedia of the Arctic*: NICKUL, KARL.

Lévesque, Esther. Département de chimie-biologie, Université du Québec a Trois-Rivières, Québec, Canada. Articles contributed to *Encyclopedia of the Arctic*: HIGH ARCTIC.

Lincoln, Amber. Independent scholar, Fairbanks, Alaska Articles contributed to *Encyclopedia of the Arctic*: ALASKA ESKIMO WHALING COMMISSION (AEWC); NATIVE CORPORATIONS.

Lincoln, Tamara. Elmer E. Rasmuson Library, University of Alaska Fairbanks. Articles contributed to *Encyclopedia of the Arctic*: LABOR CAMPS.

Lindsay, Ronald. Polar Science Center, Applied Physics Laboratory, University of Washington, Seattle. Articles contributed to *Encyclopedia of the Arctic*: CLIMATE OSCILLATIONS; ENERGY BALANCE.

Lindsey, Gillian. Writer and editor, New York. Articles contributed to *Encyclopedia of the Arctic*: BARENTS SEA; GAS HYDRATES; GREENLAND HALIBUT; HOPSON, EBEN; ILULISSAT; INVERTEBRATES, AQUATIC; MOLLOY DEEP; NELSON ISLAND; NORTHERN SEA ROUTE; NUNIVAK ISLAND; PRIMARY PRODUCTION, MARINE; PROTECTED AREAS; TATSHENSHINI/ALSEK; UNIVERSITY OF THE ARCTIC; VAIGACH.

Livingstone, Roxanne. News reporter and writer, Yukon, Canada. Articles contributed to *Encyclopedia of the Arctic*: ADAMSON, SHIRLEY.

Lomagin, Nikita A. School of Economics, St Petersburg State University, Russia. Articles contributed to *Encyclopedia of the Arctic*: ARMS CONTROL; MILITARIZATION OF THE ARCTIC IN RUSSIA; MURMANSK SPEECH (1987).

Long, Maureen. Northern Research Institute, Yukon College, Whitehorse, Canada. Articles contributed to *Encyclopedia of the Arctic*: MOWAT, FARLEY; SERVICE, ROBERT.

Lyck, Lise. Department of Management, Politics and Philosophy, Copenhagen Business School, Denmark. Articles contributed to *Encyclopedia of the Arctic*: AIR ROUTES; ECONOMIC DEVELOPMENT; ECONOMIC POLICY; GREENLAND TECHNICAL ORGANIZATION (GTO); MINING; TRADE; TRANSPORT.

Maas, David. Professor (Emeritus) of Political Science, University of Alaska Anchorage. Articles contributed to *Encyclopedia of the Arctic*: ALASKA NATIONAL INTEREST LANDS CONSERVATION ACT (ANILCA); ALASKA NATIVE REVIEW COMMISSION.

MacDonald, John. Igloolik Research Centre, Nunavut Research Institute, Canada. Articles contributed to *Encyclopedia of the Arctic*: IGLOOLIK; PIUGAATTUK, NOAH.

MacDonald, Robert. Department of Fisheries and Oceans, Canada, the Institute of Ocean Sciences, Sidney, British Columbia. Articles contributed to *Encyclopedia of the Arctic*: BEAUFORT SEA.

Machino, Yoichi. Independent researcher, Grenoble, France. Articles contributed to *Encyclopedia of the Arctic*: ARCTIC CHAR.

MacPherson, Ian. British Columbia Institute for Co-operative Studies, University of Victoria, Canada. Articles contributed to *Encyclopedia of the Arctic*: CO-OPERATIVES.

Malcolm, David. University of Alberta, Canada. Articles contributed to *Encyclopedia of the Arctic*: CANADA.

Martin, Cyd. National Park Service, Alaska. Articles contributed to *Encyclopedia of the Arctic*: CLOTHING.

Martin, Thibault. Department of Sociology, University of Winnipeg, Canada. Articles contributed to *Encyclopedia of the Arctic*: METIS NATIONAL COUNCIL; QUÉBEC.

Maschner, Herbert D. G. Department of Anthropology, Idaho State University. Articles contributed to *Encyclopedia of the Arctic*: ALEUTIAN TRADITION; WARFARE, HISTORICAL.

Mason, Arthur. University of California, Berkeley. Articles contributed to *Encyclopedia of the Arctic*: GAS EXPLORATION.

Mazhitova, Galina. Institute of Biology, Komi Science Centre, Ural Division of Russian Academy of Sciences, Russia. Articles contributed to *Encyclopedia of the Arctic*: KOMI REPUBLIC; MAGADAN; SOILS; SYKTYVKAR; VORKUTA.

Mazourov, Yuri. Heritage Institute, Russian Academy of Sciences, Moscow. Articles contributed to *Encyclopedia of the Arctic*: ARKHANGEL'SKAYA OBLAST; KAMCHATSKAYA OBLAST'; KARELIA; MAGADANSKAYA OBLAST; NATIONAL PARKS AND PROTECTED AREAS: RUSSIA; RUSSIA.

McCann, Doris. Athabasca University, and Nunavut Arctic College, Canada. Articles contributed to *Encyclopedia of the Arctic*: COURNOYEA, NELLIE; INDIAN AND NORTHERN AFFAIRS CANADA (INAC); INUVIALUIT FINAL AGREEMENT; NUNAVUT TUNNGAVIK INC.

McConnell, Joseph R. Hydrologic Sciences Division, Desert Research Institute, Nevada. Articles contributed to *Encyclopedia of the Arctic*: ICE CORE RECORD.

McCormick, Floyd. Yukon Legislative Assembly, Whitehorse, Yukon, and Arts and Sciences Division, Yukon College, Whitehorse, Yukon, Canada. Articles contributed to *Encyclopedia of the Arctic*: COMMITTEE FOR ORIGINAL PEOPLES' ENTITLEMENT (COPE); COUNCIL FOR YUKON INDIANS UMBRELLA FINAL AGREEMENT; MACKENZIE VALLEY PIPELINE; ROYAL CANADIAN MOUNTED POLICE (RCMP); SCHULTZ, ED.

McDonald, James Andrew. Department of Anthropology, University of Northern British Columbia, Canada. Articles contributed to *Encyclopedia of the Arctic*: ASSOCIATION OF CANADIAN UNIVERSITIES FOR NORTHERN STUDIES (ACUNS); TSIMSHIAN.

McEwen, Donald. Professor Emeritus, Department of Physics and Engineering Physics, University of Saskatchewan, Canada. Articles contributed to *Encyclopedia of the Arctic*: AURORA.

McRoy, C. Peter. School of Fisheries and Ocean Sciences, University of Alaska Fairbanks. Articles contributed to *Encyclopedia of the Arctic*: NORTH PACIFIC.

Meek, Chanda. Regional Resilience and Adaptation Program, Institute of Arctic Biology, University of Alaska Fairbanks. Articles contributed to *Encyclopedia of the Arctic*: POLITICAL ISSUES IN RESOURCE MANAGEMENT.

Meyer-Rochow, Benno. School of Engineering and Science, International University Bremen, Germany. Articles contributed to *Encyclopedia of the Arctic*: FINLAND; HIBERNATION; MAMMOTH; NOCTILUCENT CLOUD FORMATION; SNOW HOUSE; ULTRAVIOLET-B RADIATION.

Mit'ko, Valery. Director on Science and Projects of Saint Petersburg State Organization, Secretariat of the Northern Forum, St. Petersburg, Russia. Articles contributed to *Encyclopedia of the Arctic*: ALPHA RIDGE; AMUNDSEN BASIN; ARCTIC MID-OCEAN RIDGE; CANADIAN BASIN; CHUKCHI PLATEAU; CHUKCHI SEA; LOMONOSOV RIDGE; NANSEN BASIN; PEVEK; PROVIDENIYA.

Montgomerie, Robert. Department of Biology, Queen's University, Kingston, Canada. Articles contributed to *Encyclopedia of the Arctic*: BUNTINGS AND LONGSPURS; PTARMIGAN AND GROUSE.

Moore, Carol J. Sociology and Politics Department, Anglia Polytechnic University, Cambridge, England. Articles contributed to *Encyclopedia of the Arctic*: LEADERSHIP.

Morrow, Phyllis. Dean of the College of Liberal Arts, University of Alaska Fairbanks. Articles contributed to *Encyclopedia of the Arctic*: BLADDER CEREMONY; MESSENGER FEAST; YUPIIT.

Morton, Anne. Hudson's Bay Company Archives, Archives of Manitoba, Canada. Articles contributed to *Encyclopedia of the Arctic*: KENNEDY, WILLIAM.

Mousalimas, S.A. Oxford University, England. Articles contributed to *Encyclopedia of the Arctic*: ARCHBISHOP INNOCENT (IVAN VENIAMINOV); SHAMANISM; SHIROKOGOROV, SERGEY MIKHAILOVICH.

Mueller, Derek. Département de biologie, Université Laval, Canada. Articles contributed to *Encyclopedia of the Arctic*: CURLEY, TAGAK; INUIT TAPIRIIT KANATAMI; MICROBIAL MATS.

Muir, Magdalena. Arctic Institute of North America, University of Calgary, Canada. Articles contributed to *Encyclopedia of the Arctic*: WILDLIFE MANAGEMENT: ENVIRONMENTAL INITIATIVES.

Mullington, David. Journalist, *Ottawa Citizen*, Canada (Retired). Articles contributed to *Encyclopedia of the Arctic*: OKALIK, PAUL.

Murray, Tavi. School of Geography, University of Leeds, England. Articles contributed to *Encyclopedia of the Arctic*: GLACIAL FLOW.

Myarikyanova, Elvira Throfimovna. Arctic Research Center, Institute of Humanitarian Research, Yakutsk, Russia. Articles contributed to *Encyclopedia of the Arctic*: BURYAT REPUBLIC (BURYATIYA); DEZHNEV, SEMYON.

Myers, Heather. Department of International Studies, University of Northern British Columbia, Canada. Articles contributed to *Encyclopedia of the Arctic*: ANIMAL-RIGHTS MOVEMENTS AND RENEWABLE RESOURCES; BOURQUE, JAMES W.; CONVENTION ON INTERNATIONAL TRADE IN ENDANGERED SPECIES (CITES); DEMPSTER HIGHWAY; SEAL SKIN DIRECTIVE; TRAPPING; YELLOWKNIFE.

Myerson, Ralph M. Frederick A. Cook Society, Pennsylvania. Articles contributed to *Encyclopedia of the*

Arctic: BERING STRAIT; BOOTHIA PENINSULA; DAVIS STRAIT; DE LONG ISLANDS; HAYES, ISAAC I.; LABRADOR SEA; LINCOLN SEA; MELVILLE BAY; NORWEGIAN SEA; RAE, JOHN; RICHARDSON, SIR JOHN.

Nagy, Murielle. Université Laval, Québec, Canada. Articles contributed to *Encyclopedia of the Arctic*: INTERNATIONAL ARCTIC SOCIAL SCIENCES ASSOCIATION (IASSA).

Naidu, A. Sathy. School of Fisheries and Ocean Sciences, University of Alaska Fairbanks. Articles contributed to *Encyclopedia of the Arctic*: HEAVY METALS.

Nesis, Kir N. P.P. Shirshov Institute of Oceanology, Russian Academy of Sciences, Moscow, Russia. Articles contributed to *Encyclopedia of the Arctic*: KING CRAB; MOLLUSCS; POLLOCK; SHRIMP; TANNER CRAB.

Neumann, Caryn E. Department of History, Ohio State University. Articles contributed to *Encyclopedia of the Arctic*: FISHER, ALEXANDER; SWAINE, CHARLES.

Newton, Jennifer I. M. Department of Anthropology, University of Alaska Fairbanks, and Northern Land Use Research Inc., Fairbanks, Alaska. Articles contributed to *Encyclopedia of the Arctic*: FIFTH THULE EXPEDITION; IPIUTAK CULTURE; LAGUNA, FREDERICA DE; LARSEN, HELGE; MATHIASSEN, THERKEL; OLD BERING SEA CULTURE; SAQQAQ CULTURE; THULE CULTURE.

Nielsen, Jens K. Danish Centre for Rural Research and Development, Denmark. Articles contributed to *Encyclopedia of the Arctic*: ATASSUT; INDUSTRIAL DEVELOPMENT; INFORMATION TECHNOLOGY; INUIT ATAQATIGIIT; NORDIC COUNCIL OF MINISTERS; SELF-DETERMINATION; SIUMUT; SUSTAINABLE DEVELOPMENT; URBANIZATION; WEST NORDIC COUNCIL.

Nikitin, Valery Mefodievich. Sakha State University, Yakutsk, Russia. Articles contributed to *Encyclopedia of the Arctic*: GOLD MINING.

Nikolaev, Alexander Petrovich. Institute of Humanitarian Research, Yakutsk, Russia. Articles contributed to *Encyclopedia of the Arctic*: CHURCHES IN THE RUSSIAN ARCTIC, ESTABLISHMENT OF.

Nord, Douglas. University Center for International Education, Wright University, Ohio. Articles contributed to *Encyclopedia of the Arctic*: CIRCUMPOLAR UNIVERSITIES ASSOCIATION; DEMOGRAPHY AND POPULATION.

Novgorodov, Innokentij. Institute of Humanitarian Research, Yakutsk, Russia. Articles contributed to *Encyclopedia of the Arctic*: NORTHERN ALTAIC LANGUAGES.

Novikov, Anatoly Georgiyevich. Department of History, Yakutsk State University, Russia. Articles contributed to *Encyclopedia of the Arctic*: SAKHA REPUBLIC (YAKUTIA).

Nuttall, Mark. Department of Anthropology, University of Alberta, Canada. Articles contributed to *Encyclopedia of the Arctic*: ANIMALS IN THE WORLD-VIEWS OF INDIGENOUS PEOPLES; ARCTIC: DEFINITIONS AND BOUNDARIES; ARCTIC ENVIRONMENTAL PROTECTION STRATEGY; ESKIMO; GREENLAND; GREENLAND INUIT; INDIGENOUS PEOPLES' ORGANIZATIONS AND ARCTIC ENVIRONMENTAL POLITICS; INTERNATIONAL POLAR YEARS; INUIT; MITAARNEQ; TOURISM; WHALING, SUBSISTENCE.

Odess, Dan. Curator of Archaeology Collection, University of Alaska Museum, Fairbanks. Articles contributed to *Encyclopedia of the Arctic*: ARCTIC SMALL TOOL TRADITION.

Ogden, Aynslie. Northern Research Institute, Yukon College, Whitehorse, Canada. Articles contributed to *Encyclopedia of the Arctic*: CLIMATE: ENVIRONMENTAL INITIATIVES; FENS; HUDSON BAY; INTERGOVERNMENTAL PANEL ON CLIMATE CHANGE (IPCC); KETTLES; LOESS; MACKENZIE BASIN; MARSHES; NORTHERN CLIMATE EXCHANGE; NORTHERN RESEARCH FORUM; PRECIPITATION AND MOISTURE; WEATHER; WOODLANDS.

Ogilvie, Astrid E. J. Institute of Arctic and Alpine Research, University of Colorado at Boulder. Articles contributed to *Encyclopedia of the Arctic*: EIRÍK THE RED.

Ólafsson, Haraldur. University of Iceland, Reykjavík. Articles contributed to *Encyclopedia of the Arctic*: STRATUS CLOUD.

Olson, Rachel. Department of Sociology, University of Aberdeen, Scotland. Articles contributed to *Encyclopedia of the Arctic*: ARCTIC SLOPE REGIONAL CORPORATION (ASRC); BUREAU OF LAND MANAGEMENT; COUNCIL OF TRIBAL ATHABASCAN GOVERNMENTS; GWICH'IN COUNCIL INTERNATIONAL; NORTHWEST ALASKA REGIONAL CORPORATION (NANA); PROJECT CHARIOT.

Ørbæk, Jon Børre. Norwegian Polar Institute, Norway. Articles contributed to *Encyclopedia of the Arctic*: ARCTIC HAZE; OZONE DEPLETION.

Øverland, Indra. Department of Russian Studies, Norwegian Institute of International Affairs, Oslo, Norway. Articles contributed to *Encyclopedia of the Arctic*: INDIGENOUS PEOPLES' SECRETARIAT; INTERNATIONAL WORK GROUP FOR INDIGENOUS AFFAIRS (IWGIA); KOLA SCIENCE CENTRE; LOVOZERO; MURMANSKAYA OBLAST'; SAAMI COUNCIL.

Paci, Chris. Arctic Athabaskan Council, Yellowknife, Canada. Articles contributed to *Encyclopedia of the Arctic*: COMMON PROPERTY MANAGEMENT; HUDSON'S BAY COMPANY; METIS.

Palmer, Andrew. Department of Engineering, University of Cambridge, England. Articles contributed to *Encyclopedia of the Arctic*: OIL EXPLORATION.

Pálsson, Gísli. Institute of Anthropolgy, University of Iceland, Reykjavík. Articles contributed to *Encyclopedia of the Arctic*: STEFANSSON, VILHJALMUR.

Peter, Elisa. World Wide Fund for Nature (WWF), Sweden. Articles contributed to *Encyclopedia of the Arctic*: FORESTS: ENVIRONMENTAL INITIATIVES.

Peters, Jochen. University of Tromsø, Norway. Articles contributed to *Encyclopedia of the Arctic*: FINNMARK; NORDLAND; NORWAY; SVALBARD TREATY; TROMS; TROMSØ.

Petersen, Robert. Independent scholar, Denmark. Articles contributed to *Encyclopedia of the Arctic*: THALBITZER, WILLIAM.

Petrov, Panteleimon. Department of History, Institute of Humanitarian Research, Yakutsk, Russia. Articles contributed to *Encyclopedia of the Arctic*: ATLASOV, VLADIMIR; SPERANSKII, MIKHAIL.

Plumet, Patrick. Département des sciences de la terre et de l'atmosphère Université du Québec à Montréal. Articles contributed to *Encyclopedia of the Arctic*: MIGRATION (PREHISTORY).

Pollard, Wayne. Department of Geography, McGill University, Montréal, Canada. Articles contributed to *Encyclopedia of the Arctic*: AXEL HEIBERG ISLAND; HERSCHEL ISLAND; PATTERNED AND POLYGONAL GROUND; PERIGLACIAL ENVIRONMENTS; POLAR DESERT; THERMOKARST.

Poppel, Birger. Statistics Greenland, Nuuk, Greenland. Articles contributed to *Encyclopedia of the Arctic*: BIRTHPLACE CRITERIA; G-50; G-60; HUMAN DIMENSIONS: RESEARCH PROGRAMMES.

Potter, Ben A. Department of Anthropology, University of Alaska Fairbanks. Articles contributed to *Encyclopedia of the Arctic*: ALASKA NATIVE LANGUAGE CENTER; AMERICAN PALEO-ARCTIC TRADITION; NORTHERN ARCHAIC PERIOD.

Potter, Russell A. Department of English, Rhode Island College, Providence. Articles contributed to *Encyclopedia of the Arctic*: FRANKLIN, LADY JANE; FRANKLIN, SIR JOHN; OPEN POLAR SEA; ROSS, SIR JOHN.

Powell, Richard C. Department of Geography, University of Cambridge, England. Articles contributed to *Encyclopedia of the Arctic*: POLAR CONTINENTAL SHELF PROJECT (PCSP); RESOLUTE BASE.

Pretes, Michael. Department of Geography and Environmental Studies, University of Hawaii at Hilo. Articles contributed to *Encyclopedia of the Arctic*: ALASKA; ALASKA NATIVE CLAIMS SETTLEMENT ACT (ANCSA); LONDON, JACK.

Proppe, Hulda. Department of Anthropology, University of Iceland, Reykjavík. Articles contributed to *Encyclopedia of the Arctic*: GENDER.

Radionov, Vladimir Fedorovich. International Arctic Research Centre, University of Alaska Fairbanks. Articles contributed to *Encyclopedia of the Arctic*: DRIFTING STATIONS.

Rasmussen, Rasmus Ole. Department of Geography and International Development Studies, University of Roskilde, Denmark. Articles contributed to *Encyclopedia of the Arctic*: AASIAAT; COMMISSION FOR SCIENTIFIC RESEARCH IN GREENLAND; FISH FARMING; GREENLAND HUNTERS AND FISHERS ASSOCIATION (KNAPK); GREENLAND SEAFISHERY AND EXPORT ASSOCIATION; IVITTUT; MAARMORILIK; NANORTALIK; NORTH ATLANTIC FISHERIES ORGANIZATION (NAFO); NUUK; QAQORTOQ; ROYAL GREENLAND; SHEEP FARMING; TASIILAQ; UPERNAVIK; UUMMANNAQ.

Razzhivin, Volodya. Department of Vegetation of the Far North, Komarov Botanical Institute, St Petersburg, Russia. Articles contributed to *Encyclopedia of the Arctic*: ANADYR RIVER; CHUKOTSKOYA RANGE; DRY TUNDRA; DWARF-SHRUB HEATHS; MESIC TUNDRA; SHRUB TUNDRA; SNOW PATCHES; TUSSOCK TUNDRA; WRANGEL ISLAND.

Reedy-Maschner, Katherine. Department of Anthropology, Idaho State University. Articles contributed to *Encyclopedia of the Arctic*: ALEUT; ALEUT CORPORATION; ALEUT INTERNATIONAL ASSOCIATION; ALEUTIAN/PRIBILOF ISLANDS ASSOCIATION.

Rees, Gareth. Scott Polar Research Institute, University of Cambridge, England. Articles contributed to *Encyclopedia of the Arctic*: ALBEDO; NORIL'SK; SATELLITE REMOTE SENSING; SNOW; WINDCHILL.

Reiersen, Lars-Otto. Arctic Monitoring and Assessment Programme (AMAP), Oslo, Norway. Articles contributed to *Encyclopedia of the Arctic*: LOCAL AND TRANSBOUNDARY POLLUTION.

Rethmann, Petra. Department of Anthropology, McMaster University, Hamilton, Canada. Articles contributed to *Encyclopedia of the Arctic*: IOKHEL'SON, VLADIMIR IL'ICH; KORYAK; RUSSIAN ASSOCIATION OF INDIGENOUS PEOPLES OF THE NORTH (RAIPON).

Rex, Markus. Alfred Wegener Institute for Polar and Marine Research (AWI), Potsdam, Germany. Articles contributed to *Encyclopedia of the Arctic*: POLAR STRATOSPHERIC CLOUDS; POLAR VORTEX.

Rice, Keren. Department of Linguistics, University of Toronto, Canada. Articles contributed to *Encyclopedia of the Arctic*: NORTHERN ATHAPASKAN LANGUAGES.

Richling, Barnett. Sociology/Anthropology Department, Mount Saint Vincent University, Nova Scotia, Canada. Articles contributed to *Encyclopedia of the Arctic*: CZAPLICKA, MARIE ANTOINETTE; JENNESS, DIAMOND; LABRADOR INUIT; NEWFOUNDLAND AND LABRADOR; SETTLERS (LABRADOR).

Riffenburgh, Beau. Scott Polar Research Institute, University of Cambridge, England. Articles contributed to *Encyclopedia of the Arctic*: BENNETT, JAMES GORDON JR; EXPLORATION OF THE ARCTIC; TORRELL, OTTO.

Rigor, Ignatius. Polar Science Center, Applied Physics Laboratory, University of Washington, Seattle. Articles contributed to *Encyclopedia of the Arctic*: LAPTEV SEA; METEOROLOGICAL STATIONS; SEA ICE.

Robinson, Deborah B. Institute of Arctic Studies, Dartmouth College, New Hampshire. Articles contributed to *Encyclopedia of the Arctic*: ALUTIIT; CREE; FUR TRADE; GRAND COUNCIL OF THE CREE; PULLAR, GORDON.

Robinson, Michael. Central Connecticut State University. Articles contributed to *Encyclopedia of the Arctic*: COOK, FREDERICK A.; GRINNELL, HENRY.

Roepstorff, Andreas. Afdeling for Etnografi og Socialantropologi, Aarhus Universitet, Denmark. Articles contributed to *Encyclopedia of the Arctic*: BIRKET-SMITH, KAJ.

Rogacheva, Helene V. Institute of Ecology and Evolution, Russian Academy of Sciences, Moscow, Russia. Articles contributed to *Encyclopedia of the Arctic*: ENETS; KHATANGA; KHATANGA RIVER; YENISEY RIVER.

Rogne, Odd. International Arctic Science Committee (IASC), Oslo, Norway. Articles contributed to *Encyclopedia of the Arctic*: INTERNATIONAL ARCTIC SCIENCE COMMITTEE (IASC).

Romanenko, Fedor. Department of Geography, Moscow State University Lomonosov, Russia. Articles contributed to *Encyclopedia of the Arctic*: ARCTIC OCEAN HYDROGRAPHICAL EXPEDITION, 1909[-]1915; GEOMORPHOLOGY; NEW SIBERIAN ISLANDS; NORTH POLE AIR EXPEDITION, 1937; RUSSIAN POLAR EXPEDITION, 1900[-]1901; TOLL, BARON EDWARD VON.

Ross, William G. Department of Geography, Bishop's University, Quebec, Canada (Retired Faculty). Articles contributed to *Encyclopedia of the Arctic*: COMER, GEORGE; LOW, ALBERT PETER; PENNY, WILLIAM.

Rybakov, Felix F. Faculty of Economics, St Petersburg State University, Russia. Articles contributed to *Encyclopedia of the Arctic*: MURMANSK.

Sannikova, Yana Mikhailovna. Institute of Humanitarian Research, Yakutsk, Russia. Articles contributed to *Encyclopedia of the Arctic*: NORTHERN FORUM.

Savchenko, Andrew. Independent scholar, Providence, Rhode Island. Articles contributed to *Encyclopedia of the Arctic*: SAKHALIN ISLAND.

Sawtell, Shirley. Scott Polar Research Institute, University of Cambridge, England. Articles contributed to *Encyclopedia of the Arctic*: POND INLET.

Schledermann, Peter. Arctic Institute of North America, University of Calgary, Canada. Articles contributed to *Encyclopedia of the Arctic*: ARCHAEOLOGY OF THE ARCTIC: CANADA AND GREENLAND; MIKKELSEN, EJNAR; NORTH WEST PASSAGE, EXPLORATION OF; ROSS, SIR JAMES; SKRAELING ISLAND.

Schmidlin, Thomas W. Department of Geography, Kent State University, Ohio. Articles contributed to *Encyclopedia of the Arctic*: ALEUTIAN RANGE; CHUGACH MOUNTAINS; DAWSON; DENMARK STRAIT; KODIAK ISLAND; KUSKOKWIM MOUNTAINS; MELVILLE PENINSULA; NOME.

Schoenfuss, Heiko L. Department of Biological Sciences, St. Cloud State University, Minnesota. Articles contributed to *Encyclopedia of the Arctic*: MARINE MAMMALS: RESEARCH PROGRAMMES.

Schweitzer, Peter. Department of Anthropology, University of Alaska Fairbanks. Articles contributed to *Encyclopedia of the Arctic*: BEAR CEREMONIALISM; BOGORAZ, VLADIMIR GERMANOVICH; COLLINS, HENRY B.; DOLGIKH, BORIS; KINSHIP; RUSSIAN "OLD SETTLERS"; RUSSIAN GEOGRAPHICAL SOCIETY; SIBERIAN (CHUKOTKAN) YUPIK.

Sergeyev, Igor. Archangel'skaya, Russia. Articles contributed to *Encyclopedia of the Arctic*: DIKSON; PECHORA RIVER; SEVERNAYA DVINA.

Shabaev, Yuri. Komi Science Centre, Syktyvkar, Russia. Articles contributed to *Encyclopedia of the Arctic*: KHANTY; KOMI; NARYAN-MAR; NORTHERN URALIC LANGUAGES.

Shannon, Kerrie Ann. Department of Sociology, University of Aberdeen, Scotland. Articles contributed to *Encyclopedia of the Arctic*: DOG SLEDGE IN INUIT CULTURE; PLANT GATHERING.

Shin, Kyung-Hoon. International Arctic Research Center, University of Alaska Fairbanks. Articles contributed to *Encyclopedia of the Arctic*: FRESHWATER HYDROLOGY; OCEANOGRAPHY: RESEARCH PROGRAMMES.

Shirina, Danara Antonovna. Institute of Humanitarian Research, Yakutsk, Russia. Articles contributed to *Encyclopedia of the Arctic*: BILLINGS, JOSEPH; JESUP NORTH PACIFIC EXPEDITION.

Shishigina, Anna Nikolaevna. Institute of Humanitarian Research, Yakutsk, Russia. Articles contributed to *Encyclopedia of the Arctic*: CHELYUSKIN, SEMYON; CHIRIKOV, ALEXEI; LAPTEV, DMITRIY; LAPTEV, KHARITON.

Sidorov, Boris Ignatievich. Department of Biology and Geography, Yakutsk State University, Russia. Articles contributed to *Encyclopedia of the Arctic*: RAVEN.

Sillanpää, Lennard. Aleksanteri Institute, University of Helsinki, Finland. Articles contributed to *Encyclopedia of the Arctic*: ARCTIC RESEARCH POLICY ACT; ILO CONVENTION NO. 107; ILO CONVENTION NO. 169; NORDIC SAAMI INSTITUTE; SAAMI PARLIAMENTS.

Sirina, Anna A. Institute of Ethnology and Anthropology, Russian Academy of Sciences, Moscow, Russia. Articles contributed to *Encyclopedia of the Arctic*: EVENKI AUTONOMOUS OKRUG; KAMCHATKA PENINSULA; KAMCHATKA RIVER; KORYAK AUTONOMOUS OKRUG; SHTERNBERG, LEV YAKOVLEVICH; TOFALARS; UDEGE.

Sittler, Benoît. Institut für Landespflege, Universität Freiburg, Germany. Articles contributed to *Encyclopedia of the Arctic*: MICROTINES (LEMMINGS, VOLES); OWL.

Slobodin, Sergei B. Northeastern Interdisciplinary Scientific Research Institute, Russian Academy of Sciences, Magadan, Russia. Articles contributed to *Encyclopedia of the Arctic*: BEL'KACHI CULTURE; DIKOV, NIKOLAY; DYUKTAI CULTURE; OLD ITEL'MEN CULTURE; OLD KORYAK CULTURE; SIBERDIK CULTURE; SUMNAGIN CULTURE; SYALAKH CULTURE; TARYA CULTURE; TEIN, TASYAN; WRANGEL PALEO-ESKIMO CULTURE; YMYAKHTAKH CULTURE.

Smith, Samantha. World Wide Fund for Nature (WWF) International Arctic Programme, Oslo, Norway. Articles contributed to *Encyclopedia of the Arctic*: WORLD WIDE FUND FOR NATURE (WWF) INTERNATIONAL ARCTIC PROGRAMME.

Smyth, Steve. Department of Environment, Government of Yukon, and Yukon College, Canada. Articles contributed to *Encyclopedia of the Arctic*: WHITEHORSE; YUKON TERRITORY.

Sørensen, Axel. History Department, Aarhus Universitet, Denmark. Articles contributed to *Encyclopedia of the Arctic*: BANG, JETTE; CHEMNITZ, LARS; HØEGH, ERLING; RINK, HINRICH JOHANNES; ROYAL GREENLAND TRADE COMPANY (KGH).

Stam, Deirdre C. New York Center for Books and Reading, Palmer School of Library and Information Science, Long Island University, New York. Articles contributed to *Encyclopedia of the Arctic*: INUIT ART FOUNDATION.

Steele, Michael. Polar Science Center, Applied Physics Laboratory, University of Washington, Seattle. Articles contributed to *Encyclopedia of the Arctic*: COLD HALOCLINE.

Steele, Peter. Author, Whitehorse, Canada. Articles contributed to *Encyclopedia of the Arctic*: BACK, SIR GEORGE.

Stenbæk, Marianne. McGill University, Montreal, Canada. Articles contributed to *Encyclopedia of the Arctic:* BIRTHPLACE CRITERIA; HUMAN DIMENSIONS: RESEARCH PROGRAMMES.

Stern, Harry L. Polar Science Center, Applied Physics Laboratory, University of Washington, Seattle. Articles contributed to *Encyclopedia of the Arctic*: ARCTIC CIRCLE; CONCENTRIC SPHERES AND POLAR VOIDS, THEORY OF; NORTH POLE; UNITED STATES OF AMERICA.

Stern, Pamela. Department of Anthropology, University of Waterloo, Ontario, Canada. Articles contributed to *Encyclopedia of the Arctic*: COLLINSON, RICHARD; INUVIALUIT SETTLEMENT REGION; KROEBER, ALFRED.

Stone, I. R. Author, Isle of Man, England. Articles contributed to *Encyclopedia of the Arctic*: INGLEFIELD, EDWARD A.; SABINE, EDWARD.

Sutyrin, Sergei. Department of World Economy, St Petersburg State University, Russia. Articles contributed to *Encyclopedia of the Arctic*: GLOBALIZATION AND THE ARCTIC.

Svoboda, Josef. Department of Biology, University of Toronto at Mississauga, Ontario, Canada. Articles contributed to *Encyclopedia of the Arctic*: PRIMARY PRODUCTION.

Syroechkovski, Eugene E. Institute of Ecology and Evolution, Russian Academy of Sciences, Moscow, Russia. Articles contributed to *Encyclopedia of the Arctic*: KET; NGANASAN.

Tammiksaar, Erki. Karl Ernst von Baer Museum of the Institute of Zoology and Botany, Estonian Agricultural University. Articles contributed to *Encyclopedia of the Arctic*: BAER, KARL VON; BUNGE, ALEXANDER VON; CASTREN, ALEXANDR MATHIAS; KOTZEBUE, OTTO VON; MAAK, RIKHARD KARLOVICH.

Teilmann, Jonas. National Environmental Research Institute, Roskilde, Denmark. Articles contributed to *Encyclopedia of the Arctic*: HUMPBACK WHALE.

Tertitski, Grigori. Institute of Geography, Russian Academy of Sciences, Moscow, Russia. Articles contributed to *Encyclopedia of the Arctic*: DUDINKA; KHANTY-MANSI AUTONOMOUS OKRUG; KRASNOYARSK KRAY; SOLOVETSKI ISLANDS; TAYMYR (DOLGAN-NENETS) AUTONOMOUS OKRUG; TAZ RIVER; TYUMEN OBLAST; YAMAL PENINSULA.

Tester, Frank James. School of Social Work and Family Studies, University of British Columbia, Vancouver, Canada. Articles contributed to *Encyclopedia of the Arctic*: GRISE FIORD; RESOLUTE BAY.

Tews, Joerg. Institute of Biochemistry and Biology, University of Potsdam, Germany. Articles contributed to *Encyclopedia of the Arctic*: BACK RIVER; BIODIVERSITY; CASSIOPE HEATHS; EMPETRUM HEATHS.

Thomas, Robert H. EG&G Services, NASA Wallops Flight Facility, Virginia. Articles contributed to *Encyclopedia of the Arctic*: GREENLAND ICE SHEET.

Thompson, Niobe. Scott Polar Research Institute, University of Cambridge, England. Articles contributed to *Encyclopedia of the Arctic*: CHUKCHI AUTONOMOUS OKRUG (CHUKOTKA).

Thuesen, Søren. Department of Eskimology, University of Copenhagen, Denmark. Articles contributed to *Encyclopedia of the Arctic*: ESKIMOLOGY.

Tinsley, Clayton. Stefansson Arctic Institute, Iceland. Articles contributed to *Encyclopedia of the Arctic*: NORTH ATLANTIC BIOCULTURAL ORGANIZATION (NABO).

Traeger, Verena. Institut für Ethnologie, Kultur- und Sozialanthropologie, Universität Wien, Austria. Articles contributed to *Encyclopedia of the Arctic*: AASIVIK; CRANTZ, DAVID; ELLIS, HENRY; HOLM, GUSTAV; KLUTSCHAK, HENRY WENZEL; NY HERRNHUT; OLEARIUS, ADAM; QILAKITSOQ MUMMIES; RASMUSSEN, HENRIETTE; TUPILAK.

Turner, John. British Antarctic Survey, Cambridge, England. Articles contributed to *Encyclopedia of the Arctic*: POLAR LOWS.

Van der Wal, René. Centre for Ecology and Hydrology, Banchory, England. Articles contributed to *Encyclopedia of the Arctic*: PLANT-ANIMAL INTERACTIONS.

Vasil`eva, Maya Ivanovna. Institute of Humanitarian Research, Yakutsk, Russia. Articles contributed to *Encyclopedia of the Arctic*: DOLGAN; EVENKI; EVENS.

Vasiliev, Vladimir. Northern Forum Academy, Sakha Republic, Russia. Articles contributed to *Encyclopedia of the Arctic*: ARCTIC GROUND SQUIRREL; RESEARCH STATIONS; TIKSI; YAKUTSK.

Vasilieva, Nina Dmitrievna. Institute of Humanitarian Research, Yakutsk, Russia. Articles contributed to *Encyclopedia of the Arctic*: COMMITTEE OF THE NORTH; SIBIRYAKOV, ALEXANDER.

Vaté, Virginie. Université Paris X-Nanterre, France. Articles contributed to *Encyclopedia of the Arctic*: ANADYR; CHUKCHI; ITEL'MEN; RYTKHEU, YURI.

Veen, C.J. van der. Department of Geological Sciences, and Byrd Polar Research Center, Ohio State University. Articles contributed to *Encyclopedia of the Arctic*: GLACIER ICE; GLACIER MASS BALANCE; GLACIOLOGY.

Vick-Westgate, Ann. Author, Boston, Massachusetts. Articles contributed to *Encyclopedia of the Arctic*: EDUCATION.

Vikør, Lars Sigurdsson. University of Oslo, Norway. Articles contributed to *Encyclopedia of the Arctic*: ALPHABETS AND WRITING, SCANDINAVIA AND ICELAND; SCANDINAVIAN LANGUAGES.

Vilhjálmsson, Hjálmar. Marine Research Institute, Iceland. Articles contributed to *Encyclopedia of the Arctic*: FISHERIES (COMMERICAL).

Vinokurova, Lilia. Institute of humanitarian research, Yakutsk, Russia. Articles contributed to *Encyclopedia of the Arctic*: INSTITUTE FOR NORTHERN MINORITIES' PROBLEMS; INSTITUTE OF PEOPLES OF THE NORTH; UNIVERSITIES AND HIGHER EDUCATION ESTABLISHMENTS, RUSSIA.

Vogel, Hal. College of Communication, Rowan University, New Jersey. Articles contributed to *Encyclopedia of the Arctic*: BYRD, RICHARD; DE LONG, GEORGE WASHINGTON; GREELY, ADOLPHUS W.

Vorobieva, Irina V. Department of World Economy, St Petersburg State University, Russia. Articles contributed to *Encyclopedia of the Arctic:* GLOBALIZATION AND THE ARCTIC.

Voronin, Vadim. Archive Department, Russian State Museum of the Arctic and Antarctic (RSMAA), St Petersburg, Russia. Articles contributed to *Encyclopedia of the Arctic*: KUCHIEV, YURI SERGEEVICH; VORONIN, VLADIMIR IVANOVICH.

Wadhams, Peter. Department of Applied Mathematics and Theoretical Physics, University of Cambridge, England. Articles contributed to *Encyclopedia of the Arctic*: ARCTIC OCEAN; SIKUSSAK.

Walker, H. Jesse. Professor Emeritus, Department of Geography and Anthropology, Louisiana State University. Articles contributed to *Encyclopedia of the Arctic*: COLVILLE RIVER; RIVER AND LAKE ICE.

Wallace, Birgitta. Archaeologist Emerita, Parks Canada. Articles contributed to *Encyclopedia of the Arctic*: VIKINGS; VINLAND.

Wamsley, Doug. Independent scholar, Bergen County, New Jersey. Articles contributed to *Encyclopedia of the Arctic*: ROYAL GEOGRAPHICAL SOCIETY.

Watson, Annette. Department of Geography, University of Minnesota, Twin Cities. Articles contributed to *Encyclopedia of the Arctic*: ALEUTIAN ISLANDS; COMMANDER ISLANDS; COOK, JAMES; NUCLEAR TESTING; SCORESBY, WILLIAM; WESTERN TELEGRAPH EXPEDITION.

Ween, Gro. Institute of Anthropology, University of Oslo, Norway. Articles contributed to *Encyclopedia of the Arctic*: ALTA/KAUTOKEINO DEMONSTRATIONS; ARCTIC ATHABASCAN COUNCIL; ARCTIC PEOPLES' CONFERENCE; ASSOCIATION OF WORLD REINDEER HERDERS; INUIT CIRCUMPOLAR YOUTH COUNCIL (ICYC); MAGGA, OLE HENRIK.

Welch, Harold. Freshwater Institute, Canada Department of Fisheries and Oceans, Manitoba (Retired). Articles contributed to *Encyclopedia of the Arctic*: SECONDARY PRODUCTION.

Weller, Gunter. Cooperative Institute for Arctic Research, University of Alaska Fairbanks. Articles contributed to *Encyclopedia of the Arctic*: CLIMATE; GLOBAL WARMING; GREENHOUSE GAS EMISSIONS; IMPACTS OF CLIMATE CHANGE; MICROCLIMATES; URBAN CLIMATES.

Wenzel, George. Department of Geography, McGill University, Montréal, Canada. Articles contributed to *Encyclopedia of the Arctic*: SHARING.

West, Janet. Scott Polar Research Institute, University of Cambridge, England. Articles contributed to *Encyclopedia of the Arctic*: SCRIMSHAW.

Wheelersburg, Robert. Department of Sociology & Anthropology, Elizabethtown College, Pennsylvania. Articles contributed to *Encyclopedia of the Arctic*: PASTORALISM.

Willerslev, Rane. Department of Anthropology and Ethnography, University of Aarhus, Denmark. Articles contributed to *Encyclopedia of the Arctic*: FUR TRADE, HISTORY IN RUSSIA; YUKAGIR.

Williams, Meredith. Department of Geomatics, University of Newcastle upon Tyne, England. Articles contributed to *Encyclopedia of the Arctic*: FRANZ JOSEF LAND; GLACIER GROWTH AND DECAY; NOVAYA ZEMLYA; SEVERNAYA ZEMLYA.

Wilson, John. Writer and researcher, Lantzville, Canada. Articles contributed to *Encyclopedia of the Arctic*: BYLOT, ROBERT; CROZIER, FRANCIS; HUDSON, HENRY; WEYMOUTH, GEORGE.

Wolken, Gabriel. Department of Earth and Atmospheric Science, University of Alberta, Edmonton, Canada. Articles contributed to *Encyclopedia of the Arctic*: LITTLE ICE AGE.

Woo, Ming-Ko. School of Geography and Geology, McMaster University, Hamilton, Canada. Articles contributed to *Encyclopedia of the Arctic*: PERMAFROST HYDROLOGY.

Yates, James. Department of English and Foreign Language, Northwestern Oklahoma State University. Articles contributed to *Encyclopedia of the Arctic*: MCCLINTOCK, FRANCIS LEOPOLD; NOBILE, UMBERTO; PARRY, SIR WILLIAM EDWARD.

Yurchenko, Alexei Y. Center for Environmental and Technological History, European University at St. Petersburg, Russia. Articles contributed to *Encyclopedia of the Arctic*: KRASHENINNIKOV, STEPAN; LITKE, FEDOR; POMOR.

Zakharova, Veronika. Russian State Museum of the Arctic and Antarctic, St Petersburg, Russia. Articles contributed to *Encyclopedia of the Arctic*: CHEREVICHNY, IVAN IVANOVICH; SOMOV, MIKHAIL MIKHAILOVICH.

Zeeb, Barbara. Environmental Sciences Group, Royal Military College of Canada, Kingston. Articles contributed to *Encyclopedia of the Arctic*: CONTAMINANTS; HYDROCARBON CONTAMINATION; OCEAN DUMPING.

Zen'ko, Alexey. Articles contributed to *Encyclopedia of the Arctic*: CHERNETSOV, VALERY; MANSI; NENETS; RUDENKO, SERGEI.

Zhirkov, Innokenty. Geography Department, Sakha State University, Yakutsk, Russia. Articles contributed to *Encyclopedia of the Arctic*: KOLYMA RIVER; OLENEK RIVER; OKHOTSK, SEA OF; SUBARCTIC; TAIGA; YANA RIVER.

Zhu, Lie. Center for Atmospheric and Space Sciences, Utah State University. Articles contributed to *Encyclopedia of the Arctic*: SUBSTORMS.

Zhukova, Ludmila Nikolayevna. Department of Philology, Yakutsk State University, Russia. Articles contributed to *Encyclopedia of the Arctic*: ALPHABETS AND WRITING, RUSSIA.

Index

INDEX

INDEX

INDEX

INDEX